PRENTICE HALL FINANCE SERIES

Personal Finance
Keown, *Personal Finance: Turning Money into Wealth*
Trivoli, *Personal Portfolio Management: Fundamentals & Strategies*
Winger/Frasca, *Personal Finance: An Integrated Planning Approach*

Investments
Alexander/Sharpe/Bailey, *Fundamentals of Investments*
Fabozzi, *Investment Management*
Fischer/Jordan, *Security Analysis and Portfolio Management*
Haugen, *Modern Investment Theory*
Haugen, *The New Finance*
Haugen, *The Beast on Wall Street*
Haugen, *The Inefficient Stock Market*
Sharpe/Alexander/Bailey, *Investments*
Taggart, *Quantitative Analysis for Investment Management*
Winger/Frasca, *Investments*

Portfolio Analysis
Alexander/Sharpe/Bailey, *Fundamentals of Investments*
Fischer/Jordan, *Security Analysis and Portfolio Management*
Haugen, *Modern Investment Theory*
Sharpe/Alexander/Bailey, *Investments*

Options/Futures/Derivatives
Hull, *Fundamentals of Futures and Options Markets*
Hull, *Options, Futures, and Other Derivatives*

Risk Management/Financial Engineering
Hull, *Risk Management and Financial Engineering – Coming in 2001*
Mason/Merton/Perold/Tufano, *Cases in Financial Engineering*

Fixed Income Securities
Handa, *FinCoach: Fixed Income (software)*
Van Horne, *Financial Market Rates and Flows*

Bond Markets
Fabozzi, *Bond Markets, Analysis and Strategies*
Van Horne, *Financial Market Rates and Flows*

Capital Markets
Fabozzi/Modigliani, *Capital Markets: Institutions and Instruments*
Van Horne, *Financial Market Rates and Flows*

Corporate Finance, Survey of Finance, & Financial Economics
Bodie/Merton, *Finance*
Emery/Finnerty/Stowe, *Principles of Financial Management*
Emery/Finnerty, *Corporate Financial Management*
Gallagher/Andrew, *Financial Management: Principles and Practices*
Haugen, *The New Finance: The Case Against Efficient Markets*
Keown/Martin/Petty/Scott, *Financial Management*
Keown/Martin/Petty/Scott, *Foundations of Finance: The Logic and Practice of Financial Management*
Shapiro/Balbirer, *Modern Corporate Finance: A Multidisciplinary Approach to Value Creation*
Van Horne, *Financial Management and Policy*
Van Horne/Wachowicz, *Fundamentals of Financial Management*

Finance Center
For downloadable supplements and much more … visit us at www.prenhall.com/financecenter

Twelfth Edition

FINANCIAL MANAGEMENT AND POLICY

James C. Van Horne
Stanford University

Prentice Hall, Upper Saddle River, New Jersey 07458

To My Family

Library of Congress Cataloging-in-Publication Data

Van Horne, James C.
 Financial management and policy / James C. Van Horne. — 12th ed.
  p. cm.
 Includes bibliographical references and index.
 ISBN 0-13-032657-7
 1. Corporations—Finance. I. Title.

 HG4011 .V34 2001
 658.15—dc21   00-051656
                                                    CIP

Senior Editor: Maureen Riopelle
Editor-in-Chief: P.J. Boardman
Managing Editor (Editorial): Gladys Soto
Assistant Editor: Cheryl Clayton
Editorial Assistant: Melanie Olsen
Marketing Manager: Joshua McClary
Marketing Assistant: Lauren Tarino
Production Manager: Gail Steier de Acevedo
Production Editor: Maureen Wilson
Permissions Coordinator: Suzanne Grappi
Associate Director, Manufacturing: Vincent Scelta
Manufacturing Buyer: Natacha St. Hill Moore
Cover Design: Joseph Sengotta
Cover Illustration/Photo: Marjory Dressler
Full-Service Project Management: Impressions Book and Journal Services, Inc.
Printer/Binder: Courier-Westford, Kendallville

10 9 8 7 6
ISBN 0-13-032657-7

Brief Contents

v

Contents

Preface

This edition remains dedicated to showing how a rich body of financial theory can be applied to corporate decision making, whether it be strategic, analytical, or simply the routine decisions a financial manager faces everyday. The landscape of finance has changed a good deal since the last edition, and in this edition I try to capture the changing environment. In this regard, it is useful to review the important changes.

One change you will note is the inclusion of a number of sidebars in the margins of chapters. These sidebars define important terms as well as give alternative explanations and embellishment. Nine new boxed presentations appear, mostly of an international nature, which add practical interest to various aspects of corporate finance. Three new cases are in this edition, and an existing case has been revised. In total there now are eight cases, covering major issues in financial analysis, valuation, and financing. Extensive references to the literature, many of which are new, appear at the end of each chapter.

By chapter, the important changes follow. In Chapter 1, a new vignette on Gillette appears, as do quotes on what companies say about their corporate objectives. The chapter has been streamlined. In Chapter 3, efficient markets are better explained. An improved treatment of the tax effect appears in Chapter 4, "Multivariable and Factor Valuation." In Chapter 6, the use of EBITDA in analyzing an acquisition candidate is presented. A number of changes appear in Chapters 8 and 9, which deal with required rates of return and capital structure. Such things as market value added, adjusting costs of capital, and the discipline of the capital markets on management appear. In Chapter 10, the EBIT/EPS breakeven analysis section has been redone.

Chapter 11, "Dividends and Share Repurchase: Theory and Practice," has been substantially revised. There is a new and extended treatment of share repurchase and its important and changing effect. The review of empirical evidence is largely redone, and there is an extended treatment of the managerial implications for dividends and share repurchase. Chapters 12 and 13, "Financial Ratio Analysis" and "Financial Planning," have been moved from the back of the book to precede chapters on working capital management and financing. Chapter 14 contains a new discussion of electronic funds transfers, and Chapter 15 has new sections dealing with credit scoring, outsourcing credit and collection procedures, and B2B exchanges for acquiring inventories in the overall management of the supply chain.

Chapter 16, "Liability Management and Short/Medium-Term Financing," consolidates and streamlines two previous chapters. In addition, there is new discussion of loan pricing. In Chapter 17, the section on inflation and interest rates has been redone. The tax treatment of lease financing has been changed in Chapter 18 to reflect the current situation. Also in this chapter, the lease versus buy/borrow example is completely redone. Finally, there is more emphasis on how changing tax rates and residual values affect the relative value of a lease contract. In Chapter 19, "Issuing Securities," there is a new section on SEC registration procedures and an entirely new treatment of venture capital and its role in financing the new enterprise.

The high-yield debt section in Chapter 20 has been extensively revised, in keeping with changing conditions. The bond refunding example in this chapter has been changed, and there is a revised treatment of private placements. Finally, there is a new section on the tax treatment of preferred-stock dividends and on tax-deductible preferred stock. Chapter 21, "Hybrid Financing through Equity-Linked Securities," is importantly changed. A major new section on more exotic securities used in corporate finance has been written, which includes PERCS, DECS, CEPPS, YEELDS, LYONs, and CEPS. In addition, the growth option as it relates to the value of a convertible security is explored, and there is a crisper treatment of the option value of the stock component. Chapter 22 contains an important new section on credit derivatives. Also in this chapter, the interest-rate swap example has been changed, and there is additional discussion of replacement risk.

The last three chapters of the book have been extensively revised as well. In Chapter 23, "Mergers and the Market for Corporate Control," new sections appear on control premiums and on valuation analyses to determine the worth of a prospective acquisition. There is a new treatment of anti-takeover amendments, with particular attention to the poison pill. Many new empirical studies on acquisitions are explored. In Chapter 24, the sections on spin-offs and on equity carve-outs have been largely rewritten. Also in this chapter, many changes have been made to the section on leveraged buyouts. With respect to distress restructuring, there is a new section on the role played by "vulture" capitalists. The last chapter of the book, "International Financial Management," has a new section on economic exposure to unexpected currency movements and how to analyze the direction and magnitude of the effect. There is a new treatment of currency forward and futures contracts. A new example of interest-rate parity and covered interest arbitrage appear in this chapter as well.

Although these are the important changes, all materials have been updated and there are a number of minor changes in presentation. Collectively, these should make the book more readable and interesting.

ANCILLARY MATERIALS

A number of materials supplement the main text. For the student, select end-of-chapter problems are set up in Excel format and are available from the Prentice Hall Web site: www.prenhall.com/financecenter. These problems are denoted by the computer symbol. In addition, each chapter, save for the first, contains self-correction problems. In a handful of chapters, reference is made to FinCoach exercises. This math practice software program is available for viewing and purchase at the PH Web site: www.prenhall.com/financecenter. A new Power Point feature will be available off the PH Web site. The presentation has been credited by Richard Gendreau, Bemidji State University, and can be accessed under student Resources. At the end of each chapter, I make reference to John Wachowicz's wonderful Web site: www.prenhall.com/wachowicz. He is a co-author of mine for another text, and his constantly revised site provides links to hundreds of financial management Web sites, grouped according to major subject areas. Extensive references to other literature also appear at the end of each chapter. Finally, Craig Holden, Indiana University, provides students with instructions for building financial models through his Spreadsheet Modeling book and CD series. Spreadsheet Modeling comes as a book and a browser-accessed CD-ROM that teaches students how to build financial models in Excel. This saleable product will be shrink-wrapped with the text or available on its own.

For the instructor, there is a comprehensive Instructor's Manual, which contains suggestions for organizing the course, solutions to all the problems that appear at the end of the chapters, and teaching notes for the cases. Also available in the Instructor's Manual are transparency masters of most of the figures in the text (these also are available through the aforementioned Prentice Hall Web site). Solutions to the Excel problems in the text are available on the Prentice Hall Web site under Instructor Resources. These Excel problems and solutions have been updated by Marbury Fagan, University of Richmond. Another aid is a Test-Item File of extensive questions and problems. This is available in both hard copy and custom computerized test bank format, revised by Sharon H. Garrison, University of Arizona, through your Prentice Hall sales representative.

The finance area is constantly changing. It is both stimulating and far reaching. I hope that *Financial Management and Policy,* 12th edition, imparts some of this excitement and contributes to a better understanding of corporate finance. If so, I will regard the book as successful.

JAMES C. VAN HORNE
Palo Alto, California

The author wishes to acknowledge the work of the following people in the creation of this book.

Dr. Gautam Vora	*University of New Mexico –*
	Anderson School of Management
Dr. Glenn L. Stevens	*Franklin and Marshall College*
Dr. Andrew L.H. Parkes	*East Central University*

Part I

FOUNDATIONS OF FINANCE

■ **VIGNETTE:** *Problems at Gillette*

Through most of the 1990s Gillette was a growth stock par excellence, attracting such legendary investors as Warren Buffett. From 1995 to 1998, share price increased threefold, compared with "only" a doubling of the Standard & Poor's 500 stock index. Its businesses were not high tech: razor blades and toiletries; stationery products (Parker, Waterman and Paper Mate pens and pencils); Braun electric shaver, toothbrush, hair dryer, and coffee maker lines; and Duracell batteries. The latter company was acquired by Gillette in 1996 for nearly $8 billion, a large sum in relation to profits and cash flow. Gillette seemed to be on a roll, and its expected growth resulted in a high ratio of share price to earnings—the P/E ratio. Management was acclaimed for its vision and efficiency in creating value for its shareholders. Products were distributed in over 200 countries. Gillette was consistently on the list of *Fortune*'s most admired companies.

But there were problems lurking beneath the surface. Profit margins and asset turnover were beginning to erode. Certain noncore product lines acquired in the past to diversify away from razor blades were not earning their economic keep. In 1999 profits declined by 12 percent from the prior year, the first time this had occurred in modern memory. The downward earnings trend continued in 2000, and share price declined by nearly 50 percent in a little over one year. To add insult to injury, Gillette was rumored to be vulnerable to a takeover bid by Colgate-Palmolive. Previously, Gillette had a market capitalization (share price multiplied by number of shares outstanding) of $70 billion, double that of Colgate-Palmolive. By mid-2000, however, the market capitalizations of the two companies were nearly the same. Once growth begins to falter, the effect on the present value of expected future earnings (share price) takes a real hit, and Gillette experienced the full brunt of this shift.

What to do? A reorientation to value creation was compelling. Management efficiency needed to occur as well as a restructuring to get back to core competence where returns could be earned in excess of what the financial markets required. A new CEO, Michael C. Hawley, was appointed in 1999. His efforts were directed to reducing bloated receivable and inventory positions, which were roughly $1 billion in excess of what reasonable turnover ratios would suggest. The stationery products division and the household products division were put up for sale. These divisions provided only meager profitability. Getting back to core competence meant a focus on razors and blades, associated grooming products, Braun oral care products, and Duracell batteries. The fruits of this redirection will not be apparent until 2001 and beyond.

Throughout this book, many of the themes as to value creation and asset management efficiency taken up in this vignette will be explored.

1

Goals and Functions of Finance

The modern-day financial manager is instrumental to a company's success. As cash flows pulsate through the organization, this individual is at the heart of what is happening. If finance is to play a general management role in the organization, the financial manager must be a team player who is constructively involved in operations, marketing, and the company's overall strategy. Where once the financial manager was charged only with such tasks as keeping records, preparing financial reports, managing the company's cash position, paying bills, and, on occasion, obtaining funds, the broad domain today includes (1) investment in as-

sets and new products and (2) determining the best mix of financing and dividends in relation to a company's overall valuation.

Investment of funds in assets and people determines the size of the firm, its profits from operations, its business risk, and its liquidity. Obtaining the best mix of financing and dividends determines the firm's financial charges and its financial risk; it also impacts its valuation. All of this demands a broad outlook and an alert creativity that will influence almost all facets of the enterprise.

Introductions are meant to be short and sweet, and so too will be this chapter. ■

CREATION OF VALUE

The objective of a company must be to create value for its shareholders. Value is represented by the market price of the company's common stock, which, in turn, is a function of the firm's investment, financing, and dividend decisions. The idea is to acquire assets and invest in new products and services where expected return exceeds their cost, to finance with those instruments where there is particular advantage, tax or otherwise, and to undertake a meaningful dividend policy for stockholders.

Throughout this book, the unifying theme is value creation. This occurs when you **do something for your shareholders that they cannot do for themselves.** It may be that a company enjoys a favorable niche in an attractive industry, and this permits it to earn returns in excess of what the financial markets require for the risk involved. Perhaps the financial manager is able to take advantage of imperfections in the financial markets and acquire capital on favorable terms. If the financial markets are highly efficient, as they are in many countries, we would expect the former to be a wider avenue for value creation than the latter. Most

Financial goal
is to maximize shareholder wealth.

3

shareholders are unable to develop products on their own, so value creation here certainly is possible. Contrast this with diversification, where investors are able to diversify the securities they hold. Therefore, diversification by a company is unlikely to create much, if any, value.

Profit Maximization versus Value Creation

Frequently, maximization of profits is regarded as the proper objective of the firm, but it is not as inclusive a goal as that of maximizing shareholder value. For one thing, total profits are not as important as earnings per share. Even maximization of earnings per share, however, is not fully appropriate because it does not take account of the timing or duration of expected returns. Moreover, earnings per share are based on accounting profits. Though these are certainly important, many feel that operating cash flows are what matter most.

Another shortcoming of the objective of maximizing earnings per share is that it does not consider the risk or uncertainty of the prospective earnings stream. Some investment projects are far more risky than others. As a result, the prospective stream of earnings per share would be more uncertain if these projects were undertaken. In addition, a company will be more or less risky depending on the amount of debt in relation to equity in its capital structure. This financial risk is another uncertainty in the minds of investors when they judge the firm in the marketplace. Finally, an earnings per share objective does not take into account any dividend the company might pay.

For the reasons given, an objective of maximizing earnings per share usually is not the same as maximizing market price per share. The market price of a firm's stock represents the value that market participants place on the company.

Agency Problems

The objectives of management may differ from those of the firm's stockholders. In a large corporation, the stock may be so widely held that stockholders cannot even make known their objectives, much less control or influence management. Often ownership and control are separate, a situation that allows management to act in its own best interests rather than those of the stockholders.

Agency costs
involve conflicts between stakeholders—equity holders, lenders, employees, suppliers, etc.

We may think of management as agents of the owners. Stockholders, hoping that the agents will act in the stockholders' best interests, delegate decision-making authority to them. Jensen and Meckling were the first to develop a comprehensive **agency theory** of the firm.[1] They show that the principals, in our case the stockholders, can assure themselves that the agent (management) will make optimal decisions only if appropriate incentives are given and only if the agent is monitored. Incentives include stock options, bonuses, and perquisites, and they are directly related to how close management decisions come to the interests of stockholders.

Monitoring can be done by bonding the agent, systematically reviewing management perquisites, auditing financial statements, and explicitly limiting management decisions. These monitoring activities necessarily involve costs, an

---

[1]Michael C. Jensen and William H. Meckling," Theory of the Firm: Managerial Behavior, Agency Costs and Ownership Structure," *Journal of Financial Economics*, 3 (October 1976), 305–60.

inevitable result of the separation of ownership and control of a corporation. The less the ownership percentage of the managers, the less the likelihood that they will behave in a manner consistent with maximizing shareholder wealth and the greater the need for outside stockholders to monitor their activities.

Agency problems also arise in creditors and equityholders having different objectives, thereby causing each party to want to monitor the others. Similarly, other stakeholders—employees, suppliers, customers, and communities—may have different agendas and may want to monitor the behavior of equityholders and management. Agency problems occur in investment, financing, and dividend decisions by a company, and we will discuss them throughout the book.

A Normative Goal

Share price embraces risk and expected return.

Because the principle of maximization of shareholder wealth provides a rational guide for running a business and for the efficient allocation of resources in society, we use it as our assumed objective in considering how financial decisions *should* be made. The purpose of capital markets is to allocate savings efficiently in an economy, from ultimate savers to ultimate users of funds who invest in real assets. If savings are to be channeled to the most promising investment opportunities, a rational economic criterion must govern their flow. By and large, the allocation of savings in an economy occurs on the basis of expected return and risk. The market value of a company's stock, embodying both of these factors, therefore reflects the market's trade-off between risk and return. If decisions are made in keeping with the likely effect on the market value of its stock, a firm will attract capital only when its investment opportunities justify the use of that capital in the overall economy. Any other objective is likely to result in the suboptimal allocation of funds and therefore lead to less than optimal capital formation and growth in the economy.

What Companies Say About Their Corporate Goal

"There is a partnership between the board and its executives that is truly focused on our prime purpose of building long-term shareowner wealth."
Source: Campbell Soup Company Annual Report.

"Our mission is to maximize share-owner value over time."
Source: The Coca-Cola Company Annual Report.

"Our key objective is to increase share-holder value."
Source: CSX Corporation Annual Report.

"That EquiFax brings value to every part of the equation is evident in the success we have recorded over the last century. This success has been driven by one overriding goal:

to create long-term value for our shareholders who have entrusted their capital to us. Our strategic plans, capital investments, acquisitions, new business initiatives, and compensation plans are all aimed at this goal. It is the force behind everything we do."
Source: EquiFax Annual Report.

"The Georgia-Pacific Group continues to focus on creating long-term shareholder value."
Source: Georgia-Pacific Corporation—Georgia-Pacific Group, Annual Report.

"Our ultimate goal is to continuously increase shareholder value over time."
Source: The Quaker Oats Company, Annual Report.

Social Responsibility   This is not to say that management should ignore social responsibility, such as protecting consumers, paying fair wages, maintaining fair hiring practices and safe working conditions, supporting education, and becoming actively involved in environmental issues like clean air and water. Stakeholders other than stockholders can no longer be ignored. These stakeholders include creditors, employees, customers, suppliers, communities in which a company operates, and others. The impact of decisions on them must be recognized. Many people feel that a company has no choice but to act in socially responsible ways; they argue that shareholder wealth and, perhaps, the corporation's very existence depend on its being socially responsible. Because criteria for social responsibility are not clearly defined, however, it is difficult to formulate a consistent objective. When society, acting through Congress and other representative bodies, establishes the rules governing the trade-off between social goals and economic efficiency, the task for the corporation is clearer. The company can be viewed as producing both private and social goods, and the maximization of shareholder wealth remains a viable corporate objective.

> **Social goals** and economic efficiency can work together to benefit multiple stakeholders.

Functions of Finance   The functions of finance involve three major decisions a company must make: the investment decision, the financing decision, and the dividend/share repurchase decision. Each must be considered in relation to our objective; an optimal combination of the three will create value.

INVESTMENT DECISION

The **investment decision** is the most important of the three decisions when it comes to the creation of value. Capital investment is the allocation of capital to investment proposals whose benefits are to be realized in the future. Because the future benefits are not known with certainty, investment proposals necessarily involve risk. Consequently, they should be evaluated in relation to their expected return and risk, for these are the factors that affect the firm's valuation in the marketplace. Included also under the investment decision is the decision to reallocate capital when an asset no longer economically justifies the capital committed to it. The investment decision, then, determines the total amount of assets held by the firm, the composition of these assets, and the business-risk complexion of the firm as perceived by suppliers of capital. The theoretical portion of this decision is taken up in Part II. Using an appropriate acceptance criterion, or required rate of return, is fundamental to the investment decision. Because of the paramount and integrative importance of this issue, we shall pay considerable attention to determining the appropriate required rate of return for an investment project, for a division of a company, for the company as a whole, and for a prospective acquisition.

> **Investments** in capital projects should provide expected returns in excess of what financial markets require.

In addition to selecting new investments, a company must manage existing assets efficiently. Financial managers have varying degrees of operating responsibility for existing assets; they are more concerned with the management of current assets than with fixed assets. In Part V we explore ways in which to manage current assets efficiently to maximize profitability relative to the amount of funds tied up in an asset. Determining a proper level of liquidity is very much a part of this management, and its determination should be in keeping with the company's overall valuation. Although financial managers have little or no operating responsibility for fixed assets and inventories, they are instrumental in allocating capital to these assets by virtue of their involvement in capital investment.

In Parts II and VII, we consider mergers and acquisitions from the standpoint of an investment decision. These external investment opportunities can be evaluated in the same general manner as an investment proposal that is generated internally. The market for corporate control is ever present in this regard, and this topic is taken up in Part VII. Growth in a company can be internal, external, or both, domestic, and international. Therefore, Part VII also considers growth through international operations. With the globalization of finance in recent years, this book places substantial emphasis on international aspects of financial decision making.

FINANCING DECISION

Capital structure involves determining the best mix of debt, equity, and hybrid securities to employ.

In the second major decision of the firm, the financing decision, the financial manager is concerned with determining the best financing mix or capital structure. If a company can change its total valuation by varying its capital structure, an optimal financing mix would exist, in which market price per share could be maximized. In Chapters 9 and 10 of Part III, we take up the financing decision in relation to the overall valuation of the company. Our concern is with exploring the implications of variation in capital structure on the valuation of the firm. In Chapter 16, we examine short- and intermediate-term financing. This is followed in Part VI with an investigation of the various methods of long-term financing. The emphasis is on not only certain valuation underpinnings but also the managerial aspects of financing, as we analyze the features, concepts, and problems associated with alternative methods.

Part VI also investigates the interface of the firm with the capital markets, the ever-changing environment in which financing decisions are made, and how a company can manage its financial risk through various hedging devices. In Part VII, corporate and distress restructuring are explored. Although aspects of restructuring fall across all three major decisions of the firm, this topic invariably involves financing, either new sources or a rearrangement of existing sources.

DIVIDEND/SHARE REPURCHASE DECISION

Excess cash can be distributed to stockholders directly through dividends or indirectly via share repurchase.

The third important decision of a company is the amount of cash to distribute to stockholders, which is examined in Chapter 11. There are two methods of distribution: cash dividends and share repurchase. Dividend policy includes the percentage of earnings paid to stockholders in cash dividends, the stability of absolute dividends about a trend, stock dividends, and stock splits. Share repurchase allows the distribution of a large amount of cash without tax consequence to those who choose to continue to hold their shares. The dividendpayout ratio and the number of shares repurchased determine the amount of earnings retained in a company and must be evaluated in light of the objective of maximizing shareholder wealth. The value, if any, of these actions to investors must be balanced against the opportunity cost of the retained earnings lost as a means of equity financing. Both dividends and share repurchases are important financial signals to the market, which continually tries to assess the future profitability and risk of a corporation with publicly traded stock.

BRINGING IT ALL TOGETHER

The purpose of this book is to enable readers to make sound investment, financing, and dividend/share repurchase decisions. Together, these decisions determine the value of a company to its shareholders. Moreover, they are interrelated. The decision to invest in a new capital project, for example, necessitates financing the investment. The financing decision, in turn, influences and is influenced by the dividend/share repurchase decision, for retained earnings used in internal financing represent dividends forgone by stockholders. With a proper conceptual framework, joint decisions that tend to be optimal can be reached. The main thing is that the financial manager relate each decision to its effect on the valuation of the firm.

Financial management endeavors to make optimal investment, financing and dividend/share repurchase decisions.

Because valuation concepts are basic to understanding financial management, these concepts are investigated in depth in Chapters 2 through 5. Thus, the first five chapters serve as the foundation for the subsequent development of the book. They introduce key concepts: the time value of money, market efficiency, risk–return trade-offs, valuation in a market portfolio context, and the valuation of relative financial claims using option pricing theory. These concepts will be applied in the remainder of the book.

In an endeavor to make optimal decisions, the financial manager makes use of certain analytical tools in the analysis, planning, and control activities of the firm. Financial analysis is a necessary condition, or prerequisite, for making sound financial decisions; we examine the tools of analysis in Part IV. One of the important roles of a chief financial officer is to provide accurate information on financial performance, and the tools taken up will be instrumental in this regard.

Questions

1. Why should a company concentrate primarily on wealth maximization instead of profit maximization?
2. "A basic rationale for the objective of maximizing the wealth position of the stockholder as a primary business goal is that such an objective may reflect the most efficient use of society's economic resources and thus lead to a maximization of society's economic wealth." Briefly evaluate this observation.
3. Beta-Max Corporation is considering two investment proposals. One involves the development of 10 discount record stores in Chicago. Each store is expected to provide an annual after-tax profit of $35,000 for 8 years, after which the lease will expire and the store will terminate. The other proposal involves a classical record of the month club. Here, the company will devote much effort to teaching the public to appreciate classical music. Management estimates that after-tax profits will be zero for 2 years, after which they will grow by $40,000 a year through year 10 and remain level thereafter. The life of the second project is 15 years. On the basis of this information, which project do you prefer? Why?
4. What are the major functions of the financial manager? What do these functions have in common?
5. Should the managers of a company own sizable amounts of stock in the company? What are the pros and cons?
6. In recent years, there have been a number of environmental, pollution, hiring, and other regulations imposed on businesses. In view of these changes, is maximization of shareholder wealth still a realistic objective?

7. As an investor, do you believe that some managers are paid too much? Do not their rewards come at your expense?

8. How does the notion of risk and reward govern the behavior of financial managers?

Selected References

ALLEN, FRANKLIN, and ANDREW WINSTON, "Corporate Financial Structure, Incentives and Optimal Contracting," in R. A. Jarrow, V. Maksimovic, and W. T. Ziemba, editors, *North-Holland Handbook of Operations Research and Management Science: Finance.* Amsterdam: North Holland, 1995, Chap. 22.

ANG, JAMES S., REBEL A. COLE, and JAMES WUH LIN, "Agency Costs and Ownership Structure," *Journal of Finance,* 55 (February 2000), 81–106.

BERNSTEIN, PETER L., *Capital Ideas.* New York: Free Press, 1992.

BRENNAN, MICHAEL J., "Corporate Finance over the Past 25 Years," *Financial Management,* 24 (Summer 1995), 9–22.

COCHRANE, JOHN H., "NEW FACTS IN FINANCE," working paper, *National Bureau of Economic Research* (June 1999).

DEMIRGUC-KUNT, ASLI, and VOJISLAV MAKSIMOVIC, "Law, Finance, and Firm Growth," *Journal of Finance,* 53 (December 1998), 2107–37.

HART, OLIVER, *Firms, Contracts and Financial Structure.* Oxford: Oxford University Press, 1995.

JENSEN, MICHAEL C., and WILLIAM H. MECKLING, "Theory of the Firm: Managerial Behavior, Agency Costs and Ownership Structure," *Journal of Financial Economics,* 3 (October 1976), 305–60.

MEGGINSON, WILLIAM L., *Corporate Finance Theory.* Reading, Mass.: Addison-Wesley, 1997.

MYERS, STEWART C., "Outside Equity," *Journal of Finance,* 55 (June 2000), 1005–38.

RAJAN, RAGHURAM, and LUIGI ZINGALES, "Financial Dependence and Growth," *American Economic Review,* 88 (June 1998), 559-87.

RAPPAPORT, ALFRED, *Creating Shareholder Value.* New York: Free Press, 1998.

TREYNOR, JACK L., "The Financial Objective in the Widely Held Corporation," *Financial Analysts Journal,* 37 (March–April 1981), 68–71.

ZINGALES, LUIGI, "In Search of New Foundations," Working paper, *National Bureau of Economic Research* (May 2000).

Wachowicz's Web World is an excellent overall Web site produced and maintained by my co-author of *Fundamentals of Financial Management,* John M. Wachowicz Jr. It contains descriptions of and links to many finance Web sites and articles. *www.prenhall.com/wachowicz.*

2

Concepts in Valuation

To make itself as valuable as possible to shareholders, a firm must choose the best combination of decisions on investment, financing, and dividends. If any of these decisions are part of your job, you will have a hand in shaping your company's *return–risk character* and your firm's value in the eyes of suppliers of capital. *Risk* can be defined as the possibility that the actual return will deviate from that which was expected. Expectations are continually revised on the basis of new information about the investment, financing, and dividend decisions of the firm. In other words, on the basis of information about these three decisions, investors formulate expectations as to the return and risk involved in holding a common stock.

Common stocks are going to be important in this chapter and the next two, as we study the valuation of financial market instruments. These are groundwork chapters on which we will later base our analyses of decisions on investment, financing, and dividends. We shall consider the expected return from a security and the risk of holding it. Assuming that investors are reasonably well diversified in their security holdings, we can ultimately value a firm; but first we must consider the time value of money and how to calculate the terminal value, the present value, and the internal rate of return from an investment. These considerations involve principles that we will use repeatedly throughout the book in valuing stocks, bonds, and other securities. ■

THE TIME VALUE OF MONEY

Now we look at one of the most important principles in all of finance, the relationship between $1 in the future and $1 today. For most of us, $1 in the future is less valuable. Moreover, $1 two years from now is less valuable than $1 one year from now. We will pay more for an investment that promises returns over years 1 to 5 than we will pay for an investment that promises identical returns for years 6 through 10. This relationship is known as **the time value of money**, and it permeates almost every nook and cranny of finance. Let us see what is involved.

Compound Interest and Terminal Values

The notion of compound interest is central to understanding the mathematics of finance. The term itself merely implies that interest paid on a loan or an investment is added to the principal. As a result, interest is earned on interest. This concept can be used to solve a class of problems illustrated in the following examples. To begin with, consider a person who has $100 in an account. If the interest rate is 8

percent compounded annually, how much will the $100 be worth at the end of a year? Setting up the problem, we solve for the terminal value (or future value as it is also known) of the account at the end of the year (TV_1):

$$TV_1 = \$100(1 + .08) = \$108$$

For an investment of 2 years, the $100 initial investment will become $108 at the end of the first year at 8 percent interest. Going to the end of the second year, $108 becomes $116.64, as $8 in interest is earned on the initial $100, and $.64 is earned on the $8 interest paid at the end of the first year. In other words, interest is earned on previously earned interest, hence the name *compound interest*. The terminal value at the end of the second year is $100 times 1.08 squared, or 1.1664. Thus,

$$TV_2 = \$100(1.08)^2 = \$116.64$$

At the end of 3 years, the person would have

$$TV_3 = \$100(1 + .08)^3 = \$125.97$$

Looked at in a different way, $100 grows to $108 at the end of the first year if the interest rate is 8 percent, and when we multiply this amount by 1.08 we obtain $116.64 at the end of the second year. Multiplying $116.64 by 1.08 we obtain $125.97 at the end of the third year.

Similarly, at the end of *n* years, the terminal value is

$$TV_n = X_o(1+r)^n \qquad (2\text{-}1)$$

where X_o is the amount invested at the beginning and r is the interest rate. A calculator makes the equation very simple to use, and one application is illustrated in the appendix to this chapter.

Interest on Interest   Table 2-1, showing the terminal values for our example problem at the end of years 1 through 10, illustrates the concept of interest being earned on interest. Equation (2-1) is our fundamental formula for calculating terminal values. Obviously, the greater the interest rate r and the greater the number of periods n, the greater the terminal value.

Although our concern has been with interest rates, the concept involved applies to compound growth of any sort. Suppose the earnings of a firm are $100,000 but we expect them to grow at a 10 percent compound rate. At the end of years 1 through 5 they will be as follows:

Compound interest means interest earned on interest.

Terminal value is the value at some future time of a present amount of money.

Year	Growth Factor	Expected Earnings
1	1.10	$110,000
2	$(1.10)^2$	121,000
3	$(1.10)^3$	133,100
4	$(1.10)^4$	146,410
5	$(1.10)^5$	161,051

TABLE 2-1
Illustration of Compound Interest with $100 Initial Investment and 8 Percent Interest

Period	Beginning Value	Interest Earned During Period (8 Percent of Beginning Value)	Terminal Value
1	$100.00	$ 8.00	$108.00
2	108.00	8.64	116.64
3	116.64	9.33	125.97
4	125.97	10.08	136.05
5	136.05	10.88	146.93
6	146.93	11.76	158.69
7	158.69	12.69	171.38
8	171.38	13.71	185.09
9	185.09	14.81	199.90
10	199.90	15.99	215.89

Similarly, we can determine the level at the end of so many years for other problems involving compound growth. The principle is particularly important when we consider certain valuation models for common stock, as we will do later in this chapter.

Tables of Terminal Values Using Eq. (2-1), we can derive tables of terminal values (also known as future values). Table 2-2 is an example showing interest rates of 1 to 15 percent. In the 8 percent column, note that the terminal values shown for $1 invested at this compound rate correspond to our calculations for $100 in Table 2-1. Notice, too, that in rows tabulating two or more years, the proportional increase in terminal value becomes greater as the interest rate rises. This heightened growth is impressive when we look a century ahead. A dollar invested today will be worth only $2.70 if the interest rate is 1 percent, but it will fatten to $1,174,313 if the interest rate is 15 percent. Behold (or let your heirs behold) the wonders of compound interest.

Compounding More Than Once a Year

Up to now, we have assumed that interest is paid annually. Although this assumption is easiest to work with, we consider now the relationship between terminal value and interest rates for different periods of compounding. To begin, suppose interest is paid semiannually and $100 is deposited in an account at 8 percent. This means that for the first 6 months the return is one half of 8 percent, or 4 percent. Thus, the terminal value at the end of 6 months will be

$$TV_{1/2} = \$100\left(1 + \frac{.08}{2}\right) = \$104.00$$

TABLE 2-2
Terminal Value of $1 at the End of N Years

Year	1%	2%	3%	4%	5%	6%
1	1.0100	1.0200	1.0300	1.0400	1.0500	1.0600
2	1.0201	1.0404	1.0609	1.0816	1.1025	1.1236
3	1.0303	1.0612	1.0927	1.1249	1.1576	1.1910
4	1.0406	1.0824	1.1255	1.1699	1.2155	1.2625
5	1.0510	1.1041	1.1593	1.2167	1.2763	1.3382
6	1.0615	1.1262	1.1941	1.2653	1.3401	1.4185
7	1.0721	1.1487	1.2299	1.3159	1.4071	1.5036
8	1.0829	1.1717	1.2668	1.3686	1.4775	1.5938
9	1.0937	1.1951	1.3048	1.4233	1.5513	1.6895
10	1.1046	1.2190	1.3439	1.4802	1.6289	1.7908
11	1.1157	1.2434	1.3842	1.5395	1.7103	1.8983
12	1.1268	1.2682	1.4258	1.6010	1.7959	2.0122
13	1.1381	1.2936	1.4685	1.6651	1.8856	2.1329
14	1.1495	1.3195	1.5126	1.7317	1.9799	2.2609
15	1.1610	1.3459	1.5580	1.8009	2.0789	2.3966
20	1.2202	1.4859	1.8061	2.1911	2.6533	3.2071
25	1.2824	1.6406	2.0938	2.6658	3.3864	4.2919
50	1.6446	2.6916	4.3839	7.1067	11.4674	18.4201
100	2.7048	7.2446	19.2186	50.5049	131.5010	339.3014

and at the end of a year it will be

More compounding in a year results in a higher terminal value.

$$TV_1 = \$100\left(1 + \frac{.08}{2}\right)^2 = \$108.16$$

This amount compares with $108.00 if interest were paid only once a year. The $.16 difference is attributable to the fact that during the second 6 months, interest is earned on the $4.00 in interest paid at the end of the first 6 months. The more times during a year that interest is paid, the greater the terminal value at the end of a given year.

The general formula for solving for the terminal value at the end of year n where interest is paid m times a year is

$$TV_n = X_0\left(1 + \frac{r}{m}\right)^{mn} \tag{2-2}$$

Quarterly Compounding   To illustrate, suppose that in our previous example interest were paid quarterly and that we wished again to know the terminal value at the end of 1 year. It would be

$$TV_1 = \$100\left(1 + \frac{.08}{4}\right)^4 = \$108.24$$

7%	8%	9%	10%	12%	15%
1.0700	1.0800	1.0900	1.1000	1.1200	1.1500
1.1449	1.1664	1.1881	1.2100	1.2544	1.3225
1.2250	1.2597	1.2950	1.3310	1.4049	1.5209
1.3108	1.3605	1.4116	1.4641	1.5735	1.7490
1.4026	1.4693	1.5386	1.6105	1.7623	2.0114
1.5007	1.5869	1.6771	1.7716	1.9738	2.3311
1.6058	1.7138	1.8280	1.9487	2.2107	2.6600
1.7182	1.8509	1.9926	2.1436	2.4760	3.0590
1.8385	1.9990	2.1719	2.3579	2.7731	3.5179
1.9672	2.1589	2.3674	2.5937	3.1058	4.0456
2.1049	2.3316	2.5804	2.8531	3.4785	4.6524
2.2522	2.5182	2.8127	3.1384	3.8960	5.3503
2.4098	2.7196	3.0658	3.4523	4.3635	6.1528
2.5785	2.9372	3.3417	3.7975	4.8871	7.0757
2.7590	3.1722	3.6425	4.1772	5.4736	8.1371
3.8697	4.6610	5.6044	6.7275	9.6463	16.3665
5.4274	6.8485	8.6231	10.8347	17.0001	32.9190
29.4570	46.9016	74.3575	117.3907	289.0022	1,083.6574
867.7149	2,199.7569	5,529.0304	13,780.5890	83,522.2657	1,174,313.4510

which, of course, is higher than it would have been with semiannual or annual compounding.

The terminal value at the end of 3 years for the example with quarterly interest payments is

$$TV_3 = \$100 \left(1 + \frac{.08}{4}\right)^{12} = \$126.82$$

compared to a terminal value with semiannual compounding of

$$TV_3 = \$100 \left(1 + \frac{.08}{2}\right)^{6} = \$126.53$$

and with annual compounding of

$$TV_3 = \$100 \left(1 + \frac{.08}{1}\right)^{3} = \$125.97$$

The greater the number of years, the greater the difference in terminal values arrived at by two different methods of compounding.

Infinite Compounding As m approaches infinity, the term $(1 + r/m)^{mn}$ approaches e^{rn}, where e is approximately 2.71828 and is defined as

$$e = \lim_{m \to \infty} \left(1 + \frac{1}{m}\right)^m \tag{2-3}$$

with ∞ being the sign for infinity. To see that e approaches 2.71828 as m increases, simply increase m in expression (2-3) from, say, 5 to 10 to 100 and solve for e. The terminal value at the end of n years of an initial deposit of X_0 where interest is compounded continuously at a rate of r is

$$TV_n = X_0 e^{rn} \tag{2-4}$$

For our example problem, the terminal value at the end of 3 years would be

$$TV_3 = \$100(2.71828)^{(.08)(3)} = \$127.12$$

This compares to terminal values with annual, semiannual, quarterly, and monthly compounding of \$125.97, \$126.53, \$126.82, and \$127.02, respectively. Thus, continuous compounding results in the maximum possible terminal value at the end of n periods for a given rate of interest. As m is increased in Eq. (2-2), the terminal value increases at a decreasing rate until ultimately it approaches the terminal value achieved with continuous compounding. Again these problems can easily be solved using a calculator with the proper power function.

PRESENT VALUES

Present value is a future amount discounted to the present by some required rate.

Not all of us live by the credit card alone; some like to save now and buy later. For a \$700 purchase 1 year from now, how much will you have to put aside in an institution paying 8 percent on 1-year deposits? If we let A_1 represent the amount of money you wish to have 1 year from now, PV the amount saved, and k the annual interest rate, we have

$$A_1 = PV(1 + k) \tag{2-5}$$

For our example problem, this becomes

$$\$700 = PV(1.08)$$

Solving for PV, we obtain

$$PV = \frac{\$700}{1.08} = \$648.15$$

Deposit \$648.15 today and take home \$700 1 year hence. Stated another way, \$648.15 is the **present value** of \$700 to be received at the end of 1 year when the interest rate involved is 8 percent.

Beyond One Period

The present value of a sum to be received 2 years from now is

$$PV = \frac{A_2}{(1 + k)^2} \qquad (2\text{-}6)$$

which, for our example problem, would be

$$PV = \frac{\$700}{(1.08)^2} = \frac{\$700}{1.1664} = \$600.14$$

Thus, $700 two years from now has a lower present value than $700 one year from now. That is the whole idea of the time value of money.

In solving present-value problems, it is useful to express the interest factor separately from the amount to be received in the future. For example, our problem can be expressed as

$$PV = \$700 \left[\frac{1}{(1.08)^2} \right] = \$600.14$$

In this way, we are able to isolate the interest factor, and this isolation facilitates present-value calculations. In such calculations, the interest rate is known as the discount rate, and henceforth, we will refer to it as such.

So far we have considered present-value calculations for amounts of money to be received only 1 and 2 years in the future; however, the principles are the same for amounts to be received further in the future. The present value of $1 to be received at the end of *n* years is

$$PV = \frac{\$1}{(1 + k)^n} \qquad (2\text{-}7)$$

The present value of $1 to be received 5 years from now, when the discount rate is 10 percent, is

$$\$1 \left[\frac{1}{(1.10)^5} \right] = \$.62092$$

The dollar we shall get 5 years from now is worth approximately 62 cents today if the discount rate is 10 percent.

If we had an uneven series of cash flows—$1 one year hence, $3 two years hence, and $2 three years from now—we would set up our calculator to solve the following equation assuming a discount rate of 10 percent:

$$PV = \frac{\$1}{1.10} + \frac{\$3}{(1.10)^2} + \frac{\$2}{(1.10)^3} = \$4.89$$

For other problems of this sort we can set up our calculator or computer to solve for present values quickly.

Present Value of an Annuity

A series of even cash flows is known as an annuity. Suppose $1 is to be received at the end of each of the next 3 years. The calculation of the present value of this stream, using a 10 percent discount rate, is

An annuity

is an even series of future cash flows.

$$
\begin{array}{ll}
PV \text{ of } \$1 \text{ to be received in 1 year} & = \$\ .90909 \\
PV \text{ of } \$1 \text{ to be received in 2 years} = & .82645 \\
PV \text{ of } \$1 \text{ to be received in 3 years} = & \underline{.75131} \\
\text{Present value of series} & = \$2.48685
\end{array}
$$

With an even series of future cash flows, it is unnecessary to go through these calculations. The discount factor, 2.48685, can be applied directly. Simply multiply $1 by 2.48685 to obtain $2.48685.

Present-value tables for even series of cash flows allow us to look up the appropriate compound discount factor (see Table B at the back of the book). We note that the discount factor for an even series of cash flows for 3 years, using a 10 percent discount rate, is 2.4868, as we calculated. Thus, for an even series of cash flows, we simply multiply the appropriate discount factor by the cash flow. If the discount rate is 8 percent and a $5 cash flow is to be received at the end of each year during the next 4 years, we multiply

$$\$5(3.3121) = \$16.56$$

Using such a table enables us to quickly determine the value of an annuity, sometimes quicker than we can with a calculator or computer.

Relationship between *PV* and *k*   We know that the higher the discount rate, the lower the present value. However, the relationship is not linear. Rather, the present value of an amount of money to be received in the future decreases at a decreasing rate as the discount rate increases. The relationship is illustrated in Fig. 2-1. At a zero rate of discount, the present value of $1 to be received in the future is $1. In other words, there is no time value of money. As the discount rate increases, however, the present value declines but at a decreasing rate. As the discount rate approaches infinity, the present value of the future $1 approaches zero.

FIGURE 2-1

Relationship between present value and the discount rate

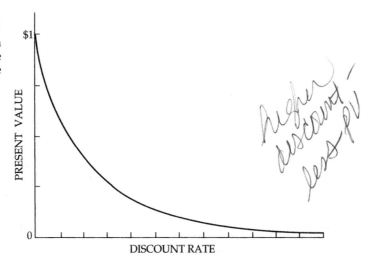

Value decreases as the required return increases, but at a decreasing rate.

With most calculators, it is possible to solve for present and terminal values, either directly or indirectly. The more sophisticated calculators have built-in functions, so one can solve directly; otherwise, one must make calculations for each cash flow and store them in memory. In addition to calculators, computer-based spreadsheet programs have present- and terminal-value functions built in that allow solution of the numbers inputted.

Amortizing a Loan

An important use of present-value concepts is in determining the payments required under an installment type of loan. Installment payments are prevalent in mortgage loans, auto loans, consumer loans, and certain business loans. The distinguishing feature is that the loan is repaid in equal periodic payments that embody both interest and principal. These payments can be made monthly, quarterly, semiannually, or annually.

To illustrate with the simplest case of annual payments, suppose you borrow $22,000 at 12 percent to be repaid over the next 6 years. Equal installment payments are required at the end of each year, and these payments must be sufficient in amount to repay the $22,000 together with providing the lender a 12 percent return. To determine the amount of payment, we set up the problem as follows:

$$\$22,000 = \sum_{t=1}^{6} \frac{x}{(1.12)^t} \tag{2-8}$$

Amortization is the reduction of a loan's principal amount through equal payments, which embrace both interest and principal.

Looking in Table B at the back of the book, we find that the discount factor for a 6-year annuity with a 12 percent discount rate is 4.1114. Solving for x in Eq. (2-8), we have

$$\$22,000 = 4.1114x$$

$$x = \frac{\$22,000}{4.1114} = \$5,351$$

Thus, annual payments of $5,351 will completely amortize a $22,000 loan in 6 years. Each payment consists partly of interest and partly of principal repayment. The amortization schedule is shown in Table 2-3. We see that annual interest is determined by multiplying the principal amount outstanding at the beginning of the year by 12 percent. The amount of principal payment is simply the total installment payment minus the interest payment. Notice that the proportion of the installment payment composed of interest declines over time, whereas the proportion composed of principal increases. At the end of 6 years, a total of $22,000 in principal payments will have been made and the loan will be completely amortized. Later in the book, we derive amortization schedules for loans of this type. The breakdown between interest and principal is important because only the former is deductible as an expense for tax purposes. Spreadsheet programming can be used to set up an amortization schedule of the sort illustrated in Table 2-3, and Excel and Lotus have embedded programs that enable you to do so easily.

Present Value When Interest Is Compounded More Than Once a Year

When interest is compounded more than once a year, the formula for calculating present values must be revised along the same lines as for the calculation of termi-

TABLE 2-3
Amortization Schedule for Illustrated Loan

End of Year	(1) Installment Payment	(2) Principal Amount Owing at Year End	(3) Annual Interest $(2)_{t-1} \times .12$	(4) Principal Payment (1)–(3)
0	—	$22,000	—	—
1	$ 5,351	19,289	$ 2,640	$ 2,711
2	5,351	16,253	2,315	3,036
3	5,351	12,853	1,951	3,400
4	5,351	9,044	1,542	3,809
5	5,351	4,778	1,085	4,266
6	5,351	0	573	4,778
	$32,106		$10,106	$22,000

nal value. Instead of dividing the future cash flow by $(1 + k)^n$ as we do when annual compounding is involved, the present value is determined by

$$PV = \frac{A_n}{\left(1 + \dfrac{k}{m}\right)^{mn}}$$ (2-9)

where, as before, A_n is the cash flow at the end of year n, m is the number of times a year interest is compounded, and k is the discount rate. The present value of $100 to be received at the end of year 3, the discount rate being 10 percent compounded quarterly, is

$$PV = \frac{\$100}{\left(1 + \dfrac{.10}{4}\right)^{(4)(3)}} = \$74.36$$

The present value of $100 at the end of 1 year with a discount rate of 100 percent compounded monthly is

$$PV = \frac{\$100}{\left(1 + \dfrac{1}{12}\right)^{12}} = \$38.27$$

Continuous Compounding When interest is compounded continuously, the present value of a cash flow at the end of the year n is

$$PV = \frac{A_n}{e^{rn}}$$ (2-10)

where e is approximately 2.71828. The present value of $100 to be received at the end of 3 years with a discount rate of 10 percent compounded continuously is

$$PV = \frac{\$100}{2.71828^{(.10)(3)}} = \$74.08$$

More compounding
in a year results in a
lower present value.

On the other hand, if the discount rate is compounded only annually, we have

$$PV = \frac{\$100}{1.10^3} = \$75.13$$

Thus, the fewer times a year the discount rate is compounded, the greater the present value. This relationship is just the opposite of that for terminal values. To illustrate the relationship between present value and the number of times a year the discount rate is compounded, consider again our example involving $100 to be received at the end of 3 years with a discount rate of 10 percent. The following present values result from various compounding intervals.[1]

Compounding	Present Value
Annually	$75.13
Semiannually	74.62
Quarterly	74.36
Monthly	74.17
Continuously	74.08

We see that the present value decreases but at a decreasing rate as the compounding interval shortens, the limit being continuous compounding.

INTERNAL RATE OF RETURN OR YIELD

The internal rate of return or yield for an investment is the discount rate that equates the present value of the expected cash outflows with the present value of the expected inflows. Mathematically, it is represented by that rate, r, such that

$$\sum_{t=0}^{n} \left[\frac{A_t}{(1+r)^t} \right] = 0 \qquad (2\text{-}11)$$

where A_t is the cash flow for period t, whether it be a net cash outflow or inflow, n is the last period in which a cash flow is expected, and Σ denotes the sum of discounted cash flows at the end of periods 0 through n. If the initial cash outlay or cost occurs at time 0, Eq. (2-11) can be expressed as

$$A_0 = \frac{A_1}{1+r} + \frac{A_2}{(1+r)^2} + \cdots + \frac{A_n}{(1+r)^n} \qquad (2\text{-}12)$$

---

[1] For semiannual compounding, m is 2 in Eq. (2-9) and mn is 6. With monthly compounding, m is 12 and mn is 36.

Thus, r is the rate that discounts the stream of future cash flows (A_1 through A_n) to equal the initial outlay at time 0—A_0. We implicitly assume that the cash inflows received from the investment are reinvested to realize the same rate of return as r. More will be said about this assumption in Chapter 6, but keep it in mind.

Illustration

To illustrate the use of Eq. (2-12), suppose we have an investment opportunity that calls for a cash outlay at time 0 of $18,000 and is expected to provide cash inflows of $5,600 at the end of each of the next 5 years. The problem can be expressed as

$$\$18,000 = \frac{\$5,600}{1 + r} + \frac{\$5,600}{(1 + r)^2} + \frac{\$5,600}{(1 + r)^3} + \frac{\$5,600}{(1 + r)^4} + \frac{\$5,600}{(1 + r)^5} \qquad (2\text{-}13)$$

Solving for the internal rate of return, r, usually can be done with a calculator or a computer program, such as Excel or Lotus, that has embedded in it an IRR function. Without such a feature, you have to go through a more laborious manual process. To illustrate this approach, suppose we start with three discount rates— 14 percent, 16 percent, and 18 percent—and calculate the present value of the cash-flow stream. Using the different discount factors shown in Table B at the back of the book, we find

Discount Rate	Discount Factor	Cash Flow Each Year	Present Value of Stream
18%	3.1272	$5,600	$17,512.32
16	3.2743	5,600	18,336.08
14	3.4331	5,600	19,225.36

When we compare the present value of the stream with the initial outlay of $18,000, we see that the internal rate of return necessary to discount the stream to $18,000 falls between 16 and 18 percent, being closer to 16 percent than to 18 percent. To approximate the actual rate, we interpolate between 16 and 17 percent as follows:

	Discount Rate	Present Value
	16%	$18,336.08
	17	17,916.08
Difference	1%	$ 420.00

$$\frac{336.08}{420.00} = .80 \qquad 16\% + .80\% = 16.8\%$$

Thus, the internal rate of return necessary to equate the present value of the cash inflows with the present value of the outflows is approximately 16.8 percent. Interpolation gives only an approximation of the exact percent; the relationship between the two discount rates is not linear with respect to present value.

In Chapter 6 we compare the present-value and internal-rate-of-return methods for determining investment worth and go deeper into the subject. With what we have learned so far, we are able to proceed with our examination of the valuation of financial instruments.

BOND RETURNS

The first instrument to consider is a bond. It calls for a stated amount of money to be paid to the investor either at a single future date, maturity, or at a series of future dates, including final maturity. The first situation is a pure discount bond, or zero coupon bond as it is known, whereas the second corresponds to a coupon bond. In what follows, we present the rudiments of bond valuation. A detailed exposition is found in a supplementary text.[2]

Pure Discount (Zero Coupon) Bonds

A pure discount bond is one where the issuer promises to make a single payment at a specified future date. This single payment is the same as the *face value* of the instrument, usually expressed as $100.[3] The present value of a zero coupon bond is

$$P = \frac{\$100}{\left(1 + \dfrac{r}{2}\right)^{2n}} \tag{2-14}$$

where P is the present market price of the bond, $100 is its face value, r is the yield to maturity, and n is the maturity. The yield is simply the internal rate of return discussed earlier. The normal pricing convention is to use semiannual compounding as shown, as opposed to annual compounding. As with solving for present values illustrated earlier, one can solve such an equation easily with most calculators.

Suppose Betatron Corporation issued a zero coupon bond with a face value of $100 and a maturity of 10 years and that the yield to maturity is 12 percent. This implies a market price of

A bond's price is the present value of future coupon payments and face value, discounted by the bond's yield.

$$P = \frac{\$100}{(1.06)^{20}} = \$31.18$$

The investor puts up $31.18 today for the promise to receive $100 in 10 years. The return of 12 percent compounded semiannually is embraced in the discount from face value—$31.18 versus $100 10 years hence.

---

[2]James C. Van Horne, *Financial Market Rates and Flows*, 6th ed. (Upper Saddle River, NJ: Prentice Hall, 2001).

[3]The actual face value of virtually all bonds is $1,000 per bond. However, the pricing convention is in terms of $100.

If the price were $35 and we wished to solve for the yield, we would set up the problem as follows:

$$\$35 = \frac{\$100}{\left(1 + \dfrac{r}{2}\right)^{20}}$$

We then solve for the rate of discount that equates $35 today with $100 twenty periods hence. This is done in the same manner as illustrated for internal-rate-of-return calculations. When we do so, we find this rate to be 5.39 percent. Doubling this percent to put things on an annual basis, the yield to maturity is 10.78 percent. The lesser discount from face value, $35 versus $31.18 in our earlier example, results in a lower yield.

Bond yield

is simply a bond's internal rate of return.

Coupon Bonds

Most bonds are not of a pure discount variety, but rather pay a semiannual interest payment along with a final principal payment of $100 at maturity. To determine the return here, we solve the following equation for r, the yield to maturity:

$$P = \frac{C/2}{\left(1 + \dfrac{r}{2}\right)} + \frac{C/2}{\left(1 + \dfrac{r}{2}\right)^2} + \cdots + \frac{C/2}{\left(1 + \dfrac{r}{2}\right)^{2n}} + \frac{\$100}{\left(1 + \dfrac{r}{2}\right)^{2n}} \tag{2-15}$$

where P is the present market price of the bond, C is the annual coupon payment, and n is the number of years to maturity.

To illustrate, if the 8 percent coupon bonds of UB Corporation have 13 years to maturity and the current market price is $96 per bond, Eq. (2-15) becomes

$$\$96 = \frac{\$4}{\left(1 + \dfrac{r}{2}\right)} + \frac{\$4}{\left(1 + \dfrac{r}{2}\right)^2} + \cdots + \frac{\$4}{\left(1 + \dfrac{r}{2}\right)^{26}} + \frac{\$100}{\left(1 + \dfrac{r}{2}\right)^{26}}$$

When we solve for r, we find the yield to maturity of the bond to be 8.51 percent.

Given any three of the following four factors—coupon rate, final maturity, market price, and yield to maturity—we are able to solve for the fourth. Fortunately, elaborate bond value tables are available, so we need not go through the calculations. These tables are constructed in exactly the same manner as present-value tables. The only difference is that they take account of the coupon rate and of the fact that the face value of the bond will be paid at the final maturity date.

Relationship between Price and Yield   Were the market price $105, so that the bond traded at a premium instead of at a discount, the yield to maturity—substituting $105 for $96 in the equation—would be 7.39 percent. On the basis of these calculations, several observations are in order:

1. When a bond's market price is less than its face value of $100 so that it sells at a **discount**, the yield to maturity exceeds the coupon rate.
2. When a bond sells at a **premium**, its yield to maturity is less than the coupon rate.
3. When the market price equals the face value, the yield to maturity equals the coupon rate.

Holding-Period Return   The yield to maturity, as calculated above, may differ from the holding-period yield if the security is sold prior to maturity. The holding-period yield is the rate of discount that equates the present value of interest payments, plus the present value of terminal value at the end of the holding period, with the price paid for the bond. For example, suppose the above bond were bought for $105, but interest rates subsequently increased. Two years later the bond has a market price of $94, at which time it is sold. The holding-period return is

$$\$105 = \frac{\$4}{\left(1 + \dfrac{r}{2}\right)} + \frac{\$4}{\left(1 + \dfrac{r}{2}\right)^2} + \frac{\$4}{\left(1 + \dfrac{r}{2}\right)^3} + \frac{\$4}{\left(1 + \dfrac{r}{2}\right)^4} + \frac{\$94}{\left(1 + \dfrac{r}{2}\right)^4}$$

Here r is found to be 2.48 percent. While the bond originally had a yield to maturity of 7.39 percent, the subsequent rise in interest rates resulted in its being sold at a loss. Although the coupon payments more than offset the loss, the holding-period yield was low.

Perpetuities

It is conceivable that we might be confronted with an investment opportunity that, for all practical purposes, is a perpetuity. With a perpetuity, a fixed cash inflow is expected at equal intervals forever. The British consol, a bond with no maturity date, carries the obligation of the British government to pay a fixed coupon perpetually. If the investment required an initial cash outflow at time 0 of A_0 and were expected to pay A^* at the end of each year forever, its yield is the discount rate, r, that equates the present value of all future cash inflows with the present value of the initial cash outflow

A perpetuity involves periodic cash inflows of an equal amount forever.

$$A_0 = \frac{A^*}{1 + r} + \frac{A^*}{(1 + r)^2} + \cdots + \frac{A^*}{(1 + r)^n} \qquad (2\text{-}16)$$

In the case of a bond, A_0 is the market price of the bond and A^* the fixed annual interest payment. When we multiply both sides of Eq. (2-16) by $(1 + r)$, we obtain

$$A_0(1 + r) = A^* + \frac{A^*}{1 + r} + \frac{A^*}{(1 + r)^2} + \cdots + \frac{A^*}{(1 + r)^{n-1}} \qquad (2\text{-}17)$$

Subtracting Eq. (2-16) from Eq. (2-17), we get

$$A_0(1 + r) - A_0 = A^* - \frac{A^*}{(1 + r)^n} \qquad (2\text{-}18)$$

As n approaches infinity, $A^*/(1 + r)^n$ approaches 0. Thus

$$A_0 r = A^* \qquad (2\text{-}19)$$

and

$$r = \frac{A^*}{A_0} \qquad (2\text{-}20)$$

Here r is the yield on a perpetual investment costing A_0 at time 0 and paying A^* at the end of each year forever. Suppose that for $100 we could buy a security that was expected to pay $12 a year forever. The yield of the security would be

$$r = \frac{\$12}{\$100} = 12\%$$

Another example of a perpetuity is a preferred stock. Here a company promises to pay a stated dividend forever. (See Chapter 20 for the features of preferred stock.) If Zeebok Shoes Inc. had a 9 percent, $50 face value preferred stock outstanding and the appropriate yield in today's market were 10 percent, its value per share would be

$$A_0 = \frac{\$4.50}{.10} = \$45$$

This is known as capitalizing the $4.50 dividend at a 10 percent rate.

Duration of Debt Instrument

Instead of maturity, bond investors and portfolio managers frequently use the duration of the instrument as a measure of the average time to the various coupon and principal payments. More formally, duration is

$$D = \sum_{t=1}^{n} \frac{C_t \times t}{(1 + r)^t} \bigg/ P$$

where

C_t = interest and/or principal payment at time t
t = length of time to that payment
n = length of time to final maturity
r = yield to maturity
P = value or market price of the bond

Suppose a 9 percent bond with 4 years to maturity paid interest annually. Its yield to maturity is 10 percent and its market value is $96.83 per bond. The duration of the instrument is

$$D = \frac{\dfrac{\$9 \times 1}{1.10} + \dfrac{\$9 \times 2}{(1.10)^2} + \dfrac{\$9 \times 3}{(1.10)^3} + \dfrac{\$109 \times 4}{(1.10)^4}}{\$96.83}$$

$$= 3.52 \text{ years}$$

This represents the weighted average time to the interest and principal payments. Notice in the formula that the higher the coupon rate, the less the duration, all other things the same.

This is merely to say that more of the total return is received early on as opposed to what would be the case with a low coupon bond. For a zero coupon, there is but one payment at maturity, and the duration of the bond equals its maturity. For coupon bonds, duration is less than maturity.*

One of the reasons that duration is widely used in the investment community is that the volatility of a bond's price is related to it. Under certain idealized circumstances (which we will not probe), the percentage change in price is proportional to duration times the percentage change in 1 plus the yield:

$$\frac{\Delta P}{P} = -D \frac{\Delta r}{1 + r}$$

Suppose in our example interest rates increased from 10 percent to 11.1 percent. This corresponds to a 1 percent increase in $1 + r$, as 1.10 goes to 1.111. The predicted change in price would be

$$-3.52 \frac{.011}{1.10} = -.0352$$

In other words, the price of the bond would be expected to decline by 3.52 percent.

---

*Duration tends to increase at a decreasing rate with maturity, but there can be peculiarities in the case of discount bonds of long maturity. For a detailed analysis of duration and maturity, see Van Horne, *Financial Market Rates and Flows*.

RETURN FROM A STOCK INVESTMENT

The common stockholders of a corporation are its residual owners; their claim to income and assets comes after creditors and preferred stockholders have been paid in full. As a result, a stockholder's return on investment is less certain than the return to a lender or to a preferred stockholder. On the other hand, the return to a common stockholder is not bounded on the upside as are returns to the others.

Some Features of Common Stock

The corporate charter of a company specifies the number of **authorized** shares of common stock, the maximum that the company can issue without amending its charter. Although amending the charter is not a difficult procedure, it does require the approval of existing stockholders, which takes time. For this reason, a company usually likes to have a certain number of shares that are authorized but unissued. When authorized shares of common stock are sold, they become *issued* stock. **Outstanding** stock is the number of shares issued and actually held by the public; the corporation can buy back part of its issued stock and hold it as **Treasury stock.**

A share of common stock can be authorized either with or without **par value**. The par value of a stock is merely a stated figure in the corporate charter and is of little economic significance. A company should not issue stock at a price less than par value, because stockholders who bought stock for less than par would be liable to creditors for the difference between the below-par price they paid and the par value. Consequently, the par values of most stocks are set at fairly low figures relative to their market values. Suppose a company sold 10,000 shares of new common stock at $45 a share and the par value of the stock was $5 per share. The equity portion of the balance sheet would be

Common stock ($5 par value)	$ 50,000
Additional paid-in capital	400,000
Shareholders' equity	$450,000

The **book value** of a share of stock is the shareholders' equity of a corporation less the par value of preferred stock outstanding divided by the number of shares outstanding. Suppose in the case above the company is now 1 year old and has generated $80,000 in after-tax profit but pays no dividend. Shareholders' equity is now $450,000 + $80,000 = $530,000, and book value per share is $530,000/10,000 = $53.

Although one might expect the book value of a share of stock to correspond to the liquidating value (per share) of the company, frequently it does not. Often assets are sold for less than their book values, particularly when liquidating costs are involved. In some cases certain assets—notably land and mineral rights—have book values that are modest in relation to their market values. For the company involved, liquidating value may be higher than book value. Thus, book value may not correspond to liquidating value, and, as we shall see, it often does not correspond to market value. What, then, determines market value?

Return on Investment

When people buy common stock, they give up current consumption in the hope of attaining increased future consumption. They expect to collect dividends and eventually sell the stock at a profit. But this is only one part of a lifetime of consumption, and wealth has to be allocated accordingly. A colleague of mine once remarked that he'd like to use his money in such a way that it would be completely spent when he died. If the person could know how long he was going to live, he could apportion his wealth so that it would give him maximum satisfaction from present and future consumption. He would know the exact returns available from investment and the timing of these returns, as well as future income from noninvestment sources. Investment would be merely a means of balancing present against future consumption.

Not knowing what lies ahead, investors are unable to plan lifetime consumption patterns with certainty. Because the returns from investment and the timing of those returns are uncertain, they compensate for the lack of certainty by requiring an expected return sufficiently high to offset it. But what constitutes the return on a common stock? For a 1-year holding period, the benefits associated with ownership include the cash dividends paid during the year together with an appreciation in market price, or capital gain, realized at the end of the year. More formally, the one-period return is

$$r = \frac{\text{Dividends} + (\text{Ending price} - \text{Beginning price})}{\text{Beginning price}} \tag{2-21}$$

where the term in parentheses in the numerator is the capital gain or loss during the holding period.

Solving for the Return   Suppose you were to purchase a share of stock of a corporation for $50. The company is expected to pay a $2 dividend at the end of the year, and its market price after the payment of the dividend is expected to be $55 a share. Thus, your expected return would be

Stock return is the discount rate which equates the present value of the dividend stream and ending price with the purchase price.

$$r = \frac{\$2.00 + (\$55.00 - \$50.00)}{\$50.00} = .14$$

where r is the expected return. Another way to solve for r is

$$\$50.00 = \frac{\$2.00}{1 + r} + \frac{\$55.00}{1 + r}$$

When we solve for the rate of discount that equates the present value of the dividend and the terminal value at the end of 1 year with the purchase price of the stock at time 0, we find it to be 14 percent. You expect a 14 percent return on your investment.

Now suppose that instead of holding the security 1 year, you intend to hold it 2 years and sell it at the end of that time. Moreover, you expect the company to pay a $2.70 dividend at the end of year 2 and the market price of the stock to be $60 after the dividend is paid. Your expected return can be found by solving the following equation for r:

$$\$50.00 = \frac{\$2.00}{1 + r} + \frac{\$2.70}{(1 + r)^2} + \frac{\$60.00}{(1 + r)^2}$$

When we solve for r by the method described earlier, we find it to be 14 percent also. For general purposes, the formula can be expressed as

$$P_0 = \sum_{t=1}^{2} \frac{D_t}{(1 + r)^t} + \frac{P_2}{(1 + r)^2} \qquad (2\text{-}22)$$

where P_0 is the market price at time 0, D_t is the expected dividend at the end of period t, and P_2 is the expected terminal value at the end of period 2. Σ denotes the sum of discounted dividends at the end of periods 1 and 2.

If your holding period were 10 years, the expected rate of return would be determined by solving the following equation for r:

$$P_0 = \sum_{t=1}^{10} \frac{D_t}{(1 + r)^t} + \frac{P_{10}}{(1 + r)^{10}} \qquad (2\text{-}23)$$

But if a perpetual trust fund had bought the stock, and the trustee expected to hold it forever, the expected return would consist entirely of cash dividends and perhaps a liquidating dividend. Thus, the expected rate of return would be determined by solving the following equation for r:

$$P_0 = \sum_{t=1}^{\infty} \frac{D_t}{(1 + r)^t} \qquad (2\text{-}24)$$

where ∞ is the sign for infinity.[4] What we are saying here is that the formula takes account of all possible future dividends that might be paid.

Are Dividends the Foundation?

It is clear that the intended holding periods of different investors will vary greatly. Some will hold a stock for only a few days; others might expect to hold it forever. Investors with holding periods shorter than infinity expect to be able to sell the stock at a price higher than they paid for it. This assumes, of course, that at that time there will be investors willing to buy it. As buyers, they will, in turn, judge the stock on expectations of future dividends and future terminal value beyond that point. That terminal value, however, will depend on other investors at that time being willing to buy the stock. The price they are willing to pay will depend on their expectations of dividends and terminal value. And so the process goes through successive investors. Note that the total cash return to all successive investors in a stock is the sum of distributions by the company, whether they be regular cash dividends, liquidating dividends, or share repurchases. (See Chapter 11 for a discussion of share repurchase as part of an overall dividend decision.) Thus, cash distributions are all that stockholders as a whole receive from their invest-

The foundation of value is cash payments to the shareholder.

---

[4]For longer holding periods, portfolio theorists usually work with continuously compounded rates of return. The assumption is that the portfolio's return follows a lognormal distribution. Although the expression of returns on a continuously compounded basis is preferred, it is difficult for the reader to follow in a basic finance course. For ease of understanding, we work with returns based on discrete time periods. If you are interested in continuously compounded returns, see the last section of Chapter 5, where they are employed in connection with option valuation.

ment; they are all the company pays out. Consequently, the foundation for the valuation of common stock must be dividends. These are construed broadly to mean any cash distribution to shareholders, including share repurchases.

The logical question to be raised is, why do the stocks of companies that pay no dividends have positive, often quite high, values? The answer is that investors expect to be able to sell the stock in the future at a price higher than they paid for it. Instead of dividend income plus terminal value, they rely only on the terminal value. In turn, terminal value will depend on the expectations of the marketplace at the end of the horizon period. The ultimate expectation is that the firm eventually will pay dividends, broadly defined, and that future investors will receive a cash return on their investment. In the interim, however, investors are content with the expectation that they will be able to sell the stock at a subsequent time because there will be a market for it. In the meantime, the company is reinvesting earnings and, it is hoped, enhancing its future earning power and ultimate dividends.

DIVIDEND DISCOUNT MODELS

We saw in Eq. (2-24) that the return on investment is the rate of discount that equates the present value of the stream of expected future dividends with the current market price of the stock. Dividend discount models are designed to compute this implied stock return under specific assumptions as to the expected growth pattern of future dividends. Merrill Lynch, First Boston, and a number of other investment banks routinely publish such calculations for a large number of stocks, based on their particular model and security analysts' estimates of future earnings and dividend-payout ratios. In what follows we examine such models, beginning with the simplest one.

Perpetual Growth Model

If dividends of a company are expected to grow at a constant rate, the calculation of the implied return is an easy matter. If this constant rate is g, Eq. (2-24) becomes

$$P_0 = \frac{D_0(1 + g)}{1 + r} + \frac{D_0(1 + g)^2}{(1 + r)^2} + \cdots + \frac{D_0(1 + g)^\infty}{(1 + r)^\infty} \qquad (2\text{-}25)$$

where D_0 is the dividend per share at time 0. Thus, the dividend expected in period n is equal to the most recent dividend times the compound growth factor $(1 + g)^n$.

Assuming r is greater than g, Eq. (2-25) can be expressed as[5]

---

[5]If we multiply both sides of Eq. (2-25) by $(1 + r)/(1 + g)$ and subtract Eq. (2-25) from the product, we obtain

$$\frac{P_0(1 + r)}{1 + g} - P_0 = D_0 - \frac{D_0(1 + g)^\infty}{(1 + r)^\infty}$$

Because r is greater than g, the second term on the right side will be zero. Consequently,

$$P_0\left[\frac{1 + r}{1 + g} - 1\right] = D_0$$

$$P_0\left[\frac{(1 + r) - (1 + g)}{1 + g}\right] = D_0$$

$$P_0(r - g) = D_0(1 + g)$$

$$P_0 = \frac{D_1}{r - g}$$

If r is less than g, it is easy to determine that the market price of the stock would be infinite. See David Durand, "Growth Stocks and the Petersburg Paradox," *Journal of Finance*, 12 (September 1957), 348–63.

$$P_0 = \frac{D_1}{r - g} \tag{2-26}$$

where D_1 is the dividend per share at time 1. Rearranging, the expected return becomes

$$r = \frac{D_1}{P_0} + g \tag{2-27}$$

Perpetual growth assumes the dividend one period in the future grows at a constant rate in perpetuity.

The critical assumption in this valuation model is that dividends per share are expected to grow perpetually at a compound rate of g. For some companies, this assumption may be a fair approximation of reality. To illustrate the use of Eq. (2-27), suppose A & G Company's dividend per share at $t = 1$ was expected to be $3, to grow at a 7 percent rate forever, and the current market price was $50 a share. The expected return would be

$$r = \frac{\$3}{\$50} + .07 = 13\%$$

and this return would be expected in every future period. For companies in the mature stage of their life cycle, the perpetual growth assumption is not unreasonable.

Conversion to a Price/Earnings Ratio With the perpetual growth model, we can easily go from dividend valuation, Eq. (2-26), to price/earnings ratio valuation. Suppose a company retained a constant portion of its earnings each year, call it b. The dividend-payout ratio (dividends per share divided by earnings per share) also would be constant:

$$1 - b = \frac{D_1}{E_1} \tag{2-28}$$

where E_1 is earnings per share in period 1. Equation (2-26) can be expressed as

$$P_0 = \frac{(1 - b)E_1}{r - g} \tag{2-29}$$

Rearranging, this becomes

$$\frac{P_0}{E_1} = \frac{1 - b}{r - g} \quad \text{constant} \tag{2-30}$$

where P_0/E_1 is the price/earnings ratio based on expected earnings in period 1. In our earlier example, suppose A & G Company had a retention rate of 40 percent. Therefore

$$\frac{P_0}{E_1} = \frac{1 - .40}{.13 - .07} = 10 \text{ times}$$

With a $50 share price, expected earnings in period 1 would be $5 per share.

Retained Earnings and Dividend Growth Without external financing, the source of dividend growth is the retention of earnings and the return on this retention, namely, the return on equity (ROE). By retaining earnings, a company is able to invest the funds and, as a result, would be expected to earn more than it did the year before. In turn, a higher dividend would be expected to be paid. If there were no retention and all earnings were paid out as dividends, there would be no net investment. In our idealized world, we implicitly assume that an amount equal to depreciation is invested to maintain the earnings of the company (no growth). Net investment is investment over and above depreciation, and it is possible only with retention.

If expected ROE is constant over time, growth in dividends, g, can be expressed as

$$g = b \times \text{ROE} \tag{2-31}$$

where b is a constant retention rate. As before, $1 - b$ is the dividend-payout ratio.

To illustrate, suppose Gonzalez Freight Company earned $5.00 per share last year. Its retention rate is 60 percent, so it paid out $5.00(1 - .60) = $2.00 in dividends per share. The historical ROE of the company is 15 percent. If things do not change, this implies that earnings per share for this period, E_1, will be

$$E_1 = \$5.00 + \$5.00(.60).15 = \$5.45$$

and that dividends per share, D_1, will be

$$D_1 = \$5.45(1 - .60) = \$2.18$$

Thus, the dividend is increased from $2.00 to $2.18 per share on the basis of the additional earnings made possible by retaining a portion of last year's earnings. The growth rate in dividends per share is

$$g = \$2.18/\$2.00 - 1 = 9\%$$

which, of course, is the same as that determined through Eq. (2-31):

$$g = .60 \times 15\% = 9\%$$

In subsequent years, dividends per share also would be expected to grow by 9 percent.

Is such growth realistic? It depends on the opportunities available for investment and their likely return. For most companies, a perpetual growth model is inappropriate. Typically, both the rate of return on equity and the retention rate change over time. The import of the above, however, is that the retention of earnings permits growth of future earnings and dividends. It is not the only source of growth; external financing and increased returns on equity through better capital investment opportunities also are sources. In Chapter 8 we discuss how to create value through capital investments. For now, we merely need to be mindful that retention is an important source of growth.

Growth Phases

When the pattern of expected growth is such that a perpetual growth model is not appropriate, modifications of Eq. (2-29) can be used. A number of valuation models are based on the premise that the growth rate will taper off eventually. For example, the transition might be from a present above-normal growth rate to one that is considered normal. If dividends per share were expected to grow at a 14 percent compound rate for 10 years and then grow at a 7 percent rate, Eq. (2-29) would become

$$P_0 = \sum_{t=1}^{10} \frac{D_0(1.14)^t}{(1+r)^t} + \sum_{t=11}^{\infty} \frac{D_{10}(1.07)^{t-10}}{(1+r)^t} \tag{2-32}$$

Phased growth allows for a nonlinear growth in expected future dividends.

Note that the growth in dividends in the second phase uses the expected dividend in period 10 as its foundation. Therefore, the growth-term exponent is $t - 10$, which means that in period 11 it is 1, in period 12 it is 2, and so forth.

The transition from an above-normal to a normal rate of growth could be specified as more gradual than the rate just given. For example, we might expect dividends to grow at a 14 percent rate for 5 years, followed by an 11 percent rate for the next 5 years, and a 7 percent growth rate thereafter. The more growth segments that are added, the more closely the growth in dividends will approach a curvilinear function. But even Microsoft cannot grow at an above-normal rate forever. Typically, companies grow at a very high rate initially, after which their growth opportunities slow down to a rate that is normal for companies in general.

Summing the Parts   Share price, then, is the summation of the present values of expected future dividends in each of the growth phases:

$$P_0 = PV(\text{phase 1}) + PV(\text{phase 2}) + \cdots + PV(\text{phase } n) \tag{2-33}$$

In this three-phase example, suppose the present dividend is $2 per share and the present market price is $40. Therefore,

$$\$40 = \sum_{t=1}^{5} \frac{\$2(1.14)^t}{(1+r)^t} + \sum_{t=6}^{10} \frac{D_t(1.11)^{t-5}}{(1+r)^t} + \sum_{t=11}^{\infty} \frac{D_{10}(1.07)^{t-10}}{(1+r)^t} \tag{2-34}$$

In a multiphase growth situation like this, solving for the rate of return that equates the stream of expected future dividends with the current market price is arduous. If you have a lot of problems to solve, it is worthwhile to program the computer with an algorithm to solve for r. In the absence of such, one must resort to trial and error similar to that illustrated for the internal rate of return. The difficulty, of course, is in knowing where to begin. With a three-phase situation, we might start by employing the middle growth rate in a perpetual growth model to approximate the actual r. With an initial growth of 14 percent, the expected dividend at the end of year 1 is $2(1.14) = $2.28. Using 11 percent as our perpetual growth rate, $r = (\$2.28/\$40) + .11 = 16.7\%$. If we then employ 16 percent as a starting discount rate, the present value of the right-hand side of Eq. (2-34) is as shown in Table 2-4.

For the last growth phase, the perpetual growth model can be used to derive expected share price at the end of year 10, based on constantly growing dividends thereafter. The resulting market price of $77.16 shown in the table is then discounted at 16 percent to its present value at time 0. When this amount is added to the total present value of dividends, we obtain an overall present value of $35.04. As this amount is less than the share price of $40, we must try a lower discount rate. Repeating the calculations for 15 percent, we obtain the results shown in

TABLE 2-4
Present Value of Multiphased Growth Problem, 16 Percent

Time	Dividend	Present Value of Dividend (16%)	Present Value of Year 10 Market Price (16%)
1	$2.28	$1.97	
2	2.60	1.93	
3	2.96	1.90	
4	3.38	1.87	
5	3.85	1.83	
6	4.27	1.75	
7	4.74	1.68	
8	5.27	1.61	
9	5.84	1.54	
10	6.49	1.47	
		$17.55	

$$P_{10} = \frac{\$6.49(1.07)}{.16 - .07} = \$77.16 \qquad PV \qquad \longrightarrow \$17.49$$

Total present value (dividends + ending price) = $17.55 + $17.49 = $35.04

Table 2-5. As $39.81 is almost $40, we know that r is slightly less than 15 percent. Therefore, the expected rate of return that equates the stream of expected future dividends with the market price is approximately 15 percent.[6]

For any stream of expected future dividends, we can solve for the rate of discount that equates the present value of this stream with the current share price. Although this is tedious when there is multiphased growth, the calculations can be streamlined. If enough computations are involved, it is worthwhile to program a computer algorithm. The rate of discount for which we solve is, by definition, the expected return on investment in the stock. However, we must be mindful that the accuracy of this estimate depends on the precision with which we are able to forecast expected future dividends.

Approximation Model for Three-Phase Growth   Fuller and Hsia have derived an approximation formula for determining the required rate of return when the dividend discount model involves three phases of growth.[7] They call their formula the H model, where the required return is expressed as

$$r = (D_0/P_0)[(1+g_3) + H(g_1 - g_3)] + g_3 \qquad (2\text{-}35)$$

---

[6]The precise discount rate is 14.96 percent, but to avoid further tediousness, we do not interpolate for it.

[7]Russell J. Fuller and Chi-Cheng Hsia, "A Simplified Common Stock Valuation Model," *Financial Analysts Journal*, 40 (September–October 1984), 40–56.

TABLE 2-5
Present Value of Multiphased Growth Problem, 15 Percent

Time	Dividend	Present Value of Dividend (15%)	Present Value of Year 10 Market Price (15%)
1	$2.28	$1.98	
2	2.60	1.97	
3	2.96	1.95	
4	3.38	1.93	
5	3.85	1.91	
6	4.27	1.85	
7	4.74	1.78	
8	5.27	1.72	
9	5.84	1.66	
10	6.49	1.60	
		$18.35	

$$P_{10} = \frac{\$6.49(1.07)}{.15 - .07} = \$86.80 \qquad \text{—} PV@15\% \quad \$21.46$$

Total present value (dividends + ending price) = $18.35 + $21.46 = $39.81

where

D_0 = present dividend per share
P_0 = present market price per share
g_3 = long-run growth rate in final phase
$H = (A + B)/2$, where A is the number of years in phase 1 and B is the end of phase 2
g_1 = growth rate in phase 1

For our previous example, this formula is expressed as

$$r = (\$2/\$40)[1.07 + 7.5(.14 - .07)] + .07 = 14.975\%$$

This percentage is very close to that solved for above. The H model is particularly useful when the first two growth phases are relatively short in number of years, the first growth rate does not exceed r, and the growth rate for the second phase is about halfway between the growth rates for the first and last phases. The further a situation is from these conditions, the poorer the approximation. However, for many situations involving three-phase growth, the H model provides a quick and reasonably accurate approximation of the discount rate.

Price/Earnings Horizon Value

For our earlier growth-phase example, a perpetual dividend growth assumption was invoked to obtain a terminal value at the end of the horizon—10 years. Another way to estimate the terminal value is by assuming a price/earnings ratio at the horizon and multiplying earnings per share by it. To do so, we disaggregate dividends into earnings per share and the dividend-payout ratio. To illustrate, suppose earnings per share for a company were expected to grow at a 25 percent rate the first 4 years, 15 percent the next 4, and 8 percent thereafter. Moreover, the dividend-payout ratio is expected to increase with the transition from the initial growth phase to the eventual mature phase of the company.

As a result, we might have the following for the three phases:

Terminal value of a stock can be based on perpetual growth beyond the terminal year or on a price/earnings ratio multiplied by terminal-year + 1 earnings.

Phase	EPS Growth	Dividend-Payout Ratio
1–4 years	25%	20%
5–8 years	15%	26%, 32%, 38%, 44%
Year 9 and beyond	8%	50%

Suppose the price/earnings ratio at the end of year 8 were expected to be 10 times. Suppose further that this ratio is based on expected earnings per share in year 9. If present earnings per share (at time 0) are $3.00, the expected cash flows to the investor are as shown in Table 2-6. In the table we see that the terminal value at the end of year 8 is determined by multiplying expected earnings per share in year 9 by the price/earnings ratio of 10 to obtain $138.30.

TABLE 2-6
Expected Dividend and Terminal Value Cash Flows for Example

Time	Earnings per Share	Dividend Payout	Dividend per Share	Cash Flow to Investor
1	$ 3.75	.20	$ .75	$ .75
2	4.69	.20	.94	.94
3	5.86	.20	1.17	1.17
4	7.32	.20	1.46	1.46
5	8.42	.26	2.19	2.19
6	9.69	.32	3.10	3.10
7	11.14	.38	4.23	4.23
8	12.81	.44	5.64	5.64

$$\text{Year 9 EPS} = \$12.81(1.08) = \$13.83$$
$$P_8 = \$13.83 \times 10 \text{ PE} = \$138.30$$
$$\text{Terminal value} = \$138.30$$

To determine the implied expected return to the investor, we solve for the rate of discount that equates the cash-flow stream shown in the last column with the market price per share at time 0. If this price were $52, the implied return would be 15.59 percent when we solve for the internal rate of return. If we knew the required rate of return and wished to determine the present value of the cash-flow stream, we would simply present value each of the cash flows in the table and sum them. If the required return were 17 percent, the present value would be $47.45 per share. With these examples, we illustrate the mechanics by which dividend discount models may be used to determine either the expected return or the present value for a stock.

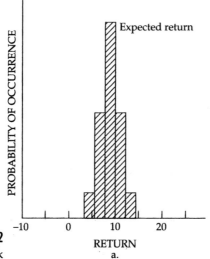
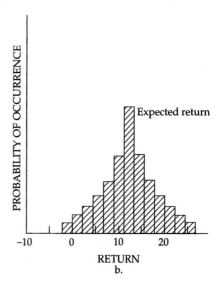

FIGURE 2-2
Illustration of risk

MEASURING RISK: STANDARD DEVIATION

So far we have worked with only the expected return from holding a security. In a world of uncertainty, this return may not be realized. Risk can be thought of as the possibility that the actual return from holding a security will deviate from the expected return. The greater the magnitude of deviation and the greater the probability of its occurrence, the greater is said to be the risk of the security. Figure 2-2 shows the probability distributions of possible returns for two securities.

Because the actual return of security B has a greater likelihood of deviating from its expected return than that of security A, we say that it has greater risk. Although the investor is principally concerned with downside risk, or the possibility of a negative return, for ease of use our measure of risk takes into account all divergence of the actual return from that which was expected.

To illustrate this measure, suppose an investor believed that the possible 1-year returns from investing in a particular common stock were those shown in Table 2-7. This probability distribution can be summarized in terms of two parameters: the *expected return* and the *standard deviation*. The expected return is[8]

Standard deviation is a measure of the relative dispersion of a probability distribution.

$$\overline{R} = \sum_{i=1}^{n} R_i P_i \qquad (2\text{-}36)$$

where R_i is the return for the *i*th possibility, P_i is the probability of concurrence of that return, and *n* is the total number of possibilities. The standard deviation is

---

[8]The average shown is an arithmetic mean that is appropriate as a measure of central tendency of a probability distribution. If we were concerned with the rate of wealth accumulation over time that arose from a security investment, however, the measure would not be appropriate. Here the average return is a multiplicative function of the returns realized each year. A geometric average annual return should be used, and it is

$$\overline{R} = \sqrt[m]{(1 + R_1)(1 + R_2)(1 + R_3) \cdots (1 + R_m)} - 1$$

where *m* is the total number of years involved, $\sqrt[m]{}$ is the *m*-root sign, and R_t is the return on investment in year *t*. This measure gives us the average compound rate of growth of wealth from beginning to end, time 0 to time *m*.

$$\sigma = \sqrt{\sum_{i=1}^{n} (R_i - \overline{R})^2 P_i} \tag{2-37}$$

where $\sqrt{}$ represents the square root. It also can be expressed as $[]^{1/2}$. The square of the standard deviation, σ^2, is known as the variance of the distribution.

To illustrate these measures, consider again the distribution of possible returns shown in Table 2-7. The expected return is

$$\begin{aligned}\overline{R} = {}& -.10(.05) - .02(.10) + .04(.20) + .09(.30) + .14(.20) \\ & + .20(.10) + .28(.05) \\ = {}& 9\%\end{aligned}$$

The standard deviation is

$$\begin{aligned}\sigma = {}& [(-.10 - .09)^2 (.05) + (-.02 - .09)^2 (.10) + (.04 - .09)^2 (.20) \\ & + (.09 - .09)^2 (.30) + (.14 - .09)^2 (.20) + (.20 - .09)^2 (.10) \\ & + (.28 - .09)^2 (.05)]^{1/2} \\ = {}& [.00703]^{1/2} \\ = {}& 8.38\%\end{aligned}$$

Use of Standard Deviation Information

The trade-off between expected return and risk (standard deviation) is a key factor throughout all of finance.

When we deal with *discrete* probability distributions, we do not have to calculate the standard deviation to determine the probability of specific outcomes. To determine the probability of the actual return in our example being less than zero, we look at Table 2-7 and see that the probability is 15 percent. When we deal with *continuous* distributions, the procedure is slightly more complex.

TABLE 2-7
Probability Distribution of Possible Returns for a 1-Year Holding Period

Probability of occurrence	.05	.10	.20	.30	.20	.10	.05
Possible return	−.10	−.02	.04	.09	.14	.20	.28

For the normal bell-shaped probability distribution, .68 of the distribution falls within one standard deviation of the expected value, .95 falls within two standard deviations, and over .99 within three standard deviations. By expressing differences from the expected value in terms of standard deviations, we are able to determine the probability that the actual return will be greater than or less than such and such an amount.

Suppose our distribution had been a *normal* distribution with an expected return equal to 9 percent and a standard deviation of 8.38 percent and we wished to determine in this case, also, the probability that the actual return would be less than zero. Standardizing the deviation from the expected value, we have 9%/8.38% = 1.07 standard deviations. Turning to the normal probability distribution Table C at the back of the book, we find that there is approximately a 14 percent probability that the actual return will be more than 1.07 standard deviations

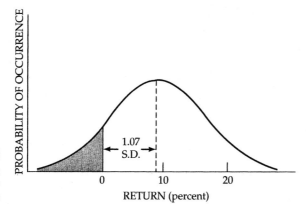

FIGURE 2-3
Probability distribution
of possible returns for
example

from the mean of the distribution. Therefore, there is a 14 percent likelihood that the actual return on investment will be zero or less. The probability distribution is illustrated in Fig. 2-3. The shaded area represents 1.07 standard deviations to the left of the mean, and, as indicated, this area represents 14 percent of the total distribution.

Thus, the dispersion, or wideness, of the probability distribution of possible returns reflects the degree of the investor's uncertainty. A distribution with a small standard deviation relative to its expected value indicates little dispersion and a high degree of confidence in the outcome. A distribution with a large standard deviation relative to its expected value indicates a high degree of uncertainty about the possible return on investment. In the immediate discussion, we assume that probability distributions can be summarized in terms of two parameters: the expected return and the standard deviation.

In the chapter that follows, we assume that investors select stocks according to the principle of maximizing expected utility. Expected utility is determined on the basis of the probability distribution of possible returns from an investment. We also assume that investors can summarize their beliefs about the probability distribution of possible returns from an investment or portfolio of investments in terms of two parameters of the distribution. These parameters are the expected return and the standard deviation, both illustrated earlier. In Chapter 3 we follow up on these ideas by showing how the utility preferences of investors can be applied to the selection of portfolios of securities.

 Summary

Investment, financing, and dividend decisions have significant impact on the firm's valuation. A key concept underlying valuation is the time value of money. In considering this topic, the determination of both terminal values and present values was illustrated. Both formulas may

be modified for compounding more than once a year. Using present-value techniques, we are able to isolate differences in the timing of cash flows for various investments. Also using these techniques, we showed how to amortize a loan and how to compute the internal rate of return on an investment. Frequent use of present values and internal rates of return will occur in subsequent chapters.

Bonds can be either pure discount ones, where only one payment is made at maturity, or coupon bonds, where interest payments are made semiannually through maturity, at which time the bond's face value is paid as well. Yield-to-maturity is the rate of discount that equates the present value of promised future payments to investors with the current market price of the bond. Formulas were presented for solving for market price, given the yield, or for yield, given the market price. In addition, the valuation of perpetuities was addressed, one example of which is preferred stock.

In purchasing a common stock, the investor gives up present consumption with the expectation of increasing future consumption. The expected return is the rate of discount that equates the present market value of the stock with the present value of the stream of expected future dividends. Because cash dividends are all that investors as a whole receive from their investment, these dividends are the foundation for valuation. A dividend valuation model is consistent with the fact that many investors expect to sell their stock in the future and realize a capital gain. Given the basic valuation model, we saw how it could be modified to solve for different expectations of future growth, be they for perpetual growth or for phased growth. With respect to the latter, a terminal value is determined at some horizon, by assuming either a perpetual growth dividend situation or a price/earnings ratio multiple.

In addition to the expected return on investment, we are concerned with risk. For our purposes, *risk* is defined as the deviation of the actual return from that which was expected. To measure the wideness of the distribution of possible returns, the standard deviation is computed. By relating the standard deviation to a specific difference from the expected return, we are able to determine the probability of occurrence of that outcome. Investors attempt to maximize their expected utility, which is a function of expected return and standard deviation. In the subsequent chapter, we show how these concepts are applied to the selection of a portfolio of securities and the implications of such selection for the required rate of return and valuation of the individual firm.

FINCOACH EXERCISES

FinCoach on the Prentice Hall Finance Center CD-ROM (Practice Center) has the following categories of practice exercises, which pertain to things taken up in this chapter: 1. Valuation of Single Cash Flows; 2. Valuation of Multiple Cash Flows; 3. Valuation of Infinitely Many Cash Flows; 4. Bond Valuation; and 5. Stock Valuation. These exercises can be used to supplement the problems that follow.

Self-Correction Problems

1. The following cash-flow streams need to be analyzed:

Cash Flow Stream	End of Year:				
	1	2	3	4	5
1	$100	$200	$200	$300	$300
2	600	—	—	—	—
3	—	—	—	—	1,200
4	200	—	500	—	300

    a. Calculate the terminal value of each stream at the end of year 5 with an interest rate of 10 percent.

    b. Compute the present value of each stream if the discount rate is 14 percent.

    c. Compute the internal rate of return of each stream if the initial investment at time 0 were $600.

2. Sanchez Hydraulics Company has outstanding a 14 percent coupon bond with 3 years to maturity. Interest payments are made semiannually. Assume a face value of $100.

    a. (1) If the market price of the bond is $104, what is the yield to maturity? (2) If it were $97, what would be the yield? (3) if it were $100?

    b. (1) If the bond's yield were 12 percent, what would be its price? (2) if it were 15 percent? (3) if it were 14 percent?

    c. Instead of a coupon bond, suppose it were a zero coupon, pure discount instrument. If the yield were 14 percent, what would be the market price? (Assume semiannual compounding.)

3. Delphi Products Corporation currently pays a dividend of $2 per share and this dividend is expected to grow at a 15 percent annual rate for 3 years, then at a 10 percent rate for the next 3 years, after which it is expected to grow at a 5 percent rate forever.

    a. What value would you place on the stock if an 18 percent rate of return were required?

    b. Would your valuation change if you expected to hold the stock only 3 years?

4. For Delphi Products Corporation in Problem 3, suppose the company were expected to have a price/earnings ratio of 8 times at the end of year 6. Moreover, earnings per share in year 7 are expected to be $7.50. If the present market price per share is $35, what is the expected return on investment? (Assume that terminal value at the end of year 6 is based on year 7 earnings.)

5. Fox River Associates is analyzing a new line of business and estimates the possible returns on investment as

Probability	.1	.2	.4	.2	.1
Possible return	−10%	5%	20%	35%	50%

a. What are the expected return and standard deviation?

b. Assume that the parameters in part a pertain to a normal probability distribution. What is the probability the return will be (1) zero or less? (2) less than 10 percent? (3) more than 40 percent?

■ Problems

1. The following are exercises in terminal values.

   a. At the end of 3 years, how much is an initial deposit of $100 worth, assuming an annual interest rate of (1) 10 percent? (2) 100 percent? (3) 0 percent?

   b. At the end of 3 years, how much is an initial deposit of $100 worth, assuming a quarterly compounded interest rate of (1) 10 percent? (2) 100 percent?

   c. Why does your answer to part b differ from that to part a?

   d. At the end of 10 years, how much is an initial deposit of $100 worth, assuming an interest rate of 10 percent compounded (1) annually? (2) semiannually? (3) quarterly? (4) continuously?

2. The following are exercises in present values.

   a. $100 at the end of 3 years is worth how much today, assuming a discount rate of (1) 10 percent? (2) 100 percent? (3) 0 percent?

   b. What is the aggregate present value of $500 received at the end of each of the next 3 years, assuming a discount rate of (1) 4 percent? (2) 25 percent?

   c. $100 is received at the end of 1 year, $500 at the end of 2 years, and $1,000 at the end of 3 years. What is the aggregate present value of these receipts, assuming a discount rate of (1) 4 percent? (2) 25 percent?

   d. $1,000 is to be received at the end of 1 year, $500 at the end of 2 years, and $100 at the end of 3 years. What is the aggregate present value of these receipts, assuming a discount rate of (1) 4 percent? (2) 25 percent?

   e. Compare your solutions in part c with those in part d and explain the reason for the differences.

3. The following are exercises on internal rates of return (IRRs).

   a. An investment of $1,000 today will return $2,000 at the end of 10 years. What is its IRR?

   b. An investment of $1,000 today will return $500 at the end of each of the next 3 years. What is its IRR?

   c. An investment of $1,000 today will return $1,000 at the end of 1 year, $500 at the end of 2 years, and $100 at the end of 3 years. What is its IRR?

   d. An investment of $1,000 will return $60 per year forever. What is its IRR?

4. Graph the present value of $1 per year for 5, 10, 15, 20, and 25 years at 0, 10, 20, 30, and 40 percent rates of discount. Explain the difference in the slopes of the curves.

5. Selyn Cohen is 70 years old and recently retired. He wishes to provide retirement income for himself and is considering an annuity contract with Monument Life Insurance Company. Such a contract pays him an equal amount each year he lives. For this cash-flow stream, he must put up so much money at the beginning. According to actuarial tables, his life expectancy is 15 years, and that is the duration on which the insurance company bases its calculations regardless of how long Cohen actually lives.

   a. If Monument Life uses an interest rate of 5 percent in its calculations, what must Cohen pay at the outset for an annuity providing him $10,000 per year? (Assume annual payments are at the end of each of the 15 years.)

   b. What would be the purchase price if the interest rate were 10 percent?

   c. If Cohen had $30,000 to put into an annuity, how much would he receive each year if the insurance company used (1) a 5 percent interest rate in its calculations? (2) a 10 percent rate?

6. On a contract, you have a choice of receiving $25,000 six years from now or $50,000 twelve years hence. What is the implied discount rate that equates these two amounts?

7. You borrow $10,000 at 14 percent for 4 years. The loan is repayable in four equal installments at year ends.

   a. What is the annual payment that will completely amortize the loan over 4 years? (You may wish to round to the nearest dollar.)

   b. Of each payment, what is (1) the amount of interest? (2) the amount of principal?

8. Establish a loan amortization schedule for the following loan to the nearest cent. (See Table 2-3 for an example.) This problem should be done only with a spreadsheet program. Situation: A 36-month loan of $8,000 with equal installment payments at the end of each month. The interest rate is 1 percent per month.

9. Barquez Mines, Inc., is considering investing in Chile. It makes a bid to the government to participate in the development of a mine, the profits of which will be realized at the end of 5 years. The mine is expected to produce $5 million in cash to Barquez at that time. Other than the bid at the outset, no other cash flows will occur, as the government will reimburse the company for all costs. If Barquez requires a return of 20 percent, what is the maximum bid it

should make for the participation right if interest is compounded (a) annually? (b) semiannually? (c) quarterly? (d) continuously?

10. Booker Brown, Inc., has a 10 percent bond outstanding with 7 years remaining to maturity. Interest payments are semiannual, and the instrument's face value is $100.

    a. What is the bond's market price if the yield to maturity is (1) 11.6 percent? (2) 9.2 percent?

    b. What would be the yield to maturity if the market price were (1) $110? (2) $94?

11. Kerby Manufacturing Corporation sells a zero coupon bond for $38 with 8 years to maturity. At maturity the company will pay the bond's holder $100. What is the bond's yield to maturity if a semiannual convention to valuation is employed?

12. Caroline Islands Resorts has 1,750,000 shares of authorized common stock having a $1 par value. Over the years it has issued 1,532,000 shares, but presently 63,000 are held as Treasury stock. The paid-in capital of the company is presently $5,314,000.

    a. How many shares are now outstanding?

    b. If the company were able to sell stock at $19 per share, what would be the maximum amount it could raise under its existing authorization, including Treasury shares?

    c. What would be its common stock and paid-in capital accounts after the financing?

13. The stock of the Health Corporation is currently selling for $20 and is expected to pay a $1 dividend at the end of the year. What will be the rate of return to investors who buy the stock now and sell it for $23 after collecting the dividend?

14. North Great Timber Company will pay a dividend of $1.50 next year. After this, earnings and dividends are expected to grow at an 8 percent annual rate indefinitely. Investors now require a rate of return of 12 percent. The company is considering several business strategies and wishes to determine the effect of these strategies on the market price per share of its stock.

    a. Continuing the present strategy will result in the expected growth rate and required rate of return shown.

    b. Expanding timber holdings and sales will increase the expected dividend growth rate to 10 percent but will increase the risk of the company. As a result, the rate of return required by investors will increase to 15 percent.

    c. Integrating into retail stores will increase the dividend growth rate to 9 percent and increase the required rate of return to 13 percent.

From the standpoint of market price per share, which strategy is best?

15. Zachery Zorro Company presently pays a dividend of $1.60 per share and the market price per share is $30. The company expects to increase the dividend at a 20 percent annual rate the first 4 years, at a 13 percent rate the next 4 years, and then grow the dividend at a 7 percent rate thereafter. This phased-growth pattern is in keeping with the expected life cycle of earnings. What is the stock's expected return on investment?

16. Northern California Fruit Company's latest earnings are $2.00 per share. Earnings per share are expected to grow at a 20 percent compound annual

rate for 4 years, at a 12 percent annual rate for the next 4 years, and at 6 percent thereafter. The dividend-payout ratio is expected to be 25 percent the first 4 years, 40 percent the next 4 years, and 50 percent thereafter. At the end of year 8, the price/earnings ratio for the company is expected to be 8.5 times, where year 9's expected earnings per share are used in the denominator.

    a.   If the required rate of return is 14 percent, what is the present market price per share?

    b.   If the present market price per share is $30, what is the stock's expected return?

17.   Wally Whittier is considering investing in a security that has the following distribution of possible returns:

Probability	.10	.20	.30	.30	.10
Possible return	−.10	.00	.10	.20	.30

    a.   What is the expected value of return and standard deviation associated with the investment?

    b.   Is there much downside risk? How can you tell?

18.   Shirley Batavia is analyzing an investment in a shopping center. The expected return on investment is 20 percent. The probability distribution of possible returns is a normal bell-shaped distribution with a standard deviation of 15 percent.

    a.   What are the chances that the investment will result in a negative return?

    b.   What is the probability that the return will be greater than (1) 10 percent? (2) 20 percent? (3) 30 percent? (4) 40 percent? (5) 50 percent?

Solutions to Self-Correction Problems

1.   a.   Terminal value of each cash flow and total future value of the stream:

Cash Flow Stream	Year					Total Terminal Value
	1	2	3	4	5	
1	$146.41	$266.20	$242	$330	$300	$1,284.61
2	878.46	—	—	—	—	878.46
3	—	—	—	—	1,200	1,200.00
4	292.82	—	605	—	300	1,197.82

b. Present value of each cash flow and total present value of stream:

Cash Flow Stream	Year					Total Present Value
	1	2	3	4	5	
1	$ 87.72	$153.89	$134.99	$177.62	$155.81	$710.03
2	526.31	—	—	—	—	526.31
3	—	—	—	—	623.24	623.24
4	175.44	—	337.49	—	155.81	668.74
Discount factor	.87719	.76947	.67497	.59208	.51937	

c. Internal rates of return: 1, 20.20 percent; 2, 0 percent (a $600 outlay followed by a $600 receipt results in a zero IRR); 3, 14.87 percent; 4, 18.34 percent. To illustrate cash-flow stream 4 by trial and error:

Year	Cash Flow	18% Discount Factor	18% Present Value	19% Discount Factor	19% Present Value
0	−$600	1.00000	−$600.00	1.00000	−$600.00
1	200	.84746	169.49	.84034	168.07
3	500	.60863	304.32	.59342	296.71
5	300	.43711	131.13	.41905	125.72
			$ 4.94		−$ 9.50

$$IRR = .18 + \frac{\$4.94}{\$4.94 + \$9.50} = 18.34\%$$

2. a. (1) Setting up the problem in keeping with Eq. (2-15) and solving for r, the yield to maturity is found to be 12.36 percent. The yield is less than the coupon rate when the bond trades at a price premium above its face value. (2) The yield here is 15.72 percent. Yield is more than the coupon rate for a bond trading at a discount. (3) Whenever the market price equals the face value, yield equals the coupon rate, 14 percent in this case.

b. (1) Setting up this problem again in keeping with Eq. (2-15) and solving for price, we find it to be $104.92. (2) In this case, price is found to be $97.65. (3) Price equals the face value of $100 when yield equals the coupon rate.

c. $P = \$100/(1.07)^6 = \$66.63$.

3. a.

End of Year:	Dividend	Present Value of Dividends, 18%
1	$2.00 (1.15) = $2.30	× .84746 = $ 1.95
2	2.00 (1.15)² = 2.64	× .71818 = 1.90
3	2.00 (1.15)³ = 3.04	× .60863 = 1.85
4	3.04 (1.10) = 3.35	× .51579 = 1.73
5	3.04 (1.10)² = 3.68	× .43711 = 1.61
6	3.04 (1.10)³ = 4.05	× .37043 = 1.50
		$10.54

Year 7 dividend = $4.05(1.05) = $4.25.

Market value at end of year $6 = 4.25/(.18 - .05) = 32.69. $PV = 12.11. Value = $10.54 + $12.11 = $22.65.

b.   Present value of market value at end of year 3 = $1.73 + $1.61 + $1.50 + $12.11 = $16.95. Present value of expected dividend to be received at end of years 1, 2, and 3 = $1.95 + $1.90 + $1.85 = $5.70. Total value = $16.95 + $5.70 = $22.65. Thus, the value is the same for an investor with a 3-year time horizon.

4. Terminal value at the end of year 6 equals $7.50 EPS × 8 *P/E* ratio = $60.00. The expected cash flows to the investor are (in dollars):

Year	0	1	2	3	4	5	6
Cash flow	−35.00	2.30	2.64	3.04	3.35	3.68	64.05

Solving for the rate of discount that equates the present values of the cash inflows with the cash outflow of $35 at time 0, we find it to be 16.50 percent.

5. a.   By visual inspection of a symmetrical distribution, the expected value of return is seen to be 20 percent. (This can easily be confirmed mathematically.) The standard deviation is

$$SD = [(-.10 - .20)^2 (.1) + (.05 - .20)^2 (.2) + (.20 - .20)^2 (.4)$$
$$+ (.35 - .20)^2(.2) + (.50 - .20)^2(.1)]^{1/2}$$
$$= 16.43\%$$

b.   (1) For a zero or less return, standardizing the deviation from the expected value of return one obtains $(0 - 20\%)/16.43\% = -1.217$ standard deviations. Turning to Table C at the back of the book, 1.217 falls between standard deviations of 1.20 and 1.25. These standard deviations correspond to areas under the curve of .1151 and .1056, respectively. Interpolating

$$.1151 - (.1151 - .1056)\left(\frac{1.217 - 1.20}{1.25 - 1.20}\right) = .1118$$

This means there is approximately an 11.18 percent probability the actual return will be zero or less. (2) For a 10 percent or less return, standardizing the deviation we obtain $(10\% - 20\%)/16.43\% = -.609$ standard deviation. Referring to Table C at the back of the book and going through the same computations as above, we obtain

$$.2743 - (.2743 - .2578)\left(\frac{.609 - .60}{.65 - .60}\right) = .2713$$

Here there is approximately a 27.13 percent probability the actual return will be 10 percent or less. (3) For a 40 percent or more return, standardizing we obtain $(40\% - 20\%)/16.43\% = 1.217$ standard deviations. This is the same as in our first instance involving a zero return or less, except that it is to the right as opposed to the left of the mean. Therefore, the probability of a 40 percent or more return is approximately 11.18 percent.

 Selected References

DURAND, DAVID, "What Price Growth?" *Journal of Portfolio Management*, 18 (Fall 1992), 84–91.

FAIRFIELD, PATRICIA M., "P/E, P/B and the Present Value of Future Dividends," *Financial Analysts Journal*, 50 (July–August 1994), 23–31.

FULLER, RUSSELL J., and CHI-CHENG HSIA, "A Simplified Common Stock Valuation Model," *Financial Analysts Journal*, 40 (September–October 1984), 49–56.

PETERS, D. J., "Valuing a Growth Stock," *Journal of Portfolio Management*, 17 (Spring 1991), 49–51.

TAGGART, ROBERT A., "Using Excel Spreadsheet Functions to Understand and Analyze Fixed Income Security Prices," *Journal of Financial Education*, 25 (Spring 1999), 46–63.

VAN HORNE, JAMES C., *Financial Market Rates and Flows*, 6th ed. Upper Saddle River, NJ: Prentice Hall, 2001.

WOOLRIDGE, J. RANDALL, "Do Stock Prices Reflect Fundamental Values?" *Journal of Applied Corporate Finance*, 8 (Spring 1995), 64–69.

Wachowicz's Web World is an excellent overall Web site produced and maintained by my coauthor of *Fundamentals of Financial Management*, John M. Wachowicz Jr. It contains descriptions of and links to many finance Web sites and articles. *www.prenhall.com/wachowicz*.

Market Risk and Returns

Prospective investors are consumers, shopping. They are influenced by advertising, by the company's image, and, predominantly, by price. Investors usually do not fill their shopping bags with only one investment opportunity, and they try to be sophisticated shoppers when they select a portfolio of securities. Like consumer researchers, let us follow them around to see how they make their choices, how the individual firm is valued in the market, and how market equilibrium is achieved. ■

EFFICIENT FINANCIAL MARKETS

Market efficiency, an underlying idea in this chapter, means that the market price of a security represents the market's consensus estimate of the value of that security. If the market is efficient, it uses all information available to it in setting a price. Investors who choose to hold a security are doing so because their information leads them to think that the security is worth at least its current market price. Those who do not purchase the stock interpret their information as a lower appraisal.

An efficient financial market exists when security prices reflect all available public information about the economy, financial markets, and the specific company involved. The implication is that market prices of individual securities adjust very rapidly to new information. As a result, security prices are said to fluctuate randomly about their "intrinsic" values. New information can result in a change in the "intrinsic" value of a security, but subsequent security price movements will follow what is known as a *random walk* (changes in price will not follow any pattern).[1] Contrary to often-quoted passages of Shakespeare and Santayana, history—at least in the stock market—is not repetitious or helpful. This simply means that one cannot use past security prices to predict future prices in such a way as to profit on average. Moreover, close attention to news releases will be for naught. Alas, by the time you are able to take action, security price adjustments will already have occurred, according to the efficient market notion.

---

[1]For a formalized presentation of this condition, see Eugene F. Fama, "Efficient Capital Markets: A Review of Theory and Empirical Work," *Journal of Finance,* 25 (May 1970), 384–87. See also Fama, "Efficient Capital Markets: II," *Journal of Finance,* 46 (December 1991), 1575–1615.

Stages of Efficiency

Expressed more formally, market efficiency means that the unanticipated portion of the return earned on a security is unpredictable and, over a sufficient number of observations, does not differ systematically from zero. The unanticipated portion is simply the actual return less that which was expected based on some fundamental analysis (e.g., its "intrinsic" value). Put differently, it is the surprise element. Using the definitions of Fama, **weak-form market efficiency** means that the unanticipated return is not correlated with previous unanticipated returns. In other words, the market has no memory. Knowing the past does not help you earn future returns. **Semistrong-form market efficiency** means it is not correlated with any publicly available information. Finally, with **strong-form market efficiency**, the unanticipated return is not correlated with any information, be it publicly available or insider.

On balance, the evidence indicates that the market for stocks, particularly those listed on the New York Stock Exchange, is reasonably efficient. Security prices appear to be a good reflection of available information, and market prices adjust quickly to new information. Market participants seem to be ready to seize on any recurring price pattern; and in doing so, they drive price changes about a security's "intrinsic" value to a random walk. About the only way one can consistently profit is to have insider information; that is, information about a company known to officers and directors but not to the public. If security prices impound all available public information, they tell us a good deal about the future. In efficient markets, one can hope to do no better.

The hypothesis that stock markets are efficient will be true only if a sufficiently large number of investors disbelieve its efficiency and behave accordingly. In other words, the theory requires that there be a sufficiently large number of market participants who, in their attempts to earn profits, promptly receive and analyze all the information that is publicly available concerning companies whose securities they follow. Should this considerable effort devoted to data accumulation and evaluation cease, financial markets would become markedly less efficient.

Arbitrage Efficiency

Efficient markets embrace all information. Arbitrage opportunities do not exist.

Another definition of market efficiency has to do with arbitrage. **Arbitrage** simply means finding two things that are essentially the same and buying the cheaper and selling, or selling short, the more expensive. Suppose there exist two risk-free bonds: Bond 1 is priced at $1,000 and pays $100 at the end of year 1 and $1,100 at the end of year 2; bond 2 costs $800 and pays $1,000 at the end of year 2. Presently you own 8 of bond 1. If you continue to hold them, you will receive $800 at the end of year 1. If a risk-free party were to pay you 10 percent for the use of these funds from the end of year 1 to the end of year 2, the $800 would grow to $880. The total amount of funds you would have at the end of year 2 would be $880 plus ($8 × $1,100), or $9,680. For bond 2, $8,000 invested today would grow to $10,000 at the end of year 2. Clearly, you should sell your holdings in bond 1 for $8,000 and invest in bond 2.

As others recognize this arbitrage opportunity, they will do the same. Selling bond 1, of course, exerts downward pressure on its price, while buying bond 2 brings upward pressure on its price. Arbitrage actions will continue until the two bonds provide the same funds at the end of year 2. The simple but powerful notion here is that security prices adjust as market participants search for arbitrage profits. When such opportunities have been exhausted, security prices are said to be in equilibrium. In this context a definition of market efficiency is the absence of arbitrage opportunities, their having been eliminated by arbitragers.

Does Market Efficiency Always Hold?

Anyone who experienced the stock market crash on October 19, 1987, when it went into a free fall losing 20 percent in a few hours, is inclined to question the efficiency of financial markets. We know that stock markets tend to increase over time in relatively small increments, but when they decline it is with a vengeance. We are left with the uneasy feeling that although market efficiency is a good explainer of market behavior most of the time and securities seem to be efficiently priced relative to each other, there are exceptions. These exceptions call into question market prices embodying all available information. Although the **efficient market hypothesis (EMH)** will underlie a good deal of our discussion, we must be mindful of evidence that suggests exceptions.

SECURITY PORTFOLIOS

In Chapter 2, we measured the expected return and risk for a single security. For a portfolio of two or more securities, things are different. The expected return, r_p, is straightforward:

$$r_p = \sum_{j=1}^{m} r_j A_j \tag{3-1}$$

where r_j is the expected return on security j, A_j is the proportion of total funds invested in security j, and m is the total number of securities in the portfolio. The Greek sigma denotes the summation from security 1 through security m. Equation (3-1) merely says that *the expected return for a portfolio is a weighted average of expected returns for securities making up that portfolio.*

Portfolio Risk

The risk of a portfolio is not a simple weighted average of the standard deviations of the individual securities. Portfolio risk depends not only on the riskiness of the securities constituting the portfolio but also on the relationships among those securities.

By selecting securities that have little relationship with each other, an investor is able to reduce relative risk. **Diversification,** combining securities in a way that will reduce relative risk, is illustrated in Fig. 3-1. Here the returns over time for security A are cyclical in that they move with the economy in general. Returns for security B, however, are mildly countercyclical. Equal amounts invested in both securities will reduce the dispersion of the return on total investment.

In another example involving less than countercyclical behavior, two securities have one-period returns under three possible states of nature:

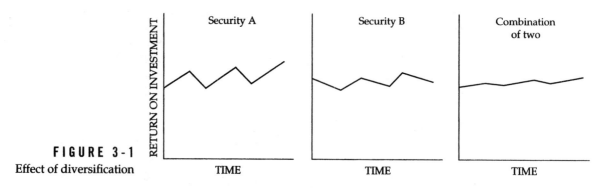

FIGURE 3-1
Effect of diversification

Diversification
of securities held
reduces relative
risk because
individual returns
do not move in
concert.

State	Probability of State Occurring	Return on Security A	Return on Security B
Boom	.25	28%	10%
Normal	.50	15	13
Recession	.25	−2	10

The expected return and standard deviation of the probability distribution of possible returns for the two securities are[2]

	Security A	Security B
Expected return	14.0%	11.5%
Standard deviation	10.7	1.5

If equal amounts of money are invested in the two securities, the expected return of the portfolio is 14.0%(.5) + 11.5%(.5) = 12.75%. The weighted average of the individual standard deviations is simply 10.7%(.5) + 1.5%(.5) = 6.1 percent.

However, this is not the standard deviation of the overall portfolio. The returns for a portfolio consisting of equal investments in both securities are

State	Probability of State Occurring	Return on Portfolio
Boom	.25	19%
Normal	.50	14
Recession	.25	4

---

[2]The expected return and standard deviation are determined by using Eqs. (2-36) and (2-37) in Chapter 2.

where the return on the portfolio is simply the weighted average of the returns on the individual securities. The expected return for the portfolio is 19%(.25) + 14%(.50) + 4%(.25) = 12.75%, the same as before. However, the standard deviation of the portfolio is

$$[(.19 - .1275)^2(.25) + (.14 - .1275)^2(.50) + (.04 - .1275)^2(.25)]^{1/2} = 5.4\%$$

where the exponent $\frac{1}{2}$ for the outside brackets means the square root. We see that the portfolio standard deviation is less than the weighted average of the individual standard deviations, 6.1 percent. The reason why the weighted average of the standard deviations fails to give the correct standard deviation of the portfolio is that it ignores the relationship, or covariance, between the returns of the two securities.

Covariance of Returns

It is clear that one cannot in general calculate the standard deviation of a portfolio's returns simply by taking the weighted average of the standard deviations for the individual securities. Instead, the standard deviation of a probability distribution of possible portfolio returns is

$$\sigma_p = \sqrt{\sum_{j=1}^{m} \sum_{k=1}^{m} A_j A_k \sigma_{jk}} \qquad (3\text{-}2)$$

where m is the total number of securities in the portfolio, A_j is the proportion of the total funds invested in security j, A_k is the proportion invested in security k, and σ_{jk} is the covariance between possible returns for securities j and k. (The covariance term will be illustrated shortly.)

The two Σs mean that we consider the covariances for all possible pairwise combinations of securities in the portfolio. For example, suppose m were 4. The matrix of covariances for possible pairwise combinations would be

$$
\begin{matrix}
\sigma_{1,1} & \sigma_{1,2} & \sigma_{1,3} & \sigma_{1,4} \\
\sigma_{2,1} & \sigma_{2,2} & \sigma_{2,3} & \sigma_{2,4} \\
\sigma_{3,1} & \sigma_{3,2} & \sigma_{3,3} & \sigma_{3,4} \\
\sigma_{4,1} & \sigma_{4,2} & \sigma_{4,3} & \sigma_{4,4}
\end{matrix}
$$

The combination in the upper left-hand corner is 1, 1, which means that $j = k$ and that our concern is with the variance of security 1. That is, $\sigma_1 \sigma_1 = \sigma_1^2$ in Eq. (3-2), or the standard deviation squared. As we trace down the diagonal, there are four situations in all where $j = k$, and we would be concerned with the variances in all four. The second combination in row 1 is $\sigma_{1,2}$, which signifies the covariance between possible returns for securities 1 and 2. Note, however, that the first combination in row 2 is $\sigma_{2,1}$, which signifies the covariance between securities 2 and 1. In other words, we count the covariance between securities 1 and 2 twice. Similarly, we count the covariances between all other combinations not on the diagonal twice. The double summation signs in Eq. (3-2) simply mean that we sum all variances and covariances in the matrix of possible pairwise combinations. In our matrix, it is 16, represented by 4 variances and 6 covariances counted twice.

Covariance Formulation   The covariance of the possible returns of two securities is a measure of the extent to which they are expected to vary together rather

Expected rate of return × st deviation

Covariance
measures how closely security returns move together.

than independently of each other. More formally, the covariance term in Eq. (3-2) is

$$\sigma_{jk} = r_{jk}\sigma_j\sigma_k \qquad (3-3)$$

where r_{jk} is the expected correlation between possible returns for securities j and k, σ_j is the standard deviation for security j, and σ_k is the standard deviation for security k. The standard deviations of the probability distributions of possible returns for securities j and k are determined by the methods taken up in the preceding chapter. When $j = k$ in Eq. (3-3), the correlation coefficient is 1.0, and $\sigma_j\sigma_k$ becomes σ_j^2. That is, we are concerned only with the own variance of securities along the diagonal of the matrix.

The formula in Eq. (3-2) makes a very fundamental point. The standard deviation for a portfolio depends not only on the variances of the individual securities but on the covariances between various pairs. As the number of securities in a portfolio increases, the covariance terms become more important relative to the variance terms. This can be seen by examining the matrix. In a two-security portfolio, there are two own variance terms along the diagonal, $\sigma_{1,1}$ and $\sigma_{2,2}$, and two covariance terms, $\sigma_{1,2}$ and $\sigma_{2,1}$. For a four-security portfolio, there are 4 own variance terms and 12 covariance terms. For a large portfolio, then, total variance depends primarily on the covariances among securities. For example, with a 30-security portfolio, there are 30 own variance terms in the matrix and 870 covariance terms. As a portfolio expands further to include all securities, only covariance is important.

Correlation coefficient

Range of Correlation The value of a correlation coefficient always lies in the range from -1 to $+1$. A correlation coefficient of 1.00 indicates that an increase in the return for one security is always associated with a proportional increase in the return for the other security, and similarly for decreases. A correlation coefficient of -1.00 indicates that an increase in the return for one security is always associated with a proportional decrease in the return for the other security, and vice versa. A zero coefficient indicates an absence of correlation, so that the returns of each security vary independently of the other. However, most stock returns tend to move together, so the correlation coefficient between two stocks is positive.

Illustration of Calculations

To illustrate the determination of the parameters of a two-security portfolio, suppose Simplicity Foods, Inc.'s stock has an expected return of 12 percent and a standard deviation of 11 percent, while that of Fast Eddys Electronics Company has an expected return of 18 percent and a standard deviation of 19 percent. The expected correlation between the two security returns is .20. By investing equal portions in each of the two stocks, the expected return for the portfolio is

$$R_p = 12\%(.50) + 18\%(.50) = 15\%$$

This, of course, is simply a weighted average.

If we calculate a weighted average of the standard deviations, we find it to be 15 percent. In fact, this would be the portfolio standard deviation if the correlation coefficient were 1.0. However, Eq. (3-2) tells us the standard deviation is lower when the correlation coefficient is less than 1.0. For a correlation coefficient of .20, the standard deviation is

$$\sigma_p = [(.5)^2\,(1.00)\,(.11)^2 + (2)\,(.5)\,(.5)\,(.20)\,(.11)\,(.19) + (.5)^2\,(1.00)(.19)^2]^{1/2}$$
$$= 11.89\%$$

From Eq. (3-2) we know that the covariance between the two stocks must be counted twice. Therefore, we multiply the covariance by two. When $j = 1$ and $k = 1$ for stock 1, the proportion invested (.5) must be squared, as must the standard deviation (.11). The correlation coefficient, of course, is 1.00. The same thing applies to stock 2 when $j = 2$ and $k = 2$. The important principle to grasp is that as long as the correlation coefficient between two securities is less than 1.00, the standard deviation of the portfolio will be less than the weighted average of the two individual standard deviations.

Two-Security Efficient Set

We see this is the case when the equal investments are made in Simplicity Foods and Fast Eddys Electronics. The standard deviation is 11.89 percent versus 15.00 percent if the correlation coefficient is 1.0. The difference is due to the diversification effect. For other combinations of our two securities, we have the following, again using Eqs. (3-1) and (3-2) to make the calculations:

Portfolio	Proportion Simplicity	Proportion Fast Eddys	Portfolio Return	Portfolio Standard Deviation
1	1.0	0	12.0%	11.0%
2	.8	.2	13.2	10.26
3	.6	.4	14.4	11.02
4	.4	.6	15.6	13.01
5	.2	.8	16.8	15.79
6	0	1.0	18.0	19.00

To visualize things graphically, Fig. 3-2 describes the relationship between expected return and risk when the proportions invested in each security are var-

FIGURE 3-2

Opportunity set for investment in a two-security portfolio

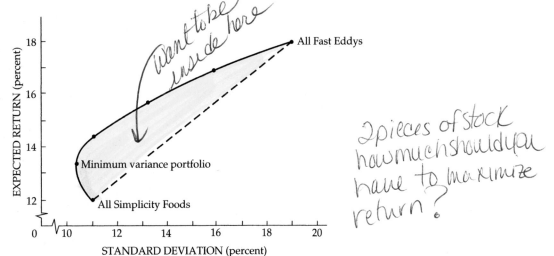

ied. The dots correspond to the six portfolios described above. The curve that connects them is known as the **opportunity set,** and it depicts the risk-return trade-off. Several features in the figure are important.

Diversification Properties   First, the diversification effect is seen by comparing the curved line with the straight dashed line, which connects an all Simplicity Foods investment (portfolio 1) with an all Fast Eddys Electronics investment (portfolio 6). The straight line would describe the opportunity set if perfect positive correlation prevailed—that is, if the correlation coefficient were 1.0. With a correlation coefficient of only .20, a considerable diversification effect is evidenced by the distance between the two lines.

Second, it is possible to reduce the standard deviation from what occurs with a 100 percent investment in Simplicity Foods by investing in the riskier security, Fast Eddys Electronics. This counterintuitive result is due to the diversification effect. Unexpected returns from one security often are offset by opposite movements in returns for the other security. On average, the two-security returns move in the same direction, but with a correlation coefficient of only .20 there are offsets. By investing a moderate amount in Fast Eddys Electronics, one can lower the standard deviation. Therefore, the opportunity set curve is backward bending for a while.

Third, the portfolio depicted farthest to the left is known as the **minimum variance portfolio.** It is the one with the lowest standard deviation that comes about by varying the mix of securities held. In our case, the minimum variance portfolio consists of 80 percent in Simplicity Foods and 20 percent in Fast Eddys Electronics. Using Eq. (3-2), one finds that a 19 percent investment in Fast Eddys Electronics or a 21 percent investment results in a slightly higher standard deviation. The minimum variance portfolio is 80–20. It should be noted that backward bending does not necessarily occur with diversification. It depends on the correlation coefficient, as we will illustrate in the next section.

Fourth, no one would want to own a portfolio with a lower expected return than that provided by the minimum variance portfolio. Therefore, the backward-bending portion of the opportunity set curve is infeasible. The *efficient set* is the portion of the curve going from the minimum variance portfolio, number 2, to the one with the maximum expected return, number 6, consisting of all Fast Eddys Electronics stock.

Fifth, it is only possible to be on the opportunity set line, not above or below it. With only two securities, altering the proportions held affects only one's position on the line.

Different Correlations

With higher correlation between returns, the diversification effect is lower. Figure 3-3 depicts the opportunity set curve for our example when the correlation coefficient is .60, in addition to .20 and 1.00. As seen, the distance from the straight line, representing perfect positive correlation, is lessened. Also, there is no backward bend to the curve. Any investment in Fast Eddys Electronics results in a higher standard deviation than occurs with a 100 percent investment in the safer stock, Simplicity Foods. Therefore, the minimum variance portfolio consists of all funds being invested in Simplicity Foods. The efficient set now is represented by the entire opportunity set line. As seen in the figure, the lower the correlation coefficient between security returns, the more bowed the opportunity set curve and the greater the diversification effect.

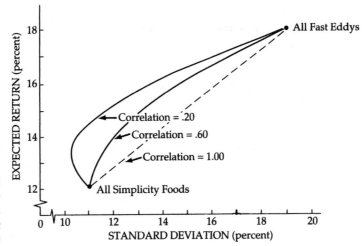

FIGURE 3-3

Opportunity sets for two-security portfolios with different correlation coefficients

The example suggests that by diversifying one's holdings to include securities with less than perfect positive correlation among themselves, the investor is able to reduce the standard deviation of the probability distribution of possible returns relative to the expected return. In other words, risk is lowered relative to expected return.

MULTIPLE SECURITY PORTFOLIO ANALYSIS AND SELECTION

The same principles hold when we go to portfolios containing more than two securities. An example of the opportunity set here is shown in Fig. 3-4. This set is based on the subjective probability beliefs of an individual investor. It reflects all possible portfolios of securities as envisioned by the investor, every point in the shaded area representing a portfolio that is attainable. Note that this opportunity set is different from that for a two-security portfolio, as illustrated in Fig. 3-2. In that figure, we saw that all possible combinations of the two securities fell on a single line. In Fig. 3-4, they fall within a rather large area. As the number of securities

FIGURE 3-4
Hypothetical opportunity set

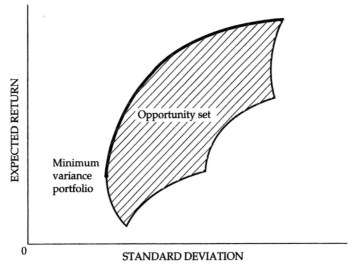

available for investment increases, the number of pairwise and multiple combinations increases geometrically.

The Efficient Set

Efficient set is the combination of securities with the highest expected return for a given standard deviation.

As before, the minimum variance portfolio is the one farthest to the left, possessing the lowest standard deviation. Notice in the figure that the outward edge of the opportunity set is backward bending for a while. This occurs for the same reason that it did for our two-security portfolio example—the diversification effect of offsetting returns. The efficient set, or efficient frontier, as it also is called, is described by the dark line at the top of the opportunity set. It goes from the minimum variance portfolio to the portfolio with the highest expected return.

According to the Markowitz mean-variance maxim, an investor should seek a portfolio of securities that lies on the efficient set.[3] A portfolio is not efficient if there is another portfolio with a higher expected return and a lower standard deviation, a higher expected return and the same standard deviation, or the same expected return but a lower standard deviation. If your portfolio is not efficient, you can increase the expected return without increasing the risk, decrease the risk without decreasing the expected return, or obtain some combination of increased expected return and decreased risk by switching to a portfolio on the efficient frontier. As can be seen, the efficient set is determined on the basis of dominance. Portfolios of securities tend to dominate individual securities because of the reduction in risk obtainable through diversification. As discussed before, this reduction is evident when one explores the implications of Eqs. (3-2) and (3-3).

Utility Functions and Investor Choice

Indifference curves map an investor's utility with respect to expected return and risk.

The best mix of expected return and standard deviation for a security portfolio depends on the investor's utility function. If you are a risk-averse investor who associates risk with divergence from expected value of return, your utility function might be depicted graphically as in Fig. 3-5. The expected return is plotted on the vertical axis, and the standard deviation is along the horizontal. The curves are known as **indifference curves;** the investor is indifferent between any combination of expected return and standard deviation on a particular curve. In other words, a curve is defined by those combinations of expected return and standard deviation that result in a fixed level of expected utility.

The greater the slope of the indifference curves, the more averse the investor is to risk. As we move to the left in Fig. 3-5, each successive curve represents a higher level of expected utility. It is important to note that the exact shape of the indifference curves will not be the same for different investors. While the curves for all risk-averse investors will be upward sloping, a variety of shapes are possible, depending on the risk preferences of the individual. As an investor, you want to hold that portfolio of securities that places you on the highest indifference curve.

Risk-Free Asset In addition to portfolios of risky securities along the efficient set in Fig. 3-4, you will usually be able to invest in a risk-free security that yields a certain future return. This security might be a Treasury security that is held to maturity. Although the expected return may be low, relative to other securities, there is complete certainty of return. Suppose for now that you can not only lend at the

---

[3]Harry M. Markowitz, *Portfolio Selection: Efficient Diversification of Investments* (New York: Wiley, 1959), chaps. 7 and 8.

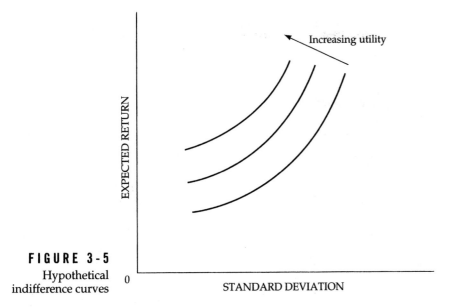

FIGURE 3-5

Hypothetical indifference curves

risk-free rate but borrow at it as well. (We relax this assumption later.) To determine the optimal portfolio under these conditions, we first draw a line from the risk-free rate, R_f, on the *expected return* axis through its point of tangency with the opportunity set of portfolio returns, as illustrated in Fig. 3-6. This line then becomes the new efficient frontier. Note that only one portfolio of risky securities—namely, m—would be considered; it now dominates all others, including those on the efficient frontier of the opportunity set.

FIGURE 3-6

Selection of optimal portfolio when risk-free asset exists

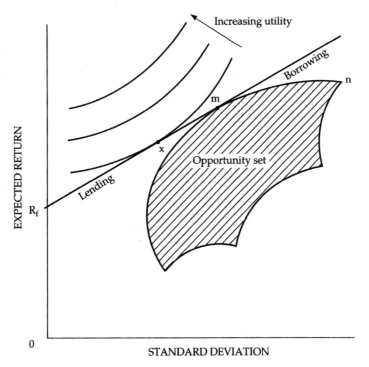

Any point on the straight line tells us the proportion of the risky portfolio, *m*, and the proportion of loans or borrowings at the risk-free rate. To the left of point *m*, you would hold both the risk-free security and portfolio *m*. To the right, you would hold only portfolio *m* and would borrow funds, in addition to your initial investment funds, in order to invest further in it. The farther to the right in the figure, the greater borrowings will be. The overall expected return = (*w*) (expected return on risky portfolio) + (1 − *w*) (risk-free rate), where *w* is the proportion of total wealth invested in portfolio *m*, and 1 − *w* is the proportion invested in the risk-free asset. If lending were involved, *w* would be less than 1.0; if borrowing occurred, it would be greater than 1.0. The overall standard deviation is simply *w* times the standard deviation of the risky portfolio. No account is taken of the risk-free asset because its standard deviation is zero.

Optimal Selection   The optimal investment policy is determined by the point of tangency between the straight line in Fig. 3-6 and the highest indifference curve. As shown in the figure, this point is portfolio *x*, and it consists of lending at the risk-free rate and investing in the risky security portfolio, *m*. If borrowing were prohibited, the efficient set would no longer be a straight line throughout but would consist of line $R_f mn$. The optimal portfolio would be determined in the same manner as before, namely, the tangency of the efficient set with the highest indifference curve.

If market participants have homogeneous expectations, in market equilibrium point *m* represents a portfolio of all securities available in the market, weighted by their respective total market values. By definition, this weighted average portfolio is the **market portfolio**. The straight line in the figure describes the trade-off between expected return and risk for various holdings of the risk-free security and the market portfolio. Thus, two things are involved: the price of time and the price of risk. The former is depicted by the intercept of the line on the vertical axis. The risk-free rate, then, can be thought of as the reward for waiting. The slope of the line represents the market price of risk. It tells us the amount of additional expected return that is required for an increment in standard deviation.

Separation Theorem

The attitude of individual investors toward bearing risk affects only the amount that is loaned or borrowed. It does not affect the optimal portfolio of risky assets. Turning to Fig. 3-6, we would select portfolio *m* of risky assets no matter what the nature of our indifference curves. The reason is that when a risk-free security exists, and borrowing and lending are possible at that rate, the market portfolio dominates all others. As long as they can freely borrow and lend at the risk-free rate, two investors with very different preferences will both choose portfolio *m*.

Thus, the individual's utility preferences are independent of or separate from the optimal portfolio of risky assets. This condition is known as the **separation theorem**.[4] Put another way, it states that the determination of an optimal portfolio of risky assets is independent of the individual's risk preferences. Such a determination depends only on the expected returns and standard deviations for the various possible portfolios of risky assets. In essence, the individual's approach to in-

Separation
of portfolio
selection from
lending/borrowing
permits an investor
greater utility.

---

[4]This theorem was originally stated by J. Tobin, "Liquidity Preference as Behavior towards Risk," *Review of Economic Studies*, 25 (February 1958), 65–86.

vesting is two phased: First determine an optimal portfolio of risky assets; then determine the most desirable combination of the risk-free security and this portfolio. Only the second phase depends on utility preferences. The separation theorem is very important in finance. As we will see, it allows the management of a corporation to make decisions without reference to the attitudes toward risk of individual owners. Rather, security price information can be used to determine required returns, and decisions will be so guided.

Global Diversification

By investing across world financial markets, one can achieve greater diversification than by investing in a single country. As we discuss in Chapter 25, the economic cycles of different countries are not completely synchronized. A weak economy in one country may be offset by a strong economy in another. Moreover, exchange-rate risk and other risks discussed in that chapter add to the diversification effect. The correlation of foreign stock returns with U.S. stock returns historically has been about .30 for Japan, .40 for other East Asian countries, .40 for Continental European countries collectively, .50 for the United Kingdom, and .70 for Canada. It is not always necessary to invest directly in foreign stocks to achieve international diversification. Many foreign equities are traded in the United States under what is known as American Depository Receipts (ADRs). **ADRs** represent certificates of ownership in a foreign company, and they are issued by U.S. banks. Also, numerous mutual funds are dedicated to international stocks; they can be easily purchased by the individual investor.

Back to international diversification. The situation is illustrated in Fig. 3-7. Here the opportunity set of risky securities for the United States is shown by the lightly shaded area. The global opportunity set is superimposed on this, and the increment is shown by the dark shaded area. We see that the outer edge of the global opportunity set is backward bending in the lower left-hand

FIGURE 3-7
Effect of global diversification

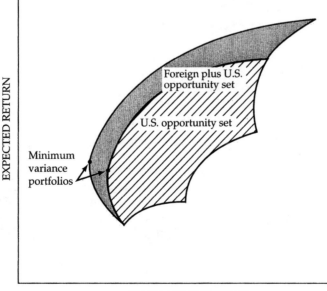

portion of the figure. Although on average foreign stocks have a higher standard deviation than U.S. stocks, the diversification effect offsets this more for moderate increments of foreign stocks into one's portfolio. As a result of greater backward bending, the global minimum variance portfolio has less risk than the domestic minimum variance portfolio. At the other end of the efficient set, the increased number of possible portfolio combinations, some of which have higher expected returns and risk, results in an extension up and to the right. Finally, higher expected foreign returns result in a higher efficient set than occurs with only U.S. stocks.

Several caveats are in order. Just because foreign-stock returns have been good in the past does not mean that this will occur in the future. Second, as financial markets of the world become increasingly integrated, the diversification effect is lessened. Expressed differently, the less segmented the international capital markets, the less opportunity there is to reduce variance. With the unrelenting globalization of finance, the darker shaded area in Fig. 3-7 becomes smaller.

CAPITAL ASSET PRICING MODEL

CAPM is an equilibrium model of the trade-off between expected portfolio return and unavoidable risk.

theoretical

Based on the behavior of the risk-averse investor, there is implied an equilibrium relationship between risk and expected return for each security. In market equilibrium, a security will be expected to provide a return commensurate with its **unavoidable risk**. This is simply the risk that cannot be avoided by diversification. The greater the unavoidable risk of a security, the greater the return that investors will expect from the security. The relationship between expected return and unavoidable risk, and the valuation of securities that follows, is the essence of the capital asset pricing model (CAPM). This model was developed by William F. Sharpe (1990 Nobel Prize winner in economics) and John Lintner in the 1960s, and it has had important implications for finance ever since.[5] Though other models also attempt to capture market behavior, the capital asset pricing model is simple in concept and has real-world applicability.

As with any model, there are assumptions to be made. First, we assume that capital markets are highly efficient where investors are well informed, transaction costs are zero, there are negligible restrictions on investment and no taxes, and no investor is large enough to affect the market price of the stock. We assume also that investors are in general agreement about the likely performance and risk of individual securities and that their expectations are based on a common holding period, say, 1 year. Under these conditions, all investors will perceive the opportunity set of risky securities in the same way and will draw their efficient frontiers in the same place.

There are two types of investment opportunities with which we will be concerned. The first is a risk-free security whose return over the holding period is known with certainty. Frequently, the rate on a Treasury security is used as surrogate for the risk-free rate. The second investment opportunity with which we are concerned is the market portfolio of common stocks. It is represented by all available stocks, weighted according to their market values outstanding. As the market portfolio is a somewhat unwieldy thing with which to work, most people use a surrogate, such as Standard & Poor's 500-Stock Index.

---

[5]See William F. Sharpe, "Capital Asset Prices: A Theory of Market Equilibrium under Conditions of Risk," *Journal of Finance,* 19 (September 1964), 425–42; John Lintner, "The Valuation of Risk Assets and the Selection of Risky Investments in Stock Portfolios and Capital Budgets," *Review of Economics and Statistics,* 47 (February 1965), 13–37; and Eugene P. Fama, "Risk, Return, and Equilibrium: Some Clarifying Comments," *Journal of Finance,* 23 (March 1968), 29–40.

The Characteristic Line

Now we are in a position to compare the expected return for an individual stock with the expected return for the market portfolio. In our comparison, it is useful to deal with returns in excess of the risk-free rate. The *excess return* is simply the expected return less the risk-free return. If the expected relationship is based on past experience, excess returns would be calculated from historical data. Suppose we felt that monthly returns over the last 5 years were a good proxy for the future. For each of the last 60 months we then would compute excess returns for the particular stock involved and for the market portfolio, as represented by Standard & Poor's 500-Stock Index. The monthly return for both is the ending price minus the beginning price plus any dividend that was paid, all over the beginning price. From these returns, the monthly risk-free rate is subtracted to obtain excess returns.

Instead of using historical returns, one might obtain future return estimates from security analysts who follow the stock. Here the focus is on the stock's likely future return *conditional* on a specific market return. For example, if the market return for next period is *x* percent, what is likely to be the stock's return? By posing the question in this way for various market returns, conditional estimates are obtained for a range of possible stock returns. An added refinement might be to ask for some measure of the analyst's uncertainty about the conditional estimates. This might be accomplished simply by requesting a pessimistic estimate, a most likely estimate, and an optimistic estimate, again conditional on a given market return. Thus, there are two ways to go about determining the relationship between excess returns for a stock and excess returns for the market portfolio. We can use historical data, under the assumption that the relationship will continue into the future, or we can go to security analysts to obtain future estimates. As the second approach usually is restricted to investment organizations with a number of security analysts, we will illustrate the relationship using the historical approach.

Having calculated historical excess returns for the stock and for the market portfolio, we plot them. Figure 3-8 compares expected excess returns for a stock with those for the market portfolio. The dots represent the monthly plots of the ex-

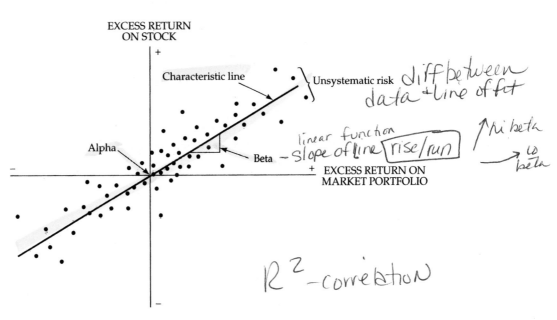

FIGURE 3-8

Relationship between excess returns for stock and excess returns for market portfolio

cess returns, 60 in all. The colored line fitted to the dots describes the historical relationship between excess returns for the stock and excess returns for the market portfolio. This line is known as the **characteristic line,** and it is used as a proxy for the expected relationship between the two sets of excess returns.

A Security's Alpha

The graph reveals that the greater the expected excess return for the market, the greater the expected excess return for the stock. Three measures are important. The first is known as the **alpha,** and it is simply the intercept of the characteristic line on the vertical axis. If the excess return for the market portfolio were expected to be zero, the alpha would be the expected excess return for the stock. In theory, the alpha for an individual stock should be zero.

If it were less than zero, as a rational investor you would avoid the stock because you could do better with some combination of risk-free asset and the market portfolio (minus the stock). If enough people avoid it, of course, the price will decline and the expected return will increase. How long will this go on? In theory, until the alpha rises to zero. One can visualize the equilibration process by supposing the characteristic line in Fig. 3-8 were below but parallel to the line shown. As the security declines in price, its expected return rises and the characteristic line shifts upward to where eventually it passes through the origin. If the alpha were positive, the opposite equilibrium process would occur; people would rush to buy the security, and this would cause the price to rise and the expected return to decline.[6] We assume, then, that the alpha for a particular stock is zero.

The Systematic Risk as Measured by Beta

The second measure with which we are concerned, and most important for our purposes, is the **beta.** The beta is simply the slope of the characteristic line. It depicts the sensitivity of the security's excess return to that of the market portfolio. If the slope is 1, it means that excess returns for the stock vary proportionally with excess returns for the market portfolio. In other words, the stock has the same unavoidable or systematic risk as the market as a whole. A slope steeper than 1 means that the stock's excess return varies more than proportionally with the excess return of the market portfolio. Put another way, it has more systematic risk than the market as a whole. This type of stock is often called an "aggressive" investment. A slope less than 1, as is the case in Fig. 3-8, means that the stock has less unavoidable or systematic risk than does the market as a whole. This type of stock is often called a "defensive" investment.

Amplification of Risk   The greater the slope of the characteristic line for a stock, as depicted by its beta, the greater its systematic risk. This means that for both upward and downward movements in market excess returns, movements in excess returns for the individual stock are greater or less, depending on its beta. If the beta for a particular stock were 1.70 and the market excess return for a specific month were −2.00 percent, this would imply an expected excess return for the stock of −3.40 percent. Thus, the beta represents the systematic risk of a stock due to underlying movements

The beta of a stock is the slope of the characteristic line between returns for the stock and those for the market.

---

[6]The alpha for the market portfolio is simply a weighted average of the alphas for the individual stocks making up the portfolio. In efficient markets, rational investors seize on any deviation from zero of the alpha of an individual stock. As the alphas of individual stocks will be driven to zero, the weighted average of alphas of stocks comprising the market portfolio also must be zero. It should be pointed out that some empirical tests have shown positive alphas for low-beta stocks and negative alphas for high-beta stocks. Various reasons have been advanced for this occurrence.

in security prices. This risk cannot be diversified away by investing in more stocks because it depends on such things as changes in the economy and in the political atmosphere, which affect all stocks. In summary, the beta of a stock represents its contribution to the risk of a highly diversified portfolio of stocks.

Systematic risk is the variability of a security's return with that of the overall stock market.

Empirical work on the stability of historical beta information over time suggests that past betas are useful in predicting future betas; however, the ability to predict seems to vary with the size of the portfolio. The larger the number of securities in a portfolio, the greater the stability of the beta for that portfolio over time. Even for the individual stock, however, past beta information has been found to have reasonable predictive value. In addition to portfolio size, betas tend to show greater stability as longer time intervals are studied.

Obtaining Betas   A number of organizations regularly compute and publish betas for actively traded stocks. The better-known services include Merrill Lynch and Value Line. The typical analysis involves either monthly or weekly returns on the stock and on the market index for 3 to 5 years in the past. For example, Merrill Lynch uses monthly returns for 5 years in the past, whereas Value Line uses weekly returns, again for 5 years in the past. The interval employed seems to make a difference. Weekly calculated betas tend to be less than monthly calculated betas for high beta levels, but higher for low levels of beta.[7] Thus, one must be mindful of the return interval used in the calculations, for calculated betas of high-risk and of low-risk securities change differently as the interval is increased.

Because beta information is readily available from various services, one is saved the task of computing it. An example of betas for a sample of companies using weekly returns is shown in Table 3-1. The betas of most stocks range from .7 to 1.4, though some are lower and some are higher. If the past systematic risk of a stock seems likely to prevail in the future, the historical beta can be used as a proxy for the expected beta coefficient.

Adjusting Historical Betas   There appears to be a tendency for the measured betas of individual securities to revert eventually toward the beta of the market portfolio, 1.0, or toward the beta of the industry of which the company is a part. This tendency may be due to economic factors affecting the operations and financing of the firm and perhaps to statistical factors. To adjust for this tendency, Merrill Lynch, Value Line, and certain others calculate an **adjusted beta.** To illustrate, suppose the reversion process were toward the market beta of 1.0. If the measured beta were 1.5 and a .70 weight were attached to it and .30 to the market beta, the adjusted beta would be 1.5(.70) + 1.0(.30) = 1.35. The same could be done if the reversion process were toward an industry average beta of, say, 1.2. As one is concerned with the beta of a security in the future, it may be appropriate to adjust the measured beta if the reversion process just described is clear and consistent.

Unsystematic Risk

The last of the three measures with which we are concerned is the unsystematic, or avoidable, risk of a security. Unsystematic risk derives from the variability of the stock's excess return *not* associated with movements in the excess return of the

---

[7]Frank K. Reilly and David J. Wright, "A Comparison of Published Betas," *Journal of Portfolio Management,* 14 (Spring 1988), 64–69; and Puneet Handa, S. P. Kothari, and Charles Wasley, "The Relation between the Return Interval and Betas," *Journal of Financial Economics,* 23 (June 1989), 79–100. The reasoning of the latter is that a security's return covariance with the market return and market's return variance may not change proportionately as the return interval is increased.

TABLE 3-1
Some Betas (July 2000)

Company	Beta
AMR Corp. (Airline)	1.35
Battle Mountain Gold Company	.50
CMGI (Internet holdings)	1.80
Caterpillar, Inc.	1.10
Cisco Systems	1.35
Coca-Cola	1.00
Diamond Offshore (Oil drilling)	1.10
Exxon-Mobil Corporation	.80
The Gap, Inc. (Clothing retailer)	1.50
General Electric	1.25
IDACORP (Utility)	.50
Intel Corporation	1.10
Johnson & Johnson (Pharmaceuticals)	.95
Kaufman & Broad Home	1.45
Kellogg	.75
Merrill Lynch & Company	1.85
Office Depot	1.25
Oshkosh B'Gosh (Clothing)	.90
Procter & Gamble	.85
Safeway	.80
Telefonos de Mexico	1.20
Tootsie Roll Industries	.70
Yahoo!	1.60

market as a whole. This risk is described by the dispersion of the estimates involved in predicting a stock's characteristic line. In Fig. 3-8, the unsystematic risk is represented by the relative distance of the dots from the solid line. The greater the dispersion, the greater the unsystematic risk of a stock. By diversification of stocks in our portfolio, however, we can reduce unsystematic risk.

Thus, the total risk involved in holding a stock is comprised of two parts:

Unsystematic risk
is the amount of a stock's variance unexplained by overall market movements. It can be diversified away.

$$\text{Total risk} = \underset{\substack{\text{(nondiversifiable} \\ \text{or unavoidable)}}}{\text{Systematic risk}} + \underset{\substack{\text{(diversifiable} \\ \text{or avoidable)}}}{\text{Unsystematic risk}} \qquad (3\text{-}4)$$

The first part is due to the overall market risk—changes in the nation's economy, tax reform by Congress, a change in the world energy situation—risks that affect securities overall and, consequently, cannot be diversified away. In other words, even the investor who holds a well-diversified portfolio will be exposed to this type of risk. The second risk component, however, is unique to a particular company, being independent of economic, political, and other factors that affect securities in a systematic manner. A wildcat strike may affect only one company; a new competitor may begin to produce essentially the same product; a technological breakthrough can make an existing product obsolete. However, by diversification this kind of risk can be reduced and even eliminated if diversification is efficient. Therefore, not all of the risk involved in holding a stock is relevant; part of it can be diversified away.

Adding Securities to a Portfolio Unsystematic risk is reduced at a decreasing rate toward zero as more randomly selected securities are added to the portfolio. Various studies suggest that 15 to 20 stocks selected randomly are sufficient to eliminate most of the unsystematic risk of a portfolio. Thus, a substantial reduction in unsystematic risk can be achieved with a relatively moderate amount of diversification. Conceptually, diversification can be viewed in the manner portrayed in Fig. 3-9. As the number of randomly selected securities held in the portfolio is increased, the total risk of the portfolio is reduced in keeping with the reduction of unsystematic risk. Such a reduction is at a decreasing rate, however. Efficient diversification reduces the total risk of the portfolio to the point where only systematic risk remains.

For the typical stock, unsystematic risk accounts for around 75 percent of the total risk or variance of the stock. Expressed differently, systematic risk explains only about 25 percent of the total variability of an individual stock. The proportion of total risk explained by movements of the market is represented by the R-square statistic for the regression of excess returns for a stock against excess returns for the market portfolio. (R-square measures the proportion of the total variance of the dependent variable that is explained by the independent variable; it is simply the correlation coefficient squared.) The proportion of total risk unique to the stock is one minus R-square.

Unsystematic Risk Is Stock Specific The proportion of systematic risk to total risk depends on the particular stock. The excess-return relationship depicted in Fig. 3-8 is an example of relatively little unsystematic risk; the observations are tightly clustered around the characteristic line. Contrast this with a more typical situation,

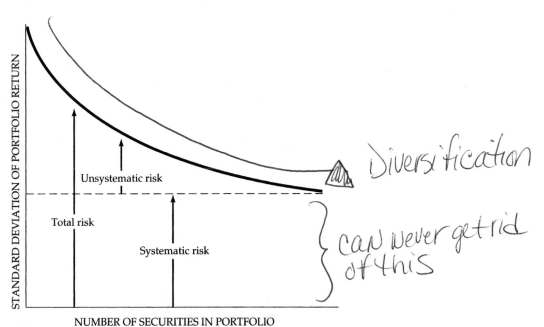

FIGURE 3-9
Total, unsystematic, and systematic risk

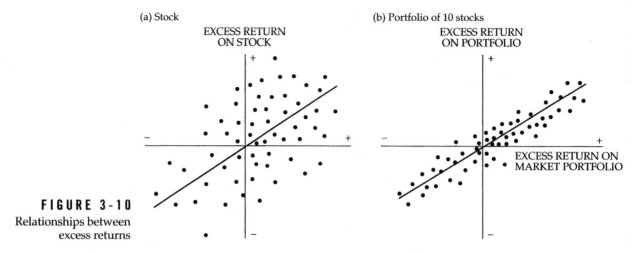

(a) Stock

EXCESS RETURN
ON STOCK

(b) Portfolio of 10 stocks

EXCESS RETURN
ON PORTFOLIO

EXCESS RETURN ON
MARKET PORTFOLIO

FIGURE 3-10
Relationships between
excess returns

such as that shown in panel (a) of Fig. 3-10. Here the observations are scattered rather widely around the characteristic line, indicating a good deal of unsystematic risk. However, this variability can be reduced through diversification. Suppose you diversify by investing in 10 stocks whose weighted average beta is the same as the slope of the characteristic line in panel (a). The result might be that shown in panel (b). We see that with reasonable diversification, the scatter of excess-return observations about the characteristic line is reduced considerably. It is not eliminated because it would take more stocks to do that. However, the scatter is much less than it is for the individual security, and this is the essence of diversification.

The CAPM assumes that all risk other than systematic risk has been diversified away. Stated differently, if capital markets are efficient and investors at the margin are well diversified, the important risk of a stock is its unavoidable or systematic risk. The risk of a well-diversified portfolio is a value-weighted average of the systematic risks (betas) of the stocks comprising that portfolio. Unsystematic, or diversifiable, risk plays no role.

EXPECTED RETURN FOR INDIVIDUAL SECURITY

For the individual security, then, the relevant risk is not the standard deviation of the security itself (total risk), but the marginal effect the security has on the standard deviation of an efficiently diversified portfolio (systematic risk). As a result, a security's expected return should be related to its degree of systematic risk, not to its degree of total risk. Systematic risk is the thing that matters to an investor holding a well-diversified portfolio. If we assume that unsystematic risk is diversified away, the expected rate of return for stock j is

$$\overline{R}_j = R_f + (\overline{R}_m - R_f)\beta_j \qquad (3\text{-}5)$$

where again R_f is the risk-free rate, $\overline{R}_m$ is the expected overall return for the market portfolio, and β_j is the beta coefficient for security j as defined earlier. The greater the beta of a security, the greater the risk and the greater the expected return required. By the same token, the lower the beta, the lower the risk, the more valuable it becomes, and the lower the expected return required.

Illustration   Put another way, the expected rate of return for a stock is equal to the return required by the market for a riskless investment plus a risk premium. In turn, the risk premium is a function of (1) the expected market return less the risk-free rate, which represents the risk premium required for the typical stock in the market; and (2) the beta coefficient. Suppose the expected return on Treasury securities is 6 percent, the expected return on the market portfolio is 11 percent, and the beta of Pro-Fli Corporation is 1.3. The beta indicates that Pro-Fli has more systematic risk than the typical stock. Given this information and using Eq. (3-5), we find that the expected return for Pro-Fli's stock would be

Expected return in a CAPM context is the risk-free rate plus a premium for systematic risk based on beta.

$$\overline{R}_j = .06 + (.11 - .06)(1.3) = 12.5\%$$

What this tells us is that, on average, the market expects Pro-Fli to show a 12.5 percent annual return. Because Pro-Fli has more systematic risk than the typical stock in the marketplace, its expected return is higher. Suppose now that we are interested in a defensive stock, First Safety Inc., whose beta coefficient is only .7. Its expected return is

$$\overline{R}_j = .06 + (.11 - .06)(.7) = 9.5\%$$

Because this stock has less systematic risk than the typical stock in the market, its expected return is less. Therefore, different stocks will have different expected returns, depending on their betas.

Betas Are Additive   The beta of a portfolio is simply a weighted average of the betas of the securities comprising the portfolio. If a portfolio consisted of .60 of Pro-Fli Corporation and .40 of First Safety Inc., the beta of the portfolio would be

$$\beta_p = .60(1.3) + .40(.7) = 1.06$$

If the risk-free rate and expected market return were the same as above, the portfolio's expected return would be

$$\overline{R}_p = .06 + (.11 - .06)(1.06) = 11.3\%$$

This is the same as the weighted average of the two expected returns previously calculated.

Expected Return Expressed Differently

Equation (3-5) can be expressed in a different way.[8] If we go back to our discussion of the calculation of covariance, we know that the beta of a security is a measure of the responsiveness of its excess returns to those of the market portfolio. Mathematically, this responsiveness is nothing more than the covariance between possible returns for security *j* and the market portfolio divided by the variance of the probability distribution of possible returns for the market portfolio. Therefore, the beta of security *j* can be expressed as

$$\beta_j = \frac{(r_{jm}\sigma_j\sigma_m)}{\sigma_m^2} \qquad (3\text{-}6)$$

---

[8]This section can be passed over without loss of continuity by those not interested in a mathematical representation of expected return.

where $(r_{jm}\sigma_j\sigma_m)$ is the covariance of returns for security j with those of the market. In turn, it embodies r_{jm}, the expected correlation between possible returns for security j and the market portfolio; σ_j, the standard deviation of the probability distribution of possible returns for security j; and σ_m, the standard deviation of the probability distribution of possible returns for the market portfolio. Finally, σ_m^2 is the variance of the market portfolio.

Substituting Eq. (3-6) into Eq. (3-5), we obtain

$$\overline{R}_j = R_f + \frac{\overline{R}_m - R_f}{\sigma_m^2}(r_{jm}\sigma_j\sigma_m) \tag{3-7}$$

In Eq. (3-7) it is possible to cancel by σ_m in the last term, leading to the equation

$$\overline{R}_j = R_f + \frac{\overline{R}_m - R_f}{\sigma_m}(r_{jm}\sigma_j) \tag{3-8}$$

This equation may be interpreted in the following way: The expected return of security j consists of the risk-free rate and a risk premium represented by the remaining term on the right-hand side. This risk premium term can be analyzed further: σ_j represents the total risk of security j, but of this total risk, only a fraction measured by r_{jm} is systematic. In other words, the diversified investor can avoid a fraction $(1 - r_{jm})$ of the risk represented by σ_j. The fraction $(\overline{R}_m - R_f)/\sigma_m$ represents the market relationship between systematic risk and the risk premium required by the market. It can be thought of as the market price of systematic risk and is equal to the slope of the line in Fig. 3-6. The risk premium, or return in excess of the risk-free rate, is equal to the product of the systematic risk $(r_{jm}\sigma_j)$ and the market price of that risk, $(\overline{R}_m - R_f)/\sigma_m$.

The systematic risk of security j, measured in absolute terms, is $(r_{jm}\sigma_j)$. Alternatively, we may choose to measure the systematic risk in relative terms by relating it to the risk of the market portfolio, σ_m. If we divide $(r_{jm}\sigma_j)$ by the measure of market risk, σ_m, we obtain the beta of security j:

$$\beta_j = \frac{(r_{jm}\sigma_j)}{\sigma_m} \tag{3-9}$$

We can therefore use β_j as a measure of the relative systematic risk of security j.

The Security Market Line

Security market line
describes the market
price of risk in the
capital markets.

In market equilibrium, the relationship between an individual security's expected rate of return and its systematic risk, as measured by beta, will be linear. The relationship is known as the **security market line,** and it is illustrated in Fig. 3-11. Under the assumptions of the CAPM, all securities lie along this line. The figure shows that the expected return on a risky security is a combination of the risk-free rate plus a premium for risk. This risk premium is necessary to induce risk-averse investors to buy a risky security. We see that the expected return for the market portfolio is $\overline{R}_m$, consisting of the risk-free rate, R_f, plus the risk premium, $\overline{R}_m - R_f$. Inasmuch as the unsystematic risk of a security can be eliminated by the well-diversified investor, investors overall are not compensated for bearing such risk according to the CAPM. The investor in only a single security will be exposed to both systematic and unsystematic risk but will be rewarded for only the systematic risk that is borne.

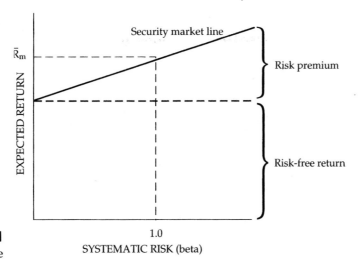

FIGURE 3-11
Security market line

Total versus Systematic Risk   In fact, it is possible for a security with a great deal of total risk to have actually lower systematic risk than a security with only a moderate amount of total risk. Take the case of a new mining company endeavoring to discover gold and silver in the Rocky Mountains. Though the total risk of the company is considerable, the finding of gold and silver deposits is almost a chance event. As a result, the security's return bears little relation to the market overall. In a well-diversified portfolio, its unsystematic risk is unimportant. Only its systematic risk matters, and this by definition is low, say, a beta of .4. On the other hand, the return from a stock of a large consumer company, such as Coca-Cola Corporation, is closely tied to the overall economy. Such stocks have only moderate unsystematic risk, so that their total risk may be less than that of the new mining company. Their systematic risk, however, is approximately that of the market as a whole, say, a beta of 1.0.

As an individual security, the mining company may be considerably more risky than Coca-Cola, but as part of a well-diversified portfolio, it is less risky. Consequently, its expected or required return in the market will be less. This counterintuitive example points to the importance of differentiating systematic risk from total risk. Although there is a tendency for stocks with large systematic risk to have large unsystematic risk as well, there can be exceptions to this generalization.

Under- and Overvaluations   Thus, in market equilibrium the CAPM implies an expected return–risk relationship for all individual securities (the security market line). If an individual security has an expected return–risk combination that places it above the security market line, it will be undervalued in the market. That is, it provides an expected return in excess of that required by the market for the systematic risk involved: $\overline{R}_j > R_f + (\overline{R}_m - R_f)\beta_j$. As a result, the security will be attractive to investors. According to the theory, the increased demand will cause the price to rise. How far? Until the expected return declines sufficiently for the security to lie on the security market line and, thereby, for $R_j = R_f + (\overline{R}_m - R_f)\beta_j$. An overvalued security is characterized by an expected return–risk combination that places it below the security market line. This security is unattractive, and investors holding it will sell it and those not holding it will avoid it. The price will fall and expected return will rise until there is consistency with the security market line and with equilibrium pricing.

Implications for the Valuation of the Firm

We have explored some of the foundations of valuation in a market context. Our exploration has not been complete, but we are getting a background for a deeper look into the valuation implications of decisions by the individual firm. As we have seen, value depends not only on the security or firm itself but also on other securities available for investment. By analyzing decisions in relation to their likely effect on expected return and systematic risk, we are able to judge their effect on valuation. According to the presentation so far, unsystematic risk or risk unique to the firm is not important because it can be diversified away. More will be said about this shortly.

In keeping with the CAPM and the separation theorem, we are able to make certain generalizations about the valuation of a company, without having to determine directly the risk preferences of investors. If management wishes to act in the best interests of the owners, it will attempt to maximize the market value of the stock. Recall from Chapter 2 that the market value per share can be expressed as the present value of the stream of expected future dividends:

$$P_0 = \sum_{t=1}^{\infty} \frac{D_t}{(1 + k)^t} \tag{3-10}$$

where P_0 is the market price per share at time 0, D_t is the expected dividend at the end of period t, and k is the required rate of return. The CAPM approach allows us to determine the appropriate discount rate to employ in discounting expected dividends to their present value. That rate will be the risk-free rate plus a premium sufficient to compensate for the systematic risk associated with the expected dividend stream. The greater the systematic risk, of course, the greater the risk premium and the return required and the lower the value of the stock, all other things being the same. Thus, we are pointed toward determining required rates of return for individual securities.

Seemingly, all decisions of the firm should be judged in a market context, using the CAPM. Recall, however, that the model presented has a number of simplifying assumptions, some of them untenable in the real world. To the extent that they do not hold, unique or unsystematic risk may become a factor affecting valuation. Indeed, a good portion of our discussion in Parts II and III is devoted to exploring market imperfections that make unsystematic risk a factor of importance.

CERTAIN ISSUES WITH THE CAPM

To put across important concepts, we have presented the capital asset pricing model (CAPM) without a number of issues surrounding its usefulness. To better understand the model, we explore certain problem areas in this section. Further extensions are described in Chapter 4.

Maturity of Risk-Free Security

There is agreement that the risk-free rate used in the CAPM should be a Treasury security, which is free of default risk at least in nominal terms. There is disagreement as to the maturity. The CAPM is a one-period model. As a result, many advocate the use of an interest rate on a short-term government security, like a Treasury bill. Others reason that the purpose of determining a required equity return is to judge whether long-term capital investments are worthwhile (see Chapter 8). Therefore, a long-term rate, like that on Treasury bonds, should be used. Still others argue for use of an intermediate-term rate, like that on 3-year Treasury securities. This rate fluctuates less than the Treasury bill rate, and its use recognizes that many capital investment projects are intermediate term in nature.

Which maturity is used may make a difference in the required return calculated. This is due to long-term interest rates usually exceeding intermediate-term rates, which, in turn, exceed short-term rates. If the beta of a security is less than 1.0, a higher calculated required equity return will be obtained if a long-term Treasury rate is used. It often is the situation that in public utility rate cases the public utility commission, which wants a low measured equity cost so that low utility rates can be justified, argues for use of the Treasury bill rate. On the other hand, the public utility, which wants a high measured cost, advocates use of a long-term Treasury bond rate. The reason is that most utility stocks have betas significantly less than 1.0.

Equity Risk Premium

The expected **equity risk premium**, $\overline{R}_m - R_f$, has ranged from 3 to 7 percent in recent years. It tends to be larger when interest rates are low and smaller when they are high. The equity risk premium also can change over time with changes in investor risk aversion. In turn, this is a function of economic and interest-rate cycles. We know also that it matters whether a short-term, an intermediate-term, or a long-term interest rate is used for the risk-free rate.

The expected risk premium is *not* the equity risk premium realized historically. As compiled by Ibbotson Associates, stock returns exceeded the return on Treasury bills by 9.5 percent for the 1926–1999 period, using the arithmetic average.[9] Put differently, the investor was rewarded with an excess return above the Treasury bill rate of 9.5 percent on average for the 74-year time frame. For long-term government bond rates, the excess for common stocks was 7.8 percent, and for intermediate-term governments it was 7.9 percent. For geometric averages, the excess common stock returns were 7.5 percent over Treasury bills, 6.2 percent over long-term government bond rates, and 6.1 percent over intermediate-term government bond rates. For cumulative wealth changes over long sweeps of time, many consider the geometric average to be better. It tells you the amount of wealth you will have at the end, given the annual returns. The arithmetic average best expresses the excess return for a single year. Obviously, it makes a difference which average is used.

For both averages, there is the question of whether past realized returns are a good proxy for the future. After all, they are backward looking. Involved is a time period marked by the stock market crash of 1929, the Great Depression, World War II, the Cold War, and many other conflicts. Many of us consider the true risk for investing in stocks to be higher for this time frame than it is at present. Therefore, higher returns would be in order for the past compared with the present.

Thus, there is disagreement as to what is the appropriate market risk premium. My preference is an ex ante, beforehand estimate by investment analysts and economists, as opposed to an ex post, backward-looking return. This allows for a change

---

[9]*Stocks, Bonds, Bills and Inflation 2000 Yearbook* (Chicago: Ibbotson Associates, 2000).

in the risk premium over time. The issue will be addressed further in Chapter 8, when we consider required rates of return for capital investments by corporations. For now, bear in mind the controversy on which reasonable people differ.

Faulty Use of the Market Index

There are problems in the use of any index as a proxy for the overall market portfolio. The "true" market portfolio consists of all assets—stocks, bonds, real estate, and human capital. Richard Roll has analyzed the problem of using the wrong security market line and has categorized errors that can occur.[10] Roll does not suggest that the capital asset pricing model is somehow devoid of meaning but that tests of it are suspect and must be evaluated with caution. Unless the true market portfolio is known and employed, tests of the CAPM are likely to result in faulty measurement of security performance. As the proxy market index is only a subset of the true market portfolio, it is unlikely to capture the basis of the underlying market equilibration process. Therefore, the measurement of security performance for various investment strategies will be ambiguous. In addition to Roll's criticism, it is bothersome that a stock's beta shows considerable variation depending on whether the New York Stock Exchange Index, the Standard & Poor's 500-Stock Index, Wilshire's 5,000 Stock Index, or some other index is employed.

Fama–French and Beta as a Risk Measure

As we know, the key ingredient in the CAPM is the use of beta as a measure of risk. Early empirical studies showed beta to have reasonable predictive power as to return, particularly the return on a portfolio of stocks. For sharp downside movements in stock prices, beta was an effective predictor of riskiness. Increasingly, however, there were challenges, not only for the reasons previously discussed, but for others.

For one thing, several anomalies were observed that the CAPM could not explain. While anomalies will be explored in Chapter 4, we must mention two now. One is a *small stock effect*. It has been found that stocks with small market capitalizations (share price times the number of shares outstanding) provide higher returns than high capitalization stocks, holding constant the effect of beta. Another anomaly is that stocks with *low price/earnings and market-to-book-value ratios* do better than stocks with high ratios. Again this is after the effect of beta is held constant.

In a provocative article, Fama and French (FF) empirically test the relationship between stock returns and market capitalization (size), market-to-book value, and beta.[11] They found the first two variables to be powerful predictors of average stock returns, having significant negative relationships with average returns. Moreover, when these variables were used first (in a regression), beta was found to have little explanatory power. This led Professor Fama, a highly respected researcher, to separately proclaim that beta as the sole variable explaining returns was dead!

---

[10]Richard Roll, "A Critique of the Asset Pricing Theory Tests," *Journal of Financial Economics*, 4 (March 1977), 129–76; and "Performance Evaluation and Benchmark Errors," *Journal of Portfolio Management*, 6 (Summer 1980), 5–12.

[11]Eugene F. Fama and Kenneth R. French, "The Cross-Section of Expected Stock Returns," *Journal of Finance*, 47 (June 1992), 427–65. See also FF, "Common Risk Factors in the Returns on Stocks and Bonds," *Journal of Financial Economics*, 33 (February 1993), 3–56.

Thus, FF launched a powerful attack on the ability of the CAPM to explain stock returns, suggesting that size and market-to-book value are the appropriate proxies for risk. However, market value is embraced in both variables, and it is market-value changes, together with dividends, which the regressions try to explain. As market value appears in the dependent as well as the independent variables, this is bound to result in explanatory power. A number of critics have attacked FF's methodology with varying degrees of support for the CAPM. (See references at the end of the chapter.)

Fama–French do not really focus on risk, but rather on realized returns. No theoretical foundation is offered for the findings they discover. Although beta may not be a good indicator of the returns to be realized from investing in stocks, it remains a reasonable measure of risk. To the extent investors are risk averse, beta gives information as to the underlying minimum return that should be earned. This return may or may not be realized by investors.

Some Final Observations

Despite challenges, the CAPM is widely used because it is a practical equilibrium model.

The CAPM is intuitively appealing in that expected return logically follows from the risk a security adds to an overall portfolio. Because of its simplicity, the CAPM is widely used, both in the securities industry and in corporate finance. A workable alternative with superior empirical support has not been advanced. We recognize that the market equilibration process is complex and that the CAPM cannot give a precise measurement of the required return for a particular company. Still the CAPM trade-off between risk and return is a useful guide for approximating capital costs and thereby allocating capital to investment projects.

However, the model has a number of challenges, as we have discovered in this section.[12] Extensions of the CAPM and alternative models are being actively developed. These models, where multiple variables and factors are employed, are examined in the next chapter.

■ Summary

Capital markets are said to be efficient when security prices fully reflect all available information. In such a market, security prices adjust very rapidly to new information. Another definition of market efficiency is the lack of security arbitrage opportunities, their having been eliminated by arbitragers.

The risk of a portfolio depends not only on the standard deviations of the individual se-

curities comprising the portfolio but also on the correlation of possible returns. For a two-security portfolio, an opportunity set line describes the risk–return trade-off for various combinations. The diversification effect sometimes causes the opportunity set line to bend backward, with the minimum variance portfolio having a lower standard deviation than that of the least-risky security. The efficient set is the

---

[12]An additional challenge to the traditional capital asset pricing model is a consumption-based CAPM, where markets equilibrate in terms of people's desires for real consumption and investment (inflation adjusted). See Douglas T. Breeden, "An Intertemporal Asset Pricing Model with Stochastic Consumption and Investment Opportunities," *Journal of Financial Economics*, 7 (September 1979), 265–96; and Douglas T. Breeden, Michael R. Gibbons, and Robert H. Litzenberger, "Empirical Tests of the Consumption Oriented CAPM," *Journal of Finance*, 44 (June 1989), 231–62.

portion of the opportunity set line going from the minimum variance portfolio to the one with the highest expected return.

By diversifying our holdings to include securities that are not perfectly correlated with each other, we can reduce risk relative to expected return. We wish to maximize utility as depicted by our indifference curves in relation to the opportunity set of risky securities available. With the existence of a risk-free security, the focus becomes a line from the risk-free rate to the point of tangency with the opportunity set. This point is the market portfolio, given our assumptions. The most desirable combination of risk-free security and market portfolio is determined by the point of tangency of investors' indifference curves with the capital market line. This two-phased approach to investing constitutes the separation theorem.

The capital asset pricing model allows us to draw certain implications about the expected return of a specific security. The key assumptions in the model are that perfect capital markets exist and that investors have homogeneous expectations. In this context, the relevant risk of a security is its undiversifiable risk. This risk is described by the slope of the characteristic line, where security returns in excess of the risk-free rate are related to excess returns for the market portfolio. Known also as beta, it is used as a measure of the systematic risk of a security. The total risk of a security can be divided into systematic and unsystematic components. Systematic risk is risk that cannot be diversified away, for it affects all securities in the market. Unsystematic risk is unique to the particular security and can be eliminated with efficient diversification.

The market equilibrium relationship between systematic risk (beta) and expected return is known as the security market line. With this approach, we are able to estimate required rates of return for individual securities. A number of problems plague the CAPM, including the maturity of the risk-free asset, whether the market risk premium should be the expected or the historical, the faulty use of a market index, and whether beta is the appropriate risk measure. However, the CAPM is practical and widely used. In Chapter 4 we explore alternative valuation models. In yet other parts of the book, we draw implications of the CAPM and of other models for financial decisions.

FINCOACH EXERCISES

FinCoach on the Prentice Hall Finance Center CD-ROM (Practice Center) has the following categories of practice exercises, which pertain to things taken up in this chapter: 5. Stock Valuation; 7. Portfolio Diversification; and 8. CAPM.

Self-Correction Problems

1. You are able to both borrow and lend at the risk-free rate of 9 percent. The market portfolio of securities has an expected return of 15 percent and a standard deviation of 21 percent. Determine the expected return and standard deviations of the following portfolios.
   a. All wealth is invested in the risk-free asset.
   b. One-third is invested in the risk-free asset and two-thirds in the market portfolio.

    c. All wealth is invested in the market portfolio. Furthermore, you borrow an additional one-third of your wealth to invest in the market portfolio.

2. Zwing-Zook Enterprises has a beta of 1.45. The risk-free rate is 6 percent and the expected return on the market portfolio is 10 percent. The company presently pays a dividend of $2 a share and investors expect it to experience a growth in dividends of 7 percent per annum for many years to come.

    a. What is the stock's required rate of return according to the CAPM?

    b. What is the stock's present market price per share, assuming this required return?

3. The common stocks of Blatz Company and Stratz, Inc., have expected returns of 15 percent and 20 percent, respectively, while the standard deviations are 20 percent and 40 percent. The expected correlation coefficient between the two stocks is .36. What is the expected value of return and standard deviation of a portfolio consisting of (a) 40 percent Blatz and 60 percent Stratz? (b) 40 percent Stratz and 60 percent Blatz?

Problems

1. Rosita Ramirez invests the following sums of money in common stocks having expected returns as follows:

Security	Amount Invested	Expected Return
Morck Drug	$ 6,000	14%
Kota Chemical	11,000	16
Fazio Electronics	9,000	17
Northern California Utility	7,000	13
Grizzle Restaurants	5,000	20
Pharlap Oil	13,000	15
Excell Corporation	9,000	18

    a. What is the expected return (percentage) on her portfolio?

    b. What would be her expected return if she quadrupled her investment in Grizzle Restaurants while leaving everything else the same?

2. Securities D, E, and F have the following characteristics with respect to expected return, standard deviation, and the correlation between them:

| Company | R | SD | Correlation Coefficients | | |
			D–E	D–F	E–F
D	.08	.02	.4	.6	
E	.15	.16	.4		.8
F	.12	.08		.6	.8

What is the expected return and standard deviation of a portfolio composed of equal investments in each?

3. Dot Thermal Controls Company's common stock has an expected return of 20 percent and a standard deviation of 22 percent. Sierra Nevada Electric Company's stock has an expected return of 12 percent and a standard deviation of 11 percent. The correlation coefficient between returns for the two stocks is .30.

    a. What portfolio expected returns and standard deviations arise from investing varying proportions of your funds in these two stocks? Vary your proportions in increments of .10, going from 1.00 in Sierra Nevada Electric and 0 in Dot Thermal Controls to .90 and .10, to .80 and .20, and so forth.

    b. (1) Approximately what is the minimum variance portfolio? (2) What is the efficient set?

    c. If the correlation coefficient were .70, what would happen to the diversification effect and to the minimum variance portfolio?

4. The following portfolios are available in the market:

		Portfolio			
	A	**B**	**C**	**D**	**E**
Expected return	.15	.07	.13	.17	.11
Standard deviation	.11	.02	.08	.15	.05

    a. Assume that you can invest in only one of these portfolios; that is, it is not possible to mix portfolios. Plot the risk–return trade-off. Which portfolio do you prefer?

    b. Assume now that you are able to borrow and lend at a risk-free rate of 6 percent. Which portfolio is preferred? Would you borrow or lend at the risk-free rate to achieve a desired position? What is the effect of borrowing and lending on the expected return and on the standard deviation?

5. Suppose the market portfolio had an expected return of 20 percent and a standard deviation of 15 percent. The risk-free rate is 10 percent, and all the assumptions of the capital asset pricing model hold. What is the expected return and standard deviation if you invest your wealth (a) entirely in the risk-free asset? (b) one half in the risk-free asset and one half in the market portfolio? (c) all in the market portfolio? (d) all in the market portfolio and borrow half again as much for additional investment in the market portfolio?

6. On the basis of an analysis of past returns and of inflationary expectations, Marta Gomez feels that the expected return on stocks in general is 14 percent. The risk-free rate on Treasury securities is now 8 percent. Gomez is particularly interested in the return prospects for Kessler Electronics Corporation. Based on monthly data for the past 5 years, she has fitted a characteristic line to the responsiveness of excess returns of the stock to excess returns of Standard & Poor's 500-Stock Index and has found the slope of the line to be 1.67. If financial markets are believed to be efficient, what return can she expect from investing in Kessler?

7. For the past two years, Natchez Steamboat Company and Standard & Poor's 500-Stock Index have had the following excess monthly returns:

	Natchez Steamboat	Standard & Poor's 500-Stock Index
January 20X1	−4%	−2%
February	−5	−6
March	2	−1
April	1	3
May	7	5
June	−1	2
July	−1	−3
August	8	4
September	3	1
October	−10	−5
November	2	1
December	4	4
January 20X2	3	2
February	−3	−4
March	1	1
April	5	3
May	8	7
June	0	−1
July	−1	−2
August	−7	−4
September	2	3
October	−2	1
November	−5	−5
December	−3	−1

    a. Plot these observations on graph paper and fit a characteristic line to them by eye.

    b. What is the approximate beta for Natchez Steamboat Company?

    c. Does the stock present much unsystematic risk? How can you tell?

8. Jane Leslie Richardson, manager of stock investments for the Delta Pension Fund, detects a tendency in the betas of certain stocks to regress toward the average beta of the industry of which they are a part. She is considering weighting factors of .60, .70, and .80 for the measured betas. The following information is available:

	Measured Beta	Industry Beta
Red Rocker Homes	1.40	1.80
Zaleski Electronics	1.50	1.10
Fairgold Foods	1.00	.90
Pottsburg Water Distilling	.80	1.10

For each of the three weighting factors, what is the adjusted beta for these stocks?

9. In the context of the CAPM, what is the expected return of security *j* if it has the following characteristics and if the following information holds for the market portfolio?

Standard deviation, security *j*	.20
Standard deviation, market portfolio	.15
Expected return, market portfolio	.13
Correlation between possible returns for security *j* and the market portfolio	.80
Risk-free rate	.07

   a. What would happen to the required return if the standard deviation of security *j* were higher?

   b. What would happen if the correlation coefficient were less?

   c. What is the functional relationship between the required return for a security and market risk?

10. At present, suppose the risk-free rate is 10 percent and the expected return on the market portfolio is 15 percent. The expected returns for four stocks are listed together with their expected betas.

Stock	Expected Return	Expected Beta
Stillman Zinc Corporation	17.0%	1.3
Union Paint Company	14.5	.8
National Automobile Company	15.5	1.1
Parker Electronics, Inc.	18.0	1.7

   a. On the basis of these expectations, which stocks are overvalued? Which are undervalued?

   b. If the risk-free rate were to rise to 12 percent and the expected return on the market portfolio rose to 16 percent, which stocks would be (1) overvalued? (2) undervalued? (Assume the expected returns and the betas stay the same.)

11. Corliss Services, Inc., provides maintenance services to commercial buildings. Presently, the beta on its stock is 1.08. The risk-free rate is now 10 percent; the expected return for the market portfolio is 15 percent. Corliss is expected to pay a $2 per share dividend at the end of the year and to grow in nominal terms at a rate of 11 percent per annum for many years to come. Based on the CAPM and other assumptions you might make, what is the market price per share of the stock?

12. The following stocks are available for investment:

Stock	Beta
Zeebock Enterprises	1.40
Topaz Jewels, Inc.	.80
Yum Yum Soups Company	.60
Fitzgerald Securities Company	1.80
Ya Hoo Fisheries	1.05
Square Deal Services	.90

a. If you invest 20 percent of your funds in each of the first four securities, and 10 percent in each of the last two, what is the beta of your portfolio?

b. If the risk-free rate is 8 percent and the expected return on the market portfolio is 14 percent, what will be the portfolio's expected return?

Solutions to Self-Correction Problems

1. The expected return is $(w)R_m + (1 - w)R_f$ and the standard deviation is $(w)\sigma_m$, where w is the proportion of total wealth invested in the risky market portfolio of securities, m, and R_f is the risk-free rate.

   a. $R_p = (0)(.15) + (1.0)(.09) = 9\%$

   $\sigma_p = (0)(.21) = 0\%$

   b. $R_p = \left(\tfrac{2}{3}\right)(.15) + \left(\tfrac{1}{3}\right)(.09) = 13\%$

   $\sigma_p = \left(\tfrac{2}{3}\right)(.21) = 14\%$

   c. $R_p = \left(\tfrac{4}{3}\right)(.15) - \left(\tfrac{1}{3}\right)(.09) = 17\%$

   $\sigma_p = \left(\tfrac{4}{3}\right)(.21) = 28\%$

   Both expected return and standard deviation increase linearly with increases in the proportion of wealth invested in the risky market portfolio of securities.

2. $R_{zz} = 6\% + (10\% - 6\%)1.45 = 11.8\%$. If we use the perpetual dividend growth model, we would have

$$P_0 = \frac{D_1}{R_{zz} - g} = \frac{\$2(1.07)}{.118 - .07} = \$44.58$$

3. a. $R_p = .4(15\%) + .6(20\%) = 18\%$

   $\sigma_p = [(.4)^2(1.0)(.2)^2 + 2(.4)(.6)(.36)(.2)(.4) + (.6)^2(1.0)(.4)^2]^{1/2}$

   $= [.0778]^{1/2} = 27.9\%$

   For the standard deviation, the middle term denotes the covariance $(.36)(.2)(.4)$ times the weights of .4 and .6, all of which is counted twice—hence, the 2 in front. For the first and last terms, the correlation coefficients for these own variance terms are 1.0.

b. $R_p = .6(15\%) + .4(20\%) = 17\%$

$\sigma_p = [(.6)^2(1.0)(.2)^2 + 2(.6)(.4)(.36)(.2)(.4) + (.4)^2(1.0)(.4)^2]^{1/2}$

$= [.0538]^{1/2} = 23.2\%$

The lesser proportional investment in the riskier asset, Stratz, results in a lower expected return as well as a lower standard deviation.

Selected References

BLACK, FISCHER, "Beta and Return," *Journal of Portfolio Management*, 23 (Fall 1993), 8–18.

BLUME, MARSHALL E., "Betas and Their Regression Tendencies," *Journal of Finance*, 30 (June 1975), 785–96.

BODIE, ZVI, *Finance*. Upper Saddle River, NJ: Prentice Hall, 2000.

BRENNAN, MICHAEL J., TARUN CHORDIA, and AVANIDHAR SUBRAHMANYAM, "Alternative Factor Specifications, Security Characteristics, and the Cross-section of Expected Stock Returns," *Journal of Financial Economics*, 49 (September 1998), 345–73.

CAMPBELL, JOHN Y., "Have Individual Stocks Become More Volatile? An Empirical Exploration of Idiosyncratic Risk," Working paper, National Bureau of Economic Research (March 2000).

FAMA, EUGENE F., "Efficient Capital Markets: A Review of Theory and Empirical Work," *Journal of Finance*, 25 (May 1970), 383–417.

———, "Efficient Capital Markets: II," *Journal of Finance*, 46 (December 1991), 1575–615.

———, "Market Efficiency, Long-term Returns, and Behavioral Finance," *Journal of Financial Economics*, 49 (September 1998), 283–306.

FAMA, EUGENE F., and KENNETH R. FRENCH, "Common Risk Factors in the Returns on Stocks and Bonds," *Journal of Financial Economics*, 33 (February 1993), 3–56.

———, "The Cross-Section of Expected Stock Returns," *Journal of Finance*, 47 (June 1992), 427–65.

———, "Value versus Growth: The International Evidence," *Journal of Finance*, 53 (December 1998), 1975–99.

GRUNDY, KEVIN, and BURTON G. MALKIEL, "Reports of Beta's Death Have Been Greatly Exaggerated," *Journal of Portfolio Management*, 22 (Spring 1996), 36–44.

HARRIS, ROBERT S., and FELICIA C. MARSTON, "Estimating Shareholder Risk Premia Using Analysts' Growth Forecasts," *Financial Management*, 21 (Summer 1992), 63–70.

———, "Value versus Growth Stocks: Book-to-Market, Growth, and Beta," *Financial Analysts Journal*, 50 (September–October 1994), 18–24.

JAGANNATHAN, RAVI, and ELLEN R. McGRATTAN, "The CAPM Debate," *Quarterly Review of the Federal Reserve Bank of Minneapolis*, 19 (Fall 1995), 2–17.

KNEZ, PETER J., and MARK J. READY, "On the Robustness of Size and Book-to-Market in Cross-Sectional Regressions," *Journal of Finance*, 52 (September 1997), 1355–82.

KOTHARI, S. P., and JAY SHANKEN, "In Defense of Beta," *Journal of Applied Corporate Finance*, 8 (Spring 1995), 53–58.

LEWELLEN, JONATHAN, "The Time-Series Relations among Expected Return, Risk, and Book-to-Market," *Journal of Financial Economics*, 54 (October 1999), 5–43.

MARKOWITZ, HARRY M., *Portfolio Selection: Efficient Diversification of Investments*. New York: Wiley, 1959.

ROLL, RICHARD, "A Critique of the Asset Pricing Theory Tests. Part I: On Past and Potential Testability of the Theory," *Journal of Financial Economics*, 4 (March 1977), 129–76.

———, "Performance Evaluation and Benchmark Errors," *Journal of Portfolio Management*, 6 (Summer 1980), 5–12.

ROLL, RICHARD, and STEPHEN A. ROSS, "On the Cross-Sectional Relation between Expected Returns and Betas," *Journal of Finance*, 49 (March 1994), 101–22.

SHARPE, WILLIAM F., "A Simplified Model for Portfolio Analysis," *Management Science*, 10 (January 1963), 277–93.

———, "Capital Asset Prices: A Theory of Market Equilibrium under Conditions of Risk," *Journal of Finance*, 19 (September 1964), 425–42.

SHARPE, WILLIAM F., and GORDON J. ALEXANDER, *Investments*, 5th ed. Upper Saddle River, NJ: Prentice Hall, 1995.

SHARPE, WILLIAM F., GORDON J. ALEXANDER, and JEFFERY V. BAILEY, *Investments*, 6th ed. Upper Saddle River, NJ: Prentice Hall, 1999.

TOBIN, JAMES, "Liquidity Preference as Behavior towards Risk," *Review of Economic Studies*, 25 (February 1958), 65–86.

VAN HORNE, JAMES C., *Financial Market Rates and Flows*, 6th ed. Upper Saddle River, NJ: Prentice Hall, 2001, Chap. 3.

WOOLRIDGE, J. RANDALL, "Do Stock Prices Reflect Fundamental Values?" *Journal of Applied Corporate Finance*, 8 (Spring 1995), 64–69.

Wachowicz's Web World is an excellent overall Web site produced and maintained by my coauthor of *Fundamentals of Financial Management*, John M. Wachowicz Jr. It contains descriptions of and links to many finance Web sites and articles. *www.prenhall.com/wachowicz.*

Multivariable
and Factor Valuation

I n the preceding chapter, prospective investors were seen to be consumers shopping. The product attribute of importance was the relationship of a security's return with that of the overall market. Other attributes, however, may influence the perceived risk of a security to our shopper and, hence, its price in the marketplace. The purpose of this chapter is to explore things additional to beta that may provide a better explanation of the risk–return trade-off for securities. We begin with extensions to the capital asset pricing model (CAPM) and then move on to factor models in general. Finally, we consider the arbitrage pricing theory (APT), which involves multiple factors, as an alternative model to the CAPM. ■

EXTENDED CAPM

The capital asset pricing model (CAPM) is a single-factor model where expected return is related to beta. As we know from Chapter 3, beta is the reaction coefficient of a security's return to that of the overall market, as typified by some broad index such as Standard & Poor's 500-Stock Index. To repeat what was in Chapter 3, a security's expected return, $\overline{R}_j$, is

$$\overline{R}_j = R_f + (\overline{R}_m - R_f)\beta_j \tag{4-1}$$

where R_f is the risk-free rate, $\overline{R}_m$ is the expected return on the market portfolio, and β_j is the security's beta. By adding additional variables to this equation, one hopes to obtain not only higher explanatory power but also insight into other influences on security returns. In turn, these influences affect financial decision making, the thrust of this book. In what follows we present various extensions to the CAPM.

Extended CAPM
adds variables
additional to beta
to the model.

Allowance for a Tax Effect

The return that an investor realizes from holding a stock is composed of two parts: (1) dividends, if any, received during the holding period and (2) the capital gain or loss that occurs when the stock is sold. If all investors paid either no taxes or the same taxes on dividends and capital gains, the CAPM generalizations made about an individual stock would be unaffected by whether the company paid high or low dividends. In many countries, capital gains are taxed at a more favorable rate than dividends. Moreover, the tax on capital gains income is deferred until the security is actually sold. If held until death, the capital gain is largely unrecognized. Therefore, there are present-value advantages to capital gains over and above any **tax wedge** between capital gains and dividend income.

Illustration   Suppose we expect Alpha Company to have a 12 percent dividend yield for the year (dividends divided by initial value) and a 3 percent capital gain on initial value, while Baker Company is expected to have a 2 percent dividend yield and a $12\frac{1}{2}$ percent capital gain. The expected before-tax return of Alpha Company, 15 percent, is higher than that of Baker Company, $14\frac{1}{2}$ percent. If an investor is in a 30 percent tax bracket, but the tax on capital gains is 20 percent, the after-tax returns are as follows:

	Alpha Company			Baker Company		
	BEFORE TAXES	TAX EFFECT	AFTER TAXES	BEFORE TAXES	TAX EFFECT	AFTER TAXES
Dividend yield	12%	1−.30	8.4%	2.0%	1−.30	1.4%
Capital gain	3	1−.20	2.4	12.5	1−.20	10.0
Expected return	15%		10.8%	14.5%		11.4%

We see that despite the lower expected return before taxes, the expected after-tax return is higher for Baker Company, owing to a greater portion of the return being realized in capital gains. On the other hand, a tax-exempt investor, such as a pension fund, would prefer Alpha Company, with its higher before-tax expected return, all other things being the same.

Systematic Bias Effect   Whether there is a systematic preference in the market as a whole for capital gains over dividends is a subject that must await a more detailed exploration in Chapter 11. In this chapter we wish to explore only the implications for the CAPM if such a preference is assumed. Most significant is that holding risk constant, high-dividend stocks may have to provide higher expected returns before taxes than will lower-dividend stocks, in order to offset the tax effect.

   If this is so, and again we emphasize the unsettled nature of the argument, the expected before-tax return on security j would be a function of both the stock's beta and its dividend yield:

$$\overline{R}_j = R_f + b\beta_j + t(d_j - R_f) \qquad (4\text{-}2)$$

where R_f = risk-free rate
   b = coefficient indicating the relative importance of beta
   β_j = the security's beta
   t = coefficient indicating the relative importance of the tax effect
   d_j = dividend yield on security j

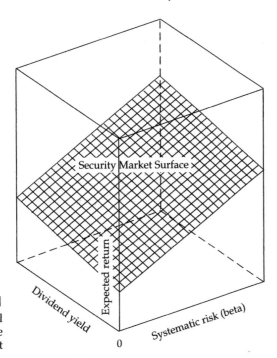

FIGURE 4-1
Three-dimensional
security market surface
illustrating a tax effect

Yield tilt implies
investors demand
higher expected
before-tax returns
the higher
the dividend.

This equation tells us that the greater the dividend yield, d_j, the greater the expected before-tax return that investors require. If t were .1 and the dividend yield were to rise by 1.0 percent, the expected return would have to increase by .1 percent to make the stock attractive to investors. Put another way, the market trade-off would be $1.00 of dividends for $.90 of capital gains.

If there is a systematic bias in the market in favor of capital gains, the expected return on a stock would depend on both its beta and its dividend yield. Instead of the two-dimensional (expected-return beta) security market line in Fig. 3-11 in Chapter 3, we need a three-dimensional surface of the sort shown in Fig. 4-1. We see that expected return is on the vertical axis, whereas beta and dividend yield are on the other axes. Looking at expected return and dividend yield, we see that the higher the dividend yield, the higher the expected return. Similarly, the higher the beta, the higher the expected return. Instead of a security market line, we have a security market surface, depicting the three-dimensional relationship among expected return, beta, and dividend yield.

Dividend and Tax Effects   The use of a trade-off surface depends on higher returns being required by the market the greater the dividend yield. The conceptual and empirical ramifications of this notion must await our overall treatment of dividend policy in Chapter 11, which brings in a number of considerations additional to the tax effect. Our purpose here is only to show the direction of the effect in the context of an extended CAPM approach.

The Presence of Inflation

In our presentation of valuation principles, we implicitly assumed that market equilibration occurred in nominal terms; however, we know that investors are concerned with **inflation**, and they factor this into account when making an investment decision. The realized real return for a security can be expressed as

$$R_j^r = R_j - \rho \tag{4-3}$$

where R_j^r is the return for security j in real terms, R_j is the return for security j in nominal terms, and ρ is the inflation during the period. If inflation is highly predictable, investors simply will add an inflation premium on to the real return they require, and markets will equilibrate in the manner described earlier in the chapter. As long as inflation is predictable, it is not a source of uncertainty. Therefore, the risk of a security can be described by its systematic and unsystematic risk, regardless of whether these risks are measured in real or nominal terms.[1]

Unanticipated Changes   When inflation is uncertain, however, things are different. By uncertainty, we mean that the market does not anticipate changes that occur in the rate of inflation. Whether uncertain inflation is good or bad for a stock depends on the covariance of this uncertainty with that of the stock. If the return on a stock increases with unanticipated increases in inflation, this desirable property reduces the systematic risk of the stock in real terms and provides a hedge. Contrarily, if the stock's return goes down when unanticipated inflation occurs, then it is undesirable because it increases the systematic risk of the stock in real terms.

> **Covariance** with unexpected inflation is desirable from the standpoint of the investor.

We would expect that the greater the covariance of the return of a stock with unanticipated changes in inflation, the lower the expected nominal return the market will require. If this is so, one could express the expected nominal return of a stock as a positive function of its beta and a negative function of its covariance with unanticipated inflation. We might have

$$\overline{R}_j = R_j + b\beta_j - i\,\frac{\text{inflation covariance}}{\sigma_i^2} \tag{4-4}$$

where i is a coefficient indicating the relative importance of a security's covariance with inflation, σ_i^2 is the variance of inflation, and the other variables are the same as defined for Eq. (4-2). In effect, the last variable is a beta for the sensitivity of security returns to changes in inflation. By dividing by inflation's variance, things are expressed on a relative as opposed to an absolute basis.

Adding an Inflation Variable   Similar to the dividend-yield case, we could construct a three-dimensional security market surface. This surface would have nominal security returns increasing with beta and decreasing with relative inflation covariance. In other words, covariance with inflation may be a desirable property and lower the return that investors require. Many stocks have negative covariances; their returns tend to decline with unanticipated increases in inflation, and vice versa. This may be an undesirable characteristic, and such a security may require a higher return, all other things the same. Though all of this is simple enough in concept, it is difficult to predict the sensitivity of an individual stock (or even stocks overall) to unanticipated changes in inflation. Efforts to do so often result in no additional predictive ability for the model.

---

[1]See James C. Van Horne, *Financial Market Rates and Flows*, 6th ed. (Upper Saddle River, NJ: Prentice Hall, 2001), chap. 5.

Market Capitalization Size

Extensions other than dividend and inflation effects have been made to the CAPM. One of these is **size**, as measured by the market capitalization of a company relative to that for other companies. Market capitalization is simply the number of shares outstanding multiplied by share price. From time to time, a "small stock effect" appears, where small capitalization stocks provide a higher return than large capitalization stocks, holding other things constant. Presumably, small stocks provide less utility to the investor and require a higher return. Often the size variable is treated as the decile in which the company's market capitalization falls relative to the market capitalizations of other companies.

Price/Earnings
and Market-to-Book Value Effects

At certain times, a **price/earnings** ratio effect has been observed. Holding constant beta, observed returns tend to be higher for low P/E ratio stocks and lower for high P/E ratio stocks. Expressed differently, low P/E ratio stocks earn excess returns above what the CAPM would predict, and high P/E ratio stocks earn less than what the CAPM would predict. This is a form of mean reversion, and it adds explanatory power to the CAPM. With only this variable added, the model becomes

$$\overline{R}_j = R_f + b\beta_j - p\,(P/E_j - P/E_m) \qquad (4\text{-}5)$$

where p is a coefficient reflecting the relative importance of a security's price/earnings ratio, P/E_j is the price/earnings ratio of that security, and P/E_m is the weighted average price/earnings ratio for the market portfolio. We should point out that this is only one of a number of ways to express the variable.

As with the other additional variables, we can construct a three-dimensional security market surface with the price/earnings ratio along one of the axes. This is shown in Fig. 4-2, and we see that expected return increases with beta and decreases with the P/E ratio. The addition of this variable has been found at times to be important in tempering return estimates derived from the CAPM. Expressed differently, beta does not capture all the risk associated with holding a stock, and additional explanatory power may come from including the price/earnings ratio.

Value stocks have lower P/E and M/B ratios, and some investors seek such.

Similar to the use of the price/earnings ratio, the ratio of market-to-book value (M/B) has been used to explain security returns. Generally, either one ratio or the other is employed, not both. The M/B ratio is the market value of all claims on a company, including those of stockholders, divided by the book value of its assets. Holding beta constant, observed returns tend to be higher for low M/B ratio stocks than for high M/B ratio stocks. This is the same relative relationship as for stock returns and the P/E ratio.

Fama and French argue that size and the market-to-book value ratio are all that are necessary to explain stock returns. It is claimed that beta does not give explanatory power additional to these two variables. This argument was examined at length in Chapter 3, substantial empirical work being at odds with this hypothesis.

Final Observations

As variables additional to beta are used to approximate the expected return from a security, we have what is known as the extended CAPM. Of the variables used to extend the CAPM, size and the price/earnings ratio or the market-to-book value

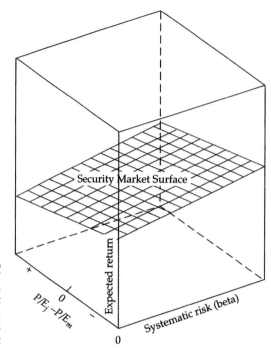

FIGURE 4-2

Three-dimensional
security market
surface illustrating a
price/earnings
ratio effect

ratio (one or the other) have been found to be the most consistent and significant in their effect. The dividend-yield effect is the most controversial, as we shall see in Chapter 11. For multiple variables,

$$\bar{R}_j = R_f + b\beta_j + c \text{ (variable 2)} + d \text{ (variable 3)} \qquad (4\text{-}6)$$
$$+ e \text{ (variable 4)} + \cdots + m \text{ (variable } n)$$

where, again, b, c, d, e, and m are coefficients reflecting the relative importance of the variable involved. When variables other than beta are added, a better data fit generally is obtained. These variables have been found to successfully explain some of a security's total return not explained by beta.

The extensions to the CAPM taken up in this section do not negate the model's underlying importance. They simply permit more precise measurement of the required return for a particular stock, as well as provide a richer, more realistic description of the market equilibrium process. However, beta still remains the dominant determinant of security returns. Of course, this is due in part to the way the extended CAPM is constructed. We turn now to models that may supplant beta.

FACTOR MODELS IN GENERAL

Perhaps the most important challenge to the CAPM is the arbitrage pricing theory (APT). As this theory involves a **factor model** approach, we first consider such models in general. Like the extended CAPM, factor models suggest that expected returns are affected by a number of risks. Such models assume that security returns are generated by a set of underlying factors, often economic. The extended CAPM may include economic variables. However, the key variable is beta, which is not necessarily the case with factor models of the sort we consider now. The difference is subtle, but important.

Two-Factor Model

To illustrate a two-factor model, suppose the actual return on a security, R_j, can be explained by the following:

$$R_j = a + b_{1j}F_1 + b_{2j}F_2 + e_j \qquad (4\text{-}7)$$

where a is the return when all factors have zero values, F_n is the value (uncertain) of factor n, b_{nj} is the reaction coefficient depicting the change in the security's return to a one-unit change in the factor, and e_j is the error term. The error term is security specific, or unsystematic.

Factor models approach required returns by relating them to unexpected changes in multiple factors, which represent broad risks in the economy.

As with our discussion in Chapter 3, unsystematic risk can be diversified away by holding a broad portfolio of securities as opposed to only one. With a portfolio, security-specific risk is not a thing of value. The error terms of individual securities are unrelated to each other; that is, their correlation coefficients are zero. Under these circumstances, only the factor risks are important. They represent unavoidable risk, whereas unsystematic risk can be avoided by diversification.

Unanticipated Changes Count   For the factors, it is the unanticipated or "surprise" element that matters. For example, an announcement of a change in commodity price levels is comprised of two parts: the expected and the unanticipated. If inflation is a factor affecting expected returns, the expected component already is embraced in security prices. It is the unanticipated that causes equilibrium conditions to be upset and for security prices to change. Thus,

$$\begin{array}{c} \text{Announcement of} \\ \text{change in factor} \end{array} = \begin{array}{c} \text{Expected} \\ \text{component} \end{array} + \begin{array}{c} \text{Unanticipated} \\ \text{component} \end{array} \qquad (4\text{-}8)$$

To repeat, the second component is the surprise element and the thing that moves security prices, which, in turn, allows us to study the process. The expected component already is discounted in the sense that a security's price reflects it. Put another way, it is the unanticipated that constitutes risk, not the expected. Therefore, the factors in Eq. (4-7) relate to unanticipated changes.

Expected Return   The expected return on a security, in contrast to the actual return in Eq. (4-7), is

$$(E)\overline{R}_j = \lambda_0 + \lambda_1 b_{1j} + \lambda_2 b_{2j} \qquad (4\text{-}9)$$

The λ_0 parameter corresponds to the return on a risk-free asset. The other λ parameters represent risk premiums for the types of risk associated with particular factors. For example, λ_1 is the expected excess return (above the risk-free rate) when $b_{1j} = 1$ and $b_{2j} = 0$. The parameters can be positive or negative. A positive λ reflects risk aversion by the market to the factor involved. A negative parameter indicates value being associated with the factor, in the sense of a lesser return being required.

Suppose Torquay Resorts Limited's stock is related to two factors where the reaction coefficients, b_{1j} and b_{2j}, are 1.4 and .8, respectively. If the risk-free rate is 8 percent, and λ_1 is 6 percent and λ_2 is −2 percent, the stock's expected return is

$$(E)\overline{R}_j = .08 + .06(1.4) - .02(.8) = 14.8\%$$

The first factor reflects risk aversion and must be compensated for with a higher expected return, whereas the second is a thing of value to investors and lowers the return they expect. Thus, the λ's represent market prices associated with factor risks.

Two Factors Graphically   Figure 4-3 illustrates a two-factor model where the lambdas are both positive. The reaction coefficients for the two factors are shown along two axes, and expected return is along the vertical axis. The market price, λ_1, is the angle of the security market surface to the b_{1j} line, while λ_2 is the angle of the surface to the b_{2j} line. The error term, e_j, is illustrated by the distance off the surface. This is a random occurrence, by definition. If persistent, we would expect it to be eliminated by arbitrage, to be illustrated shortly.

Now you might ask, How does this differ from the three-dimensional figures used to illustrate the extended CAPM? Both involve two-factor models, but with Figs. 4-1 and 4-2, one of the factors was beta.

More Than Two Factors

The same principles hold when we go to more than two factors. Here the expected return is

$$(E)\overline{R}_j = \lambda_0 + \lambda_1 b_{1j} + \lambda_2 b_{2j} + \cdots + \lambda_n b_{nj} \tag{4-10}$$

where the number of factors is n. Again, each λ represents a market price of risk. For example, λ_1 represents the expected return in excess of the risk-free rate when the reaction coefficient for the first factor, b_{1j}, is 1.0, and the b's for all other factors are zero. Each factor is an undiversifiable, or unavoidable, risk. The greater a security's reaction coefficient with respect to a factor, the more the risk and the higher the required return. Thus, Eq. (4-10) tells us that a security's expected return is the risk-free rate, λ_0, plus risk premiums for each of the n factors.

FIGURE 4-3

Three-dimensional illustration of a two-factor model

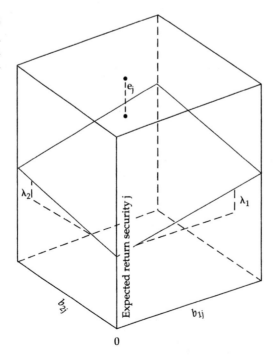

Thus the overall risk premium on a security, $(\bar{R}_j - R_f)$, depends on the expected risk premiums for each of the factors. If in Eq. (4-10) the values of all the b's were zero, the overall expected risk premium would be zero and the security would be essentially risk free. Therefore, it need provide an expected return of no more than the risk-free rate. As one or more b's in Eq. (4-10) take on nonzero values, the security must provide an expected return in excess of the risk-free rate.

Factor models are based on the idea that security prices move together or apart in reaction to common forces as well as by chance. The objective is to isolate the noise, or chance element, to get at the common forces. One way to do so is with a statistical technique called *factor analysis*. Here actual returns on securities are analyzed as to their covariances to see if any common factors can explain them. The factors that emerge are examined to see if they correspond to economic or behavioral variables that may or may not be suggested by theory. Another approach is to specify various factors on the basis of theory and then proceed to test them. This leads us to the much acclaimed arbitrage pricing theory.

ARBITRAGE PRICING THEORY

Like the CAPM, **arbitrage pricing theory (APT)** is an equilibrium model as to how security prices are determined. Originally developed by Stephen A. Ross, this theory is based on the idea that in competitive financial markets arbitrage will ensure that riskless assets provide the same expected return.[2] Arbitrage simply means finding two things that are essentially the same and buying the cheaper and selling, or selling short, the more expensive. The model is based on the simple notion that security prices adjust as investors form portfolios in search of arbitrage profits. When such profit opportunities have been exhausted, security prices are said to be in equilibrium. In this context, a definition of market efficiency is the absence of arbitrage opportunities, their having been eliminated by arbitragers.

The APT suggests that the market equilibration process is driven by individuals eliminating arbitrage profits across these multiple factors. The model does not tell us what the factors are or why they are economically or behaviorally relevant. It merely states that there is a relationship between security returns and a limited number of factors. That is, security returns move together because of some common attributes. One of the factors might be the market return, as in the CAPM, but this need not be the case.

The Arbitrage Process

According to the APT, two securities with the same reaction coefficients, the b's in Eq. (4-10), should provide the same expected return. What happens if this is not the case? Investors rush in to buy the security with the higher expected return and sell, or sell short, the security with the lower expected return.

Suppose returns required in the market by investors are a function of two factors according to the following equation, where the risk-free rate is 7 percent:

$$(E)\bar{R}_j = .07 + .04(b_{1j}) - .01(b_{2j}) \tag{4-10a}$$

Quigley Manufacturing Company and Zolotny Basic Products Corporation both

---

[2]Stephen A. Ross, "The Arbitrage Theory of Capital Asset Pricing," *Journal of Economic Theory*, 13 (December 1976), 341–60.

have the same reaction coefficients to the factors, such that $b_{1j} = 1.3$ and $b_{2j} = .9$. Therefore, the required return for both securities is

$$(E)\overline{R}_j = .07 + .04(1.3) - .01(.9) = 11.3\% \tag{4-10b}$$

However, Quigley's stock is depressed, so its expected return is 12.8 percent, whereas Zolotny's share price is relatively high; its expected return is only 10.6 percent. A clever arbitrager should buy Quigley and sell or sell short Zolotny. If she has things right and the only risks of importance are captured by factors 1 and 2, the two securities have the same overall risk. Yet because of mispricing, one security provides a higher expected return than its risk would dictate, while the other provides a lower return. This is a money game, and our clever arbitrager will want to exploit the opportunity as long as possible.

As arbitragers recognize the mispricing and engage in the transactions suggested, price adjustments will occur. The price of Quigley stock will rise, and its expected return will fall, while the price of Zolotny stock will fall, and its expected return will rise. This will continue until both securities have an expected return of 11.3 percent.

According to the APT, rational market participants will exhaust all opportunities for arbitrage profits. Market equilibrium will occur when expected returns for all securities bear a linear relationship to the various reaction coefficients, the b's. Thus, the foundation for equilibrium pricing is arbitrage. The APT implies that market participants act in a manner consistent with general agreement as to what are the relevant risk factors that move security prices. Whether this assumption is a reasonable approximation of reality is a subject of much controversy.

Arbitrage pricing theory has markets equilibrating across stocks via arbitragers driving out mispricing.

Roll–Ross and Their Five Factors

Roll and Ross believe the truth lies in five specific factors.[3] They suggest that different securities have different sensitivities to these systematic factors and that the major sources of security portfolio risk are captured in them. The five factors are (1) changes in expected inflation, (2) unanticipated changes in inflation, (3) unanticipated changes in industrial production, (4) unanticipated changes in the yield differential between low- and high-grade bonds (the default-risk premium), and (5) unanticipated changes in the yield differential between long-term and short-term bonds (the term structure of interest rates). The first three factors affect primarily the cash flows of the company and, hence, its dividends and growth in dividends. The last two affect the market capitalization, or discount, rate.

Substituting into Eq. (4-10), the **Roll–Ross model** may be expressed as

Roll–Ross factors of importance: inflation, economic activity, bond risk, and the term structure.

$$\begin{aligned} (E)\overline{R}_j = \lambda_0 &+ \lambda_1(b_{1j}E\Delta \text{ inflation}) + \lambda_2(b_{2j}U\Delta \text{ inflation}) \\ &+ \lambda_3(b_{3j}U\Delta \text{ industrial production}) \\ &+ \lambda_4(b_{4j}U\Delta \text{ bond risk premium}) \\ &+ \lambda_5(b_{5j}U\Delta \text{ long minus short rate}) \end{aligned} \tag{4-11}$$

where $E\Delta$ is an expected change, $U\Delta$ represents an unanticipated change, and the other symbols are the same as before. According to this equation, the expected return on a security, $(E)\overline{R}_j$, exceeds the risk-free rate by the sum of the products of

---

[3]Richard Roll and Stephen A. Ross, "An Empirical Investigation of the Arbitrage Pricing Theory," *Journal of Finance*, 35 (December 1980), 1073–103; Richard Roll and Stephen A. Ross, "The Arbitrage Pricing Theory Approach to Strategic Portfolio Planning," *Financial Analysts Journal*, 40 (May–June 1984); and Nai-Fu Chen, Richard Roll, and Stephen A. Ross, "Economic Forces and the Stock Market," *Journal of Business*, 59 (July 1986), 383–403.

the market prices of risk, the λ's, and the sensitivity coefficients, the b's. The sensitivity coefficients simply tell us the average response of the security's return to an unanticipated change in a factor, holding other factors constant.

Implications of the Model According to this model, investors are characterized as having risk preferences along five dimensions. Each investor would formulate a portfolio of securities depending on his or her desired risk exposure to each of the factors. Different investors will have different risk attitudes. For example, some may want little inflation risk but be willing to tolerate considerable productivity risk and default risk. Roll–Ross argue that the CAPM beta is too restricted a measure of risk. Several stocks may have the same beta but vastly different factor risks. If investors in fact are concerned with these factor risks, the CAPM beta would not be a good indicator of the expected return for a stock.

What would be? According to the Roll–Ross version of the arbitrage pricing theory, or similar versions, knowing the λ's (the market prices of various risks, expressed in terms of premiums above the risk-free rate) and the b's (the response coefficients for specific security returns to changes in factors) in Eq. (4-11) would be sufficient. In an empirical study, Chen, Roll, and Ross estimate the following parameters for *monthly* returns:[4]

$$(E)\overline{R}_j = .00412 - .00013(b_{1j}E\Delta \text{ inflation}) - .00063(b_{2j}U\Delta \text{ inflation})$$
$$+ .01359(b_{3j}U\Delta \text{ industrial production})$$
$$+ .00721(b_{4j}U\Delta \text{ bond risk premium}) \quad\quad (4\text{-}12)$$
$$- .00521(b_{5j}U\Delta \text{ long minus short rate})$$

Suppose the b's for CRR Corporation are $b_1 = 1.8$, $b_2 = 2.4$, $b_3 = .9$, $b_4 = .5$, and $b_5 = 1.1$. Under these conditions, the expected return for the stock is

$$(E)\overline{R}_{crr} = .00412 - .00013(1.8) - .00063(2.4) + .01359(.9)$$
$$+ .00721(.5) - .00521(1.1)$$
$$= 1.25\%$$

Remember that this expected return, 1.25 percent, is a monthly as opposed to an annual return.

Other Empirical Testing

If the parameters for this or some other model could be estimated with reliability and we were confident that we had specified the risk factors of importance, it would be an easy matter to determine the expected return for a security. As illustrated for the Roll–Ross model, we would simply multiply the λ's by the b's and sum them. This weighted product would represent the total risk premium for security j, to which we would add the risk-free rate to obtain the expected return.

But life is not so simple. There is not agreement as to the risk factors of importance or the number that should be used. Moreover, empirical testing of the APT has been inconclusive. As many of the articles referenced at the end of the chapter attest, disagreement abounds as to the factor structure and as to parameter estimate consistency from test to test and over time. It can never be conclusively demonstrated that the APT is superior to the CAPM, or vice versa. Both models in-

---

[4]Chen, Roll, and Ross, "Economic Forces and the Stock Market," *Journal of Business*, 59 (July 1986), 383–403.

volve expectations of risks and of returns. Such expectations are not directly observable but must be estimated, and these estimates are subject to wide error.

Implications of the APT for This Book

Because multiple risks are considered, the APT is intuitively appealing. We know that different stocks may be affected differently by different risks. A retailing company may have more exposure to unanticipated inflation than does a basic foods company. A machine tool company may be dramatically affected by what happens to industrial production, whereas a utility may be little affected. By relating security returns to underlying risk factors, we can better understand the economic forces that affect share price. In Chapter 8, which deals with required rates of return, we probe further into the use of multifactor valuation models.

For a number of stocks, a multifactor model gives a better estimate of the required return on equity than does the one-factor CAPM. For other stocks, such as the broadly based American Home Products Corporation, the CAPM has high explanatory power and additional factors contribute little. For this reason, some of the more "practical" uses of the APT begin with a CAPM estimate and then add other risk factors to get more explanatory power. This, of course, is a variant of the extended CAPM.

In the chapters that follow, we look to the CAPM as one means for describing the equilibrium behavior of security prices. This is due to its wide acceptance. Where appropriate, we will describe the implications that arise when an APT approach is used. Whether the APT should replace the CAPM is a subject of debate. Some of it is warranted, but some is not because the two models are compatible.

 ## Summary

The capital asset pricing model may be extended to include variables other than beta. Whether expected return is comprised of dividends or capital gains may make a difference in valuation. If there is a systematic bias in favor of capital gains, the required return on a high-dividend-paying stock will be greater than that on a low-paying one. Whether this is the case is controversial, and we address this controversy in Chapter 11. To the extent investors are concerned with inflation, they may value the security whose returns covary with unanticipated changes in inflation and, accordingly, require a lower return, all other things the same. Market capitalization size of a company may be a desirable characteristic and requires a lower return.

A price/earnings ratio effect may occur where observed returns are higher for low P/E ratio stocks than beta alone would predict, and vice versa. Expressed differently, the expected return on a high P/E ratio stock would be less than that on a low P/E ratio stock, holding beta constant. Similarly, the return on a high market-to-book value stock may be less than that on a low M/B ratio stock. Of the variables used to extend the CAPM, market capitalization size and either the P/E ratio or the M/B ratio are the most important. Multiple variables added to beta increase the explanatory power of the model.

Like the extended CAPM, factor models relate expected returns to multiple risks. The idea is to capture unavoidable risk in the factors employed. Here risk relates to unanticipated changes in the factors. The lambda parameters reflect the market prices of risk for the various factors. One benefit of a factor model is that it allows analysis of the way different risks affect a particular security. The factors employed may arise from a statistical technique called factor analysis or from specification on the basis of theory.

The arbitrage pricing theory (APT) is an equilibrium model based on individuals arbitraging across multiple factors. By eliminating arbitrage opportunities, arbitragers make the market efficient. Roll and Ross have specified five factors that they think capture unavoidable risk, and their model has enjoyed good usage. Still there is not agreement as to the factors that are important, nor has empirical testing produced parameter stability and consistency over time. The APT has not displaced the CAPM in use, but it holds promise for corporate finance.

■ Self-Correction Problems

1. Rubinstein Robotics Corporation has a beta of 1.25. The risk-free rate is 8 percent and the expected return on the market portfolio is 15 percent. Share price is $32, earnings per share $2.56, and dividends per share $1.28.

   a. What is the expected return using the CAPM without extension?

   b. If dividends increase the required return on stocks with the result that the t coefficient in Eq. (4-2) is .10 while the b coefficient is .075, what is the stock's expected return if we assume the equation holds?

   c. The price/earnings ratio for the market portfolio is 11, the p coefficient in Eq. (4-5) is –.006, and the b coefficient is .075. What is the stock's expected return if that equation holds?

2. The return on Hendershott Hinge Company's stock is related to factors 1 and 2 as follows:

   $$(E)\overline{R}_j = \lambda_0 + .6\lambda_1 + 1.3\lambda_2$$

   where .6 and 1.3 are sensitivity, or reaction, coefficients associated with each of the factors as defined in the chapter. If the risk-free rate is 7 percent, the λ_1 risk premium is 6 percent, and λ_2 is 3 percent, what is Hendershott's expected return?

3. Suppose a three-factor APT model holds and the risk-free rate is 6 percent. There are two stocks in which you have a particular interest: Montana Leather Company and Bozeman Enterprises. The market-price lambdas and reaction coefficients for the two stocks are as follows:

Factor	λ	b_{ML}	b_{BE}
1	.09	.5	.7
2	–.03	.4	.8
3	.04	1.2	.2

   What would be the expected return on your portfolio if you were to invest (a) equally in the two securities? (b) one-third in Montana Leather Company and two-thirds in Bozeman Enterprises?

Problems

1. Perez Paint Company pays a dividend of $3 per share and share price is $40. Presently the risk-free rate is 5 percent and the expected return on the market portfolio is 12 percent. The company's beta is .80. The *b* coefficient in Eq. (4-2) is .07 and the *d* coefficient is .10.

   a. What is the expected return for the company's stock if the equation holds?

   b. What would happen if the *b* coefficient were .08 and the *d* coefficient were .25? Under what circumstances would this occur?

2. Norway Fiord Boat Company has a beta of 1.40. The risk-free rate is presently 8 percent, and the inflation extension to the CAPM, Eq. (4-4), holds. The *b* coefficient in the equation is .075, and the *i* coefficient is .03. The inflation covariance/variance ratio for the company is .25.

   a. What is the stock's expected return?

   b. In words, what would happen if negative instead of positive covariance occurred?

3. Suppose the expected return for a stock were a function of beta and size according to the following formula:

$$\overline{R}_j = R_f + .08(\beta_j) - .002 \text{ (size decile)}$$

   where size is the decile in which security *j* falls with respect to total market capitalization, 10 being the largest. The risk-free rate is presently 9 percent.

   a. Tobias Tire Company has a beta of 1.10 and is in the second decile with respect to market capitalization size. What is its expected return?

   b. Cooper Chemical Company has a beta of 1.12 and is in the ninth decile with respect to size. What is the expected return of this company's stock? Why does it differ from that of Tobias Tire Company?

4. Fullerton-Bristol, Inc., has a beta of .90, a market price per share of $27.20, and earnings per share of $3.40. The risk-free rate is 6 percent, the price/earnings ratio for the market portfolio is 12 times, and Fullerton-Bristol is in the sixth decile with respect to market capitalization (10 is the largest). Suppose the expected return for a security is expressed as

$$\overline{R}_j = R_f + .08(\beta_j) - .001(P/E_j - P/E_m) - .002 \text{ (size)}$$

   where P/E_m is the price/earnings ratio of the market portfolio and size is the decile of market capitalization. What is the stock's expected return?

5. Leeny Kelly Company's stock is related to the following factors with respect to actual return:

$$R_j = a + .8(F_1) + 1.2(F_2) + .3(F_3) + e_j$$

a. Suppose that the *a* term for the stock is 14 percent and that for the period the unanticipated change in factor 1 is 5 percent, factor 2 minus 2 percent, and factor 3 minus 10 percent. If the error term is zero, what would be the stock's actual return for the period?

b. Now suppose that we wish to solve for the expected return. If the risk-free rate is 8 percent, $\lambda_1 = 4$ percent, $\lambda_2 = 2$ percent, and $\lambda_3 = 6$ percent, what is the stock's expected return?

6. Security returns are generated by factors according to the following formula:

$$R_j = R_f + b_{1j}F_1 + b_{2j}F_2 + b_{3j}F_3 + e_j$$

Assume $R_f = 5$ percent, $F_1 = 6$ percent, $F_2 = 7$ percent, and $F_3 = 8$ percent. Assume also the following for two securities, *X* and *Y*:

$b_{1x} = .10$	$b_{1y} = .80$
$b_{2x} = 1.20$	$b_{2y} = .20$
$b_{3x} = .90$	$b_{3y} = .40$

What actual return would you forecast for the two securities?

7. Based on their present share prices and expected future dividends, Bosco Enterprises, Target Markets, Inc., and Selby Glass Company have expected returns of 16 percent, 14 percent, and 20 percent, respectively. The risk-free rate presently is 7 percent. Required returns on investment are determined according to the following factor model:

$$(E)\overline{R}_j = \lambda_0 + .12(b_{1j}) + .04(b_{1j})$$

The reaction coefficients for the companies are as follows:

	B_{1j}	B_{2j}
Bosco	.80	.20
Target	.10	1.10
Selby	1.20	.40

a. (1) Which securities are overpriced in the sense of the required return being more than the expected return? (2) Which are underpriced?

b. As an arbitrager, what would you do and for how long?

8. The expected return for Sawyer Coding Company's stock is described by the Roll–Ross model. Sawyer's reaction coefficients are as follows: $b_1 = 1.4$, $b_2 = 2.0$, $b_3 = .7$, $b_4 = 1.2$, and $b_5 = .8$. Using the lambda estimates of Chen, Roll, and Ross, what is the expected monthly return for this security?

9. How does the arbitrage pricing theory (APT) differ from the capital asset pricing model (CAPM)? What are the similarities of the two models?

Solutions to Self-Correction Problems

1. a. $R_{rrc} = .08 + 1.25(.15 - .08) = 16.75\%$

   b. The dividend yield for Rubinstein Robotics Corporation is $1.28/$32 = 4.00%.

   $$R_{rrc} = .08 + .075(1.25) + .1(.04 - .08) = 16.98\%$$

   The equation implies that dividend income is not as attractive as capital gains. Therefore, a higher return is required for the high-dividend-paying stock. In this case, dividend yield is less than the risk-free rate, so the effect is negative.

   c. The price/earnings ratio of the stock is $32/$2.56 = 12.5 times.

   $$R_{rrc} = .08 + .075(1.25) - .006(12.5 - 11.0) = 16.48\%$$

   A higher than average price/earnings ratio implies an expectation of a lower expected return than the CAPM without extension would predict.

2. The expected return for Hendershott Hinge stock using a factor model is

   $$(E)\overline{R}_i = .07 + (.6).06 + (1.3).03 = 14.5\%$$

3. $(E)\overline{R}_{ML} = .06 + .09(.5) - .03(.4) + .04(1.2) = 14.1\%$
   $(E)\overline{R}_{BE} = .06 + .09(.7) - .03(.8) + .04(.2) = 10.7\%$

   a. Portfolio expected return where the two investments are equally weighted:

   $$(E)\overline{R}_p = .5(14.1\%) + .5(10.7\%) = 12.4\%$$

   b. Portfolio expected return with one-third invested in Montana Leather Company and two-thirds in Bozeman Enterprises:

   $$(E)\overline{R}_p = .333(14.1\%) + .667(10.7\%) = 11.83\%$$

   The return may be higher or lower because we cannot reduce unsystematic risk to zero with so small a portfolio.

Selected References

BERRY, MICHAEL A., EDWIN BURMEISTER, and MARJORIE B. MCELROY, "Sorting Out Risks Using Known APT Factors," *Financial Analysts Journal*, 44 (March–April 1988), 29–42.

BRENNAN, MICHAEL J., TARUN CHORDIA, and AVANDIDHAR SUBRAHMANYAM, "Alternative Factor Specifications, Security Characteristics, and the Cross-Section of Expected Stock Returns," *Journal of Financial Economics*, 49 (September 1998), 345–73.

CHEN, NAI-FU, "Some Empirical Tests of the Theory of Arbitrage Pricing," *Journal of Finance*, 38 (December 1983), 1194.

CHEN, NAI-FU, RICHARD ROLL, and STEPHEN A. ROSS, "Economic Forces and the Stock Market," *Journal of Business*, 59 (July 1986), 383–403.

CONNOR, GREGORY, and ROBERT A. KORAJCZYK, "Risk and Return in an Equilibrium APT: Application of a New Test Methodology," *Journal of Financial Economics*, 21 (September 1988), 255–90.

———, "A Test for the Number of Factors in an Approximate Factor Model," *Journal of Finance*, 48 (September 1993) 1263–91.

DAVIS, JAMES L., EUGENE F. FARNA, and KENNETH R. FRENCH, "Characteristics, Covariances, and Average Returns," *Journal of Finance*, 55 (February 2000), 389–406.

FAMA, EUGENE F., and KENNETH R. FRENCH, "The Cross-Section of Expected Stock Returns," *Journal of Finance*, 47 (June 1992), 427–65.

———, "Common Risk Factors in the Returns on Stocks and Bonds," *Journal of Financial Economics*, 33 (February 1993), 3–56.

———, "Multifactor Explanations of Asset Pricing Anomalies," *Journal of Finance*, 51 (March 1996), 55–84.

FERSON, WAYNE E., and ROBERT A. KORAJCZYK, "Do Arbitrage Pricing Models Explain the Predictability of Stock Returns?" *Journal of Business*, 68, No. 3 (1995), 309–49.

KEIM, DONALD B., "The CAPM and Equity Return Regularities," *Financial Analysts Journal*, 42 (May–June 1986), 19–34.

KNEZ, PETER J., and MARK J. READY, "On the Robustness of Size and Book-to-Market in Cross-Sectional Regressions," *Journal of Finance*, 52 (September 1997), 1355–82.

LEWELLEN, JONATHAN, "The Tune-series Relations among Expected Return, Risk, Book-to-Market," *Journal of Financial Economics*, 54 (October 1999), 5–43.

LITZENBERGER, ROBERT H., and KRISHNA RAMASWAMY, "The Effect of Personal Taxes and Dividends on Capital Asset Prices," *Journal of Financial Economics*, 7 (June 1979), 163–95.

MACKINLAY, A. CRAIG, "Multifactor Models Do Not Explain Deviations from the CAPM," *Journal of Financial Economics*, 38 (May 1995), 3–28.

NARANJO, ANDY, M. NIMALENDRAN, and MIKE RYNGAERT, "Stock Returns, Dividend Yields, and Taxes," *Journal of Finance*, 53 (December 1998), 2029–57.

ROLL, RICHARD, and STEPHEN A. ROSS, "An Empirical Investigation of the Arbitrage Pricing Theory," *Journal of Finance*, 35 (December 1980), 1073–103.

———, "The Arbitrage Pricing Theory Approach to Strategic Portfolio Planning," *Financial Analysts Journal*, 40 (May–June 1984), 14–26.

———, "On the Cross-Sectional Relation between Expected Returns and Betas," *Journal of Finance*, 49 (March 1994), 101–21.

ROSS, STEPHEN A., "The Arbitrage Theory of Capital Asset Pricing," *Journal of Economic Theory*, 13 (December 1976), 341–60.

TRZCINKA, CHARLES, "On the Number of Factors in the Arbitrage Pricing Model," *Journal of Finance*, 41 (June 1986), 347–68.

Wachowicz's Web World is an excellent overall Web site produced and maintained by my coauthor of *Fundamentals of Financial Management*, John M. Wachowicz Jr. It contains descriptions of and links to many finance Web sites and articles. *www.prenhall.com/wachowicz*.

Option Valuation

S o far our discussion of valuation has involved actual securities. We now consider a financial instrument that derives its value from an underlying security, such as a stock, a bond, or a mortgage. An *option* is one of a number of derivative securities. It gives the holder the right but not the obligation to buy or sell a designated security at a specific price. Other derivative securities are taken up in Chapter 21, hedging interest-rate risk, and Chapter 25, currency hedging devices. For now our focus is on stock options, but the foundations in this chapter are used again and again. The applications are numerous: convertible securities, warrants, callable bonds, debt holders versus equity holders in an option pricing context, rights offerings, executive stock options, loan guarantees, standby agreements, interest-rate caps, and insurance contracts.

A **call option** gives the holder the right to buy a security at a specified **exercise, or strike, price**. We might have a call option to buy one share of ABC Corporation's common stock at $10 through December 21 of the current year. Thus, the option has an exercise price of $10 through December 21, which is the expiration date. In contrast, a **put option** gives the holder the right to sell a share of stock at a specified price up to the expiration date; it is the mirror image of a call option. More complex options may involve combinations of the call and put options. With so many options being traded, active options markets developed. The Chicago Board Options Exchange was the first of these, and it is the largest. The exchange-traded option contract is standardized, and the Options Clearing Corporation (OCC) is interposed between a buyer and seller, thereby facilitating the mechanics. ■

EXPIRATION DATE VALUE OF AN OPTION

A **European option** can be exercised only at its expiration date; an **American option** can be exercised at any time up to and including the expiration date. We shall begin by assuming that we have a European option on a stock that does not pay dividends. Later, we relax both assumptions.

The value of the call option at its expiration date is simply

$$V_o = \max (V_s - E, 0) \tag{5-1}$$

where V_s is the market price of one share of stock, E is the **exercise price** of the option, and max means the maximum value of $V_s - E$ or zero, whichever is greater. To illustrate the formula, suppose one share of Sanchez Corporation's stock is $25 at the expiration date, and the exercise price of a call option is $15. Therefore, the value of the option is $25 - $15 = $10. Note that the value of the option is

An option gives the holder the right to acquire a valuable asset when circumstances turn favorable.

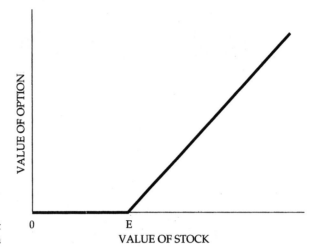

FIGURE 5-1
Value of option at expiration

determined solely by the value of the stock less the exercise price; however, the option cannot have a negative value. When the value of the stock is below the exercise price, the value of the option is zero. If the stock value in the example above were $12, the value of the option would not be $12 − $15 = − $3, but rather, it would be zero.

In Fig. 5-1, the value of the stock is on the horizontal axis, and the value of the option at the expiration date is on the vertical axis. When the value of the stock exceeds the exercise price, the option has a positive value and increases in a linear one-to-one manner with increases in the value of the stock. When the value of the stock equals or is less than the exercise price, the option has a value of zero.

Gain or Loss

The premium is the cost of acquiring an option.

To determine whether an investor holding an option gains or loses, we must take account of the price, or **premium**, paid for the option. If we disregard, for the moment, the time value of money and transaction costs, the investor's gain or loss is simply the value of the option at the expiration date less the price paid for it. To break even, the value of the stock must exceed the exercise price by an amount equal to the premium paid for the option. This is illustrated in the top panel in Fig. 5-2. Here we see that the investor suffers a loss until the stock rises in price to the point where it equals the exercise price of the option plus the premium. After that, as the stock rises in price, the holder of the option gains.

For the **writer**, or seller, of the option, the opposite picture emerges. In the lower panel of the figure, the writer receives the premium and realizes a gain as long as the value of the stock at the expiration date is less than the exercise price plus the premium. If it is more, the seller loses, and losses deepen with increases in the value of the stock. In options, then, the expiration date gain or loss to the investor and to the writer of the option are mirror images of each other. It is a zero-sum game where one can gain only at the expense of the other.

VALUATION WITH ONE PERIOD
TO EXPIRATION: GENERAL CONSIDERATION

Consider now the option with one period to expiration. Again we assume a European option, which can be exercised only at the expiration date. Although we do not know the value of the stock at the expiration date, we assume that we are able to formulate probabilistic beliefs about its value one period hence.

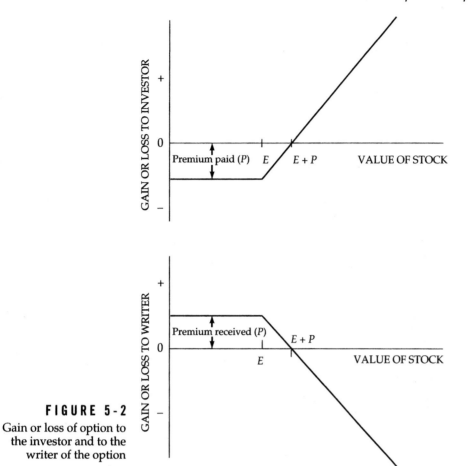

FIGURE 5-2

Gain or loss of option to the investor and to the writer of the option

Figure 5-1 illustrates the theoretical relationship between the beginning of period price of a share of common stock and the price of an option to buy that stock. The 45° line represents the theoretical value of the option. It is simply the current stock price less the exercise price of the option. When the price of the stock is less than the exercise price of the option, the option has a zero theoretical value; when more, it has a theoretical value on the line.

Market versus Theoretical Value

As long as there is some time to expiration, it is possible for the market value of an option to be greater than its theoretical value. The reason for this is the very nature of the contract: It is an option that affords the holder flexibility with respect to the purchase of stock. Suppose the current market price of ABC Corporation's stock is $10, which is equal to the exercise price. Theoretically, the option has no value; however, if there is some probability that the price of the stock will exceed $10 before expiration, the option has a positive value, inasmuch as it *may* permit the holder to exercise it advantageously. Suppose further that the option has 30 days to expiration and that there is a .3 probability that the stock will have a market price of $5 per share at the end of 30 days, .4 that it will be $10, and .3 that it will be $15. The expected value of the option at the end of 30 days is thus

$$0(.3) + 0(.4) + (\$15 - \$10)(.3) = \$1.50$$

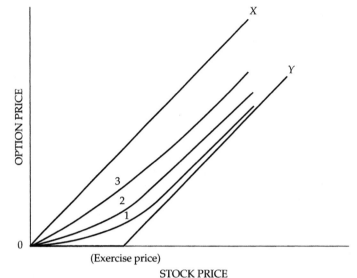

FIGURE 5-3

Relation between stock price and option price for various expiration dates

It is therefore possible for an option to have a positive value even if it is on stock valued less than or equal to the exercise price. Because the option cannot go below zero in value, even when the stock price less the exercise price is negative, the option is frequently worth more than its theoretical value. How much more depends in part on the time to expiration. Figure 5-3 illustrates the general relationship between stock prices and option prices for various terms to expiration.[1]

Boundaries for Option Valuation

The highest value the option can take is the value of the stock, represented by the 45° line X. This value can be reached, presumably, only if the option has a very long time to expiration, perhaps forever, and if the option is not expected to be exercised until far into the future. Under these circumstances, the present value of the exercise price to be paid in the future approaches zero. As a result, the value of the option approaches the value of the associated stock. The lowest value the option can take, of course, is its theoretical value, represented in the figure by zero up to the exercise price and by line Y for values of the stock greater than the exercise price. One might think of the theoretical value line as representing the values of an option with only a moment to expiration. Thus, lines X and Y constitute the boundaries for the value of the option in relation to the value of the associated stock.

For most options, however, the relationship lies between these two boundaries. In general, it can be described by a **convex relationship** in which the value of the option commands the greatest premium over its theoretical value at the exercise price, and the premium declines with increases in the value of the stock beyond that point. If the stock price is less than the exercise price in the figure, the option is said to be trading **out of the money.** The farther to the left, the deeper the

---

[1]Perhaps the first to draw attention to this type of presentation was Paul A. Samuelson, "A Rational Theory of Warrant Pricing," *Industrial Management Review*, 6 (Spring 1965), 103–32

option is out of the money, and the less likelihood it will have value at the expiration date. If the current stock price exceeds the exercise price, the option is said to be trading **in the money,** whereas if it equals the exercise price, the option is trading **at the money.**

Time to Expiration

In general, the longer the time to **expiration**, the greater the value of the option relative to its theoretical value. One reason for this is that there is more time in which the option may have value. Moreover, the greater the time to expiration, the lower the present value of the exercise price to be paid in the future; this, too, enhances the value of the option, all other things staying the same. As the expiration date of an option approaches, however, the relationship between the option value and the stock value becomes more convex. In Fig. 5-3, line 1 represents an option with a shorter time to expiration than that for line 2; and line 2, an option with a shorter time to expiration than that for line 3.

It is never optimal for an option holder to exercise early. This is evident in Fig. 5-3, where the actual option value lines exceed the theoretical value line, the "hockey stick" line commencing at zero and then going along the horizontal axis to the exercise price and then up and to the right along line Y. At expiration, of course, the option is worth only its theoretical value. This is dictated by the stock price which prevails at that time. Prior to expiration, the option's value usually exceeds its theoretical value. With an American option, which allows for early exercise, the holder should always preserve his or her option. Exercising early results in only the theoretical value being realized, whereas the market ascribes a higher value to the option. Contrarily, the writer of the option has an incentive to try to take the option away from the holder as soon as possible.

Interest Rate

Another feature of option valuation is the time value of money. When you acquire a stock by means of an option, you make an initial down payment in the price you pay for the option. Your "final" payment is not due until you exercise the option sometime in the future. This delay (to the time you pay the exercise price) is more valuable the higher interest rates are in the market. This is simply to say that the present value of the future exercise price is less, the greater the interest rate. Thus, an option will be more valuable the longer the time to expiration and the higher the interest rate.

Volatility of the Stock

The main driver of option valuation is the volatility of returns for the associated asset.

Usually the most important factor in the valuation of options is the **price volatility** of the associated security. More specifically, the greater the possibility of extreme outcomes, the greater the value of the option to the holder, all other things being the same. The greater the volatility, the higher the market line curve in Fig. 5-3. If a stock is not likely to change much in price, an option on it is worth little, and the curve will be very near the lower boundary, Y. With volatility, the option will be valuable. We may, at the beginning of a period, be considering options on the two stocks shown in Table 5-1. The expected value of stock price at the end of the period is the same for both stocks: $40. For stock B, however, there is a much larger dispersion of possible outcomes. Suppose the exercise prices of options to purchase stock A and stock B at the end of the period are the same, $38. Thus, the two stocks have the same expected values at the end of the period, and the options have the same exercise price.

TABLE 5-1
Probability Distributions of Two Stocks at the End of the Period

	Probability of Occurrence				
Price	**.10**	**.25**	**.30**	**.25**	**.10**
Stock A	$30	$36	$40	$44	$50
Stock B	20	30	40	50	60

The expected value of the option for stock A at the end of the period, however, is

$$\text{Option A} = 0(.10) + 0(.25) + (\$40 - \$38)(.30) + (\$44 - \$38)(.25)$$
$$+ (\$50 - \$38)(.10)$$
$$= \$3.30$$

whereas that for stock B is

$$\text{Option B} = 0(.10) + 0(.25) + (\$40 - \$38)(.30) + (\$50 - \$38)(.25)$$
$$+ (\$60 - \$38)(.10)$$
$$= \$5.80$$

Value of Dispersion   Thus, the greater dispersion of possible outcomes for stock B leads to a greater expected value of option price on the expiration date. In turn, this is due to the fact that the value of an option cannot be less than zero. As a result, the greater the dispersion, the greater the magnitude of favorable outcomes as measured by the stock price minus the exercise price. Increases in the volatility of the stock therefore increase the magnitude of favorable outcomes for the option buyer and, hence, increase the value of the option.

This is illustrated in Fig. 5-4, where two stocks with different end-of-period share price distributions are shown. The exercise price, *E*, is the same, so the lower

FIGURE 5-4
Volatility and option values for two stocks

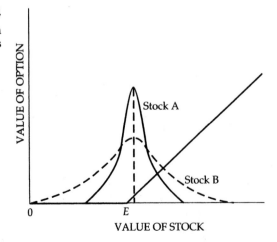

boundary for expiration-date option values is also the same. This is shown by the dark "hockey stick" line at the bottom of the figure. The probability distribution of end-of-period share price is wider for stock B than it is for stock A, reflecting greater volatility. As stock B provides a greater chance for a big payoff, its option is worth more.

Volatility Is What Counts   We shall see later in the chapter that the value of an option does not depend on the expected value of the stock price. Suppose there are two stocks with equal volatility and option features, but one stock has a greater expected future value than the other. Despite the higher expected return on this stock, the option values for the two are the same. It is the variance, or volatility, of the stock price that is important. This statement is a fundamental proposition of option valuation, and it will permeate our application of this concept to various problems in financial management. Our example has been kept purposely simple in looking at the value of the option at the end of the period. The determination of value at the beginning of the period involves the present value of outcomes at the end of the period and is more complicated. We explore this determination in the sections that follow; however, the fundamental importance of the volatility of security price in the valuation of options continues to hold as in our example.

Recapitulation

To summarize where we are up to now, the value, or price, of a call option will change as follows when the variables listed below increase:

Increase in Variable	Option Value Change
Stock volatility	Increase
Time to expiration	Increase
Interest rate	Increase
Exercise price	Decrease
Current stock price	Increase

Keeping these relationships in mind will help us as we probe deeper into option valuation.

BINOMIAL OPTION PRICING OF A HEDGED POSITION

Having two related financial assets—a stock and the option on that stock—we can set up a risk-free hedged position. In this way, price movements in one of the financial assets will be offset by opposite price movements in the other. Consider again a European option, 1 year to expiration, on a stock that pays no dividend. Moreover, assume that there are no transaction costs involved in buying and selling stock or in buying or writing options. In addition to the return on the option and the return on the stock, the opportunity cost of funds is important when it comes to establishing a hedged position. We assume this cost is the risk-free rate, denoted by r, perhaps the rate of return on Treasury bills.

Illustration of Hedging

Binomial pricing maps probabilities as a branching process.

Consider now a time-branching process where at the end of the year there are two possible values for the common stock. One value is higher than the current value of the stock, and it is denoted by uV_s. The other is a lower value, denoted by dV_s. Because V_s represents the current value of the stock, u represents one plus the percentage increase in value of the stock from the beginning of the period to the end, and d represents 1 minus the percentage decrease in the value of the stock.[2] Associated with the upward movement of the stock is a probability of q, and with the downward movement, a probability of $1 - q$.

Figure 5-5 gives some numbers and probabilities to these symbols. There is a two-thirds probability that the stock will increase in value by 20 percent and a one-third probability that it will decline in value by 10 percent. The expected value of stock price at the end of the period is $55, which, on the basis of a $50 investment, represents a return of 10 percent. Assume now that the risk-free rate, r, is 5 percent and that the exercise price of the option is $50. With this information, we see in the lower right-hand column of the figure that the value of the option at the end of the period is either $10 or 0, depending on whether the stock rises or falls in value.

FIGURE 5-5
Hedged position example

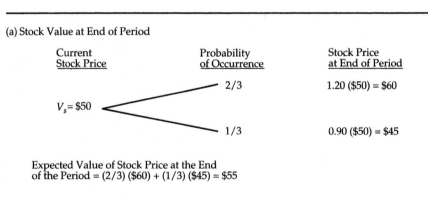

(a) Stock Value at End of Period

Current Stock Price	Probability of Occurrence	Stock Price at End of Period
	2/3	1.20 ($50) = $60
V_s = $50		
	1/3	0.90 ($50) = $45

Expected Value of Stock Price at the End
of the Period = (2/3) ($60) + (1/3) ($45) = $55

(b) Option Value at End of Period

Stock Price at End of Period	Probability of Occurrence	Option Value at End of Period
$60	2/3	Max. ($60 – $50, 0) = $10
$45	1/3	Max. ($45 – $50, 0) = 0

Expected Value of Option Value at End
of the Period = (2/3) ($10) + (1/3) (0) = $6.667

---

[2]In order that pure arbitrage opportunities not exist, u must exceed and d must be less than 1 plus the risk-free rate. This example is based in part on John Cox, "A Discrete Time, Discrete State Option Pricing Model," unpublished teaching note, Graduate School of Business, Stanford University.

Option Delta

In this situation, a hedged position can be established by buying the stock (holding it long) and by writing options. In our example, the idea is to establish a riskless hedged position. The appropriate **hedge ratio** of stock to options is known as the **option delta.** It can be determined by

$$\text{Option delta} = \frac{\text{Spread of possible option prices}}{\text{Spread of possible stock prices}} \qquad (5\text{-}2)$$

For our example, the option delta is

$$\text{Option delta} = \frac{uV_o - dV_o}{uV_s - dV_s} = \frac{\$10 - 0}{\$60 - \$45} = \frac{2}{3}$$

where uV_o is the end-of-period value of the option when the stock price, uV_s, is $60 at the end of the period, and dV_o is the value of the option when the stock price, dV_s, is $45 at the end of the period. This hedge ratio means that the person who wishes to hedge should purchase two shares of stock (the long position) and write three options (the short position).

By undertaking such transactions, the end-of-period values for the two future states will be

Stock Price at End of Period	Value of Long Position in Stock	Value of Short Position in Option	Value of Combined Hedged Position
$60	2($60) = $120	− 3($10) = −$30	$90
45	2(45) = 90	− 3(0) = 0	90

We see that when the stock price at the end of the period is $60, the value of two shares of stock is $120. However, we must subtract from this value the negative value of our short position in options of $30 to get the overall value of our hedged position. When the stock price is $45, two shares are worth $90, and in this case there is no loss on the short position. Therefore, the overall position is perfectly hedged in the sense of providing the same value at the end of the period, regardless of the stock price outcome.

In summary, the hedge ratio, or option delta, is the ratio of the number of shares of stock to the number of options necessary to get offsetting price movements. These movements are such that the net value of the hedged position remains unchanged.

Determining the Value of the Option

The return on this hedged position depends on the value of the option, or the premium, at the beginning of the period. Because the hedged position is riskless, in efficient financial markets we would expect the return on this position to equal the risk-free rate, or 5 percent. We know that the ending value of the hedged position is $90 and that the investment in the two shares of stock at the beginning of the period is $100. The overall investment in the hedged position at the beginning of the period is $100 less the price received on the three options that are written. In other words, the short position results in a cash inflow, whereas the long position results in a cash outflow. Our concern is with the net position.

The value of the option at the beginning of the period, which must prevail if the overall return is to be 5 percent, can be determined by solving the following equation for V_{oB}:

$$[\$100 - 3(V_{oB})]\,1.05 = \$90$$
$$3.15V_{oB} = \$105 - \$90$$
$$V_{oB} = \frac{\$15}{3.15}$$
$$V_{oB} = \$4.762$$

A hedged position should provide only a risk-free return in market equilibrium.

Thus, the overall investment in the hedged position at the beginning of the period is $100 − 3($4.762) = $85.714. The return on this hedged position is ($90 − $85.714)/$85.714 = 5 percent, or the risk-free rate. In other words, the return on the hedged position is the same as that which could be realized by investing $85.714 in a risk-free asset. As both investments are risk free, they should promise the same rate of return.

Implications of Hedged Positions In summary, the option should be priced so that when it is combined with the stock in a hedged position, the return on the position equals the risk-free rate. To the extent that excess returns are available on a fully hedged position, people will have an incentive to take such positions. The impact of their transactions on relative prices will drive out any excess returns that might be earned. As a result, prices will adjust until the return on the hedged position is the risk-free rate and the option is neither overpriced nor underpriced. In the appendix to this chapter, we show market equilibration across call options, shares of stock, and put options, employing what is known as the **put–call parity** theorem. This should give the interested reader a better understanding of how arbitrage works to bring about market equilibrium.

So far, we have worked with simple examples to provide a basic understanding of option pricing. A number of restrictive assumptions were imposed, and the derivation of the option's value was relevant for only the example presented. In the next section we consider a more exacting option valuation framework.

THE BLACK–SCHOLES OPTION MODEL

In a seminal paper, Black and Scholes developed a precise model for determining the equilibrium value of an option.[3] They then went on to observe that the option pricing concepts can be used to value other contingent claims. In particular, the model provides rich insight into the valuation of debt relative to equity. This application and others are taken up later in the book, after we have the foundations provided in this chapter. The **Black–Scholes model** has been extended and refined in major ways, and new applications are unfolding. The model has both theoretical importance for valuing contingent claims and practical importance for identifying overvalued and undervalued options in the market.

---

[3]Fischer Black and Myron Scholes, "The Pricing of Options and Corporate Liabilities," *Journal of Political Economy*, 81 (May–June 1973), 637–54.

The Model in General

A number of assumptions are in order before we can discuss the model:

Black and Scholes are two financial economists who modeled option valuation with a simple, widely used formula.

1. Only European options are considered; that is, options that can be exercised only at expiration.
2. There are no transaction costs. Options and stocks are infinitely divisible, and information is available to all without cost.
3. No imperfections exist in writing an option or selling a stock short.
4. The short-term interest rate is known and constant throughout the duration of the option contract. Market participants can both borrow and lend at this rate.
5. The stock pays no dividend.
6. Stock prices behave in a manner consistent with a random walk in continuous time.
7. The probability distribution of stock returns over an instant of time is normal.
8. The variance of the return is constant over the life of the option contract and is known to market participants.

Given these assumptions, we can determine the equilibrium value of an option. Should the actual price of the option differ from that given by the model, we could establish a riskless hedged position and earn a return in excess of the short-term interest rate in the manner illustrated in the previous section. As arbitragers entered the scene, the excess return would eventually be driven out and the price of the option would equal that value given by the model.

Illustration   To illustrate a hedged position, suppose the appropriate relationship between the option and the stock of XYZ Corporation were that shown in Fig. 5-6. Suppose further that the current market price of the stock were $20 and the price

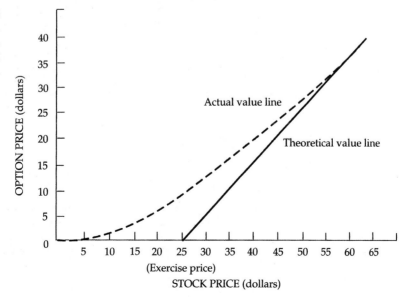

FIGURE 5-6

Relation between the option price and the stock price for XYZ Corporation of the option $7. At $20 a share, the slope of the line in Fig. 5-6 is one half. A hedged position could be undertaken by buying a share of stock for $20 and writing two options at $7 each. The "net money" invested in this position is $20 − 2($7) = $6.

The *option delta* in this example is one half. As defined in the previous section, it tells us that we can replicate the expected payoff in the stock by purchasing two options. Conversely, you can manufacture a "homemade" option by buying one-half share of stock.

Approximate Hedge The combination of holding one share of stock long and two options short leaves us essentially hedged with respect to risk. If the stock drops slightly in value, the value of the short position goes up by approximately an equal amount. We say *approximately* because with changes in the price of the common and with changes in time, the ideal hedge ratio changes. With a stock price increase, for example, the slope of the line in Fig. 5-6 increases. Therefore, fewer options would need to be written. If the stock price declines, the slope decreases and more options must be written to maintain a hedge. As a general rule, the higher the stock price relative to the exercise price, the less risky the option and the fewer options that must be used in a hedge. In addition to stock price changes, the actual value line in Fig. 5-6 will shift downward as time goes on and the expiration date approaches. Thus, one's position must be continually adjusted for changes in the stock price and for changes in time if a riskless hedged position is to be maintained.

The Specific Model

In this context, the equilibrium value of an option, V_o, that entitles the holder to buy one share of stock is shown by Black and Scholes to be

$$V_o = V_s N(d_1) - \frac{E}{e^{rt}} N(d_2) \tag{5-3}$$

where V_s = current price of the stock

$N(d)$ = cumulative normal probability density function

E = exercise price of the option

e = 2.71828, the base of natural logarithms

r = short-term annual interest rate continuously compounded

t = length of time in years to the expiration of the option

$$d_1 = \frac{\ln(V_s/E) + [r + \frac{1}{2}(\sigma^2)]t}{\sigma\sqrt{t}} \tag{5-3a}$$

$$d_2 = \frac{\ln(V_s/E) + [r - \frac{1}{2}(\sigma^2)]t}{\sigma\sqrt{t}} \tag{5-3b}$$

ln = natural logarithm

σ = standard deviation of the annual rate of return on the stock continuously compounded

Interpreting the Formula This formula may seem hopelessly complicated, but it has a rather straightforward interpretation. In the equation, $N(d_1)$ represents the delta, or hedge ratio of shares of stock to options necessary to maintain a fully hedged position. In keeping with our earlier discussion, the option holder can be viewed as a levered investor. He or she borrows an amount equal to the exercise price, E, at an interest rate of r. Therefore, the second term on the right of Eq. (5-3) represents the loan, the present value of the exercise price times an adjustment factor of $N(d_2)$. Thus, Eq. (5-3) represents the following:

$$\begin{matrix} \text{Option} \\ \text{value} \end{matrix} = \left(\begin{matrix} \text{Option} \\ \text{delta} \end{matrix} \times \begin{matrix} \text{Share} \\ \text{price} \end{matrix} \right) - \begin{matrix} \text{Loan} \\ \text{adjusted} \end{matrix} \qquad (5\text{-}4)$$

The important implication of the Black–Scholes model is that the value of an option is a function of the short-term interest rate, of the time to expiration, and of the variance rate of return on the stock, but it is not a function of the expected return on the stock. The value of the option in Eq. (5-3) increases with the increase of either or all of the terms: for duration to expiration of the option, t, for the variance rate, σ^2, and for the short-term interest rate, r. The reasons for these relationships were discussed earlier in the chapter. Of the three factors affecting the value of the option, however, the short-term interest rate generally has the least impact. With increases in t, r, and σ^2 in Eq. (5-3), the value of the option approaches the value of a share of stock as a limit.

Solving the Formula

In solving the formula, we know four of the five variables: the current stock price, the time to expiration of the option, the exercise price, and the short-term interest rate. The key unknown, then, is the standard deviation of the stock price. Black and Scholes assume that the stock's continuously compounded rate of return is normally distributed with constant variance.[4] The usual approach to the problem is to use the recent past volatility of the stock as a proxy for its volatility during the life of the option. We might use weekly observations of stock prices over the last year and derive the annualized standard deviation of the natural logarithm of price relatives.[5] There are other ways to estimate volatility, but we will not get into them as they are beyond the scope of this chapter.

Illustration To illustrate the use of the Black–Scholes option pricing formula, suppose that on the basis of an analysis of past volatility we found the standard deviation of the stock's continuously compounded return to be .40. By referring to a financial newspaper, we are able to look up the other four terms necessary to solve the option pricing formula. Suppose we find the following:

Stock price, $V_s = \$30$

Exercise price option, $E = \$28$

Short-term annual rate of interest continuously compounded, $r = .10$

Time to expiration, $t = .50$ ($\frac{1}{2}$ year)

---

[4]Although this assumption is open to question, solving the problem without a stationarity assumption is exceedingly complex. The valuation formula is very sensitive to the standard deviation employed as an estimate of the volatility of the stock.

[5]A *price relative* is simply the stock price this week divided by the stock price last week. If the stock price this week is $33 and the price last week was $31.50, the price relative is $33/31.50 = 1.04762. The natural logarithm of this number is .04652, and it can be found in a natural log table or on a calculator equipped with this function. Given a listing of 52 price relatives and their natural logarithms, we can easily derive the standard deviation (52 weeks to the year). To annualize this weekly standard deviation, it must be multiplied by the square root of 52.

Solving first for d_1 and d_2, we obtain

$$d_1 = \frac{\ln(30/28) + [.10 + \frac{1}{2}(.40)^2](.50)}{.40\sqrt{.50}} = \frac{.158993}{.282843} = .562$$

$$d_2 = \frac{\ln(30/28) + [.10 - \frac{1}{2}(.40)^2](.50)}{.40\sqrt{.50}} = \frac{.078993}{.282843} = .279$$

The expression $\ln(30/28)$ can be solved either by using a calculator having such a function or by looking it up in a natural log table. In our example, $\ln(30/28) = .068993$.

Cumulative Probabilities   In Eq. (5-3), $N(d_1)$ and $N(d_2)$ are the probabilities that a random variable with a standardized normal distribution will take on values less than d_1 and less than d_2. With the bell-shaped normal distribution, slightly over two-thirds of the distribution falls within one standard deviation on either side of the mean, 95 percent within two standard deviations, and 99.7 percent within three standard deviations. In Table C at the back of the book, an abbreviated table for the normal distribution tells us the area of the distribution that is so many standard deviations to the left or to the right of the mean. A d_1 of .562 lies between the standard deviations of .55 and .60 shown in the table, corresponding to .2912 and .2743 areas of the distribution, respectively. Interpolating, we come up with

$$.2912 - \left(\frac{.12}{.50}\right)(.2912 - .2743) = .287$$

This represents the area of a normal distribution that is .562 or more standard deviations greater than the mean. To determine the area of the normal distribution that is less than .562 standard deviation, we merely subtract .287 from 1.[6] Therefore,

$$N(d_1) = N(.562) = 1 - .287 = .713$$

For the d_2 of .279, we see in Table C that it lies between the standard deviations of .25 and .30. Interpolating here, we obtain

$$.4013 - \left(\frac{.29}{.50}\right)(.4013 - .3821) = .390$$

Therefore,

$$N(d_2) = N(.279) = 1 - .390 = .610$$

Putting It Together   Given $N(d_1)$ and $N(d_2)$ together with the information on the stock price, the exercise price, the interest rate, and the length of time to expiration

---

[6]If the value of d_1 were negative, we would be concerned with the area of the distribution that was to the left of the standard deviation. As a result, we would not subtract it from 1. It is only with positive values that we subtract the area of the normal distribution from 1.

of the option, we are able to compute the equilibrium value of the option using Eq. (5-3). For our example problem,[7]

$$V_o = \$30(.713) - \frac{\$28}{e^{(.10)(.50)}} (.610) = \$5.14$$

Thus, the Black–Scholes option pricing model suggests that an option to buy one share of stock having the characteristics specified is worth $5.14. Rather than solve for this value by hand, computer programs are available that will do it for you. Still, it is useful to see how these programs, both embedded and specialized, go about the task of calculation.

The Hedge Ratio to Use   The value of $N(d_1)$ tells us the appropriate hedge ratio to employ. In our example, the ratio is .713. This means that a movement in the stock price will be accompanied by a .713 movement in the option price. To hedge, the individual should purchase .713 shares of stock for each option that is written. With these proportions, price movements of the two financial assets will be offsetting. The equation above also tells us that if the actual market price is more or less than $5.14, it is over- or undervalued. However, caution is necessary in interpreting the results because our estimate of the stock's future volatility is based on its past volatility. This may or may not be an accurate proxy for the future. As the formula is quite sensitive to the standard deviation employed, caution is necessary in judging whether an option is over- or undervalued. In Table 5-2, Black–Scholes option values are shown for other assumptions concerning the standard deviation, stock price, exercise price, interest rate, and the time to expiration.

Some Refinements

As previously mentioned, the delta hedge ratio of stocks and options must be adjusted as prices and volatility change. In theory, continuous adjustment is necessary to maintain a risk-free hedge. Such continuous changes do not occur in practice. There are delays in execution and there are transaction costs. These factors must be weighted against the benefits. Most people who use the Black–Scholes model, or a similar one, adjust the hedge ratio every so often, perhaps once a week. When prices are changing rapidly, more frequent adjustment is necessary than in a stable market period. In practice, one cannot obtain a perfect hedge, only approximate it.

Other Parameters   Our focus in this chapter has been on the effect of delta, the hedge ratio, on the equilibration process between the value of an option and the price of the associated stock. This is the first derivative. Added precision to the Black–Scholes formula sometimes can be gained by knowing other parameters. These include (1) **gamma**, the second derivative of option value with respect to share price; (2) **theta**, the first derivative of option value with respect to the time to expiration; (3) **rho**, the first derivative with respect to the interest rate; and (4) **vega**, the first derivative with respect to volatility. Exploration into these factors is beyond the scope of this book, but you should be mindful of the terms in

---

[7]In the equation, $e = 2.71828$, as stated earlier. Many calculators have this function, which allows for easy solution to the problem. Without this help, we must resort to a table of natural logarithms.

TABLE 5-2
Option Prices from Black–Scholes Equation for Various Parameter Values (Price of Underlying Stock = $40)

Standard Deviation	Exercise Price	r = 5%		
		t = 1 MONTH	*t* = 4 MONTHS	*t* = 7 MONTHS
.20	$35	5.15	5.77	6.42
.20	40	1.00	2.18	3.02
.20	45	.02	.51	1.11
.30	35	5.22	6.26	7.19
.30	40	1.46	3.08	4.20
.30	45	0.16	1.26	2.24
.40	35	5.39	6.90	8.11
.40	40	1.92	3.99	5.38
.40	45	.42	2.11	3.44

Implied from Black–Scholes is volatility, or any other variable, if we know four of the five variables in the equation.

case you come across them in the future. Reference to the several books on options listed at the end of the chapter will give you an understanding.

Implied Volatility With the Black–Scholes formula, we can estimate the volatility of a stock if we know the other variables. Assuming equilibration between the stock and options markets, the estimated variability of the stock can be backed out of the formula. In other words, if we know the market price of the stock, the market price of the option, the expiration and exercise price of the option, and the short-term interest rate, we can solve the formula for the standard deviation of return for the stock. In practice, much attention is paid to the variance assumption involved in the associated asset. In valuing an option or a contract with option features, often it will be prefaced by saying "value is based on a 23 percent standard deviation assumption," or something to this effect.

The Black–Scholes formula, extensions of it, and other formulas of the same general sort are widely used on Wall Street. In recent years, the avenues for shifting risk have expanded enormously—options markets on stocks and fixed-income securities, futures markets on financial assets and commodities, and currency markets. With combinations of securities held outright, securities sold short, options contracts, futures contracts, and currency contracts, it is possible to derive myriad "synthetic" securities. With precision, the investment or financial manager can lay off the desired degree of risk. In Chapter 21, we probe the various ways by which this can be done and see that options play an integral role.

AMERICAN OPTIONS

In the preceding section we assumed a European option on a stock paying no dividends and then proceeded to value it in a hypothetical example of the stock's volatility, its price, the exercise price of the option, the length of time to expiration,

$r = 10\%$			$r = 15\%$		
$t = 1$ MONTH	$t = 4$ MONTHS	$t = 7$ MONTHS	$t = 1$ MONTH	$t = 4$ MONTHS	$t = 7$ MONTHS
5.30	6.29	7.26	5.44	6.81	8.11
1.09	2.54	3.67	1.19	2.94	4.38
.03	.65	1.47	.03	.82	1.91
5.36	6.72	7.92	5.50	7.18	8.66
1.55	3.42	4.79	1.64	3.78	5.42
.18	1.45	2.66	.20	1.67	3.12
5.52	7.31	8.76	5.65	7.73	9.42
2.00	4.31	5.94	2.09	4.65	6.52
.45	2.33	3.87	.48	2.57	4.34

American options can be exercised at any time up to expiration.

and the short-term interest rate. We now need to determine the effect on the value of an option when we drop the assumptions of a European option and no dividends.

An American option can be exercised by the holder any time up to the expiration date. Because the American option provides all the rights of a European option plus the ability to exercise it before the expiration date, its value must be at least that of an identical European option. In certain cases, it will be worth more. However, it has been demonstrated that an American option on a nondividend-paying stock should not be exercised before the expiration date. This is in keeping with our earlier rule that the option holder should never exercise early. He or she gives up not only the option but also the time value of money in paying the exercise price early. Without early exercise, the American and European options will be priced the same if they are alike in all other respects. Only for options on dividend-paying stocks is the distinction between the European and the American option important. To this issue we now turn.

The Effect of Dividends

Cash dividends work to the disadvantage of the option holder vis-à-vis the stockholder.

A cash dividend on a common stock tends to lower the value of the option on that stock. The higher the dividend, the lower the option's value, all other things staying the same. In essence, a cash dividend represents the partial liquidation of a company to which the stockholders, but not the option holders, are entitled. With a complete liquidating dividend, the price of the stock will go to zero, as will the price of the option. When a stock goes ex-dividend,[8] the market price of the stock will drop by an amount somewhat less than that of the dividend, depending on

---

[8]In declaring a dividend, the board of directors specifies an ex-dividend date. At that date, the stock trades ex-dividend in that investors who purchase it are not entitled to the declared dividend. See Chapter 11 for a discussion of the ex-dividend behavior of common stocks in relation to taxes.

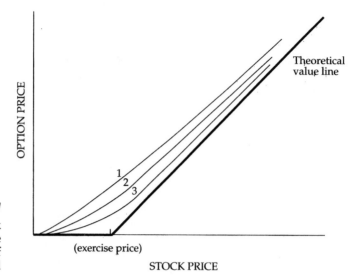

FIGURE 5-7

Relation between stock price and option price for different levels of dividend

the tax effect. The greater the present value of cash dividends likely to be paid prior to the expiration of the option, the lower its value, all other things staying the same. This relationship is illustrated in Fig. 5-7. The curved lines represent actual option values for different levels of dividend. The greater the dividend, as represented by a higher number, the lower the value of the option relative to its theoretical value, all other things staying the same.

PV of Dividends Adjustment   A cash dividend may affect the timing in exercising an American option, since there is an obvious advantage in buying the stock in time to receive the dividend. The disadvantage in early exercise of the option is the opportunity cost of the interest that would have been earned on the exercise price. Dividend and interest become a trade-off in choosing the optimal time to exercise the option. One way to adjust for the presence of dividends in the Black–Scholes option pricing model is to treat all expected future dividends up to the expiration date as though they will happen. The present value of these dividends is subtracted from the current price of the stock. The option pricing formula then is based on this **adjusted stock price**, as opposed to the actual price of the stock. This, of course, sidesteps the possibility of early exercise, which remains a problem.

More Sophisticated Approaches   Roll, followed by Geske and modified slightly by Whaley, develops a formal model to deal with call options on stocks with known dividends.[9] Essentially, the model is a modification of the Black–Scholes model that incorporates the dividend, the time to the ex-dividend date, and the decline in stock price on this date as a proportion of the dividend. Empirical tests of the model show a lower prediction error for dividend-paying stocks, particu-

[9]Richard Roll, "An Analytic Formula for Unprotected American Call Options on Stocks with Known Dividends," *Journal of Financial Economics*, 5 (November 1977), 251–58; Robert Geske, "A Note on an Analytical Valuation Formula for Unprotected American Call Options on Stocks with Known Dividends," *Journal of Financial Economics*, 7 (December 1979), 375–80; and Robert E. Whaley, "On the Valuation of American Call Options on Stocks with Known Dividends," *Journal of Financial Economics*, 9 (June 1981), 207–11.

larly where the dividend is large, than occurs with the Black–Scholes model adjusted by deducting the present value of dividend payment from the stock price.[10] However, there still is a tendency for the model to overestimate values of options written on high-variance stocks and underpredict values of options written on low-variance stocks as well as overestimate values for "in the money" options and underestimate values for "out of the money" options.

Although the presence of cash dividends complicates the picture, the basic tenets of the Black–Scholes option pricing model continue to hold. For many options, the expiration date is relatively near, and the quarterly dividends likely to be paid on the stock before the option's expiration are not material. In situations of this sort, it may not be worthwhile to make a dividend adjustment, particularly if the next ex-dividend date is some time away. For applications of the model later in this book, no dividend adjustments will be made because our focus will be on the conceptual insights provided by the model.

DEBT AND OTHER OPTIONS

In addition to stock options, there are options on other securities. Rather than an option on a specific stock, one might prefer an **index option**. Here an option is written on a broad portfolio of stocks, such as Standard & Poor's 500-Stock Index or the New York Stock Exchange Index. The option written pertains to the level of stock prices in general.

Another type of option is a **debt option**. This may be on an actual debt instrument or on an interest-rate futures contract. Either way, this type of option provides a means for protection against adverse interest-rate movements. Debt options are examined in Chapter 21, once we have covered interest-rate futures contracts as part of overall risk management. Finally, there are **foreign currency options**. Here an option is written on the number of units of a foreign currency that a U.S. dollar will buy. It could be British pounds, Euros, or Japanese yen. This type of option is discussed in Chapter 25, when we take up international financial management.

Stock options are perhaps the most important category, but there are other options.

In all our subsequent discussion involving the principles of options, we draw on the foundations of this chapter. This discussion includes the two options mentioned above, as well as warrants, convertible securities, call options, other option features embedded in securities, and the treatment of equity as an option on the total value of the firm that is written by debt holders.

---

[10]See William E. Sterk, "Comparative Performance of the Black–Scholes and Roll–Geske–Whaley Option Pricing Models," *Journal of Financial and Quantitative Analysis*, 18 (September 1983), 345–54. Also see Robert E. Whaley, "On the Valuation of American Call Options on Stocks with Known Dividends," *Journal of Financial Economics*, 9 (June 1981), 207–11; and "Valuation of American Call Options on Dividend-Paying Stocks: Empirical Tests," *Journal of Financial Economics*, 10 (March 1982), 29–58.

Summary

A call option gives the holder the right to buy a share of stock at a specified price, the exercise price. A European option can be exercised only at the expiration date, whereas an American option can be exercised any time up to and in-

cluding the expiration date. The value of the option at the expiration date is the value of the stock minus the exercise price, or it may be zero. It cannot be a negative value. The most important factor affecting the value of the option is the price volatility of the stock; the greater the volatility, the more valuable the option, all other things staying the same. In addition, the longer the time to the expiration date and the higher the interest rate, the greater the value of the option, all other things staying the same.

With a stock and an option on the stock, it is possible to establish a riskless hedged position by buying the stock and by writing options or selling them short. The option's delta, or hedge ratio, determines the portion of stock held long in relation to the options in the short position. (A riskless hedge could be established also by buying options and selling the stock short.) With a discrete time example, we showed how the value of the hedged position was the same regardless of the stock price outcome. In efficient financial markets, the rate of return on a perfectly hedged position would be the risk-free rate. If this is the case, it is possible to determine the appropriate value of the option at the beginning of the period.

The Black–Scholes option pricing model provides an exact formula for determining the value of an option based on the volatility of the stock, the price of the stock, the exercise price of the option, the time to expiration of the option, and the short-term interest rate. With an example, we showed how this formula could be used, and we discussed some of the problems. The model is based on the notion that investors are able to maintain reasonably hedged positions over time and that arbitrage will drive the return on such positions to the risk-free rate. As a result, the option price will bear a precise relationship to the stock price. The Black–Scholes model provides considerable insight into the valuation of contingent claims, and certain refinements of it were examined.

In comparing American and European options, we found that an American option on a stock that pays a dividend may have less value than a European option on a stock that does not pay a dividend. Finally, there are a number of options and option applications additional to stock options—index options, debt options, currency options, warrants, convertibles, and options embedded in securities. This chapter serves as a foundation for their later examination.

Appendix: Put–Call Parity

In the equilibration process driven by arbitrage, there is a relationship between put, call, and stock prices. To illustrate, assume European type put and call options where both have the same exercise price, $30, and the same expiration date. Suppose our strategy is to sell one put option and to buy one call option. If we ignore for now the premiums earned and paid, the expiration date values of the two options are as shown in Fig. 5A-1. We see that the expiration date value of our put–call strategy is the stock price less the exercise price of $30, described by the diagonal line throughout. Now suppose we buy the stock and borrow the exercise price of the options with a loan maturing at the expiration date. The expiration date value of our position, ignoring interest, is also the stock price minus $30. Thus, the two strategies produce the same result.

In market equilibrium with zero arbitrage opportunity, there will be a precise relationship between the market values of the put and the call options and the stock. We have established that the payoff from a strategy of buying a call and selling a put is the same as that from buying the stock and borrowing the exercise price. Taking account of the time value of money, the relationship can be expressed as

$$V_c - V_p = V_s - PV(E) \qquad (5A\text{-}1)$$

where V_c is the value of call option, V_p is the value of put option, V_s is the value of share of stock, $PV(E)$ is the present value of the exercise price, where the time interval is the time to expiration of the options.

Rearranging Eq. (5A-1), we obtain

$$-V_s + PV(E) + V_c - V_p = 0 \qquad (5A\text{-}2)$$

which is the put–call parity theorem. This basic expression can be rearranged further to

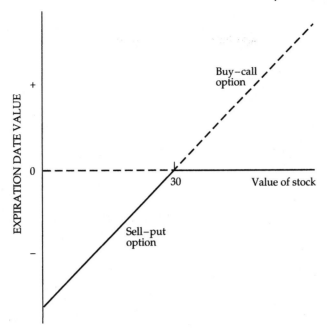

FIGURE 5A-1

Expiration date values
of put and call options

solve for any one of the four values, given the other three. For the value of the call, it is

$$V_c = V_s + V_p - PV(E) \qquad \text{(5A-3)}$$

For the value of the put, it is

$$V_p = -V_s + V_c + PV(E) \qquad \text{(5A-4)}$$

and for the value of the stock

$$V_s = V_c - V_p + PV(E) \qquad \text{(5A-5)}$$

Suppose a put option had a value of $3, both options had an exercise price of $30 and 6 months to expiration, the interest rate was 4 percent for 6 months, and share price was $35.

If there were no opportunities for arbitrage, the value of the call option would be

$$V_c = \$35 + \$3 - \$28.80 = \$9.20$$

If the call option value were other than this, there would be opportunity for arbitrage.

Thus, the put–call parity theorem may be used to determine whether the stock and the options are priced correctly. Zero arbitrage opportunity means that there is market equilibrium in the prices of all three securities, as was the case in the chapter discussion for the call option and the stock. The most practical implication of put–call parity is that in equilibrium the option value equals the option delta (hedge ratio) times share price.

Self-Correction Problems

1. Loco Baking Company's common stock has a present market price per share of $28. A 6-month call option has been written on the stock with an exercise price of $30. Presently the option has a market value of $3. At the end of 6 months, you estimate the market price of the stock to be $24 per share with a probability of .1, $28 with a probability of .2, $32 with a probability of .4, $37 with a probability of .2, and $43 with a probability of .1.

   a. What is the expected value of share price 6 months hence? What is the expiration value of the option if that expected value of share price should prevail?

    b. What is the expected value of option price at expiration, assuming that the option is held to this time? Why does it differ from the option value determined in part a?

    c. Presently, what is the theoretical value of the option? Why does it have a positive value?

2. Prudencio Jiminez Company's share price is now $60. Six months from now, it will be either $75 with probability .70 or $50 with probability .30. A call option exists on the stock that can be exercised only at the end of 6 months at an exercise price of $65.

    a. If you wished to establish a perfectly hedged position, what would you do on the basis of the facts just presented?

    b. Under each of the two possibilities, what will be the value of your hedged position?

    c. What is the expected value of option price at the end of the period?

3. A call option enables the holder to acquire one share of stock at $45 a share for each option held. The option has 6 months until its expiration. The market price of the stock is currently $40 a share, and the expected standard deviation of its continuously compounded return over the near future is .30. The short-term annual interest rate is 10 percent.

    a. On the basis of this information, what is the proper value of the option using the Black–Scholes option pricing model? (The calculations can be made with a reasonably sophisticated calculator or with an ordinary calculator and various tables.)

    b. What is the appropriate hedge ratio, and how does it work?

Problems

1. Given the following data, determine the value of the call options at their expiration dates.

Option	Market Price per Share at the Expiration Date	Exercise Price of the Option
A	$10	$12
B	25	21
C	48	52
D	7	5

2. The X-Gamma Company and the X-Theta Company have actively traded options on their stocks with the same exercise price, $30. The current market prices of the two stocks are the same, $27 per share, yet the current market price of the X-Gamma option is $2.25, and that of the X-Theta option is $3.90. How can this difference in option prices occur?

3. Julia Malone is considering writing a 30-day option on Video Sonics Corporation, which is currently trading at $60 per share. The exercise price will also be $60 per share, and the premium received on the option will be $3.75. At what common stock prices will she make money, at what price will she begin to lose money, and at what prices will she lose $5 and $10 on each option that is written?

4. The stocks of Carson Can Company and Tahoe Forest Products Company are expected to have the following probability distributions with respect to market price per share 6 months hence.

Probability of Occurrence	Carson Can	Tahoe Forest Products
.15	$34	$22
.20	38	28
.30	40	36
.20	42	44
.15	46	50

Options exist for each of these stocks, and both have an exercise price of $38 and an expiration date 6 months from now.

   a. What is the expected value of market price per share 6 months hence for the two companies?
   b. What is the expected value of option price for the two options at expiration, assuming the options are held to this time?
   c. Reconcile your answers to parts a and b.

5. Shinto Carbon Steel Company's stock price at the beginning of a 6-month period is $40 per share. At the end of the period, there is a 50 percent chance that the stock will increase in value to $50 and a 50 percent chance that it will fall in value to $38 per share. An option on the stock can be exercised only at the end of the period and at an exercise price of $41. The risk-free rate is now 5 percent per period.

   a. How would you establish a perfectly hedged position, using the stock and the option?
   b. Show how the value of your position will be the same regardless of the stock price outcome.

6. In Problem 5, what will be the market price of the option at the beginning of the period if financial markets are efficient and rational? What would happen if the actual market price of the option were in excess of the price you compute? What would happen if it were less?

7. Zilcon Laboratories, Inc., is a new high-technology company whose common stock sells for $23 per share. A call option exists on this stock with 3 months to expiration. It has an exercise price of $18 and sells for $5.30. You have made a careful study of the stock's volatility and conclude that a standard deviation of .50 is appropriate for the next 3 months. Currently, the annual rate on short-term Treasury bills is 6 percent.

   a. Using the Black–Scholes option pricing model, is the option overvalued, undervalued, or priced just right? (These calculations are possible with a reasonably sophisticated calculator or with a plain calculator and various tables.)

   b. If you believe in these numbers, what should you do?

8. For Zilcon Laboratories, Inc., in Problem 7, determine the value of the option with the following changes, holding all else constant, and explain why the change in the value of the option occurs.

   a. The length of time to expiration is 1 year instead of 3 months.

   b. The short-term interest rate is 8 percent instead of 6 percent.

   c. The standard deviation is .10 instead of .50.

9. A 6-month call option on the stock of Costello Equipment Company permits the holder to acquire one share at $30. Presently, share price is $25, and the expected standard deviation of its continuously compounded return is .20. The short-term annual interest rate is 8 percent.

   a. What is the value of the option according to the Black–Scholes formula?

   b. What would be the value if the current share price were $30? $35? How do these premiums over lower boundary theoretical values compare with that when share price is $25? Why the differences?

   c. Suppose now that the original conditions hold, but we do not know the standard deviation. If the option price is $2, what is the implied standard deviation? (*Note*: This question should be undertaken only if you have a computer program at your disposal.)

Appendix Problem

1. A put and a call option each have an expiration date 6 months hence and an exercise price of $10. The interest rate for the 6-month period is 3 percent.

   a. If the put has a market price of $2 and stock is worth $9 per share, what is the value of the call?

   b. If the put has a market price of $1 and the call $4, what is the value of the stock per share?

   c. If the call has a market value of $5 and market price of the stock is $12 per share, what is the value of the put?

Solutions to Self-Correction Problems

1.   a. *EV* of share price = $24(.1) + $28(.2) + $32(.4) + $37(.2) + $43(.1) = $32.50; option value = $32.50 − $30.00 = $2.50.

      b. *EV* of option price = 0(.1) + 0(.2) + ($32 − $30)(.4) + ($37 − $30)(.2) + ($43 − $30)(.1) = $3.50. At values of share price less than $30, the option has zero value, as opposed to a negative value. This boundary on the downside results in a higher expected value of option price than in part a, where the implicit assumption is a negative option price when share price is either $24 or $28.

 c. Theoretical value of option = max ($28 − $30, 0) = 0. The option has a positive value because the probability distribution of possible share prices 6 months hence is relatively wide. If the market's assessment corresponds to yours, that would explain the positive option price.

2. a. Hedge ratio $= \dfrac{uV_o - dV_o}{uV_s - dV_s} = \dfrac{\$10 - 0}{\$75 - \$50} = .4$

This hedge ratio means that you should purchase two shares of stock in a long position for every five options you write (your short position). By doing so, you will have established a perfectly hedged position.

 b. This hedged position may be illustrated by determining the value of your position under each of the two possibilities:

Stock Price	Value of Long Position in Stock	Value of Short Position in Option	Value of Combined Hedged Position
$75	2($75) = $150	− 5($10) = − $50	$100
50	2(50) = 100	− 5(0) = 0	100

Thus, the value of the hedged position is the same regardless of the stock outcome.

 c. *EV* of option price = ($75 − $65)(.70) + 0(.30) = $7

3. a. $d_1 = \dfrac{\ln(40/45) + [.10 + \frac{1}{2}(.30)^2].50}{.30\sqrt{.50}} = -.213$

$d_2 = \dfrac{\ln(40/45) + [.10 - \frac{1}{2}(.30)^2].50}{.30\sqrt{.50}} = -.426$

$N(d_1) = N(-.213) = .416$

$N(d_2) = N(-.426) = .335$

$V_o = \$40(.416) - \dfrac{\$45}{e^{(.10)(.50)}}(.335) = \$2.30$

Because d_1 and d_2 are negative, we do not subtract them from 1 as we do when they are positive.

 b. The appropriate hedge ratio is $N(d_1) = .416$. This means that for every option written or sold short, the individual should buy .416 share of common stock.

Selected References

BAKSHI, GURDIP, and DILIP MADAN, "Spanning and Derivative-Security Valuation," *Journal of Financial Economics*, 55 (February 2000), 205–38.

BARTH, MARY E., WAYNE R. LANDSMAN, and RICHARD J. RENDLEMAN JR., "Option-Pricing-Based Bond Value Estimates and a Fundamental Components Approach to Account for Corporate Debt," Working paper, Stanford Business School (September 1997).

BLACK, FISCHER, "How to Use the Holes in Black-Scholes," *Journal of Applied Corporate Finance*, 1 (Winter 1989), 67–73.

BLACK, FISCHER, and MYRON SCHOLES, "The Pricing of Options and Corporate Liabilities," *Journal of Political Economy*, 81 (May–June 1973), 637–54.

BUHLER, WOLFGANG, MARLIESE UHRIG-HOMBURG, ULRICH WALTER, and THOMAS WEBER, "An Empirical Comparison of Forward-rate and Spot-rate Models for Valuing Interest-Rate Options," *Journal of Finance*, 54 (February 1999), 269–305.

CAMPBELL, JOHN Y., ANDREW W. LO, and A. CRAIG MACKINLAY, *The Econometrics of Financial Markets*. Princeton, NJ: Princeton University Press, 1997. Chap. 9.

CHANCE, DON M., "Translating the Greek: The Real Meaning of Call Option Derivatives," *Financial Analysts Journal*, 50 (July/August 1994), 43–49.

DUMAS, BERNARD, JEFF FLEMING, and ROBERT E. WHALEY, "Implied Volatility Functions: Empirical Tests," *Journal of Finance*, 53 (December 1998), 2059–106.

FABOZZI, FRANK J., *Bond Markets, Analysis and Strategies, 4th ed.* Upper Saddle River, NJ: Prentice Hall, 2000. Chap. 22.

GESKE, ROBERT, "A Note on an Analytical Valuation Formula for Unprotected American Call Options on Stocks with Known Dividends," *Journal of Financial Economics*, 7 (December 1979), 375–80.

GESKE, ROBERT, and RICHARD ROLL, "On Valuing American Call Options with the Black-Scholes European Formula," *Journal of Finance*, 39 (June 1984), 443–55.

HULL, JOHN, *Options, Futures and Other Derivative Securities, 4th ed.* Upper Saddle River, NJ: Prentice Hall, 2001.

JARROW, ROBERT, and STUART TURNBULL, *Derivative Securities. 2nd ed.* Cincinnati, OH: South-Western, 2000.

MERTON, ROBERT C., "A Rational Theory of Option Pricing," *Bell Journal of Economics*, 4 (Spring 1973), 141–82.

ROLL, RICHARD, "An Analytic Valuation Formula for Unprotected American Call Options with Known Dividends," *Journal of Financial Economics*, 5 (November 1977), 251–58.

SHARPE, WILLIAM F., GORDON J. ALEXANDER, and JEFFERY V. BAILEY, *Investments, 6th ed.*, Upper Saddle River, NJ: Prentice Hall, 1999. Chap. 19.

VAN HORNE, JAMES C., *Financial Market Rates and Flows*, 6th ed. Upper Saddle River, NJ: Prentice Hall, 2001.

WHALEY, ROBERT E., "On the Valuation of American Call Options on Stocks with Known Dividends," *Journal of Financial Economics*, 9 (June 1981), 207–11.

———, "Valuation of American Call Options on Dividend-Paying Stocks: Empirical Tests," *Journal of Financial Economics*, 10 (March 1982), 29–58.

———, "On Valuing American Futures Options," *Financial Analysis Journal*, 42 (May–June 1986), 49–59.

Wachowicz's Web World is an excellent overall Web site produced and maintained by my coauthor of *Fundamentals of Financial Management*, John M. Wachowicz Jr. It contains descriptions of and links to many finance Web sites and articles. *www.prenhall.com/wachowicz*.

Part II

INVESTMENT IN ASSETS AND REQUIRED RETURNS

■ **CASE:** *Fazio Pump Corporation*

In January 2001, Sophia Ferrara, marketing vice president of Fazio Pump Corporation, was faced with an important sales management challenge involving capital investment by the company's customers. During 2000, the company reported pump sales of $177 million, primarily to the petroleum refining and chemical industries. Sales were organized through a system of salaried sales representatives who sold directly to industrial users. These representatives were highly knowledgeable about the specifications and uses of the company's pump lines. For many years they had performed effectively on the basis of technical competence, well-developed contacts with purchasing agents, and with the backing of a strong service organization.

INTRODUCTION OF A NEW PUMP

In 2000, the research and development team of Fazio made a significant technological breakthrough, which had dramatic implications for the future growth of the company. They developed a large, powerful, computer-directed switching pump that, it appeared, might make obsolete many other pumps in their hydraulic pump line. The new pump, called Faz-Power III, had tentatively been priced at $260,000 per unit. The advantage of the new pump was that it required significantly less labor, including maintenance and monitoring, than did other combinations of pumps and control devices. This had the effect of reducing costs by approximately $60,000 in the first year. With inflation, these savings were expected to increase at a 4 percent compound rate per year. In other words, year 2 expected savings would be $62,400, year 3, $64,896, and so forth. For calculation purposes, it was assumed that for the pumps Faz-Power III replaced, the cost of removal and disposal offset any salvage value. As a result, no residual value was assumed. Also, the old pumps were assumed to have no further remaining depreciation.

The new pump had an economic life of 8 years. At the end of its useful life, year 8, it was expected to have a value of $30,000. Ms. Ferrara assumed that all of the company's customers used the modified accelerated cost recovery system (MACRS) for depreciation purposes. The pump falls into the 5-year property class with respect to cost recovery. As a result, the schedule permits depreciation of 20.00 percent in the first year, 32.00 percent in the second year, 19.20 percent in the third year, 11.52 percent in both the fourth and the fifth years, and 5.76 percent in the sixth year. As the pump will be fully depreciated after $5\frac{1}{2}$ years, the salvage value realized at the end of 8 years must be treated as a recapture of depreciation for tax purposes. Consequently, the estimated salvage value will be taxed at the ordinary income tax rate. For purposes of analysis, Ms. Ferrara assumed that customers of Fazio paid an effective corporate tax rate (federal and state) of 38 percent. Finally, all cash flows were assumed to occur at the end of the year, whereas the initial outlay was assumed to occur entirely at time 0.

MARKETING THE PUMP

The challenge facing Fazio and its sales management was that virtually all of their existing pumps were priced under $40,000 and were purchased by plant manager customers without the bother of a full capital expenditure analysis. With a $260,000 purchase, however, most customers had to prepare a full capital expenditure analysis, which was sent to headquarters for approval. Since the plant managers whom Fazio sales representatives met were uncomfortable with these reports, they tended to shy away from "big ticket" items. Instead, they had a preference for less expensive equipment that did not necessitate so much paperwork and the bothersome justification procedures. Unless sales representatives could demonstrate the discounted cash flow advantage of the pump and help customers prepare capital budgeting forms for upper-level approval, the prospects for the new pump were not bright. Ms. Ferrara was faced with bringing the company's sales representatives up to speed in capital budgeting as quickly and as simply as possible. Otherwise, they would be at a loss in trying to sell the new pump.

DISCOUNT RATE AND PRICING

Another consideration was whether the price of the new pump should be adjusted downward from the tentative price to meet the prevailing return requirements of 13 percent after taxes for the middle-market companies to which Fazio typically sold pumps. Prices of new Fazio products had traditionally been "cost determined." That is, a desired profit margin was added to cost per unit. In the case of the Faz-Power III pump, management wished to experiment with a "market-determined" price, based on the value of the product to the customer. One member of the finance department even thought that the tentative price of $260,000 should be increased if the actual rate of return was greater than the 13 percent target rate of many customers. However, other people were concerned with leaving customers some profits, whereas yet others worried that all customers might not adjust upward for inflation-expected savings in year 2 and beyond.

Exhibit 1

Faz-Power III Pump

1.	Cost	$260,000
2.	Life	8 years
3.	Depreciation	Modified accelerated cost recovery applied to a 5-year asset class
4.	Savings	$60,000 in the first year, which increases by 4 percent per year through year 8
5.	Salvage value	$30,000 at the end of year 8
6.	Tax rate for customer	38 percent of pretax profits
7.	Required rate of return	13 percent after taxes

Principles of Capital Investment

When a business firm makes a capital investment, it incurs a current cash outlay for benefits to be realized in the future. We know that we must judge a proposed investment by its expected return. How close will it come to the return required by investors? The answer to that question relates the effect of an investment decision to the price of the stock. Although our objective in the subsequent two chapters is to come to grips with this issue, first we must take up certain fundamental concepts, and that is the purpose of this chapter.

To simplify the presentation of these basics, we assume for now that the required rate of return on investment projects is given and is the same for all projects. This assumption necessitates our holding constant the financing and dividend decisions of the firm. Moreover, it implies that the selection of any investment project or combination of projects does not alter the business-risk complexion of the firm as perceived by suppliers of capital.

It is important to stress that in the next chapters we relax these assumptions. By that time, we shall understand the rudiments of capital budgeting. ■

ADMINISTRATIVE FRAMEWORK

Successful administration of capital investments by a company involves

1. Generation of investment proposals
2. Estimation of cash flows for the proposals
3. Evaluation of cash flows
4. Selection of projects based on an acceptance criterion
5. Continual reevaluation of investment projects after their acceptance

The first four are examined in this chapter, although the fourth is analyzed in much greater depth in Chapter 8. The fifth is taken up in Chapter 7 when we consider the question of divestiture. With respect to this point, postcompletion audits of projects are essential to provide information on forecasting biases, to serve financial control purposes, and to guide future capital investment decisions as to which types of projects are desirable and which are not. Although many companies have sophisticated capital budgeting procedures, fewer have systematic post audits of projects previously accepted.

Depending on the firm involved, investment proposals can emanate from various sources. For purposes of analysis, projects may be classified into one of five categories:

1. New products or expansion of existing products
2. Replacement of equipment or buildings
3. Research and development
4. Exploration
5. Others

The fifth category comprises miscellaneous items, such as the expenditure of funds to comply with certain health standards or the acquisition of a pollution-control device. For a new product, the proposal usually originates in the marketing department. On the other hand, a proposal to replace a piece of equipment with a more sophisticated model usually emanates from the operations area of the firm. In each case, efficient administrative procedures are needed for channeling investment requests.

Multiple Screens

Most firms screen proposals at multiple levels of authority. For a proposal originating in the production area, the hierarchy of authority might run from (1) section chiefs to (2) plant managers to (3) the vice president of operations to (4) a capital expenditures committee under the financial manager to (5) the president to (6) the board of directors. How high a proposal must go before it is finally approved usually depends on its size. The greater the capital outlay, the greater the number of screens usually required. Plant managers may be able to approve moderate-sized projects on their own, but only higher levels of authority approve larger ones. Because the administrative procedures for screening investment proposals vary greatly from firm to firm, it is not possible to generalize. The best procedure will depend on the circumstances.

The level and type of capital expenditure appear to be important to investors, as they convey information about the expected future growth of earnings. McConnell and Muscarella test this notion with respect to the level of expenditures of a company. They find that an increase in capital expenditure intentions, relative to prior expectations, results in increased stock returns around the time of the announcement, and vice versa for an unexpected decrease.[1]

Cash-Flow Forecasts

One of the most important tasks in capital budgeting is estimating **future cash flows** for a project. The final results we obtain are really only as good as the accuracy of our estimates. Because cash, not income, is central to all decisions of the firm, we express whatever benefits we expect from a project in terms of cash flows rather than income. The firm invests cash now in the hope of receiving cash returns in a greater amount in the future. Only cash receipts can be reinvested in the firm or paid to stockholders in the form of dividends. In capital budgeting, good guys may get credit, but effective managers get cash. In setting up the cash

---

[1]John J. McConnell and Chris J. Muscarella, "Corporate Capital Expenditure Decisions and the Market Value of the Firm," *Journal of Financial Economics*, 14 (September 1985), 399–422.

flows for analysis, a computer spreadsheet program is invaluable. It allows one to change assumptions and quickly produce a new cash-flow stream.

Incremental Cash Flows   For each investment proposal, we need to provide information on expected future cash flows on an after-tax basis. In addition, the information must be provided on an **incremental** basis, so that we analyze only the difference between the cash flows of the firm with and without the project. For example, if a firm contemplates a new product that is likely to compete with existing products, it is not appropriate to express cash flows in terms of the estimated sales of the new product. We must take into account some probable "cannibalization" of existing products, and we must make our cash-flow estimates on the basis of incremental sales. The key is to analyze the situation with and without the new investment. Only *incremental* cash flows matter.

Ignore Sunk Costs   In this regard, sunk costs must be ignored. One is concerned with incremental costs and benefits: The recovery of past costs is irrelevant. They are bygones and should not enter into the decision process. Also, we must be mindful that certain costs do not necessarily involve a dollar outlay. If we have allocated plant space to a project and this space can be used for something else, its opportunity cost must be included in the project's evaluation. If a presently unused building can be sold for $1.3 million, that amount should be treated as a cash outlay at the outset of the project. Thus, in deriving cash flows we must consider appropriate opportunity costs.

Capital budgeting evaluates expected future cash flows in relation to cash put out today.

Illustration   To illustrate the information needed for a capital budgeting decision, consider the following situation. Dilly Duck Apparel Company is considering the introduction of a new clothing line. To launch the product line, the company will need to spend $150,000 for special equipment and the initial advertising campaign. The marketing department envisions the product life to be 6 years and expects incremental sales revenue to be

Year	1	2	3	4	5	6
Inflow	$60,000	$120,000	$160,000	$180,000	$110,000	$50,000

Cash outflows include labor and maintenance costs, material costs, and various other expenses associated with the product. As with sales, these costs must be estimated on an incremental basis. In addition to these outflows, the company will need to pay higher taxes if the new product generates higher profits, and this incremental outlay must be included. Cash outflows *should not* include interest costs on debt employed to finance the project. Such costs are embodied in the required rate of return to be discussed in Chapter 8. To deduct interest charges from net cash flows would result in double counting.

Suppose that on the basis of these considerations, Dilly Duck Apparel estimates total incremental cash outflows to be

Year	1	2	3	4	5	6
Outflow	$40,000	$70,000	$100,000	$100,000	$70,000	$40,000

Because depreciation is a noncash expense, it is not included in these outflows. The expected net cash flows from the project are

	Initial Cost	Year					
		1	2	3	4	5	6
Cash inflow		$60,000	$120,000	$160,000	$180,000	$110,000	$50,000
Cash outflow	$150,000	40,000	70,000	100,000	100,000	70,000	40,000
Net cash flow	−$150,000	$20,000	$ 50,000	$ 60,000	$ 80,000	$ 40,000	$10,000

Thus, for an initial cash outflow of $150,000 the company expects to generate net cash flows of $20,000, $50,000, $60,000, $80,000, $40,000, and $10,000 over the next 6 years. These cash flows represent the relevant information we need to judge the attractiveness of the project. The development of cash-flow data of this sort is facilitated greatly by the use of a spreadsheet program.

Patterns of Cash Flows   The net cash flows for this example are plotted in the top panel of Fig. 6-1. We notice that the initial cash outlay, or investment, is followed by positive and increasing net cash flows through year 4, after which they drop off as the project becomes older. Many other patterns are possible, both with respect to the life of the project and to the annual cash flows. In the middle panel, the initial cash outlay is followed by a stream of eight equal net cash inflows. From Chapter 2 we recognize this pattern to be an **annuity**. In the bottom panel, two distinct investment phases are shown. The first is at time 0 and continues into year 1 where there are heavy advertising and promotion expenses. In year 4, additional investment is needed to upgrade production capability and to promote the product some more. These outlays more than offset operating cash inflows, so there is a net cash outflow for the year. In the next two years, the project generates net cash inflows. Finally, the project terminates at the end of year 7. At that time, a salvage value is realized that results in a higher net cash inflow than in year 6. These examples illustrate that the patterns of expected net cash flows can vary considerably over time, depending on the project.

Replacement Decisions and Depreciation

To go to a somewhat more complicated replacement decision example involving taxes, suppose we are considering the purchase of a new machine to replace an old one, and we need to obtain cash-flow information to evaluate the attractiveness of this project. The purchase price of the new machine is $18,500, and it will require an additional $1,500 to install, bringing the total cost to $20,000. We can sell the old machine for its depreciated book value of $2,000. The initial net cash outflow for the investment project, therefore, is $18,000. The new machine should cut labor and maintenance costs and effect other cash savings totaling $7,100 a year before taxes for each of the next 5 years, after which it will probably not provide any savings, nor will it have a salvage value. These savings represent the net savings to the firm if it replaces the old machine with the new. In other words, we are concerned with the difference between the cash flows result-

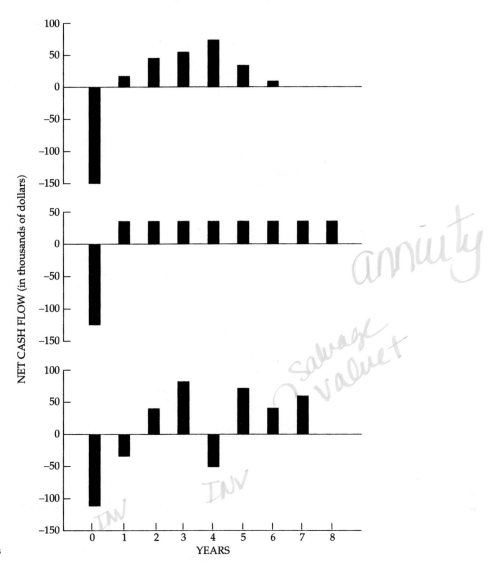

FIGURE 6-1
Patterns of cash flows

ing from the two alternatives: continuing with the old machine or replacing it with a new one.

Depreciation Effect   Because a machine of this sort has a useful life in excess of 1 year, we cannot charge its cost against income for tax purposes but must depreciate it. We then deduct depreciation from income in order to compute taxable income. Under the tax laws when this edition was written, capital assets fall into defined cost recovery classes depending on their nature. These classes of property have periods, or depreciable lives, of 3, 5, 7, 10, 15, 20, $27\frac{1}{2}$, and 39 years. A general description of the classes follows shortly. For now, suppose the machine we are considering falls into the 5-year property class for cost recovery (depreciation) purposes. Later in the chapter we consider the exact depreciation that may be deducted under existing tax law. For simplicity of illustration now, we assume straight-line depreciation.

Depreciation is a noncash expense that affects the taxes paid in cash.

As a result, the annual depreciation charge is 20 percent of the total depreciable cost of $20,000, or $4,000 a year. Assume additionally that the corporate income tax rate is 40 percent. Moreover, assume that the old machine has a remaining depreciable life of 5 years, that there is no expected salvage value at the end of this time, and that the machine also is subject to straight-line depreciation. Thus, the annual depreciation charge on the old machine is 20 percent of its depreciated book value of $2,000, or $400 a year. Because we are interested in the incremental impact of the project, we must subtract depreciation charges on the old machine from depreciation charges on the new one to obtain the incremental depreciation charges associated with the project. Given the information cited, we now are able to calculate the expected net cash flow (after taxes) resulting from the acceptance of the project.

	Book Account	Cash-Flow Account
Annual cash savings	$ 7,100	$ 7,100
Depreciation on new machine	4,000	
Less: Depreciation on old machine	400	
Additional depreciation charge	$ 3,600	
Additional income before taxes	3,500	
Income tax (40%)	1,400	1,400
Additional income after taxes	$ 2,100	
Annual net cash flow		$ 5,700

Putting It Together   In figuring the net cash flow, we simply deduct the additional cash outlay for federal income taxes from the annual cash savings. The expected annual net cash inflow for this replacement proposal is $5,700 for each of the next 5 years; this figure compares with additional income after taxes of $2,100 a year. The cash-flow and net profit figures differ by the amount of additional depreciation. As our concern is not with income as such, but with cash flows, we are interested in the right-hand column. For an initial cash outlay of $18,000, then, we are able to replace an old machine with a new one that is expected to result in net cash savings of $5,700 a year over the next 5 years. As in the previous example, the relevant cash-flow information for capital budgeting purposes is expressed on an incremental, after-tax basis.

METHODS FOR EVALUATION

Once we have collected the necessary information, we are able to evaluate the attractiveness of the various investment proposals under consideration. Because our purpose in this chapter is to examine the basic concepts of capital budgeting, we assume that the risk or quality of all investment proposals under consideration does not differ from the risk of existing investment projects of the firm and that the acceptance of any proposal or group of investment proposals does not change the relative business risk of the firm. The investment decision will be either to accept or to reject the proposal. In this section, we evaluate four methods of capital budgeting:

1. Average rate of return
2. Payback
3. Internal rate of return
4. Net present value

The first two are approximate methods for assessing the economic worth of a project. For simplicity, we assume throughout that the expected cash flows are realized at the end of each year.

Average Rate of Return

This accounting measure represents the ratio of the average annual profits after taxes to the investment in the project. In the previous example of the new machine, the average annual book earnings for the 5-year period are $2,100, and the initial investment in the project is $18,000. Therefore,

$$\text{Average rate of return} = \frac{\$2,100}{\$18,000} = 11.67\% \qquad (6\text{-}1)$$

If income were variable over the 5 years, an average would be calculated and employed in the numerator. Once the average rate of return for a proposal has been calculated, it may be compared with a required rate of return to determine if a particular proposal should be accepted or rejected.

The principal virtue of the average rate of return is its simplicity; it makes use of readily available accounting information. Once the average rate of return for a proposal has been calculated, it may be compared with a required, or cutoff, rate of return to determine if a particular proposal should be accepted or rejected. The principal shortcomings of the method are that it is based on accounting income rather than on cash flows and that it fails to take account of the timing of cash inflows and outflows. The time value of money is ignored: Benefits in the last year are valued the same as benefits in the first year.

Payback

The **payback** period of an investment project tells us the number of years required to recover our initial cash investment. It is the ratio of the initial fixed investment over the annual cash inflows for the recovery period. For our example

$$\text{Payback period} = \frac{\$18,000}{\$5,700} = 3.16 \text{ years} \qquad (6\text{-}2)$$

If the annual cash inflows are not equal, the job of calculation is somewhat more difficult. Suppose annual cash inflows are $4,000 in the first year, $6,000 in the second and third years, and $4,000 in the fourth and fifth years. In the first 3 years, $16,000 of the original investment will be recovered, followed by $4,000 in the fourth year. With an initial cash investment of $18,000, the payback period is 3 years + ($2,000/$4,000), or $3\frac{1}{2}$ years.

Shortcomings If the payback period calculated is less than some maximum acceptable payback period, the proposal is accepted; if not, it is rejected. If the required payback period were 4 years, the project in our example would be ac-

Payback is a
popular
(but crude)
measure of liquidity.

cepted. The major shortcoming of the payback method is that it fails to consider cash flows after the payback period; consequently, it cannot be regarded as a measure of profitability. Two proposals costing $10,000 each would have the same payback period if they both had annual net cash inflows of $5,000 in the first 2 years; but one project might be expected to provide no cash flows after 2 years, whereas the other might be expected to provide cash flows of $5,000 in each of the next 3 years. Thus, the payback method can be deceptive as a yardstick of profitability. In addition to this shortcoming, the method does not take account of the magnitude or timing of cash flows during the payback period. It considers only the recovery period as a whole.

Popularity of Payback   The payback method continues in use, nevertheless, frequently as a supplement to other, more sophisticated methods. It does afford management limited insight into the risk and liquidity of a project. The shorter the payback period, supposedly, the less risky the project and the greater its liquidity. The company that is cash poor may find the method to be very useful in gauging the early recovery of funds invested. There is some merit to its use in this regard, but the method does not take into account the dispersion of possible outcomes — only the magnitude and timing of the expected value of these outcomes relative to the original investment. Therefore, it cannot be considered an adequate indicator of risk. When the payback method is used, it is more appropriately treated as a constraint to be satisfied than as a profitability measure to be maximized.

Internal Rate of Return

Because of the various shortcomings in the average rate of return and payback methods, it generally is felt that **discounted cash-flow methods** provide a more objective basis for evaluating and selecting investment projects. These methods take account of both the magnitude and the timing of expected cash flows in each period of a project's life. The two discounted cash-flow methods are the internal-rate-of-return and the present-value methods described in Chapter 2. Recall that the **internal rate of return** for an investment proposal is the discount rate that equates the present value of the expected cash outflows with the present value of the expected inflows. It is represented by the rate, r, so that

IRR, the rate
of discount that equates
the PV of cash
inflows with the PV
of cash outflows.

$$\sum_{t=0}^{n}\left[\frac{A_t}{(1 + r)^t}\right] = 0 \tag{6-3}$$

where A_t is the cash flow for period t, whether it be a net cash outflow or inflow, and n is the last period in which a cash flow is expected. If the initial cash outlay or cost occurs at time 0, Eq. (6-3) can be expressed as

$$A_0 = \frac{A_1}{1 + r} + \frac{A_2}{(1 + r)^2} + \cdots + \frac{A_n}{(1 + r)^n} \tag{6-4}$$

and r is the rate that discounts the stream of future cash flows — A_1 through A_n — to equal the initial outlay at time 0, A_0. For our example, the problem can be expressed as

$$\$18,000 = \frac{\$5,700}{1 + r} + \frac{\$5,700}{(1 + r)^2} + \frac{\$5,700}{(1 + r)^3} + \frac{\$5,700}{(1 + r)^4} + \frac{\$5,700}{(1 + r)^5} \tag{6-5}$$

Solving for *r* by calculator or embedded computer routine as described in Chapter 2, we find the internal rate of return for the project to be 17.57 percent.

Acceptance Criterion   The acceptance criterion generally employed with the internal-rate-of-return method is to compare the internal rate of return with a required rate of return, known also as the cutoff, or hurdle, rate. If the internal rate of return exceeds the required rate, the project is accepted; if not, it is rejected. If the required rate of return is 12 percent and this criterion is used, the investment proposal being considered will be accepted. Accepting a project with an internal rate of return in excess of the required rate of return should result in an increase in the market price of the stock, because the firm accepts a project with a return greater than that required to maintain the present market price per share. Chapter 8 will say much more about relating the investment decision to the objective of the firm. We assume for now that the required rate of return is given.

Recognize, however, that capacity-expanding investment projects may differ from cost-reduction projects and, hence, require a different return. Miller reasons that capital-expanding projects are highly related to the level of economic activity, producing sizable cash flows when the economy is prosperous.[2] Drawing on concepts presented in Chapter 3, the systematic risk of the project would be high. Replacement projects, on the other hand, are cost reducing and would likely produce benefits across more states of the economy. As a result, they would possess lower systematic risk and require a lower return to satisfy investors.

Net Present Value

Net present value, what remains after discounting all cash flows by the required rate of return.

Like the internal-rate-of-return method, the **net-present-value** method is a discounted cash-flow approach to capital budgeting. With the present-value method, all cash flows are discounted to present value, using the required rate of return. The net present value of an investment proposal is

$$NPV = \sum_{t=0}^{n} \frac{A_t}{(1 + k)^t} \tag{6-6}$$

where *k* is the required rate of return. If the sum of these discounted cash flows is zero or more, the proposal is accepted; if not, it is rejected. Another way to express the acceptance criterion is to say that the project will be accepted if the present value of cash inflows exceeds the present value of cash outflows. The rationale behind the acceptance criterion is the same as that behind the internal-rate-of-return method. If the required rate of return is the return investors expect the firm to earn on the investment proposal, and the firm accepts a proposal with a net present value greater than zero, the market price of the stock should rise. Again, the firm is taking on a project with a return greater than that necessary to leave the market price of the stock unchanged.

---

[2]Edward M. Miller, "On the Systematic Risk of Expansion Investment," *Quarterly Review of Economics and Business*, 28 (Autumn 1988), 67–77.

Example Results If we assume a required rate of return of 12 percent after taxes, the net present value of our example problem is

$$NPV = -\$18,000 + \frac{\$5,700}{1.12} + \frac{\$5,700}{(1.12)^2} + \frac{\$5,700}{(1.12)^3} + \frac{\$5,700}{(1.12)^4} + \frac{\$5,700}{(1.12)^5}$$

$$= -\$18,000 + \$20,547 \tag{6-7}$$

$$= \$2,547$$

One can solve the problem by calculator or by embedded routines in spreadsheet programs. When we do so, we find *NPV* to be $2,547. Inasmuch as this value is greater than 0, the project should be accepted using the net-present-value method.

With the internal-rate-of-return method, we are given the cash flows, and we solve for the rate of discount that equates the present value of the cash inflows with the present value of the outflows. We then compare the internal rate of return with the required rate of return to determine whether the proposal should be accepted. With the present-value method, we are given the cash flows and the required rate of return, and we solve for the net present value. The acceptability of the proposal depends on whether the net present value is zero or more.

Profitability Index

The profitability index, or benefit/cost ratio, of a project is the present value of future net cash flows over the initial cash outlay. It can be expressed as

$$PI = \frac{\sum_{t=1}^{n} \dfrac{A_t}{(1 + k)^t}}{A_0} \tag{6-8}$$

For our example,

$$PI = \frac{\$20,547}{\$18,000} = 1.14 \tag{6-9}$$

As long as the profitability index is 1.00 or greater, the investment proposal is acceptable. For any given project, the net-present-value method and the profitability index give the same accept-reject signals. If we must choose between mutually exclusive projects, the net-present-value measure is preferred because it expresses in absolute terms the expected economic contribution of the project. In contrast, the profitability index expresses only the relative profitability.

Mutual Exclusion and Dependency

In evaluating a group of investment proposals, we must determine whether the proposals are independent of each other. A proposal is **mutually exclusive** if the acceptance of it precludes the acceptance of one or more other proposals. For example, if the firm is considering investment in one of two temperature-control systems, acceptance of one system will rule out acceptance of the other. Two mutually exclusive proposals cannot both be accepted.

A **contingent** proposal depends on the acceptance of one or more other proposals. The addition of a large machine may necessitate construction of a new wing to house it. Contingent proposals must be part of our thinking when we consider the original, dependent proposal. Recognizing the dependency, we can make investment decisions accordingly.

NPV VERSUS IRR

In general, the net-present-value and internal-rate-of-return methods lead to the same acceptance or rejection decision. In Fig. 6-2, we illustrate graphically the two methods applied to a typical investment project. The figure shows the curvilinear relationship between the net present value of a project and the discount rate employed. When the discount rate is 0, net present value is simply the total cash inflows less the total cash outflows of the project. Assuming that total inflows exceed total outflows and that outflows are followed by inflows, the typical project will have the highest net present value when the discount rate is 0. As the discount rate increases, the present value of future cash inflows decreases relative to the present value of outflows. As a result, *NPV* declines. The crossing of the *NPV* line with the 0 line establishes the internal rate of return for the project.

If the required rate of return is less than the internal rate of return, we would accept the project, using either method. Suppose that the required rate were 10 percent. As seen in Fig. 6-2, the net present value of the project then would be *Y*. Inasmuch as *Y* is greater than 0, we would accept the project, using the present-value method. Similarly, we would accept the project using the internal-rate-of-return method because the internal rate of return exceeds the required rate. For required rates greater than the internal rate of return, we would reject the project under either method. Thus, we see that the internal-rate-of-return and present-value methods give us identical answers with respect to the acceptance or rejection of an investment project.

FIGURE 6-2
Relation between discount rate and net present value

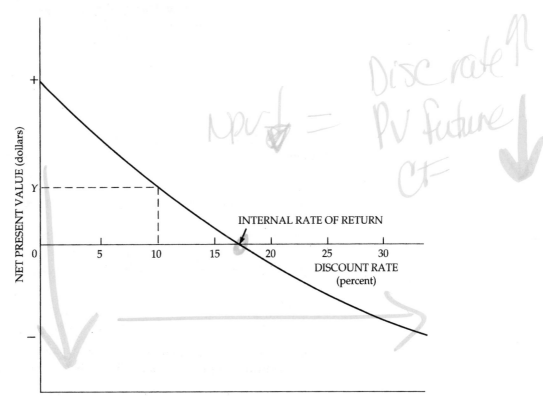

Compounding Rate Differences

We must, however, identify important differences between the methods. When two investment proposals are mutually exclusive, so that we can select only one, the two methods may give contradictory results. To illustrate the nature of the problem, suppose a firm had two mutually exclusive investment proposals that were expected to generate the following cash flows.

Proposal	Cash Flow for Year:				
	0	**1**	**2**	**3**	**4**
A	−$23,616	$10,000	$10,000	$10,000	$10,000
B	−23,616	0	5,000	10,000	32,675

Internal rates of return for proposals A and B are 25 percent and 22 percent, respectively. If the required rate of return is 10 percent, however, and we use this figure as our discount rate, the net present values of proposals A and B are $8,083 and $10,347, respectively. Thus, proposal A is preferred if we use the internal-rate-of-return method, whereas proposal B is preferred if we use the present-value method. If we can choose but one of these proposals, we obviously have a conflict.

  The conflict between these two methods is due to differences in the implicit compounding of interest. The IRR method implies that funds are compounded at the internal rate of return. For proposal A, the assumption is that $23,616 invested at 25 percent will compound in a way that will release $10,000 at the end of each of the next 4 years. The present-value method implies compounding at the required rate of return used as the discount rate. For proposal A, the assumption is that the $8,083 present value plus the $23,616 initial outflow, or $31,699, invested at 10 percent will compound in such a way that it will release $10,000 at the end of each of the next 4 years. Only if the required rate of return were 16.65 percent would the net present value of the two proposals be the same, $4,006. Below 16.65 percent, proposal B has a higher *NPV*; above, proposal A has the higher *NPV*.

Reinvestment of interim cash flows at the IRR is implied by the IRR method.

Scale of Investment

In addition to the problem of different implicit compounding rates, a problem arises if the initial cash outlays are different for two mutually exclusive investment proposals. Because the results of the internal-rate-of-return method are expressed as a percentage, the scale of investment is ignored. Without allowance for this factor, a 50 percent return on a $100 investment would always be preferred to a 25 percent return on a $500 investment. In contrast, the results of the present-value method are expressed in absolute terms. If the investment proposals were each for 1 year, we would have the following, assuming a required rate of return of 10 percent:

Proposal	Cash Flow for Year:		IRR	NPV (10%)
	0	**1**		
X	−$100	$150	50%	$36.36
Y	−500	625	25	68.18

With respect to absolute returns, the second proposal is superior, despite the fact that its internal rate of return is less. The reason is that the scale of investment is greater, which affords a greater net present value.

Multiple Rates of Return

A final problem with the internal-rate-of-return method is that multiple IRRs are possible. A necessary, but not sufficient, condition for this occurrence is that the cash-flow stream changes sign more than once. All of our examples depicted situations where a cash outflow was followed by one or more cash inflows. In other words, there was only one change in sign, which ensured a unique internal rate of return. However, some projects involve multiple changes in sign. At the end of the project, there may be a requirement to restore the environment. This often happens in the extractive industry where the land must be reclaimed at the end of the project. With a chemical plant, there are sizable dismantling costs. Whatever the cause, these costs result in a cash outflow at the end of the project and, hence, in more than one change in sign in the cash-flow series.

Whether these changes in sign cause more than one IRR depends also on the magnitudes of the cash flows. As the relationship is complicated and requires illustration, we address the problem in detail in the appendix to this chapter. Though most projects have but one change in sign in the cash-flow stream, some have more. When this occurs, the financial manager must be alert to the possibility of multiple internal rates of return. As shown in the appendix, no one internal rate of return makes sense economically when there are multiple IRRs, and an alternative method of analysis must be used.

With multiple IRR situations, calculators and computer programs often are fooled and produce only one IRR. Perhaps the best way to determine if a problem exists is to calculate the net present value of a project at various discount rates. If the discount rate were increased from zero in 25 percent increments up to, say, 1,000 percent, *NPV* could be plotted on a graph similar to that shown in Fig. 6-2. If the *NPV* line connecting the dots crosses the zero *NPV* line more than once, you have a multiple IRR problem.

Summary of the Shortcomings of the IRR Method

Despite shortcomings, the IRR is popular and usually reliable.

We have seen that the present-value method always provides correct rankings of mutually exclusive investment projects, whereas the internal-rate-of-return method sometimes does not. With the IRR method, the implied reinvestment rate will differ, depending on the cash-flow stream for each investment proposal under consideration. For proposals with a high internal rate of return, a high reinvestment rate is assumed; for proposals with a low internal rate of return, a low reinvestment rate is assumed. Only rarely will the internal rate of return calculated represent the relevant rate for reinvestment of intermediate cash flows. With the present-value method, however, the implied reinvestment rate—namely, the required rate of return—is the same for each proposal. In essence, this reinvestment rate represents the minimum return on opportunities available to the firm.

In addition, the net-present-value method takes account of differences in the scale of investment. If our objective is truly value maximization, the only theoretically correct opportunity cost of funds is the required rate of return. It is consistently applied with the net-present-value method, thereby avoiding the reinvestment rate and scale of investment problems. Finally, the possibility of multiple rates of return hurts the case for the IRR method.

With all of these criticisms, why is it used at all? The reason is that many managers find the IRR easier to visualize and interpret than they do the *NPV* measure. One does not have to specify a required rate of return in the calculations. To the extent that the required rate of return is only a rough estimate, the internal-rate-of-return method may permit a more satisfying comparison of projects for the typical manager. Put another way, they feel comfortable with a return measure as opposed to an absolute *NPV*. As long as the company is not confronted with many mutually exclusive projects or with unusual projects having multiple sign changes in the cash-flow stream, the IRR method may be used with reasonable confidence. When such is not the case, the shortcomings noted must be kept in mind. Either modifications in the IRR method or a switch to the *NPV* method needs to occur.

DEPRECIATION AND OTHER REFINEMENTS IN CASH-FLOW INFORMATION

In our machine replacement example, we assumed straight-line depreciation, the depreciable life of the asset equaling its economic life, no salvage value, and no working capital requirement. Our purpose was to keep the example simple so that we could analyze the methods for evaluating expected profitability. We shall now digress for a while to examine the effect of these real-world considerations on the magnitude and timing of cash flows.

Method of Depreciation

Accelerated depreciation has a present-value advantage in postponing taxes.

In our earlier example, we assumed straight-line depreciation when computing cash flows. However, a more advantageous method of depreciation is available for tax purposes in the United States. Known as the modified accelerated cost recovery system (MACRS), and pronounced "makers," there are eight property classes for depreciation purposes. The property category in which an asset falls determines its depreciable life for tax purposes.

- *3-Year class:* includes property with a midpoint life of 4 years or less. The midpoint life of various types of assets is determined by the Treasury Department under the asset depreciation range (ADR) system.
- *5-Year class:* includes property with an ADR midpoint life of 4 to 10 years. Included in this class are most machinery, automobiles, light trucks, most technological and semiconductor equipment, switching equipment, small power production facilities, and research and experimental equipment.
- *7-Year class:* includes property with an ADR midpoint of 10 to 16 years and railroad track and single-purpose agriculture structures.
- *10-Year class:* includes property with an ADR midpoint life of 16 to 20 years.
- *15-Year class:* includes property with a midpoint of 20 to 25 years and telephone distribution plants.
- *20-Year class:* includes property with an ADR midpoint of 25 years or more, other than real property described below.
- $27\frac{1}{2}$-*Year class:* includes residential rental property.
- *39-Year class:* other real estate.

For the 3-year, 5-year, 7-year, and 10-year property classes, the method of depreciation is the 200 percent declining-balance method. This method switches to straight line in the year that provides the quickest write-off. Moreover, a half-year convention is used in the first year and in the year following the last year. For the

15-year and 20-year property classes, 150 percent declining-balance depreciation is used with subsequent switching to straight line. Finally, for the $27\frac{1}{2}$-year and 39-year classes, straight-line depreciation is used throughout.

Rather than having to make these calculations oneself, the Treasury publishes depreciation percentages of original cost for each property class. For the first four property categories, they are

Recovery Year	3-Year	5-Year	7-Year	10-Year
1	33.33%	20.00%	14.29%	10.00%
2	44.45	32.00	24.49	18.00
3	14.81	19.20	17.49	14.40
4	7.41	11.52	12.49	11.52
5		11.52	8.93	9.22
6		5.76	8.93	7.37
7			8.92	6.55
8			4.46	6.55
9				6.56
10				6.55
11				3.28

These percentages correspond to the principles taken up in our previous calculations, and they should be used for determining depreciation.

Setting Up the Cash Flows

In most cases, the capital recovery (depreciation) period is shorter than the economic life of the asset. To illustrate how we might go about using depreciation tables and setting up the cash flows for analysis, suppose a company were considering an asset costing $100,000 that fell in the 5-year property class. The asset was expected to produce annual before-tax cash savings of $32,000 in each of the first 2 years, $27,000 in each of the next 2 years, $22,000 in both the fifth and the sixth years, and $20,000 in the seventh and last year. Assume further a 40 percent tax rate (federal and state) and no salvage value. Setting up the cash flows is facilitated greatly with a spreadsheet program. The annual net cash flows are as follows:

	0	1	2	3	4	5	6	7
1. Cost	($100,000)							
2. Annual savings		$32,000	$32,000	$27,000	$27,000	$22,000	$22,000	$20,000
3. Depreciation		20,000	32,000	19,200	11,520	11,520	5,760	
4. Income		$12,000	0	$7,800	$15,480	$10,480	$16,240	$20,000
5. Taxes (40%)		4,800	0	3,120	6,192	4,192	6,496	8,000
6. Net cash flow (1) + (2) − (5)	($100,000)	$27,200	$32,000	$23,880	$20,808	$17,808	$15,504	$12,000

We see that the tax shield occurs only in the first 6 years, after which the full cash savings are subject to taxation. As a result, the cash flow is lower. This shift in timing over what would occur with straight-line depreciation has a favorable present-value effect. To determine the net present value of the project, we discount the cash flows shown in row 6 by the required rate of return and sum them. If the required rate of return were 12 percent, the net present value would be $3,405 and the internal rate of return 13.25 percent, both measures indicating acceptance of the project. Cash flows for other projects can be set up similarly.

Salvage Value and Taxes

The cash-flow pattern will change toward the better if the asset is expected to have salvage, or scrap, value at the end of the project. As the asset will be fully depreciated at that time, the salvage value realized is subject to taxation at the ordinary income tax rate. Suppose the asset were sold for $10,000 at the end of year 7. With a 40 percent tax rate, the company will realize cash proceeds of $6,000 at the end of the last year. This amount then would be added to the net cash inflow previously determined to give the total cash flow in the last year.

If the asset is sold before it is fully depreciated, the tax treatment is different. In general, if an asset is sold for more than its depreciated book value but for less than its cost, the firm pays taxes at the full corporate rate. If the asset is sold for more than its cost, this excess is subject to the capital-gains tax treatment, which sometimes is more favorable. As such calculations are complicated, the reader is referred to the tax code and/or to a tax attorney when faced with the tax treatment of a sale of an asset.

Working Capital Requirement

In addition to the investment in a fixed asset, it is sometimes necessary to carry additional cash, receivables, or inventories. This investment in working capital is treated as a cash outflow at the time it occurs. For example, if $15,000 in working capital is required in connection with our example, there would be an additional cash outflow of $15,000 at time 0, bringing the total outflow to $115,000. At the end of the project's life, the working capital investment presumably is returned. Therefore, there would be a $15,000 cash inflow at the end of year 7. As a result, the cash inflow in that year would be $27,000 instead of $12,000.

This switching of cash flows obviously is adverse from a present-value standpoint: $15,000 is given up at time 0 and is not gotten back until 7 years later. Again using 12 percent as the required rate of return, the net present value of row 6 of our previous example, rearranged as suggested, is −$4,810. The IRR is now 10.57 percent. These figures compare with $3,405 and 13.25 percent determined before. Thus, an initial working capital investment of $15,000 causes the project to be unacceptable, whereas before it was acceptable. While total cash flows are not affected, their timing is affected.

Increases and decreases in working capital investment are not confined to the beginning and the end of the project. They can occur at any time. It is important that incremental working capital needs are treated as cash outflows when they occur and that any subsequent reductions in these needs are recorded as cash inflows.

WHAT HAPPENS WHEN CAPITAL IS RATIONED?

Capital rationing occurs any time there is a budget ceiling, or constraint, on the amount of funds that can be invested during a specific period of time, such as a year. Such constraints are prevalent in a number of firms, particularly in those that have a policy of financing all capital expenditures internally. Another example of capital rationing occurs when a division of a large company is allowed to make capital expenditures only up to a specified budget ceiling, over which the division usually has no control. With a capital rationing constraint, the firm attempts to select the combination of investment proposals that will provide the greatest profitability.

Your firm may have the following investment opportunities, ranked in descending order of profitability indexes (the ratio of the present value of future net cash flows over the initial cash outlay):

	Proposal						
	4	**7**	**2**	**3**	**6**	**5**	**1**
Profitability index	1.25	1.19	1.16	1.14	1.09	1.05	0.97
Initial outlay	$400,000	$100,000	$175,000	$125,000	$200,000	$100,000	$150,000

If the budget ceiling for initial outlays during the present period is $1 million, and the proposals are independent of each other, you would select proposals in descending order of profitability until the budget was exhausted. With capital rationing, you would accept the first five proposals, totaling $1 million in initial outlays. In other words, you do not necessarily invest in all proposals that increase the net present value of the firm; you invest in an acceptable proposal only if the budget constraint allows such an investment. You will not invest in proposal 5, even though the profitability index in excess of 1.00 would suggest its acceptance. The critical aspect of the capital rationing constraint illustrated is that capital expenditures during a period are strictly limited by the budget ceiling, regardless of the number of attractive investment opportunities.

Selection Criterion

Under capital rationing, the objective is to select the combination of investment proposals that provides the highest net present value, subject to the budget constraint for the period. If this constraint is strictly enforced, it may be better to accept several smaller, less profitable proposals that allow full utilization of the budget than to accept one large proposal that results in part of the budget's being unused. Admittedly, a fixed one-period constraint is highly artificial. Companies engaging in capital rationing seldom will set a budget so rigidly that it does not provide for some flexibility. In addition, the cost of certain investment projects may be spread over several years. Finally, a one-period analysis does not take account of intermediate cash flows generated by a project. Some projects provide relatively high net cash flows in the early years; these cash flows serve to reduce the budget constraints in the early years because they may be used to finance other investment projects. For the reasons discussed, when capital is rationed, management should consider more than one period in the allocation of limited capital to investment projects.

Problems Incurred

A budget ceiling carries its cost, too, when it bars us from taking advantage of an opportunity that provides a return in excess of that required. In our first example, the opportunity forgone by the $1 million budget ceiling is proposal 5, which has a profitability index of 1.05. Though all cash flows are discounted at the required rate of return, we do not necessarily accept proposals that provide positive net present values. We see which proposals we can accept before we exhaust the budget. In so doing, we may reject projects that provide positive net present values, as was shown with proposal 5.

Rationing capital usually is suboptimal.

Capital rationing usually results in an investment policy that is less than optimal. In some periods, the firm accepts projects down to its required rate of return; in others, it rejects projects that would provide returns substantially in excess of the required rate. If the required rate of return corresponds to the project's cost of capital, and the firm actually can raise capital at that approximate cost, should it not invest in all projects yielding more than the required rate of return? If it rations capital and does not invest in all projects yielding more than the required rate, is it not forgoing opportunities that would enhance the market price of its stock?

In the final analysis, the firm should accept all proposals yielding more than their required rates of return. By so doing, it will increase the market price per share, because it is taking on projects that will provide a return higher than necessary to maintain the present market price per share. Certainly, there are circumstances that complicate the use of this rule. In general, however, this policy should tend to maximize the market price of the stock over the long run.

INFLATION AND CAPITAL BUDGETING

In general, an inflationary economy distorts capital budgeting decisions. For one thing, depreciation charges are based on original rather than replacement costs. As income grows with inflation, an increasing portion is taxed, with the result that real cash flows do not keep up with inflation. Consider an investment proposal costing $24,000 under the assumption that no inflation is expected, that depreciation is straight line over 4 years, and that the tax rate is 40 percent. The following cash flows are expected to occur.

Year	Cash Savings	Depreciation	Taxes	Cash Flow after Taxes
1	$10,000	$6,000	$1,600	$8,400
2	10,000	6,000	1,600	8,400
3	10,000	6,000	1,600	8,400
4	10,000	6,000	1,600	8,400

Depreciation is deducted from cash savings to obtain taxable income, on which taxes of 40 percent are based. Without inflation, depreciation charges represent the "cost" of replacing the investment as it wears out. Because nominal income on which taxes are paid represents real income, the last column represents real cash flows after taxes. The internal rate of return that equates the present value of the cash inflows with the cost of the project is 14.96 percent.

Inflation's Effect on Results

Consider now a situation in which inflation is at a rate of 7 percent per annum and cash savings are expected to grow at this overall rate of inflation. The after-tax cash flows become

Year	Cash Savings	Depreciation	Taxes	Cash Flow after Taxes
1	$10,700	$6,000	$1,880	$ 8,820
2	11,449	6,000	2,180	9,269
3	12,250	6,000	2,500	9,750
4	13,108	6,000	2,843	10,265

Although these cash flows are larger than before, they must be deflated by the inflation rate if one is concerned with the real as opposed to the nominal rate of return. Therefore, the last column becomes

Year	1	2	3	4
Real after-tax cash flow	$8,243	$8,096	$7,959	$7,831

As we see, the real after-tax cash flows are less than before and decline over time. The reason is that depreciation charges do not change in keeping with inflation, so that an increasing portion of the cash savings is subject to taxation. As taxes increase at a rate faster than inflation, real after-tax cash flows must decline. The internal rate of return based on real after-tax cash flows is 12.91 percent, compared with 14.96 percent without inflation.

The presence of inflation therefore results in lower real rates of return and less incentive for companies to undertake capital investments. The cash-flow situation is improved with accelerated depreciation, but the same unfavorable comparisons hold. There simply is a disincentive for companies to undertake capital expenditures, so they typically invest less, seek investments with faster paybacks (shorter economic lives), and become less capital intensive during periods of inflation.

Bias in Cash-Flow Estimates

In estimating cash flows, it is important that the individual company take anticipated inflation into account. Often there is a tendency to assume that price levels will remain unchanged throughout the life of the project. Frequently, this assumption is imposed unknowingly; future cash flows simply are estimated on the basis of existing prices. A bias arises in the selection process, however, in that the required rate of return for the project is usually based on current capital costs, which in turn embody a premium for anticipated inflation.[3] This is known as the *nominal* required return, as distinguished from the *real* required return, which abstracts from inflation.

There is general agreement that security prices are influenced by inflation. As we will discover in Chapter 8, the relationship is far from simple and is not stable over time. Rather than get into these arguments now, we simply assume that capital costs embrace in them some kind of premium for inflation.

---

[3]This section is based on James C. Van Horne, "A Note on Biases in Capital Budgeting Introduced by Inflation," *Journal of Financial and Quantitative Analysis*, 6 (January 1971), 653–58.

If the required rate of return used as the acceptance criterion includes a premium for anticipated inflation, the estimated cash flows also must reflect inflation. Such cash flows are affected in several ways. Inflows may rise if they come from products sold at higher prices; outflows may increase with higher wages and materials costs. But future inflation does not affect depreciation charges on existing assets. Once the asset is acquired, these charges are known with certainty. The effect of anticipated inflation on cash inflows and cash outflows will vary with the nature of the project. In some cases, cash inflows, through price increases, will rise faster than cash outflows; in other cases, the opposite will hold. No matter what the relationship, it is important that it be embodied in the cash-flow estimates.

Inflation makes it important to adjust cash-flow estimates.

If the cash flows are not adjusted for inflation, real cash flows are discounted with a nominal required return. There is a bias toward rejection, because a rate higher than the real required return is used as the acceptance criterion. It is essential, then, to compare apples with apples and oranges with oranges. If a nominal required return is used, nominal cash flows (inflation adjusted) should be employed. If a real required rate of return is used, the cash-flow estimates should not be adjusted for inflation. Consistency is critical. As measurement of nominal required returns is easier than that of real required returns for a host of reasons we will not go into at this juncture, the usual comparison is nominal with nominal.

INFORMATION TO ANALYZE AN ACQUISITION

Investment proposals under consideration are not necessarily generated internally. A proposal can consist of the acquisition of a company or a portion thereof. The topic of acquisitions is treated in Chapter 23; in the present chapter and in Chapter 8 we consider the capital budgeting aspects of the problem. In principle, the prospective acquisition is much the same as any investment proposal; there is an initial outlay of cash or stock, followed by expected future benefits. The major difference is that, with an acquisition, the initial cost may not be established; indeed, it frequently is subject to bargaining. The framework for analyzing the expected return involved with an acquisition is similar to that discussed earlier. The critical thing is the accurate measurement of incremental cash flows, a topic to which we now turn.

Measuring Free Cash Flows

To consider an acquisition in a capital budgeting framework, expected future cash flows must be expressed on a basis consistent with those for investment proposals generated internally. In evaluating the prospective acquisition, the buying company should first estimate the future cash income that the acquisition is expected to add. Because we are interested in the marginal impact of the acquisition, these estimates should embody any expected economies, known as **synergism,** that are involved in the merger. (In Chapter 23 we explore synergy in greater detail.)

In an acquisition, there are the usual problems in estimating future cash flows. The process may be somewhat easier than for a capital budgeting proposal, however, because the company being acquired is a going concern. The acquiring company buys more than assets; it buys experience, an organization, and proven performance. The estimates of sales and costs are based on past results; consequently, they are likely to be more accurate than the estimates for a new investment proposal.

Free cash flows are what remain after all necessary expenditures, and they determine an acquisition's value.

We are interested in what is known as **free cash flows.** These are the cash flows that remain after we subtract from expected revenues expected costs and the capital expenditures necessary to sustain and hopefully improve the cash flows. For each future period, we begin with the *incremental* expected operating cash flow before interest and taxes. This is known as *EBITDA*, earnings before interest, taxes, depreciation, and amortization. From the EBITDA estimate, we subtract three things: (1) expected taxes to be paid; (2) likely future capital expenditures, and (3) expected net additions to working capital, that is, receivable and inventories. The residual represents the free cash flow for the period.

In making the various estimates, we isolate from consideration the capital structure that results from the merger. The reason is that once the merger is consummated, the buying company can modify the capital structure that immediately results. Therefore, incremental cash flows should be estimated value before interest charges.

TABLE 6-1
Illustration of Incremental Cash Flows from an Acquisition

	Average (in thousands) for Years:				
	1–5	*6–10*	*11–15*	*16–20*	*21–∞*
Incremental EBITDA	$3,500	$4,000	$4,400	$4,700	$5,000
Minus:					
Taxes	500	700	800	900	1,000
Capital expenditures	1,500	1,600	1,750	1,850	1,950
Working-capital additions	200	250	290	320	350
Incremental free cash flow	$1,300	$1,450	$1,560	$1,630	$1,700

Preparing the Cash Flows for Analysis

To illustrate the information needed, suppose the incremental cash flows shown in Table 6-1 were expected from an acquisition. In the case of an acquisition investment, the life of the project is indefinite. In many cases, analysts assume some horizon, such as 20 years, beyond which incremental cash flows are not estimated. Although the present-value effect of these distant cash flows usually is not material, we choose to show cash flows into perpetuity, denoted by ∞, so that the valuation of a merger is consistent with the valuation of a common stock. In addition to expected free cash flows, the acquiring firm may wish to specify other possible cash-flow series. This can be done with a probability tree of possible free cash flows, a method taken up in Chapter 7.

The free cash flows for our example are shown at the bottom of the table, and these are the basis on which value is judged. If such cash flows were discounted at an appropriate required return (discussed in Chapter 8), we would obtain the expected present value of the acquisition. If the cash price to be paid is known, it should be subtracted from the expected present value to obtain the expected *net present value*. With this information, one is able to evaluate the acquisition in the same manner as described earlier. In most cases, however, the price to be paid is not set and must be negotiated.

Noncash Payments and Liability Assumption

Now what if the acquisition were for other than cash? In many cases, the buyer assumes the liabilities of the company it acquires. Moreover, payment to the acquired company's stockholders may involve common stock, preferred stock, debt, cash, or some combination. Does not this complicate the matter? It does, but we must keep our eye on the overriding valuation principle, that is, the value of the incremental free cash flows. The present-value figure obtained in the cash-flow format illustrated represents the maximum "cash-equivalent" price to be paid. If securities other than cash are used in the acquisition, they should be converted to their cash-equivalent market values. If the acquiring firm assumes the liabilities of the acquired company, these too should be converted to their market values. Thus, the present value of incremental free cash flows sets an upper limit on the market value of all securities, including cash, used in payment, together with the market value of any liabilities assumed in the acquisition. In this way, we are able to separate the investment worth of an acquisition from the way it is financed.

In Chapter 8 we investigate the question of whether an acquisition should be evaluated in isolation or as one of many companies whose stocks are publicly traded. Our concern in this chapter has been with the information needed for the various types of evaluation possible. We leave until later the valuation principles inherent in this problem.

■ Summary

Capital budgeting involves the outlay of current funds in anticipation of future cash-flow benefits. Collection of cash-flow information is essential for the evaluation of investment proposals. The key is to measure incremental cash flows with and without the investment proposal being analyzed. Depreciation under the accelerated cost recovery system has a significant effect on the pattern of cash flows and, hence, on present value. Also affecting the pattern of cash flows is the presence of salvage value and a working capital requirement.

Capital budgeting methods, including the average-rate-of-return and payback methods, were examined under the assumption that the acceptance of any investment proposal does not change the business-risk complexion of the firm as perceived by suppliers of capital. The two discounted cash-flow methods—internal rate of return and net present value—are the only appropriate means by which to judge the economic contribution of an investment proposal. The important distinctions between the internal-rate-of-return method and the present-value method involve the implied compounding rate, the scale of investment, and the possibility of multiple internal rates of return. Depending on the situation, contrary

answers can be given with respect to the acceptance of mutually exclusive investment proposals. On theoretical grounds, a case can be made for the superiority of the present-value method, though in practice the IRR is popular.

Capital rationing is likely to result in investment decisions that are less than optimal. Inflation creates a disincentive for capital investment because depreciation charges do not reflect replacement costs, and a firm's taxes grow at a faster rate than inflation. In estimating cash flows, one should take account of anticipated inflation. Otherwise, a bias arises in using an inflation-adjusted required return and non-inflation-adjusted cash flows, and there is a tendency to reject some projects that should be accepted.

In general, we can evaluate an acquisition in much the same manner and with much the same kind of information that we use for evaluating an investment proposal generated internally. Free cash flows, after capital expenditures, are estimated taking account of likely synergies. The present value of these cash flows sets an upper limit on the market value of all securities, including cash, to be paid together with the market value of any liabilities assumed.

Appendix: Multiple Internal Rates of Return

Lorie and Savage were the first to point out that certain configurations of cash-flow streams have more than one internal rate of return.[4] To illustrate the problem, suppose we had the following stream of cash flows corresponding to the "pump" proposal of Lorie and Savage:

Year	0	1	2
Cash flow	−$1,600	$10,000	−$10,000

In this example, a new, more effective pump is substituted for an existing pump. On an incremental basis, there is an initial outlay followed by net cash inflows resulting from the increased efficiency of the new pump. If the quantity of oil, for example, is fixed, the new pump will exhaust this supply quicker than the old pump would. Beyond this point of exhaustion, the new pump alternative would result in an incremental outflow, because the old pump would still be productive.

---

[4]See James H. Lorie and Leonard J. Savage, "Three Problems in Rationing Capital," *Journal of Business*, 28 (October 1955), 229–39.

When we solve for the internal rate of return for the above cash-flow stream, we find that it is not one rate but two: 25 percent and 400 percent. This unusual situation is illustrated in Fig. 6A-1, where the discount rate is plotted along the horizontal axis and net present value along the vertical axis. At a 0 rate of discount, the net present value of the project is simply the sum of all the cash flows. It is −$1,600 because total cash outflows exceed total cash inflows. As the discount rate increases, the present value of the second-year outflow diminishes with respect to the first-year inflow and the present value of the proposal becomes positive when the discount rate exceeds 25 percent. As the discount rate increases beyond 100 percent, the present value of all future cash flows (years 1 and 2) diminishes relative to the initial outflow of −$1,600. At 400 percent, the present value of all cash flows again becomes 0.

This type of proposal differs from the usual case, shown in Fig. 6-2, in which net present value is a decreasing function of the discount rate, and in which there is but one internal rate of return that equates the present value of all inflows with the present value of all outflows. An investment proposal may have

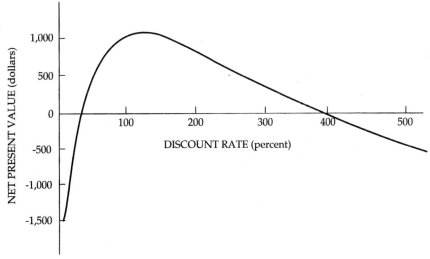

FIGURE 6A-1
Dual rates of return

any number of internal rates of return, depending on the cash-flow pattern. Consider the following series of cash flows:

Year	0	1	2	3
Cash flow	−$1,000	$6,000	−$11,000	$6,000

In this example, discount rates of 0, 100, and 200 percent result in the net present value of all cash flows equaling 0.

The number of internal rates of return is limited to the number of reversals of sign in the cash-flow stream. In the example, we have three reversals and three internal rates of return. Although a multiple reversal in signs is a necessary condition for multiple internal rates of return, it is not sufficient for such an occurrence. The occurrence of multiple internal rates of return also depends on the magnitude of cash flows. For the following series of cash flows, there is but one internal rate of return (32.5 percent), despite two reversals of sign

Year	0	1	2
Cash flow	−$1,000	$1,400	−$100

We note that the equation for solving for the internal rate of return, Eq. (6-3), is an nth degree polynomial, having n years in which cash flows occur. Therefore, the formula has n roots. For conventional investment proposals, only one of the roots is positive and $n − 1$ roots are negative or imaginary. As a result, the proposal is said to have a *unique* internal rate of return. In other words, the net-present-value line in Fig. 6-2 crosses the zero line only once. With a nonconventional investment proposal, such as those illustrated, more than one of the roots are real numbers, and the present-value line crosses the zero line more than once. For dual rates of return, for example, two of the roots are positive numbers.

When confronted with a proposal having multiple rates of return, how does one decide which is the correct rate? In our dual-rate example, is the correct rate 25 percent or 400 percent? Actually, neither rate is correct, because neither is a measure of investment worth. In essence, the firm has "borrowed" $10,000 from the project at the end of year 1 and will pay it back at the end of year 2. The relevant question is, What is it worth to the firm now to have the use of $10,000 for 1 year beginning at the end of year 1? This question, in turn, depends on the investment opportunities available to the firm for that period of time. If the firm could earn $2,000 on the use of these funds and realize these earnings at the end of the period, the value of this opportunity would be $2,000, to be received at the end of year 2. This amount would then be compared with the initial outlay of $1,600 to determine whether the project is worthwhile. Similarly, other proposals can be evaluated in this manner to determine whether they are worthwhile.

In general, holding risk constant, a company wishes to lend at as high a rate as possible and to borrow at as low a rate as possible. In the case of a project having multiple changes in signs, both lending and borrowing are involved. The best way to tackle the problem is to separate cash flows into their lending and borrowing components and then to use the net-present-value approach. In this way, the appropriate minimum required rate of return can be used on the lending side and the appropriate borrowing rate on that side.

FINCOACH EXERCISES

FinCoach on the Prentice Hall Finance Center CD-ROM (Practice Center) has the following categories of practice exercises that pertain to things taken up in this chapter: 2. Valuation of Multiple Cash Flows; and 9. Project and Firm Valuation. These exercises can be used to supplement the problems that follow.

Self-Correction Problems

1. Briarcliff Stove Company is considering a new product line to supplement its range line. It is anticipated that the new product line will involve cash investments of $700,000 at time 0 and $1.0 million in year 1. After-tax cash inflows of $250,000 are expected in year 2, $300,000 in year 3, $350,000 in year 4, and $400,000 each year thereafter through year 10. Although the product line might be viable after year 10, the company prefers to be conservative and end all calculations at that time.

   a. If the required rate of return is 15 percent, what is the net present value of the project? Is it acceptable?

   b. What is its internal rate of return?

   c. What would be the case if the required rate of return were 10 percent?

   d. What is the project's payback period?

2. Carbide Chemical Company is considering the replacement of two old machines with a new, more efficient machine. The old machines could be sold for $70,000 in the secondary market. Their depreciated book value is $120,000 with a remaining useful and depreciable life of 8 years. Straight-line depreciation is used on these machines. The new machine can be purchased and installed for $480,000. It has a useful life of 8 years, at the end of which a salvage value of $40,000 is expected. The machine falls into the 5-year property class for accelerated cost recovery (depreciation) purposes. Due to its greater efficiency, the new machine is expected to result in incremental annual savings of $120,000. The company's corporate tax rate is 34 percent, and if a loss occurs in any year on the project it is assumed that the company will receive a tax credit of 34 percent of such loss.

   a. What are the incremental cash inflows over the 8 years and what is the incremental cash outflow at time 0?

   b. What is the project's net present value if the required rate of return is 14 percent?

3. The Platte River Perfect Cooker Company is evaluating three investment situations: (1) produce a new line of aluminum skillets, (2) expand its existing cooker line to include several new sizes, and (3) develop a new, higher-quality line of cookers. If only the project in question is undertaken, the expected present values and the amounts of investment required are

Project	Investment Required	Present Value of Future Cash Flows
1	$200,000	$290,000
2	115,000	185,000
3	270,000	400,000

If projects 1 and 2 are jointly undertaken, there will be no economies; the investments required and present values will simply be the sum of the parts. With projects 1 and 3, economies are possible in investment because one of the machines acquired can be used in both production processes. The total investment required for projects 1 and 3 combined is $440,000. If projects 2 and 3 are undertaken, there are economies to be achieved in marketing and producing the products but not in investment. The expected present value of future cash flows for projects 2 and 3 is $620,000. If all three projects are undertaken simultaneously, the economies noted will still hold. However, a $125,000 extension on the plant will be necessary, as space is not available for all three projects. Which project or projects should be chosen?

4. Insell Corporation is considering the acquisition of Fourier-Fox, Inc., which is in a related line of business. Fourier-Fox presently has a cash flow of $2 million per year. With a merger, synergism would be expected to result in a growth rate of this cash flow of 15 percent per year for 10 years, at the end of which level cash flows would be expected. To sustain the cash-flow stream, Insell will need to invest $1 million annually. For purposes of analysis and to be conservative, Insell limits its calculations of cash flows to 25 years.

    a.   What expected annual cash flows would Insell realize from this acquisition?

    b.   If its required rate of return is 18 percent, what is the maximum price Insell should pay?

Problems

1. Lobears, Inc., is considering two investment proposals, labeled project A and project B, with the characteristics shown in the accompanying table.

	Project A			Project B		
Period	Cost	Profit after Taxes	Net Cash Flow	Cost	Profit after Taxes	Net Cash Flow
0	$9,000	—	—	$12,000	—	—
1		$1,000	$5,000		$1,000	$5,000
2		1,000	4,000		1,000	5,000
3		1,000	3,000		4,000	8,000

For each project, compute its average rate of return, its payback period, and its net present value, using a discount rate of 15 percent.

2. What criticisms may be offered against the average-rate-of-return method as a capital budgeting technique? What criticisms may be offered against the payback method?

3. Zaire Electronics can make either of two investments at time 0. Assuming a required rate of return of 14 percent, determine for each project (a) the payback period; (b) the net present value; (c) the profitability index; and (d) the internal rate of return. Assume the accelerated cost recovery system for depreciation and that the asset falls in the 5-year property class and the corporate tax rate is 34 percent.

		Period						
Project	Cost	1	2	3	4	5	6	7
A	$28,000	$8,000	$8,000	$8,000	$8,000	$8,000	$8,000	$8,000
B	20,000	5,000	5,000	6,000	6,000	7,000	7,000	7,000

4. Two mutually exclusive projects have projected cash flows as follows:

		Period			
Project	**0**	**1**	**2**	**3**	**4**
A	−$10,000	$5,000	$5,000	$5,000	$ 5,000
B	− 10,000	0	0	0	30,000

   a. Determine the internal rate of return for each project.
   b. Assuming a required rate of return of 10 percent, determine the net present value for each project.
   c. Which project would you select? What assumptions are inherent in your decision?

5. The city of San Jose needs a number of new special-purpose trucks. It has received several bids and has closely evaluated the performance characteristics of the various trucks. Each Patterbilt truck costs $74,000, but it is "top-of-the-line" equipment. The truck has a life of 8 years, assuming that the engine is rebuilt in the fifth year. Maintenance costs of $2,000 a year are expected in the first 4 years, followed by total maintenance and rebuilding costs of $13,000 in the fifth year. During the last 3 years, maintenance costs are expected to be $4,000 a year. At the end of 8 years, the truck will have an estimated scrap value of $9,000.

   A bid from Bulldog Trucks, Inc., is for $59,000 a truck; however, maintenance costs for this truck will be higher. In the first year, they are expected to be $3,000, and this amount is expected to increase by $1,500 a year through the eighth year. In year 4, the engine will need to be rebuilt, and this will cost the company $15,000 in addition to maintenance costs in that year. At the end of 8 years, the Bulldog truck will have an estimated scrap value of $5,000.

   The last bidder, Best Tractor and Trailer Company, has agreed to sell San Jose trucks at $44,000 each. Maintenance costs in the first 4 years are expected to be $4,000 the first year and to increase by $1,000 a year. For San Jose's purposes, the truck has a life of only 4 years. At that time it can be traded in for a new Best truck, which is expected to cost $52,000. The likely trade-in value of the old truck is $15,000. During years 5 through 8, the second truck is expected to have maintenance costs of $5,000 in year 5, and these are expected to increase by $1,000 each year. At the end of 8 years, the second truck is expected to have a resale or salvage value of $18,000.

   a. If the city of San Jose's cost of funds is 8 percent, which bid should it accept? Ignore any tax consideration, as the city pays no taxes.
   b. If its opportunity cost were 15 percent, would your answer change?

6. Thoma Pharmaceutical Company may buy DNA testing equipment costing $60,000. This equipment is expected to reduce clinical staff labor costs by $20,000 annually. The equipment has a useful life of 5 years, but falls in the 3-year property class for cost recovery (depreciation) purposes. No salvage value is expected at the end. The corporate tax rate for Thoma is 38 percent, and its required rate of return is 15 percent. (If profits before taxes on the project are negative in any year, the firm will receive a tax credit of 38 percent of

the loss in that year.) On the basis of this information, what is the net present value of the project? Is it acceptable?

7. In Problem 6, suppose 6 percent inflation in labor cost savings is expected over the last 4 years, so that savings in the first year are $20,000, savings in the second year are $21,200, and so forth.

   a. If the required rate of return is still 15 percent, what is the net present value of the project? Is it acceptable?

   b. If the working capital requirement of $10,000 were required in addition to the cost of the equipment and this additional investment were needed over the life of the project, what would be the effect on net present value? (All other things are the same as in part a.)

8. The Lake Tahoe Ski Resort is studying a half-dozen capital improvement projects. It has allocated $1 million for capital budgeting purposes. The following proposals and associated profitability indexes have been determined. The projects themselves are independent of one another.

Project	Amount	Profitability Index
Extend ski lift 3	$500,000	1.21
Build a new sports shop	150,000	.95
Extend ski lift 4	350,000	1.20
Build a new restaurant	450,000	1.18
Add to housing complex	200,000	1.20
Build an indoor skating rink	400,000	1.05

   a. With strict capital rationing, which of these investments should be undertaken?

   b. Is this an optimal strategy?

9. The R.Z. Frank Company may acquire Aziz Car Leasing Company. Frank estimates that Aziz will provide incremental net income after taxes of $2 million in the first year, $3 million the second, $4 million the third, $5 million in each of the years 4 through 6, and $6 million annually thereafter. Owing to the need to replenish the fleet, heavier than usual investments are required in the first 2 years. Capital investments and depreciation charges are expected to be (in millions):

	Year						
	1	2	3	4	5	6	7 ON
Capital investment	$5	$5	$4	$4	$4	$4	$4
Depreciation	3	4	4	4	4	4	4

The overall required rate of return is 15 percent. Compute the present value of the acquisition based on these expectations. If you had a range of possible outcomes, how would you obtain the information necessary to analyze the acquisition?

10. An investment has an outlay of $800 today, an inflow of $5,000 at the end of 1 year, and an outflow of $5,000 at the end of 2 years. What is its internal rate

of return? If the initial outlay were $1,250, what would be its IRR? (*Hint:* This case is an exception rather than the rule.)

11. An investment has an inflow of $200 today, an outflow of $300 at the end of 1 year, and an inflow of $400 at the end of 2 years. What is its internal rate of return? (*Hint:* Try calculating NPVs for a wide range of required returns.)

Solutions to Self-Correction Problems

1. a.

Year	Cash Flow	Discount Factor (15%)	Present Value
0	$ (700,000)	1.00000	$(700,000)
1	(1,000,000)	.86957	(869,570)
2	250,000	.75614	189,035
3	300,000	.65752	197,256
4	350,000	.57175	200,113
5–10	400,000	2.1638*	865,520
		Net present value =	$(117,646)

*5.0188 for 10 years − 2.8550 for 4 years.

As the net present value is negative, the project is unacceptable.

b. *IRR* = 13.20%

c. The project would be acceptable.

d. Payback period = 6 years:

$$- \$700,000 - \$1,000,000 + \$250,000 + \$300,000 + \$350,000$$
$$+ \$400,000 + \$400,000 = 0$$

2. a. Incremental cash inflows:

	1	2	3	4	5	6	7	8
1. Savings	$120,000	$120,000	$120,000	$120,000	$120,000	$120,000	$120,000	$120,000
2. Depreciation, new	96,000	153,600	92,160	55,296	55,296	27,648		
3. Depreciation, old	15,000	15,000	15,000	15,000	15,000	15,000	15,000	15,000
4. Incremental depreciation	$ 81,000	$138,600	$ 77,160	$ 40,296	$ 40,296	$ 12,648	$ (15,000)	$ (15,000)
5. Profit before tax (1) − (4)	39,000	(18,600)	42,840	79,704	79,704	107,352	135,000	135,000
6. Taxes (34%)	13,260	(6,324)	14,566	27,099	27,099	36,500	45,900	45,900
7. Operating cash flow (1) − (6)	$106,740	$126,324	$105,434	$ 92,901	$ 92,901	$ 83,500	$ 74,100	$ 74,100
8. Salvage value × (1 − .34)								26,400
9. Net cash flow	$106,740	$126,324	$105,434	$ 92,901	$ 92,901	$ 83,500	$ 74,100	$100,500

Incremental cash outflow:

Cost − Sale of old machines − Tax savings on book loss
$480,000 − $70,000 − .34 ($120,000 − $70,000) = $393,000

b. Net present value of $393,000 outflow and the cash inflows on line 9 above at 14 percent = $75,139. The project is acceptable.

3.

Project	Investment Required	Present Value of Future Cash Flows	Net Present Value
1	$200,000	$290,000	$ 90,000
2	115,000	185,000	70,000
3	270,000	400,000	130,000
1 and 2	315,000	475,000	160,000
1 and 3	440,000	690,000	250,000
2 and 3	385,000	620,000	235,000
1, 2, and 3	680,000	910,000	230,000

Projects 1 and 3 should be chosen, as they provide the highest net present value.

4. a.

Year	Cash Flow	Investment	Net Cash Flow	Present Value of Net Cash Flow (18%)
1	$2,300,000	$1,000,000	$1,300,000	$ 1,101,698
2	2,645,000	1,000,000	1,645,000	1,181,406
3	3,041,750	1,000,000	2,041,750	1,242,670
4	3,498,013	1,000,000	2,498,013	1,288,450
5	4,022,714	1,000,000	3,022,714	1,321,259
6	4,626,122	1,000,000	3,626,122	1,343,224
7	5,320,040	1,000,000	4,320,040	1,356,147
8	6,118,046	1,000,000	5,118,046	1,361,605
9	7,035,753	1,000,000	6,035,753	1,360,821
10–25	8,091,116	1,000,000	7,091,116	8,253,350
			Total present value =	$19,810,630

b. The maximum price that is justified is approximately $19.8 million. It should be noted that these calculations use present-value tables. For cash flows going from years 10 to 25, we subtract the discount factor for 9 years of annuity payments, 4.3030, in Table B at the back of the book from that for 25 years, 5.4669. The difference 5.4669 − 4.3030 = 1.1639 is the discount factor for cash flows for an annuity starting in year 10 and going through year 25. If a present-value function of a calculator is used, a slightly different total may be given due to rounding in the present-value tables.

Selected References

BALDWIN, CARLISS Y., and KIM B. CLARK, "Capabilities and Capital Investment: New Perspectives on Capital Budgeting," *Journal of Applied Corporate Finance*, 5 (Summer 1992), 67–82.

CLEARY, SEAN, "The Relationship between Firm Investment and Financial Status," *Journal of Finance*, 54 (April 1999), 673–92.

GOMBOLA, MICHAEL J., and GEORGE P. TSETSEKOS, "The Information Content of Plant Closing Announcements: Evidence from Financial Profiles and the Stock Price Reaction," *Financial Management*, 21 (Summer 1992), 31–40.

HARRIS, MILTON, and ARTUR RAVIV, "The Capital Budgeting Process: Incentives and Information," *Journal of Finance*, 51 (September 1996), 1139–74.

———, "Capital Budgeting and Delegation," *Journal of Financial Economics*, 50 (December 1998), 259–89.

MCCONNELL, JOHN J., and CHRIS J. MUSCARELLA, "Corporate Capital Expenditure Decisions and the Market Value of the Firm," *Journal of Financial Economics*, 14 (September 1985), 399–422.

MILLER, EDWARD M., "On the Systematic Risk of Expansion Investment," *Quarterly Review of Economics and Business*, 28 (Autumn 1988), 67–77.

SCHWAB, BERNHARD, and PETER LUSZTIG, "A Comparative Analysis of the Net Present Value and the Benefit-Cost Ratios as Measures of the Economic Desirability of Investments," *Journal of Finance*, 24 (June 1969), 507–16.

SMITH, KIMBERLY J., "Postauditing Capital Investments," *Financial Practice and Education*, 4 (Spring–Summer 1994), 129–37.

VAN HORNE, JAMES C., "A Note on Biases in Capital Budgeting Introduced by Inflation," *Journal of Financial and Quantitative Analysis*, 6 (January 1971), 653–58.

———, "Capital Budgeting under Conditions of Uncertainty as to Project Life," *Engineering Economist*, 17 (Spring 1972), 189–99.

———, "The Variation of Project Life as a Means for Adjusting for Risk," *Engineering Economist*, 21 (Spring 1976), 151–58.

ZHANG, GUOCHANG, "Moral Hazard in Corporate Investment and the Disciplinary Role of Voluntary Capital," *Management Science*, 43 (June 1997), 737–50.

Wachowicz's Web World is an excellent overall Web site produced and maintained by my co-author of *Fundamentals of Financial Management*, John M. Wachowicz Jr. It contains descriptions of and links to many finance Web sites and articles. *www.prenhall.com/wachowicz.*

Risk and Real Options in Capital Budgeting

U p to now we have worked with expected cash flows when assessing the worth of an investment project. In so doing, we ignored a fact of life. Expectations may not be realized. There is risk associated with the cash-flow estimates as, alas, there is risk associated with most elements of our lives. In the eyes of investors and creditors, a company's business-risk complexion may change as a result of the investments it chooses. The valuation impact of uncertain investments is going to occupy us for two chapters, beginning with this one, in which we take up the information necessary to make intelligent evaluations.

In addition to risk, investment projects sometimes embody in them options for subsequent management decisions. Once a project is accepted, management may have the flexibility to make changes that will affect subsequent future cash flows and/or the project's life. We call this ability a *real, or managerial,* option, to distinguish it from a *financial* option, presented in Chapter 5. However, the same valuation principles are at work. Thus, this chapter deals with how risk and real options may alter the treatment of capital budgeting taken up in Chapter 6. ■

QUANTIFYING RISK AND ITS APPRAISAL

From Chapter 2, recall that **risk** was defined as the variability of possible outcomes from that which was expected. Put another way, it is the surprise element in the actual return, the other element being the expected outcome. As in Chapter 2, we will use the standard deviation as a measure of risk. This measure gives us information about the tightness of the probability distribution of possible outcomes. If investors and creditors are risk averse—and all available evidence suggests that they are—it behooves management to incorporate the risk of an investment proposal into its analysis of the proposal's worth. Otherwise, capital budgeting decisions are unlikely to be in accord with an objective of maximizing share price.

Risk is the variability of possible outcomes.

We begin by considering a single project in which the cash flows are independent from period to period. Our concern is with measuring the overall riskiness of an investment proposal when the probability distributions of cash-flow outcomes for different periods are not necessarily the same. Figure 7-1 illustrates this idea; both the expected cash flow and the dispersion of the probability distribution change over time. Once we have presented the basic method of analysis under the

165

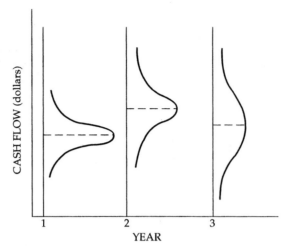

FIGURE 7-1

Illustration of changing risk over time

assumption of independent probability distributions, we shall move on to consider varying degrees of correlation of cash flows over time.

Assumption of Independence

With independence of cash flows over time, the outcome in period t does not depend on what happened in period $t - 1$. Stated differently, there is no causative relationship between cash flows from period to period. The mean of the probability distribution of possible net present values for a proposal is

$$NPV = \sum_{t=0}^{n} \frac{\overline{A}_t}{(1 + R_f)^t} \tag{7-1}$$

where $\overline{A}_t$ is the expected net cash flow in period t, R_f is the risk-free rate, and n the number of periods over which cash flows are expected.

Risk-Free Rate for Discounting   The risk-free rate is used at this time as the discount rate because we attempt to isolate the time value of money. To include a premium for risk in the discount rate would result in double counting with respect to our analysis. The required rate of return for a project embodies a premium for risk. If this rate is used as the discount rate, we would be adjusting for risk in the discounting process itself. (The greater the discount rate, the greater the risk adjustment, assuming a constant risk-free rate.) We then would use the probability distribution of net present values to judge the risk of the proposal. However, the probability distribution is obtained using a risk-adjusted discount rate. (The greater the risk premium, and hence discount rate, the less the standard deviation computed in the formulas that follow.) In essence, we would adjust for risk a second time in our analysis of the dispersion of the probability distribution of possible net present values. Because of the problems inherent in double counting for risk, we take account only of the time value of money in the discounting process.[1]

---

[1] This is not to say that to accept or reject a proposal we should discount at the risk-free rate the mean cash flows. Indeed, in Chapter 8, we show that the appropriate discount rate is the required rate of return, which embodies a premium for the project's risk. For discounting the dispersion of the distribution, however, we use the risk-free rate for the foregoing reasons.

TABLE 7-1

Expected Cash Flows for Example Problem

Period 1		Period 2		Period 3	
PROBABILITY	**NET CASH FLOW**	**PROBABILITY**	**NET CASH FLOW**	**PROBABILITY**	**NET CASH FLOW**
.10	$3,000	.10	$2,000	.10	$2,000
.25	4,000	.25	3,000	.25	3,000
.30	5,000	.30	4,000	.30	4,000
.25	6,000	.25	5,000	.25	5,000
.10	7,000	.10	6,000	.10	6,000

Standard Deviation   Given the assumption of **serial independence** of cash flows for various future periods, the standard deviation of the probability distribution of net present values is

$$\sigma = \sqrt{\sum_{t=0}^{n} \frac{\sigma_t^2}{(1 + R_f)^{2t}}} \qquad (7\text{-}2)$$

where σ_t is the standard deviation of the probability distribution of possible net cash flows in period t. To illustrate the calculations involved with Eqs. (7-1) and (7-2), suppose we had an investment proposal costing $10,000 at time 0 and expected to generate net cash flows during the first three periods with the probabilities shown in Table 7-1. The means of net cash flows for periods 1, 2, and 3 are $5,000, $4,000, and $4,000, respectively. The standard deviation of possible cash flows for period t, σ_t, is computed by

$$\sigma_t = \sqrt{\sum_{x=1}^{5} (A_{xt} - \overline{A}_t)^2 P_{xt}} \qquad (7\text{-}3)$$

where A_{xt} is the xth possible net cash flow, $\overline{A}_t$ is the mean net cash flow for period t, and P_{xt} is the probability of occurrence of A_{xt}.

In the example, the standard deviation of possible net cash flows for period 1 is

$$\sigma_1 = [.10(3{,}000 - 5{,}000)^2 + .25(4{,}000 - 5{,}000)^2 + .30(5{,}000 - 5{,}000)^2$$
$$+ .25(6{,}000 - 5{,}000)^2 + .10(7{,}000 - 5{,}000)^2]^{1/2}$$
$$= \$1{,}140$$

Final Calculations   Because the probability distributions for periods 2 and 3 have the same dispersion about their expected values as that for period 1, σ_2 and σ_3 are $1,140 also. Given this information, we are able to calculate the net present value for the proposal as well as the standard deviation. If we assume a risk-free rate of 6 percent, the net present value for the proposal is

$$NPV = -10{,}000 + \frac{5{,}000}{1.06} + \frac{4{,}000}{(1.06)^2} + \frac{4{,}000}{(1.06)^3} = \$1{,}635$$

Using Eq. (7-2), under the assumption of mutual independence of cash flows over time, the standard deviation is

$$\sigma = \sqrt{\frac{1{,}140^2}{(1.06)^2} + \frac{1{,}140^2}{(1.06)^4} + \frac{1{,}140^2}{(1.06)^6}} = \$1{,}761$$

Standardizing the Dispersion

The expected value and the standard deviation of the probability distribution of possible net present values give us a considerable amount of information by which to evaluate the risk of the investment proposal. If the probability distribution is approximately normal (bell-shaped), we are able to calculate the probability of a proposal's providing a net present value of less than or more than a specified amount. The probability is found by determining the area under the curve to the left or to the right of a particular point of interest.

To go to our previous illustration, suppose we want to determine the probability that the net present value will be zero or less. To determine this probability, we first calculate the difference between zero and the net present value for the project. In our example, this difference is −$1,635. We then **standardize** this difference by dividing it by the standard deviation of the probability distribution of possible net present values. The formula is

$$S = \frac{X - NPV}{\sigma} \tag{7-4}$$

where X is the outcome in which we are interested, NPV the mean of the probability distribution, and σ the standard deviation. In our case

$$S = \frac{0 - 1{,}635}{1{,}761} = -.928$$

This figure tells us that a net present value of zero lies .928 standard deviation to the left of the mean of the probability distribution of possible net present values.

Determining Probabilities of Adverse Events To determine the probability that the net present value of the project will be zero or less, we consult the normal probability distribution table (Table C) at the back of the book. (More detailed tables are found in most statistics texts.) With respect to the problem at hand, we find with interpolation that there is a .177 probability that an observation will be less than −.928 standard deviations from the mean of that distribution. Thus, there is a .177 probability that the net present value of the proposal will be zero or less. Put another way, there is a .177 probability that the internal rate of return of the project will be less than the risk-free rate. If we assume a continuous distribution, the probability density function of our example problem can be shown as in Fig. 7-2.

The mean of the probability distribution of possible net present values is $1,635. One standard deviation on either side of the mean gives us net present values of −$126 and $3,396. With a normal distribution, .683 of the distribution or area under the curve falls within one standard deviation on either side of the mean.[2]

Standardizing deviations from the mean allows us to assess the probability of adversity.

---

[2]Approximately .954 of a normal distribution falls within two standard deviations on either side of the mean and .997 within three standard deviations.

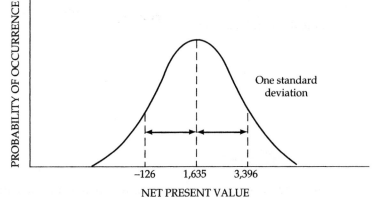

FIGURE 7-2

Probability density function for the example problem

Thus, we know that there is approximately a two-thirds probability that the net present value of the proposal examined will be between −$126 and $3,396. We know also that there is a .177 probability that the net present value will be less than zero and a .823 probability that it will be greater than zero. By expressing differences from the mean in terms of standard deviations, we are able to determine the probability that the net present value for an investment proposal will be greater than or less than a particular amount.

Knowledge of these probabilities is fundamental for a realistic assessment of risk. Suppose the firm is considering another mutually exclusive investment project, proposal Y. The probability density function for this proposal is shown in Fig. 7-3, as is that for our example problem, proposal X. We see that the mean net present value for proposal Y, $2,500, is higher than that for proposal X, $1,635, but there is also greater dispersion of the probability distribution. If risk is directly related to dispersion, proposal Y has both a higher expected profitability and a greater risk than does proposal X.

Information Generated

The approach just outlined can be adapted to internal rates of return. What is involved is expression of the distribution in terms of possible internal rates of return as opposed to net present values. By varying the discount rate, R_f, in Eq. (7-2), we obtain standard deviations for different discount rates. For each standard devia-

FIGURE 7-3

Probability distribution of net present values for proposals X and Y

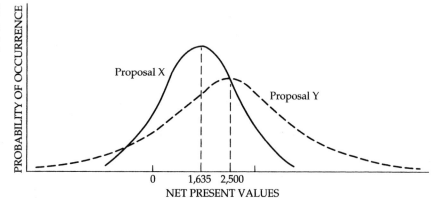

tion, the probability that net present value will be zero or less can be computed. These probabilities then are plotted with the discount rate along the horizontal axis in ascending order and with the corresponding probabilities on the vertical axis. A probability distribution of possible internal rates of return emerges from which the mean and standard deviation can be computed. Using the standard deviation together with the mean of possible internal rates of return, one is able to perform the same type of analysis as before.

Nonnormal Distributions   In the examples, we have assumed normal probability distributions. Although this property is desirable for purposes of calculation, it is not a necessary condition for the use of the foregoing approach. Even when the distribution is not normal, we usually are able to make reasonably strong probability statements by using Tchebycheff's inequality. This approach is based on the fact that regardless of the form of the distribution, there is a close relationship between the magnitude of deviations from the mean of the distribution and probability. Again, we are interested in the area under the curve, or probability density function, that is to the left or right of a particular net present value or internal rate of return. By computing this area, we are able to determine the probability that the index will be greater than or less than a particular amount and judge the risk of the project accordingly.

Biases in Obtaining Information   Before closing this section, we must point out that the main difficulty associated with risky investments lies in obtaining cash-flow estimates from people, not in the mathematical manipulation of the data obtained. People being what they are, biases invariably creep into the process. Sometimes the incentive compensation of managers is linked to the return on assets relative to some standard. If this standard is based on the expected return for investment projects, managers are likely to bias their estimates downward. In this way they are more likely to be able to exceed the standard. To ensure unbiased cash-flow forecasts, it is essential that the compensation of those doing the forecasting is divorced from subsequent performance.

In the adjustment for biases, one problem faced in any organization is overadjustment. Sam makes a forecast that he regards as unbiased and sends it up through the chain of command for final project approval. Linda believes Sam to be consistently biased and adjusts the forecast before sending it forward. Pete does not trust Linda's adjusted forecast, so he makes an adjustment to correct for the perceived bias. So the process goes until the information finally reviewed by top management bears little resemblance to that originally provided by Sam. Also, there is the problem of accountability. Because capital investment projects involve returns over many years, it is difficult to go back to the person who made the forecast with the actual results. That person often has been transferred or has left the company. Although the best approach to correcting biases may be to present a forecaster with the actual results for a number of projects and to compare these results with the forecasts, this often is not possible for long-lived projects.

In addition to the biases described, others also are possible. Although the focus of this chapter is on the quantitative organization of data, we must be mindful of the fact that the accuracy of the final results depends heavily on behavioral considerations. Every effort must be made to provide an environment conducive to the unbiased forecasting of project cash flows.

Dependence of Cash Flows over Time

Independent cash flows over time are less risky than dependent cash flows.

In the preceding section, we assumed serial independence of cash flows from one future period to another. For most investment proposals, however, the cash flow in one future period depends in part on the cash flows in previous periods. If an investment proposal turns bad in the early years, the probability is high that cash flows in later years also will be lower than originally expected. To assume that an extremely unfavorable or favorable outcome in the early life of an investment proposal will not affect the later outcome is unrealistic in most investment situations. The consequence of cash flows being correlated over time is that the standard deviation of the probability distribution of possible net present values or possible internal rates of return is larger than it would be if we assumed independence. The greater the degree of correlation, the greater the dispersion of the probability distribution. The mean net present value, however, is the same, regardless of the degree of correlation over time. In this section, we explore varying degrees of **dependence** of cash flows over time.

Perfect Correlation   Cash flows are **perfectly correlated** over time if they deviate in exactly the same relative manner—if actual cash flows for all periods show the same relative deviation from the means of their respective probability distributions of expected cash flows. In other words, the cash flow in period t depends entirely on what happened in previous periods. If the actual cash flow in period t is X standard deviations to the right of the mean of the probability distribution of possible cash flows for that period, actual cash flows in all other periods will be X standard deviations to the right of the means of their respective probability distributions. Stated differently, the cash flow in any period is a linear function of the cash flows in all other periods. The formula for the standard deviation of a perfectly correlated stream of cash flows over time is

$$\sigma = \sum_{t=0}^{n} \frac{\sigma_t}{(1 + R_f)^t} \tag{7-5}$$

To illustrate its use, consider the same example as before. The standard deviation for the proposal, using Eq. (7-5), is

$$\sigma = \frac{1,140}{1.06} + \frac{1,140}{(1.06)^2} + \frac{1,140}{(1.06)^3} = \$3,047$$

This compares with a standard deviation of \$1,761 when we used Eq. (7-2) under the assumption of serial independence over time. Thus, the standard deviation for a perfectly correlated stream of cash flows is significantly greater than the standard deviation for the same stream under the assumption of mutual independence. The standard deviation for a less than perfectly correlated stream of cash flows will be somewhere between these two values.[3] The probabilistic analysis of a

---

[3]Frederick S. Hillier, "The Derivation of Probabilistic Information for the Evaluation of Risky Investments," *Management Science*, 9 (April 1963), 443–57, combines the assumptions of mutual independence and perfect correlation of cash flows in developing a model to deal with mixed situations. Essentially, the overall cash flows of the firm are separated and classified as either independent or perfectly correlated over time. A formula is derived for calculating the standard deviation.

project with a perfectly correlated stream of cash flows over time is the same as that illustrated previously for a project with an uncorrelated stream.

Most projects have cash flows that are moderately correlated over time.

Moderate Correlation   Where the cash flows of the firm are neither approximately independent nor perfectly correlated over time, the classification of the cash-flow stream as one or the other is not appropriate. One method for dealing with the problem of moderate correlation is with a series of **conditional probability distributions.** Suppose the investment in a project costing $10,000 at time 0 is expected to generate net cash flows in periods 1, 2, and 3 with the probabilities in Table 7-2. The table shows 27 possible cash-flow series. The last column depicts the joint probability of occurrence of a particular cash-flow series. For series 1, the joint probability of a −$6,000 cash flow in period 1 being followed by cash flows of −$2,000 and $5,000 in periods 2 and 3, respectively, is .25 × .30 × .25 = .01875. Similarly, joint probabilities for the other cash-flow series can be determined in this manner.

The use of conditional probability distributions enables us to take account of the correlation of cash flows over time. In the above example, the cash flow in period 3 depends on what happened in periods 1 and 2; however, the correlation of cash flows over time is not perfect. With a given cash flow in period 1, the cash flow in period 2 can vary within a range. Similarly, the cash flow in period 3 can vary within a range, depending on the outcomes in periods 1 and 2.

The calculation of the mean net present value using this approach is the same as in Eq. (7-1). The standard deviation may be determined mathematically for the simple case by

$$\sigma = \sqrt{\sum_{x=1}^{l} (NPV_x - \overline{NPV})^2 \, P_x} \tag{7-6}$$

where NPV_x is the net present value for series x of net cash flows, covering all periods, $\overline{NPV}$ is the mean net present value of the proposal, and P_x is the probability of occurrence of that series. For the example, there are 27 possible series of cash flows, so that $l = 27$. The first series is represented by a net cash flow of −$10,000 at time 0, −$6,000 at time 1, −$2,000 at time 2, and $5,000 at time 3. The probability of occurrence of that series is .01875.

Simulation   Unfortunately, for complex situations the mathematical calculation of the standard deviation is unfeasible. For these situations, we can *approximate* the standard deviation by means of **simulation.** With this method, we use random sampling to select cash-flow series for evaluation and calculate the net present value or internal rate of return for each selected series. When a random sample of sufficient size has been built up in this way, the mean and standard deviation of the probability distribution are estimated from the sample; this information is then analyzed in much the same manner as before.[4]

We have seen that our assumption as to the degree of correlation of cash flows over time is important. If cash flows are highly correlated over time, the

---

[4]The first comprehensive simulation of investment project risk was by David B. Hertz, "Risk Analysis in Capital Investment," *Harvard Business Review,* 42 (January–February 1964), 95–106. This modeling of new product risk remains a classic.

TABLE 7-2
Illustration of Conditional Probability Distribution Approach

Period 1		Period 2		Period 3			
INITIAL PROBABILITY P(1)	**NET CASH FLOW**	**CONDITIONAL PROBABILITY P(2/1)**	**NET CASH FLOW**	**CONDITIONAL PROBABILITY P(3/2,1)**	**NET CASH FLOW**	*Cash-Flow Series*	*Joint Probability P(1,2,3)*
				.25	$ 5,000	1	.01875
		.30	−$2,000	.50	7,000	2	.03750
				.25	9,000	3	.01875
				.25	7,000	4	.02500
.25	−$6,000	.40	1,000	.50	9,000	5	.05000
				.25	11,000	6	.02500
				.25	9,000	7	.01875
		.30	4,000	.50	11,000	8	.03750
				.25	13,000	9	.01875
				.30	10,000	10	.03750
		.25	3,000	.40	12,000	11	.05000
				.30	14,000	12	.03750
				.30	12,000	13	.07500
.50	−4,000	.50	6,000	.40	14,000	14	.10000
				.30	16,000	15	.07500
				.30	14,000	16	.03750
		.25	9,000	.40	16,000	17	.05000
				.30	18,000	18	.03750
				.25	15,000	19	.01875
		.30	8,000	.50	17,000	20	.03750
				.25	19,000	21	.01875
				.25	17,000	22	.02500
.25	−2,000	.40	11,000	.50	19,000	23	.05000
				.25	21,000	24	.02500
				.25	19,000	25	.01875
		.30	14,000	.50	21,000	26	.03750
				.25	23,000	27	.01875

risk of a project will be considerably greater than if they are mutually independent, all other things being the same. Although independence often is assumed for ease of calculation, this assumption greatly underestimates project risk if in fact the cash flows are highly correlated over time. Thus, it is important to give careful consideration to the likely degree of dependence of cash flows over time. Otherwise, the assessment of risk may well be distorted. Of the approaches for dealing with the problem, the use of conditional probabilities is the most accurate, although the most difficult to implement. Other approaches to moderately correlated cash flows could be illustrated, but the discussion in this section as well as in the next is sufficient to give a flavor of how to go about it.

TOTAL RISK FOR MULTIPLE INVESTMENTS

We have been measuring risk for a single investment project. When multiple investment projects are involved, the measurement may differ from that for a single project, owing to the properties of diversification.[5] Diversification of securities was discussed in Chapter 3, and this concept applies also to capital assets. However, it is noteworthy that investment in capital assets differs from investment in securities. For one thing, capital assets typically are not divisible, whereas securities are. Moreover, it usually is much more costly, and sometimes impossible, to divest oneself of a capital asset, whereas selling a marketable security is relatively easy. Finally, there is the problem of mutual exclusion and contingency that does not occur with securities. All of these factors make diversification with respect to capital assets more "lumpy" than diversification with securities. Whether diversification of capital assets is a thing of value for the firm is a subject of considerable controversy, one that will be analyzed in Chapter 8. Our purpose here is only to show how to measure risk for combinations of risky investments, not to ponder whether such measurement is worthwhile. That comes later.

Standard Deviation

Total risk is the sum of systematic and unsystematic risk.

As was true earlier, the two pieces of information we seek are the mean and standard deviation of the probability distribution of possible net present values for the combination of projects being analyzed. The mean usually is simply a weighted average for the projects making up the combination. From Chapter 3, we know that the total variance, or risk, of a combination of risky investments depends to a large extent on the degree of correlation between the investments. The standard deviation of the probability distribution of possible net present values for a portfolio of capital investments can be expressed as

$$\sigma = \sqrt{\sum_{j=1}^{m} \sum_{k=1}^{m} r_{jk}\sigma_{j}\sigma_{k}} \qquad (7\text{-}7)$$

where m is the total number of assets in the portfolio, r_{jk} is the expected correlation between the net present values for investments j and k, σ_{j} is the standard deviation for investment j, and σ_{k} is the standard deviation for investment k.

Equation (7-7) indicates that the standard deviation, or risk, of a portfolio of projects depends on (1) the degree of correlation between various projects and (2) the standard deviation of possible net present values for each project. We note

---

[5]The development of this section assumes that the reader has studied portfolio selection in Chapter 3.

that the higher the degree of positive correlation, the greater the standard deviation of the portfolio of projects, all other things remaining constant. Moreover, the greater the standard deviations of the individual projects, the greater the standard deviation of the portfolio, if the correlation is positive. The standard deviations of the individual investment projects, necessary for the calculation of Eq. (7-7), are obtained through the methods presented earlier in the chapter.

Correlation between Projects

As was the case with a portfolio of securities discussed in Chapter 3, the correlation between expected net present values of two projects may be positive, negative, or zero, depending on the nature of the association. A correlation coefficient of 1.00 indicates that the net present values of two investment proposals vary directly in the same proportional manner; a correlation coefficient of -1.00 indicates that they vary inversely in the same proportional manner; and a zero correlation coefficient usually indicates that they are independent.

Range of Correlation For most pairs of investment projects, the correlation coefficient lies between 0 and 1.00. The lack of negatively correlated projects is due to most investments being correlated positively with the economy. Still, it is possible to find projects having low or moderate degrees of correlation. Projects in the same general line of business tend to be highly correlated with each other, whereas projects in essentially unrelated lines of business tend to have low degrees of correlation.

Illustration To illustrate calculations with Eq. (7-7), suppose a firm has a single existing investment project, 1, and it is considering an additional project, 2. The projects have the following expected net present values, standard deviations, and correlation coefficients:

Project	Expected Net Present Value	Standard Deviation	Correlation Coefficient
1	$12,000	$14,000	1.00
2	8,000	6,000	1.00
1 and 2			.40

The expected net present value of the combination of projects is simply the sum of the two separate net present values:

$$NPV = \$12{,}000 + \$8{,}000 = \$20{,}000$$

The standard deviation for the combination, using Eq. (7-7), is

$$\sigma = \sqrt{r_{11}\sigma_1^2 + 2r_{12}\sigma_1\sigma_2 + r_{22}\sigma_2^2}$$
$$= \sqrt{(1.00)(14{,}000)^2 + (2)(.40)(14{,}000)(6{,}000) + (1.00)(6{,}000)^2}$$
$$= \$17{,}297$$

Thus, the expected net present value of the firm increases from $12,000 to $20,000, and the standard deviation of possible net present values from $14,000 to $17,297 with the acceptance of project 2. As the number of projects increases, the calculations become more cumbersome. Fortunately, computer programs exist that can readily solve for the standard deviation.

Feasible Combinations and Dominance

With the foregoing procedures, you can determine the mean and the standard deviation of the probability distribution of possible net present values for a combination of investments. A combination includes all existing investment projects and one or more proposals under consideration. We assume that a firm has existing investment projects generating expected future cash flows and that disinvestment with respect to these projects is not possible. Existing projects comprise a subset that is included in all combinations. Proposals under consideration are assumed to represent all future proposals on the investment horizon.

Dominance
determines the
efficient frontier of
projects.

Evaluating Feasible Combinations   The next step involves analyzing feasible combinations of existing projects and proposals under consideration according to their net present values, and standard deviations, to see which combinations dominate. In Fig. 7-4, a scatter diagram, the expected net present value is along the vertical axis; the standard deviation is on the horizontal axis. Each dot represents a feasible combination of proposals under consideration and existing investment projects for the firm.

Collectively, the dots represent the total set of feasible combinations of investment opportunities available to the firm. This set corresponds to the opportunity set of security portfolios discussed in Chapter 3, the major difference being that combinations of investment projects are not as divisible as portfolios of securities. Certain dots in Fig. 7-4 dominate others in the sense that they represent a higher net present value and the same standard deviation, a lower standard deviation and the same net present value, or both a higher net present value and a lower standard deviation. The dots that dominate others are those that are farthest to the left, and they correspond to the efficient frontier for an opportunity set of security portfolios.

Relation to Existing Portfolio   If *E* represents the existing portfolio of investment projects, it is dominated by combination *P* with respect to net present value, by

FIGURE 7-4
Opportunity set and
project portfolio

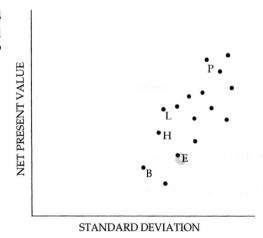

NET PRESENT VALUE

STANDARD DEVIATION

combination *B* with respect to standard deviation, and by combinations *H* and *L* with respect to both net present value and standard deviation. Other dots dominate *E*, but these are not on the frontier. With the type of information in Fig. 7-4, most combinations of investment proposals can be eliminated simply because they are dominated by other combinations. In Chapter 8, we take up the evaluation of this information and the acceptance criterion. Our purpose in this chapter is only to present the measurement of portfolio risk.

We observe that the combination of projects ultimately chosen determines the new investment proposal or proposals that will be accepted. An exception occurs only when the portfolio selected is composed of existing projects. In this situation, no investment proposals under consideration would be accepted. In our case, the portfolio of existing projects is represented by dot *E* in Fig. 7-4. Therefore, the selection of any of the four outlying portfolios would imply the acceptance of one or more new investment proposals. Those investment proposals under consideration but not in the portfolio finally selected would be rejected, of course. The incremental standard deviation and net present value can be determined by measuring on the horizontal and vertical axes the distance from dot *E* to the dot representing the combination finally selected.

REAL OPTIONS IN CAPITAL INVESTMENTS

For the capital budgeting projects so far considered, cash flows were assumed out to some horizon and then discounted to present value. Investment projects are not necessarily set in concrete once they are accepted. Managers can, and often do, make changes that affect subsequent cash flows and/or the life of the project. These **real, or managerial, options** are embedded in the investment project. Slavish devotion to discounted cash-flow methods (DCF) often ignores these options and the future managerial flexibility that accompanies them, that is, the flexibility to alter old decisions when conditions change.

Valuation in General

The presence of real options enhances the worth of an investment project. Its worth can be viewed as the net present value of the project, calculated in the usual way, together with the value of the option(s).

The option to change at mid-stream is valuable.

$$\text{Project worth} = NPV + \text{Option value} \tag{7-8}$$

The greater the number of options and the greater the uncertainty surrounding their use, the greater the second term in the equation and the greater the project's worth.

Types of Real Options   The types of real options available include

1. The option to **vary output.** An important option is to expand production if conditions turn favorable and to contract production if conditions turn bad. The former is sometimes called a growth option, and the latter may actually involve the shutdown of production.
2. The option to **abandon.** If a project has abandonment value, this effectively represents a put option to the project's owner.
3. The option to **postpone,** also known as an investment timing option. For some projects there is the option to wait, thereby obtaining new information.

Sometimes these options are treated informally as qualitative factors when judging the worth of a project. It may be no more than "if such and such occurs, we will have the opportunity to do this." Real options are more difficult to value than are financial options; the option formulas taken up in Chapter 5 often do not work. Rather, resort must be made to decision trees, simulations, and ad hoc approaches.

Although the three real options listed above are the most important, there are others. Sometimes a company will have flexibility in its production process. It may wish to build in the capability to change technology, depending on future input costs. In other situations there may be output flexibility, in that a production facility can produce multiple products. The ability to shift the mix of output in response to market demand is a real option that surely has value.[6]

The Option to Expand

For a manufacturing plant, management often has the option to make a follow-on investment. Gummy Glue Company is evaluating a new, revolutionary glue. It can build a plant that is capable of producing 25,000 cans a month. That level of production is not economical, from either a manufacturing or a marketing standpoint. As a result, the project's net present value is expected to be −$3 million. According to classical DCF analysis, the project should be rejected.

However, the new glue could be a winner. If it takes off, Gummy Glue Company could then invest in a new plant, say two years hence, which would triple output and be highly efficient. However, the opportunity for this level of demand is not available unless an initial investment is made. (Without the initial investment, the company would not have first-mover advantage.)

There is a 50–50 chance the market will take off. If it does, the net present value of the new investment at the end of year 2 will be $15 million. When discounted at the required rate of return, *NPV* at time 0 is $11 million. If the market does not take off, the company will not invest further and incremental *NPV* at the end of year 2, by definition, is zero. The situation is depicted in Fig. 7-5.

FIGURE 7-5
Gummy Glue
Company option to
expand

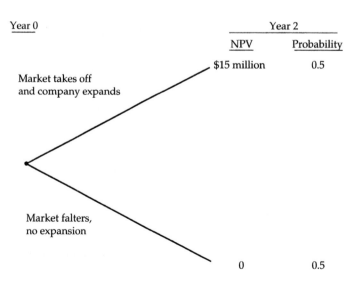

---

[6]See Nalin Kulatilaka and Alan J. Marcus, "Project Valuation under Uncertainty: When Does DCF Fail?" *Journal of Applied Corporate Finance*, 5 (Fall 1992), 92–100, for a discussion of these and other real options.

The mean of the distribution of possible *NPV* values associated with the option is .5($11 million) + .5(0) = $5.5 million. Using Eq. (7-8) gives

$$\text{Project worth} = -\$3 \text{ million} + \$5.5 \text{ million}$$
$$= \$2.5 \text{ million}$$

Even though the initial project has a negative *NPV* value, the option to expand more than offsets it. Because it embraces a valuable option, the project should be accepted. For sequential decisions of this sort, a **decision tree** allows analysis of the subsequent chance events.

Initial Regional versus National Distribution

A variation of this theme involves new product distribution. Major Munch Cereal Company is considering the introduction of a new cereal, honey-coated oat flakes. Initially, it must decide whether to distribute the product in the Midwest or nationally. Regional distribution will require an expenditure of $1 million for a new plant and for the initial marketing effort. Depending on demand during the first 2 years, the company then would decide whether or not to expand to national distribution. If it goes from regional to national distribution, it will need to spend an additional $3 million for expansion of the existing plant and to make an additional marketing effort. Of course, Major Munch can distribute nationally from the very outset. If it does, it will cost $3 million to construct a plant and to launch the marketing of the product. We see that there are economies associated with distributing nationally at the outset. For one thing, building a large plant is less expensive than building a small one and having to enlarge it later. Moreover, there are economies in marketing.

Decision trees are a method for valuing real options.

Decision Tree Approach Thus, the $1 million initial investment buys Major Munch Cereal Company an option to be exercised at the end of two years either to distribute nationally or to continue regional distribution. The nature of the option is illustrated graphically by the decision tree shown in Fig. 7-6. The squares represent decision points. The first decision is whether to distribute regionally or nationally. The circles represent chance event nodes. If the company decides to distribute nationally at the outset, there is .4 probability that demand will prove to be high, .4 that demand will turn out to be medium, and .2 that it will be low. On the other hand, if the company distributes regionally, there is .5 probability that demand will be high, .3 probability that it will be medium, and .2 probability that it will be low. At the end of year 2, the company must decide whether to continue to distribute regionally, in which case demand will continue to be high, low, or medium, or whether it should distribute nationally, in which case the national demand is shown by the subsequent chance events in the figure.

The expected net present values for the various branches are shown in Table 7-3. This information is derived from the expected cash-flow streams for each branch using the risk-free rate as the discount rate. If Major Munch switches from regional to national distribution at the end of year 2, there is a cash expenditure of $3 million, and this represents a negative cash flow at that time. This outflow is in addition to the cash outflow of $1 million at time 0 for the regional plant. We need now to incorporate these net present values into our decision tree. In Fig. 7-7, they

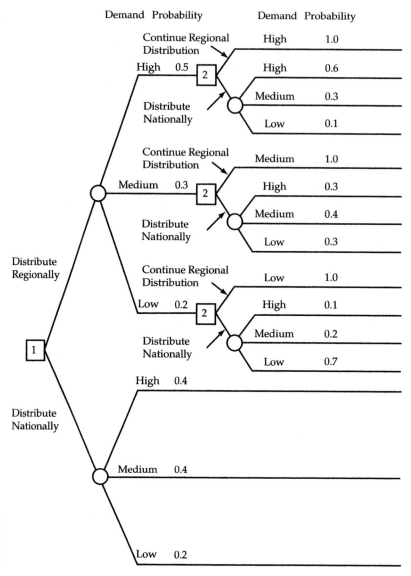

FIGURE 7-6
Decision tree: national
versus regional
distribution

are shown at the branch tips indicating the expected net present values associated
with the sequence of decisions and chance events comprising the branch.

Optimal Set of Decisions   You may determine the optimal sequence of decisions
by "rolling back" the tree from the right-hand side. In other words, first appraise
the most distant decisions—namely, the choice of whether or not to switch from
regional to national distribution. To do so, determine the mean net present value
for national distribution, given that demand for the regional distribution proves to
be high, medium, or low. The mean net present value is simply the net present values at the branch tips times the probabilities of occurrence. For high regional demand, the net present value for subsequent national distribution is

$$NPV = .6(4,096.9) + .3(1,573.1) + .1(-704.1) \tag{7-9}$$
$$= \$2,859.6$$

TABLE 7-3

Expected Net Present Values for Various Branches of Decision Tree (in Thousands)

	Net Present Value
Regional distribution throughout	
High demand	$ 947.4
Medium demand	136.2
Low demand	−637.1
Regional distribution followed by national distribution	
High regional–high national demand	4,096.9
High regional–medium national demand	1,573.1
High regional–low national demand	−704.1
Medium regional–high national demand	3,377.4
Medium regional–medium national demand	932.6
Medium regional–low national demand	−1,426.8
Low regional–high national demand	2,411.2
Low regional–medium national demand	51.9
Low regional–low national demand	−2,307.5
National distribution throughout	
High demand	3,830.5
Medium demand	851.6
Low demand	−1,927.3

This amount appears at the chance event node for national distribution, given high regional demand.

In a similar fashion, the means of net present value for national distribution, given medium and low regional demands, are computed and shown at the appropriate chance event nodes. We note in Fig. 7-7 that the net present value for national distribution, given low regional demand, is −$1,363,800. This figure compares with an expected net present value of −$637,100 if the company continues with regional distribution. Thus, if regional demand is low, the company should not distribute nationally but should continue to distribute regionally. On the other hand, if regional demand turns out to be either high or medium, Major Munch should go to national distribution, for the net present value is higher than it is if the firm continues with regional distribution. By backward induction, then, you are able to determine the optimal decision at the most distant decision point.

Comparing NPVs The next step is to determine the optimal decision at the first decision point; that is, to decide whether to distribute nationally or regionally at the outset. The mean net present value for regional distribution, given optimal decisions at decision point 2, is

$$NPV = .5(2,859.6) + .3(958.2) + .2(-637.1) = \$1,589.8 \qquad (7\text{-}10)$$

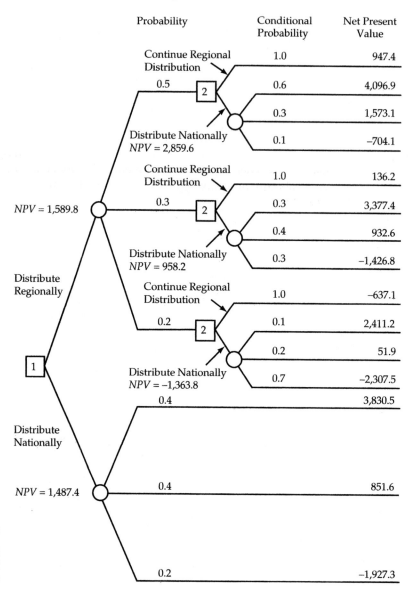

	Probability	Conditional Probability	Net Present Value
Continue Regional Distribution	1.0		947.4
0.5		0.6	4,096.9
		0.3	1,573.1
Distribute Nationally NPV = 2,859.6		0.1	−704.1
Continue Regional Distribution	1.0		136.2
0.3		0.3	3,377.4
		0.4	932.6
Distribute Nationally NPV = 958.2		0.3	−1,426.8
Continue Regional Distribution	1.0		−637.1
0.2		0.1	2,411.2
		0.2	51.9
Distribute Nationally NPV = −1,363.8		0.7	−2,307.5

NPV = 1,589.8

Distribute Regionally

NPV = 1,487.4

Distribute Nationally

0.4		3,830.5
0.4		851.6
0.2		−1,927.3

FIGURE 7-7
Decision tree: net present values of branches

Note that if regional demand is high or medium, we use the net present value associated with subsequent national distribution. If regional demand is low, we use the net present value associated with continuing regional distribution. The net present value for initial national distribution is

$$NPV = .4(3,830.5) + .4(851.6) + .2(-1,927.3) \qquad (7\text{-}11)$$
$$= \$1,487.4$$

Thus, the mean net present value for initial regional distribution exceeds that for initial national distribution. This occurs despite the fact that it is more economical to build the plant and initiate the marketing effort all at once. However, initial regional distribution gives the company the option to expand only if demand proves strong. The mean of the distribution of NPVs is $102,400 higher, after recovery of the $1 million "cost" of the managerial option to expand.

The Option to Abandon

A second option is to abandon a project after it is undertaken. This may consist of selling the asset, where a company realizes cash upon its disposal. However, an asset does not have to be sold to realize abandonment value. It simply may be employed in another area of the enterprise. In either case, an abandonment value can be estimated. Effectively, the ability to abandon a project represents a put option for the company.

Abandonment value provides a safety net of sorts for projects that go awry.

The economic rationale for abandonment is the same as that for capital budgeting. Funds should be removed from a project, or disinvested, whenever the project does not economically justify their use. In general, an investment project should be abandoned when (1) its abandonment value exceeds the present value of the project's subsequent future cash flows and (2) it is better to abandon then than in the future. With the ability to abandon, the worth of an investment project may be enhanced.

$$\text{Project worth} = \begin{matrix} NPV \text{ without} \\ \text{abandonment} \\ \text{option} \end{matrix} + \begin{matrix} \text{Value of} \\ \text{abandonment} \\ \text{option} \end{matrix} \qquad (7\text{-}12)$$

The recognition of later abandonment may have a significant effect on project selection.

Taking Account of Present and Future   The abandonment rule posed can be expressed more formally as[7]

1. Compute the present value of the sum of cash flows expected to be generated from the project and the expected abandonment value at the end of the holding period. If there were n years remaining in the life of the project, we would have the following formula:

$$PV_{\tau \cdot a} = \sum_{t=\tau+1}^{a} \frac{A_t}{(1+k)^{t-\tau}} + \frac{AV_a}{(1+k)^{a-\tau}} \qquad (7\text{-}13)$$

    where

    $PV_{\tau \cdot a}$ = present value at time τ of expected future net cash flows through period a, plus the present value of the expected abandonment value at the end of period a

    a = period in which the project is abandoned

    A_t = expected net cash flow of the project in period t

    k = required rate of return

    AV_a = expected abandonment value at the end of period a

2. For $a = n$, compute $PV_{\tau \cdot a}$. If $PV_{\tau \cdot n}$ is greater than the current abandonment value, AV_τ, we continue to hold the project and evaluate it at time $\tau + 1$, based on our expectations at that time.

---

[7]See Alexander A. Robichek and James C. Van Horne, "Abandonment Value and Capital Budgeting," *Journal of Finance*, 22 (December 1967), 557–89; Edward A. Dyl and Hugh W. Long, "Comment," *Journal of Finance*, 24 (March 1969), 88–95; and Robichek and Van Horne, "Reply," *ibid.*, pp. 96–97.

3. If $PV_{\tau \cdot n}$ is less than or equal to AV_τ, we compute $PV_{\tau \cdot a}$ for $a = n - 1$. If $PV_{\tau \cdot n - 1}$ is greater than AV_τ, we continue to hold the project as in item 2. If $PV_{\tau \cdot n - 1} \leq AV_\tau$, we compute $PV_{\tau \cdot a}$ for $a = n - 2$ and compare it with AV_τ. This procedure is continued until either a decision to hold the project is reached or $a = \tau + 1$.

4. If $PV_{\tau \cdot a} \leq AV_\tau$ for all $\tau + 1 \leq a \leq n$, then we would abandon the project at time τ.

In other words, these steps would have us abandon a project only if the present value of possible future benefits is less than the current abandonment value and if it appears better to abandon now than in the future. When the above rules suggest that a project should be given up, we would make less than optimum use of capital if we continued.

Illustration Wonka Tractor Company is considering a new plant to produce the Wonka III lawn tractor. This tractor will be produced for only 1 or 2 years, as the Wonka IV, now on the drawing board, will replace it. The proposal costs $3 million, and the cash flows and their probabilities of occurrence are shown as a series of conditional probabilities in Table 7-4. For simplicity of illustration, we assume that after the second year, the proposal is not expected to provide any cash flow or residual value. We also assume an expected abandonment value of $1.5 million at the end of the first period. There are nine possible series of cash flows over the 2-year period, the first series representing a cash flow of $1 million in period 1, followed by a cash flow of 0 in period 2. The joint probability of each series of cash flows is shown in the last column of the table; for the first series, it is $.25 \times .25 = .0625$.

TABLE 7-4
Conditional Probability Distribution Series for Abandonment Example

	Period 1		Period 2		
CASH FLOW (IN THOUSANDS)	**INITIAL PROBABILITY P(1)**		**CASH FLOW (IN THOUSANDS)**	**CONDITIONAL PROBABILITY P(2/1)**	*Joint Probability P(1,2)*
			$ 0	0.25	0.0625
$1,000	0.25		1,000	0.50	0.1250
			2,000	0.25	0.0625
			1,000	0.25	0.1250
2,000	0.50		2,000	0.50	0.2500
			3,000	0.25	0.1250
			2,000	0.25	0.0625
3,000	0.25		3,000	0.50	0.1250
			3,500	0.25	0.0625
Abandonment value $1,500					

If we assume a required rate of return of 10 percent and use this rate as our discount factor, we are able to determine the expected net present value of the proposal without abandonment by (1) computing the net present value for each cash-flow series, (2) obtaining the expected net present value for each series by multiplying the computed net present value by the probability of occurrence of that series, and (3) adding the expected net present values of all sequences. Carrying out these computations, we find the mean net present value to be $445,246.

Abandonment Option Makes Situation Better   When we allow for the possibility of abandonment, however, the results change dramatically. Following the decision rules specified earlier, Wonka Tractor would divest itself of the project if its abandonment value at the end of period 1 exceeded the expected cash flows for the subsequent period, discounted at 10 percent. Because cash flows are expected for only two periods, the possibility of abandoning the project beyond period 1 does not exist. Consequently, a number of the computational steps involved in the abandonment decision rules discussed are not applicable in this case. Referring again to Table 7-4, we find that we should abandon the project at the end of the first period if the cash flow in that period turns out to be $1 million. The reason is that the mean present value of possible cash flows in period 2, discounted to period 1, $909,091, is less than the abandonment value at the end of the period, $1.5 million. If the cash flow in period 1 turns out to be either $2 million or $3 million, however, abandonment would not be worthwhile because the mean present value of period 2 cash flows discounted to period 1 exceeds $1.5 million.

When we allow for abandonment, the expected cash flows shown in Table 7-4 must be revised; these revisions are shown in Table 7-5. Recalculating the mean net present value for the proposal, based on the information, we find it to be

TABLE 7-5
Conditional Probability Distribution Series for Revised Case

Period 1		Period 2		
CASH FLOW (IN THOUSANDS)	INITIAL PROBABILITY P(1)	CASH FLOW (IN THOUSANDS)	CONDITIONAL PROBABILITY P(2/1)	*Joint Probability* P(1,2)
$2,500	0.25	$ 0		0.2500
		1,000	0.25	0.1250
2,000	0.50	2,000	0.50	0.2500
		3,000	0.25	0.1250
		2,000	0.25	0.0625
3,000	0.25	3,000	0.50	0.1250
		3,500	0.25	0.0625

$579,544. A significant improvement occurs because a portion of the downside is eliminated if the project is abandoned when events turn unfavorable.[8]

The option to abandon is more valuable the greater the volatility of cash flows for a project. The abandonment option, like other real options, lets the good times roll while mitigating the effect of bad outcomes by exercise of the option. To the extent the option has value, it may change a reject signal for a project into an accept signal.

Ongoing Abandonment Evaluations In addition to evaluating new investment proposals, the procedure outlined above can be used for continually evaluating existing investment projects, deciding whether it is better to continue with the project or to abandon it and employ the funds elsewhere. Even though the project is profitable, it may make sense to abandon it if the abandonment value is sufficiently high. In other words, the optimal time to abandon is the point where the combination of expected future cash flows and future abandonment value has the highest present value. Through the continual assessment of projects, a company is able to weed out those that no longer are economically viable.

The Option to Postpone or Time

For some investment projects, there is the option to wait. That is, the project does not have to be undertaken immediately. By waiting, you obtain new information on the market, on prices, on costs, and perhaps on other things. However, you give up the interim cash flows and, possibly, "first mover" advantage in the marketplace.

A mining operation, where the site is owned, involves a decision to begin extraction now or to wait. Here the new information has largely to do with the price of the metal. The cost of exercising the option is the extraction cost. With commodities, such as metals, the value of the option depends importantly on the volatility of commodity price. In other words, the mine is an option on the commodity contained therein. With an operating mine, there is the option to shut it down if price goes too low. This does not mean abandonment, as the mine continues to be owned and can be reopened. Brennan and Schwartz derive optimal points at which to open or shut a gold mine, depending on the price of gold.[9] They treat the problem as a complex option.

Noncommodity Situations Most business decision situations do not hinge on the price of a commodity. As a result, they do not lend themselves to formulation in the option pricing context presented in Chapter 5. Still, the principles are similar, though improvisation is necessary. Consider a new product decision where management has the option to launch now or to defer. If the product is launched now,

---

[8]In studying plant closings, Michael J. Gambola and George P. Tsetkos, "The Information Content of Plant Closing Announcements: Evidence from Financial Profiles and the Stock Price Reaction," *Financial Management*, 21 (Summer 1992), 31–40, find a negative stock market reaction to the announcement consistent with a decline in profitability.

[9]Michael J. Brennan and Eduardo S. Schwartz, "A New Approach to Evaluating Natural Resource Investments," *Midland Corporate Finance Journal*, 3 (Spring 1985), 37–47. Additionally, see Robert L. McDonald and Daniel R. Siegel, "Investment and the Valuation of Firms When There Is an Option to Shut Down," *International Economic Review*, 26 (June 1985), 331–49; Robert L. McDonald and Daniel R. Siegel, "The Value of Waiting to Invest," *Quarterly Journal of Economics*, 101 (November 1986), 707–27; and Avinash K. Dixit, "Entry and Exit Decisions under Uncertainty," *Journal of Political Economy*, 97 (June 1989), 620–38.

the company will realize cash flows earlier than if it waits. This is like having an option on a dividend-paying stock. Exercise now and you get the near future dividends, but you give up the option. If you wait, you may be able to exercise to more advantage. The greater the volatility of possible outcomes, of course, the greater the value of the option.

If the option value for a new product is large, management may want to defer product launch even though the project has a positive net present value if undertaken now. However, one must make sure the option remains open. Much can change in the new product area, and you lose first mover advantage. These considerations may temper the value associated with waiting. Still, the greater the uncertainty, the greater the incentive to wait, thereby keeping the option alive.[10]

Final Observations on Real Options

The real options discussed—varying output, abandonment, and postponement or timing—have a common thread. Because they limit the downside, the greater the variance or uncertainty associated with the future, the more valuable these options. As our preceding discussion reflects, there are differences between financial options and real options. Option pricing theory tells us an exact relationship between the value of an option and the price of the associated asset, based on the idea that a riskless hedged position should provide a return no more than or less than the risk-free rate. Market equilibration depends on highly efficient, arbitrage-driven financial markets. Because product markets are not nearly so efficient, real options are different.

You cannot use risk neutrality to factor out implied variances, as you can with financial options. The exercise price of a real option can change over time. Moreover, volatility is difficult to measure, as you seldom have past market value changes on which to base an estimate. The opportunity cost to waiting to exercise a real option is not nearly as precise as giving up dividends on a dividend-paying stock. These and other differences cause a real option to be much more difficult to value than a financial option.

Still, the overall option pricing framework can be applied to real options, despite the difficulty in measurement. Recognition of management flexibility can alter an initial decision to accept or reject a project. A reject decision using classical DCF analysis can be reversed if the option value is high enough. An accept decision can be turned into a postponement decision if the option value more than offsets the early cash flows. Though a DCF approach to determining net present value is an appropriate starting place, in many cases it needs to be modified for real options.

In the context of our discussion of risk in the first part of the chapter, more uncertainty was a negative. In the context of real options, however, more uncertainty is a positive. Volatility makes the option more valuable as long as the option remains open. Thus, we have two distinctly different considerations of risk in this chapter. Which dominates depends on the situation.

---

[10]Avinash K. Dixit and Robert S. Pindyck, "The Options Approach to Capital Investment," *Harvard Business Review*, 73 (May–June 1995), 105–15.

Summary

Because investment proposals entail differing degrees of business risk, we must analyze not only their expected profitability but also the possible deviations from that expectation. Risk is expressed in terms of the dispersion of the probability distribution of possible net present values or possible internal rates of return and is measured by the standard deviation.

By measuring the standard deviation under a variety of assumptions and using it in relation to the expected value of the distribution, we try to determine the probability that certain events will occur. Risk can be measured under the assumptions of serial independence of cash flows over time or their dependence. For dealing with situations of moderate correlation of cash flows over time, probability trees are useful. Simulation techniques often can be applied to the problem of how to analyze risky investments. Although the portfolio approach has merit only under certain circumstances, it is one way to measure the marginal risk of a project in relation to others that exist or are being considered.

Real options often are important in capital budgeting. This term simply means flexibility of management to alter a previous decision. An in-vestment project's worth can be viewed as its net present value, calculated using classical dis-counted cash-flow analysis, together with the value of the option. The greater the uncertainty surrounding the use of the option, the greater its value. Real options include the option to vary out-put, expanding or contracting depending on de-mand, the option to abandon, and the option to postpone, or time, investment. Consideration of these various options can cause a reject decision on a capital budgeting project to turn into an ac-cept decision and an accept decision to turn into a decision to postpone. In analyzing managerial op-tions, decision trees often are used to come to grips with the sequential nature of the problem.

In the next chapter, we consider the evalua-tion of investments when we have information about risk and expected return developed in this chapter. We shall investigate the acceptance or rejection of risky investments in relation to the objective of maximizing share price. Our discus-sion will involve us in the valuation of the firm and in the considerable theoretical controversy that surrounds the question of risky investments and acquisitions. Again, we point out that Chap-ters 7 and 8 must be treated as a package.

Self-Correction Problems

1. Gomez Drug Products Company could invest in a new drug project with an estimated life of 3 years. If demand for the new drug in the first period is fa-vorable, it is almost certain that it will be favorable in periods 2 and 3. By the same token, if demand is low in the first period, it will be low in the two sub-sequent periods as well. Owing to this likely demand relationship, an assump-tion of perfect correlation of cash flows over time is appropriate. The cost of the project is $1 million, and possible cash flows for the three periods are:

Period 1		*Period 2*		*Period 3*	
PROBABILITY	CASH FLOW	PROBABILITY	CASH FLOW	PROBABILITY	CASH FLOW
.10	$ 0	.15	$ 100,000	.15	$ 0
.20	200,000	.20	400,000	.20	150,000
.40	400,000	.30	700,000	.30	300,000
.20	600,000	.20	1,000,000	.20	450,000
.10	800,000	.15	1,300,000	.15	600,000

   a. Assuming that the risk-free rate is 8 percent and that it is used as the discount rate, calculate the expected value and standard deviation of the probability distribution of possible net present values.

   b. Assuming a normal distribution, what is the probability of the project providing a net present value of (1) zero or less? (2) $300,000 or more? (3) $1,000,000 or more?

   c. Is the standard deviation calculated larger or smaller than it would be under an assumption of independence of cash flows over time?

2. Zello Creamery Company would like a new product line—puddings. The expected value and standard deviation of the probability distribution of possible net present values for the product line are $12,000 and $9,000, respectively. The company's existing lines are ice cream, cottage cheese, and yogurt. The expected values of net present value and standard deviations for these product lines are:

	Net Present Value	σ
Ice cream	$16,000	$8,000
Cottage cheese	20,000	7,000
Yogurt	10,000	4,000

The correlation coefficients between products are:

	Ice Cream	Cottage Cheese	Yogurt	Pudding
Ice cream	1.00			
Cottage cheese	.90	1.00		
Yogurt	.80	.84	1.00	
Pudding	.40	.20	.30	1.00

   a. Compute the expected value and the standard deviation of the probability distribution of possible net present values for a combination consisting of existing products.

   b. Compute the expected value and standard deviation for a combination consisting of existing products plus pudding. Compare your results in parts a and b. What can you say about the pudding line?

3. Feldstein Drug Company is considering a new drug, which would be sold over the counter without a prescription. To develop the drug and to market it on a regional basis will cost $12 million over the next 2 years, $6 million in each year. Expected cash inflows associated with the project for years 3 through 8 are $1 million, $2 million, $4 million, $4 million, $3 million, and $1 million, respectively. If the project is successful, at the end of year 5 the company will have the option to invest an additional $10 million to secure a national market. The probability of success is .60; if not successful, the company will not invest the $10 million and there will be no incremental expected cash flows. If successful, however, cash flows are expected to be $6 million higher in each of the years 6 through 10 than

would otherwise be the case with a probability of .50, and $4 million higher with a probability of .50. The company's required rate of return for the project is 14 percent.

a. What is the net present value of the initial project? Is it acceptable?

b. What is the worth of the project if we take account of the option to expand? Is the project acceptable?

Problems

1. The probability distribution of possible net present values for project X has an expected value of $20,000 and a standard deviation of $10,000. Assuming a normal distribution, calculate the probability that the net present value will be zero or less; that it will be greater than $30,000; and that it will be less than $5,000.

2. The Dewitt Corporation has determined the following discrete probability distributions for net cash flows generated by a contemplated project:

Period 1		Period 2		Period 3	
PROBABILITY	CASH FLOW	PROBABILITY	CASH FLOW	PROBABILITY	CASH FLOW
.10	$1,000	.20	$1,000	.30	$1,000
.20	2,000	.30	2,000	.40	2,000
.30	3,000	.40	3,000	.20	3,000
.40	4,000	.10	4,000	.10	4,000

a. Assume that probability distributions of cash flows for future periods are independent. Also, assume that the risk-free rate is 7 percent. If the proposal will require an initial outlay of $5,000, determine the mean net present value.

b. Determine the standard deviation about the mean.

c. If the total distribution is approximately normal and assumed continuous, what is the probability of the net present value being zero or less?

d. What is the probability that the net present value will be greater than zero?

e. What is the probability that the profitability index will be 1.00 or less?

f. What is the probability that the profitability index will be greater than 2.00?

3. Ponape Lumber Company is evaluating a new saw with a life of 2 years. The saw costs $3,000, and future after-tax cash flows depend on demand for the

company's products. The probability tree of possible future cash flows associated with the new saw is:

Year 1		Year 2		
INITIAL PROBABILITY	CASH FLOW	CONDITIONAL PROBABILITY	CASH FLOW	*Branch*
		.3	$1,000	1
.4	$1,500	.4	1,500	2
		.3	2,000	3
		.4	$2,000	4
.6	$2,500	.4	2,500	5
		.2	3,000	6

a. What are the joint probabilities of occurrence of the various branches?

b. If the risk-free rate is 10 percent, what are the mean and standard deviation of the probability distribution of possible net present values?

c. Assuming a normal distribution, what is the probability the actual net present value will be less than zero?

4. Xonics Graphics is evaluating a new technology for its reproduction equipment. The technology will have a 3-year life and cost $1,000. Its impact on cash flows is subject to risk. Management estimates that there is a 50–50 chance that the technology will either save the company $1,000 in the first year or save it nothing at all. If nothing at all, savings in the last 2 years would be zero. Even worse, in the second year an additional outlay of $300 may be required to convert back to the original process, for the new technology may result in less efficiency. Management attaches a 40 percent probability to this occurrence, given the fact that the new technology "bombs out" in the first year. If the technology proves itself, second-year cash flows may be either $1,800, $1,400, or $1,000, with probabilities of .20, .60, and .20, respectively. In the third year, cash inflows are expected to be $200 greater or $200 less than the cash flow in period 2, with an equal chance of occurrence. (Again, these cash flows depend on the cash flow in period 1 being $1,000.) All the cash flows are after taxes.

a. Set up a probability tree to depict the foregoing cash-flow possibilities.

b. Calculate a net present value for each three-year possibility, using a risk-free rate of 5 percent.

c. What is the risk of the project?

5. The Hume Corporation is faced with several possible investment projects. For each, the total cash outflow required will occur in the initial period. The cash outflows, expected net present values, and standard deviations are as follows. (All projects have been discounted at a risk-free rate of 8 percent, and it is assumed that the distributions of their possible net present values are normal.)

Project	Cost	Net Present Value	σ
A	$100,000	$10,000	$20,000
B	50,000	10,000	30,000
C	200,000	25,000	10,000
D	10,000	5,000	10,000
E	500,000	75,000	75,000

a. Determine the coefficient of variation for each of these projects. (Use cost plus net present value in the denominator of the coefficient.)

b. Ignoring size, do you find some projects clearly dominated by others?

c. May size be ignored?

d. What is the probability that each of the projects will have a net present value greater than 0?

e. What decision rule would you suggest for adoption of projects within this context? Which (if any) of the foregoing projects would be adopted under your rule?

6. The Windrop Company will invest in two of three possible proposals, the cash flows of which are normally distributed. The expected net present value (discounted at the risk-free rate) and the standard deviation for each proposal are given as follows:

Proposal	1	2	3
Expected net present value	$10,000	$8,000	$6,000
Standard deviation	4,000	3,000	4,000

Assuming the following correlation coefficients for each possible combination, which two proposals dominate?

Proposal	1	2	3	1 and 2	1 and 3	2 and 3
Correlation coefficient	1.00	1.00	1.00	.60	.40	.70

7. The Plaza Corporation is confronted with several combinations of risky investments.

Old Portfolio	Net Present Value	σ
A	$100,000	$200,000
B	20,000	80,000
C	75,000	100,000
D	60,000	150,000
E	50,000	20,000
F	40,000	60,000

New Portfolio	Net Present Value	σ
G	$120,000	$170,000
H	90,000	70,000
I	50,000	100,000
J	75,000	30,000

a. Plot the portfolios.

b. Which portfolios dominate?

8. The Ferret Pet Company is considering a new location. If it constructs an office and 100 cages, the cost will be $100,000 and the project is likely to produce net cash flows of $17,000 per year for 15 years, after which the leasehold on the land expires and there will be no residual value. The company's required return is 18 percent. If the location proves favorable, Ferret Pet will be able to expand by another 100 cages at the end of 4 years. The cost per cage would be $200. With the new cages, incremental net cash flows of $17,000 per year for years 5 through 15 would be expected. The company believes there is a 50–50 chance that the location will prove to be a favorable one.

   a. Is the initial project acceptable?

   b. What is the value of the option? the worth of the project with the option? Is it acceptable?

9. The Kazin Corporation is introducing a new product, which it can distribute initially either in the state of Georgia or in the entire Southeast. If it distributes in Georgia alone, plant and marketing will cost $5 million, and Kazin can reevaluate the project at the end of 3 years to decide whether to go regional. To go regional at the end of the 3 years would cost another $10 million. To distribute regionally from the outset would cost $12 million. The risk-free rate is 4 percent. In either case, the product will have a life of 6 years, after which the plant will be worthless. Given the graphical information in Figure 7-8 and the following data, what policy should Kazin adopt?

Expected Cash Flows (in Thousands)

Branch	0	1	2	3	4	5	6
			Year				
1	$ −5,000	$1,000	$ 3,000	$ 5,000	$ 7,000	$ 4,000	$2,000
2	−5,000	1,000	3,000	−7,000	10,000	20,000	8,000
3	−5,000	1,000	3,000	−7,000	8,000	6,000	4,000
4	−5,000	200	400	1,000	2,000	1,000	200
5	−5,000	200	400	−11,000	8,000	15,000	5,000
6	−5,000	200	400	−11,000	3,000	4,000	4,000
7	−12,000	3,000	10,000	15,000	20,000	12,000	5,000
8	−12,000	1,000	2,000	3,000	4,000	3,000	1,000

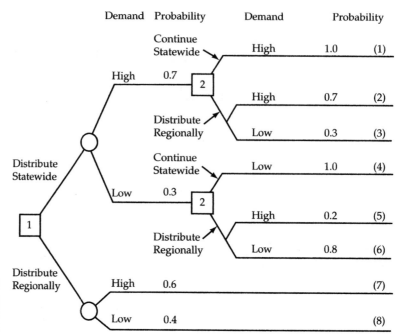

FIGURE 7-8

Decision tree: statewide versus regional distribution

10. ABC Corporation is ordering a special-purpose piece of machinery costing $9,000 with a life of 2 years, after which there is no expected salvage value. The possible incremental net cash flows are:

	Year 1		Year 2	
CASH FLOW	PROBABILITY	CASH FLOW	CONDITIONAL PROBABILITY
$6,000	.3	$2,000	.3
		3,000	.5
		4,000	.2
7,000	.4	4,000	.3
		5,000	.4
		6,000	.3
8,000	.3	6,000	.2
		7,000	.5
		8,000	.3

The company's required rate of return for this investment is 8 percent.

    a. Calculate the mean of the probability distribution of possible net present values.

    b. Suppose now that the possibility of abandonment exists and that the abandonment value of the project at the end of year 1 is $4,500. Calculate the new mean *NPV*, assuming the company abandons the project if it is worthwhile to do so. Compare your calculations with those in part a. What are the implications?

Solutions to Self-Correction Problems

1.   a. The expected values of the distributions of cash flows for the three periods are $400,000, $700,000, and $300,000. The standard deviations of the cash flows for the three periods are

$$\sigma_1 = [.1(0 - 400{,}000)^2 + .2(200{,}000 - 400{,}000)^2$$
$$+ .2(600{,}000 - 400{,}000)^2 + .1(800{,}000 - 400{,}000)^2]^{1/2}$$
$$= [48{,}000{,}000{,}000]^{1/2} = \$219{,}089$$
$$\sigma_2 = [.15(100{,}000 - 700{,}000)^2 + .2(400{,}000 - 700{,}000)^2$$
$$+ .2(1{,}000{,}000 - 700{,}000)^2 + .15(1{,}300{,}000 - 700{,}000)^2]^{1/2}$$
$$= [144{,}000{,}000{,}000]^{1/2} = \$379{,}474$$
$$\sigma_3 = [.15(0 - 300{,}000)^2 + .2(150{,}000 - 300{,}000)^2$$
$$+ .2(450{,}000 - 300{,}000)^2 + .15(600{,}000 - 300{,}000)^2]^{1/2}$$
$$= [36{,}000{,}000{,}000]^{1/2} = \$189{,}737$$

    b. The standard deviation of the probability distribution of possible net present values under the assumption of perfect correlation of cash flows over time is

$$\sigma = \frac{\$219{,}089}{1.08} + \frac{\$379{,}474}{(1.08)^2} + \frac{\$189{,}737}{(1.08)^3} = \$678{,}818$$

The mean net present value of the project is

$$NPV = -\$1{,}000{,}000 + \frac{\$400{,}000}{1.08} + \frac{\$700{,}000}{(1.08)^2} + \frac{\$300{,}000}{(1.08)^3} = \$208{,}659$$

The standardized differences for zero, $300,000, and $1 million are:

For zero or less

$$S = \frac{0 - 208{,}659}{678{,}818} = .307$$

For $300,000 or more

$$S = \frac{300{,}000 - 208{,}659}{678{,}818} = .135$$

For $1,000,000 or more

$$S = \frac{1,000,000 - 208,659}{678,818} = 1.166$$

c. From Table C, these standardized differences correspond to probabilities of approximately .38, .45, and .12, respectively. The standard deviation calculated under this assumption is much larger than it would be under an assumption of independence of cash flows over time.

2.   a. Net present value   = $16,000 + $20,000 + $10,000 = $46,000

Standard deviation = $[(8,000)^2 + (2)(.9)(8,000)(7,000)$
$+ (2)(.8)(8,000)(4,000) + (7,000)^2$
$+ (2)(.84)(7,000)(4,000) + (4,000)^2]^{1/2}$
$= [328,040,000]^{1/2} = $18,112$

b. Net present value   = $46,000 + $12,000 = $58,000

Standard deviation = $[328,040,000 + (9,000)^2$
$+ (2)(.4)(9,000)(8,000) + (2)(.2)(9,000)(7,000)$
$+ (2)(.3)(9,000)(4,000)]^{1/2} = [513,440,000]^{1/2}$
$= $22,659$

The coefficient of variation of existing projects $(\sigma/NPV) = 18,112/46,000 = .39$. The coefficient of variation for existing projects plus puddings = $22,659/58,000 = .39$. Although the pudding line has a higher coefficient of variation $(9,000/12,000 = .75)$ than existing products, indicating a higher degree of risk, the correlation of this product line with existing lines is sufficiently low as to bring the coefficient of variation for all products including puddings in line with that for only existing products.

3.

		Cash Flow (in Millions)	
Time	**INITIAL PROJECT**	**SCENARIO 1 PROBABILITY = .3**	**SCENARIO 2 PROBABILITY = .3**
1	−$6		
2	−6		
3	1		
4	2		
5	4	−$10	−$10
6	4	6	4
7	3	6	4
8	1	6	4
9		6	4
10		6	4
NPV (14%)	−$2.57	$5.51	$1.94

a. At time 0, the initial project has an *NPV* of –\$2.57 million, and it would be rejected.

b. Option value $= .3(\$5.51) + .3(\$1.94) + .4(0)$

$= \$2.23$ million

Worth of project $= -\$2.57 + \$2.23 = -\$.34$ million

While the option value raises the worth of the project substantially, it does not entirely offset the initial project's negative *NPV*. Therefore, we still would reject the project.

Selected References

AGGARWAL, RAJ, and LUC A. SOENEN, "Project Exit Value as a Measure of Flexibility and Risk Exposure," *Engineering Economist*, 35 (Fall 1989), 39–54.

BERGER, PHILIP G., ELI OFEK, and ITZHAK SWARY, "Investor Valuation of the Abandonment Option," *Journal of Financial Economics*, 42 (October 1996), 257–87.

BRENNAN, MICHAEL J., "Latent Assets," *Journal of Finance*, 45 (July 1990), 709–30.

BRENNAN, MICHAEL J., and EDUARDO S. SCHWARTZ, "A New Approach to Evaluating Natural Resource Investments," *Midland Corporate Finance Journal*, 3 (Spring 1985), 37–47.

DIXIT, AVINASH K., "Entry and Exit Decisions under Uncertainty," *Journal of Political Economy*, 97 (June 1989), 620–38.

DIXIT, AVINASH K., and ROBERT S. PINDYCK, "The Options Approach to Capital Investment," *Harvard Business Review*, 73 (May–June 1995), 105–15.

FAMA, EUGENE F., "Discounting under Uncertainty," *Journal of Business*, 69, No. 4 (1996), 415–28.

HERTZ, DAVID B., "Risk Analysis in Capital Investment," *Harvard Business Review*, 42 (January–February 1964), 95–106.

INGERSOLL, JONATHAN E., JR., and STEPHEN A. ROSS, "Waiting to Invest: Investment and Uncertainty," *Journal of Business*, 65, No. 1 (1992), 1–29.

MCDONALD, ROBERT L., and DANIEL R. SIEGEL, "Investment and the Valuation of Firms When There Is an Option to Shut Down," *International Economic Review*, 26 (June 1985), 331–49.

———, "The Value of Waiting to Invest," *Quarterly Journal of Economics*, 101 (November 1986), 707–27.

MILLER, EDWARD M., "Uncertainty Induced Bias in Capital Budgeting," *Financial Management*, 7 (Autumn 1978), 12–18.

PINDYCK, ROBERT S., "Irreversibility, Uncertainty, and Investment," *Journal of Economic Literature*, 29 (September 1991), 1110–52.

———, "Investments of Uncertain Cost," *Journal of Financial Economics*, 34 (August 1993), 53–76.

QUIGG, LAURA, "Empirical Testing of Real Option-Pricing Models," *Journal of Finance*, 48 (June 1993), 621–40.

ROBICHEK, ALEXANDER A., and JAMES C. VAN HORNE, "Abandonment Value and Capital Budgeting," *Journal of Finance*, 22 (December 1967), 557–89; Edward A. Dyl and Hugh W. Long, "Comment," *Journal of Finance*, 24 (March 1969), 88–95; and Robichek and Van Horne, "Reply," *Ibid.*, pp. 96–97.

ROSS, STEPHEN A., "Uses, Abuses, and Alternatives to the Net Present Value Rule," *Financial Management*, 24 (Autumn 1995), 96–101.

VAN HORNE, JAMES C., "Capital-Budgeting Decisions Involving Combinations of Risky Investments," *Management Science*, 13 (October 1966), 84–92.

———, "The Analysis of Uncertainty Resolution in Capital Budgeting for New Products," *Management Science*, 15 (April 1969), 376–86.

———, "The Variation of Project Life as a Means for Adjusting for Risk," *Engineering Economist*, 21 (Spring 1976), 151–58.

Wachowicz's Web World is an excellent overall Web site produced and maintained by my coauthor of *Fundamentals of Financial Management*, John M. Wachowicz Jr. It contains descriptions of and links to many finance Web sites and articles. *www.prenhall.com/wachowicz*.

Creating Value through Required Returns

Our eyes are still on the stockholders and the maximization of their value. By investing monies in products and projects, a company creates value if the expected return exceeds the return required by the financial markets for the risk involved. In previous chapters, we measured the risk of individual and combined investments. But knowing how risky is not enough; we must know how costly the risk is — that is, its market price. The idea is a simple one; we try to determine the opportunity cost of a capital investment by relating it to a financial market investment with the same risk. We want to better understand why companies like Cisco Systems (U.S.), Hennes & Mauritz (Sweden), Aegon Insurance (Netherlands), and Nokia (Finland) have such extraordinary growth in market capitalization, healthy cash flow margins, and accounting returns on equity capital. ■

FOUNDATIONS OF VALUE CREATION

In general, corporations that are situated in attractive industries and/or attain a sustainable competitive advantage within an industry are able to earn excess returns and create value. These are the things that give rise to positive net-present-value projects, ones that provide expected returns in excess of what the financial markets require.

Industry Attractiveness

At an annual meeting of Berkshire Hathaway, renowned investor Warren Buffett said, "It is better to be an average management in a wonderful business than a marvelous management in a lousy business." Favorable industry characteristics include the growth phase of a product cycle, barriers to entry, and other protective devices such as patents, temporary monopoly power, and/or oligopoly pricing where nearly all competitors are profitable. Probably the most important of these are explicit, as well as implicit, barriers to entry. **Industry attractiveness** has to do with the relative position of an industry in the spectrum of return-generating possibilities.

Competitive Advantage

Competitive advantage involves the relative position of a company within an industry. The company could be multidivisional, in which case competitive advantage needs to be judged industry by industry. The avenues to competitive advantage are several: cost advantage, marketing and price advantage, and superior organizational capability (corporate culture).[1] Cost advantage has to do with the

---

[1]For an extensive discussion of this concept and much more, see Michael E. Porter, *Competitive Advantage* (New York: Free Press, 1985).

The bedrock of excess returns resides in industry attractiveness and competitive advantage within an industry.

relative cost of producing and distributing a product or service, as well as with the utilization of assets (receivables, inventories, and fixed assets) through better asset turnover. Marketing and price advantage involves successfully rolling out new products or services, differentiating them in the marketplace, and picking the proper price point on the demand curve. Organizational capability transcends cost and marketing advantage, recognizing that certain executives simply are better able to manage people and to get the most from them. Competitive advantage is eroded with competition. Relative cost or marketing superiority, for example, is conspicuous and will be attacked. The mark of a successful company is one that continually identifies and exploits opportunities for excess returns. Only with a sequence of short-run advantages can any overall competitive advantage be sustained.

Thus, industry attractiveness and competitive advantage are principal sources of value creation. The more favorable these are, the more likely the company is to have expected returns in excess of what the financial markets require for the risk involved.

Valuation Underpinnings

We can think of the required return as the cost of obtaining and retaining capital from investors. As we know, most investors are concerned with unavoidable risk, the risk that cannot be avoided by diversification of the stocks, bonds, and other financial assets they hold. The required rate of return on investment is the return on a risk-free asset plus the market price of risk to the investor due to one or more factors. The required return can be expressed in terms of a factor model using multiple risk components to characterize unavoidable risk (Chapter 4), in terms of the single-factor capital asset pricing model (CAPM) where the factor is the return on the market portfolio (Chapter 3), or the CAPM extended to include additional variables (Chapter 4). As these models were previously discussed, we do not dwell on them here.

Whatever the valuation model, for a given degree of risk the financial markets expect a company to earn a minimum required return commensurate with the risk involved. The greater the systematic, or unavoidable, risk, the greater the return the financial markets expect of an investment opportunity. If product markets were perfect, one could not expect to find opportunities providing returns in excess of the return required by the financial markets. With imperfect product markets, however, it may be possible to find projects providing excess returns. In the parlance of economists, these excess returns are economic rents. Although competition among firms tends to drive economic rents to zero, sufficient lags may allow them to be earned temporarily.

These opportunities may arise anywhere along the risk spectrum—in a safe, mature business or in a risky, growth-oriented business. As long as we have the required return right for project acceptance, value will be created. There is nothing magical about growth per se; it is the expected return of a project *relative* to the standard imposed by the financial markets that matters.

Separation of Required Return and the Firm   Another implication is that the required rate of return for the project does not depend on the company undertaking the investment. Given the project's systematic risk, the market requires a single return. Therefore, the required rate of return on the project is the same for any firm that might invest in it. Stated differently, the systematic risk of a project is the same for all companies; therefore, the project's required return is the same. This is not to say that the project is equally valuable to all firms. Some companies will derive greater incremental cash flows from it than will others. Because of differences in expertise, management efficiency, synergism, and so forth, the expected return can vary among companies. Consequently, the project will be more valuable to some firms than to others, but the acceptance standard will be the same for all firms considering the project.

Red Herring's 50 Most Important Public Companies in the World

Red Herring, *a magazine devoted to technology, presented in the June 2000 issue the 100 brightest stars of the digital universe. Of these, 50 were private companies and 50 were public. Criteria used to determine inclusion were the company's strategy, its execution, its products and services, its brand value, its financing, and its competition. The public companies on the list were:*

Akamai Technologies, U.S.	Lucent Technologies, U.S.
Amazon.com, U.S.	MCI WorldCom, U.S
American Online, U.S.	Microsoft, U.S.
Apple Computer, U.S.	Millennium Pharmaceuticals, U.S.
Applied Materials, U.S.	Morgan Stanley Dean Witter, U.S.
ARM Holdings, U.K.	Nokia, Finland
AT&T, U.S.	Nortel Networks, Canada
Broadcom, U.S.	NTT DoCoMo, Japan
BroadVision, U.S.	Oracle, U.S.
Charles Schwab, U.S.	Pacific Century CyberWorks, China
Cisco Systems, U.S.	Palm, U.S.
CMGI, U.S.	PE Corporation, U.S.
Commerce One, U.S.	PMC-Sierra, Canada
Dell Computers, U.S.	Red Hat, U.S.
eBay, U.S.	Sapient, U.S.
EMC Corporation, U.S.	Siebel Systems, U.S.
Exodus Communications, U.S.	Sony, Japan
Ford Motor, U.S.	Sun Microsystems, U.S.
Goldman Sachs, U.S.	Taiwan Semiconductor, Taiwan
Hughes Electronics, U.S.	Texas Instruments, U.S.
IBM, U.S.	United Parcel Service, U.S.
Immunex, U.S.	Ventro.com, U.S.
Inktomi, U.S.	VeriSign, U.S.
Intel, U.S.	Vodafone/Air Touch, U.K.
JDS Uniphase, U.S. & Canada	Yahoo, U.S.

Though Red Herring's *center of interest obviously is the United States, their notions as to the movers and shakers in the digital economy and valuation are interesting.*

REQUIRED MARKET-BASED RETURN FOR A SINGLE PROJECT

Having discussed value creation in general, we want to know how to go about establishing the return the financial markets require. First we examine the required return for a single project. This will be followed by the required return for a division of a company with projects/products having similar risks. Finally, we consider the overall company and its weighted average cost of capital.

To make matters easier, assume initially that a project is financed entirely by equity and that all financial market information pertains to unlevered situations. (Modification for leverage comes later.) Under these circumstances, the required rate of return for the project can be expressed as a function of its beta, in a CAPM context, or of its factor risks, in an APT factor model context (see Chapters 3 and 4). Note that the required return derived is market based, using tradable securities. The return on investment for capital projects, however, usually is expressed in terms of the internal rate of return. This measure is based on the time-magnitude relationship between cash inflows and the initial cash outflow. It does not take account of the changes in market value of the project from period to period. Thus, there is a problem of incompatibility between the return measure for a security and that for a capital project.

Proxy Company Estimates

In many cases, a project is similar to a company whose stock is publicly traded. This is particularly true of new product decisions. If a publicly traded company, or companies, can be identified, we can use market information on these companies to derive a surrogate required return on equity capital.

Proxy companies are stand-alone companies with publicly traded stock that engage in businesses like the project or division.

Suppose a chemical company with a beta of 1.10 is considering the formation of a real estate subsidiary. The relevant required rate of return is not for the chemical company but for other real estate firms. Stated differently, the market views the chemical company's venture in the same way it views other firms engaged solely in real estate. By concentrating on companies in the same line of business as the firm desires to enter, we can find surrogates that approximate the systematic risk of the project. Exact duplication of the project's risk is unlikely, but reasonable approximations are possible.

The search for similar companies usually is industry based. In that regard, one can turn to the SIC (Standard Industrial Classification) code to determine an initial sample.[2] From the sample of proxy companies, their betas are arrayed. If outliers are felt not to be comparable with the project in question, they should be culled.

Deriving Surrogate Returns   The steps needed to derive a surrogate required rate of return on equity are:

1. Determine a sample of companies that replicate as nearly as possible the business in which an investment is being contemplated. The matching will only be approximate.
2. Obtain the betas for each proxy company in the sample, if the CAPM is being used. These betas can be obtained from a number of services, in-

---

[2]Michael C. Ehrhardt and Yatin N. Bhagwat, "A Full-Information Approach for Estimating Divisional Betas," *Financial Management*, 20 (Summer 1991), 60–69, present a framework for determining industry betas when betas for companies in an industry are weighted by relative sales.

cluding Merrill Lynch, Credit Suisse-First Boston, Goldman Sachs, and Value Line Investment Survey.

3. Calculate the central tendency of the betas of the companies in the sample. Often the median is the best measure to use, because the arithmetic average is distorted by outliers. Sometimes a modal value will be best. In still other cases you may wish to weight the betas on the basis of the relative market capitalizations of the proxy companies (share price times the number of shares outstanding).

4. Derive the required rate of return on equity using the proxy beta obtained in step 3, together with the expected return on the market portfolio, $\overline{R}_m$, and the risk-free rate, R_f.

To illustrate, suppose that 1.60 is the median beta for a sample of real estate companies. We use this beta as a surrogate for the beta of the project contemplated by our chemical company. If the expected return on the market portfolio is 11 percent and the risk-free rate 6 percent, the required return on the project will be

$$R_k = .06 + (.11 - .06)1.60 = 14.0\%$$

Therefore, 14 percent is used as the required rate of return for the project. If the real estate venture is expected to provide an internal rate of return in excess of this rate, the project should be accepted according to this line of reasoning. (Remember, there is no leverage.) If not, it should be rejected.

Risk-Free Rate and Market Return

In addition to beta, it is important that the numbers used for the market return and for the risk-free rate be the best estimates of the future possible. The issues involved and the sources of information were discussed at length in Chapter 3, but it is useful to briefly review a couple of points.

The risk-free rate is controversial, not as to the security that should be used but the maturity. All agree that the proper instrument is a Treasury security. But the proper maturity is another matter. As the market models are one period, some contend a short-term rate, such as that for a Treasury bill, should be used. Others argue that because capital investment projects are long-lived, a long-term Treasury bond rate should be used. Still others, myself included, feel more comfortable with an intermediate-term rate, such as that on three-year Treasury notes. This middle position recognizes that a number of capital equipment investments are intermediate term in nature, and also that the intermediate-term rate fluctuates less than the short-term rate.

For the expected return on the market portfolio of stocks, as depicted by Standard & Poor's 500-Stock Index or the New York Stock Exchange Index, one can use consensus estimates of security analysts, economists, and others who regularly predict such returns. Credit Suisse-First Boston, Goldman Sachs, Merrill Lynch, and other investment banks make these predictions, often on a monthly basis. The estimated annual returns are for the immediate future.

The expected return on the market portfolio has exceeded the risk-free rate by anywhere from 3 to 7 percent in recent decades. The magnitude of this **equity risk premium** depends on which maturity is used for the risk-free security and on risk aversion by investors. The equity risk premium measure we employ is ex ante, or forward looking, as opposed to ex post, or backward looking at what happened in the past. Although some use the historical risk premium, I prefer the ex ante approach for the reasons taken up in Chapter 3. In what follows, however, either measure could be employed.

APT Factor Model Approach

Market models include the CAPM, extended CAPM, and the APT.

For use of factor models, computations are more involved. If you are confident in the factor risks specified and in the consistency of parameter estimates, we learned in Chapter 4 that it is straightforward to solve for the required rate of return for a proxy company. You do the following: (1) take the firm's reaction coefficients to the various factor risks; (2) multiply them by their respective lambdas, the market prices of the factor risks; (3) sum the products; and (4) to this sum add the risk-free rate.

Suppose the risk factors of importance are unexpected changes in inflation, unexpected changes in overall economic output, and unexpected changes in default risk premiums between low- and high-grade bonds. Some proxy companies will have greater sensitivity to inflation than they do to the other factors. Other companies are more sensitive to default risk, and so forth. All of this was discussed in Chapter 4. The import is that APT factor models allow determination of the underlying sensitivities of an asset to broad economic and financial factors. These factors represent unavoidable (systematic) risk for the asset.

Instead of risk being captured by the proxy company's beta, it is a function of the responsiveness coefficients for each of the factors of importance. If these coefficients were readily available, as are betas for stocks, if the lambda risk premiums (market prices of risk) were known, and if we were confident that the factors specified were the appropriate ones, there would be no problem. As discussed in Chapter 4, however, there is not agreement as to what factors are important. Moreover, empirical inconsistencies appear in the measurement of the responsiveness coefficients. The APT factor model approach is going through refinement, but it has found considerable application in security analysis. It has potential for corporate finance, but as yet it has not been widely used.

Use of Accounting Betas

Another approach to calibrating risk is to develop betas for a company, or part thereof, based on accounting data. Here an accounting measure of return for a company or project, such as the return on assets, is related to an economywide index of returns, such as the average return on assets for nonfinancial corporations. Regressing the former on the latter, a beta or regression coefficient is determined that is said to depict the systematic risk of returns for the company or division. The procedure for determining and evaluating accounting betas is analogous to that used for market betas previously illustrated. The appeal of this approach is that it does not require data on market returns for the project. Such data often are difficult, if not impossible, to obtain. In contrast, data on accounting returns are readily available.

In Lieu of Market Information In developing countries without vibrant stock markets, obtaining proxy-company market information may be impossible. Here, too, accounting data may be useful. For example, we might regress accounting returns for a line of business against changes in the gross domestic product of the country. Both measures may be in nominal terms or, where inflation is a matter of concern, in real terms. The important thing is that both be on the same basis.

Calculating Betas Manually

The beta of a stock is simply the slope of the regression line when excess returns (above the risk-free rate) for the stock are regressed against excess returns for the market portfolio. The least squares method fits a regression line to the observations so that the sum of the squares of the deviations from that line is as small as possible. Beta information is available from a number of services, as we have mentioned. To illustrate the manual calculation of a beta, suppose Standard & Poor's 500-Stock Index returns for each of the past 10 quarters are those shown in column (1) of Table 8-1. The risk-free rate is shown in column (2). In column (3) of the table, the excess return for the market index is determined simply by subtracting the risk-free rate from the market return. In the next column, this excess return is squared and the sum appears at the bottom.

TABLE 8-1

Computation of Excess Returns for a Market Index and Project and Cross Product

Quarter	(1) Market Return R_{mt}	(2) Risk-Free Rate	(3) Excess Market Return (M) (1)−(2)	(4) Excess Market Return Squared (M)² (3)²	(5) Stock Return R_{jt}	(6) Excess Return Stock (J) (5)−(2)	(7) Cross Product Excess Returns (MJ) (3) × (6)
1	.11	.05	.06	.0036	.091	.041	.0025
2	.17	.07	.10	.0100	.110	.040	.0040
3	(.02)	.06	(.08)	.0064	.024	(.036)	.0029
4	.25	.08	.17	.0289	.234	.154	.0262
5	.18	.06	.12	.0144	.132	.072	.0086
6	.28	.07	.21	.0441	.275	.205	.0431
7	(.08)	.07	(.15)	.0225	.121	.051	(.0077)
8	.27	.09	.18	.0324	.292	.202	.0364
9	.14	.07	.07	.0049	.105	.035	.0025
10	.00	.08	(.08)	.0064	.077	(.003)	.0002
	1.30	.70	.60	.1736	1.461	.761	.1187
Average return			.06			.076	

The return on the stock for the 10 quarters is shown in column (5). In column (6), the stock's excess return above the risk-free rate is determined. In the last column, the cross product is calculated by multiplying the excess return for the market by the excess return for the stock. At the bottom of the columns, the sums of the numbers in the columns are determined, and in the next row, the average for two of them is computed. The average is simply the total divided by the number of quarters, which is 10.

The beta, or slope of the regression line, is determined by the following formula:

$$Beta = \frac{\sum MJ - n\overline{M}\overline{J}}{\sum M^2 - n\overline{M}^2}$$

where $\sum MJ$ is the sum of the cross products, n is the number of observations, $\overline{M}$ is the average excess market return, $\overline{J}$ is the average excess stock return, and $\sum M^2$ is the sum of the squares of excess market returns. For our example in Table 8-1, the beta is

$$Beta = \frac{.1187 - (10)(.06)(.076)}{.1736 - (10)(.06)^2} = \frac{.0731}{.1376} = .53$$

A beta of .53 suggests that the stock has only moderate systematic risk. Again we stress that computer routines can easily solve for the slope of a linear regression line, but it is useful to understand how they work.

Recognizing the advantages of data availability, we question only whether accounting betas are good surrogates for market betas. Although various empirical studies show a significant statistical association between accounting and market betas for companies, the explanatory power is only moderate. For the individual company, the ability to predict market betas on the basis of accounting betas is too low to make the approach anything but a crude approximation; therefore, we concentrate on developing market return information.

MODIFICATION FOR LEVERAGE

So far we have assumed all equity financing and that the beta employed pertains to an unlevered situation. It is appropriate now to modify the approach for leverage. The beta, and hence the required return of a project, is a function of both business risk and the degree of leverage. If the tenets of the capital asset pricing model hold, the relationship shown in Fig. 8-1 will prevail. As a company increases its degree of debt financing, the project's beta and required return increase in the linear manner shown. With respect to leverage, it is important that the beta used for the project corresponds with the way the firm intends to finance.

If a proxy company is used to determine the project's beta, and it has significant leverage while we do not, the use of its beta will bias things toward a higher required return on equity than is justified. This occurrence can be seen in the figure, where we assume the proxy company has leverage of x. As a result, its required return is r_x. Now if we employ no leverage, our true required return for the project is r_0. By using the proxy company's beta, however, we end up with a much higher required return. The difference between r_x and r_0 is due solely to differences in leverage. In essence, the firm unnecessarily penalizes itself in the return it requires. As can easily be visualized, the opposite occurs if the proxy company uses no leverage and we are levered.

FIGURE 8-1

Relationship between the required return on equity and leverage

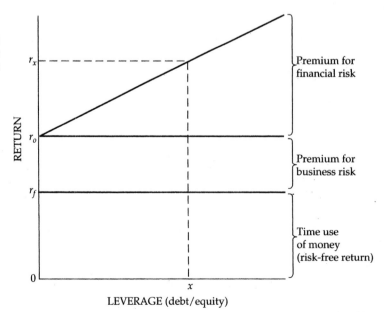

Adjusting the Beta for Leverage

When the leverage of the proxy company differs significantly from the leverage the firm wishes to employ, it may be desirable to adjust the beta of the proxy company. The procedure presented below takes as a given the assumptions of the capital asset pricing model. In the end, we shall qualify the results for the considerations to be taken up in Chapter 9, where the question of capital structure is examined in depth.

With corporate income taxes, interest payments are deductible for tax purposes. Under these circumstances, Hamada, as well as others, has demonstrated that the required rate of return for a stock is[3]

$$R_j = R_f + \left(\frac{\overline{R}_m - R_f}{\sigma_m^2}\right)(r_{ju,m}\sigma_{ju}\sigma_m)\left[1 + \frac{D}{S}(1 - T_c)\right] \tag{8-1}$$

where R_f = risk-free rate

$\overline{R}_m$ = the expected return on the market portfolio

σ_m = standard deviation of the probability distribution of possible market returns

$r_{ju,m}$ = correlation coefficient between returns for security *j in the absence of leverage* and the market portfolio

σ_{ju} = standard deviation of the probability distribution of possible returns for security *j in the absence of leverage*

D/S = debt-to-equity ratio in market value terms

T_c = corporate tax rate

The important thing to note is that the covariance between returns, which is the second bracketed term in the equation, is as if the company had an all-equity capital structure.

Rearranging the Formula   Equation (8-1) can be expressed in terms of the more familiar beta:

$$R_j = R_f + (\overline{R}_m - R_f)\beta_{ju}\left[1 + \frac{D}{S}(1 - T_c)\right] \tag{8-2}$$

where β_{ju} is the beta measuring the responsiveness of the excess return for the security *in the absence of leverage* to the excess return for the market portfolio. Thus, the overall required rate of return is composed of the risk-free rate, R_f, plus a premium for business risk, $(\overline{R}_m - R_f)\beta_{ju}$, and a premium for financial risk:

$$(\overline{R}_m - R_f)\beta_{ju}\left[\frac{D}{S}(1 - T_c)\right]$$

The measured, or observed, beta for the stock, β_j, embodies both risks and is simply

$$\beta_j = \beta_{ju}\left[1 + \frac{D}{S}(1 - T_c)\right] \tag{8-3}$$

---

[3]Robert S. Hamada, "Portfolio Analysis, Market Equilibrium and Corporation Finance," *Journal of Finance*, 24 (March 1969), 19–30.

Beta modification
for leverage first
unlevers the proxy
company's beta and
then relevers it for a
different degree of
leverage.

Rearranging the beta for the stock *in the absence of leverage* is

$$\beta_{ju} = \frac{\beta_j}{1 + \dfrac{D}{S}(1 - T_c)} \qquad (8\text{-}4)$$

Illustration   Given these expressions, we are able to derive the beta *in the absence of leverage* for a particular stock. Suppose the measured beta, β_j, for security j were 1.4; the debt-to-equity ratio in market value terms, D/S, were .70; and the tax rate were 40 percent (federal and state). Therefore, the unlevered beta would be

$$\beta_{ju} = \frac{1.4}{1 + .7(.6)} = .99$$

If we now wanted to determine the beta for a different amount of leverage, we would use Eq. (8-3). Suppose we were interested in using security j as a proxy for the systematic risk of our project. However, we employ a debt-to-equity ratio of 0.3 as opposed to the 0.7 for security j, and our marginal tax rate is 35 percent instead of 40 percent. Therefore, the adjusted beta is

$$\text{Adjusted } \beta_j = .99[1 + .3(.65)] = 1.18$$

This beta contrasts with .99 for security j *in the absence of leverage* and with 1.40 for security j with a debt-to-equity ratio of 0.7. Note that to determine beta *in the absence of leverage* we use the debt-to-equity ratio and tax rate for the proxy company, whereas to calculate the adjusted beta we use our own debt-to-equity ratio and tax rate.

Important Caveats   In summary, we are able to derive an adjusted beta for a security under the assumption of a different proportion of debt than what occurs. We first estimate the beta for the stock *in the absence of leverage* and then adjust this figure for the proportion of leverage we wish to employ. The final result is an approximation of the beta that would prevail if the external company were to employ the desired proportion of debt. Again, it should be emphasized that the beta adjustment procedure is crude.

It assumes that capital markets are perfect except for the presence of corporate taxes. Indeed, the only adjustment, and a linear one at that, is for corporate taxes. Different imperfections will affect the beta adjustment formula differently, most reducing the adjustment made. Rather than get into the effect of these imperfections now, in Chapter 9 we assess the overall impact of capital structure on valuation. Until then, keep in mind the caveats, particularly when large beta adjustments are involved.

WEIGHTED AVERAGE REQUIRED RETURN

The final step is to use the adjusted beta to determine the cost of equity capital for the project and then to go on to determine a **weighted average required return**. Consider now a situation where a company finances with instruments additional to equity. We need to bring their costs into a blended required rate of return. This return is a function not only of the business risk of the company but also of the way in which it chooses to finance itself.

Separation of Investment from Financing

For the single project, as well as for portfolios of projects, we separate the investment from the financing decision. By its very nature, financing is "lumpy." On one occasion we may finance with debt, on another occasion we may draw upon retained earnings that reside in cash, and on yet another we may employ lease financing. By using only debt financing now, we draw on the overall debt capacity of the firm. There is an opportunity cost and that cost is the restoration of the equity base in future financings. The proportions of financing methods over time are what matter, not the specific financing of a given capital investment project. The blended required return embraces the explicit and opportunity costs of various forms of financing over time. Assumed then is a target capital structure, so that the discount rate employed to judge the merits of a risky capital investment is independent of the immediate means of financing.

Thus, the required return is the blended cost of acquiring various types of capital from lenders and investors. We consider now the costs of such, with the exception of the cost of equity, which we already have discussed.

Cost of Debt

To derive the explicit cost of debt, we solve for the discount rate, k, that equates the net proceeds of the debt issue with the present value of interest plus principal payments. Then we adjust the explicit cost obtained for the tax effect. If we denote the after-tax cost of debt by k_i, it can be approximated by

$$k_i = k(1 - t) \tag{8-5}$$

where k is the internal rate of return or yield and t is the marginal tax rate. Because interest charges are tax deductible, the after-tax cost of debt is substantially less than the before-tax cost. If a company were able to sell a new issue of 20-year bonds with an 8 percent coupon rate and realize net proceeds (after underwriting expenses) of $1,000 for each $1,000 face value bond, k would be 8 percent. If the income tax rate were 40 percent,

$$k_i = 8.0(1 - .40) = 4.8\%$$

We note that the 4.8 percent after-tax cost in our example represents the marginal, or incremental, cost of additional debt. It does not represent the cost of debt already employed.

Uncertain Future Tax Rate   The adjustment downward in the cost of debt funds for taxes holds only if the company has now and will have in the future a marginal tax rate of t. An unprofitable company that pays no taxes would have a cost of debt equal to the before-tax cost, k. Therefore, if interest payments on debt are to be entirely and immediately deductible for tax purposes, reported earnings must be zero or positive. If not, the loss may be carried back 3 years and applied to taxes previously paid. If reported earnings are sufficient in those years, the firm receives a tax refund, and the cash-flow effect is nearly the same as that which occurs if operations in the current year are profitable. If reported earnings in the prior 3 years do not offset the current year loss, however, the residual is carried forward to be applied to reported profits during the subsequent 15 years. In this case, part or all of the interest tax subsidy is postponed. In addition to the uncertainty regarding reported income, there is uncertainty regarding the corporate tax rate itself. Congress may change it, as we all know.

Because interest payments may not be tax deductible, their full burden could fall on a company's cash flow. Consequently, it may be inappropriate to treat the cost of debt as the interest rate times one minus the tax rate. Assuming there are time states during the life of the instrument in which the tax shield is not entirely applicable, this computation understates the cost of debt financing. The greater the number of time states in which the tax shield cannot be used, the more important it becomes to consider this factor in cost of debt analyses.

Cost of Preferred Stock

The cost of preferred stock is a function of its stated dividend. As we discuss in Chapter 20, this dividend is not a contractual obligation of the firm but is payable at the discretion of the board of directors. Consequently, unlike debt, it does not create a risk of legal bankruptcy. To holders of common stock, however, preferred stock is a security interest that takes priority over theirs. Most corporations that issue preferred stock intend to pay the stated dividend. As preferred stock has no maturity date, its cost may be represented as

$$k_p = \frac{D}{I_0} \tag{8-6}$$

where D is the stated annual dividend and I_0 represents the proceeds of the preferred stock issue. If a company were to sell an 8.4 percent preferred stock issue ($50 par value) and realize net proceeds of $48.37 a share, the cost of the preferred stock would be $4.20/$48.37=8.68 percent. Note that this cost is not adjusted for taxes, because the preferred stock dividend is paid after taxes. Thus, the explicit cost of preferred stock usually is greater than that for debt.

However, the preferred stock has a desirable feature to the corporate investor. The tax law provides that 70 percent of the dividends received by one corporation from another is exempt from taxation. This attraction on the demand side usually results in yields on preferred stocks being slightly below those on bonds of the same company. It is only after taxes that debt financing becomes more attractive.

Other Types of Financing

Although equity, debt, and preferred stock are the major sources, other types of financing include leasing, convertible securities, warrants, and other options. Because determining the costs of these types of financing involves some special and rather complex valuation issues, we postpone their treatment until Chapters 18, 21, and 22. Also, we ignore payables, accruals, and deferred taxes, not because they are unimportant sources of financing, but because they have no explicit interest cost. For our purposes in this chapter, knowing the costs of equity, debt, and preferred stock financing is sufficient for illustrating the overall required return for a company. When costs are later determined for other types of financing, they can be inserted in the weighting scheme about to be discussed.

Weighting the Costs

Once we have computed costs of individual components of the capital structure, we need to weight them according to some standard and calculate a **weighted average cost of capital (WACC)**. The weights should correspond to market values of the various forms of financing that we, the corporation, intend to employ. Because we are trying to maximize the value of the firm to our shareholders, market-value weights, as opposed to book-value weights, are consistent with this objective. Suppose that these weights are as follows:

Source	Proportion
Debt	30%
Preferred stock	10
Common-stock equity	60
	100%

To continue with our illustration, we previously determined that the after-tax cost of debt funds was 4.80 percent and the cost of preferred stock 8.68 percent. If the required return on the market portfolio, $\overline{R}_m$, is 11 percent, the risk-free rate, R_f, is 6 percent, and the proxy company beta, adjusted for leverage, is 1.10, then the **required return on equity** is

$$k_e = 6\% + (11\% - 6\%)1.10 = 11.50\%$$

Therefore, the weighted average required return on investment is

Source	Proportion	After-Tax Cost	Weighted Cost
Debt	30%	4.80%	1.44%
Preferred stock	10	8.68	.87
Common-stock equity	60	11.50	6.90
			9.21%

WACC is a blended required return of the various capital costs making up capital structure.

Thus, with the assumptions of this example, 9.21 percent represents the weighted average cost of the component methods of financing where each component is weighted according to market-value proportions.

Some Limitations

With the calculation of a weighted average cost of capital, the critical question is whether the figure represents the "true" cost of capital. The answer to this question depends on how accurately we have measured the individual marginal costs, on the weighting system, and on certain other assumptions. Assume for now that we are able to measure accurately the marginal costs of the individual sources of financing; let us examine the importance of the weighting system.

Marginal Weights   The critical assumption in any weighting system is that the firm will in fact raise capital in the proportions specified. Because the firm raises capital *marginally* to make a *marginal* investment in new projects, we need to work with the marginal cost of capital. This rate depends on the package of funds employed to finance investment projects. In other words, our concern is with new or incremental capital, not with capital raised in the past. For the weighted average cost of capital to represent a marginal cost, the weights employed must be marginal; that is, the weights must correspond to the proportions of financing inputs the firm intends to employ. If they do not, capital is raised on a marginal basis in proportions other than those used to calculate this cost.

As we have said, raising capital is "lumpy," and strict proportions cannot be maintained. Over time, however, most firms are able to finance in roughly a proportional manner. It is in this sense that we try to measure the marginal cost of capital for the package of financing employed. In other words, weighted average cost of capital calculations should ignore temporary deviations from a target capital structure. It is the target, or anticipated, capital structure that should be used to calculate the weighted average required return.

Flotation Costs   Flotation costs involved in the sale of common stock, preferred stock, or a debt instrument affect the profitability of a firm's investments. In many cases, the new issue must be priced below the market price of existing financing; in addition, there are out-of-pocket flotation costs. Owing to flotation costs, the amount of funds the firm receives is less than the price at which the issue is sold. The presence of flotation costs in financing requires that an adjustment be made in the evaluation of investment proposals.

That adjustment is made by adding flotation costs of financing to the project's initial cash outlay. Suppose an investment proposal costs $100,000, and to finance the project the company must raise $60,000 externally. Both debt and common stock are involved, and after-tax flotation costs come to $4,000. Therefore, $4,000 should be added to $100,000, bringing the total initial outlay to $104,000. In this way, the proposal is properly "penalized" for the flotation costs associated with its financing. The expected future cash flows associated with the project are discounted at the weighted average cost of capital. If the project were expected to provide annual cash inflows of $12,000 forever and the weighted average cost of capital were 10 percent, the project's net present value would be

$$NPV = \frac{\$12,000}{.10} - \$104,000 = \$16,000$$

This amount contrasts with a net present value of $20,000 if no adjustment is made for flotation costs.

Thus, the adjustment for flotation costs is made in the project's cash flows and not in the cost of capital. A second approach calls for an upward adjustment in the discount rate when flotation costs are present. Under this procedure, each component cost of capital would be recalculated by finding the discount rate that equates the present value of cash flows to suppliers of capital with the net proceeds of the security issue. The resulting component costs then would be weighted and combined to produce an overall "adapted" cost of capital for the firm. *NPVs* calculated using this method generally will be higher than those calculated when we adjust the initial outlay for flotation costs. It has been shown that adjusting the cost of capital for flotation costs results in a biased estimate of "true" value.[4] We agree with the arguments and favor the adjustment of initial outlay method.

---

[4]For a defense of the procedure, see Simon E. Keane, "The Investment Discount Rate: In Defense of the Market Rate on Interest," *Accounting and Business Research* (Summer 1976), 234; and John R. Ezzell and R. Burr Porter, "Flotation Costs and the Weighted Average Cost of Capital," *Journal of Financial and Quantitative Analysis*, 11 (September 1976), 403–13. For additional refinements, see F. K. Wright, "New-Issue Costs and Capital Budgeting," *Journal of Business Finance and Accounting*, 14 (Summer 1987).

Rationale for Weighted Average Cost

The rationale behind the use of a weighted average cost of capital is that by financing in the proportions specified and accepting projects yielding more than the weighted average required return, the firm is able to increase the market price of its stock. This increase occurs because the investment projects accepted are expected to return more on their equity-financed portions than the cost of equity capital, k_e. Once these expectations are apparent to the marketplace, the market price of the stock should rise, all other things remaining the same. The firm has accepted projects that are expected to provide a return greater than that required by investors at the margin, based on the risk involved.

Laddering of Returns Required To see this concept in the context of the capital asset pricing model, refer to Fig. 8-2. Here we have the familiar security market line with the required returns on debt, preferred stock, and common stock for a particular company. The cost of capital of the company is a weighted average of the required rates of return of the various components. If projects are accepted with a systematic risk of X and an expected return of k_o, the expected return will be just sufficient to compensate the various security holders at their required rates of return: k_i, k_p, and k_e. As a result, the investment will leave share price unchanged. If the expected return from the project is higher than k_o, with systematic risk the same, then this return will be more than sufficient to compensate debt holders, preferred stockholders, and common stockholders. The maximum claims of debt holders and preferred stockholders being fixed, most of the benefit will accrue to the common stockholders. In other words, their expected return will be in excess of that required, k_e. As a result, share price will increase as investors bid up the price of the stock until equilibrium is restored.

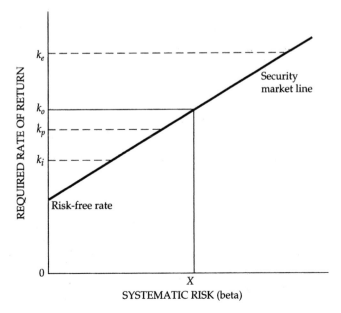

FIGURE 8-2

Required rates of return for debt (k_i), preferred stock (k_p), common stock equity (k_e), and the overall cost of capital (k_o) for an individual company

Economic Value Added and Market Value Added

Another way of expressing a company earning more than the financial markets require is through **economic value added (EVA),** which is a trademark of Stern Stewart Management Services, Inc. This financial consulting firm actively promotes the use of the concept in its engagements. Basically, EVA is the residual income a company earns after capital costs are deducted. More specifically, it is operating profits minus the required dollar-amount return for the capital employed. Suppose a company has operating profits of $35 million. It employs net assets of $180 million and the market-determined required return (WACC) is 12 percent. Therefore, the cost of capital is $180 million × .12 = $21.6 million. As a result (in millions):

EVA subtracts a capital charge, in dollars, from operating profits.

Operating profits	$35.0
Capital costs	21.6
EVA	$13.4

EVA enjoys popularity, as many executives prefer to have a dollar amount charge for the use of capital as opposed to a percent cost. The underlying idea is not new; it is simply the notion of earning returns in excess of what the financial markets require. To the extent a company finds that the concept better links corporate strategy and investments with shareholder value, it is a useful device. It does force attention to the balance sheet and the use of assets in support of operations. There are a number of variations of this theme. Clorox Company has derived a "Clorox Value Measure" to calibrate changes in the economic value of the firm and to serve as a report card of progress.

A related measure of wealth enhancement is the **market value added (MVA).** This is the difference between a company's total market value (debt and equity) at a point in time minus the total capital invested in the company since its origin. In another version of MVA only the common stock is considered; that is, the market value of the common stock less invested equity capital. This measure is related to the market-to-book value (M/B) ratio, in that the same data are used to calculate both the MVA and the M/B.

Both the EVA and MVA measures use accounting book values as measures of invested capital. Efforts are made to adjust these values for such things as goodwill amortization, bad-debt reserves, deferred tax reserves, LIFO versus FIFO inventory valuation differences, and other things of this sort. The idea is to add (and sometimes subtract) these adjustments to/from accounting book-value figures to better approximate the cash invested in a company over the years. Notwithstanding these adjustments, the calculated capital employed is still basically a historical, sunk cost. Though investors pay attention to returns on book-value measures, their principal focus is on the expected return on the current market value of a company. For these reasons, one must be careful in interpreting EVA and MVA results.

ADJUSTED PRESENT VALUE

An alternative to the WACC is the **adjusted present-value method (APV),** first proposed by Stewart C. Myers.[5] With an APV approach, project cash flows are

---

[5]Stewart C. Myers, "Interactions of Corporate Financing and Investment Decisions: Implications for Capital Budgeting," *Journal of Finance,* 29 (March 1974), 1–25.

broken down into two components: unlevered operating cash flows and those associated with financing the project. These components then are valued so that

$$APV = \frac{\text{Unlevered}}{\text{value}} + \frac{\text{Value of}}{\text{financing}} \qquad (8\text{-}7)$$

The disaggregation of cash flows is undertaken so that different discount rates may be used. As operating cash flows are more risky, they are discounted at a higher rate.

More formally, the adjusted present value is

$$APV = \sum_{t=0}^{n} \frac{OC_t}{(1 + k_u)^t} + \sum_{t=0}^{n} \frac{Int._t (T_c)}{(1 + k_i)^t} - F \qquad (8\text{-}8)$$

where OC_t = after-tax operating cash flow in period t
k_u = required rate of return in the absence of leverage (all-equity financing)
$Int._t$ = interest payment on debt in period t
T_c = corporate tax rate
k_i = cost of debt financing, and
F = after-tax flotation cost associated with financing (debt, equity, or both)

APV breaks down overall cash flows into operating and financing components and discounts them at different rates.

The first component on the right-hand side of the equation represents the net present value of operating cash flows discounted at the unlevered cost of equity capital. The second component is the present value of the interest tax shield on any debt employed to finance the project. The discount rate is the corporate cost of borrowing, the idea being that the realization of the tax shield bears a risk comparable to that embraced in the cost of debt funds. Finally, any flotation costs are subtracted from the sum of the first two components.

Illustration

Gruber-Elton Paper Company is considering a new production machine costing $2 million that is expected to produce after-tax cash savings of $400,000 per year for 8 years. The required rate of return on unlevered equity is 13 percent. If this was all there was, the net present value of the project would be (in thousands):

$$NPV = -\$2,000 + \sum_{t=1}^{8} \frac{\$400}{(1.13)^t} = -\$80$$

Under these circumstances, the project would be rejected. Ned Gruber and Martin Elton, the founders of the company, are heartbroken, as they really wanted the machine.

But all is not lost! After all, it is the policy of the company to finance capital investment projects with 50 percent debt, as that is the target debt-to–total capitalization of the company. Gruber-Elton Paper Company is able to borrow $1 million at 10 percent interest to finance the new machine in part. (The balance will come from equity funds.) The principal amount of the loan will be repaid in equal year-end installments of $125,000 through the end of year 8. If the company's tax rate

TABLE 8-2

Present Value of Interest Tax Shield
for Gruber-Elton Paper Company (in thousands)

Year	(1) Debt at Beginning of Year	(2) Interest (1) × 10%	(3) Tax Shield (2) × 40%	(4) Present Value at 10% Discount Rate
1	$1,000	$100	$40	$ 36
2	875	88	35	29
3	750	75	30	23
4	625	62	25	17
5	500	50	20	12
6	375	38	15	8
7	250	25	10	5
8	125	12	5	2
				$132

(federal and state) is 40 percent, we can compute the interest tax shield and its present value, and they are shown in Table 8-2. We see in column (4) that the present value of the interest tax shield is $132 (in thousands).

The adjusted present value of the project is now (in thousands)

$$APV = -\$80 + \$132 = \$52$$

Gruber and Elton are happy because the project is now acceptable and they can bask in the glory of a shiny new, softly purring machine.

But what about flotation costs? These are the costs of lawyers, investment bankers, printers, and other fees involved in issuing securities. They pertain to both new debt and equity, with those for the latter usually being higher. Suppose in our example the company incurs after-tax flotation costs of $40,000. These reduce the company's cash flows so the adjusted present value becomes

$$APV = -\$80 + \$132 - \$40 = \$12$$

The project is still acceptable, but it provides less benefit than in the absence of flotation costs.

WACC versus APV

We have presented two methods for determining the value of a project, the weighted average cost of capital and the adjusted present-value method. The APV method is a general theoretical rule that embraces the WACC method as a subcase. In his article, Myers shows certain biases involved in the WACC method, and there have been a number of challenges and counterchallenges.[6]

Whenever a capital investment occurs, there is an interaction of investment and financing. As a general rule, as long as the firm maintains a relatively constant

---

[6]See James A. Miles and John R. Ezzell, "The Weighted Average Cost of Capital, Perfect Capital Markets, and Proj-ect Life: A Clarification," *Journal of Financial and Quantitative Analysis*, 15 (September 1980), 719–30; and Robert A. Taggert Jr., "Consistent Valuation and Cost of Capital Expressions with Corporate and Personal Taxes," working paper, National Bureau of Economic Research (August 1989).

debt ratio over time and invests in projects like those it already owns, the WACC method gives an accurate portrayal of the project's worth. This is merely to say that financial risk and business risk are relatively invariant over time. If a company should depart radically from previous financing patterns and/or invest in an entirely new line of business (like widgets when it is a seed company), then the APV approach provides a more accurate answer theoretically.

The advantages of the WACC method are that it is easy to understand and widely used. The APV method is pleasing to many academics but is not widely used in business. The APV method is not without its difficulties. Implied is that there are no imperfections other than corporate taxes and flotation costs. In other words, the interest tax shield and flotation costs are all that matter when it comes to financing. We explore other imperfections in Chapter 9, when we evaluate capital structure decisions from a broader perspective. For now recognize the differences in approach, but also the fact that for most situations the two approaches give identical accept/reject decisions.

DIVISIONAL REQUIRED RETURNS

Nowhere is the proxy company approach illustrated earlier more applicable than it is to the required returns for various **divisions** of a company. By *division*, we mean some subunit of a company that carries on a set of activities that can be differentiated from the other activities of the firm. Usually these activities are differentiated along product or service lines as well as along management lines. Henceforth, we will refer to these subunits as divisions, whether they are called subsidiaries, divisions, business units, or whatever.

Each division employs in it assets that must be financed. The question is, What is an appropriate acceptance criterion? Again the key is homogeneity. If the products or services involved are homogeneous with respect to risk, and new investment proposals are of the same sort, a case can be made for a divisional cost of capital as the acceptance criterion. It represents the transfer price of capital from the company to the division. Stated differently, it is the minimum rate of return the company expects the division to earn on its capital investments.

The Proxy Company Approach Once More Lightly

As discussed earlier, proxy companies may largely mirror the risk of the division. As a result, the proper required rate of return for the division will be related to the systematic risk of the proxy companies. In the case of a division, sometimes a mutual fund exists for a specific industry. Here one might use the beta of the mutual fund to capture the systematic risk of the division.

Solving for Beta In summary, there usually are companies that carry on activities similar to those of the division. The principal exception would be an industry composed entirely of multidivision companies. Even here, it may be possible to glean information on systematic risk, provided that the multidivision companies are not the same in what they do. Suppose Katz Enterprises, a multidivision company, has a division similar in business to your division, but it also has two other divisions. You know Katz's overall beta. If proxy companies (pure plays) are available for its two other divisions, you can obtain betas for them. These betas then are weighted by the values of the divisions. Given the overall beta of Katz Enterprises, you can solve for the beta of the division in question. This is due to the fact that betas are additive. The derived estimate will be crude, but it may be better than estimates based on things other than stock valuation.[7] If there is more than one unknown, we might solve a system of simultaneous equations across multiple companies for beta. Although feasible in concept, such efforts bog down in measurement problems.

Once betas are calculated for all divisions of a company, a check for internal consistency compares the sum of the parts with the whole. That is, the sum of the proxy betas for each division, multiplied by the market value weights of the divisions, should equal the beta of the overall company.[8] When this is not the case, something is wrong. It may be in the sample or in the modification of the sample company betas for leverage. It may be in the weighting. It is difficult to assign a market value to a division of a multidivision company. As a surrogate, you might use operating profits or sales to determine the weighting. Or you might use the market-to-book value ratio for the sample and multiply this by the book value of the division to obtain an estimate of the division's market value. The same thing might be done for the price/earnings ratio. Despite efforts to unravel the problem, it may be that reconciliation is impossible. The proxy company beta approach should not be used if the sum of the parts is significantly different from the whole.

Cost and Proportion of Debt Funds

The amount of **nonequity financing assigned** to a division is an important consideration. For the foregoing procedure to hold, it should approximate the same relative amount as that used by the proxy company. In other words, the proportion of nonequity financing allocated to a division cannot be significantly out of line with that of the external company being used. Otherwise, one will not get a reasonable proxy for the systematic risk of the division. Where the proportions are not nearly the same, the proxy company's beta should be adjusted before it is used in determining the cost of equity capital for the division. The procedure for adjusting the beta for leverage was described earlier.

Cost of Debt For the cost of debt for a division, many use the company's overall borrowing cost. Even here adjustments can and should be made if a division has significantly more or less risk than the company as a whole. The notion that equity costs differ according to a division's systematic risk applies to debt costs as well. The greater the risk, the greater the interest rate that will be required. While a case can be made for differentiating debt costs among divisions according to their systematic risks, few companies do it. For one thing, there are mechanical difficulties in computing the beta, for the market index must include debt instruments. It is possible to make adjustments in interest rates based on the relative debt capacities of the various divisions of a company. However, the division itself is not ultimately responsible for its debt. The company as a whole is responsible. Because of diversification of cash flows among divisions, the probability of payment for the whole may be greater than the sum of the parts. For these reasons,

---

[7]A variation of this approach is found in Mark K. Krueger and Charles M. Linke, "A Spanning Approach for Estimating Divisional Cost of Capital," *Financial Management*, 23 (Spring 1994), 64–70.

[8]Russell J. Fuller and Halbert S. Kerr, "Estimating the Divisional Cost of Capital: An Analysis of the Pure-Play Technique," *Journal of Finance*, 36 (December 1981), 997–1009, collected proxy company betas for the various divisions of some 60 multidivision firms. The authors found that an appropriately weighted average of the betas of the proxy firms closely approximated the beta of the multidivision firm. Although an adjustment for leverage was made, the results here did not provide as good an estimate of the multidivision firm beta as did the unadjusted betas.

few companies have tried to apply a market model to divisional debt costs as they have to equity costs. Still, a case can be made for varying divisional debt costs in keeping with their risk, even though the adjustment is partly subjective.

Proportion of Debt Funds   When different divisions are allocated significantly different proportions of nonequity funds, determining the overall required return for a division is complicated. If one division is allocated a much higher proportion of debt, it will have a lower overall required return on paper. But is it truly lower? Should one division be allowed to significantly lower its required return simply by taking on more leverage? Is this fair to other divisions? Apart from the incentive issue, what are the problems to the company as a whole?

High leverage for one division may cause the cost of debt funds for the over-all company to rise. This marginal increase should not be allocated across divisions; rather, it should be pinpointed to the division responsible. Second, the high leverage incurred by the division may increase the uncertainty of the tax shield associated with debt for the company as a whole. As discussed earlier in this chapter, if the firm's earnings should decline so that the tax deductibility of interest payments is postponed or lost, the cost of debt funds to the company overall rises dramatically. Finally, high leverage for one division increases the volatility of returns to stockholders of the company, together with the possibility of insolvency and bankruptcy costs being incurred. In turn, this will cause them to increase the required return on equity to compensate for the increased risk. (The way this comes about is taken up in Chapter 9.) For these reasons, the "true" cost of debt for the high-leverage division may be considerably greater than originally imagined.

Adjusting Both Costs   Thus, both the cost of debt funds and the proportion assigned to a division can be varied. The greater the systematic business risk of a division, the higher the interest cost and/or the lower the proportion of debt assigned to that division. With financial institutions, the lever used is the proportion of equity funds assigned to a business unit. The idea is to obtain uniformity in measuring returns on risk-adjusted capital for the various business units making up the financial institution. The riskier the business, the more equity required to support the activities of that business unit. With nonfinancial corporations, we typically work with the proportion of debt assigned to a division, whereas with financial institutions it is the proportion of equity.

Alternative Approach

In the weighted average required return approach described, costs of equity capital are derived from proxy companies, whereas costs of debt and the weighting of capital costs are decisions of the company itself. An alternative approach is to determine the overall cost of capital, composed of both debt and equity funds, of proxy companies. This approach takes as given the costs of debt and equity funds, together with the weights employed. The median weighted average cost of capital of the sample companies (or some other measure of central tendency) then is used as the required rate of return for the division.

Thus, both external capital costs and financing weights are applied to the division. The problem, of course, is when a division uses a significantly different proportion of nonequity funds than the proxy companies. When this occurs, adjustments need to be made. However, they need to be made in the previous approach. Both approaches have shortcomings, so the use of one or the other depends on the situation.

Implications for Project Selection

With one of the two methods described, an overall divisional required return is estimated. We then allocate or transfer capital throughout the firm on a risk-adjusted return basis. The higher the systematic risk of a division, the higher the required rate of return. This approach provides a consistent framework for allocating capital among divisions with greatly different risks. Too often in a multidivision firm, a single cutoff rate is used for project selection. An edict comes from above stating that "no project shall be undertaken unless it provides a return of 15 percent!" The problem is that certain "safe" projects with little systematic risk are rejected because they do not provide a return above the company's stated goal. Yet some of these projects may provide expected returns greater than the "true" cost of capital for the division. In contrast, divisions characterized by large systematic risk may accept projects with expected returns higher than the companywide norm but lower than they should earn, considering the systematic risk involved.

Divisional Hurdle versus WACC   Figure 8-3 illustrates this problem. The horizontal dashed line is the company's overall cost of capital, and the bars represent the required returns for the various divisions of the company, based on their systematic risk. The *x*'s and *o*'s represent investment projects of the type described. The expected returns of the *x*'s are below the company's overall cost of capital but above the division's required return. The *o*'s have expected returns above the company's cost of capital but below the division's required return. The rejection of the *x* projects and acceptance of the *o*'s is suboptimal. The *x*'s provide expected returns in excess of the returns required by the market for the systematic risk involved; the *o*'s provide expected returns lower than those required. The problem may seem obvious, but this very thing happens either directly or indirectly in many a multidivision company.

Adverse Incentives   The incentives in such a company are such that divisions with low systematic risk often are too conservative in project generation and selec-

FIGURE 8-3

Comparison of companywide cost of capital and divisional required returns

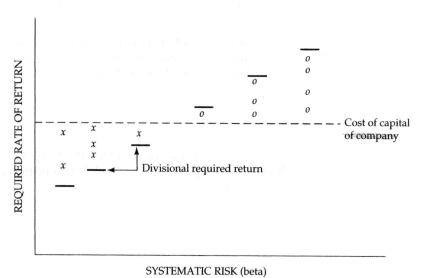

tion, while divisions with large systematic risk are too aggressive. Too often a company puts money in those divisions providing the greatest growth opportunities and rations capital to other divisions, so that they will accept only projects consistent with the overall growth objectives. Frequently, the high-growth divisions have a license to do almost anything they want, as long as the expected returns on the projects selected are above the company's overall required return. When some of the projects selected provide too low an expected return for the systematic risk involved, the company may become riskier without commensurate increases in expected return.

Divisional return allocations of capital are based on higher returns being required for divisions with greater risk.

The incentive scheme is skewed in the direction of growth and the acceptance of risky projects. "Safe" divisions may be starved for capital, even though they are able to generate investment proposals that are expected to provide returns in excess of those required for the systematic risk involved. The problem is a mistaken belief that growth in itself is the panacea for all problems. The value of a corporation rests on two foundations: expected return and risk. Growth in the former is good, but growth in the latter is bad. Whether the overall result is good or bad depends on the combined effect of these two factors.

Risk-Adjusted Returns What is needed is a system for allocating capital to divisions on a risk-adjusted return basis. The approach presented provides such a means. As long as investment proposals emanating from the division are homogeneous with respect to systematic risk, the approach will result in consistent investment decisions being made among the divisions of a company. When investment proposals are not homogeneous, management should evaluate them on a proposal-by-proposal basis, using the methods taken up earlier.

COMPANY'S OVERALL COST OF CAPITAL

When the risks of various investment projects undertaken by a firm do not differ materially from each other, it is unnecessary to derive separate project or divisional required rates of return. With homogeneous risk across investments, it is appropriate to use the firm's overall required rate of return as the acceptance criterion. The derivation of a weighted average cost of capital is the same as illustrated earlier in the chapter.

Here the cost of equity capital is the minimum rate of return that a company must earn on the equity-financed portion of its investments in order to leave unchanged the market price of its stock. This cost can be estimated using a market model: CAPM, extended CAPM, or APT multifactor.

Dividend Discount Model Approach (DDM)

Dividend discount models equate share price with the present value of expected future dividends.

Another way to estimate the required rate of return on equity for a company overall is with the dividend discount model (DDM). With the DDM, we solve for the rate of discount that equates the present value of the stream of expected future dividends with the current market price of the stock.

Briefly recalling Chapter 2, we can view the value of a share of stock to investors as the present value of the expected future stream of income paid to them. Because dividends are all that stockholders as a whole receive from their investment, this stream of income is the cash dividends paid in future periods and, perhaps, a final liquidating dividend. At time 0, the value of a share of stock is

$$P_0 = \frac{D_1}{1 + k_e} + \frac{D_2}{(1 + k_e)^2} + \cdots + \frac{D_\infty}{(1 + k_e)^\infty} \qquad (8\text{-}9)$$

$$= \sum_{t=1}^{\infty} \frac{D_t}{(1 + k_e)^t}$$

where P_0 is the value of a share of stock at time 0, D_t is the dividend per share expected to be paid in period t, and k_e is the appropriate rate of discount.

We suggested in Chapter 2 that investors formulate subjective probability distributions of dividends per share expected to be paid in various future periods. For the individual investor, the D_t in Eq. (8-9) are the expected values, or means, of these probability distributions. For the market as a whole, the D_t represent the expected values for investors at the margin, and k_e is the market discount factor appropriate for the risk involved. The *cost of equity capital* is defined as the market rate of discount, k_e, that equates the present value of all expected future dividends per share with the current market price of the stock. This cost is found by solving Eq. (8-9) for k_e.

Perpetual Growth Situation If dividends per share are expected to grow at a constant rate, g, and k_e is greater than g, we discovered in Chapter 2 that

$$P_0 = \frac{D_1}{k_e - g} \qquad (8\text{-}10)$$

where D_1 is the dividend per share expected to be paid at the end of period 1. Thus, the cost of equity capital would be

$$k_e = \frac{D_1}{P_0} + g \qquad (8\text{-}11)$$

The critical assumption, of course, is that dividends per share are expected to grow at a compound rate of g forever.

Growth Phases When the expected growth in dividends per share is other than perpetual, a modification of Eq. (8-9) can be used. As shown in Chapter 2, a number of valuation models assume that the growth rate will eventually taper off. Frequently, the transition is from an above-normal growth rate to one that is considered normal. If dividends were expected to grow at a 15 percent compound rate for 5 years, at a 10 percent rate for the next 5 years, and then grow at a 5 percent rate, we would have

$$P_0 = \sum_{t=1}^{5} \frac{D_0(1.15)^t}{(1 + k_e)^t} + \sum_{t=6}^{10} \frac{D_5(1.10)^{t-5}}{(1 + k_e)^t} + \sum_{t=11}^{\infty} \frac{D_{10}(1.05)^{t-10}}{(1 + k_e)^t} \qquad (8\text{-}12)$$

We see that the current dividend, D_0, is the base on which the expected growth in future dividends is built. By solving for k_e, we obtain the cost of equity capital as defined. One would use the method illustrated in Chapter 2 to solve for k_e. For example, if the current dividend, D_0, were $2 a share and market price per share, P_0, were $70, k_e in Eq. (8-12) would be 10.42 percent. For other patterns of expected future growth, the equation can be easily modified to deal with the situation.

The more growth segments we specify, of course, the more the growth pattern will approximate a curvilinear relationship. From Chapter 2 we learned how to determine the terminal value at the beginning of the last growth segment. This terminal value can be based on expected future dividends, as in Eq. (8-12), in which case the perpetual dividend growth model is used, or on earnings per share multiplied by an assumed price/earnings ratio.

For all growth situations, the important thing is to solve for the k_e that equates the current market price of the stock with the expected future dividends perceived by investors at the margin. Because the expected growth in dividends is not directly observable, we must estimate it. Herein lies the major difficulty involved in estimating the cost of equity capital. For reasonably stable patterns of past growth, one might project this trend into the future. However, we must temper the projection to take account of current market sentiment. Insight into such sentiment can come from investment advisors who have made analyses of the industry and company and from articles about the company in financial newspapers and magazines.

DDM *versus Market Model Approaches*

If measurement were exact and certain assumptions held, the discount rate determined by this method would be the same as the required rate of return determined by a market model approach. When assumptions underlying a market model do not seem appropriate, the second approach serves as a useful benchmark for adjusting the required rate of return. By now it should be apparent that measuring the cost of equity capital of a company is an inexact science. We can only hope to approximate it as carefully as possible.

The methods suggested enable us to make such an approximation more or less accurately, depending on the situation. For a large company whose stock is actively traded and whose systematic risk is close to that of the market as a whole, we can usually estimate more confidently than we can for a moderate-sized company whose stock is inactively traded in the over-the-counter market and whose systematic risk is large. We must live with the inexactness involved in the measurement process and try to do as good a job as possible.

When the cost of equity capital is blended with other capital costs, we obtain the weighted average cost of capital for the company overall. This rate then is used as the acceptance criterion for projects that are homogeneous with respect to risk. But what does it tell us about which risk, systematic or total, is important?

DIVERSIFICATION OF ASSETS AND TOTAL RISK ANALYSIS

We know from Chapter 3 that the total risk of an investment is the sum of both systematic and unsystematic risks. The latter is the risk that can be diversified away. If the assumptions of the CAPM or APT factor model hold, this risk does not matter to investors. As a result, diversification of assets by a company in an effort to reduce volatility would not be a thing of value. To create value you must do something for your shareholders that they cannot do for themselves. Clearly, they can diversify, and probably they can diversify more effectively than the company can for them.

Now one could argue that while investors are able to diversify across companies whose stocks are publicly traded, they cannot diversify across capital assets held by these companies. In other words, they purchase shares in the income stream of the company as a whole, not in the income streams of the individual assets of the company.

Investors Diversifying across Capital Assets

Diversification of assets by the firm usually is not a thing of value. Shareholders can do this on their own.

Investors do not need to acquire direct claims on capital assets, however, in order to accomplish such diversification. As long as there is information available about the actual returns on individual assets, investors can effectively diversify across capital assets of individual companies. In essence, an investor can replicate the return stream of the individual capital asset held by a firm.[9] Suppose a firm holds three productive assets, A, B, and C, and complete information exists about the actual ex post returns on these assets. To "invest" in asset A but not in assets B and C, the investor could buy x percent of the stock of the company. He then would sell claims against himself based on promises to pay x percent of the future income streams associated with assets B and C. That is, in a particular year, if asset B were to provide a $100 return and asset C a $200 return, he would pay $100x$ and $200x$ to the holders of the claims. In this way, the investor effectively replicates the income stream of a single capital asset of a firm, that of asset A in our example.

It is in this sense that investors are able to diversify effectively across capital assets of individual companies. Some companies have **tracking stocks** for certain stand-alone business units, a device that makes for transparency. Such stocks permit investors to buy a particular part of the enterprise, in the sense of participating in the income stream, but not necessarily the overall enterprise. Though tracking-stock investors do not have a claim on the business unit's assets, because those belong to the parent, they participate in the value creation of the business unit. The **value additive principle** states that the value of the whole is equal to the sum of the separate asset parts. As a result of this principle, the firm is said not to be able to do something for investors through diversification of capital assets that they cannot do for themselves. Various empirical studies confirm that diversified companies are less valued than are more focused companies.[10] According to the notions advanced so far, projects would be evaluated only on the basis of their systematic risk.

Imperfections and Unsystematic Risk

Recognize, however, that the variability of cash flows of a company depends on total risk, not just systematic risk. As we know from Chapter 3, total risk is

$$\text{Total risk} = \begin{array}{c}\text{Systematic} \\ \text{risk} \\ \text{(Unavoidable)}\end{array} + \begin{array}{c}\text{Unsystematic} \\ \text{risk} \\ \text{(Avoidable)}\end{array} \tag{8-13}$$

The probability of a company becoming insolvent is a function of its total risk. How does this relate to doing something for its shareholders that they cannot do for themselves?

Bankruptcy Costs A crucial assumption in the market models is that the cost of insolvency or bankruptcy is zero. If a firm fails, assets presumably can be sold for their economic value. No legal or selling costs are incurred. After creditors have been paid, the residual proceeds are distributed to stockholders. As long as assets

[9]See Lawrence D. Schall, "Asset Valuation, Firm Investment, and Firm Diversification," *Journal of Business*, 45 (January 1972), 13–21, for amplification on this point as well as proof of the irrelevancy of diversification decisions by the firm.

[10]See, for example, Philip G. Berger and Eli Ofek, "Diversifications's Effect on Firm Value," *Journal of Financial Economics*, 37 (January 1995), 39–65; and Robert Comment and Gregg A. Jarrell, "Corporate Focus and Stock Returns," *Journal of Financial Economics*, 37 (January 1995), 67–87.

can be sold at their economic value in a frictionless world, investors can effectively diversify their risk. Under real-world conditions, however, assets often have to be sold in bankruptcy at distress prices. Moreover, there are selling costs, legal fees, and other out-of-pocket costs. Finally, and probably most important, there are a number of delays and inefficiencies involved in the process of going through a bankruptcy. Impending bankruptcy repels suppliers, who fear that the company may not be able to pay them. Employees leave in anticipation of doom. Sales drop off as customers worry about the reliability of the product and service. These developments make operations inefficient, to say the least.

A cumbersome bankruptcy process delays creditor takeover, during which asset values deteriorate. All of this becomes a "drain on the system" to suppliers of capital, and it works either directly or indirectly to the detriment of stockholders, the residual owners of the firm. The idea is that there are a number of stakeholders in the company—debt holders and common stockholders to be sure, but also customers, employees, governments, and people in communities where facilities are located. When total risk increases, the cost of doing business rises. In turn, this weakens the company's chances for survival. If there were no costs to bankruptcy and the firm could go through a costless reorganization or liquidation, stockholders might not care as long as the firm were committed to doing those things that it did best. However, with significant bankruptcy costs, stockholders will be affected and may view diversification of assets in a different light.

The probability of a firm's becoming insolvent depends on its *total* risk, not just on its *systematic* risk; therefore, a case can be made for choosing projects in light of their effect on both the systematic and the total (systematic plus unsystematic) risk of the firm. Put another way, when insolvency or bankruptcy costs are significant, investors may well be served by the firm's paying attention to the total risk of the firm, not just to its systematic risk. Risky capital budgeting proposals can alter the total risk of the firm apart from their effect on its systematic risk. To the extent that unsystematic risk is a factor of at least some importance, total risk should be evaluated.

Evaluation of Combinations of Risky Investments

From Chapter 7 we know that the marginal risk of an individual proposal to the firm as a whole depends on its correlation with existing projects as well as its correlation with proposals under consideration that might be accepted. The appropriate information is the standard deviation and expected value of the probability distribution of possible net present values for all feasible combinations of existing projects and investment proposals under consideration. Now we must select the most desirable combination. Shortly, we shall ask the fundamental question: Should a portfolio approach be used at all? We assume now that management is interested only in the marginal impact of an investment proposal on the risk complexion of the firm as a whole.

Selecting the Best Combination   The selection of the most desirable combination of investments will depend on management's utility preferences with respect to net present value and variance, or standard deviation. If management is averse to risk and associates risk with the variance of net present value, its utility function may be similar to that shown in Fig. 8-4. As discussed in Chapter 3, the curves in the figure are indifference curves; management is indifferent to any combination of expected value of net present value and standard deviation on a

Sidebar (left margin):
Bankruptcy costs are the principal imperfection that may make firm diversification a thing of value.

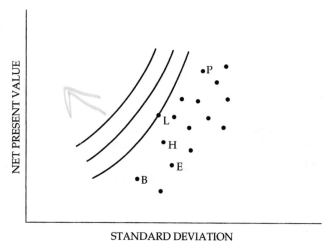

FIGURE 8-4
Selection of the best
portfolio

particular curve. Thus, a specific curve portrays the trade-off between the two parameters for a particular company.

As we move to the left and up in Fig. 8-4, each successive curve represents a higher level of utility. Thus, management would choose the combination of investments that lies on the highest indifference curve, the one farthest to the left, because this curve represents the greatest utility. This combination is determined by the intersection of a dot, point *L*, with the highest indifference curve. Point *L* represents the portfolio of existing projects and proposals offering the most desirable combination of expected net present value and risk.

Project Combination Dominance   The framework for evaluating combinations of risky investments just developed is useful, even if management's utility function is not defined. With the information shown by the dots in Fig. 8-4, management can eliminate most combinations, simply because they are dominated by other combinations. Unless management is quite averse to risk, it probably would consider only four portfolios of risky investments: *B, H, L,* and *P.* From these, management would choose the one that appeared to offer the best combination of expected return and risk.

This selection determines which new investment proposals to accept, but if the portfolio contained only existing projects, no investment proposals would be accepted. If the portfolio of existing projects were represented by portfolio *E* in Fig. 8-4, however, the selection of any of the four portfolios would imply the acceptance of one or more new investment proposals. Proposals not in the portfolio finally selected would be rejected, of course. This evaluation implies that the total risk of the firm is what is important; therefore, investment decisions should be made in light of their marginal impact on total risk. The evaluation is firm-risk oriented in the sense that management does not consider explicitly the impact of the project on investors' portfolios, only on the portfolio of assets of the firm.

When Should We Take
Account of Unsystematic Risk?

We have explored two ways to evaluate risky investments: (1) evaluate a project in relation to its systematic risk, the **market model approach**; and (2) analyze the incremental impact of the project on the business-risk complexion of the firm as a whole, the **total variability approach**. If both approaches give clear accept or reject signals, we should act on them. The obvious problem is when one approach gives an accept signal and the other a reject signal. When this occurs, management needs to assess which approach is more applicable. If the common stock of the company involved is publicly held, if the possibility of insolvency is remote, and if the firm can realistically express expected project returns in terms of changes in market-based capitalized values, a strong case can be made for the signal given by a market model.

Total risk is relevant only if imperfections are important.

If the stock is traded in a market with high transaction and information costs, if the possibility of insolvency or bankruptcy is significant, and if the expression of project returns in terms of market-based returns is crude, greater reliance should be placed on the total variability approach. Even here, however, a portion of the residual risk can be diversified away.

Obviously, the methods proposed are not operationally perfect. Still, they represent a means for judging risky investments. It is clear that the impact of a project on risk is important and must be considered if the firm is to make investment decisions that maximize shareholder wealth. It also is clear that management must consider the effect of a project not only on the risk complexion of the firm but on the systematic risk to investors. The idea that the market for common stocks is relatively efficient forces a company in this direction if its objective is truly one of maximizing shareholder wealth.

EVALUATION OF ACQUISITIONS

We saw in Chapters 6 and 7 that we can analyze an acquisition according to its expected return and risk in the same manner as we analyze any capital investment. The relevant expected future cash flows are **free cash flows**, those left over after making all investments necessary to produce the expected cash-flow stream. In the same manner as before we examine the issue under the assumptions of a market model and then under conditions in which unsystematic risk might be a factor of at least some importance.

Acquisitions are treated in two parts. In this chapter we cover valuation issues surrounding an investment in assets, following up on concepts already developed. In Chapter 23, we delve into mergers and takeovers more globally, including empirical evidence on valuation.

Market Model Implications

Given the assumptions of a market model (CAPM or APT factor), it is clear that investors are able to achieve the same diversification as the firm can achieve for them. This point is particularly apparent in the acquisition of a company whose stock is publicly held. In fact, the investor has an advantage in being able to diversify by buying only a few shares of stock, whereas the acquisition for the buying company is much more "lumpy." Thus, the acquiring firm is unable to do something for investors that they cannot do for themselves at least as efficiently. Therefore, pure diversification by a company through acquisitions is not a thing of value. The acquiring company must be able to effect operating economies, distribution economies, or other synergies if the acquisition is to be a thing of value.

However, an acquisition can enhance the value of the company to its shareholders. Indeed, economies may be involved that benefit the acquiring firm and its stockholders. The prospect of synergism may make a prospective acquisition more attractive to one company than to another, but diversification itself would not be

Synergy means efficiency gains such that the whole is worth more than the sum of the parts.

beneficial. Conglomerate mergers for the sole purpose of diversification would be suspect; they would not enhance shareholder wealth. If an acquisition is to be worthwhile, there must be the prospect of synergism. In other words, the acquiring company must be able to effect operating economies, distribution economies, or other things of this sort if the acquisition is to be a thing of value.

Purchase Price and Required Return It is an easy matter to measure the required rate of return for the acquisition of a company whose stock is publicly traded. Direct market information is available, so one is able to calculate the required rate of return on equity using the procedures illustrated earlier. No proxy company is necessary. If the acquisition involves taking on the selling company's debt, this debt must be taken into account. The purchase price we use in evaluating a prospective acquisition is the market value of its debt plus the amount paid to the stockholders of the selling company. Suppose Magna Corporation is considering acquiring Carta Company by paying the stockholders of Carta $3 million. Magna will assume Carta's debts, which have a market value of $2 million. For purposes of calculation, the purchase price of this acquisition is $5 million.

Against this purchase price, one must balance the expected incremental free cash flows arising from the acquisition. Remember from Chapter 6 that these are operating cash flows (earnings before interest, taxes, depreciation, and amortization) minus taxes, minus necessary capital expenditures, and minus additions to working capital necessary to produce the expected stream of operating cash flows. The appropriate discount rate is a weighted average required return for the selling company. The cost of equity is computed directly from market information, as discussed earlier. The cost of debt is the current yield in the marketplace for the selling company's debt, multiplied by 1 minus the tax rate. For our example, Carta Company employs two parts of debt for every three parts of equity, so these weights would be used in determining a weighted average required return. The expected after-tax cash flows from the acquisition then are discounted at the weighted average required return. If the present value of these cash flows exceeds the purchase price, the acquisition is worthwhile; if not, it should be rejected. All of this follows from our earlier study of the rules of project acceptability.

Importance of Operating Efficiencies The important thing to remember is that under the assumptions of a market model, the present value of cash flows will exceed the purchase price only if there are operating economies and/or improved management. Stated differently, in the absence of cash-flow improvements such that $2 + 2 = 5$, called synergy, the expected return arising from the acquisition will be no more than the required return. This suggests that the analysis of a prospective acquisition should focus on the likelihood of economies. For the acquiring company, this usually means doing those things that it does well. Acquiring a company in an unrelated line of business in which management has no expertise is unlikely to produce economies. Too many companies have done that, mistakenly believing that it is the only way to achieve growth. When inefficiencies develop, the acquiring company earns an incremental return less than that required by the market for the systematic risk involved. As a result, the market price of the stock drops below the price it would have sold for if the acquisition had not been made.

Acquisitions create value only if likely synergies more than offset the premium paid.

If the stock of the prospective acquisition is priced efficiently in the market, the acquiring company will pay at least what the company is worth as an independent entity. If a premium is paid—and it usually must be paid—then the acquiring company pays more than the acquisition is worth as an independent operation. This premium, however, can be offset by economies, so that the acquisition provides an incremental expected return equal to or greater than that required by the market, given the systematic risk involved. In evaluating an acquisition, one should concentrate on the prospect of operating economies. We will discover in Chapter 23 that other considerations come into play—information effects, tax reasons, wealth transfers, and personal agendas. However, the bedrock of value creation is operating economies.

A Diversification Effect?

If unsystematic risk is felt to be important or if management is concerned only with the impact of an acquisition on the expected risk and return of the firm as a whole, the evaluation process needs to be altered. One can evaluate an acquisition from the standpoint of the "portfolio" effect on the firm. This was illustrated earlier, and the procedures are the same for an acquisition. To reiterate briefly in this context, recall how we derived a probability distribution of possible incremental present values arising from an investment in Chapter 7. If the price to be paid for an acquisition has been established, it should be subtracted from the expected present value to obtain the expected net present value. The next step is to estimate the correlation coefficients for the relationship between the net present value for the prospective acquisition and the net present values for existing projects and investment proposals under consideration.

Effect on Total Risk   The acquisition then becomes one more investment proposal in a portfolio of projects to be considered. The methods of analysis and selection are the same as those employed earlier in this chapter. Management chooses the best combination of expected net present value and risk. If the portfolio of projects represented by this combination includes the prospective acquisition, the firm should acquire the company involved. In this way, an acquisition is evaluated in the same manner as any internally generated investment proposal. A decision is made with attention to the marginal impact of the acquisition on the total risk of the firm.

Whether a market model approach is altered depends on the importance of the diversification effect. In turn, its importance depends on imperfections in the capital markets, which we took up in the preceding section. The same arguments hold for an acquisition as they do for any asset that reduces the relative total risk of a company. As we know, bankruptcy costs are the principal imperfection that affects diversification-of-asset decisions.

■ Summary

Value is created through capital investments by exploiting opportunities for excess returns, those providing returns in excess of what the financial markets require for the risk involved. The avenues to value creation are industry attractiveness and competitive advantage within an industry. These things give rise to positive net-present-value projects. In evaluating risky investment opportunities, a market model (CAPM or APT factor) relates the acceptance of a project to its systematic, or unavoidable, risk

to investors. The required rate of return is the risk-free rate plus a premium for the systematic risk of the project.

To determine the systematic risk of a project, one can look at similar companies whose stocks are publicly traded. A surrogate required rate of return on equity is derived using the betas of the proxy companies. The same principle is applicable to an APT factor model approach; here proxy company parameters for the risk factors would be used. When the leverage of the firm is significantly different from that of the proxy companies, the CAPM beta should be adjusted using a well-known formula. Once the relevant cost of equity capital has been determined, it is blended with other costs of financing. The calculation of a weighted average cost of capital (WACC) was illustrated, and the rationale for and limitations to its use explained.

In addition to the weighted average cost of capital, the adjusted present value (APV) method was considered. In the latter approach, project-operating cash flows are discounted at the unlevered cost of equity, interest tax shields at the cost of borrowing, and flotation costs are subtracted from the sum of the present values. The idea is that there are two components to a project: its unlevered value and the net value of financing. The differences between the APV and WACC methods were explored, and it was determined that imperfections other than corporate taxes cloud the issue.

The proxy company approach to determining required rates of return is particularly appropriate when it comes to divisions of a multibusiness company. If the products/projects of a division are relatively homogeneous with respect to risk, the required return derived for the division becomes its transfer price of capital. Certain problems arising from the differential utilization of nonequity financing among divisions were explored, and an alternative method of using proxy companies' overall costs of capital was investigated.

When the various businesses of a company do not differ materially in systematic risk, it is unnecessary to derive individual project or division required returns. Instead the overall required return of a company, its WACC, can be used as the acceptance criterion for capital investments.

The diversification of assets by a company is not a thing of value if the assumptions of the market models hold. Investors can diversify on their own and do not need the company to do it for them. The probability of insolvency is a function of total risk or variability of a company, the sum of both its systematic and unsystematic risks. If bankruptcy costs are significant and there is some probability of insolvency, a company may wish to pay attention to the impact of project selection on total risk. In a portfolio framework, the trade-off between risk and expected *NPV* for different combinations of investments can be analyzed.

In the final section we took up the evaluation of acquisitions using the same framework as for investment projects. If most of the assumptions of a market model hold, diversification by the firm in acquisitions would not be a thing of value. This argues that a company should focus its analysis on the likelihood of operating economies when studying prospective acquisitions. Only operating economies will result in incremental value being gained. As with other capital investments, however, diversification may be a thing of value if there are sizable bankruptcy costs.

FINCOACH EXERCISES

FinCoach on the Prentice Hall Finance Center CD-ROM (Practice Center) has the following categories of practice exercises that pertain to things taken up in this chapter: 5. Stock Valuation; 6. Cost of Capital; 7. Portfolio Diversification; and 8. CAPM. These exercises can be used to supplement the problems that follow.

 ## Self-Correction Problems

1. Determine the required return on equity for the following project situations, using the capital asset pricing model.

Situation	Expected Return Market Portfolio	Risk-Free Rate	Beta
1	15%	10%	1.00
2	18	14	.70
3	15	8	1.20
4	17	11	.80
5	16	10	1.90

What generalizations can you make?

2. Silicon Wafer Company presently pays a dividend of $1. This dividend is expected to grow at a 20 percent rate for 5 years and at 10 percent per annum thereafter. The present market price per share is $20. Using a dividend discount model approach to estimating capital costs, what is the company's expected, or required, return on equity?

3. Novus Nyet Company has two divisions: Health Foods and Specialty Metals. Each of these divisions employs debt equal to 30 percent of its total requirements, with equity capital used for the balance. The current borrowing rate is 8 percent, and the company's tax rate is 40 percent. Novus Nyet wishes to establish a minimum return standard for each division based on the risk of that division. This standard then would serve as the transfer price of capital to the division.

    The company has thought about using the capital asset pricing model in this regard. It has identified two samples of companies, with the following mode-value characteristics:

	Beta	Debt/Total Capitalization Ratio	Tax Rate
Health Foods	.90	.50	.40
Specialty Metals	1.25	.30	.40

    The risk-free rate presently is 6 percent, and the expected return on the market portfolio 11 percent. Using the CAPM approach, what required returns on investment would you recommend for these two divisions?

4. You are evaluating two separate projects as to their effect on the total risk and return of your corporation. The projects are expected to result in the following (in thousands):

	Net Present Value of Company	Standard Deviation
Existing projects only	$6,000	$3,000
Plus project 1	7,500	4,500
Plus project 2	8,200	5,000
Plus projects 1 and 2	9,700	6,100

a. Would you invest in one or both projects?

b. What would you do if a CAPM approach to the problem suggested a different decision?

5. The Williams Warbler Company is contemplating acquiring the Acme Brass Company. Incremental cash flows arising from the acquisition are expected to be the following (in thousands):

	Average of Years		
	1–5	**6–10**	**11–∞**
Cash flow after taxes	$100	$150	$200
Investment required	50	60	70
Net cash flow	$ 50	$ 90	$130

Acme has an all-equity capital structure. Its beta is .80, based on the past 60 months of data relating its excess return to that of the market. The risk-free rate is 9 percent, and the expected return on the market portfolio is 14 percent.

a. What is the maximum price that Williams Warbler Company might pay for Acme?

b. On what assumptions does a price that high depend?

Problems

1. Acosta Sugar Company has estimated that the overall return for Standard & Poor's 500-Stock Index will be 15 percent over the next 10 years. The company also feels that the interest rate on Treasury securities will average 10 percent over this interval. The company is thinking of expanding into a new product line: almonds. It has had no experience in this line but has been able to obtain information on various companies involved in producing and processing nuts. Although no company examined produces only almonds, Acosta's management feels that the beta for such a company would be 1.10 once the almond operation was ongoing. There is some uncertainty about the beta that will actually prevail. Management has attached the following probabilities to possible outcomes:

Probability	.2	.3	.2	.2	.1
Beta	1.00	1.10	1.20	1.30	1.40

a. What is the required rate of return for the project using the mode beta of 1.10?

b. What is the range of required rates of return?

c. What is the expected value of required rate of return?

2. Willie Sutton Bank Vault company has a debt-to-equity ratio (market value) of .75. Its present cost of debt funds is 15 percent, and it has a marginal tax rate of 40 percent. Willie Sutton Bank Vault is eyeing the automated bank

teller business, a field that involves electronics and is considerably different from its own, so the company is looking for a benchmark or proxy company. The Peerless Machine Company, whose stock is publicly traded, produces only automated teller equipment. Peerless has a debt-to-equity ratio of .25, a beta of 1.15, and an effective tax rate of 40 percent.

    a. If Willie Sutton Bank Vault Company wishes to enter the automated bank teller business, what systematic risk (beta) is involved if it intends to employ the same amount of leverage in the new venture as it presently employs?

    b. If the risk-free rate presently is 13 percent and the expected return on the market portfolio is 17 percent, what return should the company require for the project if it uses a CAPM approach?

3. On March 10, International Copy Machines (ICOM), one of the "favorites" of the stock market, was priced at $300 per share. This price was based on an expected annual growth rate of at least 20 percent for quite some time in the future. In July, economic indicators turned down, and investors revised downward to 15 percent their estimate for growth of ICOM. What should happen to the price of the stock? Assume the following:

    a. A perpetual-growth valuation model is a reasonable representation of the way the market values ICOM.

    b. The firm does not change its dividend, the risk complexion of its assets, or its degree of financial leverage.

    c. The dividend next year will be $3 per share.

4. Zosnick Poultry Corporation has launched an expansion program that, in 6 years, should result in the saturation of the Bay Area marketing region of California. As a result, the company is predicting a growth in earnings of 12 percent for 3 years, 6 percent for years 4 through 6, then constant earnings for the foreseeable future. The company expects to increase its dividend per share, now $2, in keeping with this growth pattern. Currently, the market price of the stock is $25 per share. Estimate the company's cost of equity capital.

5. Assuming that a firm has a tax rate of 30 percent, compute the after-tax cost of the following assets:

    a. A bond, sold at par, with a 10.40 percent coupon.

    b. A preferred stock, sold at $100 with a 10 percent coupon and a call price of $110, if the company plans to call the issue in 5 years (use an approximation method).

    c. A common stock selling at $16 and paying a $2 dividend, which is expected to be continued indefinitely.

    d. The same common stock if dividends are expected to grow at the rate of 5 percent per year and the expected dividend in year 1 is $2.

6. The Kalog Precision Tool Company was recently formed to manufacture a new product. The company has the following capital structure in market value terms:

13% debentures of 2005	$ 6,000,000
12% preferred stock	2,000,000
Common stock (320,000 shares)	8,000,000
Total	$16,000,000

The common stock sells for $25 a share, and the company has a marginal tax rate of 40 percent. A study of publicly held companies in this line of business suggests that the required return on equity is about 17 percent for a company of this sort.

    a. Compute the firm's present weighted average cost of capital.

    b. Is the figure computed an appropriate acceptance criterion for evaluating investment proposals?

7. The Tumble Down D Ranch in Montana is considering investing in a new mechanized barn, which will cost $600,000. The new barn is expected to save $90,000 in annual labor costs indefinitely (for practical purposes of computation, forever). The ranch, which is incorporated and has a public market for its stock, has a weighted average cost of capital of 14.5 percent. For this project, Howard Kelsey, the president, intends to use $200,000 in retained earnings and to finance the balance half with debt and half with a new issue of common stock. After-tax flotation costs on the debt issue amount to 2 percent of the total debt raised, whereas flotation costs on the new common stock issue come to 15 percent of the issue. What is the net present value of the project after allowance for flotation costs? Should the ranch invest in the new barn?

8. Grove Plowing, Inc., is considering investing in a new snowplow truck costing $30,000. The truck is likely to provide a cash return after taxes of $10,000 per year for 6 years. The unlevered cost of equity capital of the company is 16 percent. The company intends to finance the project with 60 percent debt, which will bear an interest rate of 12 percent. The loan will be repaid in equal annual principal payments at the end of each of the 6 years. Flotation costs on financing amount to $1,000, and the company is in a 30 percent tax bracket.

    a. What is the adjusted present value (APV) of the project? Is the project acceptable?

    b. What would happen if expected after-tax cash flows were $8,000 per year instead of $10,000?

9. Ponza International, Inc., has three divisions. One is engaged in leisure wear, one in graphics, and one in household paint. The company has identified proxy companies in these lines of business whose stocks are publicly traded. Neither Ponza International nor the proxy companies employ debt in their capital structures. On the basis of analyzing these stocks in relation to the market index, Ponza has estimated that the systematic risks of its three divisions are as follows:

Division	Leisure	Graphics	Paint
Beta	1.16	1.64	.70

The expected return on the market index is 13 percent in the foreseeable future, and the risk-free rate is currently 7 percent. The divisions are evaluating a number of projects, which have the following expected returns:

Project	Division	Expected Return
1	Graphics	18%
2	Paint	12
3	Paint	10
4	Leisure	26
5	Leisure	13
6	Graphics	21
7	Paint	14
8	Graphics	16

    a. Which projects should be accepted and which rejected?

    b. What are the assumptions involved in your acceptance criterion?

10.   a. In your answer to Problem 9a, what would happen if Ponza International had a debt-to-total-capitalization ratio of 40 percent and intended to finance each of the projects with 40 percent debt, at a 6 percent after-tax interest cost, and 60 percent equity? (Assume that everything else was the same, with the exception that the proxy companies now have debt ratios corresponding to that of Ponza.)

    b. In words, what would happen to your answer to Problem 9a if market imperfections made unsystematic risk a factor of importance?

11. The Empire Mining Company's existing portfolio of assets has an expected net present value of $30 million and a standard deviation of $20 million. The company is considering four new explorations. The 16 possible portfolios have the following characteristics (in millions):

Possible Portfolio	Expected Net Present Value	Standard Deviation
1. Existing assets (EA) only	$30	$20
2. EA plus 1	33	23
3. EA plus 2	32	21
4. EA plus 3	35	24
5. EA plus 4	34	25
6. EA plus 1 and 2	35	23
7. EA plus 1 and 3	38	25
8. EA plus 1 and 4	37	26
9. EA plus 2 and 3	37	24
10. EA plus 2 and 4	36	25
11. EA plus 3 and 4	39	28
12. EA plus 1, 2, and 3	40	26
13. EA plus 1, 2, and 4	39	27
14. EA plus 1, 3, and 4	42	30
15. EA plus 2, 3, and 4	41	28
16. EA plus 1, 2, 3, and 4	44	31

   a. Plot these various portfolio possibilities on graph paper.

   b. With a firm-risk approach to evaluating risky investments, which portfolio do you prefer?

12. Cougar Pipe Company is considering the cash acquisition of Red Wilson Rod, Inc., for $750,000. The acquisition is expected to result in incremental cash flows of $125,000 in the first year, and this amount is expected to grow at a 6 percent compound rate. In the absence of the acquisition, Cougar expects net cash flows of $600,000 this coming year (after capital expenditures), and these are expected to grow at a 6 percent compound rate forever. At present, investors and creditors require a 14 percent overall rate of return for Cougar Pipe Company. Red Wilson Rod is much more risky, and the acquisition of it will raise the company's overall required return to 15 percent.

   a. Should Cougar Pipe Company acquire Red Wilson Rod, Inc.?

   b. Would your answer be the same if the overall required rate of return stayed the same?

   c. Would your answer be the same if the acquisition increased the surviving company's growth rate to 8 percent forever?

13. The North Bend Bait Company is contemplating an investment to get it into the production and sale of spinning rods and reels. Heretofore, it has produced only artificial baits. The financial manager of the company, Bruno Litzenberger, feels that the only way to analyze the merit of the project is with a capital asset pricing model approach. Fortunately, Super Splash Spinning Corporation, a publicly held company, produces only spinning fishing equipment. Litzenberger feels it appropriate to use this company as a benchmark for measuring risk. Neither North Bend Bait nor Super Splash employs any leverage. The actual returns to investors in Super Splash over the last 10 years were those shown in the following table. Also shown are 1-year returns for Standard & Poor's 500-Stock Index and the risk-free rate.

| | Annual Return | | |
Year End	Super Splash	Market Index	Risk-Free Rate
20X0	.14	.11	.05
20X1	.21	.17	.07
20X2	(.06)	(.02)	.06
20X3	.30	.25	.08
20X4	.24	.18	.06
20X5	.34	.28	.07
20X6	(.12)	(.08)	.07
20X7	.32	.27	.09
20X8	.19	.14	.07
20X9	(.10)	.00	.08
Average return	.146	.13	.07

Litzenberger believes that the average annual return for the market index and the average annual return for the risk-free rate over the 10-year period are reasonable proxies for the returns likely to prevail in the future.

    a.   Compute the beta for Super Splash Spinning Corporation.

    b.   What is the required return for the project? What assumptions are critical?

(*Note:* To solve, you may use the technique described in the special section "Calculating Betas Manually.")

Solutions to Self-Correction Problems

1.

Situation	Equation	Required Return
1	10% + (15% − 10%)1.00	15.0%
2	14% + (18% − 14%).70	16.8
3	8% + (15% − 8%)1.20	16.4
4	11% + (17% − 11%).80	15.8
5	10% + (16% − 10%)1.90	21.4

The greater the risk-free rate, the greater the expected return on the market portfolio and the greater the beta, the greater will be the required return on equity, all other things being the same. In addition, the greater the market risk premium ($\bar{R}m - R_f$), the greater the required return, all other things being the same.

2.   Through trial and error, one ends up using 18 percent and 19 percent as discount rates.

End of Year	Dividend per Share	Present Value at 18%	Present Value at 19%
1	$1.20	$1.02	$1.01
2	1.44	1.03	1.02
3	1.73	1.05	1.03
4	2.07	1.07	1.03
5	2.49	1.09	1.04
	Present value, 1–5 years =	$5.26	$5.13

Year 6 dividend = $2.49(1.10) = $2.74

Market prices at the end of year 5 using a perpetual growth dividend valuation model:

$$P_5 = \frac{\$2.74}{.18 - .10} = \$34.25 \qquad P_5 = \frac{\$2.74}{.19 - .10} = \$30.44$$

Present value at time 0 for amounts received at end of year 5:

$$\$34.25 \text{ at } 18\% = \$14.97 \qquad \$30.44 \text{ at } 19\% = \$12.76$$

	18%	19%
Present value of 1–5 years	$ 5.26	$ 5.13
Present value of 6–∞ years	14.97	12.76
Present value of all dividends	$20.23	$17.89

Therefore, the discount rate is closer to 18 percent than it is to 19 percent. Interpolating

$$k_e = 18\% + \frac{.23}{20.23 - 17.89} = 18.10\%$$

and this is the estimated return on equity that the market requires.

3. If the proxy companies are used in a CAPM approach, it is clear that different systematic risks are involved in the two divisions. The proxy companies in the health food business have more debt than Novus Nyet Company. In this case, the beta probably should be adjusted for leverage, using the technique presented in the chapter. The beta in the absence of leverage would be

$$\beta_u = \frac{.90}{\left[1 + \left(\frac{.50}{.50}\right)(1 - .4)\right]} = .5625$$

where (.50/.50) is the debt-to-equity ratio. The adjusted beta for the proportion of debt Novus Nyet employs in its division is

$$\text{Adjusted } \beta = .5625\left[1 + \left(\frac{.30}{.70}\right)(1 - .4)\right] = .7071$$

or, with rounding, .71. Given an adjusted proxy beta of .71 for health foods and a proxy beta of 1.25 for specialty metals, the required returns on equity become

	Equation	Required Equity Return
Health Foods	6% + (5%).71	9.55%
Specialty Metals	6% + (5%)1.25	12.25

The after-tax cost of debt funds for both divisions is 8%(1 − .4) = 4.80%. The weighted average required return for each division becomes

	Debt Cost	Weight	Equity Cost	Weight	Weighted Average Required Return
Health Foods	4.80	.3	9.55	.7	8.13%
Specialty Metals	4.80	.3	12.25	.7	10.02

The figures in the last column would be used as minimum, or required, returns for the two divisions.

4. a. The coefficients of variation (standard deviation/*NPV*) for the alternatives are

Existing projects	.50
Plus project 1	.60
Plus project 2	.61
Plus projects 1 and 2	.63

The coefficient of variation increases with either or both investments. A reasonably risk-averse decision maker will prefer the existing projects to any combination of new project additions to existing projects. If this is the case, both new projects will be rejected. The actual decision will depend on your risk preferences. Presumably, these preferences will be influenced by the presence of bankruptcy costs.

b. If the CAPM approach gives an opposite decision, the key to deciding would be the importance of market imperfections. As indicated earlier, if a company's stock is traded in imperfect markets, if the possibility of insolvency is substantive, and if bankruptcy costs are significant, more reliance should be placed on a total variability approach because it recognizes residual plus systematic risk. If things point in the opposite direction, more reliance should be placed on the CAPM results.

5. a. The estimated required rate of return for the acquisition is

$$R_{Acme} = R_f + (\overline{R}_m - R_f)\beta_{Acme}$$

$$= .09 + (.14 - .09)(.80) = .13$$

Using this rate to discount the net cash flows, we obtain

Years	Net Cash Flow		Present-Value Factor		Present Value
1–5	$ 50	×	3.5172	=	$175,860
6–10	90	×	(5.4262 − 3.5172)	=	171,810
11–∞	130	×	[(1/.13) − 5.4262]	=	294,594
					$642,264

The maximum price that should be paid is $642,264.

b. To pay this price, the assumptions of the CAPM must hold. The company is being valued according to its systematic risk only. The effect of the acquisition on the total risk of Williams Warbler Company is assumed not to be a factor of importance to investors. Additionally, we assume that the measurement of beta is accurate and that the estimates of R_f and $\overline{R}_m$ are reasonable.

Selected References

ARDITTI, FRED D., and HAIM LEVY, "The Weighted Average Cost of Capital as a Cutoff Rate: A Critical Analysis of the Classical Textbook Weighted Average," *Financial Management*, 6 (Fall 1977), 24–34.

BEAVER, WILLIAM, and JAMES MANEGOLD, "The Association between Market-Determined and Accounting-Determined Measures of Systematic Risk: Some Further Evidence," *Journal of Financial and Quantitative Analysis*, 10 (June 1975), 231–59.

BERGER, PHILIP G., and ELI OFEK, "Diversification's Effect on Firm Value," *Journal of Financial Economics*, 37 (January 1995), 39–65.

COMMENT, ROBERT, and GREGG A. JARRELL, "Corporate Focus and Stock Returns," *Journal of Financial Economics*, 37 (January 1995), 67–87.

DENIS, DAVID J., DIANE K. DENIS, and ATULYA SARIN, "Agency Problems, Equity Ownership, and Corporate Diversification," *Journal of Finance*, 52 (March 1997), 135–60.

EHRBAR, AL, *EVA, The Real Key to Creating Wealth*. New York: John Wiley, 1998.

FAMA, EUGENE F., and KENNETH R. FRENCH, "The Corporate Cost of Capital and the Return on Corporate Investment," *Journal of Finance*, 54 (December 1999), 1939–68.

FULLER, RUSSELL J., and HALBERT S. KERR, "Estimating the Divisional Cost of Capital: An Analysis of the Pure-Play Technique," *Journal of Finance*, 36 (December 1981), 997–1009.

HAMADA, ROBERT S., "Portfolio Analysis, Market Equilibrium and Corporation Finance," *Journal of Finance*, 24 (March 1969), 13–31.

INDRO, DANIEL C., and WAYNE Y. LEE, "Biases in Arithmetic and Geometric Averages as Estimates of Long-Run Expected Returns and Risk Premia," *Financial Management*, 26 (Winter 1997), 81–90.

KRUEGER, MARK K., and CHARLES M. LINKE, "A Spanning Approach for Estimating Divisional Cost of Capital," *Financial Management*, 23 (Spring 1994), 64–70.

MILES, JAMES A., and JOHN R. EZZELL, "The Weighted Average Cost of Capital, Perfect Capital Markets, and Project Life: A Clarification," *Journal of Financial and Quantitative Analysis*, 15 (September 1980), 719–30.

———, "Reformulating Tax Shield Valuation: A Note," *Journal of Finance*, 40 (December 1985), 1485–92.

MYERS, STEWART C., "Outside Equity," *Journal of Finance*, 55 (June 2000), 1005–37.

MYERS, STEWART C., and STUART M. TURNBULL, "Capital Budgeting and the Capital Asset Pricing Model: Good News and Bad News," *Journal of Finance*, 32 (May 1977), 321–32.

PASTOR, LUBOS, and ROBERT F. STAMBAUGH, "Costs of Equity Capital and Model Mispricing," *Journal of Finance*, 54 (February 1999), 67-121.

RAJAN, RAGHURAM, HENRI SERVAES, and LUIGI ZINGALES, "The Cost of Diversity: The Diversification Discount and Inefficient Investment," *Journal of Finance*, 55 (February 2000), 35–80.

RAPPAPORT, ALFRED, *Creating Shareholder Value*. New York: Free Press, 1998.

SCHALL, LAWRENCE D., "Asset Valuation, Firm Investment, and Firm Diversification," *Journal of Business*, 45 (January 1972), 11–28.

STEIN, JEREMY C., "Rational Capital Budgeting in an Irrational World," *Journal of Business*, 69, No. 4 (1996), 429–55.

VAN HORNE, JAMES C., "Capital-Budgeting Decisions involving Combinations of Risky Investments," *Management Science*, 13 (October 1966), 84–92.

———, "The Analysis of Uncertainty Resolution in Capital Budgeting for New Products," *Management Science*, 15 (April 1969), 376–86.

———, "Optimal Initiation of Bankruptcy Proceedings by Debt Holders," *Journal of Finance*, 31 (June 1976), 897–910.

———, "An Application of the Capital Asset Pricing Model to Divisional Required Returns," *Financial Management*, 9 (Spring 1980), 14–19.

See Chapter 23 for additional references on acquisitions.

Wachowicz's Web World is an excellent overall Web site produced and maintained by my coauthor of *Fundamentals of Financial Management*, John M. Wachowicz Jr. It contains descriptions of and links to many finance Web sites and articles. *www.prenhall.com/wachowicz*.

■ **CASE:** *National Foods Corporation*

In early 1994, Prentice Quick, executive vice president and chief financial officer of National Foods Corporation, was reviewing capital expenditure procedures for the major divisions of the company. This was in anticipation of management presenting the annual capital budget to the board of directors in March. He was concerned about the allocation of capital process among divisions and believed that the underlying standards might need to be changed. Heretofore, the principal objectives of the company had been competitive advantage and growth in the product areas in which National Foods chose to compete.

The company used a single after-tax cost of capital for a hurdle rate, regardless of the division from which a capital proposal emanated. In the low inflationary environment of the mid-1990s, the minimum acceptable return was 13 percent. This minimum return recently had been lowered from 15 percent, but the basis for the reduction was largely subjective. The president of the company, Roscoe Crutcher, simply felt the growth objectives of the company were hampered by a 15 percent rate. Mr. Quick was uneasy not only about the overall required rate of return but also about allocating capital at this single rate.

As a result, he and Laura Atkinson, vice president and treasurer, commissioned a study of the transfer prices of capital among divisions. The study itself was undertaken by Wendell Levine, manager of the corporate analysis and control office, who reported directly to Atkinson. However, Atkinson frequently reviewed the study and together she and Levine proposed the use of multiple required rates of return. As the March board of directors meeting was less than two months away, Mr. Quick and others in senior management needed to come forth with a proposal.

COMPANY BACKGROUND

National Foods Corporation is headquartered in Chicago, with roots going back to the late nineteenth century when it began as a processor of corn and wheat. The company became a public corporation in 1924, and its business gradually changed from commodity-type products to branded items. Presently, the company has three major divisions: agricultural products, bakery products, and restaurants. The fastest growing is restaurants, which continually needs more capital for expansion.

The agricultural products division traces its origin to the very beginning of the company. For many years the company was only a grain processor. In the 1920s, it began to brand certain wheat and corn products for sale to consumers. These included flour, margarine, and corn meal, followed by cake and biscuit mixes. From time to time, the division acquired other enterprises, the most recent being a vitamin supplement feedstock company in 1974. However, this business did not do well in the depressed agricultural marketplace of the 1980s. As a result of this and the consultant report, the business was divested in 1985. Also divested in the mid-1980s were certain pure commodity types of businesses: bean cleaning and wholesaling; the distribution of corn for hog and cattle feeding; and the distribution of wheat to other food processors. Though a few commodity operations remain, the emphasis is on branded agricultural products.

The bakery products division consists entirely of branded products, with many of them enjoying dominant positions in particular product markets. Products include bread, rolls, biscuits, muffins, pizza crusts, some crackers, and an extensive line of cookies. Competition is intense in this industry, but National Foods has achieved product dominance in a number of lines. However, it is concerned about the cracker and cookie lines where the "monster," Nabisco, has been dominant and aggressive. Nonetheless, the bakery products division is profitable, and many lines enjoy considerable promise. Most food industry observers feel that the agricultural commodity price declines during the 1980s and 1990s have been helpful to food processors. Many companies have plowed back their profits into research, development, and marketing, thereby strengthening their franchises.

The last division of National Foods, the restaurant division, has enjoyed impressive growth in recent years. The division has several types of fast food outlets, but the hamburger chain has grown the most dramatically. As the U.S. population has changed demographically as well as employment-wise over the past 20 years, expenditures for food away from the home have increased. This was particularly true in the 1970s and early 1980s. Throughout this time frame there was a rapid expansion of new units, and National Foods' restaurant division was among the leaders. By the early 1990s, this rapid expansion resulted in overcapacity. However, different companies were affected differently, and the restaurant division of National Foods continues to enjoy success. The division itself is operated as an independent entity and is extremely aggressive. Headquartered in Miami, Robert Einhart, the president of the division, has plotted a high growth path for the division. At times, he and other division personnel clash with people from headquarters and from the other divisions. Given to splashy advertising and promotion devices, the division's overall culture is different from that of the company. Management of the bakery products division feels that the new headquarters building in Miami, which is bright orange, is an embarrassment to others who carry the National Foods banner.

With the rapid growth of the restaurant division, it has become a larger part of total sales and operating profit. For 1993, restaurants accounted for 40 percent of the sales and 50 percent of the operating profits of the overall company. In 1985, in contrast, the restaurant division accounted for less than 10 percent of sales and profits. National Foods President Roscoe Crutcher was aware of the rivalry among divisions but felt that it was healthy as long as it was kept in balance. Many in the agricultural products and bakery products divisions did not think that things were in balance. They felt that they would ultimately end up working for a restaurant company headed by Mr. Einhart. Mr. Crutcher was not about to give up the restaurant division, yet he wanted it to play a healthy, stimulating role in the evolution of National Foods. Nowhere did the rivalry become more focused than in the capital allocation process, where the restaurant division requested ever-increasing capital to serve its expansion needs

CAPITAL INVESTMENT PROCEDURES AND FINANCING

Like most companies, National Foods Corporation has layered levels of approval, with the largest projects being approved only by the board of directors. Each division was charged with preparing capital budgeting requests, item by item. Routine types of expenditures could be lumped together. However, any major expenditure had to be documented as to expected cash flows, payback, internal rate of return,

Exhibit 1

National Foods Corporation Consolidated Balance Sheet (in millions)

Assets	OCTOBER 31 1993	OCTOBER 31 1992	OCTOBER 31 1991
Current assets			
Cash and marketable securities	$ 109.5	$ 87.7	$ 65.1
Receivables	536.9	505.1	484.9
Inventories	413.5	374.5	356.6
Other current assets	23.0	45.2	32.3
Total current assets	$1,082.9	$1,012.5	$938.9
Long-term assets			
Land, buildings, and equipment	1,234.4	1,082.4	1,073.3
Less accumulated depreciation	462.6	389.0	342.7
Net land, buildings, and equipment	$771.8	$ 693.4	$ 730.6
Other tangible assets	58.0	10.8	22.2
Intangible assets	121.2	125.2	115.1
Total assets	$2,033.9	$1,841.9	$1,806.8

Liabilities and Shareholders' Equity			
Current liabilities			
Short-term debt	$ 275.6	$ 144.9	$ 214.3
Current portion of long-term debt	26.1	23.1	2.8
Accounts payable	204.3	179.1	196.1
Taxes payable	42.4	50.0	11.9
Accruals	237.7	214.7	197.0
Total current liabilities	$ 786.1	$ 611.8	$ 622.1
Long-term debt	160.9	168.2	200.1
Other liabilities	48.7	59.9	62.1
Deferred income taxes	207.1	177.2	163.9
Total liabilities	$1,202.8	$1,017.1	$1,048.2
Preference stock	—	37.9	38.5
Shareholders' equity			
Common stock	210.0	210.0	105.0
Paid-in capital	0.6	3.4	26.3
Retained earnings	847.7	728.4	703.2
Cumulative exchange adjustment	(87.9)	(103.2)	(89.9)
Treasury stock, at cost	(139.3)	(51.7)	(24.5)
Total shareholders' equity	$ 831.1	$ 786.9	$ 720.1
Total liabilities and equity	$2,033.9	$1,841.9	$1,806.8

and a qualitative assessment of the risk involved. These proposals were reviewed by the corporate analysis and control office, headed by Wendell Levine. While neither he nor his boss, Laura Atkinson, had final authority, they made recommendations on each of the larger projects.

Projects fell into one of two categories: profit-adding and profit-sustaining. The profit-adding projects were those where the cash flows could be estimated and discounted cash flow methods employed. The profit-sustaining projects were those that did not provide a measurable return. Rather, they were projects necessary to keep the business going; for example, environmental and health controls as well as

Exhibit 2

National Foods Corporation Consolidated Statement of Earnings (in millions)

	FISCAL YEAR		
	1993	*1992*	*1991*
Net sales	$3,670.7	$3,520.1	$3,344.1
Gross profit	1,551.5	1,387.1	1,271.0
Profit before taxes	321.0	292.7	260.1
Taxes	141.4	136.1	121.4
Profit after taxes	$ 179.6	$ 156.6	$ 138.7
Dividends (common and preferred)	57.6	54.1	48.3
Earnings per share (in dollars)	$4.49	$3.76	$3.35
Dividends per common share (in dollars)	1.40	1.24	1.10

certain corporate assets. Approximately 20 percent of the projects proposed and accepted, in dollar volume, were profit-sustaining in nature. For profit-adding projects, the 13 percent required rate of return was used as the hurdle rate. Projects that fell below this return simply were not sent forward. The use of this discount rate was supplemented by the financial goal of "achieving growth in sales and earnings per share without undue diminution in the quality of the earnings stream." This objective was sufficiently "fuzzy" that most did not take cognizance of it in the capital budgeting process. Rather, the 13 percent return was the key variable. It was simply assumed that if projects provided returns in excess of this figure, they would give the company a continuing growth in "quality" earnings per share.

Overall, the company has a total debt-to-equity ratio of 1.45. However, much of the total debt is represented by accounts payable and accruals. All borrowings are controlled at the corporate level, and there is no formal allocation of debt or equity funds to the individual divisions. Everything is captured in the minimum hurdle rate, 13 percent. However, the restaurant division is characterized by having to undertake a number of lease contracts in order to expand outlets. Although many of the outlets are owned outright, others are leased. National Foods does not monitor the number of leases being undertaken by the restaurant division, but it does monitor expansion plans by the division. While the required rate of return of the company once represented a blending of the costs of debt and equity financing, this no longer is the case. In recent years it has been adjusted on a subjective basis, in keeping with returns earned by competitors in the industry. National Foods has little difficulty financing itself. It enjoys an A investment rating by both Moody's and Standard & Poor's. In addition, it has ample lines of credit with commercial banks.

REQUIRED RATES OF RETURN

Mr. Levine's office was charged with determining what would happen if the company moved from a single required rate of return to multiple hurdle rates. His group focused on using external market valuations for the required rates of return of the various divisions. For debt capital, it proposed using the company's overall rate of interest on bonds. In early 1994, this rate was approximately 8 percent. The company faced a tax rate of approximately 40 percent, when both federal and state income taxes were taken into account.

Exhibit 3

National Foods Corporation Segment Analysis (in millions)

	FISCAL YEAR		
	1993	*1992*	*1991*
Sales			
Agricultural products	$ 710	$ 855	$ 819
Bakery products	1,487	1,384	1,416
Restaurants	1,474	1,281	1,109
	$3,671	$3,520	$3,344
Operating profit			
Agricultural products	69	75	51
Bakery products	148	123	136
Restaurants	219	161	129
	$ 436	$ 359	$ 316
Identifiable assets			
Agricultural products	241	301	353
Bakery products	589	560	549
Restaurants	799	619	538
Corporate	405	362	367
	$2,034	$1,842	$1,807

For the required return on equity capital, the study group used the capital asset pricing model (CAPM). In this context the measure of risk is beta, the covariability of a stock's return with that of the overall market as represented by Standard & Poor's 500-Stock Index. The return on equity is simply

$$R_j = R_j(\overline{R}_m - R_f)\beta_j$$

where R_j is the risk-free rate, $\overline{R}_m$ is the return required on the market portfolio, as represented by the S&P 500-Stock Index, and β_j is the beta of security j. In early 1994, 3-month Treasury bills yielded approximately 3.1 percent, 3-year Treasury notes 4.6 percent, 5-year Treasury notes 5.4 percent, and long-term Treasury bonds 7.0 percent. Because the typical investment project had an "average life" of 5 years, Mr. Levine's group proposed using the 5-year Treasury rate as the risk-free rate in their calculations. Estimates by various investment banks of the required return on the overall market portfolio of common stocks averaged 11.0 percent in early 1994.

To determine the betas for the divisions, Mr. Levine and his staff proposed the use of proxy, or "pure play" companies, that is, companies that were closely identified with the business of the division, but that had publicly traded stocks. After extensive study, Mr. Levine and his staff proposed the list of companies shown in Exhibit 4. For the restaurant division there were a reasonable number of proxy companies. This was not the case for agricultural products or for bakery products. Unfortunately for bakery products, some of the larger businesses were divisions of multidivision companies. In particular, Nabisco was part of R.J.R. Nabisco and could not be differentiated. For agricultural products, some of the largest grain processors are privately owned, so that they do not appear in the sample. However, the study group felt that the proxy companies were representa-

Exhibit 4
National Foods Corporation
Financial Information on Proxy Companies

	BETA	LONG-TERM LIABILITIES TO CAPITALIZATION
Agricultural products		
American Maize Products	.90	.45
Archer Daniels, Inc.	1.05	.30
Conagra, Inc.	.76	.42
Staley Continental	1.20	.51
Average	.98	.42
Bakery products		
American Bakeries	.85	.38
Flowers Industries	.75	.46
Interstate Bakeries	.85	.31
Average	.82	.38
Restaurants (fast foods)		
Carl Karcher Enterprises	1.10	.55
Chi Chi's	1.35	.43
Church's Fried Chicken	1.24	.15
Collins Foods	1.35	.48
Jerrico, Inc.	1.10	.30
McDonald's Corporation	1.10	.49
Ponderosa, Inc.	1.30	.30
Sizzler Restaurants	1.60	.40
Vicorp Restaurants	1.40	.56
Wendy's International	1.15	.36
Average	1.27	.40

tive, and that the summary information was useful. For the betas, the group proposed using a simple average for each category of proxy companies. This meant a beta of .98 for agricultural products, .82 for bakery products, and 1.27 for restaurants.

Concerning the debt employed to get blended costs of capital, National Foods recently established a target long-term liabilities-to-capitalization ratio of 40 percent. Capitalization consisted of all long-term liabilities (including the current portion of long-term debt), plus shareholders' equity. The target of 40 percent was somewhat higher than the existing ratio. For capital expenditure purposes the relevant financing vehicles were felt to be long-term liabilities and equity, not short-term debt, payables, and accruals.

The agricultural products and the bakery products divisions did not need that much in debt funds, as their internal cash flows were sufficient to finance most capital expenditures. (The agricultural products division uses short-term debt to carry inventories.) Originally, Mr. Levine proposed that for calculation purposes these two divisions have long-term liability-to-capitalization ratios of .35. Given the growth in and demands of the restaurant division, he proposed that this division have a ratio of .45. The representative for the restaurant division objected to this percentage, claiming that it should be higher. When Mr. Einhart learned of this he went directly to Mr. Levine and Ms. Atkinson. He claimed that if the restaurant division were stand-alone, it could command a ratio of at least .60, based on its real estate value. In order to compete, he claimed that he must have a debt ratio consistent with the more aggressive companies in the industry. Mr. Einhart threatened to take the matter directly to Roscoe Crutcher, the president, unless he got his way. Eventually, Einhart, Atkinson, and Levine struck a compromise and agreed to a long-term liability-to-capitalization ratio of .50 for the restaurant division. To accommodate this change within the overall capital structure objectives of the company, Mr. Levine cut the agricultural products and the bakery products divisions ratios to .30.

In order to allow for profit-sustaining projects, Mr. Levine proposed grossing up the divisional required returns. With 20 percent of the projects on average being profit-sustaining, which were presumed to have a zero percent expected return, the "gross-up" multiplier was 1.25. That is, if a division were found to have an overall after-tax required return of 9.6 percent, it would be grossed up to be 9.6%(1.25) = 12.0 percent. As profit-sustaining projects were a cost of doing business, profit-adding projects had to earn enough to carry them. The simple gross-up was easiest to apply, and Mr. Levine proposed that it be the same for all divisions.

When Laura Atkinson, vice president and treasurer, was talking with Mr. Levine, she reminded him that the question of single versus multiple required returns was not resolved. Therefore, it would be useful to calculate a required return for the overall company in the same manner as was to be done for the divisions. The beta for National Foods Corporation in early 1994 was 1.05, and it had been relatively stable in recent years. It was felt that a target long-term liabilities-to-capitalization ratio of .40 should be employed.

THE MEETING

As the required returns report would be completed shortly, Prentice Quick, the CFO, needed to arrange a meeting among himself, other members of senior management, and the presidents of the three divisions. He asked Laura Atkinson to present the report to management.

The meeting would be an important one, because the decisions reached would determine the method by which capital would be allocated to the various divisions both now and in the future. It also would establish the standard for judging return-on-asset performance. Mr. Crutcher was anxious to get the matter resolved so that management would be on a solid footing when it went to the board of directors in March for capital allocations. While Mr. Einhart, president of the restaurant division, was familiar with the report, the other divisional presidents were not. Mr. Einhart made it known to Mr. Crutcher that although he could live with the system proposed in the report, he felt it much simpler to have a single required rate of return for all the divisions. "If your objective is competitive advantage and growth, you have to keep your eye on the fundamentals of the business. These financial whizzes don't produce value for the shareholders—we do. Don't shackle us with too many constraints," was a statement he made in passing to Mr. Crutcher.

Part III

FINANCING AND DIVIDEND POLICIES

■ **CASE:** *Restructuring the Capital Structure at Marriott*

On October 5, 1992, Marriott Corporation announced a plan to restructure the company by splitting itself into two parts. The announcement caused immediate and opposite price movements for its stock and its bonds. Stockholders were happy and bondholders were in a furor, particularly those who had bought a new issue of bonds in April.

RESTRUCTURING PLAN

The two separate companies were to be Marriott International and Host Marriott. The former company would manage/franchise over 700 hotels and motels. In addition, it would manage food and facilities for several thousand businesses, schools, and health-care providers. Finally, it would manage 14 retirement homes under contract. For these businesses, 1991 sales amounted to $7.4 billion. J. Willard Marriott Jr., chairman of Marriott Corporation, was to become chairman of Marriott International.

Host Marriott was to own most of the hard assets. More specifically, it would own 139 hotels or motels, 14 retirement communities, and nearly 100 restaurants/shops at airports and along toll roads. For these businesses, 1991 sales were $1.7 billion. Operating cash flows for these businesses approximated 40 percent of total Marriott Corporation operating cash flows, pre-restructuring. Richard Marriott, vice chairman of Marriott Corporation, was to become chairman of this company.

The key element in the restructuring plan was that Host Marriott was to keep the debt associated with these assets, approximately $2.9 billion. In contrast, Marriott International would have only modest debt after the restructuring. The bond indenture was felt not to preclude such a transfer of assets and debt. Known as event risk to bondholders, there were numerous cases of this in the 1980s with the leveraged buyout movement. Bondholder wealth was expropriated in favor of

249

equity holders, and the Marriott restructuring was felt to be a variation of the same theme. While Marriott International was to provide a $630 million line of credit to Host Marriott, the expiration date of the line was sooner than the maturities of many of the bond issues outstanding.

Merrill Lynch was advisor to Marriott on the restructuring plan, and Marriott's new chief financial officer, Stephen Bollenbach, was instrumental in the development of the restructuring plan. It called for stockholders of Marriott Corporation to receive one share of stock in each of the new companies for each share of stock previously held. Technically, the transaction represents a spin-off. The Marriott family owned approximately 25 percent of the shares before, and would initially own the same percent in each of the two companies afterward.

THE COMPANY'S DEBT STRUCTURE

Year-end balance sheets for 1991 and 1990 are shown in Exhibit 1, and long-term debt at January 3, 1992, is seen to be $3.2 billion. This debt included some dozen bond issues with a total face value of $2\frac{1}{4}$ billion. Maturities ranged from 1 to 15 years, and all issues were rated BBB by Standard & Poor's. This rating was later lowered to single B, which remained the bond rating for the new Host Marriott. In contrast, Marriott International received a rating of single A, an increase over the rating for the pre-restructured company.

The company's legacy of debt came from aggressive expansion of hotels and motels in the 1980s. With depressed real estate conditions in the early 1990s, the company was unable/unwilling to sell off certain assets and reduce its debt. The company's strategy was to manage properties, not necessarily to own them. For the most part, ownership was viewed as only a temporary phenomenon during initial development.

SECURITY PRICE REACTIONS AND GOING FORWARD

Exhibit 3 shows the prices of Marriott Corporation's common stock and two of its bond issues around the time of the restructuring announcement. The stock increased sharply in price, while the bonds dropped. These reactions are consistent with a wealth transfer, recognizing that other things were not held constant. Still the bond and the stock markets voted with their feet. The initial reaction of bondholders was to call "foul." Those that bought the April 1992 bond issue were even more vocal, citing the legal words *fraudulent conveyance*. The good company/bad company syndrome was invoked.

Marriott management tried to assure bondholders that it was their intent to service all debt on time and that the interest and principal payments promised would be delivered. Therefore, bondholders should not worry. Stockholders, in the meantime, were elated with the restructuring plan. All three parties to the transaction—bondholders, stockholders, and management—needed to plot their next steps.

Exhibit 1

Marriott Corporation Consolidated Balance Sheets,
1991 and 1990 Year Ends (in millions)

	JANUARY 3 1992	DECEMBER 28 1990
Cash and cash equivalents	$ 36	$ 283
Accounts receivable	524	654
Inventories	243	261
Prepayments	220	230
Current assets	$1,023	$1,428
Investment in affiliates	455	462
Net property, plant and equipment	2,485	2,774
Assets held for sale	1,524	1,274
Goodwill	476	494
Other assets	437	494
Total assets	$6,400	$6,926
Current maturities, LTD	$ 52	$ 75
Accounts payable	579	675
Accruals	704	887
Current liabilities	$1,335	$1,637
Long-term debt	3,189	3,598
Deferred taxes	614	584
Deferred income	232	312
Other liabilities	351	388
Preferred stock	200	—
Common shareholders' equity	479	407
Total liabilities and equity	$6,400	$6,926

E x h i b i t   2

Marriott Corporation Statements of Income,
1991 and 1990 Fiscal Years (in millions)

	JANUARY 2 1992	DECEMBER 28 1990
Net sales	$ 8,331	$7,646
Costs and expenses	7,692	7,069
Depreciation and amortization	272	208
Other income	43	47
Interest expense	320	324
Restructuring costs	—	153
Other income	55	141
Income before taxes	$ 145	$ 80
Income taxes	63	33
Income after taxes	$ 82	$ 47
Dividends	$ 27	$ 27
Earnings per share	.80	.46
Dividends per share	.28	.28

E x h i b i t   3

Marriott Corporation Security Prices
around Time of Restructuring Announcement

	9 3/8% OF 6/15/1997	9 1/2% OF 5/1/2002	COMMON SHARES
October 1, 1992	$111.0	$108.0	$ 17 1/8
October 2	111.2	108.2	17 1/8
October 5 (announcement)	89.3	83.6	19 1/4
October 6	83.9	83.1	19 1/8
October 7	79.4	82.7	19 1/8
October 8	80.3	82.7	18 1/2
October 9	83.1	83.2	18 5/8
October 30	88.9	87.4	20
November 30	89.2	91.3	20 3/8
December 31	94.7	93.6	20 3/4

9

Theory of Capital Structure

In Part II we looked into allocating capital to investment proposals, when we had a given financing mix. In this chapter and the next, we are going to find out whether the way in which investment proposals are financed matters, and if it does, what the optimal capital structure might be. If we finance with one mix of securities rather than another, is the market price of the stock affected? If a company can affect the market price of its stock by its financing decision, it will want to undertake a financing policy that will maximize its valuation. For simplicity, we examine the question of capital structure in terms of the proportion of debt to equity; however, the principles taken up in this chapter can be easily expanded to include consideration of the specific type of security being issued. ■

INTRODUCTION TO THE THEORY

Even a casual review of the literature brings one quickly to the key question of whether or not **capital structure** matters. Can a company affect its total valuation and its required return by changing its financing mix? In this section, we are going to find out what happens to the total valuation of the firm and to its cost of capital when the ratio of debt to equity, or degree of leverage, is varied. We use a capital market equilibrium approach because it allows us to abstract from factors other than leverage that affect valuation.

Capital structure is the proportions of debt instruments and preferred and common stock on a company's balance sheet.

Assumptions and Definitions

To present the analysis as simply as possible, we make the following assumptions:

1. There are no corporate or personal income taxes and no bankruptcy costs. (Later, we remove these assumptions.)
2. The ratio of debt to equity for a firm is changed by issuing debt to repurchase stock or issuing stock to pay off debt. In other words, a change in capital structure is effected immediately. In this regard, we assume no transaction costs.
3. The firm has a policy of paying 100 percent of its earnings in dividends. Thus, we abstract from the dividend decision.

4. The expected values of the subjective probability distributions of expected future operating earnings for each company are the same for all investors in the market.

5. The operating earnings of the firm are not expected to grow. The expected values of the probability distributions of expected operating earnings for all future periods are the same as present operating earnings.

Given these assumptions, we are concerned with the following three rates:

$$k_i = \frac{F}{B} = \frac{\text{Annual interest charges}}{\text{Market value of debt outstanding}} \qquad (9\text{-}1)$$

In this equation, k_i is the yield on the company's debt, assuming this debt to be perpetual.

$$k_e = \frac{E}{S} = \frac{\text{Earnings available to common stockholders}}{\text{Market value of stock outstanding}} \qquad (9\text{-}2)$$

The earnings/price ratio is the required rate of return for investors in a company whose earnings are not expected to grow and whose dividend-payout ratio is 100 percent. With our restrictive assumptions, then, the earnings/price ratio represents the market rate of discount that equates the present value of the stream of expected future dividends with the current market price of the stock. It should not be used as a general rule to depict the required return on equity, for with expected growth it is a biased and low estimate (see Chapter 8 on measuring capital costs). We use it only because of its simplicity in illustrating the theory of capital structure. The final rate we consider is

$$k_o = \frac{O}{V} = \frac{\text{Net operating earnings}}{\text{Total market value of the firm}} \qquad (9\text{-}3)$$

where $V = B + S$. Here, k_o is an overall capitalization rate for the firm. It is defined as the weighted average cost of capital and may also be expressed as

WACE

$$k_o = k_i\left(\frac{B}{B+S}\right) + k_e\left(\frac{S}{B+S}\right) \qquad (9\text{-}4)$$

We want to know what happens to k_i, k_e, and k_o when the degree of leverage, as denoted by the ratio B/S, increases.

Net Operating Income Approach

One approach to the valuation of the earnings of a company is known as the **net operating income approach**. To illustrate it, assume that a firm has $1,000 in debt at 10 percent interest, that the expected value of annual net operating earnings is $1,000, and that the overall capitalization rate, k_o, is 15 percent. Given this information, we may calculate the value of the firm as follows:

O	Net operating income	$1,000
k_o	Overall capitalization rate	.15
V	Total value of firm	$6,667
B	Market value of debt	1,000
S	Market value of stock	$5,667

WACC

The earnings available to common stockholders, E, is simply net operating income minus interest payments, or $1,000 − $100 = $900. The implied required return on equity is

$$k_e = \frac{E}{S} = \frac{\$900}{\$5,667} = 15.88\%$$

With this approach, net operating income is capitalized at an overall capitalization rate to obtain the total market value of the firm. The market value of the debt then is deducted from the total market value to obtain the market value of the stock. Note that with this approach the overall capitalization rate, k_o, as well as the cost of debt funds, k_i, stay the same regardless of the degree of leverage. The required return on equity, however, increases linearly with leverage.

To illustrate, suppose the firm increases the amount of debt from $1,000 to $3,000 and uses the proceeds of the debt issue to repurchase stock. The valuation of the firm then is

O	Net operating income	$1,000
k_o	Overall capitalization rate	.15
V	Total value of firm	$6,667
B	Market value of debt	3,000
S	Market value of stock	$3,667

Debt + Stock = total value

The implied required return on equity is

$$k_e = \frac{E}{S} = \frac{\$700}{\$3,667} = 19.09\%$$

We see that the required equity return, k_e, rises with the degree of leverage. This approach implies that the total valuation of the firm is unaffected by its capital structure. Figure 9-1 shows the approach graphically. Not only is the total value of the company unaffected, but so too is share price. To illustrate, assume in our example that the firm with $1,000 in debt has 100 shares of common stock outstanding. Thus, the market price per share is $56.67 ($5,667/100). The firm issues $2,000 in additional debt and, at the same time, repurchases $2,000 of stock at $56.67 per share, or 35.29 shares in total if we permit fractional shares. It then has 100 − 35.29 shares = 64.71 shares outstanding. We saw in the example that the total market value of the firm's stock after the change in capital structure is $3,667. Therefore, the market price per share is $3,667/64.71 = $56.67, the same as before the increase in leverage and recapitalization.

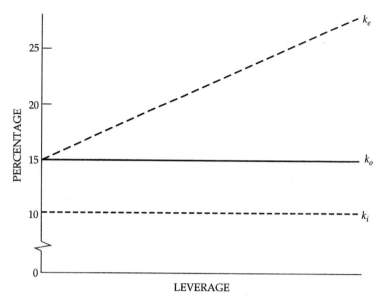

FIGURE 9-1

Capital costs: net operating income approach

Important Assumptions The critical assumption with this approach is that k_o is constant, regardless of the degree of leverage. The market capitalizes the value of the firm as a whole; as a result, the breakdown between debt and equity is unimportant. An increase in the use of supposedly "cheaper" debt funds is offset exactly by the increase in the required equity return, k_e. Thus, the weighted average of k_e and k_i remains unchanged for all degrees of leverage. As the firm increases its degree of leverage, it becomes increasingly more risky. Investors penalize the stock by raising the required equity return directly in keeping with the increase in the debt-to-equity ratio. As long as k_i remains constant, k_e is a constant linear function of the debt-to-equity ratio. Because the cost of capital of the firm, k_o, cannot be altered through leverage, the net operating income approach implies that there is no one optimal capital structure.

So far our discussion of the net operating income approach has been purely definitional; it lacks behavioral significance. Modigliani and Miller, in their famous 1958 article, offered behavioral support for the independence of the total valuation and the cost of capital of the firm from its capital structure.[1] Before taking up the implications of their position, however, we examine the traditional approach to valuation.

Traditional Approach

The **traditional approach** to valuation and leverage assumes that there is an optimal capital structure and that the firm can increase the total value of the firm through the judicious use of leverage. The approach suggests that the firm initially can lower its cost of capital and raise its total value through leverage. Although investors raise the required rate of return on equity, the increase in k_e does not offset entirely the benefit of using "cheaper" debt funds. As more leverage occurs, investors increasingly penalize the firm's required equity return until eventually this effect more than offsets the use of "cheaper" debt funds.

[1]Franco Modigliani and Merton H. Miller, "The Cost of Capital, Corporation Finance and the Theory of Investment," *American Economic Review,* 48 (June 1958), 261–97.

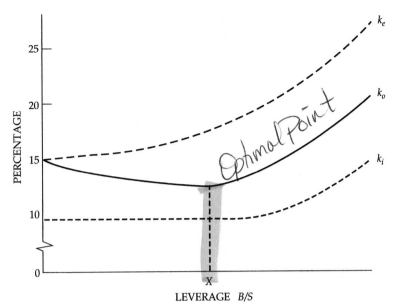

FIGURE 9-2
Traditional approach

In one variation of the traditional approach, shown in Fig. 9-2, k_e is assumed to rise at an increasing rate with leverage, whereas k_i is assumed to rise only after significant leverage has occurred. At first, the weighted average cost of capital declines with leverage because the rise in k_e does not entirely offset the use of cheaper debt funds. As a result, the weighted average cost of capital, k_o, declines with moderate use of leverage. After a point, however, the increase in k_e more than offsets the use of cheaper debt funds in the capital structure, and k_o begins to rise. The rise in k_o is supported further once k_i begins to rise. The optimal capital structure is the point at which k_o bottoms out. In the figure, this optimal capital structure is point X. Thus, the traditional position implies that the cost of capital is not independent of the capital structure of the firm and that there is an optimal capital structure.

MODIGLIANI–MILLER POSITION   IN A PERFECT WORLD — THEORETICAL!

Modigliani and Miller are two economists who demonstrated that with perfect financial markets capital structure is irrelevant.

Modigliani and Miller (MM) in their original position advocate that the relationship between leverage and the cost of capital is explained by the net operating income approach. They make a formidable attack on the traditional position by offering behavioral justification for having the cost of capital, k_o, remain constant throughout all degrees of leverage. As their assumptions are important, it is necessary to spell them out.

1. Capital markets are perfect. Information is costless and readily available to all investors. There are no transactions costs, and all securities are infinitely divisible. Investors are assumed to be rational and to behave accordingly.

2. The average expected future operating earnings of a firm are represented by subjective random variables. It is assumed that the expected values of the probability distribution of all investors are the same. The MM illustration implies that the expected values of the probability distributions of

expected operating earnings for all future periods are the same as present operating earnings.

3. Firms can be categorized into "equivalent return" classes. All firms within a class have the same degree of business risk. As we shall see later, this assumption is not essential for their proof.

4. The absence of corporate income taxes is assumed. MM remove this assumption later.

Simply put, the Modigliani–Miller position is based on the idea that no matter how you divide up the capital structure of a firm among debt, equity, and other claims, there is a conservation of investment value.[2] That is, because the total investment value of a corporation depends on its underlying profitability and risk, it is invariant with respect to relative changes in the firm's financial capitalization. Thus, the total pie does not change as it is divided into debt, equity, and other securities. The sum of the parts must equal the whole; so regardless of financing mix, the total value of the firm stays the same, according to MM. The idea is illustrated with the two pies in Fig. 9-3. Different mixes of debt and equity do not alter the size of the pie—total value stays the same.

Homemade Leverage

The support for this position rests on the idea that investors are able to substitute personal for corporate leverage, thereby replicating any capital structure the firm might undertake. Because the company is unable to do something for its stockholders (leverage) that they cannot do for themselves, capital structure changes are not a thing of value in the perfect capital market world that MM assume. Therefore, two firms alike in every respect except capital structure must have the same total value. If not, arbitrage will be possible, and its occurrence will cause the two firms to sell in the market at the same total value.

Illustration   Consider two firms identical in every respect except that company A is not levered, while company B has $30,000 of 12 percent bonds outstanding. According to the traditional position, company B may have a higher total value and

FIGURE 9-3
Illustration of capital structure irrelevancy

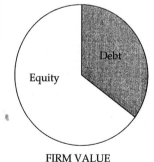

FIRM VALUE

FIRM VALUE

[2]This idea was first espoused by John Burr Williams, *The Theory of Investment Value* (Amsterdam: North-Holland, 1938), pp. 72–73.

lower average cost of capital than company A. The valuation of the two firms is assumed to be the following:

Homemade leverage can replicate the firm's capital structure, thereby causing investors to be indifferent to it.

		Company A	Company B
O	Net operating income	$10,000	$10,000
F	Interest on debt		3,600
E	Earnings available to common stockholders	$10,000	$ 6,400
k_e	Required equity return	.15	.16
S	Market value of stock	$66,667	$40,000
B	Market value of debt		30,000
V	Total value of firm	$66,667	$70,000
k_o	Implied overall capitalization rate	15%	14.3%
B/S	Debt-to-equity ratio	0	75.0%

MM maintain that this situation cannot continue, for arbitrage will drive the total values of the two firms together. Company B cannot command a higher total value simply because it has a financing mix different from company A's. MM argue that by investing in company A, investors in company B are able to obtain the same dollar return with no increase in financial risk. Moreover, they are able to do so with a smaller investment outlay.[3] Because investors would be better off with the investment requiring the lesser outlay, they would sell their shares in company B and buy shares in company A. These **arbitrage transactions** would continue until company B's shares declined in price and company A's shares increased in price enough to make the total value of the two firms identical.

Arbitrage Steps   If you are a rational investor who owns 1 percent of the stock of company B, the levered firm, worth $400 (market value) you should

1. Sell the stock in company B for $400.
2. Borrow $300 at 12 percent interest. This personal debt is equal to 1 percent of the debt of company B, your previous proportional ownership of the company.
3. Buy 1 percent of the shares of company A, the unlevered firm, for $666.67.

Prior to this series of transactions, your expected return on investment in company B's stock was 16 percent on a $400 investment, or $64. Your expected return on investment in company A is 15 percent on a $666.67 investment, or $100.

---

[3]This arbitrage proof appears in Franco Modigliani and Merton H. Miller, "Reply to Heins and Sprenkle," *American Economic Review,* 59 (September 1969), 592–95.

From this return you must deduct the interest charges on your personal borrowings, so your net dollar return is

Return on investment in company A	$100
Less: interest ($300 × .12)	36
Net return	$ 64

Arbitrage efficiency means all opportunities for arbitrage profit have been driven out.

Your net dollar return, $64, is the same as it was for your investment in company B; however, your cash outlay of $366.67 ($666.67 less personal borrowings of $300) is less than the $400 investment in company B, the levered firm. Because of the lower investment, you would prefer to invest in company A under the conditions described. In essence, you "lever" the stock of the unlevered firm by taking on personal debt.

The action of a number of investors undertaking similar arbitrage transactions will tend to drive up the price of company A shares, lower its k_e, drive down the price of company B, and increase its k_e. This arbitrage process will continue until there is no further opportunity for reducing one's investment outlay and achieving the same dollar return. At this equilibrium, the total value of the two firms must be the same. The principle involved is simply that investors are able to replicate any capital structure the firm might undertake through personal leverage. Unless a company is able to do something for investors that they cannot do for themselves, value is not created.

Irrelevance in a CAPM Framework

It is important to realize that MM's proof of the proposition that leverage is irrelevant does not depend on the two firms' belonging to the same risk class. This assumption was invoked for easier illustration of the arbitrage process. However, equilibrium occurs across securities of different companies on the basis of expected return and risk. If the assumptions of the capital asset pricing model hold, as they would in perfect capital markets, the irrelevance of capital structure can be demonstrated using the CAPM.

Consider the expected return and systematic risk of a levered company. The firm's expected return is simply a weighted average of the expected returns for the debt and equity securities.

$$k_o = \left(\frac{B}{B + S}\right)k_i + \left(\frac{S}{B + S}\right)k_e \tag{9-5}$$

where, as before, B is the market value of debt, S is the market value of stock, k_i is now the expected return on the firm's debt, and k_e is the expected return on its stock. Rearranging this equation and canceling out, we obtain[4]

---

[4]The rearrangement to obtain Eq. (9-6) is

$$k_e = \frac{k_o - \left(\frac{B}{B + S}\right)k_i}{\frac{S}{B + S}} = \left(\frac{B + S}{S}\right)k_o - \left(\frac{B}{S}\right)k_i = k_o + \frac{B}{S}(k_o - k_i)$$

$$k_e = k_o + \frac{B}{S}(k_o - k_i) \tag{9-6}$$

Here we see that the expected return on the stock increases in proportion to increases in the debt-to-equity ratio.

As described by beta, the systematic risk of the overall firm is simply a weighted average of the betas of the individual securities of the firm.

$$\beta_{firm} = \left(\frac{B}{B + S}\right)\beta_{debt} + \left(\frac{S}{B + S}\right)\beta_{stock} \tag{9-7}$$

Rearranging and canceling out as we did before, we obtain

$$\beta_{stock} = \beta_{firm} + \frac{B}{S}\left(\beta_{firm} - \beta_{debt}\right) \tag{9-8}$$

Thus, an increase in the debt-to-equity ratio increases not only the expected return of a stock but also its beta. With perfect capital markets, both increase proportionally, so that they offset each other with respect to their effect on share price. The increase in return is just sufficient to offset the additional return required by investors for the increment in beta. Therefore, share price being invariant with respect to leverage can be shown in the context of the CAPM equilibrating process of risk and expected return.

TAXES AND CAPITAL STRUCTURE

The irrelevance of capital structure rests on an absence of market imperfections. No matter how one slices the corporate pie between debt and equity, there is a conservation of value, so that the sum of the parts is always the same. In other words, nothing is lost or gained in the slicing. To the extent that there are capital market imperfections, however, changes in the capital structure of a company may affect the total size of the pie. That is to say, the firm's valuation and cost of capital may change with changes in its capital structure. One of the most important imperfections is the presence of taxes. In this regard, we examine the valuation impact of corporate taxes in the absence of personal taxes and then the combined effect of corporate and personal taxes.

Corporate Taxes

The advantage of debt in a world of **corporate taxes** is that interest payments are deductible as an expense. They elude taxation at the corporate level, whereas dividends or retained earnings associated with stock are not deductible by the corporation for tax purposes. Consequently, the total amount of payments available for both debt holders and stockholders is greater if debt is employed.

To illustrate, suppose the earnings before interest and taxes are $2,000 for companies X and Y, and they are alike in every respect except in leverage. Company Y has $5,000 in debt at 12 percent interest, whereas company X has no debt. If the tax rate (federal and state) is 40 percent for each company, we have

	Company X	Company Y
Earnings before interest and taxes	$2,000	$2,000
Interest, income to debt holders	0	600
Profit before taxes	$2,000	$1,400
Taxes	800	560
Income available to stockholders	$1,200	$ 840
Income to debt holders plus income to stockholders	$1,200	$1,440

Corporate taxes
create an incentive
for debt through the
deduction of interest
as an expense.

Thus, total income to both debt holders and stockholders is larger for levered company Y than it is for unlevered company X. The reason is that debt holders receive interest payments without the deduction of taxes at the corporate level, whereas income to stockholders is after corporate taxes have been paid. In essence, the government pays a subsidy to the levered company for the use of debt. Total income to all investors increases by the interest payment times the tax rate. In our example, this amounts to $600 \times .40 = \$240$. This figure represents a tax shield that the government provides the levered company. If the debt employed by a company is permanent, the present value of the tax shield using the perpetuity formula is

$$\text{Present value of tax shield} = \frac{t_c rB}{r} = t_c B \qquad (9\text{-}9)$$

where t_c is the corporate tax rate, r the interest rate on the debt, and B the market value of the debt. For company Y in our example

$$\text{Present value of tax shield} = .40(\$5,000) = \$2,000$$

Components of Overall Value   What we are saying is that the tax shield is a thing of value and that the overall value of the company will be $2,000 more if debt is employed than if the company has no debt. This increased valuation occurs because the stream of income to all investors is $240 per year greater. The present value of $240 per year discounted at 12 percent is $240/.12 = \$2,000$. Implied is that the risk associated with the tax shield is that of the stream of interest payments, so the appropriate discount rate is the interest rate on the debt. Thus, the value of the firm is

$$\text{Value of firm} = \begin{array}{c} \text{Value if} \\ \text{unlevered} \end{array} + \begin{array}{c} \text{Value of} \\ \text{tax shield} \end{array} \qquad (9\text{-}10)$$

For our example, suppose the required equity return for company X, which has no debt, is 16 percent. Therefore, the value of the firm if it were unlevered would be $1,200/.16 = \$7,500$. The value of the tax shield is $2,000, so the total value of company Y, the levered firm, is $9,500.

We see in Eq. (9-9) that the greater the amount of debt, the greater the tax shield and the greater the value of the firm, all other things the same. Thus, the original MM proposition as subsequently adjusted for corporate taxes suggests that an optimal strategy is to take on a maximum amount of leverage.[5] Clearly, this is not consistent with the behavior of corporations, and alternative explanations must be sought.

Uncertainty of Tax Shield

As pointed out in Chapter 8, the tax savings associated with the use of debt are not certain. If reported income is consistently low or negative, the tax shield on debt, as denoted by t_cB in Eq. (9-9), is reduced or even eliminated. As a result, the near full or full cash-flow burden of interest payments would be felt by a company. If the firm should go bankrupt and liquidate, the potential future tax savings associated with debt would stop altogether. We must recognize also that Congress can change the corporate tax rate. Finally, the greater the possibility of going out of business, the greater the probability the tax shield will not be effectively utilized. All of these things make the tax shield associated with debt financing less than certain.

Redundancy   Another argument in this vein is by De Angelo and Masulis, and it has to do with tax shelter redundancy.[6] The notion here is that companies have ways other than interest on debt to shelter income—leasing, foreign tax shelters, investment in intangible assets, and the use of option and future contracts, to name a few. If earnings in a given year are sufficiently low, these other tax shields may entirely use up the earnings at hand. As a result, the tax liability would be zero, and the company would be unable to utilize interest payments as a tax deduction. De Angelo and Masulis reason that as a company takes on more debt, it increases the probability that earnings in some years will not be sufficient to offset all the tax deductions. Some of them may be redundant, including the tax deductibility of interest.

The New Value Equation   The uncertain nature of the interest tax shield, together with the possibility of at least some tax shelter redundancy, may cause firm value to rise less with leverage than the corporate tax advantage alone would suggest. This is illustrated in Fig. 9-4, where the corporate tax effect is shown by the top line. As leverage increases, the uncertainty associated with the interest tax shield comes into play. At first, the diminution in value is slight. As more leverage occurs, tax shield uncertainty causes value to increase at an ever-decreasing rate and perhaps eventually to turn down. Thus, the more uncertain the corporate tax shield the less attractive debt becomes. The value of the firm now can be expressed as

$$\begin{matrix} \text{Value of} \\ \text{firm} \end{matrix} = \begin{matrix} \text{Value if} \\ \text{unlevered} \end{matrix} + \begin{matrix} \text{Pure value of} \\ \text{corporate tax} \\ \text{shield} \end{matrix} - \begin{matrix} \text{Value lost through} \\ \text{tax shield} \\ \text{uncertainty} \end{matrix} \qquad (9\text{-}11)$$

The last two factors combined give the present value of the corporate tax shield. The greater the uncertainty associated with the shield, the less important it becomes.

---

[5]Franco Modigliani and Merton H. Miller, "Corporate Income Taxes and the Cost of Capital: A Correction," *American Economic Review,* 63 (June 1963), 433–42.

[6]Harry De Angelo and Ronald W. Masulis, "Optimal Capital Structure under Corporate and Personal Taxation," *Journal of Financial Economics,* 8 (March 1980), 3–29.

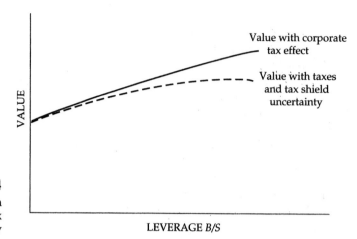

FIGURE 9-4
Value of firm with
corporate taxes and tax
shield uncertainty

Corporate Plus Personal Taxes

Apart from tax shield uncertainty, the presence of taxes on personal income may reduce or possibly eliminate the corporate tax advantage associated with debt. If returns on debt and on stock are taxed at the same personal tax rate, however, the corporate tax advantage remains. This can be seen by taking our earlier example and applying a 30 percent personal tax rate to the debt and stock returns:

Personal taxes
reduce the corporate
tax advantage.

	Company X	Company Y
Debt income	$ 0	$ 600
Less: Personal taxes of 30%		−180
Debt income after personal taxes	0	420
Income available to stockholders	$1,200	$ 840
Less: Personal taxes of 30%	−360	−252
Stockholders' income after personal taxes	$ 840	$ 588
Income to debt holders and stockholders after personal taxes	$ 840	$1,008

Although the total after-tax income to debt holders and stockholders is less than before, the tax advantage associated with debt remains.

Looking at the matter as we did in our earlier discussion, we discover that the present value of the corporate tax shield would be the following when personal taxes are present:

$$\text{Present value of tax shield} = \left[1 - \frac{(1 - t_c)(1 - t_{ps})}{1 - t_{pd}} \right] B \qquad (9\text{-}12)$$

where t_c and B, as before, are the corporate tax rate and market value of the firm's debt; t_{ps} is the personal income tax applicable to common stock income; and t_{pd} is the personal tax rate applicable to debt income.[7] If the return on debt is taxed at the same personal tax rate as that on stock, we have $t_{pd} = t_{ps}$. As a result, these two terms cancel out in Eq. (9-12), and the present value of the corporate tax shield becomes

$$\text{Present value of tax shield} = t_c B$$

which is the same as Eq. (9-9). Therefore, the corporate tax advantage of debt remains exactly the same if debt income and stock income are taxed at the same personal tax rate.

Dividends versus Capital Gains   We know that stock income is composed both of dividends and capital gains, however. Dividend income by and large is taxed at the same personal tax rate as interest income. Capital gains often are taxed at a lower rate. Sometimes the differential is explicit in that the tax rate is less. Even when capital gains are taxed at the same rate as ordinary income, however, there is an advantage to the capital gain. For one thing, it is postponed until the security is sold. For those who give appreciated securities as gifts to charitable causes, the tax may be largely avoided, as it is if a person dies. For these reasons, the effective tax on capital gains in a present-value sense is less than that on interest and dividend incomes. As a result, the corporate tax advantage associated with debt is reduced. To illustrate, we begin with an extreme assumption. All stock income is realized as capital gains and the tax rate on such gains is zero; therefore, t_{ps} is equal to zero. Assume, however, that the personal tax rate applicable to debt income, t_{pd}, is positive.

Debt or Stock Income?   In this situation, a company will need to decide whether to finance with debt or with stock. If a dollar of operating earnings is paid out as interest to debt holders, the company pays no corporate tax on it because interest is deductible as an expense. Therefore, the income to the investor after personal taxes are paid is

$$\text{After-tax income for debt holders} = \$1(1 - t_{pd})$$

If the dollar of operating earnings is directed instead to stockholders, the company pays a tax on those earnings at the corporate tax rate. The residual would be in-

---

[7]To see why this is so, we know that the total income available to both stockholders and debt holders is

$$[(\text{EBIT} - rB)(1 - t_c)(1 - t_{ps})] + [rB(1 - t_{pd})]$$

where the after-tax income to stockholders is depicted by the first major bracketed term and that to debt holders by the second, and EBIT is earnings before interest and taxes. Rearranging, we obtain

$$\text{EBIT} (1 - t_c)(1 - t_{ps}) + rB (1 - t_{pd})\left[1 - \frac{(1 - t_c)(1 - t_{ps})}{1 - t_{pd}}\right]$$

The first part of this equation is the income from an unlevered company after corporate and personal taxes have been paid. If an individual buys a bond for B, he or she receives, in the construct of our previous examples, $rB(1 - t_{pd})$ annually forever. Therefore, the value of the last part of the second equation is

$$\left[1 - \frac{(1 - t_c)(1 - t_{ps})}{1 - t_{pd}}\right] B$$

which is Eq. (9-12).

come to stockholders; and because we assume that the personal tax rate on stock income is zero, it would go directly to them. Therefore

$$\text{After-tax income for stockholders} = \$1(1 - t_c)$$

If the company is concerned with only after-tax income to the investor, it would finance either with debt or with stock, depending on the relative values of t_{pd} and t_c. If the personal tax rate on debt income exceeds the corporate tax rate, the company would finance with stock, because the after-tax income to the investor would be higher. If t_{pd} is less than t_c, however, it would finance with debt, because after-tax income to the investor would be greater here. If t_{pd} equals t_c, it would be a matter of indifference whether debt or stock were employed.

Merton Miller's Equilibrium

In a provocative presidential address to the American Finance Association, Miller proposed that with both corporate and personal taxes, capital structure decisions by the firm were irrelevant.[8] That is, changes in capital structure have no effect on the firm's total valuation. This position is the same as Modigliani–Miller's original proposition in a world of no taxes, but it contrasts sharply with their 1959 corporate tax adjustment article, in which they found that debt had substantial advantage. Simply put, Miller's model suggests that in market equilibrium personal and corporate tax effects cancel out. He assumes that the personal tax rate on stock income, t_{ps}, is zero. Accordingly, his model implies that at the margin, the personal tax rate on debt income, t_{pd}, must equal the corporate tax rate, t_c. As illustrated in the previous section, when $t_{pd} = t_c$, changes in the proportion of debt in the capital structure do not change the total after-tax income to investors. As a result, capital structure decisions by the corporation would be irrelevant.

Investor Clienteles and Market Equilibrium   Different investors, however, have different personal tax rates. Some investors, such as pension funds, are tax exempt; others, such as high-income individuals, are in high tax brackets. Holding risk constant, the tax-exempt investor would want to invest in debt; the high tax bracket investor would want to hold the company's stock. Miller's position is based on the idea that when the market is in disequilibrium, corporations alter their capital structures to take advantage of clienteles of investors in different tax brackets. If there is an abundance of tax-exempt investors, a company will increase the supply of its debt to appeal to this clientele. As companies increase the supply of debt, however, the tax-exempt clientele's ability to absorb more debt is exhausted, and further debt must be sold to higher tax bracket clienteles. Companies will stop issuing debt when the marginal personal tax rate of a clientele investing in the instrument equals the corporate tax rate. At this point, the market for debt and stock is said to be in equilibrium, and an individual company no longer can increase its total value by increasing or decreasing the amount of debt in its capital structure.

Completing the Market   One can think of the equilibration process as corporations marketing their securities in much the same way as they market their products. They identify an unsatisfied demand and then design a product to fit this

---

[8]Merton H. Miller, "Debt and Taxes," *Journal of Finance*, 32 (May 1977), 266–68.

market niche. In the case of capital structure, the product is a financial instrument and the niche is an unsatisfied investor clientele. This clientele is unsatisfied simply because there are not enough securities available of the type necessary to satisfy its tax motivated investment desires. The market is **incomplete**, and corporations should seek to offer those securities in excess demand. Thus, as total debt rises the effective tax rate of the marginal investor (lender) rises and the marginal corporate tax rate declines. Market equilibrium occurs when the total debt issued causes the two marginal tax rates to be the same.

Miller's equilibrium has the personal tax effect entirely offsetting the corporate tax advantage.

Note that for all companies there is a total optimal capital structure that depends on the tax brackets of different clienteles of investors and the amounts of funds these clienteles have to invest. Corporations overall will want to issue enough debt to satisfy the total demand of investors in tax brackets less than the corporate tax rate. One implication is that if the corporate tax rate were to increase relative to the personal tax rate, the equilibrium would be upset, and the new equilibrium would call for higher total debt-to-equity ratios for companies overall. If the personal tax rate were increased relative to the corporate tax rate, the new equilibrium would involve lower debt-to-equity ratios for companies overall. If the two sets of tax rates go up or down proportionally, there will be no effect. Once the new equilibrium is achieved, however, Miller's position is that the individual firm cannot alter its capital structure to advantage.

Counterarguments So far we have taken as given Miller's assumption that the personal tax rate on stock income is effectively zero. We know from Treasury tax data, however, that most individuals pay taxes on dividends. Moreover, companies do pay dividends, so some of the return on stock is taxed at essentially the same rate as that for interest income. Furthermore, some capital gains are realized, and taxes are paid on these gains, so the assumption of a zero personal tax on stock income is suspect.

Also disturbing is the relationship between corporate debt and stock returns and returns available on tax-exempt municipal bonds. If the tax rate on stock income is zero, we would expect there to be an equilibration of returns between common stocks and tax-exempt bonds, because the tax rate on municipal debt income is zero. Typically, the yield on municipal debt is between 75 and 80 percent of that of corporate debt of the same quality rating, implying a tax rate of 20 to 25 percent for the marginal investor. This implied rate is less than the top corporate tax rate, which should prevail on municipal securities if the market equilibrating process advanced by Miller holds. On the supply side of the equation, we know that different corporations have different effective tax rates at the margin. This makes the market equilibration process two-sided and more likely that there will be a net tax effect associated with corporate leverage.

Recapitulation

The Miller proposition is provocative and certainly has led us to a better understanding of how taxes affect capital structure. In addition to the arguments presented, theoretical arguments can be marshaled against the idea that the presence of personal taxes completely offsets the corporate tax effect.[9] My own view is that the personal tax effect does not entirely offset the corporate tax effect and that

---

[9]Robert H. Litzenberger and James C. Van Horne, "Elimination of the Double Taxation of Dividends and Corporate Financial Policy," *Journal of Finance,* 33 (June 1978), footnote 10, demonstrate that Miller's position is inconsistent with market clearing and that a tax advantage of debt remains.

there is a tax advantage to borrowing for the typical corporation. This is particularly true for companies having only moderate amounts of debt and where tax shield uncertainty is not great. Still, there would appear to be some lessening of the corporate tax effect owing to personal taxes.

Perhaps this can best be visualized if we reconsider Eq. (9-12). We suggested earlier that if the personal tax rate on stock income, t_{ps}, equaled that on debt income, t_{pd}, the present value of the tax shield associated with leverage would be $t_c B$, which is the corporate tax rate times the market value of the debt. If t_{ps} is less than t_{pd}, the tax advantage associated with debt is less than $t_c B$. Suppose the marginal corporate tax rate is 35 percent, the marginal personal tax rate on debt income is 30 percent, and the market value of DSS Corporation's perpetual debt is $1 million. Now suppose the effective marginal personal tax rate on stock income is 28 percent. As a result, the present value of the tax shield is

$$\text{Present value of tax shield} = \left[1 - \frac{(1 - .35)(1 - .28)}{1 - .30} \right] \$1 \text{ million}$$
$$= \$331,429$$

If the effective personal tax rate on stock income is .20 instead of .28, we have

$$\text{Present value of tax shield} = \left[1 - \frac{(1 - .35)(1 - .20)}{1 - .30} \right] \$1 \text{ million}$$
$$= \$257,143$$

Thus, the greater the tax "wedge" between debt income and stock income, the lower the overall tax shield. Expressed differently, personal tax effects increasingly offset the corporate tax shield advantage as the tax rate on stock income declines relative to that on debt income.

EFFECT OF BANKRUPTCY COSTS

Another important imperfection affecting capital structure decisions is the presence of **bankruptcy costs**. We know from earlier chapters that bankruptcy costs are more than legal and administrative expenses of bankruptcy; they involve inefficiencies in operating a company when it is about to go bankrupt as well as liquidation of assets at distress prices below their economic values.

If there is a possibility of bankruptcy, and if administrative and other costs associated with bankruptcy are significant, the levered firm may be less attractive to investors than the unlevered one. With perfect capital markets, zero bankruptcy costs are assumed. If the firm goes bankrupt, assets presumably can be sold at their economic values with no liquidating or legal costs involved. Proceeds from the sale are distributed according to the claim on assets described in Chapter 24. If capital markets are less than perfect, however, there are administrative costs to bankruptcy, and assets may have to be liquidated at less than their economic values.[10] These costs and the shortfall in liquidating value from economic value represent a drain in the system from the standpoint of debt holders and equity holders.

---

[10]See Brian L. Betker, "The Administrative Costs of Debt Restructurings," *Financial Management*, 26 (Winter 1997), 56–68, as well as references in Chapter 24, which deals with financial distress.

Relationship to Leverage

Bankruptcy costs are a dead weight loss to suppliers of capital.

In the event of bankruptcy, security holders as a whole receive less than they would in the absence of bankruptcy costs. To the extent that the levered firm has a greater possibility of bankruptcy than the unlevered one has, the levered firm would be a less attractive investment, all other things the same. The possibility of bankruptcy usually is not a linear function of the debt-to-equity ratio, but it increases at an increasing rate beyond some threshold. As a result, the expected cost of bankruptcy increases in this manner and would be expected to have a corresponding negative effect on the value of the firm and on its cost of capital. Creditors bear the ex post cost of bankruptcy, but they will probably pass on the ex ante cost to stockholders in the form of higher interest rates. Hence, the stockholders would bear the burden of ex ante bankruptcy costs and the subsequent lower valuation of the company. Because bankruptcy costs represent a "dead weight" loss, investors are unable to diversify away these costs even though the market equilibration process is assumed to be efficient.

As a result, investors are likely to penalize the price of the stock as leverage increases. The nature of the penalty is illustrated for a no-tax world in Fig. 9-5. Here the required rate of return for investors, k_e, is broken into its component parts. There is the risk-free rate, R_f, plus a premium for business risk. This premium is depicted on the vertical axis by the difference between the required rate of return for an all-equity capital structure and the risk-free rate. As debt is added, the required rate of return rises, and this increment represents a financial risk premium. In the absence of bankruptcy costs, the required return would rise in a linear manner in our no-tax world. However, with bankruptcy costs and an increasing probability of bankruptcy with leverage, the required rate of return would be expected to rise at an increasing rate beyond some point. At first there might be a negligible probability of bankruptcy, so there would be little or no penalty. As leverage increases, so does the penalty; for extreme leverage, the penalty becomes very substantial indeed.

FIGURE 9-5
Required rate of return for equity capital when bankruptcy costs exist but there are no taxes

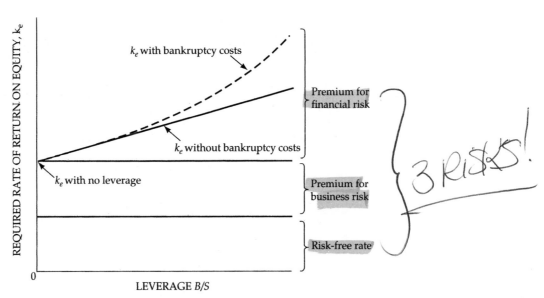

Can't determine where you should be (handwritten margin note)

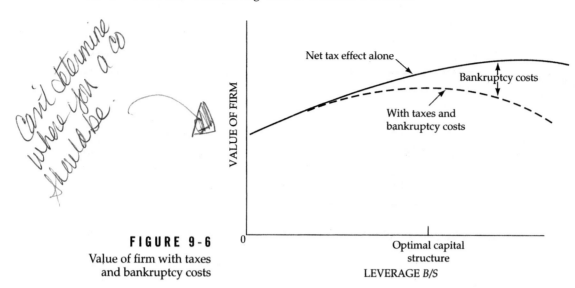

FIGURE 9-6
Value of firm with taxes
and bankruptcy costs

Taxes and Bankruptcy Costs

Our earlier discussion of taxes and capital structure concluded that leverage is likely to result in a net tax advantage (the corporate tax effect offset by the personal tax effect). As the company increases its leverage, the present value of the tax shield will increase, at least for a while. If we allow for bankruptcy costs and if the probability of bankruptcy increases at an increasing rate with leverage, high leverage will be penalized by investors. In a world of both taxes and bankruptcy costs, there will be an optimal capital structure. Whereas the net tax effect will have a positive influence on value, at least for moderate amounts of leverage, bankruptcy costs and tax shield uncertainty exert a negative influence. The value of the firm will increase as leverage is first employed because of the tax advantage of debt. Gradually, however, the prospect of bankruptcy will become increasingly important. This, together with tax shield uncertainty, will cause the value of the firm to increase at a decreasing rate and eventually to decline. We can express the above as

$$\begin{array}{ccc} & \text{Value as} & \text{Present value} & \text{Present value} \\ \text{Value of firm} = & \text{unlevered} + & \text{of net tax} - & \text{of bankruptcy} \\ & \text{firm} & \text{shield on debt} & \text{costs} \end{array} \quad (9\text{-}13)$$

The joint effect of taxes and bankruptcy costs is illustrated in Fig. 9-6. The net tax effect line is shown to taper off as more leverage is undertaken, in keeping with the mathematics and with tax shield uncertainty. However, bankruptcy costs are what cause value to decline sharply with extreme leverage. The optimal capital structure by definition is the point at which the value of the firm is maximized. Thus, we have a trade-off between the tax effects associated with leverage and the bankruptcy costs that come when leverage is pushed beyond a point. Although taxes and bankruptcy costs are probably the most important imperfections when it comes to capital structure decisions, there are others that bear on the problem.

OTHER IMPERFECTIONS

Other capital market imperfections impede the equilibration of security prices according to their expected returns and risks. As a result, these imperfections may result in leverage having an effect on the value of the firm apart from taxes and bankruptcy costs. The imperfections must be not only material but also one-directional. We know that transaction costs restrict the arbitrage process described earlier, but the net effect of this imperfection is not predictable as to direction if, in fact, there is a net effect at all. In what follows, we examine certain additional imperfections that may have a predictable effect on the capital structure question.

Corporate and Homemade Leverage Not Being Perfect Substitutes

The perceived risks of personal leverage and corporate leverage may differ. For one thing, if investors borrow personally and pledge their stock as collateral, they are subject to possible margin calls. Many investors view this possibility with alarm. Moreover, personal leverage involves a certain amount of inconvenience for investors, which they do not experience with corporate leverage. In addition, stockholders have limited liability with a stock investment, whereas their liability with personal loans is unlimited. Moreover, the cost of borrowing may be higher for the individual than for the corporation. This argument suggests that there are advantages to the corporation borrowing instead of the individual investor.

However, arbitrage can occur without the individual actually borrowing. The same thing may be accomplished by changing one's holdings of corporate bonds held. Moreover, the arbitrage process is not confined to individuals. If opportunities for profit exist, financial intermediaries may enter the scene and replicate the financial claims of either the levered or the unlevered company and buy the stock of the other. The free entry of financial intermediaries without cost will ensure the efficient functioning of the arbitrage process, which in turn will result in the irrelevance of corporate leverage. Therefore, we are inclined to discount the importance of this argument.

Institutional Restrictions

Imperfections cause interior, nonextreme solutions to the capital structure issue.

Restrictions on investment behavior may retard the arbitrage process. Many institutional investors, such as pension funds and life insurance companies, are not allowed to engage in the "homemade" leverage that was described. Regulatory bodies often restrict stock and bond investments to a list of companies meeting certain quality standards, such as only a "safe" amount of leverage. If a company breaches that amount, it may be removed from the acceptable list, thereby precluding certain institutions from investing in it. This reduction in investor demand can have an adverse effect on the market value of the company's financial instruments.

With institutional restrictions on loans to levered companies, the point at which the firm value line turns down with leverage in Fig. 9-6 may be sooner than depicted. The greater the importance of the other imperfections we have discussed, the less effective the MM arbitrage process becomes, and the greater the case that can be made for an optimal capital structure.

INCENTIVE ISSUES AND AGENCY COSTS

Agency costs arise when different stakeholders monitor each other's behavior.

Capital structure decisions lead to a number of incentive issues among equity holders, debt holders, management, and other stakeholders in the corporation. In this section we examine these issues, followed by the question of financial signaling. These considerations can, and often do, influence the choice of security used in financing, as well as whether to finance, and invest, at all. To begin, we look at debt versus equity in an option pricing model framework. This serves as a foundation for the subsequent discussion.

Debt Holders versus Equity Holders[11]

Using the concepts developed in Chapter 5, the equity of a firm can be viewed as a **call option on the firm's total value**, the value being the associated or underlying asset of the option. The writers of the option are the debt holders. For simplicity, assume that debt is represented by discount bonds that pay only at maturity. We can then view stockholders as having sold the firm to the debt holders with an option to buy it back at a specified price. The option has an exercise price equal to the face value of debt, and its expiration date is the maturity of the debt.

Option price portrayal of debt versus equity is a zero-sum game.

The value of the option at the expiration date, which by definition is the value of the stock, is

$$V_o = \max{(V_f - D, 0)} \tag{9-14}$$

where V_f is the value of the firm at the expiration date; D is the face value of the debt, which is the exercise price of the option; and max means the maximum value of $V_f - D$ or zero, whichever is greater. The value of the debt at the expiration date is simply

$$V_d = \min{(V_f, D)} \tag{9-15}$$

where min means V_f or D, whichever is less. In other words, if V_f is greater than D, the debt holders are entitled only to the face value of the debt, and the stockholders exercise their option. If V_f is less than D, the debt holders as owners of the firm are entitled to its full value. The stockholders receive nothing. Note that the value of their option at expiration cannot be negative, because they have limited liability.

These notions are illustrated in Fig. 9-7, where in the left panel the value of debt is shown and in the right panel the value of equity. The value of the firm at the expiration date of the debt is shown along the horizontal axis in both panels, with the face value of the debt again being represented by D. Depending on whether the value of the firm is above or below D, equity and debt values will be those shown. We see, then, that the debt holder–stockholder relationship can be pictured in an option pricing framework.

FIGURE 9-7

Value of debt and equity at the debt's expiration date

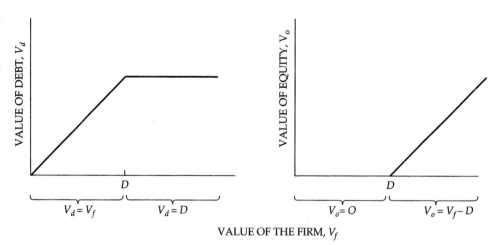

VALUE OF THE FIRM, V_f

---

[11]Unless the reader has covered Chapter 5 this section should be passed over.

Effect of Variance
and the Riskiness of Assets

We know from Chapter 5 that the greater the variance or volatility in value of the underlying asset, the greater the value of the option, all other things the same. Therefore, it is in the interest of the option holders, in this case the stockholders, to increase the variance of the firm. With a given exercise price of D, an increase in the dispersion of the probability distribution of possible firm values increases the value of their option. Thus, by increasing the riskiness of the assets of the firm, stockholders can increase the value of their option. This works to the disadvantage of the debt holders because there will be a corresponding decrease in the market value of their investment.

To illustrate, we use the Black–Scholes option pricing model from Chapter 5. Suppose that the total value of Belgrazia Tube Company is $4 million, and it has just issued debt with a face value of $3 million payable entirely at the end of 5 years. At present the standard deviation of the continuously compounded rate of return on the overall value of the company is .12. Also, the short-term, risk-free rate is 6 percent. Given this information, we first solve for d_1 and d_2 in the Black–Scholes option pricing formula.

$$d_1 = \frac{\ln (\$4/\$3) + [.06 + 1/2(.12)^2]5}{.12\sqrt{5}} = \frac{.623682}{.268328} = 2.32$$

In the equation, ln refers to the natural log and 5 to the length of time to the expiration of the option. For d_2, we have

$$d_2 = \frac{\ln (\$4/\$3) + [.06 - 1/2(.12)^2]5}{.12\sqrt{5}} = \frac{.551682}{.268328} = 2.06$$

In Table C at the back of the book, the area of a normal distribution to the right of 2.30 standard deviations is .0107 and to the right of 2.35 standard deviations, .0094. Interpolating, we find that 2.32 standard deviations correspond to .0102. Therefore, the area of the distribution less than 2.32 standard deviations to the right of the mean is $1 - .0102 = .9898$. For the area 2.06 standard deviations to the right of the mean, we find by interpolating that this standard deviation corresponds to .0197. The area of the distribution less than 2.06 standard deviations is $1 - .0197 = .9803$. Therefore, $N(d_1) = .9898$, and $N(d_2) = .9803$. Solving for the option pricing formula, Eq. (5-3) in Chapter 5, we obtain

$$V_o = \$4 \text{ million} (.9898) - \frac{\$3 \text{ million}}{e^{(.06)(5)}} (.9803) = \$1,780,526$$

where $e = 2.71828$ and the exponent is the interest rate times the length of time to expiration. Thus, the value of the stock is $1,780,526, and the value of the debt is $4,000,000 - \$1,780,526 = \$2,219,474$.

Suppose now that Belgrazia Tube Company dramatically increases the riskiness of its business so that the standard deviation of its continuously compounded rate becomes .36 in contrast to .12 before. Going through the same kind of calculations as before, the value of the stock is found to be $2,084,431. This contrasts with

$1,780,526 before. The value of the debt is $4,000,000 − $2,084,431 = $1,915,569, in contrast to $2,219,474 before.

By increasing the riskiness of the company, stockholders are thus able to increase the value of their stock at the direct expense of the debt holders. The reason for this occurrence is that stockholders have an option on the total value of the firm. As with any option, increased variance of the underlying asset increases the option's value.

Changing the Proportion of Debt

With the perfect market assumptions of the option pricing model, changing the proportion of debt in the capital structure will not affect the total value of the firm. In other words, the Modigliani–Miller irrelevance proposition holds. Such a change will affect the relative valuations of the debt and of the equity, however. We know that the option pricing formula can be used to determine the value of the common stock and that by deducting this value from the value of the total firm we can determine the value of the debt. By comparing values for different proportions of debt, we are able to determine the relationship between the proportion of debt and valuation.

To understand this, use our last example but assume that the face value of the debt is $1 million instead of $3 million. Putting these numbers into the Black–Scholes formula, the value of the stock is found to be $3,266,681. The value of the debt is $4,000,000 − $3,266,681 = $733,319. Recall from our previous example that with $3 million in debt, these values were $2,084,431 and $1,915,569, respectively. The percentage increases for the debt are

			Percentage Change
Face value of debt	$1,000,000	$3,000,000	200%
Value of debt	733,319	1,915,569	161

Thus, the increase in the face value of the debt is accompanied by a smaller percentage increase in the value of the debt, holding constant the total value of the firm. The reason is that the probability of default has increased, and with the greater default risk, the value of the debt (per dollar of face value) is reduced.

In the context of the option pricing model, issuing debt and retiring stock— thereby increasing the proportion of debt in the capital structure—will result in a decline in the price of the existing debt (per dollar of face value) and an increase in share price. If the face value of each bond were $1,000, there would be 1,000 bonds outstanding at $1 million in debt and 3,000 bonds outstanding at $3 million in debt. The value per bond at the lower level of debt is $733,319/1,000 = $733.32 per bond. At the higher level, it is $1,915,569/3,000 = $638.52. In essence, the stockholders have expropriated some of the wealth of the existing debt holders. The new debt holders are not hurt, because they lend money on the basis of the default risk associated with the new capital structure. In our example, they would lend $638.52 for each $1,000 face value bond. Only the old debt holders suffer. Similar to a change in the overall risk of the firm in our previous discussion, wealth transfers from the old debt holders to the stockholders.

Protective Covenants

Debt holders can protect themselves against expropriation by imposing constraints on the company at the time the loan is made. Known as protective covenants, these covenants may be used to restrict the stockholders' ability to increase the asset riskiness of the company and/or its leverage. In Chapter 16, we describe protective covenants in detail and show how they may be used in an option pricing model context. The reputation of the borrower may affect the terms of the loan. New borrowers with short track records generally face more restrictions and monitoring than does a company with a long-standing, high credit rating.[12]

The Modigliani–Miller argument for the irrelevance of capital structure requires that security holders protect themselves against capital structure changes that work to erode their position. "Me-first" rules ensure that one party cannot gain at the expense of the other. Although stockholders usually gain and old debt holders usually lose, it is possible for the reverse to occur. With certain protective covenants, debt holders might obtain a claim on future retained earnings at the expense of stockholders. Therefore, stockholders also must assure themselves that their position is not eroded without compensation. To the extent that "me-first" rules are not effective, capital structure decisions may be relevant even in the absence of taxes and bankruptcy costs.

The Underinvestment Problem

Underinvestment is the result of equity holders not wishing to invest when the rewards favor debt holders.

When a company finances with debt, there may be an incentive problem concerning capital investments. We have argued that a positive net-present-value project should be accepted, but this may not always happen. Suppose the project works more to the benefit of debt holders than to that of stockholders. An example might be a project that lowers the relative risk of the firm because of diversification properties. This may enhance debt holder wealth, but only at the expense of stockholders. The decline in stockholder value via the risk dimension may more than offset any favorable cash-flow characteristics. As a result, the project will be rejected by management, on behalf of stockholders, even though it has a positive NPV to security holders overall.[13]

An analogy is that of a levered farmer who decides not to buy crop insurance. Whereas a farmer without debt might purchase such insurance, the levered farmer may well reason that lenders will benefit much more in the event of a payoff.

The underinvestment proposition can be put in an option pricing model framework. Stockholders can be thought of as having an option to buy back the company from debt holders (the option writer) if its total value exceeds the face value of the debt. As with any option, its value increases as the variability of the associated asset, in this case the value of the overall firm, increases and declines when variability decreases. A possible remedy is for investors to own both stocks and bonds in the company. If the incentives of debt holders and stockholders can somehow be brought together by this means or by contracting between the two parties, the underinvestment problem disappears. In a practical world where this does not occur, the problem can arise.

---

[12]Douglas W. Diamond, "Reputation Acquisition in Debt Markets," *Journal of Political Economy*, 97, No. 4 (1989), 828–62.

[13]The underinvestment problem was first identified by Stewart C. Myers, "Determinants of Corporate Borrowing," *Journal of Financial Economics*, 5 (November 1977), 147–75.

Agency Costs More Broadly Defined

The expropriation of wealth and the "me-first" rules illustrate the need for debt holders to monitor the actions of equity holders. Monitoring requires the expenditure of resources, and the costs involved are one form of **agency costs**. As discussed in Chapter 1, Jensen and Meckling have expounded a theory of agency costs.[14] Among other things, they show that regardless of who makes the monitoring expenditures, the cost is borne by stockholders. Debt holders, anticipating monitoring costs, charge higher interest. The higher the probable monitoring costs, the higher the interest rate and the lower the value of the firm to its shareholders, all other things the same.

Complete protection would require the specification of extremely detailed protective covenants and extraordinary enforcement costs. Virtually every decision of the firm would need to be monitored. Not only would there be substantial legal and enforcement costs, but the firm would operate inefficiently. All of these agency costs go to reduce the overall value of the firm. As residual owners of the firm, stockholders have an incentive to see that such monitoring costs are minimized—up to a point. There is a trade-off. In the absence of any protective covenants, debt holders may charge very high interest rates, and these rates may cost stockholders more than the agency costs associated with reasonable protective covenants.

Stockholders Bear Monitoring Costs It is not that monitoring costs per se are bad for the owners of a company; it is that monitoring needs to be efficient. As more and more safeguards and enforcement procedures are imposed, debt holders' protection rises, but at a decreasing rate. Beyond a point, the reduction in interest rate is more than offset by escalating agency costs, which ultimately are borne by the stockholders. An optimal balance needs to be struck between monitoring costs and the interest rate charged on a debt instrument at the time it is sold. Some activities of the firm are relatively inexpensive to monitor; others are expensive. Dividend and financing decisions can be monitored with only moderate cost, whereas the production and investment decisions of the firm are much more costly to monitor. The relative costs of monitoring need to be taken into account in determining the protective covenants that should be used. As stockholders ultimately bear the costs of monitoring, it is important to them that monitoring be efficient.

Like bankruptcy costs, monitoring costs may limit the amount of debt that is optimal for a firm to issue. It is likely that beyond a point the amount of monitoring required by debt holders increases with the amount of debt outstanding. When there is little or no debt, lenders may engage in only limited monitoring, whereas with a great deal of debt outstanding they may insist on extensive monitoring. In turn, this monitoring may involve considerable costs. As a result, Fig. 9-6, showing the relationship among taxes, bankruptcy costs, and firm value, would need to be modified. Monitoring costs would act as a further factor decreasing firm value for extreme leverage. The situation is illustrated in Fig. 9-8. The optimal capital structure occurs at point *x*, somewhat before that which occurs with taxes and bankruptcy costs alone, point *y*.

---

[14]Michael C. Jensen and William H. Meckling, "Theory of the Firm: Managerial Behavior, Agency Costs and Ownership Structure," *Journal of Financial Economics*, 3 (October 1976), 305–60.

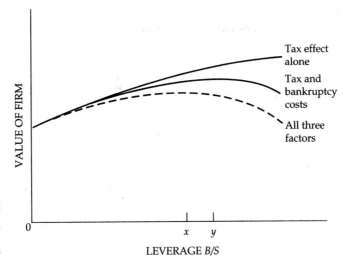

FIGURE 9-8
Value of firm with
taxes, bankruptcy costs,
and monitoring costs

Organizational Incentives to Manage Efficiently

Working in the other direction is the notion that high debt levels create incentives for management to be more efficient. Jensen's free-cash-flow theory alleges that if managements are left to their own devices they will invest in capital projects and acquisitions that do not provide sufficient expected returns.[15] Moreover, they will squander funds on unnecessary perquisites and other things. According to Jensen there is a need to incent management to disgorge free cash flow to stockholders, the rightful owners of excess liquidity. Only in this way can the agency problem be resolved.

By taking on the cash-flow obligation to service debt, it is claimed that "management's feet are held close to the fire." As a result, there is said to be an incentive not to squander funds in wasteful activities, whether it be an investment, a perquisite, a company plane, or whatever. The idea is that levered companies may be leaner because management cuts the fat. Contrarily, the company with little debt and significant free cash flow, after investing in all worthwhile projects, may have a tendency to squander funds. In the absence of other incentives, "running scared" to make debt payments may have a salutary effect on efficiency.[16]

More generally, debt brings capital-market discipline to management's table. Executives bent on entrenchment often seek to minimize debt.[17] By doing this, they face less pressure and intrusion into matters of their competency, performance, and compensation. The ultimate discipline in the market for corporate control is the hostile takeover, but stockholders may suffer a good deal of suboptimal performance before this occurs. From their standpoint, a moderate amount of debt may be the necessary disciplinary medicine.

[15]Michael C. Jensen, "Agency Costs of Free Cash Flow, Corporate Finance, and Takeovers," *American Economic Review,* 76 (May 1986), 323–29.

[16]For empirical support for debt improving managerial efficiency, see Michael T. Maloney, Robert E. McCormick, and Mark L. Mitchell, "Managerial Decision Making and Capital Structure," *Journal of Business,* 66, No. 2 (1993), 189–217; and Gordon Hanka, "Debt and the Terms of Employment," *Journal of Financial Economics,* 48 (June 1998), 245–82.

[17]Philip G. Berger, Eli Ofek, and David L. Yermack, "Managerial Entrenchment and Capital Structure Decisions," *Journal of Finance,* 52 (September 1997), 1411–38, empirically document this relationship.

FINANCIAL SIGNALING

Closely related to monitoring costs and agency relationships is the notion of signaling. Because strict managerial contracts are difficult to enforce, managers may use capital structure changes to convey information about the profitability and risk of the firm. The implication is that insiders know something about the firm that outsiders do not. As a manager, your pay and benefits may depend on the firm's market value. That gives you an incentive to let investors know when the company is undervalued. You could make an announcement, "Our company is undervalued," but you are more sophisticated than that, and you know that investors would probably be as convinced as if you were boasting about your child. So you alter your company's capital structure by issuing more debt. Increased leverage implies a higher probability of bankruptcy, and since you would be penalized contractually if bankruptcy occurred, investors conclude that you have good reason to believe that things really are better than the stock price reflects. Your actions speak louder than words. Increased leverage is a positive sign.

Asymmetric Information

Credibility of a financial signal depends on asymmetric information.

More formally, a signaling effect assumes there is information asymmetry between management and stockholders. When financing an investment project, management will want to issue the overvalued security if it is acting in the interests of current stockholders. As Myers and Majluf suggest, it will issue stock if it believes the existing stock is overvalued and debt if it believes the stock is undervalued.[18] However, investors are not unmindful of this phenomenon, so debt issues are regarded as "good news" and stock issues as "bad news."

The greater the asymmetry in information between insiders (management) and outsiders (security holders), the greater the likely stock price reaction to a financing announcement. In general, empirical evidence is consistent with the asymmetry of information idea. Around the time of the announcement, leverage-increasing transactions tend to result in positive excess returns to stockholders, whereas leverage-decreasing transactions result in the opposite. The evidence overall is consistent with a financial signaling effect accompanying the choice of security employed in the capital structure.

From Where Does Value Cometh?

This is not to say that capital structure changes cause changes in valuation. Rather, it is the signal conveyed by the change that is significant. This signal pertains to the underlying profitability and risk of the firm, as that is what is important when it comes to valuation. Financial signaling is a topic of considerable interest in the writing on finance, but the various models are difficult to evaluate. Unless the managerial contract is very precise, the manager is tempted to give false signals. Moreover, there simply may be more effective and less costly ways to convey information than by altering a company's capital structure. We shall have more to say about this phenomenon when we consider dividend policy in Chapter 11.

---

[18]Stewart C. Myers and Nicholas S. Majluf, "Corporate Financing and Investment Decisions When Firms Have Information That Investors Do Not Have," *Journal of Financial Economics*, 13 (June 1984), 187–222.

Summary

A great deal of controversy has developed over whether the capital structure of a firm, as determined by its financing decision, affects its overall value. Traditionalists argue that the firm can lower its cost of capital and increase market value per share by the judicious use of leverage. Modigliani and Miller, on the other hand, argue that in the absence of taxes and other market imperfections, the total value of the firm and its cost of capital are independent of capital structure. This position is based on the notion that there is a conservation of investment value. No matter how you divide the pie between debt and equity claims, the total pie or investment value of the firm stays the same. Therefore, leverage is said to be irrelevant. We saw that behavioral support for the MM position was based on the arbitrage process.

In a world of corporate income taxes, there is a substantial advantage to the use of debt; and we showed how the present value of the tax shield might be measured. This advantage is lessened with tax shield uncertainty, particularly if leverage is high. When we allow for personal income taxes and a higher personal tax rate on debt income than on stock income, we find the tax advantage of debt to be further reduced. Miller argues that it is zero, and his argument, as well as certain refuting evidence, were examined. Bankruptcy costs work to the disadvantage of leverage, particularly extreme leverage. A combination of net tax effect with bankruptcy costs will result in an optimal capital structure. Other market imperfections—such as institutional restrictions on lender and stock investor behavior—impede the equilibration of security prices according to expected return and risk. As a result, leverage may affect the value of the firm.

One can analyze the capital structure problem in an option pricing model framework giving stockholders an option to buy back the firm at the maturity of the debt. As with any option, an increase in the variance of the associated asset—in this case, the value of the firm—will increase the value of the option. It is to the stockholders' advantage to increase variance, either by increasing the riskiness of the assets of the firm or by increasing the proportion of debt. Debt holders can protect themselves against this occurrence by imposing protective covenants. This protection involves monitoring costs, which are a form of agency costs. Stockholders, who ultimately bear the cost of monitoring, have an incentive to see that it is efficient. Beyond some threshold, monitoring costs are likely to increase at an increasing rate with leverage. Like bankruptcy costs, monitoring costs may limit the amount of debt in an optimal capital structure. In the context of agency costs, other incentive issues affecting capital structure decisions were analyzed.

Financial signaling occurs when capital structure changes convey information to security holders. It assumes an asymmetry in information between management and stockholders. Management behavior results in debt issues being regarded as good news by investors and stock issues as bad news. Empirical evidence seems to be consistent with this notion. In the next chapter, we shall find out how a firm can choose an appropriate capital structure.

Self-Correction Problems

1. Abacus Calculation Company and Zoom Calculators, Inc., are identical except for capital structures. Abacus has 50 percent debt and 50 percent equity, whereas Zoom has 20 percent debt and 80 percent equity. (All percentages are in market-value terms.) The borrowing rate for both companies is 8 percent in a no-tax world, and capital markets are assumed to be perfect.

a. (1) If you own 2 percent of the stock of Abacus, what is your dollar return if the company has net operating income of $360,000 and the overall capitalization rate of the company, k_o, is 18 percent? (2) What is the implied required rate of return on equity?

b. Zoom has the same net operating income as Abacus. (1) What is the implied required equity return of Zoom? (2) Why does it differ from that of Abacus?

2. Massey-Moss Corporation has earnings before interest and taxes of $3 million and a 40 percent tax rate. Its required rate of return on equity in the absence of borrowing is 18 percent.

a. In the absence of personal taxes, what is the value of the company in an MM world (1) with no leverage? (2) with $4 million in debt? (3) with $7 million in debt?

b. Personal as well as corporate taxes now exist. The marginal personal tax rate on common stock income is 25 percent, and the marginal personal tax rate on debt income is 30 percent. Determine the value of the company using Eq. (9-12) for each of the three debt alternatives in part a. Why do your answers differ?

3. L'Etoile du Nord Resorts is considering various levels of debt. Presently, it has no debt and a total market value of $15 million. By undertaking leverage, it believes that it can achieve a net tax advantage (corporate and personal combined) equal to 20 percent of the amount of the debt. However, the company is concerned with bankruptcy and agency costs as well as lenders increasing their interest rate if it borrows too much. The company believes that it can borrow up to $5 million without incurring any of these costs. However, each additional $5 million increment in borrowing is expected to result in the three costs cited being incurred. Moreover, they are expected to increase at an increasing rate with leverage. The present-value cost is expected to be the following for various levels of debt:

Debt (in millions)	$5	$10	$15	$20	$25	$30
PV cost of bankruptcy, agency, and increased interest rate (in millions)	0	.6	1.2	2.0	3.2	5.0

Is there an optimal amount of debt for the company?

Problems

1. The Malock Company has net operating earnings of $10 million and $20 million of debt with a 7 percent interest charge. In all cases, assume no taxes.

a. Using the net operating income approach and an overall capitalization rate of 11 percent, compute the total market value, the stock market value, and the implied required return on equity for the Malock Company prior to the sale of additional debt.

b. Determine the answers to part a if the company were to sell the additional $10 million in debt.

2. The Kelly Company and the Green Company are identical in every respect except that the Kelly Company is not levered, while the Green Company has $2 million in 12 percent bonds outstanding. There are no taxes, and capital markets are assumed to be perfect. The valuation of the two firms is the following:

	Kelly	Green
Net operating income	$ 600,000	$600,000
Interest on debt	0	240,000
Earnings to common	$ 600,000	$ 360,000
Required equity rate	.15	.16
Market value of stock	$4,000,000	$2,250,000
Market value of debt	0	2,000,000
Total value of firm	4,000,000	4,250,000
Implied overall capitalization rate, k_o	15.00%	14.12%
Debt-to-equity ratio, B/S	0	.89

a. You own $22,500 worth of Green stock. Show the process and the amount by which you could reduce your outlay through the use of arbitrage.

b. When will this arbitrage process cease?

3. The Blalock Corporation has a $1 million capital structure and will always maintain this book-value amount. Blalock currently earns $250,000 per year before taxes of 50 percent, has an all-equity capital structure of 100,000 shares, and pays all earnings in dividends. The company is considering issuing debt in order to retire stock. The cost of the debt and the price of the stock at various levels of debt are given in the accompanying table. It is assumed that the new capital structure would be reached all at once by purchasing stock at the current price. In other words, the table is a schedule at a point in time.

Amount of Debt	Average Cost of Debt	Price of Stock per Share
—	—	$10.00
$100,000	10.0%	10.50
200,000	10.0	10.80
300,000	10.5	11.00
400,000	11.0	11.15
500,000	12.0	10.50
600,000	14.0	9.50

a. By observation, what do you think is the optimal capital structure?

b. Construct a graph in terms of k_e, k_i, and k_o based on the data given.

c. Are your conclusions in part a confirmed?

4. Zapatta Cottonseed Oil Company has $1 million in earnings before interest and taxes. Currently it is all equity financed. It may issue $3 million in per-

petual debt at 15 percent interest to repurchase stock, thereby recapitalizing the corporation. There are no personal taxes.

    a. If the corporate tax rate is 40 percent, what is the income to all security holders (1) if the company remains all equity financed? (2) if it is recapitalized?

    b. What is the present value of the debt tax shield?

    c. The required return on equity for the company's stock is 20 percent while it remains all equity financed. What is the value of the firm? What is the value if it is recapitalized?

5. Loveless Electrical Products Company has $4 million in debt outstanding. The corporate income tax rate is 35 percent. In an extensive study of investors, G. Rosenberg and Associates, an outside consulting firm, has estimated that the marginal personal tax rate on common stock income for investors overall is 25 percent. Dividends and capital gains are both included in this income. The firm also has estimated that the marginal personal tax rate on debt income is 30 percent.

    a. Determine the tax advantage to Loveless Electrical Products Company for the use of debt under the assumption of corporate income taxes but no personal income taxes. (Assume the debt is perpetual and that the tax shield will be the same throughout.)

    b. Determine the tax advantage with both corporate and personal income taxes. Why does your answer to part b differ from that to part a?

    c. What would be the tax advantage if the personal tax rate on common stock income were (1) 30 percent? (2) 20 percent? (Assume that all else stays the same.)

6. Petroles Vintage Wine Company is presently family owned and has no debt. The Petroles family is considering going public by selling some of their stock in the company. Investment bankers tell them the total market value of the company is $10 million if no debt is employed. In addition to selling stock, the family wishes to consider issuing debt that, for computational purposes, would be perpetual. The debt then would be used to purchase stock, so the size of the company would stay the same. Based on various valuation studies, the net tax advantage of debt is estimated at 22 percent of the amount borrowed when both corporate and personal taxes are taken into account. The investment banker has estimated the following present values for bankruptcy costs associated with various levels of debt:

Debt (in Millions)	Present Value of Bankruptcy Costs
$1	0
2	$ 50,000
3	100,000
4	200,000
5	400,000
6	700,000
7	1,100,000
8	1,600,000

Given this information, what amount of debt should the family choose?

7. Acme-Menderhall Corporation is trying to determine an appropriate capital structure. It knows that as its leverage increases, its cost of borrowing will eventually increase, as will the required rate of return on its common stock. The company has made the following estimates for various leverage ratios:

| | | Required Rate of Return on Equity | |
| | | --- | --- |
Debt/(Debt + Equity)	*Interest Rate on Borrowings*	**WITHOUT BANKRUPTCY AND AGENCY COSTS**	**WITH BANKRUPTCY AND AGENCY COSTS**
0	—	10%	10%
.10	8%	$10\frac{1}{2}$	$10\frac{1}{2}$
.20	8	11	$11\frac{1}{4}$
.30	$8\frac{1}{2}$	$11\frac{1}{2}$	12
.40	9	$12\frac{1}{4}$	13
.50	10	$13\frac{1}{4}$	$14\frac{1}{2}$
.60	11	$14\frac{1}{2}$	$16\frac{1}{4}$
.70	$12\frac{1}{2}$	16	$18\frac{1}{2}$
.80	15	18	21

   a. (1) At a tax rate of 50 percent (federal and state), what is the weighted average cost of capital of the company at various leverage ratios in the absence of bankruptcy and agency costs? (2) What is the optimal capital structure?

   b. With bankruptcy and agency costs, what is the optimal capital structure?

8. Mohave Sand and Transit Company currently has an overall value of $8 million. The debt has a face value of $4 million and is represented by discount bonds that mature in 3 years. The standard deviation of the continuously compounded rate of return on overall value is 20 percent. The short-term risk-free rate is currently 6 percent.

   a. Treating the stock as an option and using the Black–Scholes option model, Eq. (5-3) in Chapter 5, determine the value of the equity and the value of debt.

   b. If the company were to increase the riskiness of its business so that the standard deviation became 50 percent, what would happen to the value of the stock and to the value of the debt?

   c. Does one party gain at the expense of the other? If this is the case, how can the other party protect itself?

9. Suppose in Problem 8 that Mohave Sand and Transit Company decided to issue $2 million in additional debt (face value) with a 3-year maturity and to repurchase $2 million in stock.

   a. What is the effect on the value of the stock and on the value of the debt if the standard deviation is 50 percent?

   b. Does the value of the debt increase proportionally with the increase in its face value? Why or why not?

10. Archer-Deloitte Company wishes to finance a $15 million expansion program and is trying to decide between debt and equity. Management believes the market does not appreciate the company's profit potential and that the stock is undervalued. What security do you suppose it will use in financing, and what will be the market's reaction? What if management felt the stock were overvalued?

Solutions to Self-Correction Problems

1. a. (1)

Net operating income	$ 360,000
Overall capitalization rate	.18
Total value of firm	$2,000,000
Market value of debt (50%)	1,000,000
Market value of stock (50%)	$1,000,000
Net operating income	$ 360,000
Interest on debt (8%)	80,000
Earnings to common	$ 280,000

2% of $280,000 = $5,600

(2) Implied required equity return = $280,000/$1,000,000 = 28%

b. (1)

Total value of firm	$2,000,000
Market value of debt (20%)	400,000
Market value of equity (80%)	$1,600,000
Net operating income	$ 360,000
Interest on debt (8%)	32,000
Earnings to common	$ 328,000

Implied required equity return = $328,000/$1,600,000 = 20.5%

(2) It is lower because Zoom uses less debt in its capital structure. As the equity capitalization is a linear function of the debt-to-equity ratio when we use the net operating income approach, the decline in required equity return offsets exactly the disadvantage of not employing so much in the way of "cheaper" debt funds.

2. a. (1) Value if unlevered (in thousands):

EBIT	$ 3,000	
Profit before taxes	3,000	
Taxes	1,200	
Profit after taxes	$ 1,800	
÷ required equity return	.18	
Value if unlevered	$10,000	($10 million)

(2) Value with $4 million in debt:

$$\text{Value} = \text{Value if unlevered} + \text{Value of tax shield}$$
$$\text{Value} = \$10,000 + .40(\$4,000) = \$11,600$$

(3) Value with $7 million in debt:

$$\text{Value} = \$10,000 + .40(\$7,000) = \$12,800$$

Due to the tax subsidy, the firm is able to increase its value in a linear manner with more debt.

b. (1) Value if unlevered (in thousands): the same as before, namely, $10,000 (10 million).

(2) Value with $4 million in debt:

$$\text{Value} = \$10,000 + \left[1 - \frac{(1 - .40)(1 - .25)}{1 - .30}\right]\$4,000$$
$$= \$11,429$$

(3) Value with $7 million in debt:

$$\text{Value} = \$10,000 + \left[1 - \frac{(1 - .40)(1 - .25)}{1 - .30}\right]\$7,000$$
$$= \$12,500$$

The presence of personal taxes reduces the tax advantage associated with corporate debt. As long as the personal tax on stock income is less than that on debt income, however, the net tax advantage to debt is positive. As a result, the value of the firm rises with more debt, but not as rapidly as if there were no personal taxes or if the personal tax rate on stock and debt income were the same.

3. (In millions):

(1)	(2)	(3)	(4)	
		PV of Tax	PV of Bankruptcy,	Value of
Level of	Firm Value	Shield	Agency, and Increased	Firm
Debt	Unlevered	(1) × 0.20	Interest Cost	(2) + (3) − (4)
0	$15	0	0	$15.0
$ 5	15	$1	0	16.0
10	15	2	$ .6	16.4
15	15	3	1.2	16.8
20	15	4	2.0	17.0
25	15	5	3.2	16.8
30	15	6	5.0	16.0

The market value of the firm is maximized with $20 million in debt.

Selected References

BARCLAY, MICHAEL J., CLIFFORD W. SMITH, and ROSS L. WATTS, "The Determinants of Corporate Leverage and Dividend Policies," *Journal of Applied Corporate Finance,* 7 (Winter 1995), 4–19.

BAXTER, NEVINS D., "Leverage, Risk of Ruin, and the Cost of Capital," *Journal of Finance,* 22 (September 1967), 395–404.

BERGER, PHILIP G., ELI OFEK, and DAVID L. YERMACK, "Managerial Entrenchment and Capital Structure Decisions," *Journal of Finance,* 52 (September 1997), 1411–38.

BETKER, BRIAN L., "The Administrative Costs of Debt Restructurings," *Financial Management,* 26 (Winter 1997), 56–68.

BLACK, FISCHER, and MYRON SCHOLES, "The Pricing of Options and Corporate Liabilities," *Journal of Political Economy,* 81 (May–June 1973), 637–54.

DE ANGELO, HARRY, and RONALD W. MASULIS, "Optimal Capital Structure under Corporate and Personal Taxation," *Journal of Financial Economics,* 8 (March 1980), 3–29.

DIAMOND, DOUGLAS W., "Reputation Acquisition in Debt Markets," *Journal of Political Economy,* 97, No. 4 (1989), 828–62.

DICHEV, ILIA, "Is the Risk of Bankruptcy a Systematic Risk?" *Journal of Finance,* 53 (June 1998), 1131–47.

FAMA, EUGENE F., and KENNETH R. FRENCH, "Taxes, Financing Decisions, and Firm Value," *Journal of Finance,* 53 (June 1998), 819–43.

GRAHAM, JOHN R., "Debt and the Marginal Tax Rate," *Journal of Financial Economics,* 41 (May 1996), 41–73.

HARRIS, MILTON, and ARTUR RAVIV, "The Theory of Capital Structure," *Journal of Finance,* 46 (March 1991), 297–355.

JENSEN, MICHAEL C., and WILLIAM E. MECKLING, "Theory of the Firm: Managerial Behavior, Agency Costs and Ownership Structure," *Journal of Financial Economics,* 3 (October 1976), 305–60.

KIM, E. HAN, "A Mean-Variance Theory of Optimal Structure and Corporate Debt Capacity," *Journal of Finance,* 33 (March 1978), 45–64.

KIM, E. HAN, JOHN J. MCCONNELL, and IRWIN SILBERMAN, "Capital Structure Rearrangements and Me-First Rules in an Efficient Capital Market," *Journal of Finance,* 32 (June 1977), 789–810.

KRAUS, ALAN, and ROBERT H. LITZENBERGER, "A State-Preference Model of Optimal Financial Leverage," *Journal of Finance,* 28 (September 1973), 911–22.

LANG, LARRY, ELI OFEK, and RENE M. STULZ, "Leverage, Investment, and Firm Growth," *Journal of Financial Economics,* 40 (January 1996), 3–29.

LELAND, HAYNE E., "Corporate Debt Value, Bond Covenants, and Optimal Capital Structure," *Journal of Finance,* 49 (September 1994), 1213–52.

MALONEY, MICHAEL T., ROBERT E. MCCORMICK, and MARK L. MITCHELL, "Managerial Decision Making and Capital Structure," *Journal of Business,* 66, No. 2 (1993), 189–217.

MCCONNELL, JOHN J., and HENRI SERVAES, "Equity Ownership and the Two Faces of Debt," *Journal of Financial Economics,* 39 (September 1995), 131–57.

MELLO, ANTONIO S., and JOHN E. PARSONS, "Measuring the Agency Cost of Debt," *Journal of Finance,* 47 (December 1992), 1887–904.

MILLER, MERTON H., "Debt and Taxes," *Journal of Finance,* 32 (May 1977), 261–78.

———, "The Modigliani-Miller Propositions after Thirty Years," *Journal of Economic Perspectives,* 2 (Fall 1988), 99–120.

MODIGLIANI, FRANCO, and M. H. MILLER, "The Cost of Capital, Corporation Finance and the Theory of Investment," *American Economic Review,* 48 (June 1958), 261–97.

———, "The Cost of Capital, Corporation Finance and the Theory of Investment: Reply," *American Economic Review,* 48 (September 1958), 665–69; "Taxes and the Cost of Capital: A Correction," *Ibid.,* 53 (June 1963), 433–43; "Reply," *Ibid.,* 55 (June 1965), 524–27; "Reply to Heins and Sprenkle," *Ibid.,* 59 (September 1969), 592–95.

MYERS, STEWART C., "Determinants of Corporate Borrowing," *Journal of Financial Economics,* 5 (November 1977), 147–75.

———, "Capital Structure Puzzle," *Journal of Finance,* 39 (July 1984), 575–92.

MYERS, STEWART C., and NICHOLAS S. MAJLUF, "Corporate Financing and Investment Decisions When Firms Have Information That Investors Do Not Have," *Journal of Financial Economics,* 13 (June 1984), 187–222.

OPLER, TIM C., and SHERIDAN TITMAN, "Financial Distress and Corporate Performance," *Journal of Finance,* 49 (July 1994), 1015–40.

ROSS, STEPHEN A., "The Determination of Financial Structure: The Incentive-Signalling Approach," *Bell Journal of Economics,* 8 (Spring 1977), 23–40.

SHAH, KSHITIJ, "The Nature of Information Conveyed by Pure Capital Structure Changes," *Journal of Financial Economics*, 36 (August 1994), 89–126.

VAN HORNE, JAMES C., "Optimal Initiation of Bankruptcy Proceedings by Debt Holders," *Journal of Finance*, 31 (June 1976), 897–910.

Wachowicz's Web World is an excellent overall Web site produced and maintained by my coauthor of *Fundamentals of Financial Management*, John M. Wachowicz Jr. It contains descriptions of and links to many finance Web sites and articles. *www.prenhall.com/wachowicz*.

10

Making Capital Structure Decisions

N ow let us put ourselves in the role of financial manager seeking an appropriate capital structure for our firm. We may use various methods of analysis—none completely satisfactory in itself, but taken collectively, they give us enough information to make a rational decision. Like all financial managers, we shall not be able to identify the precise percentage of debt that will maximize share price, but we must try to determine an approximate proportion of debt to employ for that objective. In this regard, we are mindful of the theoretical framework presented in Chapter 9. We also explore the questions of timing and flexibility of a single security issue, followed by consideration of the "pecking order" hypothesis of the preferred method of financing. Finally, a checklist of things to consider when approaching a financing decision is presented. First, however, we want to look at the effect of a financing method on earnings per share. ■

EBIT-EPS ANALYSIS

One means of examining the effect of leverage is to analyze the relationship between earnings before interest and taxes **(EBIT)** and earnings per share **(EPS)**. Essentially, the method involves the comparison of alternative methods of financing under various assumptions as to EBIT.

Calculation of Earnings per Share

To illustrate an EBIT-EPS analysis of leverage, suppose Cherokee Tire Company, with long-term capitalization of $18 million consisting of $5 million in debt bearing an average interest rate of 9 percent and $13 million in shareholders' equity, wishes to raise another $5 million for expansion. It is looking at three possible financing plans: (1) common stock that can be sold at $50 per share (100,000 new shares), (2) debt at 8 percent interest, and (3) preferred stock with a 7.6 percent dividend. Present annual earnings before interest and taxes are $3 million, the tax rate for Cherokee is 40 percent, and 400,000 shares of common stock are now outstanding.

To determine the **EBIT indifference points** between the various financing alternatives, we begin by calculating earnings per share for some hypothetical level of EBIT. Suppose we wished to know what earnings per share would be under the three financing plans if EBIT were $4 million. The calculations are shown in Table

TABLE 10-1

Calculations of Earnings per Share under Three Financing Alternatives

	Common Stock	Debt	Preferred Stock
Earnings before interest and taxes (hypothetical)	$4,000,000	$4,000,000	$4,000,000
Interest on existing debt	450,000	450,000	450,000
New debt interest	—	400,000	—
Earnings before taxes	3,550,000	3,150,000	3,550,000
Taxes (40%)	1,420,000	1,260,000	1,420,000
Earnings after taxes	$2,130,000	$1,890,000	$2,130,000
Preferred dividend	—	—	380,000
Earnings available to common stockholders	$2,130,000	$1,890,000	$1,750,000
Number of shares	500,000	400,000	400,000
Earnings per share	$4.26	$4.73	$4.38

10-1. We note that interest on debt is deducted before taxes, whereas preferred stock dividends are deducted after taxes. As a result, earnings available to common stockholders are higher under the debt alternative than they are under the preferred stock alternative, despite the fact that the interest rate on debt is higher than the preferred stock dividend rate.

EBIT-EPS analysis focuses on the EBIT indifference between financing methods with respect to EPS.

Break-Even, or Indifference, Analysis

Given the information in Table 10-1, we are able to construct a break-even, or indifference, chart. On the horizontal axis we plot earnings before interest and taxes and on the vertical axis, earnings per share. For each financing alternative, we must draw a straight line to reflect EPS for all possible levels of EBIT. To do so, we need two datum points for each alternative. The first is the EPS calculated for some hypothetical level of EBIT. For $4 million in EBIT, we see in Table 10-1 that earnings per share are $4.26, $4.73, and $4.38 for the common stock, debt, and preferred stock financing alternatives. We simply plot these earning per share at the $4 million mark in EBIT. Technically it does not matter which hypothetical level of EBIT we choose for calculating EPS. On good graph paper, one level is as good as the next.

The second datum point is simply the EBIT necessary to cover all fixed financial costs for a particular financing plan, and it is plotted on the horizontal axis. For the common stock alternative, we must have $450,000 in EBIT to cover interest on existing debt. At that level, earnings available to common stockholders will be zero, and so will EPS. The intercept on the horizontal axis then is $450,000 for the common stock alternative. For the debt alternative, the intercept is existing interest of $450,000 plus new interest of $400,000 to give $850,000 in total. For the preferred stock alternative, we must divide total annual dividends by 1 minus the tax rate to obtain the EBIT necessary to cover these dividends. Thus, we need $380,000/(1 − .40) = $633,333 in EBIT to cover the dividends and $450,000 to cover interest on existing debt. Therefore, the intercept on the horizontal axis is $1,083,333 for the preferred stock alternative. Given the horizontal axis intercepts and earnings per share for some hypothetical level of EBIT, we draw a straight line through the two sets of points. The break-even, or indifference, chart for Cherokee Tire Company is shown in Fig. 10-1.

We see from the figure that the earnings per share indifference point between the debt and common stock financing alternatives is $2.45 million in EBIT. If EBIT is below

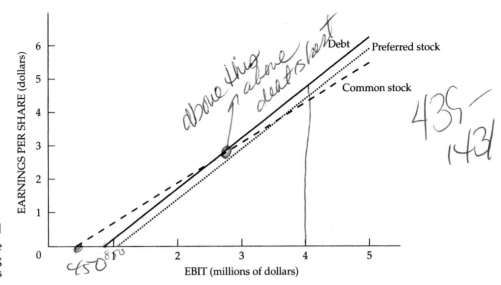

FIGURE 10-1
EBIT-EPS indifference
chart for three financing
alternatives

that point, the common stock alternative will provide higher earnings per share; above
that point the debt alternative is best. The indifference point between the preferred stock
and the common stock alternatives is $3.62 million in EBIT. Above that point, the pre-
ferred stock alternative is favored with respect to earnings per share; below it, the common stock alternative is best. Note that there is no indifference point between the debt
and preferred stock alternatives. The debt alternative dominates for all levels of EBIT
and by a constant amount of earnings per share: $0.35.

Indifference Point Mathematically   The indifference point between two methods
of financing can be determined mathematically by

$$\frac{EBIT^* - C_1}{S_1} = \frac{EBIT^* - C_2}{S_2} \tag{10-1}$$

where EBIT* is the EBIT indifference point between the two methods of financing
for which we solve, C_1, C_2 are the annual interest expenses or preferred stock dividends on a before-tax basis for financing methods 1 and 2, and S_1, S_2 are the number
of shares of common stock to be outstanding after financing for methods 1 and 2.

Suppose we wished to determine the indifference point between the common
stock and the debt-financing alternatives in our example. We would have

$$\frac{EBIT^* - 450,000}{500,000} = \frac{EBIT^* - 850,000}{400,000} \tag{10-2}$$

Rearranging, we obtain

$$(EBIT^*)(400,000) - (450,000)(400,000) = (EBIT^*)(500,000) - (850,000)(500,000)$$
$$100,000\ EBIT^* = 245,000,000,000$$
$$EBIT^* = \$2,450,000$$

The indifference point in EBIT, where earnings per share for the two methods of financing are the same, is $2.45 million. This amount can be verified graphically in Fig.
10-1. Thus, indifference points for financial leverage can be determined either graphically or mathematically.

Use of EBIT-EPS Information

Constructing an EBIT-EPS chart shows the financial manager how alternative methods of financing have different impacts on earnings per share. Insight comes in comparing the indifference point between two financing alternatives, like debt versus common-stock financing, with the existing and expected **level of EBIT**. The higher the level of EBIT in relation to the indifference point, the stronger the case that can be made for debt financing, all other things being the same. The lower the level of EBIT is in relation to the indifference point, the stronger the case is for common-stock financing. This is particularly true when the indifference point is below the existing level of EBIT.

In addition, the financial manager should assess the **likelihood of EBIT falling below the indifference point**. If the probability is negligible, the use of the debt alternative would be supported. On the other hand, if EBIT is now only slightly above the indifference point and the probability of EBIT's falling below this point is high, we may conclude that the debt alternative is too risky. In summary, the greater the level of EBIT and the lower the probability of downside fluctuation, the stronger the case that can be made for the use of debt. To facilitate the evaluation of downside fluctuations, you may wish to superimpose the probability distribution of possible EBIT on the indifference chart, like the one shown in Fig. 10-1. For our example, the present level of EBIT is $3 million. Though this is above the indifference point of $2.45 million, we would want to assess the business risk of Cherokee Tire Company to determine the probability that EBIT might fall below $2.45 million.

Financial leverage magnifies the underlying business risk of the firm when it comes to the variability of earnings per share. EBIT-EPS break-even analysis gives us insight into the return–risk trade-off that governs valuation. However, no one method of analysis of leverage is satisfactory by itself. When several methods of analysis are undertaken simultaneously, generalizations are possible.

CASH-FLOW ABILITY TO SERVICE DEBT

When considering the appropriate capital structure, we should analyze also the cash-flow ability of the firm to service fixed charges. The greater the dollar amount of senior securities a company issues and the shorter their maturity, the greater the fixed charges of that company. These charges include principal and interest payments on debt, lease payments, and preferred stock dividends. Before assuming additional fixed charges, the firm should analyze its expected future cash flows, for fixed charges must be met with cash. The inability to meet these charges, with the exception of preferred stock dividends, may result in financial insolvency. The greater and more stable the expected future cash flows of the firm, the greater the debt capacity of the company.

Times Interest Earned

Coverage of interest by earnings is an important test of creditworthiness.

Among the ways we can gain knowledge about the debt capacity of a firm is through the use of coverage ratios. In the computation of these ratios, one typically uses earnings before interest and taxes as a rough measure of the cash flow available to cover debt-servicing obligations. Perhaps the most widely used coverage ratio is times interest earned, which is simply

$$\text{Times interest earned} = \frac{\text{EBIT}}{\text{Interest on debt}} \tag{10-3}$$

Suppose the most recent annual earnings before interest and taxes for a company were $6 million, and interest payments on all debt obligations were $1.5 million.

Therefore, times interest earned would be four times. This tells us that EBIT can drop by as much as 75 percent and the firm still will be able to cover its interest payments out of earnings.

A coverage ratio of only one indicates that earnings are *just* sufficient to satisfy the interest burden. Although generalizations about what is an appropriate interest coverage ratio are difficult, one usually is concerned when the ratio gets much below three to one. If a company is below this ratio, for example, it is very difficult to achieve an investment-grade credit rating on any new debt that is issued.

Debt-Service Coverage

Note that the times interest earned ratio tells us nothing about the ability of the firm to meet principal payments on its debt. The inability to meet a principal payment constitutes the same legal default as failure to meet an interest payment. Therefore, it is useful to compute the coverage ratio for the full debt-service burden. This ratio is

$$\text{Debt service coverage} = \frac{\text{EBIT}}{\text{Interest} + \dfrac{\text{Principal payments}}{1 - \text{Tax rate}}} \tag{10-4}$$

Here principal payments are adjusted upward for the tax effect. The reason is that EBIT represents earnings before taxes. Because principal payments are not deductible for tax purposes, they must be paid out of after-tax earnings. Therefore, we must adjust principal payments so that they are consistent with EBIT. If principal payments in our previous example were $1 million per annum and the tax rate were 40 percent, the debt-service coverage ratio would be

$$\text{Debt service coverage} = \frac{\$6 \text{ million}}{\$1.5 \text{ million} + \dfrac{\$1 \text{ million}}{1 - .4}} = 1.89$$

A coverage ratio of 1.89 means that EBIT can fall by 47 percent before earnings coverage is insufficient to service the debt.[1] Obviously the closer the ratio is to 1.0, the worse things are, all other things the same. Even with a coverage ratio of less than one, a company may still meet its obligations if it can renew some of its debt when it comes due.

The financial risk associated with leverage should be analyzed on the basis of the firm's ability to service total fixed charges. While lease financing is not debt per se, its impact on cash flows is exactly the same as the payment of interest and principal on a debt obligation. (See Chapter 18 for an analysis of lease financing.) Annual lease payments, therefore, should be added to the numerator and denominator of Eq. (10-4) to properly reflect the total cash-flow burden associated with financing.

Debt Service and Business Risk   As with the times interest earned ratio, there are no exact rules of thumb for what constitutes a good or bad debt-service ratio. It varies according to the business risk of the firm. This is illustrated in Fig. 10-2, which shows the probability distributions of EBIT for two hypothetical companies. The expected value of EBIT is the same for both companies, as is the debt-service burden as described by the denominator in Eq. (10-4). Therefore, the debt-service coverage ratios also are the same, $100/$60 = 1.67. Company A, however, has

---

[1] The percentage is determined by $1 - (1/1.89) = .47$.

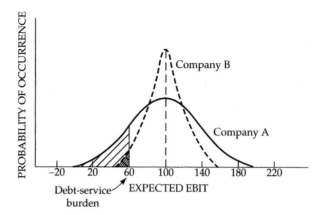

FIGURE 10-2
Possible EBIT in
relation to
debt-service burden

much more business risk. The probability that EBIT will fall below the debt-service burden is depicted by the shaded areas in the figure. We see that this probability is much greater for company A than it is for company B. Although a debt-service coverage ratio of 1.67 may be appropriate for company B, it may not be appropriate for company A. Simply put, a company with stable cash flows is able to take on relatively more fixed charges. This explains why electric utility companies have low coverage ratios when compared with manufacturing companies.

Earnings before Interest, Taxes, Depreciation, and Amortization

Instead of focusing on EBIT in the coverage ratio, some analysts add back depreciation and amortization. **EBITDA** is earnings before interest, taxes, depreciation, and amortization, and it portrays the total operating cash flow of a company. To the extent that all such cash flow can be dedicated to debt service, EBITDA is appropriate to use in the numerator of the coverage ratio. However, certain capital expenditures may be necessary to keep the business operating. To the extent that these expenditures approximate depreciation and amortization, EBITDA is not a good measure of the cash available for debt service. Under these circumstances, it is better to use EBIT in the numerator of the coverage ratio.

Probability of Cash Insolvency

The vital question for the firm is not so much whether a coverage ratio will fall below one, but what the **chances of insolvency** are. The answer depends on whether all sources of payment—EBITDA, cash, a new financing arrangement, or the sale of assets—are collectively deficient. A coverage ratio tells only part of the story. To address the broader question of cash insolvency, we must obtain information on the possible deviation of actual cash flows from those expected. As we discuss in Chapter 13, cash budgets can be prepared for a range of possible outcomes, with a probability attached to each. This information is valuable to the financial manager in evaluating the ability of the firm to meet fixed obligations. Not only expected earnings are taken into account in determining this ability, but other factors as well: the purchase or sale of assets, the liquidity of the firm, dividends, seasonal patterns, and any other factors impacting on cash flows. Given the probabilities of particular cash-flow sequences, the financial manager is able to determine the amount of fixed charges and debt the company can undertake while still remaining within the insolvency limits tolerable to management.

Management may feel that a 5 percent probability of being out of cash is the maximum it can tolerate, and that this probability corresponds to a cash budget prepared under pessimistic assumptions. In this case, debt might be undertaken up to the point where the cash balance under the pessimistic cash budget is just sufficient to cover the fixed charges associated with the debt. In other words, debt would be increased to the point at which the additional cash drain would cause the probability of cash insolvency to equal the risk tolerance specified by management. It is not necessary that debt be increased to this point, of course. Note that the method of analysis simply provides a means for assessing the effect of increases in debt on the risk of cash insolvency. On the basis of this information, management would determine the most appropriate level of debt.

Donaldson Approach

Gordon Donaldson has proposed a similar type of analysis.[2] He suggests that the ultimate concern of a company is whether cash balances during some future period will be involuntarily reduced below zero. Therefore, he advocates examining the cash flows of the company under the most adverse circumstances; that is, in his definition, under recession conditions. These conditions may or may not be the most adverse; however, in keeping with the spirit of his proposal, the firm should evaluate its cash flows under adverse circumstances. Donaldson defines the net cash balance in a recession as

$$CB_r = CB_0 + NCF_r \qquad (10\text{-}5)$$

where CB_0 is the cash balance at start of recession and NCF_r is the net cash flow during a recession. Donaldson then calculates a probability distribution of expected net cash flows and analyzes the cash-flow behavior of a firm during a recession.[3] Combining the beginning cash balance, CB_0, with the probability distribution of recession cash flows, NCF_r, he prepares a probability distribution of cash balances in the recession—CB_r.

Debt Capacity To ascertain its debt capacity, a company first would calculate the fixed charges associated with additional increments of debt. For each addition, the firm then would determine the probability of being out of cash, based on the probability distribution of cash balances during the recession. As before, management could set tolerance limits on the probability of being out of cash. Suppose the firm were considering issuing $20 million in additional debt, and the annual fixed charges were $3 million. By subtracting $3 million from the expected cash balances shown for the probability distribution of CB_r, we obtain the probability of distribution of CB_r with the addition of $20 million in debt. If the probability of being out of cash with this increment of debt is negligible, Donaldson would contend that the company has unused debt capacity. Therefore, it would be possible to increase the amount of debt until the probability of being out of cash equaled the risk tolerance of management.

Donaldson extends his analysis to calculate the probability of **cash inadequacy**. Our discussion before was in terms of **cash insolvency**, which is defined as lack of cash after all nonessential expenditures have been cut. Cash inadequacy is said to occur if the firm is out of cash after making certain desired expenditures such as dividends, R&D expenditures, and capital expenditures. Thus, cash insolvency is the extreme form of cash inadequacy. In all cases, the firm should take

---

[2]Gordon Donaldson, *Corporate Debt Capacity* (Boston: Division of Research, Harvard Business School, 1961). See also Donaldson, "Strategy for Financial Emergencies," *Harvard Business Review*, 47 (November–December 1969), 67–79.

[3]The determinants of net cash flows with which he works are sales collections, other cash receipts, payroll expenditures, raw materials expenditures, and nondiscretionary cash expenditures. By analyzing each of these determinants, he determines the range and probability of recession net cash flows.

stock of the resources it has at its disposal to meet an unexpected cash drain. Typically, a number of alternatives are available, ranging from the use of surplus cash to the sale of fixed assets at distress prices.

EFFECT ON DEBT RATIOS

Pro forma debt ratios should be computed for various financing alternatives under consideration. For the debt alternative, new debt is simply added to the old debt and the combined amount then is used to calculate a debt-to-equity ratio or a debt-to-capitalization ratio. The new debt ratios then can be compared with past ratios in a trend analysis (see Chapter 12).

Also, the new debt ratios should be compared with other companies having similar business risk, such as those in the same industry. If a company is contemplating a capital structure significantly out of line with that of similar companies, it is conspicuous in the marketplace. This is not to say that the firm is wrong. Other companies in the industry may be too conservative in their use of debt. The optimal capital structure for all companies in the industry might call for a higher proportion of debt to equity than the industry average. As a result, the firm may well be able to justify more debt than the industry average. Because investment analysts and creditors tend to evaluate companies by industry, a company should be prepared to justify its position if its capital structure is noticeably out of line in either direction. (See Chapter 12 for a discussion of the comparison of financial ratios with industry averages.)

EFFECT ON SECURITY RATING

The financial manager must consider the effect of a financing alternative on its security rating. Whenever a company sells a debt or preferred stock issue to public investors, as opposed to private lenders such as banks, it must have the issue rated by one or more rating services. The principal rating agencies are Moody's Investors Service and Standard & Poor's. The issuer of a new corporate security contracts with the agency to evaluate and rate the issue as to quality as well as to update the rating throughout the life of the instrument. For this service, the issuer pays a fee. In addition, the rating agency charges subscribers to its rating publications. Though the assignment of a rating for a new issue is current, changes in ratings of existing securities tend to lag the events that prompt the change.

Security ratings indicate the creditworthiness of a borrower.

Both agencies use much the same letter grading. The ratings used by Moody's and Standard & Poor's, as well as brief descriptions, are shown in Table 10-2. In their ratings, the agencies attempt to rank issues according to their probability of default. The first four grades are considered investment-grade issues, whereas other rated securities are considered speculative grade. The highest grade securities, whose risk of default is felt to be negligible, are rated triple A. For each rating category one of three modifiers is applied. For example, Aa-1, using Moody's, means that a security is in the higher end of the Aa rating category. Baa-3 indicates that the security is in the lower end of the Baa category, whereas a modifier of 2 indicates it is in the middle. Standard & Poor's uses modifiers of +, no modifier, and −, to indicate the area of a rating category in which a security falls.

The rating agencies look at a number of things before assigning a grade: trends in ratios of liquidity, debt, profitability, and coverage; the firm's business risk, both historically and expected; present and likely future capital requirements;

TABLE 10-2
Ratings by Investment Agencies

Moody's Investors Service		Standard & Poor's	
Aaa	Best quality	AAA	Highest rating; extremely strong capacity to pay interest and principal
Aa	High quality	AA	Very strong capacity to pay
A	Upper medium grade	A	Strong capacity to pay
Baa	Medium grade	BBB	Adequate capacity to pay
Ba	Possess speculative elements	BB	Uncertainties that could lead to inadequate capacity to pay
B	Generally lacks characteristics of desirable investment	B	Greater vulnerability to default, but currently has capacity to pay
Caa	Poor standing; may be in default	CCC	Vulnerable to default
		CC	For debt subordinated to that with CCC rating
Ca	Highly speculative; often in default	C	For debt subordinated to that with CCC–rating; or bankruptcy petition has been filed
C	Lowest grade; extremely poor prospects	D	In payment default

Junk Bonds

Note: The top four categories indicate "investment-grade quality" securities; the categories below the dashed line are reserved for speculative-grade securities.

specific features associated with the instrument being issued; the relative proportion of debt; and, perhaps most important, the cash-flow ability to service principal and interest payments. If a public security offering is contemplated, the financial manager must be mindful of ratings when determining how much leverage is appropriate. If taking on additional debt lowers your firm's security ratings from an investment- to a speculative-grade category (junk bonds)—thus making the security ineligible for investment by many institutional investors—you will want to factor this into account before making a decision.

TIMING AND FLEXIBILITY

Once a company has determined an appropriate capital structure, it still has the problem of **timing** security issues. When external financing is required, a company often faces the question of how to time an issue appropriately and whether to use debt or common stock. Because financing is "lumpy," it is difficult for a company to maintain strict proportions in its capital structure. Frequently, it must decide whether to finance now with a stock issue and later with a debt issue, or vice versa. Consequently, it is forced to evaluate the alternative methods of financing in light of general market conditions and expectations for the company itself.

If the future were certain, it would be an easy matter to determine today an optimal financing sequence for many years to come. The sequence would be timed to take advantage of known future changes in the stock market and in the market for fixed-income securities. Unfortunately, prices in financial markets, particularly in the equity market, are unstable. Instead of making decisions based on a sure thing, decisions must be based on management's best estimate of the future. In addition, there are the financial signaling and incentive issues taken up in the last chapter. Usually, the announcement of a debt issue has a favorable impact on share price, as we know from that discussion.

If a firm chooses this alternative, however, it may sacrifice a certain amount of flexibility. By **flexibility**, we simply mean that today's financing decision will keep open future financing options. Remember that a company cannot issue debt continually without building its equity base. It is neither desirable, given our discussion in the preceding chapter, nor possible, once default risk becomes too great. Therefore, the equity base must be increased over time, and this is where flexibility becomes important. If a company undertakes a substantial debt issue and things take a turn for the worse, it may be forced to issue stock on unfavorable terms in the future. To preserve its flexibility in tapping the capital markets, it may be better for a firm to issue stock now so that it will have unused debt capacity for future needs. The preservation of unused debt capacity can be a consideration of consequence for the company whose funds requirements are sudden and unpredictable. It gives the company financial maneuverability by virtue of leaving the options open.

We must bear in mind that if the financial markets are efficient, all available information is reflected in the price of the security. Under these circumstances, the market price of the security is the market's best estimate of the value of that security. If management is no better than the average investor at forecasting future market prices, efforts by a company to time security offerings will be for naught. In other words, management will be wrong about as often as it is right. If timing is to be a thing of value, management's expectations must be more correct than those of the market. In Part V, we examine specific methods of long-term financing, the timing of a specific security issue, and the flexibility afforded by the instrument.

Flexibility as to financing is important when future external financing will be necessary.

A PECKING ORDER OF FINANCING?

Donaldson followed by Myers suggests that management follows a preference ordering when it comes to financing.[4]

(1) Internal financing of investment opportunities is preferred, in part because it avoids the outside scrutiny of suppliers of capital. Also, there are no flotation costs associated with the use of retained earnings. A target dividend-payout ratio is set in keeping with long-run investment opportunities. Management wishes to avoid sudden changes in dividends. When cash flows are insufficient to fund all desirable investment opportunities, and a "sticky" dividend policy precludes a dividend cut, resort must be made to external financing.

(2) Here straight debt is preferred. Not only does debt result in less intrusion into management by suppliers of capital, but flotation costs are less than with other types of external financing. Also, asymmetric information and financial signaling considerations come into play. As taken up in the previous chapter (and again in Chapter 19 on issuing securities), debt issues are regarded as "good news" by investors. The reason is the belief that management will never issue an undervalued security. If debt is issued, this means management believes the stock is undervalued and the debt either overvalued or valued fairly by the market.

(3) Next in order of financing preference is preferred stock, which has some of the features of debt. Donaldson in particular makes a strong case for its usefulness.

---

[4]Gordon Donaldson, *Corporate Debt Capacity*; Stewart C. Myers, "The Capital Structure Puzzle," *Journal of Finance*, 39 (July 1984), 575–92; Myers, "Still Searching for Optimal Capital Structure," *Journal of Applied Corporate Finance*, 6 (Spring 1993), 4–14; and Lakshmi Shyam-Sunder and Stewart C. Myers, "Testing Static Tradeoff Against Pecking Order Models of Capital Structure," *Journal of Financial Economics*, 51 (February 1999), 219–44.

(4) This is followed by the various hybrid securities, like conver
(5) Finally, the least desirable security to issue is straight equity.
investors the most intrusive, but flotation costs are higher than w
methods of financing and there is likely to be an adverse signaling
ing to the pecking order hypothesis, equity is issued only as a last resort.

The pecking order story is mainly a behavioral explanation of why certain companies finance the way they do. It is consistent with some rational arguments, such as asymmetric information and signaling, as well as with flotation costs. Moreover, it is consistent with the observation that the most profitable companies within an industry tend to have the least amount of leverage. However, the pecking order hypothesis suggests that corporations do not have a well-thought-out capital structure. Rather, a company finances over time with the method providing the least resistance to management, and there is little in the way of capital market discipline on management's behavior. The capital structure that results is a by-product and changes whenever there is an imbalance between internal cash flows and capital investments. As interesting as the pecking order hypothesis is, my view is that financing decisions should be based on rigorous analysis embracing valuation.

Managers sometimes have a preference ordering as to types of financing.

CHECKLIST WHEN IT COMES TO FINANCING

We have discovered a number of methods of analysis that can be brought to bear on the question: What is appropriate capital structure for our company? In particular we are concerned with the mix of debt and equity, saving for later chapters specific features of an instrument as well as the more exotic instruments. It is useful now to provide a practical checklist of things that should be considered, drawing from both Chapter 9 and from this chapter.

1. TAXES
The degree to which a company is subject to taxation is very important. Much of the advantage of debt is tax related. If, because of marginal profitability, a company pays little or no taxes, debt is far less attractive than it is for the company subject to the full corporate tax rate.

2. EXPLICIT COST
The higher the interest rate on debt, the higher the preferred stock dividend rate, and the higher implicit interest cost in such things as lease financing, the less attractive that method of financing, all other things the same.

3. AGENCY COSTS AND INCENTIVE ISSUES
Does one type of financing expropriate value from other security holders? This is part and parcel of the issue of management taking on risk to expropriate value from existing debt holders, and how the latter can protect themselves. Will management be more efficient if saddled with the obligation to service debt? These and other questions of this sort need to be addressed.

4. FINANCIAL SIGNALING
What is likely to be the stock market reaction to a particular financing decision and why? An effect, if any, is based on asymmetric information between management and security holders.

5. CASH FLOW ABILITY TO SERVICE DEBT
This is probably the most important analytical tool in determining the debt capacity of a corporation. The analysis here brings together the business and financial risk of a company. It allows you to address the likelihood of insolvency and the cost therein.

6. EBIT-EPS ANALYSIS

At what point in earnings before interest and taxes (EBIT) are the earnings per share (EPS) of a company the same under alternative methods of financing? How does this relate to the existing level of EBIT and what is the probability of falling below the indifference point?

7. DEBT RATIOS

What effect does a method of financing have on the company's debt ratios? How do the new debt ratios compare with other companies' in the industry? What is the likely effect on investment analysts and lenders?

8. SECURITY RATING

Is a particular method of financing likely to result in a downgrade or upgrade of the company's security rating? No financial manager can ignore this consideration, though it should not necessarily be a binding constraint.

9. TIMING

Is it a good time to issue debt? to issue equity? Whenever securities are to be issued, the vitality of the debt and stock markets must be addressed. This consideration is taken up in later chapters.

10. FLEXIBILITY

If a company needs to finance on a continuing basis over time, how does the method chosen this time affect future financing? How important is it that a company have flexibility to tap the debt markets in the future?

These important questions must be addressed when considering the appropriate degree of leverage for a company. By undertaking a variety of analyses, the financial manager should be able to determine, within some range, the appropriate capital structure for his or her company. The final decision is somewhat subjective, but it can be based on the best information available. Hopefully, this decision will be consistent with maximizing shareholder wealth.

Summary

In choosing an appropriate capital structure, the financial manager should consider a number of factors. Considerable insight can be gained from an analysis of the cash-flow ability of the firm to service fixed charges associated with debt, preferred stock, and leasing. One way to determine this ability is through the analysis of the times interest earned ratio and the debt-service coverage ratio. However, these ratios consider only the earnings of a company as a means to service debt. A more inclusive analysis involves the probability of cash insolvency and takes into account all resources available to service debt. Using this type of analysis, the financial manager is better able to estimate the debt capacity of the firm.

Another method for gaining insight into the question of the appropriate capital structure involves analyzing the relationship between earnings before interest and taxes (EBIT) and earnings per share for alternative methods of financing. When this analysis is expanded to consider the level of and likely fluctuations in EBIT, light is shed on the question of financial risk.

In addition, the financial manager can learn much from a comparison of capital structure ratios for similar companies. Security ratings on public issues of debt and preferred stock necessarily are of concern to the financial manager and are a part of any decision. We examined also the question of timing a debt or equity issue. Where sequential financing is involved, the choice of debt or equity influences the future financial flexibility of the firm.

It has been argued that management follow a pecking order when it comes to the method of financing. Most desirable, because it is safest and least intrusive, is internal financing. The least desirable alternative is equity. The pecking order hypothesis is mainly behavioral in connotation, though issues of asymmetric information, signaling, and flotation costs come into play.

Finally, we presented a checklist of things to consider when approaching a financing decision. These practical and conceptual considerations draw from both this chapter and the preceding one. Hopefully, they will guide you in determining a capital structure.

Self-Correction Problems

1. Dorsey Porridge Company presently has $3.6 million in debt outstanding bearing an interest rate of 10 percent. It wishes to finance a $4 million expansion program and is considering three alternatives: additional debt at 12 percent interest, preferred stock with an 11 percent dividend, and the sale of common stock at $16 per share. The company presently has 800,000 shares of common stock outstanding and is in a 40 percent tax bracket.

   a. If earnings before interest and taxes are presently $1.5 million, what would be earnings per share for the three alternatives, assuming no immediate increase in profitability?

   b. Develop an indifference chart for these alternatives. What are the approximate indifference points? To check one of these points, what is the indifference point mathematically between debt and common?

   c. Which alternative do you prefer? How much would EBIT need to increase before the next alternative would be best?

2. Torstein Torque and Gear Company has $7.4 million in long-term debt having the following schedule:

	AMOUNT (IN THOUSANDS)
8% serial bonds, payable $100,000 in principal annually	$2,400
10% first mortgage bonds, payable $150,000 in principal annually	3,000
12% subordinated debentures, interest only until maturity in 10 years	2,000
	$7,400

Torstein's common stock has a book value of $8.3 million and a market value of $6.0 million. The corporate tax rate is 30 percent. Torstein is in a cyclical business: Its expected EBIT is $2.0 million with a standard deviation of $1.5 million. The average debt-to-equity ratio of other companies in the industry is .47.

   a. Determine the times interest earned and the debt-service coverage of the company at the expected EBIT.

   b. What are the probabilities these two ratios will go below one-to-one?

   c. Does Torstein have too much debt?

3. Sowla Electronics currently has $2 million in cash and marketable securities, a $3 million bank line of credit of which $1.3 million is in use, pays a cash dividend on its stock of $1.2 million annually, plans capital expenditures of $4 million a year, and devotes $2 million a year to advertising and special promotions. In addition, it spends $2 million a year on research and development. The company's sales are highly correlated with swings in sales of integrated circuits. Currently, the firm is enjoying good times with annual after-tax profits and depreciation (cash flow) totaling $7 million. As it sells mainly to jobbers, finished goods inventories are minimal.

   a. If the integrated circuit cycle moves into a recession and cash flow drops by $5 million, what would you do? Do you have proper flexibility now for the unforeseen?

   b. What if a negative cash flow of $9 million per annum were experienced?

Problems

1. The Lemaster Company is a new firm that wishes to determine an appropriate capital structure. It can issue 16 percent debt or 15 percent preferred stock. Moreover, common stock can be sold at $20 per share. In all cases, total capitalization of the company will be $5 million, and it is expected to have a 30 percent tax rate. The possible capital structures are

Plan	Debt	Preferred	Equity
1	0%	0%	100%
2	30	0	70
3	50	0	50
4	50	20	30

   a. Construct an EBIT-EPS chart for the four plans.
   b. Determine the relevant indifference points.
   c. Using Eq. (10-1), verify the indifference points on your graph for the dominant plans.
   d. Which plan is best?

2. Gallatin Quarter Company makes saddles. During the preceding calendar year, it earned $200,000 after taxes. The company is in a 40 percent tax bracket, it had no debt outstanding at year end, and it has 100,000 shares of common stock outstanding. At the beginning of the current year, it finds that it needs to borrow $300,000 at an interest rate of 10 percent in order to expand its operations.

   a. What are earnings per share before and after financing if EBIT stays the same?

   b. What are the absolute and percentage increases in earnings per share if EBIT increases by 50 percent?

3. Hi Grade Regulator Company currently has 100,000 shares of common stock outstanding with a market price of $60 per share. It also has $2 million in 6 percent debt. The company is considering a $3 million expansion program that it can finance with (1) all common stock at $60 a share, (2) straight bonds at 8 percent interest, (3) preferred stock at 7 percent, or (4) half common stock at $60 per share and half 8 percent bonds.

   a. For a hypothetical EBIT level of $1 million after the expansion program, calculate the earnings per share for each of the alternative methods of financing. Assume a corporate tax rate of 50 percent.

   b. Construct an EBIT-EPS chart. What are the indifference points between alternatives? What is your interpretation of them?

4. Hi Grade Regulator Company (see Problem 3) expects the EBIT level after the expansion program to be $1 million, with a two-thirds probability that it will be between $600,000 and $1,400,000.

   a. Which financing alternative do you prefer? Why?

   b. Suppose the expected EBIT level were $1.5 million and there were a two-thirds probability that it would be between $1.3 million and $1.7 million. Which financing alternative would you prefer? Why?

5. Fazio Pump Corporation presently has 1.1 million shares outstanding and $8 million in debt bearing an interest rate of 10 percent on average. It is considering a $5 million expansion program financed with either (1) common stock at $20 per share being realized, (2) debt at an interest rate of 11 percent, or (3) preferred stock with a 10 percent dividend rate. Earnings before interest and taxes after the new funds are raised are expected to be $6 million, and the company's tax rate is 35 percent.

   a. Determine likely earnings per share after financing for each of the three alternatives.

   b. What would happen if EBIT were (1) $3 million? (2) $4 million? (3) $8 million?

   c. What would happen under the original conditions (1) if the tax rate were 46 percent? (2) if the interest rate on new debt were 8 percent and the preferred stock dividend rate were 7 percent? (3) if the common could be sold for $40 per share?

6. The Power Corporation currently has 2 million shares outstanding at a price of $20 each and needs to raise an additional $5 million. These funds could be raised with stock or 10 percent debentures. Expected EBIT after the new funds are raised will be normally distributed with a mean of $4 million per year forever and a standard deviation of $2 million. Power Corporation has a 50 percent tax rate. What is the probability that the debt alternative is superior with respect to earnings per share?

7. Cornwell Real Estate Speculators, Inc., and the Northern California Electric Utility Company have the following EBITs and debt-servicing burdens:

	Cornwell	Northern California
Expected EBIT	$5,000,000	$100,000,000
Annual interest	1,600,000	45,000,000
Annual principal payments on debt	2,000,000	35,000,000

The tax rate for Cornwell is 40 percent; for Northern California Electric Utility, 36 percent. Compute the times interest earned ratio and the debt-service coverage ratio for the two companies. With which company would you feel more comfortable if you were a lender? Why?

8. Gamma Tube Company plans to undertake a $7.5 million capital improvement program and is considering how much debt to use. It feels that it could obtain debt financing at the following interest rates (assume that this debt is perpetual):

Amount	First $3 million	Next $2 million	Next $1.5 million	Next $1 million
Interest cost	10 percent	11 percent	12 percent	13 percent

The company has made projections of its net cash flows (exclusive of new financing) during a period of adversity such as a recession. In a recession, it expects a net cash flow of $3 million with a standard deviation of $2 million (assume a normal distribution). Its beginning cash balance is $1 million. If the company is willing to tolerate only a 5 percent probability of running out of cash during a recession, what is the maximum proportion of the $7.5 million capital improvement program that can be financed with debt? (Ignore any tax considerations.)

Solutions to Self-Correction Problems

1.   a. (in thousands):

	Debt	Preferred Stock	Common Stock
EBIT	$1,500	$1,500	$1,500
Interest on existing debt	360	360	360
Interest on new debt	480	—	—
Profit before taxes	$ 660	$1,140	$1,140
Taxes	264	456	456
Profit after taxes	$ 396	$ 684	$ 684
Preferred stock dividend	—	440	—
Earnings available to common stockholders	$ 396	$ 244	$ 684
Number of shares	800	800	1,050
Earnings per share	$ .495	$ .305	$ .651

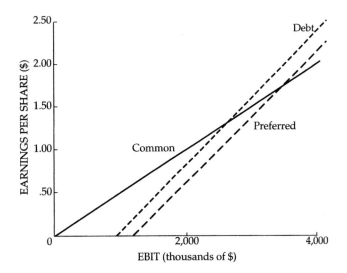

b. Approximate indifference points: debt and common, $2.4 million in EBIT; preferred and common, $3.3 million in EBIT; debt dominates preferred by the same margin throughout, there is no indifference point. Mathematically, the indifference point between debt and common is (in thousands):

$$\frac{\text{EBIT}^* - \$840}{800} = \frac{\text{EBIT}^* - \$360}{1,050}$$

$$\text{EBIT}^*(1,050) - \$840(1,050) = \text{EBIT}^*(800) - \$360(800)$$

$$250\text{EBIT}^* = \$594,000$$

$$\text{EBIT}^* = \$2,376$$

Note that for the debt alternative, the total before-tax interest is $840, and this is the intercept on the horizontal axis. For the preferred stock alternative, we divide $440 by (1 − .40) to get $733. When this is added to $360 in interest on existing debt, the intercept becomes $1,093.

c. For the present EBIT level, common is clearly preferable. EBIT would need to increase by $2,376 − $1,500 = $876 before an indifference point with debt is reached. One would want to be comfortably above this indifference point before a strong case for debt should be made. The lower the probability that actual EBIT will fall below the indifference point, the stronger the case that can be made for debt, all other things the same.

2. a. Total annual interest (in thousands):

Serial bonds, 8% on $2,400	$192
Mortgage bonds, 10% on $3,000	300
Subordinated debentures, 12% of $2,000	240
	$732

Total annual principal payments : $100 + $150 = $250

EBIT necessary to service: $250 (1 − .30) = $175.

$$\text{Times interest earned:} \frac{\$2,000}{\$732} = 2.73$$

$$\text{Debt-service coverage:} \frac{\$2,000}{\$1,089} = 1.84$$

b. Deviation from mean before ratio is one to one:

Times interest earned: $2,000 − $732 = $1,268

Debt-service coverage: $2,000 − $1,089 = $911

Standardizing the deviations:

$$\text{Times interest earned:} \frac{1,268}{1,500} = .845$$

$$\text{Debt-service coverage:} \frac{911}{1,500} = .607$$

Using Table C, these standardized deviations correspond to probabilities of the two ratios being less than one to one of approximately 20 percent and 27 percent, respectively. (These probabilities assume that the distribution of possible EBITs is normal.)

c. There is a significant probability, 27 percent, that the company will fail to cover its interest and principal payments. Its debt ratio of $7.4 million/$8.3 million = .89 is much higher than the industry norm of .47. Its book value of debt to market value of stock ratio is even higher. Although the information is limited, it would appear that Torstein is pushing out on the risk spectrum as it has to do with debt. Still its times interest earned approaches 3, and the situation would not yet appear to be critical.

3. a. There is not a precise solution to this problem; rather, it is a judgment call. In the problem are listed various possibilities for coming to grips with the cash-flow shortfall. In addition, there may be others, such as the sale of plant and equipment. A cash flow of $7 million is $1.8 million more than capital expenditures and the dividend. If the cash flow were to fall by $5 million, this annual surplus would disappear. In addition, other things must give. One probably would use most of the cash and marketable securities, but not all. The bank line should be fully utilized, or nearly so. In a slack period, it may be possible to cut capital expenditures. Due to competition, the company probably should maintain advertising and promotion expenses at approximately the same level. Otherwise, sales may suffer even more. To build for the future, the company probably should not cut its R&D expenditures, although something could give here. The dividend may be reduced, but there will be an adverse informational effect (see Chapter 11). If the recession is expected to be short, many firms will try to maintain their dividend.

Based on this discussion, a possible proposal to offset the $5 million in reduced cash flow might be (in thousands):

Elimination of previous annual surplus	$1,800
Decrease in cash and marketable securities	900
Additional borrowings under line of credit	1,700
Capital expenditure reduction	600
	$5,000

Again, there is no right or wrong solution. If $5 million is the maximum decline in cash flow and the industry recession is expected to be short in duration, the firm probably has adequate financial flexibility. Once in a recession, however, it should try to negotiate a larger line of credit so that it has some margin for error.

b. If the cash-flow shortfall is $9 million, the solution must be harsher. Capital expenditures will need to be cut further, and all other items will need to be cut. The dividend, if maintained at all, will be sharply reduced. Indeed, survival becomes the theme. If the bank line cannot be increased, a possible remedy might be (in thousands):

Elimination of previous surplus	$1,800
Decrease in cash and marketable securities	1,000
Additional borrowings under line of credit	1,700
Capital expenditures reduction	2,000
Reduction in R&D expenditures	800
Reduction in advertising and promotions	800
Reduction of dividend	900
	$9,000

Obviously, the company has utilized a good deal of its resources to stem the cash-flow decline. Further cuts will be needed if the recession continues. Additional financing will need to be sought, as the firm is completely inflexible after one really bad year. Again, these are only examples of solutions.

Selected References

CLEARY, SEAN, "The Relationship between Firm Investment and Financial Status," *Journal of Finance*, 54 (April 1999), 673–92.

DIAMOND, DOUGLAS W., "Reputation Acquisition in Debt Markets," *Journal of Political Economy*, 97, No. 4 (1989), 828–62.

DONALDSON, GORDON, *Corporate Debt Capacity*. Boston: Division of Research, Harvard Business School, 1961.

———, "Strategy for Financial Emergencies," *Harvard Business Review*, 47 (November–December 1969), 67–79.

GUEDES, JOSE, and TIM OPLER, "The Determinants of the Maturity of Corporate Debt Issues," *Journal of Finance*, 51 (December 1996), 1809–33.

JUNG, KOOYUL, YONG-CHEOL KIM, and RENE M. STULZ, "Timing, Investment Opportunities, Managerial Discretion, and the Security Issue Decision," *Journal of Financial Economics*, 47 (October 1996), 159–85.

LEVY, HAIM, and ROBERT BROOKS, "Financial Break-Even Analysis and the Value of the Firm," *Financial Management*, 15 (Autumn 1986), 22–26.

MYERS, STEWART C., "Capital Structure Puzzle," *Journal of Finance*, 39 (July 1984), 575–92.

———, "Still Searching for Optimal Capital Structure," *Journal of Applied Corporate Finance*, 6 (Spring 1993), 4–14.

PIPER, THOMAS R., and WOLF A., WEINHOLD, "How Much Debt Is Right for Your Company," *Harvard Business Review*, 60 (July–August 1982), 106–14.

RAJAN, RAGHURAM G., and LUIGI ZINGALES, "What Do We Know about Capital Structure? Some Evidence from International Data," *Journal of Finance*, 50 (December 1995), 1421–60.

SHYAM-SUNDER, LAKSHMI, and STEWART C. MYERS, "Testing Static Tradeoff Against Pecking Order Models of Capital Structure," *Journal of Financial Economics*, 51 (February 1999), 219–44.

Wachowicz's Web World is an excellent overall Web site produced and maintained by my coauthor of *Fundamentals of Financial Management*, John M. Wachowicz Jr. It contains descriptions of and links to many finance Web sites and articles. *www.prenhall.com/wachowicz.*

Dividends and Share Repurchase: Theory and Practice

he third major decision of a company is the distribution of cash to its stockholders. This can take two forms: dividends and share repurchase. In a typical year the aggregate amount of dividends paid by American corporations exceeds the amount of funds devoted to share repurchase, but the latter has risen dramatically in relative importance. In keeping with this shift, the proportion of U.S. companies paying cash dividends has declined over time to where now it is only about one-quarter.

Dividends and share repurchase, of course, reduce the amount of earnings retained in a company and affect the total amount of internal financing. Consequently, they must be considered in relation to a company's overall financing decision. We begin our inquiry by looking at the percentage of earnings a company pays out in cash dividends to its stockholders. Known as the dividend payout ratio, like the other major decisions of the firm—the investment and the financing decisions—it has both theoretical and managerial facets. This chapter—structured much the same as Chapter 9 on capital structure—begins with dividend payout under perfect capital-market assumptions. There follows a systematic analysis of the implications of various market imperfections and financial signaling.

Our attention is then directed to share repurchase as a substitute for cash dividends in the distribution of excess cash, using the framework developed earlier. This is followed by the special topic of stock dividends and stock splits. Finally, the chapter itemizes what a company in practice should analyze in approaching dividend and share repurchase decisions. Before delving into the heart of the matter, we need to understand certain procedures. ■

PROCEDURAL ASPECTS OF PAYING DIVIDENDS

When the board of directors of a corporation declares a cash dividend, it specifies a **date of record**. At the close of business that day, a list of stockholders is drawn up from the stock transfer books of the company. Stockholders on the list are entitled to the dividend, whereas stockholders who come on the books after the date of record are not entitled to the dividend. When the board of directors of United Chemical Company met on May 8, it declared a dividend of 25 cents a share payable June 15 to stockholders of record on May 31. Jennifer Doakes owned the stock well before May 31, so she is entitled to the dividend, even though she might sell her stock prior to the dividend actually being paid on June 15.

Sight liquidating (handwritten in margin)

The buyer and the seller of a stock have 3 business days to settle the transaction. Therefore, new stockholders are entitled to dividends only if they buy the stock 3 or more business days before the date of record. If the stock is bought after that time, the stockholder is not entitled to the dividend. The date itself is known as the **ex-dividend date.** A company cannot pay a dividend if it impairs capital. Capital impairment rules vary according to state laws, but most consider impairment to occur when a dividend reduces the common-stock account (at par) or reduces common stock plus additional paid-in capital.

Once a dividend is declared, stockholders become general creditors of the company until the dividend is actually paid; the declared but unpaid dividend is a current liability of the company coming out of retained earnings. Most companies that pay dividends do so on a quarterly basis, though semiannual or even annual intervals are sometimes used.

DIVIDEND PAYOUT IRRELEVANCE

To begin our inquiry into dividend payout (dividends/earnings), let us see what happens when perfect market assumptions hold. If dividend payout is a matter of indifference to investors, the corporation will treat retained earnings simply as a means of financing.

Dividends as a Residual

Under these circumstances, each period the company must decide whether to retain its earnings or to distribute part or all of them to stockholders as cash dividends. (We rule out share repurchase for now.) As long as there are investment projects with returns exceeding those that are required, it will use retained earnings, and the amount of senior securities the increase in equity base will support, to finance these projects. If the firm has retained earnings left over after financing all acceptable investment opportunities, these earnings then will be distributed to stockholders in the form of cash dividends. If not, there will be no dividends.

When we treat dividend policy as strictly a financing decision, the payment of cash dividends is a **passive residual.** The amount of dividend payout will fluctuate from period to period in keeping with fluctuations in the amount of acceptable investment opportunities available to the firm. If these opportunities abound, the percentage of dividend payout is likely to be zero. On the other hand, if the firm is unable to find profitable investment opportunities, dividend payout will be 100 percent. For situations between these two extremes, the payout will be a fraction between zero and one.

Residual dividend policy pays out only excess cash.

The treatment of dividend policy as a passive residual determined solely by the availability of acceptable investment proposals implies that dividends are irrelevant; the investor is indifferent between dividends and retention by the firm. If investment opportunities promise a return greater than their required return, the investor is happy to have the company retain earnings. Contrarily, if the return is less than the required return, the investor prefers dividends. A residual theory of dividend policy does not necessarily mean that dividends need fluctuate from period to period in keeping with fluctuations in investment opportunities. A firm may smooth out actual payments by saving some funds in surplus years, in anticipation of deficit years. If forecasting is relatively accurate, the firm can establish its dividend payment at a level at which the cumulative distribution over time corresponds to cumulative residual funds over the same period. The fact that dividends do not correspond to residual funds period by period does not negate the residual theory of dividends.

Modigliani and Miller Position

Our friends from Chapter 9 on capital structure, **Modigliani and Miller**, have moved on to dividend payout.[1] Not surprisingly, they make a comprehensive argument for irrelevancy. They assert that, given the investment decision of the firm, the dividend-payout ratio is a mere detail. It does not affect the wealth of shareholders. MM argue that the value of the firm is determined by the earning power of the firm's assets or its investment policy and that the manner in which the earnings stream is split between dividends and retained earnings does not affect this value. The critical assumptions are:

1. Perfect capital markets in which all investors are rational. Information available to all at no cost, instantaneous transactions without cost, infinitely divisible securities, and no investor large enough to affect the market price of a security.
2. An absence of flotation costs on securities issued by the firm.
3. A world of no taxes.
4. A given investment policy for the firm, not subject to change.
5. Perfect certainty by every investor as to future investments and profits of the firm. (MM drop this assumption later.)

Dividends versus Terminal Value

The crux of MM's position is that the effect of dividend payments on shareholder wealth is offset exactly by other means of financing. Consider first selling additional stock in lieu of retained earnings. When the firm has made its investment decision, it must decide whether to retain earnings or to pay dividends and sell new stock in the amount of these dividends to finance the investments. MM suggest that the sum of the discounted value per share after financing and dividends paid is equal to the market value per share before the payment of dividends. In other words, the stock's decline in market price because of external financing offsets exactly the payment of the dividend. Thus, the stockholder is said to be indifferent between dividends and the retention of earnings and subsequent capital gains.

The market price of a share of stock at the beginning of a period is defined as equal to the present value of the dividend paid at the end of the period plus the market price at the end of the period. Thus

$$P_0 = \frac{1}{1+p}(D_1 + P_1) \tag{11-1}$$

where P_0 is the market price per share at time 0, p is the capitalization rate for firm in that risk class (this rate is assumed to be constant throughout time), D_1 is the dividend per share at time 1, and P_1 is the market price per share at time 1.

Assume that n is the number of shares of record at time 0 and that m is the number of new shares sold at time 1 at a price of P_1. Equation (11-1) then can be rewritten as

---

[1]Merton H. Miller and Franco Modigliani, "Dividend Policy, Growth, and the Valuation of Shares," *Journal of Business*, 34 (October 1961), 411–33.

$$nP_0 = \frac{1}{1 + p}[nD_1 + (n + m)P_1 - mP_1] \qquad (11\text{-}2)$$

In words, the total value of all shares outstanding at time 0 is the present value of total dividends paid at time 1 on those shares plus the total value of all stock outstanding at time 1, less the total value of the new stock issued. The total amount of new stock issued is

$$mP_1 = I - (X - nD_1) \qquad (11\text{-}3)$$

where I is the total new investments during period 1 and X is the total new profit of firm for the period. Equation (11-3) merely states that the total sources of funds must equal total uses. That is, net profit plus new stock sales must equal new investments plus dividends.

Financing/Dividend Forgone Indifference   The total amount of financing by the sale of new stock is determined by the amount of investments in period 1 not financed by retained earnings. By substituting Eq. (11-3) into Eq. (11-2), MM find that the nD_1 term cancels out and

$$nP_0 = \frac{1}{1 + p}[(n + m)P_1 - I + X] \qquad (11\text{-}4)$$

Because D_1 does not appear directly in the expression and because X, I, $(n + m)P_1$, and p are assumed to be independent of D_1, MM conclude that the current value of the firm is independent of its current dividend decision. What is gained by stockholders in increased dividends is offset exactly by the decline in the terminal value of their stock. MM go on to show that nP_0 is unaffected not only by current dividend decisions but by future dividend decisions as well. Under the assumption of perfect certainty by all investors, the price of the stock at time 1, time 2, and time n is determined solely by Eq. (11-4). Thus, **stockholders are indifferent** between retention and the payment of dividends (and concurrent stock financing) in all future periods. As a result, stockholder wealth is unaffected by current and future dividend decisions; it depends entirely on the expected future earnings stream of the firm.

If both leverage and dividends are irrelevant, the firm would be indifferent to whether investment opportunities were financed with debt, retained earnings, or a common stock issue. One method of financing would be as satisfactory as the next. Now one might ask, How does this correspond to our earlier chapters when we said that dividends are the foundation for the valuation of common stocks? Although it is true that the market value of a share of stock is the present value of all expected future dividends, the timing of the dividends can vary. The irrelevance position simply argues that the present value of future dividends remains unchanged even though dividend policy changes their timing. It does not argue that dividends, including liquidating dividends, are never paid, only that their postponement is a matter of indifference when it comes to market price per share.

Irrelevance under Uncertainty

In a world of perfect capital markets and the absence of taxation, dividend payout would be a matter of irrelevance even with uncertainty. This argument involves the same reasoning as that for the irrelevance of capital structure and for the irrelevance of diversification of corporate asset decisions. Investors are able to replicate any dividend stream the corporation might pay. If dividends are less than desired, investors can sell portions of their stock to obtain the desired cash distribution. If dividends are more than desired, investors can use dividends to purchase additional shares in the company. Thus, investors are able to manufacture **"homemade" dividends** in the same way they devise "homemade" leverage in capital structure decisions.

For a corporate decision to be a thing of value, the company must be able to do something for stockholders that they cannot do for themselves. Because investors can manufacture "homemade" dividends, which are perfect substitutes for corporate dividends under the above assumptions, dividend policy is irrelevant. As a result, one dividend policy is as good as the next. The firm is unable to create value simply by altering the mix of dividends and retained earnings. As in capital structure theory, there is a conservation of value so that the sum of the parts is always the same. The total size of the pie is what is important, and it is unchanged in the slicing.

ARGUMENTS FOR DIVIDEND PAYOUT MATTERING

The irrelevance of dividend argument assumes an absence of market imperfections. To the extent imperfections exist, they may support the contrary position, namely, that dividends are relevant. We shall examine various imperfections bearing on the issue, beginning with taxes. After we consider the theory, we look at various empirical evidence bearing on the topic.

Unimportance of Corporate Income Taxes

Unlike the capital structure decision, corporate income taxes have no bearing on dividend relevance. Under present law, earnings of a company are taxed at the corporate level, regardless of whether or not a dividend is paid. In other words, it is the profit after corporate taxes that is divided between dividends and retained earnings. Corporate income taxes could affect dividend relevance if tax laws were changed, as would occur under various methods to eliminate the double taxation of dividends.

Taxes on the Investor and Negative Dividend Effect

Tax wedge is the difference in tax rates on dividends and on capital gains.

Taxes paid by the investor are another matter. To the extent that the personal tax rate on capital gains is less than that on dividend income, there may be an advantage to the retention of earnings. Apart from explicit tax rates, the capital gains tax is deferred until the actual sale of stock. Effectively, the stockholder is given a valuable timing option when the firm retains earnings as opposed to paying dividends.

As we described in Chapter 4, a differential tax on dividends and capital gains may result in a **yield tilt.** That is, a dividend-paying stock will need to provide a higher expected before-tax return than will a non-dividend-paying stock of the same risk. This is said to be necessary to offset the tax effect on dividends. According to this notion, the greater the dividend yield of a stock, the higher its expected before-tax return, all other things being the same. Thus, security markets would equilibrate in terms of systematic risk, dividend yield, and, perhaps, other factors.

However, different types of investors experience different taxation on the two types of income. Institutional investors, such as retirement and pension funds, pay no tax on either dividends or capital gains. Corporate investors enjoy what is known as the **intercorporate dividend exclusion**. Presently, 70 percent of any dividend received by one corporation from another is not subject to taxation. As a result, the effective tax rate on dividends is less than that on capital gains. For example, if Laurel Corporation owns 100 shares of Hardy Corporation, which pays $1 per share dividend, 70 percent of the dividend income is tax exempt. In other words, Laurel Corporation would pay taxes on $30 of dividend income at the corporate tax rate. The overall tax effect will be less than if Hardy Corporation had share appreciation of $100 and all of this were taxed at the capital gains rate. Accordingly, there may be a preference for current dividends on the part of the corporate investors.

Despite these exceptions, for many investors there exists a differential in tax rate between a dollar of dividend and a dollar of retained earnings. If these investors dominated at the margin, there would need to be an inducement to them to accept dividends. This inducement is simply a higher before-tax return so that after taxes they are as well off. According to this notion, paying dividends has a "negative" effect on value.

Dividend Neutrality

Even with a **tax wedge** between dividend and capital-gains income, it is not clear that investors at the margin are those who prefer capital gains to dividends. With different tax situations, clienteles of investors may develop with distinct preferences for dividend- or non-dividend-paying stocks. Many corporate investors will prefer dividend-paying stocks, whereas wealthy individual investors may prefer stocks that pay no dividends. Tax-exempt investors will be indifferent, all other things the same. If dividend-paying stocks were priced in the marketplace to provide a higher return than non-dividend-paying stocks, however, they would not be indifferent. They would prefer dividend-paying stocks.

Completing markets implies that corporations tailor dividend payout to the unfilled desires of investors.

If various clienteles of investors have dividend preferences, corporations should adjust their dividend payout to take advantage of the situation. Expressed differently, **corporations should tailor their dividend policies** to the unfulfilled desires of investors and thereby take advantage of an incomplete market. Suppose two-fifths of all investors prefer a zero dividend payout, one-fifth prefer a 25 percent payout, and the remaining two-fifths prefer a 50 percent payout. If most companies pay out 25 percent of their earnings in dividends, there will be excess demand for the shares of companies paying zero dividends and for the shares of companies whose dividend-payout ratio is 50 percent. Presumably, a number of companies will recognize this excess demand and adjust their payout ratios in order to increase share price. The action of these companies eventually will eliminate the excess demand.

In equilibrium, the dividend payouts of corporations will match the desires of investor groups. At this point, no company would be able to affect its share price by altering its dividend. As a result, even with taxes, dividend payout would be irrelevant. The **neutral position** is largely based on corporations adjusting the supply of dividends to take advantage of any mispricing of stocks in the marketplace.[2]

However, another argument against clientele effects is that investors can use combinations of put and call options to isolate movements in stock price. By so doing, the investor effectively strips the dividend from the capital gains component

---

[2] For an excellent synthesis of these arguments together with a review of the empirical evidence, see Franklin Allen and Roni Michaely, "Dividend Policy," in R. A. Jarrow, V. Maksimovic, and W. T. Ziemba, editors, *North-Holland Handbook of Operations Research and Management Science: Finance*. Amsterdam: North-Holland, 1995.

of the stock. If investors are able to separate dividends from capital gains to suit their needs, the tax-induced clientele argument for a particular stock is weakened. Thus, both supply and demand forces may drive the equilibrium toward investors at the margin being indifferent, taxwise, between dividends and capital gains.

Positive Dividend Effect

Apart from tax issues, we must recognize an argument for a positive dividend effect. This is the possibility of a preference for dividends on the part of a sizable number of investors for **behavioral reasons**. For one thing, the payment of dividends may resolve uncertainty in the minds of some. Also, such payments may be useful in diversification of investments in an uncertain world. If in fact investors can manufacture homemade dividends, such a preference is irrational. Nonetheless, sufficient statements from investors make it difficult to dismiss the argument. Perhaps, for either psychological or inconvenience reasons, investors are unwilling to manufacture homemade dividends.

Behavioral reasons could produce a net preference for dividends.

Shefrin and Statman reason that some investors are reluctant to sell shares because they will experience regret if the stock subsequently rises in price.[3] For them, dividends and the sale of stock for income are not perfect substitutes. A second argument the authors advance is that although many investors are willing to consume out of dividend income they are unwilling to "dip into capital" to do so. Again, dividends and the sale of stock are not perfect substitutes for these investors. For behavioral reasons, then, certain investors prefer dividends. Whether they are numerous enough to make a difference is the question.

Ultimately, the question of whether a negative, neutral, or positive dividend effect prevails is an empirical matter. We investigate this later in the chapter. First, however, we need to consider other influences on dividends.

Impact of Other Imperfections

Although the factors we have examined are the most important when it comes to establishing whether or not dividend payout matters, there are other imperfections.

Flotation Costs The irrelevance of dividend payout is based on the idea that in accordance with the investment policy of the firm, funds paid out by a company must be replaced by funds acquired through external financing. The introduction of flotation costs favors the retention of earnings in the company. Flotation costs are the legal, investment banking, and other costs incurred by the corporation in a security issue. This means that for each dollar paid out in dividends, the company nets less than a dollar after flotation costs per dollar of external financing. Moreover, the smaller the size of the issue, the greater in general the flotation costs as a percentage of the total amount of funds raised. In addition, stock financing is "lumpy" in the sense that small issues are difficult to sell even with high flotation costs.

Transaction Costs and Divisibility of Securities Transaction costs involved in the sale of securities tend to restrict the arbitrage process in the same manner as that described for debt. Stockholders who desire current income must pay brokerage fees on the sale of portions of their stock if the dividend paid is not sufficient to satisfy their current desire for income. This fee varies inversely, per dollar of

---

[3]Hersh M. Shefrin and Meir Statman, "Explaining Investor Preferences for Cash Dividends," *Journal of Financial Economics*, 13 (June 1984), 253–82.

stock sold, with the size of the sale. For a small sale, the brokerage fee can be a rather significant percentage. Because of this fee, stockholders with consumption desires in excess of current dividends will prefer that the company pay additional dividends. Perfect capital markets also assume that securities are infinitely divisible. The fact that the smallest integer is one share may result in "lumpiness" with respect to selling shares for current income. This, too, acts as a deterrent to the sale of stock in lieu of dividends. On the other hand, stockholders not desiring dividends for current consumption purposes will need to reinvest their dividends. Here again, transaction costs and divisibility problems work to the disadvantage of the stockholder, although in the opposite direction. Thus, transaction costs and divisibility problems cut both ways, and one is not able to draw directional implications about dividends versus retained earnings.

Institutional Restrictions Certain institutional investors are restricted in the types of common stock they can buy or in the portfolio percentages they can hold in these types. The prescribed list of eligible securities is determined in part by the duration over which dividends have been paid. If a company does not pay a dividend or has not paid dividends over a sufficiently long period of time, certain institutional investors are not permitted to invest in the stock.

Universities, on the other hand, sometimes have restrictions on the expenditure of capital gains from their endowment. Also, a number of trusts have a prohibition against the liquidation of principal. In the case of common stocks, the beneficiary is entitled to the dividend income, but not to the proceeds from the sale of stock. As a result of this stipulation, the trustee who manages the investments may feel constrained to pay particular attention to dividend yield and seek stocks paying reasonable dividends.

If institutional investors are better monitors of corporate performance than are individual investors, their presence may help ensure that the company is managed efficiently. In this context, paying dividends would be a positive signal to the market because such dividends will attract institutional investors seeking investment in quality companies.[4] From the standpoint of increased demand for the stock and signaling, the argument works in the direction of a preference for dividends as opposed to retention and capital gains.

FINANCIAL SIGNALING

Signaling may occur if the dividend is more or less than expected.

Cash dividends, then, may be viewed as a signal to investors. Presumably, companies with good news about their future profitability will want to tell investors. Rather than make a simple announcement, dividends may be increased to add conviction to the statement. When a firm has a target-payout ratio that is stable over time and it changes this ratio, investors may believe that management is announcing a change in the expected future profitability of the firm. The signal to investors is that management and the board of directors truly believe things are better than the stock price reflects. In this vein, Miller and Rock suggest that investors draw inferences about the firm's internal operating cash flows from the dividend announcement.[5] The notion is based on asymmetric information. Management

---

[4]This argument is made by Franklin Allen, Antonio Bernardo, and Ivo Welch, "A Theory of Dividends Based on Tax Clienteles," working paper, Wharton School (May 1999).

[5]Merton H. Miller and Kevin Rock, "Dividend Policy under Asymmetric Information," *Journal of Finance*, 40 (September 1985), 1031–51. The authors also analyze management trying to fool the market by increasing dividends and the implications of such an expectation for stockholders and for the equilibrating mechanism.

knows more about the true state of the company's earnings than do outside investors.

Accordingly, the price of the stock may react to any unanticipated change in dividends. To the extent dividends provide information on economic earnings not provided by reported accounting earnings and other information, share price will respond. Put another way, dividends speak louder than words under these circumstances. The rationale behind a dividend signaling effect is similar to that of a capital structure signaling effect described in Chapter 9. However, it generally is agreed that the effect is more important for dividends than it is for capital structure.

EMPIRICAL TESTING AND IMPLICATIONS FOR PAYOUT

While we have seen that a number of factors may explain dividends' impact on valuation, many are difficult to test. Most empirical testing has concentrated on the tax effect and on financial signaling. This is not to say that such things as flotation costs, transaction costs, institutional restrictions, and preference for dividends have no effect; only that whatever effect they might have is swamped by the two effects discussed. Empirical testing has taken several forms.

Ex-dividend Day Tests

One of the mainstays has involved the **ex-dividend behavior** of common stock prices. Investors buying the stock before that date are entitled to the dividend declared; purchases on or after the ex-dividend date are not entitled to the dividend. In a nontaxable world, the stock should drop in value by the amount of the dividend on the ex-dividend day. If you are a taxable investor, however, and buy the stock before the ex-dividend day, you will need to pay taxes on the dividend. In contrast, if you wait until the ex-dividend day to buy the stock, you will pay no taxes on the dividend, since there is no dividend, and any price movement presumably is subject only to the capital-gains tax. A number of authors reason that if there is a tax effect, owing to capital gains being taxed at a lower rate than dividend income, a stock should decline in price by less than the dividend on the ex-dividend day. Expressed differently, investors would value a dollar of dividends less than they would a dollar of capital gains.

An early study of the phenomenon was by Elton and Gruber.[6] In a sample of companies, they found that on average a stock declined by .78 of the dividend on the ex-dividend date. They interpret this result as consistent with a clientele effect where investors in high tax brackets show a preference for capital gains over dividends, and vice versa.

There have been a number of other studies of share price behavior on the ex-dividend day.[7] In a number of these studies, the evidence is consistent with the

---

[6]Edwin J. Elton and Martin J. Gruber, "Marginal Stockholder Tax Rates and the Clientele Effect," *Review of Economics and Statistics*, 52 (February 1970), 68–74.

[7]Avner Kalay, "The Ex-Dividend Day Behavior of Stock Prices: A Re-examination of the Clientele Effect," *Journal of Finance*, 37 (September 1982), 1059–70; Kenneth M. Eades, Patrick J. Hess, and E. Han Kim, "On Interpreting Security Returns during the Ex-Dividend Period," *Journal of Financial Economics*, 13 (March 1984), 3–34; Patrick J. Hess, "The Ex-Dividend Day Behavior of Stock Returns: Further Evidence on Tax Effects," *Journal of Finance*, 37 (May 1982), 445–56; James M. Poterba and Lawrence H. Summers, "New Evidence That Taxes Affect the Valuation of Dividends," *Journal of Finance*, 39 (December 1984), 1397–1416; Costas P. Kaplanis, "Options, Taxes and Ex-Dividend Day Behavior," *Journal of Finance*, 41 (June 1986), 411–24; Michael J. Barclay, "Dividends, Taxes and Common Stock Prices: The Ex-Dividend Day Behavior of Common Stock Prices before the Income Tax," *Journal of Financial Economics*, 19 (September 1987), 31–44; Roni Michaely, "Ex-Dividend Day Stock Price Behavior," *Journal of Finance*, 46 (July 1991), 845–59; and John H. Boyd and Ravi Jagannathan, "Ex-Dividend Price Behavior of Common Stocks," *Review of Financial Studies*, 7 (Winter 1994), 711–41.

foregoing, namely, that stock prices decline on the ex-dividend day but by less than the amount of the dividend. Such findings are consistent with a tax effect where dividends are taxed more heavily than are capital gains, and stock prices reflect this differential. This, of course, is in accord with dividends having a negative effect on value. Other studies look at market microstructure considerations, such as the minimum tick size in a transaction, and find that when these considerations are taken into account the drop in stock price approximates the dividend amount.[8] Findings of this sort support the dividend neutrality argument.

Dividend-Yield Approach

A second approach to the tax effect question is to study the relationship between dividend yields and stock returns, where other influences on returns are isolated. If higher-dividend-yielding stocks provide higher returns to investors, this would be consistent with a negative effect of dividends on value. For the most part, there is not evidence of a significant relationship between stock returns and dividend yield.[9] A lack of relationship is consistent with dividend neutrality. The evidence is not unambiguous, however. Naranjo, Nimalendran, and Ryngaert find a significant positive relationship between stock returns and dividend yields.[10] Moreover, this effect appears to be unrelated to the tax rate of the corporation—the yield tilt hypothesis previously described.

Financial Signaling Studies

Testing for a financial signaling effect has involved a different methodology. Typically, an event study is employed where daily share price changes, relative to the market, are analyzed around the announcement of a dividend change. A number of studies report findings consistent with a dividend announcement effect: increases in dividend leading to positive excess returns and decreases leading to negative excess returns.[11] The effect seems to be more pronounced for companies

---

[8]See Rakesh Bali and Gailen L. Hite, "Ex Dividend Day Stock Price Behavior: Discreteness or Tax-Induced Clienteles?" *Journal of Financial Economics*, 47 (February 1998), 127–59; Murray Frank and Ravi Jagannathan, "Why Do Stock Prices Drop by Less than the Value of the Dividend? Evidence from a Country without Taxes," *Journal of Financial Economics*, 47 (February 1998), 161–88; and M. Ameziane Lasfer, "Ex-Day Behavior: Tax or Short-Term Trading Effects," *Journal of Finance*, 50 (July 1995), 875–97.

[9]See Fischer Black and Myron Scholes, "The Effects of Dividend Yield and Dividend Policy on Common Stock Prices and Returns," *Journal of Financial Economics*, 1 (May 1974), 1–22; Robert H. Litzenberger and Krishna Ramiswamy, "The Effect of Personal Taxes and Dividends on Capital Asset Prices," *Journal of Financial Economics*, 7 (June 1979), 163–95; Nai Fu Chen, Bruce Grundy, and Robert F. Stambaugh, "Changing Risk Premiums and Dividend Yield Effects," *Journal of Business*, 63 (Spring 1990), 51–70; William G. Christie, "Dividend Yield and Expected Returns: The Zero Dividend Puzzle," *Journal of Financial Economics*, 28 (November–December 1990), 95–126; and Allen and Michaely, "Dividend Policy."

[10]Andy Naranjo, M. Nimalendran, and Mike Ryngaert, "Stock Returns, Dividend Yields, and Taxes," *Journal of Finance*, 53 (December 1998), 2029–57.

[11]See, for example, Joseph Aharony and Itzhak Swary, "Quarterly Dividend and Earnings Announcements and Stockholders' Returns: An Empirical Analysis," *Journal of Finance*, 35 (March 1980), 1–12; Kenneth M. Eades, Patrick H. Hess, and E. Han Kim, "Market Rationality and Dividend Announcements," *Journal of Financial Economics*, 14 (December 1985), 581–604; Aharon R. Ofer and Daniel R. Siegel, "Corporate Financial Policy, Information, and Market Expectations: An Empirical Investigation of Dividends," *Journal of Finance* (September 1987), 889–911; Paul M. Healy and Krishna G. Palepu, "Earnings Information Conveyed by Dividend Initiations and Omissions," *Journal of Financial Economics*, 21 (September 1988), 149–75; Paul Asquith and David W. Mullins Jr., "The Impact of Initiating Dividend Payments on Shareholders' Wealth," *Journal of Business*, 56 (January 1983), 77–96; Larry H. P. Lang and Robert H. Litzenberger, "Dividend Announcements: Cash Flow Signalling vs. Free Cash Flow Hypothesis," *Journal of Financial Economics*, 24 (September 1989), 181–91; Chihwa Kao and Chunchi Wu, "Tests of Dividend Signaling Using the Marsh-Merton Model: A Generalized Friction Approach," *Journal of Business*, 67, No. 1 (1994), 45–68; and Roni Michaely, Richard H. Thaler, and Kent Womack, "Price Reactions to Dividend Initiations and Omissions: Overreaction or Drift?" *Journal of Finance*, 50 (June 1995), 573–608.

that previously overinvested free cash flow in projects with returns less than what the financial markets require. After all, those cash flows belong to stockholders and should not be invested in negative NPV projects. The signaling effect is particularly pronounced for companies that initiate dividends for the first time or after a long hiatus (positive share price effect) and for companies that omit dividends (negative effect). The two effects are not symmetric: Omitted dividends have a greater negative effect than the positive effect associated with dividend initiations.

Conceptually, dividend changes should provide information about future cash flows and earnings of a company. In an interesting article Benartzi, Michaely, and Thaler find little evidence of a positive relationship between dividend changes and earnings changes 2 years out.[12] Expressed differently, dividends do not appear to contain information about future earnings. At the time of the dividend change, however, the authors find that there is a significant earnings change.

Implications for Corporate Policy

> **Excess cash**
> belongs to the
> shareholders and
> should be
> distributed to them.

As reflected in the foregoing discussion, the empirical evidence is mixed as to there being a tax effect that requires a higher before-tax return the greater the dividend. In recent years, however, the evidence is largely consistent with a dividend neutrality. No studies of recent vintage support a positive dividend effect. In contrast to the mixed results for a tax effect, most empirical studies suggest that dividends convey information and that there is a signaling effect. Where does this leave us with respect to directions for a corporation?

A company should endeavor to establish a dividend policy that will maximize shareholder wealth. Almost everyone agrees that if a company does not have sufficiently profitable investment opportunities, it should **distribute excess funds** to its stockholders. As we have said before, these funds belong to them, not to management to squander on wasteful expenditures. The firm need not pay out the exact unused portion of earnings every period. Indeed, it may wish to stabilize the absolute amount of dividends paid from period to period. But over the longer run the total earnings retained, plus the senior securities the increasing equity base will support, will correspond to the amount of profitable investment opportunities. Dividend policy still would be a passive residual determined by the amount of investment opportunities.

For the firm to be justified in paying a dividend larger than that dictated by the amount left over after profitable investment opportunities, there must be a net preference for dividends in the market. It is difficult to "net out" the arguments just discussed to arrive at the bottom line. Only institutional restrictions and some investors' preference for dividends argue for dividends. The other arguments suggest either a neutral effect or a bias favoring retention. There does appear to be some positive value associated with a modest dividend as opposed to none at all. This occurrence may be due to institutional demand and/or a signaling effect.

Beyond that, the picture is cloudy, and some argue that even a modest dividend has no effect on valuation. Few academic scholars argue that dividends significantly in excess of what a passive policy would dictate will lead to share price improvement. This is particularly true when there is information asymmetry between management and investors, as the excess dividend ultimately must be replaced with a stock offering. Still, many corporations pay out a significant portion

---

[12]Shlomo Benartzi, Roni Michaely, and Richard Thaler, "Do Changes in Dividends Signal the Future or the Past?" *Journal of Finance*, 52 (July 1997), 1007–34.

of their earnings, and many high-taxed stockholders receive and pay taxes on these dividends. These facts are difficult to reconcile with the theory.

SHARE REPURCHASE

Share repurchase has increased in importance relative to dividends.

In recent years, the repurchase of stock by corporations has grown dramatically. When you look at the total cash distributed to shareholders—cash dividends, **share repurchases,** and cash tender offers in connection with acquisitions—dividends remain the primary mechanism for such distribution but have diminished relative to the other two. Stock repurchase often is used as part of an overall corporate restructuring, a topic taken up in Chapter 24. In this chapter, our focus is on stock repurchase as a substitute for cash dividends.

Employee Stock Options and Share Repurchase

Stock repurchases often occur in conjunction with stock options granted to employees as part of a total compensation package. Some companies, like Microsoft, roughly match share repurchases with the number of options awarded to employees. In this way the number of shares outstanding remains relatively constant over time. Share repurchase in this context is not so much a means for distributing excess cash as it is a means to compensate employees.

When the choice is one of distributing excess cash either by dividends or by share repurchase, management and employees with existing stock options prefer the latter. All other things being the same, cash dividends reduce the value of a stock option for the reasons discussed in Chapter 5. With stock repurchase, share value will increase, all other things remaining the same, and this will benefit the option holder. To the extent a CEO and others in top management strongly influence the choice between dividends and share repurchase at the board level, personal compensation considerations may tilt the balance in favor of share repurchase. The greater the relative number of stock options owned by management, the more likely there is to be a share repurchase in lieu of an increase in cash dividends.[13]

Method of Repurchase

There are three principal methods of repurchase: a fixed-price tender offer, a dutch-auction tender offer, and open-market repurchases. Brennan and Thakor advance a theory of corporate cash disbursement, suggesting that cash dividends are likely to be preferred for small distributions whereas tender offer repurchases dominate for large distributions.[14] Open-market repurchases are suitable in the intermediate range. The authors formulate their theory based on less informed shareholders being vulnerable to expropriation by the better informed. With a fixed cost of information, it pays larger shareholders to become informed when a repurchase offer comes along. As a result, unless their tax rates are high, smaller stockholders are said to prefer dividends.

With a **fixed-price tender offer,** the company makes a formal offer to stockholders to purchase so many shares, typically at a set price. This bid price is above

---

[13]For empirical support of this hypothesis, see Eli Bartov, Itzhak Krinsky, and Jason Lee, "Evidence on How Companies Choose between Dividends and Open-Market Stock Repurchases," *Journal of Applied Corporate Finance,* 11 (Spring 1998), 89–96.

[14]Michael J. Brennan and Anjan V. Thakor, "Shareholder Preferences and Dividend Policy," *Journal of Finance,* 45 (September 1990), 993–1018.

the current market price; stockholders can elect either to sell their stock at the specified price or continue to hold it. Typically, the tender offer period is between 2 and 3 weeks. If stockholders tender more shares than originally sought by the company, the company may elect to purchase all or part of the excess. It is under no obligation to do so. In general, the transaction costs to the firm in making a tender offer are much higher than those incurred in the purchase of stock in the open market.

With a **dutch-auction tender offer,** each shareholder is given the opportunity to submit to the company the number of shares he or she is willing to sell at a particular price. In advance, the company specifies the number of shares it wishes to repurchase as well as a minimum and a maximum price it will entertain. Typically, the minimum price is slightly above the current market price. Upon receipt of all the self tenders, the company arrays them from low to high within the range. It then determines the lowest price that will result in the full repurchase of shares specified. This price is paid to all shareholders who tendered shares at that price or below. (The purchase of shares from those submitting the cutoff price is on a pro rata basis.) The fact that the price is the same may encourage certain shareholders to submit low ask prices, which may work to the advantage of the company.

Unlike a fixed-price tender offer, the company does not know the eventual repurchase price. In both cases, it is uncertain as to the number of shares that will be tendered, either at the fixed price or at or above the minimum price in the case of the dutch auction. The dutch-auction tender offer has increased dramatically in use and is now the dominant form of tender offer. Though smaller companies still use the fixed-price tender offer, larger ones tend to use the dutch auction.

In **open-market repurchases,** a company buys its stock as any other investor does—through a brokerage house but at a negotiated fee. If the repurchase program is gradual, its effect is to drive up the price of the stock. Also, certain Securities and Exchange Commission rules restrict the manner in which a company bids for its shares. As a result, it takes an extended period of time for a company to accumulate a relatively large block of stock. For these reasons, the tender offer is more suitable when the company seeks a large amount of stock.

Before the company repurchases stock, stockholders must be informed of the company's intentions. In a tender offer, these intentions are announced by the offer itself. Even here, the company must not withhold other information. It would be unethical for a mining company, for example, to withhold information of a substantial ore discovery while making a tender offer to repurchase shares. In open-market purchases especially, it is necessary to disclose a company's repurchase intentions. Otherwise, stockholders may sell their stock not knowing about a repurchase program that will increase earnings per share. Given full information about the amount of repurchase and the objective of the company, the stockholders can sell their stock if they choose. Without proper disclosure, the selling stockholder may be penalized. When the amount of stock repurchased is substantial, a tender offer is particularly suitable, for it gives all stockholders equal treatment.

Repurchasing as Part of a Dividend Decision

If a firm has excess cash and insufficient profitable investment opportunities to justify the use of these funds, it is in the shareholders' interests to distribute the funds. The distribution can be accomplished either by the repurchase of stock or by paying the funds out in increased dividends. In the absence of personal income taxes and transaction costs, the two alternatives, theoretically, should make no difference to stockholders. With repurchase, fewer shares remain outstanding, and earnings per share and, ultimately, dividends per share rise. As a result, the market price per share should rise as well. In theory, the capital gain arising from repurchase should equal the dividend that otherwise would have been paid.

Equilibrium Formula   What repurchase price per share should a company offer to achieve this balance, assuming a fixed-price tender offer? It depends on the current share price and the proportion of shares a company wishes to repurchase. The idea is to establish such a price that shareholders who do not tender will be no better or worse off than shareholders who tender, and vice versa. The equilibrium share repurchase price, P^*, a company should offer is

$$P^* = \frac{S \times P_c}{S - n} \tag{11-5}$$

where S is the number of shares outstanding prior to the distribution, P_c is the current market price per share prior to the distribution, and n is the number of shares to be repurchased.

Illustration   To illustrate, suppose Apollo Products Inc. has 8 million shares outstanding whose current market price is $36 per share, and the company wishes to repurchase 1 million shares. The equilibrium share repurchase price offered should be

$$P^* = \frac{8{,}000{,}000 \times \$36}{8{,}000{,}000 - 1{,}000{,}000} = \$41.14$$

If the offer price were $44, shareholders who tendered their shares would gain at the expense of those who continued to hold the stock. Contrarily, if the offer price were $38, selling stockholders would lose and continuing stockholders would gain. At $41.14, both parties are treated equally.

Recognize that this formula does not take account of the opportunity cost associated with using liquidity to repurchase shares. However, we assume that this liquidity is excess and should be distributed to stockholders. It is merely a question of dividends or share repurchase being the vehicle. With respect to monies realized, stockholders presumably would be indifferent. The equilibrium price established in Eq. (11-5), or by some other equilibrium formula, often is used as the maximum price specified in a dutch-auction tender offer.

Personal Tax Effect   With a differential tax rate on dividends and capital gains, however, repurchase of stock offers a tax advantage over payment of dividends to the taxable investor. The market price increase resulting from a repurchase of stock is subject to the capital gains tax, whereas dividends are taxed at the ordinary income tax rate. With a share repurchase, the stockholder has a timing option. He or she can accept the share repurchase offer or reject it and continue to hold the stock. With a cash dividend, there is no such option.

It is important to recognize that if an investor manufactures a homemade dividend by selling off sufficient stock to match the cash dividend that otherwise would have been paid, the proceeds realized are not entirely subject to the capital gains tax. Only the excess of the price realized over original cost is subject to taxation. Capital gains arising from the repurchase are not taxed on the remainder of the investor's holdings until the remaining stock is sold. In essence, the bulk of the capital gains tax is postponed. For tax reasons, then, most taxable investors are better off financially if the firm elects to distribute unused funds via the stock repurchase route rather than via cash dividends.

The repurchase of stock seems particularly appropriate when the firm has a large amount of unused funds to distribute. To pay the funds out through an extra dividend would result in a nonpostponable tax to stockholders. The tax effect could be alleviated somewhat by paying the funds out as extra dividends over a period of time, but this action might result in investors' counting on the extra dividend. The firm must be careful not to undertake a steady program of repurchase in lieu of paying dividends. The Internal Revenue Service may regard such a program as dividend income and not allow stockholders redeeming their shares the capital gains tax advantage.[15]

Signaling Effect

Stock repurchases may have a **signaling effect**. For example, a positive signal might be sent to the market if management believed the stock were undervalued and they were constrained not to tender shares they owned individually. In this context, the premium in repurchase price over existing market price would reflect management's belief about the degree of undervaluation. The idea is that concrete actions, such as repurchase, stock dividends and splits, as well as capital structure changes and cash dividend changes, speak louder than words.

Empirical studies support the signaling effect in different ways.[16] For fixed-price tender offers in particular, there is a significant positive share price effect around the time of the announcement. The evidence is less compelling for open-market purchases. The last study cited in the footnote finds that stocks with low market values in relation to book values (known as "value" stocks) enjoy superior performance in the 4 years after the open-market repurchase announcement. This suggests undervaluation, which is recognized only slowly over time, that is, not completely at the time of the repurchase announcement. For most firms repurchasing their stock, there does not appear to be an improvement in operating performance following the repurchase. The exception is low-growth firms, which have been found to redeploy their existing assets more efficiently following repurchase.[17] Finally, dutch-auction tender offers appear to provide somewhat less in-

---

[15]The tax consequences involved in the repurchase of stock are complex and, in places, ambiguous. In most cases, the monies received by stockholders tendering their shares are subject to the capital gains tax. Under certain circumstances, however, the distribution can be treated as ordinary income to the redeeming stockholder.

[16]Larry Y. Dann, "Common Stock Repurchases: An Analysis of Returns to Bondholders and Stockholders," *Journal of Financial Economics*, 9 (June 1981), 113–38; Theo Vermaelen, "Common Stock Repurchases and Market Signalling," *Journal of Financial Economics*, 9 (June 1981), 139–83; Paul Asquith and David W. Mullins Jr., "Signalling with Dividends, Stock Repurchases, and Equity Issues," *Financial Management*, 15 (Autumn 1986), 27–44; Robert Comment and Gregg A. Jarrell, "The Relative Signalling Power of Dutch-Auction and Fixed-Price Self-Tender Offers and Open-Market Share Repurchases," *Journal of Finance*, 46 (September 1991), 1243–71; Laurie Simon Bagwell, "Dutch Auction Repurchases: An Analysis of Shareholder Heterogeneity," *Journal of Finance*, 47 (March 1992), 71–105; Erik Lie and John J. McConnell, "Earnings Signals in Fixed-Price and Dutch Auction Self-Tender Offers," *Journal of Financial Economics*, 49 (August 1998), 161–86; Bartov, Krinsky, and Lee, "Evidence on How Companies Choose Between Dividends and Open-Market Stock Repurchases"; and David Ikenberry, Josef Lakonishok, and Theo Vermaelen, "Market Underreaction to Open Market Share Repurchases," *Journal of Financial Economics*, 39 (October–November 1995), 181–208.

[17]See Tom Nohel and Vefa Tarhan, "Share Repurchases and Firm Performance: New Evidence on the Agency Costs of Free Cash Flow," *Journal of Financial Economics*, 49 (August 1998), 187–222.

formation content than do fixed-price tender offers but more than open-market repurchase programs. Thus, the credibility of the signal as to undervaluation differs with the method of repurchase.

STOCK DIVIDENDS AND STOCK SPLITS

In an economic sense, stock dividends and stock splits are very similar, although typically used for different purposes. Only from an accounting standpoint is there a significant difference.

Stock Dividends

A stock dividend is simply the payment of additional stock to stockholders. It represents nothing more than a recapitalization of the company; a stockholder's proportional ownership remains unchanged. Chen Industries had the following capital structure before issuing a stock dividend:

Stock splits and dividends are alike in principle, but not in accounting treatment.

Common stock ($5 par, 400,000 shares)	$ 2,000,000
Additional paid-in capital	1,000,000
Retained earnings	7,000,000
Shareholders' equity	$10,000,000

Chen pays a 5 percent stock dividend, amounting to 20,000 additional shares of stock. The fair market value of the stock is $40 a share. For each 20 shares of stock owned, the stockholder receives an additional share. The balance sheet of the company after the stock dividend is

Common stock ($5 par, 420,000 shares)	$ 2,100,000
Additional paid-in capital	1,700,000
Retained earnings	6,200,000
Shareholders' equity	$10,000,000

With a stock dividend, $800,000 is transferred ($40 × 20,000 shares) from retained earnings to the common stock and paid-in capital accounts. Because the par value stays the same, the increase in number of shares is reflected in a $100,000 increase in the common stock account ($5 par × 20,000 shares). The residual of $700,000 goes into the paid-in capital account. Shareholders' equity of the company remains the same.

Because the number of shares outstanding is increased by 5 percent, earnings per share of the company are reduced proportionately. Total net profit after taxes is $1 million. Before the stock dividend, earnings per share were $2.50 ($1 million/400,000). After the stock dividend, earnings per share are $2.38 ($1 million/420,000). Thus, stockholders have more shares of stock but lower earnings per share. The proportion of total earnings available to common stockholders remains unchanged.

Accounting Treatment Differences   The accounting treatment portrayed holds for what is known as **small-percentage stock dividends**, usually a distribution of 20 percent or less of the number of common shares already outstanding. Because larger stock dividends will materially reduce share price, the accounting authorities usually require that capitalization changes be in terms of the par value of the additional shares issued. (For small-percentage dividends, market value per share is employed.) Suppose in our example that Chen Industries declared a 50 percent stock dividend, amounting to 200,000 additional shares. The capitalization accounts after a **large-percentage stock dividend** of this sort are

Common stock ($5 par, 600,000 shares)	$ 3,000,000
Additional paid-in capital	1,000,000
Retained earnings	6,000,000
Shareholders' equity	$10,000,000

Thus, retained earnings are reduced by only the par value of new shares issued.

Stock Splits

With a stock split, the number of shares is increased through a proportional reduction in the par value of the stock. The capital structure of a pharmaceutical company before a 2-to-1 stock split was

Common stock ($5 par, 400,000 shares)	$ 2,000,000
Additional paid-in capital	1,000,000
Retained earnings	7,000,000
Shareholders' equity	$10,000,000

After the split, the capital structure is

Common stock ($2.50 par, 800,000 shares)	$ 2,000,000
Additional paid-in capital	1,000,000
Retained earnings	7,000,000
Shareholders' equity	$10,000,000

With a stock dividend, the par value is not reduced, whereas with a split, it is. As a result, the common stock, paid-in capital, and retained earnings accounts remain unchanged. Shareholders' equity, of course, also stays the same; the only change is in the par value of the stock. Except in accounting treatment, the stock dividend and stock split are very similar. A stock split, however, is usually reserved for occasions when a company wishes to achieve a substantial reduction in the market price per share.

Value to Investors
of Stock Dividends and Splits

Theoretically, a stock dividend or stock split is not a thing of value to investors. They receive additional stock certificates, but their proportionate ownership of the company is unchanged. The market price of the stock should decline proportionately, so that the total value of their holdings stays the same. To illustrate with a stock dividend, suppose you held 100 shares of stock worth $40 per share, or $4,000 in total. After a 5 percent stock dividend, share price should drop by $40(1 − 1.00/1.05), or $1.90. The total value of your holdings then would be $38.10 × 105, or $4,000. Under these conditions, the stock dividend does not represent a thing of value to you. You merely have an additional stock certificate evidencing ownership. In theory, the stock dividend or split is purely cosmetic.

To the extent that the investor wishes to sell a few shares of stock for income, the stock dividend may make it easier to do so. Without the stock dividend, of course, stockholders could also sell a few shares of their original holdings for income. In either case, the sale of stock represents the sale of principal and is subject to the capital gains tax. Some investors, however, may not look on the sale of a stock dividend as a sale of principal. To them, the stock dividend represents a windfall gain; they can sell it and still retain their original holdings. The stock dividend may have a favorable behavioral effect on these stockholders. In efficient markets, however, we would not expect a favorable impact on share price.

Effect on Cash Dividends   The stock dividend or stock split may be accompanied by an increased cash dividend. For the former, suppose an investor owns 100 shares of a company paying a $1 dividend. The company declares a 10 percent stock dividend and, at the same time, announces that the cash dividend per share will remain unchanged. The investor then will have 110 shares, and total cash dividends will be $110 rather than $100, as before. In this case, a stock dividend increases the total cash dividends. Whether this increase in cash dividend has a positive effect on shareholder wealth will depend on the valuation of dividends, which we discussed earlier. Clearly, the stock dividend in this case represents a decision by the firm to increase modestly the amount of cash dividends. However, it does not need the stock dividend to do so.

Sometimes a stock dividend is employed to conserve cash. Instead of increasing the cash dividend as earnings rise, a company may desire to retain a greater portion of its earnings and declare a modest stock dividend. The decision then is to lower the dividend-payout ratio, for as earnings rise and total cash dividends remain approximately the same, the payout ratio will decline. Whether shareholder wealth is increased by this action will depend on considerations taken up in an earlier section. The decision to retain a higher proportion of earnings, of course, could be accomplished without a stock dividend. However, the stock dividend may tend to please certain investors by virtue of its psychological impact. But the substitution of stock for cash dividends involves a sizable administrative cost. Stock dividends simply are much more costly to administer than are cash dividends, and this out-of-pocket expense works to their disadvantage.

More-Popular Trading Range   A stock split and, to a lesser extent, a stock dividend are used to place the stock in a lower, more-popular trading range. By so doing, more buyers may be attracted, increasing the number of individual holders. Whether this wider ownership is a thing of value is another matter.

Since 1982, the United States has had a huge run-up in its overall stock market. Yet few companies have share prices in excess of $80. The reason is simply that stock splits and, to a lesser extent, stock dividends are used to keep share price at what many regard as an appropriate trading range. (The notable exception is Berkshire Hathaway, which under Warren Buffet has never split its stock and has reached a high of $81,000 per share!) Finally, trading volume tends to increase after a stock split or dividend, giving the stock more liquidity. For these reasons, the "more-popular trading range" motivation for stock splits and dividends is widely supported.

Informational or Signaling Effect

The declaration of a stock dividend or a stock split may convey information about future earnings to investors. As taken up earlier in this chapter and in the previous chapter, there may be asymmetric information between management and investors. As with capital-structure and cash dividend changes, a stock dividend or split may connote more convincingly management's belief about the favorable prospects of the company. In this sense, the stock dividend or split is an attention-getting device.

Whether these signals are more convincing is an empirical question. Here there have been a number of event type of studies.[18] As we know, such studies attempt to isolate the abnormal return associated with a particular event—in this case, a stock dividend or split. The abnormal return is simply the residual after risk-adjusted market movements (beta), and perhaps other factors, have been taken into account. If stock dividends and splits have a positive signaling effect, a plot of the cumulative residuals might look like that shown in Fig. 11-1. In the sev-

FIGURE 11-1

Cumulative daily abnormal returns around stock dividend or stock split announcement

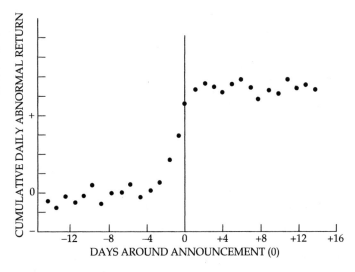

[18]A classic earlier study is by Eugene F. Fama, Lawrence Fisher, Michael Jensen, and Richard Roll, "The Adjustment of Stock Prices to New Information," *International Economic Review*, 10 (February 1969), 1–21. Subsequent studies include Mark S. Grinblatt, Ronald W. Masulis, and Sheridan Titman, "The Valuation Effects of Stock Splits and Stock Dividends," *Journal of Financial Economics*, 13 (December 1984), 461–90; Christopher G. Lamoreux and Percy Poon, "The Market Reaction to Stock Splits," *Journal of Finance*, 42 (December 1987), 1347–70; Michael J. Brennan and Thomas E. Copeland, "Stock Splits, Stock Prices and Transaction Costs," *Journal of Financial Economics*, 22 (October 1988), 83–101; Maureen McNichols and Ajay Dravid, "Stock Dividends, Stock Splits, and Signaling," *Journal of Finance*, 45 (July 1990), 857–79; Eugene Pilotte and Timothy Manuel, "The Market's Response to Recurring Events: The Case of Stock Splits," *Journal of Financial Economics*, 41 (May 1996), 111–27; and Robert M. Conroy and Robert S. Harris, "Stock Splits and Information: The Role of Share Price," *Financial Management*, 28 (Autumn 1999), 28–40.

eral days surrounding the announcement, there is a run-up in the cumulative abnormal return, after which the higher level of security price persists owing to the favorable information effect. The larger the announced stock split, in relation to that which was anticipated, the greater the abnormal return.

The empirical evidence is consistent with an information or signaling effect; namely, that the stock is undervalued and should be priced higher. Of course, the company must eventually deliver improved earnings if the stock is to remain higher. The underlying cause for the increase in market price is perceived future earnings, not the stock dividend or split itself.

Reverse Stock Splits

Rather than increase the number of shares of stock outstanding, a company may want to reduce the number. It can accomplish this with a *reverse split*. In our stock split example before, had there been a 1-to-4 reverse split instead of the 2-to-1 straight stock split, for each four shares held the stockholder would have received one share in exchange. The par value per share would become $20, and there would be 100,000 shares outstanding rather than 400,000. Reverse stock splits are employed to increase the market price per share when the stock is considered to be selling at too low a price. Many companies have an aversion to seeing their stock fall below $10 per share. If financial difficulty or some other depressant lowers the price into this range, it can be increased with a reverse split.

As with stock dividends and straight stock splits, there is likely to be an information or signaling effect associated with the announcement. Usually the signal is negative, such as would accompany the admission by a company that it is in financial difficulty. A healthy company simply wanting to place its stock in a higher trading range should think twice before undertaking a reverse stock split. There are too many bad apples in the barrel not to be tainted by association.

MANAGERIAL CONSIDERATIONS AS TO DIVIDEND/SHARE REPURCHASE POLICY

Many practical things influence the dividend/share repurchase decision.

A number of things come into play when a company is trying to determine the appropriate amount of cash to distribute to stockholders and whether it should be dividends or share repurchase. These considerations should be related back to the theory we have discussed pertaining to the valuation of a company. In what follows, we take up various factors that financial managers in practice should analyze.

Funds Needs of the Firm

Perhaps the place to begin is with an assessment of the funds needs of the firm. In this regard, cash budgets and projected source and use of funds statements (topics taken up in Chapter 13) are of particular use. The key is to determine the likely cash flows and cash position of the company in the absence of a change in dividend/share repurchase. In addition to looking at expected outcomes, we should factor in business risk, so that we may obtain a range of possible cash-flow outcomes. The procedure is spelled out in Chapter 13, so we need not dwell on it here.

In keeping with our earlier discussion of the theory of dividend payout, the firm wishes to determine if anything is left over after servicing its funds needs, including profitable investment projects. In this regard, a company should look at its situation over a reasonable number of future years to iron out fluctuations. On the basis of this analysis, a company can determine its likely future residual funds that are available for distribution to stockholders.

With respect to dividends, we would expect no dividends to be paid in the early life of a company. As it matures and begins to generate excess cash, dividends may be paid—a token dividend at first, but bigger ones as relatively fewer productive investment opportunities are found. The dividend may be supplemented or supplanted by share repurchase. In the late stages of a company's life cycle, "harvesting" may occur. Here a company self-liquidates by paying substantial dividends to its stockholders or, more usually, engaging in substantial stock repurchase. For dividend payout, the life-cycle notion is illustrated in Fig. 11-2.

Ability to Borrow

A liquid position is not the only way to provide for flexibility and thereby protect against uncertainty. If a firm has the ability to borrow on comparatively short notice, it may be relatively flexible. This ability to borrow can be in the form of a line of credit or a revolving credit from a bank or simply the informal willingness of a financial institution to extend credit. In addition, flexibility can come from the ability of a company to go to the capital markets with a bond issue. The larger and more established a company, the better its access to capital markets. The greater the ability of the firm to borrow, the greater its flexibility and the greater its ability to pay a cash dividend or engage in share repurchase.

Assessment of Any Valuation Information

To the extent that there are insights into the effect of a dividend on valuation, they should be gathered. Most companies look at the dividend-payout ratios of other companies in the industry, particularly those having about the same growth. It may not matter that a company is out of line with similar companies, but it will be conspicuous; and usually a company will want to justify its position. Also, a company should judge the informational effect of a dividend or share repurchase. What do investors expect? Here security analysts and security reports are useful. The company should ask itself what information it is conveying with its present dividend and/or share repurchase program and what it would convey with a possible change.

Control

If a company pays substantial dividends or engages in substantial share repurchase, it may need to raise capital at a later time through the sale of stock. Under such circumstances, the controlling interest of the company may be diluted if controlling stockholders do not or cannot subscribe for additional shares. These stock-

FIGURE 11-2

Dividends and the company life cycle

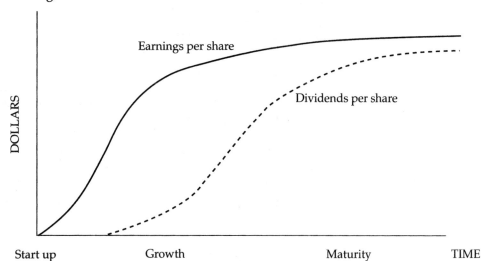

holders may prefer a low dividend payout/share repurchase program and the financing of investment needs with retained earnings. Control can work two ways, however. When a company is being sought by another company or by individuals, a low dividend payout may work to the advantage of the "outsiders" seeking control. The outsiders may be able to convince stockholders that the company is not maximizing shareholder wealth and that they (the outsiders) can do a better job. Consequently, companies in danger of being acquired may establish a high dividend payout in order to please stockholders.

Nature of Stockholders

When a company is closely held, management usually knows the dividend desires of its stockholders in relation to their share repurchase desires and may act accordingly. If most stockholders are in high tax brackets and prefer capital gains to current income, the firm can establish a low, or even zero, dividend payout and use share repurchase as a way to distribute excess cash. The corporation with a large number of stockholders can judge their desires for dividends only in a market context.

Liquidity

The **liquidity** of a company is a consideration in many dividend/share repurchase decisions. As they represent a cash outflow, the greater the cash position and overall liquidity of a company, the greater its ability to pay a dividend or engage in a share repurchase program. A company that is growing and profitable may not be liquid, for its funds may go into fixed assets and permanent additions to current assets. Because the management of such a company usually desires to maintain some liquidity cushion, it may be reluctant to jeopardize this position in order to pay a large dividend or engage in a substantial share buyback.

Restrictions in Bond Indenture or Loan Agreement

The protective covenants in a bond indenture or loan agreement often include a restriction on payment of dividends and share repurchase. The restriction is employed by the lenders to preserve the company's ability to service debt. Usually, it is expressed as a maximum percentage of cumulative earnings. When such a restriction is in force, it naturally influences dividends and share repurchases.

Dividend Stability

The financial manager must be concerned with the stability of dividends to investors. By **stability**, we mean maintaining a position in relation to a dividend trend line, preferably one that is upward sloping. It would appear that investors value stability.

As we have said, dividends may serve to resolve uncertainty. When earnings drop and a company does not cut its dividend, the market may have more confidence in the stock than it would have if the dividend were cut. The stable dividend may convey management's view that the future of the company is better than the drop in earnings suggests. Thus, management may be able to influence the expectations of investors through the informational content of dividends. Management will not be able to fool the market permanently. If there is a downward trend in earnings, a stable dividend will not convey forever an impression of a rosy future.

Investors who desire a specific periodic income will prefer a company with stable dividends to one with unstable dividends, even though both companies may have the same pattern of earnings and long-run dividend payout. Although investors can always sell portions of their stock for income when the dividend is not sufficient to meet their current needs, many investors have an aversion to dipping into principal and to transaction and inconvenience costs.

Finally, dividend stability may be important from the standpoint of permitting certain institutional investors to buy the stock. Various governmental bodies prepare lists of securities in which pension funds, trustees, insurance companies, and certain others may invest. To qualify, a company often must have an uninterrupted pattern of dividends. A cut in dividends or their omission may result in the removal of a company from these lists.

Target-Payout Ratios

A number of companies appear to follow the policy of a **target dividend-payout ratio** over the long run. Lintner contends that dividends are adjusted to changes in earnings, but only with a lag.[19] When earnings increase to a new level, a company increases dividends only when it feels it can maintain the increase in earnings. Companies are also reluctant to cut the absolute amount of their cash dividend. Both of these factors explain the lag in dividend changes behind changes in earnings. In an economic upturn, the lag relationship becomes visible when retained earnings increase in relation to dividends. In a contraction, retained earnings grow at a slower rate than dividends.

However, a company cannot pay dividends indefinitely unless there is profitability. In an empirical test, DeAngelo, DeAngelo, and Skinner find that 51 percent of companies experiencing losses reduce their dividend in the initial loss year.[20] They claim that a loss is a necessary condition for dividend reductions, but not a sufficient reason. Income adjusted for unusual items is a critical determinant of dividend changes. The authors view the evidence as supporting Lintner's target-payout notion. Rather than omit dividends in the face of financial distress, the majority of companies reduce them, indicating managerial reluctance to do away with a dividend.

Some Final Observations

In determining a dividend payout and/or share repurchase program, the typical company will analyze a number of factors already described. These factors largely dictate the boundaries within which a dividend can be paid or shares repurchased. When a company pays a dividend in excess of its residual funds, it implies that management and the board of directors believe the payment has a favorable effect on shareholder wealth. The frustrating thing is that we have so little in the way of clear generalizations from the empirical evidence. The lack of firm footing for predicting the long-run effect of a specific dividend policy on valuation makes the dividend decision more difficult in many ways than either the investment or financing decisions.

Considerations taken up in the section above allow a company to determine with reasonable accuracy what would be an appropriate passive dividend strategy. An active dividend policy involves an act of faith, because it demands that a portion of the cumulative dividends ultimately be replaced with common stock financing. Such a strategy is undertaken in a foggy area, but one in which most academics have difficulty believing shareholder wealth will be enhanced. Notwithstanding, many companies profess a belief that dividend payout affects share price and behave in a manner consistent with dividends mattering.

When a company has a sizable amount of excess funds to transmit to shareholders, a strong case can be made for the repurchase of stock as opposed to cash dividends. This alternative results in capital gains income as opposed to dividend income.

---

[19]See John Lintner, "Distribution of Income of Corporations among Dividends, Retained Earnings, and Taxes," *American Economic Review*, 46 (May 1956), 97–113.

[20]Harry DeAngelo, Linda DeAngelo, and Douglas J. Skinner, "Dividends and Losses," *Journal of Finance*, 48 (December 1992), 1837–63. See also DeAngelo and DeAngelo, "Dividend Policy and Financial Distress: An Empirical Investigation of Troubled NYSE Firms," *Journal of Finance*, 45 (December 1990), 1415–31.

Summary

The distribution of excess cash to shareholders can take two forms: dividends and/or share repurchase. In recent years the latter has become increasingly more important, though in the aggregate dividends are larger.

The critical question in dividend policy is whether dividends have an influence on the value of the firm, given its investment decision. If dividends are irrelevant, as Modigliani and Miller believe, the firm should retain earnings only in keeping with its investment opportunities. If there are not sufficient investment opportunities providing expected returns in excess of the required return, the unused funds should be paid out as dividends.

The key issue is whether dividends are more than just a means of distributing unused funds. With perfect capital markets and an absence of taxes, stockholders can manufacture homemade dividends and make dividend payout irrelevant. Only market imperfections will result in relevancy. With imperfections, there are three possibilities: (1) dividends have a negative effect on value, (2) dividends are neutral in effect, and (3) dividends have a positive effect.

With differential taxes on dividends and capital gains, there seemingly is a bias in favor of retention. This is a negative dividend effect where dividend-paying companies must provide a higher before-tax expected return, resulting in a yield tilt. However, different investors are affected differently by taxes, and a clientele theory would suggest that corporations alter the supply of dividends in keeping with the tax situation of investor clienteles. This could well result in dividend neutrality. For behavioral reasons, certain investors may prefer dividends to the retention of earnings and capital gains. Though not necessarily rational, this could result in a positive dividend effect. Financial signaling implies that dividends may be used to convey information. That information, rather than the dividend itself, affects valuation.

Empirical testing of dividend policy has focused on whether there is a tax effect and whether dividends serve as signals in conveying information. The evidence is conflicting with respect to the former, but the preponderance of recent evidence is consistent with dividend neutrality. There seems to be agreement that dividends provide financial signals. In final analysis, we are unable to state whether the dividend payout of the firm should be more than a passive decision variable. Most academics think not.

Instead of dividends, a company can repurchase its own stock. Employees with stock options have a decided preference for share repurchase. There are three methods of share repurchase: (1) fixed-price tender offers; (2) dutch-auction tender offers, the most widely used method; and (3) open-market purchases. In the absence of a tax differential between dividends and capital gains, the monetary value of share repurchase or cash dividends should be the same. A formula for determining the equilibrium fixed-price tender offer was presented. Tender offer repurchases appear to have a positive and significant signaling effect, though more so for fixed-price tender offers than for dutch-auction repurchases.

A stock dividend pays additional stock to stockholders. Theoretically, it is not a thing of value to the stockholder unless cash dividends per share remain unchanged or are increased. Stock dividends may serve to keep the market price per share in a popular trading range. A more effective device for reducing market price per share is a stock split. Both stock dividends and stock splits appear to have an informational or signaling effect. When other things are held constant, share price tends to rise around the time of the announcement, consistent with a positive signal. In a reverse stock split, the number of shares outstanding is reduced and the signal to the market usually is negative.

In the preceding section we examined various managerial considerations when a company is faced with a dividend and/or share repurchase decision. These factors include the funds needs of the firm, liquidity, ability to borrow, assessment of any valuation information, control and the nature of stock-holders, and restrictions in bond indenture or loan agreement. Dividend stability is thought by many to be important to investors. Many companies appear to follow the policy of a target dividend-payout ratio, increasing dividends only when they feel that an increase in earnings can be sustained.

Self-Correction Problems

1. The Beta-Alpha Company expects with some degree of certainty to generate the following net income and to have the following capital expenditures during the next 5 years (in thousands):

Year	1	2	3	4	5
Net income	$2,000	$1,500	$2,500	$2,300	$1,800
Capital expenditures	1,000	1,500	2,000	1,500	2,000

The company currently has 1 million shares of common stock outstanding and pays dividends of $1 per share.

   a. Determine dividends per share and external financing required in each year if dividend policy is treated as a residual decision.

   b. Determine the amounts of external financing in each year that will be necessary if the present dividend per share is maintained.

   c. Determine dividends per share and the amounts of external financing that will be necessary if a dividend-payout ratio of 50 percent is maintained.

   d. Under which of the three dividend policies are (1) aggregate dividends maximized? (2) external financing minimized?

2. Do-Re-Mi Corporation makes musical instruments and experiences only moderate growth. The company has just paid a dividend and is contemplating a dividend of $1.35 per share 1 year hence. The present market price per share is $15, and stock price appreciation of 5 percent per annum is expected.

   a. (1) If the required return on equity were 14 percent and we lived in a no-tax world, what would be the market price per share at the end of the year using the Modigliani-Miller model? (2) What would be the price if no dividend were paid?

   b. Jose Hernandez, a stockholder, is in a 30 percent tax bracket for ordinary income, but his effective tax rate for capital gains is 20 percent. If he were to hold the stock 1 year, what would be his expected after-tax return in dollars for each share held?

3. Le Pomme de Terre Corporation has enjoyed considerable recent success because Brazil placed a huge order for potatoes. This business is not expected to be repeated, and Le Pomme de Terre has $6 million in excess funds. The company wishes to distribute these funds via the repurchase of stock. Presently, it has 2,400,000 shares outstanding, and the market price per share is $25. It wishes to repurchase 10 percent of its stock, or 240,000 shares.

a. Assuming no signaling effect, at what share price should the company offer to repurchase?

b. In total, how much will the company be distributing through share repurchase?

c. If the company were to pay out the funds through cash dividends instead, what would be the market price per share after the distribution? (Ignore tax considerations.)

4. The Kleidon King Company has the following shareholders' equity account:

Common stock ($8 par value)	$ 2,000,000
Additional paid-in capital	1,600,000
Retained earnings	8,400,000
Shareholders' equity	$12,000,000

The current market price of the stock is $60 per share.

a. What will happen to this account and to the number of shares outstanding with (1) a 20 percent "small-percentage" stock dividend? (2) a 2-for-1 stock split? (3) a 1-for-2 reverse stock split?

b. (1) In the absence of an informational or signaling effect, at what share price should the common sell after the 20 percent stock dividend? (2) What might happen if there were a signaling effect?

5. For each of the companies described below, would you expect it to have a medium/high or a low dividend-payout ratio? Explain why.

a. A company with a large proportion of inside ownership, all of whom are high-income individuals.

b. A growth company with an abundance of good investment opportunities.

c. A company experiencing ordinary growth that has high liquidity and much unused borrowing capacity.

d. A dividend-paying company that experiences an unexpected drop in earnings from a trend.

e. A company with volatile earnings and high business risk.

 Problems

1. Malkor Instruments Company treats dividends as a residual decision. It expects to generate $2 million in net earnings after taxes in the coming year. The company has an all-equity capital structure, and its cost of equity capital is 15 percent. The company treats this cost as the opportunity cost of retained earnings. Because of flotation costs and underpricing, the cost of common stock financing is higher. It is 16 percent.

a. How much in dividends (out of the $2 million in earnings) should be paid if the company has $1.5 million in projects whose expected return exceeds 15 percent?

b. How much in dividends should be paid if it has $2 million in projects whose expected return exceeds 15 percent?

c. How much in dividends should be paid if it has $3 million in projects whose expected return exceeds 16 percent? What else should be done?

2. The Mann Company belongs to a risk class for which the appropriate required equity return is 15 percent. It currently has outstanding 100,000 shares selling at $100 each. The firm is contemplating the declaration of a $5 dividend at the end of the current fiscal year, which just began. Answer the following questions based on the Modigliani and Miller model and the assumption of no taxes.

a. (1) What will be the price of the stock at the end of the year if a dividend is not declared? (2) What will it be if one is?

b. Assuming that the firm pays the dividend, has net income of $1 million, and makes new investments of $2 million during the period, how many new shares must be issued?

c. Is the MM model realistic with respect to valuation? What factors might mar its validity?

3. The University of Northern California pays no taxes on the dividend income and capital gains received on its various endowment funds. Over the years, it has steadily bought the stock of IVM Corporation for its alumni fellowship fund. The alumni campaign is such that the bulk of alumni giving occurs in the months of June and December. Coincidentally, IVM pays a semiannual dividend in these months. In the past, the university has not paid attention to whether it bought the stock before or after the ex-dividend dates of June 10 and December 10. (Before the ex-dividend date, investors are entitled to the dividend; after, they are not.) The feeling has been that the stock will decline by the amount of the dividend on the ex-dividend date, so it really does not matter when the stock is purchased. Shirley McDonald, the finance officer of the university, has just completed a study showing that over the years IVM's stock price on average declined by only 90 percent of the dividend per share on the ex-dividend date. She attributes this occurrence to the fact that a number of investors are interested in capital gains. As a result, these investors buy the stock after the ex-dividend date, and the impact of their purchases causes the stock to decline by less than the amount of the dividend. In view of this finding, should the university change the timing of its purchase of IVM stock? If so, how should it change?

4. The Xavier Industrial Coating Company has hired you as a financial consultant to advise the company with respect to its dividend policy. The coating industry has been very stable for some time, and the firm's stock has not appreciated significantly in market value for several years. The rapidly growing Southeastern market provides an excellent opportunity for this old, traditionally Midwestern coating manufacturer to undertake a vigorous expansion program. To do so, the company has decided to sell common stock for equity capital in the near future. The company expects its entrance into the Southeastern market to be extremely profitable, returning approximately 25 percent

on investment each year. Data on earnings, dividends, and common stock prices are given in the following table.

	20x1	20x2	20x3	20x4	Anticipated 20x5
Earnings/share	$4.32	$4.17	$4.61	$4.80	$4.75
Cash available/share	$6.00	$5.90	$6.25	$6.35	$6.25
Dividend/share	$2.90	$2.80	$3.00	$3.20	?
Payout ratio	67%	67%	65%	67%	?
Average market price	$60.00	$58.00	$60.00	$67.00	$66.00
P/E ratio	14/1	14/1	13/1	14/1	14/1

What dividend policy recommendations would you make to the company? Specifically, what payout would you recommend for 19x5? Justify your position.

5. In October, Baxter Lorry Company was in a flush cash position and repurchased 100,000 shares of its 1.8 million shares outstanding at a price of $42.50 per share. Immediately prior to the share repurchase announcement, share price was $37.00. The company was surprised that nearly 1 million shares were tendered by stockholders wanting to sell. The company had to repurchase the 100,000 shares on a pro-rata basis according to the number of shares tendered.

   a. Why did so many stockholders tender their shares? At what price should the company have made its repurchase offer?

   b. Who gained from the offer? Who lost?

6. Singleton Electronics Company repurchased 1 million of 14 million shares outstanding at $98 a share. Immediately before the announcement, market price per share was $91.

   a. Was the offer price by the company the correct repurchase price?

   b. After the repurchase, share price went to $105. What would explain this rise if there were no other information concerning the company or stocks in general?

7. Zoppo Manufacturers shareholders' equity, December 30:

Common stock ($100 par, 300,000 shares)	$ 30,000,000
Additional paid-in capital	15,000,000
Retained earnings	55,000,000
Shareholders' equity	$100,000,000

On December 31, Zoppo split the stock 2-for-1 and then declared a 10 percent stock dividend. The price of the stock on December 30 was $500. Reformulate the stockholders' capitalization accounts of the firm.

8. Johore Trading Company has 2.4 million shares of common stock outstanding, and the present market price per share is $36. Its equity capitalization is as follows:

Common stock, $2.00 par	$ 4,800,000
Additional paid-in capital	5,900,000
Retained earnings	87,300,000
Shareholders' equity	$98,000,000

   a. What would happen to these accounts if the company were to declare (1) a 12 percent stock dividend? (2) a 5 percent stock dividend?
   b. What would happen to the accounts if the company declared (1) a 3-for-2 stock split? (2) a 2-for-1 stock split? (3) a 3-for-1 split?
   c. What would happen if there were a reverse stock split of (1) 1-for-4? (2) 1-for-6?

9. The Canales Copper Company declared a 25 percent stock dividend on March 10 to stockholders of record on April 1. The market price of the stock is $50 per share. You own 160 shares of the stock.
   a. If you sold your stock on March 20, what would be the price per share, all other things the same? (No signaling effect.)
   b. After the stock dividend is paid, how many shares of stock will you own?
   c. At what price would you expect the stock to sell on April 2, all other things the same? (No signaling effect.)
   d. What will be the total value of your holdings before and after the stock dividend, all other things the same?
   e. If there were an informational or signaling effect, what would be the effect on share price?

10. Darcy Dip Doodle Company's earnings per share over the last 10 years were the following:

Year	1	2	3	4	5	6	7	8	9	10
EPS ($)	1.70	1.82	1.44	1.88	2.18	2.32	1.84	2.23	2.50	2.73

   a. Determine annual dividends per share under the following policies:
      (1) A constant dividend-payout ratio of 40 percent (to the nearest cent).
      (2) A regular dividend of $.80 and an extra dividend to bring the payout ratio to 40 percent if it otherwise would fall below.

(3) A stable dividend that is occasionally raised. The payout ratio may range between 30 percent and 50 percent in any given year, but should average approximately 40 percent.

    b. What are the valuation implications of each of these policies?

11. Forte Papers Corporation and Great Southern Paper Company are in the same industry, both are publicly held with a large number of stockholders, and they have the following characteristics (in thousands):

	Forte	Great Southern
Expected annual cash flow	$ 50,000	$35,000
Standard deviation of cash flow	30,000	25,000
Annual capital expenditures	42,000	40,000
Cash and marketable securities	5,000	7,000
Existing long-term debt	100,000	85,000
Unused short-term line of credit	25,000	10,000
Flotation costs and underpricing on common-stock issues as a percent of proceeds	.05	.08

On the basis of this information, which company is likely to have the higher dividend-payout ratio? Why?

Solutions to Self-Correction Problems

1.   a.

Year	Income Available for Dividends	Dividends Per Share	External Financing
1	$1,000	$1.00	0
2	0	0	0
3	500	.50	0
4	800	.80	0
5	0	0	$200
	$2,300		$200

b.

Year	(1) Net Income	(2) Dividends	(3) Capital Expenditures	(4) External Financing (2) + (3) − (1)
1	$2,000	$1,000	$1,000	0
2	1,500	1,000	1,500	$1,000
3	2,500	1,000	2,000	500
4	2,300	1,000	1,500	200
5	1,800	1,000	2,000	1,200
		$5,000		$2,900

c.

Year	(1) Net Income	(2) Dividends	(3) Dividends Per Share	(4) Capital Expenditures	(5) External Financing (2) + (4) − (1)
1	$2,000	$1,000	$1.00	$1,000	0
2	1,500	750	.75	1,500	$ 750
3	2,500	1,250	1.25	2,000	750
4	2,300	1,150	1.15	1,500	350
5	1,800	900	.90	2,000	1,100
		$5,050			$2,950

d. Aggregate dividends are highest under alternative c, which involves a 50 percent dividend payout. However, they are only slightly higher than that which occurs under alternative b. External financing is minimized under alternative a, the residual dividend policy.

2.   a. Using Eq. (11-1) and rearranging, $P_1 = P_0(1 + p) - D_1$

(1) With a dividend,

$$P_1 = \$15(1 + .14) - \$1.35 = \$15.75$$

(2) Without a dividend,

$$P_1 = \$15(1 + .14) - 0 = \$17.10$$

The investor would have the same total value (share price plus dividend of $1.35) either way.

b.

	Amount	Tax Rate	Tax	A.T. Amount
Dividend	$1.35	30%	$.405	$ .945
Capital gain	.75	20	.150	.600
Total after-tax return				$1.545

3.   a. $P* = \dfrac{S \times P_c}{S - n}$

$$= \dfrac{2,400,000 \times \$25}{2,400,000 - 240,000} = \$27.78$$

      b. $240,000 \times \$27.78 = \$6,667,200$

      c. $\$6,667,200/2,400,000$ shares $= \$2.778$ cash dividend

Share price after dividend $= \$25 - \$2.778$

$$= \$22.222$$

	(1) Stock Dividend	(2) Stock Split	(3) Reverse Split
Common stock (par)	$ 2,400,000 ($8)	$ 2,000,000 ($4)	$ 2,000,000 ($16)
Additional paid-in capital	4,200,000	1,600,000	1,600,000
Retained earnings	5,400,000	8,400,000	8,400,000
Shareholders' equity	$12,000,000	$12,000,000	$12,000,000
Number of shares	300,000	500,000	125,000

4.   a.   Present number of common shares = $2,000,000/$8 par value = 250,000.

      b.   (1) The total market value of the firm before the stock dividend is $60 × 250,000 shares = $15 million. With no change in the total value of the firm, market price per share after the stock dividend should be $15 million/300,000 shares = $50 per share. (2) If there is a signaling effect, the total value of the firm might rise and share price be somewhat higher than $50 per share. The magnitude of the effect probably would be no more than several dollars a share, based on empirical findings.

5. The answers assume all things are held constant other than the item in question.

      a.   Low payout ratio. Highly taxed owners probably will want to realize their returns through capital gains.

      b.   Low payout ratio. There will be no residual funds.

      c.   Medium or high payout ratio. There are likely to be funds left over after funding capital expenditures. Moreover, the liquidity and access to borrowing give the company considerable flexibility.

      d.   Medium or high payout ratio. Unless the company cuts its dividend, which probably is unlikely in the short run, its payout ratio will rise with the drop in earnings.

      e.   Low payout ratio. The company will probably wish to retain earnings to build its financial strength in order to offset the high business risk.

Selected References

ALLEN, FRANKLIN, and RONI MICHAELY, "Dividend Policy," in R. A. Jarrow, V. Maksimovic, and W. T. Ziemba, editors, *North-Holland Handbook of Operations Research and Management Science: Finance.* Amsterdam: North-Holland, 1995.

ASQUITH, PAUL, and DAVID W. MULLINS JR., "The Impact of Initiating Dividend Payments on Shareholders' Wealth," *Journal of Business*, 56 (January 1983), 77–96.

———, "Signalling with Dividends, Stock Repurchases, and Equity Issues," *Financial Management*, 15 (Autumn 1986), 27–44.

BAGWELL, LAURIE SIMON, "Dutch Auction Repurchases: An Analysis of Shareholder Heterogeneity," *Journal of Finance*, 47 (March 1992), 71–105.

BAGWELL, LAURIE SIMON, and JOHN B. SHOVEN, "Cash Distributions to Shareholders," *Journal of Economic Perspectives*, 3 (Summer 1989), 129–40.

BALI, RAKESH, and GAILEN L. HITE, "Ex Dividend Day Stock Price Behavior: Discreteness or Tax-Induced Clienteles?" *Journal of Financial Economics*, 47 (February 1998), 127–59.

BARCLAY, MICHAEL J., and CLIFFORD W. SMITH, "The Determinants of Corporate Leverage and Dividend Policies," *Journal of Applied Corporate Finance*, 7 (Winter 1995), 4–19.

BARTOV, ELI, ITZHAK KRINSKY, and JASON LEE, "Evidence on How Companies Choose Between Dividends and Open-Market Stock Repurchases," *Journal of Applied Corporate Finance*, 11(Spring 1998), 89–96.

BENARTZI, SHLOMO, RONI MICHAELY, and RICHARD THALER, "Do Changes in Dividends Signal the Future or the Past?" *Journal of Finance*, 52 (July 1997), 1007–34.

BLACK, FISCHER, "The Dividend Puzzle," *Journal of Portfolio Management*, 2 (Winter 1976), 5–8.

BLACK, FISCHER, and MYRON SCHOLES, "The Effects of Dividend Yield and Dividend Policy on Common Stock Prices and Returns," *Journal of Financial Economics*, 1 (May 1974), 1–22.

BOYD, JOHN H., and RAVI JAGANNATHAN, "Ex-Dividend Price Behavior of Common Stocks," *Review of Financial Studies*, 7 (Winter 1994), 711–41.

BRENNAN, MICHAEL J., and THOMAS E. COPELAND, "Stock Splits, Stock Prices and Transaction Costs," *Journal of Financial Economics*, 22 (October 1988), 83–101.

BRENNAN, MICHAEL J., and ANJAN V. THAKOR, "Shareholder Preferences and Dividend Policy," *Journal of Finance*, 45 (September 1990), 993–1018.

COMMENT, ROBERT, and GREGG A. JARRELL, "The Relative Signalling Power of Dutch-Auction and Fixed-Price Self-Tender Offers and Open-Market Share Repurchases," *Journal of Finance*, 46 (September 1991), 1243–71.

CONROY, ROBERT M., and ROBERT S. HARRIS, "Stock Splits and Information: The Role of Share Price," *Financial Management*, 28 (Autumn 1999), 28–40.

DANN, LARRY Y., "Common Stock Repurchases: An Analysis of Returns to Bondholders and Stockholders," *Journal of Financial Economics*, 9 (June 1981), 113–38.

ELTON, EDWIN J., and MARTIN J. GRUBER, "The Effect of Share Repurchases on the Value of the Firm," *Journal of Finance*, 23 (March 1968), 135–50.

———, "Marginal Stockholder Tax Rates and the Clientele Effect," *Review of Economics and Statistics*, 52 (February 1970), 68–74.

FAMA, EUGENE F., LAWRENCE FISHER, MICHAEL JENSEN, and RICHARD ROLL, "The Adjustment of Stock Prices to New Information," *International Economic Review*, 10 (February 1969), 1–21.

Financial Management, 27 (Autumn 1998), special issue on dividends.

FRANK, MURRAY, and RAVI JAGANNATHAN, "Why Do Stock Prices Drop by Less than the Value of the Dividend? Evidence from a Country without Taxes," *Journal of Financial Economics*, 47 (February 1998), 161–88.

HALL, ROBERT E, "The Stock Market and Capital Accumulation," working paper, National Bureau of Economic Research (June 1999).

HARRIS, TREVOR S., R. GLENN HUBBARD, and DEEN KEMSLEY, "The Share Price Effects of Dividend Taxes and Tax Imputation Credits," working paper, National Bureau of Economic Research (December 1999).

HEALY, PAUL M., and KRISHNA G. PALEPU, "Earnings Information Conveyed by Dividend Initiations and Omissions," *Journal of Financial Economics*, 21 (September 1988), 149–75.

IKENBERRY, DAVID, JOSEF LAKONISHOK, and THEO VERMAELEN, "Market Underreaction to Open Market Share Repurchases," *Journal of Financial Economics*, 39 (October–November 1995), 181–208.

KALAY, AVNER, "The Ex-Dividend Day Behavior of Stock Prices: A Re-examination of the Clientele Effect," *Journal of Finance*, 37 (September 1982), 1059–70.

LAKONISHOK, JOSEF, and THEO VERMAELEN, "Anomalous Price Behavior around Repurchase Tender Offers," *Journal of Finance*, 45 (June 1990), 455–78.

LAMONT, OWEN, "Earnings and Expected Returns," *Journal of Finance*, 33 (October 1998), 1563–88.

LAPORTA, RAFAEL, FLORENCIO LOPEZ-DE-SILANES, ANDREI SHLEIFER, and ROBERT W. VISHNY, "Agency Problems and Dividend Policies around the World," *Journal of Finance*, 55 (February 2000), 1–33.

LASFER, M. AMEZIANE, "Ex-Day Behavior: Tax or Short-Term Trading Effects," *Journal of Finance*, 50 (June 1995), 875–97.

LIE, ERIK, and JOHN J. MCCONNELL, "Earnings Signals in Fixed-Price and Dutch Auction Self-Tender Offers," *Journal of Financial Economics*, 49 (August 1998), 161–86.

LINTNER, JOHN, "Distribution of Income of Corporations among Dividends, Retained Earnings, and Taxes," *American Economic Review*, 46 (May 1956), 97–113.

LITZENBERGER, ROBERT H., and KRISHNA RAMISWAMY, "The Effect of Personal Taxes and Dividends on Capital Asset Prices," *Journal of Financial Economics*, 7 (June 1979), 163–95.

LITZENBERGER, ROBERT H., and JAMES C. VAN HORNE, "Elimination of the Double Taxation of Dividends and Corporate Financial Policy," *Journal of Finance*, 33 (June 1978), 737–49.

MCNALLY, WILLIAM J., "Open Market Stock Repurchase Signaling," *Financial Management*, 28 (Summer 1999), 55–67.

MCNICHOLS, MAUREEN, and AJAY DRAVID, "Stock Dividends, Stock Splits, and Signaling," *Journal of Finance*, 45 (July 1990), 857–79.

MICHAELY, RONI, RICHARD H. THALER, and KENT WOMACK, "Price Reactions to Dividend Initiations and Omissions: Overreaction or Drift?" *Journal of Finance*, 50 (June 1995), 573–608.

MILLER, MERTON H., and FRANCO MODIGLIANI, "Dividend Policy, Growth, and the Valuation of Shares," *Journal of Business*, 34 (October 1961), 411–33.

MILLER, MERTON H., and KEVIN ROCK, "Dividend Policy under Asymmetric Information," *Journal of Finance*, 40 (September 1985), 1031–51.

MYERS, STEWART C., "Outside Equity," *Journal of Finance*, 55 (June 2000), 1005–37.

NARANJO, ANDY, M. NIMALENDRAN, and MIKE RYNGAERT, "Stock Returns, Dividend Yields and Taxes," *Journal of Finance*, 53 (December 1998), 2029–57.

NOHEL, TOM, and VEFA TARHAN, "Share Repurchases and Firm Performance: New Evidence on the Agency Costs of Free Cash Flow," *Journal of Financial Economics*, 49 (August 1998), 187–222.

PILOTTE, EUGENE, and TIMOTHY MANUEL, "The Market's Response to Recurring Events: The Case of Stock Splits," *Journal of Financial Economics*, 41 (May 1996), 111–27.

SHEFRIN, HERSH M., and MEIR STATMAN, "Explaining Investor Preferences for Cash Dividends," *Journal of Financial Economics*, 13 (June 1984), 253–82.

VERMAELEN, THEO, "Common Stock Repurchases and Market Signalling," *Journal of Financial Economics*, 9 (June 1981), 139–83.

Wachowicz's Web World is an excellent overall Web site produced and maintained by my coauthor of *Fundamentals of Financial Management*, John M. Wachowicz Jr. It contains descriptions of and links to many finance Web sites and articles. *www.prenhall.com/wachowicz.*

Part IV

TOOLS OF
FINANCIAL ANALYSIS
AND CONTROL

■ **CASE:**   *Morley Industries, Inc.*

January 2000, Sarah Quintrod, vice president and treasurer of Morley Industries, was working on a loan request to be presented to the company's bank of account, First Security Bank. Ms. Quintrod had to determine how large a loan to request, as well as the length and type of loan, and to appraise the likelihood of the bank's granting the loan.

Morley Industries is a manufacturer of architectural aluminum products and a major producer of aluminum frame windows. Founded in 1970, the company has experienced considerable growth in sales. Operations have been consistently profitable, except for three years when small losses were incurred. Recent balance sheets and income statements are shown in Exhibits 1 and 2. Morley Industries sells most of its products directly to construction firms, although an increasing portion of its sales are to distributors of construction products and to distributors to home building centers.

During the past 3 years, Morley had undertaken a major expansion and modernization program aimed at providing the efficient production facilities its management considered vital to the company's survival in a competitive environment. In anticipation of growth in the demand for aluminum products, plant capacity had been increased to a point sufficient to handle a volume of $75 million per year. It was anticipated that the company's expansion program would be completed in March 2000 with the installation of new equipment costing $3.2 million.

The expansion had been timely because Morley was hoping to increase its market share in 2000 with an all-out marketing and selling effort. Management estimates the company will reach $54 million in sales in 2000. Further sales growth of $5 to $7 million per year is expected in 2001–3.

The company's sales, like those of the industry as a whole, are highly seasonal. Over two-thirds of annual sales usually comes during the first 6 months of the year. Exhibit 3 shows forecasted monthly sales for 2000; the pattern is similar to that in previous years. On the other hand, production is held relatively steady through the year. This policy is necessary to give employment to and thereby retain the skilled workforce required in the company's manufacturing operation. Additional economies come in better utilization of equipment.

Morley Industries had borrowed seasonally from First Security Bank for 8 years. These loans occurred under a line of credit arranged annually in January. The bank requires that the loan be completely repaid and "off the books" for 2 months during the year. In previous years, Morley had not experienced difficulty in obtaining seasonal loans and meeting loan requirements. First Security Bank had always granted the company's seasonal needs, which in 1999 had amounted to $8.1 million at the peak.

Normally, the company began borrowing in early January and repaid its loans by mid June. However, in 1999 the company had been unable to liquidate its loan until mid-September and by early November had again required a bank loan. At the end of 1999, the bank loan outstanding amounted to nearly $4.5 million. Although the bank had not hesitated to extend the credit, its officers expressed disappointment at not being given greater forewarning of the continued need, particularly at a time when the federal bank examiners were conducting an examination and were critical of aberrations of this sort. They suggested that it would be helpful if Ms. Quintrod could plan Morley's requirements more carefully for 2000.

Ms. Quintrod also was disturbed by the unexpected increase in borrowing and what it might mean in terms of future requirements. Therefore, she began collecting data that might be helpful in making plans for 2000. These plans would need to be cleared with the company's founder and president, Roger Morley, before presentation to the bank.

The company's nominal terms of sales were net 30 days. However, for competitive reasons, these terms were not strictly enforced, and the average collection period had recently slipped to around 40 days. All sales are credit sales, and Ms. Quintrod feels that a 40-day average period to collection is a reasonable estimate for 2000. There had been a deterioration in collection experience through 1999, but she is confident the downtrend has been arrested. (Of November 1999 sales of $1,683,000, $1,122,000 was collected in December; none of the December sales was collected in that month. All of October and earlier sales had been collected by December 31, 1999.)

Production is scheduled to be fairly level throughout 2000, except for 2 weeks beginning Monday, August 7, when it is planned to shut down the plant for the annual paid vacation period. Also, in February through June, production is scheduled to be moderately higher. Material purchases are scheduled as follows:

November (actual)	$1,430,000
December (actual)	1,473,000
January (forecast)	1,503,000
February	1,583,000
March	1,583,000
April	1,583,000
May	1,583,000

June	1,583,000
July	1,503,000
August	907,000
September	1,503,000
October	1,503,000
November	1,503,000
December	1,503,000

The company purchases its materials on varying terms, depending on the supplier, but on average pays for them in 33 days. Depreciation of $2.6 million is forecast for the year and is included in cost of goods sold. For simplicity in preparing a pro forma balance sheet, it is assumed that the entire depreciation burden is allocated to inventory. Cash disbursements related to labor and other overhead (not including depreciation, a noncash charge) are planned at $1,480,000 per month throughout 2000, except for the months of February through June when $1,512,000 per month is planned. It should be noted that planned production not only embraces that associated with estimated sales but also reflects a moderate build-up in inventory.

General and administrative expenses are estimated to total $10,632,000 in 2000. Disbursements for these expenses are expected to run fairly evenly through the year. Twenty-five percent of the estimated income taxes for 2000 are to be paid quarterly in March, June, September, and December. New equipment costing $3.2 million is to be delivered in March. It will be paid for in five equal monthly installments, beginning in March. Advertising and promotion expenditures, not included elsewhere, are forecast at $50,000 per month in January and February, $30,000 per month in March through August, and $65,000 per month in September through December 2000.

In 1997, Morley Industries borrowed $12 million from a life insurance company under a 16-year mortgage loan, secured by the entire plant and certain equipment. The loan is repayable in equal semiannual principal installments in June and December each year. Interest at the rate of 10 percent per annum on the unpaid balance is also payable on these dates. In her financial forecasting, Ms. Quintrod planned to treat differently the interest payments on the mortgage loan and on the bank loan. The two mortgage interest payments due in 2000 would be shown separately in the cash flow and income projections. In contrast, bank loan interest payments had been roughly estimated and included in the total general and administrative expenses estimate of $10,632,000.

In 2000, sales are forecast at $54 million, costs of goods sold (including depreciation) at 70 percent, and general and administrative expenses at $10,632,000. Advertising and promotion expenses (not included elsewhere) are expected to total $540,000. Additional expenses of $1,031,000 (rounded to the nearest thousand) for mortgage interest result in an estimated profit before taxes of $3,997,000. The effective tax rate for 2000 is estimated at 35 percent.

In 1999, the company raised its common stock dividend to $0.10 per share, per quarter, payable in March, June, September, and December. Ms. Quintrod knew that the directors of Morley Industries would be reluctant to raise the dividend in 2000. However, maintenance of the present dividend was essential. The company was not well known, and directors hoped that with another several years of profitable operations and stable dividends an equity issue might be feasible.

As chief financial officer of Morley Industries, Ms. Quintrod had given considerable thought to the optimum cash position of the company. She had concluded that cash and cash equivalents of at least $1.5 million should be maintained at all times. This will take care of transactions needs and provide a moderate amount of liquidity for emergencies.

On the basis of the plans outlined above, Ms. Quintrod asked her assistant treasurer to prepare a monthly cash budget for 2000, which she hopes will indicate the amount and timing of the bank credit that Morley Industries will require. She also asked the assistant treasurer to prepare a pro forma income statement for the year and a pro forma balance sheet for December 31, 2000. She suggested that the assistant assume no change in "other assets" or in "accruals" from the amounts shown at year end 1999.

E x h i b i t 1
Morley Industries, Inc.
Balance Sheets as of December 31, 1997–99
(Dollar Figures in Thousands)

ASSETS	1997	1998	1999
Cash and cash equivalents	$9,564	$2,187	$1,524
Accounts receivable	2,633	2,908	3,779
Inventories	4,632	5,547	7,280
Total current assets	$16,829	$10,642	$12,583
Property, plant, and equipment (net)	18,207	24,300	26,979
Other assets	806	1,065	1,110
Total assets	$35,842	$36,007	$40,672
LIABILITIES AND SHAREHOLDERS' EQUITY			
Bank loan	$0	$0	$4,478
Accounts payable	1,417	1,564	1,616
Accruals	837	906	867
Mortgage, current portion	750	750	750
Total current liabilities	$3,004	$3,220	$7,711
Mortgage payable	$11,250	$10,500	$9,750
Common stock (3,000,000 shares @ $2 par value)	6,000	6,000	6,000
Retained earnings	15,588	16,287	17,211
Total liabilities and equity	$35,842	$36,007	$40,672

E x h i b i t 1
Morley Industries, Inc.
Income Statements
(Dollar Figures in Thousands)

	1997	1998	1999
Net sales	$34,788	$38,373	$44,466
Cost of goods sold*	24,838	27,175	30,930
Gross profit	9,950	11,198	13,536
General and admin. expenses	6,755	7,433	9,147
Interest expense	1,056	1,181	1,106
Profit before taxes	2,139	2,584	3,283
Income taxes	813	925	1,159
Net profit	$ 1,326	$ 1,659	$2,124
Common dividends	960	960	1,200
Change in retained earnings	$366	$699	$924

*Includes depreciation of $1,657, $2,223, and $2,469, respectively.

E x h i b i t 1
Morley Industries, Inc.
Estimated Monthly Sales for 2000
(Dollar Figures in Thousands)

	Net Sales
November, 1999 actual	$ 1,683
December, 1999 actual	3,218
January 2000	3,720
February	5,250
March	7,410
April	7,650
May	8,550
June	4,830
July	4,020
August	3,360
September	1,920
October	1,800
November	1,890
December	3,600
Total	$54,000

Financial Ratio Analysis

To make rational decisions in keeping with the objectives of the firm, the financial manager must have analytical tools. The more useful tools of financial analysis are the subjects of this chapter and the next. The company itself and outside suppliers of capital—creditors and investors—all undertake financial analysis. The firm's purpose is not only internal control but also better understanding of what capital suppliers seek in financial condition and performance from it. After all, the public company is in a fish bowl always subject to credit and investor analyses. ■

INTRODUCTION TO FINANCIAL ANALYSIS

The type of analysis varies according to the specific interests of the party involved. Trade creditors are interested primarily in the liquidity of a firm. Their claims are short term, and the ability of a firm to pay these claims is best judged by means of a thorough analysis of its liquidity. The claims of bondholders, on the other hand, are long term. Accordingly, they are more interested in the cash-flow ability of the company to service debt over the long run. The bondholder may evaluate this ability by analyzing the capital structure of the firm, the major sources and uses of funds, its profitability over time, and projections of future profitability.

Investors in a company's common stock are concerned principally with present and expected future earnings and the stability of these earnings about a trend, as well as their covariance with the earnings of other companies. As a result, investors might concentrate their analysis on a company's profitability. They would be concerned with its financial condition insofar as it affects the ability of the company to pay dividends and to avoid bankruptcy. In order to bargain more effectively for outside funds, the management of a firm should be interested in all aspects of financial analysis that outside suppliers of capital use in evaluating the firm. Management also employs financial analysis for purposes of internal control. In particular, it is concerned with profitability on investment in the various assets of the company and in the efficiency of asset management.

Use of Financial Ratios

To evaluate the financial condition and performance of a company, the financial analyst needs certain yardsticks. The yardstick frequently used is a ratio, or index, relating two pieces of financial data to each other. Analysis and interpretation of various ratios should give experienced, skilled analysts a better understanding of the financial condition and performance of the firm than they would obtain from analysis of the financial data alone.

Financial ratios
help us size up a
company as to trends
and relative to others.

Trend Analysis   The analysis of **financial ratios** involves two types of comparison. First, the analyst can compare a present ratio with past and expected future ratios for the same company. The current ratio (the ratio of current assets to current liabilities) for the present year end could be compared with the current ratio for the preceding year end. When financial ratios are arrayed on a spreadsheet over a period of years, the analyst can study the composition of change and determine whether there has been an improvement or a deterioration in the financial condition and performance over time. Financial ratios also can be computed for projected, or pro forma, statements and compared with present and past ratios. In the comparisons over time, it is best to compare not only financial ratios but also the raw figures.

Comparison with Others   The second method of comparison involves comparing the ratios of one firm with those of similar firms or with industry averages at the same point in time. Such a comparison gives insight into the relative financial condition and performance of the firm. Financial ratios for various industries are published by Robert Morris Associates, by Dun & Bradstreet, by Prentice Hall (*Almanac of Business and Industrial Financial Ratios*), by the Federal Trade Commission–Securities and Exchange Commission, and by various credit agencies and trade associations.[1] Sometimes a company will not fit neatly into an industry category. In such situations, one should try to develop a set, albeit usually small, of peer firms for comparison purposes.

Some Caveats

The analyst should avoid using rules of thumb indiscriminately for all industries. For example, the criterion that all companies should have at least a 2-to-1 current ratio is inappropriate. The analysis must be in relation to the type of business in which the firm is engaged and to the firm itself. The true test of liquidity is whether a company has the ability to pay its bills on time. Many sound companies, including electric utilities, have this ability despite current ratios substantially below 2 to 1. It depends on the nature of the business. Only by comparing the financial ratios of one firm with those of similar firms can one make a realistic judgment.

Similarly, analysis of the deviation from the norm should be based on some knowledge of the distribution of ratios for the companies involved. If the company being studied has a current ratio of 1.4 and the industry norm is 1.8, one would like to know the proportion of companies whose ratios are below 1.4. If it is only 2 percent, we are likely to be much more concerned than if it is 25 percent. There-

---

[1]Robert Morris Associates, an association of bank credit and loan officers, publishes industry averages based on financial statements supplied to banks by borrowers. Sixteen ratios are computed annually for over 150 lines of business. In addition, each line of business is divided into four size categories. Dun & Bradstreet calculates annually 14 important ratios for over 100 lines of business. The *Almanac of Business and Industrial Financial Ratios* (Upper Saddle River, NJ: Prentice Hall, 2001) shows industry averages for 22 financial ratios. Approximately 170 businesses and industries are listed, covering the complete spectrum. The data for this publication come from U.S. corporate tax filings with the Internal Revenue Service. The *Quarterly Financial Report of Manufacturing Corporations* is published jointly by the Federal Trade Commission and the Securities and Exchange Commission. This publication contains balance sheet and income statement information by industry groupings and by asset-size categories.

fore, we need information on the dispersion of the distribution to judge the significance of the deviation of a financial ratio for a particular company from the industry norm.

Comparisons with the industry must be approached with caution. It may be that the financial condition and performance of the entire industry is less than satisfactory, and a company's being above average may not be sufficient. The company may have a number of problems on an absolute basis and should not take refuge in a favorable comparison with the industry. The industry ratios should not be treated as target asset and performance norms. Rather, they provide general guidelines. For benchmark purposes, a set of firms displaying "best practices" should be developed.

In addition, the analyst should realize that the various companies within an industry grouping may not be homogeneous. Companies with multiple product lines often defy precise industry categorization. They may be placed in the most "appropriate" industry grouping, but comparison with other companies in that industry may not be consistent. Also, companies in an industry may differ substantially in size.

Because reported financial data and the ratios computed from these data are numerical, there is a tendency to regard them as precise portrayals of a firm's true financial status. Accounting data such as depreciation, reserve for bad debts, and other reserves are estimates at best and may not reflect economic depreciation, bad debts, and other losses. To the extent possible, accounting data from different companies should be standardized. Compare apples with apples and oranges with oranges; even with standardized figures, however, the analyst should use caution in interpreting the comparisons.

Types of Ratios

For our purposes, financial ratios can be grouped into five types: **liquidity, debt, profitability, coverage,** and **market-value** ratios. No one ratio gives us sufficient information by which to judge the financial condition and performance of the firm. Only when we analyze a group of ratios are we able to make reasonable judgments. We must be sure to take into account any seasonal character of a business. Underlying trends may be assessed only through a comparison of raw figures and ratios at the same time of year. We would not compare a December 31 balance sheet with a May 31 balance sheet, but we would compare December 31 with December 31.

Although the number of financial ratios that might be computed increases geometrically with the amount of financial data, we concentrate only on the more important ratios in this chapter. Computing unneeded ratios adds both complexity and confusion to the problem. To illustrate the ratios discussed in this chapter, we use the balance sheet and income statements of the Aldine Manufacturing Company shown in Tables 12-1 and 12-2. A third accounting statement required in the presentation of audited financial results, a statement of cash flows, is taken up in Chapter 13.

LIQUIDITY RATIOS

Liquidity ratios are used to judge a firm's ability to meet short-term obligations. From them, much insight can be obtained into the present cash solvency of a company and its ability to remain solvent in the event of adversities. Essentially, we wish to compare short-term obligations with the short-term resources available to meet these obligations.

TABLE 12-1
Aldine Manufacturing Company Balance Sheet (in thousands)

	March 31, 2002	March 31, 2001
Assets		
Cash and short-term investments	$ 177,689	$ 175,042
Accounts receivable	678,279	740,705
Inventories	1,328,963	1,234,725
Prepaid expenses	20,756	17,197
Deferred income taxes	35,203	29,165
Current assets	$2,240,890	$2,196,834
Property, plant, and equipment	1,596,886	1,538,495
Less: Accumulated depreciation	856,829	791,205
	$ 740,057	$ 747,290
Investment, long term	65,376	—
Other assets	205,157	205,624
Total assets	$3,251,480	$3,149,748
Liabilities and shareholders' equity		
Bank loans and notes payable	$ 448,508	$ 356,511
Accounts payable	148,427	136,793
Income taxes payable	36,203	127,455
Accruals	190,938	164,285
Current liabilities	$ 824,076	$ 785,044
Long-term debt	630,783	626,460
Shareholders' equity		
Common stock ($5 par value)	420,828	420,824
Additional paid-in capital	361,158	361,059
Retained earnings	1,014,635	956,361
Total shareholders' equity	$1,796,621	$1,738,244
Total liabilities and equity	$3,251,480	$3,149,748

Current Ratio

One of the most general and most frequently used of these ratios is the **current ratio:**

$$\frac{\text{Current assets}}{\text{Current liabilities}} \tag{12-1}$$

For Aldine, the ratio for the 2002 year end is

$$\frac{\$2,240,890}{\$824,076} = 2.72$$

TABLE 12-2

Aldine Manufacturing Company Statement of Earnings (in thousands)

	Year Ended March 31, 2002	Year Ended March 31, 2001
Net sales	$3,992,758	$3,721,241
Cost of goods sold	2,680,298	2,499,965
Selling, general, and administrative expenses	801,395	726,959
Depreciation	111,509	113,989
Interest expense	85,274	69,764
Earnings before taxes	$ 314,282	$ 310,564
Provision for taxes	113,040	112,356
Earnings after taxes	$ 201,242	$ 198,208
Cash dividends	142,968	130,455
Retained earnings	$ 58,274	$ 67,753

The higher the ratio, supposedly, the greater the ability of the firm to pay its bills. The ratio must be regarded as a crude measure of liquidity, however, because it does not take into account the liquidity of the individual components of the current assets. A firm having current assets composed principally of cash and current receivables is generally regarded as more liquid than a firm whose current assets consist primarily of inventories.[2] Consequently, we must turn to "finer" tools of analysis if we are to evaluate critically the liquidity of the firm.

Liquidity ratios allow assessment of whether a company is likely to be able to pay its bills.

Quick Ratio

A somewhat more accurate guide to liquidity is the **quick,** or **acid-test, ratio:**

$$\frac{\text{Current assets less inventories}}{\text{Current liabilities}} \qquad (12\text{-}2)$$

For Aldine, this ratio is

$$\frac{\$2,240,890 - \$1,328,963}{\$824,076} = 1.11$$

This ratio is the same as the current ratio, except that it excludes inventories—presumably the least liquid portion of current assets—from the numerator. The ratio concentrates on cash, marketable securities, and receivables in relation to current obligations and thus provides a more penetrating measure of liquidity than does the current ratio.

---

[2] We have defined *liquidity* as the ability to realize value in money, the most liquid of assets. Liquidity has two dimensions: (1) the time required to convert the asset into money and (2) the certainty of the price realized. To the extent that the price realized on receivables is as predictable as that realized on inventories, receivables would be a more liquid asset than inventories, owing to the shorter time required to convert the asset into money. If the price realized on receivables is more certain than is that on inventories, receivables would be regarded as being even more liquid.

Liquidity of Receivables

When there are suspected imbalances or problems in various components of the current assets, the financial analyst will want to examine these components separately in assessing liquidity. Receivables, for example, may be far from current. To regard all receivables as liquid when in fact a sizable portion may be past due, overstates the liquidity of the firm being analyzed. Receivables are liquid assets only insofar as they can be collected in a reasonable amount of time. For our analysis of receivables, we have two basic ratios, the first of which is the **average collection period:**

$$\frac{\text{Receivables} \times \text{Days in year}}{\text{Annual credit sales}} \qquad (12\text{-}3)$$

If we assume for Aldine that all sales are credit sales, this ratio is

$$\frac{\$678,279 \times 365}{\$3,992,758} = 62 \text{ days}$$

The average collection period tells us the average number of days receivables are outstanding, that is, the average time it takes to convert them into cash.

The second ratio is the **receivable turnover ratio:**

$$\frac{\text{Annual credit sales}}{\text{Receivables}} \qquad (12\text{-}4)$$

For Aldine, this ratio is

$$\frac{\$3,992,758}{\$678,279} = 5.89$$

These two ratios are reciprocals of each other. The number of days in the year, 365, divided by the average collection period, 62 days, gives the receivable turnover ratio, 5.89. The number of days in the year divided by the turnover ratio gives the average collection period. Thus, either of these two ratios can be employed.

Year-End versus Average Receivables   The receivable figure used in the calculation ordinarily represents year-end receivables. When sales are seasonal or have grown considerably over the year, using the year-end receivable balance may not be appropriate. With seasonality, an average of the monthly closing balances may be the most appropriate figure to use. With growth, the receivable balance at the end of the year will be deceptively high in relation to sales. The result is that the collection period calculated is a biased and high estimate of the time it will take for the receivable balance at year end to be collected. In this case, an average of receivables at the beginning and at the end of the year might be appropriate if the growth in sales were steady throughout the year. The idea is to relate the relevant receivable position to the relevant credit sales so that apples are compared with apples.

Interpreting the Information   The average collection period ratio or the receivable turnover ratio indicates the slowness of receivables. Either ratio must be analyzed in relation to the billing terms given on the sales. If the average collection period is 45 days and the terms are 2/10, net 30,[3] the comparison would indicate that a sizable proportion of the receivables is past due beyond the final due date of 30 days. On the other hand, if the terms are 2/10, net 60, the typical receivable is being collected before the final due date. Too low an average collection period may suggest an excessively restrictive credit policy. The receivables on the books may be of prime quality, yet sales may be curtailed unduly—and profits less than they might be—because of this policy. In this situation, credit standards for an acceptable account should be relaxed somewhat. On the other hand, too high an average collection period may indicate too liberal a credit policy. As a result, a large number of receivables may be past due—some uncollectible. Here, too, profits may be less than those possible, because of bad-debt losses and the need to finance a large investment in receivables. In this case, credit standards should be raised. All of this is in keeping with a much deeper analysis of credit policy in Chapter 15.

Aging of Accounts   Another means by which we can obtain insight into the liquidity of receivables is through an **aging of accounts.** With this method, we categorize the receivables at a moment in time according to the proportions billed in previous months. We might have the following hypothetical aging of accounts receivable at December 31:

Month	December	November	October	September	August and before	Total
Proportion of receivables billed	67%	19%	7%	2%	5%	100%

If the billing terms are 2/10, net 30, this aging tells us that 67 percent of the receivables at December 31 are current, 19 percent are up to 1 month past due, 7 percent are 1 to 2 months past due, and so on. Depending on the conclusions drawn from our analysis of the aging, we may want to examine more closely the credit and collection policies of the company. In the example, we might be prompted to investigate the individual receivables that were billed in August and before, in order to determine if any should be charged off. The receivables shown on the books are only as good as the likelihood that they will be collected. An aging of accounts receivables gives us considerably more information than the calculation of the average collection period because it pinpoints the trouble spots more specifically.

Duration of Payables

From a creditor's standpoint, it would be desirable to obtain an aging of accounts payable. However, few customers are willing to provide such information, and many will resent being asked. Nonetheless, we often are able to compute the average age of a company's accounts payable. The **average payable period** is

$$\frac{\text{Accounts payable} \times 365}{\text{Purchases}} \tag{12-5}$$

---

[3]The notation means that the supplier gives a 2 percent discount if the receivable invoice is paid within 10 days and that payment is due within 30 days if the discount is not taken.

where accounts payable is the average balance outstanding for the year and the denominator is external purchases during the year.

When information on purchases is not available, one can occasionally use the cost of goods sold in the denominator. A department store chain, for example, typically does no manufacturing. As a result, the cost of goods sold consists primarily of purchases. However, in situations where there is sizable value added, such as with a manufacturer, the use of the cost of goods sold is inappropriate. One must have the amount of purchases if the ratio is to be used. Another caveat has to do with growth. As with receivables, the use of a year-end payable balance will result in a biased and high estimate of the time it will take a company to make payment on its payables if there is strong underlying growth. In this situation, it may be better to use an average of payables at the beginning of the year and at the end.

The average payable period is valuable in evaluating the probability that a credit applicant will pay on time. If the average age of payables is 48 days, and the terms in the industry are net 30, we know that a portion of the applicant's payables are not being paid on time. A credit check of other suppliers will give insight into the severity of the problem.

Liquidity of Inventories

We may compute the **inventory turnover ratio** as an indicator of the liquidity of inventory

$$\frac{\text{Cost of goods sold}}{\text{Average inventory}} \tag{12-6}$$

For Aldine, the ratio is

$$\frac{\$2,680,298}{(\$1,328,963 + \$1,234,725)/2} = 2.09$$

Inventory turns tell us the funds being tied up in inventories as well as give us a hint as to possible obsolescence.

The figure for cost of goods sold used in the numerator is for the period being studied—usually 1 year; the average inventory figure used in the denominator typically is an average of beginning and ending inventories for the period. The inventory turnover ratio tells us the rapidity with which the inventory is turned over into receivables through sales. This ratio, like other ratios, must be judged in relation to past and expected future ratios of the firm and in relation to ratios of similar firms, the industry average, or both.

Generally, the higher the inventory turnover, the more efficient the inventory management of a firm. Sometimes a relatively high inventory turnover ratio may be the result of too low a level of inventory and frequent stockouts. It might also be the result of too many small orders for inventory replacement. Either of these situations may be more costly to the firm than carrying a larger investment in inventory and having a lower turnover ratio. Again, caution is necessary in interpreting the ratio. When the inventory turnover ratio is relatively low, it indicates slow-moving inventory or obsolescence of some of the stock. Obsolescence may necessitate substantial write-downs, which, in turn, would negate the treatment of inventory as a liquid asset. Because the turnover ratio is a somewhat crude measure, we would want to investigate any perceived inefficiency in inventory management. In this regard, it is helpful to compute the turnover of the major categories of inventory to see if there are imbalances, which may indicate excessive investment in specific components of the inventory. Once we have a hint of a problem, we must investigate it more specifically to determine its cause.

DEBT RATIOS

Extending our analysis to the long-term liquidity of the firm (that is, its ability to meet long-term obligations), we may use several debt ratios. The **debt-to-equity ratio** is computed by simply dividing the total debt of the firm (including current liabilities) by its shareholders' equity:

$$\frac{\text{Total debt}}{\text{Shareholders' equity}} \qquad (12\text{-}7)$$

For Aldine, the ratio is

$$\frac{\$1,454,859}{\$1,796,621} = .81$$

When intangible assets are significant, they frequently are deducted from shareholders' equity.

Debt ratios
reflect the relative
proportion of debt
funds employed.

The ratio of debt to equity varies according to the nature of the business and the volatility of cash flows. An electric utility, with very stable cash flows, usually will have a higher debt ratio than will a machine tool company, whose cash flows are far less stable. A comparison of the debt ratio for a given company with those of similar firms gives us a general indication of the creditworthiness and financial risk of the firm.

In addition to the ratio of total debt to equity, we may want to compute the following ratio, which deals with only the **long-term capitalization** of the firm:

$$\frac{\text{Long-term debt}}{\text{Total capitalization}} \qquad (12\text{-}8)$$

where total capitalization represents all long-term debt, preferred stock, and shareholders' equity. For Aldine, the ratio is

$$\frac{\$630,783}{\$2,427,404} = .26$$

This measure tells us the relative importance of long-term debt in the capital structure. The ratios computed here have been based on book-value figures; it is sometimes useful to calculate these ratios using market values. In summary, debt ratios tell us the relative proportions of capital contribution by creditors and by owners.

Cash Flow to Debt and Capitalization

A measure of the ability of a company to service its debt is the relationship of annual cash flow to the amount of debt outstanding. The cash flow of a company often is defined as the cash generated from the operation of the company. This is defined as earnings before interest, taxes, depreciation, and amortization **(EBITDA)**. The **cash-flow-to-total-liabilities ratio** is simply

$$\frac{\text{Cash flow (EBITDA)}}{\text{Total liabilities}} \qquad (12\text{-}9)$$

For Aldine, the ratio is

$$\frac{\$511{,}065}{\$1{,}454{,}859} = .35$$

The cash flow is composed of earnings before taxes, $314,282, plus interest, $85,274, and depreciation, $111,509. This ratio is useful in assessing the creditworthiness of a company seeking debt funds.

Another ratio is the **cash-flow-to-long-term-debt ratio:**

$$\frac{\text{Cash flow (EBITDA)}}{\text{Long-term debt}} \qquad (12\text{-}10)$$

Here we have the following for Aldine:

$$\frac{\$511{,}065}{\$630{,}783} = .81$$

This ratio is used to evaluate the bonds of a company. The two cash-flow ratios just described have proven useful in predicting the deteriorating financial health of a company.

This is particularly helpful in corporate restructuring, where heavily levered transactions occur. Another ratio often used in this regard is total interest-bearing debt plus equity in relation to operating cash flows. Known as the **enterprise value-to-EBITDA ratio**, it can be expressed as

$$\frac{\text{Total borrowings} + \text{Equity}}{\text{Cash flow (EBITDA)}} \qquad (12\text{-}11)$$

For Aldine, this ratio is

$$\frac{\$2{,}875{,}912}{\$511{,}065} = 5.63$$

where bank loans, notes payable, and long-term debt represent total borrowings. The higher this ratio, the greater the value that is being placed on the securities. Lenders in highly levered transactions become concerned when the ratio exceeds 8, as the possibility of default has been found to be significant at this point.

COVERAGE RATIOS

Coverage ratios are designed to relate the financial charges of a firm to its ability to service them. Bond-rating services, such as Moody's Investors Service and Standard & Poor's, make extensive use of these ratios.

Interest Coverage Ratio

One of the most traditional of the coverage ratios is the **interest coverage ratio,** simply the ratio of earnings before interest and taxes for a particular reporting period to the amount of interest charges for the period. We must differentiate which interest charges should be used in the denominator. The **overall coverage method** stresses a company's meeting all fixed interest, regardless of the seniority of the claim. We have the following financial data for a hypothetical company:

Average earnings before interest and taxes	$2,000,000
Interest on senior 7% bonds	− 400,000
	$1,600,000
Interest on junior 8% bonds	160,000

The overall interest coverage would be $2,000,000/$560,000, or 3.57. This method implies that the creditworthiness of the senior bonds is only as good as the firm's ability to cover all interest charges.

Of the various coverage ratios, the most objectionable is the **prior deductions method**. Using this method, we deduct interest on the senior bonds from average earnings and then divide the residual by the interest on the junior bonds. We find that the coverage on the junior bonds in our example is 10 times ($1,600,000/$160,000). Thus, the junior bonds give the illusion of being more secure than the senior obligations. Clearly, this method is inappropriate. The **cumulative deduction method,** perhaps, is the most widely used method of computing interest coverage. Under this method, coverage for the senior bonds would be 5 times. Coverage for the junior bonds is determined by adding the interest charges on both bonds and relating the total to average earnings. Thus, the coverage for the junior bonds would be $2,000,000/$560,000 = 3.57 times.

Cash-Flow Coverage Ratios

Coverage ratios give insight into the ability of a company to service its debt.

Cash-flow coverage ratios involve the relation of earnings before interest, taxes, depreciation, and amortization (EBITDA) to interest and to interest plus principal payments. For the **cash-flow coverage of interest** we have

$$\frac{\text{EBITDA}}{\text{Annual interest payments}} \qquad (12\text{-}12)$$

This ratio is very useful in determining whether a borrower is going to be able to service interest payments on a loan. Even for highly levered transactions, lenders want a coverage ratio comfortably above 2.0. The EBITDA interest coverage ratio is highly correlated with bond ratings and the market's assessment of risk.[4] To be investment grade, that is, AAA, AA, A, or BBB, the ratio for an industrial corporation usually must be above 4.0.

One of the shortcomings of an interest coverage ratio is that a firm's ability to service debt is related to both interest and principal payments. Moreover, these payments are not met out of earnings per se, but out of cash. Hence, a more appropriate coverage ratio relates the cash flow of the firm to the sum of interest and principal payments. The **cash-flow coverage of interest and principal ratio** may be expressed as

$$\frac{\text{EBITDA}}{\text{Interest} + \text{Principal payments }[1/(1-t)]} \qquad (12\text{-}13)$$

---

[4]Gregory W. Foss, "Quantifying Risk in the Corporate Bond Markets," *Financial Analysts Journal*, 51 (March–April 1995), 29–34.

where t is the income tax rate and principal payments are annual. Because principal payments are made after taxes, it is necessary to gross them up so that they correspond to interest payments, which are made before taxes. If the tax rate were 40 percent and annual principal payments $120,000, before-tax earnings of $200,000 would be needed to cover these payments. If the company has preferred stock outstanding, the stated dividend on this stock, grossed up by 1 minus the tax rate, should appear in the denominator of Equation 12-13.

In assessing the financial risk of a firm, then, the financial analyst should first compute the debt ratios as a rough measure of financial risk. Depending on the payment schedule of the debt and the average interest rate, debt ratios may or may not give an accurate picture of the ability of the firm to meet its financial obligations. Therefore, it is necessary to analyze additionally the cash-flow ability of the company to service debt. This is done by relating cash flow not only to the amount of debt outstanding but also to the amount of financial charges. Neither debt ratios nor coverage ratios are sufficient by themselves.

PROFITABILITY RATIOS

Profitability ratios are of two types: those showing profitability in relation to sales, and those showing profitability in relation to investment. Together these ratios indicate the firm's efficiency of operation.

Profitability in Relation to Sales

The first ratio we consider is the **gross profit margin:**

$$\frac{\text{Sales less cost of goods sold}}{\text{Sales}} \qquad (12\text{-}14)$$

Net profit margin is a combination of the gross profit margin and SG&A-to-sales.

For Aldine, the gross profit margin is

$$\frac{\$1,312,460}{\$3,992,758} = 32.9\%$$

This ratio tells us the profit of the firm relative to sales after we deduct the cost of producing the goods sold. It indicates the efficiency of operations as well as how products are priced. A more specific ratio of profitability is the **net profit margin:**

$$\frac{\text{Net profits after taxes}}{\text{Sales}} \qquad (12\text{-}15)$$

For Aldine, this ratio is

$$\frac{\$201,242}{\$3,992,758} = 5.04\%$$

The net profit margin tells us the relative efficiency of the firm after taking into account all expenses and income taxes, but not extraordinary charges.

By considering both ratios jointly, we are able to gain considerable insight into the operations of the firm. If the gross profit margin is essentially unchanged over a period of several years, but the net profit margin has declined over the same period, we know that the cause is either higher selling, general, and administrative expenses (SG&A) relative to sales or a higher tax rate. On the other hand, if the gross profit margin falls, we know that the cost of producing the goods relative to sales has increased. This occurrence, in turn, may be due to problems in pricing or costs.

In many situations, it is useful to compute the ratio of **SG&A to sales**:

$$\frac{\text{Selling, general \& administrative expenses}}{\text{Sales}} \qquad (12\text{-}16)$$

For Aldine, we have for the most recent fiscal year

$$\frac{\$801,395}{\$3,992,758} = 20.1\%$$

With growth, we might expect this percent to decline over time as economies of scale occur. When the SG&A-to-sales increases over time and/or is large relative to peer companies it gives us cause for concern.

In summary, there are any number of combinations of changes possible in the gross and net profit margins. Indications of the sort illustrated here tell us where we should investigate further. In our analysis, it is useful to examine over time each of the individual expense items as a percentage of sales. By so doing, we can pick out specific areas of deterioration or improvement.

Profitability in Relation to Investment

The second group of profitability ratios relates profits to investments. One of these measures is the **rate of return on equity,** or the ROE:

$$\frac{\text{Net profits after taxes} - \text{Preferred stock dividend}}{\text{Shareholders' equity}}$$

For Aldine, the rate of return is

$$\frac{\$201,242}{\$1,796,621} = 11.2\%$$

This ratio tells us the earning power on shareholders' book investment and is frequently used in comparing two or more firms in an industry. The figure for shareholders' equity used in the ratio may be expressed in terms of market value instead of book value. When we use market value, we obtain the earnings/price ratio of the stock.

A more general ratio used in the analysis of profitability is the **return on assets,** or the ROA:

$$\frac{\text{Net profits after taxes}}{\text{Total assets}} \qquad (12\text{-}17)$$

For Aldine, the ratio is

$$\frac{\$201,242}{\$3,251,480} = 6.19\%$$

This ratio is somewhat inappropriate, inasmuch as profits are taken after interest is paid to creditors. Because these creditors provide means by which part of the total assets are supported, there is a fallacy of omission. When financial charges are significant, it is preferable, for comparative purposes, to compute a net operating profit rate of return instead of a return on assets ratio. The **net operating profit rate of return** may be expressed as

$$\frac{\text{Earnings before interest and taxes}}{\text{Total assets}} \tag{12-18}$$

Using this ratio, we are able to abstract from differing financial charges (interest and preferred stock dividends). Thus, the relationship studied is independent of the way the firm is financed.

Turnover and Earning Power

Frequently, the financial analyst relates total assets to sales to obtain the **asset turnover ratio:**

$$\frac{\text{Sales}}{\text{Total assets}} \tag{12-1}$$

Higher asset turnover means less investment in assets is necessary to produce sales.

Aldine's turnover for the 2002 fiscal year was

$$\frac{\$3,992,758}{\$3,251,480} = 1.23$$

This ratio tells us the relative efficiency with which the firm utilizes its resources in order to generate output. It varies according to the type of company being studied. A food chain has a considerably higher turnover, for example, than does an electric utility. The turnover ratio is a function of the efficiency with which the various asset components are managed: receivables as depicted by the average collection period, inventories as portrayed by the inventory turnover ratio, and fixed assets as indicated by the throughput of product through the plant or the sales to net fixed asset ratio.

When we multiply the asset turnover of the firm by the net profit margin, we obtain the return on assets ratio, or **earning power** on total assets:

$$\text{Earning power} = \frac{\text{Sales}}{\text{Total assets}} \times \frac{\text{Net profits after taxes}}{\text{Sales}} \tag{12-20}$$

$$= \frac{\text{Net profits after taxes}}{\text{Total assets}}$$

For Aldine, we have

$$\frac{\$3,992,758}{\$3,251,480} \times \frac{\$201,242}{\$3,992,758} = 6.19\%$$

Neither the net profit margin nor the turnover ratio by itself provides an adequate measure of operating efficiency. The net profit margin ignores the utilization of assets, whereas the turnover ratio ignores profitability on sales. The return on assets ratio, or earning power, resolves these shortcomings. An improvement in the earning power of the firm will result if there is an increase in turnover, an increase in the net profit margin, or both. Two companies with different asset turnovers and net profit margins may have the same earning power. Firm A, with an asset turnover of 4 to 1 and a net profit margin of 3 percent, has the same earning power—12 percent—as firm B, with an asset turnover of $1\frac{1}{2}$ to 1 and a net profit margin of 8 percent.

Another way to look at the return on equity (ROE) is

$$\text{ROE} = \text{Earning power} \times \left(1 + \frac{Debt}{Equity}\right) \qquad (12\text{--}21)$$

In this equation, earning power is grossed up by the equity multiplier associated with the use of debt. For Aldine,

$$\text{ROE} = 6.19\% \times 1.81 = 11.20\%$$

or the same as we determined earlier when we computed it directly.

With all the profitability ratios, comparing one company with similar companies is valuable. Only by comparison are we able to judge whether the profitability of a particular company is good or bad, and why. Absolute figures provide insight, but relative performance is most revealing.

MARKET-VALUE RATIOS

There are several widely used ratios that relate the market value of a company's stock to profitability, to dividends, and to book equity. Although these ratios have been taken up in Parts II and III, for the sake of completeness it is useful to present them here.

Price/Earnings Ratio

The price/earnings ratio of a company is simply

$$\text{P/E ratio} = \frac{\text{Share price}}{\text{Earnings per share}} \qquad (12\text{--}22)$$

where earnings per share (EPS) usually are the trailing 12 months of earnings. However, security analysts sometimes use estimated EPS for the next 12 months. Suppose Aldine Manufacturing Company has a share price of $38. With a par value of $5 per share at 2002 fiscal year end in Table 12–1, there are 84,165,600 shares outstanding. Therefore, earnings per share are earnings after taxes divided

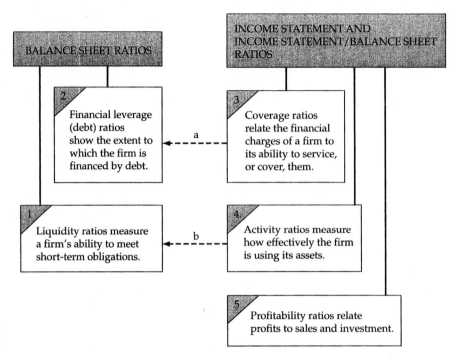

FIGURE 12-1
Financial ratio
implications

by number of shares outstanding, or $201,242,000/84,165,600 = $2.39. The P/E ratio for Aldine is

$$\frac{\$38.00}{\$2.39} = 15.9 \text{ times}$$

Price/earnings, dividend yield, and market/book give indication of the relative valuation of a stock.

In earlier chapters, the P/E ratio was described as one measure of relative value. The higher this ratio, the more the value of the stock that is being ascribed to future earnings as opposed to present earnings. That is to say, likely future growth is what is being valued. During the last 20 years, the P/E ratio for Standard & Poor's 500 stock index has ranged from 8 to 28. The ratio reflects a number of things including interest rates, growth expectations for stocks in general, and investor risk aversion, all of which were taken up in Parts I and II.

Dividend Yield

The **dividend yield** for a stock relates the annual dividend to share price. Therefore,

$$\text{Dividend yield} = \frac{\text{Dividends per share}}{\text{Share price}} \tag{12–23}$$

Going to Tables 12–1 and 12–2, we determine that dividends per share for the 2002 fiscal year are $1.70. Therefore, the dividend yield for Aldine is

$$\frac{\$1.70}{\$38.00} = 4.47\%$$

Typically companies with good growth potential retain a high proportion of earnings and have a low dividend yield, whereas companies in more mature industries pay out a high portion of their earnings and have a relatively high dividend yield (see Chapter 11). Aldine falls in the latter category.

Market-to-Book Ratio

The final market-value ratio we consider relates market value per share to book value

$$\text{M/B ratio} = \frac{\text{Share price}}{\text{Book value per share}} \quad (12\text{–}24)$$

where M/B ratio is the market-to-book value ratio. Going again to Table 12–1, we divide shareholders' equity by the number of shares outstanding to get a book value per share of $21.35. Therefore, for Aldine we have

$$\text{M/B ratio} = \frac{\$38.00}{\$21.35} = 1.78$$

The market-to-book value ratio is a relative measure of how the growth option for a company is being valued vis-à-vis its physical assets. The greater the expected growth and value placed on such, the higher this ratio. M/B ratios for established companies range from as little as .5 to as high as 8.0. The former often is associated with a company that earns less than what the financial markets require, a harvest situation, and the latter with a company that earns substantially more through industry attractiveness and/or competitive advantage (see Chapter 8).

Another ratio that is used from time to time is **Tobin's Q ratio** named after its original proponent, the famous economist James Tobin. This ratio is

$$\text{Q ratio} = \frac{\text{Market value of company}}{\text{Replacement costs of assets}} \quad (12\text{–}25)$$

The market value of a company is the sum of the market values of all debt instruments plus the total market value of the stock. Similar to the discussion above, companies with Q ratios of less than 1.0 often are harvest situations that are worth more dead than alive. The higher the Q ratio, the greater the industry attractiveness and/or competitive advantage.

PREDICTIVE POWER OF FINANCIAL RATIOS

In the previous sections, we presented the principal ratios used in financial analysis. Reliance on certain ratios depends on the analyst's perception of their predictive power relative to the problem at hand—a perception based on either subjective beliefs or empirical analysis. In predicting the future value of a stock, an investor might feel that the return on investment ratio and various profit margin ratios would be the greatest help. Most estimates of the predictive power of financial ratios are based on the analyst's past experience with them. By their very nature, then, these estimates tend to be subjective and differ from one analyst to the next.

A number of empirical studies have tested the predictive power of financial ratios. In many of these studies, financial ratios are used to predict business failure. Others have tested the power of financial ratios to predict corporate bond ratings. With these ratios as the dependent variable, regression analysis and discriminant analysis have been employed, using various financial ratios for a sample of companies. The best ratios for predictive purposes are debt-to-equity, cash-flow-to-debt, net operating profit margin, debt coverage and its stability, return on investment, size, and earnings stability. On the basis of these studies, it appears that a handful of ratios can be used to predict the long-term credit standing of a firm.

Predicting Financial Distress

For our purposes, financial distress is the event of particular interest. Beaver was first to use statistical techniques to predict corporate failure.[5] He found that financial ratios for failed companies deteriorated markedly as failure approached. In a similar type of study, Altman employed multiple discriminant analysis to predict bankruptcy, using various financial ratios.[6] (This statistical technique is described in the appendix to Chapter 15.) He found that five financial ratios were able to discriminate rather effectively between bankrupt and nonbankrupt companies, beginning up to 5 years prior to the bankruptcy event.

The Z-score model itself was the following:

$$Z = 1.2X_1 + 1.4X_2 + 3.3X_3 + .6X_4 + 1.0X_5 \qquad (12\text{--}26)$$

where X_1 = working capital to total assets
X_2 = cumulative retained earnings to total assets
X_3 = earnings before interest and taxes to total assets
X_4 = market value of equity to book value of total liabilities
X_5 = sales to total assets

The Z ratio is the overall index of the multiple discriminant function. Altman found that companies with Z scores below 1.81 (including negative amounts) always went bankrupt, whereas Z scores above 2.99 represented healthy firms. Firms with Z scores in between were sometimes misclassified, so this represents an area of gray. On the basis of these cutoffs, Altman suggests that one can predict whether or not a company is likely to go bankrupt in the near future.

This model was expanded by Altman and others into what is known as the **Zeta model.** This model is more accurate in prediction, but unfortunately the coefficients are not published. It was developed for private sale by ZETA Services, Inc., and the output consists of Zeta scores for thousands of companies. As a result of this and other work, financial ratio analysis has become more scientific and objective. It now focuses on those ratios that really have underlying predictive ability. Expert systems have been developed on the basis of such models, where computer software mimics the reasoning process of experienced financial analysts.

Ratios have predictive power when it comes to financial distress.

---

[5]William H. Beaver, "Financial Ratios as Predictors of Failure," *Empirical Research in Accounting: Selected Studies,* supplement to *Journal of Accounting Research,* 41 (1966), 71–111.

[6]Edward I. Altman, "Financial Ratios, Discriminant Analysis and the Prediction of Corporate Bankruptcy," *Journal of Finance,* 23 (September 1968), 589–609.

COMMON SIZE AND INDEX ANALYSES

It is often useful to express balance sheet and income statement items as percentages. The percentages can be related to totals, such as total assets or total sales, or to some base year. Called **common size analysis** and **index analysis,** respectively, the evaluation of trends in financial statement percentages over time affords the analyst insight into the underlying improvement or deterioration in financial condition and performance. Though a good portion of this insight is revealed in the analysis of financial ratios, a broader understanding of the trends is possible when the analysis is extended to include the foregoing considerations. To illustrate these two types of analyses, we shall use the balance sheet and income statement of Riker Electronics Corporation for the 20x1 through 20x4 fiscal years. These statements are shown in Tables 12-3 and 12-4.

Common size expresses assets and liabilities as a percent of total assets, and expenses and profits as a percent of sales.

TABLE 12-3
Riker Electronics Corporation Balance Sheet (in thousands)

	20x1	*20x2*	*20x3*	*20x4*
Assets				
Cash	$ 2,507	$ 4,749	$ 11,310	$ 19,648
Accounts receivable	70,360	72,934	85,147	118,415
Inventory	77,380	86,100	91,378	118,563
Other current assets	6,316	5,637	6,082	5,891
Current assets	$156,563	$169,420	$193,917	$262,517
Fixed assets, net	$ 79,187	$ 91,868	$ 94,652	$115,461
Other long-term assets	4,695	5,017	5,899	5,491
Total assets	$240,445	$266,305	$294,468	$383,469
Liabilities and shareholders' equity				
Accounts payable	$ 35,661	$ 31,857	$ 37,460	$ 62,725
Notes payable	20,501	25,623	14,680	17,298
Other current liabilities	11,054	7,330	8,132	15,741
Current liabilities	$ 67,216	$ 64,810	$ 60,272	$ 95,764
Long-term debt	888	979	1,276	1,917
Total liabilities	$ 68,104	$ 65,789	$ 61,548	$ 97,681
Preferred stock	0	0	0	2,088
Common stock	12,650	25,649	26,038	26,450
Additional paid-in capital	36,134	33,297	45,883	63,049
Retained earnings	123,557	141,570	160,999	194,201
Shareholders' equity	$172,341	$200,516	$232,920	$285,788
Total liabilities and equity	$240,445	$266,305	$294,468	$383,469

TABLE 12-4
Riker Electronics Corporation Income Statement (in thousands)

	20x1	20x2	20x3	20x4
Sales	$323,780	$347,322	$375,088	$479,077
Cost of goods sold	148,127	161,478	184,507	223,690
Gross profit	$175,653	$185,844	$190,581	$255,387
Selling expenses	$ 79,399	$ 98,628	$103,975	$125,645
General and administrative expenses	43,573	45,667	45,275	61,719
Total expenses	$122,972	$144,295	$149,250	$187,364
Earnings before interest and taxes	$ 52,681	$ 41,549	$ 41,331	$ 68,023
Other income	1,757	4,204	2,963	3,017
Earnings before taxes	$ 54,438	$ 45,753	$ 44,294	$ 71,040
Taxes	28,853	22,650	20,413	32,579
Earnings after taxes	$ 25,585	$ 23,103	$ 23,881	$ 38,461

Statement Items as Percentages of Totals

In common size analysis, we express the various components of a balance sheet as percentages of the total assets of the company. In addition, this can be done for the income statement, but here items are related to sales. The gross and net profit margins, taken up earlier, are examples of this type of expression; and it can be extended to all the items on the income statement. The expression of individual financial items as percentages of totals usually permits insights not possible from a review of the raw figures themselves.

To illustrate, common size balance sheet and income statements are shown in Tables 12-5 and 12-6 for Riker Electronics Corporation for the fiscal years 20x1 through 20x4. In the first of the two tables, we see that over the 4 years the percentage of current assets increased and that this was particularly true of cash. In addition, we see that accounts receivable showed a relative increase from 20x3 to 20x4. On the liability and shareholders' equity side of the balance sheet, the debt of the company declined on a relative basis from 20x1 to 20x3. With the large absolute increase in assets that occurred in 20x4, however, the debt ratio increased from 20x3 to 20x4. This is particularly apparent in accounts payable, which increased substantially in both absolute and relative terms.

The common size income statement in Table 12-6 shows the gross profit margin fluctuating from year to year. When this is combined with selling, general, and administrative expenses, which also fluctuate over time, the end result is a net profit picture that varies from year to year. Although 20x4 shows a sharp improvement over 20x3 and 20x2, it still is not as good as 20x1 on a before-tax relative basis.

TABLE 12-5
Riker Electronics Corporation Common Size Balance Sheet

	20x1	20x2	20x3	20x4
Assets				
Cash	1.0	1.8	3.8	5.1
Accounts receivable	29.3	27.4	28.9	30.9
Inventory	32.2	32.3	31.0	30.9
Other current assets	2.6	2.1	2.1	1.5
Current assets	65.1	63.6	65.9	68.5
Fixed assets, net	32.9	34.5	32.1	30.1
Other long-term assets	2.0	1.9	2.0	1.4
Total assets	100.0	100.0	100.0	100.0
Liabilities and shareholders' equity				
Accounts payable	14.8	12.0	12.7	16.4
Notes payable	8.5	9.6	5.0	4.5
Other current liabilities	4.6	2.8	2.8	4.1
Current liabilities	28.0	24.3	20.5	25.0
Long-term debt	.4	.4	.4	.5
Total liabilities	28.3	24.7	20.9	25.5
Preferred stock	.0	.0	.0	.5
Common stock	5.3	9.6	8.8	6.9
Additional paid-in capital	15.0	12.5	15.6	16.4
Retained earnings	51.4	53.2	54.7	50.6
Shareholders' equity	71.7	75.3	79.1	74.5
Total liabilities and equity	100.0	100.0	100.0	100.0

TABLE 12-6
Riker Electronics Corporation Common Size Income Statement

	20x1	20x2	20x3	20x4
Sales	100.0	100.0	100.0	100.0
Cost of goods sold	45.7	46.5	49.2	46.7
Gross profit	54.3	53.5	50.8	53.3
Selling expenses	24.5	28.4	27.7	26.2
General and administrative expenses	13.5	13.1	12.1	12.9
Total expenses	38.0	41.5	39.8	39.1
Earnings before interest and taxes	16.3	12.0	11.0	14.2
Other income	.5	1.2	.8	.6
Earnings before taxes	16.8	13.2	11.8	14.8
Taxes	8.9	6.5	5.4	6.8
Earnings after taxes	7.9	6.7	6.4	8.0

Statement Items
as Indexes Relative to a Base Year

The common size balance sheet and income statement can be supplemented by the expression of items as trends from a base year. For Riker Electronics Corporation, the base year is 20x1, and all financial statement items are 100.0 for that year. Items for the 3 subsequent years are expressed as an index relative to that year. If a statement item were $22,500 compared with $15,000 in the base year, the index would be 150. Tables 12-7 and 12-8 are an indexed balance sheet and an indexed income statement. In the first of these two tables, the buildup in cash from the base year is particularly apparent, and this agrees with our previous assessment. Note also the large increase in accounts receivable and inventories from 20x3 to 20x4. The latter was not apparent in the common size analysis. To a lesser extent, there was a sizable increase in fixed assets. On the liability side of the balance sheet, we note the large increase in accounts payable as well as in other current liabilities that occurred from 20x3 to 20x4. This, coupled with retained earnings and the sale of common stock, financed the large increase in assets that occurred between these two points in time.

TABLE 12-7

Riker Electronics Corporation Indexed Balance Sheet

Index analysis expresses balance sheet and income statement items in index form relative to a base year.

	20x1	20x2	20x3	20x4
Assets				
Cash	100.0	189.4	451.1	783.7
Accounts receivable	100.0	103.7	121.0	168.3
Inventory	100.0	111.3	118.1	153.2
Other current assets	100.0	89.2	96.3	93.3
Current assets	100.0	108.2	123.9	167.7
Fixed assets, net	100.0	116.0	119.5	145.8
Other long-term assets	100.0	106.9	125.6	117.0
Total assets	100.0	110.8	122.5	159.5
Liabilities and shareholders' equity				
Accounts payable	100.0	89.3	105.0	175.9
Notes payable	100.0	125.0	71.6	84.4
Other current liabilities	100.0	66.3	73.6	142.4
Current liabilities	100.0	96.4	89.7	142.5
Long-term debt	100.0	110.2	143.7	215.9
Total liabilities	100.0	96.6	90.4	143.4
Preferred stock	0.0	0.0	0.0	100.0
Common stock	100.0	202.8	205.8	209.1
Additional paid-in capital	100.0	92.1	127.0	174.5
Retained earnings	100.0	114.6	130.3	157.2
Shareholders' equity	100.0	116.3	135.2	164.3
Total liabilities and equity	100.0	110.8	122.5	159.5

TABLE 12-8
Riker Electronics Corporation Indexed Income Statement

	20x1	20x2	20x3	20x4
Sales	100.0	107.3	115.8	148.0
Cost of goods sold	100.0	109.0	124.6	151.0
Gross profit	100.0	105.8	108.5	145.4
Selling expenses	100.0	124.2	131.0	158.2
General and administrative expenses	100.0	104.8	103.9	141.6
Total expenses	100.0	117.3	121.4	152.4
Earnings before interest and taxes	100.0	78.9	78.5	129.1
Other income	100.0	239.3	168.6	171.7
Earnings before taxes	100.0	84.0	81.4	130.5
Taxes	100.0	78.5	70.7	112.9
Earnings after taxes	100.0	90.3	93.3	150.3

The indexed income statement in Table 12-8 gives much the same picture as the common size income statement, namely, fluctuating behavior. The sharp improvement in 20x4 profitability is more easily distinguished, and the indexed statement gives us information on the magnitude of absolute change in profits and expenses. With the common size statement, we have no information about how total assets or total sales change over time.

In summary, the standardization of balance sheet and income statement items as percentages of totals and as indexes to a base year often gives us insights additional to those obtained from analysis of financial ratios. Common size and index analyses are much easier when a computer spreadsheet program is employed. The division calculations by rows or by columns can be done quickly and accurately with such a program.

Summary

Financial ratios can be derived from the balance sheet and the income statement. They are categorized into five types: liquidity, debt, coverage, profitability, and market value. Each type has a special use for the financial or security analyst. The usefulness of the ratios depends on the ingenuity and experience of the financial analyst who employs them. By themselves, financial ratios are fairly meaningless; they must be analyzed on a comparative basis.

A comparison of ratios of the same firm over time uncovers leading clues in evaluating changes and trends in the firm's financial condition and profitability. The comparison may be historical and predictive. It may include an analysis of the future based on projected financial statements. Ratios may also be judged in comparison with those of similar firms in the same line of business and, when appropriate, with an industry average. From empirical testing in recent years, it appears that financial ratios can be used successfully to predict certain events, bankruptcy in particular. With this testing, financial ratio analysis has become more scientific and objective than ever before, and we can look to further progress in this regard.

Additional insight often is obtained when balance sheet and income statement items are expressed as percentages. The percentages can be in relation to total assets or total sales or to some base year. Called common size analysis and index analysis, respectively, the idea is to study trends in financial statement items over time.

Self-Correction Problems

1. High-Low Plumbing Company sells plumbing fixtures on terms of 2/10, net 30. Its financial statements over the last 3 years follow:

	20x1	20x2	20x3
Cash	$ 30,000	$ 20,000	$ 5,000
Accounts receivable	200,000	260,000	290,000
Inventory	400,000	480,000	600,000
Net fixed assets	800,000	800,000	800,000
	$1,430,000	$1,560,000	$1,695,000
Accounts payable	$ 230,000	$ 300,000	$ 380,000
Accruals	200,000	210,000	225,000
Bank loan, short term	100,000	100,000	140,000
Long-term debt	300,000	300,000	300,000
Common stock	100,000	100,000	100,000
Retained earnings	500,000	550,000	550,000
	$1,430,000	$1,560,000	$1,695,000
Sales	$4,000,000	$4,300,000	$3,800,000
Cost of goods sold	3,200,000	3,600,000	3,300,000
Net profit	300,000	200,000	100,000

Using the ratios taken up in the chapter, analyze the company's financial condition and performance over the last 3 years. Are there any problems?

2. Using the following information, complete this balance sheet.

Long-term debt to net worth	.5 to 1
Total asset turnover	2.5×
Average collection period*	18 days
Inventory turnover	9×
Gross profit margin	10%
Acid-test ratio	1 to 1

*Assume a 360-day year and all sales on credit.

Cash	$_____	Notes and payables	$100,000
Accounts receivable	_____	Long-term debt	_____
Inventory	_____	Common stock	100,000
Plant and equipment	_____	Retained earnings	100,000
Total assets	$_____	Total liabilities and equity	$_____

3. Stella Stores, Inc., has sales of $6 million, an asset turnover ratio of 6 for the year, and net profits of $120,000.

    a. What is the company's return on assets or earning power?

    b. The company will install new point-of-sales cash registers throughout its stores. This equipment is expected to increase efficiency in inventory control, reduce clerical errors, and improve record keeping throughout the system. The new equipment will increase the investment in assets by 20 percent and is expected to increase the net profit margin from 2 percent now to 3 percent. No change in sales is expected. What is the effect of the new equipment on the return on assets ratio or earning power?

4. Kedzie Kord Company had the following balance sheets and income statements over the last 3 years (in thousands):

	20x1	20x2	20x3
Cash	$ 561	$ 387	$ 202
Receivables	1,963	2,870	4,051
Inventories	2,031	2,613	3,287
Current assets	$ 4,555	$ 5,870	$ 7,540
Net fixed assets	2,581	4,430	4,364
Total assets	$ 7,136	$10,300	$11,904
Payables	$ 1,862	$ 2,944	$ 3,613
Accruals	301	516	587
Bank loan	250	900	1,050
Current liabilities	$ 2,413	$ 4,360	$ 5,250
Long-term debt	500	1,000	950
Shareholders' equity	4,223	4,940	5,704
Total liabilities and equity	$ 7,136	$10,300	$11,904
Sales	$11,863	$14,952	$16,349
Cost of goods sold	8,537	11,124	12,016
Selling, general, and administrative expenses	2,349	2,659	2,993
Profit before taxes	$ 977	$ 1,169	$ 1,340
Taxes	390	452	576
Profit after taxes	$ 587	$ 717	$ 764

Using common size and index analyses, evaluate trends in the company's financial condition and performance.

■ **Problems**

1. Cordillera Carson Company has the following balance sheet and income statement for 20x2 (in thousands):

Balance Sheet			
Cash	$ 400	Accounts payable	$ 320
Accounts receivable	1,300	Accruals	260
Inventories ($1,800 for 20x1)	2,100	Short-term loans	1,100
Current assets	$3,800	Current liabilities	$1,680
Net fixed assets	3,320	Long-term debt	2,000
		Shareholders' equity	3,440
Total assets	$7,120	Total liabilities and equity	$7,120

Income Statement	
Net sales (all credit)	$12,680
Cost of goods sold*	8,930
Gross profit	$ 3,750
Selling, general, and admin. expenses	2,230
Interest expense	460
Profit before taxes	$ 1,060
Taxes	390
Profit after taxes	$ 670

*Includes depreciation of $480.

On the basis of this information, compute (a) the current ratio, (b) the acid-test ratio, (c) the average collection period, (d) the inventory turnover ratio, (e) the debt-to-net-worth ratio, (f) the long-term-debt-to-total-capitalization ratio, (g) the gross profit margin, (h) the net profit margin, (i) the rate of return on common stock equity, and (j) the ratio of cash flow to long-term debt.

2. Parker Phial Company has current assets of $1 million and current liabilities of $600,000.

   a. What is the company's current ratio?
   b. What would be its current ratio if each of the following occurred, holding all other things constant?
      (1) A machine costing $100,000 is paid for with cash.
      (2) Inventories of $120,000 are purchased and financed with trade credit.
      (3) Accounts payable of $50,000 are paid off with cash.

    (4) Accounts receivable of $75,000 are collected.

    (5) Long-term debt of $200,000 is raised for investment in inventories ($100,000) and to pay down short-term borrowings ($100,000).

3. A company has total annual sales (all credit) of $400,000 and a gross profit margin of 20 percent. Its current assets are $80,000; current liabilities, $60,000; inventories, $30,000; and cash, $10,000.

    a. How much average inventory should be carried if management wants the inventory turnover to be 4? (Assume a 360-day year for calculations.)

    b. How rapidly (in how many days) must accounts receivable be collected if management wants to have only an average of $50,000 invested in receivables? (Assume a 360-day year.)

4. The data for various companies in the same industry and of about the same size follow (in millions):

			Company			
	A	**B**	**C**	**D**	**E**	**F**
Sales	$10	$20	$8	$5	$12	$17
Total assets	8	10	6	2.5	4	8
Net income	0.7	2.0	0.8	0.5	1.5	1.0

Determine the asset turnover, net profit margin, and earning power for each of the companies.

5. The long-term debt section of the balance sheet of the Diters Corporation appears as follows:

$9\frac{1}{4}$% mortgage bonds	$2,500,000
$12\frac{3}{8}$% second-mortgage bonds	1,500,000
$10\frac{1}{4}$% debentures	1,000,000
$14\frac{1}{2}$% subordinated debentures	1,000,000
	$6,000,000

    a. If the average earnings before interest and taxes of the Diters Corporation are $1.5 million, what is the overall interest coverage?

    b. Using the cumulative deduction method, determine the coverage for each issue.

6.

U.S. Republic Corporation Balance Sheet, December 31, 20x3

Assets		Liabilities and Stockholders' Equity	
Cash	$ 500,000	Notes payable	$ 2,000,000
Accounts receivable	2,500,000	Accounts payable	1,000,000
Inventory*	3,500,000	Accrued wages and taxes	1,000,000
Fixed assets, net	7,500,000		
Excess over book value of assets acquired (intangible assets)	1,000,000	Long-term debt	6,000,000
		Preferred stock	2,000,000
		Common stock	1,000,000
		Retained earnings	2,000,000
Total assets	$15,000,000	Total liabilities and equity	$15,000,000

*Inventory at December 31, 20x2 = $1,500,000.

U.S. Republic Corporation Statement of Income and Retained Earnings, Year Ended December 31, 20x3

Net sales		
Credit		$ 8,000,000
Cash		2,000,000
Total		$10,000,000
Costs and expenses		
Costs of goods sold	$6,000,000	
Selling, general, and administrative expenses	1,100,000	
Depreciation	700,000	
Interest on long-term debt	600,000	8,400,000
Net income before taxes		$ 1,600,000
Taxes on income		600,000
Net income after taxes		$ 1,000,000
Less: Dividends on preferred stock		120,000
Net income available to common		880,000
Add: Retained earnings 1/1/x3		1,300,000
Subtotal		$ 2,180,000
Less: Dividends paid on common		180,000
Retained earnings at 12/31/x3		$ 2,000,000

a. Fill in the 20x3 column using the data presented.

U.S. Republic Corporation

Ratio	20x1	20x2	20x3	Industry 20x3
1. Current ratio	250%	200%		225%
2. Acid-test ratio	100%	90%		110%
3. Receivables turnover	5.0×	4.5×		6.0×
4. Inventory turnover	4.0×	3.0×		4.0×
5. Long-term debt to capitalization	35%	40%		33%
6. Gross profit margin	39%	41%		40%
7. Net profit margin	17%	15%		15%
8. Rate of return on equity	15%	20%		20%
9. Return on tangible assets	15%	12%		10%
10. Tangible asset turnover	.9×	.8×		1.0×
11. Overall interest coverage	11×	9×		10×
12. Cash flow to long-term debt	.66	.59		.60

b. Evaluate the position of the company from the table. Cite specific ratio levels and trends as evidence.

c. Indicate which ratios would be of most interest to you and what your decision would be in each of the following situations:

   (1) U.S. Republic wants to buy $500,000 worth of raw materials from you, with payment to be due in 90 days.

   (2) U.S. Republic wants you, a large insurance company, to pay off its note at the bank and assume it on a 10-year maturity basis at the current coupon of 14 percent.

   (3) There are 100,000 shares outstanding, and the stock is selling for $80 a share. The company offers you an opportunity to buy 50,000 additional shares at this price.

7. The following information is available on the Vanier Corporation. Assuming sales and production are steady throughout the year and a 360-day year, complete the balance sheet and income statement for Vanier Corporation.

Balance Sheet, December 31, 20x2 (in thousands)

Cash and marketable securities	$500	Accounts payable	$ 400
Accounts receivable	?	Bank loan	?
Inventories	?	Accruals	200
Current assets	?	Current liabilities	?
		Long-term debt	?
Net fixed assets	?	Common stock and retained earnings	3,750
Total assets	?	Total liabilities and equity	?

Income Statement for 20x2 (in thousands)

Credit sales	$8,000
Cost of goods sold	?
Gross profit	?
Selling and administrative expenses	?
Interest expense	400
Profit before taxes	?
Taxes, at 44%	?
Profit after taxes	?

Other information

Current ratio	3 to 1
Depreciation	$500
Net profit and depreciation to long-term debt	.40
Net profit margin	7%
Total liabilities to net worth	1 to 1
Average collection period	45 days
Inventory turnover ratio	3 to 1

8. Susan Doherty Designs has 1.64 million shares outstanding, shareholders' equity of $36.4 million, earnings of $4.7 million during the last 12 months during which it paid dividends of $1.1 million, and a share price of $59.
    a. What is the price/earnings ratio?
    b. What is the dividend yield?
    c. What is the ratio of market-to-book value per share?
    d. From this information, what can you say about the expected growth of the company?

9. Tic Tac Homes has had the following balance sheet statements during the past 4 years (in thousands):

	20x1	20x2	20x3	20x4
Cash	$ 214	$ 93	$ 42	$ 38
Receivables	1,213	1,569	1,846	2,562
Inventories	2,102	2,893	3,678	4,261
Net fixed asset	2,219	2,346	2,388	2,692
Total assets	$5,748	$6,901	$7,954	$9,553
Accounts payable	$1,131	$1,578	$1,848	$2,968
Notes payable	500	650	750	750
Accruals	656	861	1,289	1,743
Long-term debt	500	800	800	800
Common stock	200	200	200	200
Retained earnings	2,761	2,812	3,067	3,092
Total liabilities and shareholders' equity	$5,748	$6,901	$7,954	$9,553

Using index analysis, what are the major problems in the company's financial condition?

10. Two companies have the following financial characteristics (in thousands):

	Zoom Company	Zing Company
Working capital	$10,500	–$ 1,600
Total assets	50,000	21,000
Total liabilities	22,000	13,000
Equity value (market)	38,000	5,100
Retained earnings	19,000	3,000
Sales	86,000	23,000
Earnings before interest and taxes	12,000	1,300

Using Altman's model for predicting bankruptcy presented in this chapter, determine the Z-score index for each company. On the basis of these indexes, is either company likely to go into bankruptcy? Why?

Solutions to Self-Correction Problems

1.

	20x1	20x2	20x3
Current ratio	1.19	1.25	1.20
Acid-test ratio	.43	.46	.40
Average collection period	18	22	27
Inventory turnover	NA*	8.2	6.1
Total debt to net worth	1.38	1.40	1.61
Long-term debt to total capitalization	.33	.32	.32
Gross profit margin	.200	.163	.132
Net profit margin	.075	.047	.026
Asset turnover	2.80	2.76	2.24
Return on assets	.21	.13	.06

*NA, not applicable.

The company's profitability has declined steadily over the period. As only $50,000 is added to retained earnings, the company must be paying substantial dividends. Receivables are growing slower, although the average collection period is still very reasonable relative to the terms given. Inventory turnover is slowing as well, indicating a relative buildup in inventories. The increase in receivables and inventories, coupled with the fact that net worth has increased very little, has resulted in the total debt-to-worth ratio increasing to what would have to be regarded on an absolute basis as a high level.

The current and acid-test ratios have fluctuated, but the current ratio is not particularly inspiring. The lack of deterioration in these ratios is clouded by the relative buildup in both receivables and inventories, evidencing a deterioration in the liquidity of these two assets. Both the gross profit and net profit margins have declined substantially. The relationship between the two suggests that the company has reduced relative expenses in 20x3 in particular. The buildup in inventories and receivables has resulted in a decline in the asset turnover ratio, and this, coupled with the decline in profitability, has resulted in a sharp decrease in the return on assets ratio.

2. $$\frac{\text{Long-term debt}}{\text{Net worth}} = .5 = \frac{\text{Long-term debt}}{200,000} \qquad \text{Long-term debt} = \$100,000$$

Total liabilities and net worth = $400,000

Total assets = $400,000

$$\frac{\text{Sales}}{\text{Total assets}} = 2.5 = \frac{\text{Sales}}{400,000} \qquad \text{Sales} = \$1,000,000$$

Cost of goods sold = (.9)($1,000,000) = $900,000

$$\frac{\text{Cost of goods sold}}{\text{Inventory}} = \frac{900,000}{\text{Inventory}} = 9 \qquad \text{Inventory} = \$100,000$$

$$\frac{\text{Receivables} \times 360}{1,000,000} = 18 \text{ days} \qquad \text{Receivables} = \$50,000$$

$$\frac{\text{Cash} + 50,000}{100,000} = 1 \qquad \text{Cash} = \$50,000$$

Plant and equipment = $200,000

Balance Sheet

Cash	$ 50,000	Notes and payables	$100,000
Accounts receivable	50,000	Long-term debt	100,000
Inventory	100,000	Common stock	100,000
Plant and equipment	200,000	Retained earnings	100,000
		Total liabilities	
Total assets	$400,000	and equity	$400,000

---

3. a.   Total assets = Sales/turnover = $6 million/6 = $1 million

Earning power = Net profits/total assets

= $120,000/$1 million = 12%

    b.   Total assets = $1 million × 1.2 = $1.2 million

Earning power = Turnover × Net profit margin

$$= \frac{\$6 \text{ million}}{\$1.2 \text{ million}} \times 3\% = 15\%$$

4. The common size analysis shows that receivables are growing faster than total assets and current assets, while cash declined dramatically as a percentage of both. Net fixed assets surged in 20x2, but then fell back as a percentage of the total to almost the 20x1 percentage. The absolute amounts suggest that the company spent less than its depreciation on fixed assets in 20x3. With respect to financing, shareholders' equity has not kept up, so the company has had to use somewhat more debt percentagewise. It appears to be leaning more on the trade as payables increased percentagewise. Bank loans and long-term debt also increased sharply in 20x2, no doubt to finance the bulge in net fixed assets. The bank loan remained about the same in 20x3 as a percentage of total liabilities and equity, while long-term debt declined as a percentage. Profit after taxes slipped slightly as a percentage of sales over the 3 years. In 20x2, this decline was a result of the cost of goods sold, as expenses and taxes declined as a percentage of sales. In 20x3, cost of goods sold declined as a percentage of sales, but this was more than offset by increases in expenses and taxes as percentages of sales.

	20x1	20x2	20x3
	Common Size Analysis		
Cash	7.9%	3.8%	1.7%
Receivables	27.5	27.8	34.0
Inventories	28.4	25.4	27.6
Current assets	63.8%	57.0%	63.3%
Net fixed assets	36.2	43.0	36.7
Total assets	100.0%	100.0%	100.0%
Payables	26.1%	28.6%	30.4%
Accruals	4.2	5.0	4.9
Bank loan	3.5	8.7	8.8
Current liabilities	33.8%	42.3%	44.1%
Long-term debt	7.0	9.7	8.0
Shareholders' equity	59.2	48.0	47.9
Total liabilities and equity	100.0%	100.0%	100.0%
Sales	100.0%	100.0%	100.0%
Cost of goods sold	72.0	74.4	73.5
Selling, general, and administrative expenses	19.8	17.8	18.3
Profit before taxes	8.2%	7.8%	8.2%
Taxes	3.3	3.0	3.5
Profit after taxes	4.9%	4.8%	4.7%
	Index Analysis		
Cash	100.0	69.0	36.0
Receivables	100.0	146.2	206.4
Inventories	100.0	128.7	161.8
Current assets	100.0	128.9	165.5
Net fixed assets	100.0	171.6	169.1
Total assets	100.0	144.3	166.8
Payables	100.0	158.1	194.0
Accruals	100.0	171.4	195.0
Bank loan	100.0	360.0	420.0
Current liabilities	100.0	180.7	217.6
Long-term debt	100.0	200.0	190.0
Shareholders' equity	100.0	117.0	135.1
Total liabilities and equity	100.0	144.3	166.8
Sales	100.0	126.0	137.8
Cost of goods sold	100.0	130.3	140.8
Selling, general, and administrative expenses	100.0	113.2	127.4
Profit before taxes	100.0	119.7	137.2
Taxes	100.0	115.9	147.7
Profit after taxes	100.0	122.2	130.2

Index analysis shows much the same picture. Cash declined faster than total assets and current assets, and receivables increased faster than these two benchmarks. Inventories fluctuated but were about the same percentagewise to total assets in 20x3 as they were in 20x1. Net fixed assets increased more sharply than total assets in 20x2 and then fell back into line in 20x3. The sharp increase in bank loans in 20x2 and 20x3 and the sharp increase in long-term debt in 20x2 are evident. Equity increased less than total assets, so debt increased more percentagewise. With respect to profitability, net profits increased less than sales, for the reasons indicated earlier.

Selected References

Almanac of Business and Industrial Financial Ratios. Upper Saddle River, NJ: Prentice Hall, 2001.

ALTMAN, EDWARD I., "Financial Ratios, Discriminant Analysis and the Prediction of Corporate Bankruptcy," *Journal of Finance*, 23 (September 1968), 589–609.

ALTMAN, EDWARD I., and ROBERT HALDEMAN, "Corporate Credit Scoring Models: Approaches and Standards for Successful Implementation," working paper, New York University Stern School of Business (1995).

ALTMAN, EDWARD I., ROBERT G. HALDEMAN, and P. NARAYANAN, "Zeta Analysis: A New Model to Identify Bankruptcy Risk of Corporations," *Journal of Banking and Finance*, 1 (June 1977), 29–54.

AZIZ, ABDUL, and GERALD H. LAWSON, "Cash Flow Reporting and Financial Distress Models: Testing of Hypotheses," *Financial Management*, 18 (Spring 1989), 55–63.

BEAVER, WILLIAM H., "Financial Ratios as Predictors of Failure," *Empirical Research in Accounting: Selected Studies*, supplement to *Journal of Accounting Research* (41) (1966), 71–111.

CUNNINGHAM, DONALD F., and JOHN T. ROSE, "Industry Norms in Financial Statement Analysis: A Comparison of RMA and D&B Benchmark Data," *The Credit and Financial Management Review* (1995), 42–48.

FOSS, GREGORY W., "Quantifying Risk in the Corporate Bond Markets," *Financial Analysts Journal*, 51 (March–April 1995), 29–34.

FRASER, LYN M., and AILEEN ORMISTON, *Understanding Financial Statements*, 5th ed. Upper Saddle River, NJ: Prentice Hall, 1998.

HELFERT, ERICH A., *Techniques of Financial Analysis*, 9th ed. Boston: Irwin McGraw-Hill, 1997.

HIGGINS, ROBERT C., *Analysis for Financial Management*, 4th ed. Boston: Irwin McGraw-Hill, 1998.

MANESS, TERRY S., and JOHN T. ZIETLOW, *Short-Term Financial Management*. New York: Dryden Press, 1997.

MATSUMOTO, KEISHIRO, MELKOTE SHIVASWAMY, and JAMES P. HOBAN JR., "Security Analysts' Views of the Financial Ratios of Manufacturers and Retailers," *Financial Practice and Education*, 5 (Fall–Winter 1995), 44–55.

Wachowicz's Web World is an excellent overall Web site produced and maintained by my coauthor of *Fundamentals of Financial Management*, John M. Wachowicz Jr. It contains descriptions of and links to many finance Web sites and articles. *www.prenhall.com/wachowicz*.

■ CASE: *Financial Ratios and Industries*

The ratios and balance-sheet percentages presented are computed from 1996 financial statements for companies in the following industries:

1. Advertising
2. Airline
3. Aluminum/packaging manufacturing
4. Commercial banking
5. Computer software development
6. Electric and gas utility
7. Employment services and temporary help
8. Food retailing
9. Hotel supply business
10. Integrated oil production
11. Laundry detergents and other consumer products
12. News and information publishing
13. Pharmaceutical manufacturing
14. Tools and process/environmental controls manufacturing
15. Wholesaling of electronic and computer products

Certain industries are characterized by high or low financial ratios and/or balance-sheet percentages, and often can be identified on the basis of there being an outlier across one or more dimensions. Match the industries with the lettered columns of financial ratios and balance-sheet percentages.

	Company*							
	A	**B**	**C**	**D**	**E**	**F**	**G**	**H**
Financial ratios								
Current ratio	1.1	1.0	1.6	1.3	.6	1.1	1.1	1.5
Quick ratio	.6	.8	1.6	1.0	.6	1.1	1.1	.8
Average collection period (days)	55.2	24.0	69.5	57.4	43.6	NA	50.5	51.8
Inventory turns	6.2	5.2	NA	7.9	NA	NA	NA	6.5
Total debt/equity	1.5	1.5	2.3	1.0	.6	10.0	4.7	2.0
LTD/capitalization	.3	.4	.1	.2	.1	.2	.3	.4
Sales/total assets	1.0	.4	3.6	1.0	.9	.1	.5	.9
Gross profit margin	30.1%	30.8%	18.3%	55.0%	46.8%	50.8%	NA	20.4%
Net profit margin	7.3%	13.2%	2.3%	10.1%	8.3%	14.2%	6.0%	5.4%
Dividends/net income	4.3%	68.2%	7.9%	50.9%	47.0%	52.8%	35.5%	21.8%
Balance sheet percentages								
Cash and investments	.5%	.2%	9.4%	7.2%	.5%	6.6%	10.7%	.5%
Receivables	15.1	2.6	68.8	16.4	10.5	71.2	54.5	13.5
Inventories	13.6	2.0	NA	6.3	.5	NA	NA	11.5
Other current assets	2.1	6.1	6.0	1.6	2.8	17.4	4.6	.5
Net PP&E	19.7	66.7	7.1	27.5	26.6	1.7	6.6	41.7
Other assets and goodwill	49.0	22.4	8.7	41.0	59.1	3.1	23.6	32.3
Total assets	100.0%	100.0%	100.0%	100.0%	100.0%	100.0%	100.0%	100.0%
Payables and accruals	26.1%	3.2%	46.9%	18.7%	9.1%	74.4%	59.8%	11.4%
Notes payable	1.0	6.5	2.6	6.1	.2	10.8	3.8	2.7
Other current liabilities	.0	1.1	1.7	.3	13.1	.5	2.8	3.5
LTD and capital leases	18.1	29.1	4.1	13.3	9.8	3.0	6.6	24.0
Other liabilities	15.3	19.8	14.7	12.1	6.2	2.2	9.4	24.6
Preferred stock	.0	.7	.0	.0	.0	.3	.0	6.5
Shareholders' equity	39.5	39.6	30.0	49.5	61.6	8.8	17.6	27.3
Total liabilities and equity	100.0%	100.0%	100.0%	100.0%	100.0%	100.0%	100.0%	100.0%

*NA, not applicable.

Continued on following page

				Company*			
	I	**J**	**K**	**L**	**M**	**N**	**O**
Financial ratios							
Current ratio	4.2	1.1	2.4	.8	1.8	1.5	.8
Quick ratio	4.1	.2	1.2	.7	1.0	1.2	.7
Average collection period (days)	35.7	NA	58.0	10.1	65.6	54.6	39.5
Inventory turns	9.2	13.4	5.5	14.8	4.8	4.2	16.8
Total debt/equity	.3	.9	1.3	1.3	1.4	1.0	1.4
LTD/capitalization	.0	.3	.3	.3	.3	.1	.2
Sales/total assets	.8	2.6	2.2	.9	1.7	.7	1.1
Gross profit margin	85.7%	24.0%	17.4%	41.1%	23.4%	55.3	25.1%
Net profit margin	24.5%	2.7%	3.4%	6.4%	3.2%	20.0%	5.3%
Dividends/net income	.0%	25.2%	.0%	3.2%	.0%	46.2%	64.0%
Balance sheet percentages							
Cash and investments	65.9%	.7%	3.5%	9.8%	1.9%	14.1%	4.1%
Receivables	8.1	1.6	34.8	2.4	30.0	13.5	11.7
Inventories	1.2	16.5	38.5	1.3	29.6	10.9	4.7
Other current assets	2.8	1.4	1.2	1.1	2.4	3.9	2.5
Net PP&E	16.5	65.9	4.3	85.4	29.8	24.1	63.2
Other assets and goodwill	5.5	13.9	17.7	.1	6.3	33.5	13.8
Total assets	100.0%	100.0%	100.0%	100.0%	100.0%	100.0%	100.0%
Payables and accruals	9.6%	16.5%	28.5%	14.3%	32.7%	13.0%	13.3%
Notes payable	.0	1.3	4.3	.4	2.5	1.8	11.1
Other current liabilities	9.1	.0	.0	4.1	.0	9.1	3.1
LTD and capital leases	.0	22.9	20.3	20.3	21.9	5.8	13.2
Other liabilities	7.3	5.4	2.6	17.1	2.0	21.1	17.5
Preferred stock	.0	.0	.0	.0	.0	.0	.0
Shareholders' equity	74.0	53.9	44.3	43.8	40.9	49.2	41.8
Total liabilities and equity	100.0%	100.0%	100.0%	100.0%	100.0%	100.0%	100.0%

*NA, not applicable.

Financial Planning

F inancial planning involves analyzing the financial flows of a company; forecasting the consequences of various investment, financing, and dividend decisions, and weighing the effects of various alternatives. The idea is to determine where the firm has been, where it is now, and where it is going—not only the most likely course of events, but deviations from the most likely outcome. The advantage of financial planning is that it forces management to take account of possible deviations from the company's anticipated path.

The planning horizon depends on the company. Most firms have a horizon of at least 1 year. Many will produce detailed plans for 1 year and more general financial plans for 3 to 5 years. Some companies will plan ahead 10 or even more years. Public utilities and energy companies, having very long lead times for capital projects, make much longer financial plans than do most companies. ∎

METHODS OF ANALYSIS

This chapter looks through the tool kit for financial planning and the analysis of past financial progress. One of the valuable aids we find is a **funds-flow statement,** with which a financial manager or a creditor may evaluate how a firm uses funds and may determine how these uses are financed. In addition to studying past flows, the analyst can evaluate future flows by means of a funds statement based on forecasts. Such a statement provides an efficient method for the financial manager to assess the growth of the company and its resulting financial needs as well as to determine the best way by which to finance those needs. In particular, funds statements are very useful in planning intermediate- and long-term financing.

In the analysis of future funds flows, we have the **cash budget** and **pro forma** statements. The cash budget is indispensable to the financial manager in determining the short-term cash needs of the firm and, accordingly, in planning its short-term financing. When cash budgeting is extended to include a range of possible outcomes, the financial manager can evaluate the business risk and liquidity of the company and plan a realistic margin of safety. This margin of safety might come from adjusting the firm's liquidity cushion, rearranging the maturity structure of its debt, arranging a line of credit with a bank, or a combination of the three. Cash budgets prepared for a range of possible outcomes are valuable also in appraising the ability of the company to adjust to unexpected changes in cash flows. The preparation of pro forma balance sheets and income statements enables the financial manager to analyze the effect of various policy decisions on the future financial condition and performance of the firm.

The final method of analysis involves **sustainable growth modeling.** Here we determine whether the sales growth objectives of the company are consistent with its operating efficiency and with its financial ratios. This powerful tool of analysis allows us to simulate the likely effects of changes in target ratios when we move from a steady state environment. The integration of marketing, operational, and financial objectives permits better management of growth.

SOURCE AND USE OF FUNDS

The flow of funds in a firm may be visualized as a continuous process. For every use of funds, there must be an offsetting source. In a broad sense, the assets of a firm represent the net uses of funds: its liabilities and net worth represent net sources. A funds-flow cycle for a typical manufacturing company is illustrated in Fig. 13-1. For the going concern, there is really no starting or stopping point. A finished product is a variety of inputs—namely, raw material, fixed assets, and labor—ultimately paid for in cash. The product then is sold either for cash or on credit. A credit sale involves a receivable, which, when collected, becomes cash. If the selling price of the product exceeds all costs (including depreciation on assets) for a period of time, there is a profit for the period; if not, there is a loss. The reservoir of cash, the focal point in the figure, fluctuates over time with the production schedule, sales, collection of receivables, capital expenditures, and financing. On the other hand, reservoirs of raw materials, work in process, finished goods inventory, accounts receivable, and trade payables fluctuate with sales, the production schedule, and policies on managing receivables, inventories, and trade payables.

The **funds statement** is a method by which we study the net funds flow between two points in time. These points conform to beginning and ending financial statement dates for whatever period of examination is relevant—a quarter, a year, or 5 years. We must emphasize that the funds statement portrays net rather than gross changes between two comparable financial statements at different dates. For example, gross changes might be thought to include all changes that occur between the two statement dates, rather than the sum of these changes—the net change as defined. Although an analysis of the gross funds flow of a firm over time would be much more revealing than an analysis of net funds flow, we are usually constrained by the financial information available, namely, balance sheets and income statements that span particular periods of time. Funds may be defined in several different ways, depending on the purpose of the analysis. Although they are often defined as cash, many analysts treat funds as working capital, a somewhat broader definition. Other definitions are possible, although the two described are the most common by far.

In what follows, we present two similar but somewhat different approaches to analyzing funds flows on a cash basis. The first is a traditional way used by many financial analysts. The second is an accounting statement of cash flows required in the presentation of audited financial results. This statement supplements the balance sheet and income statement.

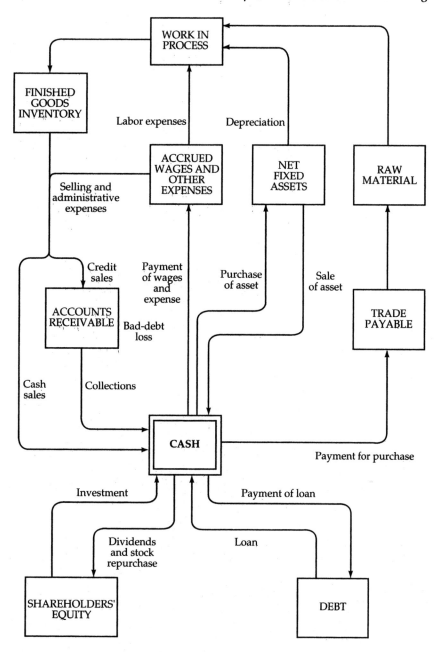

FIGURE 13-1
Funds flow within
the firm

Funds Statement on a Cash Basis

Basically, one prepares a funds statement on a cash basis by (1) classifying net balance sheet changes that occur between two points in time: changes that increase cash and changes that decrease cash; (2) classifying, from the income statement and the shareholders' equity statement, the factors that increase cash and the factors that decrease cash; and (3) consolidating this information in a source and use of funds statement form. In the first of these steps, we simply place one balance sheet beside the other and compute the changes in the various accounts.

Sources of funds that increase cash are

1. A net decrease in any asset other than cash or fixed assets
2. A gross decrease in fixed assets
3. A net increase in any liability
4. Proceeds from the sale of preferred or common stock
5. Funds provided by operations

Funds provided by operations usually are not expressed directly on the income statement. To determine them, one must add back depreciation to net income after taxes. For Aldine Manufacturing Company, our example in the preceding chapter, we have (in thousands):

Funds flows
ultimately
impact cash.

Net income after taxes	$201,242
Add noncash expenses: depreciation	111,509
Funds provided by operations	$312,751

Thus, the net income of Aldine understates funds provided by operations by $111,509. Depreciation is not a source of funds, for funds are generated only from operations. If operating losses before depreciation are sustained, funds are not provided regardless of the magnitude of depreciation charges.

Uses of funds include

1. A net increase in any asset other than cash or fixed assets
2. A gross increase in fixed assets
3. A net decrease in any liability
4. A retirement or purchase of stock
5. Cash dividends

To avoid double counting, we compute gross changes in fixed assets by adding depreciation for the period to net fixed assets at the ending financial statement date and subtract from this amount net fixed assets at the beginning financial statement date. The residual represents the gross change in fixed assets for the period. If the residual is positive, as is usually the case, it represents a use of funds; if negative, it represents a source.

Categorizing the Changes Once all sources and uses are computed, they may be arranged in statement form, so that we can analyze them better. Table 13-1 shows a source and use of funds statement for the Aldine Manufacturing Company for the fiscal year ended March 31, 2002. The balance sheet and income statement for this corporation, on which the funds statement is based, are shown in Tables 12-1 and 12-2. When we subtract the total uses of funds in Table 13-1 from the total sources, the difference should equal the actual change in cash between the two statement dates. If it does not, then the analyst must search for the cause of the discrepancy. Frequently, discrepancies will be due to equity adjustments, and the analyst should be alert to this possibility.

In Table 13-1, we see that the principal uses of funds for the 2002 fiscal year were additions to fixed assets, increases in inventories and in investments, and a siz-

TABLE 13-1

Aldine Manufacturing Company Sources and Uses of Funds March 31, 2001, to March 31, 2002 (in thousands)

Sources		Uses	
Funds provided by operations			
Net profit	$201,242	Dividends	$142,968
Depreciation	111,509	Additions to fixed assets	104,276
Decrease, accounts		Increase, inventories	94,238
receivable	62,426	Increase, prepaid expenses	3,559
Decrease, other assets	467		
Increase, bank loans	91,997	Increase, deferred income	
		taxes	6,038
Increase, accounts payable	11,634	Increase, investments	65,376
Increase, accruals	26,653	Decrease, income taxes	
		payable	91,252
Increase, long-term debt	4,323		
Increase, common stock and			
paid in capital	103	Increase, cash position	2,647
Total sources	$510,354	Total uses	$510,354

Source and use statements tell us the major uses of funds and how those uses have been financed over time.

able decrease in taxes payable. These uses were financed primarily by funds provided by operations in excess of dividends; by a decrease in accounts receivable; and by increases in bank loans, payables, and accruals. As sources exceeded slightly the uses of funds, cash and short-term investments rose by $2,647. In a sources and uses of funds analysis, it is useful to place cash dividends opposite net profits and additions to fixed assets opposite depreciation. Doing this allows the analyst to evaluate easily both the amount of dividend payout and the increase in fixed assets.

Accounting Statement of Cash Flows

A statement of cash flows (using the "indirect" method employed by most firms) is shown in Table 13-2. Again, this statement is derived from balance sheet and income statement information in Tables 12-1 and 12-2. Notice that changes that increase cash, all other things the same, are shown as positive numbers, whereas changes that decrease cash are shown as negative numbers, and that they all appear in a single column. This contrasts with the presentation in Table 13-1, where positive changes are shown in the sources column and negative changes in the uses column.

Moreover, changes in Table 13-2 are categorized into operating activities, investing activities, and financing activities. For many analysts, this categorization is helpful; no such categorization occurs in Table 13-1. A third difference is that the accounting statement of cash flows records gross investment in not only property, plant, and equipment (fixed assets) but also dispositions. The two are combined in Table 13-1. While not shown in Table 13-2, because there were none, repurchase of stock is a separate item in the accounting statement of cash flows. In the approach shown in Table 13-1, only the net change in stock is shown.

TABLE 13-2

Aldine Manufacturing Company Statement of Cash Flows March 31, 2001, to March 31, 2002 (in thousands)

	Year Ended March 31, 2002
Cash flows from operating activities:	
Net earnings	$201,242
Adjustments to reconcile net earnings to cash provided by operating activities	
Depreciation	111,509
Changes in assets and liabilities	
Accounts receivable	62,426
Inventories	(94,238)
Prepaid expenses	(3,559)
Deferred income taxes	(6,038)
Accounts payable	11,634
Income taxes payable	(91,252)
Accruals	26,653
	$218,377
Cash flows from investing activities:	
Investment in property, plant, and equipment	($113,730)
Disposition of property, plant, and equipment	9,454
Purchase of long-term investments	(65,376)
Other	467
	($169,185)
Cash flows from financing activities:	
Increase (decrease) short-term borrowings	$ 91,997
Increase (decrease) long-term debt	4,323
Issuance of common stock	103
Dividends	(142,968)
	($ 46,545)
Increase (decrease) in cash and short-term investments	$ 2,647
Cash and short-term investments at beginning of year	175,042
Cash and short-term investments at end of year	$177,689

Having explained the differences, there are a number of similarities, as the reader can appreciate when comparing the two statements. The final reconciliation, the change in cash position, +$2,647, is the same. Which approach, or both, the analyst uses is a matter of taste. The accounting statement of cash flows appears in audited statements and does not have to be derived. This obviously is an advantage. The same generalizations are possible with either format. The important thing is to be able to quickly identify the major uses of funds and how those uses were financed.

Implications

The analysis of funds statements gives us a rich insight into the financial operations of a firm—an insight that will be especially valuable to you as a financial manager analyzing past and future expansion plans of the firm and the impact of these plans on liquidity. You can detect imbalances in the uses of funds and undertake appropriate actions. An analysis spanning the past several years might reveal a growth in inventories out of proportion with the growth of other assets and with sales. Upon analysis, you might find that the problem was due to inefficiencies in inventory management. Thus, a funds statement alerts you to problems that you can analyze in detail and take proper actions to correct. When a company has a number of divisions, individual funds statements may prove useful. These statements enable top management to appraise the performance of divisions in relation to the funds committed to them.

Another use of funds statements is in the evaluation of the firm's financing. An analysis of the major sources of funds in the past reveals what portion of the firm's growth was financed internally and what portion externally. Funds statements are also useful in judging whether the company has expanded too fast and whether financing is strained. You can determine if trade credit has increased out of proportion to increases in current assets and sales. It is also revealing to analyze the mix of short- and long-term financing in relation to the funds needs of the firm. If these needs are primarily for fixed assets and permanent increases in working capital, you might be disturbed if a significant portion of total financing came from short-term sources.

CASH BUDGETING

A **cash budget** is arrived at through a projection of future cash receipts and cash disbursements of the firm over various intervals of time. It reveals the timing and amount of expected cash inflows and outflows over the period studied. With this information, the financial manager is better able to determine the future cash needs of the firm, plan for the financing of these needs, and exercise control over its cash and liquidity. Though cash budgets may be made for almost any interval of time, monthly projections for a year are most common. This enables analysis of seasonal variations in funds flows. When cash flows are volatile, however, the interval may be shortened to a week.

> **Cash budgets** are indispensible as a planning tool when you manage a seasonal business for cash.

Preparation of the Cash Budget: Receipts

The key to the accuracy of most cash budgets is the **forecast of sales.** This forecast can be based on an internal analysis, an external one, or both. With an internal approach, sales representatives are asked to project sales for the forthcoming period. The product sales managers screen these estimates and consolidate them into sales estimates for product lines. The estimates for the various product lines then are combined into an overall sales estimate for the firm. The basic problem with an internal approach is that it can be myopic. Significant trends in the economy and in the industry are often overlooked.

For this reason, many companies use an external analysis as well. With an external approach, economic analysts make forecasts of the economy and of industry sales for several years to come. They may use regression analysis to estimate the association between industry sales and the economy in general. After these basic predictions of business conditions and industry sales, the next step is to estimate market share by individual products, prices that are likely to prevail, and the expected reception of new products. Usually, these estimates are made in conjunction with marketing managers, but the ultimate responsibility should lie with the economic forecasting department. From this information, an external forecast of sales can be prepared.

When the internal forecast of sales differs from the external one, as it is likely to do, a compromise must be reached. Past experience will show which of the two forecasts is more accurate. In general, the external forecast should serve as the foundation for the final sales forecast, often modified by the internal forecast. A final sales forecast based on both internal and external analyses is usually more accurate than either an internal or an external forecast by itself. The final sales forecast should be based on prospective demand, not modified initially by internal constraints, such as physical capacity. The decision to remove these constraints will depend on the forecast. The value of accurate sales forecasts cannot be overestimated for most of the other forecasts, in some measure, are based on expected sales.

Sales to Cash Receipts   With the sales forecast out of the way, the next job is to determine the cash receipts from these sales. For cash sales, cash is received at the time of the sale; for credit sales, receipts do not come until later. How much later will depend on the billing terms given, the type of customer, and the credit and collection policies of the firm. The Continental Sheetmetal Company offers terms of net 30, meaning that payment is due within 30 days after the invoice date. In the company's experience, 90 percent of receivables are collected, on the average, 1 month from the date of the sale, and 10 percent are collected 2 months from the date of the sale, with no bad-debt losses. Moreover, on the average, 10 percent of total sales are cash sales.

If the sales forecasts are those shown in the first line of Table 13-3, we can compute a schedule of the expected sales receipts based on the foregoing assumptions. This schedule appears in Table 13-3. For January, we see that total sales are estimated to be $250,000, of which $25,000 are cash sales. Of the $225,000 in credit sales, 90 percent, or $202,500, are expected to be collected in February, and 10 percent, or $22,500, are expected to be collected in March. Similarly, sales in other months are estimated according to the same percentages. The firm should be ready to change its assumptions with respect to collections when there is an underlying shift in the payment habits of its customers.

From this example, it is easy to see the effect of a variation in sales on the magnitude and timing of cash receipts, all other things being held constant. For most companies, there is a degree of correlation between sales and collection experience. In times of recession and sales decline, the average collection period is likely to lengthen; bad-debt losses are likely to increase. Thus, the collection experience of a firm may reinforce a decline in sales and magnify the downward impact on total sales receipts.

Other Receipts   In addition to the collection of sales from a product or service, cash receipts may arise from the sale of assets, from sale of stock, from a debt issue, from a tax refund, and from fee income. For the most part, things of this sort are planned in advance and are predictable for purposes of cash budgeting. Suppose that Continental Sheetmetal intends to sell $40,000 of used equipment in February. As a result, cash receipts in that month are $254,000 from Table 13-3 plus $40,000, or $294,000 in total.

TABLE 13-3
Schedule of Sales Receipts (in thousands)

	Nov.	Dec.	Jan.	Feb.	Mar.	Apr.	May	June
Total sales	$300.0	$350.0	$250.0	$200.0	$250.0	$300.0	$350.0	$380.0
Credit sales	270.0	315.0	225.0	180.0	225.0	270.0	315.0	342.0
Collections, 1 month		243.0	283.5	202.5	162.0	202.5	243.0	283.5
Collections, 2 months			27.0	31.5	22.5	18.0	22.5	27.0
Total collections			$310.5	$234.0	$184.5	$220.5	$265.5	$310.5
Cash sales			25.0	20.0	25.0	30.0	35.0	38.0
Total sales receipts			$335.5	$254.0	$209.5	$250.5	$300.5	$348.5

Receivable Collection Period

Digressing for the moment, consider now how collection forecasts might be set up for cash budgeting purposes. In our example, we assumed 90 percent of credit sales in a given month was collected 1 month later and that 10 percent was collected 2 months later. If credit sales are steady throughout the month and each month has 30 days, this corresponds to an average collection period of 33 days (the weighted average of 30 and 60 days). If the average collection period were 30 days, all credit sales would be collected 1 month later. That is, the $315,000 in December credit sales would be collected in January, and so forth. If the average collection period were 60 days, of course, collections would be lagged 2 months, so that the $315,000 in December would be collected in February.

> **Different lags** in the collections of sales result when the average collections period assumption is changed.

If the average collection period were 45 days, however, one-half of December credit sales, or $157,500, would be collected in January and the other half in February. The assumption is that credit sales billed in the first half of December will be collected in the last half of January, and sales billed in the last half of December will be collected in the first half of February. Other months will reflect this lag structure as well. If the average collection period were 40 days, it is implied that two-thirds of December sales, or $210,000, will be collected in January and that one-third, or $105,000, will be collected in February. The weighted average of $(\frac{2}{3} \times 30 \text{ days}) + (\frac{1}{3} \times 60 \text{ days})$ equals 40 days.

By similar reasoning, an average collection period of 50 days means that one-third of December credit sales, or $105,000, will be collected in January and two-thirds, or $210,000, will be collected in February. Similarly, the 30-day month can be divided into fifths, sixths, tenths, fifteenths, and thirtieths to come to grips with other average collection periods. The situation for tenths was illustrated in our example. Finally, if the average collection period were 37 days, the implication is that 23/30 of December credit sales, or $241,500, will be collected in January, while 7/30, or $73,500, will be collected in February. These are enough examples to illustrate the effect of a change in average collection period assumptions on collections. With a computer-based spreadsheet program, it is an easy matter to set up lagged collections for credit sales.

Forecasting Disbursements

Next comes a forecast of cash disbursements. Given the sales forecast, management may choose to gear production closely to seasonal sales, to produce at a relatively constant rate over time, or to have a mixed production strategy. Once a production schedule has been established, estimates can be made of the needs in materials, labor, and additional fixed assets. As with receivables, there is a lag between the time a purchase is made and the time of actual cash payment. If suppliers give average billing terms of net 30 and the company's policy is to pay its bills at the end of this period, there is approximately a 1-month lag between a purchase and the payment. If the production program of Continental Sheetmetal calls for the manufacture of goods in the month preceding forecasted sales, we might have a schedule like that in Table 13-4. As we see, there is a 1-month lag between the time of purchase and the payment for the purchase. As with the collection of receivables, payment for purchases can be lagged for other average payable periods. The setup is the same as illustrated for collections, and the lagged structure is facilitated using a computer-based spreadsheet program.

Wages are assumed to increase with the amount of production. Generally, wages are more stable over time than are purchases. When production dips slightly, workers usually are not laid off. When production picks up, labor becomes more efficient with relatively little increase in total wages. Only after a certain point is overtime work required or do new workers have to be hired to meet the increased production schedule. Included in other expenses are general, administrative, and selling expenses; property taxes; interest expenses; power, light, and heat expenses; maintenance expenses; and indirect labor and material expenses. These expenses tend to be reasonably predictable over the short run.

In addition to cash expenses, we must take into account capital expenditures, dividends, federal income taxes, and any other cash outflows. Because capital expenditures are planned in advance, they usually are predictable for the short-term cash budget. As the forecast becomes more distant, however, prediction of these expenditures becomes less certain. Dividend payments for most companies are stable and are paid on specific dates. Estimation of federal income taxes must be based on projected profits for the period under review. Other cash outlays might consist of the repurchase of stock or payment of long-term debt. These outlays are combined with total cash expenses to obtain the schedule of total cash disbursements shown in Table 13-5.

TABLE 13-4
Schedule of Disbursements for Purchases and Expenses (in thousands)

	Dec.	Jan.	Feb.	Mar.	Apr.	May	June
Purchases	$100	$ 80	$100	$120	$140	$150	$150
Cash payment for purchases		100	80	100	120	140	150
Wages		80	80	90	90	95	100
Other expenses		50	50	50	50	50	50
Total cash expenses		$230	$210	$240	$260	$285	$300

TABLE 13-5
Schedule of Cash Disbursements (in thousands)

	Jan.	Feb.	Mar.	Apr.	May	June
Total cash expenses	$230	$210	$240	$260	$285	$300
Capital expenditures		150	50			
Dividend payments				20		20
Income taxes	30			30		
Total cash disbursements	$260	$360	$310	$290	$285	$320

Net Cash Flow and Cash Balance

Once we are satisfied that we have taken into account all foreseeable cash inflows and outflows, we combine the cash receipts and cash disbursements schedules to obtain the net cash inflow or outflow for each month. The net cash flow may then be added to beginning cash in January, which is assumed to be $100,000, and the projected cash position computed month by month for the period under review. This final schedule is shown in Table 13-6.

The cash budget shown indicates that the company is expected to have a cash deficit in April and May. Its deficit is caused by a decline in collections through March, capital expenditures totaling $200,000 in February and March, and a cash dividend of $20,000 in March. With the increase in collections in May and June, the cash balance without financing rises to $13,500 in June. The cash budget indicates that peak cash requirements occur in April. If the firm has a policy of maintaining a minimum cash balance of $75,000 and of borrowing from its bank to maintain this minimum, it will need to borrow an additional $66,000 in March. Additional borrowings will peak at $105,500 in April, after which they will decline to $61,500 in June, if all goes according to prediction.

Alternative means of meeting the cash deficit are available. The firm may be able to delay its capital expenditures or its payments for purchases. Indeed, one of the principal purposes of a cash budget is to determine the timing and magnitude of prospective financing needs, so that the most appropriate method of financing can be arranged. When financing is not needed, the cash budget enables one to plan for the efficient transfer of excess funds from cash to marketable securities.

TABLE 13-6
Net Cash Flow and Cash Balance (in thousands)

	Jan.	Feb.	Mar.	Apr.	May	June
Total cash receipts	$335.5	$294.0*	$ 209.5	$250.5	$300.5	$348.5
Total cash disbursements	260.0	360.0	310.0	290.0	285.0	320.0
Net cash flow	$ 75.5	$ (66.0)	$(100.5)	$ (39.5)	$ 15.5	$ 28.5
Beginning cash without financing	100.0	175.5	109.5	9.0	(30.5)	(15.0)
Ending cash without financing	175.5	109.5	9.0	(30.5)	(15.0)	13.5

*Includes sales receipts of $254,000 and cash sale of assets of $40,000.

Deviations from Expected Cash Flows

Often there is a tendency to place considerable faith in the cash budget simply because it is expressed in numbers. We stress again that a cash budget represents merely an *estimate* of future cash flows. Depending on the care devoted to preparing the budget and the volatility of cash flows resulting from the nature of the business, actual cash flows will deviate more or less widely from those that were expected. In the face of uncertainty, we must provide information about the range of possible outcomes. Analyzing cash flows under only one set of assumptions, as is the case with conventional cash budgeting, results in a faulty perspective of the future.

To take into account deviations from expected cash flows, it is desirable to work out additional cash budgets. We might want to base one cash forecast on the assumption of a maximum probable decline in business and another on the assumption of the maximum probable increase in business. With a spreadsheet program, it is a simple matter to change assumptions and produce a new ending cash row in Table 13-6.

The final product of these simulations might be a series of distributions of end-of-the-month cash without financing. Figure 13-2 shows relative frequency distributions for the months of January through June. Bar graphs are used, as these are usually the product of a simulation. The most likely values of ending cash are depicted by the highest bar; these conform with the values shown in Table 13-6. We note that although several of the distributions are reasonably symmetrical, others are skewed. In particular, the distributions for March and April are skewed to the left. As a result, the need for cash during these months might be considerably greater than that depicted in Table 13-6. It is clear that the type of information portrayed in Fig. 13-2 better enables management to plan for contingencies than does information giving only single-point estimates of monthly cash flows.

From the standpoint of internal planning, it is far better to allow for a range of possible outcomes than to rely solely on the expected outcome. This allowance is particularly necessary for firms whose business is relatively unstable. If a company bases its plans on only expected cash flows, it is likely to be caught flat-footed if there is a significant deviation from the expected outcome. An unforeseen deficit in cash may be difficult to finance on short notice. Therefore, it is essential for the firm to be honest with itself and attempt to minimize the costs associated with deviations from expected outcomes. It may do this by taking the steps necessary to ensure accuracy and by preparing additional cash budgets to take into account the range of possible outcomes.

PRO FORMA STATEMENTS

Pro forma statements project forward the balance sheet and income statement.

In addition to projecting the cash flow of a firm over time, it often is useful to prepare a projected, or **pro forma,** balance sheet and income statement for selected future dates. A cash budget gives us information about only the prospective future cash positions of the firm, whereas pro forma statements embody forecasts of all assets and liabilities as well as of income statement items. Much of the information that goes into the preparation of the cash budget, however, can be used to derive a pro forma statement. As before, the key to accuracy is the sales forecasts.

Pro Forma Income Statement

The pro forma income statement is a projection of income for a period of time in the future. As was true of our cash budget, the sales forecast is the key to scheduling production and estimating production costs. The analyst may wish to evaluate each component of the cost of goods sold. A detailed analysis of purchases, pro-

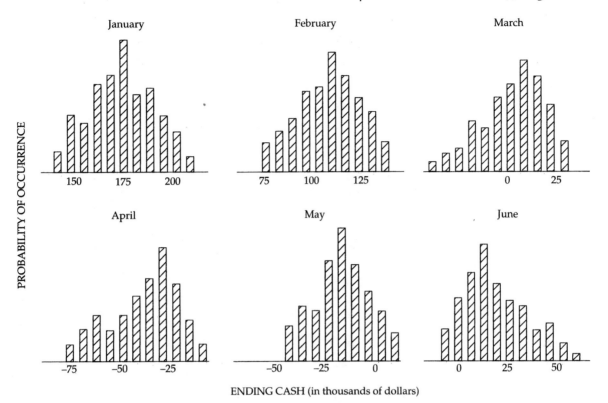

FIGURE 13-2
Distribution of ending cash

duction wages, and overhead costs is likely to produce the most accurate forecasts. Often, however, costs of goods sold are estimated on the basis of past ratios of costs of goods sold to sales.

Selling, general, and administrative expenses are estimated next. Because these expenses usually are budgeted in advance, estimates of them are fairly accurate. Typically, these expenses are not overly sensitive to changes in sales in the very short run, particularly to reductions in sales. Next, we estimate other income and expenses as well as interest expenses to obtain net income before taxes. Income taxes are then computed—based on the applicable tax rate—and deducted, to arrive at estimated net income after taxes. All of these estimates are then combined into an income statement.

Continuing Our Illustration To illustrate for Continental Sheetmetal Company, suppose projected sales for January through June in Table 13-3 are $1,730,000, as reflected in our cash budget in Table 13-3. In the cash budget, the cost of goods sold is not depicted directly. However, we know that purchases fall into this category. For financial statement purposes, the purchases associated with January through June sales are those for December through May, because production occurs in the month preceding forecasted sales. Purchases are shown in Table 13-4, and they total $690,000 for December through May. Wages also are a cost of goods sold, and here, too, the relevant period for financial statement purposes is December through May. For this period, wages totaling $505,000 are expected to be paid (see Table 13-4). We stated earlier that depreciation of $110,000 was expected for the January–June period. Other expenses (selling, general, and administrative) are expected to be $50,000 a month and are also shown in Table 13-4. For the 6-month period they total $300,000. Finally, assume an income tax rate of 40 percent. Given this information, we can derive a **pro forma income statement** for the January–June period (in thousands):

Sales		$1,730
Cost of goods sold		
Purchases	$690	
Wages	505	
Depreciation	110	$1,305
Gross profit		425
Selling, general, and administrative		
expenses		300
Profit before taxes		125
Taxes		50
Profit after taxes		$ 75

The pro forma income statement need not be based on a cash budget. Instead, one can make direct estimates of all the items. By first estimating a sales level, one can multiply historical ratios of cost of goods sold and various expense items by the level in order to derive the statement. Where historical ratios are no longer appropriate, new estimates should be employed.

Pro Forma Balance Sheet

Let us prepare a pro forma balance sheet for Continental Sheetmetal for June 30. The company has the following balance sheet at December 31 (in thousands):

Assets		Liabilities	
Cash	$ 100	Bank borrowings	$ 50
Receivables	342	Accounts payable	200
Inventory	350	Accrued wages and expenses	250
Current assets	$ 792	Income taxes payable	70
		Current liabilities	$ 570
Net fixed assets	800	Shareholders' equity	1,022
Total assets	$1,592	Total liabilities and equity	$1,592

Receivables at June 30 can be estimated by adding to the receivable balance at December 31 the total projected credit sales from January through June, less total projected credit collections for the period. On the basis of the information in the cash budget, receivables at June 30 would be $342,000 + $31,500, or $373,500.

Estimates Based on Turnover If a cash budget is not available, the receivable balance may be estimated on the basis of a turnover ratio. This ratio, which depicts the relationship between credit sales and receivables, should be based on past experience. To obtain the estimated level of receivables, projected sales are simply divided by the turnover ratio. If the sales forecast and turnover ratio are realistic, the method will produce a reasonable approximation of the receivable balance. The estimated investment in inventories at June 30 may be based on the production schedule, which, in turn, is based on the sales forecast. This schedule should show expected purchases, the expected use of inventory in production, and the expected level of finished goods. On the basis of this information, together with the beginning inventory level, a pro forma estimate of inventory can be made.

Rather than use the production schedule, estimates of future inventory can be based on a turnover ratio of cost of goods sold to inventory. This ratio is applied in the same manner as for receivables, except that we solve for the ending inventory position that emanates from the average. We have

$$\frac{\text{Cost of goods sold}}{(\text{Beginning} + \text{Ending inventory})/2} = \frac{\text{Turnover}}{\text{ratio}} \qquad (13\text{-}1)$$

Given an assumed turnover ratio and assumed cost of goods sold figure, and knowing the beginning inventory, we rearrange the equation to solve for the unknown:

$$\text{Ending inventory} = \frac{2(\text{C of GS})}{\text{Turnover ratio}} - \text{Beginning inventory}$$

If the estimated inventory turnover ratio in our example were 3.39 and the estimated cost of goods sold were $1,305,000, we would have (with rounding)

$$\text{Ending inventory} = \frac{2(1,305,000)}{3.39} - 350,000 = \$420,000$$

Thus, $420,000 would be our estimate of inventory on June 30, a figure that represents a moderate increase over the inventory level of December 31, in keeping with the buildup in sales.

Fixed Asset Estimate   Future net fixed assets are estimated by adding planned expenditures to existing net fixed assets and subtracting from this sum depreciation for the period, plus any sale of fixed assets at book value. From the cash budget, we note that capital expenditures are estimated at $200,000 over the period and that $40,000 in fixed assets will be sold at what we assume to be their depreciated book values. If depreciation for the period is expected to be $110,000, the expected net addition to fixed assets would be $50,000, ($200,000 − $40,000 − $110,000), and projected net fixed assets at June 30 would be $850,000. Because capital expenditures are planned in advance, fixed assets generally are fairly easy to forecast.

Liability Estimates   Turning now to the liabilities, we estimate accounts payable by adding total projected purchases for January through June, less total projected cash payments for purchases for the period, to the December 31 balance. Our estimate of accounts payable, therefore, is $200,000 + $50,000, or $250,000. The calculation of accrued wages and expenses is based on the production schedule and the historical relationship between these accruals and production. We assume the estimate of accrued wages and expenses to be $240,000. Income taxes payable are estimated by adding to the current balance taxes on forecasted income for the 6-

month period, less the actual payment of taxes. If income taxes for the period are forecast at $50,000, and Continental Sheetmetal is scheduled to make $60,000 in actual payments, estimated accrued income taxes at June 30 would be $60,000 ($70,000 beginning balance + $50,000 − $60,000).

Equity, Cash, and Borrowing Estimates   Shareholders' equity at June 30 would be that at December 31 plus profits after taxes for the period, less the amount of cash dividends to be paid. Assuming $75,000 in after-tax profits from the pro forma income statement, shareholders' equity at June 30 would be $1,022,000 plus $75,000 minus dividends of $40,000, or $1,057,000. Two items remain: cash and bank loans. We see from the cash budget that estimated cash at June 30 would be $13,500 without additional financing. If the firm has the policy of maintaining a minimum cash balance of $75,000, and borrowing from its bank to maintain this balance, cash at June 30 would be $75,000, and bank borrowings would increase by $61,500 to $111,500. In general, cash and notes payable serve as balancing factors in the preparation of pro forma balance sheets, whereby assets and liabilities plus shareholders' equity are brought into balance.

Putting It Together   Once we have estimated all the components, they are combined into a balance sheet format. The pro forma balance sheet at June 30 for Continental Sheetmetal is (in thousands)

Assets		Liabilities	
Cash	$ 75.0	Bank borrowings	$ 111.5
Receivables	373.5	Accounts payable	250.0
Inventory	420.0	Accrued wages and expenses	240.0
		Income taxes payable	60.0
Current assets	$ 868.5	Current liabilities	$ 661.5
Net fixed assets	850.0	Shareholders' equity	1,057.0
Total	$1,718.5	Total	$1,718.5

Use of Ratios and Implications

As before, the cash budget method is but one way to prepare a pro forma statement. One can also make direct estimates of all the items on the balance sheet by projecting financial ratios into the future and then making estimates on the basis of these ratios. Receivables, inventories, accounts payable, and accrued wages and expenses are frequently based on historical relationships to sales and production when a cash budget is not available. For example, if the average collection period is 45 days, turnover would be eight times a year. If receivables were $500,000 but the firm were predicting a $2 million increase in sales for the coming year, it would take approximately $2 million/8 = $250,000 in additional receivables to support the added sales. Thus, the level of receivables 1 year hence might be forecast at $750,000.

Pro forma statements allow us to study the composition of expected future balance sheets and income statements. Financial ratios may be computed for analysis of the statements; these ratios and the raw figures may be compared with those for present and past balance sheets. Using this information, the financial manager can analyze the direction of change in the financial condition and performance of the firm over the past, present, and future. If the firm is accustomed to making accurate estimates, the preparation of a cash budget, pro forma statements, or both literally forces it to plan ahead and to coordinate policy in the various areas of operation. Continual revision of these forecasts keeps the firm alert to changing conditions in its environment and in its internal operations. Again, it is useful to prepare more than one set of pro forma statements to take into account the range of possible outcomes.

SUSTAINABLE GROWTH MODELING

Sustainable growth rate is the maximum percent increase in sales that is possible, given a set of target financial and operating ratios.

The management of growth requires careful balancing of the sales objectives of the firm with its operating efficiency and financial resources. Many a company overreaches itself financially at the altar of growth; the bankruptcy courts are filled with such cases. The trick is to determine what sales growth rate is consistent with the realities of the company and of the financial marketplace. In this regard, sustainable growth modeling is a powerful planning tool and has found enthusiastic use in companies like Hewlett-Packard. In the way of definition, the **sustainable growth rate (SGR)** is the maximum annual percentage increase in sales that can be achieved based on target operating, debt, and dividend-payout ratios. If actual growth exceeds the SGR, something must give, and frequently it is the debt ratio. By modeling the process of growth, we are able to make intelligent trade-offs.

Steady-State Model

To illustrate the calculation of a sustainable growth rate, we begin with a steady-state model where the future is exactly like the past with respect to balance sheet and performance ratios. Assumed also is that the firm engages in no external equity financing; the equity account builds only through earnings retention. Both of these assumptions will later be relaxed when we consider sustainable growth modeling under changing assumptions.

Variables Employed In a steady-state environment, the variables necessary to determine the sustainable growth rate are

$$A/S = \text{total assets-to-sales ratio}$$
$$NP/S = \text{net profit margin (net profits divided by sales)}$$
$$b = \text{retention rate of earnings } (1 - b \text{ is the dividend-payout ratio})$$
$$D/Eq. = \text{debt-to-equity ratio}$$
$$S_0 = \text{most recent annual sales (beginning sales)}$$
$$\Delta S = \text{absolute change in sales from the most recent annual sales}$$

The first four variables are target variables. The total assets-to-sales ratio is a measure of operating efficiency, the reciprocal of the traditional asset turnover ratio. The lower the ratio, the more efficient the utilization of assets. In turn, this ratio is a composite of (1) receivable management, as depicted by the average collection period; (2) inventory management, as indicated by the inventory turnover ratio; (3) fixed-asset management, as reflected by the throughput of product through the plant; and (4) liquidity management, as suggested by the proportion of and return on liquid assets. For purposes of illustration, we assume liquid assets are kept at moderate levels.[1]

---

[1]If this is not the case, it may be better to use the operating-assets-to-sales ratio.

The net profit margin is a relative measure of operating efficiency, after taking account of all expenses and income taxes. Though both the assets-to-sales ratio and the net profit margin are affected by the external product markets, they largely capture internal management efficiency. The earnings retention rate and the debt ratio should be determined in keeping with dividend and capital structure theory and practice. They are influenced importantly by the external financial markets. Our purpose is not to touch on how they are established, as that is done elsewhere in this book, but to incorporate them in the planning model presented.

Sustainable Growth Rate With these variables, we can derive the sustainable growth rate (SGR). The idea is that an increase in assets (a use of funds) must equal the increase in liabilities and shareholders' equity (a source of funds). The increase in assets can be expressed as ΔS (A/S), the change in sales times the total assets-to-sales ratio. The increase in shareholders' equity (through retained earnings) is $b(NP/S)(S_0 + \Delta S)$, or the retention rate times the net profit margin times total sales. Finally, the increase in total debt is simply the equity increase multiplied by the target debt-to-equity ratio, or $[b(NP/S)(S_0 + \Delta S)]\, D/Eq.$ Putting these things together, we have[2]

$$\Delta S\left(\frac{A}{S}\right) = b\left(\frac{NP}{S}\right)(S_0 + \Delta S) + \left[b\left(\frac{NP}{S}\right)(S_0 + \Delta S)\right]\frac{D}{Eq.} \qquad (13\text{-}2)$$

Asset   Retained
increase   earnings   Increase in
increase   debt

By rearrangement, this equation can be expressed as[3]

$$\frac{\Delta S}{S_0} \text{ or SGR} = \frac{b\left(\dfrac{NP}{S}\right)\left(1 + \dfrac{D}{Eq.}\right)}{\left(\dfrac{A}{S}\right) - \left[b\left(\dfrac{NP}{S}\right)\left(1 + \dfrac{D}{Eq.}\right)\right]} \qquad (13\text{-}3)$$

---

[2]This is the same formulation as in Robert C. Higgins, *Analysis for Financial Management* (Homewood, IL: Richard D. Irwin, 1984), chap. 5.

[3]Equation (13-2) can be expressed as

$$\Delta S\left(\frac{A}{S}\right) = b\left(\frac{NP}{S}\right)(S_0 + \Delta S)\left(1 + \frac{D}{Eq.}\right)$$

$$\Delta S\left(\frac{A}{S}\right) = b\left(\frac{NP}{S}\right)\left(1 + \frac{D}{Eq.}\right)S_0 + b\left(\frac{NP}{S}\right)\left(1 + \frac{D}{Eq.}\right)\Delta S$$

$$\Delta S\left(\frac{A}{S}\right) - b\left(\frac{NP}{S}\right)\left(1 + \frac{D}{Eq.}\right)\Delta S = b\left(\frac{NP}{S}\right)\left(1 + \frac{D}{Eq.}\right)S_0$$

$$\Delta S\left[\left(\frac{A}{S}\right) - b\left(\frac{NP}{S}\right)\left(1 + \frac{D}{Eq.}\right)\right] = b\left(\frac{NP}{S}\right)\left(1 + \frac{D}{Eq.}\right)S_0$$

$$\frac{\Delta S}{S_0} = \frac{b\left(\dfrac{NP}{S}\right)\left(1 + \dfrac{D}{Eq.}\right)}{\left(\dfrac{A}{S}\right) - \left[b\left(\dfrac{NP}{S}\right)\left(1 + \dfrac{D}{Eq.}\right)\right]}$$

TABLE 13-7

Initial Inputs and Variables Used to Illustrate Sustainable Growth Rates

Symbol	Initial Input and/or Variable	
$Eq._0$	Beginning equity capital (in millions)	$100
$Debt_0$	Beginning debt (in millions)	$ 80
$Sales_0$	Sales the previous year (in millions)	$300
b	Target earnings retention rate	.70
NP/S	Target net profit margin	.04
$D/Eq.$	Target debt-to-equity ratio	.80
A/S	Target assets-to-sales ratio	.60

This is the maximum rate of growth in sales that is consistent with the target ratios. Whether or not this growth rate can be achieved, of course, depends on the external product markets and on the firm's marketing efforts. A particular growth rate may be feasible financially, but the product demand simply may not be there. Implicit in the formulations presented is that depreciation charges are sufficient to maintain the value of operating assets. A final caveat has to do with interest on new borrowings. The implicit assumption is that all interest expenses are incorporated in the target net profit margin. Although it would be possible to specify interest costs separately, it complicates the modeling considerably with simultaneous equations. As sustainable growth modeling is a broad-gauged planning tool, we will skirt this dimension.

Illustration Suppose a company were characterized by the data shown in Table 13-7. If this were the case, the sustainable growth rate would be

$$SGR = \frac{.70(.04)(1.80)}{.60 - [.70(.04)(1.80)]} = 9.17\%$$

Thus, 9.17 percent is the sales growth rate consistent with the steady-state variables shown in Table 13-7. It can be demonstrated that initial equity increases by 9.17 percent to $109.17 and that debt grows by 9.17 percent to $87.34, as everything increases in stable equilibrium. If the actual growth rate is other than 9.17 percent, however, one or more of the variables must change. In other words, operating efficiency, leverage, or earnings retention must change or there must be the sale or repurchase of stock.

Modeling under Changing Assumptions

Most situations do not conform to steady-state modeling, so year-by-year modeling is in order.

To see what happens when we move from steady state, and variables change from year to year, we must model sustainable growth in a different way. In effect, the sales the previous year and equity at the previous year end serve as foundations on which to build **year-by-year modeling.** Also, we express dividends in terms of the absolute amount that a company wishes to pay, as opposed to a payout ratio. Finally, we allow for the sale of common stock in a given year, though this can be specified as zero.

With these variables, the sustainable growth rate in sales for the next year, SGR in decimal form, becomes

$$SGR = \left[\frac{(Eq._0 + \text{New Eq.} - \text{Div.})\left(1 + \dfrac{D}{Eq.}\right)\left(\dfrac{S}{A}\right)}{1 - \left[\left(\dfrac{NP}{S}\right)\left(1 + \dfrac{D}{Eq.}\right)\left(\dfrac{S}{A}\right)\right]} \right]\left[\frac{1}{S_0}\right] - 1 \qquad (13\text{-}4)$$

where New Eq. is the amount of new equity capital raised, Div. is the absolute amount of annual dividend, and S/A is the sales-to-total-assets ratio. The latter is simply the reciprocal of the assets-to-sales ratio that we used before. Intuitively, the numerator in the first bracket in Eq. (13-4) represents the sales that could occur on the basis of existing capital plus any change occasioned by common stock sales or dividends. The equity base is expanded by the debt employed and then multiplied by the sales-to-asset ratio. The denominator in the first bracket is 1 minus the target earning power of the company, $(NP/S)\,(S/A)$, magnified by the proportion of debt employed. When the numerator is divided by the denominator, we obtain the new level of sales that can be achieved. In the last bracket, we divide this new level by beginning sales to determine the change in sales that is sustainable for the next year.

Our Earlier Illustration   To illustrate, suppose the target dividend were $3.93 million, no new equity issuance was planned, and the other variables in Table 13-7 held. The sustainable growth rate, using Eq. (13-4), is

$$SGR = \left[\frac{(100 - 3.93)\,(1.80)\,(1.6667)}{1 - [(.04)\,(1.80)\,(1.6667)]}\right]\left[\frac{1}{300}\right] - 1 = 9.17\%$$

This is exactly the same as computed with the steady-state model, Eq. (13-3), because a dividend of $3.93 million corresponds to an earnings retention rate of .70. Note also that an assets-to-sales ratio of .60 is the same as a sales-to-assets ratio of 1.6667.

Varying Our Assumptions   Suppose now that the target assets-to-sales ratio is .55 (a sales-to-assets ratio of 1.8182) instead of .60. Moreover, the target net profit margin is also better, .05 instead of .04. Finally, the target debt-to-equity ratio is moved from .80 to 1.00. Assuming a dividend of $4 million, the sustainable growth rate becomes

$$SGR = \left[\frac{(100 - 4)\,(2.00)\,(1.8182)}{1 - [(0.5)\,(2.00)\,(1.8182)]}\right]\left[\frac{1}{300}\right] - 1 = 42.22\%$$

This substantial increase in SGR is due to improved operating efficiency, which generates more retained earnings, and a higher debt ratio. It is important to recognize that the sales growth rate possible is for 1 year only. Even if operating efficiency continues on an improved basis, the debt ratio would have to increase continually to generate an SGR of 42.22 percent. The change in debt ratio affects all assets, not just the growth component.

To illustrate, suppose the debt-to-equity ratio were to remain at 1.00 and the other ratios also stayed the same. At the end of the year, we would be building from higher equity and sales bases:

$$S_1 = \$300\,(1.4222) = \$426.66$$
$$E_1 = \$300\,(1.4222)\,.05 - \$4 + 100 = \$117.33$$

The SGR for year 2 becomes

$$SGR_2 = \left[\frac{(117.333 - 4)\,(2.00)\,(1.8182)}{1 - [(.05)\,(2.00)\,(1.8182)]} \right] \left[\frac{1}{426.66} \right] - 1 = 18.06\%$$

Thus, the model produces the SGR year by year in a changing environment. Just because a high SGR is possible one year does not mean that this growth rate is sustainable in the future. In fact, it will not be sustainable unless further variable changes in the same direction occur. In this sense, it represents a one-shot occurrence.

Let us return to our earlier example that produced a 9.17 percent SGR under the assumptions of

$$NP/S = .04 \qquad S/A = 1.6667 \qquad D/Eq. = .80 \qquad Div. = \$3.93$$

If the company were to raise \$10 million in new equity capital, we would have

$$SGR = \left[\frac{(100 + 10 - 3.93)\,(1.80)\,(1.6667)}{1 - [(.04)\,(1.80)\,(1.6667)]} \right] \left[\frac{1}{300} \right] - 1 = 20.54\%$$

This SGR value is higher than earlier because of the new equity infusion, which, again, may be a one-shot occurrence. In summary, sustainable growth modeling year by year is considerably different from steady-state modeling.

Solving for Asset Turnover

With any five of the six variables, together with beginning equity and beginning sales, it is possible to solve for the sixth. For example, suppose we wished to determine the **assets-to-sales ratio** consistent with a growth in sales of 25 percent next year and the following other target variables:

$$NP/S = .05 \qquad D/Eq. = .50 \qquad Div. = \$4 \qquad New\ Eq. = \$10$$

The relevant formula is

$$\frac{S}{A} = \frac{(1 + SGR)S_0}{\left[1 + \dfrac{D}{Eq.} \right]\left[Eq._0 + New\ Eq. - Div. + \left(\dfrac{NP}{S} \right)(1 + SGR)\,S_0 \right]} \qquad (13\text{-}5)$$

and solving for our example, we have

$$\frac{S}{A} = \frac{(1.25)300}{[1.50]\,[100 + 10 - 4 + (.05)\,(1.25)\,300]} = 2.00$$

$$\frac{A}{S} = 1/2.00 = .50$$

This suggests that the company will need to have an assets-to-sales ratio of .50 if it is to grow at a 25 percent rate next year. This assumes a 5 percent net profit margin and the sale of \$10 million in new equity capital.

Assets-to-sales is a sensitive driver of the sustainable growth rate for capital-intensive businesses.

Solving for the Debt Ratio

If a sales growth rate of 25 percent is again desired but a sales-to-assets ratio of 1.70 is all that is likely (assets-to-sales ratio of .5882), we might be interested in the **debt-to-equity ratio** consistent with this and the other variables. The relevant formula is

$$\frac{D}{Eq.} = \frac{(1 + SGR)\, S_0}{\left[Eq._0 + \text{New Eq.} - \text{Div.} + \left(\frac{NP}{S}\right)(1 + SGR)\, S_0 \right]\left[\frac{S}{A}\right]} - 1 \qquad (13\text{-}6)$$

For our example

$$\frac{D}{Eq.} = \frac{(1.25)\, 300}{[100 + 10 - 4 + (.05)\,(1.25)\,300]\,[1.70]} - 1 = .7682$$

If the sales-to-assets ratio were 1.70 instead of 2.00, an increase in debt ratio from .50 to .7682 would be necessary to sustain a growth in sales of 25 percent next year. Thus, the sales-to-assets ratio and the debt-to-equity ratio have powerful effects on the results.

Solving for the Net Profit Margin

Suppose the company wished to grow at 20 percent in sales, raise no new equity capital, and had other target variables of

$$S/A = 1.90 \qquad D/Eq. = .60 \qquad \text{Div.} = \$4$$

It now wishes to determine the **net profit margin** it would need to achieve to make this happen. The formula is

$$\frac{NP}{S} = 1 \bigg/ \left(1 + \frac{D}{Eq.}\right)\left(\frac{S}{A}\right) - \frac{(Eq._0 + \text{New Eq.} - \text{Div.})}{(1 + SGR)\, S_0} \qquad (13\text{-}7)$$

which, for our example, becomes

$$\frac{NP}{S} = \frac{1}{(1.60)\,(1.90)} - \frac{(100 - 4)}{(1.20)\,300} = .0623$$

To achieve a 20 percent growth in sales in the face of no new equity financing, the net profit margin needs to be 6.23 percent.

Solving for the Dividend

The **dividend,** if treated as a residual in a sustainable growth model, can be determined with the following formula:

$$\text{Div.} = \left[Eq._0 + \left(\frac{NP}{S}\right)(1 + SGR)S_0 + \text{New Eq.} \right] - \frac{(1 + SGR)S_0}{\left(1 + \frac{D}{Eq.}\right)\left(\frac{S}{A}\right)} \qquad (13\text{-}8)$$

Suppose that our company wishes to grow sales by 25 percent and has the following other target variables:

$$S/A = 1.85 \qquad D/Eq. = .70 \qquad NP/S = .05 \qquad \text{New Eq.} = \$10$$

Using Eq. (13-8), the dividend possible is

$$\text{Div.} = 100 + (.05)(1.25)\,300 + 10 - \frac{(1.25)\,300}{(1.70)\,1.85}$$

$$= \$9.51$$

With new equity of \$10, the company would be able to pay a dividend of almost this amount.

Solving for New Equity

For the sake of completeness, we consider the remaining variable, the sale of **new equity.** Like the dividend, this becomes a residual once we know the other five. The formula is

$$\text{New Eq.} = \frac{(1 + \text{SGR})S_0}{\left(1 + \dfrac{D}{Eq.}\right)\left(\dfrac{S}{A}\right)} - Eq._0 - \left(\frac{NP}{S}\right)(1 + \text{SGR})S_0 + \text{Div.} \qquad (13\text{-}9)$$

Suppose the company still wanted to grow at a 25 percent rate, but the other target variables were

$$S/A = 1.8 \qquad D/Eq. = .60 \qquad NP/S = .04 \qquad \text{Div.} = \$4$$

Solving for new equity required to sustain sales growth while being consistent with the other target variables

$$\text{New Eq.} = \frac{(1.25)\,300}{(1.6)(1.8)} - 100 - [(.04)(1.25)\,300] + 4 = \$19.21$$

Thus, a sizable equity infusion is necessary to sustain a 25 percent increase in sales. This is due to a lower debt/equity ratio, a slightly lower asset turnover, and a lower net profit margin than were assumed in the dividend example.

Implications

By simulation, then, one is able to gain insight into the sensitivity of certain variables in the overall growth picture. By programming the formulas presented, these simulations can be made with ease. For most situations we are interested in the first four target variables and their sensitivity. Usually, the dividend and any new equity are taken as given. When not, we can solve for them in the manner illustrated. In Table 13-8, certain simulations are shown where the missing variables for which we solve are boxed.

To grow in a stable, balanced way, the equity base must grow proportionally with sales. When this is not the case, one or more of the financial ratios must change in order for the divergence in the two growth rates to be accommodated. By putting things into a sustainable growth model, we are able to check the consistency of various growth plans. Often in corporate planning the company wants a number of good things: high sales growth, manufacturing flexibility, moderate use of debt, and high dividends. However, these things may be inconsistent with one another.

TABLE 13-8
Simulations Using Sustainable Growth Modeling*

Variable	1	2	3	4	5	6	7	8	9	10	11	12	13
A/S	.60	.60	.55	.50	.65	.70	.50	.4292	.5263	.60	.5882	.60	.60
NP/S	.04	.04	.05	.05	.035	.03	.05	.04	.0623	.0538	.05	.04	.04
D/E	.80	.80	1.00	.50	.80	.80	.50	.50	.60	1.00	.7682	1.0272	1.1659
Div.	4.00	4.00	4.00	4.00	4.00	4.00	4.00	4.00	4.00	4.00	4.00	4.00	4.00
New Eq.	0	10.00	0	0	5.00	0	10.00	0	0	0	10.00	0	0
SGR	.0909	.2046	.4222	.1294	.0325	−.1083	.25	.30	.20	.30	.25	.25	.35

*Beginning sales = $300, beginning equity = $100.

Sustainable growth modeling enables one to check for such inconsistency. In this way, more informed and wiser marketing, finance, and manufacturing decisions can be reached. Sustainable growth modeling provides an integrative tool for helping the decision-making process. With the current emphasis in corporations on return on assets and on asset management, such modeling can play an integral part.

Summary

Continuing our examination of the analytical tools of the financial manager, we looked at source and use of funds statements, the cash budget, pro forma statements, and sustainable growth modeling. The funds statement on a cash basis (either a traditional sources and uses statement or an accounting statement of cash flows) gives the financial analyst considerable insight into the uses of funds and how these uses are financed over a specific period of time. Funds-flow analysis is valuable in analyzing the commitment of funds to assets and in planning the firm's intermediate- and long-term financing. The flow of funds studied, however, represents net rather than gross transactions between two points in time.

A cash budget is a forecast of the future cash receipts and cash disbursements of a firm. This forecast is particularly useful to the financial manager in determining the probable cash balances of a company in the near future and in planning for the financing of prospective cash needs. In addition to analyzing expected cash flows, the financial manager should take into account possible deviations from the ex-

pected outcome. An analysis of the range of possible outcomes enables management to better assess the efficiency and flexibility of the firm and to determine the appropriate margin of safety.

We considered the preparation of pro forma balance sheets and income statements. These statements give financial managers insight into the prospective future financial condition and performance of the firm, giving them yet another tool for financial planning and control.

Finally, we took up sustainable growth modeling and learned that it is a powerful tool for checking the consistency between sales growth goals, operating efficiency, and financial objectives. Two variations of the model exist; steady state, where the equity base and sales grow in concert; and unbalanced growth, where the ratios and growth change from year to year. With the latter, the sustainable growth rate is determined year by year. Given a desired growth in sales, through simulation, one is able to determine the operating and financial variables necessary to achieve it.

Self-Correction Problems

1. Serap-Jones, Inc., had the following financial statements for 20x1 and 20x2.

   a. Prepare a source and use of funds statement on a cash basis.

   b. Prepare an accounting statement of cash flows.

   c. Evaluate your findings.

	20x1	20x2
Assets		
Cash and cash equivalents	$ 140,000	$ 31,000
Accounts receivable	346,000	528,000
Inventories	432,000	683,000
Current assets	$ 918,000	$1,242,000
Net fixed assets	1,113,000	1,398,000
Total	$2,031,000	$2,640,000
Liabilities and equity		
Accounts payable	$ 413,000	$ 627,000
Accruals	226,000	314,000
Bank borrowings	100,000	235,000
Current liabilities	$ 739,000	$1,176,000
Common stock	100,000	100,000
Retained earnings	1,192,000	1,364,000
Total	$2,031,000	$2,640,000

Note: Depreciation was $189,000 for 20x2 and no dividends were paid.

2. Consider the balance sheet of Rodriguez Malting Company at December 31 (in thousands). The company has received a large order and anticipates the need to go to its bank to increase its borrowings. As a result, it has to forecast its cash requirements for January, February, and March. Typically, the company collects 20 percent of its sales in the month of sale, 70 percent in the subsequent month, and 10 percent in the second month after the sale. All sales are credit sales.

Cash	$ 50	Accounts payable		$ 360
Accounts receivable	530	Bank loan		400
Inventories	545	Accruals		212
Current assets	$1,125	Current liabilities		$ 972
Net fixed assets	1,836	Long-term debt		450
		Common stock		100
		Retained earnings		1,439
Total assets	$2,961	Total liabilities and equity		$2,961

Purchases of raw materials to produce malt are made in the month prior to the sale and amount to 60 percent of sales in the subsequent month. Payments for these purchases occur in the month after the purchase. Labor costs, including overtime, are expected to be $150,000 in January, $200,000 in February, and $160,000 in March. Selling, administrative, taxes, and other cash expenses are expected to be $100,000 per month for January through March. Actual sales in November and December and projected sales for January through April are as follows (in thousands):

November	$500	January	$ 600	March	$650
December	600	February	1,000	April	750

On the basis of this information:

    a. Prepare a cash budget for the months of January, February, and March.

    b. Determine the amount of additional bank borrowings necessary to maintain a cash balance of $50,000 at all times.

    c. Prepare a pro forma balance sheet for March 31.

3. Zippo Industries has equity capital of $12 million, total debt of $8 million, and sales last year of $30 million.

    a. It has a target assets-to-sales ratio of .6667, a target net profit margin of .04, a target debt-to-equity ratio of .6667, and a target earnings retention rate of .75. In steady state, what is its sustainable growth rate?

    b. Suppose, now, the company has established for next year a target assets-to-sales ratio of .62, a target net profit margin of .05, and a target debt-to-equity ratio of .80. It wishes to pay an annual dividend of $.3 million and raise $1 million in equity capital next year. What is its sustainable growth rate for next year? Why does it differ from that in part a?

Problems

1. Galow Fish Canning Company reports the following changes from the preceding year end. Categorize each change as either a source of funds or a use of funds.

Item	Change
Cash	−$100
Accounts receivable	700
Inventory	−300
Gross fixed assets	900
Depreciation	1,000
Accounts payable	300
Accruals	−100
Long-term debt	−200
Net profit	600
Dividends	400

2. Kohn Corporation comparative balance sheets at December 31 (in millions):

Assets	20x1	20x2	Liabilities and Equity	20x1	20x2
Cash	$ 5	$ 3	Notes payable	$20	$ 0
Accounts receivable	15	22	Accounts payable	5	8
Inventories	12	15	Accrued wages	2	2
Fixed assets, net	50	55	Accrued taxes	3	5
Other assets	8	5	Long-term debt	0	15
			Common stock	20	26
			Retained earnings	40	44
			Total liabilities		
Total assets	$90	$100	and equity	$90	$100

Kohn Corporation statement of income and retained earnings year ended December 31, 20x2:

Net sales		$48,000,000
Expenses		
Cost of goods sold	$25,000,000	
Selling, general, and administrative	5,000,000	
Depreciation	5,000,000	
Interest	2,000,000	37,000,000
Net income before taxes		$11,000,000
Less: Taxes		4,000,000
Net income		$ 7,000,000
Add: Retained earnings at 12/31/x1		40,000,000
Subtotal		$47,000,000
Less: Dividends		3,000,000
Retained earnings at 12/31/x2		$44,000,000

a. Prepare a source and use of funds statement on a cash basis for 20x2 for the Kohn Corporation.

b. Prepare an accounting statement of cash flows.

c. Prepare a source and use of working capital statement for 20x2.

3. Financial statements for the Sennet Corporation follow:

Sennet Corporation Balance Sheet, December 31 (in millions)

	20x1	20x2		20x1	20x2
Cash	$ 4	$ 5	Accounts payable	$ 8	$10
Accounts receivable	7	10	Notes payable	5	5
Inventory	12	15	Accrued wages	2	3
Current assets	$23	$30	Accrued taxes	3	2
Net plant	40	40	Current liabilities	$18	$20
			Long-term debt	20	20
			Common stock	10	10
			Retained earnings	15	20
			Total liabilities		
Total assets	$63	$70	and equity	$63	$70

Sennet Corporation Income Statement, 20x2 (in millions)

Sales		$95
Cost of goods sold	$50	
Selling, general, and administrative expenses	15	
Depreciation	3	
Interest	2	70
Net income before taxes		$25
Taxes		10
Net income		$15

a. Prepare a source and use of funds statement for Sennet.
b. Prepare a source and use of working capital statement.

4. Prepare a cash budget for the Ace Manufacturing Company indicating receipts and disbursements for May, June, and July. The firm wishes to maintain a minimum cash balance of $20,000 at all times. Determine whether or not borrowing will be necessary during the period, and if it is, when and for how much. As of April 30, the firm had a balance of $20,000 in cash.

Actual Sales		Forecasted Sales	
January	$50,000	May	$ 70,000
February	50,000	June	80,000
March	60,000	July	100,000
April	60,000	August	100,000

Accounts receivable: 50 percent of total sales are for cash. The remaining 50 percent will be collected equally during the following 2 months (the firm incurs a negligible bad-debt loss).

Cost of goods manufactured: 70 percent of sales; 90 percent of this cost is paid during the first month after incurrence, the remaining 10 percent is paid the following month.

Sales and administrative expenses: $10,000 per month plus 10 percent of sales.

All of these expenses are paid during the month of incurrence.

Interest payments: Semiannual interest of $18,000 is paid during July. An annual $50,000 sinking-fund payment is also made at that time.

Dividends: A $10,000 dividend payment will be declared and made in July.

Capital expenditures: $40,000 will be invested in plant and equipment in June.

Taxes: Income tax payments of $1,000 will be made in July.

5. Downeast Nautical Company expects sales of $2.4 million next year and expects sales of the same amount the following year. Sales are spread evenly throughout the year. On the basis of the following information, prepare a pro forma balance sheet and income statement for year end:

Cash	=	minimum of 4 percent of annual sales
Accounts receivable	=	60-day average collection period based on annual sales
Inventories	=	turnover of 8 times a year
Net fixed assets	=	$500,000 now; capital expenditures are equal to depreciation
Accounts payable	=	1 month's purchases
Accruals	=	3 percent of sales
Bank borrowings	=	$50,000 now; can borrow up to $250,000
Long-term debt	=	$300,000 now; $75,000 payable at year end
Common stock	=	$100,000; no additions planned
Retained earnings	=	$500,000 now
Net profit margin	=	8 percent of sales
Dividends	=	none
Cost of goods sold	=	60 percent of sales
Purchases	=	50 percent of cost of goods sold
Income taxes	=	50 percent of before-tax profits

6. Given the information that follows, prepare a cash budget for the Central City Department Store for the first 6 months of 20x2 under the following assumptions:

   a. All prices and costs remain constant.

   b. Sales are 75 percent for credit and 25 percent for cash.

   c. In terms of credit sales, 60 percent are collected in the month after the sale, 30 percent in the second month, and 10 percent in the third. Bad-debt losses are insignificant.

   d. Sales, actual and estimated, are

October 20x1	$300,000	March 20x2	$200,000
November 20x1	350,000	April 20x2	300,000
December 20x1	400,000	May 20x2	250,000
January 20x2	150,000	June 20x2	200,000
February 20x2	200,000	July 20x2	300,000

e. Payments for purchases of merchandise are 80 percent of the following month's anticipated sales.

f. Wages and salaries are

January	$30,000	March	$50,000	May	$40,000
February	40,000	April	50,000	June	35,000

g. Rent is $2,000 a month.

h. Interest of $7,500 is due at the end of each calendar quarter.

i. A tax prepayment on 20x2 income of $50,000 is due in April.

j. A capital investment of $30,000 is planned in June.

k. The company has a cash balance of $100,000 at December 31, 20x1, which is the minimum desired level for cash. Funds can be borrowed in multiples of $5,000 on a monthly basis. (Ignore interest on such borrowings.)

7. Use the cash budget worked out in Problem 6 and with the following additional information prepare a pro forma income statement for the first half of 20x2 for the Central City Department Store.

a. Inventory at December 31, 20x1, was $200,000.

b. Depreciation is taken on a straight-line basis on $250,000 of assets with an average remaining life of 10 years and no salvage value. It is recorded as an operating expense apart from cost of goods sold.

c. The tax rate is 40 percent.

8. Liz Clairson Industries has $40 million in shareholders' equity and sales of $150 million last year.

a. Its target ratios are: assets-to-sales ratio, .40; net profit margin, .07; debt-to-equity ratio, .50; and earnings retention, .60. If these ratios correspond to steady state, what is its sustainable growth rate?

b. If instead of these ratios, what would be the sustainable growth rate next year if the company moved from steady state and had the following targets? Assets-to-sales ratio, .42; net profit margin, .06; debt-to-equity ratio, .45; dividend of $5 million; and no new equity financing.

9. Hildebrand Hydronics Corporation wishes to achieve a 35 percent increase in sales next year. Sales last year were $30 million, and the company has equity capital of $12 million. It intends to raise $.5 million in new equity by sale of stock to officers. No dividend is planned. Tentatively, the company has set the following targets: assets-to-sales ratio, .67; net profit margin, .08; and debt-to-equity ratio, .60. The company has determined that these ratios are not sufficient to produce a growth in sales of 35 percent.

a. Holding the other two target ratios constant, what assets-to-sales ratic would be necessary to attain the 35 percent sales increase?

b. Holding the other two ratios constant, what net profit margin would be necessary?

c. Holding the other two ratios constant, what debt-to-equity ratio would be necessary?

Solutions to Self-Correction Problems

1. a.

Source and Use of Funds Statement for Serap-Jones, Inc. (in thousands)

Sources		Uses	
Funds provided by operations			
Net profit	$172		
Depreciation	189	Addition to fixed assets	$474
	$361		
		Increase, accounts receivable	182
Increase, accounts payable	214		
Increase, accruals	88	Increase, inventories	251
Increase, bank borrowings	135		
Decrease, cash	109		
Total sources	$907	Total uses	$907

b.

Statement of Cash Flows for Serap-Jones, Inc. (in thousands)

Cash flows from operating activities:	
Net earnings	$172
Adjustments to reconcile net earnings to cash provided by operating activities	
Depreciation	189
Changes in assets and liabilities	
Accounts receivable	(182)
Inventories	(251)
Accounts payable	214
Accruals	88
	$230
Cash flows from investing activities:	
Investment in fixed assets	($474)
Cash flows from financing activities:	
Increase (decrease) short-term borrowings	$135
Increase (decrease) in cash and cash equivalents	($109)
Cash and cash equivalents at beginning of year	140
Cash and cash equivalents at end of year	$ 31

c. The company has had substantial capital expenditures and increases in accounts receivable and inventories. To finance this growth, which is greatly in excess of the growth in equity base, the company has leaned on the trade, has increased its accruals, and has increased its bank borrowings significantly. This has not been enough; there was a substantial draw down of the cash position. The financing is short term in nature, but it is being used mostly for long-term build-ups in assets.

2.   a.   Cash budget (in thousands):

	Nov.	Dec.	Jan.	Feb.	Mar.	Apr.
Sales	$500	$600	$600	$1,000	$650	$750
Collections, current month's sales			120	200	130	
Collections, previous month's sales			420	420	700	
Collections, previous 2 months' sales			50	60	60	
Total cash receipts			$590	$ 680	$890	
Purchases		$360	$600	$390	$450	
Payment for purchases			360	600	390	
Labor costs			150	200	160	
Other expenses			100	100	100	
Total cash disbursements			$610	$ 900	$650	
Receipts less disbursements			($ 20)	($ 220)	$240	

b.

	Jan.	Feb.	Mar.
Additional borrowings	$ 20	$220	($240)
Cumulative borrowings	420	640	400

The amount of financing peaks in February owing to the need to pay for purchases made the previous month and higher labor costs. In March, substantial collections are made on the prior month's billings, causing a large net cash inflow sufficient to pay off the additional borrowings.

c.   Pro forma balance sheet, March 31 (in thousands):

Cash	$ 50	Accounts payable	$ 450
Accounts receivable	620	Bank loan	400
Inventories	635	Accruals	212
Current assets	$1,305	Current liabilities	$1,062
Net fixed assets	1,836	Long-term debt	450
		Common stock	100
		Retained earnings	1,529
Total assets	$3,141	Total liabilities and equity	$3,141

Accounts receivable = Sales in March × .8 + Sales in February × .1

Inventories = $545 + Total purchases January through March − Total sales January through March × .6

Accounts payable = Purchases in March

Retained earnings = $1,439 + Sales − Payment for purchases − Labor costs and − Other expenses, all for January through March

3. a. $\text{SGR} = \dfrac{.75\,(.04)\,(1.6667)}{.6667 - [.75(.04)(1.6667)]} = 8.11\%$

  b. $\text{SGR} = \left[\dfrac{(12 + 1 - 0.3)\,(1.80)\,(1.6129)}{1 - [(.05)(1.80)(1.6129)]} \right] \left[\dfrac{1}{30} \right] - 1 = 43.77\%$

The company has moved from steady state with higher target operating efficiency, a higher debt ratio, and the sale of common stock. All of these things permit a high rate of growth in sales next year. Unless further changes in these directions occur, the SGR will decline in future years.

Selected References

FRASER, LYN M., and AILEEN ORMISTON, *Understanding Financial Statements*, 5th ed. Upper Saddle River, NJ: Prentice Hall, 1998.

HELFERT, ERICH A., *Techniques of Financial Analysis*, 9th ed. Boston: Irwin McGraw-Hill, 1997.

HIGGINS, ROBERT C., "Sustainable Growth under Inflation," *Financial Management*, 10 (Autumn 1981), 36–40.

———, *Analysis for Financial Management*, 4th ed. Boston: Irwin McGraw-Hill, 1998.

JENSEN, MICHAEL C., and WILLIAM H. MECKLING, "Specific Knowledge and Divisional Performance Measurement," *Journal of Applied Corporate Finance*, 12 (Summer 1999), 8–17.

KAPLAN, ROBERT S., and ROBIN COOPER, *Cost and Effect*. Boston: Harvard Business School Press, 1997.

PARKER, GEORGE G. C., "Financial Forecasting," in Edward I. Altman, editor, *Handbook of Corporate Finance*. New York: Wiley, 1986, Chap. 2.

VAN HORNE, JAMES C., "Sustainable Growth Modeling," *Journal of Corporate Finance*, 1 (Winter 1988), 19–25.

Wachowicz's Web World is an excellent overall Web site produced and maintained by my coauthor of *Fundamentals of Financial Management*, John M. Wachowicz Jr. It contains descriptions of and links to many finance Web sites and articles. *www.prenhall.com/wachowicz.*

Part V

LIQUIDITY AND WORKING CAPITAL MANAGEMENT

■ **CASE:** *Caceres Semilla S.A. de C.v.*

Prudencio Jimenez B., chief administrative and financial officer of Caceres Semilla S.A. de C.V., was concerned about forthcoming negotiations with the company's bank, Banco Popular de Santa Fe. To renew a lending arrangement, he has to present a financial plan to the bank for fiscal year 2000. In July 1998, during the past fiscal year, the company had overdrawn its account and Jimenez had received a reprimand from the general manager of the bank, Carlos Fernandez Cristobal, with whom the company has done business for a number of years. The problem arose because of inefficient bookkeeping at the company, together with a big account delaying payment beyond a promised date. As the fiscal year just ended was February 28, 1999, negotiations over lending arrangements take place in March.

THE COMPANY AND ITS BACKGROUND

The company, located in Esperanza, Argentina, was founded in 1888 by Jaime Caceres Iturriaga to sell corn seed to local farmers in the area. The company is still family run with Josefina Caceres G. as general manager and her son, Juan Pablo Caceres, as associate general manager and, effectively, chief operating officer. Another family member, Joaquin Estaban C., is the nephew of Josefina and participates in strategy sessions as well as in sales during peak periods. However, his principal business is steer manure used for fertilizer, which he collects from outlying ranches, dries, and packages. His aversion to *la bano* results in minimum contact with other family members, but certain customers seem to like him. Jimenez reports directly to Juan Pablo Caceres.

Esperanza is located in La Pampa, the rich agricultural heartland of Argentina and the land of the legendary *gaucho*. The area of La Pampa occupies about a quarter of the country to the west of Buenos Aires. Extensive fields of alfalfa, maize (corn), sorghum, wheat, and sunflowers thrive in the fertile environ-

421

ment. The green grasslands of the prairies provide the mainstay for cattle for which Argentina is famous. Esperanza, in the province of Santa Fe, is approximately 400 kilometers northwest of Buenos Aires. The nearest large city is Santa Fe, the capital of the province. In this city, the Constitution of 1853 was declared. The province has an agricultural heritage, with some historians claiming that in Esperanza ranching and farming as we know it today began in the 1800s.

Throughout the years the Caceres company, a limited liability company with variable capital, has had reasonable success. Initially, and throughout most of the twentieth century, it specialized only in corn seed. In the 1960s, it began to contract for and sell alfalfa seed. Alfalfa is the most important of the hayseeds, the others being clover, alsike, and timothy. The output of the seed, baled hay, is sold to ranchers and dairy farmers to feed cattle. Presently, the company sells more alfalfa seed than it does corn seed.

For both types of seed, the seed is purchased from growers in the local area primarily in the summer and autumn (opposite to that in the Northern Hemisphere). Most of the growers from whom Caceres purchases seed are under contract to the company, with additional demand being satisfied by purchases in the spot market. The company has two buyers, whose sole responsibility is working with contract growers and purchasing seed. A great deal of emphasis is placed on quality; in corn, hybrid seeds are grown to resist diseases peculiar to the area. With contract growers, Caceres furnishes the grower with the initial, or stock, seed. By carefully monitoring the progress of each grower, the company is able to assure high quality. While quality is high with contract growers, control is more difficult with seed purchased in the spot market.

After the seed is purchased by the company from growers, it is sent to the plant in Esperanza for processing. First the seed must be dried. Essentially this involves circulating hot air through the seeds, which are placed in specially constructed open bins. Cleaning comes next, and this requires a special type of blowing equipment. In this procedure, it is important not to mix different types of corn seed and hayseed. To do so will result in customer dissatisfaction along with the occasional lawsuit. Next the seed must be sorted and bad seed eliminated. Electronic sorting machines do most of the work, but some of it still must be done by hand. It then is necessary to test the seed for purity, durability, and germination. Finally, the seed is packaged in various sized boxes and bags. Once packaged, the seed is stored in warehouses. For the most part, warehousing is done on site, but occasionally the company must use a public warehouse, which is more expensive and less efficient.

DEMAND FOR PRODUCT AND RISKS

The ultimate demand for the seed is from farmers, but Caceres does not distribute directly to them. Rather, distribution is through grain elevators, farm and ranch cooperatives, fertilizer and hardware stores, farm implement dealers, and assorted other retail outlets. Caceres employs five salespeople, who cover the provinces of Santa Fe, Cordoba, San Luis, and La Rioja, and report directly to Juan Pablo Ca-ceres. For distribution reasons, it does not sell product in other provinces. During the autumn months in particular, salespeople are active in booking advance orders from customers. By close coordination between the sales people and the seed buyers, the company attempts to closely tailor its purchases to demand. They keep in close touch by phone, fax, and email, carefully checking seed bookings and the latest prices.

Although the company is able to vary its purchases to some extent, it is obligated to its contract growers to buy a minimum amount of seed each year.

Should demand fall below the minimum amount of purchases required under contract, the seed needs to be carried over to the next selling period. In turn, this affects the quality. The principal appeal of Caceres seed is its purity and heartiness, as well as the fact that the company has been in business for over 110 years. To stimulate retail demand from farmers, the company has spot radio commercials in the provinces served as well as advertisements in selected farm journals and manuals.

In the 1980s, sales grew rapidly in keeping with an aggressive marketing effort. The company relied on purchasing seed in the spot market to satisfy excess demand. By 1987, contract growers accounted for only 47 percent of seed purchases. During this time, quality problems developed and certain farmers experienced inferior crops. The dissatisfaction caused Josefina Caceres to scale back the sales drive and to increase the number of contract growers. Gradually, the problem was ameliorated, and customers once again came to regard Caceres as synonymous with quality. Presently, 86 percent of the seed purchased is from contract growers.

The quality edge is essential to sales. When compared with the total cost of farming, the cost of seed is a minor component. Therefore, good seed is a good, value-added investment by the farmer. Other than the quality of the product itself, the other major business risk is fluctuations in the market for hay and for corn. While customers commit in advance to buy seed from the company, they cannot be held to these commitments. If demand should falter, Caceres would end up with substantial inventories. In addition, the prices of seed would fall. Despite efforts by Caceres and other seed companies to differentiate their products, to some extent they are commodities when it comes to pricing. For this reason, the company pays close attention to the price of hay and corn in La Pampa and changes in demand. Presently both markets are reasonably robust, but cycles in agricultural products are notorious.

There is considerable competition in the seed business. The principal competitor, of course, is the farmer who holds back seed from one harvest to plant in the next. The packaged seed companies must compete on the basis of greater yield and disease resistance. The farmer must be willing to incur the added expense to achieve greater yield, for "own seed" is always cheapest. Depending on the state of the farm economy, the percentage of "own seed" versus packaged seed increases or decreases. Of the packaged seeds sold, Caceres has the number one position in the Province of Santa Fe with a 19 percent market share. In the provinces of Cordoba, San Luis and La Rioja, it is number 3, with an 8 percent market share overall. For the most part, distribution of product to customers is by company-owned trucks. Occasionally, deliveries are delayed by truck breakdown or by road conditions in certain outlying areas where roads are not good. This causes a degree of customer irritation but is not a serious problem.

THE COMPANY'S FINANCING

In recent years, the company financing has consisted of a long-term mortgage loan as well as bank loans. In the 1970s, some equity capital was raised from extended family members. In 1993, the company completely rebuilt its plant in Esperanza. The old plant was constructed in 1924 with add-ons over the years. By having all equipment in carefully arranged, contiguous space, seed processing efficiency was greatly enhanced. Caceres Semilla financed the plant with a 3 million peso mortgage loan from an insurance company in Buenos Aires. The loan bears a fixed rate of 13 percent and was originally for 20 years, 3 months. For the first 5 fiscal years, principal payments of P120,000 were due semiannually in June and December. For fiscal year 1999 and beyond, principal payments of P60,000 are due semiannually. The loan is secured by the plant and 218 hectares of land, which comprise the estancia Caceres, on which the plant occupies 5 hectares. Although the interest rate is fixed, it is essentially dollar denominated. Should the 1-to-1 peso/dollar exchange rate regime change with the peso weakening, the loan covenants require principal payments in pesos to increase proportional to the dollar strengthening.

For over a half century, the company has banked with Banco Popular de Santa Fe. The bank has accommodated the company with seasonal credit as well as occasional transactions loans of a term nature. For the unsecured, seasonal credit accommodation, interest is at the reference (floating) rate, presently 12.5 percent. The bank had hoped to arrange the 1993 mortgage loan, taking the early maturities and syndicating the rest. Carlos Fernandez Cristobal, the banker, was irritated when the company took the deal to the Buenos Aires insurance company. However, the bank continued to accommodate the company's seasonal borrowing needs under a line of credit. For the past fiscal year (1999), the line was for 4.8 million pesos. The company was out of bank debt in March 1998 of that fiscal year. However, in August 1998 Senor Jimenez sent in a loan note, which took total borrowings to slightly above 5.0 million pesos. As this had not been discussed in advance, Senor Fernandez was upset.

Although the overage was approved, it was not without reprimand. Senor Fernandez demanded a meeting with Senor Jimenez, Josefina Caceres, and Juan Pablo Caceres. At the meeting in September, he expressed concern with the growth of receivables, inventories, and fixed assets resulting in the overage. He suggested that a term loan would make sense and that Banco Popular would be willing to consider such but at a floating rate $1\frac{1}{2}$ percent higher than the rate under the seasonal line of credit. Prudencio Jimenez assured him that they would not exceed the maximum credit limit in the future and that there was no need for a term loan. Senor Fernandez also expressed concern that he had heard that Juan Pablo was diverting attention away from the business to his hobby of raising mules. Juan Pablo assured him that this was not the case and that the "mule thing" was done in his spare time. When discussing the matter of "other assets" on the balance sheet suddenly increasing by P105,000, Josefina Caceres reluctantly explained that it represented a direct investment in the steer manure business of her nephew, Joaquin Estaban C. Senor Fernandez said he did not care for this diversion of funds and that he should have been consulted prior to the investment. The meeting ended on a frosty note.

FINANCIAL PLANNING REQUIRED FOR FY2000

In preparation for the meeting in March 1999 with Banco Popular, Prudencio Jimenez was required by the bank to prepare pro forma statements for fiscal year 2000. Such forecasts had not previously been required. With help from a local accountant, Jimenez undertook the task. The important assumptions follow. An overall sales increase of 22.7 percent is projected. Of this increase, price increases are expected to account for 6 percent and volume increases for the remainder. Market share is expected to increase, not only as a result of an aggressive marketing effort but also because one significant competitor in the province of Cordoba recently went into bankruptcy. Interest expenses are incorporated in the overall "general and administrative expense" category. Because Caceres Semilla S.A. de

C.V. is a family-run business, it does not accrue taxes month by month. Rather, it pays taxes quarterly based on projected profits for the year. As to dividends, Josefina Caceres wants to double the dividend paid. Profitability has improved, and she feels a sense of obligation to extended family members who are not active in management. After all, when profits declined in fiscal years 1997 and 1998 she asked them to go without dividends in order to build for the future.

After much effort and consultation with members of management, Senor Jimenez produced the pro forma income statements shown in Exhibit 3. While nothing is certain, the company is reasonably confident it will be able to meet these projections with respect to both revenues and expenses.

Given the sales forecast, accounts receivable, inventories, accounts payable, and accruals are driven off this schedule. The average collection period assumed is 1 month after sales, whereas purchases are assumed to be paid for with a lag of 2 months. Some of the growers are upset with the 2 months, and a further stretching of payables is not possible. However, the Caceres buyers have been largely successful in keeping growers happy despite the stretching, which gives the company 2 months of free financing.

On the basis of these assumptions, Prudencio Jimenez was able to produce the pro forma balance sheets shown in Exhibit 4. However, he did not know how to determine the cash position and the bank loan. Given the overdraft last July, Jimenez felt the company needed to maintain a cash position of P200,000 or more at all times. Inadvertently, he left out the retained earnings row in Exhibit 4. As the meeting with Banco Popular de Santa Fe is the next day, he will try to remedy these matters in the evening.

THE MEETING

Prior to meeting with the banker, Senor Fernandez, in the afternoon, Prudencio Jimenez will brief Josefina Caceres and Juan Pablo Caceres in the morning. On the morning agenda will be whether the company should be proactive in proposing a specific financing plan or reactive to the thoughts of the banker on the matter of financing. Whichever approach is taken, Senor Jimenez will need to be thoroughly prepared to defend the numbers.

Exhibit 1

Caceres Semilla S.A. de C.V.
Balance Sheets at 28 February
(in thousands of pesos)

Assets	1996	1997	1998	1999
Cash	648	276	246	138
Accounts receivable	1,374	1,446	1,506	2,106
Inventories	1,638	1,974	2,364	3,408
Total current assets	3,660	3,696	4,116	5,652
Net fixed assets	3,678	3,966	4,074	4,404
Other assets	306	444	522	654
Total assets	7,644	8,106	8,712	10,710
Liabilities & equity				
Accounts payable	1,488	1,572	1,608	2,202
Accruals	714	768	774	1,176
Current portion, LTD	240	240	240	120
Bank loan			252	900
Total current liabilities	2,442	2,580	2,874	4,398
Long-term debt	2,040	1,800	1,560	1,440
Common stock	192	192	192	192
Paid-in capital	534	534	534	534
Retained earnings	2,436	3,000	3,552	4,146
Total liabilities and equity	7,644	8,106	8,712	10,710

Exhibit 2

Income Statements (in thousands of pesos)

	1996	1997	1998	1999
Net sales	18,037	17,082	17,916	20,538
Cost of goods sold	11,064	10,572	10,530	12,198
Gross profit	6,973	6,510	7,386	8,340
Depreciation	276	294	342	378
Processing and storing expenses	1,987	1,896	2,178	2,454
Selling and delivery expenses	2,262	2,118	2,436	2,598
General and administration expenses	1,359	1,386	1,632	1,818
Profits before taxes	1,089	816	798	1,092
Income taxes	378	252	246	378
Profits after taxes	711	564	552	714
Dividends	120	0	0	120

Exhibit 3
Caceres Semilla S.A. de C.V. Pro forma Income Statements FY2000

	March	April	May	June	July	Aug.	Sep.	Oct.	Nov.	Dec.	Jan.	Feb.	FY2000
Net sales	1,680	1,260	1,260	1,680	1,680	2,400	3,300	3,000	1,320	2,100	3,000	2,520	25,200
Cost of goods sold	1,008	756	756	1,008	1,008	1,440	1,980	1,800	792	1,260	1,800	1,512	15,120
Gross profit	672	504	504	672	672	960	1,320	1,200	528	840	1,200	1,008	10,080
Depreciation	31	31	31	32	32	32	32	33	33	34	34	35	390
Procession and storing expenses	150	150	204	204	288	396	360	156	252	360	300	240	3,060
Selling and delivery expenses	216	162	162	216	216	312	432	390	174	276	390	330	3,276
General and administrative expenses	151	158	185	199	200	202	201	192	175	174	171	164	2,172
Profits before taxes	124	3	(78)	21	(64)	18	295	429	(106)	(4)	305	239	1,182
Income taxes	96			110			110			110			426
Profits after taxes	28	3	(78)	(89)	(64)	18	185	429	(106)	(114)	305	239	756
Dividends				120						120			240

427

Exhibit 4
Pro Forma Balance Sheets for FY2000

	March	April	May	June	July	Aug.	Sep.	Oct.	Nov.	Dec.	Jan.	Feb.
Cash												
Accounts receivable	1,626	1,206	1,206	1,626	1,626	2,346	3,246	2,946	1,266	2,046	2,946	2,466
Inventories	5,877	6,888	7,434	7,728	7,557	6,954	5,811	4,848	4,893	4,935	4,437	4,692
Total current assets												
Net fixed assets	4,385	4,366	4,479	4,459	4,439	4,419	4,399	4,498	4,597	4,695	4,793	4,770
Other assets	654	654	654	660	660	670	670	680	680	680	680	680
Total assets												
Accounts payable	4,713	4,794	2,619	2,154	1,689	1,224	759	387	852	1,689	2,154	2,619
Accruals	1,059	954	1,059	1,164	1,326	1,723	1,885	1,408	1,176	1,583	1,688	1,455
Current portion, LTD	120	120	120	120	120	120	120	120	120	120	120	120
Bank loan												
Total current liabilities												
Long-term debt	1,440	1,440	1,440	1,380	1,380	1,380	1,380	1,380	1,380	1,320	1,320	1,320
Common stock	192	192	192	192	192	192	192	192	192	192	192	192
Paid-in capital	534	534	534	534	534	534	534	534	534	534	534	534
Retained earnings												
Total liabilities and equity												

428

Liquidity, Cash, and Marketable Securities

So far, we have endeavored to understand the valuation of a company under varying assumptions as to the perfection of capital markets. Though our concerns were with investment in assets and financing in general, the focus really was on property, plant and equipment, and long-term financing. In this part, we shift our focus to current assets and to short- and intermediate-term financing. We begin by taking up the most liquid assets of a company, cash and near cash. ▪

LIQUIDITY AND ITS ROLE

The term **liquid assets** is used to describe money and assets that are readily convertible into money. Different assets may be said to exhibit different degrees of liquidity. Money itself is, by definition, the most liquid of assets; other assets have varying degrees of liquidity, depending on the ease with which they can be turned into cash. For assets other than money, liquidity has two dimensions: (1) the time necessary to convert the asset into money and (2) the degree of certainty associated with the conversion ratio, or price, realized for the asset. Although most assets have a degree of liquidity, we shall focus on the most liquid assets of the firm: cash and marketable securities.

Liquidity When Perfect Capital Markets Exist

We have seen that under the assumptions of perfect capital markets, a firm could not alter its value by varying its capital structure, its dividend policy, or the diversification of the assets it holds. If we invoke these assumptions again, the degree of liquidity of the firm would be a matter of indifference to equity holders. Presumably, investors would manage their portfolios of common stocks and other assets, as well as their liabilities, in a way that satisfied their utility for liquidity. As a result, the liquidity of individual firms would not be a factor enhancing shareholder wealth. In essence, the argument is that the firm is unable to do something for investors that they cannot do for themselves.

In this context, excess cash cannot be justified. It is the equity holders' money, and management is only their steward. If the company cannot employ the funds in

429

Perfect markets imply liquidity is not a thing of value. Investors can produce homemade liquidity.

projects providing expected returns no less than those required by the financial markets, such excess liquidity should be distributed. Put another way, allow the equity holders to use the funds for investment in other endeavors providing appropriate returns.

The assumptions of perfect capital markets imply that if the firm becomes technically insolvent and unable to pay its bills, creditors will be able to step in instantaneously and realize value either by liquidating assets, by running the company themselves, or by effecting a costless reorganization. If the assets are sold, they are assumed to be employed productively without delay or inefficiency in other areas of the economy. When we allow for market imperfections, liquidity may become a desirable characteristic affecting value.

Liquidity Management with Imperfections

Chapter 9 pointed out two dimensions of bankruptcy costs. The first is the "shortfall," arising from the liquidation of assets at "distress" prices below their economic values, as well as the productivity lost in going into bankruptcy. The second is the out-of-pocket fees paid to lawyers, trustees in bankruptcy, referees, receivers, liquidators, and so forth. Embodied in the shortfall phenomenon are considerable delays in bankruptcy proceedings, during which the firm and its value can continue to deteriorate.

In effect, bankruptcy costs represent a drain in the system to suppliers of capital. This drain works to the disadvantage of equity holders, who have a residual claim on assets in liquidation. Higher interest rates are another result as creditors seek ways of passing on all or part of the ex ante costs of bankruptcy. This obviously also works to the disadvantage of equity holders. Investors are unable to diversify away the costs of bankruptcy. The firm can reduce the probability of bankruptcy, however, by maintaining liquidity. Making bankruptcy less probable now and in the future may bestow some benefits on stockholders as residual owners of a company. It may be able to do something for stockholders that they cannot do for themselves, which we know from earlier chapters is what creates value.

Another imperfection has to do with contracting costs of managers, workers, suppliers, and customers. If these parties are unable to diversify their claims on the firm properly, they may require additional incentive the riskier the firm.[1] This incentive, whether it be higher compensation, higher prices to suppliers, or lower prices to customers, represents a cost to the firm's equity holders. By increasing liquidity, the risk to these parties can be reduced and the aforementioned costs lowered.

Benefits Relative to Cost

Against the benefits associated with maintaining liquidity, one must balance the cost. Liquid assets, like all other assets, have to be financed. Accordingly, the cost of liquidity may be thought of as the differential in interest earned on the investment of funds in liquid assets and the cost of financing. If the firm could both borrow and lend at the same interest rate, there would be no "cost" to maintaining whatever level of liquidity was desired to reduce the probability of technical insolvency. If imperfections in the capital markets result in the borrowing rate exceeding the lending rate, there is a "cost" to maintaining liquidity. Under these condi-

---

[1]This argument is made by Clifford W. Smith and Rene M. Stulz, "The Determinants of Firms' Hedging Policies," *Journal of Financial and Quantitative Analysis*, 20 (December 1985), 391–405.

tions, a trade-off exists between the benefits associated with liquidity and the cost of maintaining it. The optimal level of liquidity then could be determined by marginal analysis.

Quantification of this trade-off is complex. Our purpose has been to explore the problem in concept. The important thing in establishing a case for a company maintaining any liquidity is the presence of market imperfections that make liquidity a thing of value. Then the question is whether liquidity should be held in the form of transactions balances or marketable securities.

CASH MANAGEMENT AND COLLECTIONS

The cash cycle begins with the payment for purchases and services and ends with the collection of receivables.

Cash management involves managing the monies of the firm to maximize cash availability and interest income on any idle funds. At one end, the function starts when a customer writes a check to pay the firm on its accounts receivable. The function ends when a supplier, an employee, or the government realizes collected funds from the firm on an account payable or accrual. All activities between these two points fall within the realm of cash management. The firm's efforts to get customers to pay their bills at a certain time fall within accounts receivable management. On the other hand, the firm's decision about when to pay its bills involves accounts payable and accrual management.

The various **collection and disbursement methods** by which a firm can improve its cash management efficiency constitute two sides of the same coin. They exercise a joint impact on the overall efficiency of cash management. The idea is to collect accounts receivable as soon as possible, but pay accounts payable as late as is consistent with maintaining the firm's credit standing with suppliers.

We consider first the acceleration of collections, which simply means reducing the delay between the time customers pay their bills and the time the checks are collected and become usable funds for the firm. A number of methods are designed to speed up this collection process by doing one or all of the following: (1) speed the mailing time of payments from customers to the firm, (2) reduce the time during which payments received by the firm remain uncollected funds, and (3) speed the movement of funds to disbursement banks.

The second item, representing **float**, has two aspects. The first is the time it takes a company to process checks internally. This interval extends from the moment a check is received to the moment it is deposited with a bank for credit to the company's account. The second aspect of float involves the time consumed in clearing the check through the banking system. Float is important, because usually a company cannot make withdrawals on a deposit until the checks in that deposit are collected. As the name of the game is usable funds, the financial manager wants to reduce the float as much as possible.

Transferring Funds

Increasing cash availability also involves moving funds among banks. There are two principal methods: (1) wire transfers and (2) electronic depository transfer checks. With a **wire transfer**, funds are immediately transferred from one bank to another. Wire transfers can be through the Federal Reserve Bank's wire transfer service (Fedwire) or the Clearing House Interbank Payments System (CHIPS). With an **electronic depository transfer check (DTC)** arrangement for the movement of funds, an electronic check image is processed through an automatic clearinghouse. The funds become available one business day later. Depository transfer checks also can be physically transported, but electronic processing has largely displaced the mail-based DTC. The advantage of the electronic DTC over the wire transfer is cost. The former is only about one-quarter as expensive, but it involves a one-day delay versus none at all. For small transfers, a wire transfer may be too costly.

Concentration Banking

Concentration banking is a means of accelerating the flow of funds of a firm by establishing strategic collection centers. Instead of a single collection center located at the company headquarters, multiple collection centers are established. The purpose is to shorten the period between the time customers mail in their payments and the time when the company has use of the funds. Customers in a particular geographic area are instructed to remit their payments to a collection center in that area. Location of the collection centers usually is based on the geographic areas served and the volume of billings in an area. When payments are received, they are deposited in the collection center's local bank. Surplus funds are then transferred from these local bank accounts to a concentration bank or banks. A bank of concentration is one with which the company has a major account—usually a disbursement account.

The advantage of a system of decentralized billings and collections over a centralized system is twofold. (Remember that we are comparing a system of multiple collection centers with a single collection center located at company headquarters.)

1. The time required for mailing is reduced. Because the collection center bills customers in its area, these customers usually receive their bills earlier than if bills were mailed from the head office. In turn, when customers pay their bills, the mailing time to the nearest collection center is shorter than the time required for the typical remittance to go to the head office.

2. The time required to collect checks is reduced because remittances deposited in the collection center's local bank usually are drawn on banks in that general area.

Profits from the investment of the released funds must be compared with any additional costs of a decentralized system over a centralized one. Also consider any differences between the two systems in total compensating balances. The greater the number of collection centers, the greater the number of local bank accounts that must be maintained.

Lockbox System

Another means of accelerating the flow of funds is a **lockbox** arrangement. With concentration banking, a collection center receives remittances, processes them, and deposits them in a bank. The purpose of a lockbox arrangement is to eliminate the time between the receipt of remittances by the company and their deposit in the bank. A lockbox arrangement usually is on a regional basis, the company choosing regional banks according to its billing patterns. Before determining the regions to be used, a feasibility study is made of the availability of checks that would be deposited under alternative plans vis-à-vis their costs. If a company divided the country into five sections on the basis of a feasibility study, it might pick New York City for the Northeast, Atlanta for the Southeast, Chicago for the Midwest, Dallas for the Southwest, and San Francisco for the West Coast.

International Cash Management

The payments systems for various countries differ. For example, the lockbox system so widely used in the United States is not well developed in other countries. A foreign lockbox arrangement generally is more costly than is a U.S. arrangement. As lockbox networks are developed in Europe and in Asia, however, the cost should come down. Now the cost/benefit ratio is not as favorable as typically occurs in the U.S.

Many payments in Europe are through a postal clearing service. In this regard, the *giro* system permits automatic payments through the postal service. The service is instructed by the payer to transfer funds to a payee's account, and advices are sent to both parties. No physical check is used. This service is apart from the banking system.

Checks on the banking system also are used for payments, and their use is growing. However, for recurring payments the giro payments system is the most widely used. Payments also can be through wire transfers, usually with a 1-day lag in availability of funds if domestic currency is involved and 2-day if the currency is foreign.

For multinational companies, cash and marketable securities may be kept in multiple currencies. Many companies maintain liquidity in the country where investment takes place and/or where the sourcing of a product occurs. The marketable securities position of such a company is part of a broader management of currency risk exposure, which we address in Chapter 24.

It is important that the financial manager understand the many differences in institutional aspects of overseas payment and investment of excess funds. We have touched on only a few, but the globalization of business and finance dictates a familiarity if the company is to compete in the world arena.

The company rents a local post office box and authorizes its bank in each of these cities to pick up remittances in the box. Customers are billed with instructions to mail their remittances to the lockbox. The bank picks up the mail several times a day and deposits the checks in the company's account. The checks are recorded and cleared for collection. The company receives a deposit slip and a list of payments, together with any material in the envelope. This procedure frees the company from handling and depositing the checks.

The main advantage of a lockbox system is that checks are deposited at banks sooner and become collected balances sooner than if they were processed by the company prior to deposit. In other words, the lag between the time checks are received by the company and the time they actually are deposited at the bank is eliminated. The principal disadvantage of a lockbox arrangement is the cost. The bank provides a number of services additional to the usual clearing of checks and requires compensation for them, usually preferring increased deposits. Because the cost is almost directly proportional to the number of checks deposited, lockbox arrangements usually are not profitable if the average remittance is small.

Preauthorized Checks

A **preauthorized check (PAC)** arrangement is sometimes used to reduce mailing and processing time. It works well for certain large customers where payments of a fixed amount are required. The PAC is like an ordinary check, but it does not require the drawer to sign it. Rather, the customer has given legal authorization to the vendor to draw checks on its bank account. The bank then honors the PAC and pays the vendor. Records are kept, obviously, and there are controls. The PAC system works only when both the customer and the vendor are well known to each other and completely creditworthy.

CONTROL OF DISBURSEMENTS

Effective control of disbursements can also result in more availability of cash. Whereas the underlying objective of collections is maximum acceleration, the objective in disbursements is to slow them down as much as possible. The combination of fast collections and slow disbursements will result in maximum availability of funds.

One way of maximizing cash availability is "playing the float." For disbursements, float is the difference between the total dollar amount of checks drawn on a bank account and the balance shown on the bank's books. It is possible, of course, for a company to have a negative balance on its books and a positive bank balance, because checks outstanding have not been collected from the account on which they are drawn. If the size of float can be estimated accurately, bank balances can be reduced and the funds invested to earn a positive return.

Accelerating collections and slowing disbursements shorten the cash cycle and result in more usable funds.

Mobilizing Funds and Slowing Disbursements

A company with multiple banks should be able to shift funds quickly to banks from which disbursements are made, to prevent excessive balances from building up temporarily in a particular bank. The idea is to have adequate cash at the various banks, but not to let excessive balances build up. This requires daily information on collected balances. Excess funds then are transferred to the disbursement banks, either to pay bills or to invest in marketable securities. Many companies have developed sophisticated computer systems to provide the necessary information and to transfer excess funds automatically.

A means for delaying disbursements is through the use of **payable-through drafts**. Unlike an ordinary check, the draft is not payable on demand. When it is presented to the issuer's bank for collection, the bank must present it to the issuer for acceptance. The funds then are deposited by the issuing firm to cover payment of the draft. The advantage of the draft arrangement is that it delays the time the firm actually has to have funds on deposit to cover the draft. When a company has multiple bank accounts throughout the country, the opportunities for "playing the float" expand. Taking advantage of inefficiencies in the check-clearing processes, a company can pay suppliers with checks drawn on remote banks.

By maximizing disbursement float, the firm can reduce the amount of cash it holds and employ these funds in more profitable ways. One firm's gain, however, is another firm's loss. Maximizing disbursement float means that suppliers will not have collectible funds as early as would otherwise be the case. To the extent that they look with disfavor on such payment habits, supplier relations may be hurt. Some suppliers may simply raise prices to compensate; others may let service slip because the buyer is no longer a favored customer.

Zero Balance Account

To make transfers automatically into a payroll, dividend, or other special account, some companies employ a **zero balance account (ZBA)**. The ZBA is offered by a number of banks, and it eliminates the need to estimate and fund each disbursement account. Rather, one master disbursing account services all subsidiary accounts. At the end of each day, the bank automatically transfers just enough funds to cover the checks presented for collection. As a result, a zero balance is maintained in each of the special disbursing accounts. While balances must be maintained in the master account, increased efficiency works to reduce the total balances that must be maintained.

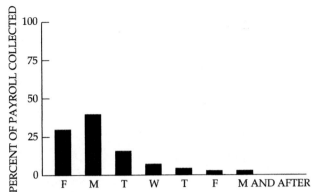

Payroll and Dividend Disbursements

Many companies maintain a separate account for payroll disbursements. In order to minimize the balance in this account, one must predict when the payroll checks issued will be presented for payment. If payday falls on a Friday, not all of the checks will be cashed on that day. Consequently, the firm need not have funds on deposit to cover its entire payroll. Even on Monday, some checks will not be presented, owing to delays in their deposit. Based on its experience, the firm should be able to construct a distribution of when, on average, checks are presented for collection. An example is shown in Fig. 14-1. With this information, the firm can approximate the funds it needs to have on deposit to cover payroll checks. Many firms establish a separate account for dividends, similar to the payroll account. Here, too, the idea is to predict when such checks will be presented for payment, to minimize the cash balance in the account.

Electronic Funds Transfers

Accelerating collections and slowing disbursements increasingly are being done electronically. This is illustrated in Fig. 14-2. The supplier, company Y, sends an invoice to its customer, company X. On the appropriate payment date, company X instructs its bank to pay its supplier via a prearranged procedure. The instructions can be transmitted by central computer, terminal, or some other means. The bank then debits company X's account and either credits directly or wire transfers the credit to company Y's bank, along with communicating electronically the supporting information. The latter bank then credits company Y's account, sending it the supporting information, again electronically. Company Y is then in a position to update its accounts receivable ledgers. In addition to paying bills, electronic funds transfers (EFTs) can be used to deposit payrolls automatically in employee accounts, to pay taxes, and to make dividend and other payments.

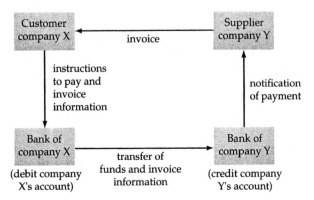

Electronic funds transfer is a subset of electronic commerce, the exchange of business information in an electronic format. Internationally, EFTs may be affected through CHIPS, the Clearinghouse Interbank Payments System, which we mentioned for domestic transfers, and through SWIFT, the Society of Worldwide Interbank Financial Telecommunications.

Because electronic funds transfer is capital intensive, the cost per transaction is reduced as volume increases. Indeed, this has occurred in recent years, and much of the savings is passed along to users of financial services. The customer benefits from the intense competition among financial institutions and large retailers that provide financial services. For the firm, electronic banking means less time in the collection of receivables, more efficient control of cash, and perhaps a reduction in servicing costs.

Because of lack of size or efficiency, some companies outsource their payable operation, including electronic funds transfers. Indeed, **outsourcing** is increasingly occurring in the finance function as companies focus on their core competencies in finance. All other essential but noncore areas of business are candidates for outsourcing. Outsourcing can be applied to collections as well as to payables.

INVESTMENT IN MARKETABLE SECURITIES

Marketable securities serve the liquidity needs of the firm.

The financial manager will want to invest the portion of liquid assets in excess of transactions cash needs. Yields on marketable securities vary with differences in default risk, in marketability, in length of time to maturity, in coupon rate, and in taxability. Before discussing these factors, we must mention that for accounting purposes marketable securities and time deposits are shown as "cash equivalents" on the balance sheet if their original maturity is 3 months or less. Other marketable securities are shown as "short-term investments," assuming their maturity is less than 1 year. In what follows, we will not concern ourselves with this accounting distinction.

Credit Risk

When we speak of credit, or default, risk, we mean the risk that the borrower will not satisfy the contractual obligation to make principal and interest payments. Investors are said to demand a risk premium to invest in other than default-free securities.[2] The greater the possibility that the borrower will default, the greater the financial risk and the premium demanded by the marketplace. Treasury securities are usually regarded as default free, and other securities are judged in relation to them. U.S. government agency issues might be rated next to Treasury securities in creditworthiness. For all practical purposes, these securities are default free. The creditworthiness of other obligations is frequently judged on the basis of security ratings. Moody's Investors Service and Standard & Poor's grade the quality of corporate and municipal securities, for example (see Chapter 20 for a discussion). The greater the default risk of the borrower, the greater the yield of the security should be, all other things held constant. By investing in riskier securities, the firm can achieve higher returns, but it faces the familiar trade-off between expected return and risk.

Marketability

Marketability of a security relates to the ability of the owner to convert it into cash. There are two dimensions: the price realized and the amount of time required to sell the asset. The two are interrelated in that it is often possible to sell an asset in a

---

[2]For an extended discussion of default risk and of the other topics taken up in this section, see James C. Van Horne, *Financial Market Rates and Flows*, 6th ed. (Upper Saddle River, NJ: Prentice Hall, 2001).

short period of time if enough price concession is given. For financial instruments, marketability is judged in relation to the ability to sell a significant volume of securities in a short period of time without significant price concession. The more marketable the security, the greater the ability to execute a large transaction near the quoted price. In general, the lower the marketability of a security, the greater the yield necessary to attract investors.

Maturity

Credit risk and maturity are the two most important features when it comes to investment.

The relationship between yield and maturity can be studied graphically by plotting yield and maturity for securities differing only in the length of time to maturity. In practice, this means holding constant the degree of default risk. Generally, when interest rates are expected to rise, the yield curve is upward sloping, whereas it is humped and somewhat downward sloping when they are expected to fall significantly. However, there is a tendency toward positive-sloped yield curves. Most economists attribute this tendency to the presence of risk for those who invest in long-term securities vis-à-vis short-term securities. In general, the longer the maturity, the greater the risk of fluctuation in the market value of the security. Consequently, investors need to be offered a risk premium to induce them to invest in long-term securities. Only when interest rates are expected to fall significantly are they willing to invest in long-term securities yielding less than short- and intermediate-term securities. In Part VI we look deeper into yield curves and their relevance to financing decisions.

Coupon Rate

In addition to maturity, price fluctuations also depend on the level of the coupon. For a given fixed-income security, the lower the coupon rate, the greater the price change for a given shift in interest rates. The reason for this is that with lower coupons, more of the total return to the investor is reflected in the principal payment at maturity as opposed to interest payments that are discounted from nearer coupon dates. In effect, investors realize their return sooner with high-coupon bonds than with low-coupon ones. Thus, the volatility of a security depends on the combined effect of maturity and coupon rate. To come to grips with this combined effect, the duration measure explained in Chapter 2 is used.

Taxability

Another factor affecting observed differences in market yields is the differential impact of taxes. The interest income on all but one category of securities is taxable to taxable investors. Interest income from state and local government securities is tax exempt; as a result, they sell in the market at lower yields to maturity than Treasury and corporate securities of the same maturity. For corporations located in states with income taxes, interest income on Treasury securities is exempt from state income taxes. As a result, such instruments may hold an advantage over the debt instruments of corporations or of banks where the interest income is fully taxable at the state level. Under present tax law, capital gains arising from the sale of a security at a profit are taxed at the full corporate tax rate.

Types of Marketable Securities

Money markets include instruments of shorter maturity, which are liquid.

In this section, we describe briefly the more prominent marketable securities available for investment. Space prohibits the discussion of longer-term investments, although corporations do invest excess funds in long-term securities that are about to reach maturity. The vast majority of corporations invest in the instruments about to be described, mostly money market instruments, which, by definition, are highly marketable and subject to little default risk. Also, the usual definition restricts maturity of a money market instrument to less than a year.

Treasury Securities   U.S. Treasury obligations constitute the largest segment of the money markets. The principal securities issued are **bills**, tax anticipation bills, **notes**, and **bonds**. The Treasury auctions bills weekly with maturities of 91 days and 182 days. In addition, 9-month and 1-year bills are sold every month. All sales by the Treasury are by auction. Smaller investors can enter a "noncompetitive" bid, which is filled at the market clearing price. Treasury bills carry no coupon but are sold on a discount basis. Denominations range from $10,000 to $1 million. These securities are popular with some companies as short-term investments, in part because of the large amount outstanding. The market is very active and transaction costs are small in the sale of Treasury bills in the secondary market.

The original maturity on Treasury notes is 1 to 10 years, whereas the original maturity on Treasury bonds is over 10 years. With the passage of time, of course, a number of these securities have maturities of less than 1 year and serve the needs of short-term investors. Notes and bonds are coupon issues, and there is an active market for them. Overall, Treasury securities are the safest and most marketable investments. Consequently, they provide the lowest yield for a given maturity of the various instruments we consider. Though the interest income on these securities is taxed at the federal level, it is exempt from state income taxes.

FIGURE 14-3
Cash and marketable securities management

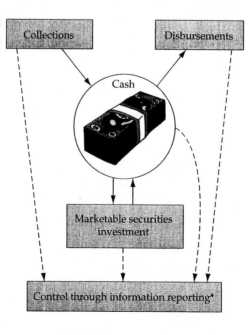

◄——— Funds flow   ◄– – – Information flow

*With timely information reporting, a firm can generate significant income by properly managing collections, disbursements, cash balances, and marketable securities investment.

Repurchase Agreements   In an effort to tap important sources of financing, government security dealers offer repurchase agreements to corporations. The repurchase agreement, or **repo**, is the sale of short-term securities by the dealer to the investor, whereby the dealer agrees to repurchase the securities at a specified future time. The investor receives a given yield while holding the security. The length of the holding period itself is tailored to the needs of the investor. It can be as little as "overnight," meaning a 1-day holding period, or it may run several days to a week or more. Thus, repurchase agreements give the investor a great deal of flexibility with respect to maturity. Rates on repurchase agreements are related to the rates on Treasury bills, federal funds, and loans to government security dealers by commercial banks. There is little marketability to the instrument, but the usual maturity is either overnight or only a few days. Because the instrument involved is a U.S. Treasury security, the default risk depends solely on the financial condition and reliability of the dealer.

Agency Securities   Obligations of various agencies of the federal government are guaranteed by the agency issuing the security, but not by the U.S. government as such. Principal **agencies** issuing securities include the Federal Housing Administration and the Government National Mortgage Association (Ginnie Mae). In addition, there are a number of **government-sponsored enterprises (GSEs)**. Their securities are not guaranteed by the federal government, nor is there any stated "moral" obligation, but there is an implied backing. It would be hard to imagine the federal government allowing them to fail. Major government-sponsored agencies include the Farm Credit System and the Federal National Mortgage Association (Fannie Mae). Agency issues typically provide a modest yield advantage over Treasury securities of the same maturity, and they have a fairly high degree of marketability. Although interest income on these securities is subject to federal income taxes, issues of the Farm Credit agencies are not subject to state and local income taxes. Maturities range from several days to approximately 15 years. About half of the securities outstanding mature in less than a year.

Bankers' Acceptances   Bankers' acceptances are drafts that are accepted by banks, and they are used in financing foreign and domestic trade. The creditworthiness of bankers' acceptances is judged by the bank accepting the draft, not the drawer. Acceptances generally have maturities of less than 6 months and are of high quality. They are traded in an over-the-counter market dominated by five principal dealers. The rates on bankers' acceptances tend to be slightly higher than rates on Treasury bills of like maturity, and both are sold on a discount basis. Bankers' acceptances can be on both domestic banks and on large foreign banks.

Commercial Paper   Commercial paper consists of short-term unsecured promissory notes issued by finance companies and certain industrial concerns. Commercial paper can be sold either directly or through dealers. Many large sales finance companies have found it profitable, because of the volume, to sell their paper directly to investors, thus bypassing dealers. Among companies selling paper on this basis are the General Electric Credit Corporation and the Ford Motor Credit Company. Paper sold through dealers is issued by industrial companies and smaller finance companies. Dealers very carefully screen the creditworthiness of potential issuers. In a sense, dealers stand behind the paper they place with investors.

Rates on commercial paper are somewhat higher than rates on Treasury bills of the same maturity and about the same as the rates available on bankers' acceptances. Paper sold directly generally commands a lower yield than paper sold through dealers. Usually, commercial paper is sold on a discount basis, and maturities generally range from 30 to 270 days. Most paper is held to maturity, for there is essentially no secondary market. Often, direct sellers of commercial paper will repurchase the paper on request. Arrangements may also be made through dealers for repurchase of paper sold through them. Commercial paper is sold only in large denominations, usually $100,000.

Certificates of Deposit A short-term investment, the certificate of deposit (CD) is evidence of the deposit of funds at a commercial bank for a specified period of time and at a specified rate of interest. The most common denomination is $100,000, so its appeal is limited to large investors. Money market banks quote rates on CDs; these rates are changed periodically in keeping with changes in other money market rates. Yields on CDs are greater than those on Treasury bills and repos and about the same as those on bankers' acceptances and commercial paper. Original maturities of CDs generally range from 30 to 360 days. A good secondary market has developed for the CDs of the large money market banks. Default risk is that of the bank failing. Like bankers' acceptances, corporations buy domestic as well as CDs of large foreign banks. The latter are known as "Yankee" CDs, and they typically carry a higher expected return.

Eurodollars Although most Eurodollars are deposited in Europe, the term applies to any dollar deposit in foreign banks or in foreign branches of U.S. banks. There exists a substantial, very active market for the deposit and lending of Eurodollars. This market is a wholesale one in that the amounts involved are at least $100,000. Moreover, the market is free of government regulation, as it is truly international in scope. The rates quoted on deposits vary according to the maturity of the deposit, while the rates on loans depend on maturity and default risk. For a given maturity, the lending rate always exceeds the deposit rate. The bank makes its money on the spread. The benchmark rate in this market is the 3-month London interbank offer rate (LIBOR). This is the rate at which banks make loans to each other. All other borrowers are quoted rates in excess of this rate, such as LIBOR $+\frac{1}{2}$ percent.

As a marketable security, the Eurodollar time deposit is like a negotiable certificate of deposit. Most deposits have a maturity of less than a year, and they can be sold in the market prior to maturity. Call money deposits are available, allowing investors to get their money back on demand, and there are 1-day (overnight) deposits. For the large corporation with ready contact with international money centers, the Eurodollar deposit usually is an important investment.

Short-Term Municipals State and local governments are increasingly providing securities tailored to the short-term investor. One is a commercial paper type of instrument, where the interest rate is reset every week. That is, the security is essentially a floating rate where the weekly reset ensures that market value will vary scarcely at all. Some corporations invest in longer-term municipal securities, but the maturity usually is kept within 1 or 2 years. A problem with longer-term instruments is that marketability is only fair. Shorter-term instruments designed for the corporate treasurer and for municipal money market mutual funds have much better marketability and price stability.

Floating-Rate Preferred Stock Straight preferred stock is a perpetual security where the dividend can be omitted by the issuer when its financial condition deteriorates (see Chapter 20). For these reasons, we usually do not think of it as being suitable for the marketable security portfolio of a corporation. However, the corporate investor gains a considerable tax advantage, in that 70 percent of the preferred stock dividend is exempt from federal taxation. (The full dividend is subject to state income taxation.) *Floating-rate preferred stock,* as the name implies, provides a yield that goes up or down with money market rates. It also permits the corporate investor to reap the advantage of the 70 percent dividend exclusion for federal tax purposes. One product in this vein is money market preferred stock (MMP). How does it work?

With MMP, an auction is held every 49 days. This provides the investor with liquidity and relative price stability as far as interest-rate risk goes. It does not protect the investor against default risk. The new auction rate is set by the forces of supply and demand in keeping with interest rates in the money market. A typical rate might be .75 times the commercial paper rate, with more creditworthy issuers commanding an even greater discount. As long as enough investors bid at each auction, the effective maturity date is 49 days. As a result, there is little variation in the market price of the instrument over time, and this represents a substantial advantage. In a failed auction where there are insufficient bidders, there is a default dividend rate for one period that is frequently 110 percent of the commercial paper rate. In addition, the holder has the option to redeem the instrument at its face value. These provisions are attractive to the investor as long as the company is able to meet the conditions. If the company should altogether default, however, the investor loses. There have been only a few instances of failed auctions and default.

Portfolio Management

The decision to invest excess cash in marketable securities involves not only the amount to invest but also the type of security in which to invest. To some extent, the two decisions are interdependent. Both should be based on an evaluation of expected net cash flows and the uncertainty associated with these cash flows. If future cash-flow patterns are known with reasonable certainty and the yield curve is upward sloping in the sense of longer-term securities yielding more than shorter-term ones, a company may wish to arrange its portfolio so that securities will mature approximately when the funds will be needed. Such a cash-flow pattern gives the firm a great deal of flexibility in maximizing the average return on the entire portfolio, for it is unlikely that significant amounts of securities will have to be sold unexpectedly.

If the yield curve is downward sloping, the maturity matching strategy outlined above may not be appropriate. The company may wish to invest in securities having maturities shorter than the intended holding period, then to reinvest at maturity. In this way, it can avail itself of the higher initial yield on shorter-term securities, but it does not know what the securities will yield on reinvestment at maturity. Another key factor is the degree of certainty one has in the cash-flow projections. With a high degree of certainty, the maturity of a marketable security becomes its most important characteristic.[3] If future cash flows are fairly uncertain, the most important characteristics of a security become its marketability and risk with respect to fluctuations in market value. Treasury bills and short-term repos

---

[3]This statement assumes that all the securities considered are of reasonably high quality from the standpoint of default risk. Otherwise, they would not fall within the usual definition of a marketable security.

are perhaps best suited for the emergency liquidity needs of a firm. Higher yields can be achieved by investing in longer-term, less marketable securities with greater risk.

For multinational companies, cash and marketable securities may be kept in multiple currencies. Many companies maintain liquidity in the country where investment takes place and/or where the sourcing of a product occurs. The marketable securities position of such a company is part of a broader management of currency risk exposure. As that topic is addressed in Chapter 25, we do not take it up here.

Later in the book we devote a chapter to financial risk management. There we will see how risk of various sorts—interest rate, default, currency, and commodity—can be hedged. The laying off of risk, for a price, results in the corporation keeping only the appropriate risk. The art of hedging and the instruments used to accomplish that purpose are applicable to marketable security management.

Summary

Under perfect market assumptions, liquidity is not a thing of value. Stockholders personally could replicate any liquidity a company might hold. Only with imperfections, such as bankruptcy costs, can corporate liquidity be a thing of value. We take liquidity to be cash and marketable securities.

In the management of cash, we should attempt to accelerate collections and handle disbursements so that maximum cash is available. Collections can be accelerated by means of concentration banking, a lockbox system, and certain other procedures. Disbursements should be handled to give maximum transfer flexibility and the optimum timing of payments, being mindful, however, of supplier relations. Several methods for controlling disbursements

were described. Electronic funds transfers are becoming increasingly important, and most corporations use such transfers in one way or another.

The company can invest excess cash in a number of marketable securities. These securities can be evaluated in relation to their default risk, marketability, maturity, coupon rate, and taxability. Depending on the cash-flow pattern of the company and other considerations, a portfolio can be selected in keeping with these characteristics. Specific securities considered included Treasury securities, repurchase agreements, government agency securities, bankers' acceptances, commercial paper, certificates of deposit, Eurodollars, short-term municipals, and floating-rate preferred stock.

Self-Correction Problems

1. The Zakuta Fish Company is in a cyclical, risky business. By maintaining liquidity, it lowers the possibility of going into bankruptcy. It is estimated that if bankruptcy were to occur, there would be a $100,000 present-value shortfall in what suppliers of capital would realize from the going concern value of the assets. This "cost" of bankruptcy is attributable to legal expenses and the sale of assets at distress prices. By maintaining the following levels of liquidity, the probabilities of bankruptcy occurring are:

Level of Liquidity	Probability of Bankruptcy
$ 25,000	.30
50,000	.20
75,000	.15
100,000	.12
125,000	.10
150,000	.08
175,000	.06
200,000	.05
225,000	.04
250,000	.03

Liquidity is increased by borrowing, and it is held in the form of marketable securities. Marketable securities yield less than the interest rate the company must pay on short-term borrowings. The present-value differential amounts to $1,500 for each $25,000 borrowed. If we assume no taxes and no other explicit or implicit costs associated with debt, what is the optimal level of liquidity?

2. The Zindler Company currently has a centralized billing system. Payments are made by all customers to the central billing location. It requires, on the average, 4 days for customers' mailed payments to reach the central location. An additional $1\frac{1}{2}$ days are required to process payments before a deposit can be made. The firm has a daily average collection of $500,000. The company has recently investigated the possibility of initiating a lockbox system. It has estimated that with such a system, customers' mailed payments would reach the receipt location $2\frac{1}{2}$ days sooner. Further, the processing time could be reduced by 1 additional day, because each lockbox bank would pick up mailed deposits twice daily.

   a. Determine the reduction in cash balances that can be achieved through the use of a lockbox system.

   b. Determine the opportunity cost of the present system, assuming a 5 percent return on short-term instruments.

   c. If the annual cost of the lockbox system were $75,000, should such a system be initiated?

3. Over the next year, El Pedro Steel Company, a California corporation, expects the following returns on continual investment in marketable securities:

Treasury bills	8.00%
Commercial paper	8.50
Floating-rate preferred stock	7.00

The company's marginal tax rate for federal income tax purposes is 30 percent (after allowance for the payment of state income taxes), while its marginal, incremental tax rate with respect to California income taxes is 7 percent. On the basis of after-tax returns, which is the most attractive investment? Are there other considerations?

Problems

1. Speedway Owl Company franchises Gas and Go stations in North Carolina and Virginia. All payments by franchisees for gasoline and oil products are by check, which average in total $420,000 a day. At present, the overall time between a check being mailed by the franchisee to Speedway Owl and the company having available funds at its bank is 6 days.

    a. How much money is tied up in this interval of time?

    b. To reduce this delay, the company is considering daily pickups from the stations. In all, two cars would be needed and two additional people hired. The cost would be $93,000 annually. This procedure would reduce the overall delay by 2 days. Currently, the opportunity cost of funds is 9 percent, that being the interest rate on marketable securities. Should the company inaugurate the pickup plan?

    c. Rather than mail checks to its bank, the company could deliver them by messenger service. This procedure would reduce the overall delay by 1 day and cost $10,300 annually. Should the company undertake this plan?

2. The List Company, which can earn 7 percent on money market instruments, currently has a lockbox arrangement with a New Orleans bank for its southern customers. The bank handles $3 million a day in return for a compensating balance of $2 million.

    a. The List Company has discovered that it could divide the southern region into a southwestern region (with $1 million a day in collections, which could be handled by a Dallas bank for a $1 million compensating balance) and a southeastern region (with $2 million a day in collections, which could be handled by an Atlanta bank for a $2 million compensating balance). In each case, collections would be one-half day quicker than with the New Orleans arrangement. What would be the annual savings (or cost) of dividing the southern region?

    b. In an effort to retain the business, the New Orleans bank has offered to handle the collections strictly on a fee basis (no compensating balance). What would be the maximum fee the New Orleans bank could charge and still retain List's business?

3. The Frazini Food Company has a weekly payroll of $150,000, paid on Friday. On average, its employees cash their checks in the following manner:

Day Check Cleared on Company's Account	Percent of Checks Cashed
Friday	20
Monday	40
Tuesday	25
Wednesday	10
Thursday	5

    As treasurer of the company, how would you arrange your payroll account? Are there any problems involved?

4. Topple Tea Houses, Inc., operates seven restaurants in the state of Pennsylvania. The manager of each restaurant transfers funds daily from the local bank

to the company's principal bank in Harrisburg. There are approximately 250 business days during a year in which transfers occur. Several methods of transfer are available. A wire transfer results in immediate availability of funds, but the local banks charge $5 per wire transfer. A transfer through an automatic clearinghouse involves next-day settlement, or a 1-day delay, and costs $3 per transfer. Finally, a mail-based depository transfer check arrangement costs $.30 per transfer, and mailing times result in a 3-day delay on average for the transfer to occur. (This experience is the same for each restaurant.) The company presently uses depository transfer checks for all transfers. The restaurants have the following daily average remittances:

Restaurant	1	2	3	4	5	6	7
Remittance	$3,000	$4,600	$2,700	$5,200	$4,100	$3,500	$3,800

    a. If the opportunity cost of funds is 10 percent, which transfer procedure should be used for each of the restaurants?

    b. If the opportunity cost of funds were 5 percent, what would be the optimal strategy?

5. Research Project: Examine quotations in the *Wall Street Journal* for each of the following money market instruments:

    a. Treasury bills

    b. Bankers' acceptances

    c. Certificates of deposit

    d. Commercial paper

    e. Government agency issues

    f. Eurodollars

Evaluate the yield–risk trade-off for each instrument. Consider the appropriateness of each of these securities for the corporation's short-term investment account.

Solutions to Self-Correction Problems

1.

(1) Level of Liquidity	(2) Probability of Bankruptcy	(3) Expected Cost of Bankruptcy (2) × $100,000	(4) Change in (3)
$ 25,000	.30	$30,000	—
50,000	.20	20,000	−$10,000
75,000	.15	15,000	−5,000
100,000	.12	12,000	−3,000
125,000	.10	10,000	−2,000
150,000	.08	8,000	−2,000
175,000	.06	6,000	−2,000
200,000	.05	5,000	−1,000
225,000	.04	4,000	−1,000
250,000	.03	3,000	−1,000

As the marginal present-value cost of each $25,000 increment of liquidity is $1,500, the optimal level of liquidity is $175,000. At this level, there is a 6 percent chance that bankruptcy will occur.

2. a. Total time savings = $3\frac{1}{2}$ days

    Time savings $\times$ Daily average collection = Reduction in cash balances achieved

    $3\frac{1}{2} \times \$500,000 = \$1,750,000$

    b. $5\% \times \$1,750,000 = \$87,500$

    c. Since the opportunity cost of the present system ($87,500) exceeds the cost of the lockbox system ($75,000), the system should be initiated.

3.

Security	Federal Tax	State Tax	Combined Effect	After-Tax Expected Return
Treasury bills	.30	0	.30	$(1 - .30)8.00\% = 5.60\%$
Commercial paper	.30	.07	.37	$(1 - .37)8.50\% = 5.36\%$
Floating-rate preferred stock	$(1 - .70).30$ $= .09$	.07	.16	$(1 - .16)7.00\% = 5.88\%$

The floating-rate preferred is the most attractive after taxes, owing to the 70 percent exemption for federal income tax purposes. Commercial paper is less attractive than Treasury bills because of the state income tax from which Treasury bills are exempt. (In states with no income taxes, the after-tax yield on commercial paper would be higher.) Preferred stock may not be the most attractive investment when risk is taken into account.

■ Selected References

BAUMOL, WILLIAM J., "The Transactions Demand for Cash: An Inventory Theoretic Approach," *Quarterly Journal of Economics*, 65 (November 1952), 545–56.

FREEMAN, TOM, "Transforming the Finance Function for The New Millennium," *Corporate Controller*, 11 (May/June 1998), 23–29.

HILL, NED C., and WILLIAM L. SARTORIS, *Short-Term Financial Management: Text and Cases*, 2nd ed. New York: Macmillan, 1992.

KALLBERG, JARL G., and KENNETH L. PARKINSON, *Corporate Liquidity: Management and Measurement*. Homewood, IL: Irwin, 1993.

KIM, CHANG-SOO, DAVID C. MAUER, and ANN E. SHERMAN, "The Determinants of Corporate Liquidity: Theory and Evidence," *Journal of Financial and Quantitative Analysis*, 33 (September 1998), 335–59.

KNEZ, PETER J., ROBERT LITTERMAN, and JOSE SCHEINKMAN, "Explorations into Factors Explaining Money Market Returns," *Journal of Finance*, 49 (December 1994), 1861–82.

LACKER, JEFFREY M., "The Check Float Puzzle," *Economic Quarterly of the Federal Bank of Richmond*, 83 (Summer 1997), 1–25.

MILLER, MERTON H., and DANIEL ORR, "A Model of the Demand for Money by Firms," *Quarterly Journal of Economics*, 80 (August 1966), 413–35.

MORRIS, JAMES R., "Role of Cash Balances in Firm Valuation," *Journal of Financial and Quantitative Analysis*, 18 (December 1983), 533–46.

OPLER, TIM, LEE PINKOWITZ, RENE STULZ, and RO-HAN WILLIAMSON, "The Determinants and Implications of Corporate Cash Holdings," *Journal of Financial Economics*, 52 (April 1999), 3–46.

PHILLIPS, AARON L., "Migration of Corporate Payments from Check to Electronic Format," *Financial Management*, 27 (Winter 1998), 92–105.

STONE, BERNELL K., "Design of a Receivable Collection System," *Management Science*, 27 (August 1981), 866–80.

VAN HORNE, JAMES C., "A Risk–Return Analysis of a Firm's Working-Capital Position," *Engineering Economist*, 14 (Winter 1969), 71–89.

———, *Financial Market Rates and Flows*, 6th ed. Upper Saddle River, NJ: Prentice Hall, 2001.

Wachowicz's Web World is an excellent overall Web site produced and maintained by my coauthor of *Fundamentals of Financial Management*, John M. Wachowicz Jr. It contains descriptions of and links to many finance Web sites and articles. *www.prenhall.com/wachowicz.*

Management of Accounts Receivable and Inventories

F or most companies, accounts receivable and inventories are very important investments, often dominating fixed-asset investments. With the concern for return on assets expressed by many companies in recent years, there has come ever-increasing focus on the funds committed to receivables and inventories. Whether these current assets are managed efficiently influences very strongly the amount of funds invested. In this chapter we explore the key variables involved in efficiently managing receivables and inventories. In both situations, the optimal investment is determined by comparing benefits to be derived from a particular level of investment with the costs of maintaining that level. We consider first the credit and collection policies of the firm as a whole and then discuss procedures for the individual account. The last part of the chapter investigates techniques for efficiently managing inventories. The cash-flow cycle involves inventories being acquired ahead of sales, whereas receivables are generated at the time of sales and become cash only after a further lapse of time. Measures by which to judge the turnover of receivables and inventories were taken up in Chapter 12 on financial ratios. This chapter assumes a familiarity with such. ∎

CREDIT POLICIES

Economic conditions and the firm's credit policies are the chief influences on the level of a firm's accounts receivable. Economic conditions, of course, are largely beyond the control of the financial manager. As with other current assets, however, the manager can vary the level of receivables in keeping with the trade-off between profitability and risk. Lowering quality standards may stimulate demand, which, in turn, should lead to higher profits. But there is a cost to carrying the additional receivables, as well as a greater risk of bad-debt losses. It is this trade-off that we wish to examine.

We must emphasize that the credit and collection policies of one firm are not independent of those of other firms. If product and capital markets are reasonably competitive, the credit and collection practices of one company will be influenced by what other companies are doing. Such practices are related to the pricing of the product or service and must be viewed as part of the overall competitive process. Our examination of certain policy variables implies that the competitive process is accounted for in the specification of the demand function as well as in the opportunity cost associated with taking on additional receivables. The policy variables we consider include the quality of the trade accounts accepted, the length of the

449

Credit policy
embraces terms of sale and quality standards for acceptance.

credit period, the cash discount, any special terms—such as seasonal datings—and the collection program of the firm. Together, these elements largely determine the average collection period and the proportion of bad-debt losses.

Credit Standards

Credit policy can have a significant influence on sales. In theory, the firm should lower its quality standard for accounts accepted as long as the profitability of sales generated exceeds the added costs of the receivables. What are the costs of relaxing credit standards? Some arise from an enlarged credit department, the clerical work of checking additional accounts, and servicing the added volume of receivables. We assume for now that these costs are deducted from the profitability of additional sales to give a net profitability figure for computational purposes. Another cost comes from the increased probability of bad-debt losses. We postpone consideration of this cost to a subsequent section; we assume for now that there are no bad-debt losses.

Our focus is on the carrying cost of the additional receivables, which result from increased sales and a slower average collection period. If new customers are attracted by the relaxed credit standards, collecting from these customers is likely to be slower than collecting from existing customers. In addition, a more liberal extension of credit may cause certain existing customers to be less conscientious in paying their bills on time.

Illustration   To assess the profitability of a more liberal extension of credit, we must know the profitability of additional sales, the added demand for products arising from the relaxed credit standards, the increased slowness of the average collection period, and the required return on investment. Suppose a firm's product sells for $10 a unit, of which $8 represents variable costs before taxes, including credit department costs. The firm is operating at less than full capacity, and an increase in sales can be accommodated without any increase in fixed costs. Therefore, the contribution margin of an additional unit of sales is the selling price less variable costs involved in producing the unit, or $10 − $8 = $2.

The longer the credit period, the more funds that are tied up in receivables.

At present, annual credit sales are running at a level of $2.4 million, and there is no underlying trend in such sales. The firm may liberalize credit, which will result in an average collection experience of new customers of 2 months.[1] Existing customers are not expected to alter their payment habits and continue to pay in 1 month. The relaxation in credit standards is expected to produce a 25 percent increase in sales, to $3 million annually. This $600,000 increase represents 60,000 additional units if we assume that the price per unit stays the same. Finally, assume that the opportunity cost of carrying additional receivables is 20 percent before taxes.

This information reduces our evaluation to a trade-off between the added profitability on the additional sales and the opportunity cost of the increased investment in receivables. The increased investment arises solely from new, slower-paying customers; we have assumed existing customers continue to pay in 1 month. With the additional sales of $600,000 and receivable turnover of 6 times a

---

[1]It should be pointed out that if there is either an upward or a downward trend in sales, the average collection period and receivable turnover ratio will not provide an accurate estimate of the new level of receivables outstanding. This problem was investigated at length in Chapter 12, where we explore the use of the average collection period and aging of accounts receivable. For ease of understanding of our example, we assume that there is no trend in sales either before a credit policy decision or after the decision.

year (12 months divided by the average collection period of 2 months), the additional receivables are $600,000/6 = $100,000. For these additional receivables, the firm invests the variable costs tied up in them. For our example, $.80 of every $1.00 in sales represents variable costs. Therefore, the added investment in receivables is .80 × $100,000 = $80,000. With these inputs, we are able to make the calculations shown in Table 15-1. Inasmuch as the profitability on additional sales, $120,000, far exceeds the required return on the additional investment in receivables, $16,000, the firm would be well advised to relax its credit standards. An optimal credit policy would involve extending trade credit more liberally until the marginal profitability on additional sales equals the required return on the additional investment in receivables.

Some Qualifications   Obviously there are many practical problems in effecting a change in credit policy, particularly in estimating the outcomes. In our example, we have worked with only the expected values of additional demand and of the slowing of the average collection period. It is possible and desirable to attach probability distributions to the increased demand and to the increased slowness in receivables and to evaluate a range of possible outcomes. For simplicity of discussion, we shall not incorporate these dimensions into our example.

   Another assumption is that we can produce 60,000 additional units at a variable cost of $8 a unit; that is, we do not have to increase our plant. After some point, we are no longer able to meet additional demand with existing plant and would need to add plant. This occurrence would necessitate a change in analysis, for there would be a large block of incremental costs at the point where the existing plant could produce no more units. One implication to all this is that the firm should vary its credit quality standards in keeping with the level of production. As capacity is approached, quality standards might be increased. When production sags and the firm operates at a level below capacity, the lowering of credit quality standards becomes more attractive, all other things the same.

   The credit standards of the firm may affect the level of inventories maintained. Easier standards leading to increased sales may require more inventories. If so, the calculations shown in Table 15-1 overstate the profitability of change in credit standards. In order to correct for this overstatement, the additional inventories associated with a new credit policy should be added to the additional receivables, and the opportunity cost should be computed on the basis of the combined increase. Our analysis also implies that the conditions described will be permanent. That is, increased demand as a function of lowering credit quality standards as well as price and cost figures will remain unchanged. If the increase in sales that

TABLE 15-1

Profitability versus Required Return, Credit Standard Change

Profitability of additional sales	= $2 × 60,000 units = $120,000
Additional receivables	= (Additional sales/Receivable turnover) $600,000/6 = $100,000
Investment in additional receivables	= (Variable costs/Sales price) (Additional receivables) (.80) ($100,000) = $80,000
Required return on additional investment	= .20 × $80,000 = $16,000

results from a change in credit policy were a one-shot as opposed to a continuing occurrence, we would need to modify our analysis accordingly.

Credit Period

Credit terms involve both the length of the credit period and the discount given. The term "2/10, net 30" means that a 2 percent discount is given if the bill is paid before the tenth day after the date of invoice; payment is due by the thirtieth day. The credit period, then, is 30 days. Although the customs of the industry frequently dictate the terms given, the credit period is another means by which a firm may be able to affect product demand, hoping to increase demand by extending the credit period. As before, the trade-off is between the profitability of additional sales and the required return on the additional investment in receivables.

Increasing the Period   Let us say that the firm in our example increases its credit period from 30 days to 60 days. The average collection period for existing customers goes from 1 month to 2 months. The more liberal period results in increased sales of $360,000, and these new customers also pay, on average, in 2 months. The total additional receivables are composed of two parts. The first part represents the receivables associated with the increased sales. In our example, there are $360,000 in additional sales. With a receivable turnover of 6 times a year, the additional receivables associated with the new sales are $360,000/6 = $60,000. For these additional receivables, the investment by the firm is the variable costs tied up in them. For our example, we have ($8/$10)($60,000) = $48,000.

The second part of the total additional receivables represents the slowing in collections associated with original sales. The old receivables are collected in a slower manner, resulting in a higher receivable level. With $2.4 million in original sales, the firm's level of receivables with a turnover of 12 times a year is $2,400,000/12 = $200,000. The new level with a turnover of 6 times a year is $2,400,000/6 = $400,000. Thus, there are $200,000 in additional receivables associated with the original sales. For this addition, the relevant investment using marginal analysis is the full $200,000. In other words, the use of variable costs pertains only to new sales. The incremental $200,000 in receivables on original sales would have been collected earlier had it not been for the change in credit standards. Therefore, the firm must increase its investment in receivables by $200,000.

New and Original Sales Results   Based on these inputs, our calculations are shown in Table 15-2. The appropriate comparison is the profitability of additional sales with the opportunity cost of the additional investment in receivables. Inasmuch as the profitability on additional sales, $72,000, exceeds the required return on the investment in additional receivables, $48,000, the change in credit period from 30 to 60 days is worthwhile. The profitability of the additional sales more than offsets the added investment in receivables, the bulk of which comes from existing customers slowing their payments.

Discount Given

Varying the discount given involves an attempt to speed up the payment of receivables. To be sure, the discount also may have an effect on demand and bad-debt

TABLE 15-2
Profitability versus Required Return, Credit Period Change

Profitability of additional sales	= \$2 × 36,000 units = \$72,000
Additional receivables associated with new sales	= (New sales/Receivable turnover) \$360,000/6 = \$60,000
Additional investment in receivables associated with new sales	= (Variable costs/Sales price)(Additional receivables) (.80)(\$60,000) = \$48,000
Present level of receivables	= (Annual sales/Receivable turnover) \$2.4 million/12 = \$200,000
New level of receivables associated with original sales	= \$2.4 million/6 = \$400,000
Additional investment in receivables associated with original sales	= \$400,000 − \$200,000 = \$200,000
Total additional investment in receivables	= \$48,000 + \$200,000 = \$248,000
Carrying cost of additional investment	= .20 × \$248,000 = \$49,600

losses. We assume that the discount is not regarded as a means of cutting price and thereby affecting demand, and that the discount offered does not affect the amount of bad-debt losses. Holding constant these factors, we must determine whether a speedup in collections would more than offset the cost of an increase in the discount. If it would, the present discount policy should be changed.

Illustration Suppose the firm has annual credit sales of \$3 million and an average collection period of 2 months, and the sales terms are net 45 days, with no discount given. Consequently, the average receivable balance is \$500,000. By instigating terms of 2/10, net 45, the average collection period can be reduced to 1 month, as 60 percent of the customers (in dollar volume) take advantage of the 2 percent discount. The opportunity cost of the discount to the firm is .02 × .6 × \$3 million, or \$36,000 annually. The turnover of receivables has improved to 12 times a year, so that average receivables are reduced from \$500,000 to \$250,000.

Thus, the firm realizes \$250,000 from accelerated collections. The value of the funds released is their opportunity cost. If we assume a 20 percent rate of return, the opportunity saving is \$50,000. In this case, the opportunity saving arising from a speedup in collections is greater than the cost of the discount. The firm should adopt a 2 percent discount. If the speedup in collections had not resulted in sufficient opportunity savings to offset the cost of discount, the discount policy should not be changed. It is possible, of course, that discounts other than 2 percent may result in an even greater difference between the opportunity savings and the cost of the discount.

Seasonal Datings
During periods of slack sales, firms will sometimes sell to customers without requiring payment for some time to come. This seasonal dating can be tailored to

the cash flow of the customer and may stimulate demand from customers who cannot pay until later in the season. Again, we should compare the profitability of additional sales with the required return on the additional investment in receivables to determine whether datings are appropriate terms by which to stimulate demand.

Datings also can be used to avoid inventory carrying costs. If sales are seasonal and production is steady throughout the year, there will be buildups in finished goods inventory during certain times of the year. Storage involves warehousing costs that might be avoided by giving datings. If warehousing costs plus the required rate of return on investment in inventory exceed the required rate of return on the additional receivables, datings are worthwhile.

Default Risk

In the foregoing examples, we assumed no bad-debt losses. Our concern in this section is not only with the slowness of collection but also with the portion of the receivables defaulting. Different credit standard policies will involve both of these factors. Suppose we are considering the present credit standard policy (sales of $2,400,000) together with two new ones, and these policies are expected to produce the following results:

	Present Policy	Policy A	Policy B
Demand (sales)	$2,400,000	$3,000,000	$3,300,000
Default losses on incremental sales (percentage)	2	10	18
Average collection period on incremental sales	1 month	2 months	3 months

We assume that after 6 months an account is turned over to a collection agency and that, on average, 2 percent of the original sales of $2.4 million is never received by the firm, 10 percent is never received on the $600,000 in additional sales under policy A, and 18 percent on the $300,000 in additional sales under policy B is never received. Similarly, the 1-month average collection period pertains to the original sales, 2 months to the $600,000 in additional sales under policy A, and 3 months to the $300,000 in additional sales under policy B. These numbers of months correspond to annual receivable turnovers of 12 times, 6 times, and 4 times, respectively.

The incremental profitability calculations associated with these two new credit standard policies are shown in Table 15-3. We would want to adopt policy A but would not want to go as far as policy B in relaxing our credit standards. The marginal benefit is positive in moving from the present policy to policy A, but negative in going from policy A to policy B. It is possible, of course, that a relaxation of credit standards that fell on one side or the other of policy A would provide an even greater marginal benefit; the optimal policy is the one that provides the greatest marginal benefit.

TABLE 15-3

**Profitability versus Required Return,
Bad-Debt Losses and Collection Period Changes**

	Policy A	Policy B
1. Additional sales	$600,000	$300,000
2. Profitability of additional sales (20%)	120,000	60,000
3. Additional bad-debt losses (additional sales × bad-debt percentage)	60,000	54,000
4. Additional receivables (additional sales/receivables turnover)	100,000	75,000
5. Investment in additional receivables (.8 × additional receivables)	80,000	60,000
6. Required return on additional investment (20 percent)	16,000	12,000
7. Bad-debt losses plus additional required return	76,000	66,000
8. Incremental profitability, line 2 – line 7	44,000	(6,000)

COLLECTION POLICY

The firm determines its overall collection policy by the combination of collection procedures it undertakes. These procedures include telephoning the customer, sending a letter, resending the invoice, sometimes paying a person a visit, and legal action. After a point in time, often 90 days past due, many companies turn the account over to a collection agency. Here fees run up to 50 percent of the amount collected. In collections, one of the principal policy variables is the amount expended on collection procedures. Within a range, the greater the relative amount expended, the lower the proportion of bad-debt losses and the shorter the average collection period, all other things the same.

The relationships are not linear. Initial collection expenditures are likely to cause little reduction in bad-debt losses. Additional expenditures begin to have a significant effect up to a point; then they tend to have little effect in further reducing these losses. The hypothesized relationship between expenditures and bad-debt losses is shown in Fig. 15-1. The relationship between the average collection period and the level of collection expenditures is likely to be similar to that shown in the figure.

The Trade-off

If sales are independent of the collection effort, the appropriate level of collection expenditure again involves a trade-off—this time between the level of expenditure on the one hand and the reduction in the cost of bad-debt losses and reduction in receivables on the other. Suppose we are comparing the present collection program with two new ones, and the programs are expected to produce these results:

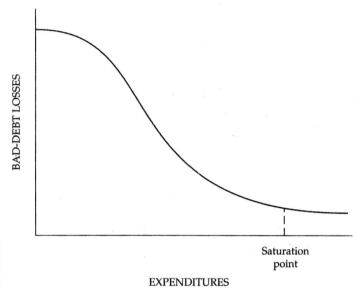

FIGURE 15-1
Relationship between amount of bad-debt losses and collection expenditures

BAD-DEBT LOSSES

Saturation point

EXPENDITURES

Collection efforts provide diminishing returns beyond some point.

	Present Program	Program A	Program B
Annual collection expenditures	$116,000	$148,000	$200,000
Average collection period, all accounts	2 months	1½ months	1 month
Percentage of default, all accounts	3%	2%	1%

Assume that present sales are $2.4 million and that they are not expected to change with changes in the collection effort. If we go through the same type of reasoning we used for the discount policy where receivables were reduced and for bad-debt losses based on changes in the default percentages for all accounts, we obtain the results in Table 15-4. We see that the opportunity saving resulting from a speedup in collections plus the reduction in bad-debt losses exceeds the additional collection expenditures in going from the present program to program A, but not in going from program A to program B. As a result, the firm should adopt program A but not increase collection expenditures to the extent of program B.

Other Considerations

In the example we have assumed that demand is independent of the collection effort. In most cases, though, sales are likely to be affected adversely if the collection efforts of the firm become too intense and customers become increasingly irritated. If they do, we must take into account the relationship between the collection effort and demand. Reduction in demand can be incorporated into the marginal analysis of collection expenditures in the same manner as was the increase in demand accompanying a relaxation in credit standards. In addition, if the collection effort has an effect on the percentage of total sales taking a cash discount, this factor must be considered. With increased collection efforts, more customers might take the cash discount.

TABLE 15-4
Evaluation of Collection Programs

	Present Program	Program A	Program B
Annual sales	$2,400,000	$2,400,000	$2,400,000
Turnover of receivables	6	8	12
Average receivables	400,000	300,000	200,000
Reduction in receivables from present level		100,000	
Reduction in receivables from program A level			100,000
Return on reduction in receivables (20 percent)		20,000	20,000
Bad-debt losses (percent of annual sales)	72,000	48,000	24,000
Reduction in bad-debt losses from present losses		24,000	
Reduction in bad-debt losses from program A losses			24,000
Opportunity saving on reduced receivables plus reduction in bad-debt losses		44,000	44,000
Additional collection expenditures from present expenditures		32,000	
Additional collection expenditures from program A expenditures			52,000

Summary of Credit and Collection Policies

We see that the credit and collection policies of a firm involve several decisions: (1) the quality of account accepted, (2) the credit period, (3) the cash discount given, (4) any special terms such as seasonal datings, and (5) the level of collection expenditures. In each case, the decision should involve a comparison of possible gains from a change in policy and the cost of the change. Optimal credit and collection policies would be those that resulted in the marginal gains equaling the marginal costs.

To maximize profits arising from credit and collection policies, the firm should vary these policies jointly until it achieves an optimal solution. That solution will determine the best combination of credit standards, credit period, cash discount policy, special terms, and level of collection expenditures. Sensitivity analysis might be used to judge the impact of a change in policies on profits. Once functional relationships have been specified for the relationship between a particular policy and marginal sales, average collection period, and bad-debt losses, the policy can be varied from one extreme to the other, holding constant other factors. This variation gives insight into the impact of a change in policy on profits.

Effects of Changing Credit Standards For most policy variables, profits increase at a decreasing rate up to a point and then decrease as the policy is varied from no

Collection Periods Differ Internationally

The most typical credit terms in the United States involve net 30 days, which means payment is due by 30 days after invoice. This does not necessarily mean that the average collection period for a company is 30 days or less. In fact, it is more for most industries. Robert Morris Associates' financial ratio data suggest that the average collection period for manufacturing industries is approximately 44 days.

However, credit terms, payment habits, and legal redress are different in other countries. Though the average collection period is not substantially different for countries in Europe, it is for Latin American and African countries. According to data from the Finance, Credit & International Business subsidiary of the National Association of Credit Management, the average collection period is approximately 110 to 120 days for such Latin American countries as Argentina, Chile, Ecuador, and Uruguay whereas it is approximately 100 to 140 days for such African countries as Algeria, Cameroon, Ethiopia, Kenya, and Morocco.

When doing business internationally, the financial manager must recognize different payment traditions depending on the country involved. If you wish to do business in a particular country, it may be difficult to impose home-country credit and collection procedures. Recognizing this reality is essential before entering such a market.

effort to an extreme effort. Figure 15-2 depicts this relationship with the quality of account rejected. When there are no credit standards, when all applicants are accepted, sales are maximized, but they are offset by large bad-debt losses as well as by the opportunity cost of carrying a very large receivable position. As credit standards are initiated and applicants are rejected, revenue from sales declines, but so do the average collection period and bad-debt losses. Because the latter two de-

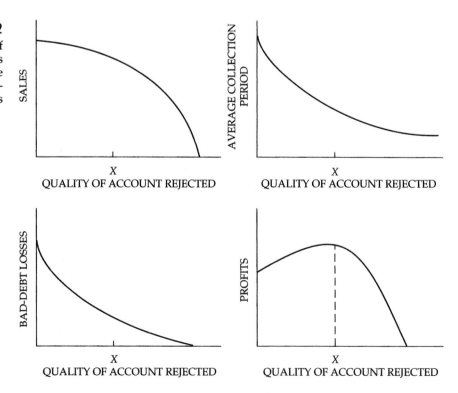

FIGURE 15-2
How the quality of account rejected relates to sales, average collection period, bad-debt losses, and profits

cline initially at a faster rate than do sales, profits increase. As credit standards are tightened increasingly, sales revenue declines at an increasing rate. At the same time, the average collection period and bad-debt losses decrease at a decreasing rate. Fewer and fewer bad credit risks are eliminated. Because of the combination of these influences, total profits of the firm increase at a diminishing rate with stricter credit standards up to a point, after which they decline. The optimal policy with respect to credit standards is represented by point *X* in the figure. In turn, this policy determines the level of accounts receivable held by the firm.[2]

When some of the underlying parameters change, sensitivity analysis proves valuable in formulating new credit and collection policies. If the marginal profit per unit of sales declines because of increased competition, the optimal set of policies is likely to change. Lower profits per unit of sale may not justify the present level of receivables carried or the present loss rate. As a result, new credit and collection policies might be in order. Through sensitivity analysis, management could determine the new set of policies that will maximize profit.

EVALUATING THE CREDIT APPLICANT

Having established the terms of sale to be offered, the firm must evaluate individual credit applicants and consider the possibilities of a bad debt or slow payment. The credit evaluation procedure involves three related steps: obtaining information on the applicant, analyzing this information to determine the applicant's creditworthiness, and making the credit decision. The credit decision, in turn, establishes whether credit should be extended and what the maximum amount of credit should be.

Sources of Information

A number of sources supply credit information, but for some accounts, especially small ones, the cost of collecting it may outweigh the potential profitability of the account. The firm extending credit may have to be satisfied with a limited amount of information on which to base a decision. In addition to cost, the firm must consider the time it takes to investigate a credit applicant. A shipment to a prospective customer cannot be delayed unnecessarily, pending an elaborate credit investigation. Thus, the amount of information collected needs to be considered in relation to the time and expense required. Depending on these considerations, the credit analyst may use one or more of the following sources of information.

Financial Statement   At the time of the prospective sale, the seller may request a financial statement, one of the most desirable sources of information for credit analysis. Frequently, there is a correlation between a company's refusal to provide a statement and its weak financial position. Audited statements are preferable; when possible, it is helpful to obtain interim statements in addition to year-end figures, particularly for companies having seasonal patterns of sales.

Credit Ratings and Reports   In addition to financial statements, credit ratings are available from various mercantile agencies. Dun & Bradstreet, Inc., is perhaps the best known and most comprehensive of these agencies. It provides credit ratings

---

[2]For a present-value approach to evaluating credit policy decisions, see Yong H. Kim and Joseph C. Atkins, "Evaluating Investments in Accounts Receivable: A Wealth Maximizing Framework," *Journal of Finance,* 33 (May 1978), 403–12.

to subscribers for a vast number of business firms. These ratings range from high to limited and are arrayed according to various net worth ranges. D&B also provides credit reports containing a brief history of a company and its principal officers, the nature of the business, certain financial information, and a trade check of suppliers—the length of their experience with the company and whether payments are discount, prompt, or past due. The quality of the D&B reports varies with the information available externally and the willingness of the company being checked to cooperate with the D&B reporter. The report itself can be accessed via a computer terminal if so desired. The typical D&B contract with a creditor involves a price for a minimum number of reports, with further inquiries bearing an incremental charge.

SR Research, Experian (formerly TRW) has developed a business-credit database on some 10 million businesses. Experian collects and processes data to produce risk management and credit-evaluation services. Typically, the information is not as extensive as that of Dun & Bradstreet, but it does offer a comprehensive alternative for credit analysis. Experian's commercial credit services are available in a variety of formats, including online delivery via computer, CD-ROM, and regional reference guides. Finally, the Credit Interchange Service of the National Association of Credit Management serves as a clearinghouse for credit information.

Bank Checking Another source of information for the firm is a credit check through a bank. Many banks have large credit departments that undertake credit checks as a service for their customers. By calling or writing a bank in which the credit applicant has an account, a firm's bank is able to obtain information on the average cash balance carried, loan accommodations, experience, and sometimes financial information. Because banks generally are more willing to share information with other banks than with a direct inquirer, it usually is best for the firm to initiate the credit check through its own bank rather than to inquire directly.

Trade Checking Credit information is frequently exchanged among companies selling to the same customer. Through various credit organizations, credit people in a particular area become a closely knit group. A company can ask other suppliers about their experiences with an account. Useful information includes the length of time they have had the account, the maximum credit extended, the amount of the line of credit, and whether payments are prompt or slow.

The Company's Own Experience A study of the promptness of past payments, including any seasonal patterns, is very useful. Frequently, the credit department will make written assessments of the quality of the management of a company to whom credit may be extended. These assessments are very important, for they pertain to the first of the famous "four C's" of credit: *character, collateral, capital,* and *capacity.* The person who made the sale to a prospective customer frequently can offer useful impressions of the management and operations. Caution is necessary in interpreting this information, because a salesperson has a natural bias toward granting credit and making the sale.

Credit Analysis

Having collected credit information, a company must make a credit analysis of the applicant and determine if the company falls above or below the minimum quality standard. If financial statements are provided, the analyst should undertake a ratio analysis, a source and use of funds analysis, and perhaps other analyses, as described in Chapters 12 and 13. The analyst will be particularly interested in the applicant's liquidity and ability to pay bills on time. Such ratios as the quick ratio, receivable and inventory turnovers, the average payable period, debt-to-net-worth ratio, and cash-flow coverage ratio are particularly germane.

In addition to analyzing financial statements, the credit analyst will consider the character and strength of the company and its management, the business risk associated with its operation, and various other matters. Then the analyst attempts to determine the ability of the applicant to service trade credit and the probability of an applicant's not paying on time and of a bad-debt loss. On the basis of this information, together with information about the profit margin of the product or service being sold, a decision is reached on whether or not to extend credit.

Credit Scoring   Discriminant analysis, a statistical technique described in the appendix to this chapter, is used to determine a **credit score** for a credit applicant. On the basis of a weighted overall score provided by this technique, an applicant is judged to be a "good" or a "bad" credit risk. Discriminant analysis has been used with success in consumer credit and other forms of installment lending in which various characteristics of an individual are quantitatively rated and a credit decision is made on the basis of the total score. The plastic credit cards many of us carry often are given out on the basis of a credit scoring system that takes into account such things as age, occupation, duration of employment, home ownership, years of residence, telephone, and annual income.

Numerical rating systems also are used by companies extending trade credit. With the overall growth of trade credit, a number of companies are finding it worthwhile to screen out "clear" accept and reject applicants. In other words, routine credit decisions are made on the basis of a numerical score. Marginal applicants, who fall between "clear" accept or reject signals, can then be analyzed in detail by the credit analyst. In this way, a company is able to achieve greater efficiency in its credit investigation process. It uses trained credit analysts to the best advantage. Credit scoring is used not only when trying to determine whether to accept or reject a new customer but also when a current customer wishes credit beyond its existing credit limit.

A company does not have to develop a credit scoring system itself. Many use an outside vendor, which models the customer base either generically or specifically. In addition, these vendors can process the credit applicants. Providers of credit scoring services include Credit & Management Systems, Inc.; Dun & Bradstreet; Fair Isaac & Company; SR Research, Experian; and Trans Union. In the appendix to this chapter, discriminant analysis as applied to business credit decisions is illustrated.

Sequential Investigation Process   The amount of information collected should be determined in relation to the expected profit from an order and the cost of investigation. More sophisticated analysis should be undertaken only when there is a chance that a credit decision based on the previous stage of investigation will be changed. If an analysis of a Dun & Bradstreet report resulted in an extremely unfavorable picture of the applicant, an investigation of the applicant's bank and its trade suppliers might have little prospect of changing the reject decision. Therefore, the added cost associated with this stage of investigation would not be worthwhile. With incremental stages of investigation each having a cost, they can be justified only if the information obtained has value in changing a prior decision.[3]

---

[3]For such an analysis, see Dileep Mehta, "The Formulation of Credit Policy Models," *Management Science*, 15 (October 1968), 30–50.

The value of more information must be balanced against its cost.

Figure 15-3 is a graphic representation of a sequential approach to credit analysis. The first stage is simply consulting past experience to see if the firm has sold previously to the account and, if it has, whether that experience has been satisfactory. Stage 2 might involve ordering a Dun & Bradstreet report on the applicant and evaluating it. The third, and last, stage could be credit checks of the applicant's bank and creditors. Each stage costs more. The expected profit from accepting an order will depend on the size of the order, as will the opportunity cost associated with its rejection. Rather than perform all stages of investigation, regardless of the size of the order and the firm's past experience, the firm should investigate in stages and go to a new stage only when the expected net benefits of the additional information exceed the cost of acquiring it. When past experience has been favorable, there may be little need for further investigation. In general, the riskier the applicant, the greater the desire for more information. By balancing the costs of information with the likely profitability of the order, as well as with information from the next stage of investigation, added sophistication is introduced only when it is beneficial.

The Credit Decision

Once the credit analyst has marshaled the necessary evidence and has analyzed it, a decision must be reached on the disposition of the account. In an initial sale, the

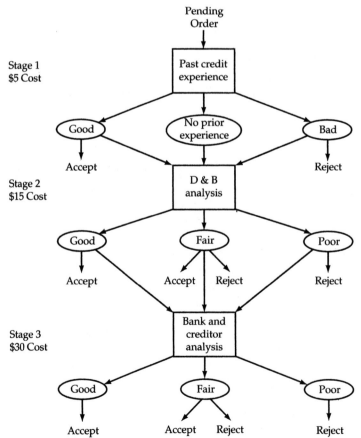

FIGURE 15-3
Sequential investigation process

first decision to be made is whether or not to ship the goods and extend credit. If repeat sales are likely, the company will probably want to establish procedures so that it does not have to evaluate the extension of credit each time an order is received. One means for streamlining the procedure is to establish a **line of credit** for an account. A line of credit is a maximum limit on the amount the firm will permit to be owing at any one time. In essence, it represents the maximum risk exposure that the firm will allow itself to undergo for an account. In the sequential investigation method illustrated, single orders were evaluated. With a line of credit, multiple orders are assumed. The principle is the same. Likely profits from present and future sales must be balanced against the likely collection period, collection costs, and probability of bad-debt losses over time. Those last three balancing factors depend on the magnitude of the line of credit offered rather than on the size of order. As before, probability concepts can be applied to analyze the trade-off between expected benefits and expected costs and to determine an appropriate line of credit for the customer.

The establishment of a credit line streamlines the procedure for shipping goods. One need only determine whether an order brings the amount owed by a customer in excess of the line. If not, the order is shipped; if so, an incremental credit decision must be reached. The line itself must be reevaluated periodically in order to keep abreast of developments in the account. A satisfactory risk exposure today may be more or less than satisfactory a year from today. Despite comprehensive credit procedures, there will always be special cases that must be dealt with individually. Here, too, the firm can streamline the operation by defining responsibilities clearly.

Outsourcing Credit and Collections

The entire credit/collection function can be **outsourced**. A number of third parties, like Dun & Bradstreet, offer complete or partial services to corporations. Credit scoring models, together with other information, are used in deciding on whether credit will be granted. Ledgers are maintained, and payments processed in an orderly manner. Collection efforts on tardy accounts are initiated on a timely basis. As with the outsourcing of any business function, it is a question of core competence. Where such competency does not exist or is inefficient, the "make or buy" decision may be slanted toward buying the service on the outside. For small- and medium-sized companies, credit and collection may be too costly to do on one's own. Even larger companies will outsource when core competency is stronger in other areas of the enterprise.

INVENTORY MANAGEMENT AND CONTROL

Inventories form a link between production and sale of a product. A manufacturing company must maintain a certain amount of inventory during production, the inventory known as work in process (WIP). Although other types of inventory—namely, raw materials and finished goods—are not necessary in the strictest sense, they allow the company to be flexible. Raw materials inventory gives the firm flexibility in its purchasing. Finished goods inventory allows the firm flexibility in its production scheduling and in its marketing. Production does not need to be geared directly to sales. Large inventories also allow efficient servicing of customer demands. If a product is temporarily out of stock, present as well as future sales may be lost. Thus, there is an incentive to maintain large stocks of all three types of inventory.

Benefits versus Costs

The advantages of increased inventories, then, are several. The firm can effect economies of production and purchasing and can fill orders more quickly. In short, the firm is more flexible. The obvious disadvantages are the total cost of holding the inventory, including storage and handling costs, and the required return on capital tied up in inventory. An additional disadvantage is the danger of obsolescence. Because of the benefits, however, the sales manager and production manager are biased toward relatively large inventories. Moreover, the purchasing manager often can achieve quantity discounts with large orders, and there may be a bias here as well. It falls on the financial manager to dampen the temptation for large inventories. This is done by forcing consideration of the cost of funds necessary to carry inventories as well as perhaps the handling and storage costs.

Like accounts receivables, inventories should be increased as long as the resulting savings exceed the total cost of holding the added inventory. The balance finally reached depends on the estimates of actual savings, the cost of carrying additional inventory, and the efficiency of inventory control. Obviously, this balance requires coordination of the production, marketing, and finance areas of the firm in keeping with an overall objective. Our purpose is to examine various principles of inventory control by which an appropriate balance might be achieved.

Economic Order Quantity

The **economic order quantity** (EOQ) is an important concept in the purchase of raw materials and in the storage of finished goods and in-transit inventories. In our analysis, we wish to determine the optimal order quantity for a particular item of inventory, given its forecasted usage, ordering cost, and carrying cost. Ordering can mean either the purchase of the item or its production. Assume for the moment that the usage of a particular item of inventory is known with certainty. This usage is stationary or steady throughout the period of time being analyzed. In other words, if usage is 2,600 items for a 6-month period, 100 items would be used each week.

Ordering Costs We assume that ordering costs, O, are constant, regardless of the size of the order. In the purchase of raw materials or other items, these costs represent the clerical costs involved in placing an order as well as certain costs of receiving and checking the goods once they arrive. For finished goods inventories, ordering costs involve scheduling a production run. These costs are known as setup costs. For WIP inventories, ordering costs are likely to involve nothing more than record keeping. The total ordering cost for a period is simply the number of orders for that period times the cost per order.

Carrying Costs Carrying costs per period, C, represent the cost of inventory storage, handling, and insurance, together with the required rate of return on the investment in inventory. These costs are assumed to be constant per unit of inventory, per unit of time. Thus, the total carrying cost for a period is the average number of units of inventory for the period times the carrying cost per unit. In addition, we assume for now that inventory orders are filled without delay. Because out-of-stock items can be replaced immediately, there is no need to maintain a buffer or safety stock. Though the assumptions made up to now may seem overly restrictive, they are necessary for an initial understanding of the conceptual framework that follows. Subsequently, we shall relax some of them.

If the usage of an inventory item is perfectly steady over a period of time and there is no safety stock, average inventory (in units) can be expressed as

$$\text{Average inventory} = \frac{Q}{2} \tag{15-1}$$

where Q is the quantity (in units) ordered and is assumed to be constant for the period. This problem is illustrated in Fig. 15-4. Although the quantity demanded is a step function, we assume for analytical purposes that it can be approximated by a straight line. We see that zero inventory always indicates that further inventory must be ordered.

Total Costs The carrying cost of inventory is the carrying cost per unit times the average number of units of inventory, or $CQ/2$. The total number of orders for a period of time is simply the total usage (in units) of an item of inventory for that period, S, divided by Q. Consequently, total ordering costs are represented by the ordering cost per order times the number of orders, or SO/Q. Total inventory costs, then, are the carrying costs plus ordering costs, or

$$T = \frac{CQ}{2} + \frac{SO}{Q} \tag{15-2}$$

We see from Eq. (15-2) that the higher the order quantity, Q, the higher the carrying costs but the lower the total ordering costs. The lower the order quantity, the lower the carrying costs but the higher the total ordering costs. We are concerned with the trade-off between the economies of increased order size and the added cost of carrying additional inventory.

FIGURE 15-4
Order quantity example

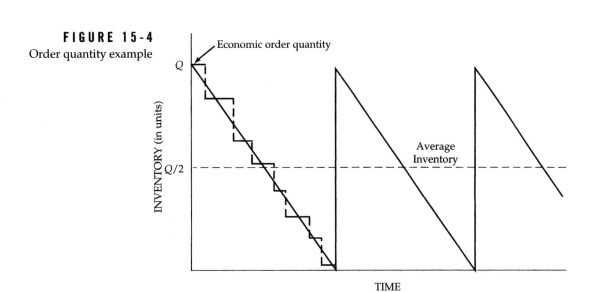

EOQ: The Famous Formula   To determine the optimal order quantity, Q^*, we differentiate Eq. (15-2) with respect to Q and set the derivative equal to zero, obtaining[4]

$$Q^* = \sqrt{\frac{2SO}{C}} \tag{15-3}$$

This equation, known as the economic order formula, is perhaps the best known formula in management. To illustrate its use, suppose that usage of an inventory item is 2,000 units during a 100-day period, ordering costs are $100 an order, and the carrying costs are $10 per unit per 100 days. The optimal economic order quantity, then, is

EOQ balances fixed ordering costs against variable carrying costs.

$$Q^* = \sqrt{\frac{2(2,000)(100)}{10}} = 200 \text{ units}$$

With an order quantity of 200 units, the firm would order (2,000/200), or 10 times, during the period under consideration, or every 10 days. We see from Eq. (15-3) that Q^* varies directly with total usage, S, and order cost, O, and inversely with the carrying cost, C. The relationship is dampened by the square root sign in both cases. As usage increases, the optimal order size and the average level of inventory increase by a lesser percentage. In other words, economies of scale are possible.

In our example, we have assumed that inventory can be ordered and received without delay. Usually, there is a time lapse between placement of a purchase order and receipt of the inventory, or in the time it takes to manufacture an item after an order is placed. This lead time must be considered. If it is constant and known with certainty, the optimal order quantity is not affected. In the above example, the firm would still order 200 units at a time and place 10 orders during the specified time period, or every 10 days. If the lead time for delivery were 3 days, the firm simply would place its order 7 days after the delivery of the previous order.

Putting It Together   The EOQ function is illustrated in Fig. 15-5. In the figure, we plot ordering costs, carrying costs, and total costs—the sum of the first two costs. We see that whereas carrying costs vary directly with the size of the order, ordering costs vary inversely with the size of the order. The total cost line declines at first as the fixed costs of ordering are spread over more units. The total cost line begins to rise when the decrease in average ordering cost is more than offset by the additional carrying costs. Point X, then, represents the economical order quantity, which minimizes the total cost of inventory.

---

[4]These steps are

$$\frac{dT}{dQ} = \frac{C}{2} - \frac{SO}{Q} = 0$$
$$CQ^2 - 2SO = 0$$
$$Q^2 = \frac{2SO}{C}$$
$$Q = \sqrt{\frac{2SO}{C}}$$

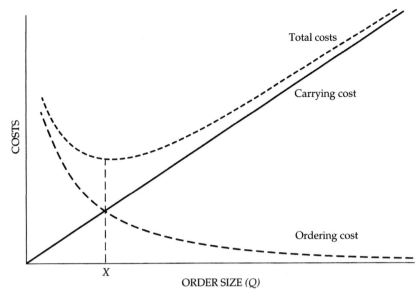

FIGURE 15-5
Economic order
quantity relationship

UNCERTAINTY AND SAFETY STOCK

In practice, the demand or usage of inventory generally is not known with certainty; usually it fluctuates during a given period of time. Typically, the demand for finished goods inventory is subject to the greatest uncertainty. In general, the use of raw materials inventory and in-transit inventory, both of which depend on the production scheduling, is more predictable. In addition to demand, the lead time required to receive delivery of inventory once an order is placed usually is subject to some variation. Owing to these fluctuations, it is not feasible usually to allow expected inventory to fall to zero before a new order is anticipated, as the firm could do when usage and lead time were known with certainty. A safety stock is necessary.

Order Point and Safety Stock

When we allow for uncertainty in demand for inventory as well as in lead time, a safety stock becomes advisable. The concept is illustrated in Fig. 15-6. In panel a of the figure, we show what would happen if the firm had a safety stock of 100 units and if expected demand of 200 units every 10 days and lead time of 5 days were to occur. Note that with a safety stock of 100 units, the order point must be set at 200 units of inventory on hand as opposed to the previous 100 units. In other words, the order point determines the amount of safety stock held.

Actual versus Expected Panel b of Fig. 15-6 shows the actual experience for our hypothetical firm. In the first segment of demand, we see that actual usage is somewhat less than expected. (The slope of the line is less than the expected demand line in the upper panel.) At the order point of 200 units of inventory held, an order is placed for 200 units of additional inventory. Instead of taking the expected 5 days for the inventory to be replenished, we see that it takes only 4 days. The second segment of usage is much greater than expected and, as a result, inventory is rapidly used up. At 200 units of remaining inventory, a 200-unit order again is

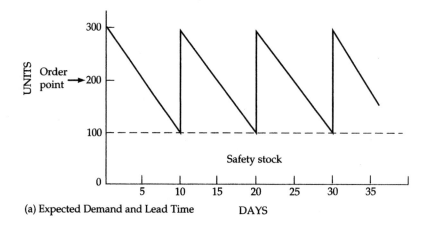

(a) Expected Demand and Lead Time

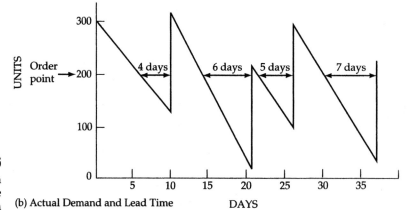

FIGURE 15-6
Safety stock when
demand and lead time
are uncertain

(b) Actual Demand and Lead Time

placed, but here it takes 6 days for the inventory to be received. As a result of both of these factors, heavy inroads are made into the safety stock.

In the third segment of demand, usage is about the same as expected; that is, the slopes of expected and actual usage lines are about the same. Because inventory was so low at the end of the previous segment of usage, an order is placed almost immediately. The lead time turns out to be 5 days. In the last segment of demand, usage is slightly greater than expected. The lead time necessary to receive the order is 7 days, much longer than expected. The combination of these two factors again causes the firm to go into its safety stock. The example illustrates the importance of safety stock in absorbing random fluctuations in usage and in lead times. Without such stock, the firm would have run out of inventory on two occasions.

The Amount of Safety Stock

The proper amount of safety stock to maintain depends on several things. The greater the uncertainty associated with forecasted demand for inventory, the greater the safety stock the firm will wish to carry, all other things the same. Similarly, the greater the uncertainty of lead time to replenish stock, the greater the risk of running out of stock, and the more safety stock a company will wish to maintain, all other things being equal. Another factor influencing the safety stock decision is the cost of running out of inventory. The cost of being out of raw materials and inventories is a delay in production. How much does it cost when production closes down temporarily? Where fixed costs are large, this cost will be quite high, as can be imagined in the case of an aluminum extrusion plant. The cost of running out of finished goods is customer dissatisfaction. Not only will the immediate sale be lost, but future sales will be endangered if customers take their business elsewhere. Although this opportunity cost is difficult to measure, it must be recognized by management and incorporated into the safety stock decision. The greater the costs of running out of stock, of course, the greater the safety stock management will wish to maintain, all other things being the same.

The cost of carrying additional inventory is crucial. If it were not for this cost, a firm could maintain whatever safety stock was necessary to avoid all possibility of running out of inventory. The greater the cost of carrying inventory, the more costly it is to maintain a safety stock, all other things being equal. Determination of the proper amount of safety stock involves balancing the probability and cost of a stockout against the cost of carrying enough safety stock to avoid this possibility. Ultimately, the question reduces to the probability of inventory stockout that management is willing to tolerate.

Just-in-Time Inventory Control and the Internet

The management of inventory has become very sophisticated in recent years. In certain industries, the production process lends itself to **"just-in-time" (JIT)** inventory control. As the name implies, the idea is that inventories are acquired and inserted in production at the exact times they are needed. This requires efficient purchasing, very reliable suppliers, and an efficient inventory-handling system. One thing that has made this possible is the advent of instant information through sophisticated computer networks. The coordination of various suppliers in an efficient manner is known as **supply chain management**.

For standard inventory items, the use of the Internet has greatly facilitated supply chain management. A number of exchanges have developed for business-to-business **(B2B)** types of transactions. If you need to purchase a certain type of chemical for use in your production process, you can specify your exact need on an Internet chemical exchange. Various suppliers then will bid for the contract. This auction technique significantly reduces the paperwork and other costs involved in searching for best price. This, together with competition among suppliers, may reduce your costs by 15 percent or so. A number of B2B exchanges already exist for a wide variety of products, and new ones are developing all the time. Again, the raw material in question must be relatively standardized for an Internet exchange to work well for you.

In the context of the EOQ model, the idea with JIT is to minimize setup costs, O in the formula. Not only can certain traditional fixed costs be reduced, but through changing the work environment some can be transformed to variable costs. One example is in machine tool shops. With computer aided manufacturing, the setup for a new production run can be accomplished in a matter of minutes and with only a fraction of the cost that occurred when it was all manual. As a result, the "spindle time" of a lathe or milling machine is increased significantly. When the order costs in the EOQ formula are reduced, the economic order quantity drops and less average inventory needs to be maintained.

A company can reduce its work in process (WIP) through managing more efficiently. This is an internal improvement. Raw materials also can be reduced by internal efficiency, but, as we have discussed, reductions here also depend on external suppliers. Finished goods are another matter, because satisfaction of customers comes into play. However, JIT should result in faster production runs. If finished goods can be replenished quickly, the cost of "running out of stock" is reduced and less finished-goods inventories need be maintained. Though inventories can never be reduced to zero, the notion with JIT is one of extremely tight control so as to minimize inventories. How close a company comes to the ideal depends on the type of production process and the nature of supplier industries, but it is a worthy objective for almost all companies.

INVENTORY AND THE FINANCIAL MANAGER

The inventory control methods described in this chapter give us a means for determining an optimal level of inventory, as well as how much should be ordered and when. These tools are necessary for managing inventory efficiently and balancing the advantages of additional inventory against the cost of carrying it.

A financial manager's concern is with inventory turns and monies tied up in inventories.

Monitoring Amounts Tied Up in Inventories

Although inventory management is not the direct operating responsibility of the financial manager, the investment of funds in inventory is an important aspect of financial management. Consequently, the financial manager must be familiar with ways to control inventories effectively, so that capital may be allocated efficiently. It is very important for the financial manager to watch the inventory turnover ratio, which we took up in Chapter 12. A deteriorating trend over time (decreasing inventory turns from one period to the next) should set off an alarm. More and more funds are being tied up in inventory. The greater the opportunity cost of funds invested in inventory, the more serious this becomes. Also, a deteriorating turnover ratio may indicate obsolescence problems in addition to the cost of carrying inventories. Perhaps write-offs are necessary. Whenever financial ratios indicate a potential problem, serious inquiry should follow and remedies be put into place.

Watching Inventory Risks

Thus, the financial manager is concerned not only with the cost of carry but with the risks involved in carrying inventory. The major risk is that the market value of specific inventories will be less than the value at which they were acquired. Certain types of inventory are subject to obsolescence, whether it be in technology or in consumer tastes. A change in technology may make an electronic component worthless. A change in style may cause a retailer to sell dresses at substantially reduced prices. Other inventories, such as agricultural products, are subject to physical deterioration. With deterioration, of course, inventories will have to be sold at lower and lower prices, all other things being the same. In other situations, the principal risk is that of fluctuations in market price. Some items of inventory, such as copper, are subject to rather wide price swings. The financial manager is perhaps in the best place to make an objective analysis of the risks associated with the firm's investment in inventories. These risks must be considered in determining the appropriate level of inventory the firm should carry.

The opportunity cost of funds is the link by which the financial manager ties inventory management to the overall objective of the firm. In this regard, inventory can be treated as an asset to which capital is committed, as in any capital budgeting project. Different items of inventory may involve different risks, and these differences can be incorporated into an analysis of risk similar to that for capital budgeting. Our discussion in this chapter has focused on determining an optimal level of investment. We know that the greater the efficiency with which the firm manages its inventory, the lower the required investment and the greater the shareholder wealth, all other things being the same.

Summary

Credit and collection policies encompass the quality of accounts accepted, the credit period extended, the cash discount given, certain special terms, and the level of collection expenditures. In each case, the credit decision involves a trade-off between the additional profitability and the cost resulting from a change in any of these elements. By liberalizing the quality requirements for accounts, the firm hopes to make more on additional sales than it spends to carry the additional receivables plus the additional bad-debt losses. To maximize profits arising from credit and collection policies, the firm should vary these policies jointly until an optimal solution is obtained. This variation can be accomplished through simulation, once the functional relationships are specified. The firm's credit and collection policies, together with its credit and collection procedures, determine the magnitude and quality of its receivable position.

In evaluating a credit applicant, the credit analyst obtains financial and other information about the applicant, analyzes this information, and reaches a credit decision. In a sequential analysis process, the firm can decide whether to accept an order, reject it, or obtain additional information. More information is justified only when the expected benefits of the information exceed its cost. In turn, expected benefits arise only if the information allows us to correct a previously wrong decision. If the account is new, the firm must decide whether or not to accept the order. Credit scoring, using a statistical technique, can be used in the decision-making process. With repeat orders, a company must

decide on the maximum credit to extend, known as a line of credit. Increasingly, companies are outsourcing all or part of the credit and collection function.

The optimal level of inventories should be judged in relation to the flexibility inventories afford. If we hold constant the efficiency of inventory management, the lower the level of inventories, the less the flexibility of the firm. In evaluating the level of inventories, management must balance the benefits of economies of production, purchasing, and increased product demand against the cost of carrying the additional inventory. Of particular concern to the financial manager is the cost of funds invested in inventory, which is a function of the risk of the specific inventories involved.

In this chapter, we examined several tools of inventory control. One is the economic order quantity (EOQ), whereby we determine the optimal size of order to place, on the basis of the demand or usage of the inventory, the ordering costs, and the carrying costs. Under conditions of uncertainty, the firm usually must provide for a safety stock, owing to fluctuations in demand for inventory and lead times. By varying the point at which orders are placed, one varies the safety stock that is held. The movement toward "just-in-time" inventory control has reduced the amount of inventory many companies hold. The role of the financial manager is to monitor the monies tied up in inventories and the risks therein. Efficient inventory management means less to finance and write off, thereby enhancing shareholder wealth.

■ Appendix: Application of Discriminant Analysis to the Selection of Accounts

Discriminant analysis is a statistical tool that can help us decide which prospective accounts to accept or reject on the basis of certain relevant variables. This type of analysis is similar to regression analysis but assumes that the observations come from two or more different universes. In our case, these universes consist of good and bad accounts. Let us start with an evaluation of only two characteristics of trade credit applicants: the quick, or acid-test, ratio and the ratio of net worth to total assets. For purposes of experiment, we extend open-book credit to all new credit applicants for a sample period. We record the quick ratio of each account, its net-worth-to-total-assets ratio, and whether or not after a length of time it defaults on payment. If the account defaults, it is classified as a bad account; if it pays in a reasonable period of time, it is classified as a good account. With this information, we are able to undertake a linear discriminant analysis with two independent variables. We wish to determine the predictive value of these variables for the behavior of the dependent variable, whether the account is good or bad.

We plot quick ratios and net worth/total assets ratios for each account on a scatter diagram, obtaining the results shown in Fig. 15A-1.

The circles represent bad accounts; the squares represent good accounts. Using the two independent variables, we try to find the linear boundary line that discriminates best between good and bad accounts. We need to find the parameters, or weights, of the following discriminant function:

$$f_i = a_1(X_1) + a_2(X_2) \qquad (15A\text{-}1)$$

where X_1 is the quick ratio of the firm, X_2 is its net-worth-to-total-assets ratio, and a_1 and a_2 are the parameter values such that the average or mean value of f_g in Eq. (15A-1) for good accounts will be significantly larger than the average value of f_b for bad accounts. This notion is illustrated in Fig. 15A-2, where the discriminant function value is along the horizontal axis, and the probability of occurrence is along the vertical. In the figure, two universes of credit applicants are shown: good to the right and bad to the left. The average value, f_b, for bad accounts is much lower than the average value, f_g, for good accounts, but the two universes overlap. In general, the smaller the area of overlap, the better the ability of discriminant analysis to predict good and bad accounts. In other words, it is desirable that the averages or

FIGURE 15A-1
Discriminant analysis of accounts receivable

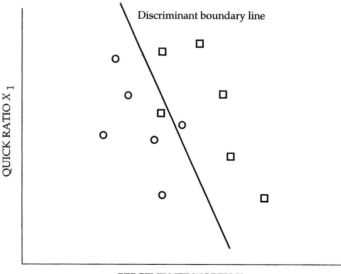

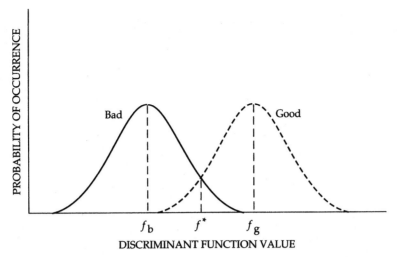

FIGURE 15A-2
Universes of good and
bad accounts

means of the two distributions, f_b and f_g, be as far apart as possible.

The coefficients a_1 and a_2 in Eq. (15A-1) can be computed mathematically from the sample data by

$$a_1 = \frac{Szz\,dx - Sxz\,dz}{SzzSxx - Sxz^2} \quad (15A\text{-}2)$$

$$a_2 = \frac{Sxx\,dz - Sxz\,dx}{SzzSxx - Sxz^2} \quad (15A\text{-}3)$$

where Sxx and Szz represent the variances of variables X_1 and X_2, respectively, and Sxz is the covariance of variables X_1 and X_2. The difference between the average of X_1's for good accounts and the average of X_1's for bad accounts is represented by dx. Similarly, dz represents the difference between the average of X_2's for good accounts and the average of X_2's for bad accounts. When we solve for a_1 and a_2, we obtain the parameters of the linear discriminant function in Eq. (15A-1). The ratio a_1/a_2 determines the slope of the discriminant boundary line.

We now need to determine the minimum cutoff value of the function. The idea is to refuse credit to those accounts with values of f below the cutoff value and extend credit to those with f values above the cutoff value. In theory we wish to find the discriminant function value denoted by f^* in Fig. 15A-2. Using this value for cutoff purposes will minimize the prediction of good accounts when they are bad and the prediction of bad accounts when they are good. To determine the cutoff value in practice, we start by calculating the f_i for each account, given the parameters of Eq. (15A-1). For our example, suppose we obtained the f_i values, arranged in ascending order or magnitude, shown in Table 15A-1.

We see that there is an area of overlap for accounts 6, 12, 11, and 4. We know that the cutoff value must lie between 1.65 and 1.91. For simplicity, we may want to use the midpoint, 1.78, as our cutoff value. Given the cutoff value, we are able to draw the discriminant boundary line in Fig. 15A-1 that discriminates best between good and bad accounts. We note that two of the accounts, 11 and 12, are misclassified, given this cutoff value. Account 11

TABLE 15A-1

Values of f_i

Account number	7	10	2	3	6	12	11	4	1	8	5	9
Good or bad	B	B	B	B	B	G	B	G	G	G	G	G
f_i	.81	.97	1.36	1.44	1.65	1.77	1.83	1.91	2.12	2.19	2.34	2.48

is classified as a good account when, in fact, it was bad; account 12 is classified as a bad account when, in fact, it was good. Rather than assign a strict cutoff value, it may be better to allow for misclassification and designate the area between 1.65 and 1.91 as uncertain, requiring further analysis. In theory, this area would correspond to the area of overlap in Fig. 15A-2.

If we have reason to believe that new credit applicants will not differ significantly from the relationships found for the sample accounts, discriminant analysis can be used as a means for selecting and rejecting credit sale customers. If we use a minimum cutoff value, we will reject all sales in which the f_i value for the credit applicant is less than 1.78 and accept all sales in which the f_i value exceeds 1.78. If a range is used, we will accept all sales in which the prospective customer has an f_i value in excess of 1.91 and reject applicants with f_i values below 1.65. For applicants with f_i values lying between these two values, we might want to obtain additional credit information, along with information as to the profitability of the sale, before making a decision.

Although the example we used is simple, it illustrates the potential of discriminant analysis in selecting or rejecting credit applicants. Discriminant analysis can be extended to include a number of other independent variables. In fact, additional independent variables should be added as long as the benefits of greater predictability exceed the costs of collecting and processing the additional information. As before, the idea with more than two independent variables is to determine a set of weights, $a_1, a_2, a_3, \ldots, a_n$, for the various independent variables employed, so that the weighted average, or total score,

$$f_i = a_1X_1 + a_2X_2 + a_2X_3 + \cdots + a_nX_n \quad \text{(15A-4)}$$

for the good accounts is as different as possible from that for the bad accounts. Given the optimal set of weights or parameters, one then calculates the total score, f^*, which best discriminates between good and bad accounts.

Assume that we are concerned with four independent variables: the quick ratio, X_1; the net-worth-to-total-assets ratio, X_2; the cash-

flow-to-total-debt ratio, X_3; and the net profit margin ratio, X_4. The optimal parameters, or weights, for $a_1, a_2, a_3,$ and a_4 were found to be 2, 5, 13, and 22, respectively. If a new credit applicant had a quick ratio of 1.5, a net worth to total assets ratio of .4, a cash-flow-to-total-debt ratio of .2, and a net profit margin of .05, its total credit score would be

$$f_i = 2(1.5) + 5(.4) + 13(.2) + 22(.05) = 8.7$$

This score is then compared with the optimal discriminant function, or cutoff, value determined on the basis of a sample. If 8.7 exceeds the predetermined cutoff value, the account is accepted. If 8.7 is less than the cutoff value, the account is rejected. Thus, the general approach is the same, whether two independent variables are used or more than two are used.

For discriminant analysis to have predictive value, the credit applicants being analyzed must correspond to the sample applicants on which the discriminant function parameters are based. With the passage of time, the underlying characteristics change. What was once an important financial ratio for predictive purposes may be less important today. In most applications, there is a decay in the validity of the discriminant function over time. As the system decays, there is a tendency to extend credit to more bad customers and to reject more potentially good customers. After a point, the discriminant function system is no longer worthwhile from the standpoint of credit decisions, and the firm would be better off with no system. Therefore, as experience provides new information it is important to assess the validity of the parameters or weights. Where the parameters are no longer realistic, a new sample should be drawn and new parameters generated.

In summary, discriminant analysis is a flexible and practical means for evaluating new credit applicants and monitoring existing accounts. Because the information is processed on a high-speed computer, time spent on clerical work and credit analysis can be reduced. Credit analysts can concentrate on only those marginal accounts falling in an uncertain area. Discriminant analysis offers an efficient means by which a company can meet the mounting demands on its credit department.

Self-Correction Problems

1. Durham-Feltz Corporation presently gives terms of net 30 days. It has $60 million in sales, and its average collection period is 45 days. To stimulate demand, the company may give terms of net 60 days. If it does instigate these terms, sales are expected to increase by 15 percent. After the change, the average collection period is expected to be 75 days, with no difference in payment habits between old and new customers. Variable costs are $.80 for every $1.00 of sales, and the company's required rate of return on investment in receivables is 20 percent. Should the company extend its credit period? (Assume a 360-day year.)

2. Matlock Gauge Company makes wind and current gauges for pleasure boats. The gauges are sold throughout the southeast to boat dealers, and the average order size is $50. The company sells to all registered dealers without a credit analysis. Terms are net 45 days, and the average collection period is 60 days, which is regarded as satisfactory. Jane Sullivan, vice-president of finance, is now uneasy about the increasing number of bad-debt losses on new orders. With credit ratings from local and regional credit agencies, she feels she would be able to classify new orders into one of three risk categories. Past experience shows the following:

	Order Category		
	LOW RISK	MEDIUM RISK	HIGH RISK
Bad-debt loss	1%	4%	24%
Percent of category orders to total orders	30	50	20

The cost of producing and shipping the gauges and of carrying the receivables is 78 percent of sales. The cost of obtaining credit-rating information and of evaluating it is $4 per order. Surprisingly, there does not appear to be any association between the risk category and the collection period; the average for each of the three risk categories is around 60 days. Based on this information, should the company obtain credit information on new orders instead of selling to all new accounts without credit analysis?

3. Vostick Filter Company is a distributor of air filters to retail stores. It buys its filters from several manufacturers. Filters are ordered in lot sizes of 1,000, and each order costs $40 to place. Demand from retail stores is 20,000 filters per month, and carrying cost is $.10 a filter per month.
   a. What is the optimal order quantity with respect to so many lot sizes?
   b. What would be the optimal order quantity if the carrying cost were $.05 a filter per month?
   c. What would be the optimal order quantity if ordering costs were $10?

4. To reduce production start-up costs, Bodden Truck Company may manufacture longer runs of the same truck. Estimated savings from the increase in ef-

ficiency are $260,000 per year. However, inventory turnover will decrease from eight times a year to six times a year. Costs of goods sold are $48 million on an annual basis. If the required rate of return on investment in inventories is 15 percent, should the company instigate the new production plan?

Problems

1. To increase sales from their present annual $24 million, Jefferson Knu Monroe Company, a wholesaler, may try more liberal credit standards. Currently, the firm has an average collection period of 30 days. It believes that with increasingly liberal credit standards, the following will result:

Credit policy	A	B	C	D
Increase in sales from previous level (in millions)	$2.8	$1.8	$1.2	$.6
Average collection period for incremental sales (days)	45	60	90	144

The price of its products average $20 per unit, and variable costs average $18 per unit. No bad-debt losses are expected. If the company has a pretax opportunity cost of funds of 30 percent, which credit policy should be pursued? (Assume a 360-day year.)

2. Upon reflection, Jefferson Knu Monroe Company has estimated that the following pattern of bad-debt losses will prevail if it initiates more liberal credit terms:

Credit policy	A	B	C	D
Bad-debt losses on incremental sales	3%	6%	10%	15%

Given the other assumptions in Problem 1, which credit policy should be pursued?

3. Recalculate Problem 2, assuming the following pattern of bad-debt losses:

Credit policy	A	B	C	D
Bad-debt losses on incremental sales	1.5%	3.0%	5.0%	7.5%

Which policy now is best?

4. The Chickee Corporation has a 12 percent opportunity cost of funds and currently sells on terms of net 10, EOM. This means that goods shipped before the end of the month must be paid for by the tenth of the following month. The firm has sales of $10 million a year, which are 80 percent on credit and spread evenly over the year. Currently, the average collection period is 60

days. If Chickee offered terms of 2/10, net 30, 60 percent of its customers would take the discount, and the collection period would be reduced to 40 days. Should Chickee change its terms from net/10, EOM to 2/10, net 30? (Assume a 360-day year.)

5. Porras Pottery Products, Inc., spends $220,000 per annum on its collection department. The company has $12 million in credit sales, its average collection period is $2\frac{1}{2}$ months, and the percentage of bad-debt losses is 4 percent. The company believes that if it were to double its collection personnel, it could bring down the average collection period to 2 months and bad-debt losses to 3 percent. The added cost is $180,000, bringing total expenditures to $400,000 annually. Is the increased effort worthwhile if the opportunity cost of funds is (a) 20 percent? (b) 10 percent? (Assume a 360-day year.)

6. The Pottsville Manufacturing Corporation is considering extending trade credit to the San Jose Company. Examination of the records of San Jose has produced the following financial statements:

San Jose Company Balance Sheet (in millions)

	20x1	20x2	20x3
Assets			
Current assets			
Cash	$ 1.5	$ 1.6	$ 1.6
Receivables	1.3	1.8	2.5
Inventories (at lower of cost or market)	1.3	2.6	4.0
Other	.4	.5	.4
Total current assets	$ 4.5	$ 6.5	$ 8.5
Fixed assets			
Buildings (net)	2.0	1.9	1.8
Machinery and equipment (net)	7.0	6.5	6.0
Total fixed assets	$ 9.0	$ 8.4	$ 7.8
Other assets	1.0	.8	.6
Total assets	$14.5	$15.7	$16.9
Liabilities and shareholders' equity			
Current liabilities			
Notes payable	$ 2.1	$ 3.1	$ 3.8
Trade payables	.2	.4	.9
Other payables	.2	.2	.2
Total current liabilities	$ 2.5	$ 3.7	$ 4.9
Term loan	4.0	3.0	2.0
Total liabilities	$ 6.5	$ 6.7	$ 6.9
Shareholders' equity			
Common stock	5.0	5.0	5.0
Preferred stock	1.0	1.0	1.0
Retained earnings	2.0	3.0	4.0
Total liabilities and equity	$14.5	$15.7	$16.9

The San Jose Company has a Dun & Bradstreet rating of 4A-2. Inquiries into its banking disclosed balances generally in the low seven figures. Five suppliers to San Jose revealed that the firm takes its discounts from the three offering 2/10, net 30 terms, and it is about 15 days late in paying the two firms offering terms of net 30.

**San Jose Company Income
Statement (in millions)**

	20x1	20x2	20x3
Net credit sales	$15.0	$15.8	$16.2
Cost of goods sold	11.3	12.1	13.0
Gross profit	$ 3.7	$ 3.7	$ 3.2
Operating expenses	1.1	1.2	1.2
Net profit before taxes	$ 2.6	$ 2.5	$ 2.0
Taxes	1.3	1.2	1.0
Profit after taxes	$ 1.3	$ 1.3	$ 1.0
Dividends	.3	.3	.0
Total income	$ 1.0	$ 1.0	$ 1.0

Analyze the San Jose Company's application for credit. What positive factors are present? What negative factors are present?

7. The Quigley Company sells and installs ski lifts. It has received an order from Alpine Ski Resort for a $2.3 million system. The production and installation costs of this system amount to 69.6 percent of the total selling price. Because Alpine wishes to go through a full season before paying for the system, it has asked for credit terms of 1 year. Quigley estimates that there is an 80 percent probability that Alpine will pay in full and a 20 percent chance that it will go bankrupt and pay nothing at the end of the year. Alpine's hill will be filled with this installation, so there is no prospect for repeat orders. Quigley's opportunity cost of carrying the receivable at its stated value of $2.3 million is 15 percent per annum.

   a. On the basis of this information, should Quigley accept the order?

   b. (1) If its costs were 74 percent of the selling price, would the order be accepted? (2) If 65 percent?

8. A college bookstore is attempting to determine the optimal order quantity for a popular book on psychology. The store sells 5,000 copies of this book a year at a retail price of $12.50, although the publisher allows the store a 20 percent discount on this price. The store figures that it costs $1 per year to carry a book in inventory and $100 to prepare an order for new books.

   a. Determine the total costs associated with ordering 1, 2, 5, 10, and 20 times a year.

   b. Determine the economic order quantity.

9. The Hedge Corporation manufactures only one product: planks. The single raw material used in making planks is the dint. For each plank manufactured, 12 dints are required. Assume that the company manufactures 150,000 planks per year, that demand for planks is perfectly steady throughout the year, that it costs $200 each time dints are ordered, and that carrying costs are $8 per dint per year.

   a. Determine the economic order quantity of dints.

   b. What are total inventory costs for Hedge (carrying costs plus ordering costs)?

   c. How many times per year would inventory be ordered?

10. Favorite Foods, Inc., buys 50,000 boxes of ice cream cones every 2 months to service steady demand for the product. Order costs are $100 per order, and carrying costs are $.40 per box.

   a. Determine the optimal order quantity.

   b. The vendor now offers Favorite Foods a quantity discount of $.02 per box if it buys cones in order sizes of 10,000 boxes. Should Favorite Foods avail itself of the quantity discount? (*Hint:* Determine the increase in carrying cost and decrease in ordering cost relative to your answer in part a. Compare these with the total savings available through the quantity discount.)

11. Fouchee Scents, Inc., makes various scents for use in the manufacture of food products. Although the company does maintain a safety stock, it has a policy of "lean" inventories, with the result that customers sometimes must be turned away. In an analysis of the situation, the company has estimated the cost of being out of stock associated with various levels of safety stock:

Safety Stock Level	Level of Safety Stock (in Gallons)	Annual Cost of Stockouts
Present	5,000	$26,000
New level 1	7,500	14,000
New level 2	10,000	7,000
New level 3	12,500	3,000
New level 4	15,000	1,000
New level 5	17,500	0

Carrying costs are $.65 per gallon per year. What is the best level of safety stock for the company?

Solutions to Self-Correction Problems

1. Receivable turnover $= 360/75 = 4.8$

   Profitability of additional sales $= \$9 \text{ million} \times .2 = \$1,800,000$

   Additional receivables associated with the new sales

   $$= \$9 \text{ million}/4.8 = \$1,875,000$$

   Additional investment in receivables associated with the new sales

   $$= \$1,875,000 \times .8 = \$1,500,000$$

   New level of receivables associated with the original sales

   $$= \$60 \text{ million}/4.8 = \$12,500,000$$

   Old level of receivables associated with the original sales

   $$= \$60 \text{ million}/8 = \$7,500,000$$

   Incremental receivable investment, original sales

   $$= \$5,000,000$$

Total increase in receivable investment
$$= \$1.5 \text{ million} + \$5 \text{ million} = \$6,500,000$$
Carrying cost of additional investment $= .20 \times \$6.5 \text{ million} = \$1,300,000$

As the incremental carrying cost is less than the incremental profitability, the company should lengthen its credit period from 30 to 60 days.

2. As the bad-debt loss ratio for the high-risk category exceeds the profit margin of 22 percent, it would be desirable to reject orders from this risk class if such orders could be identified. However, the cost of credit information, as a percentage of the average order, is $4/$50 = 8%, and this cost is applicable to all new orders. As the high-risk category is one-fifth of sales, the comparison would be $5 \times 8\% = 40\%$ relative to the bad-debt loss of 24%. Therefore, the company should not undertake credit analysis of new orders.

An example can better illustrate the solution. Suppose new orders were $100,000. The following would then hold:

| | Order Category | | |
	LOW RISK	MEDIUM RISK	HIGH RISK
Total orders	$30,000	$50,000	$20,000
Bad-debt loss	300	2,000	4,800

Number of orders $= \$100,000/\$50 = 2,000$; credit analysis cost $= 2,000 \times \$4 = \$8,000$.

To save $4,800 in bad-debt losses by identifying the high-risk category of new orders, the company must spend $8,000. Therefore, it should not undertake the credit analysis of new orders. This is a case where the size of the order is too small to justify credit analysis. After a new order is accepted, the company will gain experience and can reject subsequent orders if its experience is bad.

3.   a.

$$Q^* = \sqrt{\frac{2(20)(40)}{100}} = 4$$

Carrying costs $= \$.10 \times 1,000 = \$100$. The optimal order size would be 4,000 filters, which represents five orders a month.

b.

$$Q^* = \sqrt{\frac{2(20)(40)}{50}} = 5.66$$

Since the lot size is 1,000 filters, the company would order 6,000 filters each time. The lower the carrying cost, the more important ordering costs become relatively, and the larger the optimal order size.

c.

$$Q^* = \sqrt{\frac{2(20)(10)}{100}} = 2$$

The lower the order cost, the more important carrying costs become relatively and the smaller the optimal order size.

4. Inventories after change = $48 million/6 = $8 million

   Present inventories = $48 million/8 = $6 million

   Additional inventories = $2 million

   Opportunity cost = $2 million × .15 = $300,000

The opportunity cost is greater than the savings. Therefore, the new production plan should not be undertaken.

Selected References

BRENNAN, MICHAEL J., VOJISLAV MAKSIMOVIC, and JOSEF ZECHNER, "Vendor Financing," *Journal of Finance*, 43 (December 1988), 1127–41.

DeCROIX, GREGORY, and ANTONIO ARREOLA-RISA, "Optimal Production and Inventory Policy for Multiple Products under Resource Constraints," *Management Science*, 44 (July 1998), 950–61.

FREEMAN, TOM, "Transforming the Finance Function for the New Millennium," *Corporate Controller*, 11 (May/June 1998), 23–29.

GUEDES, JOSE, and TIM OPLER, "The Determinants of the Maturity of Corporate Debt Issues," *Journal of Finance*, 51 (December 1996), 1809–33.

HORNSTEIN, ANDREAS, "Inventory Investment and the Business Cycle," *Economic Quarterly of the Federal Reserve Bank of Richmond*, 84 (Spring 1998), 49–71.

JOY, MAURICE O., and JOHN O. TOLLEFSON, "On the Financial Applications of Discriminant Analysis," *Journal of Financial and Quantitative Analysis*, 10 (December 1975), 723–40.

KALLBERG, JARL G., and KENNETH L. PARKINSON, *Corporate Liquidity: Management and Measurement*. Homewood, IL.: Richard D. Irwin, 1993.

KIM, YONG H., and JOSEPH C. ATKINS, "Evaluating Investments in Accounts Receivable: A Wealth Maximizing Framework," *Journal of Finance*, 33 (May 1978), 403–12.

KIM, YONG H., and KEE H. CHUNG, "Inventory Management under Uncertainty: A Financial Theory for the Transactions Motive," *Managerial and Decision Economics* (1989).

LONG, MICHAEL S., ILEEN B. MALITZ, and S. ABRAHAM RAVID, "Trade Credit, Quality Guarantees, and Product Marketability," *Financial Management*, 22 (Winter 1993), 117–27.

MEHTA, DILEEP, "The Formulation of Credit Policy Models," *Management Science*, 15 (October 1968), 30–50.

MESTER, LORETTA J., "What's the Point of Credit Scoring?" *Business Review of the Federal Reserve Bank of Philadelphia* (September/October 1997), 3–16.

MIAN, SHEHZAD, and CLIFFORD W. SMITH JR., "Accounts-Receivable Management Policy: Theory and Evidence," *Journal of Finance*, 47 (March 1992), 169–200.

NG, CHEE K., JANET KIHOLM SMITH, and RICHARD L. SMITH, "Evidence on the Determinants of Credit Terms Used in Interfirm Trade," *Journal of Finance*, 54 (June 1999), 1109–29.

OH, JOHN S., "Opportunity Cost in the Evaluation of Investment in Accounts Receivable," *Financial Management*, 5 (Summer 1976), 32–36.

PARKINSON, KENNETH L., and JOYCE R. OCHS, "Using Credit Screening to Manage Credit Risk," *Business Credit*, 100 (March 1998), 22–27.

PETERSEN, MITCHELL A., and RAGHURAM G. RAJAN, "Trade Credit: Theories and Evidence," *Review of Financial Studies*, 10 (June 1997), 661–91.

SCHERR, FREDERICK C., "Optimal Trade Credit Limits," *Financial Management*, 25 (Spring 1996), 71–85.

SRINIVASAN, VENKAT, and YONG H. KIM, "Credit Granting: A Comparative Analysis of Classification Procedures," *Journal of Finance*, 42 (July 1987), 665–81.

STOHS, MARK HOVEN, and DAVID C. MAUER, "The Determinants of Corporate Debt Maturity Structure," *Journal of Business*, 69 (July 1996), 279–312.

Wachowicz's Web World is an excellent overall Web site produced and maintained by my coauthor of *Fundamentals of Financial Management*, John M. Wachowicz Jr. It contains descriptions of and links to many finance Web sites and articles. *www.prenhall.com/wachowicz*.

Liability Management and Short/Medium-Term Financing

For most companies, short- and medium-term financing is the principal means by which assets are funded. There are numerous types, ranging from spontaneous credit in the form of accounts payable and accruals to negotiated, interest-bearing debt. The proportion of short-term versus longer-term financing is a function of a company's funds requirements, seasonal versus more permanent, as well as of the aggressiveness of management in matching its financing with its funds requirements. Before considering various types of financing, we need to sketch out a conceptual framework for addressing the liability structure of a company. This will help us better understand how the firm can choose between various types of financing described in this and subsequent chapters. ■

LIABILITY STRUCTURE OF A COMPANY

If perfect and complete financial markets existed, not only would capital structure be irrelevant, as we discovered in Chapter 9, but so would be the maturity and other conditions of the debt. Other conditions include such things as whether or not the debt is secured, the presence or absence of a call feature and/or sinking fund, and the coupon rate. The corporation could not hope to profit by issuing debt instruments with different maturities and other conditions. One type of instrument would be as good as the next.

Imperfections and Incompleteness

With imperfections and/or incompleteness in financial markets, stockholders will benefit from the firm's "packaging" its debt instruments in a way that takes advantage of these circumstances. The imperfections that most affect debt financing are flotation costs, bankruptcy costs, costs of information, and restrictions on lenders. Since these imperfections were described earlier in Parts II and III, we touch now on their implications for the problem at hand.

If flotation costs are fixed, either in whole or in part, they create a bias toward less frequent financing, larger offerings of debt each time, and longer maturities. In other words, the presence of fixed costs results in economies of scale in debt offerings. Bankruptcy costs create a bias in favor of lower levels of debt obligations coming due in the near future; that is, longer maturities. To the extent that there

483

Liability management
matters when there are
imperfections and in-
complete markets.

are costs of information, they affect the sources of financing the firm is able to tap. If the cost of information is somewhat fixed to either the lender or the borrower, it creates a tendency toward less diversity in debt arrangements. A medium-sized firm may be unable to sell its debt in a public offering simply because the cost of information to ultimate investors is so high that it makes debt issues of less than $10 million infeasible. Instead, the firm will go to a commercial bank or an institutional lender, such as an insurance company, where it need negotiate with only one party. If the relationship is continuous over time, the cost of information per financing can be reduced. Thus, economies of scale in information affect the sources of debt financing.

Restrictions, or institutional constraints, on lenders affect the type of loans they can make. These constraints may be caused by things such as legal restrictions or tax differences, or they may simply be self-imposed. Commercial banks tend to make short- to intermediate-term loans, for example, owing to regulations on their investment behavior. Small firms, limited to bank financing because of the cost of information, may be restricted to shorter-term debts. Other examples of imperfections could be cited, but these examples point to the direction of their impact. If financial markets are incomplete with respect to the types of securities offered, the firm may wish to tailor its debt issues to the unfilled desires of investors. By appealing to this excess demand, there will be an interest-cost saving, all other things staying the same.

In this part, we assume that imperfections and/or incompleteness exist in financial markets, even though they may not be substantial. As a result, the way the firm "packages" its debt financing is important. That is, by varying the maturity composition and conditions of its debt, the firm may be able to affect its value, although the impact is likely to be modest. For our purposes in this chapter, the most important aspect of a firm's debt is its maturity.

Permanent and Temporary Financing

If the firm adopts a **hedging** approach to financing, each asset would be offset with a financing instrument of the same approximate maturity. A firm incurs short-term debt to finance short-term or seasonal variations in current assets; it uses long-term debt or equity to finance the permanent component of current assets. The situation is illustrated in Fig. 16-1.

If current assets fluctuate in the manner shown in the figure, only the temporary fluctuations shown at the top of the figure would be financed with temporary debt. To finance short-term requirements with long-term debt would necessitate the payment of interest for the use of funds during times when they were not needed. This occurrence can be illustrated by drawing a straight line to represent the total amount of long-term debt and equity across the seasonal humps in Fig. 16-1. It is apparent that financing would be employed in periods of seasonal lull when it was not needed. With a hedging approach to financing, the borrowing and payment schedule for short-term financing would be arranged to correspond to the expected swings in current assets. Fixed assets and the permanent component of current assets would be financed with long-term debt, equity, and the permanent component of current liabilities.

A hedging approach to financing suggests that apart from current installments on long-term debt, a firm would show no current borrowings at the seasonal troughs in Fig. 16-1. Short-term borrowings would be paid off with surplus cash. As the firm moved into a period of seasonal funds needs, it would borrow on a short-term basis, again paying off the borrowings as surplus cash was generated. In this way, financing would be employed only when it was needed. In a growth

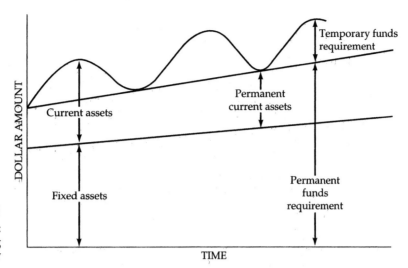

FIGURE 16-1

Funds requirement:
hedging financing
policy

situation, permanent financing would be increased in keeping with underlying increases in permanent funds requirements.

Maturity of Debt

Although an exact synchronization of the schedule of expected future net cash
flows and the payment schedule of debt is appropriate under conditions of certainty, it usually is not appropriate under uncertainty. Net cash flows will deviate
from expected flows in keeping with the business risk of the firm. As a result, the
schedule of debt maturities is important in assessing the risk-profitability trade-
off. We assume that the firm will not arrange its debt obligations so that the composite maturity schedule calls for payments of principal and interest before expected net cash flows are available. The question is, What margin of safety should
be built into the maturity schedule to allow for adverse fluctuations in cash flows?
This depends on the trade-off between risk and profitability.

Maturity: The Risks Involved

In general, the shorter the maturity schedule of a firm's debt obligations, the
greater the risk that it will be unable to meet principal and interest payments. On
the other hand, the longer the maturity schedule, the less risky the financing of the
firm, all other things the same.

Suppose a company borrows on a short-term basis to build a new plant. The
short-term cash flows from the plant are not sufficient in the short run to pay off
the loan. As a result, the company bears the risk that the lender may not renew the
loan at maturity. This risk is accentuated if there is a financial institution crisis, and
the borrower must search for a new lender. The risk of nonrenewal can be reduced
by financing the plant on a long-term basis, the expected cash flows being sufficient to retire the debt in an orderly manner. Thus, committing funds to a long-
term asset and borrowing short carries the risk that the firm may not be able to renew its borrowings. If the company should fall on hard times, creditors may
regard renewal as too risky and may demand immediate payment. This, in turn,
will cause the firm to either retrench or go into bankruptcy.

In addition to this sort of risk, there is also the uncertainty associated with interest costs. When the firm finances with long-term debt, it knows precisely what

its interest costs will be over the time period it needs the funds. If it finances with short-term debt, it is uncertain of the interest costs on refinancing. In a sense, then, the uncertainty of interest costs represents risk to the borrower. We know that short-term interest rates fluctuate more than long-term interest rates. A firm forced to refinance its short-term debt in a period of rising interest rates may pay an over-all interest cost on short-term debt that is higher than it would have been on long-term debt. Therefore, the absence of knowledge of future short-term interest costs represents a risk to the company.

A mitigating factor is the possible covariance of short-term interest costs with operating income. With covariance, when operating income is high it will be offset by higher interest costs, thereby dampening the rise in net income. When operating income is low, net income will benefit from the lower interest costs at that time.[1] Net income therefore would be somewhat lower in periods of economic prosperity and somewhat higher in periods of economic contraction than it would be if constant interest had been paid on long-term debt. It is only if the financing is short-term and rolled over at maturity that interest costs vary over time and there is the possibility for covariance with the firm's operating income.

Taking all the foregoing factors into account, we can say that for most companies the longer the maturity schedule of a firm's debt in relation to its expected net cash flows, the less the risk. The major risk in this regard is the possible inability to refinance short-term debt at its maturity. There is also the uncertainty associated with interest costs on the rollover of short-term borrowings, which can either dampen or accentuate fluctuations in the firm's operating income.

In the margin: **Debt maturity** involves a tradeoff between interest cost and the risk of a crisis at maturity.

Maturity: The Cost Trade-off

Differences in risk between short- and long-term financing must be balanced against differences in interest costs. The longer the maturity schedule of a firm's debt, the more costly the financing is likely to be. For one thing, the expected cost of long-term financing usually is more than that of short-term financing. In periods of high interest rates, the rate on short-term corporate borrowings may exceed that on long-term borrowings; but over an extended period of time, the firm typically pays more for long-term borrowings. In addition to the higher expected costs of long-term borrowings, a company may pay interest on debt over periods of time when the funds are not needed. Thus, there usually is an inducement to finance funds requirements on a short-term basis.

Consequently, we have the familiar trade-off between risk and profitability. The margin of safety, or lag between expected net cash flows and payments on debt, will depend on the risk preferences of management. In turn, its decision on the maturity composition of the firm's debt will determine the portion of current assets financed by current liabilities and the portion financed on a long-term basis.

To allow for a margin of safety, management might decide on the proportions of short-term and long-term financing shown in Fig. 16-2. Here we see that the firm finances a portion of its expected seasonal funds requirement on a long-term basis. If the expected net cash flows do occur, it will pay interest on debt during seasonal troughs when the funds are not needed. During these troughs, moreover, it will be financing with the higher expected cost of long-term debt. If there is a shortfall in net cash flows, the firm will have in place a cushion of long-term financing with which it hopes to cover its permanent funds requirements. If the

---

[1]This proposition is advanced by James R. Morris, "On Corporate Debt Maturity Strategies," *Journal of Finance*, 31 (March 1976), 29–37.

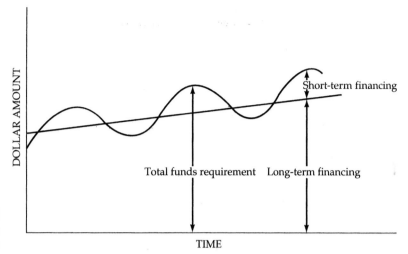

FIGURE 16-2

Funds requirement:
margin of safety

shortfall is great enough, it will need to resort to short-term financing or other measures. These examples are sufficient to show that the firm can reduce the risk of cash insolvency by increasing the maturity schedule of its debt. In testing corporate debt maturity, Stohs and Mauer find that average maturity is greater the larger the size of a company, the longer term the company's assets, and the greater the quality of the earnings (less risky).[2]

Agency and Signaling Issues

Debt maturity may be influenced by other theoretical considerations. Recall the underinvestment problem described in Chapter 9, where companies have a disincentive to invest in certain profitable investment opportunities because such projects work more to the benefit of debt holders than of stockholders. This problem is exacerbated by projects with considerable growth options; that is, projects where important benefits and opportunities are expected to occur in the far as opposed to the near future.

Myers, who first advanced the underinvestment problem, suggests that the problem can be reduced, among other ways, by a company using short- as opposed to long-term debt in its financing.[3] If the growth options materialize beyond the debt's maturity, the debt holders will not participate in them and the disincentive to stockholders to invest disappears. Other ways to control the underinvestment problem include the provision of protective covenants in the debt contract and the use of secured as opposed to unsecured debt.

As in capital structure and dividend decisions, the maturity of the debt a company employs may have a signaling effect. If there is asymmetric information between investors and management, the latter will want to issue short-term debt if it believes the firm is undervalued. The reason is that once expectations are realized, the company will be able to refinance at more favorable rates, whereas if it finances initially with long-term debt, the interest cost is locked in. The market will

[2]Mark Hoven Stohs and David C. Mauer, "The Determinants of Corporate Debt Maturity Structure," *Journal of Business,* 69 (July 1996), 279–312.

[3]Stewart C. Myers, "Determinants of Corporate Borrowing," *Journal of Financial Economics,* 5 (November 1977), 147–75.

come to associate the issuance of short-term debt with undervaluation and long-term debt with overvaluation and respond accordingly to these signals.[4]

With this general framework in mind, we are now able to examine in detail specific methods of short- and medium-term financing. The major sources are trade credit, accruals, commercial paper, unsecured and secured short-term loans, and various types of intermediate-term loans. We wish to see how sources of short-term financing may be used for seasonal and temporary fluctuations in funds requirements, as well as the more permanent needs of the firm.

TRADE CREDIT FINANCING

Trade credit is a form of short-term financing common to almost all businesses. In fact, it is the largest source of short-term funds for business firms collectively. In an advanced economy, most buyers are not required to pay for goods on delivery but are allowed a short deferment period before payment is due. During this period, the seller of the goods extends credit to the buyer. Because suppliers generally are more liberal in the extension of credit than are financial institutions, small companies in particular rely on trade credit.

Terms of Sale

When a product or service is sold, the seller sends the buyer an invoice that specifies the goods or service, the price, the total amount due, and the terms of the sale. These terms fall into several broad categories according to the net period within which payment is expected and according to the terms of the cash discount.

COD and CBD—No Extension of Credit   COD terms mean *cash on delivery* of the goods. The only risk the seller undertakes in this type of arrangement is that the buyer may refuse the shipment. Under such circumstances, the seller will be stuck with the shipping costs. Occasionally, a seller might ask for cash before delivery (CBD) to avoid all risk. Under either COD or CBD terms, the seller does not extend credit. CBD terms must be distinguished from progress payments, which are common in certain industries. With progress payments, the buyer pays the manufacturer at various stages of production prior to actual delivery of the finished product. Because large sums of money are tied up in work in progress, aircraft manufacturers request progress payments from airlines in advance of the actual delivery of aircraft.

Net Period—No Cash Discount   When credit is extended, the seller specifies the period of time allowed for payment. The terms, net 30, indicate that the invoice or bill must be paid within 30 days. If the seller bills on a monthly basis, it might require such terms as net/15 EOM, which means that all goods shipped before the end of the month must be paid for by the fifteenth of the following month.

Net Period with Cash Discount   In addition to extending credit, the seller may offer a cash discount if the bill is paid during the early part of the net period. The

---

[4]See Douglas W. Diamond, "Debt Maturity Structure and Liquidity Risk," *Quarterly Journal of Economics*, 106 (1991), 709–37; Diamond, "Seniority and Maturity of Debt Contracts," *Journal of Financial Economics*, 33 (June 1993), 341–68; Mark J. Flannery, "Asymmetric Information and Risky Debt Maturity Choice," *Journal of Finance*, 41 (March 1996), 19–37; Michael J. Barclay and Clifford W. Smith Jr., "The Maturity Structure of Corporate Debt," *Journal of Finance*, 50 (June 1995), 609–31; and Stohs and Mauer, "The Determinants of Corporate Debt Maturity Structure." The last two articles offer a mixed empirical picture to the relationship between corporate debt maturity and growth options.

terms 2/10, net 30 indicate that the seller offers a 2 percent discount if the bill is paid within 10 days; otherwise, the buyer must pay the full amount within 30 days. Usually, a cash discount is offered as an incentive to the buyer to pay early. In Chapter 15, we discussed the optimal cash discount the seller might offer. A cash discount differs from a trade discount and from a quantity discount. A trade discount is greater for one class of customers (e.g., wholesalers) than for others (e.g., retailers). A quantity discount is offered on large shipments.

Datings In a seasonal business, sellers frequently use datings to encourage customers to place their orders before a heavy selling period. A manufacturer of lawn mowers may give seasonal datings specifying that any shipment to a dealer in the winter or spring does not have to be paid for until summer. Earlier orders benefit the seller, who can gauge the demand more realistically and schedule production more efficiently. Also, the seller does not have to store finished goods inventory. The buyer has the advantage of not having to pay for the goods until the height of the selling period. Under this arrangement, credit is extended for a longer than normal period of time.

Trade Credit as a Means of Financing

We have seen that trade credit is a source of funds, because the buyer does not have to pay for goods until after they are delivered. If the firm automatically pays its bills a certain number of days after the date of invoice, trade credit becomes a built-in source of financing that varies with the production cycle. As the firm increases its production and corresponding purchases, accounts payable increase and provide part of the funds needed to finance the increase in production. As production decreases, accounts payable tend to decrease. Under these circumstances, trade credit is not a discretionary source of financing. It is entirely dependent on the purchasing plans of the firm, which, in turn, are dependent on its production cycle. In examining trade credit as a discretionary form of financing, we want to consider situations in which (1) a firm does not take a cash discount but pays on the last day of the net period and (2) a firm pays its bills beyond the net period.

Payment on the Final Due Date

Assume that a company forgoes a cash discount but pays its bill on the final due date of the net period. If no cash discount is offered, there is no cost for the use of credit during the net period. By the same token, if a firm takes the discount, there is no cost for the use of trade credit during the discount period. If a cash discount is offered but not taken, there is a definite opportunity cost. If the terms of sale are 2/10, net 30, the firm has the use of funds for an additional 20 days if it does not take the cash discount but pays on the final day of the net period. For a $100 invoice, it would have the use of $98 for 20 days. The approximate (noncompounded) annual interest cost is

$$\frac{2}{98} \times \frac{365}{20} = 37.2\% \tag{16-1}$$

Thus, we see that trade credit can be a very expensive form of short-term financing when a cash discount is offered.

The cost of trade credit declines as the net period becomes longer in relation to the discount period. Had the terms in the above example been 2/10, net 60, the annual interest cost would have been

The longer the time between the discount date and the time of payment, the lower the cost of discount forgone.

$$\frac{2}{98} \times \frac{365}{50} = 14.9\% \qquad (16\text{-}2)$$

The relationship between the annual interest cost of trade credit and the number of days between the end of the discount period and the end of the net period is shown in Fig. 16-3. In the figure, we assume 2/10 discount terms. We see that the cost of trade credit decreases at a decreasing rate as the net period increases. The point is that if a firm does not take a cash discount, its cost of trade credit declines with the length of time it is able to postpone payment.

Stretching Accounts Payable

In the preceding section, we assumed that payment was made at the end of the due period; however, a firm may postpone payment beyond this period. We shall call this postponement **stretching** accounts payable or **leaning on the trade**. The cost of stretching accounts payable is twofold: the cost of the cash discount forgone and the possible deterioration in credit rating. In Chapter 15, we discussed the rating system of credit agencies, such as Dun & Bradstreet. If a firm stretches its payables excessively, so that trade payables are significantly delinquent, its credit rating will suffer. Suppliers will view the firm with apprehension and may insist on rather strict terms of sale if, indeed, they sell at all. In assessing a company, banks and other lenders do not favorably regard excessive slowness in the trade. Although it is difficult to measure, there is certainly an opportunity cost to a deterioration in a firm's credit reputation.

FIGURE 16-3

Annual rate of interest on accounts payable with terms of 2/10

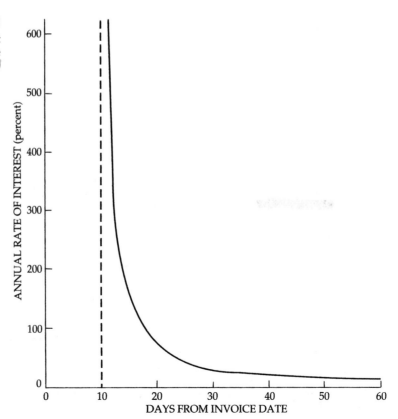

Stretching accounts payable beyond the due date is a source of funds, but at the expense of supplier relations.

Notwithstanding the possibility of a deteriorating credit rating, it may be possible to postpone certain payables beyond the net period without severe consequences. Suppliers are in business to sell goods, and trade credit may increase sales. A supplier may be willing to go along with stretching payables, particularly if the risk of bad-debt loss is negligible. If the funds requirements of the firm are seasonal, suppliers may not view the stretching of payables in an unfavorable light during periods of peak requirements, provided that the firm is current in the trade during the rest of the year. There may be an indirect charge for this extension of credit, in the form of higher prices, a possibility that the firm should carefully consider in evaluating the cost of stretching accounts payable.

Periodic and reasonable stretching of payables is not necessarily bad per se. It should be evaluated objectively in relation to its cost and in relation to alternative sources of short-term credit. When a firm does stretch its payables, an effort should be made to keep suppliers fully informed of its situation. Many suppliers will allow a firm to stretch payables if the firm is honest with the supplier and consistent in its payments.

Advantages of Trade Credit

The firm must balance the advantages of trade credit against the cost of forgoing a cash discount, the opportunity cost associated with possible deterioration in credit reputation if it stretches its payables, and the possible increase in selling price the seller imposes on the buyer. There are several advantages of trade credit as a form of short-term financing. Probably the major advantage is its ready availability. The accounts payable of most firms represent a continuous form of credit. There is no need to arrange financing formally; it is already there. If the firm is now taking cash discounts, additional credit is readily available by not paying existing accounts payable until the end of the net period. There is no need to negotiate with the supplier; the decision is entirely up to the firm. In stretching accounts payable, a company will find it necessary, after a certain degree of postponement, to negotiate with the supplier.

In most other types of short-term financing, it is necessary to negotiate formally with the lender over the terms of the loan. The lender may impose restrictions on the firm and seek a secured position. Restrictions are possible with trade credit, but they are not nearly as likely. With other sources of short-term financing, there may be a lead time between the time the need for funds is recognized and the time the firm is able to borrow them. Trade credit is a more flexible means of financing. The firm does not have to sign a note, pledge collateral, or adhere to a strict payment schedule on the note. A supplier views an occasional delinquent payment with a far less critical eye than does a banker or other lender.

The advantages of using trade credit must be weighed against the cost. As we have seen, the cost may be high when all factors are considered. Many firms utilize other sources of short-term financing in order to be able to take advantage of cash discounts. The savings in cost over other forms of short-term financing, however, must offset the flexibility and convenience of trade credit. For certain firms there are no alternative sources of short-term credit.

Who Bears the Cost?

We must recognize that trade credit involves a cost for the use of funds over time. This use is not free. The burden may fall on the supplier, on the buyer, or on both parties. The supplier of a product or service for which demand is elastic may be reluctant to increase prices and may end up absorbing most of the cost of trade credit. Under other circumstances, the supplier is able to pass the cost on to the buyer. The buyer should determine who is bearing the cost of trade credit. A buyer who is bearing the cost may shop around for a better deal. The buyer should recognize that the cost of trade credit changes over time. In periods of rising interest rates and tight money, suppliers may raise the price of their products to take account of the rising cost of carrying receivables. This rise in price should not be confused with other rises caused by changing supply and demand conditions in the product markets. Finally, it is likely that when a buyer stretches its accounts payable well beyond the net period the seller will try to recover its opportunity cost through higher prices.

ACCRUAL ACCOUNTS AS SPONTANEOUS FINANCING

Perhaps even more than accounts payable, accrual accounts represent a spontaneous source of financing. The most common accrual accounts are for wages and taxes. For both accounts, the expense is incurred or accrued but not paid. Usually a date is specified indicating when the accrual must be paid. Income taxes are paid quarterly; property taxes are paid semiannually. Wages are typically paid weekly, every other week, bimonthly, or monthly. Like accounts payable, accruals tend to expand with the scope of the operation. As sales increase, labor costs usually increase; and with them, accrued wages increase. As profits increase, accrued taxes increase.

Built-in methods of financing include payables and accruals.

Built-in Financing

In a sense, accruals represent costless financing. Services are rendered for wages, but employees are not paid and do not expect to be paid until the end or after the end of the pay period. The lapse is established by the company, although unions and competing employers in the labor market influence its length. Similarly, taxes are not expected to be paid until their due date. Thus, accruals represent an interest-free source of financing.

Unfortunately for the company, they do not represent discretionary financing. For taxes, the government is the creditor, and it likes to be paid on time. A company in extreme financial difficulty can postpone tax payment for a short while, but there is a penalty charge. It may also postpone payment of wages at the expense of employees and morale. Employees may respond with absenteeism or reduced efficiency or may seek employment elsewhere. A company must be extremely careful in postponing wages. It must fully inform employees and set a firm date for payment. Such a measure is one of last resort; nevertheless, many a company on the brink of cash-flow disaster finds itself having to postpone wages as well as all other payments.

Accrued Wages and Pay Period Changes

Accrued wages are partially discretionary in that a company can change the frequency of wage payments and thereby affect the amount of financing. If the interval of time between the last working day of a pay period and payday stays the same, the less frequent the paydays the more the financing. Suppose a company had a weekly payroll of $400,000 with an average amount accrued of $200,000. If the company were to increase its pay period from 1 to 2 weeks, the payroll at the end of the period would be $800,000. The average amount of accrued wages would now be $400,000 ($800,000 divided by 2). Therefore, the company increases its interest-free financing by $200,000.

The longer the pay period, the greater the amount of accrued wage financing. Obviously, it would be desirable from the standpoint of a company to have as long a pay period as possible, but competition for labor from other employers and union pressures limit the feasible range of options. Moreover, an increase in the pay period is usually "one-shot" in that it is not possible to repeat with a subsequent increase. In summary, then, accruals are a discretionary source of financing only within a very narrow range.

UNSECURED SHORT-TERM LOANS

For expository purposes, it is convenient to separate business loans into two categories: unsecured loans and secured loans. Almost without exception, finance companies do not offer unsecured loans, simply because a borrower who deserves unsecured credit can borrow at a lower cost from a commercial bank. Our discussion of unsecured loans will involve only commercial banks.

Short-term, unsecured bank loans typically are **self-liquidating** in that the assets purchased with the proceeds generate sufficient cash flows to pay off the loan eventually. At one time, banks confined their lending mostly to this type of loan, but they now provide a wide variety of business loans tailored to the specific needs of the borrower. Still, the short-term, self-liquidating loan is a popular source of business financing, particularly in financing seasonal buildups in accounts receivable and inventories. Unsecured short-term loans may be extended under a line of credit, under a revolving credit agreement, or on a transaction basis. The debt itself is evidenced formally by a promissory note signed by the borrower, showing the time and amount of payment and the interest to be paid.

Line of Credit

A line of credit is an arrangement between a bank and its customer, specifying the maximum amount of unsecured credit the bank will permit the firm to owe at any one time. Usually, credit lines are established for a 1-year period and are subject to 1-year renewals. Frequently, lines of credit are set for renewal after the bank receives the audited annual report and has had a chance to review the progress of the borrower. If the borrower's year-end statement date is December 31, a bank may set its line to expire some time in March. At that time, the bank and the company meet to discuss the credit needs of the firm for the coming year in light of its past year's performance. The amount of the line is based on the bank's assessment of the creditworthiness and credit needs of the borrower. Depending on changes in these conditions, a line of credit may be adjusted at the renewal date or before, if conditions necessitate a change.

Some Conditions   The cash budget (see Chapter 13) gives the best insight into the borrower's short-term credit needs. If maximum or peak borrowing needs over the forthcoming year are estimated at $800,000, a company might seek a line of credit of $1 million to give it a margin of safety. Whether the bank will go along with the request, of course, will depend on its evaluation of the creditworthiness of the company. If the bank agrees, the firm then may borrow on a short-term basis—usually 90 days—up to the full $1 million line. Because certain banks regard borrowing under lines of credit as seasonal or temporary financing, they may require that the borrower be out of bank debt at some time during the year. Frequently, the borrower will be required to **clean up** (pay off) bank debt for a period of time during the year. The cleanup period required usually is 1 or 2 months. The cleanup itself is evidence to the bank that the loan is truly seasonal in nature. If the interval during which a profitable firm were out of bank debt decreased from 4 months 2 years ago to 2 months last year and to no cleanup this year, the trend would suggest the use of bank credit to finance permanent funds requirements.

Moral, Not Legal Obligation Despite its many advantages to the borrower, a line of credit does not constitute a legal commitment on the part of the bank to extend credit. The borrower is usually informed of the line by means of a letter indicating that the bank is willing to extend credit up to a certain amount. This letter is not a legal obligation of the bank to extend credit. If the creditworthiness of the borrower should deteriorate over the year, the bank may not want to extend credit and would not be required to do so. Under most circumstances, however, a bank feels morally bound to honor a line of credit.

Revolving Credit Agreement

Revolvers are legal obligations of banks to provide credit, in contrast to lines of credit, which are a moral obligation.

A revolving credit agreement is a legal commitment by a bank to extend credit up to a maximum amount. While the commitment is in force, the bank must extend credit whenever the borrower wishes to borrow, provided total borrowings do not exceed the maximum amount specified. If the revolving credit is for $5 million, and $3 million is already owed, the borrower can borrow an additional $2 million at any time. For the privilege of having this formal commitment, the borrower usually is required to pay a commitment fee on the unused portion of the revolving credit. If the revolving credit is for $5 million, and borrowing for the year averages $2 million, the borrower will be required to pay a commitment fee on the $3 million unused portion. If the fee is $\frac{1}{2}$ percent, the cost of this privilege will be $15,000 for the year.

Revolving credit agreements frequently extend beyond 1 year, sometimes up to 3 years. The arrangement is particularly useful at times when a company is uncertain about its funds requirements. The borrower has flexible access to funds over a period of uncertainty and can make more definitive credit arrangements once the uncertainty is resolved.

Transaction Loans

Borrowing under a line of credit or under a revolving credit arrangement is not appropriate when the firm needs short-term funds for only one purpose. A contractor may borrow from a bank in order to complete a job. When the contractor receives payment for the job, the loan is paid. For this type of loan, a bank evaluates each request by the borrower as a separate transaction. In these evaluations, the cash-flow ability of the borrower to pay the loan is usually of paramount importance.

Interest Rates

Unlike interest rates on impersonal money market instruments, such as Treasury bills, bankers' acceptances, and commercial paper, most business loans are determined through personal negotiation between the borrower and the lender. In some measure, banks try to vary the interest rate charged according to the creditworthiness of the borrower; the lower the creditworthiness, the higher the interest rate. Interest rates charged also vary in keeping with money market conditions. One index used by banks for pricing business loans is the **prime rate.** This rate is set by large money market banks and tends to be uniform throughout the country. It is changed only occasionally; some contend it is effectively a cartel rate. In recent years, the prime rate has been several percentage points above the Treasury bill rate, and changes have averaged once or twice a year.

Rates other than Prime Despite the term *prime rate* implying the price a bank charges its most creditworthy customers, this has not been the recent practice. With banks becoming more competitive for corporate customers and facing extreme competition from the commercial paper market, the well-established, financially sound company is able to borrow at a rate of interest below prime. The rate charged is based on the bank's marginal **cost of funds,** as typically reflected by LIBOR or the rate paid on money market certificates of deposit. An interest-rate margin is added to the cost of funds, and the sum becomes the rate charged the customer. This rate is changed daily in keeping with changes in money market rates. The margin over the cost of funds depends on competitive conditions and on the relative bargaining power of the borrower, but it will usually be in excess of 1 percent.

Other borrowers will pay either the prime rate or a rate above prime, the bank's pricing of the loan being relative to the prime rate. A bank might extend a line of credit to a company at a rate of $\frac{1}{2}$ percent above prime. If the prime rate is 7 percent, the borrower is charged an interest rate of 7.5 percent. If the prime rate changes to 8 percent, the borrower will pay 8.5 percent. Interest-rate differentials among the various customers of a bank supposedly should reflect only differences in creditworthiness.

Other factors, however, influence the differential. Among them are the balances maintained and other business the borrower has with a bank (such as trust business). Also, the cost of servicing a loan is a factor determining the differential from prime. Because of the fixed costs involved in credit investigation and in the processing of a loan, we would expect the interest rate on small loans to be higher than the rate on large loans.

Loan pricing for floating-rate loans can be off of the prime rate or off of LIBOR.

Methods of Computing Interest Rates

There are three ways in which interest on a loan may be paid: on a collect basis, on a discount basis, and on an add-on basis. When paid on a **collect** basis, the interest is paid at the maturity of the note; when paid on a discount basis, interest is deducted from the initial loan. On a $10,000 loan at 8 percent interest for 1 year, the effective rate of interest on a collect note is

$$\frac{\$800}{\$10,000} = 8.00\% \tag{16-3}$$

On a **discount** basis, the effective rate of interest is not 8 percent but

$$\frac{\$800}{\$9,200} = 8.70\% \tag{16-4}$$

When we pay on a discount basis, we have the use of only $9,200 for the year but must pay back $10,000 at the end of that time. Thus, the effective rate of interest is higher on a discount note than on a collect note. We should point out that most bank business loans are on a collect note basis.

On installment loans, banks and other lenders usually charge interest on an **add-on** basis. This means that interest is added to the funds disbursed in order to determine the face value of the note. Suppose that an installment loan were involved with 12 equal monthly installments and that the interest rate were 12 percent. The borrower would receive $10,000, and the face value of the note would be $11,200. Thus, $1,200 in interest is paid. However, the borrower has use of the full $10,000 for only 1 month and at the end of that month must pay one twelfth of the

$11,200, or $933.33. Installments in that amount are due at the end of each of the subsequent 11 months until the note is paid. For the full year, then, the borrower has use of only about one half of the $10,000. Instead of a 12 percent rate, the effective rate is nearly double that, about 22 percent with monthly compounding. Thus, add-on interest is paid on the initial amount of the loan and not on the declining balance, as is customary with other types of loans.

SECURED LENDING ARRANGEMENTS

Many firms cannot obtain credit on an unsecured basis, either because they are new and unproven or because bankers do not highly regard the firms' ability to service debt. To make a loan, lenders require security that will reduce their risk of loss. With **security,** lenders have two sources of loan payment: the cash-flow ability of the firm to service the debt and, if that source fails for some reason, the collateral value of the security. Most lenders will not make a loan unless the firm has sufficient expected cash flows to make proper servicing of debt probable. To reduce their risk further, lenders require security.

Some Theoretical Notions

We know that secured lending arrangements are more costly to administer than unsecured loans and that the incremental cost is passed on to the borrower in the form of fees and higher interest costs than would otherwise be the case. The question that might be asked is, Why is it in either party's interest to create the additional cost? The answer is that the market for loans is a competitive one. If unsecured credit is available somewhere at less total cost, one can be sure that a borrower will go there to get it. Beyond a point in risk, however, all lenders in the market will want some type of safeguard in addition to the general credit standing of the company. This safeguard can come in the form of security or a set of protective covenants that afford the lender the ability to take corrective steps prior to maturity if the borrower's financial condition should deteriorate. We discuss protective covenants later in the chapter; our focus now is on secured loans. In both cases, we must be aware that the conditions imposed on a borrower are determined in competitive financial markets. A lender cannot demand security and expect to get it unless the borrower has no other alternatives. The use of security is negotiated in keeping with conditions in the overall market for loans.

With secured loans, a company's cash flows are segregated with respect to payments to creditors. This may reduce conflict between creditors and reduce monitoring, enforcement, and foreclosure costs, which, in turn, can work to the advantage of a company and its stockholders.[5] Stulz and Johnson portray the use of secured debt as an option to segregate the cash flows emanating from a new investment project from those arising from old projects.[6] As a result, the underinvestment problem described in Chapter 9 can be reduced. In turn, this benefits stockholders, at the expense of existing debt holders. The idea, then, is that a company plays one set of debt holders off against another, thereby extracting gain in the option pricing model context illustrated earlier in the book.

---

[5]Clifford W. Smith Jr. and Jerold B. Warner, "On Financial Contracting: An Analysis of Bond Covenants," *Journal of Financial Economics,* 7 (June 1980), 117–61. For secured receivable financing implications, see Shehzad L. Mian and Clifford W. Smith Jr., "Accounts-Receivable Management Policy: Theory and Evidence," *Journal of Finance,* 47 (March 1992), 169–200.

[6]Rene M. Stulz and Herb Johnson, "An Analysis of Secured Debt," *Journal of Financial Economics,* 14 (December 1985), 501–21.

Collateral Value

The excess of the market value of the security pledged over the amount of the loan determines the lender's margin of safety. If the borrower is unable to meet an obligation, the lender can sell the security to satisfy the claim. If the security is sold for an amount exceeding the amount of the loan and interest owed, the difference is remitted to the borrower. If the security is sold for less, the lender becomes a general, or unsecured, creditor for the amount of the difference. Because secured lenders do not wish to become general creditors, they usually seek security with a market value sufficiently above the amount of the loan to minimize the likelihood of their not being able to sell the security in full satisfaction of the loan. The degree of security protection a lender seeks varies with the creditworthiness of the borrower, the security the borrower has available, and the financial institution making the loan.

The value of the collateral to the lender varies according to several factors. Perhaps the most important is marketability. If the collateral can be sold quickly in an active market without depressing the price, the lender is likely to be willing to lend an amount that represents a fairly high percentage of the collateral's stated value. On the other hand, if the collateral is a special-purpose machine designed specifically for a company and it has no viable secondary market, the lender may choose to lend nothing at all. The life of the collateral also matters. If the collateral has a cash-flow life that closely parallels the life of the loan, it will be more valuable to the lender than collateral that is much longer-term in nature. As the collateral is liquidated into cash, the proceeds may be used to pay down the loan. Still another factor is the basic riskiness associated with the collateral. The greater the fluctuation in its market value or the more uncertain the lender is concerning market value, the less desirable the collateral from the standpoint of the lender. Thus, marketability, life, and riskiness determine the attractiveness of various types of collateral to a lender and, hence, the amount of financing available to a company.

Uniform Commercial Code   In secured lending arrangements, lenders protect themselves under Article 9 of the Uniform Commercial Code. A lender who requires collateral of a borrower obtains a **security interest** in the collateral. The collateral may be accounts receivable, inventory, equipment, or other assets of the borrower. The security interest in the collateral is created by a **security agreement,** also known as a **security device.** This agreement is signed by the borrower and the lender and contains a description of the collateral. To "perfect" a security interest in the collateral, the lender must file a copy of the security agreement or a financing statement with a public office of the state in which the collateral is located. Frequently, this office is that of the secretary of state. The filing gives public notice to other parties that the lender has a security interest in the collateral described. Before accepting collateral as security for a loan, a lender will search the public notices to see if the collateral has been pledged previously in connection with another loan. Only the lender with a valid security interest in the collateral has a prior claim on the assets and can sell the collateral in settlement of the loan.

Assignment of Accounts Receivable

Accounts receivable are one of the most liquid assets of the firm; consequently, they make desirable security for a loan. From the standpoint of the lender, the major difficulties with this type of security are the cost of processing the collateral and the risk of fraud. To illustrate the nature of the arrangement, we trace through a typical assignment of an accounts receivable loan. A company may seek a receivable loan from either a commercial bank or a finance company. Because a bank usually charges a lower interest rate than a finance company does, the firm will generally try first to borrow from a bank.

Quality and Size of Receivables In evaluating the loan request, the lender will analyze the quality of the firm's receivables to determine how much to lend against them. The higher the quality of the accounts the firm maintains, the higher the percentage the lender is willing to advance against the face value of the receivables pledged. A lender does not have to accept all the borrower's accounts receivable; usually, accounts that have low credit ratings or that are unrated will be rejected. Also, government and foreign accounts usually are ineligible unless special arrangements are made. Depending on the quality of the receivables accepted, a lender typically advances between 50 and 80 percent of their face value.

> **With an accounts receivable loan,** the lender has a lien on the collateral.

The lender is concerned not only with the quality of receivables but also with their size. The lender must keep records on each account receivable that is pledged; the smaller the average size of the accounts, the more it costs per dollar of loan to process them. Consequently, a firm that sells low-priced items on open account will generally be unable to obtain a receivable loan, regardless of the quality of the accounts. The cost of processing the loan is simply too high. Sometimes a general assignment, known also as a "floating" or "blanket" assignment, will be used to circumvent the problem of cost. With a general assignment, the lender does not keep track of the individual accounts but records only the total amounts in the accounts assigned and the payments received. Because preventing fraud is difficult with a "general" assignment, the percentage advance against the face value of receivables may be lower.

Procedure Suppose a lender has decided to extend credit to a firm on the basis of a 75 percent advance against the face value of accounts receivable assigned. The firm then sends in a schedule of accounts showing the name of the account, the date of billings, and the amounts owed. The lender will sometimes require evidence of shipment, such as an invoice. Having received the schedule of accounts, the lender has the borrower sign a promissory note and a security agreement. The firm then receives 75 percent of the face value of the receivables shown on the schedule of accounts.

A receivable loan can be on either a **nonnotification** or a notification basis. Under the former arrangement, customers of the firm are not notified that their accounts have been pledged to the lender. When the firm receives payment on an account, it forwards this payment, together with other payments, to the lender. The lender checks the payments against its record of accounts outstanding and reduces the amount the borrower owes by 75 percent of the total payments. The other 25 percent is credited to the borrower's account. With a nonnotification arrangement, the lender must take precautions to make sure the borrower does not withhold a payment check. With a **notification** arrangement, the account is notified of the assignment, and remittances are made directly to the lender. Under this arrangement, the borrower cannot withhold payments. Most firms naturally prefer to borrow on a nonnotification basis; however, the lender reserves the right to place the arrangement on a notification basis.

Advantages of the Lending Arrangement An accounts receivable loan is a more or less continuous financing arrangement. As the firm generates new receivables that are acceptable to the lender, they are assigned, adding to the security base against which the firm is able to borrow. New receivables replace the old, and the security base and the amount of loan fluctuate accordingly. A receivable loan is a very flexible means of secured financing. As receivables build up, the firm is able to borrow additional funds to finance this buildup. Thus, it has access to "built-in" financing. The interest rate charged is floating rate, typically anywhere from 1 to 4 percent above the prime rate. Also, a service fee of around 2 percent typically is charged to cover bookkeeping and other administrative costs of the lender. Finally, a "cleanup" of the loans is not required, because it is regarded as a more or less permanent source of financing.

Factoring Receivables

Factoring involves the sale of receivables to a factor.

In the assignment of accounts receivable, the firm retains title to the receivables. When a firm **factors** its receivables, it actually sells them to a factor. The sale may be either with or without recourse, depending on the type of arrangement negotiated. The factor maintains a credit department and makes credit checks on accounts. Based on its credit investigation, the factor may refuse to buy certain accounts that it deems too risky. By factoring, a firm frequently relieves itself of the expense of maintaining a credit department and making collections. Any account that the factor is unwilling to buy is an unacceptable credit risk unless, of course, the firm wants to assume this risk on its own and ship the goods. Factoring arrangements are governed by a contract between the factor and the client. The contract frequently is for 1 year with an automatic provision for renewal and can be canceled only with prior notice of 30 to 60 days. Although it is customary in a factoring arrangement to notify customers that their accounts have been sold and that payments on the account should be sent directly to the factor, in some instances notification is not made. Customers continue to remit payments to the firm, which, in turn, endorses them to the factor. These endorsements are frequently camouflaged to prevent customers from learning that their accounts have been sold.

Factoring Costs   For bearing risk and servicing the receivables, the factor receives a commission, typically 1 to 3 percent of the face value of the receivables. The commission varies according to the size of the individual accounts, the volume of receivables sold, and the quality of the accounts. Since receivables sold to the factor will not be collected from the various accounts for a period of time, the firm may wish to receive payment for the sale of its receivables before they are actually collected. On that advance, it must pay interest. Advancing payment is a lending function of the factor in addition to risk bearing and servicing the receivables. For this additional function, the factor requires compensation.

  If the receivables total \$10,000 and the factoring fee is 2 percent, the factor will credit the firm's account with \$9,800. If the firm wants to draw on this account before the receivables are collected, it will have to pay an interest charge—say, 1 percent a month—for the use of the funds. If it wishes a cash advance and the receivables are collected, on the average, in 1 month, the interest cost will be approximately $.01 \times \$9,800$, or \$98. Thus, the total cost of factoring is composed of a factoring fee plus an interest charge if the firm draws on its account before the receivables are collected. If the firm does not draw on its account until the receivables are collected, there is no interest charge. In a third alternative, the firm may leave its funds with the factor beyond the time when the receivables are collected and receive interest on the account from the factor.

Flexibility   The typical factoring agreement is continuous. As new receivables are acquired, they are sold to the factor, and the firm's account is credited. The firm then draws on this account as it needs funds. Sometimes the factor will allow the firm to overdraw its account during periods of peak needs and thereby borrow on an unsecured basis. Under other arrangements, the factor may withhold a reserve from the firm's account as a protection against losses. The principal sources of factoring are commercial banks, factoring subsidiaries of bank holding companies, and certain old-line factors. Though factoring appears to be expensive, one must remember that the factor relieves the company of credit checks, of the cost of processing receivables, and of collection expenses. As the factor has the advantage of economies of scale, it often can do the job at a lower cost. Also, the factor has access to more extensive credit information than does the individual company. This may make for better company decisions. For the small company in particular, these advantages may well outweigh the cost.

Inventory Loans

Inventory loans can be made against inventory in general or against specific inventory.

Inventories also represent a reasonably liquid asset and are therefore suitable as security for loans. As with a receivable loan, the lender determines a percentage advance against the market value of the collateral. This percentage varies according to the quality of the inventory. Certain inventories, such as grains, are very marketable and when properly stored resist physical deterioration. The margin of safety required by the lender on a loan of this sort is fairly small, and the advance may be as high as 90 percent. On the other hand, the market for a highly specialized piece of equipment may be so narrow that a lender is unwilling to make any advance against its reported market value. Thus, not every kind of inventory can be pledged as security for a loan. The best collateral is inventory that is relatively standard and for which a ready market exists apart from the marketing organization of the borrower.

Lenders determine the percentage that they are willing to advance by considering marketability, perishability, market price stability, and the difficulty and expense of selling the inventory to satisfy the loan. The cost of selling some inventory may be very high. Lenders do not want to be in the business of liquidating collateral, but they do want to assure themselves that collateral has adequate value in case borrowers default in the payment of principal or interest. As is true with most secured loans, the actual decision to make the loan will depend on the cash-flow ability of the borrower to service debt. There are a number of different ways a lender can obtain a secured interest in inventories, and we consider each in turn. In the first methods (floating lien, chattel mortgage, and trust receipt), the inventory remains in the possession of the borrower. In the last two methods (terminal warehouse and field warehouse receipts), the inventory is in the possession of a third party.

Floating Lien   Under the Uniform Commercial Code, the borrower may pledge inventories "in general" without specifying the kind of inventory involved. Under this arrangement, the lender obtains a floating lien on all inventory of the borrower. This lien by its very nature is loose, and the lender may find it difficult to police. Frequently, a floating lien is requested only as additional protection and does not play a major role in determining whether or not the loan will be made. Even if the collateral is valuable, the lender usually is willing to make only a moderate advance because of the difficulty in exercising tight control over the collateral. The floating lien can be made to cover both receivables and inventories, as

Factoring Exports

Export factoring is catching on in a big way, thanks to booming U.S. export sales and a growing demand on the part of foreign customers for shipments on open account. These days, export factoring is becoming commonplace for products as diverse as aircraft parts, surgical tools, and photo equipment.

For U.S. exporters, factoring foreign receivables has advantages over asking the buyer to open a letter of credit. The biggest is the ability to ship goods on open account without running the risk of not getting paid. By paying a fee of less than 2 percent of the value of the overseas shipment, U.S. exporters can avail themselves of an array of services, including credit checks, bill collection, bookkeeping, and cash advances of up to 90 percent of the shipment's value.

But factoring is not the answer for every exporter. Besides the transaction fee, which the exporter may not be able to pass along to the buyer, getting paid can sometimes take one or two weeks longer than with a letter of credit, exporters say.

What's more, factoring companies are reluctant to finance small shipments, generally insisting that their customers let them handle at least $2 million in transactions a year.

Export factoring typically works like this. The U.S. exporter sells or transfers title to its accounts receivable to a factoring company. The factor then assumes the credit risk and takes responsibility for all customer credit checks, billing, and collection. If the factor discovers the prospective buyer's credit is no good, the exporter will often back out of the deal or insist on cash in advance.

Despite factoring's main advantages, the financing technique has its limitations. Since factors make their money by assessing credit risk, they generally avoid doing business in developing nations and in countries on shaky economic or political ground. Another drawback is timely payment. Getting paid is usually faster if the company uses a letter of credit.

All this considered, for established exporters seeking the competitive advantage of selling on open account or the peace of mind of trusting collections to a company with international contacts and experience, export factoring is a financial technique that should not be overlooked.

Factoring Exports — sells export receivables — U.S. EXPORTER — ships on open account — Foreign Buyer — pays when receivables due, or gives cash advance — Factoring Company — collects money on shipment

Source: Adapted from Rosalind Resnick, "Taking the Bite Out of Exporting," *International Business* (April 1992), 17–18.

well as the collection of receivables. This modification gives the lender a lien on a major portion of the firm's current assets. In addition, the lien can be made to encompass almost any length of time, so that it includes future as well as present inventory as security.

Chattel Mortgage With a chattel mortgage, inventories are identified specifically by serial number or by some other means. While the borrower holds title to the goods, the lender has a lien on inventory. This inventory cannot be sold unless the lender consents. Because of the rigorous identification requirements, chattel mortgages are ill suited for inventory with rapid turnover or inventory that is not easily identified because of size or other reasons. Chattel mortgages are well suited for certain capital assets, such as machine tools.

Trust Receipt Loans Under a trust receipt financing arrangement, the borrower holds in trust for the lender the inventory and the proceeds from its sale. This type

Trust receipt loans sometimes are known as floor planning.

of lending arrangement, known also as floor planning, has been used extensively by automobile dealers, equipment dealers, and consumer durable goods dealers. An automobile manufacturer will ship cars to a dealer who, in turn, may finance the payment for these cars through a finance company. The finance company pays the manufacturer for the cars shipped. The dealer signs a trust receipt security agreement, which specifies what can be done with the inventory. The car dealer is allowed to sell the cars but must turn the proceeds of the sale over to the lender, in payment of the loan. Inventory in trust, unlike inventory under a floating lien, is specifically identified by serial number or by other means. In our example, the finance company periodically audits the cars the dealer has on hand. The serial numbers of these cars are checked against those shown in the security agreement. The purpose of the audit is to see if the dealer has sold cars without remitting the proceeds of the sale to the finance company.

As the dealer buys new cars from the automobile manufacturer, a new trust receipt security agreement is signed, taking account of the new inventory. The dealer then borrows against this new collateral, holding it in trust. Although there is tighter control over collateral with a trust receipt agreement than with a floating lien, there is still the risk of inventory being sold without the proceeds being turned over to the lender. Consequently, the lender must exercise judgment in deciding to lend under this arrangement. A dishonest dealer can devise numerous ways to fool the lender.

Many durable goods manufacturers finance the inventories of their distributors or dealers. Their purpose is to encourage dealers or distributors to carry reasonable stocks of goods. It is reasoned that the greater the stock, the more likely the dealer or distributor is to make a sale. Because the manufacturer is interested in selling its product, financing terms are often more attractive than they are with an "outside" lender.

Terminal Warehouse Receipt Loans   A borrower secures a terminal warehouse receipt loan by storing inventory with a public, or terminal, warehousing company. The warehouse company issues a warehouse receipt, which evidences title to specified goods that are located in the warehouse. The warehouse receipt gives the lender a security interest in the goods, against which a loan can be made to the borrower. Under such an arrangement, the warehouse can release the collateral to the borrower only when authorized to do so by the lender. Consequently, the lender is able to maintain strict control over the collateral and will release collateral only when the borrower pays a portion of the loan. For protection, the lender usually requires the borrower to take out an insurance policy with a loss-payable clause in favor of the lender.

Warehouse receipts may be either nonnegotiable or negotiable. A nonnegotiable warehouse receipt is issued in favor of a specific party—in this case, the lender—who is given title to the goods and has sole authority to release them. A negotiable warehouse receipt can be transferred by endorsement. Before goods can be released, the negotiable receipt must be presented to the warehouse operator. A negotiable receipt is useful when title to the goods is transferred from one party to another while the goods are in storage. With a nonnegotiable receipt, the release of goods can be authorized only in writing. Most lending arrangements are based on nonnegotiable receipts.

Field Warehouse Receipt Loans   In a terminal warehouse receipt loan, the goods are located in a public warehouse. Another arrangement, known as field ware-

Field warehousing
secures the inventory
loan on property.

housing, permits loans to be made against inventory that is located on the borrower's premises. Under this arrangement, a field warehousing company sets off a designated storage area on the borrower's premises for the inventory pledged as collateral. The field warehousing company has sole access to this area and is supposed to maintain strict control over it. (The goods that serve as collateral are segregated from the borrower's other inventory.) The field warehousing company issues a warehouse receipt as described in the preceding section, and the lender extends a loan based on the collateral value of the inventory. The field warehouse arrangement is a useful means of financing when it is not desirable, either because of the expense or because of the inconvenience, to place the inventory in a public warehouse. Field warehouse receipt lending is particularly appropriate when a borrower must make frequent use of inventory. Because of the need to pay the field warehousing company's expenses, the cost of this method of financing can be relatively high.

The warehouse receipt, as evidence of collateral, is only as good as the issuing warehousing company. When administered properly, a warehouse receipt loan affords the lender a high degree of control over the collateral; however, sufficient examples of fraud show that the warehouse receipt does not always evidence actual value. The warehouse operator must exercise strict control. A grain elevator that is alleged to be full may, in fact, be empty. Upon close examination, we may find that barrels reported to contain grain oil actually contain water.

INTERMEDIATE-TERM DEBT

Typically, intermediate-term financing is self-liquidating and in that way resembles short-term financing. However, it also can satisfy more permanent funds requirements and, in addition, it can serve as an interim substitute for long-term financing. If a firm wishes to float long-term debt or issue common stock, but conditions are unfavorable in the market, the firm may seek intermediate-term debt to bridge the gap until long-term financing can be undertaken on favorable terms. Thus, intermediate-term debt may give a firm flexibility in the timing of long-term financing. It also can provide flexibility when the firm is uncertain about the size and nature of its future funds requirements. As uncertainty is resolved, intermediate-term financing can be replaced by a more appropriate means of financing. The most important use of intermediate-term financing, however, is to provide credit when the expected cash flows of the firm are such that the debt can be retired steadily over a period of several years. Even though it is sometimes linked to a particular asset, such as a piece of equipment, intermediate-term financing must be considered in relation to the firm's total funds requirements.

Term Loans

A bank or insurance company term loan is a business loan with a final maturity of more than 1 year, repayable according to a specified schedule. Banks tend to make term loans in the 3- to 5-year maturity area, whereas insurance companies are willing to make longer loans. For the most part, term loans are repayable in periodic installments—quarterly, semiannually, or yearly. The payment schedule of the loan usually is geared to the borrower's cash-flow ability to service the debt. Typically, this schedule calls for equal periodic installments, but it may specify irregular amounts or repayment in a lump sum at final maturity. Sometimes the loan is amortized in equal periodic installments except for the final payment, known as a "balloon" payment, which is larger than any of the others.

The interest rate on a term loan can be set in one of two ways: (1) a fixed rate over the life of the loan, or (2) a floating rate, to be adjusted in keeping with changes in the prime rate, in the London interbank offer rate (LIBOR), or in some cost of funds index. Sometimes a ceiling or a floor rate is established, limiting the range within which the rate may fluctuate. In recent years the majority of bank term loans have been floating rate. In addition to interest costs, the borrower usually is required to pay a commitment fee for the time the loan is committed but not actually borrowed. A typical fee on the unused portion of a commitment is .50 percent. This means that if the commitment were $1 million, and the company took down all of the loan 3 months after the commitment, it would owe $1 million $\times$ .005 $\times$ 3/12 = $1,250.

The advantage of a term loan is flexibility. The borrower deals directly with the bank or insurance company, and the loan can be tailored to the borrower's needs through direct negotiation. Should the firm's requirements change, the terms and conditions of the loan may be renegotiated. In many instances, term loans are made to companies that do not have access to the capital markets and cannot float a public debt issue. Even for companies that can, however, some prefer the convenience and flexibility that a term loan affords. The disadvantage? Usually, a higher interest cost than could be obtained with a public issue.

Term loans can be fixed rate or floating rate.

Equipment Financing

Equipment represents another asset that may be pledged to secure a loan. If the firm either has equipment that is marketable or is purchasing such equipment, it is usually able to obtain some sort of secured financing. Because such loans usually are for more than a year, we classify them as intermediate-term financing. As with other secured loans, the lender evaluates the marketability of the collateral and will advance a percentage of the market value, depending on the quality of the equipment. Frequently, the repayment schedule for the loan is set in keeping with the economic life of the equipment. In setting the repayment schedule, the lender wants to be sure that the market value of the equipment always exceeds the balance of the loan.

The excess of the expected market value of the equipment over the amount of the loan is the margin of safety, which will vary according to the specific situation. The rolling stock of a trucking company is movable collateral and reasonably marketable. As a result, the advance may be as high as 80 percent. Less marketable equipment, such as that with a limited use, will not command as high an advance. A certain type of lathe may have a thin market, and a lender might not be willing to advance more than 40 percent of its reported market value. Some equipment is so specialized that it has no value as collateral.

Equipment varies in its desirability as collateral for a loan.

Sources of Equipment Financing Commercial banks, finance companies, and the sellers of equipment are among the sources of equipment financing. The seller of the equipment may finance the purchase either by holding the secured note or by selling the note to its captive finance subsidiary. The interest charge will depend on the extent to which the seller uses financing as a sales tool. The seller who uses financing extensively may charge only a moderate interest rate but make up for part of the cost of carrying the notes by charging higher prices for the equipment. The borrower must consider this possibility in judging the true cost of financing. Equipment loans may be secured either by a chattel mortgage or by a conditional sales contract arrangement.

Chattel Mortgage A chattel mortgage is a lien on property other than real estate. The borrower signs a security agreement that gives the lender a lien on the equipment specified in the agreement. To perfect the lien, the lender files a copy of the security agreement or a financing statement with a public office of the state in which the equipment is located. Given a valid lien, the lender can sell the equipment if the borrower defaults in the payment of principal or interest on the loan.

Conditional Sales Contract With a conditional sales contract arrangement, the seller of the equipment retains title to it until the purchaser has satisfied all the terms of the contract. The buyer signs a conditional sales contract security agreement to make periodic installment payments to the seller over a specified period of time. These payments usually are monthly or quarterly. Until the terms of the contract are satisfied completely, the seller retains title to the equipment. Thus, the seller receives a down payment and a promissory note for the balance of the purchase price on the sale of the equipment. The note is secured by the contract, which gives the seller the authority to repossess the equipment if the buyer does not meet all the terms of the contract. The seller may either hold the contract or sell it, simply by endorsing it, to a commercial bank or finance company. The bank or finance company then becomes the lender and assumes the security interest in the equipment.

Medium-Term Notes

Medium-term notes are a financing vehicle only for larger, creditworthy companies.

Unlike loans arranged with a financial institution, medium-term notes (MTNs) are sold to investors through an investment bank. For some companies, MTNs are a major funding device. An important characteristic of the MTN market is that the instrument may be offered continually. As most MTNs are unsecured, issuers typically are large and of high quality as evidenced by their credit rating. The maturity range is 9 months to 10 years. MTNs are registered with the Securities and Exchange Commission under Rule 415. The interest rate depends on the maturity and the credit risk of the borrower. Both fixed-rate and floating-rate MTNs are possible.

The major advantage of the MTN to the corporate borrower is flexibility. While the instrument is similar in some ways to a corporate bond, the borrower can raise funds in relatively small increments on either a continuous or an intermittent basis.[7] Flexibility also occurs because the maturity is not constrained to such traditional maturities as 5, 7, 10, or 30 years. The MTN affords flexibility in timing. A sizable amount of funds can be raised in a relatively short time. This is not true of a traditional corporate bond issue. If a company wishes to space its borrowings over an interval of time in order to obtain an average interest cost, it is able to do so with the MTN.

For these reasons MTNs have proven to be a popular and growing means of financing. They have displaced to some extent the use of commercial paper as well as traditional bond underwritings, the latter being explored in Chapter 19. Still the MTN market is confined to only several hundred companies that are both large and creditworthy.

---

[7]See Leland Crabbe, "Corporate Medium-Term Notes," *Journal of Applied Corporate Finance*, 4 (Winter 1992), 90–102; and Crabbe, "Anatomy of the Medium-Term Note Market," *Federal Reserve Bulletin*, 79 (August 1993), 751–68, for extensive discussions of the instrument. MTNs are issued under what is known as a shelf registration, which is explained in Chapter 19.

PROTECTIVE COVENANTS AND LOAN AGREEMENTS

When a lender makes a term loan or revolving credit commitment, it provides the borrower with available funds for an extended period of time. Much can happen to the financial condition of the borrower during that period. To safeguard itself, the lender requires the borrower to maintain its financial condition and, in particular, its current position at a level at least as favorable as when the commitment was made. The provisions for protection contained in a loan agreement are known as **protective covenants.**

Remedies under Default

The loan agreement itself simply gives the lender legal authority to step in should the borrower default under any of the provisions. Otherwise, the lender would be locked into a commitment and would have to wait until maturity before being able to effect corrective measures. The borrower who suffers losses or other adverse developments will default under a well-written loan agreement; the lender then will be able to act. The action usually takes the form of working with the company to straighten out its problems. Seldom will a lender demand immediate payment, despite the legal right to do so in cases of default. More typically, the condition under which the borrower defaults is waived or the loan agreement is amended. The point is that the lender has the authority to act.

The formulation of the different restrictive provisions should be tailored to the specific loan situation. The lender fashions these provisions for the overall protection of the loan. No one provision is able by itself to provide the necessary safeguards; but together with the other provisions, it is designed to ensure overall liquidity and ability to pay a loan. The important protective covenants of a loan agreement may be classified as follows: (1) general provisions used in most loan agreements, which are variable to fit the situation; (2) routine provisions used in most agreements, which usually are not variable; and (3) specific provisions that are used according to the situation. Although we focus on a bank loan agreement, the protective covenants used and the philosophy underlying their use are the same for a bond indenture, which is described in Chapter 19.

> **Protective covenants** allow the lender to control the situation if any are breached.

General Provisions

We begin with general provisions that are more or less universal in their use by lenders.

Working Capital The working capital requirement is probably the most commonly used and most comprehensive provision in a loan agreement. Its purpose is to preserve the company's current position and ability to pay the loan. Frequently, a straight dollar amount, such as $6 million, is set as the minimum working capital the company must maintain during the duration of the commitment. When the lender feels that it is desirable for a specific company to build working capital, it may increase the minimum working capital requirement throughout the duration of the loan. The establishment of a working capital minimum normally is based on the amounts of present working capital and projected working capital, allowing for seasonal fluctuations. The requirement should not restrict the company unduly in the ordinary generation of profit. Should the borrower incur sharp losses or spend too much for fixed assets, purchase of stock, dividends, redemption of long-term debt, and so forth, it would probably breach the working capital requirement.

Restrictions are designed to safeguard the liquidity of the borrower.

Dividends/Share Repurchase The cash dividend and repurchase of stock restriction is another major restriction in this category. Its purpose is to limit cash going outside the business, thus preserving the liquidity of the company. Most often, cash dividends and repurchase of stock are limited to a percentage of net profits on a cumulative basis after a certain base date, frequently the last fiscal year end prior to the date of the term loan agreement. A less flexible method restricts dividends and repurchase of stock to an absolute dollar amount each year. In most cases, the prospective borrower must be willing to undergo a cash dividend and repurchase of stock restriction. If tied to earnings, this restriction still will allow adequate dividends as long as the company is able to generate satisfactory profits.

Capital Expenditures The capital expenditures limitation is third in the category of general provisions. Capital expenditures may be limited to a fixed dollar amount yearly or, probably more commonly, either to depreciation or to a percentage thereof. The capital expenditures limitation is another tool the lender uses to ensure the maintenance of the borrower's current position. By limiting capital expenditures directly, the bank can be more certain that it will not have to look to liquidation of fixed assets for payment of its loan. Again, the provision should not be so restrictive that it prevents adequate maintenance and improvement of facilities.

Other Debt A limitation on other indebtedness is the last general provision. This limitation may take a number of forms, depending on the circumstances. Frequently, a loan agreement will prohibit a company from incurring any other long-term debt. This provision protects the lender, inasmuch as it prevents future lenders from obtaining a prior claim on the borrower's assets. Usually a company is permitted to borrow within reasonable limits for seasonal and other short-term purposes arising in the ordinary course of business.

Routine Provisions

The second category of restrictions includes routine, usually invariable provisions found in most loan agreements. Ordinarily, the loan agreement requires the borrower to furnish the bank with financial statements and to maintain adequate insurance. Additionally, the borrower normally must not sell a significant portion of its assets and must pay, when due, all taxes and other liabilities, except those it contests in good faith. A provision forbidding the pledging or mortgaging of any of the borrower's assets is almost always included in a loan agreement; this important provision is known as a **negative pledge clause.**

Usually, the company is required not to discount or sell its receivables. Moreover, the borrower generally is prohibited from entering into any leasing arrangement of property, except up to a certain dollar amount of annual rental. The purpose of this provision is to prevent the borrower from taking on a substantial lease liability, which might endanger its ability to pay the loan. A lease restriction also prevents the firm from leasing property instead of purchasing it and thereby getting around the limitations on capital expenditures and debt. Usually, too, there is a restriction on other contingent liabilities.

In addition to these restrictions, there typically is a restriction on the acquisition of other companies. This restriction often is a straight prohibition of such mergers unless specifically approved by the lender. The provisions in this "routine" category appear as a matter of course in most loan agreements. Although somewhat mechanical, they are necessary because they close many loopholes and provide a tight, comprehensive loan agreement.

Special Provisions

In specific loan agreements, the bank uses special provisions to achieve a desired total protection of its loan. A loan agreement may contain a definite understanding regarding the use of the loan proceeds, so that there will be no diversion of funds to purposes other than those contemplated when the loan was negotiated. If one or more executives are essential to a firm's effective operation, a bank may insist that the company carry life insurance on them. Proceeds of the insurance may be payable to the company or directly to the bank, to be applied to the loan. An agreement may also contain a management clause under which certain key individuals must remain actively employed in the company during the time the loan is owing. Aggregate executive salaries and bonuses are sometimes limited in the loan agreement to prevent excessive compensation of executives, which might reduce profits. This provision closes another loophole; it prevents large stockholders who are officers of the company from increasing their own salaries in lieu of paying higher dividends, which are limited under the agreement.

Negotiating Restrictions and the Option Pricing Theory

Option pricing can be used to model protective-covenant determination.

The provisions just described represent the most frequently used protective covenants in a loan agreement. From the standpoint of the lender, the aggregate impact of these provisions should be to safeguard the financial position of the borrower and its ability to pay the loan. Under a well-written agreement, a borrower cannot get into serious financial difficulty without defaulting under an agreement, thereby giving the lender legal authority to take action. Although the lender is instrumental in establishing restrictions, the restrictiveness of protective covenants is subject to negotiation between borrower and lender. The final result will depend on the relative bargaining power of each of the parties involved.

The OPT Setting From our discussion in Chapters 5 and 9 concerning the application of the option pricing theory, it is easy to visualize the debt holder–equity holder relationship as being essentially an option arrangement. Looking at the relationship in this manner affords a better understanding of a lender's desire for protective covenants. A firm may have a single debt issue outstanding, which is denoted by the obligation of the company to pay D at time T.[8] If total value of the company at time T, which we denote by V, exceeds D, debt holders will be paid the face value of the obligation. If V is less than D, the firm is assumed to default. Therefore, the value of the debt obligation at time T is min (D, V). This merely states that debt holders receive the lesser of the contractual amount of the debt obligation or the value of the firm if this obligation cannot be entirely paid.

---

[8]This example is based on James C. Van Horne, "Optimal Initiation of Bankruptcy Proceedings by Debt Holders," *Journal of Finance*, 31 (June 1976), 897–910. See also Fischer Black and John C. Cox, "Valuing Corporate Securities: Some Effects of Bond Indenture Provisions," *Journal of Finance*, 31 (May 1976), 351–67; Fischer Black and Myron Scholes, "The Pricing of Options and Corporate Liabilities," *Journal of Political Economy*, 81 (May–June 1973), 649–51; and Clifford W. Smith Jr. and Jerold B. Warner, "On Financing Contracting: An Analysis of Bond Covenants," *Journal of Financial Economics*, 7 (June 1979), 117–61.

On the other hand, the value of the common stock at time T is max ($V - D$, 0). Equity holders are the residual owners of the company and are entitled to any value of the firm that remains after the debt has been paid, $V - D$. In the event the debt cannot be paid in its entirety because V is less than D, they receive nothing. In this sense, the equity holders have an option on the total value of the firm at time T. If V exceeds D, they exercise this option, so to speak, by paying off the loan and they receive the total value of the firm at time T less the debt claim. (The face value of the debt can be thought of as the exercise price of the option.) If V is less than D, the option is worth zero. Now we know from Chapter 5 that with an option, the greater the variance of the distribution of possible values of the firm at time T, the greater the value of the option, all other things the same.

Equity Holder Motivation In the context of our example, it behooves the equity holders to increase the risk of the firm to increase the variance of its total value. By undertaking more risky ventures, the value of the equity holders' option increases. Though greater risk works to the advantage of equity holders, it is at the expense of the option writer, the debt holders. In fact, the increase in value of the equity holders' option means a corresponding decrease in the value of debt. Expressed differently, there is a transfer of wealth from debt holders to equity holders. The same thing occurs when the capital structure is changed by issuing new debt and repurchasing stock. As illustrated in Chapter 9, the probability of default increases and, as a result, the value of existing debt declines. In essence, the stockholders expropriate some of the wealth of the old debt holders. (New debt holders are not affected because they lend money on the basis of the new, more risky capital structure.)

Lender Restraint If a lender recognizes the possibility that the equity holders may substantially alter the riskiness of the firm or issue new debt after a loan is made, it will want to institute some safeguards against these occurrences before making the loan. This can be done by imposing protective covenants of the sort described earlier. If the firm should breach any of these restrictions, default occurs, and the lender can then declare the loan immediately payable. Protective covenants obviously give the lender the additional ability to force bankruptcy. With bankruptcy, ownership of the firm effectively passes to the debt holders, and they can seize on the value of the firm at that time. Therefore, lenders are in a position to preclude equity holders from increasing the risk of the company or issuing new debt at their expense. They have only to write protective covenants that will trigger default.

As discussed in Chapter 9, there are monitoring costs associated with the writing of protective covenants and with their enforcement. These costs ultimately are borne by the equity holders, so it is in their interest to see that monitoring activities are administered efficiently. The greater the safeguards to the lender, the greater its protection and the lower the interest rate, all other things the same; however, the incremental protection afforded the lender increases at a decreasing rate. On the other hand, monitoring costs increase, probably at an increasing rate, as more safeguards are added. It is therefore necessary to strike a balance that embraces this trade-off. The final position will be a compromise between the borrower and the lender, one that is influenced by relative conditions in the financial markets and by the costs of monitoring (see Chapter 9).

■ Summary

With perfect financial markets, the maturity and other features of debt would be irrelevant. If imperfections and/or incompleteness exist, however, the financial manager should be concerned with the type of debt that is issued. By "packaging" debt instruments to take advantage of imperfections and incompleteness, the firm can maximize shareholder wealth. A debt instrument has a number of features, but one of the most meaningful is its maturity. In general, short-term debt is less costly than long-term debt, but it is also more risky. Thus, a decision as to the maturity composition of the firm's debt involves a trade-off between profitability and risk. It also may involve agency and financial signaling considerations.

A number of types of short-term financing are available. Trade credit is the most widely used. When a cash discount is offered but not taken, the cost of trade credit is the cash discount forgone. The longer the period between the end of the discount period and the time the bill is paid, the less this opportunity cost. "Stretching" accounts payable involves postponement of payment beyond the due period. The opportunity cost of stretching payables is the possible deterioration in the firm's credit rating. The firm must balance the cost of trade credit against its advantages and the costs of other short-term credit. A major advantage of trade credit is the flexibility it gives the firm.

Like accounts payable, accruals represent a spontaneous source of financing, albeit offering a company even less discretion than it has with trade credit financing. The principal accrual items are wages and taxes, and both are expected to be paid on established dates. In the interim, interest-free financing is available to the company, and for an ongoing company, this financing is continuous. A company can increase the amount of its accrued wages by lessening the frequency of paydays.

Short-term loans can be divided into two types: unsecured and secured. Unsecured credit is usually confined to bank loans under a line of credit, under a revolving credit agreement, or on a transaction basis. Interest rates on business loans are a function of a bank's cost of funds, the existing prime rate, the creditworthiness of the borrower, and the profitability of the relationship to the bank. Interest on loans can be computed in three ways: collect, discount, or add-on used in installment loans. The "true" interest rate is lowest for the collect note and highest for the add-on, all other things the same.

Many firms unable to obtain unsecured credit are required to pledge security. In giving a secured loan, the lender looks first to the cash-flow ability of the company to service debt and, if this source of loan repayment should fail, to the collateral value of the security. To provide a margin of safety, a lender usually will advance somewhat less than the market value of the collateral. The percentage advance varies according to the quality of the collateral pledged and the control the lender has over this collateral. Accounts receivable and inventory are the principal assets used to secure short-term business loans. Receivables may either be assigned to secure a loan or sold to a factor. Inventory loans can be under a floating lien, under a trust receipt, or under terminal warehouse or field warehouse receipt arrangements.

Intermediate-term financing generally is thought to include maturities of 1 to 5 years. There are a number of sources of intermediate-term financing. Commercial banks, insurance companies, and other institutional investors make term loans to business firms.

On a secured basis, firms can obtain intermediate-term financing by pledging equipment that they own or are purchasing. Banks, finance companies, and sellers of the equipment are active in providing this type of secured financing. Finally, medium-term notes are used by large, creditworthy corporations to raise funds in the public market.

Lenders who offer unsecured credit usually impose restrictions on the borrower. These restrictions are called protective covenants and are contained in a loan agreement. If the borrower defaults under any of the provisions of the loan agreement, the lender may initiate immediate corrective measures. The use of protective covenants can be viewed in the option pricing model framework of debt holders versus equity holders. This framework was illustrated, as was the influence of monitoring costs.

Self-Correction Problems

1. The Hollezorin Company must decide among three liability strategies, which differ in maturity structure and type of securities. For each strategy, the annual interest costs, the annual flotation costs, and the annual expected bankruptcy costs (probability weighted) are estimated. On the basis of the information given, which is the best strategy? Why do the various costs change with changes in strategy?

Strategy	Maturity	Secured or Unsecured	Annual Interest Costs	All Flotation Costs	Bankruptcy Costs
A	$\frac{1}{2}$ short-, $\frac{1}{4}$ medium-, $\frac{1}{4}$ long-term debt	All unsecured	$1,400,000	$300,000	$200,000
B	$\frac{1}{3}$ short-, $\frac{1}{3}$ medium-, $\frac{1}{3}$ long-term debt	Unsecured Secured Unsecured	1,520,000	250,000	150,000
C	$\frac{1}{4}$ short-, $\frac{1}{4}$ medium-, $\frac{1}{2}$ long-term debt	Unsecured Secured Secured	1,600,000	200,000	75,000

2. The Dud Company purchases raw materials on terms of 2/10, net 30. A review of the company's records by the owner, Mr. Dud, revealed that payments are usually made 15 days after purchases are received. When asked why the firm did not take advantage of its discounts, the bookkeeper, Mr. Grind, replied that it cost only 2 percent for these funds, whereas a bank loan would cost the firm 12 percent.

   a. What mistake is Grind making?

   b. What is the real cost of not taking advantage of the discount?

   c. If the firm could not borrow from the bank and was forced to resort to the use of trade credit funds, what suggestion might be made to Grind that would reduce the annual interest cost?

3. The Halow Harp and Chime Company is negotiating a new labor contract. Among other things, the union is demanding that the company pay its workers weekly instead of twice a month. The payroll currently is $260,000 per payday, and accrued wages average $130,000. What is the annual cost of the union's demand if the company's opportunity cost of funds is 9 percent?

4. The Barnes Corporation has just acquired a large account. As a result, it needs an additional $75,000 in working capital immediately. It has been determined that there are three feasible sources of funds:

   a. Trade credit: the company buys about $50,000 of materials per month on terms of 3/30, net 90. Discounts are taken.

   b. Bank loan: the firm's bank will lend $100,000 at 13 percent. A 10 percent compensating balance will be required, which otherwise would not be maintained by the company.

   c. A factor will buy the company's receivables ($100,000 per month), which have a collection period of 60 days. The factor will advance up to 75 percent of the face value of the receivables at 12 percent on an annual basis. The factor will also charge a 2 percent fee on all receivables purchased. It has been estimated that the factor's services will save the company a credit department expense and bad-debt expenses of $1,500 per month.

   On the basis of annual percentage cost, which alternative should Barnes select?

5. The Kedzie Cordage Company needs to finance a seasonal bulge in inventories of $400,000. The funds are needed for 6 months. The company is considering the following possibilities:

   a. Terminal warehouse receipt loan from a finance company. Terms are 12 percent annualized with an 80 percent advance against the value of the inventory. The warehousing costs are $7,000 for the 6-month period. The residual financing requirement, which is $400,000 less the amount advanced, will need to be financed by forgoing cash discounts on its payables. Standard terms are 2/10, net 30; however, the company feels it can postpone payment until the fortieth day without adverse effect.

   b. A floating lien arrangement from the supplier of the inventory at an effective interest rate of 20 percent. The supplier will advance the full value of the inventory.

   c. A field warehouse loan from another finance company at an interest rate of 10 percent annualized. The advance is 70 percent, and field warehousing costs amount to $10,000 for the 6-month period. The residual financing requirement will need to be financed by forgoing cash discounts on payables as in the first alternative.

   Which is the least costly method of financing the inventory needs of the firm?

■ **Problems**

1. Mendez Metal Specialities, Inc., has a seasonal pattern to its business. It borrows under a line of credit from Central Bank at 1 percent over prime. Its total

asset requirements now (at year end) and estimated requirements for the coming year are

Time	Now	First Quarter	Second Quarter	Third Quarter	Fourth Quarter
Amount	$4,500,000	$4,800,000	$5,500,000	$5,900,000	$5,000,000

Assume that these requirements are level throughout the quarter. Presently, the company has $4,500,000 in equity capital plus long-term debt plus the permanent component of current liabilities, and this amount will remain constant throughout the year.

The prime rate presently is 11 percent, and the company expects no change in this rate for the next year. Mendez Metal Specialities is also considering issuing intermediate-term debt at an interest rate of $13\frac{1}{2}$ percent. In this regard, three alternative amounts are under consideration: zero, $500,000, and $1 million. All additional funds requirements will be borrowed under the company's bank line of credit.

    a.   Determine the total dollar borrowing costs for short- and intermediate-term debt under each of the three alternatives for the coming year. (Assume there are no changes in current liabilities other than borrowings.) Which is lowest?

    b.   Are there other considerations in addition to expected cost?

2.   Determine the annual percentage interest cost for each of the following terms of sale, assuming the firm does not take the cash discount but pays on the final day of the net period (assume a 365-day year).

    a.   1/20, net 30 ($500 invoice).

    b.   2/30, net 60 ($1,000 invoice).

    c.   2/5, net 10 ($100 invoice).

    d.   3/10, net 30 ($250 invoice).

3.   Does the dollar size of the invoice affect the percentage annual interest cost of not taking discounts? Illustrate with an example.

4.   Recompute Problem 2, assuming a 10-day stretching of the payment date. What is the major advantage of stretching? What are the disadvantages?

5.   On January 1, Faville Car Company, a large car dealer, gave its employees a 10 percent pay increase in view of the substantial profits the preceding year. Before the increase, the weekly payroll was $50,000. What is the effect of the change on accruals?

6.   The Fox Company is able to sell $1 million of commercial paper every 3 months at a rate of 10 percent and a placement cost of $3,000 per issue. The dealers require Fox to maintain bank lines of credit demanding $100,000 in bank balances, which otherwise would not be held. Fox has a 40 percent tax rate. What do the funds from commercial paper cost Fox after taxes?

7.   Commercial paper has no stipulated interest rate. It is sold on a discount basis, and the amount of the discount determines the interest cost to the issuer. On the basis of the following information, determine the percentage interest cost on an annual basis for each of the following issues.

Issue	Face Value	Price	Time to Maturity
a	$ 25,000	$24,500	60 days
b	100,000	96,500	180
c	50,000	48,800	90
d	75,000	71,300	270
e	100,000	99,100	30

8. The Sphinx Supply Company needs to increase its working capital by $10 million. It has decided that there are essentially three alternatives of financing available:

   a. Forgo cash discounts, granted on a basis of 3/10, net 30.
   b. Borrow from the bank at 15 percent. This alternative would necessitate maintaining a 12 percent compensating balance.
   c. Issue commercial paper at 12 percent. The cost of placing the issue would be $100,000 each 6 months.

   Assuming that the firm would prefer the flexibility of bank financing, provided the additional cost of this flexibility is no more than 2 percent, which alternative should Sphinx select?

9. Castellanos Company wishes to borrow $100,000 for 1 year. It must choose one of the following alternatives.

   a. 9 percent loan on a collect basis, with face value due at the end.
   b. 8.4 percent loan on a discount basis, with face value due at the end.
   c. 6 percent loan on an add-on basis, with equal quarterly payments required on the initial face value.

   Which alternative has the lowest effective yield, using annual compounding for the first two and quarterly compounding for the last?

10. Fritz-Polakoff Finance Company makes a variety of secured loans. Both the percentage of advance and the interest rate charged vary with the marketability, life, and riskiness of the collateral. It has established the following advances and interest-rate charges for certain types of equipment:

Item	Advance Against Appraisal Value	Interest Rate
Forklift truck	75%	18%
Back hoe truck	80	18
Drill press	50	20
Bottle filler	40	22
Turret lathe	60	20

L. Bradford Company has used equipment of this sort worth appraised values of $13,000, $19,000, $6,000, $38,000, and $24,000, respectively. How much can it borrow and what will be the total annual interest cost in dollars? in percentage? (Assume that the company owns only one item of each.)

11. The Selby Gaming Manufacturing Company has experienced a severe cash squeeze and must raise $200,000 over the next 90 days. The company has already pledged its receivables in support of a loan. Still, it has $570,000 in unencumbered inventories. Determine which of the following financing alternatives is better.

    a. The Cody National Bank of Reno will lend against finished goods, provided that they are placed in a public warehouse under its control. As the finished goods are released for sale, the loan is reduced by the proceeds of the sale. The company currently has $300,000 in finished goods inventories and would expect to replace finished goods that are sold out of the warehouse with new finished goods, so that it could borrow the full $200,000 for 90 days. The interest rate is 10 percent, and the company will pay quarterly warehousing costs of $3,000. Finally, it will experience a reduction in efficiency as a result of this arrangement. Management estimates that the lower efficiency will reduce quarterly before-tax profits by $5,000.

    b. The Zarlotti Finance Company will lend the company the money under a floating lien on all of its inventories. The rate is 23 percent, but no additional expenses will be incurred.

12. The Bone Company has been factoring its accounts receivable for the past 5 years. The factor charges a fee of 2 percent and will lend up to 80 percent of the volume of receivables purchased for an additional 1.5 percent per month. The firm typically has sales of $500,000 per month, 70 percent of which are on credit. By using the factor, two savings are effected:

    a. $2,000 per month that would be required to support a credit department

    b. A bad-debt expense of 1 percent on credit sales

    The firm's bank has recently offered to lend the firm up to 80 percent of the face value of the receivables shown on the schedule of accounts. The bank would charge 15 percent per annum interest plus a 2 percent monthly processing charge per dollar of receivables lending. The firm extends terms of net 30, and all customers who pay their bills do so in 30 days. Should the firm discontinue its factoring arrangement in favor of the bank's offer if the firm borrows, on the average, $100,000 per month on its receivables?

13. Vesco-Zultch Corporation is a chain of appliance stores in Chicago. It needs to finance all of its inventories, which average the following during the four quarters of the year (in thousands):

Quarters	1	2	3	4
Inventory level	$1,600	$2,100	$1,500	$3,200

Vesco-Zultch presently utilizes a finance company loan secured by a floating lien. The interest rate is the prime rate plus $7\frac{1}{2}$ percent, but no additional expenses are incurred. The Boundary Illinois National Bank of Chicago is bidding for the Vesco-Zultch business. It has proposed a trust receipt financing arrangement. The interest rate will be $2\frac{1}{2}$ percent above the prime rate, with servicing costs of $20,000 each quarter. Should the company switch financing arrangements?

14. On January 1, Sharpe Razor Corporation is contemplating a 4-year, $3 million term loan from the Fidelity First National Bank. The loan is payable at the end of the fourth year and would involve a loan agreement containing a number of protective covenants. Among these restrictions are the following: The company must maintain working capital of $3 million at all times; it cannot take on any more long-term debt; its total liabilities cannot be more than .6 of its total assets; and capital expenditures in any year are limited to depreciation plus $3 million. The company's balance sheet at December 31, before the term loan, is (in millions)

Current assets	$ 7	Current liabilities	$ 3
Net fixed assets	10	Long-term debt (due in 5 years)	5
		Shareholders' equity	9
	$17		$17

The proceeds of the term loan will be used to increase Sharpe's investment in inventories and receivables in response to introducing a new "closer-to-the-face" razor blade. The company anticipates a subsequent need to grow at a rate of 24 percent a year, equally divided between current assets and net fixed assets. Profits after taxes of $1.5 million are expected this year, and these profits are further expected to grow by $250,000 per year over the subsequent 3 years. The company pays no dividends and does not intend to pay any over the next 4 years. Depreciation in the past year was $2.5 million, and this is predicted to grow over the next 4 years at the same rate as the increase in net fixed assets. Under the loan agreement, will the company be able to achieve its growth objectives?

15. Max-Fli Toy Company currently has a total value of $10 million. The face value of the debt outstanding is $7 million, and it is represented by discount bonds that all mature in 4 years. The standard deviation of the continuously compounded rate of return on the total value of the firm is .30. The short-term risk-free rate is currently 6 percent.

   a. Using the Black–Scholes option model, Eq. (5-2) in Chapter 5, determine the value of the equity and the value of the debt.

   b. If the company goes into a new, riskier toy line that increases the standard deviation to .50, what will be the effect on the value of the debt?

   c. How can the debt holders protect themselves?

■ Solutions to Self-Correction Problems

1. The total estimated annual costs for the three strategies are

Strategy	A	B	C
Total cost	$1,900,000	$1,920,000	$1,875,000

Strategy C, involving the highest portion of long-term debt, is best, despite the higher interest cost. As we see, interest costs increase with the greater use of long-term and medium-term debt. This pattern is consistent with interest rates rising at a decreasing rate with maturity. Flotation costs decrease the longer the average maturity of the debt, which is in keeping with fewer offerings per year. Finally, expected bankruptcy costs decline the longer the average maturity. This occurrence is consistent with less uncertainty associated with long-term debt. Also, expected bankruptcy costs decline as more of the debt is made secured, and lenders can turn directly to assets for payment in cases of adversity as opposed to settlement through the bankruptcy courts.

2.   a.   Grind is confusing the percentage cost of using funds for 5 days with the cost of using funds for a year. These costs are clearly not comparable. One must be converted to the time scale of the other.

      b. $\dfrac{2}{98} \times \dfrac{365}{5} = 149.0\%$

      c.   Assuming that the firm has made the decision not to take the cash discount, it makes no sense to pay before the due date. In this case, payment 30 days after purchases are received rather than 15 would reduce the annual interest cost to 37.2 percent.

3.   New average amount of accrued wages = $(\$130,000) \left(\dfrac{1}{52}\right)\left(\dfrac{24}{1}\right)$

$$= \$60,000$$

(*Note:* Fifty-two is the number of paydays in a year if wages are paid weekly; 24 is the number if wages are paid twice a month.)

Decrease in average accrued wages = $\$130,000 - \$60,000$

$$= \$70,000$$

Cost = $\$70,000 \times .09 = \$6,300$

4.   a.   Cost of trade credit: If discounts are not taken, up to $97,000 can be raised after the second month. The cost would be

$$\frac{3}{97} \times \frac{365}{60} = 18.81\%$$

      b.   Cost of bank loan: Assuming the compensating balance would not otherwise be maintained, the cost would be

$$\frac{13}{90} = 14.44\%$$

      c.   Cost of factoring: The factor fee for the year would be

$$2\% \times \$1,200,000 = \$24,000$$

The savings effected, however, would be $18,000, giving a net factoring cost of $6,000. Borrowing $75,000 on the receivables would thus cost

$$\frac{(12\%)\,(\$75,000) + \$6,000}{\$75,000} = \frac{\$9,000 + \$6,000}{\$75,000} = 20.00\%$$

Bank borrowing would be the cheapest source of funds.

5. a. Twelve percent of 80 percent of $400,000 for 6 months = $19,200

Warehousing cost = 7,000

Cash discount forgone to extend payables
from 10 days to 40 days

$$\left(\frac{2}{98} \times \frac{365}{30} \right) (\$80,000) \left(\tfrac{1}{2} \text{ year} \right) = .2483 \times 80,000 \times .5 \qquad = \quad 9,932$$

Total cost = $36,132

b. $400,000 \times 20\% \times \tfrac{1}{2}$ year = $40,000

c. Ten percent of 70 percent of $400,000 for 6 months = $14,000

Field warehousing cost = 10,000

Cash discount forgone to extend payables
from 10 days to 40 days

$$\left(\frac{2}{98} \times \frac{365}{30} \right) (\$120,000) \left(\tfrac{1}{2} \text{ year} \right) = .2483 \times 120,000 \times .5 \qquad = \quad 14,898$$

Total cost = $38,898

The terminal warehouse receipt loan results in the lowest cost.

Selected References

ADAMS, PAUL D., STEVE B. WYATT, and YONG H. KIM, "A Contingent Claims Analysis of Trade Credit," *Financial Management*, 21 (Autumn 1992), 95–103.

BARCLAY, MICHAEL J., and CLIFFORD W. SMITH JR., "The Maturity Structure of Corporate Debt," *Journal of Finance*, 50 (June 1995), 609–31.

———, "The Priority Structure of Corporate Liabilities," *Journal of Finance*, 50 (July 1995), 899–917.

BLACK, FISCHER, and JOHN C. COX, "Valuing Corporate Securities: Some Effects of Bond Indenture Provisions," *Journal of Finance*, 31 (May 1976), 351–67.

CRABBE, LELAND, "Corporate Medium-Term Notes," *Journal of Applied Corporate Finance*, 4 (Winter 1992), 90–102.

———, "Anatomy of the Medium-Term Note Market," *Federal Reserve Bulletin*, 79 (August 1993), 751–68.

DEMIRGUC-KUNT, ASLI, and VOJISLAV MAKSIMOVIC, "Institutions, Financial Markets, and Firm Debt Maturity," *Journal of Financial Economics*, 54 (December 1999), 295–336.

DIAMOND, DOUGLAS, "Reputation Acquisition in Debt Markets," *Journal of Political Economy*, 97, No. 4 (1989), 828–62.

———, "Debt Maturity Structure and Liquidity Risk," *Quarterly Journal of Economics*, 106 (1991), 709–37.

———, "Seniority and Maturity of Debt Contracts," *Journal of Financial Economics*, 33 (June 1993), 341–68.

HO, THOMAS S. Y., and RONALD F. SINGER, "Bond Indenture Provisions and the Risk of Corporate Debt," *Journal of Financial Economics*, 10 (December 1982), 375–406.

LELAND, HAYNE E., "Corporate Debt Value, Bond Covenants, and Optimal Capital Structure," *Journal of Finance*, 49 (September 1994), 1213–52.

MANESS, TERRY S., and JOHN T. ZIETLOW, *Short-Term Financial Management*. New York: Dryden Press, 1997.

MIAN, SHEHZAD L., and CLIFFORD W. SMITH JR., "Accounts-Receivable Management Policy: Theory and Evidence," *Journal of Finance*, 47 (March 1992), 169–200.

MORRIS, JAMES R., "On Corporate Debt Maturity Strategies," *Journal of Finance*, 31 (March 1976), 29–37.

PETERSEN, MITCHELL A., and RAGHURAM G. RAJAN, "The Benefits Lending Relationships: Evidence from Small Business Data," *Journal of Finance*, 49 (March 1994), 3–37.

RAMASWAMY, KRISHNA, and SURESH M. SUNDARESAN, "The Valuation of Floating-Rate Instruments: Theory and Evidence," *Journal of Financial Economics*, 17 (December 1986), 251–72.

SCOTT, JAMES H., JR., "Bankruptcy, Secured Debt, and Optimal Capital Structure," *Journal of Finance*, 32 (March 1977), 1–19.

SHOCKLEY, RICHARD L., and ANJAN V. THAKOR, "Bank Loan Commitment Contracts," *Journal of Money, Credit and Banking*, 29 (November 1997), 515–34.

SMITH, CLIFFORD, W., JR., "A Perspective on Accounting-Based Debt Covenant Violations," *Accounting Review*, 68 (June 1993), 289–903.

SMITH, CLIFFORD, W., JR., and JEROLD B. WARNER, "On Financial Contracting: An Analysis of Bond Covenants," *Journal of Financial Economics*, 7 (June 1980), 117–61.

SNYDER, CHRISTOPHER M., "Loan Commitments and the Debt Overhang Problem," *Journal of Financial and Quantitative Analysis*, 33 (March 1998), 87–116.

STOHS, MARK HOVEN, and DAVID C. MAUER, "The Determinants of Corporate Debt Maturity Structure," *Journal of Business*, 69 (July 1996), 279–312.

STULZ, RENE M., and HERB JOHNSON, "An Analysis of Secured Debt," *Journal of Financial Economics*, 14 (December 1985), 501–21.

VAN HORNE, JAMES C., "A Linear-Programming Approach to Evaluating Restrictions under a Bond Indenture or Loan Agreement," *Journal of Financial and Quantitative Analysis*, 1 (June 1966), 68–83.

———, "Optimal Initiation of Bankruptcy Proceedings by Debt Holders," *Journal of Finance*, 31 (June 1976), 897–910.

Wachowicz's Web World is an excellent overall Web site produced and maintained by my coauthor of *Fundamentals of Financial Management*, John M. Wachowicz Jr. It contains descriptions of and links to many finance Web sites and articles. *www.prenhall.com/wachowicz.*

Part VI

CAPITAL MARKET FINANCING AND RISK MANAGEMENT

■ **CASE:** *Dougall & Gilligan Global Agency*

In early 1995, Lynne Caldwell, executive vice president and chief financial officer of the worldwide advertising agency Dougall & Gilligan, was faced with recommending a means for financing a $300 million expansion program. This program was directed primarily toward acquiring advertising agencies and developing business de novo in Southeast Asia and Latin America. The company has identified major growth areas in these regions and its strategy is to exploit such opportunities. Means of financing being contemplated are: (1) utilization of bank lines of credit, (2) a 7- to 10-year term loan through a private placement, (3) 20-year debentures, and (4) common stock financing. Although other means of financing are not precluded, Ms. Caldwell wished to focus on these means first.

THE COMPANY AND INDUSTRY

Dougall & Gilligan Global Agency (D & G), one of the larger advertising agencies in the world with over 11,000 employees, had its origin in 1912 through a predecessor firm. Through creative genius as well as through acquisitions, the company grew rapidly in the 1980s. While headquartered in New York City and strictly an "American" agency until 1960, recent growth has come primarily from foreign accounts. Foreign business now accounts for 56 percent of total commission and fee income. D & G is a broad-based agency, having clients across many industries and operating in all media. The 10 largest clients account for 23 percent of total billings. As D & G acquired other advertising agencies, it retained some of their names. Dougall & Gilligan Global Agency is the corporate umbrella under which there are five operating units, the largest of which is Dougall & Gilligan Advertising. Although each agency has its own president, operations are fairly centralized.

521

Spending for advertising is highly correlated with the level of economic activity within a country. With the pickup in economic activity in 1994 and that expected in 1995, advertising spending worldwide should increase. However, the increase will be nowhere near that which occurred in the late 1980s. With the present emphasis on "reengineering" their marketing efforts, many companies are turning to their advertising agencies for help. Part of this "help" is pressure on agencies to discount their fees or provide more services for a given fee. To prosper in the advertising industry today, cost cutting and containment are essential, painful as they may be. The client simply demands such. Competition is intense, and such firms as Foote, Cone & Belding, Interpublic Group, and Omnicom Group are relentless in the pressure they bring to bear on D & G to operate efficiently. However, there is a delicate balance between operating efficiently and maintaining a creative edge together with prospecting for new clients. The switching by clients of the advertising agency they employ is legendary, so no one can rest on past laurels.

For the overall industry, advertising revenue is forecast to increase by 9 percent for 1995. Worldwide, the increases are likely to be higher in the United States than in Western Europe. However, growth prospects for Eastern Europe, the Pacific Rim, and Latin America are the brightest of all. One of the challenges for the industry is how to come to grips with interactive communications. D & G as well as several other agencies are aggressively pursuing how to participate in the Internet and other aspects of the "information highway." These developments are making the future highly uncertain. In this changing environment, how is an advertiser to reach its marketing objectives? Advertising agencies are being called on to provide answers and to create programming that will reach the consumer through these new medias. Reinvention must take place.

Although D & G has been innovative in its pursuit of change, it is not quite at the vanguard of the two largest agencies. The present chairman and CEO, Gilbert Stein, 62, and president and COO, John Waitley, 54, have worked together in those capacities for several years. Waitley is very aggressive in new business development. Sometimes he forces client representatives to promise more than D & G can deliver. Waitley's aggressive nature is tempered by the more balanced and reflective perspective of Mr. Stein. Most stock analysts feel they make an excellent team. However, neither was satisfied with the performance of the company in 1994, when revenues and earnings dipped from the historic highs of 1993. Although the firm purposely exited two unprofitable businesses, its fifth most profitable client switched advertising firms in May. Also, D & G felt continuing pressure from clients to pare margins. Stein and Waitley hope to reverse the 1994 downturn in 1995 and to set in place a strategic plan to improve profitability in the years beyond.

PAST FINANCING

A mainstay of financing has been bank borrowings under lines of credit. These lines currently total $340 million from some 23 banks. Not only does the company use these lines to finance a moderate seasonal bulge in receivables in the latter part of the year, but also to finance underlying buildups in assets. These needs are dictated largely by the acquisition of other companies, reduced by the occasional sale of a business such as occurred in 1993. Borrowings under the bank lines are at the prime rate, presently $8\frac{1}{2}$ percent. Although the banks have accommodated the company willingly in the past, the lead bank has expressed concern with the company's occasional repurchase of stock.

Long-term debt consists entirely of term loans from institutional investors. These loans, six in all, are fixed rate with coupons ranging from $8\frac{1}{4}$ to $11\frac{1}{2}$ percent. The loans were taken out for specific purposes, such as financing an acquisition or a new building. Where fixed assets were involved as they were in two situations, a mortgage on the property afforded the lenders protection. Other term loans are unsecured, but subject to a loan agreement. Protective covenants contained therein are reasonably restrictive as to large acquisitions, further indebtedness, net worth, and investment in fixed assets. All loans involve balloon payments, with approximately $23 million coming due in 1996, $13 million in 1997, $10 million in 1998, $27 million in 1999, and $8 million in 2000, with the remaining debt coming due in the years 2001 to 2005. The life insurance companies involved have been willing to renegotiate a loan into a longer-term loan if needed, or to allow the company to prepay its debt, with a modest penalty, if it is flush with funds. This flexibility is dependent, however, on the continuing profitability of the company.

In March 1993, the company successfully placed a convertible subordinated debenture issue. Proceeds were used to pay down existing debt along with providing some funds for working capital needs. The $5\frac{3}{4}$ percent issue due March 15, 2013, has a total face value of $81 million. At the time of issue, share price was at an historic high of $98. The conversion price of the debentures is $118. They are callable any time after March 15, 1995, at an initial call price of $105.75, using the $100 face value pricing convention. Since issuance, share price rose further in 1993, eventually reaching $111 in August. As the pressure on margins and decline in 1994 revenue became apparent to the market, growth expectations were revised downward. Share price declined to where the stock now trades at $64. The debentures have dropped in price to where they now trade at $77\frac{1}{4}$ per $100 of face value. During this time, interest rates for straight fixed-income corporate debt declined through early 1994 and then rose to where they now are at levels somewhat higher than those which prevailed in March 1993. Several institutional investors have expressed displeasure with the performance of their investment during the last year and a quarter. Ms. Caldwell has felt pressure from these investors as to when performance will improve.

Finally, the company has engaged in common-stock financing, the last time being in 1992. At that time it sold 0.8 million shares of stock in a rights offering to existing stockholders at a subscription price of $71\frac{1}{2}$ per share. The net proceeds to the company of $56 million were used to finance a buildup in current assets, to fund an acquisition in part, and to offset for accounting purposes foreign exchange translation losses. In addition to this rights offering, small amounts of common stock are issued each year in connection with the exercise of stock options and various employee stock purchase and incentive plans. The performance of the stock is shown in Exhibit 3, where it is seen that share price has both risen and fallen since the 1992 offering. The stock's beta is 1.30, compared with a median beta of 1.10 for other large companies in the industry.

In addition to stock sales and the retention of earnings, total shareholders' equity is affected by stock repurchases and foreign currency translations adjustments. In 1993 and 1994, D & G engaged in moderate share repurchases, in an effort to boost share price as well as to fulfill its obligation under various compensation plans. The stronger dollar in 1992 and 1993 resulted in negative foreign translations adjustments, whereas the weaker dollar in 1994 resulted in a positive adjustment. The breakdown of the European Monetary System in 1992, the sharp appreciation of the dollar late in that year, and the lack of hedging by D & G together with some outright speculation resulted in nearly $50 million in translation losses in that year. As the functional currency for accounting purposes is local, the loss was reflected in shareholders' equity but not in the income statement.

FINANCING NEEDS

To set in motion its strategic plan for developing markets in Southeast Asia and in Latin America, $300 million is needed during 1995 and early 1996. This is in addition to the free cash flow expected to be generated from operations. Like other advertising agencies, Dougall & Gilligan attempts to bill and collect payments from its clients at about the same time it needs funds to pay the media for the ads placed. On average, commissions and fees to D & G average only 13 percent of billings. As the amounts of billings outstanding and accounts payable are large, a moderate tilt toward slower receivables vis-à-vis the times D & G must pay the media can have a pronounced effect on the company's need for cash.

Although revenues and assets have grown at a relatively slow rate during the last 4 years, D & G anticipates faster growth during the remainder of the decade. Internal goals call for underlying growth in revenues of 15 percent per annum. This is based on the higher expected growth in advertising worldwide in the later 1990s, as well as a moderate gain in market share. Ms. Caldwell felt that growth of this magnitude could be largely accommodated with internal financing, together with $300 million in external, new financing.

ALTERNATIVES FOR FINANCING

Ms. Caldwell looks first to bank lines of credit as a means for financing seasonal and special needs of a moderate size. With $340 million in lines and present borrowings of $151.9 million, there is room for additional borrowing. However, $300 million is beyond this capacity. To accommodate such needs using bank financing, the lines would need to be renegotiated. Caldwell wants to have excess borrowing capacity for emergency purposes, so $152 million plus $300 million is not sufficient. In discussions with the lead banker, Jonathan Golden, he indicated that he doubted that the consortium of banks would go along with an increase in bank lines of the sort needed to accommodate their entire needs. Golden did say that he was prepared to try to arrange an additional $80 million in bank lines to bring the total to roughly $420 million. However, this increase and concurrent heavier dependence on debt would need to be accompanied by a higher interest rate. When Caldwell asked what that meant, Golden responded that prime plus $\frac{1}{2}$ percent would be required at a minimum, compared with prime today.

A second alternative is to arrange a term loan of 7 to 10 years with the same life insurance companies from which private placements presently were arranged. These institutional investors indicated a willingness to consider the additional financing needs of D & G. Presently, the company was accorded an investment grade of BBB by these investors. With additional borrowings, this rating would slip into the speculative-grade category, probably BB. With the risk-based reserve requirements now being imposed by the National Association of Insurance Commissioners, a likely 5 to 10 percent reserve requirement, in contrast to 2 percent presently, makes new term loans to the company less attractive. To offset the increased risk, a premium interest rate would be necessary. For a 7-year term loan, the rate would be $10\frac{1}{4}$ percent, and for a 10-year term loan, $10\frac{3}{4}$ percent. In addition, the interest rates on all existing term loans would need to be reset. This would result in a weighted average rate on existing loans of 10.73 percent, compared with 10.38 percent before any new financing. As several existing term loans bear coupon rates in excess of interest rates in the current market, allowance was made for this in the reset proposed by the institutional investors. Otherwise, the net increase proposed would have been greater.

The new term loan would allow for no prepayment, unless renegotiated, and would subject D & G to a number of restrictive covenants: (1) a current ratio greater than 1:1; (2) senior interest-bearing debt (bank loans and long-term debt) not to exceed 75 percent of total capitalization (bank loans + LTD + shareholders' equity); (3) intangible assets not to exceed $450 million; (4) no further indebtedness other than bank loans for seasonal financing requirements; (5) dividends not to exceed 35 percent of consolidated net profits after January 1, 1995; (6) any additional leases subject to approval on an individual basis; and (7) a negative pledge clause. Legal and other out-of-pocket costs associated with a term loan are likely to cost D & G around $100,000.

The third alternative is a public offering of 20-year debentures. With this new debt, the likely credit rating for the company would be either Ba-2/BB or Ba-3/BB−, contrasted with Baa-2/BBB if D & G presently had public as opposed to private debt outstanding. Shirley Jackson, an investment banker with Merrill Lynch, felt that D & G could obtain a rate of $10\frac{1}{2}$ percent in the current market. However, she expected interest rates to rise and the window for lower-grade companies tapping the market eventually to close. Presently quality yield spreads between low- and high-grade corporates are narrow, particularly when contrasted with 1990–1991. She advised Caldwell to seize the opportunity with a debt issue at the earliest possible moment. "Time is of the essence," according to Ms. Jackson.

The spread between the price of the debentures to the public and the proceeds of the offering to the company (representing underwriter and selling fees) would be in the area of 2 percent. In addition, the company would probably incur legal and other out-of-pocket costs of approximately $260,000. As to call feature, Jackson estimated that the company could obtain a $\frac{1}{4}$ percent lower rate if the issue had no call provision. With a call feature, a minimum of 5 years deferred call protection to investors would be necessary to place the issue. A sinking fund would begin at the end of year 10 with annual provisions sufficient to retire one-half the bonds by maturity. As a public debenture issue is precluded under existing term loan agreements, Caldwell explored a waiver with the institutional investors at the same time that she discussed a term loan. These investors agreed with her that the expansion program would be good for the company in the long run. In the short run, their existing investment would be more risky whether the new debt took the form of a term loan or a longer-term debenture issue. They would agree to a waiver only with a higher interest rate on existing debt. The increase proposed was from a weighted average rate of 10.38 percent to 10.90 percent, somewhat higher than if the institutional investors made a new term loan.

The last financing alternative being considered is an equity offering. Presently, the company has outstanding 26,860,000 shares, with a market price per share of $64. In order to place the issue, underpricing will need to occur, with estimates running from 6 to 10 percent, depending on the size of the offering. Legal and other out-of-pocket costs borne by D & G would probably total $350,000. Mr. Waitley, president, was opposed to an equity offering because he believed the stock was significantly undervalued. "Selling stock at a price more than 40 percent below the 1993 high is not my idea of enhancing shareholder wealth. The dilution is simply too great for our public shareholders and for management owning stock and with stock options. It will only serve to depress our incentive compensation. The market doesn't understand our strategic plan to grow this company at 15 percent. If we must sell stock, let us at least wait until we are better appreciated by the market and our multiple improves."

Mr. Stein, chairman and CEO, was not opposed per se to an equity offering but was concerned with the effect it would have on convertible subordinated debenture holders who faced a conversion price of $118. "Will not they rebel if we now sell stock at little more than half that price?" One estimate of earnings growth for D & G, by Zacks, was that the company would grow earnings per share at a 13 percent annual rate during the next 5 years. This compares with a 15.3 percent average rate for other companies in the advertising industry. Price/earnings ratios for selected other companies are: Foote, Cone and Belding, 18x; Interpublic Group, 19x; Omnicom Group, 16x; and WPP Group, 27x. Because of losses, a P/E ratio for Saatchi & Saatchi is not applicable.

THE DECISION

Ms. Caldwell hoped to make a recommendation to Messrs. Stein and Waitley and to two other members of the management committee by the end of next week. She was mindful of the need to retain some financial flexibility. To end up like Saatchi & Saatchi as a highly risky company was not something that she would like to see as chief financial officer. However, she had only one voice in five on the matter. The "final" voice was that of Stein. Given management's recommendation, it would be her task to present the matter to the board of directors at its next meeting in 5 weeks. Although she had been a member of the board for over 2 years, one still needed to have structured, analytical backup for any management recommendation.

Exhibit 1

Dougall & Gilligan Global Agency Consolidated Balance Sheets (in millions)

	1991	1992	1993	1994
Cash and cash equivalents	$ 123.4	$ 147.5	$ 146.9	$ 166.7
Receivables, net	1,169.9	1,210.5	1,128.8	1,181.9
Other client billables	105.9	119.0	121.6	112.7
Other current assets	37.0	46.7	38.9	41.1
Current assets	$1,436.2	$1,523.7	$1,436.2	$1,502.4
Net fixed assets	134.1	140.1	135.3	162.5
Other assets	83.1	86.0	97.2	119.1
Intangible assets, net	284.8	338.5	298.9	368.3
Total assets	$1,938.2	$2,088.3	$1,967.6	$2,152.3
Bank notes payable	$ 123.8	$ 155.3	$ 108.4	$ 147.8
Accounts payable	1,065.7	1,068.2	998.3	1,071.3
Accruals	175.0	180.3	198.5	195.4
Current liabilities	$1,364.5	$1,403.8	$1,305.2	$1,414.5
Long-term debt	221.1	256.1	195.6	211.1
Convertible subordinated debentures			81.0	81.0
Deferred compensation and reserves	88.0	91.1	100.7	110.0
Accrued post retirement benefits		26.7	33.0	33.4
Other liabilities	21.7	20.5	18.6	29.5
Noncurrent liabilities	$ 330.8	$ 394.4	$ 428.9	$ 465.0
Total shareholders' equity	242.9	290.1	233.5	272.8
Total liabilities and equity	$1,938.2	$2,088.3	$1,967.6	$2,152.3

Exhibit 2

Dougall & Gilligan Global Agency Consolidated Income Statement (in millions)

	1991	1992	1993	1994
Commissions and fees	$1,079.6	$1,258.1	$1,392.0	$1,330.4
Salaries and benefits	587.1	660.2	744.8	700.7
Office and general expenses	364.7	433.9	466.9	462.4
Interest	28.8	40.1	38.5	36.3
Income before taxes	$ 99.0	$ 123.9	$ 141.8	$ 131.0
Provision for U.S. and foreign taxes	48.4	57.8	62.5	56.5
Net income	$ 50.6	$ 66.1	$ 79.3	$ 74.5
Dividends	$ 17.6	$ 20.3	$ 22.3	$ 24.9

Exhibit 3

Dougall & Gilligan Global Agency
Earnings, Dividends, and Market Price Per Share

	1990	1991	1992	1993	1994
Earnings per share	$ 2.13	$ 2.07	$ 2.33	$ 3.14	$ 2.77
Dividend per share	.72	.72	.80	.88	.92
Share price, high	$72.50	$63.25	$86.37	$111.12	$84.50
Share price, low	44.87	36.75	53.12	77.25	58.87

17

Foundations for Longer-Term Financing

N ow that we have covered short- and intermediate-term financing, it is appropriate to lay out some foundations for long-term financing. Long-term interest rates behave differently than short-term rates. For one thing they appear to be more strongly influenced by inflation expectations. Debt instruments of corporations often are priced off the Treasury yield curve, so we need to understand the relevance of yield curves for a financing decision.

One can hardly open the financial section of a newspaper today without reading about rapidly changing financial markets. Like it or not, the financial services industry is in a period of rapid change. Deregulation, globalization, volatile interest rates and currency exchange rates, and heightened competition are some of the reasons. Today the financial manager of any medium to large corporation must search for "best price" across a wide spectrum of possibilities, both domestic and global. In what immediately follows, we investigate the purpose of financial markets and the ever-changing environment in which capital is raised. ■

PURPOSE AND FUNCTION OF FINANCIAL MARKETS

Financial assets exist in an economy because the savings of various individuals, corporations, and governments during a period of time differ from their investment in real assets. By real assets, we mean things such as houses, buildings, equipment, inventories, and durable goods. If savings equaled investment in real assets for all economic units in an economy over all periods of time, there would be no external financing, no financial assets, and no money and capital markets. Each economic unit would be self-sufficient; current expenditures and investment in real assets would be paid for out of current income. A financial asset is created only when the investment of an economic unit in real assets exceeds its savings, and it finances this excess by borrowing or issuing equity securities. Of course, another economic unit must be willing to lend. This interaction of borrowers with lenders determines interest rates. In the economy as a whole, savings-surplus economic units (those whose savings exceed their investment in real assets) provide funds to savings deficit units (those whose investment in real assets exceeds their savings). This exchange of funds is evidenced by pieces of paper representing a financial asset to the holder and a financial liability to the issuer.

529

Efficiency of Financial Markets

The purpose of financial markets in an economy is to allocate savings efficiently during a period of time—a day, a week, a month, or a quarter—to parties who use funds for investment in real assets or for consumption. If those parties that saved were the same as those that engaged in capital formation, an economy could prosper without financial markets. In modern economies, however, the economic units most responsible for capital formation—nonfinancial corporations—use more than their total savings for investing in real assets. Households, on the other hand, have total savings in excess of total investment. The more diverse the patterns of desired savings and investment among economic units, the greater the need for efficient financial markets to channel savings to ultimate users. The ultimate investor in real assets and the ultimate saver should be brought together at the least possible cost and inconvenience.

Financial Intermediaries Efficient financial markets are essential to ensure adequate capital formation and economic growth in an economy. With financial intermediaries in an economy, the flow of savings from savers to users of funds can be indirect. Financial intermediaries include institutions such as commercial banks, life insurance companies, and pension and profit-sharing funds. These intermediaries come between ultimate borrowers and lenders by transforming direct claims into indirect ones. They purchase primary securities and, in turn, issue their own securities. The primary security that a bank might purchase is a mortgage, a commercial loan, or a consumer loan; the indirect claim issued is a demand deposit, a savings account, or a certificate of deposit. A life insurance company, on the other hand, purchases corporate bonds, among other things, and issues life insurance policies.

Financial intermediaries transform funds in such a way as to make them more attractive. On one hand, the indirect security issued to ultimate lenders is more attractive than is a direct, or primary, security. In particular, these indirect claims are well suited to the small saver. On the other hand, the ultimate borrower is able to sell its primary securities to a financial intermediary on more attractive terms than it could if the securities were sold directly to ultimate lenders. Financial intermediaries provide a variety of services and economies that make the transformation of claims attractive.

1. **Transaction costs.** Because financial intermediaries are continually in the business of purchasing primary securities and selling indirect securities, economies of scale not available to the borrower or to the individual saver are possible. As a result, transaction costs and costs associated with locating potential borrowers and savers are lowered.

2. **Information production.** The financial intermediary is able to develop information on the ultimate borrower in a more efficient manner than the saver. Moreover, the intermediary may be able to reduce the moral hazard problem of unreliable information.

3. **Divisibility and flexibility.** A financial intermediary is able to pool the savings of many individual savers to purchase primary securities of varying sizes. In particular, the intermediary is able to tap small pockets of savings for ultimate investment in real assets. The offering of indirect securities of varying denomination makes financial intermediaries more attractive to the saver. Moreover, borrowers have more flexibility in deal-

ing with a financial intermediary than with a large number of lenders and are able to obtain terms better suited to their needs.

4. **Diversification and risk.** By purchasing a number of different primary securities, the financial intermediary is able to spread risk. If these securities are less than perfectly correlated with each other, the intermediary is able to reduce the risk associated with fluctuations in value of principal. The benefits of reduced risk are passed on to the indirect security holders. As a result, the indirect security provides a higher degree of liquidity to the saver than does a like commitment to a single primary security.

5. **Maturity.** A financial intermediary is able to transform a primary security of a certain maturity into indirect securities of different maturities. As a result, the maturities of the primary and the indirect securities may be more attractive to the ultimate borrower and lender than they would be if the loan were direct.

6. **Expertise and convenience.** The financial intermediary is an expert in making purchases of primary securities and in so doing eliminates the inconvenience to the saver of making direct purchases. The financial intermediary is also an expert in dealing with ultimate savers—an expertise lacking in most borrowers.

Financial intermediaries tailor the denomination and type of indirect securities they issue to the desires of savers. Their purpose, of course, is to make a profit by purchasing primary securities yielding more than the return they must pay on the indirect securities issued and on operations. In so doing, they must channel funds from the ultimate lender to the ultimate borrower at a lower cost or with more convenience or both than is possible through a direct purchase of primary securities by the ultimate lender. Otherwise, they have no reason to exist.

Disintermediation

We usually think of financial intermediation making the markets more efficient. However, this is not always the case. Sometimes the intermediation process becomes cumbersome and expensive. When this occurs, there is a reversion toward direct loans and security issues. This reversal process is known as *disintermediation*. In other words, when financial intermediation no longer makes the financial markets more efficient, disintermediation occurs. One manifestation of this phenomenon is securitization.

Securitization

Securitization involves taking an illiquid asset, such as a residential mortgage, packaging it into a pool of like assets, and then issuing securities backed by the asset pool. The investor has a direct claim on a portion of the mortgage pool. That is to say, interest and principal payments on the mortgages are passed directly along to the investor. Other securities involve bonds backed by the pool of assets. Though securitization of assets was originally confined to residential mortgages, in the mid- to late-1980s it spread to auto loans, credit card receivables, commercial mortgages, and lease contracts. The reason for its spread is that the total transaction costs of credit often are less with securitization than they are when a depository institution intermediates between borrowers and savers. When a company's assets include consumer receivables and loans, securitization may be a logical, cost effective means of financing.

Financial Innovation

Innovations in financial products, such as the securitization movement, and in processes, like the ATM machine, are the lifeblood of the financial markets. Such innovation comes about to exploit profit opportunities arising from operational inefficiencies. A second foundation is the drive for complete markets. This merely means supplying securities with the features desired by investors. In steady-state equilibrium, the financial markets would be highly efficient and reasonably complete. As a result, the financial instruments that should have been provided and the operational efficiencies that should have been achieved already will have happened.

For financial innovation to occur, there must be a change in the environment. What are some of the changes? They are (1) tax law changes; (2) technological advances; (3) changing interest rates, currency levels, and volatility; (4) changes in the level of economic activity; and (5) regulatory changes. With a change in one or more of these factors, profit opportunities arise and new financial products and processes are introduced by financial promoters to exploit the opportunity. With competition among providers, the profitability of a financial innovation to its original promoter declines over time. As this occurs, consumers of financial services increasingly benefit from the innovation.

During the last decade, literally thousands of financial innovations have occurred. The majority are in the product area and involve fixed-income securities. Financial innovation reduces the cost of financial intermediation, widens the choice of financial instruments in which to invest and which to issue, and lowers the cost of inconvenience in some cases. As long as the economic and political environment is changing, financial innovation will flourish.

Allocation of Funds

The allocation of funds in an economy occurs primarily on the basis of price, expressed in terms of expected return. Economic units in need of funds must outbid others for their use. Although the allocation process is affected by capital rationing, government restrictions, and institutional constraints, expected returns are the primary mechanism whereby supply and demand are brought into balance for a particular financial instrument across financial markets. If risk is held constant, economic units willing to pay the highest expected return are the ones entitled to the use of funds. If rationality prevails, the economic units bidding the highest prices will have the most promising investment opportunities. As a result, savings will tend to be allocated to the most efficient uses.

It is important to recognize that the equilibration process by which savings are allocated in an economy occurs not only on the basis of expected return but on the basis of risk as well. Different financial instruments have different degrees of risk. In order for them to compete for funds, these instruments must provide different expected returns, or yields.

Reasons for Yield Differentials   From our discussion of marketable securities in Chapter 14, we know that the relative risk and, hence, expected return of different financial instruments are a function of a number of things:

1.   Differences in maturity
2.   Differences in the level of coupon rate
3.   Differences in default risk

Namibia's Quest for Economic Growth

Namibia, located in southwest Africa, became an independent country in 1990. It has only 1.6 million people spread over some 325,000 square miles of mostly semi-arid land. The country has been hurt by the civil war in Angola, its northern neighbor. Mining (diamonds in particular), fishing, livestock, tourism, a major shipping port, and limited manufacturing drive the economy. While real GDP growth has averaged $3\frac{1}{2}$ percent per annum in recent years, unemployment is high and the country clearly would like to grow faster.

Public policies designed to provide stable government, infrastructure, and accommodation to business help. Financial policies encourage foreign investment. All earnings from a Namibian foreign subsidiary can be repatriated. An exporting processing zone regime exists throughout the country, providing special incentives to manufacturing companies and exporters. Though not large, Namibia has a sound and efficient banking system. The central bank does not control interest rates, nor does it overregulate the five commercial banks in the country. Exchange rate controls have been steadily reduced. In all, there is a recognition that market-driven financial markets are essential for economic growth to happen.

4. Differences in taxation of interest, dividend, and capital gains returns
5. Differences in option-type features, such as conversion rights, other equity links, call features, and sinking funds

In this chapter we explore the effect of the first three—maturity, coupon rate, and default risk. Embedded options will be taken up in other chapters in this part.

Inflation and Interest Rates   The expected return on a financial instrument depends also on expected inflation. Embraced in the nominal interest rate at a moment in time is an **inflation premium.** That is to say, the interest rate we observe on an intermediate-term note or a longer-term bond will embrace in it some multiple of the inflation the market expects to occur over the life of the instrument. In the late 1970s and early 1980s, the inflation expectation in the United States was high—double digit at one time. Not surprisingly, interest rates were high as well—16 percent for Treasury notes! Since that time inflation has dropped, with 2 percent or less being the norm in recent years. Interest rates are a good deal lower, as we would expect. The relationship between unexpected changes in inflation and interest rates is not consistent over time.[1] While we know that expected inflation is important in determining the level of interest rates, it has little effect on interest-rate differentials.

YIELD CURVES AND THEIR USE

When a financial manager taps the capital market for funds, much of the pricing of debt instruments revolves around the yield curve. This curve, or *term structure of interest rates* as it is known more formally, describes the relationship between yield and

---

[1]See James C. Van Horne, *Financial Market Rates and Flows*, 6th ed. (Upper Saddle River, NJ: Prentice Hall, 2001), Chapter 5, for an in-depth treatment of this subject and a review of the empirical evidence.

maturity on securities differing only in length of time to maturity. All factors other than maturity must be held constant if the relationship studied is to be meaningful. To hold constant default risk, Treasury securities usually are employed.

Examples of yield curves for zero coupon Treasury securities, known as STRIPS, are shown in Fig. 17–1. As discussed in Chapter 2, the return on a zero coupon bond is embraced entirely in the discount from the face value of the instrument. No interim coupon payments occur, so return is represented by the rate of discount that equates the face value of the instrument at maturity, usually $100, with the market price paid for the bond. Typically, yield curves are upward sloping, as shown in the figure. Occasionally, the yield curve is downward sloping throughout all but the early maturities. Though such a shape has been infrequent, it has occurred.

Yield curves describe the yield–maturity relationship for securities of the same default risk.

Shape of the Yield Curve

There are a number of explanations for the shape of the yield curve.[2] Perhaps the most important is **expectations** of market participants about the future course of interest rates. If they believe interest rates will rise, the yield curve will be upward sloping, all other things the same. If they believe interest rates will decline, it can be downward sloping. In the first case, investors are unwilling to buy long-term bonds that yield no more than short-term ones. They can do better by investing in short-term securities and rolling them over at maturity. Only if interest rates are expected to decline will they invest in long-term securities providing a lesser yield than short-term securities, because they can expect to do no better with a short-term strategy.

Term Premiums However, the yield curve is seldom downward sloping. Over a large number of interest-rate cycles we would expect it to be downward sloping about as much of the time as it is upward sloping, if expectations alone determine its

FIGURE 17-1

Yields on zero-coupon Treasury Securities (STRIPS)

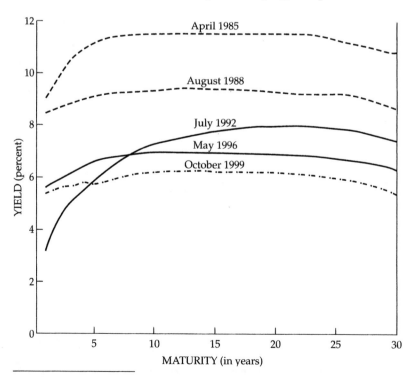

[2]See Van Horne, *Financial Market Rates and Flows*, Chapters 6 and 7, for a much deeper treatment of maturity and coupon rate effects.

shape. Most attribute the lack of downward-sloping yield curves to the presence of **term premiums.** Because long-term bond prices fluctuate more than short-term ones, lenders must be offered a yield inducement to lend on a long-term basis. The presence of a term, or liquidity, premium has been documented empirically.

Segmentation Effect   A third explanation for the shape of the yield curve is that **market segmentation** affects demand and supply. If, to some degree, the yield curve is compartmentalized into separate markets, a change in the relative supply or demand in one of these markets may change its shape. During 1991–1992 short-term interest rates dropped dramatically in the United States, while long-term rates experienced only a moderate decline. The yield curve became steeply upward sloping. Most attributed this occurrence to concerted actions by the Federal Reserve to lower interest rates, conducting open market operations in the short-term area of the yield curve to do so. The sharp change in the shape of the yield curve was consistent at least in part with a market segmentation effect, where actions in one segment of the yield curve are not fully transmitted to others.

Thus, all three explanations—expectations, term premiums, and market segmentation—seem to have explanatory power when it comes to the shape of the yield curve. From what we know empirically, the first is the most important.

Coupon Effect

We know that the longer the maturity of a debt instrument, the greater the change in price that accompanies a shift in interest rates. However, price changes also depend on the level of coupon.

When market yields change, different bonds are affected differently depending on their coupon rate and maturity. For a given bond, the lower the coupon, the greater the price change for a given shift in interest rates. This is illustrated in Table 17-1 for 10- and 20-year bonds. In the left-hand part of the table, a yield increase is assumed, while in the right-hand part a yield decline is assumed to occur. We see that the lower the coupon, the more sensitive market prices are to changes in yields. The reason for this is that with lower coupons more of the total return to the investor is reflected in the principal payment at maturity as opposed to nearer-term interest payments.

TABLE 17-1
Changes in price accompanying a shift in yield for various coupons

COUPON	Yield Increase from 8% to 10%		Yield Decrease from 8% to 6%	
	PRICE DECLINE 10-YEAR BOND	PRICE DECLINE 20-YEAR BOND	PRICE INCREASE 10-YEAR BOND	PRICE INCREASE 20-YEAR BOND
12%	−11.57%	−16.07%	13.72%	21.31%
10	−11.96	−16.52	14.23	22.07
8	−12.46	−17.16	14.88	23.11
6	−13.11	−18.11	15.73	24.67
4	−14.02	−19.68	16.89	27.28
2	−15.33	−22.80	18.61	32.37
0	−17.42	−31.80	21.32	47.18

We see also in Table 17-1 that the 20-year bond column shows more price volatility than the 10-year column, in keeping with our previous discussion. Furthermore, the percentage increase in price when yields decline is greater than the percentage decrease when yields rise. This is due to the convex relationship between price and yield, an example of which is shown in Fig. 17-2. The point of Table 17-1, however, is to emphasize that one gets very different market price movements, depending on the coupon rate. With high coupons, the total income stream (interest and principal payments) is closer to realization than it is with low coupons. The nearer the income stream, the less the present value effect, given a change in yields.

Duration   The problems associated with different market price movements for different coupon rates have led many to question the usefulness of maturity as a measure of the length of a financial instrument. Instead they suggest the use of another measure—the duration of a security, which is a weighted average of the times in the future when interest and principal payments are to be received. This measure was introduced in Chapter 2, so we do not go through the formula again. As we took up, the volatility of a bond's price is directly related to its duration.

The use of duration is particularly important to a financial manager when managing a marketable securities portfolio and/or pension fund assets. By matching the duration of the portfolio with likely future cash needs, the risk of principal loss and the risk of not knowing the reinvestment rate when coupon payments occur in the future can be largely neutralized. This is known as **immunization** and it is explained in detail in the companion text, *Financial Market Rates and Flows*, 6th ed. (Upper Saddle River, NJ: Prentice Hall, 2001, Chap. 7).

Coupon Yield Curves versus Zero Coupon Curves

There tends to be a precise relationship between Treasury yield curves based on coupon instruments and those based on zero coupon instruments. Arbitrage assures the equilibrium. The sum of the zero coupon parts, both coupon and principal payments, should equal the whole coupon bond. If the total market value of the

FIGURE 17-2

Relationship between price and yield for a long-term bond

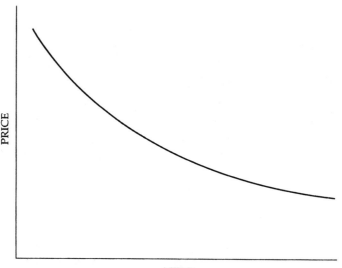

parts exceeds the whole, one would buy the parts, reconstitute a coupon bond, and sell it in the market for more than the total price paid for the parts. If the parts were more valuable than the whole, one buys the coupon bond, strips the coupon and principal payments into a series of zero coupon bonds, and sells them in the market for more than what was paid for the coupon bond. (The U.S. Treasury provides facilities both to strip bonds and to reconstitute them.) These actions continue until the two yield curves are in line and there is an absence of arbitrage opportunities.

A hypothetical, and exaggerated, example of the two yield curves is seen in Fig. 17-3. When the yield curve for coupon bonds is upward sloping, the yield curve for zero coupon bonds should be above it. This is simply to say that the endpoint (for zero coupon bonds) must be greater than the weighted average (for coupon bonds) of all the pure discount rates through the endpoint. The opposite should occur when the yield curve for coupon bonds is downward sloping. While the yield curve for coupon bonds should bear a precise relationship with the yield curve for zero coupon bonds, it will depend on the equilibration between the markets for the two types of bonds.

PRICING DEFAULT RISK OFF TREASURIES

Treasury securities are a base for pricing other bonds and loans.

Many securities are priced off of a Treasury yield curve. When a zero coupon instrument is involved, the zero-coupon Treasury yield curve is used. Given a maturity, the Treasury curve gives a base yield, to which a risk premium is added. The rate quotation might be "10-year Treasuries plus 80 basis points." This means the security is priced so as to yield the 10-year Treasury rate plus $\frac{8}{10}$ of 1 percent. If a coupon issue is involved, one would use the Treasury coupon yield curve. More specifically, it should be a curve based on Treasury bonds whose market prices approximate their face values. These bonds are referred to as "trading at par." Again, the Treasury coupon curve provides the foundation on which to determine an appropriate interest rate.

The yield spread from Treasuries reflects the default risk of the issuer. The greater the default risk, the greater the spread. Usually, default risk is based on the bond or credit rating of the company involved. As taken up in Chapter 10, these range from AAA for the highest grade through the investment grade of BBB and into the speculative grade (junk bonds), BB through D, using Standard & Poor's

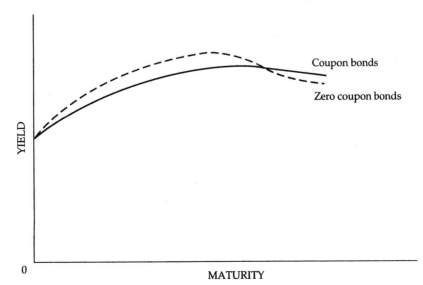

FIGURE 17-3
Hypothetical yield curves for zero coupon and coupon bonds

letters. The quality yield spread for a particular grade is not static. It varies with maturity and with the economic cycle.

Default-Risk Structure

For most corporate bonds, quality, or credit, yield spreads widen with maturity. Implicit in this statement is a market that attaches a higher probability of default the further in the future the maturity. An example of credit risk spreads varying with maturity is shown in Fig. 17-4. The baseline is the horizontal axis, which represents the Treasury yield for each maturity. The spreads above Treasuries are reflected for four grades, AAA through BBB. The lower the grade, the higher the yield required and the greater the increase in yield with maturity.

Given the information in Fig. 17-4, the yield to maturity for a corporate issue would be established in four steps:

1. Determine the maturity and credit rating of the security to be issued.
2. Find the Treasury yield for the maturity, using a yield curve like that portrayed in Fig. 17-3.
3. For this maturity, turn to Fig. 17-4 to determine the credit yield spread appropriate for the credit rating.
4. Add the risk premium to the Treasury yield to obtain the appropriate yield. In this way it is possible for the financial manager to price a debt issue in the market.[3]

FIGURE 17-4
Credit yield differentials and maturity

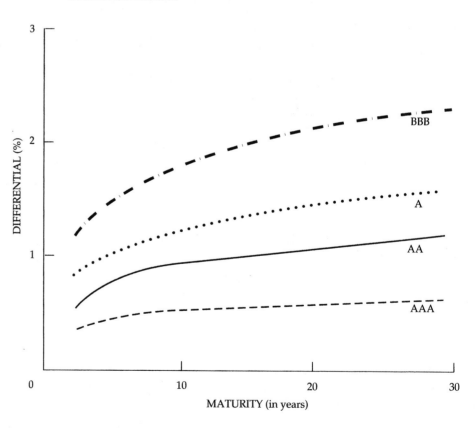

---

[3]See Robert Litterman and Thomas Iben, "Corporate Bond Valuation and the Term Structure of Credit Spreads," *Financial Analysts Journal*, 47 (Spring 1991), 52–64, for a more sophisticated application of this technique.

Cyclical Behavior of Credit Risk Spreads

Credit risk spreads are the differential in yield between a risky instrument and Treasuries.

Another aspect of credit risk spreads is their cyclical behavior over time. During periods of economic downturn they tend to widen, while during periods of economic prosperity they tend to narrow. This pattern of behavior may have to do with investors' utility preferences for bonds changing with different states of the economy. In a recession, their prime concern may be with safety. To invest in more risky bonds, the investor may have to be offered a substantial premium. On the other hand, during a period of prosperity, investors may be less concerned with safety and may be willing to bear more risk of default.

A related reason for this behavior has to do with liquidity and marketability. If liquidity is more valued in a recession than it is in a period of economic expansion, investors may seek out Treasury and other high-grade, marketable securities. In this way they achieve a high degree of liquidity. This changing preference for liquidity would tend to widen risk premiums in periods of economic contraction and narrow them in periods of economic expansion. Accentuating this phenomenon are occasional "flights to quality," when, in a chaotic and depressed market, investors seek the safest, most liquid investment, namely, Treasury securities. While flights to quality are infrequent, when they occur yield differentials mushroom.

In Fig. 17-5, the yield differential between long-term Aaa corporate bonds and Baa corporate bonds, using Moody's ratings, is shown over time. Economic recessions are denoted by the shaded areas. In the figure, we see that the yield differential between these two grades of corporate bonds widened during the reces-

FIGURE 17-5

Yield differential between Aaa corporate bonds and Baa corporate bonds, 1946–2000

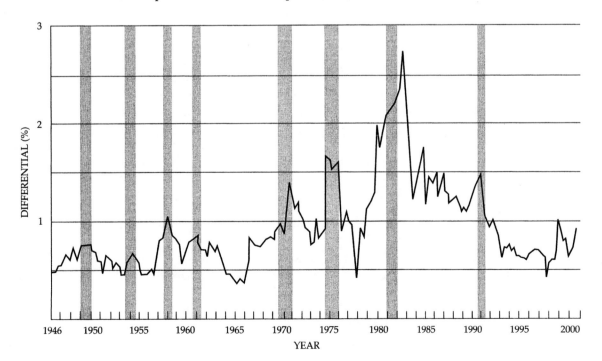

sionary periods. This widening is particularly evident in 1957–1958, 1970, 1974–1975, and 1981–1982. Moreover, during periods of economic expansion, the differential narrowed from the previous peak. From the mid 1990s into 2000, the differential fluctuated between 0.50 and 1.00 percent. With the problems in Asian financial markets in late 1998, there was a "flight to quality," and the yield differential widened. It subsequently narrowed and then widened in mid-2000.

Although maturity, coupon rate, and default risk are the most important factors explaining yield, embedded options also may affect the yield. Examples include the call feature and a sinking-fund provision. We explore these options later in this part, but you should recognize that they may have an influence on the market yield estimated with the method above.

Summary

Financial assets exist in an economy because an economic unit's investment in real assets frequently differs from its savings. The purpose of financial markets is the efficient allocation of savings to ultimate users of funds. A number of factors make financial markets efficient. Among the important is the presence of financial intermediaries. A financial intermediary transforms the direct claims of an ultimate borrower into an indirect claim, which is sold to ultimate lenders. At times, intermediation is no longer effective and is reversed either by securitization or by other means. Financial innovation, where new products and processes are introduced, occurs because of the profit motive. There are a number of causes: volatile inflation, interest rates, and currency rates; regulatory changes; tax changes; technological advances; and the business cycle.

The allocation of funds in an economy occurs primarily on the basis of expected return and risk. We reviewed the reasons for differing risks and returns on financial market instruments. An inflation premium is embraced in nominal rates of interest, which is a reflection of expected future inflation.

The yield curve, which depicts the relationship between yield and maturity, has a number of implications for the financial manager in financing and in investing funds. Either zero coupon or coupon Treasury yield curves are used, depending on the situation. The longer the maturity, the greater the volatility of bond price with a given change in yield. Also, the lower the coupon rate, the greater the volatility, holding other things constant. The duration measure combines maturity and coupon effects, and serves as a guide to bond volatility. Arbitrage assures equilibration between zero coupon and coupon yield curves.

Many times new corporate debt issues are priced off the Treasury yield curve. Quality yield differentials, or spreads from Treasuries, determine the interest rate a particular corporation will pay. These default-risk premiums tend to widen with maturity, as seen when we plot various grades of corporate bonds against maturity, and in times of recession.

Self-Correction Problems

1. Abra Axle Company has a heavy inventory position, which is on a FIFO basis. It finances this inventory with floating-rate loans. As it is in an extremely competitive business, it cannot quickly pass along cost increases to its customers in the form of higher prices. Its fixed assets are old, and it has no long-term debt. On the other hand, Elexir Extracts Company uses the LIFO method of inventory accounting. Its fixed assets are short-lived, and the company must continually replace older ones. The company has no short-term debt but does have

fixed-rate long-term debt. It is the price leader in its industry and enjoys a relatively inelastic demand for its product.

    a. If there is an unanticipated increase in inflation, what is likely to happen to the share values of these two companies? Why?

    b. If there is an unanticipated decrease, what is likely to happen?

2. For your company, how would you go about pricing a corporate bond issue off of Treasuries? What factors are involved?

Problems

1. For 20xx, suppose the following changes in the balance sheets of business firms, households, and governments in the aggregate occur (in billions):

	Business Firms	Households	Governments
Net worth (savings)	$220	$380	-$50
Real assets	275	280	
Money	5	10	2
Other financial assets	75	215	70
Financial liabilities	135	125	122

    a. Which sectors are savings-deficit sectors? savings-surplus sectors? Why?

    b. From which sector do the savings-deficit sectors finance their deficits? How is it done?

2. Zero coupon Treasury bonds of 20 years' maturity presently yield 8.50 percent. If the convention is to compound interest semiannually, what is the price of the bonds? Assume a face value of $100.

3. A coupon Treasury bond of the same maturity as in Problem 2 yields 8.00 percent. Why does it yield less than the zero coupon bond? What are the implications for the coupon yield curve being upward or downward sloping at this point? What if the coupon bond yielded 9.00 percent?

4. Fernando Baltra Company wishes to issue zero coupon straight debt with approximately a 15-year maturity. The company is rated single A by both Moody's and Standard & Poor's. How would you estimate the appropriate yield if the October 1999 yield curve in Fig. 17-1 and the spreads in Fig. 17-4 prevailed? What is the approximate yield the company would pay?

5. Lexalt Systems, Inc., has observed that computer-aided access to corporate bond price quotations and other information could be improved. Beare, Kelly and Zlotney, an investment banking firm, is particularly interested in an application proposed by Lexalt, as it wishes to introduce a new financial product—options on convertible bonds. To develop the necessary secondary market, information availability to market participants is critical. Beare, Kelly and Zlotney believe that the computer application and new financial product must be treated as a package, and the two parties have agreed to a joint venture. In words, what are the requisites for this innovation to succeed?

Solutions to Self-Correction Problems

1. a. Abra Axle Company's share price is likely to decline. Costs are likely to increase faster than prices in response to the higher inflation. The FIFO method of inventory accounting will result in higher taxes on real income. Depreciation much below replacement depreciation will also have an adverse tax effect in real terms. As it has no long-term debt and floating-rate short-term debt, it will not enjoy the benefits of existing debt values declining.

    Elexir Extracts Company's shares are likely to increase in value. It is able to pass along inflation-induced cost increases in higher prices. It may be able to raise prices even more than costs. Its LIFO method of inventory accounting and rapid replacement of fixed assets will largely shield the company from adverse tax effects. Its long-term debt will decline in value, thereby benefiting stockholders.

    b. For just the opposite reasons, Abra Axle Company's shares are likely to increase in value, while Elexir Extracts Company's shares are likely to decline in value.

2. The idea in pricing off of Treasuries is to add a credit risk premium to the Treasury yield. Given the maturity of the offering, the first job is to determine the appropriate Treasury yield using a Treasury yield curve. The credit yield spread is determined by analyzing the grade of bond of your company in relation to Treasuries. By looking at yield spreads for a particular bond grade, like Baa, one estimates the appropriate yield spread. These spreads are available through investment banks and through other sources. The combination of Treasury yield and default-risk premium give the appropriate yield. Credit risk spreads vary with maturity and with the business cycle.

Selected References

ALLEN, LINDA, *Capital Markets and Institutions: A Global View*. New York: John Wiley, 1997.

EDWARDS, FRANKLIN R., *The New Finance*. Washington, D.C.: American Enterprise Institute, 1996.

FABOZZI, FRANK J., FRANCO MODIGLIANI, and MICHAEL G. FERRI, *Foundations of Financial Markets and Institutions*, 2nd ed. Upper Saddle River, NJ: Prentice Hall, 1998.

LITTERMAN, ROBERT, and THOMAS IBEN, "Corporate Bond Valuation and the Term Structure of Credit Spreads," *Financial Analysts Journal*, 47 (Spring 1991), 52–64.

VAN HORNE, JAMES C., "Of Financial Innovation and Excesses," *Journal of Finance*, 40 (July 1985), 621–31.

——, *Financial Market Rates and Flows*, 6th ed. Upper Saddle River, NJ: Prentice Hall, 2001.

Wachowicz's Web World is an excellent overall Web site produced and maintained by my coauthor of *Fundamentals of Financial Management*, John M. Wachowicz Jr. It contains descriptions of and links to many finance Web sites and articles. *www.prenhall.com/wachowicz*.

Lease Financing

L easing is an important source of equipment financing. For some equipment, the financing is intermediate-term in nature. However, the really big financings of aircraft and power plants are long-term. As a lease contract embraces an interest-rate cost to the lessee and an interest-rate return to the lessor, effectively it is a capital market instrument. Though certain features differentiate it from other fixed-income financing, the principles by which we go about an evaluation are similar. ■

FEATURES OF A LEASE

A lease is a contract whereby the owner of an asset (the lessor) grants to another party (the lessee) the exclusive right to use the asset in return for the payment of rent. Most of us are familiar with leases of apartments, cars, and telephones. For corporate financing purposes, there is a similar obligation to make periodic lease payments, usually monthly or quarterly. Typically these payments are **in advance**, which simply means they are paid at the beginning of the period. This contrasts with **in arrears**, which is at the end of the period. Also, the lease contract specifies who is to maintain the asset. Under a **maintenance lease**, the lessor pays for maintenance, repairs, taxes, and insurance. Under a **net lease**, the lessee pays these costs.

Operating versus Financial Leases

An **operating lease** for office space, for example, is relatively short-term in length and is cancellable with proper notice. The term of this type of lease is shorter than the asset's economic life. It is only in releasing the space over and over, either to the same party or to others, that the lessor recovers its cost. Other examples of operating leases include the leasing of copying machines, certain computer hardware, word processors, and automobiles. Some operating leases are noncancellable, such as that for an aircraft on an 8-year lease. In contrast to an operating lease, a **financial lease** is longer term in nature and is noncancellable. The lessee is obligated to make lease payments until the lease's expiration, which approaches the useful life of the asset.

Operating leases are for a time shorter than the economic life of the asset.

Financial leases are for terms that approach the economic life of the asset.

543

Residual Value

Finally, the lease contract typically specifies some kind of option to the lessee at expiration. It may involve renewal, where the lessee has the right to renew the lease for another lease period, either at the same rent or at a different, usually lower, rent. The option might be to purchase the asset at expiration. For tax reasons, the purchase price must not be significantly lower than fair market value. If the lessee does not exercise its option, the lessor takes possession of the asset and is entitled to any **residual value** associated with it. As we will see, the determination of the cost of lease financing to the lessee, and return to the lessor, depends importantly on the residual value assumption. This is particularly true for operating leases.

Types of Lease Contracts

Virtually all lease financing arrangements fall into one of three types: a sale and leaseback, the direct acquisition of an asset under a lease, and leveraged leasing.

Sale and Leaseback   Under a sale and leaseback arrangement, a firm sells an asset to another party, and this party leases it back to the firm. Usually, the asset is sold at approximately its market value. The company receives the sales price in cash and the economic use of the asset during the basic lease period. In turn, it contracts to make periodic lease payments and gives up title to the asset. As a result, the lessor realizes any residual value the asset might have at the end of the lease period, whereas before, this value would have been realized by the firm. Lessors engaged in a sale and leaseback arrangement include insurance companies, other institutional investors, finance companies, and independent leasing companies.

Direct Leasing   Under direct leasing, a company acquires the use of an asset it did not own previously. A firm may lease an asset from the manufacturer: IBM leases computers; Xerox leases copiers. Indeed many capital goods are available today on a lease-financed basis. The major lessors are manufacturers, finance companies, banks, independent leasing companies, special-purpose leasing companies such as Polaris Aircraft Leasing, and partnerships. For leasing arrangements involving all but manufacturers, the vendor sells the asset to the lessor, who in turn, leases it to the lessee.

Leveraged Leasing   A special form of leasing sometimes is used in financing assets requiring large capital outlays. It is known as **leveraged leasing.** In contrast to the two parties involved in the forms of leasing previously described, there are three parties involved in leveraged leasing: (1) the lessee; (2) the lessor, or equity participant; and (3) the lender.

From the standpoint of the lessee, there is no difference between a leveraged lease and any other of type of lease. The lessee contracts to make periodic payments over the basic lease period and, in return, is entitled to the use of the asset over that period of time. The role of the lessor, however, is changed. The lessor acquires the asset in keeping with the terms of the lease arrangement and finances the acquisition in part by an equity investment of, say, 20 percent (hence the name *equity participant*). The remaining 80 percent is provided by a long-term lender or lenders. The loan is usually secured by a mortgage on the asset, as well as by the assignment of the lease and lease payments. The lessor is the borrower.

As owner of the asset, the lessor is entitled to deduct all depreciation charges associated with the asset. The cash-flow pattern for the lessor typically involves

(1) a cash outflow at the time the asset is acquired, which represents its equity participation, (2) a period of cash inflows represented by lease payments and tax benefits, less payments on the debt, and (3) a period of net cash outflows during which, because of declining tax benefits, the sum of lease payments and tax benefits falls below the debt payments due. If there is any residual value at the end of the lease period, this of course represents a cash inflow to the lessor. From the standpoint of the lessor, the reversal of signs of the cash flows from negative to positive to negative gives rise to the possibility of multiple internal rates of return. (This problem is addressed in the appendix to Chapter 6.) For this reason, it is best for the lessor to use a net-present-value approach when evaluating the situation.

Although the leveraged lease may at first seem more complicated than either the sale and leaseback arrangement or direct leasing, it reduces to certain basic concepts that, from the standpoint of the lessee, can be analyzed in the same manner as for any lease.

ACCOUNTING AND TAX TREATMENTS OF LEASES

Where once leases were not disclosed and were attractive to some as "off balance sheet" financing, this no longer is the case. Financial Accounting Standards Board Statement No. 13 requires capitalization on the balance sheet of certain types of leases. In essence, this statement says that if the lessee acquires essentially all of the economic benefits and risks of the leased property, then the value of the asset along with the corresponding lease liability must be shown on the balance sheet.

Capital and Operating Leases

Leases that conform in principle to this definition are called *capital leases*. More specifically, a lease is regarded as a capital lease if it meets any one of the following conditions:

1. The lease transfers title to the asset to the lessee by the end of the lease period.
2. The lease contains an option to purchase the asset at a bargain price.
3. The lease period is equal to, or greater than, 75 percent of the estimated economic life of the asset.
4. At the beginning of the lease, the present value of the minimum lease payments equals or exceeds 90 percent of the fair value of the leased property to the lessor.

If any of these conditions is met, the lessee is said to have acquired most of the economic benefits and risks associated with the leased property; therefore, a capital lease is involved. If a lease does not meet any of these conditions, it is classified as an *operating lease*. Essentially, operating leases give the lessee the right to use the leased property over a period of time, but they do not give the lessee all the benefits and risks associated with the asset.

Recording the Value of a Capital Lease

With a capital lease, the lessee must report the value of the leased property on the asset side of the balance sheet. The amount reflected is the present value of the minimum lease payments over the lease period. If executory costs, such as insurance, maintenance, and taxes, are a part of the total lease payment, these are deducted and only the remainder is used for purposes of calculating the present value. As required by the accounting rules, the discount rate employed is the lower of (1) the lessee's incremental borrowing rate or (2) the lessor's implicit interest rate if, in fact, that rate can be determined.

The present value of the lease payments should be recorded as an asset on the lessee's balance sheet. (If the fair value of the leased property is lower than the present value of the minimum lease payments, then the fair value would be shown.) The associated lease obligation would be shown on the liability side of the balance sheet, with the present value of payments due within 1 year being reflected as current liabilities and the present value of payments due after 1 year being shown as noncurrent liabilities. The leased property may be combined with similar information on assets that are owned, but there must be a disclosure in a footnote with respect to the value of the leased property and its amortization. A hypothetical balance sheet might look like the following:

Assets		Liabilities	
Gross fixed assets*	$3,000,000	Current	
Less: Accumulated depreciation and amortization	1,000,000	Obligations under capital leases	$ 90,000
		Noncurrent	
Net fixed assets	$2,000,000	Obligations under capital leases	$270,000

*Gross fixed assets include leased property of $500,000. Accumulated depreciation and amortization includes $140,000 in amortization associated with such property.

Capital leases appear on the balance sheet.
Operating leases appear in footnotes.

Footnote Disclosure   Here we see in the footnote that the capitalized value of leases of the company is $500,000 less $140,000 in amortization, or $360,000 in total. The liability is split with $90,000 current and $270,000 due beyond 1 year. In addition to this information, more details are required in footnotes. Relevant information here includes the gross amounts of leased property by major property categories (these can be combined with categories of owned assets), the total future minimum lease payments, a schedule by years of future lease payments required over the next 5 years, the total minimum sublease rentals to be received, the existence and terms of purchase or renewal options and escalation clauses, rentals that are contingent on some factor other than the passage of time, and any restrictions imposed in the lease agreement.

Disclosure of Operating Leases

For operating leases, as for capital leases, some of the same disclosure is required, but it can be in footnotes. For noncancellable leases having remaining terms in excess of 1 year, the lessee must disclose total future minimum lease payments, a schedule by year for the next 5 years, the total sublease rentals to be received, the basis for contingent rental payments, the existence and terms of purchase and renewal options and escalation clauses, and any lease agreement restrictions. The last two categories are included in a general description of the leasing arrangement.

Amortizing the Capital Lease and Reducing the Obligation

A capital lease must be amortized and the liability reduced over the lease period. The method of amortization can be the lessee's usual depreciation method for assets that are owned. It should be pointed out that the period of amortization is always the lease term, even if the economic life of the asset is longer. If the latter occurs, the asset would have an expected residual value, which would go to the lessor. FASB No. 13 also requires that the capital lease obligation be reduced over the lease period by the "interest" method. Under this method, each lease payment is separated into two components: the payment of principal and the payment of interest. The obligation is reduced by the amount of the principal payment.

Reporting Earnings For income-reporting purposes, FASB No. 13 requires that both the amortization of the leased property and the annual interest embodied in the lease payment be treated as an expense. This expense then is deducted in the same way that any expense is, to obtain net income. This treatment differs from that for the operating lease, for which only the lease payment itself is deductible as an expense.

Tax Treatment of Lease Contracts

Recognize that the treatment of capital leases for tax purposes differs from that for income statement purposes. For tax purposes, most companies report the lease payment as an expense. In other words, for tax purposes, a company does not deduct the amortization of the asset and the interest as the expense of a capital lease. It deducts the annual lease payment.

The Internal Revenue Service wants to be sure that the lease contract truly represents a lease and not an installment purchase of the asset. To assure itself that a true lease in fact is involved, the IRS has established a handful of guidelines.[1] The most important is that the lessor have a minimum "at-risk" investment, both at inception and throughout the lease period, of 20 percent or more of the acquisition cost of the asset. This means a residual value of at least 20 percent of initial cost. Another guideline is that the remaining life of the asset at the end of the lease period must be the longer of 1 year or 20 percent of the asset's original estimated life. There can be no bargain purchase option given to the lessee, nor can there be a loan from the lessee to the lessor. Last, there must be an expected profit to the lessor from the lease contract, apart from any tax benefits.

In essence, the IRS wants to assure itself that the lease contract is not, in effect, a purchase of the asset, for which payments are much more rapid than would be allowed with depreciation. As lease payments are deductible for tax purposes, such a contract would allow the lessor to effectively "depreciate" the asset more quickly than allowed under a straight purchase. If the lease contract meets the conditions described, the full lease payment is deductible for tax purposes. If not, the lease is regarded as a conditional-sales contract, and the rules governing a depreciable asset hold.

There are conflicts between what qualifies for a "capital" lease for accounting purposes and what qualifies for a "true" lease for tax purposes. To qualify as a true lease, there can be no transfer of ownership before expiration nor bargain pur-

---

[1]See John R. Graham, Michael L. Lemmon, and James S. Schallheim, "Debt, Leases, Taxes, and the Endogeneity of Corporate Tax Status," *Journal of Finance*, 53 (February 1998), 159–61.

chase option, two of the four accounting conditions that would qualify the contract to be treated as a capital lease. The remaining life must be 1 year or 20 percent of the acquisition cost for tax purposes, as opposed to the lease period being at least 75 percent of the economic life under FASB No. 13. Finally, the 20 percent residual value requirement for tax purposes contrasts with a 10 percent minimum requirement for accounting purposes. Thus, condition number 3, "the lease period is equal to, or greater than, 75 percent of the estimated economic life of the asset," is the sole condition under which a contract can qualify as a capital lease and still, if 80 percent or less, qualify as a true lease for tax purposes. In the examples that follow we assume a true lease for tax purposes, so the full lease payment is treated as an expense.

RETURN TO THE LESSOR

A good place to begin an analysis of a lease is with the interest return to the lessor. Obviously this is important to the lessor, but it also is useful to a potential lessee in comparing financing alternatives. The return depends on three things: (1) the length of the lease, (2) the periodic lease payment and whether it is paid at the beginning or at the end of the period, and (3) the residual value assumption. If lease payments are *in advance,* the formula for determining the implied interest return is

$$\text{Value of asset} = \sum_{t=0}^{mn-1} \frac{\text{lease payment}}{\left(1 + \dfrac{R}{m}\right)^t} + \frac{RV}{\left(1 + \dfrac{R}{m}\right)^{mn}} \tag{18-1}$$

Lessor's return is the IRR that equates the PV of lease payments and residual value with the asset's beginning value.

where value of asset = what it costs the lessor to acquire or its market value if the asset already is owned

n = length of the lease in years

m = number of times a year periodic lease payments are made

R = implicit interest rate for which we solve

RV = assumed residual value at the end of the lease term

If, instead of in advance, lease payments are at the end of the period, the Greek summation sign would begin at $t = 1$ and end at mn.

Illustration

Suppose Veritas Leasing Company will lease a computerized milling machine that costs it $140,000 to purchase. The terms of the lease call for $6,500 quarterly payments payable in advance for 6 years. At the end of 6 years, Veritas assumes the asset will have a residual value of $40,000. Given this information, we can set up the problem as follows:

$$\$140{,}000 = \sum_{t=0}^{23} \frac{\$6{,}500}{\left(1 + \dfrac{R}{4}\right)^t} + \frac{\$40{,}000}{\left(1 + \dfrac{R}{4}\right)^{24}} \tag{18-2}$$

When we solve for R, we find it to be 10.30 percent. (*Hint:* Use $140,000 – $6,500 = $133,500 on the left-hand side of the equation and $t = 1$ through 23 on the right.) The 10.30 percent solved for is the expected return to the lessor *if* the lessee makes all payments as scheduled *and* if the residual value at the end of 6 years turns out to be $40,000.

What if the milling machine ended up with a residual value of only $28,000? The return obviously declines, and when we solve for R we find it to be 8.67 percent. Differences in assumptions as to residual value can make a big difference in the return to the lessor. If you as a lessee believe the lessor has attached too high a residual value to the asset, this works to your advantage in the sense that the true implicit interest cost is lower.

As a potential lessee, it is useful to first calculate the return to the lessor. This gives you a great deal of information, because you can compare this cost with interest costs for other methods of financing. We will look at more sophisticated methods of analysis shortly, but certain deals can be ruled out merely on the basis of before-tax return calculations. Only if the before-tax cost of leasing is lower than the before-tax cost of borrowing is it usually worthwhile to go to after-tax calculations. In most cases, lease financing can be ruled out because it is dominated on a before-tax return basis.

Calculating the Lease Payment

The lessor can use Eq. (18-1) to solve for the periodic lease payment necessary to provide a given return. Suppose in the case above the lessor wanted a 12 percent return, and that the asset continued to cost $140,000 and a residual value of $40,000 was expected. Setting up the problem and solving for the necessary lease payment (L) to the nearest dollar:

$$\$140,000 = \sum_{t=0}^{23} \frac{L}{(1.03)^t} + \frac{\$40,000}{(1.03)^{24}} \tag{18-3}$$

$$\$140,000 = L + 16.4435L + .49193\ (\$40,000)$$
$$\$140,000 - \$19,677 = 17.4435L$$
$$L = \$120,323/17.4435 = \$6,898$$

In the equation, 16.4435 is the present-value discount factor for an even stream of cash flows for 23 periods, discounted at 3 percent (see Table B at the back of the book), and .49193 is the present value of a single cash flow at the end of 24 periods, again discounted at 3 percent (see Table A at the back of the book). Therefore, the quarterly lease payment necessary at the beginning of each quarter is $6,898. This will result in a return to the lessor of 12 percent on an annualized basis.

AFTER-TAX ANALYSES OF LEASE VERSUS BUY/BORROW

Where the before-tax cost of lease financing is not dominated by the before-tax cost of borrowing, it is appropriate to bring in tax effects and look at things according to discounted cash flows.

To Lease or to Buy/Borrow

Whether lease financing or buy/borrow is favored will depend on the patterns of cash outflows for each financing method and on the opportunity cost of funds.

Several different methods may be used to compare the two alternatives. Our hypothetical examples will show the more frequently used methods.

Investment Followed by Financing Decision

A decision to acquire the economic use of an asset is an investment decision. Using the discounted cash-flow methods and the required rate of return discussed in Part II, the firm will decide whether or not to accept the project. Expressed differently, the investment worthiness of the project should be evaluated separately from the specific method of financing to be employed.

Once a decision is reached to acquire the economic use of an asset, the company must decide how it is to be financed. In this regard, we assume that it has determined an appropriate capital structure and that this structure calls for financing the project with fixed-income financing of some sort. For our purposes the relevant comparison is the after-tax cost of debt financing versus that of lease financing. The company will wish to use the least costly alternative.

In the rest of this part, we present two ways in which to analyze the lease versus buy/borrow decision—the present-value method and the internal-rate-of-return method. To illustrate them, we will use a common example.

Example for Analysis

Suppose Kennedy Electronics, Inc., has decided to acquire a piece of equipment costing $148,000 to be used in the fabrication of microprocessors. If it were to lease finance the equipment, the manufacturer would provide such financing over 7 years. The terms of the lease call for the annual payment of $25,000. Lease payments are made in advance, that is, at the end of the year prior to each of the 7 years. The lessee is responsible for maintenance of the equipment, insurance, and taxes.

If the asset is purchased, Kennedy Electronics would finance it with a 7-year term loan at 10 percent. The company is in a 40 percent tax bracket. The asset falls in the 5-year property class for accelerated cost recovery (depreciation) purposes. Accordingly, the schedule discussed in Chapter 6 is used:

Buy/borrow is the purchase of an asset through debt financing.

Year	1	2	3	4	5	6
Depreciation	20.00%	32.00%	19.20%	11.52%	11.52%	5.76%

The cost of the asset is then depreciated at these rates, so that first-year depreciation is $.20 \times \$148,000 = \$29,600$, and so forth. At the end of the 7 years, the equipment is expected to have a scrap value of $15,000. If purchased, Kennedy Electronics would be entitled to this residual value, as it would be the owner of the asset.

Present-Value Analysis of Alternatives

The first method of analysis we consider is a comparison of the present values of cash outflows for each of the alternatives. According to this method, whichever alternative has the lowest present value is the most desirable. Remember that the company will make annual lease payments of $25,000 if the asset is leased. Because these payments are an expense, they are deductible for tax purposes, but only in the year for which the payment applies. The $25,000 payment at the end of year 0 represents a prepaid expense and is not deductible for tax purposes until year 1. Similarly, the other six payments are not deductible until the following year.

As leasing is analogous to borrowing, an appropriate discount rate for discounting the after-tax cash flow might be the after-tax cost of borrowing. For our example, the after-tax cost of borrowing = 10%(1 − .40) = 6.0%. The use of this rate assumes that the firm's future taxable income will be sufficient to utilize fully the tax shield associated with lease payments. It also assumes that the tax rate will not change.

Given the foregoing assumptions, we are able to derive a schedule of cash outflows after taxes and compute their present value. These computations are shown in Table 18-1. The present value of the total cash outflows under the leasing alternative is $92,109. This figure, then, must be compared with the present value of cash outflows under the borrowing alternative.

Analysis of Debt   If the asset is purchased, Kennedy Electronics is assumed to finance it entirely with a 10 percent unsecured term loan, its payment schedule of the same configuration as the lease payment schedule. In other words, loan payments are assumed to be payable at the beginning, not the end, of each year. This assumption places the loan on an equivalent basis with the lease and allows us to compare apples with apples. If the loan payments are treated as being paid at the end of the year while lease payments are at the beginning, there is a present-value bias in favor of buy/borrow. In theory, paying in advance increases the debt capacity of the company vis-à-vis paying at the end of the period. To avoid the bias described, it is important to place both methods of financing on the same footing when it comes to the time of payment. This is not a big deal if monthly payments are involved and the lease contract is reasonably long, but it is very important with annual payments.

We assume a loan of $148,000 is taken out at time 0 and is payable over 7 years with annual payments of $27,636 at the beginning of each year.[2] The proportion of interest in each payment depends on the unpaid principal amount owing during the year. The principal amount owing during year 1 is $148,000 minus the payment at the very start of the year of $27,636, which is equal to $120,364. The annual interest for the first year is $120,364 × 10% = $12,036. As subsequent pay-

TABLE 18-1
Schedule of Cash Outflows: Leasing Alternative

End of Year	(1) Lease Payment	(2) Tax Shield (1)(.40)	(3) Cash Outflow After Taxes (1)−(2)	(4) Present Value of Cash Outflows (6.0%)
0	$25,000	—	$25,000	$25,000
1–6	25,000	$10,000	15,000	73,760
7	—	10,000	(10,000)	(6,651)
				$92,109

[2]For ease of illustration, we round to the nearest dollar throughout. This results in the final debt payment in Table 18-2 being slightly more than would otherwise be the case.

TABLE 18-2
Schedule of Debt Payments

End of Year	Loan Payment	Principal Amount Owing at End of Year	Annual Interest
0	$27,636	$120,364	—
1	27,636	104,764	$12,036
2	27,636	87,604	10,476
3	27,636	68,728	8,760
4	27,636	47,965	6,873
5	27,636	25,126	4,797
6	27,639	0	2,513

ments are made, the interest component decreases. Table 18-2 shows these components over time.

Debt After-Tax Cash Flows To compute the cash outflows after taxes for the debt alternative, we must determine the tax effect. This requires knowing the amounts of annual interest and annual depreciation. Using the cost recovery schedule for the 5-year property class listed earlier, we show the annual depreciation charges in the third column of Table 18-3. Because both depreciation and interest are deductible expenses for tax purposes, they provide a tax shield equal to their sum times the tax rate of 40 percent. This is shown in column (4) of the table. When this shield is deducted from the debt payment, we obtain the cash outflow after taxes at the end of each year, column (5). At the end of the seventh year, the

TABLE 18-3
Schedule of Cash Outflows: Debt Alternative

End of Year	(1) Payment	(2) Interest	(3) Depreciation	(4) Tax Shield [(2) + (3)] .40	(5) Cash Outflow After Taxes (1) − (4)	(6) Present Value of Cash Outflow (6.0%)
0	$27,636	—	—	—	$27,636	$27,636
1	27,636	$12,036	$29,600	$16,654	10,982	10,360
2	27,636	10,476	47,360	23,134	4,502	4,007
3	27,636	8,760	28,416	14,870	12,766	10,719
4	27,636	6,873	17,050	9,569	18,067	14,311
5	27,636	4,797	17,050	8,739	18,897	14,121
6	27,639	2,513	8,524	4,415	23,224	16,372
7	(30,000)*			(12,000)	(18,000)	(11,971)
						$85,555

*Residual value inflow.

asset is expected to have a residual value of $30,000. This amount is subject to the corporate tax rate of 40 percent for the company, which leaves an expected aftertax cash inflow of $18,000. Finally, we compute the present value of all of these cash flows at a 6 percent discount rate and find that they total $85,555.

Comparing Present Values   This present value of cash outflow is less than that for the lease alternative, $92,109. Therefore, the analysis suggests that the company use debt as opposed to lease financing in acquiring use of the asset. With buy/borrow the company is able to avail itself of accelerated cost recovery depreciation, and this helps the situation from a present-value standpoint. Moreover, the residual value at the end of the project is a favorable factor, whereas this value goes to the lessor with lease financing. Another factor that favors the debt alternative is the deductibility of interest payments for tax purposes. Because the amount of interest embodied in a "mortgage-type" debt payment is higher at first and declines with successive payments, the tax benefits associated with these payments follow the same pattern over time. From a present-value standpoint, this pattern benefits the firm relative to the pattern of lease payments, which typically are constant over time.

Lower Tax Rate   If the effective tax rate were 10 percent instead of 40 percent, the present-value comparison changes. The tax shield is lower and the discount rate—the after-tax cost of borrowing—is higher, $10\%(1 - .10) = 9.0\%$. These two changes result in the present value of cash outflows for the lease alternative (Table 18-1 reworked) being $124,565, whereas that for the debt alternative (Table 18-3 reworked) is $121,507. The debt alternative still dominates, but by a lesser margin than before.

The impact of this example is that the tax rate of the lessee matters a lot. In general, as the effective tax rate declines, the relative advantage of debt versus lease financing decreases. This explains why lease financing usually is attractive only to those in low or zero tax brackets who are unable to enjoy the full tax benefits associated with owning an asset. Much more will be said about this when we explore the economics of leasing.

The greater the tax rate and the greater the residual value, the less attractive lease financing is relative to buy/borrow.

Residual Value Effect   A final consideration is the fact that the residual value is seldom known with certainty. The economic value of an asset at the end of a period of time is usually subject to considerable uncertainty, whether it be sold or continues to be employed in the firm. One way to treat the problem is with a probability distribution of residual values. Another way is to analyze the asset in terms of the value of services that are expected over its remaining life where these values are subject to a stochastic process. Such an approach is beyond the scope of this book, but we must bring residual value into our analysis. The greater the residual value assumed, of course, the more desirable buy/borrow becomes vis-à-vis lease financing.

Because of the uncertainty surrounding an asset's value, one can make an argument for discounting the net salvage value at a rate higher than the firm's after-tax cost of debt. For example, some leasing experts suggest using the company's cost of capital as a more appropriate discount rate for residual value flows under the buy/borrow alternative. In our example (Table 18-3), applying a discount rate higher than the 6 percent after-tax cost of debt to the estimated residual value will increase the present value of the net cash outflows for the debt alternative, making buy/borrow less attractive.

Internal-Rate-of-Return Analysis Instead of computing the present value of cash outflows for the two financing alternatives, we could compute the internal rate of return (IRR). This approach avoids the problem of having to choose a rate of discount.

To begin with consideration of the lease, the after-tax cost of leasing can be determined by solving the following equation for r:

$$A_0 - \sum_{t=0}^{n-1} \frac{L_t}{(1+r)^t} + \sum_{t=1}^{n} \frac{T(L_{t-1} - P_t)}{(1+r)^t} - \frac{RV(1-T)}{(1+r)^n} = 0 \qquad (18\text{-}4)$$

where A_0 = cost of the asset to be leased

n = number of periods to the end of the lease

L_t = lease payment at the end of period t

T = corporate tax rate

P_t = depreciation in period t

RV = amount of expected residual value at the end of the lease

In this construct, the cost of leasing is the rate of discount that equates the cost of the asset with the present value of lease payments, net of their tax shields, together with the present value of expected residual value after taxes. In other words, the cost of leasing includes not only the lease payments but also the depreciation tax deductions and residual value that are forgone by virtue of leasing the asset as opposed to purchasing it. The last two represent opportunity costs if the asset is leased. If there is no expected residual value, the RV term drops out of Eq. (18-4).

IRR Method Illustrated Using our previous example and drawing on Tables 18-1 and 18-2, the information necessary to solve for the after-tax cost of leasing is shown in Table 18-4. The cash-flow stream appears in the last column. When we solve for the rate of discount that equates the negative cash flows with the positive ones in column (6), we find it to be 7.73 percent. This figure then serves as the

TABLE 18-4
Schedule of Cash Flows, IRR Analysis of Lease

End of Year	(1) Cost of Asset	(2) L_t Lease Payment	(3) P_t Depreciation	(4) Tax Shield $T(L_{t-1} - P_t)$	(5) Residual Value After Taxes	(6) Cash Flow (1) − (2) + (4) − (5)
0	$148,000	$25,000	—	—	—	$123,000
1	—	25,000	$29,600	$(1,840)	—	(26,840)
2	—	25,000	47,360	(8,944)	—	(33,944)
3	—	25,000	28,416	(1,366)	—	(26,366)
4	—	25,000	17,050	3,180	—	(21,820)
5	—	25,000	17,050	3,180	—	(21,820)
6	—	25,000	8,524	6,590	—	(18,410)
7	—	—	—	10,000	$18,000	(8,000)

after-tax cost of lease financing, and it should be compared with the after-tax cost of debt financing to determine which method results in the lower cost of financing. With the before-tax interest cost of 10 percent and a tax rate of .40 for our example problem, the after-tax cost of debt financing is 6.0 percent. According to this method of analysis, then, buy/borrow is the preferred alternative because its effective yield is less than that for the leasing alternative.

In summary, the internal-rate-of-return method of analysis permits a simple comparison of the after-tax costs of the lease and borrowing alternatives. Whichever alternative has the lowest rate would be selected according to this method. Again, this assumes that decisions have already been reached with respect to acquiring the asset and to financing it with a fixed-income type of instrument—either debt or a lease.

Uncertain Borrowing Costs

Rather than a fixed-rate term loan, sometimes the debt alternative is floating rate in nature, where the rate is geared to the prime rate. Though the lease payments in the lease versus buy/borrow analysis are known and contractual, debt payments are not, owing to fluctuations in the prime rate. When confronted with a situation of this sort, most analysts employ either the present short-term borrowing rate or some average of expected future short-term borrowing rates. In such situations, sensitivity analysis may be helpful. If our evaluation using the present borrowing rate shows debt financing to be the preferred alternative, we may wish to know how much the interest rate would need to rise before lease financing were favored. Also, a time dimension may be introduced to determine not only how much but also how fast the rate must rise before we are indifferent between lease and buy/borrow. If such a rise is improbable, this will strengthen the case for buy/borrow. If it is probable, the case is weakened. Similarly, if lease financing dominates on the basis of present borrowing costs, an interesting question is how far and how quickly must interest rates decline before debt financing dominates. By employing sensitivity analysis in this manner, one can come to grips with situations where the cost of borrowing is uncertain in lease versus buy/borrow analyses.

Analysis of an Asset That Can Only Be Leased

Occasionally, a company must evaluate an asset that it can acquire only by leasing. For example, ocean freighters may use certain dock facilities only through a long-term lease. The purchase alternative is not available. In situations of this sort, the firm does not choose between leasing or borrowing; the only decision is whether or not to lease. As a result, the investment and financing decisions are inextricably intertwined.

Although no method of analysis is entirely satisfactory, perhaps the best approach is to determine the merit of the project as an investment. The first step is to compute the cash-equivalent price of the lease alternative, beginning by establishing an interest rate that is consistent with other current leasing arrangements. The cash-equivalent price is the present value of all required lease payments, discounted by this rate. The next step is to compute the present value of expected future cash benefits associated with the project, discounted at the required rate of return. Obviously these benefits should be estimated only for the duration of the lease period. If the present value of the expected future cash benefits exceeds the cash-equivalent price, the project is worthwhile, and the firm should enter into the lease. If the present value of the cash benefits is less than the cash-equivalent price, the project should be rejected.

SOURCES OF VALUE IN LEASING

Now that we have an understanding of leasing and how it might be analyzed in relation to debt financing, we focus on the factors that give rise to leasing's being a thing of value in the capital markets.

Lease Financing in Perfect Capital Markets

It is useful to begin by assuming that capital markets are perfect and complete. Discussed in Part II and other parts of the book, this implies that there are no transaction costs, information is costless and readily available to all, securities are infinitely divisible, there are no bankruptcy costs, and there are no taxes. Complete financial markets imply that the desires of borrowers are satisfied with respect to the kinds of financial instruments available in the marketplace. Under these assumptions and the implied perfect competition among financial markets that results, it can be shown that the debt and lease obligations of a firm will be valued by secured lenders and lessors in the same manner.[3] The costs of debt and lease financing will therefore be the same, and the firm would be indifferent between the two as methods of financing.

When we relax the assumptions of perfect and complete capital markets, debt and lease instruments may not be valued in the same manner. The imperfections of transaction costs, information costs, and less than infinite divisibility of securities do not have a systematic effect in the sense that they favor lease or debt financing all of the time. Rather, arbitrage between the markets is impeded; consequently, it may be possible for the firm to take "advantage" of the situation by issuing one type of instrument or the other. Because the advantage is likely to be small and difficult to predict in practice, we do not concentrate on these imperfections. In contrast, the presence of bankruptcy costs and taxes affects things in a systematic manner, and the direction of their effect is predictable.

Bankruptcy Costs to the Lender or Lessor

If a lessee or borrower liquidates, the lessor's position is somewhat superior to that of a supplier of capital. The lessor owns the asset and can retrieve it when the lessee defaults. The lender finds it more difficult and costly to gain possession when the borrower defaults, even though the loan was secured with the asset.

The riskier the firm that seeks financing, the greater the incentive for the supplier of capital to make the arrangement a lease rather than a loan. Many suppliers of capital are either lenders or lessors but not both; some, such as bank holding companies, are both. The author is familiar with situations in which loans have been converted to leases when the risk of default has increased significantly. The purpose, of course, is to improve one's position should liquidation become necessary. To the extent that any of the ex-ante costs of bankruptcy avoided by lease as opposed to debt financing are passed on to the lessee in the form of lower lease payments than otherwise would be the case, a company might have an incentive to lease as opposed to buy/borrow. However, the incentive will be modest at best.

---

[3]In James C. Van Horne, "The Cost of Leasing with Capital Market Imperfections," *Engineering Economist*, 23 (Fall 1977), 1–12, this is demonstrated, using a state-preference model. Because the model is complicated, it is not presented here; however, the conclusion logically follows from all of our earlier discussion of the impact of the perfect market assumption on the valuation of financial instruments.

Effect of Differing Taxes

The dominant economic reason for the existence of leasing is that companies, financial institutions, and individuals derive different tax benefits from owning assets. The greater the divergence in these benefits, the greater the attraction of lease financing overall, all other things staying the same. We know from our previous discussion that the tax benefit associated with owning an asset is the tax shield afforded by the deduction of depreciation over the depreciable life of the asset.

If the effective tax benefits associated with owning an asset were the same for all economic units in the economy and if capital markets were perfect in every other way, debt and lease obligations would be valued in the same manner. As a result, their costs would be the same. If the lessor did not lower lease payments to give the lessee all the tax benefits of ownership, the prospective lessee could simply purchase the asset and finance it with debt. In this way, it could avail itself of all the tax benefits. Therefore, it is not the existence of taxes per se that gives rise to leasing being a thing of value, but it is a situation in which different companies, financial institutions, and individuals have different abilities to realize the tax benefits.

Such differences are due to

1. **Different tax rates among economic units in the economy.** *Examples:* differences in personal and corporate income tax rates and differences in tax rates among various individuals and corporations.

2. **Different levels of past and current taxable income among economic units.** *Example:* a company that carries forward a tax loss and pays little or no taxes.

3. **Different effects related to the alternative minimum tax.** The presence of the alternative minimum tax (AMT) causes divergences in the ability of different corporations and individuals to fully use accelerated depreciation and the deduction of interest as an expense. *Example:* a company with redundant tax deductions will have an incentive to lease finance because the lease payment is not classified as a preference item when computing the AMT. Companies not so affected will have an incentive to act as lessors.

A company that pays little or no taxes may lease an asset from another party that pays higher taxes. The lessee gets part of the tax benefits of ownership because its lease payments are lower than they would otherwise be. In turn, the lessor is able to use the full tax credit, which might not otherwise be available to it. As a result, both parties gain.[4] We illustrated the increased benefit to the lessee when we lowered the tax rate in our lease versus buy/borrow analysis. For the lessor/lender, the relative advantage of leasing versus lending increases as the effective tax rate rises.

John R. Graham, Michael L. Lemmon, and James S. Schallheim have analyzed empirically the marginal tax rates paid by companies that lease and those that borrow.[5] The authors find a negative relation between operating lease levels

---

[4]In studying the sale and leaseback announcements, Myron B. Slovin, Marie E. Sushka, and John A. Polonchek, "Corporate Sale-and-Leasebacks and Shareholder Wealth," *Journal of Finance*, 45 (March 1990), 289–99, find a positive stock market reaction for the lessee. They interpret this as being consistent with a reduction in expected taxes.

[5]John R. Graham, Michael L. Lemmon, and James S. Schallheim, "Debt, Leases, Taxes, and the Endogeneity of Corporate Tax Status," *Journal of Finance*, 53 (February 1998), 131–62.

and tax rates and a positive relation between debt levels and tax rates. For capital leases, the relation is ambiguous. The evidence is consistent with tax-driven clienteles when it comes to the lease versus buy/borrow decision. Low tax-bracket firms lease more and borrow less than high tax-bracket firms.

Market Equilibration Process

How much realization of the tax benefits the lessee is able to achieve depends on the supply and demand conditions in the market for lease financing. A lessor is unlikely to give up all the tax benefits, because realization of such benefits depends on its favorable tax situation. By the same token, competition among lessors will ensure that part of the benefits will be transferred to the lessee in the form of lower lease payments than would otherwise be the case. The exact sharing of the tax benefits is negotiable, but it will depend on equilibrium conditions in the capital markets.

Our discussion shows that a company seeking financing should concentrate its analysis on the tax considerations when approaching the question of whether to lease or buy/borrow. For the consistently profitable company, lease financing may make little sense. Whenever a third-party lessor is involved, an added financing intermediary is introduced. This additional intermediation adds administrative costs ultimately borne by the lessee. For the marginally profitable firm or for the firm that has had a temporary setback and expects to pay little in the way of taxes in the near future, lease financing may prove very beneficial.

The economic benefits passed off to the lessee are reflected in the implied interest cost of the lease. By concentrating on this cost and the economic benefits associated with leasing relative to those for borrowing, the firm is able to determine whether lease financing is promising. It also is able to better shop around among lessors and to negotiate the lease. In this way, the decision will be grounded in sound economic reasoning, as opposed to the sales pitch used by many a leasing company to sell its financial service.

Differing tax rates between the lessor and lessee are the main source of value in leasing.

Other Alleged Advantages In addition to bankruptcy costs and differences in tax situations, there may be other reasons for the existence of lease financing. For one thing, the lessor may enjoy economies of scale in the purchase of assets that are not available to the lessee. Also, the lessor may have a different estimate of the life of the asset, of its residual value, or of the discount rate than the lessee. Moreover, the lessor may face different borrowing costs than the lessee, lower, it is hoped, if leasing is to be stimulated. Finally, the lessor may be able to provide expertise to its customers in equipment selection and maintenance. While all of these factors may give rise to leasing, we would not expect them to be nearly as important as the tax reason.

For all practical purposes, the leasing industry in the United States is an artifact of the tax laws. As these laws change the industry is impacted, often in dramatic ways. Parties that financed via the leasing route may no longer do so, where others may find it attractive. Previous lessors may step out of the business, whereas others may be able to serve this role to advantage. The greater the change in tax laws affecting asset write-offs, tax rates, and alternative minimum taxes, the greater the disequilibrium and the longer the equilibration process as parties exit or enter the market on the lessor or the lessee side.

Summary

In lease financing, the lessee agrees to pay the lessor periodically for economic use of the lessor's asset. Because of this contractual obligation, leasing is regarded as a method of financing similar to borrowing. Leasing can involve the direct acquisition of an asset under a lease, a sale and leaseback arrangement whereby the firm sells an asset it owns and leases it back from the buyer, or a leveraged lease.

The accounting treatment of leases depends on the type. Leases that convey most of the economic benefits and risks associated with ownership are known as capital leases. Non-cancellable leases not meeting this criterion are called operating leases. For a capital lease, the capitalized value of the leased property must be shown on the balance sheet as an asset, with the obligation shown as a liability. Moreover, the reported lease expense is the amortization of the lease property plus the implied interest rate embodied in the lease payments, not the amount of the lease payment. For the operating lease, the reported lease expense is the latter. For tax purposes, the lease payment is deductible as an expense provided it meets certain guidelines established by the Internal Revenue Service.

When we know the lease payment required each period, whether it is payable at the beginning or at the end of the period, the number of periods, the value of the asset, and a residual value assumption, we can calculate the implicit return to the lessor. Given the last four factors, together with the return the lessor desires, we can determine the periodic lease payments necessary to produce this return. Knowledge of the expected return to the lessor is valuable to a potential lessee, giving him or her a starting point for evaluation.

More sophisticated after-tax, cash-flow methods can be used for evaluating lease financing in relation to debt financing. Unless an asset can be used only by leasing it, the decision to lease or buy/borrow can be made on the basis of which alternative has the lowest present value of cash outflows or the lowest after-tax internal rate of return. In both cases, a key factor is the interest rate on debt funds relative to the implied discount rate embodied in the lease payments. Unless the latter is relatively low, owing to the lessor enjoying the tax and residual value benefits associated with ownership, debt financing will dominate. The decision to employ lease or debt financing occurs only after a firm decides to invest in the project.

The foundation for the growth in leasing is (1) differences in the protection afforded the lessor and the lender in the event of bankruptcy and (2) differences in the ability of companies, financial institutions, and individuals to take advantage of the tax benefits associated with owning an asset. Of the two, tax differences have by far the greater influence. Companies that pay no or low taxes may be able to realize some of the tax benefits associated with accelerated depreciation via high-tax bracketed lessors passing them off through lower lease payments.

Self-Correction Problems

1. Assuming that annual lease payments are in advance, solve for the unknown in each of the following situations

    a. Purchase price of $46,000, implicit interest rate of 11 percent, a 6-year lease period, $3,000 expected residual value; solve for the annual lease payment.

    b. Purchase price of $210,000, a 5-year lease period, annual lease payments of $45,000, an expected residual value of $25,000; solve for the implied interest rate.

c. Implied interest rate of 8 percent, a 7-year lease period, annual lease payments of $16,000, expected residual value of $10,000; solve for the purchase price.

d. Purchase price of $165,000, implied interest rate of 10 percent, annual lease payments of $24,412, no residual value; solve for the lease period.

2. Cordillera Pisco Company wishes to acquire a $100,000 press, which has a useful life of 8 years. At the end of this time, its scrap value will be $20,000. The asset falls into the 5-year property class for cost recovery (depreciation) purposes. The company can use either lease or debt financing. Lease payments of $14,000 at the beginning of each of the 8 years would be required. If debt financed, the interest rate would be 10 percent and debt payments would be due at the beginning of each of the 8 years. (Interest would be amortized as a mortgage type of debt instrument.) The company is in a 15 percent tax bracket. Which method of financing has the lower present value of cash outflows?

3. The Xenia-Youngstown Zipper Company (XYZ) has decided to invest in a computer-controlled measuring device costing $120,000. The device has an economic life of 7 years, after which no salvage value is expected. The company must determine whether it is better to finance the acquisition through debt or leasing. XYZ expects profits before taxes of $10,000 next year, $20,000 the following year, $30,000 the third year, and $40,000 each year thereafter (before depreciation on the device). It has a high degree of confidence in these estimates. The tax rate is 15 percent on the first $50,000 in profits, 25 percent on the next $25,000, and 34 percent on any profits above $75,000. The company has had break-even operations during the previous 3 years. If the machine is financed with debt, the Atticks National Bank of Youngstown is willing to extend a loan for the full purchase price at an 11 percent rate of interest payable in equal annual amounts over 7 years. The bank also has a leasing division and has indicated that it is willing to lease finance the acquisition for XYZ over the 7-year period. The bank is and has been quite profitable, and it is in a 34 percent tax bracket. Describe in words whether lease or debt financing is likely to be more favorable for XYZ. Why? Is the bank likely to want to accommodate the company more on a lease basis or on a debt basis?

Problems

1. Given the following information, compute the annual lease payment that a lessor will require. (Lease payments are in advance.)

   a. Purchase price of $260,000, interest rate of 13 percent, 5-year lease period, and no residual value.

   b. Purchase price of $138,000, interest rate of 6 percent, 9-year lease period, and a near certain residual value of $20,000.

   c. Purchase price of $773,000, interest rate of 9 percent, 10-year lease period, and no residual value.

2. Lucky Locker Corporation has just leased a metal-bending machine that calls for annual lease payments of $30,000 payable in advance. The lease period is 6 years, and the lease is classified as a capital asset for accounting purposes. The company's incremental borrowing rate is 11 percent, whereas the lessor's im-

plicit interest rate is 12 percent. Amortization of the lease in the first year amounts to $16,332. On the basis of this information, compute:

    a. The accounting lease liability that will be shown on the balance sheet immediately after the first lease payment.

    b. The annual lease expense (amortization plus interest) in the first year as it will appear on the accounting income statement. (The interest expense is based on the accounting value determined in part a.)

3. Fez Fabulous Fabrics wishes to acquire a $100,000 multifacet cutting machine. The machine has a useful life of 8 years, after which there is no expected salvage value. If it were to lease finance the machine over 8 years, annual lease payments of $16,000 would be required, payable in advance. The company also could borrow at a 12 percent rate. The asset falls in the 5-year property class for cost recovery (depreciation) purposes and the company has a 35 percent tax rate. What is the present value of cash outflows for each of these alternatives, using the after-tax cost of debt as the discount rate? Which alternative is preferred?

4. In Problem 3, suppose now the machine were expected to have a scrap value of $14,000 at the end of year 8. Using the internal-rate-of-return method of analysis, determine the best alternative. Does it differ from your answer to Problem 3?

5. Valequez Ranches, Inc., wants to acquire a mechanized feed spreader that costs $80,000. The ranch company intends to operate the equipment for 5 years, at which time it will need to be replaced. However, it is expected to have a salvage value of $10,000 at the end of the fifth year. The asset will be depreciated on a straight-line basis ($16,000 per year) over the 5 years, and Valequez Ranches is in a 30 percent tax bracket. Two means for financing the feed spreader are available. A lease arrangement calls for lease payments of $19,000 annually, payable in advance. A debt alternative carries an interest cost of 10 percent. Debt payments will be at the start of each of the 5 years using mortgage type of debt amortization.

    a. Using the present-value method, determine the best alternative.

    b. Using the internal-rate-of-return method, which is the best alternative? Does your answer differ from that to part a?

6. Pacific-Baja Shipping Company may need dock facilities in Valdez, Alaska. It would use the facilities for 4 years in connection with supplying heavy-duty equipment and other cargo to the area. The Port of Valdez Authority leases the facilities at an annual cost of $200,000 payable at the beginning of each year. Although the port authority has not stated the implied interest rate embodied in the lease payments, officials of Pacific-Baja believe a 9 percent rate would be appropriate. Over the 4 years, the company expects the project to show net cash flows of $180,000 in the first year, $250,000 in the second, $320,000 in the third, and $240,000 in the last year. (For simplicity, assume these cash flows are realized at the end of each of the years.) The project is subject to risk and it has been determined that the required after-tax rate of return is 18 percent. Should the company undertake the project and lease the dock facilities or should it reject the project?

7. Star Trac Leasing Company will lease a piece of equipment that costs it $80,000 to purchase. Quarterly lease payments of $4,400 in advance are required for 5 years. At the end of the lease, Star Trac estimates the asset will have a residual value of $20,000. What is the implicit return to the lessor embraced in these terms?

Solutions to Self-Correction Problems

1. a. Using Eq. (18-1) as the formula throughout

$$\$46{,}000 = \sum_{t=0}^{5} \frac{x}{(1.11)^t} + \frac{\$3{,}000}{(1.11)^6}$$

$$\$46{,}000 = x + 3.6959x + \$1{,}604$$

$$x = \frac{\$44{,}396}{4.6959} = \$9{,}454.20$$

   b.
$$\$210{,}000 = \sum_{t=0}^{4} \frac{\$45{,}000}{(1+x)^t} + \frac{\$25{,}000}{(1+x)^5}$$

Solving for x in the equation, it is found to be 8.26 percent.

   c.
$$x = \sum_{t=0}^{6} \frac{\$16{,}000}{(1.08)^t} + \frac{\$10{,}000}{(1.08)^7}$$
$$= \$16{,}000(1 + 4.6229) + \$5{,}835$$
$$= \$95{,}801$$

   d.
$$\$165{,}000 = \sum_{t=0}^{x} \frac{\$24{,}412}{(1.10)^t}$$

$\$165{,}000/\$24{,}412 = 6.759$

Subtracting 1 from this gives 5.759. Looking in Appendix Table B down the 10 percent column, we find that 5.759 corresponds to year 9. Therefore, the lease period is 9 + 1, or 10 years.

End of Year	(1) Lease Payment	(2) Tax Shield (1)(.15)	(3) Cash Outflow After Taxes (1)–(2)	(4) Present Value Of Cash Outflow (8.5%)
0	$14,000	—	$14,000	$14,000
1–7	14,000	$2,100	11,900	60,910
8	—	2,100	(2,100)	(1,093)
			Present value of cash outflow =	$73,817

2. Lease cash outflows:
    The discount rate is the before-tax cost of borrowing, 10 percent, times 1 minus the tax rate.

    Debt cash outflows:

$$\text{Annual debt payment: } \$100{,}000 = \sum_{t=0}^{7} \frac{x}{(1.10)^t}$$

$$\$100{,}000 = x + 4.8684x$$

$$x = \frac{\$100{,}000}{5.8684} = \$17{,}040$$

End of Year	(1) Debt Payment	(2) Amount Owing at End of Year	(3) Annual Interest
0	$17,040	$82,960	0
1	17,040	74,216	$8,296
2	17,040	64,598	7,422
3	17,040	54,018	6,460
4	17,040	42,380	5,402
5	17,040	29,578	4,238
6	17,040	15,496	2,958
7	17,046	0	1,550

The last payment is slightly higher due to rounding throughout.

End of Year	(1) Debt Payment	(2) Interest	(3) Depreciation	(4) Tax Shield $(2 + 3).15$	(5) A.T. Cash Flow $(1)-(4)$	(6) PV of Cash Flows (8.5%)
0	$17,040	0	0	0	$17,040	$17,040
1	17,040	$8,296	$20,000	$4,244	12,796	11,794
2	17,040	7,422	32,000	5,913	11,127	9,452
3	17,040	6,460	19,200	3,849	13,191	10,327
4	17,040	5,402	11,520	2,538	14,502	10,464
5	17,040	4,238	11,520	2,364	14,676	9,760
6	17,040	2,958	5,760	1,308	15,732	9,643
7	17,046	1,550	—	233	16,813	9,498
8	(20,000)	Residual value		(3,000)	(17,000)	(8,851)
				Present value of cash outflows =		$79,127

As the lease alternative has the lower present value of cash outflows, it is preferred. The low tax rate and favorable embedded lease cost explain the dominance.

3. The company is in a low tax bracket and has relatively low profits. If the asset is purchased, XYZ will be unable to utilize fully accelerated depreciation tax benefits in the early years, Finally, the applicable tax rate on XYZ's expected profits is 15 percent, very low. In contrast, the applicable tax rate for the bank is 34 percent. Moreover, it will be able to fully utilize the accelerated depreciation charges at the times they occur. As a result, ownership of the asset is more valuable to the bank than it is to XYZ. If the bank is willing to lend money at 11 percent, it should be willing to lease finance at a lower implicit rate. Therefore, lease financing is likely to be the more favorable alternative to XYZ.

Assuming that the bank does not have to pass on all the tax benefits to XYZ in the form of lower lease payments than otherwise would be the case, it should have a preference for leasing as opposed to lending. The problem serves to illustrate that with divergent tax rates and levels of profits, both parties can gain through lease as opposed to debt financing. The source of this incremental value, of course, is the government through its tax policies.

Selected References

ANG, JAMES, and PAMELA P. PETERSON, "The Leasing Puzzle," *Journal of Finance*, 39 (September 1984), 1055–66.

COPELAND, THOMAS E., and J. FRED WESTON, "A Note on the Evaluation of Cancellable Operating Leases," *Financial Management*, 11 (Summer 1982), 60–67.

GRAHAM, JOHN R., MICHAEL L. LEMMON, and JAMES S. SCHALLHEIM, "Debt, Leases, Taxes, and the Endogeneity of Corporate Tax Status," *Journal of Finance*, 53 (February 1998), 131–62.

GRENADIER, STEVEN R., "Leasing and Credit Risk," *Journal of Financial Economics*, 42 (November 1996), 333–64.

———, "Valuing Lease Contracts: A Real-Options Approach," *Journal of Financial Economics*, 38 (July 1995), 297–331.

KRISHNAN, V. SIVARAMA, and R. CHARLES MOYER, "Bankruptcy Costs and the Financial Leasing Decision," *Financial Management*, 23 (Summer 1994), 31–42.

LEWELLEN, WILBUR G., and DOUGLAS R. EMERY, "On the Matter of Parity among Financial Obligations," *Journal of Finance*, 36 (March 1981), 97–111.

McCONNELL, JOHN J., and JAMES S. SCHALLHEIM, "Valuation of Asset Leasing Contracts," *Journal of Financial Economics*, 12 (August 1983), 237–61.

MEHRAN, HAMID, ROBERT A. TAGGART, and DAVID YERMACK, "CEO Ownership, Leasing, and Debt Financing," *Financial Management*, 28 (Summer 1999), 5–14.

SCHALLHEIM, JAMES S., *Lease or Buy?* Boston: Harvard Business School Press, 1994.

SCHALLHEIM, JAMES S., RAMON E. JOHNSON, RONALD C. LEASE, and JOHN J. McCONNELL, "The Determinants of Yields on Financial Leasing Contracts," *Journal of Financial Economics*, 19 (September 1987), 45–68.

SHARPE, STEVEN A., and HIEN H. NGUYEN, "Capital Market Imperfections and the Incentive to Lease," *Journal of Financial Economics*, 39 (October–November 1995), 271–94.

SLOVIN, MYRON B., MARIE E. SUSHKA, and JOHN A. POLONCHEK, "Corporate Sale-and-Leasebacks and Shareholder Wealth," *Journal of Finance*, 45 (March 1990), 289–99.

VAN HORNE, JAMES C., "The Cost of Leasing with Capital Market Imperfections," *Engineering Economist*, 23 (Fall 1977), 1–12.

Wachowicz's Web World is an excellent overall Web site produced and maintained by my coauthor of *Fundamentals of Financial Management*, John M. Wachowicz Jr. It contains descriptions of and links to many finance Web sites and articles. *www.prenhall.com/wachowicz*.

Issuing Securities

Not all external financing is of a direct, arranged sort between the corporation and suppliers of capital, as was the case with lease financing and many aspects of short-term financing. A number of companies issue bonds and stocks to the investment public. During the last several years, corporate public security offerings have averaged in excess of $1 trillion annually. Of this, over 80 percent has involved debt instruments.

In this and the next two chapters we look at various methods of long-term financing where securities are issued. We shall see how a firm employs the various methods, their features, certain valuation concepts, information effects, and the integration of the specific methods into the theory of capital structure presented in Chapter 9. ∎

PUBLIC OFFERING OF SECURITIES

The efficient functioning of financial markets requires a number of financial institutions. One of these institutions, the investment banking firm, acts as middleman in the distribution of new securities to the public. Its principal function is to buy the securities from the company and then resell them to investors. For this service, investment bankers receive the difference, or spread, between the price they pay for the security and the price at which the securities are resold to the public. Because most companies make only occasional trips to the capital market, they are not specialists in the distribution of securities. On the other hand, investment banking firms have the expertise, the contacts, and the sales organization necessary to do an efficient job of marketing securities to investors.

There are two means by which companies offer securities to the public: a traditional underwriting and a shelf registration. In recent years, the latter has come to dominate, at least with respect to larger corporations. Let us explore the two methods for offering bonds and stocks to investors.

Traditional Underwriting
When an investment banking institution buys a security issue, it underwrites the sale of the issue by giving the company a check for the purchase price. At that time, the company is relieved of the risk of not being able to sell the issue at the

established price. If the issue does not sell well, either because of an adverse turn in the market or because it is overpriced, the underwriter, not the company, takes the loss. Thus, the investment banker insures, or underwrites, the risk of adverse market price fluctuations during the period of distribution.

Typically, the investment banking institution with whom a company discusses the offering does not handle the underwriting alone. To spread risk and obtain better distribution, it invites other investment bankers to participate in the offering. The originating house usually is the manager and has the largest participation. Other investment bankers are invited into the syndicate, and their participations are determined primarily on the basis of their ability to sell securities. With a negotiated offering, the company selects a lead investment banking firm and works directly with that firm in determining the essential features of the issue. Together, they discuss and negotiate a price for the security and the timing of the issue.

Public offering means to the general public in contrast to institutional investors.

Compensation to Investment Bankers To illustrate the compensation of investment bankers, we turn to an example. Figure 19-1 shows the essential features of a bond issue. The issue involves a syndicate of eight underwriters, with Hendershott, Kane and Kaufman being the manager that put it together. Its participation was the largest, being $22.5 million. Other participations ranged from $15 million down to $2 million. We see in the figure that the syndicate bought the bonds from the company for $74,156,250, or $988.75 per bond. In turn, it priced the bonds to the public at $997.50 a bond, or $74,812,500 in total. The spread of $8.75 per bond, or $656,250 in total, represents the gross commission to the syndicate for underwriting the issue, for selling it, and for covering the various expenses incurred.

Of the total spread of $8.75 per bond, $3.75, or 43 percent of it, is the **gross underwriting profit**. A portion of this gross goes to the originating house as manager of the offering. In our example, the manager receives a fee of $100,000, which represents approximately 15 percent of the total spread. After the bonds are sold, total underwriting profits less expenses and manager's fee are distributed to members of the syndicate on the basis of their percentage participation. It should be noted that the amount of underwriting profit to a member of a syndicate after expenses and the manager's fee is not large. In our example, it is probably less than $2 a bond.

Underwriters guarantee payment to the security issuer, regardless of the success of the offering.

With respect to underwriter risk, each member of the syndicate is liable for its percentage participation in the unsold securities of the syndicate, regardless of the number of securities the individual member sells. If a member of a syndicate has a 20 percent participation in an offering involving 40,000 bonds, and 10,000 remain unsold at the termination of the syndicate, the member would be responsible for 2,000 bonds. Its liability would be the same whether it had sold 20,000 bonds or none.

The principal reward for an investment banker participating in a syndicate comes from selling the securities to investors. As we discussed earlier, investment bankers are invited into syndicates, and their participation is determined primarily on the basis of their ability to distribute securities. For this function, an investment banker is rewarded by a **selling concession** of so many dollars a bond. In the Northern California Public Utility offering, the selling concession was $5 per bond, or 57 percent of the total spread of $8.75. The ultimate seller can be either a member of the underwriting syndicate or a qualified outside security dealer. To earn the full concession, however, the seller must be a member of the syndicate. An outside security dealer must purchase bonds from a member and will obtain only a dealer conces-

---

$75,000,000

Northern California Public Utility Company

9½% FIRST MORTGAGE BONDS DUE 2032

Interest payable September 1 and March 1. The bonds are redeemable on 30 days' notice at the option of the company at 109.5% to and including March 1, 2003, at decreasing prices thereafter to and including March 1, 2024, and thereafter at 100%. Due March 1, 2032

Application will be made to list the bonds on the New York Stock Exchange.

THESE SECURITIES HAVE NOT BEEN APPROVED OR DISAPPROVED BY THE SECURITIES AND EXCHANGE COMMISSION NOR HAS THE COMMISSION PASSED UPON THE ACCURACY OR ADEQUACY OF THIS PROSPECTUS. ANY REPRESENTATION TO THE CONTRARY IS A CRIMINAL OFFENSE.

	Price to Public (1)	Underwriting Discounts and Commissions (2)	Proceeds Company (1) (3)
Per unit	99.750%	.875%	98.875%
Total	$74,812,500	$656,250	$74,156,250

---

(1) Plus accrued interest from March 1, 2002 to date of delivery and payment.
(2) The company has agreed to indemnify the several purchasers against certain civil liabilities.
(3) Before deducting expenses payable by the company estimated at $200,000.

The new bonds are offered by the several purchasers named herein subject to prior sale, when, as and if issued and accepted by the purchasers and subject to their right to reject any orders for the purchase of the new bonds, in whole or in part. It is expected that the new bonds will be ready for delivery on or about March 12, 2002 in New York City.

HENDERSHOTT, KANE AND KAUFMAN

ELTON AND GRUBER   LITZENBERGER, MCDONALD, PARKER
AND PORTERFIELD

BRENNAN, KRAUS AND SCHWARTZ
UPSTAIRS AND DOWNING
CARLETON, PINCHES, REILLY, AND YAWITZ
BLACK, MERTON AND SCHOLES   MODIGLANI, MILLER, KIM,
ROLL AND SHARPE

The date of this prospectus is March 5, 2002

FIGURE 19-1
Cover of a prospectus

---

sion, which is less than the full selling concession. In our example, the outside dealer concession was $2.50 per bond out of a total selling concession of $5.

Best Efforts Offering Instead of underwriting a security issue, investment bankers may sell the issue on a *best efforts* basis. Under this arrangement, the investment bankers agree only to sell as many securities as they can at an established price. They have no responsibility for securities that are unsold. In other words, they bear no risk. Investment bankers frequently are unwilling to underwrite a security issue of smaller, nontechnological companies. For these companies, the only feasible means by which to place securities may be through a best efforts offering.

Making a Market On occasion, the underwriter will make a market for a security after it is issued. In the first public offering of common stock, making a market is important to investors. In making a market, the underwriter maintains a position in the stock, quotes bid and asked prices, and stands ready to buy and sell it at those prices. These quotations are based on underlying supply and demand conditions. With a secondary market, the stock has greater liquidity to investors; this appeal enhances the success of the original offering.

Shelf Registrations

The distinguishing feature of the traditional underwriting is that the registration process with the Securities and Exchange Commission (SEC) takes at least several weeks to complete. (The process itself is described at the end of this section.) Often 2 or more months elapse between the time a company decides to finance and the time the security offering actually takes place.

Shelf registrations are quicker and more efficient than traditional security offerings.

Large corporations, whose securities are listed on an exchange, are able to shortcut the registration process under Rule 415. This rule permits what is known as a **shelf registration.** Here a company files a form with the SEC describing itself, its financing needs, and the securities it is likely to issue over the next 2 years. When the company wishes to sell new securities, it files a brief amendment to its detailed SEC filing. It then is able to sell securities "off the shelf." By using a shelf registration, a company is able to go to market with a new issue in a matter of days as opposed to weeks or months. As a result, it has the flexibility to time issues to market conditions, and the issues themselves need not be large.

Flotation Costs In effect, a corporation places securities it expects to use in financing over the next 2 years on the "shelf," and from time to time it auctions off some of them. In this regard, large corporations are able to play investment bankers off against each other, and the resulting competition is felt in reduced spreads. For example, a typical spread on a traditional underwriting of corporate bonds is $7.50 or $8.75 per bond; the spread on a shelf registration might be $2 or $3 a bond. Flotation costs for a large common stock issue, again using a traditional underwriting, might run 3 to 4 percent of the gross proceeds. (For smaller issues, it will run upward to 8 percent.) With a shelf registration, these costs run about 2 percent. In addition, the fixed costs of public debt issues (legal and administrative) are lower with a shelf registration because there is only one registration. Therefore, it is not surprising that large corporations have turned to shelf registrations.

GOVERNMENT REGULATIONS

With the collapse of the stock market in 1929 and the subsequent depression, there came a cry to protect investors from misinformation and fraud. Congress undertook extensive investigations and proposed federal regulation of the securities industry. The Securities Act of 1933 dealt with the sale of new securities and required the full disclosure of information to investors. The Securities Exchange Act of 1934 dealt with the regulation of securities already outstanding. Moreover, it created the **Securities and Exchange Commission** (SEC) to enforce the two acts.

Registration Process

The purpose of registering a security offering with the SEC is to protect the investor through proper disclosure of financial and legal information about the issuing corporation. Though the registration process applies to most offerings, there is an exemption if the security is sold to a limited number of financially sophisticated investors. An example would be a private placement to a handful of institutional investors. Most corporations, however, must file a detailed registration statement, which contains information such as the nature and history of the company, the use of the proceeds of the security issue, financial statements, the management and directors and their security holdings, competitive conditions and risks, legal opinions, and a description of the security being issued. Along with the registration statement, the corporation must file a copy of the prospectus (see Fig. 19-1), which is a summary of the essential information in the registration statement. The prospectus must be available to prospective investors and others who request it.

The SEC regulates security offerings in the United States and safeguards the investor from false information.

SEC Review   Post 1929

The SEC reviews the registration statement and the prospectus to see that all the required information is presented and that it is not misleading. If the SEC is satisfied with the information, it approves the registration, and the company then is able to issue a final prospectus and sell the securities. If not, the SEC issues a *stop order*, which prevents the sale of the securities. Most deficiencies can be corrected by the company, and approval will usually be given eventually, except in cases of fraud or misrepresentation. For serious violations of the 1933 Securities Act, the SEC is empowered to go to court and seek an injunction. It should be pointed out that the SEC is not concerned with the investment value of the securities being issued, only with the presentation of complete and accurate information on all material facts regarding the security.

The minimum period required between the time a registration statement is filed and the time it becomes effective is 20 days. The usual time lapse, however, is around 40 days. As we discussed earlier, large corporations are able to use shelf registrations. Once a detailed report is filed covering a block of securities, the company is able to sell off the shelf by filing a simple amendment. The lapse in time in this case is very short—perhaps a day.

Streamlining Registration Procedures

At the time of this writing, the SEC was making significant changes in the procedures outlined above. Larger companies no longer will be required to go through the lengthy review process for each security issue. Like a shelf registration, they will be required to provide detailed information on the company on a one-time basis. When securities are subsequently issued, this information will need to be updated. The term *larger* means companies with a market capitalization of $250 million or more (share price times number of shares = market capitalization). Smaller companies will still have to provide the SEC and investors with a prospectus. In addition, companies of all sizes will face fewer restrictions in how they market and communicate with potential investors. Offering securities over the Internet will be allowed. Overall, the idea is to provide more timely and accurate information to investors about the companies in which they invest. While there will be less scrutiny by the SEC, underwriters will be required to undertake more "due diligence" in ferreting out fraud and deception. All companies still will be required to file annually with the SEC "10-K" reports on their financial condition and performance. These changes in the information age will make registration more efficient not only as to time but as to cost.

Secondary Market

The SEC regulates the sale of securities in the secondary markets in addition to the sale of new issues. In this regard, it regulates the activities of the security exchanges, the over-the-counter market, investment bankers and brokers, the National Association of Security Dealers, and investment companies. It requires monthly reports on insider stock transactions by officers, directors, and large stockholders. Whenever an investor or group obtains 5 percent or more of the stock, it must file a **form 13D**, which alerts all to the accumulation and to subsequent changes in ownership. In its regulatory capacity, the SEC seeks to prevent manipulative practices by investment dealers and by officers and directors of the company, abuses by insiders (officers and directors) in transactions involving the company's stock, fraud by any party, and other abuses affecting the investing public.

SELLING COMMON STOCK THROUGH A RIGHTS ISSUE

Instead of selling a security issue to new investors, some firms offer the securities first to existing shareholders on a **privileged subscription** basis. Sometimes the corporate charter requires that a new issue of common stock or an issue of securities convertible into common be offered first to existing shareholders because of their preemptive right.

Preemptive Right

Under a preemptive right, existing common stockholders have the right to preserve their proportionate ownership in the corporation. If the corporation issues additional common stock, they must be given the right to subscribe to the new stock so that they maintain their pro rata interest in the company. You may own 100 shares of a corporation that decides to make a new company stock offering for the purpose of increasing outstanding shares by 10 percent. If you have a preemptive right, you must be given the option to buy 10 additional shares so that you can preserve your proportionate ownership in the company.

Offering through Rights

When a company sells securities by privileged subscription, it mails to its stockholders one right for each share of stock held. With a common stock offering, the rights give stockholders the option to purchase additional shares according to the terms of the offering. The terms specify the number of rights required to subscribe for an additional share of stock, the subscription price per share, and the expiration date of the offering. The holder of rights has three choices: (1) exercise them and subscribe for additional shares, (2) sell them because they are transferable, or (3) do nothing and let them expire. Generally, the subscription period runs about 3 weeks. A stockholder who wishes to buy a share of additional stock but does not have the necessary number of rights may purchase additional rights. If you own 152 shares of stock in a company, and the number of rights required to purchase 1 additional share is 5, your 152 rights will allow you to purchase 30 full shares. If you would like to buy the 31st share, you may do so by purchasing an additional 3 rights.

Rights issues are to existing shareholders, with a subscription price below existing share price.

In a rights offering, the board of directors establishes a date of record. Investors who buy the stock prior to that date receive the right to subscribe to the new issue. The stock is said to sell with **rights-on** through the date of record. After the date of record, the stock is said to sell **ex-rights;** that is, the stock is traded without the rights attached. An investor who buys the stock after this date does not receive the right to subscribe to additional stock.

Value of Rights

The market value of a right is a function of the present market price of the stock, the subscription price, and the number of rights required to purchase an additional share of stock. The theoretical market value of one right after the offering is announced but while the stock is still selling rights-on is

$$R_0 = \frac{P_0 - S}{N + 1} \tag{19-1}$$

where R_0 is the market value of one right when stock is selling rights-on, P_0 is the market value of a share of stock selling rights-on, S is the subscription price per share, and N is the number of rights required to purchase one share of stock.

If the market price of a stock is \$100 per share, the subscription price is \$90 a share, and it takes four rights to buy an additional share of stock, the theoretical value of a right when the stock is selling rights-on is

$$R_0 = \frac{100 - 90}{4 + 1} = \$2$$

Note that the market value of the stock with rights-on contains the value of one right.

Ex-Rights Value When the stock goes ex-rights, the market price theoretically declines, for investors no longer receive the right to subscribe to additional shares. The theoretical value of one share of stock when it goes ex-rights is

$$P_x = \frac{(P_0 \times N) + S}{N + 1} \tag{19-2}$$

where P_x is the market price of the stock when it goes ex-rights. For our example

$$P_x = \frac{(100 \times 4) + 90}{4 + 1} = \$98$$

From this example we see that, theoretically, the right does not represent a thing of value to the stockholder. Before the date of record, the stock is worth \$100. After the date of record, it is worth \$98 a share but he or she realizes \$2 in value from the right. The decline in market price is offset exactly by the value of the right, so the stockholder does not benefit from the rights offering. The right represents merely a return of capital.

The theoretical value of a right when the stock sells ex-rights is

$$R_x = \frac{P_x - S}{N} \tag{19-3}$$

where R_x is the market value of one right when the stock is selling ex-rights. If, in our example, the market price of the stock is $98 when it goes ex-rights

$$R_x = \frac{98 - 90}{4} = \$2$$

or the same value as before.

Market versus Theoretical Value   We should be aware that the actual value of a right may differ somewhat from its theoretical value on account of transaction costs, speculation, and the irregular exercise and sale of rights over the subscription period. However, arbitrage limits the deviation of actual value from theoretical value. If the price of a right is significantly higher than its theoretical value, stockholders will sell their rights and purchase the stock in the market. Such action will exert downward pressure on the market price of the right and upward pressure on its theoretical value. The latter occurs because of the upward pressure on the market price of the stock. If the price of the right is significantly lower than its theoretical value, arbitragers will buy the rights, exercise their option to buy stock, and then sell the stock in the market. This occurrence will exert upward pressure on the market price of the right and downward pressure on its theoretical value. These arbitrage actions will continue as long as they are profitable.

Success of the Offering

One of the most important aspects of a successful rights offering is the subscription price. If the market price of the stock should fall below the subscription price, stockholders obviously will not subscribe to the stock, for they can buy it in the market at a lower price. Consequently, a company will set the subscription price at a value lower than the current market price, to reduce the risk of the market price's falling below it.

We know that the stock should fall in price when it goes ex-rights. Its new theoretical value is determined by Eq. (19-2), and we see that it strongly depends on N, the number of rights required to purchase one share of stock. The greater the N, the less the theoretical price decline when the stock goes ex-rights. Thus, the risk that the market price will fall below the subscription price is inversely related to N.[1] To illustrate, suppose the following were true:

	Company A	Company B
Market value per share rights-on, P_0	$60.00	$60.00
Subscription price, S	$46.00	$46.00
Number of rights needed to purchase one share, N	1	10
Theoretical value of one share ex-rights, P_x	$53.00	$58.73

[1]See Haim Levy and Marshall Sarnat, "Risk, Dividend Policy, and the Optimal Pricing of a Rights Offering," *Journal of Money, Credit, and Banking*, 3 (November 1971), 840–49.

We see that company A will have a greater decline in value per share when its stock goes ex-rights than will company B. All other things staying the same, there is a greater probability, or risk, that company A's stock will fall below the subscription price of $46 than there is that company B's stock will fall below it.

Amount of Discount   Apart from the number of rights required to purchase one share, the risk that the market price of a stock will fall below the subscription price is a function of the volatility of the company's stock, the tone of the market, expectations of earnings, and other factors. To avoid all risk, a company could set the subscription price so far below the market price that there is virtually no possibility that the market price will fall below it.

The greater the discount, however, the more shares will have to be issued to raise a given amount of money, and the greater the dilution in earnings per share. This dilution may be of practical concern, for the investment community analyzes closely the growth trend in earnings per share. Significant underpricing of the new issue will dampen the growth trend in earnings per share. Although theoretically the stockholders are equally well off regardless of the subscription price set, in practice the market value of their stock holdings may suffer if investors in any way are fooled by the dilution in reported earnings per share.

The disadvantages of underpricing must be balanced against the risk of the market price's falling below the subscription price. The primary consideration in setting the subscription price is to reduce the probability of this occurrence to a tolerable level. If, then, the subscription price appears to result in excessive dilution and this dilution seems to matter, the company should consider a public issue wherein the amount of underpricing is less. For most rights offerings, the subscription price discount ranges between 10 and 20 percent.

Other Factors   The size of the capital outlay in relation to a stockholder's existing ownership of the stock is an influence on the success of a rights offering. Stockholders are likely to be more willing to subscribe to an issue amounting to a 20 percent addition to the stock they now hold than to an issue amounting to a 50 percent addition. The mix of existing stockholders may also be a factor. If a substantial number of stockholders hold only a few shares, the success of the offering may be less than if most stockholders hold units of 100 shares. The balance between institutional and individual investors may also bear on the success of the rights offering. The current trend and tone of the stock market are influential. If the trend is upward and the market is relatively stable in this upward movement, the probability of a successful sale is high. The more uncertain the stock market, the greater the underpricing that may be necessary to sell the issue. There are times when the market is so unstable that an offering will have to be postponed.

Standby Underwriting

Standby arrangements guarantee to the issuer that the funds will be raised.

A company can ensure the complete success of a rights offering by having an investment banker or a group of investment bankers "stand by" to underwrite the unsold portion of the issue. In fact, most companies use a **standby** arrangement in a rights offering. For this standby commitment, the underwriter charges a fee that varies with the risk involved in the offering. Often the fee consists of two parts: a flat fee and an additional fee for each unsold share of stock that the underwriter has to buy. From the standpoint of the company issuing the stock, the greater the risk of an unsuccessful sale, the more desirable a standby arrangement, although it also is more costly.

In essence, the underwriter sells a put option to the firm and its shareholders. If the stock price declines below the subscription price, the stock will be put to the underwriter at the subscription price. That is bad for the underwriter, but it all is in the nature of writing options. If the stock price remains above the subscription price, rights will be exercised and the underwriter will pocket the standby fee. Because of the risk, standby fees are significant and increase with the volatility of the stock. Therefore, the company must pay for its put option.

In view of the high cost of this insurance relative to experience, it is surprising that the vast majority of companies have their rights offerings underwritten as opposed to the seemingly low-cost uninsured method. Various scholars have tried to explain this "paradox" in terms of such things as asymmetric information, financial signaling, transaction costs, flotation costs, and taxes. No explanation is entirely satisfactory, and the preponderance of underwritten rights offerings remains, to a degree, a paradox in academic finance.

Oversubscriptions

Another, less used means of increasing the probability that the entire issue will be sold is through **oversubscriptions.** This device gives stockholders not only the right to subscribe for their proportional share of the total offering but also the right to oversubscribe for any unsold shares. Oversubscriptions are then awarded on a pro rata basis relative to the number of unsold shares. Stockholders may subscribe to 460,000 shares of a 500,000-share rights offering. Perhaps some of them would like to purchase more shares, and their oversubscriptions total 100,000 shares. As a result, each stockholder oversubscribing is awarded four-tenths of a share for each share oversubscribed. This results in the entire issue being sold. Although the use of the oversubscription increases the chances that the issue will be entirely sold, it does not assure this occurrence, as does the standby agreement. It is possible that the combination of subscriptions and oversubscriptions will fall short of the amount of stock the company desires to sell.

Rights Issue versus Public Offering

By offering stock first to existing stockholders, the company taps investors who are familiar with the operations of the company. The principal sales tool is the discount from the current market price, whereas with a public issue, the major selling tool is the investment banking organization. When the issue is not underwritten with a standby arrangement, the flotation costs of a rights offering are lower than the costs of an offering to the general public. Therefore, there is less drain in the system from the standpoint of existing stockholders. Moreover, many stockholders feel that they should be given the first opportunity to buy new common shares.

Offsetting these advantages in the minds of some is that a rights offering will have to be sold at a lower price than will an issue to the general public. If a company goes to the equity market with reasonable frequency, this means that there will be somewhat more dilution with rights offerings than there will be with public issues. Even though this consideration is not relevant theoretically, many companies wish to minimize dilution. Also, a public offering tends to result in a wider distribution of shares, which may be desirable to the company.

The Puzzle Examined Further Although these factors may have an effect on shareholder wealth, we would expect their effect to be slight. The issue remains as to why so many companies incur the costs associated with underwriting when they could sell securities through a rights issue without a standby agreement at less cost. Hansen and Pinkerton contend that companies that issue securities through a rights offering have a different stockholder mix than those that use a public offering.[2] The more concentrated the ownership of a company, the lower the merchandising expense of a rights offering. These expenses include printing, mailing, stock transfer, and payment of fees to a subscription agent to promote the sale. In testing ownership patterns for a sample of stock offerings, the authors claim to find a higher concentration of ownership for companies that use rights offerings. They suggest the choice of offering is a function of the flotation cost structure of the company.

In a separate paper, Hansen finds that underwritten rights offerings are associated with a price decline of more than 4 percent just prior to the sale.[3] This contrasts with a public offering, where there is little price concession. He argues that the price dip is a transaction cost for placing new securities. Inasmuch as total transaction costs (flotation and price concession) are higher for an underwritten rights offering, he suggests it is not surprising that companies prefer public offerings.

In summary, the introduction of imperfections in the capital markets may explain the wide use of public offerings versus rights offerings. Still, the greater direct flotation cost must be weighed in reaching a financing decision, particularly if the price concession is viewed not as a transaction cost but simply as a proportional renumbering of shares within the family of stockholders. The fact that uninsured rights offerings are used only infrequently in equity financing, despite their flotation cost advantage, remains largely a paradox.

Green Shoe Provision

With a stock or convertible-security financing, underwriters often obtain an option to purchase additional securities at the offering price. Known as a **green shoe provision** (after an actual company), the option usually lasts several weeks after the offering. Often the option is for an additional 15 percent of the security offering, the maximum allowed. As with any option, the green shoe provision benefits the holder. If the security rises in price immediately after the offering, the underwriter can exercise the option and purchase additional securities, then sell them at a gain. In most situations, however, the underwriter will exercise the option in order to deliver securities against a short position. This short position is occasioned by satisfying demand for the security in the original and after-market.

FINANCING A FLEDGLING

When a company is formed, it obviously must be financed. There are a number of sources of such financing, and there has evolved in the United States and in certain other countries what is known as a **private equity market**. In this chapter, we consider several aspects of private equity. In Chapter 24, we will take up two other aspects, namely, leveraged buyouts and distress restructuring.

Founders and Angels

For some start-up companies, the founders will have sufficient resources to get things launched. They simply will cover living costs, office space rental, and other things out of their savings while they formulate a business plan for the product or

---

[2]Robert S. Hansen and John M. Pinkerton, "Direct Equity Financing: A Resolution of a Paradox," *Journal of Finance*, 37 (June 1982), 651–65.
[3]Robert S. Hansen, "The Demise of the Rights Issue," *Review of Financial Studies*, 1 (Fall 1988), 289–309.

service they intend to launch. When they have no resources or their resources dry up, they may seek funding from one or more **angel investors**. For the most part, these investors are wealthy individuals who are willing to fund what they regard as a good idea as long as it is accompanied by competent founders to bring it off. Often the investment by each angel is in the $100,000 range, and for this he or she receives a sizable equity stake. However, the founders typically retain the great majority of the equity.

The idea may not pan out, and the angel may realize a zero return. For the successful company, the return to the angel investor can be extraordinary—several hundred percent compounded annually! However, this is the exception rather than the rule. Most angel investments provide either no or negligible returns to the investor. Founder and angel capital are necessary in order to get the idea formulated, initially survey the potential market, and develop a **business plan** that sets forth the purpose of the company, its vision, how the product or service will be developed, the market, management needed to carry out the development, and the likely financing needed to bring the idea to fruition, to revenue, and ultimately to profitability. The next step is to approach venture capitalists for further funding.

> **Venture capitalists** provide early stage financing to new enterprises.

Venture Capital

Venture capital (VC) represents funds invested in an existing, relatively new enterprise. There are several stages of investment with more or less standard guidelines and expectations.

Stages of VC Financing   **Seed money** is needed to prove a concept—product or service. Although usually these needs are small—several hundred thousand dollars or less—and funded by the entrepreneur or angel investor, on occasion venture capitalists will provide such financing. The next stage is **start-up**, and this funding is used to support further research and development and to formulate initial marketing and production plans. Perhaps a prototype will be developed. **First-round** financing typically is used to initiate actual production and marketing of the product or service. **Second-round** financing provides working capital for expansion of production or of service provision. Assuming lack of profitability, receivables and inventories need to be financed. **Third-round** financing is used to further increase sales and to achieve cash-flow breakeven, assuming it has not already occurred. Finally, **bridge** financing may be necessary to carry a company to an initial public offering.

> **Staged financing** is a discipline used by the venture capitalist on the entrepreneur.

These stages vary with the situation and with the industry. Seldom will a biotech company achieve cash-flow breakeven prior to selling stock to the public. In other words, negative profitability and cash flow will occur throughout the time the company is funded by venture capitalists. Although venture capitalists would like to bring a company along to profitability, this is not always the case.

Sources of Venture Capital   The sources of venture funding are several. A venture capital firm will seek capital in advance from external investors. Such investors include (in order of importance): public pension funds, corporate pension funds, endowments and foundations, bank holding companies, wealthy families and individuals, insurance companies, and others.[4] With money and commitments in hand from

---

[4]See Stephen D. Prowse, "The Economics of the Private Equity Market," *Economic Review of the Federal Reserve Bank of Dallas* (3rd Quarter, 1998), 21–34.

external investors, together with any cash investment the VC firm may have made, the VC then goes about investing the funds. This means screening venture applicants; investigating those passing initial screens as to their merit, known as **due diligence**; and ultimately reaching a decision as to whether to fund the venture.

New venture proposals in the high-technology area are more attractive than new ventures in more mundane industries. The reason is simple. In high tech there is the perceived possibility of substantial growth and ultimate capital gains. Thus, there are a number of venture capital firms in Silicon Valley in California; in Austin, Texas; and in the greater Boston area. Whereas high-tech situations, like computer hardware and software and biotech, once were the only type of ventures funded, this is no longer the case. Some low-tech and service companies lend themselves to venture capital financing. The keys are the quality of management and the potential market niche for the product or service.

Structure of Venture-Capital Partnership   Investors in a venture capital partnership come in as **limited partners.** They sign an agreement calling for an initial investment followed by calls by the venture capitalist for additional investments up to some maximum committed amount. The venture capitalist is the **general partner** and makes all the investment decisions. As general partner, the venture capitalist receives 25 to 30 percent of the ultimate profits of the partnership, known as carried interest, together with an annual management fee, usually 2 percent of the fund. The carried-interest reward to the general partner is received only when the partnership is liquidated and distributions are made to the limited partners. Limited partners typically expect returns of 15 percent or more on their capital to compensate them for the risk and lack of liquidity. The typical venture capital partnership is liquidated in 7 to 10 years. However, partial payouts can, and usually do, occur earlier. The forms of payout include stock of the companies in the portfolio that go public and cash where the investment is sold to a strategic corporate buyer.

Financing Structure   Once the venture capitalist has decided to finance a venture, the principal vehicle is preferred stock with an equity link. This link can be warrants to buy common stock at a nominal price or a conversion feature into common (see the next two chapters). Negotiations with management focus on how much ownership management will be allowed. The venture capitalist wants to control the situation. Often, this means majority ownership and the power to replace management if necessary. Another device employed is to phase in over time the stock allocated to management. For example, management might be given one-third of its total stock allocation at the time of the financing, one-third after 5 years if it meets the goals set forth in the business plan, and one-fifteenth each year during the first 5 years as long as things are on target.

All stock held by management and the venture-capital partnership is illiquid, not being registered for a period of years. Known as **letter stock,** it cannot be sold until the issue is registered. This occurs after an initial public offering or at the time the business is sold to someone else.

If a company proves itself, initial start-up financing is followed by several rounds of expansion financing described earlier. For the venture capitalist, **staged financing** is a control device with checkpoints where go/no go decisions can be made, as opposed to giving the entrepreneur all the money at once. At each stage, the value of the equity from previous stages is marked up to what is called the **pre-offer market price.** Though the markup is only a paper entry, it affects the percentage of ownership given up with the new stage of financing. Venture capital financing may carry a company for 5 years.

Rather than entirely finance a company, venture capitalists often will join together in a **syndicate.** Not only does this spread risk, but it reduces the probability of making a mistake. Because different venture capitalists will look at the situation from different perspectives, they may discover things overlooked by any single venture capitalist. By these and the other control devices described, venture capitalists lessen agency conflicts between themselves and management.

Venture Capital Portfolio   The venture capitalist hopes that all of the companies in the partnership portfolio will do well. If a company thrives, it will be profitable enough in 4 or 5 years to sell its stock in the public market or to be sold to, or merged with, another corporation. In turn, the venture capital partnership will be able to sell/exchange its stock for many times what was paid for it. This is one scenario. Others, unfortunately, are possible. The risks associated with a new venture are many, and the frequency of failure can be high. With failure, the investor loses everything. The probability distribution of possible returns for most venture capital portfolio investments is skewed to the right. That is, there is a significant chance that investors will lose all their investment, but there also is some probability that their investment will increase in value fiftyfold. The overall portfolio return to the venture capitalist is very sensitive to those few investments that do very well, perhaps one or two in ten.

Initial Public Offerings

If the private firm is successful, usually the owners will want to take the company public with a sale of stock to outsiders. Often this is prompted by venture capitalists, who wish to realize a cash return on their investment. In other situations, the founders simply want to establish a value, and liquidity, for their stock. Whatever the motivation, a decision is reached to become a public corporation. There are exceptions; some large, successful companies choose to remain private. Bechtel Corporation is one of the largest construction and engineering companies in the world, but it is private.

Although there are advantages to being a public company, there are also disadvantages. The public company must conform to SEC requirements in having a board of directors, disclosing sensitive information, having to employ certain accounting conventions, and incurring expenses as a public company not incurred by a private one. In addition, there is an investor fixation on quarterly earnings. At times this is a hindrance to management in trying to make long-term decisions. More will be said about this in Chapter 24, when we examine public companies that go private. Suppose for now, however, that a private company has decided to go public.

Initial public offerings (IPOs) typically have a "pop" in price on the first day of trading.

Underpricing of IPO   Most initial public offerings (IPOs) are through an underwriter. Having no previous public market, there is no stock price benchmark. Consequently, there is more uncertainty than there is when a public company sells additional stock. Empirical studies suggest that on average IPOs are sold at a significant discount (over 15 percent) from the prices that prevail in the aftermarket. Several explanations have been offered. There may be an asymmetry in information between the company and the investment banker and among investors who are informed in varying degree. Beatty and Ritter posit a reputational effect

Japanese Capital Markets Open Up

Throughout history, Japanese financial markets have been heavily regulated and protected. Comfortable arrangements abounded, which assured Japanese security dealers and financial institutions reasonable margins without having to provide comparable benefits to consumers of financial services. Capital flows were strongly influenced by the government and by institutional rigidities, as opposed to the private marketplace. As a result, capital did not necessarily flow to the most productive investment opportunities.

Then in 1996 came the announcement of "big bang" deregulation of the financial services industry. The intent was to open up financial markets to competition, both foreign and domestic; reduce bureaucratic interference with the markets; and make the markets more transparent. As a result, it was hoped that financial markets would become more efficient in allocating capital, more convenient to use, and more liquid. An important milestone occurred in 2000 when NASDAQ Japan was launched. It is a joint venture between the National Association of Securities Dealers in the United States, which sponsors the NASDAQ stock market in the United States, and Softbank Corporation of Japan, a large Internet company. The lack of a viable initial public offering marketplace heretofore put a damper on start-up companies in the high-tech and biotech areas as well as on small and medium-size firms in general.

NASDAQ Japan is one manifestation of a new era in Japanese financial markets, an era of greater competition, efficiency, and vitality. Such changes should stimulate the real sector of the economy with a more efficient allocation of capital.

for the investment banker that causes him or her to seek an optimal underpricing.[5] If the issue is underpriced too much, the investment banker will lose potential future issues; if too little, potential investors. The authors test this proposition empirically and find that underwriters with the most deviation from an estimated normal underpricing lose market share.

Another reason for the discount, Ritter argues, is that there are both informed and uninformed investors in an IPO.[6] The informed investors will invest only in successful offerings where share price subsequently rises. Yet some IPOs are unsuccessful and the investor loses money. If the "average" uninformed investor is to be drawn into the market, the average return to them must be positive. But it will not be if informed investors invest only in the good deals and uninformed investors must pick up all the bad. (A winner's curse: Though they win the bid, they are cursed with the outcome.) To lure uninformed investors into the IPO market, Ritter suggests the need for a substantial discount.

For the corporation, the implication is that the initial public stock offering will need to be significantly underpriced from what is believed to be its true value. This is the price of admission to the public market. If reputational effects prevail, investment bankers should be motivated to seek a fair underpricing. Due to asymmetric information, however, significant underpricing probably will be necessary. Subsequent public offerings will not need to be underpriced as much, as a benchmark price will exist and there will be less uncertainty.

---

[5]Randolph P. Beatty and Jay R. Ritter, "Investment Banking, Reputation, and the Underpricing of Initial Public Offerings," *Journal of Financial Economics*, 15 (January–February 1986), 213–32.

[6]Jay R. Ritter, "The Costs of Going Public," *Journal of Financial Economics*, 19 (December 1987), 269–82.

While underpricing occurs with seasoned equity issues, it is not nearly as great as with an IPO.

Long-Run Underperformance   After the typical runup in price immediately after an IPO, the return to investors is not attractive on average. Relative to the overall stock market, there is underperformance in the years following the IPO.[7] Perhaps investors are excessively optimistic at the time of the IPO, and the company, venture capitalists, and underwriters seize on the opportunity by issuing stock. For high-tech and health-care stocks in particular, the cycles of receptivity in the stock market are particularly pronounced. This underperformance may mean that IPOs are not so much overpriced, as that investors in the immediate aftermarket are too optimistic. However, it has been found that most of underperformance is attributable to IPOs that are not venture capitalist–backed. VC-backed firms do not seem to significantly underperform, whereas smaller, nonventure-backed firms do.[8]

INFORMATION EFFECTS

When a public company announces a security issue, there may be an information effect that causes a stock market reaction. Holding constant market movements, scholars have found negative stock price reactions (or abnormal returns) to a common stock or convertible security issue. Straight debt and preferred stock announcements do not tend to show a statistically significant effect. A typical reaction for stock issue announcements is shown in Fig. 19-2, where days around the event are on the horizontal axis and the cumulative average abnormal return, after isolating overall market movement effects, is along the vertical axis. As seen, a stock price reduction occurs around the announcement date, and it tends to average about 3 percent.

Expectations of Future Cash Flows

Several explanations have been offered for this phenomenon. For one thing, the security issue announcement may be telling us something about future cash flows. When a company announces a security issue, the implication is that these funds will go to one or more purposes: investment in assets, reduction of debt, stock repurchase or increased dividends, or to make up for lower than expected operating cash flows. To the extent an unexpected security sale is associated with the last, the event will be bad news and the stock price accordingly may suffer. The cash-flow argument for an information effect is associated with Miller and Rock.[9]

---

[7]See Jay R. Ritter, "The Long-Run Performance of Initial Public Offerings," *Journal of Finance,* 46 (March 1991), 269–82; Tim Loughran, "NYSE vs. Nasdaq Returns: Market Microstructure or the Poor Performance of IPOs?" *Journal of Financial Economics,* 33 (April 1993), 241–60; Joshua Lerner, "Venture Capitalists and the Decision to Go Public," *Journal of Financial Economics,* 35 (June 1994), 293–316; and Loughran and Ritter, "The New Issues Puzzle," *Journal of Finance,* 50 (March 1995), 23–51.

[8]Alon Brav and Paul A. Gompers, "Myth or Reality? The Long-Run Underperformance of Initial Public Offerings: Evidence from Venture and Nonventure Capital-Backed Companies," *Journal of Finance,* 52 (December 1997), 1791–1821.

[9]Merton H. Miller and Kevin Rock, "Dividend Policy under Asymmetric Information," *Journal of Finance,* 40 (September 1985), 1031–51. In testing analysts' forecasts of earnings following announcements of equity offerings, Peter Alan Brous, "Common Stock Offerings and Earnings Expectations: A Test of the Release of Unfavorable Information," *Journal of Finance,* 47 (September 1992), 1517–36, found evidence consistent with the offerings conveying unfavorable information about the level of future earnings.

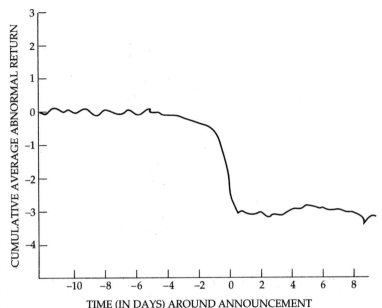

FIGURE 19-2
Relative stock returns around the announcement of a new equity offering

Asymmetric Information

Asymmetric information between investors and management is the foundation for an information effect.

A second effect has to do with asymmetric information between investors and management. In this argument, associated with Myers and Majluf, potential investors in securities have less information than management, and management tends to issue securities when the market's assessment of their value is higher than its assessment.[10] This would be particularly true with common stock, where investors have only a residual claim to income and assets. Because cash flows are affected when a new security is offered, an asymmetric information effect is difficult to sort out using new issue data.

With an exchange offering of one security for another, however, cash flows are not affected. When empirical studies on exchange offers are categorized into those that increase leverage and those that decrease leverage, the results are striking.[11] Leverage-increasing transactions are accompanied by positive abnormal stock returns in the 2 days prior to announcement, while leverage-reducing transactions are accompanied by negative returns. The effect is greatest for debt for common exchanges (positive return) and common for debt exchanges (negative re-

---

[10]Stewart C. Myers and Nicholas S. Majluf, "Corporate Financing and Investment Decisions When Firms Have Information That Investors Do Not Have," *Journal of Financial Economics*, 13 (June 1984), 187–221.

[11]See the synthesis of empirical evidence by Clifford W. Smith Jr., "Investment Banking and the Capital Acquisition Process," *Journal of Financial Economics*, 15 (January–February 1986), 3–29.

turn). Thus, the evidence is consistent with asymmetric information where managers are more likely to issue debt when they believe the common stock is underpriced in the market and to issue common when it is believed to be overpriced.

Underperformance of Seasoned Equity Offerings   This seems to be supported by empirical evidence that shows seasoned equity offerings (non-IPOs) underperforming nonissuing public corporations on average.[12] While the underperformance is not as great as that which occurs for IPOs, it is still substantial. The timing is such that management on average seems to be able to sell overvalued stock when there is opportunity to do so. Although the theory suggests that this should be done, investors should beware.

Summary

When companies finance their long-term needs externally, they may obtain funds from the capital markets. If the financing involves a public offering, the company often will use the services of an investment banking firm. The investment banker's principal functions are risk bearing, or underwriting, and selling the securities. For these functions, the investment banking firm is compensated by the spread between the price it pays for the securities and the price at which it resells the securities to investors. The offering itself can be either a traditional underwriting or, in the case of a large corporation, a shelf registration. With a shelf registration, a company sells securities "off the shelf" without the delays associated with a lengthy registration process.

A company may give its existing stockholders the first opportunity to purchase a new security issue on a privileged subscription basis. This type of issue is known as a rights offering, because existing stockholders receive one right for each share of stock they hold. A right represents an option to buy the new security at the subscription price, and it takes a specified number of rights to purchase the security. Depending on the relationship between the current market price of the stock and the subscription price, a right usually will have a market value. Security offerings to the general public and offerings on a privileged subscription basis must comply with federal and state regulations. The enforcement agency for the federal government is the Securities and Exchange Commission, whose authority encompasses both the sale of new securities and the trading of existing securities in the secondary market.

In its early stages, a company needs financing. One source is the venture capitalist who specializes in financing new enterprises, particularly if they involve high technology. If the company is successful, it often will "go public" with an initial public offering of common stock. Because there is no benchmark stock price, much uncertainty exists and the new issue usually must be sold at a sizable discount from the price that will prevail in the after-market.

The announcement of a debt or stock issue may be accompanied by a stock market reaction. For one thing, the announcement may connote information about future cash flows of the company. Or the reaction may be due to asymmetric information between investors and management. The latter presumes management will finance with stock when it believes the stock is overvalued and with debt when it is believed to be undervalued. Empirical evidence is consistent with both of these notions, so the financial manager must recognize the likelihood of an information effect when issuing securities.

---

[12]See Loughran and Ritter, "The New Issues Puzzle."

Self-Correction Problems

1. The Homex Company wishes to raise $5 million in additional equity capital through a traditional underwriting. After considering the potential difficulty of selling the shares, the investment banker decides that the selling concession should be between 3 percent and 4 percent of the value of the issue. When the risks of underwriting are evaluated, it is decided that the selling concession should constitute between 50 and 60 percent of the gross spread. If the manager's fee (which constitutes part of the underwriting profit) is taken to be 15 percent of the gross spread, answer the following questions.

   a. Assuming that the selling concession is set at 4 percent of gross proceeds and 50 percent of the gross spread, what would be the dollar value of the manager's fee, net underwriting profit, selling concession, and gross spread on the Homex underwriting?

   b. Rework part a, assuming that the selling concession was set at 3 percent of gross proceeds and 60 percent of the gross spread.

   c. Assuming that the managing underwriter underwrote 25 percent and sold 20 percent of the issue, what would be the manager's total compensation under (1) part a? (2) part b?

2. The stock of the Dunbar Company is selling for $150 per share. The company issues rights to subscribe for one additional share of stock at $125 a share, for each nine held. Compute the theoretical value of:

   a. A right when the stock is selling rights-on.

   b. One share of stock when it goes ex-rights.

   c. A right when the stock sells ex-rights and the actual market price goes to $143 per share.

Problems

1. Caldacci Copper Company, a risky company, needs to raise $75 million in long-term debt funds. The company is negotiating the offering through First Columbia Corporation. First Columbia believes it can bring together a syndicate of investment bankers to underwrite and sell the issue. The bonds will be given a coupon rate, so that they may be priced to the public at their face value of $1,000. The selling concession will be $6 per bond; in addition, administrative expenses of $115,000 will be incurred. Typically, First Columbia requires a manager's fee of 15 percent of the total spread. To sell this issue, it feels that the underwriting commission, net of expenses, and manager's fee must be 25 percent of the total spread.

   a. What will be (1) the total spread? (2) the total spread per bond?

   b. What will be the net proceeds of the issue to Caldacci Copper?

   c. What is the selling concession as a percentage of the total spread?

   d. What are the total costs of issuing the securities as a percentage of the net proceeds to the company?

2. Black Telecommunications Company needs to raise $1.8 billion (face value) of debt funds over the next 2 years. If it were to use traditional underwritings, the company would expect to have six underwritings over the 2-year span.

The underwriter spread would likely be $7.50 per bond, and out-of-pocket expenses paid by the company would total $350,000 per underwriting. With shelf registrations, the average size of offering would probably be $75 million. Here the estimated spread is $3 per bond, and out-of-pocket expenses of $40,000 per issue are expected.

a. Ignoring interest costs, what are the total absolute costs of flotation over the 2 years for the traditional underwriting method of offering securities?

b. For the shelf registration method?

c. Which is lower?

3. Two different companies are considering rights offerings. The current market price per share is $48 in both cases. To allow for fluctuations in market price, company X wants to set a subscription price of $42. Company Y feels a subscription price of $41.50 is in order. The number of rights necessary to purchase an additional share is 14 for company X and 4 for company Y.

a. Which company has the larger stock issue relatively? Is it the larger stock issue in absolute terms?

b. In which case is there less risk that the market price will fall below the subscription price?

4. The stock of the National Corporation is selling for $50 per share. The company then issues rights to subscribe to one new share at $40 for each five rights held.

a. What is the theoretical value of a right when the stock is selling rights-on?

b. What is the theoretical value of one share of stock when it goes ex-rights?

c. What is the theoretical value of a right when the stock sells ex-rights at $50?

d. Joe Speculator has $1,000 at the time National stock goes ex-rights at $50 per share. He feels that the price of the stock will rise to $60 by the time the rights expire. Compute his return on his $1,000 if he (1) buys National stock at $50, or (2) buys the rights at the price computed in part c, assuming his price expectations are valid.

5. Instead of a rights offering, National Corporation (see Problem 4) could undertake a public offering of $45 per share with a 6 percent gross spread. National currently has 1 million shares outstanding and earns $4 million a year. All earnings are paid in dividends. In either case, National would sell enough shares to raise $8 million, which would be invested at an after-tax return of 10 percent.

a. Compute the earnings per share, dividends per share, and market price of the stock (assuming a 12.5 P/E ratio) for (1) the rights offering and (2) the public offering alternatives.

b. Mr. Brown owns one share of National stock. On a rights offering, he will sell the right (assume for $2), thereby reducing his investment to $48. On a public offering, he would not buy any more shares. Compute Brown's earnings and dividend return on his investment and his price gain or loss on his investment under each of the two financing alternatives facing National.

6. Zeus Electronics Company is a new enterprise formed to exploit a technological innovation. It is to be capitalized with $6 million in equity, of which venture capitalists are being asked to provide $5.6 million. For this cash invest-

ment, venture capitalists will receive 70 percent of the common stock, with the management/founders keeping 30 percent. At the end of 6 years, management believes that the equity portion of the company is likely to be worth $50 million. At that time, it envisions an initial public offering where venture capitalists and the management/founders can sell all their stock if they so choose. For initial public offerings, a discount of 20 percent is believed to be required from the "true" worth of the company. While $50 million is the most likely "true" value of the company's stock 6 years hence, there is a 30 percent probability the company will fail and be worth nothing to stockholders and a 20 percent probability that its true worth (equity portion) will be worth $80 million.

    a.   If the most likely value prevails, what will be the compound annual return on investment to a venture capitalist who decides to sell stock at the end of 6 years?

    b.   What is the compound expected annual return based on all possibilities?

7. Doubletree Foods, Inc., is considering either a new stock issue or a new debt issue to raise capital. What are the likely information effect and stock market reaction that accompany the announcement of (a) a stock issue? (b) a debt issue? Why?

▪ Solutions to Self-Correction Problems

1.   a.

SC	= 4% of GP = 50% of GS	
GS	= 8% × $5,000,000 = $400,000	
SC	= $200,000	
MF	= $60,000	
Net UP	= $140,000	

    b.

SC	= 3% of GP = 60% of GS	
GS	= 5% × $5,000,000 = $250,000	
SC	= $150,000	
MF	= $37,500	
Net UP	= $62,500	

    c. Case A: $60,000 + .25($140,000) + .20($200,000) = $135,000

        Case B: $37,500 + .25($62,500) + .20($150,000) = $83,125

2.   a. $R_0 = \dfrac{P_0 - S}{N + 1}$

$$= \frac{\$150 - \$125}{9 + 1} = \frac{\$25}{10} = \$2.50$$

    b. $P_x = \dfrac{(P_0 \times N) + S}{N + 1} = \dfrac{(\$150 \times 9) + \$125}{9 + 1}$

$$= \frac{\$1,350 + \$125}{10} = \frac{\$1,475}{10} = \$147.50$$

    c. $P_x = \dfrac{P_x - S}{N} = \dfrac{\$143 - \$125}{9} = \dfrac{\$18}{9} = \$2$

■ Selected References

ADMATI, ANAT R., and PAUL PFLEIDERER, "Robust Financial Contracting and the Role of Venture Capitalists," *Journal of Finance,* 49 (June 1994), 371–402.

AGGARWAL, REENA, "Stabilization Activities by Underwriters after Initial Public Offerings," *Journal of Finance,* 55 (June 2000), 1075–1103.

ALLEN, FRANKLIN, and GERALD R. FAULHABER, "Signaling by Underpricing in the IPO Market," *Journal of Financial Economics,* 23 (August 1989), 303–24.

ASQUITH, PAUL, and DAVID MULLINS JR., "Equity Issues and Offering Dilution," *Journal of Financial Economics,* 15 (January–February 1986), 61–90.

———, "Signalling with Dividends, Stock Repurchases, and Equity Issues," *Financial Management,* 15 (Autumn 1986), 27–44.

BARRY, CHRISTOPHER B., "New Directions in Research on Venture Capital Finance," *Financial Management,* 23 (Autumn 1994), 3–15.

BEATTY, RANDOLPH P., and JAY R. RITTER, "Investment Banking, Reputation, and the Underpricing of Initial Public Offerings," *Journal of Financial Economics,* 15 (January–February 1986), 213–32.

BERLIN, MITCHELL, "That Thing Venture Capitalists Do," *Business Review of the Federal Reserve Bank of Philadelphia* (January/February 1998), 15–26.

BETHEL, JENNIFER E., and ERIK R. SIRRI, "Express Lane or Tollbooth in the Desert? The SEC's Framework for Security Issuance," *Journal of Applied Corporate Finance,* 11 (Spring 1998), 25–38.

BOHREN, OYVIND, B. ESPEN ECKBO, and DAG MICHALSEN, "Why Underwrite Rights Offerings? Some New Evidence," *Journal of Financial Economics,* 46 (November 1997), 223-61.

BRAV, ALON, and PAUL A. GOMPERS, "Myth or Reality? The Long-Run Underperformance of Initial Public Offerings: Evidence from Venture and Nonventure Capital-Backed Companies," *Journal of Finance,* 52 (December 1997), 1791–1821.

CARTER, RICHARD, and STEVEN MANASTER, "Initial Public Offerings and Underwriter Reputation," *Journal of Finance,* 45 (September 1990), 1045–68.

CHEN, HSUAN-CHI, and JAY R. RITTER, "The Seven Percent Solution," *Journal of Finance,* 55 (June 2000), 1105-31.

ECKBO, B. ESPEN, and RONALD W. MASULIS, "Adverse Selection and the Rights Offer Paradox," *Journal of Financial Economics,* 32 (December 1992), 293–332.

ECKBO, B. ESPEN, RONALD W. MASULIS, and OYVIND NORLI, "Seasoned Public Offerings: Resolution of the New Issues Puzzle," *Journal of Financial Economics,* 56 (May 2000), 251–91.

FENN, GEORGE W., "Speed of Issuance and the Adequacy of Disclosure in the 144A High-Yield Debt Market," *Journal of Financial Economics,* 58 (June 2000), 383–405.

GOMPERS, PAUL A., "Grandstanding in the Venture Capital Industry," *Journal of Financial Economics,* 42 (September 1996), 133–56.

———, "Optimal Investment, Monitoring, and the Staging of Venture Capital," *Journal of Finance,* 50 (December 1995), 1461–89.

GOMPERS, PAUL, and JOSH LERNER, "An Analysis of Compensation in the U.S. Venture Capital Partnership," *Journal of Financial Economics,* 51 (January 1999), 3–44.

———, "Money Chasing Deals? The Impact of Funds Inflows on Private Equity Valuations," *Journal of Financial Economics,* 55 (February 2000), 281–325.

HANLEY, KATHLEEN WEISS, and WILLIAM J. WILHELM JR., "Evidence on the Strategic Allocation of Initial Public Offerings," *Journal of Financial Economics,* 37 (February 1995), 239–56.

HANSEN, ROBERT S., "The Demise of the Rights Issue," *Review of Financial Studies,* 1 (Fall 1988), 289–309.

HANSEN, ROBERT S., and JOHN M. PINKERTON, "Direct Equity Financing: A Resolution of a Paradox," *Journal of Finance,* 37 (June 1982), 651–65.

JUNG, KOOYUL, YONG-CHEOL KIM, and RENE M. STULZ, "Timing, Investment Opportunities, Managerial Discretion, and the Security Issue Decision," *Journal of Financial Economics,* 42 (October 1996), 159–89.

KIM, MOONCHUL, and JAY R. RITTER, "Valuing IPOs," *Journal of Financial Economics,* 53 (September 1999), 409–37.

LERNER, JOSHUA, "The Syndication of Venture Capital Investments," *Financial Management,* 23 (Autumn, 1994), 16–27.

———, "Venture Capitalists and the Decision to Go Public," *Journal of Financial Economics,* 35 (June 1994), 293–316.

LOUGHRAN, TIM, and JAY R. RITTER, "The New Issues Puzzle," *Journal of Finance,* 50 (March 1995), 23–51.

———, "The Operating Performance of Firms Conducting Seasoned Equity Offerings," *Journal of Finance,* 52 (December 1997), 1823–50.

MYERS, STEWART C., and NICHOLAS S. MAJLUF, "Corporate Financing and Investment Decisions When Firms Have Information That Investors Do Not Have," *Journal of Financial Economics,* 13 (June 1984), 187–221.

PARSONS, JOHN E., and ARTUR RAVIV, "Underpricing of Seasoned Issues," *Journal of Financial Economics,* 14 (September 1985), 377–98.

PROWSE, STEPHEN D., "The Economics of the Private Equity Market," *Economic Review of the Federal Reserve Bank of Dallas* (3rd Quarter 1998), 21–34.

SUBRAHMANYAM, AVANIDHAR, and SHENDAN TITMAN, "The Going-Public Decision and the Development of Financial Markets," *Journal of Finance,* 54 (June 1999), 1045–82.

WRUCK, KAREN HOPPER, "Equity Ownership Concentration and Firm Value: Evidence from Private Equity Financings," *Journal of Financial Economics,* 23 (June 1989), 3–28.

Wachowicz's Web World is an excellent overall Web site produced and maintained by my coauthor of *Fundamentals of Financial Management,* John M. Wachowicz Jr. It contains descriptions of and links to many finance Web sites and articles. *www.prenhall.com/wachowicz.*

Fixed-Income Financing and Pension Liability

ow that we know how securities are issued and how fixed-income securities are used in general, it is time to look at specific instruments. In this chapter we take up a wide spectrum of long-term debt instruments available to a company, consider certain conceptual and valuation issues associated with them, and evaluate the use of preferred stock financing. From the standpoint of common stockholders, preferred stock represents a form of leverage and must be evaluated in much the same way as debt. This is followed by a discussion of what for many companies is their largest single liability, the obligation to pay pensions to past and present employees. ■

FEATURES OF DEBT

The holders of a company's long-term debt, of course, are creditors. Generally they cannot exercise control over the company and do not have a voice in management. If the company violates any of the provisions of the debt contract, then these holders may be able to exert some influence on the direction of the company. Holders of long-term debt do not participate in the residual earnings of the company; instead, their return is fixed. Their debt instrument has a specific maturity, whereas a share of common or preferred stock does not. In liquidation, the claim of debt holders is before that of preferred and common stockholders. Depending on the nature of the debt instrument, however, there may be differences in the priority of claim among the various creditors of a company.

Some Definitions

The fixed return of a long-term debt instrument is denoted by the **coupon rate**. A $7\frac{1}{2}$ percent debenture indicates that the issuer will pay bondholders $37.50 semiannually for every $1,000 face value bond they hold. The yield to maturity on a bond is determined by solving for the rate of discount that equates the present value of principal and interest payments with the current market price of the bond. (See Chapter 2 for the mathematics of bond interest.) The yield on a bond is the same as the internal rate of return for an investment project.

The Trustee A company issuing bonds to the public designates a qualified *trustee* to represent the interests of the bondholders. The obligations of a trustee are specified in the Trust Indenture Act of 1939, administered by the Securities and Exchange Commission. The trustee's responsibilities are to authenticate the bond issue's legality at the time of issuance, to watch over the financial condition and behavior of the borrower to make sure all contractual obligations are carried out, and to initiate appropriate actions if the borrower does not meet any of these obligations. The trustee is compensated directly by the corporation, a compensation that adds to the cost of borrowing.

Indenture The legal agreement between the corporation issuing the bonds and the trustee, who represents the bondholders, is defined in the **indenture.** The indenture contains the terms of the bond issue as well as the restrictions placed on the company. These restrictions, known as **protective covenants,** are very similar to those contained in a term loan agreement. Because we analyzed protective covenants in detail in Chapter 16, it is not necessary to describe these restrictions here. The terms contained in the indenture are established jointly by the borrower and the underwriter along with the trustee. If the corporation defaults under any of the provisions of the indenture, the trustee, on behalf of the bondholders, can take action to correct the situation. If not satisfied the trustee then can call for the immediate payment of all outstanding bonds.

Bond Ratings

The creditworthiness of a publicly traded debt instrument often is judged by investors in terms of the credit rating assigned to it by investment agencies. The principal rating agencies are Moody's Investors Service and Standard & Poor's. The issuer of a new corporate bond contracts with the agency to evaluate and rate the bond as well as to update the rating throughout the bond's life. Based on their evaluations, the agencies give their opinion in the form of letter grades, which are published for use by investors. In their ratings, the agencies attempt to rank issues according to the probability of default.

As described in Chapter 10, the highest-grade issues, whose risk of default is felt to be negligible, are rated AAA, followed by AA, A, BBB, BB, B, and so forth through C and D, which are the lowest grades of the two agencies, respectively. The first four grades mentioned are considered to represent investment-quality issues, whereas other rated bonds are considered speculative. For each rating category, a modifier is applied. For example, Aa-1 means that a security is in the higher end of the Aa rating category. A-3 indicates that a security is in the lower end of the A category, whereas A-2 reflects the midrange.

High-Yield Bonds

During the 1980s, there developed an active market for noninvestment-grade bonds. These are bonds with a grade of BB or less (Ba or less using Moody's), and they are called "junk" or "high-yield" bonds. The market was promulgated by the investment banking firm of Drexel Burnham Lambert, which dominated this market until its demise in 1990. A number of companies used the market to raise billions of dollars of funds, displacing what was previously bank and private-placement financing. In addition, high-yield bonds were used in acquisitions and leveraged buyouts (topics taken up in Chapters 23 and 24).

The principal investors in junk bonds are high-yield bond mutual funds, though other institutional investors buy them as well. A secondary market of sorts exists, but in any kind of "flight to quality" in the bond markets, such liquidity dries up. In the late 1980s, bonds issued in connection with highly leveraged transactions (i.e., leveraged buyouts) began to experience difficulty and many defaulted. Investors lost confidence, and there was a sharp drop in new issues. From the shambles of late 1990, the situation improved. Default rates abated, and junk bonds increased in price. There was a revival in junk bond financing by corporations, as investors looked for yield opportunities. As a result, substantial amounts of funds were raised in this market from 1993 to 1998. In late 1998 there developed a "flight to quality" in bond investing, and liquidity in the market for lower-grade bonds dried up. The trades that did take place were at 6 percent or more above yields for Treasury securities of the same maturity. It was very difficult for the lower-grade corporation to issue bonds to the public. By 2000, this difficulty abated and noninvestment-grade companies were able to tap this market.

High-yield debt is that rated Ba/BB or below, the speculative grades.

While high-yield bonds are a viable means of financing for some companies, it must be recognized that there are windows of opportunity. In an unstable market, few investors are to be found. A company dependent on this market will face a financing crisis at such a time.

Sinking Funds

The retirement of bonds may be accomplished in a number of ways: by payment at final maturity, by conversion if the bonds are convertible, by calling the bonds if there is a call feature, or by periodic repayment. Periodic repayment of the debt is possible if the bond issue is a sinking-fund issue. Conversion is discussed in Chapter 21, and calling is examined later in this chapter.

The majority of corporate bond issues carry a provision for a sinking fund, which requires the corporation to make periodic sinking-fund payments to a trustee, to retire a specified face amount of bonds each period. Many sinking funds begin not at the time of issuance but after a period of 5 or 10 years. The sinking-fund retirement of a bond issue can take two forms:

Sinking funds retire a portion of the bonds prior to maturity.

1. The corporation can make a cash payment to the trustee, who in turn calls the bonds for redemption at the sinking-fund call price. (This usually is lower than the regular call price of a bond, often being the face value of the instrument.) The bonds themselves are called on a lottery basis by their serial numbers, which are published in the *Wall Street Journal* and other papers.
2. The corporation can purchase bonds in the open market and pay the trustee by delivering to it a given number of bonds.

Issuer's Option The corporation should purchase the bonds in the open market as long as the market price is less than the sinking-fund call price; when the market price exceeds the call price, it should make cash payments to the trustee. In this context, the sinking fund represents a delivery option to the corporation. It can satisfy the provision by paying cash to the trustee or by repurchasing bonds in the market. Expressed differently, it has an option to retire debt at the sinking-fund call price or at the market price, whichever is lower. If interest rates increase and/or credit quality deteriorates, the bond's price will decline in relation to the sinking-fund call price. As a result, the delivery option can have significant value. As with any option, it works to the advantage of the holder, in this case the corporation, and to the disadvantage of bondholders. The greater the volatility of interest rates and/or volatility of firm value, the more valuable the option to the corporation.

However, the sinking-fund provision may benefit the bondholder. By delivering bonds whose cost is lower than the call price, the company conserves cash, which may lower the probability of default. Because of the orderly retirement of sinking-fund debt, known as the amortization effect, some feel that it has less default risk than nonsinking-fund debt. In addition, steady repurchase activity adds liquidity to the market, which may be beneficial to investors.

The two factors discussed work in opposite directions.[1] The delivery option works to the disadvantage of bondholders, but amortization and other things that reduce risk and/or increase liquidity work to their advantage. The limited empirical evidence available supports both effects, but the amortization effect somewhat more so.

Nasty Accumulators!   Some corporations, in purchasing bonds for sinking-fund payment, find that **accumulators** have gotten there first. Accumulators are institutional or other investors that buy bonds in advance of the corporation going into the market to acquire them for sinking funds. If supply is sufficiently restricted, the corporation will be able to purchase bonds only by bidding up the price. In this way, the accumulator hopes to sell the bonds at an inflated price, knowing the corporation must purchase them to satisfy the sinking-fund requirement. Imperfections allow the accumulator to partially corner the market, thereby forcing the corporation to pay the inflated price. Although perfectly legal, accumulation is not looked on with favor by financial managers. Only when the bonds sell at a discount from the sinking-fund call price, of course, does accumulation occur. Otherwise, the corporation will make a cash payment to the trustee, who will purchase the bonds at the sinking-fund call price.

Floating-Rate Notes

Instead of a fixed interest rate over the life of the debt instrument, the interest rate can float with some short-term rate, such as the London Interbank Offered Rate (LIBOR) or the Treasury bill or commercial paper rate. In a volatile interest-rate environment, corporations are reluctant to commit to long-term debt. Floating-rate notes (FRNs) are looked to as a way to reduce some of the risk of volatile interest rates. A typical FRN might have a 5-year maturity with the interest rate adjusted

---

European Corporate Bond Issuance

Until recently the European bond market was a rather inhospitable place for the corporation. It was difficult to do a large issue, like $500 million, and longer-term maturities simply were not possible. The bond market was not sufficiently developed to provide the depth and breadth necessary to be attractive to a corporate financial officer. With the advent of the Euro currency in 1999 (see Chapter 25), all of that changed. A bond issue denominated in the Euro has become the vehicle of choice for many a corporate financial officer engaged in cross-border financing.

In 1999, $150 billion in corporate bond issues occurred—2½ times the amount issued in 1998. The year 2000 was even larger. Issues of upwards to $1 billion now are possible, as are issues of 10 years or longer, both unthinkable several years ago. Whereas once only highly rated debt (triple or double A) was possible, recently about one-quarter of the debt issued has been triple B or below. The largest issuance has emanated from corporations in the United Kingdom, France, Germany, and Italy—not surprising given the economic clout of these countries. The development of a viable European corporate bond market has been a welcome addition to the flexibility accorded chief financial officers.

---

[1]For details of how they work, see Andrew J. Kalotay and George O. Williams, "The Valuation and Management of Bonds with Sinking Fund Provisions," *Financial Analysts Journal,* 48 (March–April 1992), 59–67; and Andrew Ho and Michael Zaretsky, "Valuation of Sinking Fund Bonds," *Journal of Fixed Income,* 3 (June 1993), 25–31.

every 3 months in keeping with changes in the LIBOR rate. An initial interest rate is set for the first 3 months, but after that the instrument might provide an interest rate $\frac{1}{2}$ percent above 3-month LIBOR.

Often a minimum or floor rate is specified, and there may be some special features, such as options, a declining spread, or even a fixed-rate provision after a specified change in rates. The FRN is a financial innovation that came about in response to volatile interest rates. During such times, its use is widespread.

TYPES OF DEBT FINANCING

Moving now to fixed-rate, long-term debt instruments, we consider the various kinds. With the exception of income bonds, all are widely employed.

Debentures

The term **debenture** usually applies to the unsecured bonds of a corporation. Investors look to the earning power of the corporation as their security. Because these general credit bonds are not secured by specific property, in the event of liquidation the holder becomes a general creditor. Although the bonds are unsecured, debenture holders are protected by the restrictions imposed in the indenture, particularly the **negative pledge clause,** which precludes the corporation from pledging its assets to other creditors. This provision safeguards the investor in that the borrower's assets will not be impaired in the future. Because debenture holders must look to the general credit of the borrower to meet principal and interest payments, only well-established and creditworthy companies are able to issue debentures.

Subordinated Debentures

Subordinated debentures represent debt that ranks behind debt senior to these debentures with respect to the claim on assets. In the event of liquidation, subordinated debenture holders usually receive settlement only if all senior creditors are paid the full amount owed them. These holders still would rank ahead of preferred stockholders in the event of liquidation. The existence of subordinated debentures may work to the advantage of senior holders, because senior holders are able to assume the claims of the subordinated debenture holders. To illustrate: A corporation is liquidated for $600,000. It had $400,000 in straight debentures outstanding, $400,000 in subordinated debentures outstanding, and $400,000 in obligations owed to general creditors. One might suppose that the straight debenture holders and the general creditors would have an equal and prior claim in liquidation, that each would receive $300,000. The fact is, the straight debenture holders are entitled to the subordinated debenture holders' claims, giving them $800,000 in total claims. As a result, they are entitled to two-thirds of the liquidating value, or $400,000, whereas general creditors are entitled to only one-third, or $200,000.

Because of the nature of the claim, a straight subordinated debenture issue has to provide a yield higher than a regular debenture issue in order to be attractive to investors. Frequently, subordinated debentures are convertible into common stock and therefore may sell at a yield that is less than what the company would have to pay on an ordinary debenture.

Mortgage Bonds

A mortgage bond issue is secured by a lien on specific assets of the corporation—usually fixed assets. The specific property securing the bonds is described in detail in the mortgage, which is the legal document giving the bondholder a lien on the property. As with other secured lending arrangements, the market value of the collateral should exceed the amount of the bond issue by a reasonable margin of safety. If the corporation defaults in any of the provisions of the bond indenture, the trustee, on behalf of the bondholders, has the power to foreclose. In a foreclosure, the trustee takes over the property and sells it, using the proceeds to pay the bonds. If the proceeds are less than the amount of the issue outstanding, the bondholders become general creditors for the residual amount. A company may have more than one bond issue secured by the same property. If a bond issue is secured by a *second mortgage* and the first mortgagee forecloses, the first-mortgage bondholders must be paid the full amount owed them before there can be any distribution to the second-mortgage bondholders.

Income Bonds

A company is obligated to pay interest on an income bond only when it is earned. There may be a cumulative feature in the issue where unpaid interest in a particular year accumulates. If the company does generate earnings, it will have to pay the cumulative interest to the extent that earnings permit. However, the cumulative obligation usually is limited to no more than 3 years. As should be evident, this type of security offers the investor a rather weak promise of a fixed return. Nevertheless, the income bond is still senior to preferred and common stock, as well as to any subordinated debt. Unlike preferred stock dividends, the interest payment is deductible for tax purposes. Because income bonds are not popular with investors, they have been used principally in reorganizations.

Equipment Trust Certificates

Although equipment trust financing is a form of lease financing, the certificates themselves represent an intermediate- to long-term fixed-income investment. This method of financing is used by railroads to finance the acquisition of rolling stock. Under this method, the railroad arranges with a trustee to purchase equipment from a manufacturer. The railroad signs a contract with the manufacturer for the construction of specific equipment. When the equipment is delivered, equipment trust certificates are sold to investors.

The proceeds of this sale, together with the down payment by the railroad, are used to pay the manufacturer. Title to the equipment is held by the trustee, who in turn leases the equipment to the railroad. Lease payments are used by the trustee to pay a fixed return on the certificates outstanding—actually a dividend—and to retire a specified portion of the certificates at regular intervals. Upon the final lease payment by the railroad, the last of the certificates is retired, and title to the equipment passes to the railroad.

The duration of the lease varies according to the equipment involved, but 15 years is common. Because rolling stock is essential to the operation of a railroad and it has a ready market value, equipment trust certificates enjoy a very high standing as fixed-income investments. As a result, railroads are able to acquire cars and locomotives on favorable financing terms. Airlines, too, use a form of equipment trust certificate to finance jet aircraft. Usually, airlines' certificates are sold to institutional investors; some issues are sold to the public.

Equity-Linked Debt

Sometimes the investor in the debt instruments of a company is given an option on common stock. With *debt + warrants*, the debt holder has an option to purchase the common stock of the company and he or she continues to hold the debt instrument. The warrant is an "equity sweetener" to make the instrument more attractive. A *convertible bond* is one that may be exchanged, at the option of the holder, into a certain number of shares of common stock of the corporation. The number of shares into which the bond is convertible is specified in the bond indenture, and these shares remain unissued until actual conversion. With *exchangeable debt,* the debt can be exchanged into shares of stock of another corporation. These and other equity-linked debt arrangements are considered in depth in Chapter 21.

Project Financing

The term *project financing* describes a variety of financing arrangements for large, individual investment projects. Often a separate legal entity is formed to own the project. Suppliers of capital then look at the earnings stream of the project for repayment of their loan or for the return on their equity investment. Often, the projects involve energy: not only large explorations of gas, oil, and coal but also tankers, port facilities, refineries, and pipelines. Other projects include mineral extraction operations, aluminum plants, fertilizer plants, and, very important, power plants. An example of the latter is a cogeneration project.

Relation to Sponsor Projects of this sort require huge amounts of capital, often beyond the reach of a single company. Many times a consortium of companies is formed to spread risk and to finance the project. Part of the capital comes from equity participations by the companies, and the rest comes from lenders or lessors. If the loan or lease is on a nonrecourse basis, the lender or lessor pays exclusive attention to the size of the equity participation and to the economic feasibility of the project. In other words, the lender or lessor can look only to the project for payout, so the larger the equity cushion and the greater the confidence that can be placed in the projections, the better the project. In another type of arrangement, each sponsor may guarantee its share of the project's obligations. Under these circumstances, the lender or lessor places emphasis on the creditworthiness of the sponsors as well as on the economic feasibility of the project.

Sharing Rules For the sponsors of the project there are several types of sharing rules. In a "take-or-pay" arrangement, each sponsor agrees to purchase a specific percentage of the output of the project and to pay that percentage of the operating costs of the project plus debt-servicing charges. This obligation exists whether or not output actually occurs. When pipelines are involved, the type of sharing rule is frequently a "throughput" arrangement. Here each sponsor is required to ship through the facility a certain amount, or percentage, of product. If the total shipped is insufficient to cover the expenses of running the facility, sponsors are assessed additional amounts to cover the shortfall. The amount of assessment is proportional to their participation. The maturity of the loan or lease corresponds to the likely ability of the project to generate cash over time. Although the financing need not be long term, in most cases it extends over a period of 8 or more years.

CALL FEATURE AND REFUNDING

Debt instruments often contain **embedded options.** One example is the sinking-fund provision previously considered; another is the call feature. This feature gives the issuer the option to buy back a debt instrument at a specified price before maturity. The price at which this occurs is known as the *call price.* When a bond is callable, the call price usually is above the face value of the bond and decreases

A call feature is an option to the issuer to retire the debt early; it works to the investor's disadvantage.

over time. Frequently, the call price in the first year is established at 1 year's interest above the face value of the bond. If the coupon rate is 9 percent, the initial call price may be $109 ($1,090 per $1,000 face value).

Forms of the Provision

The call feature itself may take several forms. The security may be **immediately callable,** which simply means that the instrument may be bought back by the issuer at the call price at any time. Even here, the investor is partially protected from a call because the initial call price is above the face value of the bond. Moreover, there are a number of expenses and inconveniences associated with refunding a bond issue that must be factored in by the borrower before a decision to call a bond issue is made. However, should interest rates decline significantly, the issuer may wish to call the bond. Rather than being immediately callable, the call provision may be **deferred** for a period of time. This means that the instrument cannot be called during the deferment period; thus, the investor is protected from a call.

Though many corporate bond issues have a call feature, the relative use of the provision varies over time. When interest rates are low and investors demand what corporations regard as too high a premium in yield, noncallable bonds are issued. This was the case in the 1990s, when most bond issues were noncallable. This experience contrasts with that of the 1970s, when almost all were callable. When corporate bonds are callable, they usually provide the investor with deferred call protection. For a long-term industrial bond issue, the typical deferment period is 10 years, whereas that for a public utility is 5 years.

The call provision gives the company flexibility. If interest rates should decline significantly, it can call the bonds and refinance the issue at a lower interest cost. Thus, the company does not have to wait until the final maturity to refinance. In addition, the provision may be advantageous to the company if it finds any of the protective covenants in the bond indenture to be unduly restrictive.

Refunding versus Redemption

The deferment period protects the investor from early call. However, this protection is not always what it seems. Many issues reserve the right to redeem a bond issue at any time under a set of conditions different from those that govern the call. In most bond indentures, call deferment is restricted to situations where a refunding takes place. By **refunding,** we mean refinancing the bond issue with a new bond issue at a lower interest cost.

However, many bond issues can be **redeemed** provided the source of the redemption is not a refunding. It may be the issuer has excess liquidity, or it can sell assets. It might issue common stock or be acquired in a merger. As long as the funds used to redeem the bond issue do not come from a new one, the investor has no call protection. As though this were not bad enough, the redemption price often is the face value of the bond as opposed to the higher call price. The line of demarcation between a call and a redemption is blurred. For example, if a company redeems a bond issue out of cash and later issues bonds to restore its liquidity, is it a redemption or a call? Sometimes legal redress is sought, but seldom does the investor win.

Value of Call Privilege

Although the call privilege is beneficial to the issuing corporation, it works to the detriment of investors. If interest rates fall and the bond issue is called, they can invest in other bonds only at a sacrifice in yield to maturity. Consequently, the call privilege usually does not come free to the borrower. Its cost, or value, is measured at the time of issuance by the difference in yield on the callable bond and the yield that would be necessary if the security were noncallable. This value is determined by supply and demand forces in the market for callable securities. When interest rates are high and expected to fall, the call feature is likely to have significant value. Investors are unwilling to invest in callable bonds unless such bonds yield more than bonds that are noncallable, all other things the same. In other words, they must be compensated for assuming the risk that the bonds might be called. On the other hand, borrowers are willing to pay a premium in yield for the call privilege in the belief that yields will fall and that it will be advantageous to refund the bonds.

When interest rates are low and expected to rise, the call privilege may have a negligible value in that the company might pay the same yield if there were no call privilege. The key factor is that the borrower has to be able to refund the issue at a profit and that cannot be done unless interest rates drop significantly, for the issuer must pay the call price—which is usually at a premium above face value—as well as the flotation costs involved in refinancing. If there is no probability that the borrower can refund the issue at a profit, the call privilege is unlikely to have a value.

Valuation in an Option Pricing Context   The call feature, of course, is an option given by investors to the corporation. Consequently, much of the thinking that went into our discussion of the option pricing theory in Chapter 5 applies here. Rather than the variance of a common stock's value determining the value of the option, in this case it is the variance of future interest rates. The greater the expected volatility of future interest rates, the greater the value of the call option.

More volatility increases the value of the call option.

This concept is illustrated in Fig. 20-1. In the figure we assume that the call option pertains only to a given future date. In other words, the option can be exercised at only one time, this being the option date. The value of the bond appears on the vertical axis, and the interest rate in the market on the horizontal axis. For a noncallable bond, value decreases at a decreasing rate as the interest rate increases. For a callable bond, value is constrained on the upside by the call price. This occurs for lower levels of interest rates—to the left of X on the horizontal axis. In this range, the difference between the value of a noncallable bond and the value of

FIGURE 20-1
Valuation of callable bond on the option date

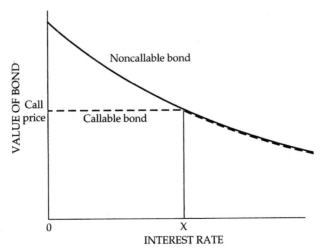

a callable bond represents the value of the option on the option date. If interest rates are such that the bond's value as a noncallable bond is less than the call price, the company obviously will not call the issue. As a result, the value of the callable bond is the same as that of a noncallable bond for interest rates higher than X on the horizontal axis. The key to valuation of the option is the likelihood that interest rates will be less than X on the horizontal axis on the option date. The greater the variance, the greater the expected value of call option to the company.

Equilibrium Pricing The equilibration mechanism for valuation is

$$\text{Callable bond} = \text{Noncallable bond} - \text{Call option} \qquad (20\text{-}1)$$

where the noncallable bond is identical to the callable bond in all respects except the call feature. The greater the value of the call feature, the lower the value of the callable bond relative to that of the noncallable one. The level and volatility of interest rates are key factors in giving value to the call feature. A sharp drop in interest rates will cause the option to have more value. In turn, such a drop is related to volatility.

Once the call option has been valued, Eq. (20-1) may be used to determine if the callable bond and the noncallable bond are mispriced. This type of analysis identifies arbitrage opportunities. For example, if it were determined that the standard deviation of bond returns necessary to bring about the equality was 26 percent, and you believed 15 percent was more realistic, you would conclude the two bonds were mispriced. More specifically, the noncallable bond in Eq. (20-1) is priced too high in relation to the callable one. This is merely to say that if the "true" standard deviation is 15 percent, then the call option is less valuable than the difference in prices of the two bonds would suggest. To arbitrage, you would buy the callable bond and sell short the noncallable bond.

Refunding a Bond Issue

Refunding is the replacement of one bond, through calling it, with another at a lower interest cost.

In this section, we analyze the profitability of a company refunding a bond issue before its maturity. By *refunding*, we mean calling the issue and replacing it with a new issue of bonds. In this regard, we focus our attention on only one reason for refunding—profitability—which, in turn, is due to interest rates having declined since the bonds were issued.

Analysis in a Capital Budgeting Framework The refunding decision can be regarded as a form of capital budgeting: There is an initial cash outlay followed by future interest savings. These savings are represented by the difference between the annual cash outflow required under the old bonds and the net cash outflow required on the new, or refunding, bonds. Calculating the initial cash outlay is more complex. Consequently, it is best to show an example of this method of evaluation.[2]

A company currently has a $20 million, 10 percent debenture issue outstanding, and the issue still has 20 years to final maturity. Because interest rates are significantly lower than at the time of the original offering, the company can now sell a $20 million issue of 20-year bonds at a coupon rate of 8 percent that will net it $19,600,000 after the underwriting spread.

---

[2]This example draws on Oswald D. Bowlin, "The Refunding Decision: Another Special Case in Capital Budgeting," *Journal of Finance*, 21 (March 1966), 55–68.

Cash Outlay For federal income tax purposes, the unamortized issuing expense of the old bonds, the call premium, and the unamortized discount of the old bonds, if they were sold at a discount, are deductible as expenses in the year of the refunding. The old bonds were sold originally at a slight discount from par value, and the unamortized portion now is $200,000. Moreover, the legal fees and other issuing expenses involved with the old bonds have an unamortized balance of $100,000. The call price on the old bonds is $109, issuing expenses on the new bonds are $150,000, the income tax rate is 40 percent, and there is a 1-month period of overlap. The period of overlap is the lag between the time the new bonds are sold and the time the old bonds are called. This lag occurs because most companies wish to have the proceeds from the new issue on hand before they call the old issue. Otherwise, there is a certain amount of risk associated with calling the old issue and being at the mercy of the bond market in raising new funds. During the period of overlap, the company pays interest on both bond issues.

With this rather involved background information in mind, we can calculate the initial cash outflow and the future cash benefits. The net cash outflow at the time of the refunding is as follows:

Cost of calling old bonds (call price $109)		$21,800,000
Net proceeds of new bond issue		19,600,000
Difference		$ 2,200,000
Expenses		
Issuing expense of new bonds	$ 150,000	
Interest expense on old bonds during		
overlap period ($20 million × 10%/12)	166,667	316,667
Gross cash outlay		$ 2,516,667
Less tax savings		
Interest expense on old bonds during		
overlap period	166,667	
Call premium	1,800,000	
Unamortized discount on old bonds	200,000	
Unamortized issuing expense on old		
bonds	100,000	
Total	$2,266,667	
Tax savings (40% of amount above)		906,667
Net cash outflow		$ 1,610,000

For ease of presentation, we ignore any interest that might be earned by investing the refunding bond proceeds in marketable securities during the 1-month period of overlap.

Net Cash Benefits The annual net cash benefits may be determined by calculating the difference between the net cash outflow required on the old bonds and the net cash outflow required on the new or refunding bonds. We assume for simplicity that interest is paid only once a year, at year end. The annual net cash outflow on the old bonds is

Interest expense (10%)		$2,000,000
Less: Tax savings		
Interest expense	$2,000,000	
Amortization of bond discount ($200,000/20)	10,000	
Amortization of issuing costs ($100,000/20)	5,000	
Total	$2,015,000	
Tax savings (40% of above amount)		806,000
Annual net cash outflow, old bonds		$1,194,000

The annual net cash outflow on the new bonds is

Interest expense (8%)		$1,600,000
Less: Tax savings		
Interest expense	$1,600,000	
Amortization of bond discount ($400,000/20)	20,000	
Amortization of issuing costs ($150,000/20)	7,500	
Total	$1,627,500	
Tax savings (40% of amount above)		651,000
Annual net cash outflow, new bonds		$ 949,000
Difference between annual net cash outflows		
($1,194,000 − $949,000)		$ 245,000

Discounting Thus, for an initial net cash outflow of $1,610,000, the company can achieve annual net cash benefits of $245,000 over the next 20 years. Because the net cash benefits occur in the future, they must be discounted back to present value. But what discount rate should be used? Certain authors advocate the use of the cost of capital. However, a refunding operation differs from other investment proposals. Once the new bonds are sold, the net cash benefits are known with certainty. From the standpoint of the corporation, the refunding operation is essentially a riskless investment project. The only risks associated with the cash flows are that of the firm defaulting in the payment of principal or interest. Because a premium for default risk is embodied in the market rate of interest, most agree that the appropriate discount rate is the after-tax cost of debt on the refunding bonds.

For our example, this is 8% $(1 - .40) = 4.8\%$. Using this as the discount rate, the net present value of the refunding is $1,495,689. As this amount is positive and relatively large, the refunding operation is quite worthwhile.

Some Qualifications Several points should be raised with respect to the calculations in our example. First, most firms refund an existing issue with a new bond issue of a longer maturity. In our example, we assumed that the new bond issue has the same maturity as that of the old bond issue. The analysis needs to be modified somewhat when the maturity dates are different. The usual procedure is to consider only the net cash benefits up to the maturity of the old bonds. A second assumption in our example was that neither issue involved sinking-fund bonds or serial bonds. If either issue calls for periodic reduction of the debt, we must adjust our procedure for determining future net cash benefits. Finally, the annual cash outflows associated with the refunding bonds usually are less than those associated with the refunded bonds. As a result, effectively there is a decrease in the leverage of the firm. Although this effect is likely to be small, leverage is not held constant. To remedy these problems, one may wish to use something different.

Timing of Refunding

We must recognize that just because a refunding operation is found to be worthwhile, it should not necessarily be undertaken right away. If interest rates are declining, and this decline is expected to continue, management may prefer to delay the refunding. At a later date, the refunding bonds can be sold at an even lower rate of interest, making the refunding operation even more worthwhile. The decision concerning timing must be based on expectations of future interest rates. In determining whether or not to postpone refunding, the financial manager should also consider the dispersion and shape of the probability distribution of possible future interest rates.

PRIVATE PLACEMENTS

Private placements of securities with institutional investors have increased in importance relative to public offerings.

Rather than sell securities to the public, a corporation can sell the entire issue to a single institutional investor or a small group of such investors. This type of sale is known as a **private placement**, for the company negotiates directly with the investor over the terms of the offering, eliminating the function of the underwriter. The typical private-placement borrower is medium size, as large firms borrow in the public bond market and smaller companies borrow from banks.[3]

Features

One of the more frequently mentioned advantages of a private placement is the speed of the commitment. A public issue must be registered with the SEC, documents prepared and printed, and extensive negotiations undertaken. All of this requires a certain lead time. With a private placement the terms can be tailored to the needs of the borrower, and the financing can be consummated quickly. (The large corporation also can quickly tap the public market through a shelf registration, described in Chapter 19.) The fact that there is only a single investor or small group of investors is attractive if it becomes necessary to change any of the terms of the issue. Renegotiation is nearly impossible with a public issue, whereas with a private one the contracting between borrower and lender is fashioned to the situation.

Another advantage of a privately placed debt issue is that the actual borrowing does not necessarily have to take place all at once. The company can enter into an arrangement whereby it can borrow up to a fixed amount over a period of time. For this nonrevolving credit arrangement, the borrower usually will pay a commitment fee. Because the private placement does not have to be registered with the SEC, the company avoids making certain detailed information available to the

---

[3]See Mark S. Carey, Stephen D. Prowse, John D. Rea, and Gregory F. Udell, "Recent Developments in the Market for Privately Placed Debt," *Federal Reserve Bulletin,* 79 (February 1993), 77–92.

public. As to costs, private placements usually bear a slightly higher interest rate than a public bond issue but lower flotation costs. Many of the fixed costs of a public bond issue are avoided with a private placement. Whether the advantages of the private placement outweigh the higher interest cost depends on the circumstances.

Developments in the Market

The private-placement market has enjoyed considerable popularity over the last two decades. Lenders can craft protective covenants that preclude the borrower from being restructured to the disadvantage of the lender, such as occurs when it takes on substantial additional debt. The expropriation of bondholder wealth, known as *event risk,* is prevalent in the public market. Under **Rule 144A** of the SEC, institutional investors are able to sell private-placement securities to other qualified institutional investors. This allowance for secondary trading brings liquidity to the market, and the distinction between private placements and public market has blurred. Further blurring is caused by the fact that securities firms now underwrite private placements. In fact, most speculative-grade (junk) bonds today are issued in the private-placement market. Known as "144A" issues, many of them are as liquid as public-bond issues. Remember that the market for corporate bonds is largely an institutional investor market, and 144A issues can now be bought and sold as easily as public issues of comparable grade and maturity. When liquidity in the overall junk market dries up from time to time, as described earlier, there is little distinction between private and publicly issued bonds.

PREFERRED STOCK

Preferred stock is a hybrid form of financing, combining features of debt and common stock. In the event of liquidation, a preferred stockholder's claim on assets comes after that of creditors but before that of common stockholders. Usually, this claim is restricted to the par value of the stock. If the par value of a share of preferred stock is $100, the investor will be entitled to a maximum of $100 in settlement of the principal amount. Although preferred stock carries a stipulated dividend, the actual payment of a dividend is a discretionary rather than a fixed obligation of the company. The omission of a dividend will not result in a default of the obligation or insolvency of the company, as will failure to make an interest payment on its debt. The board of directors has full power to omit a preferred stock dividend if the financial condition of the company should deteriorate. From the standpoint of creditors, preferred stock adds to the equity base of the company and enhances the ability of the company to borrow in the future.

> **Preferred stock** is a form of fixed-income security, but the dividend is at the discretion of the company's board.

The maximum return to preferred stockholders usually is limited to the specified dividend, and these stockholders ordinarily do not share in the residual earnings of the company. Thus, if you own 100 shares of $8\frac{1}{2}$ percent preferred stock, $50 par value, the maximum return you can expect in any one year is $425, and this return is at the discretion of the board of directors.

Cumulative Feature

Almost all preferred stocks have a cumulative feature, providing for unpaid dividends in any one year to be carried forward. Before the company can pay a dividend on its common stock, it must pay dividends **in arrears** on its preferred stock. A board of directors may omit the preferred stock dividend on a company's 8 percent cumulative preferred stock for 3 consecutive years. If the stock has a $100 par value, the company would be $24 per share in arrears on its preferred stock. Before it can pay a dividend to its common stockholders, it must pay preferred stockholders $24 for each share of preferred stock held. It should be emphasized that just because preferred stock dividends are in arrears, there is no guarantee that they will ever be paid. If the corporation has no intention of paying a common stock dividend, there is no need to clear up the arrearage on the preferred. The preferred stock dividend typically is omitted for lack of earnings, but the corporation does not have to pay a dividend if earnings are restored.

Cumulative feature appears in most all preferred stock issues.

If the preferred stock dividends are in arrears, and the company wishes to pay a common stock dividend, it may choose not to clear up the arrearage but to make an exchange offering to preferred stockholders. Say that the dividend arrearages on an issue of $100 par value preferred stock are $56 and that the market price of the stock is $61 a share. The company might offer preferred stockholders common stock in the company, valued at $110, for each share of preferred stock held. Although theoretically the preferred stockholder is asked to give up $156 ($100 par value plus $56 dividend arrearages), the exchange offering promises $110 relative to a current preferred stock market value of only $61 per share. To eliminate the preferred stock, the company must obtain the approval of a required percentage of the stock outstanding, often two-thirds. Consequently, it probably will make its exchange offering contingent on obtaining the required acceptance.

Voting Power

Because of their prior claim on assets and income, preferred stockholders normally are not given a voice in management unless the company is unable to pay preferred stock dividends during a specified period of time. Arrearages on four quarterly dividend payments might constitute such a default, and under such circumstances, preferred stockholders as a class would be entitled to elect a specific number of directors. Usually, the number of directors is rather small in relation to the total, and by the time the preferred stockholders obtain a voice in management, the company probably is in considerable financial difficulty. Consequently, the voting power that preferred stockholders are granted may be virtually meaningless.

Depending on the agreement between the preferred stockholders and the company, they may obtain voting power under other conditions as well. The company may default under restrictions in the agreement that are similar to those found in a loan agreement or a bond indenture. One of the more frequently imposed restrictions is that dividends on common stock are prohibited if the company does not satisfy certain financial ratios. We note, however, that default under any of the provisions of the agreement between the corporation and its preferred stockholders does not result in the obligation's becoming immediately payable, as does default under a loan agreement or bond indenture. The preferred stockholders merely are given a voice in management and assurance that common stock dividends will not be paid during the period of default. Thus, preferred stockholders do not have nearly the same legal power in default as do debt holders.

Retirement of Preferred Stock

The fact that preferred stock, like common stock, has no maturity does not mean that most preferred stock issues will remain outstanding forever, because provision for retirement of the stock invariably is made.

Call Feature   Almost all preferred stock issues have a stated call price, which is above the original issuance price and decreases over time. Like the call feature on bonds, the call feature on preferred stock affords the company flexibility. Because the market price of a straight preferred stock tends to fluctuate in keeping with interest-rate cycles, the value of the preferred stock call feature is determined by the same considerations as is the call feature for bonds, which we discussed earlier. Unlike preferred stock, long-term debt has a final maturity that assures the eventual retirement of the issue. Without a call feature on preferred stock, the corporation would be able to retire the issue only by the often more expensive and less efficient methods of purchasing the stock in the open market, inviting *tenders* of stock from preferred stockholders at a price above the market price, or offering the preferred stockholders another security in its place.

Sinking Fund   Many preferred stock issues provide for a sinking fund, which partially assures an orderly retirement of the stock. Like bond issues, a preferred stock sinking fund may be advantageous to investors because the retirement process exerts upward pressure on the market price of the remaining shares. However, the issuing corporation often has the option to make payment in cash or with preferred shares it purchases in the market, and this option works to the investor's disadvantage.

Convertibility   Certain preferred stock issues are convertible into common stock at the option of the holder. Upon conversion, of course, the preferred stock is retired. Because virtually all convertible securities have a call feature, the company can force conversion by calling the preferred stock if the market price of the preferred is significantly above the call price. Convertible preferred stock is used frequently in the acquisition of other companies. In part, its use stems from the fact that the transaction is not taxable for the company that is acquired or its stockholders at the time of acquisition. It becomes a taxable transaction only when the preferred stock is sold. We shall examine convertible securities in much more detail in the next chapter.

Tax Treatment of Preferred Dividend

For individual investors, the preferred stock dividend is taxed as ordinary income. If the investor is a corporation, however, 70 percent is not subject to taxation. This is known as the **intercorporate dividend exclusion**, and it is designed to reduce the triple taxation of dividends that otherwise would occur (corporation to corporation to stockholder). Suppose Barton Biggs Company owns one share of preferred stock of William Sharpe Corporation, which pays a $2 dividend on its preferred. If Barton Biggs Company is in a 34 percent tax bracket, it will pay taxes of $2(1 - .70).34 = $0.204 on the dividend received.

   For the corporation, the preferred stock dividend paid is not deductible as an expense for tax purposes. This is a major disadvantage, resulting in straight, nonconvertible preferred stock seldom being used as a means of financing.

Tax-Deductible Preferred Stock

In recent years, instruments have been devised to get around this shortcoming. These are known as **tax-deductible preferreds**; as the name implies, they allow companies issuing them to secure the tax benefits usually associated only with a debt instrument. How is this possible? A special-purpose vehicle (**SPV**) is created. The SPV can be a limited partnership, a Delaware business trust, or an offshore subsidiary. It is simply a conduit; the SPV issues preferred stock to public investors. The proceeds are loaned to the parent company. The interest paid on the loan is deductible by the parent as an expense for tax purposes. The interest is used by the SPV to pay preferred stock dividends. The loan itself is subordinated to the parent's other debt, and usually is long term (e.g., 30 years). One other wrinkle is that payment of interest on the debt can be deferred for up to some maximum length, say, 5 years. Up to this time, the SPV cannot force the parent into bankruptcy for failure to pay interest.

The SPV itself is a nontaxable entity under U.S. tax law. The par value of tax-deductible preferred stock usually is set at $25, which finds favor with retail investors. The dividend paid does not qualify for the 70 percent intercorporate dividend exclusion. Even without this feature, tax-deductible preferred stock is the method of choice when it comes to preferred stock financing. Investment banks have come out with a number of variations of the instrument. Perhaps the most widely used are MIPS and TOPrS. The first, **MIPS**, stands for monthly income preferred stock, and Goldman Sachs pioneered the product in the early 1990s. As the name implies, dividends are paid monthly. Quarterly income preferred stock, **QUIPS**, provides quarterly income. **TOPrS** stands for trust-originated preferred stock, a Merrill Lynch product. Here the dividend is paid quarterly. The popularity of tax-deductible preferred stock is due not only to the tax advantage but also to the financial flexibility preferred stock in general affords.

Auction-Rate Preferred Stock

Finally in this section on preferred stock we consider an instrument whose interest rate floats with money market rates. This is known as **auction-rate preferred stock**, and here the 70 percent intercorporate dividend exclusion does apply. Consequently, the instrument is attractive to the corporate treasurer in managing the firm's marketable security position. In one variation of auction-rate preferred stock, money market preferred stock (MMP), the rate is set by auction every 49 days, which is beyond the minimum holding period required for a corporate investor to benefit from the corporate dividend federal tax exclusion.

The rate is established by the forces of supply and demand in keeping with money rates in general. A typical rate might be .75 times the commercial paper rate, with more creditworthy issuers commanding an even greater discount. As long as enough investors bid at each auction, the effective maturity date is 49 days. As a result, there is little variation in the market price of the investment over time. A failed auction represents a risk to the investor, but to date this has been rare. The tax arbitrage involved in this instrument, which benefits both investor and issuer, is at the expense of the federal government. For the issuer, the relevant cost comparison is with the after-tax cost of other methods of short-term financing.

PENSION FUND LIABILITY

Although it does not appear on the balance sheet, many companies have a contractual obligation to make present and future pension payments. Under the Employee Retirement Income Security Act of 1974 (ERISA), this liability is every bit as binding a claim as a federal tax lien and is senior to all other claims. In other words, it is very important and goes to the head of the line of creditors if the firm were to be liquidated. For some companies, this liability exceeds tangible assets. As a financial manager, you will be involved in any pension fund your company might have, so a basic understanding is essential.

Types of Pension Plans

Defined benefit plans are a liability of the employer to provide retirement benefits.

Corporate pension plans may be one of two types. A **defined benefit plan** either pays a retired employee so many dollars per month or it pays the individual a percentage of his or her average final salary. To illustrate the former, after 25 years a participant might be entitled to $44 times the number of years of service, or $1,100 per month. This is known as a *flat benefit formula*. With respect to the latter method, a person might be paid 2 percent of his or her average salary during the last 5 years of employment multiplied by the number of years of service. If these years were 20 and average monthly salary were $4,500, the monthly pension would be $1,800. This is known as a *unit benefit formula*. Under ERISA, a person who leaves a company prior to regular retirement age will qualify for pension benefits, provided that he or she has been with the firm a sufficient time. This provision is known as *vesting*. A plan must be 100 percent vested after a certain period of employment, the maximum length of time a company may take before fully vesting an employee being 10 years.

Defined contribution plans, where the employee accumulates assets in an individual account, are growing in importance.

The second type of plan is a **defined contribution plan.** Here a company agrees to make a specified monthly or annual payment to the pension plan. All contributions to the plan are a tax-deductible expense by the corporation. (Usually, these payments may be augmented by the employee making individual contributions on a voluntary basis.) The contributions are invested, and at retirement the employee is entitled to the cumulative total of contributions plus investment earnings on those contributions. Only when the employee retires and actually receives payment are taxes paid on the benefits. In the accumulation/investment phase, no taxes are paid. Actual future benefits paid to an employee are not known with certainty; they depend on what can be earned by investing the contributions. Because many corporations wish to avoid the liability associated with a defined benefit plan, defined contribution plans are growing in importance. As we are concerned with balance-sheet liabilities, however, our focus is on the defined-benefit plan.

Funded and Unfunded Liabilities

The pension liability of a company with a defined benefit plan is composed of two parts. There is the liability to currently retired employees. The present value of this obligation depends on their average life expectancy as well as the discount rate used. The second obligation is to employees not yet retired. This obligation is further subdivided into (1) the benefits earned by employees by virtue of past employment and (2) likely benefits to be earned based on future service. The latter is a forecast, and obviously subject to error. The total pension liability of a company must be valued, usually by an actuary. The idea is to determine the amount of funds necessary for a company to be able to make good on its pension obligations. The *present value of liabilities* is calculated by discounting to present value likely future benefits to be paid, where these benefits are based on past service as well as on expected future service.

Liability Sensitivity The magnitude of present-value liability obviously is sensitive to the discount rate employed—the higher the rate, the lower the liability. However, the rate must correspond to a realistic return on investment in stocks, bonds, and other assets. Usually, actuaries are conservative in the rate they use. This may make sense, inasmuch as they typically ignore the effect of inflation on future salaries and wages. By changing actuarial assumptions, companies sometimes are able to reduce pension fund liabilities in relation to assets. However, the change is an accounting one and usually does not affect the obligation in an economic sense. Moreover, auditors and government agencies restrict the degree to which "creative" actuarial changes can occur.

Asset Valuation   Once the liabilities are valued, the assets must be valued. This valuation process also consists of two parts. The first involves past corporate contributions. These contributions are paid to a trust or insurance company and are invested in a diversified portfolio of assets. The market value of this portfolio then is its value, although some actuaries value the portfolio using historical costs. The second part involves the present value of expected future contributions by the company for future service by employees. Again this is an estimate, and this total also is sensitive to the discount rate. The present value of assets is the sum of the two parts.

Unfunded Liability   It is desirable, of course, for the present value of the assets to equal the present value of the pension liabilities. This seldom is the case. When the former is less than the latter, there is said to be an unfunded liability, which is simply

$$\text{Unfunded liability} = PV \text{ of pension liabilities} - PV \text{ of pension assets} \quad (20\text{-}2)$$

If a company has an unfunded liability, it must be reported on the balance sheet as a liability[4] (FASB No. 87). If there is a surplus, nothing appears. For some companies, the unfunded liability is large and is a matter of concern to creditors. Why? Because it represents a claim that ultimately must be paid. If the underfunded plan is terminated, the company is responsible for the deficit up to 30 percent of its shareholders' equity. Credit- and bond-rating agencies are mindful of this obligation and analyze it closely before assigning a rating.

   We must recognize that the unfunded liability of a company is not a precise figure. It is an actuary's estimate and is subject to a number of assumptions. However, suppliers of capital should watch closely a company's unfunded liability and dig into the assumptions. For many a company, it simply is too large a potential liability to be ignored, despite problems of estimation. In fact, for some companies the unfunded pension liability dwarfs all other liabilities.

Other Aspects

If a company should go into bankruptcy and there are not enough funds on hand to meet its pension obligations, the Pension Benefit Guarantee Corporation (PBGC) makes good on most of the total obligation. This government agency is funded by premiums paid to it by companies with pension plans. Because the premium is invariant with respect to default risk, there is option pricing gamesmanship to it. From the standpoint of the stockholders of a company, the bias is for the pension fund to invest in risky assets. If the investments go well, they gain in enhanced share value; if badly, the PBGC is left holding the bag. Over time, Congress has reduced some of the avenues by which companies play "games" against the PBGC.

   Throughout our discussion, we have dealt with pensions for nonunion employees. Unions have their own pension plans, and the labor contracts they negoti-

---

[4]As accountants are wont to do, smoothing is possible for companies that have a sudden change putting them in an unfunded liability position. First, they can spread the effect over several years. Second, they can record an intangible asset (for more productive employees!), which is amortized over several years.

ate with corporations include contributions to the union pension fund. Union employees look to this fund and not to the company's for their retirement income.

With respect to accounting for pension expenses, FASB No. 87 is explicit. There are four components: (1) the interest cost, which is the interest rate times the pension liability; (2) the service cost for additional benefits that employees earn during the year; (3) amortization of any accumulated deficit in the pension fund (unfunded liability); and (4) the expected investment return. The pension expense recorded is the sum of the first three components, offset by No. 4. This expense usually differs from the cash actually contributed to the plan for the year. FASB No. 87 brought a consistent treatment of pension expense accounting together with bringing pension liability firmly onto the balance sheet. This clearly has forced senior management to pay attention to the company's pension liability and pension management, which was the intent.

An important responsibility of the financial manager is to oversee the management of the pension fund's investments. This involves determining asset allocations, choosing investment managers, and monitoring their investment performance. These responsibilities are in addition to analyzing actuarial assumptions, determining the proper funding of a plan, and overseeing the record keeping.

 ## Summary

The principal features of debt include the fixed- or floating-rate return, the final maturity, the priority claim on assets, the credit quality (going from the highest investment-grade to junk bonds), the call privilege, and the presence or absence of a sinking-fund provision.

In financing with long-term debt, the company must bargain with investors over the terms of the debt instrument. If the company wishes to include terms that are not beneficial to investors, it must be prepared to pay a higher yield in order to sell the instrument. If debentures are subordinated, investors will demand a higher yield than if the issue involves straight debentures. Another interesting aspect of the bargaining process relates to the call privilege. If interest-rate expectations in the market lead investors to think that the issue may be called, the company will have to pay a higher yield for the privilege of being able to call it. As with any option, the value of it depends on variability; for the call option, the variance of future interest rates is paramount. When there is a call feature on a bond, one method for analyzing the refunding of the issue before maturity treats the refunding operation as a riskless capital budgeting project.

Rather than offer securities to the general public, a company may place them privately with an institutional investor. With a private placement, the company negotiates directly with the investor; there is no underwriting and no registration of the issue with the SEC. The private placement has the virtue of flexibility and affords the medium-sized and even the small company the opportunity to sell its securities.

Preferred stock is a hybrid form of security having characteristics of both debt and common stock. The payment of dividends is not a legal but a discretionary obligation, although many companies regard the obligation as fixed. Preferred stockholders' claims on assets and income come after those of creditors but before those of common stockholders. The return on their investment is almost always limited to the specified dividend. Because preferred stock has no final maturity, almost all issues have call features that give the corporation financial flexibility. Tax-deductible preferred stock allows the corporate issuer, through a special purpose corporation, to deduct the payment as an expense for tax purposes. Most issuers of preferred stock use this vehicle, though it does not permit the 70 percent intercorporate dividend exclusion. This exclusion does apply to auction-rate preferred stock, a floating rate instrument.

The financial manager necessarily is involved in the company's pension plan. Many corporate plans involve defined benefits, and the present value of the pension liability must be compared with the present value of assets earmarked to meet that obligation. If the former exceeds the latter, the company has an unfunded liability. The magnitude of this liability as well as the assumptions inherent in its calculation should be watched closely by suppliers of capital, for pensions are a prior claim in the event of liquidation.

■ Self-Correction Problems

1. The Lemand Corporation has $8 million of 10 percent mortgage bonds outstanding under an open-end indenture. The indenture allows additional bonds to be issued as long as all the following conditions are met:
   a. Pre-tax interest coverage [(income before taxes + bond interest)/bond interest] remains greater than 4.
   b. Net depreciated value of mortgaged assets remains twice the amount of mortgage debt.
   c. Debt-to-equity ratio remains below .5.

   The Lemand Corporation has net income after taxes of $2.4 million and a 40 percent tax rate, $40 million in equity, and $30 million in depreciated assets, covered by the mortgage. Assuming that 50 percent of the proceeds of a new issue would be added to the base of mortgaged assets and that the company has no sinking-fund payments until next year, how much more 10 percent debt could be sold under each of the three conditions? Which protective covenant is binding?

2. Northern California Public Service Company is considering refunding its preferred stock. The dividend rate on this stock is $6, and it has a par value of $50 a share. The call price is $52 a share, and 500,000 shares are outstanding. George Arroya, vice-president of finance, feels the company can issue new preferred stock in the current market at an interest rate of 11 percent. With this rate, the new issue could be sold at par; the total par value of the issue would be $25 million. Flotation costs of $780,000 are tax deductible, but the call premium is not tax deductible; the company's marginal tax rate is 30 percent. A 90-day period of overlap is expected between the time the new preferred stock is issued and the time the old preferred stock is retired. Should the company refund its preferred stock using a capital budgeting analysis of refunding?

3.
   a. Alvarez Apparel, Inc., could sell preferred stock with a dividend cost of 8 percent. If it were to sell bonds in the current market, the interest rate cost would be 9 percent. The company is in a 40 percent tax bracket. What is the after-tax cost of each of these methods of financing?
   b. Setlec Corporation holds a limited number of preferred stocks in its marketable security portfolio. It is in a 36 percent tax bracket. If it were to invest in the preferred stock of Alvarez Apparel, what would be its after-tax return? What would be its after-tax return if it were to invest in the bonds?

Problems

1. Bragon Manufacturing Company has in its capital structure $20 million of $13\frac{1}{2}$ percent sinking-fund debentures. The sinking-fund call price is $1,000 per bond, and sinking-fund payments of $1 million in face amount of bonds are required annually. Presently, the yield to maturity on the debentures in the market is 12.21 percent.

   a. To satisfy the sinking-fund payment, should the company deliver cash to the trustee or bonds?

   b. What if the yield to maturity were 14.60 percent?

2. The Hirsch Corporation is in bankruptcy. Mortgaged assets have been sold for $5 million, and other assets have yielded $10 million. Hirsch has $10 million in mortgage bonds, $5 million in subordinated (to the mortgage bonds) debentures, $15 million owed to general creditors, and $10 million par value of common stock. How would distribution of the $15 million in liquidating value be made?

3. Crakow Machine Company wishes to borrow $10 million for 10 years. It can issue either a noncallable bond at 11.40 percent interest or a bond callable at the end of 5 years for 12 percent. For simplicity, we assume that the bond will be called only at the end of year 5. The interest rate that is likely to prevail 5 years hence for a 5-year straight bond can be described by the following probability distribution:

Interest rate	9%	10%	11%	12%	13%
Probability	.1	.2	.4	.2	.1

   Issuing and other costs involved in selling a bond issue 5 years hence will total $200,000. The call price is assumed to be par.

   a. (1) What is the total absolute amount of interest payments for the noncallable issue over the 10 years? (Do not discount.) (2) What is the expected value of total interest payments and other costs if the company issues callable bonds? (Assume that the company calls the bonds and issues new ones only if there is a savings in interest costs after issuing expenses.) (3) On the basis of total costs, should the company issue noncallable or callable bonds?

   b. What would be the outcome if the probability distribution of interest rates 5 years hence were the following?

Interest rate	7%	9%	11%	13%	15%
Probability	.2	.2	.2	.2	.2

Assume that all other conditions stay the same.

4. Five years ago, Zapada International issued $50 million of 10 percent, 25-year debentures at a price of $990 per bond to the public. The call price was originally $1,100 per bond the first year after issuance, and this price declined by $10 each subsequent year. Zapada now is calling the bonds in order to refund them at a lower interest rate.

   a. Ignoring taxes, what is the bondholder's return on investment for the 5 years? (Assume that interest is paid once a year and that the investor owns one bond.)

   b. If the bondholder can now invest $1,000 in a 20-year bond of equivalent risk that provides 8 percent interest, what is his overall cash-flow return over the 25-year holding period? How does this compare with the return on the Zapada bonds had they not been called? (Assume again that interest is paid once a year.)

5. The U.S. Zither Corporation has $50 million of 14 percent debentures outstanding, which are due in 25 years. USZ could refund these bonds in the current market with new 25-year bonds, sold to the public at par ($1,000 per bond) with a 12 percent coupon rate. The spread to the underwriter is 1 percent, leaving $990 per bond in proceeds to the company. The old bonds have an unamortized discount of $1 million, unamortized legal fees and other expenses of $100,000, and a call price of $1,140 per bond ($114 on $100 face value convention). The tax rate is 40 percent. There is a 1-month overlap during which both issues are outstanding, and issuing expenses are $200,000. Compute the present value of the refunding, using the after-tax rate on the new bonds as the discount rate. Is the refunding worthwhile?

6. The Riting Railroad needs to raise $9.5 million for capital improvements. One possibility is a new preferred stock issue: 8 percent, $100 par value stock that would yield 9 percent to investors. Flotation costs for an issue this size amount to 5 percent of the total amount of preferred stock sold; these costs are deducted from gross proceeds in determining the net proceeds to the company. (Ignore any tax considerations.)

   a. At what price per share will the preferred stock be offered to investors? (Assume that the issue will never be called.)

   b. How many shares must be issued to raise $9.5 million for Riting Railroad?

7. Lost Horizon Silver Mining Company has 200,000 shares of $7 cumulative preferred stock outstanding, $100 par value. The preferred stock has a participating feature. If dividends on the common stock exceed $1 per share, preferred stockholders receive additional dividends per share equal to one-half of the excess. In other words, if the common stock dividend were $2, preferred stockholders would receive an additional dividend of $.50. The company has 1 million shares of common outstanding. What would dividends per share be on the preferred stock and on the common stock if earnings available for dividends in three successive years were (a) $1,000,000, $600,000, and $3,000,000; (b) $2,000,000, $2,400,000 and $4,600,000; and (c) $1,000,000, $2,500,000, and $5,700,000. (Assume that all the available earnings are paid in dividends, but nothing more is paid.)

8. Solie Sod and Seed Company (SSS) has a defined benefit pension plan for its salaried employees. The balance sheet of the plan has the following format:

Value of existing pension fund assets	PV of expected benefits to retired employees
PV of expected future contributions	PV of expected benefits for future service
Total assets	Total pension fund liabilities

Presently, the fund has an unfunded liability. Determine in general the effect of each of the following on the appropriate balance sheet item and on the unfunded liability:

a. Sal Zambrano joins the firm and is expected to be entitled to a pension of $25,000 a year starting in 20 years.

b. In a good earnings year, SSS buys $400,000 in bonds and contributes them to the plan over and above its regular contribution.

c. In view of inflation, SSS raises the monthly pension of existing retirees by $10 per month.

d. As interest rates have risen, the discount rate used for determining present values is raised by 1 percent.

Solutions to Self-Correction Problems

1. (Dollars in millions) Let x = the number of millions of dollars of new debt that can be issued.

a.
$$\frac{\$4.0 + \$0.8 + .10x}{\$0.8 + .10x} = 4$$
$$\$3.2 + .40x = \$4.8 + .10x$$
$$.30x = \$1.6$$
$$x = \$5.333$$

b.
$$\frac{\$30 + .5x}{\$8 + x} = 2$$
$$\$16 + 2x = \$30 + .5x$$
$$1.5x = \$14$$
$$x = \$9.333$$

c.
$$\frac{\$8 + x}{\$40} = .5$$
$$\$8 + x = \$20$$
$$x = \$12$$

Condition a is binding, and it limits the amount of new debt to $5.333 million. The advantage of an open-end mortgage is that additional debt can be issued under an existing lien, subject to limitations such as those posed in this problem.

2. Net cash outflow:

Cost of calling old preferred ($52)	$26,000,000
Net proceeds of new issue: $25 million –	
flotation costs of $780,000	24,220,000
Difference	$ 1,780,000
Preferred stock dividends on old	
preferred during overlap	750,000
Gross cash outlay	$ 2,530,000
Less: Tax savings on flotation costs	
$780,000 (.3)	234,000
Net cash outflow	$ 2,296,000
Annual net cash outflow on old preferred:	
Preferred stock dividend	$ 3,000,000
Annual net cash outflow on new preferred:	
Preferred stock dividend	$ 2,750,000
Difference	$ 250,000

Discounted at a rate of 11 percent for a perpetuity:

$$PV = \frac{\$250,000}{.11} = \$2,272,727$$

The preferred stock issue should not be refunded. The net benefit is negative ($2,272,727 − $2,296,000).

3. a. After-tax cost:

Preferred stock = 8%
Bonds = 9% (1 − .40) = 5.40%

   b. The dividend income to a corporate investor is 70 percent exempt from taxation. With a corporate tax rate of 36 percent, we have for the preferred stock:

After-tax return = 8% [1 − .3(.36)] = 7.14%
For the bonds, after-tax return = 9%(1 − .36) = 5.76%

Selected References

ALDERSON, MICHAEL J., and DONALD R. FRASER, "Financial Innovation and Excesses Revisited: The Case of Auction Rate Preferred Stock," *Financial Management*, 22 (Summer 1993), 61–75.

ANG, JAMES S., "The Two Faces of Bond Refunding," *Journal of Finance*, 20 (June 1975), 869–74.

BLACK, FISCHER, "The Tax Consequences of Long Run Pension Policy," *Financial Analysts Journal*, 36 (July–August 1980), 21–28.

BLUME, MARSHALL D., FELIX LIM, and A. CRAIG MACKINLAY, "The Declining Credit Quality of U.S. Corporate Debt: Myth or Reality?" *Journal of Finance*, 53 (August 1998), 1389–1413.

BOWLIN, MARSHALL E., FELIX LIM, and A, CRAIG MACKINLAY, "The Declining Credit Quality of U.S. Corporate Debt: Myth or Reality?" *Journal of Finance,* 53 (August 1998), 1389–1413.

CAREY, MARK "Credit Risk in Private Debt Portfolios," *Journal of Finance,* 53 (August 1998), 1363–87.

CRABBE, LELAND E., and JEAN HELWEGE, "Alternative Tests of Agency Theories of Callable Corporate Bonds," *Financial Management,* 23 (Winter 1994), 3–20.

DONALDSON, GORDON, "In Defense of Preferred Stock," *Harvard Business Review,* 40 (July–August 1962), 123–36.

DYL, EDWARD A., and MICHAEL D. JOEHNK, "Sinking Funds and the Cost of Corporate Debt," *Journal of Finance,* 34 (September 1979), 887–94.

FENN, GEORGE W., "Speed of Issuance and the Adequacy of Disclosure in the 144A High-Yield Debt Market," *Journal of Financial Economics,* 58 (June 2000), 383–405.

FRIDSON, MARTIN S., and M. CHRISTOPHER GARMAN, "Valuing Like-Rated Senior and Subordinated Debt," *Journal of Fixed Income,* 7 (December 1997), 83–93.

HAND, JOHN R. M., ROBERT W. HOLTHAUSEN, and RICHARD W. LEFTWICH, "The Effect of Bond Rating Agency Announcements on Bond and Stock Prices," *Journal of Finance,* 47 (June 1992), 733–52.

HO, ANDREW, and MICHAEL ZARETSKY, "Valuation of Sinking Fund Bonds," *Journal of Fixed Income,* 3 (June 1993), 25–31.

HO, THOMAS, and RONALD F. SINGER, "Bond Indenture Provisions and the Risk of Corporate Debt," *Journal of Financial Economics,* 10 (December 1982), 375–406.

JEWELL, JEFF, and MILES LIVINGSTON, "Split Ratings, Bond Yields, and Underwriter Spreads," *Journal of Financial Research,* 21 (Summer 1998), 185–204.

KALOTAY, ANDREW J., and GEORGE O. WILLIAMS, "The Valuation and Management of Bonds with Sinking Fund Provisions," *Financial Analysts Journal,* 48 (March–April 1992), 59–67.

KHANNA, ARUN, and JOHN J. MCCONNELL, "MIPS, QUIPS and TOPrS: Old Wine in New Bottles," *Journal of Applied Corporate Finance,* 11 (Spring 1998), 39–44.

MCCONNELL, JOHN J., and GARY G. SCHLARBAUM, "Returns, Risks, and Pricing of Income Bonds, 1956–76," *Journal of Business,* 54 (January 1981), 33–57.

MCGILL, DAN M., and DONALD S. GRUBBS JR., *Fundamentals of Private Pensions,* 7th ed. Homewood, IL: Pension Research Council, Richard D. Irwin, 1992.

MITCHELL, KARLYN, "The Call, Sinking Fund, and Term-to-Maturity Features of Corporate Bonds: An Empirical Investigation," *Journal of Financial and Quantitative Analysis,* 26 (June 1991), 201–22.

OFER, AHARON R., and ROBERT A. TAGGART JR., "Bonding Refunding: A Clarifying Analysis," *Journal of Finance,* 32 (March 1977), 21–30.

PETERSEN, MITCHELL A., "Cash Flow Variability and Firm's Pension Choice: A Role for Operating Leverage," *Journal of Financial Economics,* 36 (December 1994), 361–83.

TEPPER, IRWIN, "Taxation and Corporate Pension Policy," *Journal of Finance,* 36 (March 1981), 1–14.

VAN HORNE, JAMES C., "Implied Fixed Costs in Long-Term Debt Issues," *Journal of Financial and Quantitative Analysis,* 8 (December 1973), 821–34.

———, "Called Bonds: How Does the Investor Fare?" *Journal of Portfolio Management,* 6 (Summer 1980), 58–61.

———, *Financial Market Rates and Flows,* 6th ed. Upper Saddle River, NJ: Prentice Hall, 2001.

Wachowicz's Web World is an excellent overall Web site produced and maintained by my coauthor of *Fundamentals of Financial Management,* John M. Wachowicz Jr. It contains descriptions of and links to many finance Web sites and articles. *www.prenhall.com/wachowicz.*

Hybrid Financing through Equity-Linked Securities

I n this chapter, we explore a number of hybrid securities used in corporate finance. A hybrid has characteristics of both straight debt and straight equity, falling somewhere in between. The equity link is a form of option. We know from Chapter 5 that the value of an option should bear a relationship to certain factors. Obviously, the higher the current price of the stock and the lower the exercise price, the greater the value of the option. Increased volatility of the common stock works to the advantage of the option holder. This is because the downside risk of the option is bounded at zero. Therefore, an increase in variance expands the upside potential of the option while the downside risk continues to be bounded at zero. The longer the time to expiration of the option, the more valuable it becomes. Moreover, the higher the short-term, risk-free interest rate, the greater the value of the option. Finally, the higher the dividend on the common, the lower the value of the option.

Remembering these things, we will examine a number of equity-linked securities. We begin with the warrant, which is like a pure call option in a number of respects. Next we investigate the most widely used hybrid, the convertible security—part bond, or preferred stock, and part common stock. Depending on the stock component's value in relation to the option's exercise price, the convertible security's position in the spectrum between straight debt and straight equity will be determined. A form of convertible is the exchangeable bond, where the conversion is into the common stock of a corporation different from that of the issuer. This is followed by an examination of a representative sample of other hybrid securities, some of which are rather exotic. Hybrids other than convertibles do not account for a large percentage of financing by corporations overall, but for the individual company they can be quite important. Let us begin our inquiry. ■

USE OF WARRANTS

A **warrant** is an option to purchase a specified number of shares of common stock at a stated price. When holders exercise options, they surrender the warrants. Warrants are often employed as "sweeteners" to a public issue of bonds or debt that is privately placed. As a result, the company should be able to obtain a lower interest rate than it would otherwise. For companies that are marginal credit risks, the use of warrants may make the difference between being able and not being able to

615

raise funds through a debt issue. Occasionally, warrants are sold directly to investors for cash. On other occasions they are used in the founding of a company as compensation to underwriters and venture capitalists. Still the origin of most warrants is in connection with a debt issue, often a private placement.

Features

A warrant is an option to buy common stock, often used to "sweeten" a debt issue for the investor.

The warrant itself contains the provisions of the option. It states the number of shares the holder can buy for each warrant. Frequently, a warrant will provide the option to purchase 1 share of common stock for each warrant held, but it might be 2 shares, 3 shares, or 2.54 shares. Another important provision is the price at which the warrant is exercisable, such as $12 a share. This means that to buy one share, the warrant holder must put up $12. This exercise price may be either fixed or "stepped up" over time. For example, the exercise price might increase from $12 to $13 after 3 years and to $14 after another 3 years.

The warrant must specify the date the option expires, unless it is perpetual, having no expiration date. Because a warrant is only an option to purchase stock, warrant holders are not entitled to any cash dividends paid on the common stock, nor do they have voting power. If the common stock is split or a stock dividend is declared, the option price of the warrant usually is adjusted to take this change into account. Some warrants are callable after a period of time provided that share price exceeds some minimum price.[1]

For accounting reporting purposes, a company with warrants outstanding is required to report earnings per share in such a way that those who read the financial statement can visualize the potential dilution. More specifically, it must report earnings per share on two bases. The first is **basic earnings per share**, where earnings per share are based on only outstanding common stock. The second is **diluted earnings per share**, where earnings per share are calculated as if all potentially dilutive securities were converted or exercised. For companies with sizable financing involving potentially dilutive securities, the difference between the two earnings per share figures can be substantial.

Exercise of Warrants

When warrants are exercised, the common stock of the company is increased. Moreover, the debt that was issued in conjunction with the warrants remains outstanding. At the time of the issue of the warrants, the exercise price usually is set in excess of the market price of the common stock. The premium often is 15 percent or so above the stock's value. If the share price is $40 and the holder can purchase one share of common stock for each warrant held, this translates into an exercise price of $46.

To see how new capital can be infused with the exercise of warrants, let us take a company we shall call Western Rig. It has just raised $25 million in debt funds with warrants attached. The debentures carry a 10 percent coupon rate, and with each debenture ($1,000 face value) investors receive one warrant entitling them to purchase four shares of common stock at $30 a share. The capitalization of the company before financing, after financing, and after complete exercise of the warrants is as follows (in millions):

---

[1]Paul Schultz, "Calls of Warrants: Timing and Market Reaction," *Journal of Finance*, 48 (June 1993), 681–96.

	Before Financing	After Financing	After Exercise
Debentures		$25 ✓	$25
Common stock ($10 par value)	$10	10	11
Additional paid-in capital			2
Retained earnings	40	40	40
Shareholders' equity	$50	$50	$53
Total capitalization	$50	$75	$78

The retained earnings of the company remain unchanged, and the debenture issue has neither matured nor been called. Exercising their options, the warrant holders purchase 100,000 shares of stock at $30 a share, or $3 million in total. Consequently, the total capitalization of the company is increased by that amount.

Valuation of Warrants

The theoretical value of a warrant can be determined by

$$NP_s - E \qquad (21\text{-}1)$$

where N is the number of shares that can be purchased with one warrant, P_s is the market price of one share of stock, and E is the exercise dollar amount associated with the purchase of N shares. Note that this formula is exactly the same as that discussed in Chapter 5 for the valuation of an option where $N = 1$. Most warrants sell at prices in excess of their theoretical values. The typical relationship is shown in Fig. 21-1. The theoretical value of the warrant is represented by the solid "hockey

FIGURE 21-1

Relationship between theoretical and market values of a warrant

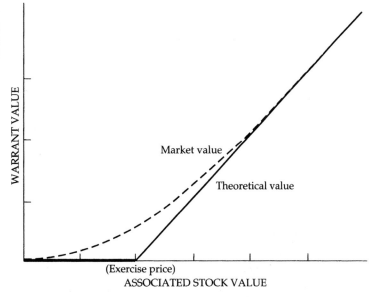

stick" line in the figure, and the actual market value of the warrant by the dashed line. When the market value of the associated stock is less than the exercise price, the theoretical value of the warrant is zero and it is said to be trading "out of the money." When the value of the associated common stock is greater than the exercise price, the theoretical value of the warrant is positive, as depicted by the solid diagonal line. Under these circumstances, the warrant is said to be trading "in the money."

The shorter the length of time to the expiration of the option, the more convex the market-value line. With only a few days to expiration, the market-value line will approach the theoretical value line. It should be noted that the typical warrant has a longer time to expiration than does the option. Because the investor in a warrant does not participate in dividends paid on the common, the greater the dividend, the less attractive the warrant in relation to its associated stock. As a result, the greater the dividend, the more the actual value line would approach the theoretical value line. All of these factors are familiar from our discussion of option valuation in Chapter 5.

Effect of Dilution

Option valuation and warrant valuation differ in one fundamental respect. With the exercise of an option, there is no change in the number of shares of stock of the company or in its net worth. Essentially, we have a side bet between two parties. With the exercise of a warrant, however, the number of shares increases, and there is a cash infusion into the firm. To illustrate, suppose Sigma Corporation has two equal owners, Gamma Jones and Delta Smith. The company owns 1 ounce of gold worth $400, so each share of stock is worth $200. Jones decides to sell an option to a third party, Alpha Brown, which enables Brown to buy Jones's share of stock for $240. If the market price of gold were to go above $480 per ounce, Brown could exercise her option at a profit. Note that if this is done, the number of total shares remains at two; Jones merely sells her stock to Brown.[2]

Cash is brought into the firm on exercise of a warrant.

How a Warrant Differs Instead of an option, suppose the company issues a warrant to Brown to buy one share of stock at $240 per share. Let us assume further that the price of gold goes to $510 per ounce and that the warrant is exercised. As a result, an additional share of stock is issued and the company receives a cash infusion of $240. The value of the company now is $510 in gold plus $240 in cash, or $750 total. Therefore, the value per share is $750/3 = $250. Thus, Brown pays out $240 to obtain a one-third interest in a larger company—larger by virtue of the exercise price paid into it. The gain to Brown is $10. Another way to look at the situation is that part of the exercise price paid in actually belongs to Brown. Effectively, she gives up only two-thirds of it, or $160. For this, she obtains a one-third interest in the gold of the company before the exercise. At $510 per ounce, this is worth $170. Therefore, Brown gains $10, the same as calculated before.

Adjustments to Pricing Formula If the Black–Scholes option pricing formula is used to value a warrant, certain adjustments are necessary if the number of new shares issued is relatively large. The exercise price used in the formula should be

---

[2]This example is based on Paul Pfleiderer, Teaching Note, Stanford Graduate School of Business, Stanford, CA. See also Fischer Black and Myron Scholes, "The Pricing of Options and Corporate Liabilities," *Journal of Political Economy*, 81 (May–June 1973), 648–49. We assume the other conditions associated with the Black–Scholes model hold, including the absence of dividends. For an empirical valuation of warrants, see Beni Lauterbach and Paul Schultz, "Pricing Warrants: An Empirical Study of Black–Scholes Model and Its Alternatives," *Journal of Finance*, 45 (September 1990), 1181–1209.

the money actually given up, or $160 in our example, not $240. The stock price employed should be the value of the equity before exercise divided by the number of shares in existence after the exercise of all warrants. Therefore, this value is $170 in our example. Finally, the variance rate used is the variance rate of return of the company's overall equity—stocks and warrants—not just its common stock. In general the same factors that affect the valuation of an option affect the valuation of a warrant, but certain adjustments are necessary if the option pricing model is used.

CONVERTIBLE SECURITIES

A convertible security is a bond or a share of preferred stock that can be converted at the option of the holder into common stock of the same corporation. The investor is provided with a fixed return from a bond or with a specified dividend from preferred stock. In addition, the investor has an option on the common stock. As a result, a company is able to sell a convertible security at a lower yield than it would have to pay on a straight bond or preferred stock issue. As the principles are nearly the same, our subsequent discussion will cover only convertible bonds.

Conversion Price/Ratio

Conversion price and conversion ratio both express the formula for conversion into common stock.

The ratio of exchange between the convertible security and the common stock can be stated in terms of either a **conversion price** or a **conversion ratio.** Suppose Zapata Corporation's 7 percent convertible subordinated debentures ($1,000 face value) have a conversion price of $43.75. To determine the conversion ratio, we merely divide $1,000 by $43.75 to get 22.86 shares. This is the number of shares of stock a holder will receive upon converting his or her debenture.

The conversion terms are not necessarily constant over time. Some convertible issues provide for increases or "step-ups" in the conversion price at periodic intervals. A $1,000 face value bond might have a conversion price of $40 a share for the first 5 years, $48 a share for the second 5 years, $56 for the third 5, and so on. In this way, the bond converts into fewer shares of common stock as time goes by. Usually, the conversion price is adjusted for any stock splits or stock dividends that occur after the securities are sold. If the common stock were split 2 for 1, the conversion price would be halved. This provision protects the convertible bondholders and is known as an antidilution clause.

Conversion Value and Premium

Conversion premium is the premium of conversion price over share price at the time of issuance.

The **conversion value** of a convertible security is the conversion ratio of the security times the market price per share of the common stock. If Zapata stock were selling for $48 per share, the conversion value of the debenture would be $22.86 \times \$48 = \$1,097$. At the time of issuance, the convertible security will be priced higher than its conversion price. The differential is known as a **conversion premium.** Zapata's share price at the time of issuance was $38. Therefore, the conversion premium was $43.75 - \$38.00 = \$5.75$. On a percentage basis, this translates into 15.1 percent. For most issues of convertibles, the conversion premium ranges from 15 to 40 percent. For a growth company, the conversion premium can be in the upper part of this range, or perhaps even higher in the case of super growth. For companies with only moderate growth, like Zapata, the conversion premium may be closer to 15 percent. The range itself is established mainly by market tradition.

Other Convertible Features

The greater the conversion premium, the less the dilution on conversion.

Almost all convertible bond issues are **subordinated** to other creditors. That fact permits the lender to treat convertible subordinated debt or convertible preferred stock as a part of the equity base when evaluating the financial condition of the issuer. In the event of liquidation, it makes no difference to the lender if the issue is actually converted. In either case, the lender has a prior claim.

The **dilution** accompanying conversion can be seen in a company that presently has outstanding $20 million in 8 percent convertible debentures where the conversion price is $25. The company has 3 million in common shares outstanding and no debt other than the convertible security. If earnings before interest and taxes are $9 million and the company's tax rate is 40 percent, earnings per share before and after conversion are:

	Debentures Unconverted	Debentures Converted
Earnings before interest and taxes	$9,000,000	$9,000,000
Interest 8% debentures	1,600,000	—
Profit before taxes	$7,400,000	$9,000,000
Taxes	2,960,000	3,600,000
Profit after taxes	$4,440,000	$5,400,000
Shares outstanding	3,000,000	3,800,000
Earning per share	$1.48	$1.42

We see that on conversion there is dilution. We note also that on conversion, the company no longer has to pay interest on the debentures: this factor has a favorable influence on earnings per share. As with warrants, it is necessary for companies to report earnings per share on a **basic** and on a **diluted** basis. Because of this accounting requirement, the common stock investor is not likely to overlook the potential dilution inherent in a company's financing with convertible securities.

Virtually all convertible securities have a **call feature.** As was true with straight debt or preferred stock, this enables the corporation to retire the security through paying the holders cash. Few convertible securities, however, are ever redeemed for cash. Instead, the purpose of the call is to force conversion when the conversion value of the security is above its call price.

Financing with Convertibles

Convertibles are delayed equity financing.

Convertible securities, in many cases, are employed as **deferred common stock financing.** Technically, these securities represent debt or preferred stock, but in essence they are delayed common stock. Companies that issue convertibles expect them to be converted in the future. By selling a convertible security instead of common stock, they create less dilution in earnings per share, both now and in the future. The reason is that the conversion price on a convertible security is higher than the issuing price on a new issue of common stock.

Less Dilution with Convertible   Recall that Zapata Corporation was able to issue a convertible debenture with a conversion price of $43.75 when its common share price was $38.00. If the company were to have issued common stock instead of the convertible debentures, it would have had to underprice the issue. Suppose the net proceeds to the company on a common issue would have been $35 per share. When we compare $43.75 with $35, we see that there is significantly less dilution with the delayed equity financing vehicle—namely, the convertible—than there is with the immediate equity issue—common stock.

Lower Yield Than Straight Debt/Preferred   Another advantage to the company in using convertible securities is that the interest rate or preferred dividend rate is lower than the rate the company would have to pay on a straight bond or a straight preferred stock issue. The conversion feature makes the issue more attractive to investors. The greater the value of the conversion feature to investors, the lower the yield the company will need to pay in order to sell the issue. The lower interest payments early on may be particularly useful to a company in a growth phase, for it allows it to keep more cash for growth.

New companies and/or ones with relatively low credit standing find it difficult if not impossible to finance with straight debt. The answer to this difficulty may be to give investors a "piece of the action." If a company has promise and is growing, this may be a valuable consideration. Indeed, the market may respond favorably to a convertible issue of these companies, not because of its quality as a bond or as preferred stock but because of its quality as common stock.

Asymmetric Information and Agency Costs   Yet another reason for convertible securities being issued is in situations where there is asymmetric information between management and investors/lenders, together with agency costs. From Chapter 19 we know that new equity issues may signal bad news to investors, in that the company finances with the overvalued security. While a debt issue may signal good news, lenders worry about the expropriation of their wealth. To mitigate such, they insist on protective covenants and costly monitoring devices. Equity holders, not wanting to have their wealth expropriated from debtholders, instigate still other protective and monitoring devices. By occupying the middle ground and issuing a hybrid security—part equity and part debt—a company may be able to reduce the need for costly monitoring.[3] After all, the convertible security holders are all in the same boat, not being at odds with each other. As a result, convertible financing may reduce agency costs.

Sequential Financing   Closely allied to the above argument is that the convertible resolves certain sequential financing problems. Where uncertainty exists as to the outcome of capital investment decisions, the convertible security is a useful financing device pending the resolution of uncertainty. When the growth option arising from a corporate investment proves valuable, the company is able to force conversion and keep the funds within the firm. If the growth option proves not to be valuable, the security will not be in the money and there will not be voluntary conversion. At maturity, funds will be returned to the bondholders. David Mayers argues that use of the convertible security controls the overinvestment problem.[4] It brings capital market discipline to management in investing/financing. If the growth option proves valuable, the company is likely to follow with incremental

---

[3]See Jeremy C. Stein, "Convertible Bonds as Backdoor Equity Financing," *Journal of Financial Economics*, 32 (August 1992), 3–21.

[4]David Mayers, "Why Firms Issue Convertible Bonds: The Matching of Financial and Real Investment Options," *Journal of Financial Economics*, 47 (January 1998), 83–102.

investment activity, which often is financed with straight debt. Mayers advocates the convertible security as a control device that economizes on issue costs.

Forcing or Stimulating Conversion

Companies usually issue convertible securities with the expectation that these securities will be converted within a certain length of time. Investors can exercise their options voluntarily at any time and exchange the convertible security for common stock; however, they may prefer to hold the security, for its price will increase as the price of the common stock increases. During this time, also, they receive regular interest payments or preferred stock dividends. For the convertible security in which the common stock pays no dividend, it is to the convertible security holder's advantage never to convert voluntarily. In other words, the investor should delay conversion as long as possible. (When a company pays a common stock dividend, it may be in the interest of the convertible security holder to convert voluntarily.)

On the other hand, it is in the company's interest, on behalf of existing stockholders, to force conversion as soon as the conversion value exceeds the call price, thereby taking the option away from the holder. In so doing, it also eliminates the cost of paying interest on the convertible debenture or dividends on the convertible preferred.[5] Only if the common dividend paid on conversion is more than the after-tax interest expense for the convertible does the issuing corporation have reason not to want to force conversion.[6]

Calling the Security To force conversion, assuming it makes sense to do so, corporations call the security, giving the holder a period of time, usually 30 days, to either convert or accept the call price. As the corporation wants investors to convert, the market price of the security must be higher than the call price. Many companies regard a 15 percent premium of conversion value over call price as a sufficient cushion for possible declines in market price and for enticing investors to convert their securities. The conversion price of a convertible debenture ($1,000 face value) might be $50 and the call price $1,060. For the conversion value of the bond to equal the call price, the market price of the stock must be $1,060/20, or $53 a share. If the bonds are called when the market price is $53, many investors might choose to accept the call price rather than convert. The company then would have to redeem many of the bonds for cash, in part defeating the purpose of the original financing. To ensure almost complete conversion, it might wait to call the debentures until the conversion value of the bond is 15 percent above the call price, a value that corresponds to a common stock market price of nearly $61.

Some companies require a greater cushion, and a few do not seem to want to ever force conversion. Such inaction is not in accord with what finance theory tells us

Forcing conversion is calling the bonds when share price is comfortably above the call price equivalent, causing investors to voluntarily convert.

---

[5]See Jonathan E. Ingersoll Jr., "A Contingent-Claims Valuation of Convertible Securities," *Journal of Financial Economics*, 4 (January 1977), 297–301; and M. J. Brennan and E. S. Schwartz, "Convertible Bonds: Valuation and Optimal Strategies for Call and Conversion," *Journal of Finance*, 32 (December 1977), 1699–1715.

[6]In a study of convertible preferred stocks, Kenneth B. Dunn and Kenneth M. Eades, "Voluntary Conversion of Convertible Securities and the Optimal Call Strategy," *Journal of Financial Economics*, 23 (August 1989), 273–301, find that a substantial number of investors do not convert voluntarily when the common dividend income they would realize as common stockholders exceeds the convertible preferred's dividend plus its premium of conversion value over call price. Under these circumstances, a company could rationally delay forcing conversion, and the authors offer this as a reason for the phenomenon observed. Similar conclusions were reached by Paul Asquith and David W. Mullins Jr., "Convertible Debt: Corporate Call Policy and Voluntary Conversion," *Journal of Finance*, 46 (September 1991), 1273–89; Cynthia J. Campbell, Louis H. Ederington, and Prashant Vankudre, "Tax Shields, Sample-Selection Bias, and the Information Content of Conversion-Forcing Bond Calls," *Journal of Finance*, 46 (September 1991), 1291–1324; and Louis H. Ederington, Gary L. Caton, and Cynthia J. Campbell, "To Call or Not to Call Convertible Debt," *Financial Management*, 26 (Spring 1997), 22–31.

should be done—seize the option from investors at the first opportunity. However, evidence suggests that most companies call their convertible issues once share price rises sufficiently to afford a moderate safety cushion over the call price.[7] For those that do not, often the explanation is that the debenture is still under deferred call protection or that there is the cash-flow advantage to delaying mentioned above.

Means for Stimulating Conversion Other means are available to a company for "stimulating," as opposed to "forcing," conversion. By establishing an acceleration or "step-up" in the conversion price at steady intervals in the future, there is persistent pressure on bondholders to convert, assuming the conversion value of the security is relatively high. If the conversion price is scheduled to increase from $50 to $56 at the end of next month, convertible bondholders have an incentive to convert prior to that time, all other things the same. If the holders wait, they receive fewer shares of stock. Be aware that the "step-up" provision must be established at the time the convertible issue is sold. It cannot be used for purposes of stimulating conversion at a particular moment in time.

Another means for stimulating conversion is to increase the dividend on the common stock, thereby making the common more attractive. If the dividend income available on the associated common exceeds interest income on the convertible security, there is particular incentive to convert. Although the two stimulants just discussed enhance conversion, invariably a portion of the convertible bondholders will not convert, owing to the downside protection of the bond, the superior legal claim on assets, and other reasons. Consequently, calling the issue may be the only means for ensuring that the issue will be substantially converted.

Overhanging Issues

As we have suggested, the investment community expects a company to be in a position to force conversion several years after issuance. To do so, the convertible security's conversion value must be in excess of its call price. In turn, this requires share price to rise sufficiently to offset not only the conversion premium at issuance but also the call premium. If after a few years share price does not rise sufficiently so the company can force conversion, the issue is said to be *overhanging*. This condition reduces a company's future financing flexibility. For all practical purposes it cannot sell another convertible security. Although straight equity issues are possible, the overhanging convertible makes marketing such issues difficult for the underwriter. It is hard to explain why the future is so much better than the past, when the stock did not perform up to the expectations of the market at the time the convertible security was issued.

VALUATION OF CONVERTIBLE SECURITIES

The view that a convertible security is the best of all things to the corporation because it requires a lower yield cost than straight debt or preferred, but involves less dilution than straight common financing, is too simplistic.

---

[7]See Paul Asquith, "Convertible Bonds Are Not Called Late," *Journal of Finance*, 50 (September 1995), 1275–89. The author finds that for a large sample the median delay before call, once the conversion price exceeds the call price, is only 77 days. With a cushion of 20 percent, the median delay is but 20 days. Thus, the evidence is consistent with most companies calling their convertible bonds as soon as possible. Further support of the safety cushion notion is found in Louis H. Ederington, Gary L. Caton, and Cynthia J. Campbell, "To Call or Not to Call Convertible Debt," *Financial Management*, 26 (Spring 1997), 22–31.

Debt Plus Option Characteristic

Convert value is straight bond value plus the value of the stock option.

The convertible bond may be viewed as straight debt plus an option to purchase common stock in the corporation. If the expiration of the option and the maturity of the convertible are the same, then the following roughly holds

$$\frac{\text{Debt}}{\text{Value}} + \frac{\text{Option}}{\text{Value}} = \frac{\text{Convertible Bond}}{\text{Value}} \tag{21-2}$$

Both the value of the debt and the value of the option components are affected by the volatility of the company's cash flows. The greater this volatility, the lower the value of the debt component but the higher the value of the option component.

Thus, risk cuts both ways. As firm risk increases, a company incurs higher interest costs on straight debt. However, with convertible debt the option component becomes more valuable. As a result, the interest rate for the convertible may not increase with more firm risk and actually could decrease. This offset means the convertible security is less affected by the issuing company's risk than are other types of securities. Put another way, differences in coupon rates and conversion premiums for the convertible debentures of companies having different risk complexions are not likely to be nearly as large as they would be for other types of securities. This suggests that when a company's future is highly uncertain, the convertible security should be the financing method of choice.

In summary, the greater the risk faced by the firm, the more difficult it is to sell straight debt and the more valuable the conversion feature becomes. In the appendix at the end of this chapter, we explore the option characteristic of a convertible issue in detail. But now we look at convertible security valuation in more traditional ways.

Bond Value

The bond value of a convertible security is the price at which a straight bond of the same company would sell in the open market. For semiannual compounding, it can be determined by solving the following equation for B:

$$B = \sum_{t=1}^{2n} \frac{I}{\left(1 + \dfrac{r}{2}\right)^t} + \frac{F}{\left(1 + \dfrac{r}{2}\right)^{2n}} \tag{21-3}$$

where B = straight bond value of the convertible
n = years to final maturity
I = semiannual interest payments determined by the coupon rate
F = face value of the bond
r = market yield to maturity on a straight bond of the same company

In the equation, we assume semiannual interest payments, which are typical with corporate bonds, so the total number of interest payments is two times the years to maturity, n, and the semiannual interest rate on a straight bond is r divided by 2. (The mathematics of bond interest are discussed in Chapter 2.)

Calculating the Floor Price   Amos White Company has outstanding a 6 percent convertible debenture with a final maturity 20 years hence. If the company is to sell a straight 20-year debenture in the current market, the yield will have to be 8 percent to be attractive to investors. For a 20-year bond with a 6 percent coupon to yield 8 percent to maturity, the bond has to sell at a discount. Using Eq. (21-3) and rounding, we have the following:

$$B = \sum_{t=1}^{40} \frac{\$30}{(1.04)^t} + \frac{\$1,000}{(1.04)^{40}} = \$802.07$$

Thus the bond-value floor of Amos White Company's convertible bonds is approximately $802. This floor suggests that if the price of the common stock were to fall sharply, the price of the convertible would fall only to $802. At that price, the security would sell as a straight bond in keeping with prevailing bond yields for that grade of security.

Changes in Floor   The bond-value floor of a convertible is not constant over time. It varies with (1) interest-rate movements in the capital markets and (2) changes in the financial risk of the company involved. If interest rates in general rise, the bond value of a convertible will decline. If the yield to maturity on a straight bond in our example increases from 8 to 10 percent, the bond value of the convertible will drop from $802 to $657. Moreover, the company's credit rating can either improve or deteriorate over time. If it improves, and the company is able to sell a straight bond at a lower yield to maturity, the bond value of the convertible security will increase, all other things held constant. If the company's credit standing deteriorates, and the yield on a straight bond increases, the bond-value floor will decline. Unfortunately for investors, when the market price of the stock falls because of poor earnings and/or increased risk, its credit standing may suffer. As a result, the straight bond value of the convertible may decline along with the decline in its conversion value, giving investors less downside protection than they might have expected originally.

Both interest-rate and credit-risk changes cause changes in the bond-value floor.

Premiums

Convertible securities frequently sell at premiums over both their bond value and their conversion value. Recall that the conversion value of a convertible is simply the current market price per share of the company's common stock times the number of shares into which the security is convertible. The fact that the convertible bond provides the investor with a degree of downside protection, given the qualifications just mentioned, often results in its selling at a market price somewhat higher than its conversion value. The difference is known as the **premium-over-conversion value.**

Moreover, a convertible bond typically will sell at a **premium-over-bond value,** primarily because of the conversion feature. Unless the market price of the stock is very low relative to the conversion price, the conversion feature usually will have value, in that investors may eventually find it profitable to convert the securities. To the extent that the conversion feature does have value, the convertible will sell at a premium over its straight bond value. The higher the market price of the common relative to the conversion price, the greater this premium.

Relation between Premiums

The trade-off between the two premiums depicts the value of the option to investors and is illustrated in Fig. 21-2. The market price of the common is on the horizontal axis; the value of the convertible security is on the vertical. It should be pointed out that the two axes are on different scales. The diagonal line, which

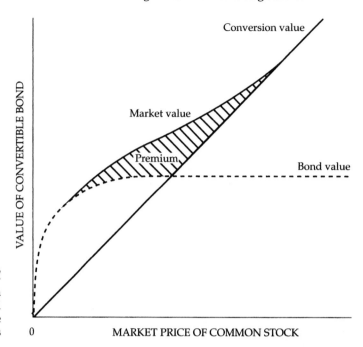

FIGURE 21-2
Relation between bond-value and conversion-value premiums

starts at the origin, represents the conversion value of the bond. It is linear, as the conversion ratio is invariant with respect to the market price of the stock.

The bond-value line, however, is related to the market price of the common. If a company is doing badly financially, the prices of both its common stock and its bonds are likely to be low. At the extreme, if the total value of the company were zero, both the bonds and the stock would have a value of zero. As the company becomes sounder financially and the common stock increases in price, bond value increases but at a decreasing rate. After a point, the bond-value line becomes flat, and further increases in common stock price are unrelated to it. At this point, the bond-value floor is determined by what other high-grade bonds sell for in the market.

Market Value Trade-Off   The upper curved line in the figure represents the market price of the convertible security. The distance between this line and the bond-value line is the premium-over-bond value, while the distance between the market-value line and the conversion-value line represents the premium-over-conversion value. We see that at relatively high common stock price levels, the value of the convertible as a bond is insignificant. Consequently, its premium-over-bond value is high, whereas its premium-over-conversion value is negligible. The security sells mainly for its stock equivalent. Investors are unwilling to pay a significant premium-over-conversion value for the following reasons. First, the greater the premium of market price of the convertible over its bond value, the less valuable the bond-value protection is to the investor. Second, when the conversion value is high, the convertible may be called; if it is, the investor will want to convert rather than redeem the bond for the call price. Upon conversion, of course, the bond is worth only its conversion value.

On the other hand, when the market value of the convertible is close to its straight bond value, the conversion feature has little value. At this level, the convertible security is valued primarily as a straight bond. Under these circumstances, the market price of the convertible is likely to exceed its conversion value by a significant premium.

Option Nature of Convertible   The shaded area of the figure reflects the option nature of the convertible bond. There is partial protection on the downside, with the "slipping" bond value floor, coupled with the upside potential of rising share price. Thus, the distribution of possible outcomes is skewed to the right, and this characteristic finds favor with investors. The greater the volatility of share price, the greater the potential for upside gain and the more valuable the option. In the context of Fig. 21-2, this greater value would be expressed as a larger shaded area in the figure. Lower volatility would cause the shaded area to be smaller.

The option value of the convertible in Eq. (21-2) can be determined using standard option pricing models (see Chapter 5). If the Black–Scholes model is used, we need to have an estimate of the stock's standard deviation. The expiration date is either the maturity of the convertible bond or the time to when the company is likely to be able to call the bonds and force conversion. In this regard, one may wish to use several expiration dates. The risk-free rate is the yield on a Treasury security with a maturity equal to that of the expiration date assumed. The exercise price is the conversion price of the bond. When a common dividend is paid, the stock price used in the Black–Scholes formula needs to be adjusted downward by the present value of the likely dividend stream through the expiration date.[8] With this information, one can solve for the option value per share. By multiplying this figure by the conversion ratio, one obtains the option value of the convertible bond. This amount then is added to the bond value in Eq. (21-2) to obtain the value of the convertible bond.

Other Factors Affecting Valuation

Although we have concentrated on the main reasons for the shaded area in Fig. 21-2, other factors have an influence on convertible security valuation. For one thing, lower transaction costs on convertible bonds relative to those on common stocks enhance the attractiveness of these bonds. By purchasing convertible bonds and converting them into common stock, investors incur somewhat lower transaction costs than they would by purchasing the stock outright. This attraction should exert upward pressure on the premiums-over-conversion value and over-bond value. Yet another influence that may raise premiums is that certain institutional investors, such as life insurance companies, are restricted with respect to investing in common stock. By investing in convertible bonds, they gain the benefits of a common stock investment without actually investing in common stock.

The length of time to expiration of the convertible option also should affect the premiums. The longer this time, the more valuable the option. Unlike other options, however, the time to expiration is uncertain, owing to the fact that the company can force conversion if the price of the common stock is high enough. The longest time to expiration is the maturity of the security, but actual expiration typically is much shorter. Another factor is the dividend on the common. The greater the dividend, the greater the attraction of common vis-à-vis the convertible security and the lower the premiums, all other things being the same. All of these influences affect the premiums at which convertible securities sell, but they are less important than the influences discussed in the preceding section.

EXCHANGEABLE DEBT

An exchangeable bond is like a convertible bond, but the common stock involved is that of another corporation. Petrie Stores issued exchangeable debt, which enabled the investor to exchange each $1,000 bond into slightly over 27 shares of common stock in Toys 'R' Us.

---

[8]See Chapter 5 for more detail.

Exchangeable debt involves an option on the stock of a company other than the issuer.

Features

Like the conversion price and conversion ratio for a convertible security, the **exchange price** and **exchange ratio** must be set at the time of issuance. The Petrie Stores' exchangeable bond had an exchange ratio of 27, which translates into an exchange price of $37.04. As with convertible bonds, there typically is a call feature and most issues are subordinated.

Use in Financing

Exchangeable bond issues usually occur only when the issuer owns common stock in the company in which the bonds can be exchanged. Petrie Stores acquired 25 percent of Toys 'R' Us common stock in a friendly takeover attempt. A primary reason for an exchangeable offer is that the company owning the stock wishes to divest.[9] A secondary offering of the stock involves more underwriting and other fees than does an exchangeable offer. Perhaps a tax advantage exists in that any dividends on the stock owned by the company prior to its being exchanged qualify for the 70 percent intercorporate dividend exclusion, whereas interest on the exchangeable debt may be deducted in its entirety for tax purposes.

Like the convertible, interest costs are lower because of the option value of the instrument. So far most companies issuing exchangeables have been large and would not have experienced difficulty financing with a straight debt issue. The attraction is a lower interest cost together with the possibility of disposing of a common stock investment at a premium above the present price. Finally, some exchangeable issues of U.S. companies have been placed with investors outside the United States.

Valuation of an Exchangeable

The valuation of an exchangeable security is identical in most respects to that of a convertible security. Exchangeable debt can be viewed as

$$\frac{\text{Debt}}{\text{Value}} + \frac{\text{Call option}}{\text{Value}} = \frac{\text{Exchangeable debt}}{\text{Value}} \tag{21-4}$$

where the call option is on the stock of the company in which the debt is exchangeable. Therefore, the investor must analyze and track the bond of one company and the stock of another.

One advantage of the exchangeable bond is diversification; the bond-value floor and the stock value are not directly linked. Poor earnings and financial performance in one company will not lead to a simultaneous decline in bond-value floor and in the stock value. If the companies are in unrelated industries, the investor achieves diversification. With market imperfections, this may lead to a higher valuation for the exchangeable than for the convertible, all other things the same.

Because option values are driven by the volatility of the associated asset, differences in volatility may affect the choice between an exchangeable and a convertible bond issue. If the stock of the company in exchange is more volatile than that of the issuer, the option value will be greater with an exchangeable bond issue than it will with a convertible bond issue, all other things the same.

A relative disadvantage to the investor has to do with taxation. The difference between the market value of the stock at the time of exchange and the cost of the bond is treated as a capital gain for tax purposes. In the case of a convertible, this gain goes unrecognized until the stock is sold. The net effect of these factors is unclear.

---

[9]This motivation is confirmed by Brad M. Barber, "Exchangeable Debt," *Financial Management*, 22 (Summer 1993), 48–60. He lists the two subsequent reasons but does not find the tax reason relevant empirically.

OTHER HYBRID SECURITIES

There are dozens of other hybrid securities, all with cute abbreviations concocted by investment-bank sponsors. Table 21-1 gives a representative sample of some of these securities. As mentioned at the outset of the chapter, these securities have characteristics that place them somewhere along the spectrum going from straight common stock to straight debt, the latter having no equity characteristics. Note that in our discussion of tax-deductible preferred stock in the last chapter we took up two of the names on the list, namely, MIPS and TOPrS. In the remainder of the chapter, we consider PERCS, DECS, CEPPPS, YEELDS, LYONs, and CEPS. First, however, we need to consider why securities of this sort come about. What is it that makes exotic (and often complicated) features attractive to investors and issuers?

Foundations for Equity-Linked Security Products

There are a number of reasons why we see products of the sort depicted in Table 21-1. The overriding foundation is **market incompleteness**, a concept explored on several other occasions. Market incompleteness exists when financial markets do not provide securities with features in demand by investors and issuers. Making the markets more complete is the simple marketing notion of tailoring a security's design to the demands of the marketplace.

Role of the Investment Bank   With respect to equity-linked securities, profitability and prestige to the promoter are the motives for financial innovation. There is a first-mover advantage that the investment bank hopes to retain. A successful product, of course, invites others to come up with substitutes. With competition, profit margins

TABLE 21-1
Some Hybrid Securities

ACES	Automatic Conversion-Rate Equity Securities
BOUNDS	Buy-Write Option Unitary Derivatives
CEPS	Convertible Exchangeable Preferred Stock
DECS	Dividend Enhanced Cumulative Stock
ELKS	Equity-Linked Securities
EPICS	Exchangeable Preferred Income Cumulative Shares
LYONs	Liquid Yield Option Notes
MIPS	Monthly Income Preferred Stock
PEPS	Premium Equity Preferred Stock
PERCS	Preferred Equity Redemption Cumulative Stock
PREPS	Preferred Equity Participation Securities
PRIDES	Preferred Redeemable Increased Dividend Equity Securities
SIRENS	Step-up Income Redeemable Equity Notes
SPINS	Standard & Poor's 500 Indexed Notes
STREPS	Structured Tradable Receipt Exchangeable for Preferred Securities
TOMCATS	Trust-Oriented Convertible Accruable Term Securities
TOPrS	Trust Originated Preferred Stock
YEELDS	Yield Enhanced Equity-Linked Debt Securities

to the original promoter may erode. However, certain products become fixtures not easily displaced and provide the investment bank with sizable profitability for many years. An example is LYONs, introduced many years ago by Merrill Lynch. As with all financial innovations, change is the important ingredient.

Regulatory and Tax Law Changes   With deregulation of financial institutions, geographical and functional boundaries are broken down and the distinction among them purposely blurred. This permits financial innovation of all sorts, including equity-linked securities. Other regulatory changes may prompt new security designs to take advantage of regulatory loopholes. Tax law changes prompt many financial product innovations. In particular, the differential taxation of interest income, dividend income, and capital gains from an investor standpoint and the corporate tax rate and timing options from the standpoint of issuer are important.

Volatility, Asymmetric Information, and Agency Costs   When volatility of stock prices, interest rates, and currency exchange rates increases or decreases sharply, the changed environment creates demand for different types of financial instruments. New vehicles arise for shifting risk. Asymmetric information as to a corporation's expected future cash flows and the variance of firm value is fertile ground for financial innovation. Certain financial products may reduce asymmetric information and the agency costs associated with such. With these foundations in mind, consider now some of the hybrids listed in Table 21-1.

Preferred Equity Redemption Cumulative Stock (PERCS)

A PERCS is a form of redeemable convertible preferred stock, originated by Morgan Stanley in the late 1980s. Typically, the PERCS is convertible into common only at a specified future date. The key feature is that the upside is capped. If the market price of the common stock is less than some specified threshold price on the exchange date, the security holder receives one common share for each PERCS share held. If more, the holder receives less than one share. Suppose X-Cell Corporation has a PERCS issue outstanding for which the specified share price 3 years hence is $56. If actual share price turns out to be $70 on that exchange date, the holder receives $56/$70 = .80 shares of common for every PERCS share held. The nature of the cap can be seen in the upper panel of Fig. 21-3, where the expiration value of the instrument is shown. If share price should decline from that which prevailed at original issuance, the holder can end up with a value less than what he or she paid for the PERCS. The "carrot" to the investor is that the PERCS pays a higher dividend than that available on the common stock. The trade-off then is higher income through the exchange date, but with a cap on the common stock equivalent. The mirror image occurs for the corporate issuer.

Effectively, the corporation has a long position in a call option on its own stock while the PERCS holder has a short position. PERCS are offered to common stockholders in exchange for common stock they hold. In other words, they are not issued to new investors. For the investor, the opportunity cost is giving up the common in exchange for the PERCS. In this context, the value of the PERCS can be thought of as

$$\text{PERCS Value} = S + PVXD - C \tag{21-5}$$

where S = Common share price with no exchange, and lower dividend.
 $PVXD$ = Present value of the incremental dividend, PERCS minus common,

PERCS cap the upside but provide a higher dividend payment.

through the exercise date.

C = Value of the call option.

The PERCS holder forgoes the upside potential, so the embedded call option given the corporation works against him or her. The exercise price of the option is the threshold price shown in the upper panel of Fig. 21-3. Standard option pricing can be used to value the PERCS. The greater the volatility, the lower the value of the PERCS, whereas the higher the stock price and the greater the differential in dividends, the higher the value.[10]

Dividend Enhanced Cumulative Stock (DECS)

The DECS is a Salomon Smith Barney product, with a different configuration than a PERCS. This profile is seen in the middle panel of Fig. 21-3. Here the security holder gives up the mid-range of share price movement, but keeps downside exposure and participates in the far upside. The "carrot" again is a higher dividend than that provided on the common stock. As with the PERCS, mandatory conversion occurs at the exchange date. Up to threshold price #1, the investor receives one share of common stock for each DECS held. At threshold price #2 and beyond, the investor might receive 0.8333 shares of common for each DECS held. Between the two thresholds, the number ranges from 1.0 down to 0.8333 shares. In this way, the payoff in the mid-range is constrained. The DECS appeal is to the income- and growth-oriented investor.

CEPPPS and YEELDS

Securities can be designed to protect the investor on the downside if the far upside is given up. In 1996, Goldman Sachs and Morgan Stanley jointly underwrote Convertible Exchangeable Principal-Protected Preferred Shares (CEPPPS) of Microsoft Corporation. In the lower panel of Fig. 21-3, the nature of the collar arrangement is shown. The floor price often is existing share price. If this price were $80, up to the first threshold the investor receives a number of shares equal to $80 divided by share price on the exchange date. If the share price were $60, he or she would receive 1.3333 shares. Through the second threshold, the investor receives one share of common for each CEPPPS held. Suppose now the second threshold were $110. Beyond this threshold, the investor receives less than one share of stock for each CEPPPS held. If share price were $140, he or she would obtain $110/$140 = 0.7857 shares. The "carrot" again is a dividend greater than that on the common. In the case of Microsoft, it was a $2\frac{3}{4}$ percent yield versus no dividend on the common. In a similar manner Yield Enhanced Equity-Linked Debt Securities (YEELDS) can be designed to provide this pattern of investor protection. However, other design patterns are also possible with YEELDS.

Liquid Yield Option Notes (LYONs)

LYONs were first developed by Merrill Lynch in the mid-1980s, and have been a very successful product. They are complicated, but there are some defining features. The security is a zero-coupon note, with maturities ranging from 10 to 20 years. They are convertible by the investor into a fixed number of shares at any time. That differs from PERCS, DECS, CEPPPS, and YEELDS, for which conversion is mandatory on a given date. Moreover, the conversion price of a LYON increases over time. The investor has a put option of the security back to the corpo-

---

[10]However, the greater the S in Eq. (21-5), the more valuable the call option. Consequently, there is some offset to an increase in S causing an increase in the value of the PERCS.

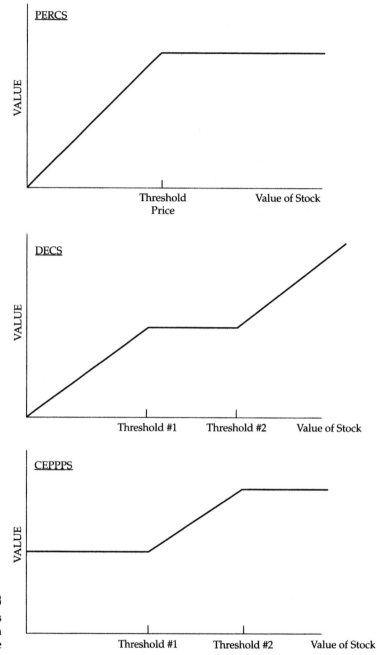

FIGURE 21-3

Expiration Date Values
of Hybrid Securities in
Relation to Share Price

LYONs embed several
different options in the
contract.

ration at increasing put prices over time. Finally, the issuer has a call option at increasing call prices over time. The initial call price typically is below the investor's
put price, but there is a crossover some time before maturity. The accreted interest
is deductible as an expense for tax purposes by the corporation, even though it is
not paid in cash. Because of the multiple embedded options, the valuation of
LYONs is difficult to model.[11] In general, the greater the volatility of stock return,
the greater the value of the LYON.

---

[11]For one approach, see John J. McConnell and Eduardo S. Schwartz, "LYON Taming," *Journal of Finance,* 41 (July
1986), 561–77.

Convertible Exchangeable Preferred Stock (CEPS)

The final hybrid we consider is CEPS, which is a variation of convertible preferred stock and was first issued in the early 1980s. In fact, it starts as convertible preferred stock with all the features taken up earlier in the chapter. The only difference is that the issuer has the option of exchanging the convertible preferred shares for convertible bonds. With respect to cash flows to the investor and conversion terms, the security exchanged is identical to the one given up. The major advantage to the corporation is a tax timing option, in being able to use the tax shield associated with debt if it becomes advantageous to do so.[12]

This concludes our inquiry into hybrid securities. Although there are many more exotics, the ones discussed here should give a flavor to many of the elements in security design.

Summary

Warrants, convertible securities, and exchangeable securities are options under which the holder can obtain common stock. The conversion or exchange feature enables the investor to transfer a debt instrument or preferred stock into common stock, whereas a warrant attached to a bond enables the holder to purchase a specified number of shares at a specified price. With a warrant, the exercise of the option does not result in the elimination of the bonds.

Normally, warrants are employed as a "sweetener" for a public or private issue of debt. They are like a call option, but the beginning time to expiration tends to be longer. Also, there is a dilution effect on value, which is not the case with call options, and money is paid into the company upon exercise of the warrant. When the market price of the stock is near the exercise price, the market value of the warrant tends to be high relative to its theoretical value. The greater the volatility of the associated stock, the more valuable the warrant. Other factors also influence the price of this type of option.

The convertible security can be viewed as a straight debt or preferred stock issue plus an option to buy common stock. For the corporation, convertibles often represent delayed common stock financing. For a given amount of financing, there will be less dilution with a convertible issue than with a common stock issue, assuming it eventually converts. As a hybrid security, the convertible security has a bond-value floor and a conversion, or stock, value. As a result, the distribution of possible returns is skewed to the right and there is a trade-off between the two factors.

The premiums at which a convertible security sells above its conversion value and above its bond value are due to the security's partial downside protection as a bond and its upside potential as stock (the same in principle as with any option), the volatility of the common stock, the dividend on the common, the duration of the convertible option, and certain institutional imperfections that affect investors. Convertibles are particularly suited as a financing vehicle when there is much uncertainty concerning the company. If things go well, the company will be in a position to force conversion by calling the issue.

An exchangeable bond may be exchanged for common stock in another corporation. It is like the convertible security in its valuation underpinnings with a few exceptions. This method of financing is applicable to companies that have stock holdings in another company.

A number of other hybrid securities exist, the foundation for which is incomplete financial markets that allow an investment bank to tailor a security's design to the unfilled desires of investors and issuers. In the case of PERCS, the equity link to common stock is capped on the upside, but the security pays a higher dividend than is available on the common. For

---

[12]For an analysis of this point and other aspects to CEPS, see Arnold R. Cowan, "Tax Options, Clienteles, and Adverse Selection: The Case of Convertible Exchangeable Preferred Stock," *Financial Management*, 28 (Summer 1999), 15–31.

DECS, the mid-range of stock price participation is constrained for the investor, but the upside and downside are not. With CEPPPS and certain types of YEELDS, there is a collar where the investor participates in stock movements only in the mid-range. LYONs are zero-coupon debt instruments convertible into common, but for which the investor has an option to put the security back to the issuer and the issuer has a call option. A CEPS is a convertible preferred stock, but the issuer has the option to exchange it for convertible debt.

Appendix: Valuing Convertible Bonds in the Face of Firm Volatility, Default Risk, and Fluctuating Interest Rates

Because a convertible bond is both a debt instrument and a stock option, its precise valuation is complex. In this chapter as well as in certain preceding chapters, we discussed the valuation of stock options and debt in an option pricing model framework. We have not put the various components together as they relate to convertible bonds, and that is the purpose of this appendix. Briefly reviewing, a convertible bond is an option to obtain stock in a corporation. As with any option, the greater the volatility of the stock and the underlying volatility of firm value, the greater the value of the option to the convertible security holder.

In Chapters 9 and 16, we saw that debt holders could be viewed as option writers and the equity holders could be viewed as holding a call option on the firm's total value. At the maturity of the debt, the equity holders have the option of buying back the firm from the debt holders at a specified price, which is the face value of the debt instrument. In this context, the greater the volatility of the value of the total firm, the greater the value of the option to the equity holders. On the other hand, the greater the volatility, the greater the default risk in the sense that the firm will be worth less than the debt's face value. If default occurs, equity holders will not exercise their option, bankruptcy by definition will occur, and debt holders will suffer a loss. In Chapter 20, we explored the valuation of the call option on straight debt. Here we found that the greater the volatility of future interest rates, the greater the value of the call option to the equity holders and the greater the value loss to the debt holders. If such interest-rate volatility is anticipated at the time of the loan, lenders will demand a higher interest rate to compensate them for the call risk.

All three factors influence the valuation of convertible bonds, and it is useful to explore the interrelationships. What will emerge is not a precise model, if indeed one were possible, but a general overview of the valuation underpinnings. To begin, let us assume that financial markets are perfect, that a firm has no debt other than convertible bonds, and that bondholders and the firm follow optimal strategies. Under these circumstances, optimal strategies consist of (1) bondholders converting their bonds into stock if the value of the convertible is less than its conversion value; (2) bondholders forcing the firm into bankruptcy and seizing its value if the value of the firm falls below the debt's face value, assuming that the ability to do so is written into the contract; and (3) the firm calling the bonds when their value equals the call price.

Given these actions, the boundaries for the valuation of convertible bonds are shown in Fig. 21A-1. If the value of bonds should exceed the call price, they will be called so their value is bounded on the upside by the call price. On the downside, bondholders will force bankruptcy, should the value of the firm fall below the total value of the bonds outstanding. Moreover, bondholders will convert if the value of their bonds falls below the conversion value, so we have another lower boundary. Finally, the total value of the bonds cannot exceed the total value of the firm. As a result of these constraints, the value of the bonds must fall within the shaded area in the figure.

Within these boundaries, certain relationships are likely to hold. For one, we would expect an inverse relationship between the risk of default and the value of the firm. That is, increases in firm value would be associated with decreases in default risk up to a point. As a result, we might expect the relationship shown in the upper panel of Fig. 21A-2. Here we see that the value of the bonds

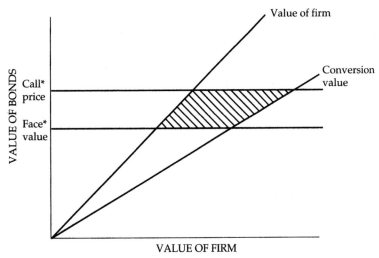

FIGURE 21A-1
Boundaries of
convertible bond
valuation

*Represents the total value of all bonds at the call price
and at face value.

FIGURE 21A-2
Convertible bond
valuation with
default risk

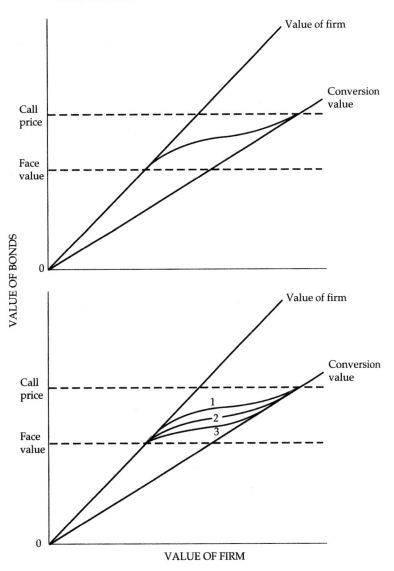

increases at a decreasing rate until the curve eventually turns up, in keeping with the change in conversion value. This phenomenon was discussed in the chapter, and we know that it embraces both default risk and firm value volatility.

For a given firm value, companies can have different business-risk strategies, which result in different default risks. Therefore, the relationship between bond value and firm value will differ, depending on the risk strategy chosen by the firm. In the bottom panel of Fig. 21A-2, risk strategy 1 is safer than strategies 2 and 3, in the sense of less volatility of firm value. Accordingly, the risk of default is less for any level of firm value, and the value of the convertible bonds is higher.

Having considered default risk, we turn now to interest rate risk. For given levels of firm value and default risk, the greater the interest rate, the lower the value of the outstanding convertible bonds. The relationship is depicted by the upper panel of Fig. 21A-3. For a hypothetical interest rate of 6 percent, the bond-value line is higher than it is for interest rates of 10 percent and 14 percent, respectively. This follows, of course, from the valuation of any fixed-income security. Apart from the expected level of interest rates, the greater the volatility of future interest rates, the greater the value of the call option to the company and the lower the value of the convertible security to the holder. This situation is depicted in the lower panel of Fig. 21A-3. Bear in mind that if the bond is called, the

FIGURE 21A-3
Convertible bond valuation and interest rates

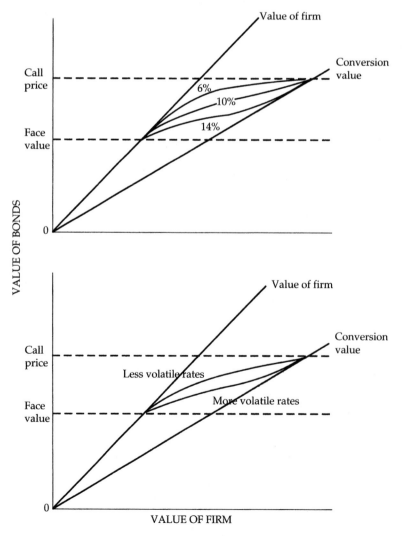

holder has the option to convert it into common stock; therefore, the impact of the call is far less than it is in the case of straight debt. Finally, we should point out that in determining whether a convertible security is called, stock price volatility usually dominates interest-rate volatility.

We have described the more important "two-way" relationships affecting the valuation of convertible bonds, but there are others that complicate the picture. For one thing, there is likely to be an association among the level of interest rates, default risk, and the value of the firm. High interest rates often are associated with periods of high and uncertain inflation. Consequently, the value of the firm will be less,

all other things staying the same, than it is in times of low inflation, moderate uncertainty, and low interest rates. Similarly, periods of high inflation, great uncertainty, and high interest rates may be characterized by greater default risk. Thus, the volatility of firm value and of interest rates are not independent, and this makes the valuation of the hybrid convertible security very complicated indeed.

Our purpose in this appendix is not to present a model but to point out the direction of bond-value changes that are likely to accompany parameter changes.[13] This discussion gives us a richer understanding of the valuation of convertible securities.

Self-Correction Problems

1. Camelot Pizza has outstanding warrants, where each warrant entitles the holder to purchase two shares of stock at $24 per share. The market price per share of stock and market price per warrant were the following over the last year:

	Observation					
	1	2	3	4	5	6
Stock price	$20	$18	$27	$32	$24	$38
Warrant price	5	3	12	20	8	29

   Determine the theoretical value per warrant for each of these observations. Plot the market value per warrant in relation to its theoretical value. At what price per common share is the warrant premium over theoretical value the greatest? Why?

2. The Charrier Boat Company has current earnings of $3 a share with 500,000 shares outstanding. The company plans to issue 40,000 shares of 7 percent, $50 par value convertible preferred stock at par. The preferred stock is convertible into two shares of common for each preferred share held. The common stock has a current market price of $21 per share.

   a. What is the preferred stock's conversion value?

   b. What is its conversion premium?

   c. Assuming that total earnings stay the same, what will be the effect of the issue on basic earnings per share (1) before conversion? (2) on a fully diluted basis?

   d. If profits after taxes increase by $1 million, what will be basic earnings per share (1) before conversion? (2) on a fully diluted basis?

---

[13]For one approach to modeling the relationships, see Michael J. Brennan and Eduardo S. Schwartz, "Analyzing Convertible Bonds," *Journal of Financial and Quantitative Analysis*, 15 (November 1980), 907–29.

3. Sadfield Manufacturing Company plans to issue $10 million in 6 percent convertible subordinated debentures. Currently, the stock price is $36 per share, and the company believes it could obtain a conversion premium (issuing price in excess of conversion value) of approximately 12 percent. The call price of the debenture in the first 10 years is $1,060 per bond, after which it drops to $1,030 in the next 10 years and to $1,000 in the last 10 years. To allow for fluctuations in the market price of the stock, the company does not want to call the debentures until their conversion value is at least 15 percent in excess of the call price. Earnings per share are expected to grow at an 8 percent compound annual rate in the foreseeable future, and the company envisions no change in its price/earnings ratio.

    a. Determine the expected length of time that must elapse before the company is in a position to force conversion.

    b. Is the issuance of a convertible security a good idea for the company?

Problems

1. Using Eq. (21-1), compute the theoretical value of each of the following warrants:

	N	P_s	E
a.	5	$100	$400
b.	10	10	60
c.	2.3	4	10
d.	3.54	27⅛	35.40

2. Max Murphy, Inc., has warrants outstanding that allow the holder to purchase 3 shares of stock for a total of $60 for each warrant. Currently, the market price per share of Max Murphy common is $18. Investors hold the following probabilistic beliefs about the stock 6 months hence:

Market price per share	$16	$18	$20	$22	$24
Probability	.15	.20	.30	.20	.15

    a. What is the present theoretical value of the warrant?

    b. What is the expected value of stock price 6 months hence?

    c. What is the theoretical value of the warrant 6 months hence?

    d. Would you expect the present market price of the warrant to equal its theoretical value? If not, why not?

3. The Beruth Company is contemplating raising $10 million by means of a debt issue. It has the following alternatives:

    a. A 20-year, 8 percent convertible debenture issue with a $50 conversion price and $1,000 face value.

    b. A 20-year, 10 percent straight bond issue.

Each $1,000 bond has a detachable warrant to purchase four shares for $50 a share. The company has a 50 percent tax rate, and its stock is currently selling at $40 a share. Its earnings before interest and taxes are a constant 20 percent of its total capitalization, which currently appears as follows:

Common stock (par $5)	$ 5,000,000
Additional paid-in capital	10,000,000
Retained earnings	15,000,000
Total	$30,000,000

    (1) Show the capitalizations resulting from each alternative, both before and after conversion or exercise (a total of four capitalizations).

    (2) Compute earnings per share currently and under each of the four capitalizations determined in part 1.

    (3) If the price of Beruth stock went to $75, determine the theoretical value of each warrant issued under alternative b.

4. The common stock of the Draybar Corporation earns $2.50 per share, has a dividend payout of two-thirds, and sells at a P/E ratio of 16. Draybar wishes to offer $10 million of 9 percent, 20-year convertible debentures with an initial conversion premium of 20 percent and a call price of 105. Draybar currently has 1 million common shares outstanding and has a 50 percent tax rate.

    a. What is the conversion price?

    b. What is the conversion ratio per $1,000 debenture?

    c. What is the initial conversion value of each debenture?

    d. How many new shares of common must be issued if all debentures are converted?

    e. If Draybar can increase operating earnings by $1 million per year with the proceeds of the debenture issue, compute the new earnings per share and earnings retained before and after conversion.

5. Assume that the Draybar Corporation (in Problem 4) could sell $10 million in straight debt at 12 percent as an alternative to the convertible issue. Compute the earnings per share and earnings retained after issuance of the straight debt under the assumption of a $1 million increase in operating earnings and compare your answers with those obtained in Problem 4e.

6. What are the straight bond values of the following convertible bonds?

    a. An 8 percent coupon convertible bond with 20 years to maturity where a straight bond of this maturity would yield 13 percent

    b. A 10 percent coupon convertible bond with 15 years to maturity where the straight bond would yield 12 percent

7. Curran Consolidated Industries has outstanding a $7\frac{3}{4}$ percent, 20-year convertible debenture issue. Each $1,000 debenture is convertible into 25 shares of common stock. The company also has a straight debt issue outstanding of

640 *Part VI Capital Market Financing and Risk Management*

the same approximate maturity, so it is an easy matter to determine the straight bond value of the convertible issue. The market price of Curran stock is volatile. Over the last year, the following was observed:

	Observation				
	1	2	3	4	5
Market price per share	$ 40	$ 45	$ 32	$ 23	$ 18
Straight bond value	690	700	650	600	550
Market price of convertible debenture	1,065	1,140	890	740	640

a. Compute the premium-over-conversion value (in dollars) and the premium-over-straight-bond value for each of the observations.

b. Compare the two premiums either visually or by graph. What do the relationships tell you with respect to the valuation of the convertible debenture?

8. The following year, Curran Consolidated Industries fell on further hard times. Its stock price drops to $10 per share, and the market price of the convertible debentures to $440 per debenture. The straight bond value goes to $410. Determine the premium-over-conversion value and the premium-over-bond value. What can you say about the bond-value floor?

9. Singapore Enterprises is considering an exchangeable bond issue, where each bond can be exchanged for $16\frac{2}{3}$ shares of Malaysian Palm Oil Company. The latter company's stock is presently selling for $50 a share. At what premium-over-exchange value will the bonds be sold if they are sold for $1,000 a bond? Are there advantages to this type of financing versus a convertible issue?

10. Fujiwara Electronics Company has a warrant outstanding that enables the holder to acquire two shares of stock for $32 a share for each warrant held. The present market price of the stock is $39 a share, and the expected standard deviation of its continuously compounded return is .20. The warrant has 3 years until expiration. The current rate on short-term Treasury bills is 5 percent.

a. If one values the warrant as a "European" option and uses the Black–Scholes option pricing model, Eq. (5-2) in Chapter 5, what is the value of the warrant? Assume that the added shares of stock on exercise of the warrants are small relative to the number of shares outstanding and that no adjustments to the Black–Scholes formula are necessary.

b. What would happen to the value of the warrant if the standard deviation were .40? Why does this occur?

Solutions to Self-Correction Problems

1. Market price of warrant and theoretical value at various common stock prices (in ascending order):

Common price	$18	$20	$24	$27	$32	$38
Warrant price	3	5	8	12	20	29
Theoretical value	0	0	0	6	16	28

When plotted, the relationship is of the same pattern as that shown in Fig. 21-1. The maximum premium over theoretical value occurs when share price is $24 and the warrant has a theoretical value of zero. Here the greatest leverage occurs, and since volatility is what gives an option value, the premium over theoretical value tends to be the greatest at this point.

2. a. Conversion ratio × market price per share = 2 × $21 = $42

    b. ($50/42) − 1 = 19.05%

    c. Earnings per share effect:

Total after-tax earnings = $3 × 500,000 shares =	$1,500,000
Preferred stock dividend	140,000
Earnings available to common stockholders	$1,360,000
Number of shares	500,000
Basic earnings per share	$2.72
Total after-tax earnings	$1,500,000
Number of shares (500,000 + 80,000)	580,000
Diluted earnings per share	$2.59

   d. Primary earnings per share effect with profit increase:

Total after-tax earnings	$2,500,000
Preferred stock dividend	140,000
Earnings available to common stockholders	$2,360,000
Number of shares	500,000
Earnings per shares	$4.72
Total after-tax earnings	$2,500,000
Number of shares (500,000 + 80,000)	580,000
Earnings per share	$4.31

3. a. Conversion price = $36 × 1.12 = $40.32

    Call price per share the first 10 years = $40.32 × 1.06 = $42.74

    Price to which the common must rise before the company will be in a position to force conversion = $42.74 × 1.15 = $49.15

    Increase from present price = $49.15/$36 = 1.365

    At an 8 percent compound growth rate, earnings per share will grow to 1.36 in 4 years. (This is simply 1.08^4.) If the price/earnings ratio stays the same, it will take approximately 4 years before the company will be in a position to force conversion.

    b. This period is somewhat longer than the 2 to 3 years that market participants have come to expect for the convertible security. Still, it is not far out of line and the company may wish to go ahead. However, if uncertainty as to earnings per share increases with the length of time in the future, there may be considerable risk of an overhanging issue.

Selected References

ARZAC, ENRIQUE R., "PERCS, DECS, and Other Mandatory Convertibles," *Journal of Applied Corporate Finance*, 10 (Spring 1997), 54–63.

ASQUITH, PAUL, "Convertible Bonds Are Not Called Late," *Journal of Finance*, 50 (September 1995), 1275–89.

ASQUITH, PAUL, and DAVID W. MULLINS JR., "Convertible Debt: Corporate Call Policy and Voluntary Conversion," *Journal of Finance*, 46 (September 1991), 1273–89.

BARBER, BRAD M., "Exchangeable Debt," *Financial Management*, 22 (Summer 1993), 48–60.

BLACK, FISCHER, and MYRON SCHOLES, "The Pricing of Options and Corporate Liabilities," *Journal of Political Economy*, 81 (May–June 1973), 637–54.

BRENNAN, M. J., and E. S. SCHWARTZ, "Convertible Bonds: Valuation and Optimal Strategies for Call and Conversion," *Journal of Finance*, 32 (December 1977), 1699–1715.

——, "The Case for Convertibles," *Journal of Applied Corporate Finance*, 1 (Summer 1988), 55–64.

BURNEY, ROBERT B., and WILLIAM T. MOORE, "Valuation of Callable Warrants," *Review of Quantitative Finance and Accounting*, 8 (January 1997), 5–18.

CAROW, KENNETH A., GAYLE R. ERWIN, and JOHN J. MCCONNELL, "A Survey of U.S. Corporate Financing Innovations," *Journal of Applied Corporate Finance*, 12 (Spring 1999), 55–69.

CHEN, ANDREW H., "Uncommon Equity," *Journal of Applied Corporate Finance*, 5 (Spring 1992), 36–43.

COWAN, ARNOLD R., "Tax Options, Clienteles, and Adverse Selection: The Case of Convertible Exchangeable Preferred Stock," *Financial Management*, 28 (Summer 1999), 15–31.

DUNN, KENNETH B., and KENNETH M. EADES, "Voluntary Conversion of Convertible Securities and the Optimal Call Strategy," *Journal of Financial Economics*, 23 (August 1989), 273–301.

EDERINGTON, LOUIS H., GARY L. CATON, and CYNTHIA J. CAMPBELL, "To Call or Not to Call Convertible Debt," *Financial Management*, 26 (Spring 1997), 22–31.

INGERSOLL, JONATHAN E., JR., "A Contingent-Claims Valuation of Convertible Securities," *Journal of Financial Economics*, 4 (January 1977), 289–321.

——, "An Examination of Corporate Call Policies on Convertible Securities," *Journal of Finance*, 32 (May 1977), 463–78.

JONES, E. PHILIP, and SCOTT P. MASON, "Equity-Linked Debt," *Midland Corporate Finance Journal*, 3 (Winter 1986), 47–58.

KANG, JUN-KOO, and YUL W. LEE, "The Pricing of Convertible Debt Offerings," *Journal of Financial Economics*, 41 (June 1996), 231–48.

KIM, YONG CHEOL, and RENE M. STULZ, "Is There a Global Market for Convertible Bonds?" *Journal of Business*, 65 (January 1992), 75–91.

MAYERS, DAVID, "Why Firms Issue Convertible Bonds: The Matching of Financial and Real Investment Options," *Journal of Financial Economics*, 47 (January 1998), 83–102.

SCHULTZ, PAUL, "Calls of Warrants: Timing and Market Reaction," *Journal of Finance*, 48 (June 1993), 681–96.

——, "Unit Initial Public Offerings: A Form of Staged Financing," *Journal of Financial Economics*, 34 (October 1993), 199–229.

STEIN, JEREMY C., "Convertible Bonds as Backdoor Equity Financing," *Journal of Financial Economics*, 32 (August 1992), 3–21.

TSIVERIOTIS, KOSTAS, and CHRIS FERNANDEZ, "Valuing Convertible Bonds with Credit Risk," *Journal of Fixed Income*, 8 (September 1998), 95–102.

VAN HORNE, JAMES C., "Warrant Valuation in Relation to Volatility and Opportunity Costs," *Industrial Management Review*, 10 (Spring 1969), 19–32.

Wachowicz's Web World is an excellent overall Web site produced and maintained by my coauthor of *Fundamentals of Financial Management*, John M. Wachowicz Jr. It contains descriptions of and links to many finance Web sites and articles. *www.prenhall.com/wachowicz.*

22

Managing Financial Risk

U nlike times in the past, the financial officer today has a be-wildering number of ways to hedge risk. If a company does not wish to bear certain types of risk, it can shift the undesir-able risk to others. This risk may have to do with interest rates, exchange rates, stock prices, or commodity prices. Some risk-shifting devices are traded on open exchanges, such as the Chicago Board of Trade, the Chicago Mercantile Exchange, the Commodity Exchange in New York, and the London International Financial Futures Exchange. Others are available in the over-the-counter market, where financial contracts are individually crafted and negotiated with an investment bank. In this chapter, we come to know these devices and what they can do for us. ■

DERIVATIVE SECURITIES

A *primary* financial instrument evidences a direct claim against some other party. These instruments often are traded in the **spot market** with prices set by the usual forces of supply and demand. In contrast, a **derivative** security derives its value from an underlying primary security. One example is the stock option, which we considered in Chapter 5. Movements in the price of the underlying asset, the stock, drive the value of the derivative instrument, the option.

Derivative securities derive their value from primary securities.

Derivative, or synthetic, securities have been around for some time, in the form of simple put and call options on stocks. These options were traded in relatively illiquid over-the-counter markets. With the tremendous financial innovation that occurred during the last 20 years (see Chapter 17), a cascade of new derivatives occurred. As long as investors have desires for particular security properties, it pays an investment bank to satisfy these desires and complete the market. Without current computer technology, much of what we observe in derivatives would not be possible. The complication of many derivative securities is simply too great to unravel without sophisticated computer programming.

Derivatives can insulate a corporation from different types of risk. For example, American Airlines may wish to hedge against rising fuel prices and does so by buying an option that rises in value with oil prices. Or Kentucky Fried Chicken may buy Japanese yen forward to protect itself against adverse currency movements affecting its many Japanese outlets. What risk should be hedged and how

645

much? There is no universal rule. However, there are certain principles of hedging that warrant exploration before we consider specific risk-shifting devices.

HEDGING RISK

Hedging is taking a derivative position opposite to your exposure.

Before risk can be hedged, it first must be identified. Exactly what kind of risk exposure is involved? Once identified, we then try to quantify it with probabilities and perhaps with simulations. The idea is to determine what is likely to happen if the underlying situation changes. For example, if the source of the risk were interest rates, we would like to know what happens to the value of our security or financing position with a change in interest rates.[1] Knowing this, the idea in hedging is to take a position *opposite* to the exposure. This can be with futures contracts, forward contracts, options, or swaps. We would like to effect a perfect hedge, but this usually is not possible. The value of our position and the value of the instrument used to hedge do not move completely in concert. Usually there are slight to moderate deviations. These deviations create **basis risk,** a phenomenon we will illustrate shortly.

Some Hedging Fundamentals

Hedge ratio is the ratio of one position relative to the other where risk is neutralized.

The principles of hedging are the same regardless of the type of hedge undertaken. Suppose you wish to hedge an asset you own with an offsetting instrument. You hope that downward price movements in the value of your asset will be offset by upward movements in the value of the instrument with which you hedge. Suppose the asset you own is X and the instrument with which you hedge, Y. The expected change in values of these two instruments can be reflected as

$$\text{Value } \overline{X} = a + \delta(\text{Value } \overline{Y}) \qquad (22\text{-}1)$$

where both changes in value are expected, a is a constant, and δ (delta) reflects the sensitivity of expected changes in X to changes in the value of Y. If δ were 0.6, it would suggest that on average X goes up or down in value by 0.6 percent with a 1 percent change in the value of Y.

The delta (δ) tells us the number of units of Y that should be used to hedge our position in X. The delta (δ) is known as the **hedge ratio.** If the delta were 0.6 as assumed above, we would make an offsetting commitment of $0.60 in Y for every $1.00 of investment in X. This delta hedge would be expected to offset the risk of holding X. However, the offset usually is not perfect, for reasons we illustrate shortly.

Dynamic Hedging

The idea, then, is to minimize risk. Because the values of the two instruments change over time, so too does the relationship between them. The delta in Eq. (22-1) is not constant over time but is ever changing. As a result, you must adjust your hedge ratio over time if risk is to be minimized. This adjustment is known as *dynamic hedging,* and it must be done with an eye to transaction costs. The higher these costs, the fewer the adjustments that should be made. The lower the transaction costs, the more that adjustments can occur and the more that risk is mini-

---

[1]See Clifford W. Smith Jr., Charles W. Smithson, and D. Sykes Wilford, *Managing Financial Risk* (New York: Harper & Row, 1990), Chaps. 2 and 17; and Tim S. Campbell and William A. Kracaw, *Financial Risk Management* (New York: HarperCollins, 1993), Chap. 8, for discussion of quantifying risk and the appropriate hedging strategy.

mized. Dynamic hedging requires continual vigilance as to underlying changes in the delta. This monitoring is essential if risk is to be controlled.

Arguments for Corporate Hedging

If financial markets are efficient and complete, why should the corporation hedge at all? With no imperfections, it would be a matter of indifference to investors whether or not the firm hedged. Whatever the company did, shareholders could replicate through "homemade" hedging on their own. As in our earlier discussion of corporate finance theory, only if you can do something for your stockholders that they cannot do for themselves do you create value.

Bankruptcy Costs With imperfections, however, hedging may be a thing of value. One imperfection is *bankruptcy costs*, which is a deadweight loss to suppliers of capital. (See Chapter 9 for amplification on this point.) The possibility of insolvency depends on total cash-flow variability. Hedging can reduce this variability and, in the process, the expected cost of bankruptcy. This is not to say that one would want to eliminate this risk altogether, but might want to reduce the chance that bankruptcy costs will be incurred. The same argument was invoked when we considered diversification of assets in Chapter 8.[2]

Agency Costs By hedging, the corporation may be able to *reduce agency costs*. The safer the company, the less creditors and others will need to monitor management and the less will be the monitoring costs borne by the corporation. Of course, such costs also can be reduced through employing less debt or by maintaining more liquidity. Still hedging is an appropriate vehicle for accomplishing this objective. In this vein, hedging may reduce the problem of *underinvestment*, where equity holders forgo positive net-present-value projects because too much of the gain from such goes to debt holders. This problem was illustrated in Chapter 9, where we saw that the greater the debt of a company the greater might be the underinvestment problem. By hedging some of the adversity associated with high leverage, a company can ameliorate the problem.[3]

Reduce Taxes *Expected taxes* may be reduced if the effective tax schedule is convex.[4] With a progressive income tax schedule, hedging might stabilize earnings in a mid-range where the tax bite is less than it is if reported earnings are more volatile. With more volatile earnings, the lesser earnings in some years do not offset the higher tax bite associated with greater earnings in other years. For this effect to be meaningful, the tax schedule must be reasonably progressive. This is not the case in the United States, except for the first $75,000 in corporate income. Still, certain tax preference items introduce a degree of progressivity into the corporate tax schedule.

---

[2]See also Clifford W. Smith Jr. and Rene M. Stulz, "The Determinants of Firms' Hedging Policies," *Journal of Financial and Quantitative Analysis*, 20 (June 1985), 391–405.

[3]See Deana R. Nance, Clifford W. Smith Jr., and Charles W. Smithson, "On the Determinants of Corporate Hedging," *Journal of Finance*, 48 (March 1993), 269–70.

[4]*Ibid.*, pp. 268–69. In testing for this effect, the authors find that firms with more convex tax schedules hedge more. Their work also supports the notion that hedging, and such financial policies as liquidity, dividend, and capital structure, are substitutes.

Regulations   Another reason to hedge may be *regulatory constraints*. Regulations and/or traditions pertaining to minimum accounting capital requirements for a financial institution or for a public utility may make the negative "penalties" associated with falling below because of poor accounting earnings greater than the positive "rewards" associated with good earnings. Hedging may serve to stabilize accounting earnings and reduce the probability of falling below some regulatory requirement. Similarly, credit and bond rating agencies pay attention to certain financial ratios being maintained. When a credit rating is in jeopardy, hedging may serve to reduce the probability of a downward rating. As with the other things mentioned, there are ways other than hedging to realize these objectives.

Operating Management Focus   Finally, hedging may *insulate operating managers* from the vagaries of interest-rate changes and currency movements. If their performance is judged on "all inclusive" results, such vagaries may distract them from operations. To the extent managers spend significant time looking over their shoulders at interest-rate changes and currency movements, operating efficiency may suffer. Under these circumstances, hedging may serve to align objectives to what is really important in creating value. If this is the case, stockholders may be better served.

A Summing Up

For the reasons examined, it may make sense for a company to hedge its risk exposure. Following up on earlier ideas, first one must identify the relevant risk and then quantify the exposure. Once these steps are undertaken, the financial manager must select the best hedging vehicle available to minimize the risk involved. In the subsequent sections of this chapter, we examine these vehicles. In the process we will come to an understanding not only of instruments themselves but also of hedging.

FUTURES MARKETS

A **futures contract** is a standardized agreement that calls for delivery of a commodity at some specified future date. In the case of financial futures, the commodity is a security. Transactions occur either on an *exchange* or through an investment bank in what is known as the *over-the-counter market*. With an exchange transaction, the clearinghouse of the exchange interposes itself between the buyer and the seller. Its creditworthiness is substituted for that of the broker on the other side of the transaction, and each exchange has a number of rules governing transactions. While the clearinghouse affords the market participant a degree of safety, if the broker should default the participant may be hurt.[5]

As in commodities, very few financial futures contracts involve actual delivery at maturity. Rather, buyers and sellers of a contract independently take offsetting positions to close out the contract. The seller cancels a contract by buying another contract; the buyer, by selling another contract. As a result, only a small percentage of contracts come to actual delivery. The **open interest** is the number of futures contracts outstanding that have not been closed.

---

[5]For an analysis of this problem, see James V. Jordan and George Emir Morgan, "Default Risk in Futures Markets: The Customer Broker Relationship," *Journal of Finance*, 45 (July 1990), 909–33.

Features of Futures Markets

Interest-rate futures markets are available for Eurodollars, federal funds, 1-month LIBOR, Treasury bills, Treasury notes, Treasury bonds, and municipal bonds. Each market is different. By far the most important, volume-wise, are Eurodollars, Treasury notes, and Treasury bonds.

Money Market Instruments To illustrate a transaction, consider first the market for Eurodollars. Each contract is for $1 million face value of Eurodollar deposits, with delivery months of March, June, September, and December (second Wednesday of the month). At present, 40 delivery months are traded, going out nearly 10 years. In the case of Eurodollars, there is no physical settlement on the delivery day. Rather, it is a cash settlement procedure against the LIBOR rate. In contrast, the Treasury bill futures market calls for the actual delivery of a 90- to 92-day bill. Cash settlements involve fewer complications concerning delivery, but the derivation of an index, such as obtaining and averaging Eurodollar quotations, also has its problems.

Margin Requirements When transacting in a futures contract, one must put up margin as a security deposit. The exchange sets the minimum margin requirement, but a brokerage firm may ask for more. Only competition limits the amount of margin a firm requires. At the time of this writing, the margin requirement on money market futures was around $2,000 per $1 million contract, whereas that on Treasury bond futures also was $2,000, but per a $100,000 contract. In general, the more volatile the futures market for a particular instrument, the higher the margin required. In putting up margin, one can use cash or an interest-bearing security such as Treasury bills. In either case, the initial margin put up earns a market rate of interest.

Margin is the amount of money that must be pledged to cover fluctuations in the market price of the contract, and it is subject to daily reset.

Both **initial** and **maintenance** margin requirements are established. Typically, the maintenance requirement is 75 to 80 percent of the initial margin requirement. The way it works is as follows. Suppose the initial and maintenance margin requirements on Treasury bond futures are $2,000 and $1,500, respectively. Initially, both the buyer and the seller (writer) of the contract put up $2,000. If interest rates rise, the value of the buyer's position declines. As long as the decline is less than $500 per $100,000 contract, the buyer is not obligated to put up additional margin. However, if the cumulative decline in value comes to $501, the buyer's margin account would stand at $1,499. He or she would get a margin call from the brokerage firm and be obligated to restore the account to the initial level, namely to $2,000. Each day, the futures contract is **marked-to-market** in the sense that it is valued at the closing price. Price movements affect the margin positions of buyers and sellers in opposite ways. Every day there is a winner and a loser, depending on the direction of price movement, for it is a zero-sum game. Margin settlements must be made in keeping with the procedures just outlined. Unlike spot market instruments, settlements occur not at the end of the contract but daily. This is a distinguishing feature of the futures markets.

Marked-to-market means daily valuation of a contract with the loser owing money to the winner.

Longer-Term Instruments The features of a longer-term contract, such as Treasury bond futures, are somewhat different from those for Eurodollars. The trading unit for a single contract is $100,000, in contrast to $1 million. Delivery months are March, June, September, and December, and contracts go out about $2\frac{1}{2}$ years. Price quotations are given as a percentage of the face value ($100) of an 8 percent coupon with 20 years to maturity. A quotation of $102\frac{4}{32}$ means $102\frac{1}{8}$ percent of $100, or $102.125.

For delivery, any Treasury bond with at least 15 years to the earliest call date or to maturity may be used. This contrasts with Treasury bills, where a specific maturity bill is stated in the contract. Because most bonds have a coupon rate other than 8 percent, the invoice is the settlement price multiplied by a **conversion factor.** Recall that the futures contract settlement price is based on a coupon rate of 8 percent. Therefore, the conversion factor is greater than 1.00 for coupon rates greater than 8 percent, 1.00 for an 8 percent coupon bond, and less than 1.00 for coupon rates less than 8 percent. The greater the deviation in coupon rate from 8 percent, the greater the deviation in conversion factor from 1.00.

Conversion factors are established for each coupon rate and time to maturity. Although a formula is used to establish them, conversion factors are readily available to market participants through tables and computer programs.

Hedging and Speculation

Hedging represents taking a futures contract position opposite to a position taken in the spot market. The purpose is to reduce risk exposure by protecting oneself from unexpected price changes. In contrast, a **speculator** takes positions in futures markets in the pursuit of profits and assumes price risk in this endeavor. In other words, a long or short position is undertaken without an offsetting position in the spot market. The speculator buys or sells futures contracts based on his or her interest-rate expectations. Why not use the spot market? Because it often is more expensive with respect to transaction costs and slower in execution than the futures market.

Long Hedges   A *long hedge* involves buying (going long in) a futures contract. It is generally employed to lock in an interest rate that is believed to be high. Suppose an investor will have $1 million to invest in Treasury bonds 2 months hence—on November 1, for example. The investor believes interest rates have peaked at present and wishes to lock in the current high rates (on September 1), even though the funds will not be available for investment for 2 months.

Suppose the conditions shown in Table 22-1 held for September 1 and November 1, respectively. In the example, we ignore transaction costs and margin deposits.

TABLE 22-1
Illustration of a Long Hedge

Cash Market	Futures Market

September 1:
  8% Treasury bond sells at $106\frac{15}{32}$
  Investor wants to lock in high yield
	September 1:
	  Buys 10 December Treasury bond
	    futures contracts at $107\frac{9}{32}$

November 1:
  Buys $1 million of 8% Treasury
    bond at $113\frac{6}{32}$
	November 1:
	  Sells 10 December bond futures
	    contracts at $113\frac{17}{32}$

Loss: $67,187.50	Gain: $62,500

We also assume the use of 8 percent coupon bonds in the spot market, so we do not need a conversion factor. The investor buys 10 futures contracts on September 1, and prices rise and yields fall as expected. By selling the contracts on November 1, the investor realizes a gain of $62,500. On the same day, the investor purchases $1 million in Treasury bonds at a higher price and lower yield than prevailed on September 1. The opportunity loss is $67,187.50. Thus, the opportunity loss is offset, but not entirely so, by the gain on the futures contracts. The hedge was less than perfect, but it was largely successful in insulating the investor from price changes.

Notice that the use of the futures market provides a **two-sided hedge.** If interest rates rise in our example, you gain in an opportunity sense on your cash-market purchase November 1, but lose on your futures market position. If interest rates fall, as they do in the example, the opposite occurs. The hedge is two-sided with respect to price risk; you merely lock in a position (except for residual risk, to be discussed shortly). This contrasts with **one-sided hedges,** such as options, which are taken up next. The transaction cost of taking a futures position, either for hedging or for speculative purposes, is relatively low. A $100,000 contract is likely to cost less than $50 to establish and settle.

Long hedges involve buying a futures contract; **short hedges**, writing a contract.

Short Hedges A *short hedge* involves the opposite sort of transactions from a long hedge. Here the idea is to sell a futures contract now because of a belief that interest rates will rise. The sale of a futures contract is used as a substitute for the sale of an actual security held. Another example of a short hedge is a corporation that needs to borrow in the future and sells a futures contract now to protect itself against an expected rise in interest rates. Suppose on February 1, a corporation knows it will need to borrow $1 million in the long-term market 3 months hence. The company feels interest rates will rise and wishes to hedge against this possibility.

Unfortunately, there is no futures market for long-term corporate bonds. Therefore, the company must look to a related market and settles on the Treasury bond futures market. While interest rates in these two markets do not move entirely in concert, there is a close relationship, so a **cross hedge** across markets makes sense. This type of hedge is shown in Table 22-2. Again we ignore transac-

TABLE 22-2
Illustration of a Short Cross Hedge

Cash Market	Futures Market
February 1:	February 1:
$7\frac{1}{2}$% high-grade, 20-year corporate bond sells at $99\frac{3}{8}$ Issuer wants to protect against rise in interest rates	Sells 12 June 8% Treasury bond futures contracts at $110\frac{2}{32}$
May 1:	May 1:
Issues $7\frac{1}{2}$% corporate bond at $91\frac{7}{8}$	Buys 12 June 8% Treasury bond futures contracts at $103\frac{14}{32}$
Loss: $75,000	Gain: $79,500

tion costs and margin deposits. Instead of selling 10 Treasury bond futures contracts, the company sells 12, to bring its total commitment to a little over $1 million in the futures market. The hedge ratio, which is greater than 1.0, is established in keeping with the considerations in the previous section. Because the cross markets do not have exactly the same price movements, a perfect hedge is not achieved. In this case, the gain in the futures market more than offsets the opportunity loss in the spot market. These examples are sufficient to illustrate the principles of hedging and some of the terms.

Basis Risk

The examples show that hedging is not perfect in eliminating all the risk of a position. In hedging, market participants are concerned with fluctuations in the **basis,** which portrays the risk to the hedger. The basis is simply

$$\text{Basis} = \text{Spot market price} - \text{Future price (adjusted by appropriate conversion factor)} \qquad (22\text{-}2)$$

Basis risk is the random fluctuation in net position that remains after hedging.

Theoretically, the spot price less the futures price should equal the *cost of carry*. The cost of carry is the cash return, or yield earned, on the asset less the net financing cost. A *positive carry* occurs when the former exceeds the latter; a *negative carry* when the opposite prevails. If there is a positive carry, the spot price should exceed the futures price; with a negative carry it should be less than the futures price.

While this is how things should work, hedgers face uncertainty as to what basis will prevail when they close out their futures contracts. This is known as **basis risk.** To illustrate this risk, suppose you hold a portfolio of corporate bonds and wish to hedge it. If interest rates rise, the value of your portfolio declines, and vice versa. This is illustrated in the top panel of Fig. 22-1. The mathematical relationship between value and interest-rate changes is given by the curvilinear line. Because the corporate bond market is subject to imperfections, there may be deviations about the line, as depicted by the scatter of dots.

To hedge a portfolio one would want to write Treasury bond futures contracts. As there is not a viable corporate bond futures market, one must resort to a cross hedge. By writing futures contracts, one offsets the long position in the spot market with a short position in the futures market. As interest rates rise, the value of the futures contract will increase and vice versa. The relationship is illustrated by the middle panel of Fig. 22-1. Here, too, there is a random component, as depicted by the scatter of dots.

On average, the long and the short positions are offsetting. As shown in the bottom panel of Fig. 22-1, the overall position (spot and futures) is insensitive to changes in interest rates. However, there is risk left over, again depicted by the dispersion of dots about the line. This basis risk arises because of somewhat divergent movements in the spot and futures markets. However, the financial manager can affect a reasonable hedge even with basis risk.

FORWARD CONTRACTS

The forward contract serves the same economic function as a futures contract but is different in the detail. With respect to interest-rate forward contracts, the **forward rate** is that rate at which two parties agree to lend and borrow money for a specified period of time in the future. For example, a forward contract might be for

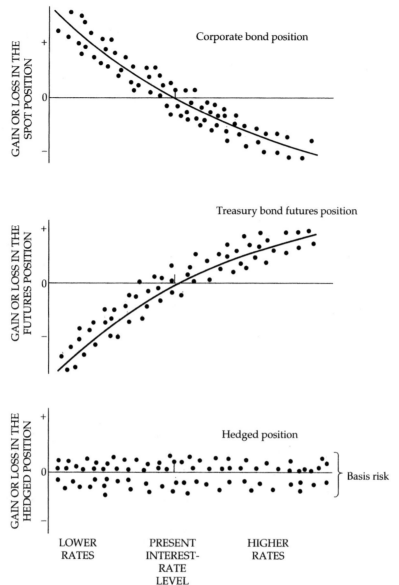

FIGURE 22-1

Illustration of basis risk in hedging a corporate bond portfolio

Forward and futures contracts are "two-sided" hedges.

a 2-year loan beginning 3 years hence. Such a contract might be arranged explicitly with an investment bank in what is known as the *over-the-counter* market. This is merely to say that it is arranged privately and not acquired on an exchange as is a futures contract.

Implicit Forward Arrangements

Rather than arrange an explicit forward contract, you can create one for yourself. Suppose you wanted to lock in a forward rate on Treasury securities, say, a 1-year return starting 2 years from now. You could manufacture your own forward contract by buying a 3-year Treasury security and selling short a 2-year security. With a *short sale*, you borrow a security and sell it in the market, both of which are through an investment bank. You have the obligation to return the security to the party from whom it was borrowed. If the security declines in value, you will be able to buy it back at a price lower than that at which it was sold. If it is higher in price, the opposite occurs. By buying the 3-year security and selling short the 2-year security you have created a forward contract that upon delivery 2 years hence provides you a 1-year security.

Embedded in yields for zero-coupon Treasury securities of various maturities are implied forward rates of interest. If we were interested in the implied forward rate for a one-period loan beginning n periods in the future, it can be derived with the following:

$$_n r_1 = \frac{(1 + R_{n+1})^{n+1}}{(1 + R_n)^n} - 1 \qquad (22\text{-}3)$$

where $_n r_1$ is the implied forward rate, R_{n+1} is the actual rate of interest for an $n + 1$ period Treasury security, and R_n is that for an n-period security. Suppose the interest rate for a 6-year zero coupon Treasury security were 6 percent, whereas that for a 5-year security were 5.7 percent. The implied 1-year forward rate 5 years hence is

$$_5 r_1 = \frac{(1.060)^6}{(1.057)^5} - 1 = 7.51\%$$

Effectively we can achieve this forward rate by buying the 6-year Treasury security and selling short the 5-year security.

Difference from a Futures Contract

Unlike a futures contract, a forward contract is nonstandardized. There is no clearinghouse and the secondary market, to the extent it exists at all, is over-the-counter as opposed to an exchange market. As a result, the forward contract is less liquid. The two contracts also differ in that there are daily settlements of a futures position, while settlement of the forward contract comes only at maturity. As discussed previously, the futures position is marked-to-market with daily settlements throughout the life of the contract. Also, the forward contract is not constrained as to contract size, such as multiples of $1 million, nor as to the starting and ending dates. Rather it can be customized to most any amount and any maturity.

Finally, futures and forward contracts may differ in default risk. The futures contract is backed by the clearinghouse involved in the transaction. Though not entirely free of risk, it tends to be safer than a forward contract arranged with an investment bank. The creditworthiness of the provider of a forward contract must be carefully monitored. Usually, this is done simply by restricting transactions to an intermediary having some minimum credit rating, such as single A or better.

Having made the case for differences between forward and futures contracts, we return to the proposition that generally the two serve the same economic function. To be sure, the details may cause you to prefer one over the other. However, both represent "two-sided" hedges and are used in the ways described in the previous section. We turn now to a risk management device that is somewhat different in economic function.

OPTION CONTRACTS

An *option* is yet another security that derives its value from that of an underlying security. As we know from Chapter 5, the option may be to acquire stock. It may be that the option is to acquire a debt instrument or an interest-rate futures position, which is somewhat like a double derivative security. Option valuation is fundamental to understanding debt options; we rely on Chapter 5 for this purpose together with applications of option pricing theory in subsequent chapters.

Debt Options

Option contracts are "one-sided" hedges.

Exchange markets for debt options began in 1982 with options on individual Treasury securities and options on interest-rate futures contracts. The former type of contract has withered on the exchange market, though option contracts can be arranged on individual Treasury securities through an investment bank. In contrast, exchange options on futures have grown dramatically, and there now are futures options on Eurodollars, Treasury notes, Treasury bonds, and on British and German long-term debt. As is the case for futures markets, volume is heaviest for options on Eurodollar futures and on Treasury bond futures.

Use of Debt Options

With a futures contract, an investor's gain or loss depends on interest-rate movements. If one wished to hedge a long position in a fixed-income security, he or she would take a short position in a futures contract; that is, a hedger would write a contract. By such action a hedger largely neutralizes risk; the remaining basis risk was described earlier. The situation is illustrated in the top panel of Fig. 22-2.

With an option, the potential loss is limited to the premium paid. This contrasts with a futures position where the loss is not so bounded. If an individual wished to hedge a long position in a fixed-income security, he or she would buy a put option. The situation is illustrated in the bottom panel of Fig. 22-2.

Options are particularly suited to hedging risk in one direction. Consider a fixed-rate loan commitment by a financial institution. If interest rates rise, a high proportion of the commitments will be taken down, necessitating the financial institution to make loans at below market rates of interest. By purchasing a put option, however, the financial institution offsets the value loss that occurs with higher interest rates. If interest rates decline, customers will renegotiate their loans at lower rates and let their commitments expire. Thus, the risk to the financial institution is **one-sided**—rising interest rates. Effectively, the financial institution has written a put option to its customers. To hedge, it may purchase a put option in the market.

So far we have discussed only put options. However, one can buy call options or write either type of option. The various configurations of price movements are shown in Fig. 22-3. The dark lines represent expiration date values of the options as interest rates change. Note that with interest rates on the horizontal axis, the lines are opposite to what would be the case if prices were used. Also, the lines are curvilinear, reflecting the relationship between value changes and interest rates. Thus, debt options can be used in a number of ways to hedge risk or place bets on the direction and/or volatility of interest rates.

Caps, Floors, and Collars

A cap is a put option on a fixed-income security's value, whereas **a floor** is a call option.

On occasion, borrowers want to **cap** their short-term, floating-rate borrowing costs. If interest rates should rise beyond some specified ceiling, the borrower pays no more. One vehicle for "manufacturing" your own cap is to purchase a put option. Should interest rates rise, you pay more on your borrowings but gain on your put position. Caps also can be arranged directly with a lender or an investment bank, for a price. Usually the price takes the form of a fee. The presence of a cap

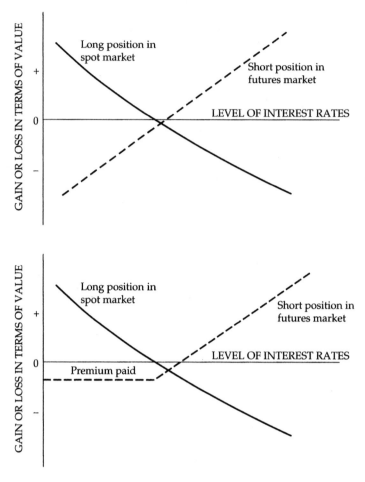

FIGURE 22-2
Hedging with interest-rate futures and options

A collar is a combination of a cap and a floor, with variation only in the mid-range.

protects the borrower, as shown in the top panel of Fig. 22-4, relative to what occurs under a straight floating-rate arrangement. The index frequently used in the cap market is the 3-month LIBOR rate.

If a borrower is willing to accept a **floor** in addition to receiving a cap, a **collar** is created. This arrangement is shown in the lower panel of Fig. 22-4. If interest rates fall below the floor, the borrower pays the floor rate. If they rise above the ceiling, the borrower pays the cap rate. Only in the intermediate range do borrowing costs vary with underlying short-term interest rates. The advantage of a collar is that the cost is much less than it is for a cap, because the lender is protected against significant declines in interest rates. The lower the present interest rate in relation to the floor, the lower the cost of the collar. If close enough, the collar will have no cost. The cap and collar markets have developed as customized derivative products, and they are available through commercial and investment banks.[6] In turn, these institutions use debt options to insulate their interest-rate risk exposure.

---

[6]For a methodology for pricing caps and collars, see Eric Briys, Michel Crouhy, and Rainer Schobel, "The Pricing of Default-Free Interest Rate Cap, Floor, and Collar Agreements," *Journal of Finance*, 46 (December 1991), 1879–92.

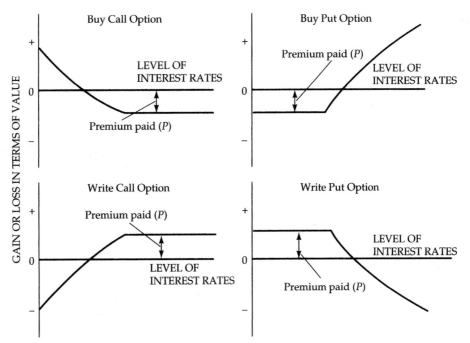

FIGURE 22-3

Profit or loss in options position with a change in interest rates

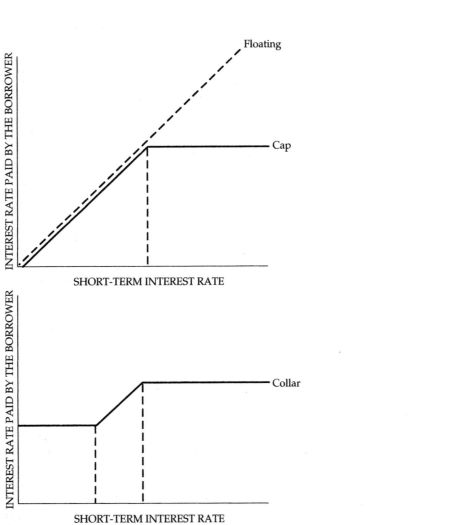

FIGURE 22-4

Illustrations of floating-rate, cap, and collar arrangements

Valuation of Debt Options

Option pricing models in the spirit of Black–Scholes may be used to value debt options (substituting futures prices and variances for stock prices and variances in the formula). As with any option, the key is the volatility of returns for the associated asset. In this case, volatility has to do with the variability of interest rates. Unlike stock options, where the return variance is assumed to be constant over time, a bond's return variance declines as maturity approaches. Although the assumption of constant variance may be reasonable over a short time span, it obviously does not hold over the long run. Variance changes over time. Another problem is the assumption of a constant short-term interest rate, implying a term structure anchored at the short end.

Because prices of fixed-income securities are bounded on the upside by their face value at maturity, there is a problem in applying standard option pricing formulas. Such formulas assume no limits for the volatility parameter, frequently expressed in terms of the log-normal price distribution. Instead of price, many scholars use yield and assume that it conforms to some type of distribution, usually log-normal, at the expiration of the option. Finally, most option models, such as Black–Scholes, are for European options, whereas debt options may be exercised up to and including the expiration date. However, adjustments can be made to come to grips with the problem of early exercise.[7] When properly modified, the Black–Scholes model gives reasonable explanations of debt option pricing. More complicated modeling is explored in a companion book.[8]

Yield Curve Options

Just as there are options on interest rates, there are options on yield spreads. The spread is simply a long-term Treasury interest rate minus a shorter-term rate. For the SYCURVE (slope of the yield curve) options of Goldman Sachs, for example, the more popular options are the 2- to 10-year spread, the 2- to 30-year spread, and the 10- to 30-year spread. There is no deliverable instrument involved; all settlements are on a cash basis, relative to the spread that prevails upon exercise of the option.

The exercise "price" is expressed in terms of basis points. Suppose the exercise, or strike, spread for a 2- to 30-year call option is 125 basis points, or $1\frac{1}{4}$ percent. If the actual yield spread turns out to be greater than 125 basis points, the option is "in the money" and can be exercised to advantage. The holder receives 1 cent per $1 of face value for every basis point above the exercise spread. If the actual spread turns out to be 144 basis points and a $1 million call option is involved, the settlement amount is

$$(144 - 125) \times .01 \times \$1 \text{ million} = \$190,000$$

Whether the option holder makes money, of course, depends on what was paid for the option. If the premium were $110,000, the net profit would be $80,000 on the contract. A put option is opposite in direction. If the actual spread is below the exercise spread, the option is "in the money."

---

[7]See Robert E. Whaley, "On Valuing American Futures Options," *Financial Analysts Journal*, 42 (May–June 1986), 49–59.

[8]James C. Van Horne, *Financial Market Rates and Flows*, 6th ed. (Upper Saddle River, NJ: Prentice Hall, 2001), Chaps. 5 and 10.

For the call option holder the bet being placed is that the term structure of interest rates will widen, whereas with a put option it will flatten. A number of applications to bond portfolio management are possible. Risk can be more effectively isolated when this financial innovation is used either by itself or in combination with other derivative securities. The greater the volatility of yield spreads, of course, the more valuable this type of option and the greater the premium charged for its use. However, volatility of a spread is different from the volatility of yield for a specific maturity instrument. As a result, the valuation of these options is more complicated even though some of the same tools are used.

INTEREST-RATE SWAPS

A swap exchanges a floating-rate obligation for a fixed-rate one, or vice versa.

When a company can borrow to advantage with one type of financing but really prefers another, it sometimes will engage in a swap. A **swap,** as the name implies, represents an exchange of obligations. There are two principal types: *currency swaps* and *interest-rate swaps.* With the former, two parties exchange interest obligations on debt denominated in different currencies. At maturity the principal amounts are exchanged, usually at a rate of exchange agreed upon in advance. With an interest-rate swap, interest-payment obligations are exchanged between two parties, but they are denominated in the same currency. Our focus in this chapter is on interest-rate swaps; in Chapter 25 we consider currency swaps. The swap can be longer term in nature than either the forward or the futures contract. Terms extend out to 15 years or more, whereas the range for forward or futures contracts is upward to 5 years, and this only for Eurodollars. The market for swaps is unregulated and began in the early 1980s.

Swap Features

The most common swap is the **floating-/fixed-rate** exchange. For example, a corporation that has borrowed on a fixed-rate, term basis may swap with a counterparty to make floating-rate interest payments. The counterparty, which has borrowed directly on a floating-rate basis, agrees to make fixed-rate interest payments in the swap. There is no transfer of principal; it is *notional* only. The interest obligation is what is exchanged, and this usually is done every 6 months. The exchange itself is on a net settlement basis. That is, the party that owes more interest than it receives in the swap pays the difference. Often, the arrangement is blind in that the counterparties do not know each other. An intermediary—often a commercial or investment bank—makes the arrangements. Sometimes the intermediary will assume the obligation of one of the counterparties, but usually this assumption is only temporary until an outside counterparty can be found.

Typically, floating-rate payments are tied to the London interbank offer rate (LIBOR), though this does not need to be the case. LIBOR is the rate for top-quality Eurodollar borrowings by banks. For standardized swaps, a secondary market of sorts developed in the mid- to late 1980s. This market allows contracts to be reversed or terminated, providing a degree of liquidity to be discussed shortly.

Though the floating-/fixed-rate swap is the most common, a *basis swap,* or floating-to-floating swap as it sometimes is called, also is used. With this type of arrangement, two floating-rate obligations are exchanged. Typically, the indices used are different for the two instruments. One might be LIBOR while the other is the 6-month Treasury bill rate. If a party's assets and liabilities are priced off of different indices, a basis swap may put them on the same footing. It is an effort to reduce basis risk; hence the name. In addition to these standard swaps, there is an array of customized swaps.

Illustration

To illustrate a basic floating-/fixed-rate swap, consider the example in Fig. 22-5. Company A has an AAA credit rating and is able to borrow directly in the market at a rate of 7 percent for a 10-year loan and at LIBOR + 0.20 percent for a floating-rate loan. Company B has a BBB credit rating and can borrow directly at interest rates of 8.20 percent term and LIBOR + 0.75 percent floating. In our example, company A borrows directly at a fixed rate of 7 percent and swaps to pay floating rate at LIBOR. It is called the **floating-rate payer**. In contrast, company B borrows directly in the floating-rate market at LIBOR + 0.75 percent, and agrees to pay a fixed rate of 7.16 percent in the swap. It is called the **fixed-rate payer**. Finally, the intermediary is interposed between the two parties. It passes the floating-rate payments through directly but retains 0.04 percent of the fixed-rate payments as its margin.

At the bottom of the figure is a recap which portrays the "alleged" savings. For company A, its all-in cost of floating-rate financing is the LIBOR rate it pays in the swap minus (7.12 percent − 7.00 percent), which represents the excess of what it receives in the swap over its fixed-rate cost of borrowing directly. As a result, it realizes an opportunity savings of 0.32 percent relative to the LIBOR + 0.20 percent it would pay to borrow directly on a floating-rate basis. Company B's all-in cost of fixed-rate financing is 7.91 percent. This is comprised of the 7.16 percent rate it pays in the swap plus (LIBOR + 0.75 percent − LIBOR), which represents the excess of its floating-rate cost of direct borrowing over what it receives in the swap. It realizes an opportunity savings of 0.29 percent, relative to the 8.20 percent it would pay to borrow directly on a fixed-rate basis. Thus, both parties as well as the intermediary seem to gain in this floating-/fixed-rate swap. From whence do these gains come?

FIGURE 22-5
Illustration of a
floating-/fixed-rate
swap

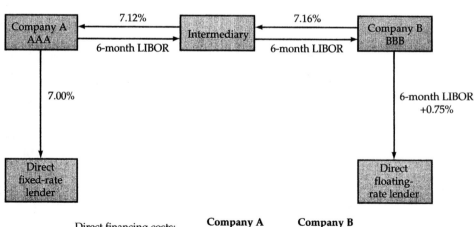

Direct financing costs:	**Company A**	**Company B**
10-year fixed rate	7.00%	8.20%
Floating rate	LIBOR+0.20%	LIBOR+0.75%
All-in cost of financing	LIBOR − 0.12%	7.91%
	floating	fixed
Savings	0.32% floating	0.29% fixed

Swap Valuation Issues

One argument is comparative advantage in financing, which rests on market segmentation occurring. It is argued that institutional restrictions (regulatory, tax, and tradition) limit the ability of a party to borrow in the way or in the currency desired. Closely allied is an argument that asymmetric information causes the opportunity. Different lenders are said to have access to different information about borrowers. As disclosure requirements are different in Europe than in the United States, for example, a potential corporate borrower may be able to borrow to better advantage in the home market where lenders have an information edge.

Comparative Advantage Illustrated   As a result of imperfections and disparate information, borrowers are said to have comparative advantage. It may be that United Fruit can borrow more effectively on a term basis in the United States than it can on a floating-rate basis either in the United States or in Europe, while Foreaux Company can place floating-rate debt more effectively in France than it can place term debt either in Europe or in the United States. If United Fruit really wants to borrow on a floating-rate basis and Foreaux really wants to borrow on a term basis it makes sense for each to borrow where it has comparative advantage. By swapping interest obligations, both parties can realize cost savings similar to those shown in Fig. 22-5, so the argument goes.

The key is whether the arbitrage opportunity persists. One would think that as more and more swaps occur, the rate differences would be reduced and eventually eliminated. In other words, any initial opportunity would be arbitraged out as the swap market seasoned. So while institutional rigidities may persist, arbitrage would eliminate savings possible from comparative advantage. Moreover, informational asymmetry would be reduced as more swaps occur, and credit rating services endeavor to fill information gaps. Thus, the comparative advantage argument is suspect.

Completing Markets   Swaps are used to manage interest-rate risk, such as a mismatch between the average duration of assets and that of funding sources. Recall from earlier chapters that a complete market is characterized by a set of available securities that spans the desires of investors. It may be that the swap market fills a gap in the overall market to hedge interest-rate risk. The futures market and the debt options market are limited in horizon to about 4 years. There is little in the way of a forward market for interest rates. In foreign countries, certain instruments simply are not available. By using the swap market, one can create a synthetic security and may be able to shift risk in ways that otherwise are not available. By exploiting market incompleteness in interest-rate management, the swap may benefit all parties.

Skirting Taxes and Regulations   In certain cases, the use of swaps allows a party to get around tax laws and regulations, a topic touched on earlier in the section on comparative advantage. Usually such skirting is possible only when the swap is across two countries. Through swaps, currency and interest-rate risk exposures can be separated, sometimes to tax advantage. In other cases, regulations in one country can be avoided by arranging a cross-border swap. Known as tax and regulatory arbitrage, the idea is simply to exploit opportunities to reduce tax and regulatory constraints.

Credit Risk

Typically the counterparties in a swap are not of equal credit risk. Default risk does not apply to principal; each party is responsible for whatever principal obligation it has incurred in direct borrowings. However, there is default risk with respect to the differential in interest payments. In the beginning, default risk was borne by the two counterparties in most swaps. However, intermediaries increasingly interposed themselves between the parties in such a way as to assume the default risk. Sometimes an intermediary will take on a swap contract without a counterparty, putting one side of the contract on its own books. While not all swap contracts are characterized by intermediary exposure, an increasing percentage involve such exposure.

Replacement Risk   If a counterparty should default on its obligation, the exposed intermediary will need to assume its position. This is known as **replacement risk.** Suppose the fixed-rate payer in the swap defaults. If interest rates decline from the time of the contract, there is a shortfall between the payment required and what could be obtained in the current swap market. The exposed intermediary must make up the difference. It can bring in another counterparty to pay the fixed rate, but it will be at a lower rate and again the intermediary must make up the differential. If interest rates rise, the intermediary will have no difficulty replacing the defaulted counterparty. Thus, fixed-rate default risk depends on two things: (1) the fixed-rate payer's defaulting and (2) interest rates declining. This combined scenario is more likely in a steep recession than it is at other times.

The condition under which an intermediary is hurt when the floating-rate payer defaults is just the opposite. Should interest rates rise, another counterparty cannot be found to accept the fixed rate contracted for in the swap. Therefore, the intermediary must make up the difference. For floating-rate default to result in a loss, again two things must happen: (1) the floating-rate payer defaults and (2) interest rates rise. For both fixed-rate payer and floating-rate payer default exposure, the intermediary can liquidate the exposed side of the contract at a loss instead of paying the interest rate differential for the remainder of the contract.

Protecting Oneself   Because there is no exchange of principal, the credit risk of a swap is much lower than that of a loan. In addition, swap positions can be sold, which gives them a degree of liquidity not found in many loans. Longer-term swaps often contain triggers to replace counterparties whose credit rating falls below A or below BBB. Because of the interlocking nature of swaps and lines of credit internationally, there is concern that several serious defaults could trigger a cascade. Others suggest that the idea of systemic risk of this sort is overdone, and that no more than 1 percent of the notional amount of swaps outstanding is subject to risk.

Increasingly, discipline is coming into play as participants turn to quality when choosing an intermediary. Those intermediaries with lower credit ratings simply are unable to do business. Even single-A intermediaries often must put up collateral or provide other credit enhancement to participate in the derivatives market. Default-prone counterparties are screened out. Swaps typically are written under a standardized contract of the **ISDA Master Agreement** (International Swaps and Derivatives Association). This contract specifies how swaps are to be liquidated in the event of default. It also allows for the netting of payments between counterparties, thereby reducing settlement risk. A problem is that plain vanilla swaps have become a commodity, with the margin to the intermediary in

Replacement risk is that of having to replace one of the counterparties in the case of default.

Only interest rate differences are at risk with a swap.

the neighborhood of .05 percent. With any defaults no matter how minor, the margin is not sufficient to compensate for the credit risk.

Secondary Market Values

Although a swap may be held to maturity, a secondary market has developed for standardized swaps. Customized swaps sometimes can be exited, but with more difficulty and price concession. In a **swap sale,** you sell your position to another party and there is no further obligation. This differs from a **swap reversal,** where you arrange a swap opposite to the one held. You now hold offsetting swaps, alike in every way except direction. Although interest-rate risk has been removed, the disadvantage of a swap reversal is that credit risk remains and on two swaps instead of one.

Price quotations in the swap market tend to be in terms of the fixed rate paid. A typical quote would be so many basis points over a Treasury security of comparable maturity. For example, the quote might be "72 basis points over 5-year Treasuries." The floating-rate quote usually is flat. That is, the floating rate is set equal to an index, such as 6-month LIBOR. In some situations, it will be LIBOR plus so many basis points, with the result that the quote is in terms of both the fixed and the floating rates. However, this is the exception.

Effect of Interest-Rate Changes   After a swap is undertaken, interest rates can and do change. As a result, the value of the swap changes. Most participants in the swap market are required to **mark-to-market** every day, similar to what occurs in the futures market. If interest rates should decline, the fixed-rate payer, company B in Fig. 22-5, will suffer a decline in the value of its swap contract. To get someone to take over the position requires that a lower fixed rate be paid. As a result, the contract is worth less. In contrast the floating-rate payer realizes a gain in value, because the stream of fixed-rate payments it receives is worth more. This is the same as with holding any fixed-income security when interest rates drop. The opposite occurs when interest rates rise. In summary, we have the following:

	Interest Rate Decline	Interest Rate Increase
Fixed-rate payer	Loses	Gains
Floating-rate payer	Gains	Loses

An analogy of this profile is found in the futures market. The floating-rate payer in the swap (who receives fixed rate) is like the buyer of an interest-rate futures contract (long position). If interest rates rise, he or she suffers a diminution in value, whereas if they fall, the value of the contract increases. Contrarily, the fixed-rate payer (who receives floating rate) is like the seller of a futures contract (short position). Here an increase in interest rates results in an increase in the value of the futures contract, whereas a decrease results in a decline in value. (See Fig. 22-1 for amplification.) Thus, an interest-rate swap is like a series of futures or forward contracts.

Swaptions

Various options exist for swap transactions, and these are known as **swaptions.** One is to *enter into a swap* at a future date. The terms of the swap are set at the time of the option, and they give the holder the right, but not the obligation, to take a swap position. A *call swaption,* if exercised, involves paying floating rate and receiving fixed rate in the swap. With a *put swaption,* assuming exercise, you would pay fixed rate and receive floating rate. A 5/2 put swaption, for example, allows you to pay fixed rate and receive floating rate in a 3-year swap that begins 2 years hence.

Suppose the yield curve is steeply upward sloping. As a financial institution, you wish to fund your assets through floating-rate debt for the time being. However, you are concerned with the yield curve flattening. To protect yourself, you buy a put swaption to swap into fixed-rate debt at a contracted interest rate. If short-term interest rates rise relative to long-term rates, and the latter remain at present levels, your swaption will be a thing of value.

While the swaption to enter into a swap is the most common type of option, there are others. There is the option to *cancel a swap* contract. Another type of option allows you to *extend an existing swap* contract. In addition, there are futures and forward contracts on swaps. Being long in such a contract is like holding a call swaption to pay floating rate and receive fixed rate in the swap. A short swap futures or forward contract is like a put swaption to pay fixed rate and receive floating rate in the swap.

A Summing Up

One reason for the rapid growth in the swap market is that it provides a hedging vehicle not otherwise available in certain maturity areas. It is like a series of forward contracts corresponding to the future settlement dates at which difference checks are paid. However, a comparable forward market does not exist, nor do lengthy futures or options contracts. As a result, the swap market serves to complete the market for risk-taking devices taken up in this chapter. Differences in default risk often are involved. To the extent that credit risk is not properly priced, swaps may give a false impression of the economic benefit depicted in Fig. 22-5.

CREDIT DERIVATIVES

Credit derivatives
unbundle default risk from
the other features of a loan.

In the recent past, markets have developed for **credit derivatives**. The idea is to unbundle the default risk of a loan or security from its other attributes. The original lender no longer needs to bear this risk; it can be transferred to others for a price, of course. The party who wishes to transfer is known as the **protection buyer**. The **protection seller** assumes the credit risk and receives a premium for providing this insurance. The premium is based on the probability and likely severity of default.

Total Return Swaps

Cash flows for a **total return swap** are illustrated in the upper panel of Fig. 22-6. The protection buyer is assumed to hold a risky debt instrument and agrees to pay out its total return to the protection seller. This return consists of the stream of interest payments together with the change in the instrument's market value. The protection seller agrees to pay some reference rate and perhaps a negative or positive spread from this rate. In the case of a floating-rate instrument, the reference rate might be LIBOR or the Treasury bill rate; for a fixed-rate instrument, it might

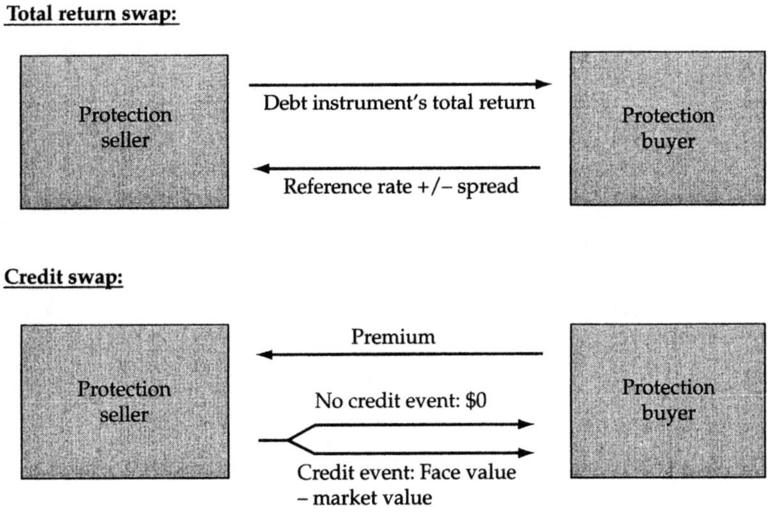

Total return swap:

Credit swap:

FIGURE 22-6
Total return
and credit swaps

The protection buyer
pays the protection seller to
assume the credit risk.

be a constant-maturity Treasury rate. The protection buyer receives a cash-flow stream commensurate with a default-free obligation, and the protection seller a stream commensurate with a risky debt instrument. The difference between the two streams represents the premium for protection.

Like other swaps, the counterparties do not exchange ownership of the underlying debt obligation. The differential in cash flows is established contractually. While the protection seller participates in the cash-flow stream of the risky debt instrument, he or she does not have to book the loan or investment. However, the protection seller bears the economic risk of default. Should actual default occur, he or she receives only the recovery amount and is out the shortfall from the instrument's face value. The protection buyer receives the full face value. If a debt instrument is downgraded, the protection seller also bears the market value decline.

An advantage of a total return swap is that credit deterioration is largely based on market price changes, not on the legality of whether or not default occurs. Though there are problems in getting quotations on certain bonds and floating-rate instruments, an underlying market discipline prevails.

Credit Swaps

A **credit swap**, sometimes known as a default swap, is similar in concept to the total-return swap, but different in the detail. Together these two types of swaps account for the majority of credit derivatives. Cash flows for a credit swap are illustrated in the lower panel of Fig. 22-6. The protection buyer pays a periodic premium to the protection seller, insurance against a risky debt instrument deteriorating in quality. This annuity premium is paid each period until the earlier of (1) the maturity of the credit swap agreement or (2) a specific **credit event** occurring, usually default. If the credit event occurs, the protection seller pays the protection buyer a **contingent amount**. This often takes the form of physical settlement, where the protection buyer "puts" the defaulted obligation to the protection seller at its face value. The economic cash flow then is the difference between the

Total-return and credit swaps are the two largest forms of credit derivatives.

face value of the instrument and its market value. Thus, the protection buyer receives payment only when a specific credit event occurs; otherwise the cash flow from the protection seller is zero.

The credit event need not be default, though that is the thing most commonly specified. It could be a credit downgrade, a merger, a corporate restructuring, or some other event that impacts the creditworthiness of the underlying debt instrument. The periodic premium paid, usually quarterly, often is called the **credit-swap spread**. This cost of protection depends on the credit rating of the company, risk migration, and likely recovery should default occur. The pricing of credit swaps and other credit derivatives has been modeled by academic scholars and practitioners.[9] At the time of this writing, a single-A industrial note had a premium, or spread, of roughly 50 basis points ($\frac{1}{2}$ percent) per annum.

Defining Default, and Liquidity in the Market

One difficulty with credit swaps is legally defining *default*. Failure to pay interest and/or principal on time, bankruptcy, receivership, and things of this sort usually are specified. However, legal wrangling being what it is, economic default may occur well before the situation is finally put in legal default. Market price triggers do not have this problem.

An over-the-counter secondary market of sorts exists for credit derivatives of a plain vanilla sort. Unlike an interest rate swap, where only the difference in fixed/floating interest payments is at risk, with a credit derivative usually the entire face value is at risk. Liquidity in the market is spotty. In the "flight to quality" of late 1998, liquidity dried up for all practical purposes. For sovereign credit derivatives in particular, there were no trades for a number of weeks. Thus, liquidity in credit derivatives is limited.

Other Credit Derivatives

There are credit derivatives other than the two described. **Spread adjusted notes** involve resets based on the spread of a particular grade of security over Treasuries. An index is specified, and quarterly or semiannual resets occur, where one counterparty must pay the other depending on whether the quality yield spread widens or narrows. Usually the spread is collared with a floor and cap. **Credit options** involve puts and calls based on a basket of corporate fixed-income securities. The strike price often is a specified spread over Treasuries. With **credit-sensitive notes**, the coupon rate changes with the credit rating of the company involved. If the company is downgraded, the investor receives more interest income; if upgraded, less interest income. Various other types of credit derivatives have been tried, but the descriptions above should give some sense of the breadth of products.

COMMODITY CONTRACTS

Some corporations find that their product and cost risks are linked to movements in commodity prices. Futures markets began in the 1800s in response to agricultural users and farmers wanting to reduce the price risk of grains, edible oils, live-

---

[9]See Darrell Duffie, "Credit Swap Valuation," *Financial Analysts Journal,* 55 (January/February 1999), 73–87; Francis A. Longstaff and Eduardo S. Schwartz, "Valuing Credit Derivatives," *Journal of Fixed Income,* 5 (June 1995), 6–12; and Robert A. Jarrow and Stuart M. Turnbull, "Pricing Derivatives on Financial Securities Subject to Credit Risk," *Journal of Finance,* 50 (March 1995), 53–85.

stock, cotton, and various food products. Contracts now exist for certain nonagricultural products—metals and petroleum products in particular.

Some Features

Unlike financial and currency contracts, physical commodities often involve storage costs and, in the case of agricultural products, perishability. The contract size varies with the commodity and is expressed in such sizes as 5,000 bushels, 20 metric tons, 40,000 pounds, 100 troy ounces, 1,000 barrels, and 42,000 gallons.

There are futures markets for commodities and options on commodity futures, but no swap market. While some contracts extend over a year, most do not. Commodity contracts are traded on a number of exchanges, and the familiar clearinghouse function is involved. In the United States the more active markets are in Chicago, which emanate historically from its location near agricultural production. The mechanics are similar to those for interest-rate futures and options, so we do not go into them here.

Use of Market

Commodity futures contracts are used by hedgers to shift price risk. The hedger can be a producer, a merchandiser, or simply a storer of commodities. In the case of agricultural crops there are seasonal production and inventory risks. As there is considerable supply immediately after harvest, this supply must be stored and worked down over time, a factor that affects the pricing. Other commodities can be produced more steadily throughout the year, and the risk for these nonseasonal commodities is that associated with the usual supply and demand forces.

Whereas hedgers try to avoid commodity price risk, speculators take on such risk by virtue of betting on the future course of prices. The bet is that the market has got the fundamentals wrong, and that likely future demand and supply for a commodity will differ from the expectations of the market. The bet may be on weather conditions, a likely labor strike, or any number of other conditions that affect commodity prices. The principles are the same as for interest-rate contracts, so we go no further with the matter.

Summary

Managing financial and other risks is critical to successful corporate finance. In this regard, a derivative security is one that derives its value from an underlying primary security. Examples include futures contracts, forward contracts, options, and swaps. To hedge risk, the financial manager must first identify the relevant risk. To the extent possible, it should be quantified. Hedging simply involves taking a position opposite to the risk exposure involved. There is no such thing as a perfect hedge; the risk that remains after a hedge is known as basis risk. A formula was presented for determining the appropriate hedge ratio. Dynamic hedging recognizes that the hedge ratio must change over time as prices and other conditions change. Various reasons that may make corporate hedging worthwhile were explored.

A futures contract is standardized and traded on an exchange; it calls for delivery of a specific instrument, one out of a basket of approved instruments, or a cash settlement based on some index, all of which pertain to a specific future date. Both the buyer and the seller of a contract must maintain margin as a security deposit. Each day, their positions are marked-to-market, with the losing party required to settle. The distinctive features of money and capital market futures markets were explored. Long hedges, short hedges, and cross hedges (across different financial instruments) were illustrated, and the reasons speculators use the futures market as opposed to the spot market investigated.

A forward contract is like a futures contract in economic function, but different in detail. It is nonstandardized and sold in the over-the-counter market as opposed to an exchange market. Settlement occurs at the end as opposed to daily. There is no standard size. Rather than buy a forward contract, one can manufacture an implicit contract by buying a Treasury security and selling short a shorter-term security.

Options permit hedging "one-sided" risk as opposed to both sides as occurs with futures and forward contracts. Through buying call or put options together with writing call or put options, a company can hedge various interest-rate movements. A variation of option has to do with caps on floating-rate borrowing costs. When a cap is combined with a floor, a collar is created where the interest paid varies only within a range. In addition to interest-rate options, there are options on yield spreads between various maturities of Treasury securities.

In interest-rate swaps, the obligation to pay interest, but not principal, is exchanged. The most common swap is floating-for-fixed rate between two counterparties, with an intermediary often between. In many swaps there seemingly are net savings to all parties. The illusion as well as substance of the savings was explored, with particular attention to credit risk. A secondary market exists for standardized swaps, and the value of a swap position changes with changes in interest rates. Several options exist for swap contracts, and they are known as swaptions.

A market is developing for credit derivatives. The idea is to unbundle and transfer the credit risk of a debt contract from its other attributes. The two most widely used credit derivative products are the total return swap and the credit, or default, swap. The features of both were explored. There is limited liquidity for credit derivative products.

Several of the contracts examined—futures, forward, options, and swaps—exist for currencies, and they are examined in Chapter 25. The corporation also may wish to manage its product price and cost risks. This may be possible through commodity futures contracts and options.

Self-Correction Problems

1. As a company you wish to hedge your product costs, which involve petrochemicals. The best vehicle for doing so is with the Natural Gas Futures contract traded on the New York Mercantile Exchange. The contract is in terms of dollars per MMBTU; the present price is $2.20.

   a. If the appropriate hedge ratio is 0.60, what is the average relationship between changes in your company's costs and this contract?

   b. If the price of gas futures should rise to $2.70, what is likely to happen to your costs if they are unhedged?

   c. How would you hedge your costs?

2. The present rate of interest on 4-year zero coupon Treasury securities is 8.00 percent and on 5-year securities, 7.80 percent.

   a. What is the implied forward rate on a 1-year loan 4 years in the future?

   b. How can you arrange for such a forward contract?

   c. Suppose interest rates decline so that the 4-year security is 5.00 percent and the 5-year security 5.40 percent. What happens to the forward rate? What overall relationship prevails between actual rates and forward rates?

3. Goyne Industries is concerned about interest rates rising. It needs to borrow in the bond markets 3 months hence. The company receives a high credit rating and believes that an option on Treasury bond futures is the best hedging device.

a. Should the company buy a put or a call option?

b. Presently the futures contract trades at $100, and 3-month put and call options both involve premiums of $1\frac{1}{2}$ percent based on this strike price. During the 3 months interest rates rise, so that the price on a Treasury bond futures contract goes to $95. What is your gain or loss on the option per $100,000 contract?

c. What would be the outcome if interest rates fell and the price went to $103?

■ Problems

1. You wish to set up a hedge using apples and oranges. You own apples but wish to use oranges to hedge your apple position. A viable derivative market exists for oranges, but not for apples. If oranges were to rise in price by 12 cents a pound, apples on average would rise by 6 cents, and vice versa. Presently apples cost $2.00 a pound and oranges $1.50 per pound. What is the appropriate hedge ratio?

2. Bo Lo Corporation wishes to hedge against interest rates rising. It has made commitments totaling $2 million that need to be financed 3 months hence. Presently the 3-month futures contract on Treasury bonds trades at $100 even. (This is based on an 8 percent coupon rate.) If the company were to borrow now, it could do so at 9 percent for 20 years.

a. What should the company do to hedge its position if the appropriate hedge ratio is 1.2?

b. Suppose interest rates rise and 3 months hence Treasury bond futures are priced at $95\frac{1}{2}$. If the company were to sell a 9 percent coupon bond of 20 years, it could do so only at a price of $94 per face value of $100. What is the outcome of your hedge?

3. If the hedge in Problem 2 was less than perfect, what are some of the reasons for such? Expressed differently, why does basis risk exist in this situation?

4. Presently the interest rate on 3-year zero coupon Treasury securities is 7.2 percent, whereas the rate on 4-year Treasuries is 8 percent.

a. What is the implied forward rate for a 1-year loan beginning 3 years in the future?

b. If the 3-year rate were 8 percent, what would be the implied forward rate?

c. If the 3-year rate were 8.5 percent? What generalizations can you make as to forward rates and actual rates of interest?

5. How does the forward contract differ from a futures contract (a) in what you wish to accomplish? (b) in form?

6. Ibanez Foods Corporation wishes to hedge against a significant drop in interest rates. It will receive a $4 million cash settlement on a contract 6 months from now, and the company will invest in Treasury securities at that time. The premium to buy/write 6-month call options is 2 percent whereas that to buy/write put options is $1\frac{1}{2}$ percent. The strike price for both options is $100, the face value of a Treasury bond futures contract.

a. Which of the four alternatives (buy call, write call, buy put, or write put) should the company undertake?

b. (1) If interest rates in fact were to fall and the futures contract were to go from a price of $100 to $106 6 months later, what would be the gain/loss on the hedge? (2) What if interest rates rose, and the price was $95?

c. If you thought interest rates would fluctuate only within a narrow range, what would you have the company do?

7. How does hedging interest-rate movements with debt options differ from using a futures or a forward contract?

8. As it borrows in the short- to intermediate-term market, Jorrell Corporation is concerned about the yield curve flattening; that is, short-term rates rising relative to long-term rates. Six-month yield-curve options are available to hedge the 2-year to 10-year spread. Presently, the spread between these two Treasury maturities is 2.10 percent, or 210 basis points. Both call and put yield-curve options are available, with an exercise, or strike, price of 200 basis points. For a $1 million contract, the call option involves a premium of $200,000, whereas that for the put option is $50,000.

a. Which option should the company use?

b. If the yield curve in fact were to flatten and the yield spread declined by $\frac{1}{2}$ percent over the 6-month interval, how much would the company gain or lose on its hedge? Assume a $1 million contract.

c. If the yield curve were to widen instead of flatten, to $2\frac{1}{4}$ percent, what would be the outcome of the hedge?

9. For the most part, Excell National Bank funds its fixed-rate loan portfolio with floating-rate debt. The average interest cost on such debt is 6-month LIBOR plus 40 basis points. Colossus Corporation borrows in the fixed-rate market at 9.10 percent, whereas Excell National Bank would pay 9.70 percent if it were to do so.

a. What happens to the two parties (1) if interest rates rise? (2) if they fall?

b. Suppose a swap could be arranged between the two parties such that Colossus swaps to pay 6-month LIBOR flat and receive 9.20 percent fixed. Borrowing directly in the floating-rate market, Colossus would pay LIBOR plus 20 basis points. Involved in the swap is an intermediary that charges 7 basis points. What are (1) the implied savings to the two parties? (2) the all-in costs of financing?

c. From where do the savings come?

10. Aluminax Conversion Corporation makes aluminum ingots, and the process requires considerable electricity. Aluminax produces its own electricity with oil-fired boilers. The company is very concerned about rising energy costs. In words, what can the company do to hedge against rising costs?

Solutions to Self-Correction Problems

1.   a. On average for every $1 rise or fall in Natural Gas futures, the company's costs go up or down by $0.60. The hedge ratio tells us this relationship, though we must recognize that it is on average. Random fluctuations cause deviations from the rule.

b. A rise to \$2.70 of 1 MMBTU of natural gas translates into a percentage increase of (\$2.70/\$2.20) $-$ 1 = 22.73 percent. With a hedge ratio of 0.6, this means a cost increase of 13.64 percent on average.

c. To hedge, the company should buy futures contracts on natural gas. If prices rise it will gain on its futures contract, but lose on rising costs, and vice versa if prices fall. Contracts are available in sizes of 10,000 MMBTU.

2. a. Implied forward rate $= \dfrac{(1.078)^5}{(1.08)^4} - 1 = 7.00\%$

b. The contract can be bought from an investment bank in the over-the-counter market. You also can manufacture your own forward contract by buying the 5-year zero coupon Treasury security and selling short the 4-year security.

c. Implied forward rate $= \dfrac{(1.054)^5}{(1.05)^4} - 1 = 7.02\%$

When the yield curve is upward sloping, the forward rate exceeds the two actual rates. When it is downward sloping, as in part a, the forward rate is less than the two actual rates.

3. a. To protect against upward movements in interest rates, and accompanying downward price movements, the company should buy a put option. See Fig. 22-3.

b. Gross gain on option = (1.00 $-$ .95) $\times$ \$100,000 = \$5,000
Premium = $1\frac{1}{2}\%$ $\times$ \$100,000 = \underline{\hspace{2cm} 1,500}
Net gain on option position \underline{\hspace{1cm} \$3,500}

c. Goyne Industries would not exercise its put option, as it is out of the money. The company would be out the \$1,500 premium paid for the option.

Selected References

ALLEN, LINDA, *Capital Markets and Institutions: A Global View.* New York: John Wiley, 1997.

ARDITTI, FRED D., *Derivatives.* Boston: Harvard Business School Press, 1996.

BLACK, FISCHER, EMANUEL DERMAN, and WILLIAM TOY, "A One-Factor Model of Interest Rates and Its Application to Treasury Bond Options," *Financial Analysts Journal*, 46 (January–February 1990), 33–39.

BODNAR, GORDON M., GREGORY S. HAYT, and RICHARD C. MARSTON, "Wharton Survey of Financial Risk Management by U.S. Non-Financial Firms," *Financial Management*, 27 (Winter 1998), 70–91.

CAMPBELL, TIM S., and WILLIAM A. KRACAW, *Financial Risk Management.* New York: HarperCollins, 1993.

CHIU, DAN, and STEVE FOERSTER, "Using Derivatives to Manage Risk," *Business Quarterly*, 6 (Spring 1997), 56–64.

DUFFIE, DARRELL, "Credit Swap Valuation," *Financial Analysts Journal*, 55 (January/February 1999), 73–87.

FABOZZI, FRANK J., *Bond Markets, Analysis and Strategies.* Upper Saddle River, NJ: Prentice Hall, 2000.

HULL, JOHN C., *Futures and Options Markets*, 3rd ed. Upper Saddle River, NJ: Prentice Hall, 1998.

———, *Options, Futures, and Other Derivatives*, 4th ed. Upper Saddle River, NJ: Prentice Hall, 2000.

JARROW, ROBERT, and STUART TURNBULL, *Derivative Securities*, 2nd ed. Cincinnati: South-Western, 2000.

LITZENBERGER, ROBERT H., "Swaps: Plain and Fanciful," *Journal of Finance*, 47 (July 1992), 831–50.

LONGSTAFF, FRANCIS A., "The Valuation of Options on Yields," *Journal of Financial Economics*, 26 (July 1990), 97–121.

———, "Hedging Interest Rate Risk with Options on Average Interest Rates," *Journal of Fixed Income*, 4 (March 1995), 37–44.

LONGSTAFF, FRANCIS A., and EDUARDO S. SCHWARTZ, "Valuing Credit Derivatives," *Journal of Fixed Income*, 5 (June 1995), 6–12.

NANCE, DEANA R., CLIFFORD W. SMITH JR., and CHARLES W. SMITHSON, "On the Determinants of Corporate Hedging," *Journal of Finance*, 48 (March 1993), 267–84.

SMITH, CLIFFORD W. JR., CHARLES W. SMITHSON, and D. SYKES WILFORD, *Managing Financial Risk*. New York: Harper & Row, 1990.

STULZ, RENE M., "Optimal Hedging Policies," *Journal of Financial and Quantitative Analysis*, 19 (March 1984), 127–40.

VAN HORNE, JAMES C., *Financial Market Rates and Flows*, 5th ed. Upper Saddle River, NJ: Prentice Hall, 1998.

Wachowicz's Web World is an excellent overall Web site produced and maintained by my coauthor of *Fundamentals of Financial Management*, John M. Wachowicz Jr. It contains descriptions of and links to many finance Web sites and articles. *www.prenhall.com/wachowicz*.

Part VII

EXPANSION AND CONTRACTION

■ **CASE:** *Rayovac Corporation*

In September 1997, Rayovac's CEO, David Jones, sat down to review the progress that he and his management team had achieved since the leveraged buyout. The stock market was red hot, and Thomas H. Lee, a leveraged buyout firm, was considering ways of realizing some of the gains on their investment. Although the company was performing ahead of expectations, it had been only 12 months since Thomas H. Lee completed the leveraged buyout, and Jones and the new management team had not implemented all of the improvements they identified at the time of the transaction. Moreover, he was concerned that the market might not value the progress made to date without a longer and more proven track record.

Thomas H. Lee recruited Jones to lead Rayovac while they were negotiating the acquisition in September 1996. Jones found the opportunity attractive for a number of reasons. First, the battery market was growing rapidly relative to other consumer products due to technological advancements and the proliferation of electronic devices. Second, Rayovac was the sleepy player in the industry with an underexploited brand and excellent manufacturing capabilities and technology. Finally, Jones believed that Rayovac presented a unique turnaround opportunity. This belief had been borne out as changes executed by Jones and the management team had reduced operating costs substantially while growing the top line. However, Jones felt as though there was still more work to be done and wondered how to deal with Thomas H. Lee's desire to realize value so soon.

This case was prepared by Darius Brooks, Bryan Locke, and Richard Peacock under the supervision of James Van Horne as the basis for class discussion rather than to illustrate effective or ineffective handling of an administrative situation.

THE COMPANY

Founded in 1906 as the French Battery Company, Rayovac is the third largest manufacturer and marketer of batteries in the United States. The company is headquartered in Madison, Wisconsin, and, as of July 1996, Rayovac employed 2,480 people. In 1996, Thomas Pyle, chairman and chief executive officer of the company, together with his family owned 91.3 percent of Rayovac's capital stock. The remainder was owned by officers of the company.

Within the general battery market, the company is the leader in a number of areas, including (1) the household rechargeable and heavy-duty battery segments, (2) hearing aid batteries, (3) lantern batteries, and (4) lithium batteries for personal computer memory back-up. In addition, Rayovac is one of the leading marketers of flashlights and other battery-powered lighting products in the United States. The company markets and sells its products in the United States, Europe, Canada, and the Far East through a variety of distribution channels, including retail, industrial, professional, and OEMs. By positioning its products as a value brand in the early 1980s, the company became the leader in the mass merchandise retail channel, a rapidly growing retail segment in the United States and Canada. Rayovac offers batteries of substantially the same quality and performance, but at lower price points than those of its competitors.

THE BATTERY INDUSTRY

In 1995, the U.S. battery industry generated $4.1 billion in sales, of which approximately $2.3 billion took place through retail channels. Between 1986 and 1995, the retail segment experienced compound annual unit sales growth in excess of 5 percent. This growth was driven by (1) the popularity of battery-powered devices, (2) the miniaturization of such devices, and (3) increased purchases of multiple battery packages for household use. This growth continued, and in 1997 the U.S. battery industry generated $4.3 billion in sales.

The U.S. battery industry is dominated by Duracell and Energizer, with Rayovac in third position. The three companies account for over 90 percent of the sales in the U.S. general retail battery market. Analysts note that the competitive structure of the battery industry will only support three manufacturers in a specific battery market. Although new players sometimes seek to enter, the substantial capital expenditures required make successful new competition difficult. In 1995, Rayovac estimated that it would require an initial investment of $120 million to build a battery manufacturing facility with five production lines. In addition to high fixed costs, industry players are heavily dependent on strong distribution channels, product differentiation, brand awareness, and access to retail shelf space.

The battery market has three submarkets: general retail, industrial, and hearing aids. The retail market is the broadest category and includes alkaline, reusable/rechargeable, and heavy-duty batteries. This segment accounted for 56 percent of all battery sales in 1995 and 1997. Zinc carbon, known as "heavy-duty" batteries were the forerunners to the alkaline technology with which most consumers are currently familiar. Though heavy-duty batteries continue to be manufactured for low- and medium-drain devices (i.e., lanterns, flashlights), sales have been declining. Alkaline batteries last four to five times longer. In the 1980s, alkaline batteries gained wide acceptance; by 1996 they accounted for approximately 86 percent of the general retail battery market. Rechargeable batteries have also increased in availability. Though they have yet to catch on, rechargeable batteries have increased in quality, offering consumers a good value in terms of cost and power.

In line with other retail trends, mass merchandisers and warehouse clubs have recorded rapid growth in battery sales in recent years. Mass merchandisers accounted for 66 percent of the total increase in general battery retail sales from 1993 to 1997. Batteries are popular with retailers because they offer attractive profit margins and consume little shelf or warehouse space.

The industrial battery market accounted for 10 percent of total U.S. sales in 1994 and 19 percent in 1997. Products in this segment include alkaline, heavy-duty, and lantern batteries sold to such consumers as government agencies, maintenance repair operations, and office product supply companies.

The hearing aid market accounted for 5 percent of the total U.S. battery market in 1997, and it has grown at a 5 percent annual rate since 1992. The U.S. hearing aid battery industry had aggregate sales of approximately $205 million in 1996 ($530 million worldwide). Rayovac estimates that there are 26 million hearing-impaired individuals in the United States, but only 5.5 million hearing aid users. The trend is miniaturization. As hearing aids become smaller, they gain wider acceptance and create demand for smaller batteries that must be changed more frequently. The combination of increasing demand and technological innovation will continue to fuel growth in this segment for years to come.

The top competitors in the U.S. battery market are Duracell and Eveready.

Duracell

Duracell is the top manufacturer of batteries in the United States with 45 percent of the alkaline market in 1996. After its buyout by Kohlberg, Kravis, Roberts and Co. in 1988, the company led the industry in an attempt to change perceptions of the consumer battery market from a commodity to a highly differentiated product. In the late 1980s, the company spent record amounts to promote its differentiated brand of battery. After rising to the top of the consumer segment in 1992, Duracell began to look abroad to generate additional growth.

In 1996, KKR began to consider exit strategies for its investment in Duracell. Recognizing the strength of batteries in the retail segment, Gillette agreed to buy Duracell for $7.8 billion. In a conference call to announce the deal Gillette CEO Alfred Zeien described Gillette's reasoning with the following: "At the checkout counter, there's going to be nobody who can touch the magnitude of what we're going to be able to do. This isn't diversification, but an additional leg of our tightly focused strategy."

Eveready

The second major player in the U.S. battery market is the Energizer/Eveready division of Ralston Purina. Eveready controlled approximately 37 percent of the alkaline market in 1996. Eveready and Duracell are archrivals. With its now famous Energizer bunny, Eveready began an all-out war with Duracell for market share in 1988. Since then the two companies have battled each other in terms of technical innovation, pricing strategy, advertising dollars, and, most important, market share.

THE BATTERY MANUFACTURING PROCESS

A battery consists of three parts: (1) a negative portion or anode, (2) a positive portion or cathode, and (3) an electrolyte, the liquid solution that aids in the flow of energy. The energy flow from the anode to the cathode continues until the anode can no longer give up electrons and the cathode can no longer accept electrons. The life of a battery depends on a number of factors, including the size and type of battery, the power demands of the device, and the frequency and length of battery use. The battery development and manufacturing process involves considerable trial and error as companies attempt to increase power while decreasing size and production costs. The key trade-off for manufacturers is between manufacturing cost and battery performance. While battery companies may be able to develop the ultimate product in terms of size, power, and reliability in the laboratory, transferring a concept to the production line is a difficult step and the point where most new battery projects fail.

In terms of costs associated with battery production, the process is material intensive. Rayovac spends 63 percent on materials (alkaline cans that form the casing for the most common batteries, zinc and zinc cans, etc.), 29 percent on overhead (allocation to manufacturing), and 8 percent on direct labor. The manufacturing process can be made less costly through the introduction of capital equipment. However, the combination of technological change (which has driven battery sizes smaller and power needs higher), production difficulties, and price competition has driven most manufacturers to focus on specific battery types to allow them to maintain profitability.

RAYOVAC'S PRODUCT LINE

General Batteries

General batteries encompass alkaline, heavy-duty, and rechargeable products. Rayovac produces a full line of alkaline batteries, including D, C, AA, AAA and nine-volt sizes for the consumer and industrial markets. Although the company does produce some batteries for private labels, they are primarily sold under the Rayovac name. For the fiscal years ending June 30, 1995 and 1996, general batteries comprised 61.9 percent and 62.3 percent of total sales, respectively. In fiscal 1996, Rayovac held 11.2 percent of the alkaline battery market and, within the mass merchandise retail channel, the company had a 19.9 percent alkaline battery market share. In addition to alkaline batteries, Rayovac manufactures heavy-duty (nonalkaline) batteries in the same sizes but sells these batteries at a lower price point. In 1996, Rayovac's market share was 44.5 percent in the heavy-duty segment. Overall, heavy-duty battery sales are shrinking as consumers switch to alkaline and rechargeable batteries.

Rayovac is the only domestic manufacturer of alkaline rechargeable batteries. This technology, which was introduced by the company under the Renewal name in 1993, allows consumers to reuse batteries up to 25 times for an aggregate electrical charge of 10 regular alkaline batteries. In addition to cost benefits, Rayovac's batteries retain their charge substantially longer than standard nickel-cadmium rechargeable batteries. Because the Renewal system does not require mercury or cadmium, it is exempt from collection and disposal legislation. The Renewal system is the highest quality, most cost-effective, and most environmentally responsible rechargeable battery for household use on the market. In 1996, Rayovac dominated the rechargeable battery segment with 64.2 percent of the market.

Specialty Batteries

For the fiscal years ending June 30, 1995 and 1996, specialty batteries comprised 29.5 percent and 28.6 percent of total sales, respectively. Rayovac is the only producer of the smallest hearing aid battery and one of only two companies manufacturing the next smallest size. Hearing aid battery consumption has grown dramatically from 134.5 million units in 1992 to 193.4 million in 1996. The company expects this growth to continue as the decreasing size of hearing aids broadens its appeal and U.S. and western European populations grow older. Rayovac holds the number one position in the hearing aid battery market with over 40 percent market share in 1996. The company produces five sizes sold under the Loud n' Clear and ProLine brand names and under several private labels, including Beltone and Miracle Ear.

Other specialty batteries include non–hearing aid button-cell and lithium coin-cell batteries. The button- and coin-cell batteries are used in a variety of electronic products, including watches, cameras, calculators, personal computers, and communication equipment. Rayovac also produces a wide range of consumer and industrial lantern batteries, and, in 1996, the company held a 47.2 percent market share of the retail lantern battery market.

Battery-Powered Lighting Devices

For the fiscal years ending June 30, 1995 and 1996, battery-powered lighting devices accounted for 8.6 percent and 9.1 percent of total sales, respectively. Rayovac is the leading marketer of battery-powered lighting devices, including flashlights, lanterns, and similar portable products for the retail and industrial market. In 1996, the company's products accounted for 9.9 percent of aggregate lighting product retail sales in the mass merchandiser market segment.

HISTORICAL PERFORMANCE THROUGH 1996

Rayovac's financial performance depends on a number of factors, including general retailing trends, the company's product mix, and the company's relative market position, which is affected by the behavior of its competitors. Its performance through fiscal 1996 was affected by (1) the expansion of production facilities, (2) the Renewal product line, and (3) seasonality. Historical financial statements are shown in Exhibits 1 and 2.

1. In 1994 and 1995 the company completed the modernization and expansion of its production lines at its Fennimore, Wisconsin, facility. The expansion more than doubled Rayovac's aggregate capacity for AA and AAA batteries and included the complete renovation of existing capacity for C and D alkaline batteries. Between 1992 and 1995, the company invested $36.7 million in new production lines that not only increased capacity but also resulted in better-performing and higher-quality alkaline batteries.

2. In connection with the introduction of the Renewal rechargeable battery in 1994, the company dramatically increased its advertising and promotional expenses to $26.0 million. By comparison, the company spent $15.7 million in fiscal 1995 and $20.3 million in fiscal 1996, with the increase in 1996 largely attributable to the new Renewal advertising campaign featuring Michael Jordan. The Renewal introduction was also responsible for the significant increase in receivables and inventories from 1993 to 1994.

3. The company's revenues are seasonal, with the highest sales occurring in its second fiscal quarter (during the Christmas holiday buying season). During the past four years, second quarter sales averaged 33 percent of annual net sales. As a result of this seasonality, the company's working capital requirements and revolving credit borrowings are typically highest in the first and second quarters of each year.

In addition to these specific developments, the company's recent financial performance has been affected by other factors. Net sales increased from $332.2 million in 1992 to $399.4 million in 1996, a compound annual growth rate of 4.7 percent. The increase in sales is largely attributable to growth in the company's alkaline, rechargeable, and hearing aid battery products, offset slightly by declines in heavy-duty batteries and lighting products. Management attributes higher gross margins in 1995 and 1996 to the renovation and expansion of the Fennimore facility. The company believes further efficiencies will be realized from this investment over the next several years. The increase in selling expenses, which peaked in 1994 at $103.8 million, is largely attributable to marketing and advertising costs related to the rollout of the Renewal rechargeable battery system.

MR. PYLE EXAMINES HIS OPTIONS

In late 1995, Rayovac's principal owner and chief executive officer, Thomas Pyle, contacted Merrill Lynch to discuss the company's strategic alternatives. As Mr. Pyle edged closer to retirement, he wished to consider the possibility of liquidating all or part of his investment in the company. When Merrill Lynch and Pyle discussed the company's options, they narrowed their search to two alternatives: a private sale to a financial buyer or a sale to a competitor, such as Duracell or Energizer. Each option had a number of implications.

- A sale to a competitor could result in a higher price, as the buyer would benefit from substantial cost savings from the elimination of redundant overhead costs and capacity rationalization. However, the likelihood that a competitor would realize these cost savings through large-scale layoffs of Rayovac employees concerned Pyle.
- Given the large market shares of Rayovac's competitors it appeared likely that any transaction would attract the attention of the Federal Trade Commission.
- A cash offer from Duracell was unlikely, as the company already carried a large debt burden, preventing it from raising additional debt to finance the transaction. A stock offer from Ralston Purina was less attractive because Pyle and other Rayovac shareholders would be subject to certain lockout provisions that limited their liquidity.
- Rayovac represented a relatively large transaction for financial buyers, limiting the number of parties that might be involved in a bidding process.

As the Merrill Lynch descriptive memorandum made its way into the hands of a number of different potential suitors, few bids were offered. Despite the fact that the deal had begun to appear as if it had been excessively "shopped," Thomas H. Lee (THL) decided that it was worth careful consideration. THL's interest was driven by a number of factors:

- The overall growth of the battery market—the U.S. retail market had grown at an average rate of 5 percent over the past 5 years and was expected to continue to grow at or above this pace over the short term.
- Despite trailing other competitors in the alkaline battery market, Rayovac had superior positions in the hearing aid, rechargeable, and lithium battery markets.
- Rayovac had invested considerably over the past 3 years to modernize its production facilities.
- The existing management team offered strong experience in the battery market.
- The company generated strong and steady cash flow.
- There was potential for significant cost savings. The expense structure of Rayovac had grown to include the company's leased aircraft, two sponsored race cars, and excess compensation.

THL also had a number of concerns, not the least of which was the business deteriorated during the time the company was up for sale. In addition, Mr. Pyle made it clear that he planned to step aside under any deal scenario. As a result, a top priority for THL was finding the right management team to take over in the event they were successful in their bid for the company.

THE MANAGEMENT

THL recruited David Jones to manage the company. Prior to the Rayovac opportunity, Jones was chief operating officer, chief executive officer, and chairman of Thermoscan, Inc., a manufacturer and marketer of infrared ear thermometers, also controlled by THL. From 1989 to 1994, Jones was president and CEO of The Regina Company, a manufacturer of vacuum cleaners and other floor care equipment. Jones had over 25 years experience working in consumer durables, involving positions in operations, manufacturing, and marketing. Merrell Tomlin and Randall Steward were also invited to leave Thermoscan and join Jones as senior vice president of sales and senior vice president and chief financial officer, respectively.

THE LEVERAGED BUYOUT

On September 12, 1996, THL came to terms with Mr. Pyle on a deal to buy a majority of Rayovac's common stock. The transaction valued Rayovac at $326 million or approximately 7.5x trailing 12 months EBITDA, a sharp discount to the 15.0x multiple Gillette had paid for Duracell just weeks earlier. In addition, it represented a deep discount from the $500 million valuation that Rayovac and Merrill Lynch had considered at the start of the process.

Simultaneous with the acquisition of the company, THL recapitalized Rayovac. As a result of the recapitalization, THL, together with David Jones, owned 80.2 percent, Pyle owned 9.9 percent, and existing management owned 9.9 percent of Rayovac's common stock. The sources and uses of funds in connection with the recapitalization are outlined below.

SOURCES	
Revolving credit facility	$ 26.0
Term loan facility	105.0
Bridge notes	100.0
Equity investment by THL	72.0
Continuing shareholders' equity investment	18.0
Foreign debt and capital leases	5.5
Total sources	$ 326.5

USES	
Retirement of Rayovac common stock[1]	$ 127.4
Purchase of newly issued common stock by THL[2]	72.0
Continuing shareholders' equity investment	18.0
Repay existing debt	85.2
Fees and expenses related to the recapitalization	18.4
Foreign debt and capital leases	5.5
Total uses	$ 326.5

AFTER THE LBO

The new management team immediately went to work implementing the plan to reduce costs and grow revenues formulated during the due diligence period. The plan focused on the following: (1) reinvigorating the Rayovac brand name through increased advertising; (2) growing market share by expanding Rayovac's presence in underrepresented retail channels, such as food stores, drugstores, and warehouse clubs; (3) reducing costs by rationalizing manufacturing and distribution, improving plant utilization, and reducing overhead; and (4) increasing worker productivity through the installation of new information systems and training. In total, Jones's near-term targets were 10 percent top-line growth and 20 percent EBIT growth per annum.

For David Jones, the most challenging assignment was reshaping the culture of Rayovac. There was a lack of effective communication among headquarters, functional heads, and manufacturing divisions as well as a management group with little experience making decisions. This complacency was also evidenced by the "womb to tomb" employment philosophy at the company. Few employees ever left Rayovac for performance reasons, and the company's employee review process was ineffective. Jones and his management team worked hard to push decision making lower into the organization and expected employees to accept responsibility. This initiative was aided by the introduction of a new incentive structure that encouraged communication across divisions, risk taking, and continuous improvement. Although many Rayovac employees prospered in the new performance-based culture, the company lost 30 to 40 percent of its corporate staff in the first year after the buyout.

---

[1] Retired Treasury stock in connection with the recapitalization.
[2] Purchase of common stock in the new recapitalized company. The acquisition of Rayovac was structured to satisfy the recapitalization requirements for accounting purposes. Goodwill is not recorded under a recapitalization.

In addition to the cultural difficulties, Rayovac's antiquated information technology systems made it difficult for management to access required data in a timely way. This made it hard to analyze the company's operations and nearly impossible to forecast performance. Jones replaced nearly 75 percent of the company's IS staff and began an extensive overhaul of Rayovac's computing infrastructure, including the installation of SAP, an inventory and material forecasting system and sales automation program.

Simultaneous with the changes noted above, Jones aggressively rationalized the company's manufacturing facilities. Through the installation of high-speed equipment and advanced computer systems, Rayovac was able to increase capacity while decreasing brick and mortar investments. In 12 months, the number of factories was reduced from eight to four while simultaneously increasing the company's total capacity. These closures resulted in a substantial reduction in overhead and working capital requirements. Jones also centralized certain functions that had previously been performed independently by each factory. For example, the adoption of a centralized purchasing strategy resulted in annual savings of 5 percent.

Jones was also focused on growing the top line. Consistent with its strategy of avoiding direct, head-to-head competition with Duracell and Energizer, Rayovac worked to expand its presence in the niche markets of hearing aid, rechargeable, lantern, and heavy-duty batteries. These markets offer higher margins than those available in the general retail category. In terms of rechargeable batteries, Rayovac focused on the promotion of its Renewal product. As the holder of the leading share in this market, management hoped to build on this position by convincing consumers of the benefits of rechargeable batteries.

Recognizing the crucial nature of the company's relationship with distributors, Jones and his team reorganized sales, marketing, and administration by distribution channel. The goal of the reorganization was to place an increased focus on Rayovac's underserved customer population through channel-specific strategies and to regain the trust of distributors who felt Rayovac had overpromised and underdelivered in the past.

To revive the business and its brand recognition, Rayovac devised a new marketing strategy. The plan included the introduction of a new and improved alkaline product called the MAXIMUM and the redesign of all product graphics and packaging to convey a high-quality image with the Rayovac brand name emphasized. In addition, the company extended Michael Jordan's contract to continue as a spokesman for Rayovac products.

At an early stage, the plan began to show results. The cost reduction plan resulted in cash cost saving of $6.3 million for fiscal 1997 and was projected to yield $8.6 million in savings on an ongoing basis. Rayovac's gross margins increased from 43.1 percent in 1996 to 45.8 percent in 1997, reflecting not only its cost reductions but also its marketing efforts and greater focus on higher-margin products. In terms of market share, Rayovac continued its domination of the rechargeable and hearing aid battery segments, in addition to achieving gains in alkaline battery sales.

EXIT ALTERNATIVES

At the inception of the Rayovac acquisition, THL's expected investment horizon was 3 to 6 years. However, in the summer of 1997 (less than 12 months after the acquisition), THL and Jones began to consider the long-term investment strategy. Among the possibilities was partial or total liquidation of their investment. A number of factors drove this consideration. First, the management team had made substantial improvements to operating performance in a short period of time. Although Jones remained enthusiastic about Rayovac's prospects, THL believed that the steps taken to date represented much of the low-hanging fruit and that future operating gains would be more difficult to identify and execute. Second, the equity investment by THL was relatively large, and there was interest in reducing its exposure to the business or in applying additional leverage to boost potential returns. Third, the run-up in the U.S. equity markets had expanded valuation multiples for public offerings as well as private acquisitions. THL was anxious to lock in some of these gains. Finally, the ability to realize value in so short a period of time would increase the fund's internal rate of return.

THL and Jones considered the following alternatives:

- **Stay the Course.** Although future operating improvements could prove more difficult, THL remained committed to the management team and believed in the company's long-term prospects. The value of the company was likely to benefit from a longer operating history, validating management's early cost-reduction and revenue-enhancement initiatives. Moreover, by remaining independent and private, Jones would avoid intrusions by outside investors and research analysts. Accordingly, the management team could focus on the long-term prospects of the company rather than quarter-to-quarter results. Jones believed that more predictable earnings could be demonstrated within 12 to 24 months.

- **Leveraged Build-Up.** A number of private equity firms had converted their investments into leveraged build-up (LBU) platforms. Though it was unlikely that THL would use Rayovac to acquire another battery business, given the size of its competitors, Rayovac could be used as a vehicle to make additional purchases of companies that would benefit from Rayovac's strategic assets and market position. For example, THL considered the possibility of targeting other consumer products companies that could benefit from Rayovac's value reputation and mass-retailer distribution power. Unfortunately, without a public currency, rising multiples would make it difficult for Rayovac to complete acquisitions.

- **IPO.** In 1997, the IPO market continued to rebound from the doldrums of the early 1990s; the general stock market's expansion had been especially dramatic. While an IPO was attractive for a number of reasons, THL and Jones also considered the costs associated with being a public company. There were a number of considerations. First, an IPO would only provide limited liquidity for THL and management, due to lock-up requirements. Second, a public offering was expensive. The cost of filing and navigating the regulatory process as well as investment banking fees were significantly higher than the costs of a private transaction. Third, there were operating costs associated with becoming public, such as the establishment of an investor relations department and annual regulatory filing fees. Fourth, a public offering would allow investors (including THL and management) to retain a substantial portion of their ownership and, consequently, to participate in the upside potential of the market and the company. Finally, an IPO would provide Rayovac with an acquisition currency. (See Exhibits 4 and 5 for relevant comparable company information and recent stock market performance.)

- **Strategic Buyer.** In 1996 and 1997, a consolidation wave began to sweep across consumer products companies. Many of these companies used acquisitions to expand their product offerings and leverage their relationship with retailers and existing distribution channels. By selling the company to a strategic buyer, THL would benefit from the recent run-up in multiples while also achieving total or near-total liquidity. In addition, Rayovac would avoid some of the recurring costs associated with a public offering. (See comparable companies and transactions in Exhibits 4 and 5.)

THE DECISION

THL, along with Jones, needed to decide on the best course of action. Although the Rayovac leveraged buyout was scarcely seasoned, it had already created value. As a result, there were viable exit alternatives. Still, it might be better to postpone exit and continue to build value.

Exhibit 1

Rayovac Corporation: Balance Sheets
(Dollars in millions)

	FY ENDED JUNE 30				FY ENDED SEPTEMBER 30
	1993	1994	1995	1996	1997
Assets					
Cash	$ 2.8	$ 2.5	$ 2.6	$ 2.2	$ 1.1
Accounts receivable	41.6	50.2	52.7	55.8	79.7
Inventory	54.6	74.5	65.6	66.9	58.6
Other current assets	9.1	11.8	11.3	13.2	15.0
Total current assets	108.1	139.0	132.2	138.1	154.4
Property, plant, and equip.	70.1	72.1	78.0	73.9	65.5
Other assets	10.1	11.3	10.4	9.8	17.0
Total assets	$ 188.3	$ 222.4	$ 220.6	$ 221.9	$ 236.9
Liabilities and equity					
Accounts payable	$ 38.3	$ 35.0	$ 39.2	$ 38.7	$ 57.3
Current portion of L.T.D.	*	*	11.9	11.6	23.9
Other current liabilities	29.0	27.8	25.2	25.3	39.4
Total current liabilities	67.3	62.8	76.3	75.7	120.6
Long-term debt	71.9	108.0	76.4	69.7	183.4
Other liabilities	10.7	12.6	14.3	14.9	13.5
Total liabilities	149.9	183.4	167.0	160.3	317.5
Shareholders' equity	38.4	39.0	53.6	61.6	(80.6)
Total liabilities and equity	$ 188.3	$ 222.4	$ 220.6	$ 221.9	$ 236.9

* Current portions of long-term debt were not available for 1993 and 1994.
Fiscal year-end changed from June 30 to September 30.

Exhibit 2

Rayovac Corporation: Statements of Income
(Dollars in millions)

	1993	1994	1995	1996	1997
		FY ENDED	JUNE 30		FY ENDED SEPTEMBER 30
Net sales	$372.4	$403.7	$415.2	$423.4	$432.6
Cost of goods sold	202.1	234.9	237.1	239.4	234.6
Gross profit	170.3	168.8	178.1	184.0	198.0
Selling expense	98.8	121.3	108.7	116.5	122.1
General and administrative, other	31.7	30.9	32.9	31.8	35.2
Research and development	5.6	5.7	5.0	5.4	6.2
Income from operations	34.2	10.9	31.5	30.3	34.5
Interest expense	6.0	7.7	8.6	8.4	24.5
Other (income) expense, net	2.2	(0.6)	0.3	0.6	0.4
Income before taxes and cumulative effect for change in accounting	26.0	3.8	22.6	21.3	9.6
Income tax expense (benefit)	10.1	(0.6)	6.2	7.0	3.4
Net income	$ 15.9	$ 4.4	$ 16.4	$ 14.3	$ 6.2
Other financial data					
Depreciation and amortization	$ 7.4	$ 10.3	$ 11.0	$ 11.9	$ 11.3
Capital expenditures	30.1	12.5	16.9	6.6	10.9
EBITDA	41.6	21.2	42.5	42.2	45.8

Exhibit 3

Rayovac Corporation:
Product Types as Percent of Sales

	FY ENDED JUNE 30		FY ENDED SEPTEMBER 30
PRODUCT TYPE	1995	1996	1997
General batteries			
Alkaline	43.4%	43.6%	45.0%
Heavy-duty	14.1%	12.2%	10.4%
Rechargeable	5.6%	7.1%	5.5%
Total	63.1%	62.9%	60.9%
Specialty batteries			
Hearing aid	12.7%	14.6%	14.8%
Other	10.0%	8.6%	9.8%
Total	22.7%	23.2%	24.6%
Lighting products and lantern batteries	14.2%	13.9%	14.5%
Total	100.0%	100.0%	100.0%

E x h i b i t 4

Rayovac Corporation: Comparable Companies
(Dollars in millions, except per share amounts)

COMPANY	EPS ESTIMATES			STOCK PRICES*		P/E		EQUITY	DEBT	ENTERPRISE VALUE	1998E	
	1996A	1997E	1998E	8/15/97	8/15/96	1997	1998				SALES	EBITDA
Sunbeam	$ (0.10)	$ 1.41	$ 2.05	$ 41.38	$ 19.95	29.3 x	20.2 x	$ 3,682.4	$ 200.6	$ 3,883.0	$ 1,427.1	$ 335.6
Revlon	0.49	1.14	1.90	53.13	28.63	46.6 x	28.0 x	2,735.9	1,506.9	4,242.8	2,631.5	361.2
Samsonite	0.96	2.05	2.65	38.88	18.50	19.0 x	14.7 x	820.3	185.7	1,006.0	818.3	134.5
Gillette	2.22	2.55	3.00	85.88	63.63	33.7 x	28.6 x	47,832.4	2,212.7	50,045.1	11,105.8	3,160.9
Ralston-Purina	n/a	n/a	3.91	87.56	66.25	n/a	22.4 x	9,342.9	2,412.9	11,755.8	5,898.3	989.9
Colgate-Palmolive	1.96	2.27	2.60	63.76	39.25	28.1 x	24.5 x	18,828.3	2,867.7	21,696.0	9,501.2	1,796.4
Clorox	2.24	2.51	2.82	64.34	44.04	25.6 x	22.8 x	6,781.6	702.2	7,483.8	2,933.0	705.2
S&P 500	41.02	45.34	48.40	900.81	662.28	19.9 x	18.6 x					
DJIA	353.88	403.33	428.33	7,694.70	5,665.80	19.1 x	18.0 x					

* Stock prices adjusted for splits. All P/E and equity value information based on stock prices as of 8/15/97.

Exhibit 5

Rayovac Corporation: Comparable Transactions
(Dollars in millions, except per share amounts)

BUSINESS SOLD:	MENNEN	NEUTROGENA	GERBER	SCOTT PAPER	ARMOR ALL	DURACELL	KIRSCH	ROLODEX	ELDON
Date of sale	Apr-92	Aug-94	Jul-94	Dec-95	Dec-96	Dec-96	Jan-97	Mar-97	May-97
Seller	Mennen	Neutrogena	Gerber	Scott Paper	McKesson	KKR	Cooper	Insilco	Rubbermaid
Purchaser	Colgate	Johnson & Johnson	Sandoz	Kimberly-Clark	Clorox	Gillette	Newell	Newell	Newell
Major brands	Mennen	Neutrogena	Gerber	Scott	Armor All	Duracell	Kirsch	Rolodex	Eldon, Micro-Computer
Price		35.25	53.00	61.23	19.09	66.88			
Shares		25.9	69.6	151.5	21.3	121.4			
Equity	$650.0	$913.0	$3,668.8	$9,276.3	$406.6	$8,118.6	$200.0	$117.0	$246.0
Debt	n/a	—	n/a	1,190.9	—	575.1	—	—	n/a
Enterprise value	650.0	913.0	3,688.8	10,467.2	406.6	8,693.7	200.0	117.0	246.0
P&L									
Sales	$550.0	$299.5	$1,200.0	$4,309.2	$189.0	$2,474.6	$250.0	$58.0	$162.0
EBIT	60.5	41.6	212.0	818.1	14.7	475.6	7.5	9.0	18.0
EBITDA	n/a	48.1	238.9	1,035.1	18.7	575.6	n/a	11.5	24.6
Net	39.3	27.1	113.6	508.1	10.0	272.1	n/a	n/a	n/a

Mergers and the Market for Corporate Control

The market for corporate control can alter dramatically the setting in which business firms compete. In an idealized world, this market is a positive thing for stockholders and for the economy as a whole. Assets, people, and products may be transferred to more productive uses. By loosening management control over these resources, higher-value employment is possible. With rapidly changing technology and product markets, what was once a viable corporate strategy may no longer be so. Yet existing management may be wedded to the old strategy and reluctant to change. Moreover, a top-heavy bureaucracy may have little incentive to run a company efficiently, enjoying high compensation and perquisites while paying insufficient attention to cost-effectiveness and competitive advantage.

Realistically, the contested takeover, the proxy contest, and institutional shareholder activism may be the only means for forcing ineffective management out and getting better utilization of corporate resources. Moreover, the ever-present threat of these things may stimulate existing management to perform better. The market for corporate control has both supporters and detractors. In this chapter, we sort out the issues as to their valuation underpinnings. We will look at mergers, tender offers, resistance to takeovers, and the empirical evidence on valuation. This will be followed in Chapter 24 by other aspects of corporate restructuring. ■

WHAT IS CONTROL WORTH?

The maximum a company is worth as a stand-alone company is its value if it were managed efficiently. The **value gap** is the difference between this value and the company's current value in the market place. This gap may be due to inefficient, sloppy management; excessive compensation levels; perquisites like expensive cars, airplanes, and club memberships; misalignment of management incentives with those of shareholders; as well as other reasons. Where there are private control benefits, such as those suggested, together with the peace of mind that comes from management entrenchment, they work to the disadvantage of public stockholders. When control has value apart from the ordinary trading of shares, outsiders may pay premiums over existing share price to wrest control from incumbent management.[1]

Apart from managing a company more efficiently, another reason to pay a premium to gain control is the **synergy** that might be achieved by combining it with another company. By effecting economies of operation and eliminating duplication of efforts and/or by producing greater revenue, synergism may be achieved such that the fused company is worth more than the sum of the parts.

> **Synergy** is economies realized through a merger.

Recall from Chapters 6 and 8 that the acquisition of another company can be treated as a capital budgeting decision. There is an initial outlay, which is expected to be followed by **free cash flows.** These are cash flows in excess of necessary investments in working capital and in fixed assets. In those earlier chapters, we developed a conceptual framework for analyzing and evaluating the likely effect of an acquisition on the value of the firm in both firm-risk and market-risk contexts.

The value of the combined company was found to be the sum of the values of the parts plus any synergy that might be involved.

$$V_{ab} = V_a + V_b + \text{Synergy} \qquad (23\text{-}1)$$

where V_{ab} is the value of company postmerger, V_a is the value of company A premerger, V_b is the value of company B premerger, and Synergy is the economies realized in the merger through increased revenues and/or cost reductions.

Thus, the maximum total value of a control change is the combination of managing the acquisition more efficiently internally and the synergism that might be achieved. With these broad foundations in place, we need to move to some definitions.

FEATURES OF A MERGER

A merger is a combination of two corporations in which only one survives. The merged corporation goes out of existence. There are some features we need to understand before we can go into the valuation underpinnings.

Purchase of Assets or Purchase of Stock

A company may be acquired either by the purchase of its assets or its common stock. The buying company may purchase all or a portion of the assets of another company and pay for them in cash or with its own stock. Frequently, the buyer acquires only the assets of the other company and does not assume its liabilities. When an acquiring company purchases the stock of another company, the latter is combined into the acquiring company. The company that is acquired ceases to exist, and the surviving company assumes all its assets and liabilities. As with a purchase of assets, the means of payment to the stockholders of the company being acquired can be either cash or stock.

Taxable or Tax-Free Transaction

If the acquisition is made with cash or with a debt instrument, the transaction is taxable to the selling company or to its stockholders at that time. This means

---

[1]For the theoretical development of private control benefits, see Sanford J. Grossman and Oliver D. Hart, "One Share–One Vote and the Market for Corporate Control," *Journal of Financial Economics*, 20 (January–March 1988), 175–202; Milton Harris and Artur Raviv, "Corporate Governance," *Journal of Financial Economics*, 20 (January–March 1988), 203–35; and Milton Harris and Artur Raviv, "The Design of Securities," *Journal of Financial Economics*, 24 (October 1989), 203–35.

that they must recognize any capital gain or loss on the sale of the assets or the sale of the stock at the time of the sale. If payment is made with voting preferred or common stock, the transaction is not taxable at the time of the sale. The capital gain or loss is recognized only when the stock is sold. In addition to the requirement of voting stock, in order for a combination to be tax free it must have a business purpose. In other words, it cannot be entirely for tax reasons. Moreover, in a purchase of assets the acquisition must involve substantially all the assets of the selling company, and no less than 80 percent of those assets must be paid for with voting stock. In a purchase of stock, the buying company must own at least 80 percent of the selling company's stock immediately after the transaction.

Accounting Treatment

At the time this edition was written, the accounting treatment of a merger was in a state of change. The issue involves whether a combination of two companies should be treated as a **purchase** or as a **pooling of interests.** In a purchase, the buyer treats the acquired company as an investment. If the buyer pays a premium above the book value of the assets, this premium must be reflected on the buyer's balance sheet. The purchase method requires tangible assets to be reported at fair market value. As a result, it may be possible to write up the acquired company's tangible assets. If such occurs, there will be higher depreciation charges.

If the premium paid exceeds the write-up, however, the difference must be reflected as **goodwill** on the buyer's balance sheet. Moreover, goodwill should be written off against future income, the logic being that it will be reflected in such income. An estimate must be made of the life of goodwill, and goodwill is amortized over this period, which cannot exceed 40 years for "financial accounting purposes." In a pooling of interests, the balance sheets of two companies are combined, with assets and liabilities simply being added together. As a result, asset writeups and/or goodwill are not reflected in the combination, and there are no charges against future income.

In the late 1990s, the Financial Accounting Standards Board (FASB), with the strong encouragement of the Securities and Exchange Commission, proposed a standard that would force companies to use purchase accounting. This would be in conformity with most other countries of the world, where pooling-of-interests accounting treatment is not possible. Though purchase accounting was made less onerous to the acquiring corporation than before, there was a considerable outcry against the virtual elimination of pooling. The new standard was to have gone into place in 2001, but at the end of 2000 the FASB proposed a new rule. This was the requirement that companies use purchase accounting for mergers, but that goodwill need be written off against future earnings only if it is "impaired." At the time of this writing, the rules for what constituted impairment were unclear. Certainly a patent would need to be amortized, but brands and "know how" were another matter. While corporate executives and investment bankers were pleased with the proposal, because it did much of what pooling did before, others were not. Where things end up in practice remains to be seen.

An Example Suppose Lambda Corporation acquires Phi Zeta, Inc. in an exchange of stock valued at $2 million. Phi Zeta had debt of $1 million and shareholders' equity of $1.2 million prior to the merger, with a net book value of its assets of $2.2 million. The larger Lambda Corporation, the acquirer, had shareholders' equity of $10 million, debt of $5 million, and assets having a net book value of $15 million prior to the merger. With purchase accounting, the total assets of the acquired company, Phi Zeta, are written up by $0.8 million, which is the price paid for the company in excess of its book value. Part of this figure, $0.3 million, can be treated as a write-up of tangible assets to their fair market value. However, the remainder, $0.5 million, must be reflected as goodwill.

Therefore, we have under purchase accounting (in thousands):

	Before Merger		After Merger
	LAMBDA	PHI ZETA	LAMBDA PZ
Net tangible assets	$15,000	$2,200	$17,500
Goodwill	0	0	500
Total assets	$15,000	$2,200	$18,000
Debt	$ 5,000	$1,000	$ 6,000
Shareholders' equity	10,000	1,200	12,000
Total liabilities and equity	$15,000	$2,200	$18,000

If no impairment is felt to occur, the $0.5 million in goodwill will remain on the balance sheet as an asset. It need not be written down against future income. If $0.2 million is viewed to be impaired over the next 10 years, Lambda PZ Corporation will need to amortize against earnings $20,000 a year. At the end of 10 years, assuming there are no other acquisitions, goodwill will be $0.3 million.

Most corporate executives will argue against goodwill impairment for the simple reason that they want future accounting earnings to be as high as possible. The challenge to the accounting profession is to come up with standards for determining impairment.

STRATEGIC ACQUISITIONS INVOLVING STOCK

Strategic acquisitions involve one company acquiring another.

A **strategic acquisition** occurs when one company acquires another as part of its overall strategy. Perhaps cost advantages result, or it may be that the target company provides revenue enhancement through product extension or market dominance. The key is that there is a strategic reason for blending two companies together. In contrast, a **financial acquisition** is where a financial promoter, such as Kohlberg, Kravis and Roberts (KKR), is the acquirer. The motivation is to sell off assets, cut costs, and operate whatever remains more efficiently than before, in the hope of producing value above what was paid. The acquisition is not strategic, for the company acquired is operated as an independent entity.

A financial acquisition invariably involves cash, and payment to the selling stockholders is funded importantly with debt. As this type of acquisition is taken up in Chapter 24, our focus is on strategic acquisitions, which can be with either stock or cash. With a stock acquisition, a ratio of exchange occurs, denoting the relative value weightings of the two companies with respect to earnings and to market prices.

Earnings Effect

Company A wishes to acquire company B with a stock offer. Financial data for the two companies are as follows:

	Company A	Company B
Present earnings	$20,000,000	$5,000,000
Shares	5,000,000	2,000,000
Earnings per share	$4.00	$2.50
Price of stock	$64.00	$30.00
Price/earnings ratio	16x	12x

The exchange ratio of shares will determine the effect on earnings per share.

Company B has agreed to an offer of $35 a share to be paid in company A stock. The exchange ratio, then, is $35/$64, or about .547 share of company A's stock for each share of company B's stock. In total, 1,093,750 shares of company A will need to be issued to acquire company B. Assuming that the earnings of the component companies stay the same after the acquisition, earnings per share of the surviving company will be

	Surviving Company A
Earnings	$25,000,000
Shares	6,093,750
Earnings per share	$4.10

Thus, there is an immediate improvement in earnings per share for company A as a result of the merger. Company B's former stockholders experience a reduction in earnings per share, however. For each share of B's stock they had held, they now hold .547 share of A. Thus, the earnings per share on each share of company B's stock they had held is (.547)(4.10), or $2.24, compared with $2.50 before.

Varying the Ratio of Exchange   Suppose now that the price agreed on for company B's stock is $45 a share. The ratio of exchange, then, is $45/$64, or about .703 share of A for each share of B. In total, 1,406,250 shares would have to be issued, and earnings per share after the merger will be

	Surviving Company A
Earnings	$25,000,000
Shares	6,406,250
Earnings per share	$3.90

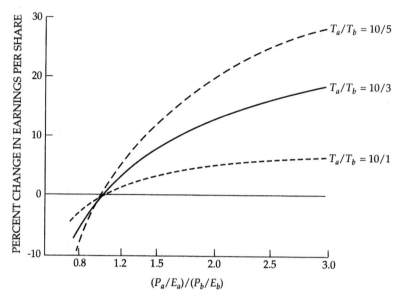

FIGURE 23-1

Earnings per share change as a function of the price/earnings ratio differential and relative earnings

In this case, there is initial dilution in company A's earnings per share on account of the acquisition of company B.[2] Dilution in earnings per share will occur any time the price/earnings ratio paid for a company exceeds the price/earnings ratio of the company doing the acquiring. In our example, the price/earnings ratio in the first case was \$35.00/\$2.50, or 14, and in the second case, it was \$45.00/\$2.50, or 18. Because the price/earnings ratio of company A was 16, there was an increase in earnings per share in the first case and a decrease in the second.

Thus, initial increases and decreases in earnings per share are both possible. The *amount* of increase or decrease is a function of (1) the differential in price/earnings ratios and (2) the relative size of the two firms as measured by total earnings.[3] The higher the price/earnings ratio of the acquiring company in relation to that of the company being acquired, and the larger the earnings of the acquired company in relation to those of the acquiring company, the greater the increase in earnings per share of the acquiring company. These relationships are illustrated in Fig. 23-1 for three different earnings relationships. The *a* subscript for total earnings, T_a, and for price/earnings ratio, P_a/E_a, denotes the acquiring company, and the *b* subscript for T_b and P_b/E_b denotes the company being acquired.

Future Earnings   If the decision to acquire another company were based solely on the initial impact on earnings per share, an initial dilution in earnings per share would stop any company from acquiring another. This type of analysis, however, does not take into account the possibility of a future growth in earnings owing to the merger. This growth may be due to the expected growth in earnings of the acquired company as an independent entity and to any synergistic effects that result from the fusion of the two companies. It is useful to graph likely future earnings per share with and without the acquisition. Figure 23-2 shows this for a hypothetical merger. The graph tells us how long it

---

[2]Company B's former stockholders obtain an improvement in earnings per share. Earnings per share on each share of stock they had held are \$2.74.

[3]See Walter J. Mead, "Instantaneous Merger Profit as a Conglomerate Merger Motive," *Western Economics Journal*, 7 (December 1969), 295–306.

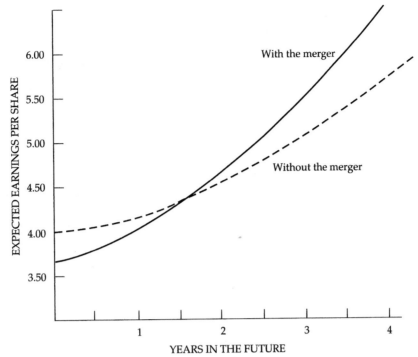

FIGURE 23-2
Expected earnings per share with and without the merger

will take for the dilution in earnings per share to be eliminated and for an accretion to take place. In this example, it is $1\frac{1}{2}$ years; earnings per share drop $.30 initially, but this relative dilution is eliminated by the middle of the second year. The greater the duration of dilution, the less desirable the acquisition is said to be from the standpoint of the acquiring company. Some companies set a ceiling on the number of years dilution will be tolerated.

Market Value Effect

The major emphasis in the bargaining process is on the ratio of exchange of market prices per share, which is simply

$$\frac{\text{Market price per share of acquiring company} \times \text{Number of shares offered}}{\text{Market price per share of acquired company}}$$

If the market price of Acquiring Company is $60 per share and that of Bought Company is $30, and Acquiring offers a half share of its stock for each share of Bought Company, the ratio of exchange is

$$\frac{\$60 \times .5}{\$30} = 1.00$$

In other words, the stocks of the two companies would be exchanged on a one-to-one market price basis. If the market price of the surviving company is relatively stable at $60 a share, stockholders of both companies are about as well off as before with respect to market value. The company being acquired finds little enticement to accept a one-to-one market-value ratio of exchange, however. The acquiring company must offer a price in excess of the current market price per share of the company it wishes to acquire. Instead of a half share of stock, Acquiring might have to offer .667 share, or $40 a share in current market value.

Bootstrapping Earnings per Share   In the absence of synergism, improved management, or the underpricing of Bought Company's stock in an inefficient market, we would not expect it to be in the interest of Acquiring's stockholders to offer a price in excess of Bought Company's current market price. Acquiring stockholders could be better off if their company's price/earnings ratio were higher than Bought Company's and if somehow the surviving company were able to keep that same higher price/earnings ratio after the merger. Perhaps Bought Company has a price/earnings ratio of 10. Acquiring Company, on the other hand, has a price/earnings ratio of 18. Assume the following financial information:

	Company A	Company B
Present earnings	$20,000,000	$6,000,000
Shares	6,000,000	2,000,000
Earnings per share	$3.33	$3.00
Market price per share	$60.00	$30.00
Price/earnings ratio	18x	10x

With an offer of .667 share of Acquiring Company for each share of Bought Company, or $40 a share in value, the market price exchange ratio of Bought Company is

$$\frac{\$60 \times .667}{\$30} = 1.33$$

Stockholders of Bought Company are being offered a stock with a market value of $40 for each share of stock they own. Obviously, they benefit from the acquisition with respect to market price, because their stock was formerly worth $30 a share. Stockholders of Acquiring Company also stand to benefit, *if the price/earnings ratio of the surviving company stays at 18.* The market price per share of the surviving company after the acquisition, all other things held constant, would be

	Surviving Company
Total earnings	$26,000,000
Number of shares	7,333,333
Earnings per share	$3.55
Price/earnings ratio	18x
Market price per share	$63.90

The reason for this apparent bit of magic whereby the stockholders of both companies benefit is the difference in price/earnings ratios.

Does Bootstrapping Pay? Under the conditions described, companies with high price/earnings ratios are able to acquire companies with lower price/earnings ratios and obtain an immediate increase in earnings per share, despite the fact that they pay a premium with respect to the market-value exchange ratio. The key is what happens to the price/earnings ratio after the merger. If it stays the same, the market price of the stock will increase. As a result, an acquiring company is able to show a steady growth in earnings per share if it acquires a sufficient number of companies over time in this manner. This increase is not the result of economies or underlying growth but is due to the "bootstrap" increase in earnings per share through acquisitions. If the marketplace values this illusory growth, a company presumably could increase shareholder wealth through acquisitions alone. In reasonably efficient capital markets, however, it is unlikely that the market will hold constant the price/earnings ratio of a company that cannot demonstrate growth potential in ways other than acquiring companies with lower price/earnings ratios.

Thus, the acquiring company must allow for the price/earnings ratio changing with an acquisition. If the market is relatively free from imperfections and if synergism and/or improved management is not anticipated, we would expect the price/earnings ratio of the surviving firm to approach a weighted average of the two previous price/earnings ratios. Under these circumstances, the acquisition of companies with lower price/earnings ratios would not enhance shareholder wealth. In fact, if the market price exchange ratio were more than one, as occurs with a premium being paid, there would be a transfer of wealth from the stockholders of the acquiring company to those of the acquired firm. Let us turn now to the fundamental valuation underpinnings of a merger.

SOURCES OR REARRANGEMENTS OF VALUE

The purpose of a merger or takeover is to create value. There are a handful of reasons why we might expect value to be created or rearranged, and we consider them in turn. Some were discussed in Chapter 8, so this treatment is an extension of those ideas together with some new ones.

Sales Enhancement
and Operating Economies

An important reason for some acquisitions is the enhancement of sales. By gaining market share, ever-increasing sales may be possible through market dominance. There may be other marketing and strategic benefits. Perhaps the acquisition will bring technological advances to the product table. Or it may be that it will fill a gap in the product line, thereby enhancing sales throughout. To be a thing of value, such sales enhancement must be cost effective.

Operating economies can often be achieved through a combination of companies. Duplicate facilities can be eliminated, and marketing, accounting, purchasing, and other operations can be consolidated. The sales force may be reduced to avoid duplication of effort in a particular territory. Physical facilities may be redundant, and economies of operation can occur through the elimination of the less efficient. The realization of increased revenue and operating efficiency is known as synergism; the fused company is of greater value than the sum of the parts, that is, $2 + 2 = 5$.

In addition to operating economies, economies of scale may be possible with a merger of two companies. Economies of scale occur when average cost declines with increases in volume. Usually, we think of economies of scale in production and overlook their possibilities in marketing, purchasing, distribution, accounting, and even finance. The idea is to concentrate a greater volume of activity into a given facility, into a given number of people, into a given distribution system, and so forth. In other words, increases in volume permit a more efficient utilization of resources. Like anything else, it has limits. Beyond a point, increases in volume may cause more problems than they remedy, and a company may actually become less efficient. Economists speak of an "envelope curve" with economies of scale possible up to some optimal point, after which diseconomies occur.

Economies can perhaps best be realized with a **horizontal merger,** combining two companies in the same line of business. The economies achieved by this means result primarily from eliminating duplicate facilities and offering a broader product line in the hope of increasing total demand. A **vertical merger,** whereby a company expands either forward toward the ultimate consumer or backward toward the source of raw material, may also bring about economies. This type of merger gives a company more control over its distribution and purchasing. There are few operating economies in a **conglomerate merger,** combining two companies in unrelated lines of business.

Improved Management

Some companies are inefficiently managed, with the result that profitability is lower than it might be. This topic was discussed at the outset of the chapter when we considered the market for corporate control. To the extent the acquirer can provide better management, an acquisition may make sense for this reason alone. While a company can change management itself, the practical realities of entrenchment may be such that an external acquisition *is* required for anything to happen. This motivation would suggest that poor-earning, low-return companies are ripe acquisition candidates, and there appears to be some evidence in support of this contention. The idea is that the external financial markets discipline management.

Information Effect

Value also could occur if new information is conveyed as a result of the merger negotiations or takeover attempt. This notion implies asymmetric information between management (or the acquirer) and the general market for the stock. To the extent a stock is believed to be undervalued, a positive signal may occur via the merger announcement, which causes share price to rise. The idea is that the merger/takeover event provides information on underlying profitability that otherwise cannot be convincingly conveyed. This argument has been examined elsewhere in the book and, in a nutshell, it is that specific actions speak louder than words.

Whether a company is truly undervalued is always questionable. Invariably management believes it is, and in certain cases it has information that is not properly reflected in market price. However, the market for acquisitions is an active one with extensive information networks being maintained by investment banks and merger brokers. Moreover, there is considerable competition among potential buyers, so the argument for sizable numbers of undervalued bargains existing is dubious.

Tax Reasons

A motivation in some mergers is tax. In the case of a tax-loss carryforward, a company with cumulative tax losses may have little prospect of earning enough in the future to utilize fully its tax-loss carryforward. By merging with a profitable company, it may be possible for the surviving company to utilize the carryforward more effectively. However, there are restrictions that limit its utilization to a percentage of the fair market value of the acquired company. Still, there can be an economic gain—at the expense of the government—that cannot be realized by either company separately. There are other tax motivations, but they tend to be of minor importance. The Tax Reform Act of 1986 sharply reduced tax-motivated mergers. The technical tax advantages that remain provide little in the way of value.

Diversification

Diversification is the motive in some mergers. By acquiring a firm in a different line of business, a company may be able to reduce cyclical instability in earnings. To the extent that investors in a company's stock are averse to risk and are concerned only with the total risk of the firm, a reduction in earnings instability would have a favorable impact on share price.

This argument assumes that investors evaluate risk solely in relation to the *total* risk of the firm. We know from Chapters 3 and 8, however, that investors are able to diversify risk on their own. If they evaluate risk in an overall market context, they will diversify at least as effectively on their own as the firm is able to do for them. Particularly when the stock of the company being acquired is publicly traded, there is no reason to believe that investors are not able to diversify their portfolios efficiently. Because the firm is unable to do something for them that they cannot do for themselves, diversification as a reason for merging usually is not a thing of value.[4] Consequently, it would not lead to an increase in share price.

Wealth Transfers

However, there may be wealth transfers from equity holders to debt holders, via diversification, when a merger occurs. To the extent the combination lowers the relative variability of cash flows, debt holders benefit from having a more creditworthy claim. As a result, the market value of their claim should increase, all other things the same. Unless equity holders protect themselves, they will lose value to debt holders in the option pricing model context illustrated in Chapter 9. In effect it is a zero-sum game, and one party gains only at the expense of the other. Equity holders can protect themselves by increasing the amount of debt or instigating "me-first" rules (see Chapter 9).

Hubris Hypothesis

Roll argues that takeovers are motivated by bidders who get caught up in believing they can do no wrong and that their foresight is perfect.[5] **Hubris** refers to an animal-like spirit of arrogant pride and self-confidence. Such individuals are said not to have the rational behavior necessary to refrain from bidding. They get

---

[4]In Chapter 8, we discussed certain conditions under which diversification through merging may have a positive effect—though minor, compared to any synergistic effect—on the total value of the firm.

[5]Richard Roll, "The Hubris Hypothesis of Corporate Takeovers," *Journal of Business*, 59 (April 1986), 197–216.

VALUATION ANALYSES FOR ACQUISITIONS

When considering a company for acquisition, it is important to place a value on it. There are a number of ratios and other considerations used to determine an appropriate value. No one method of analysis gives the answer, but together they permit some degree of closure. In all cases, the figures calculated for the potential acquiree must be compared with those for peer companies. Known as *comparables,* these companies give a relative metric around which to judge the target's worth. The following are not in order of importance but represent a checklist of things that can (and often should) be determined. In this regard, equity value = market capitalization (share price times number of shares outstanding). Enterprise capitalization = equity value + interest-bearing debt + preferred stock − cash.

1. *Equity value-to-book value of the stock.* This is simply market value in relation to book value.
2. *Enterprise Capitalization-to-sales.* A ratio that takes on much importance in certain industries like retail stores and supermarkets.
3. *Equity value-to-earnings.* This is simply the price/earnings ratio, always important.
4. *Enterprise capitalization-to-EBITDA.* The denominator is earnings before interest, taxes, depreciation, and amortization. This multiple of operating cash flows is widely used as a first cut toward valuation. The lower the better. For a mature industry with only moderate growth, a multiple of 5 is good; a multiple of 10 generally is regarded as bad. The multiple paid for companies varies with the business cycle and the exuberance in the acquisition marketplace.
5. *Effect on acquiring company's earnings per share.* Taken up in this chapter, the effect varies with whether a cash or stock offer is involved and whether the accounting treatment requires amortization of goodwill.
6. *Discounted cash flow analysis.* Free cash flows are projected out to some horizon, like 7 years, and a terminal value is estimated at that horizon. This value can be based on a multiple of earnings in the last year, a multiple of EBITDA, or the perpetual growth dividend discount model approach to valuing free cash flow beyond the horizon year. The estimated yearly free cash flows and terminal value at the horizon then are discounted at a risk-adjusted discount rate, like the weighted average cost of capital.
7. *Hidden values.* Are there hidden values in assets, like timber or minerals, or in brands?
8. *PEG ratio = P/E ratio/growth in EPS.* The growth rate employed in the denominator often is either the 5-year historical rate or the 5-year likely rate going forward. The lower this ratio, the more conservative the valuation.

Again, these ratios and considerations will not give a single answer for how much a company is worth in today's market. However, they generally permit a range of valuations. Also remember that an acquisition will involve a premium. Therefore, two sets of comparables are in order: the ratios in comparison with companies (comparables) trading in the regular marketplace and a comparison involving the prices paid for companies actually acquired. Equity values and enterprise capitalizations obviously will be higher with the latter.

caught up in the "heat of the hunt" where the prey must be had regardless of cost. As a result, bidders pay too much for their targets. The hubris hypothesis suggests that the excess premium paid for the target company benefits those stockholders, but that stockholders of the acquiring company suffer a diminution in wealth.

Management's Personal Agenda

Many reasons exist for mergers, but only some result in value creation.

Rather than hubris, it may be that the acquiring company overpays because management pursues personal as opposed to corporate wealth-maximizing goals. Sometimes management chases growth. Being larger may bring prestige, in whose glow management basks. The goal may be diversification, because with unrelated businesses and risk spread out, management jobs may be more secure. From the standpoint of the selling company, personal reasons also may come into play. In a tightly held company, the individuals who have controlling interest may want their company acquired by another company that has an established market for its stock. For estate tax purposes, it may be desirable for these individuals to hold shares of stock that are readily marketable and for which market-price quotations are available. The owners of a tightly held company may have too much of their wealth tied up in the company. By merging with a publicly held company, they obtain a marked improvement in their liquidity, enabling them to sell some of their stock and diversify their investments. All of these things are forms of agency costs, a concept explored from time to time in earlier chapters.

Now that we have explored various reasons for a merger/takeover, we need to consider corporate voting by which control is determined.

CORPORATE VOTING AND CONTROL

Inasmuch as the common stockholders of a company are its owners, they are entitled to elect a board of directors. The board, in turn, selects the management, and management actually controls the operations of the company. In a proprietorship, partnership, or small corporation, the owners usually directly control the operations of the business; in a large corporation, the owners have but an indirect and often very faint voice in the affairs of the company.

Voting Procedures

Discipline on management from the board may not be sufficient.

Depending on the corporate charter, the board of directors is elected either under a **majority voting system** or under a **cumulative voting system.** Under the majority system, stockholders have one vote for each share of stock they own, and they must vote for each director position that is open. A stockholder who owns 100 shares will be able to cast 100 votes for each director's position open. Because each person seeking a position on the board must win a majority of the total votes cast for that position, the system precludes minority interests from electing directors. If management can garner 50.1 percent of the shares voted, it can select the entire board.

Under a cumulative voting system, a stockholder is able to accumulate votes and cast them for less than the total number of directors being elected. The total number of votes is the number of shares the stockholder owns times the number of directors being elected. If you are a stockholder who owns 100 shares, and 12 directors are to be elected, you may cast 1,200 votes for any number of directors you choose, the maximum being 1,200 votes for one director.

Formula for Cumulative Voting   A cumulative voting system, in contrast to the majority system, permits minority interests to elect a certain number of directors. The minimum number of shares necessary to elect a specific number of directors is determined by

$$\frac{\text{Total shares outstanding times specific number of directors sought}}{\text{Total number of directors to be elected plus one}} + 1 \quad (23\text{-}2)$$

If there are 3 million shares outstanding, the total number of directors to be elected is 14, and if a minority group wishes to elect 2 directors, it will need at least the following number of shares:

$$\frac{3,000,000 \times 2}{14 + 1} + 1 = 400,001$$

Thwarting Minority Interests   Cumulative voting gives minority interests a better opportunity to be represented on the board of directors of a corporation. Because the system is more democratic, a number of states require that companies in the state elect directors in this way. Even with cumulative voting, however, management can reduce the number of directors and sometimes preclude minority interests from obtaining a seat on the board of directors. Suppose the minority group just described actually owns 400,001 shares. With 14 directors to be elected, the group can elect 2 directors. If the board is reduced to 6 members, the minority group can elect no directors, because the minimum number of shares needed to elect a single director is

$$\frac{3,000,000 \times 1}{6 + 1} + 1 = 428,572$$

Another method of thwarting a minority interest from obtaining representation is to stagger the terms of the directors so that only a portion is elected each year. If a firm has 12 directors and the term is 4 years, only 3 are elected each year. As a result, a minority group needs considerably more shares voted in its favor to elect a director than it would need if all 12 directors came up for election each year.

Proxies and Proxy Contests

Voting may be either in person at the stockholders' annual meeting or by proxy. As most stockholders do not attend the meeting, the latter is the mechanism by which most votes are garnered. A **proxy** is a form a stockholder signs giving his or her right to vote to another person or persons. The SEC regulates the solicitation of proxies and also requires companies to disseminate information to its stockholders through proxy mailings. Prior to the annual meeting, management solicits proxies from stockholders to vote for the recommended slate of directors and for any other proposals requiring stockholder approval. If stockholders are satisfied with the company, they generally sign the proxy in favor of management, giving written authorization to management to vote their shares. If some stockholders do not vote their shares, the number of shares voted at the meeting and the number needed to constitute a majority are lower. Because of the proxy system and the fact that management is able to mail information to stockholders at the company's expense, management has a distinct advantage in the voting process.

Proxy contests are few, owing to management having the upper hand.

But the fortress is not invulnerable. Outsiders can seize control of a company through a **proxy contest.** When an outside group undertakes a proxy raid, it is required to register its proxy statement with the Securities and Exchange Commission to prevent the presentation of misleading or false information. In a proxy contest, the odds favor existing management to win. It has both the organization and the use of the company's resources to carry on the proxy fight. Insurgents are likely to be successful only when the earnings performance of the company has been bad and management obviously ineffective. Still, the undertaking of a proxy contest often is associated with higher share price performance than otherwise would be the case around the time of the event. The challenge itself may be sufficient to change expectations about management in the future behaving more in keeping with maximizing shareholder wealth.[6]

Dual-Class Common Stock

To retain control for management, founders, or some other group, a company may have more than one class of common stock. For example, its common stock might be classified according to voting power and to the claim on income. Class A common may have inferior voting privilege but may be entitled to a prior claim to dividends, whereas the class B common has superior voting rights but a lower claim to dividends. Usually, the promoters of a corporation and its management will hold the class B common stock, whereas the class A common is sold to the public.

Suppose the class A and class B common stockholders of a company are entitled to one vote per share, but the class A stock is issued at an initial price of $20 a share. If $2 million is raised in the original offering through the issuance of 80,000 shares of class A common for $1.6 million and 200,000 shares of class B common for $400,000, the class B stockholders will have over twice as many votes as the class A holders have, despite the fact that their original investment is only one-quarter as large. Thus, the class B holders have effective control of the company. Indeed, this is the purpose of classified stock.

Perhaps the most famous example of a company with classified common stock is the Ford Motor Company. The class B stock is owned by members of the Ford family, and the class A stock is held by the general public. Regardless of the number of class A shares issued, the class B common constitutes 40 percent of the total voting power of the company. Thus, members of the Ford family retain substantial voting power in the company, despite the fact that they hold far fewer shares than does the general public.

A number of scholars have examined the valuation of dual-class stock. The superior voting-right stock tends to trade at a premium above the class of common having inferior voting power. Although one would think that announcement of a new superior voting-right stock would result in a negative stock price reaction, the empirical evidence is mixed in this regard.

TENDER OFFERS AND COMPANY RESISTANCE

Rather than a proxy contest, the threatening party can make a **tender offer** directly to stockholders of the company it wishes to acquire. A tender offer is an offer to purchase shares of stock of another company at a fixed price per share from stockholders who "tender" their shares. The tender price is usually set significantly above the present market price, as an incentive. Use of the tender offer allows the

---

[6]For empirical studies of the phenomenon, see Peter Dodd and Jerold B. Warner, "On Corporate Governance: A Study of Proxy Contests," *Journal of Financial Economics*, 11 (April 1983), 401–38; Harry DeAngelo and Linda DeAngelo, "Proxy Contests and the Governance of Publicly Held Corporations," *Journal of Financial Economics*, 23 (June 1989), 29–59; David Ikenberry and Josef Lakonishok, "Corporate Governance through the Proxy Contest: Evidence and Implications," *Journal of Business*, 66 (July 1993), 405–35; Lisa F. Borstadt and Thomas J. Zwirlein, "The Efficient Monitoring Role of Proxy Contests: An Empirical Analysis of Post-contest Control Changes and Firm Performance," *Financial Management*, 21 (Autumn 1992), 22–34; and J. Harold Mulherin and Annette B. Poulsen, "Proxy Contests and Corporate Change: Implications for Shareholder Wealth," *Journal of Financial Economics*, 47 (March 1998), 279–313.

acquiring company to bypass the management of the company it wishes to acquire and, therefore, serves as a threat in any negotiations with that management.

Use of the Tender

The tender offer can be used also when there are no negotiations but when one company simply wants to acquire another. It is not possible to surprise another company, because the Securities and Exchange Commission requires rather extensive disclosures. The primary selling tool is the premium that is offered over the existing market price of the stock. In addition, brokers are often given attractive commissions for shares tendered through them. The tender offer itself is usually communicated through financial newspapers. Direct mailings are made to the stockholders of the company being bid for if the bidder is able to obtain a list of stockholders. Although a company is legally obligated to provide such a list, it usually is able to delay delivery long enough to frustrate the bidder.

Instead of one tender offer, some bidders make a **two-tier offer.** An example of this was the bid by CSX Corporation for Consolidated Rail Corporation (Conrail) in the late 1990s. With a two-tier offer, the first tier of stock usually represents control and is more attractive in terms of price and/or the form of payment than is the second-tier offer for the remaining stock. The differential is designed to increase the probability of successfully gaining control, by providing an incentive to tender early. The two-tier offer avoids the "free-rider" problem associated with a single tender offer where individual stockholders have an incentive to hold out in the hope of realizing a higher counteroffer by someone else.

Defensive Tactics

The company being bid for may use a number of defensive tactics. Management may try to persuade stockholders that the offer is not in their best interests. Usually, the argument is that the bid is too low in relation to the true, long-run value of the firm. Hearing that, stockholders may look at an attractive premium and find the long run too long. Some companies raise the cash dividend or declare a stock split in hopes of gaining stockholder support. Legal actions are often undertaken, more to delay and frustrate the bidder than with the expectation of winning. When the two firms are competitors, an antitrust suit may prove a powerful deterrent to the bidder. As a last resort, management of the company being bid for may seek a merger with a "friendly" company, known as a **white knight.**

Indication of unusual accumulation of stock comes from watching trading volume and stock transfers. If an outside group acquires more than 5 percent, it is required to file a **13-D form** with the Securities and Exchange Commission. This form describes the people involved with the group, their holdings, and the intention of the group. Each additional 1 percent accumulation requires an amendment.

Antitakeover Amendments

In addition to the defensive tactics already described, some companies use more formal methods that are put into place prior to an actual takeover attempt. Known as antitakeover or "shark-repellent" devices, they are designed to make a takeover more difficult. Before describing them, it is useful to consider their motivation. The **managerial entrenchment hypothesis** suggests that the barriers erected are to protect management jobs and that such actions work to the detriment of stockholders. On the other hand, the **stockholders interest hypothesis** implies that corporate control contests are dysfunctional and take management time away from

Tender offers appeal directly to stockholders and are always hostile.

profit-making activities. Therefore, antitakeover devices ensure more attention being paid to these activities and are in the interest of stockholders. Moreover, the barriers erected are said to cause individual stockholders not to accept a low offer price but to join other stockholders in a cartel response to any offer. Therefore, antitakeover devices would enhance shareholder wealth, according to this hypothesis.

Voting Devices   A handful of devices exist to make it more difficult for another party to take you over. As we know, some companies **stagger the terms of their board of directors** so that fewer stand for election each year, and, accordingly, more votes are needed to elect a director. Sometimes it is desirable to **change the state of incorporation.** Charter rules differ state by state, and many companies like to incorporate in a state with few limitations, such as Delaware. By so doing, it is easier for the corporation to install antitakeover amendments as well as to defend itself legally if a takeover battle ensues. Some companies put into place a **super-majority merger approval provision.** Instead of an ordinary majority being needed for approval of a merger, a higher percentage is required, often two-thirds. The percentage may be even higher; 80 percent is used in a number of instances. The ability to install this provision depends on the state of incorporation.

The poison pill is the most effective of the antitakeover devices.

The Poison Pill   The **poison pill**—or **distribution of rights** to stockholders as it is known as formally—is the "biggie" when it comes to putting defenses in place. Many contend it is the only effective deterrent. The distribution of rights to existing stockholders allows them to purchase a new security, often a convertible preferred stock, on favorable terms. By favorable, the subscription price might be only 40 percent of the true market value. However, the security offering is triggered only if an outside party acquires some percentage, frequently 20 percent, of the company's stock. This trigger is known as the flip-in feature. The idea is to have available a security offering that is unpalatable to the acquirer. This can be with respect to a bargain subscription price, or it can be with respect to voting rights or with respect to precluding a change in control unless a substantial premium (often several hundred percent) is paid.

The rights typically have an expiration date, frequently 10 years. Upon expiration, the pill no longer is in place. To be continued a new distribution of rights must occur. Example: On October 5, 1997, Pfizer, the pharmaceutical company, issued new rights to stockholders to replace those that expired on that date issued 10 years earlier. The board of directors reserves the ability to redeem the rights at any time for a token amount. The poison pill is meant to force the potential acquirer into negotiating directly with the board as opposed to a tender offer to the shareholders. Only the board can authorize the pill being redeemed. Most companies state something to the effect that the rights are not intended to prevent an acquisition of company that is in the best interest of stockholders. Whether the board acts in the best interests of the shareholders in negotiating with a potential acquirer deterred by the pill varies from situation to situation.

Other Antitakeover Devices   A number of other shark repellents are employed, but most feel that they are far less effective deterrents than the poison pill. With a **fair merger price provision,** the bidder must pay noncontrolling stockholders a price at least equal to a "fair price," which is established in advance. Usually this minimum price is linked to earnings per share through a price/earnings ratio, but it may simply be a stated market price. Often the fair price provision is coupled with a **supermajority provision.** If the stated minimum price is not satisfied, the combination can only be approved if a supermajority of stockholders are in favor. It also is frequently accompanied with a **freeze-out provision,** which allows the transaction to proceed, at a "fair price," only after a delay of between 2 and 5 years.

A **lock-up provision** is used in conjunction with other provisions. This provision requires supermajority stockholder approval to modify the corporate charter and any previously passed antitakeover provisions. In addition to these charter amendments, many companies enter into **management contracts** with their top management. Typically, high compensation is triggered if the company is taken over. Known as a "golden parachute," these contracts effectively increase the price the acquiring company must pay in an unfriendly takeover.

Sometimes the company will negotiate a **standstill agreement** with the outside party. Such an agreement is a voluntary contract where, for a period of several years, the substantial stockholder group agrees not to increase its stock holdings. Often this limitation is expressed as a maximum percentage of stock the group may own. The agreement also specifies that the group will not participate in a control contest against management and that it gives the right of first refusal to the company if it should decide to sell its stock. The standstill agreement, together with the other provisions discussed, serves to reduce competition for corporate control.

As a last resort, some companies make a **premium buy-back offer** to the threatening party. As the name implies, the repurchase of stock is at a premium over its market price and usually is in excess of what the accumulator paid. Moreover, the offer is not extended to other stockholders. Known as **greenmail,** the idea is to get the threatening party off management's back by making it attractive for the party to leave. Of course the premium paid to one party may work to the disadvantage of stockholders left "holding the bag."

Takeover Defenses and the Courts

Whether defensive devices work for the besieged company depends in some measure on the courts. When confronted with a hostile takeover or the potential for such, a board of directors must be guided by the legal environment in which it finds itself. Doctrines of behavior involve rules of *business judgment, intrinsic fairness*, and *proportionality*. The first is that the board acts in the interests of shareholders and exercises good business judgment when it comes to a bid or to the instigation of antitakeover devices. Taken to the extreme, it says management and the board can "just say no." The second notion is that the board acts in a way that is fair to all parties, in particular to its shareholders.

The rule of proportionality is that a company's response to a takeover threat must be proportional, with respect to value, to the threat itself. For the most part, this rule has revolved around the poison pill. If an acquirer makes an offer conditional on an existing pill being removed, the company under attack must eliminate its pill or the response will be construed as not being proportional.

The principal state in which companies are incorporated is Delaware. In the 1980s and 1990s, the Delaware Supreme Court and Chancery Court made some landmark rulings. These rulings affirmed the use of the poison pill under the business judgment rule. Several rulings made the proportionality rule ambiguous in its interpretation. The present legal environment is one of management having the upper hand in control contests. One manifestation of this phenomenon is that we see fewer such challenges, but the Delaware legal environment is only one cause.

Although Delaware law is the most important—nearly half of the NYSE companies are incorporated there—companies do incorporate elsewhere. For them, other laws and rulings regulate corporate takeovers. In the 1980s, a number of state courts seemed to shift toward less protection of incumbent management. However, Indiana, Minnesota, and Pennsylvania promulgated laws making hostile takeovers difficult and limiting the personal liability of officers and directors. The purpose of these laws seems to be to preserve employment in the state as well as the independence of local companies. However, they work to the detriment of shareholders in chilling takeover activity.[7]

Shareholder Proposals and Activism

Rather than trying to seize control of a corporation, certain institutional investors and shareholder activist groups want to change the ways of governance. The end result, they hope, will be a management more responsive to shareholders and the creation of value. Proposals are initiated by these groups to be voted on by shareholders, usually in connection with the annual meeting. The changes proposed can be of a number of sorts, but they usually fall into the categories of election of directors, reduction of antitakeover devices, and management compensation and disclosure of such. Shareholder proposals usually are submitted under **Rule 14a-8** of the Securities and Exchange Commission. These must be submitted 6 months in advance of the shareholders' meeting.

The active use of shareholder proposals to prompt change began in the mid-1980s with such groups as the California Public Employees Retirement System (CALPERS), a large pension investor, and the United Shareholders Association, which is dedicated to increasing shareholder value. While the success rate of shareholder proposals is not large in the sense of a majority voting in favor, a strong minority vote may cause management to change. In general, the vote for a proposal is larger if the company has been doing poorly, if the proposal is sponsored by a large organization, if the proposal restores shareholder voting rights, and if the corporation previously enacted a significant number of takeover defenses.[8]

Though some large institutional investors are active in shareholder proposals, most are not. The reality is that very few proposals pass. Still a proposal garnering strong but not majority support puts pressure on management to reform. When activism is coordinated among institutional investors, the pressure gauge grows hotter. Less overt than a shareholder proposal, some institutional investors negotiate directly with management over corporate governance and directional matters of concern. Whether change occurs or not is correlated with the credibility of the threat of management ouster.

EMPIRICAL EVIDENCE ON MERGERS AND TAKEOVERS

In recent years, there have been a number of empirical studies on takeovers, and these studies provide a wealth of information. However, differences in samples, sample periods, and research methods render some of the valuation implications ambiguous. Nonetheless, with the ever-increasing number of studies, certain patterns emerge that make generalizations possible. In this section we review the overall evidence for valuation implications; no attempt is made to analyze the numerous empirical studies, many of which are shown in the Selected References section

---

[7]Samuel H. Szewczyk and George P. Tsetsekos, "State Intervention in the Market for Corporate Control," *Journal of Financial Economics*, 31 (February 1992), 3–23, tested the effect of the 1990 Pennsylvania law on shareholder wealth of companies incorporated in that state. They found significant negative abnormal returns using event study methodology, and estimated the cost at $4 billion overall for shareholders of Pennsylvania firms.

[8]See Lilli A. Gordon and John Pound, "Information, Ownership Structure, and Shareholder Voting: Evidence from Shareholder-Sponsored Corporate Governance Proposals," *Journal of Finance*, 48 (June 1993), 697–718.

at the end of the chapter. The implications of the studies can be categorized into those for target company stockholders and those for buying company stockholders and debt holders.

Target Company Shareholder Returns

For the successful, or completed takeover, all studies show the target company stockholders realizing appreciable increments in wealth relative to the market value of their holdings prior to any takeover activity. This wealth increment is due to the premium paid by the acquiring company, the size of which has run around 30 percent on average during the last few decades. However, premiums as high as 100 percent have occurred. The market price of the target company's stock tends to rise once information about a potential takeover becomes available or rumors of such develop. Typically the stock price improvement begins prior to the takeover announcement, perhaps 1 month in advance. The pattern usually observed for the target or selling company is shown in Fig. 23-3. However, it makes a difference whether the takeover is by tender offer or by merger agreement. Share price improvement usually is greater with a tender offer than with a merger. This difference is attributable to the competition and multiple bids often associated with a tender offer as opposed to merger negotiation with only one party.

For the unsuccessful takeover, the results are even more affected by whether a tender offer or a merger agreement is involved. With an unsuccessful tender offer, the target company's share price typically remains high after the failure announcement. The reason is the prospect of future tender offers that will enhance share price. If no subsequent acquisition attempts occur, share price usually slips and may even fall back as far as the pre-offer level. If subsequent bids occur, however, share price of the target company may show further improvement. For the unsuccessful takeover, share price tends to fall quickly to its pre-offer level, after the failure becomes evident. It also seems to matter whether cash or stock is being offered in the terminated merger, the former resulting in higher returns.

In summary, target company stockholders realize substantial gains in a successful takeover, more for a tender offer than for a merger. For the unsuccessful takeover, share price falls back toward the pre-offer level unless there is a subsequent bid. However, the fallback is slower when the initial offer is for cash than when it is for stock.

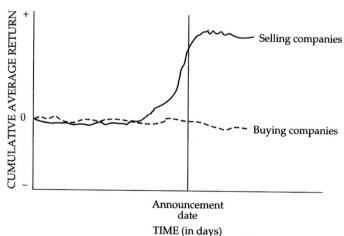

FIGURE 23-3
Relative stock returns around a successful takeover

Acquiring Company Stockholder Returns

For the buying, or acquiring, company, the evidence is less clear. In all cases of a successful takeover, a premium obviously is paid, and its justification must be expected synergy and/or more efficient management of the resources of the target company. The question is whether likely synergy and/or improved management will result in a wealth increment sufficient to offset the premium. Answers to this question from empirical studies are mixed. Some studies suggest stockholders of acquiring firms obtain a small improvement in share price while others find no effect at all. The situation of no effect is illustrated in Fig. 23-3. Still others find that stockholders of acquiring companies earn negative returns, holding constant other factors. The small negative returns observed were found in the 1980s and 1990s, but not in earlier decades.

Another explanation, of course, is that acquiring companies simply pay too much. This would agree with the hubris hypothesis, which predicts a decrease in value of the acquiring firm. In other words, potential synergy and management improvement are not enough to offset the premium paid. In certain bidding wars, the frenzy is such that rational decision making seems to disappear. In some contests, the quest of the prize is so important that the premium is bid up beyond what synergy and/or improved management will justify. Several studies show that companies that acquire others via a stock merger underperform in the postacquisition period. This contrasts with acquiring companies via a tender offer, where positive excess returns in the postacquisition period occur.[9] A possible explanation for this phenomenon is that taken up in Chapter 19 on issuing securities. With asymmetric information between investors and management, a company will acquire with stock when management believes it is overvalued and with cash, in this case through a tender offer, when the stock is believed to be undervalued. As the over- or undervaluation works itself out over time, postacquisition performance would be negative or positive relative to stocks overall. In a tender offer, management of the target usually is replaced, and this may drive efficiency gains as well.

Another cause for concern is that so many acquirers later divest themselves of the companies they acquired. More often than not the divestiture is of a diversifying acquisition as opposed to one that is in a related line of business.[10] The invariable reason for the divestiture is that the target did not live up to expectations; often the disposition involves a loss. The question remains as to why the acquirer was so eager and paid so much in the first place. Equally puzzling is why companies acquire in unrelated lines of business. On average, acquiring company stockholders experience negative returns in "conglomerate" types of acquisitions. The premium paid simply is not recovered with the limited synergism possible. Sometimes the acquiring company will get lucky and come across a truly undervalued firm, but this usually is not the case. A related line of business acquisition makes more sense.

In summary, the evidence on returns to stockholders of acquiring companies is mixed. It is difficult to make an overall case for takeovers being a thing of value to the stockholders of the acquiring company. Clearly, some acquisitions are

Target company stockholders nearly always gain via the premium paid; **acquiring company stockholders** do not, on average.

Diversifying mergers are not well regarded by the stock market.

[9]Tim Loughran and Anand M. Vijh, "Do Long-Term Shareholders Benefit from Corporate Acquisitions?" *Journal of Finance*, 52 (December 1997), 1765–90; and P. Raghavendra Rau and Theo Vermaelen, "Glamour, Value and the Post-Acquisition Performance of Acquiring Firms," *Journal of Financial Economics*, 49 (August 1998), 223–53.

[10]See Steven N. Kaplan and Michael S. Weisbach, "The Success of Acquisitions: Evidence from Divestitures," *Journal of Finance*, 47 (March 1992), 107–38, who found that 44 percent of the acquired companies in their sample were later divested.

worthwhile, because of synergy and managerial improvement, and some are bad. The key for the financial manager is to be careful because, on average, a case cannot be made for corporations overall making consistently good acquisitions. For the acquired and the acquiring companies collectively, there is an increment in wealth associated with takeovers. This is primarily the result of the premium paid to the selling company's stockholders. As long as it is not offset by a significant decline in share price of the acquiring company, wealth overall is increased.

Other Security Holder Returns

There have been only a limited number of studies dealing with what happens to debt instrument returns around the time of a merger. The results suggest that nonconvertible debt holders neither gain nor lose in a merger. For both acquiring and acquired companies, the abnormal returns at the time of the merger announcement do not differ significantly from zero. Therefore, the wealth transfer hypothesis, which suggests bondholders gain with a merger because of diversification leading to a reduction in default risk, is not supported.

Effect of Antitakeover Devices

There have been various tests of antitakeover devices, usually in conjunction with the two hypotheses discussed earlier. The managerial entrenchment hypothesis works to the detriment of present stockholders. The stockholders interest hypothesis holds that antitakeover devices benefit stockholders in ensuring management's attention to the profit-generating affairs of the company as well as giving individual stockholders a greater incentive to hold out for a high price, thereby benefiting all stockholders. The empirical evidence, which uses event study analysis, shows that for some of the devices, like the standstill agreement and greenmail, there is a negative price effect. For completed acquisitions, Robert Comment and G. William Schwert (see Selected References) find that the premium paid is higher when a poison pill is in place. At the time of the announcement of the poison pill, however, the empirical results are mixed. The same applies to other antitakeover devices.

Where a takeover attempt fails, management of the targeted company often undertakes actions that increase efficiency and shareholder wealth. These are the things that the aggressor sought to do, of course. Assem Safieddine and Sheridan Titman find that targeted companies that increase their leverage discipline themselves to make improvements.[11] Efficiencies involved include cutting some capital expenditures, selling assets, reducing employment, and increasing focus. As a result, cash flows and share-price performance are better on average than benchmarks in the 5 years following the failed takeover attempt.

Summary

The market for corporate control is one where various management teams compete to gain control of corporate resources, hoping to put them to more productive uses. One company may acquire another through the purchase of its assets or its stock, and payment can be cash or stock. Whether a combination is taxable or tax free is highly consequential to the selling company and its stockholders and, sometimes, to the buying company. Accounting considera-

---

[11]Assem Safieddine and Sheridan Titman, "Leverage and Corporate Performance: Evidence from Unsuccessful Takeovers," *Journal of Finance*, 54 (April 1999), 547–80.

tions come into play in that the merger using purchase accounting requires that any goodwill created be amortized against future earnings. If goodwill is not impaired, however, it need not be amortized.

Whenever two companies exchange stock, certain financial relationships come into prominence. Some companies focus on the impact on earnings per share. When the price/earnings ratio of the company being acquired is lower than the price/earnings ratio of the acquiring company, there is an initial improvement in earnings per share of the latter company; a dilution occurs when the price/earnings ratio is higher. In efficient financial markets and in the absence of synergism, we would expect the price/earnings ratio of the surviving company to be a weighted average of the price/earnings ratios of the two pre-merger companies.

The foundations for value creation through a merger are several. Sales enhancement, operating economies, economies of scale, and more effective management may give rise to synergy. Moreover, there may be an information effect, leading to the correction of an undervalued situation. Tax effects can lead to value creation, while diversification tends to benefit debt holders in having a more creditworthy claim. The hubris hypothesis is that acquirers become irrational in bidding wars and pay too much. Finally, personal motives of the owners of a company being sold or of the management of the acquiring company may be a reason for a merger.

Corporate voting determines who will be successful in a merger skirmish. Common stockholders elect the board of directors by proxy. These directors can be elected under a majority voting system or a cumulative voting one, the latter allowing minority interests to gain board membership. The use of different classes of common stock permits promoters and management of a corporation to retain voting control. Proxy contests are one means by which outsiders can seize corporate control. More prevalent is the tender offer to purchase shares directly from the stockholders of that company. A number of antitakeover devices exist, and they were explored, as were defenses against the takeover and the legal environment in which they hold. The deterrent regarded as the most effective is the poison pill. Shareholder proposals, their purpose, and likelihood of their success were also examined.

Certain empirical evidence indicates substantial excess returns to the stockholders of the selling company if the merger or tender offer is successful. If it fails, share price falls back to the preoffer level unless, in the case of a tender offer, there is a subsequent bid. For the acquiring company stockholders, the evidence is mixed. It is hard to make a case for positive excess returns to buying company stockholders, and some recent studies show negative excess returns. Using event study methodology, modest negative share price effects have been found around the announcement of some antitakeover amendments.

Self-Correction Problems

1. Yablonski Cordage Company is considering the acquisition of Yawitz Wire and Mesh Corporation with stock. Relevant financial information is as follows:

	Yablonski	Yawitz
Present earnings (in thousands)	$4,000	$1,000
Common shares (in thousands)	2,000	800
Earnings per share	$2.00	$1.25
Price/earnings ratio	12x	8x

Yablonski plans to offer a premium of 20 percent over the market price of Yawitz stock.

    a. (1) What is the ratio of exchange of stock? (2) How many new shares will be issued?

    b. What are earnings per share for the surviving company immediately following the merger?

    c. (1) If the price/earnings ratio stays at 12 times, what is the market price per share of the surviving company? (2) What would happen if it went to 11 times?

2. Wilson Service Corporation is engaged in electrical and fluid (mostly pumps) equipment maintenance and sales for mid-market-size companies. In this regard, it is relatively capital intensive. Its most recent year-end financial statement reflects revenues of $112 million, operating income of $28 million, depreciation of $7 million, net income after taxes of $12 million, total assets of $172 million, interest-bearing debt of $54 million, and shareholders' equity of $40 million. Its cash position is negligible. The company has 5.6 million shares outstanding and its current share price is 16\frac{1}{4}$.

    The company has attracted the attention of Keller Industries, Inc., which is considering acquiring Wilson Service. Keller Industries and its investment banker believe that by offering a premium of 40 percent that Wilson can be acquired. Presently, Wilson's free cash flow (excluding interest on debt) is the following:

Operating profits after taxes	$17 million
Depreciation	7
Total	$24
Less: capital expenditures	8
working-capital additions	3
Free cash flow	$13

Keller believes that with synergy, it can grow EBITDA by 20 percent per annum for 3 years, and then by 12 percent for the next 3 years. At the same time, it believes it can hold capital expenditures and working capital additions to a combined increase (from the present $11 million) of only $2 million per year. At the end of 6 years, Keller assumes that free cash flow will grow at 5 percent per annum into perpetuity. It also assumes that the required discount rate for such an investment is 15 percent.

    Comparable recently acquired companies have had the following median valuation ratios:

Equity value-to-book	2.9x
Enterprise value-to-sales	1.4x
Equity value-to-earnings	15.3x
Enterprise value-to-EBITDA	7.8x

You are CFO of Keller Industries. Does the acquisition of Wilson Service Corporation make sense to you? What is your recommendation?

3. Aggressive Incorporated wishes to make a tender offer for the Passive Company. Passive has 100,000 shares of common stock outstanding and earns $5.50 per share. If it were combined with Aggressive, total economies of $1.5 million could be realized. Presently the market price per share of Passive is $55. Aggressive makes a two-tier tender offer: (i) $65 per share for the first 50,001 shares tendered and (ii) $50 per share for the remaining shares.

   a. (1) If successful, what will Aggressive end up paying for Passive? (2) How much incrementally will stockholders of Passive receive for the economies?

   b. (1) Acting independently, what will each stockholder do to maximize his or her wealth? (2) What might they do if they could respond collectively as a cartel?

   c. How can a company increase the probability of individual stockholders resisting too low a tender offer?

   d. What might happen if Aggressive offered $65 in the first tier and only $40 in the second tier?

Problems

1. The following data are pertinent for companies A and B:

	Company A	Company B
Present earnings (in millions)	$20	$4
Shares (in millions)	10	1
Price/earnings ratio	18x	10x

   a. If the two companies were to merge and the exchange ratio were 1 share of company A for each share of company B, what would be the initial impact on earnings per share of the two companies? What is the market-value exchange ratio? Is a merger likely to take place?

   b. If the exchange ratio were 2 shares of company A for each share of company B, what would happen with respect to part a?

   c. If the exchange ratio were 1.5 shares of company A for each share of company B, what would happen?

   d. What exchange ratio would you suggest?

2.

	Net Income	Number of Shares	Market Price per Share	Tax Rate
Nimbus Company	$5,000,000	1,000,000	$100	50%
Noor Company	1,000,000	500,000	20	50

The Nimbus Company wishes to acquire the Noor Company. If the merger were effected through an exchange of stock, Nimbus would be willing to pay a 25 percent premium for the Noor shares. If done for cash, the terms would have to be as favorable to the Noor shareholders. To obtain the cash, Nimbus would have to sell its own stock in the market.

   a. Compute the combined earnings per share for an exchange of stock.

   b. If we assume that all Noor shareholders have held their stock for more than 1 year, have a 20 percent marginal capital gains tax rate, and paid an average of $14 for their shares, what cash price would have to be offered to be as attractive as the terms in part a? (Assume that Noor shareholders equate value per share in cash after capital gains taxes with value per share in Nimbus stock.)

3. Assume the exchange of Nimbus shares for Noor shares as outlined in Problem 2.

   a. What is the ratio of exchange?

   b. Compare the earnings per Noor share before and after the merger. Compare the earnings per Nimbus share. On this basis alone, which group fared better? Why?

   c. Why do you imagine that old Nimbus commanded a higher P/E than Noor? What should be the change in P/E ratio resulting from the merger?

   d. If the Nimbus Company were in a high-technology growth industry and Noor made cement, would you revise your answers?

   e. In determining the appropriate P/E ratio for Nimbus, should the increase in earnings resulting from this merger be added as a growth factor?

   f. In light of the foregoing discussion, do you feel that the Noor shareholders would have approved the merger if Noor stock paid a $1 dividend and Nimbus paid $3? Why?

4. Biggo Stores, Inc. (BSI), has acquired the Nail It, Glue It, and Screw It Hardware Company (NGS) for $4 million in stock and the assumption of $2 million in NGS liabilities. The balance sheets of the two companies before the merger were (in millions):

	BSI	NGS
Tangible and total assets	$10.0	$5.0
Liabilities	4.0	2.0
Shareholders' equity	$ 6.0	$3.0

Determine the balance sheet of the combined company after the merger under the purchase and pooling-of-interests methods of accounting.

5. Copper Tube Company currently has annual earnings of $10 million, with 4 million shares of common stock outstanding and a market price per share of $30. In the absence of any mergers, Copper Tube's annual earnings are expected to grow at a compound rate of 5 percent per annum. Brass Fitting Com-

pany, which Copper Tube is seeking to acquire, has present annual earnings of $2 million, 1 million shares of common outstanding, and a market price per share of $36. Its annual earnings are expected to grow at a compound annual rate of 10 percent per annum. Copper Tube will offer 1.2 shares of its stock for each share of Brass Fitting Company. No synergistic effects are expected from the merger.

    a. What is the immediate effect on the surviving company's earnings per share?

    b. Would you want to acquire Brass Fitting Company? If it is not attractive now, when will it be attractive from the standpoint of earnings per share?

6. D. Sent, a disgruntled stockholder of the Zebec Corporation, desires representation on the board. The Zebec Corporation, which has 10 directors, has 1 million shares outstanding.

    a. How many shares would Sent have to control to be assured of one directorship under a majority voting system?

    b. Recompute part a, assuming a cumulative voting system.

    c. Recompute parts a and b, assuming the number of directors was reduced to 5.

7. Joe Miller has formed a company that can earn a 12 percent return after taxes, although no investment has yet been made. Joe plans to take $1 million in $1 par value stock for his promotion efforts. All financing for the firm will be in stock, and all earnings will be paid in dividends.

    a. Joe desires to keep 50 percent control of the company after he has acquired new financing. He can do this by taking his stock in the form of $1 par value, class B, with 2 votes per share, while selling $1 par value class A stock. The investors, however, would require a dividend formula that would give them a 10 percent dividend return. (1) How many class A shares would be issued? (2) What dividend formula would meet the investors' requirements? (3) What dividend payment would be left for Joe's class B shares?

    b. If Joe were willing to accept one share–one vote, he could have just one class of common stock and sell the same amount of class A stock as in part a. The investors would require only an 8 percent dividend rate of return. (1) What would be the dividend distribution in this case? (2) Comparing this answer with that obtained in part a, what is Joe paying to retain control?

    c. Rework part b under the assumption that the investors require a 9 percent dividend return. What happens to Joe?

8. Friday Harbor Lime Company presently sells for $24 per share. Management, together with their families, controls 40 percent of the 1 million shares outstanding. Roche Cement Company wishes to acquire Friday Harbor Lime because of likely synergies. The estimated present value of these synergies is $8 million. Moreover, Roche Cement Company feels that management of Friday Harbor Lime is overpaid and "overperked." It feels that with better management motivation, lower salaries, and fewer perks for controlling management, including the disposition of two yachts, approximately $400,000 per year in expenses can be saved. This would add $3 million in value to the acquisition.

a. What is the maximum price per share that Roche Cement Company can afford to pay for Friday Harbor Lime Company?

b. At what price per share will the management of Friday Harbor Lime be indifferent to giving up the present value of their private control benefits?

c. What price per share would you offer?

 Solutions to Self-Correction Problems

1. a.

	Yablonski	Yawitz
Earnings per share	$2.00	$1.25
Price/earnings ratio	12x	8x
Market price per share	$24	$10

(1) Offer to Yawitz shareholders in Yablonski stock (including the premium) = $10 × 1.20 = $12 per share. Exchange ratio = $12/$24 = .5, or one-half share of Yablonski stock for every share of Yawitz stock.

(2) Number of new shares issued = 800,000 shares × .5 = 400,000 shares.

b.

Surviving company earnings (in thousands)	$5,000
Common shares (in thousands)	2,400
Earnings per share	$2.0833

There is an increase in earnings per share by virtue of acquiring a company with a lower price/earnings ratio.

c. (1) Market price per share $2.0833 × 12 = $25.00

(2) Market price per share $2.0833 × 11 = $22.92

In the first instance, share price rises, from $24, due to the increase in earnings per share. In the second case, share price falls owing to the decline in the price/earnings ratio. In efficient markets, we might expect some decline in price/earnings ratio if there was not likely to be synergy and/or improved management.

2. With a 40 percent premium, the offering share price is $16.25 × 1.4 = $22.75. With 5.6 million shares outstanding, the implied market capitalization of the equity is $22.75 × 5.6 million = $127.4 million. With $54 million in interest-bearing debt, the enterprise value is $181.4 million. EBITDA is $28 million + $7 million = $35 million. Therefore, the following ratios prevail:

	Wilson	Comparables
Equity value-to-book	127.4/40 = 3.2x	2.9x
Enterprise value-to-sales	181.4/112 = 1.6x	1.4x
Equity value-to-earnings	127.4/12 = 10.6x	15.3x
Enterprise value-to-EBITDA	181.4/35 = 5.2x	7.8x

As to discounted cash flow, we have the following (in millions):

	Present	Expected					
		1	2	3	4	5	6
EBITDA	$24.0	$28.8	$34.6	$41.5	$46.5	$52.0	$58.3
Cap. ex. & w.c. addn.	11.0	13.0	15.0	17.0	19.0	21.0	23.0
Free cash flow	13.0	15.8	19.6	24.5	27.5	31.0	35.3

For year 6 terminal value, we have

$$\frac{\$35.3\,(1.05)}{.15 - .05} = \$370.7$$

At a 15 percent discount rate, the present value of the expected free cash flows through year 6, together with the terminal value at the end of year 6, is $251.3 million.

Even though the equity value-to-book and the enterprise value-to-sales ratios are moderately above those for the comparable companies, the other two ratios are much better. The equity value-to-earnings, or P/E ratio, is only 10.6x in comparison with 15.3x for the comparables and enterprise value-to-EBITDA is only 5.2x, whereas the comparables have a ratio of 7.8x. These are particularly attractive. With respect to DCF, a value of $251.3 million is comfortably in excess of the enterprise value being placed on the company of $181.4 million. Based on these financial considerations only, as the CFO you should recommend the acquisition of Wilson Service Corporation at a share price of $22.75.

3. a. Value to Passive:

$$50{,}001 \text{ shares} \times \$65 = \$3{,}250{,}065$$
$$49{,}999 \text{ shares} \times \$50 = \underline{2{,}499{,}950}$$
$$\text{Total purchase price} = \$5{,}750{,}015$$

$$\text{Total value of stock before} = 100{,}000 \text{ shares} \times \$55 = \underline{5{,}500{,}000}$$
$$\text{Increment to Passive stockholders} = \underline{\$\ \ 250{,}015}$$

The total value of the economies to be realized is $1,500,000. Therefore, Passive stockholders receive only a modest portion of the total value of the economies; in contrast, Aggressive stockholders obtain a large share.

b. (1) With a two-tier offer, there is a great incentive for individual stockholders to tender early, thereby ensuring success for the acquiring firm. (2) Collectively, Passive stockholders would be better off holding out for a larger fraction of the total value of the economies. They can do this only if they act as a cartel in their response to the offer.

c. By instigating antitakeover amendments and devices, some incentives may be created for individual stockholders to hold out for a higher offer. However, in practice, it is impossible to achieve a complete cartel response.

d.   50,000 shares $\times$ \$65 = \$3,250,065
     49,999 shares $\times$ \$40 =   1,999,960
     Total purchase price = \$5,250,025

This value is lower than the previous total market value of \$5,500,000. Clearly, stockholders would fare poorly if in the rush to tender shares the offer were successful. However, other potential acquirers would have an incentive to offer more than Aggressive, even with no economies to be realized. Competition among potential acquirers should ensure counterbids, so that Aggressive would be forced to bid no less than \$5,500,000 in total, the present market value.

Selected References

BERGER, PHILIP G., ELI OFEK, and DAVID L. YERMACK, "Managerial Entrenchment and Capital Structure Decisions," *Journal of Finance*, 52 (September 1997), 1411–38.

BHAJAT, SANJAI, and RICHARD H. JEFFERIS, "Voting Power in the Proxy Process: The Case of Antitakeover Charter Amendments," *Journal of Financial Economics*, 30 (November 1991), 193–225.

BOROKHOVICH, KENNETH A., KELLY R. BRUNARSKI, and ROBERT PARRINO, "CEO Contracting and Antitakeover Amendments," *Journal of Finance*, 52 (September 1997), 1495–1517.

BRADLEY, MICHAEL, ANAND DESAI, and E. HAN KIM, "The Rationale behind Interfirm Tender Offers: Information on Synergy," *Journal of Financial Economics*, 11 (April 1983), 183–206.

BRICKLEY, JAMES A., RONALD C. LEASE, and CLIFFORD W. SMITH JR., "Corporate Voting: Evidence from Charter Amendment Proposals," *Journal of Corporate Finance*, 1 (March 1994), 5–31.

COMMENT, ROBERT, and G. WILLIAM SCHWERT, "Poison or Placebo? Evidence on the Deterrence and Wealth Effects of Modern Antitakeover Measures," *Journal of Financial Economics*, 39 (September 1995), 3–43.

COTTER, JAMES F., and MARC ZENNER, "How Managerial Wealth Affects the Tender Offer Process," *Journal of Financial Economics*, 39 (February 1994), 63–97.

DANN, LARRY Y., and HARRY DEANGELO, "Standstill Agreements, Privately Negotiated Stock Repurchases, and the Market for Corporate Control," *Journal of Financial Economics*, 11 (April 1983), 275–300.

DEANGELO, HARRY, and LINDA DEANGELO, "Managerial Ownership of Voting Rights: A Study of Public Corporations with Dual Classes of Common Stock," *Journal of Financial Economics*, 14 (March 1985), 33–70.

DEANGELO, HARRY, and EDWARD M. RICE, "Antitakeover Charter Amendments and Stockholder Wealth," *Journal of Financial Economics*, 11 (April 1983), 329–60.

DENIS, DAVID J., "Defensive Changes in Corporate Payout Policy: Share Repurchases and Special Dividends," *Journal of Finance*, 45 (December 1990), 1433–56.

DENIS, DAVID J., and JAN M. SERRANO, "Active Investors and Management Turnover Following Unsuccessful Control Contests," *Journal of Financial Economics*, 40 (February 1996), 239–66.

DODD, PETER, and JEROLD B. WARNER, "On Corporate Governance: A Study of Proxy Contests," *Journal of Financial Economics*, 11 (April 1983), 401–38.

HARFORD, JARRAD, "Corporate Cash Reserves and Acquisitions," *Journal of Finance*, 54 (December 1999), 1969–98.

IKENBERRY, DAVID, and JOSEF LAKONISHOK, "Corporate Governance through the Proxy Contest: Evidence and Implications," *Journal of Business*, 66 (July 1993), 405–35.

JARRELL, GREGG A., and ANNETTE B. POULSEN, "Shark Repellents and Stock Prices," *Journal of Financial Economics*, 19 (September 1987), 127–68.

KAPLAN, STEVEN N., and MICHAEL S. WEISBACH, "The Success of Acquisitions: Evidence from Divestitures," *Journal of Finance*, 47 (March 1992), 107–38.

LINN, SCOTT C., and JOHN J. MCCONNELL, "An Empirical Investigation of the Impact of Antitakeover Amendments on Common Stock Prices," *Journal of Financial Economics*, 11 (April 1983), 361–99.

LOUGHRAN, TIM, and ANAND M. VIJH, "Do Long-term Shareholders Benefit from Corporate Acquisitions?" *Journal of Finance*, 52 (December 1997), 1765–90.

MALATESTA, PAUL H., and RALPH A. WALKING, "Poison Pill Securities," *Journal of Financial Economics*, 20 (January–March 1988), 347–76.

MAQUIEIRA, CARLOS P., WILLIAM L. MEGGINSON, and LANCE NAIL, "Wealth Creation versus Wealth Redistributions in Pure Stock-for-Stock Mergers," *Journal of Financial Economics*, 48 (April 1998), 3–33.

MITCHELL, MARK L., and J. HAROLD MULHERIN, "The Impact of Industry Shocks on Takeover and Restructuring Activity," *Journal of Financial Economics*, 41 (June 1996), 193–229.

MULHERIN, J. HAROLD, and ANNETTE B. POULSEN, "Proxy Contests and Corporate Change: Implications for Shareholder Wealth," *Journal of Financial Economics*, 47 (March 1998), 279–313.

PARTCH, M. MEGAN, "The Creation of a Class of Limited Voting Common Stock and Shareholder Wealth," *Journal of Financial Economics*, 18 (June 1987), 313–39.

POUND, JOHN, "Proxy Contests and the Efficiency of Shareholder Oversight," *Journal of Financial Economics*, 18 (January–March 1988), 237–65.

RAU, P. RAGHAVENDRA, "Investment Bank Market Share, Contingent Fee Payments, and the Performance of Acquiring Firms," *Journal of Financial Economics*, 56 (May 2000), 293–324.

RAU, P. RAGHAVENDRA, and THEO VERMAELEN, "Glamour, Value and the Post-Acquisition Performance of Acquiring Firms," *Journal of Financial Economics*, 49 (August 1998), 223–53.

ROLL, RICHARD, "The Hubris Hypothesis of Corporate Takeovers," *Journal of Business*, 59 (April 1986), 197–216.

SAFIEDDINE, ASSEM, and SHERIDAN TITMAN, "Leverage and Corporate Performance: Evidence from Unsuccessful Takeovers," *Journal of Finance*, 54 (April 1999), 547–80.

SCHWERT, G. WILLIAM, "Markup Pricing in Mergers and Acquisitions," *Journal of Financial Economics*, 41 (June 1996), 153–92.

SHLEIFER, ANDREI, and ROBERT W. VISHNY, "A Survey of Corporate Governance," *Journal of Finance*, 52 (June 1997), 737–83.

SONG, MOON H., and RALPH A. WALKLING, "Abnormal Returns to Rivals to Acquisition Targets: A Test of the 'Acquisition Probability Hypothesis,'" *Journal of Financial Economics*, 55 (February 2000), 143–72.

SULLIVAN, MICHAEL J., MARLIN R. H. JENSEN, and CARL D. HUDSON, "The Role of Medium of Exchange in Merger Offers: Examination of Terminated Merger Proposals," *Financial Management*, 23 (Autumn 1994), 51–62.

WESTON, J. FRED, KWANG S. CHUNG, and JUAN A. SIU, *Takeovers, Restructuring, and Corporate Governance*, 2nd ed. Upper Saddle River, NJ: Prentice Hall, 1998.

Wachowicz's Web World is an excellent overall Web site produced and maintained by my coauthor of *Fundamentals of Financial Management*, John M. Wachowicz Jr. It contains descriptions of and links to many finance web sites and articles. *www.prenhall.com/wachowicz.*

Corporate and Distress Restructuring

Corporate restructuring is a broad umbrella that covers many things. One thing is the merger, or takeover, which we considered in Chapter 23. From the standpoint of the buyer, this represents expansion, whereas from the perspective of the seller it represents a change in ownership that may or may not be voluntary. In addition to mergers, takeovers, and contests for corporate control, there are other types of corporate restructuring: divestitures, rearrangements, and ownership reformulations. In this chapter we consider such things as sell-offs, spin-offs, equity carve-outs, leveraged buyouts, and leveraged recapitalizations. The name "corporate restructuring" can be construed as almost any change in capital structure, in operations, or in ownership that is outside the ordinary course of business. Stock repurchase often is part of an overall corporate restructuring plan. As this topic was addressed in Chapter 11, we do not take it up here.

The restructuring of a company in financial distress differs from the above. Here the pressure to restructure is external, from creditors. There are defined legal remedies, and in any restructuring these must be observed. Still, management often is able to influence the outcome, as we shall see. ■

DIVESTITURES IN GENERAL

Divestiture can be involuntary or voluntary. An **involuntary divestiture** usually is the result of an antitrust ruling by the government. When another company is acquired, for example, the Federal Trade Commission and/or the Justice Department sometimes will stipulate that a particular business must be divested. Otherwise undue concentration will occur. A **voluntary divestiture**, on the other hand, is a willful decision by management to divest. It presumably is based on one or more reasons. What are the possible reasons? Efficiency gains, information effects and undervaluation, wealth transfers, and tax reasons.

Efficiency Gains and Refocus

Simply put, a particular operation may be more valuable to someone else than it is to the company. With **synergy** in a merger, the whole is said to be greater than the sum of the parts: $2 + 2 = 5$. With a divestiture, reverse synergy may occur, such that $4 - 2 = 3$. That is, the operation may be more valuable to someone else in generating cash flows and positive net present value. As a result, that someone is willing to pay a higher price for the operation than its present value to you.

A related reason for divestiture is a strategic change by the company. Periodically, most companies review their long-range plans in an effort to answer the eternal question, What businesses should we be in? Strategic considerations include internal capabilities (capital, plant, and people), the external product markets, and competitors. The market, as well as the competitive advantage of a company within a market, changes over time, sometimes very quickly. New markets emerge, as do new capabilities within the firm. What was a good fit before may no longer be a good fit. As a result, a decision may be reached to divest a particular operation. It may be that past diversification programs by the company have dissipated value. To the extent that divestiture undoes past diversification mistakes and causes the company to refocus on its core competencies, value may be enhanced. Strategic realignment is the most cited reason CEOs give for divestiture.

Information Effect

A second reason for divestiture involves the information it conveys to investors. If there is asymmetric information in management having information not known by investors, the announcement of a divestiture may be interpreted as a change in investment strategy or in operating efficiency. Here the signal is positive and may boost share price. On the other hand, if the announcement is interpreted as the sale of the most marketable subsidiary to deal with adversities elsewhere in the company, the signal will be negative. Whether a good or bad signal is conveyed depends on the circumstances.

Wealth Transfers

If a company divests a portion of the enterprise and distributes the proceeds to stockholders, there will be a wealth transfer from debt holders to stockholders. The transaction reduces the probability that the debt will be paid, and it will have a lesser value, all other things the same. If the total value of the company remains unchanged, the value of the equity must rise. (Here equity value consists of the value of the shares plus the cash distribution to shareholders.) In essence, the stockholders have "stolen away" a portion of the enterprise, thereby reducing its remaining collateral value.[1] As a result, there is a wealth transfer from debt holders to stockholders.

Tax Reasons

Divestitures include sell-offs, spin-offs, and equity carve-outs.

As in mergers, sometimes tax considerations enter into a decision to divest. If a company loses money and is unable to use a tax-loss carryforward, divestiture in whole or in part may be the only way to realize the tax benefit. Where corporate restructuring involves increased leverage, there is a tax shield advantage, owing to interest payments being tax deductible. Under certain circumstances, an employee stock ownership plan (ESOP) is tax advantageous. Other, more technical tax issues also come into play.

With these four motivations in mind, we turn now to the specific divestiture techniques.

---

[1]See Dan Galai and Ronald W. Masulis, "The Option Pricing Model and the Risk Factor of Stocks," *Journal of Financial Economics*, 3 (January–March 1976), 53–81.

VOLUNTARY LIQUIDATION AND SELL-OFFS

The sale of assets can consist of the entire company or of some business unit, such as a subsidiary, a smaller business unit, or a product line.

Liquidating the Overall Firm

The decision to sell a firm in its entirety should be rooted in value creation for the stockholders. Assuming the situation does not involve financial failure, which we address later, the idea is that the assets may have a higher value in liquidation than the present value of the expected cash-flow stream emanating from them. By liquidating, the seller is able to sell the assets to multiple parties, which may result in a higher value being realized than if they had to be sold as a whole, as occurs in a merger. With a complete liquidation, the debt of the company must be paid off at its face value. If the market value of the debt was previously below this, debt holders realize a wealth gain, which ultimately is at the expense of equity holders.

Partial Sell-offs

In the case of a **sell-off,** only part of the company is sold. When a business unit is sold, payment generally is in the form of cash or securities. The decision should result in some positive net present value to the selling company. The key is whether the value received is more than the present value of the stream of expected future cash flows if the operation were to be continued. This excess value may be due to one or more of the reasons taken up in the previous section.

Empirical Studies of Liquidations/Sell-offs

There have been a handful of empirical studies of voluntary liquidations/sell-offs. Event-study methodology is employed. In this case, the event is the announcement of the sell-off. The idea is to study daily security return behavior before and after the event, holding constant overall stock market movements. For liquidation of the entire company, the results of various studies shown in selected references at the end of the chapter indicate a large abnormal return to stockholders of the liquidating company, in the area of 15 percent.

The results of partial sell-off studies indicate a modest positive (2 to 3 percent) abnormal return to the seller's stock around the announcement date. Moreover, stockholders of the buying company also seem to experience a positive abnormal return around the time of the announcement, particularly if the business purchased is similar to that of the acquirer.

SPIN-OFFS

A spin-off is a complete divestiture of a business unit to existing shareholders.

Similar to a sell-off, a **spin-off** involves a decision to divest a business unit such as a stand-alone subsidiary or division. In a spin-off, the business unit is not sold for cash or securities. Rather, common stock in the unit is distributed to the stockholders of the company on a pro rata basis, after which the operation becomes a completely separate company with its own traded stock. There is no tax to the stockholder at the time of the spin-off; taxation occurs only when the stock is sold.

Reasons for Spin-offs

The motivations for a spin-off are similar in some ways to those for a sell-off. In the case of a spin-off, however, another company will not operate it. Therefore, there is no opportunity for synergy in the usual sense of the term. It is possible that as an independent company with different management incentives, the operation will be better run. In this sense, an economic gain may be achieved from the transaction. However, costs are involved. New shares must be issued and there are the ongoing costs of servicing stockholders, together with new agency costs involving auditors and other monitoring devices. Thus, there is duplication of costs in having two public companies as opposed to one. The net case for economic gain is not clear.

It may be that there is a divergence of opinion between current owners of the company and nonowners. To the extent that some nonowners think that the value of the business unit to be spun off is higher than do the current owners, the spin-off may increase value. The greater the divergence, the greater the excess return associated with the spin-off.[2] A variation of this theme is that spin-offs may reduce information asymmetry about a company's individual business units. This may argue for highly diversified firms engaging in more spin-offs than less diversified firms.[3] It may be possible with a spin-off to obtain greater flexibility in contracting such things as labor, debt, taxes, and regulations. No longer is the subsidiary painted with the overall brush that paints the parent. Greater contracting flexibility, in turn, should lead to improved productivity. Finally, the spin-off may make the financial markets more complete. With a new publicly traded stock, the opportunity set of securities available to investors is expanded. The spin-off may have a scarcity value in the stock market and be accorded a premium.

Empirical Evidence on Spin-offs

Valuation studies of corporate spin-offs involve the same event-study methodology described for sell-offs. The studies undertaken suggest moderate, positive abnormal stock returns of around 3 percent at the time of the announcement. (See selected references at end of chapter.) However, Lane Daley, Vikas Mehrotra, and Ranjini Sivakomar find that these gains hold only for spin-offs of divisions in an industry different from that of the parent.[4] For cross-industry spin-offs, the authors found excess returns averaged 4.3 percent around the time of the announcement, whereas overall excess returns for the full sample were 3.4 percent. For own-industry spin-offs, excess returns, though mildly positive, were not significantly different from zero. The authors also found that in the postspinoff period significant increases in operating ROA occurred for cross-industry spinoffs but not for own-industry spin-offs. In a similar type of inquiry, Hemang Desai and Prem C. Jain that in the 3 years following a spin-off, focus increasing terms earn significant positive excess returns (36.4 percent), whereas nonfocus firms experience negative excess returns (–14.3 percent) on average.[5] These two sets of results are consistent with corporate focus increasing value.

---

[2]See Edward M. Miller, "Risk, Uncertainty, and Divergence of Opinion," *Journal of Finance,* 32 (September 1977), 151–68. Empirical support for the Miller hypothesis is found in Ronald J. Kudla and Thomas H. McInish, "Divergence of Opinion and Corporate Spin-offs," *Quarterly Review of Economics and Business,* 28 (Summer 1988), 20–29.

[3]Sudha Krishnaswami and Venkat Subramaniam, "Information Asymmetry, Valuation, and the Corporate Spin-off Decision," *Journal of Financial Economics,* 53 (July 1999), 73–112.

[4]Lane Daley, Vilcas Mehrotra, and Ranjini Sivakomar, "Corporate Focus and Value Creation: Evidence from Spinoffs," *Journal of Financial Economics,* 45 (August 1997), 257–81.

[5]Hemang Desai and Prem C. Jain, "Firm Performance and Focus: Long-run Stock Market Performance Following Spinoffs," *Journal of Financial Economics,* 54 (October 1999), 75–101.

Apart from event studies around the time of the announcement, Anand M. Vijh looked at what happened at the time of the ex-date and a found a 3 percent positive effect at that time.[6] As the previous announcement effect already was embraced in the stock price, the ex-date effect seemingly arises because of the completion of markets that comes with investors preferring to buy the separate shares of the parent and the subsidiary. On balance there appears to be a significant and positive stock price effect to the spin-off, which, in turn, appears to be due to the perception of greater efficiency.

EQUITY CARVE-OUTS

An **equity carve-out** is similar in some ways to the two previous forms of divestiture. However, common stock in the business unit is sold to the public. The initial public offering of the subsidiary's stock usually involves only some of it. Typically, the parent continues to have an equity stake in the subsidiary and does not relinquish immediate control. A minority interest, usually less than 20 percent, is sold in an IPO. The difference between the equity carve-out and the parent selling stock under its own name is that the claim is on the subsidiary's cash flows and assets. For the first time, the value of the subsidiary becomes observable in the marketplace.

Equity carve-outs divest part of a business unit, with an initial-public offering.

Some equity carve-outs are followed later by a spin-off of the remaining shares to the parent's stockholders. Examples of the **two-stage carve-out/spin-off** include Lucent Technologies from AT&T, Associates First Capital from Ford Motor Company, and Agilent Technologies from Hewlett-Packard.

Motivations for a Carve-out

One motivation for the equity carve-out is that with a separate stock price and public trading, managers may have more incentive to perform well. For one thing, the size of the operation is such that their efforts will not go unnoticed, as they sometimes do in a large, multibusiness company. With separate stock options, it may be possible to attract and retain better managers and to motivate them. Also, information about the subsidiary's worth to be assessed more accurately by the marketplace. Capital market discipline may have a salutary effect on overall value by eliminating the cross-subsidization of business units. Each company is on its own bottom when it comes to raising funds. If the projects to be financed are worthwhile, presumably funding will be forthcoming. If not, availability and/or cost of funding will preclude their being undertaken.

Some suggest that the equity carve-out is a favorable means for financing growth. When the subsidiary is in leading-edge technology but not particularly profitable, the equity carve-out may be a more effective vehicle for financing than financing through the parent. Another motivation may be a belief by management that though the parent's stock is undervalued, a subsidiary would not be undervalued and may even be overvalued by the market. As a result, the carve-out announcement could have a favorable information effect for the parent.[7] A final aspect is that with a separately traded subsidiary, the market may become more complete because investors are able to obtain a "pure play" investment.

---

[6]Anand M. Vijh, "The Spinoff and Merger Ex-Date Effects," *Journal of Finance*, 49 (June 1994), 581–609.

[7]Vikram Nanda, "On the Good News in Equity Carve-outs," *Journal of Finance*, 46 (December 1991), 1717–37.

Empirical Testing of Carve-out

Various event studies document an average excess return of about 2 percent around the time of a carve-out announcement, holding constant overall stock market movements. (See selected references at the end of chapter.) It appears to matter what the proceeds of the equity sale are used for by the divesting company. If they are used to pay down debt or pay dividends to stockholders, there is a significant positive information effect. If they are used primarily to increase investment in assets, there is no effect. In a study by Myron B. Slovin, Marie E. Shushka, and Steven R. Ferraro, the stock returns of competitors of the carved-out unit are investigated.[8] They find that the announcement of an equity carve-out has an average 1 percent negative effect on the rival's stock price. The implication is that the industry structure is upset by a competitor (the carve-out) that becomes more aggressive. In the 3 years following an equity carve-out, Anand M. Vigh finds that the entity on average provides a market return consistent with that of appropriate benchmarks (e.g., risk-adjusted S&P 500).[9] This contrasts with IPOs for new companies, which tend to underperform appropriate benchmarks in the post-IPO period.

In all three cases—the sell-off, the spin-off, and the equity carve-out—scholars have observed a positive share price effect. The results contrast with those for the straight sale of new equity by a company. For the reasons taken up in Chapters 9 and 20, negative abnormal returns are associated with the announcement of a stock offering by a company. For the three methods of divestiture discussed, the results are positive, which indicates a different informational effect to the event.

GOING PRIVATE AND LEVERAGED BUYOUTS

A number of well-known companies have "gone private," including Levi Strauss & Company. Going private simply means transforming a company whose stock is publicly held into a private one. The privately held stock is owned by a small group of investors, with incumbent management usually having a large equity stake. In this ownership reorganization, a variety of vehicles are used to buy out the public stockholders. Probably the most common involves cashing them out and merging the company into a shell corporation owned solely by the private investor/management group. Rather than a merger, the transaction may be treated as an asset sale to the private group. There are other ways, but the result is the same: The company ceases to exist as a publicly held entity and the stockholders receive a valuable consideration for their shares. Though most transactions involve cash, sometimes noncash compensations, such as notes, are employed.

The stockholders must agree to a company going private, and the incentive to them is the premium in price paid. Even when the majority vote in favor, other stockholders can sue, claiming the price is not high enough. Class action suits prompted by hungry lawyers are also common.

Motivations for Going Private

A number of factors may prompt management to take a company private.[10] There are costs to being a publicly held company. The stock must be registered, stock-

---

[8]Myron B. Slovin, Marie E. Sushka and Steven R. Ferraro, "A Comparison of the Information Conveyed by Equity Carve-outs, Spin-offs, and Asset Sell-offs," *Journal of Financial Economics*, 37 (January 1995), 89–104.

[9]Anand M. Vijh, "Long-term Returns from Equity Carveouts," *Journal of Financial Economics*, 51 (February 1999), 273—308.

[10]The major paper dealing with going private is by Harry DeAngelo, Linda DeAngelo, and Edward M. Rice, "Going Private: Minority Freezeouts and Stockholder Wealth," *Journal of Law and Economics*, 27 (June 1984), 367–401, where most of these motivations are discussed.

holders must be serviced, there are administrative expenses in paying dividends and sending out materials, and there are legal and administrative expenses in filing reports with the Securities and Exchange Commission and other regulators. In addition, there are annual meetings and meetings with security analysts leading to embarrassing questions that most CEOs would rather do without. All of these things can be avoided by being a private company.

With a publicly held company, some feel there is a fixation on quarterly accounting earnings as opposed to long-run economic earnings. To the extent decisions are directed more toward building economic value, going private may improve resource allocation decisions and thereby enhance value.

Another motivation is to realign and improve management incentives. With increased equity ownership by management, there may be an incentive to work more efficiently and longer. The money saved and the profits generated through more effective management largely benefit the company's management as opposed to a wide group of stockholders. As a result, they may be more willing to make the tough decisions, cut costs, reduce management "perks," and simply work harder. The rewards are linked more closely to their decisions. The greater the performance and profitability, the greater the reward. In a publicly held company, the compensation level is not so directly linked, particularly for decisions that produce high profitability. When compensation is high in a publicly held company, there are always questions from security analysts, stockholders, and the press.

Though there are a number of reasons for going private, there are some offsetting arguments. For one thing, there are transaction costs to investment bankers, lawyers, and others that can be quite substantial. A private company gives little liquidity to its owners with respect to their stock ownership. A large portion of their wealth may be tied up in the company. Management, for example, may create value for the company but be unable to realize this value unless the company goes public in the future. If the company later goes public, transaction costs are repeated—wonderful for investment bankers and lawyers but a sizable cost nonetheless.

Leveraged Buyouts

Going private can be a straight transaction, where the investor group simply buys out the public stockholders, or it can be a **leveraged buyout (LBO),** where there are third- and sometimes fourth-party investors. As the name implies, a leveraged buyout represents an ownership transfer consummated importantly with debt. Sometimes called asset-based financing, the debt is secured by the assets of the enterprise involved. Some leveraged buyouts involve the acquisition of an entire company, but many involve the purchase of a division of a company or some other subunit. Frequently, the sale is to the management of the division being sold, the company having decided that the division no longer fits its strategic objectives. Another distinctive feature is that leveraged buyouts are cash purchases, as opposed to stock purchases. Finally, the business unit involved invariably becomes a privately held, as opposed to a publicly held, company.

> **Leveraged buyouts** take a company private by buying out public stockholders, taking on a large amount of debt in the process.

Characteristics of Successful LBOs Desirable LBO candidates have certain common characteristics. Frequently, the company has a several-year window of opportunity where major expenditures can be deferred. Often, it is a company that has gone through a heavy capital expenditures program, and whose plant is modern. Companies with high R&D requirements, like drug companies, are not good LBO candidates. For the first several years, cash flows must be dedicated to debt ser-

Good LBO candidates must be able to dedicate cash flow to debt service, so competing needs for funds cannot be large.

vice. Capital expenditures, R&D, advertising, and personnel development take a back seat. If the company has subsidiary assets that can be sold without adversely impacting the core business, this may be attractive. Such asset sales provide cash for debt service in the early years.

Stable, predictable operating cash flows are prized. In this regard, consumer-branded products dominate "commodity-type" businesses. Proven historical performance with an established market position means a lot. Turn-around situations tend to be spurned. The less cyclical the company or business unit, the better. A service company, where people are the franchise value, is seldom a good LBO candidate. If the people should leave, little of value remains. As a rule, the assets must be physical assets and/or brand names. Management, however, is important. The experience and quality of senior management are critical to success. When such management is not in place, outsiders must be brought in. Finally, the absence of significant preexisting leverage is desirable. While the foregoing characteristics are not all inclusive, they give a flavor of the ingredients that make for desirable and undesirable LBO candidates.

LBO Illustration

To illustrate a typical leveraged buyout, suppose Alsim Corporation wishes to divest itself of its dairy products division. The assets of the division consist of plants, equipment, truck fleets, inventories, and receivables. These assets have a book value of $120 million. While their replacement value is $170 million, if the division were to be liquidated, the assets would fetch only $95 million. Alsim has decided to sell the division if it can obtain $110 million in cash, and it has enlisted an investment banker to assist it in the sale. After surveying the market for such a sale, the investment banker concludes that the best prospect is to sell the division to existing management. The four top divisional officers are interested and eager to pursue the opportunity. However, they are able to come up with only $3 million in personal capital among them. Obviously, more is needed.

Debt Service and Equity Commitment   The investment banker agrees to try to arrange a leveraged buyout. Financial projections and cash budgets are prepared for the division, to determine how much debt can be serviced. On the basis of these forecasts as well as the curtailment of certain capital expenditures, research and development expenses, and advertising expenses, it is felt that the likely cash throw-off is sufficient to service upwards to $100 million in debt. The reduction in expenditures is regarded as temporary for the company to service debt during the next several years. The investment banker has drawn on a limited partnership to make an additional equity investment of $23 million, bringing total equity to $26 million. For this cash contribution, the partnership is to receive 60 percent of the initial common stock, with management receiving the remainder.

Debt Financing   With this equity capital commitment, the investment banker proceeds to arrange debt financing. In a leveraged buyout, two forms of debt typically are employed: senior debt and junior subordinated debt. For the senior debt, a large New York bank, through its asset-based lending subsidiary, has agreed to provide $60 million toward the cost plus an additional $8 million revolving credit for seasonal needs. The rate on both arrangements is 2 percent over the prime rate, and the loans are secured by liens on all the assets—real estate, buildings, equipment, rolling stock, inventories, and receivables. The term of the $60 million loan is 6 years, and it is payable in equal monthly installments of principal with interest for the month being added on. All major banking will be with the bank and company receipts will be deposited into a special account at the bank for purposes of servicing the debt. In addition to the collateral, the usual protective covenants are imposed in a loan agreement.

Junior subordinated debt in the amount of $24 million has been arranged with the merger-funding subsidiary of a large finance company. This debt sometimes is referred to as **mezzanine-layer** financing, as it falls between senior debt and the equity. The loan is for 7 years with an interest rate of 11 percent being fixed throughout. Only monthly interest payments are required during the 7 years, with the full principal amount being due at the end. As the senior lender will have liens on all assets, the debt is unsecured and subordinated to the senior debt as well as to trade creditors. For this subordinated financing, the lender receives warrants exercisable for 30 percent of the stock. These warrants may be exercised any time throughout the 7 years at a price of $1 per share, quite nominal. If exercised, management's stock will go from 40 percent of the total outstanding to 28 percent, and the limited partnership from 60 percent to 42 percent. To recapitulate, the financing is as follows (in millions):

Senior debt	$ 60
Junior subordinated debt	24
Common stock	26
Total	$110

In addition, the company will have access to an $8 million revolving credit for seasonal needs.

The mezzanine layer of financing fills the gap between what senior lenders are willing to provide and what equity holders/management are able to commit. Because of the highly levered nature of the transaction, mezzanine debt invariably is rated speculative grade, Ba or lower (junk bonds). Expected returns, including the exercise of stock warrants or other equity participation, are in the 20 to 30 percent per annum range. The security itself is illiquid, so the bulk of the return comes at the end when the company goes public, is sold, or is further restructured. If the LBO is unsuccessful, of course, mezzanine lenders may lose everything. Such lenders like to see total EBIT (earnings before interest and taxes) coverage of all interest payments in the neighborhood of 1.25 to 1. For more speculative deals, coverage may be closer to 1 to 1.

In recent years, mezzanine financing has become less important. Indeed, in a number of leveraged buyouts it is not used at all. The equity and the senior debt layers simply become larger. Sometimes the seller will accept a note as partial consideration. While this note is subordinated to the senior debt, there are no warrants giving rise to future dilution. The highly levered transaction of the late 1980s, where the equity component was less than 10 percent, is largely a thing of the past. The private equity market, of which LBOs are an important part, is constantly evolving.

Empirical Evidence on LBOs

There have been a number of studies on the valuation implications of LBOs and of management buyouts (MBOs), which are shown in selected references at the end of the chapter. In a buyout, one implication is whether public stockholders realize fair value for their holdings. Depending on the study, the average premium to pre-buyout shareholders has been found to be between 25 percent and 40 percent. Thus, stockholders typically receive a sizable premium for their stock when a company goes private. This is consistent with the economic gains being shared between pre-buyout stockholders and post-buyout owners.

Operating performance and cash flows have been found to improve after the buyout, as has the productivity of capital. This gives credence to efficiency gains being one source of value. Often this is attributable to improved management incentives. Another source is tax benefits, though these were dramatically reduced with the 1986 Tax Reform Act. Wealth transfers from pre-buyout bondholders to post-buyout equity holders are also a factor. We know that when leveraged buyouts occur, bond ratings are downgraded, sometimes several notches. However, wealth transfers have been found to be small. Typically, the pre-buyout company has only a moderate amount of debt outstanding, and some of this is protected by restrictive covenants from the expropriation of value. The notion of wealth transfers from workers via lost jobs has not been supported, though administrative personnel tend to be cut. The evidence also is consistent with buyouts reducing agency problems between management and stockholders. These arise because management sometimes squanders free cash flow on wasteful expenditures when it should be directing such cash flow to stockholders.

Many LBOs return to become public companies after a period of time. The average interval appears to be between 4 and 7 years. Going public can be with an IPO or by sale to a publicly owned company. In this way the financiers and management realize value. A number of LBOs remain private, either because of performance that leaves something to be desired or because of the wishes of management or financiers.

Observations on LBOs

We see that leveraged buyouts permit going private with only moderate equity. The assets of the acquired company or division are used to secure a large amount of debt. The equity holders, of course, are residual owners. If things go according to plan and the debt is serviced according to schedule, after 5 years they will own a healthy company with moderate debt. Of course, their position will be diluted if mezzanine financing exists and such financiers exercise their warrants to purchase stock. In any leveraged buyout, the first several years are key. If the company can make its debt payments, the interest burden declines Over time as operating profits, it is hoped, improve.

There are two kinds of risk. The first is business risk. Operations may not go according to plan, and the cash-flow wherewithal to service debt may be lower than forecasted. The other risk involves changing interest rates. As the senior debt typically is floating rate and changes with the prime rate, a sharp rise in interest rates may carry the business under. By their very nature, leveraged buyouts have a modest safety cushion built into the calculations for the first several years. Even with good management of operations, a sizable increase in interest costs may eliminate this cushion and cause the firm to default. To mitigate the effect of adverse interest-rate movements, some firms hedge through interest-rate options.

Thus, the equity holders are playing a high-risk game, and the principle of leverage being a two-edged sword becomes abundantly clear. Another potential problem with the need to service debt is the focus on short-run profitability. This may work to the detriment of the long-run viability of the enterprise. If capital expenditures, research and development, and advertising are cut not only to but through the bone, the company may not be competitive once the debt is paid off. Once lost, the company may not be able to regain its competitive position despite reasonable expenditures later.

A rule of thumb is that the enterprise value placed on an LBO should be no more than six to eight times operating cash flow. From the previous chapter, we know that enterprise, or capitalization, value is common equity plus preferred stock plus interest-bearing debt minus cash. Operating cash flow is earnings before interest, taxes, depreciation, and amortization (EBITDA). If higher than eight, and if leverage is a large component of the total value assigned to the LBO, the probability of default is accentuated beyond what most would regard as reasonable. This clearly occurred in the late 1980s when multiples of 10 and above were observed. As a number of highly levered transactions defaulted in the early 1990s, rationality returned to the market. The valuation multiples of EBITDA placed on an LBO moderated, as did the use of debt. The rule of thumb can be stretched if significant growth is expected. For most LBO situations only moderate growth is in the offing and the rule holds.

LEVERAGED RECAPITALIZATIONS

Leveraged recaps
fund a large dividend to stockholders with debt, usually causing book equity to turn negative.

The LBO must be distinguished from a leveraged recapitalization, or **leveraged recap** as it is known. With an LBO, public stockholders are bought out and the company, or business unit of a company, becomes private. With a leveraged recap, a publicly traded company raises cash through increased leverage, usually massive leverage. The cash then is distributed to stockholders, often by means of a huge dividend. In contrast to an LBO, stockholders continue to hold shares in the company. The firm remains a public corporation with a traded stock.

These shares are known as "stub" shares. Obviously, they are worth a lot less per share, owing to the huge cash payout. (While a cash payout is most common, stockholders could receive debt securities or even preferred stock.) In the transaction, management and other insiders do not participate in the payout but take additional shares instead. As a result, their proportional ownership of the corporation increases sharply. For example, rather than receive one share of new stock plus a large cash dividend for each old share, management might receive five shares, but no cash dividend. Thus, management obtains a large equity stake in the company, but unlike an LBO, this stake is represented by publicly traded stock. The leveraged recap does not lend itself to a business unit, as does an LBO. It must involve the company as a whole.

The number of leveraged recaps is limited, but the ones that have occurred have been large. They include Colt Industries, Sealed Air Corporation, Owens-Corning, USG Corporation, and Harcourt Brace Jovanovich. Often leveraged recaps occur in response to a hostile takeover threat or to management's perception that the company is vulnerable even though it is not actually under attack. A leveraged recap can occur without putting the company up for sale, or "into play," as is required with an LBO. The disadvantage, relative to an LBO, is that as a public company, shareholder-servicing costs and security regulations and disclosures remain.

Valuation Implications

How do the outside, or public, stockholders fare? While the leveraged recap usually is a defensive tactic and antitakeover devices generally work to the disadvantage of stockholders, this is different. For one thing, leverage and a greater equity stake may give management more incentive to manage efficiently and to reduce wasteful expenditures. There also is the tax shield that accompanies the use of debt. Event studies, which analyze share price reaction around the time of announcement of a leveraged recap, have found excess returns somewhat in excess of 30 percent. This is in the same general area as LBOs and returns to acquired company stockholders in a takeover. By virtue of absorbing free cash flow, leverage may have a salutary effect on management efficiency. Under the discipline of debt, internal organization changes may now be possible that lead to improvements in operating performance.[11]

With the high degree of leverage, however, there is little margin for error. Not surprisingly, a number of leveraged recaps do not make it. Operating difficulties, often due to industry-wide problems beyond the control of the company, are magnified by the financial leverage.[12] When financial distress occurs, these leveraged recaps are restructured either under Chapter 11 or in other ways that we consider next.

DISTRESS RESTRUCTURING

Companies experiencing financial difficulty are often restructured. While some of the corporate restructuring devices illustrated earlier may be applicable, this usually is not the case. Instead different strategies are in order for management, for equity holders, and for creditors. As what can be done is rooted in bankruptcy law, we first consider the remedies available to a failing company. These vary in harshness according to the degree of financial difficulty.

Voluntary Settlements and Workouts

Voluntary settlements are forms of workouts. When a company fails to meet its debt obligations or violates one of its debt covenants, it may be able to negotiate a relaxation in terms with the lender(s). Though lawyers usually are involved, workouts are informal and occur outside the courts.

An **extension** involves creditors postponing the maturity of their obligations. By not forcing legal proceedings, creditors avoid considerable legal expense and the possible shrinkage of value in liquidation. As all creditors must agree to extend their obligations, the major creditors usually form a committee whose function is to negotiate with the company and to formulate a plan mutually satisfactory to all concerned.

A **composition** involves a pro rata settlement of creditors' claims in cash or in cash and promissory notes. All creditors must agree to accept this partial settlement in discharge of their entire claim. As with an extension, dissenting creditors must be either brought into the fold or paid in full.

---

[11]One example is Sealed Air Corporation, whose experience is analyzed in Karen Hopper Wruck, "Financial Policy, Internal Control, and Performance: Sealed Air Corporation's Leveraged Special Dividend," *Journal of Financial Economics,* 36 (October 1994), 193–224.

[12]See David J. Denis and Diane K. Denis, "Causes of Financial Distress Following Leveraged Recapitalizations," *Journal of Financial Economics,* 37 (February 1995), 129–57.

Voluntary liquidation represents an orderly private liquidation of a company apart from the bankruptcy courts. Not only is it likely to be more efficient, but creditors are likely to receive a higher settlement, as many of the costs of bankruptcy are avoided. However, the company and all creditors must go along. As a result, voluntary liquidations usually are restricted to companies with a limited number of creditors.

Legal Proceedings

Legal procedures undertaken in connection with a failing company fall under bankruptcy law as carried out through bankruptcy courts. While bankruptcy law has many facets, we are concerned only with the two that pertain to business failure. **Chapter 7 deals with liquidation; Chapter 11 deals with rehabilitation** of an enterprise through its reorganization. In both cases, proceedings begin with the debtor or creditors filing a petition in the bankruptcy court. When the debtor initiates the petition, it is called a voluntary proceeding; if the initiative is taken by creditors, it is said to be involuntary. In voluntary proceedings, merely filing the petition gives the debtor immediate protection from creditors. A stay restrains creditors from collecting their claims or taking actions until the court decides on the merit of the petition. The court can either accept the petition and order relief or dismiss it.

> **Chapter 7** means liquidation, whereas **Chapter 11** means reorganization.

For an involuntary bankruptcy, three or more unsecured creditors with claims totaling $5,000 or more are required. Here the petition must give evidence that the debtor has not paid debts on a timely basis or has assigned possession of most of its property to someone else. The bankruptcy court then must decide whether the involuntary petition has merit. If the decision is negative, the petition is dismissed. If the petition is accepted, the court issues an order of relief pending a more permanent solution. The idea behind this stay of creditor action is to give the debtor breathing space to propose a solution to the problem. In what follows, we observe the solutions of liquidation and the reorganization of an enterprise.

Liquidation

If there is no hope for the successful operation of a company, liquidation under Chapter 7 is the only feasible alternative. Upon petition of bankruptcy, the debtor obtains temporary relief from creditors until a decision is reached by the bankruptcy court. After issuing the order of relief, the court frequently appoints an interim trustee to take over the operation of the company and to call a meeting of creditors. The interim trustee is a "disinterested" private citizen who is appointed from an approved list and who serves until at least the first meeting of creditors. At the meeting, claims are proven, and the creditors then may elect a new trustee to replace the interim trustee. Otherwise, the interim trustee serves as the regular trustee, continuing to function in that capacity until the case is completed. The trustee has responsibility for liquidating the property of the company and distributing liquidating dividends to creditors.

Priority of Claims In distributing the proceeds of a liquidation to creditors with unsecured claims, the priority of claims must be observed. The order of distribution is as follows:

1. Administrative expenses associated with liquidating the property, including the trustee's fee and attorney fees.
2. Creditor claims that arise in the ordinary course of the debtor's business from the time the case starts to the time a trustee is appointed.
3. Wages employees earned within 90 days of the bankruptcy petition.
4. Claims for contributions to employee benefit plans for services rendered within 120 days of the bankruptcy petition.
5. Claims of customers who make money deposits for goods or services not provided by the debtor.
6. Income tax claims for 3 tax years prior to the petition, property taxes for 1 year prior to the petition, and all taxes withheld from employees' paychecks.
7. Unsecured claims either filed on time or tardily filed if the creditor did not know of the bankruptcy.
8. Unsecured claims filed late by creditors who had knowledge of the bankruptcy.
9. Fines and punitive damages.
10. Interest that accrues to claims after the date of the petition.

Claims in each of these classes must be paid in full before any payment can be made to claims in the next class. If anything is left over after all of these claims are paid in full, liquidating dividends can then be paid to subordinated debt holders, to preferred stockholders, and, finally, to common stockholders. It is unlikely, however, that common stockholders will receive any distribution from a liquidation. Special provision is made in the Bankruptcy Act for damage claims by lessors to the debtor. In general, lessors are limited to the greater of 1 year of payments or 15 percent of the total remaining payments, but not to exceed 3 years. Upon the payment of all liquidating dividends, the debtor is discharged and relieved of any further claims.

Reorganization

Conceptually, a firm should be reorganized under Chapter 11 if its economic worth as an operating entity is greater than its liquidation value. It should be liquidated if the converse is true, that is, if it is worth more dead than alive. Reorganization is an effort to keep a company alive by changing its capital structure. The motivation of management and equity holders, of course, is to keep the company alive. As long as the corporation has some option value, they may benefit in the future, whereas with liquidation they usually receive nothing. Moreover, overworked bankruptcy judges tend toward leniency and hope, allowing a company to be reorganized as opposed to liquidated. The fact that a high proportion of the companies that reorganize later must be liquidated calls into question the tendency to preserve companies. More about this later, once we have taken up some details of reorganization.

The idea behind rehabilitation through reorganization is to reduce fixed charges by substituting equity and limited-income securities for fixed-income securities. Reorganizations under Chapter 11 of bankruptcy law are initiated in the same general manner as liquidation in bankruptcy. Either the debtor or the creditors file a petition, and the case begins. The idea in a reorganization is to keep the business going. In most cases, the debtor will continue to run the business, although a trustee can assume operating responsibility of the company.

Reorganized companies should be viable when interest payments are pared. If not, liquidation should occur.

DIP financiers
move to the head of the
credit line in priority.

One of the great needs in rehabilitation is interim credit. To provide inducements, Chapter 11 gives postpetition creditors priority over prepetition creditors. This new debt is known as **debtor-in-possession (DIP)** financing. The DIP loan market is well developed, with a number of banks and other lenders eager to participate in it. The incentives are a premium interest rate and being near the head of the line in the event of liquidation. The result is that larger Chapter 11 companies are able to arrange new debt financing without significant difficulty.

Procedures Followed

Exclusivity period
gives management the
sole right to propose a
reorganization plan.

In most cases the debtor has the sole right to draw up a reorganization plan and to file it within 120 days. This is known as the **exclusivity period,** and as we shall see a bit later, it tips the scale in favor of management/equity holders. If a plan is not proposed by the company, the trustee has the responsibility for seeing that a plan is filed. It may be drawn up by the trustee, the debtor, the creditors' committee, or individual creditors, and more than one plan can be filed. All reorganization plans must be submitted to creditors and stockholders for approval. The role of the court is to review the information in the plan, to make sure disclosure is full.

In a reorganization, the plan should be **fair, equitable,** and **feasible.** This means that all parties must be treated fairly and equitably and that the plan must be workable with respect to the earning power and financial structure of the reorganized company as well as the ability of the company to obtain trade credit and, perhaps, short-term bank loans. Each class of claimholders must vote on a plan. More than one-half in number and two-thirds in amount of total claims in each class must vote in favor of the plan if it is to be accepted.

Cram downs
of reorganization
plans by judges
seldom occur.

If the reorganization plan is rejected by creditors, the bankruptcy judge will try to get the various parties to negotiate another plan. If such efforts are rejected by creditors, the judge may go with what is known as a **cram down.** Here the court imposes a plan on all claimholders, being bound by the principle that it is fair and equitable. Upon confirmation of a plan by the bankruptcy court, the debtor then must perform according to the terms of the plan. Moreover, all creditors and stockholders, including dissenters, are bound by the plan.

Reorganization Plan

The difficult aspect of a reorganization is the recasting of the company's capital structure to reduce the amount of fixed charges. In formulating a reorganization plan, there are **three steps.** First, the **total valuation** of the reorganized company must be determined. This step, perhaps, is the most difficult and the most important. The technique favored by trustees is a capitalization of prospective earnings. If future annual earnings of the reorganized company are expected to be $2 million, and the overall capitalization rate of similar companies averages 10 percent, a total valuation of $20 million would be set for the company. The valuation figure is subject to considerable variation, owing to the difficulty of estimating prospective earnings and determining an appropriate capitalization rate. Thus, the valuation figure represents nothing more than a best estimate of potential value. Although the capitalization of prospective earnings is the generally accepted approach of valuing a company in reorganization, the valuation may be adjusted upward if the assets have substantial liquidating value.

Once a valuation figure has been determined, the next step is to formulate a **new capital structure** for the company, to reduce fixed charges so that there will be an adequate coverage margin. To reduce these charges, the total debt of the firm is scaled down by being partly shifted to income bonds, preferred stock, and common stock. In addition to being scaled down, the terms of the debt may be changed. The maturity of the debt can be extended to reduce the amount of annual sinking-fund obligation. If it appears that the reorganized company will need new financing in the future, the trustee may feel that a more conservative ratio of debt to equity is needed to provide for future financial flexibility. A more conservative use of debt also tends to occur when the liquidation value of the assets is substantially less than their value in current use,[13] that is, when the current value placed on a company is importantly based on future cash flows, known as a futures option, as opposed to being based on hard asset values.

Once a new capital structure is established, the last step involves the valuation of the old securities and their exchange for new securities. In general, all senior claims on assets must be settled in full before a junior claim can be settled. In the exchange process, bondholders must receive the par value of their bonds in another security before there can be any distribution to preferred stockholders. The total valuation figure arrived at in step 1 sets an upper limit on the amount of securities that can be issued.

Reorganization Illustration

The existing capital structure of a company undergoing reorganization may be as follows (in millions):

Debentures	$ 9
Subordinated debentures	3
Preferred stock	6
Common stock equity (at book value)	10
Total	$28

If the total valuation of the reorganized company is to be $20 million, the trustee might establish the following capital structure in step 2:

Debentures	$ 3
Income bonds	6
Preferred stock	3
Common stock	8
Total	$20

Having established the "appropriate" capital structure for the reorganized company, the trustee then must allocate the new securities. In this regard, the trustee may propose that the debenture holders exchange their $9 million in debentures for $3 million in new debentures and $6 million in income bonds, that the subordinated debenture holders exchange their $3 million in securities for preferred stock, and that preferred stockholders exchange their securities for $6 million of common stock in the reorganized company. The common stockholders

---

[13]Michael J. Alderson and Brian L. Betker, "Liquidation Costs and Capital Structure," *Journal of Financial Economics*, 39 (September 1995), 45–69.

would then be entitled to $2 million in stock in the reorganized company, or 25 percent of the total common stock of the reorganized company.

Thus, each claim is settled in full before a junior claim is settled. The example represents a relatively mild reorganization. In a harsh reorganization, debt instruments may be exchanged entirely for common stock in the reorganized company, and the old common stock may be eliminated completely. Had the total valuation figure in the example been $12 million, the trustee might have proposed a new capital structure consisting of $3 million in preferred stock and $9 million in common stock. Only the straight and subordinated debenture holders would receive a settlement in this case. The preferred and the common stockholders of the old company would receive nothing.

GAMING WITH THE RULE OF ABSOLUTE PRIORITY

The rule of absolute priority often is violated.

The examples above show that the common stockholders of a company undergoing reorganization suffer under a *rule of absolute priority*, whereby claims must be settled in the order of their legal priority. This rule was upheld by the Supreme Court in 1939 (*Case v. Los Angeles Lumber Products Company*). However, the Bankruptcy Reform Act of 1978 provided a degree of flexibility, allowing for moderate deviations from this rule when it is in the interest of total value to do so. This opening and the failure of the courts to enforce strict priority of claims gives management/equity holders considerable leverage in the proceedings, which comes at the expense of creditors.[14]

Bargaining Power

Management, on behalf of equity holders, has a number of advantages. A principal one is that bankruptcy proceedings are costly and protracted. With delays, the distressed company falls further into disrepair and the total value realized by creditors declines. In most cases management has the sole right under the exclusivity rule to propose a reorganization plan during the first 120 days after the bankruptcy petition. This gives management the ability to influence the outcome, as it can threaten to downgrade the claim of a particular creditor. As each class of claimholder must vote in favor of a plan, management can argue that the total value placed on the firm, including its option value, is too low. This not only may influence the vote but also can cause considerable delay.

The delay card of management is a powerful incentive for creditor concessions.

The **threat of delay** is a powerful bargaining chip, because creditors know that there may not be much left if the company continues to decay. If bankruptcy proceedings were efficient, and bankruptcy judges were inclined to propose liquidation unless there were well-founded odds for success, creditors could not be bullied by management. However, the "delay card" is very prominent, and creditors know its cost to them. For these reasons, creditors often give ground and cut equity holders into an ownership position to which they are not entitled under the rule of absolute priority. The cut may go as high as 10 percent of the total value placed on the enterprise, although the average is less.

---

[14]For documentation of violations of absolute priority and the percentage of value equity holders extract, see Lawrence A. Weiss, "The Bankruptcy Code and Violations of Absolute Priority," *Journal of Applied Corporate Finance*, 4 (Summer 1991), 71–78; Julian R. Franks and Walter N. Torous, "A Comparison of Financial Recontracting in Distressed Exchanges and Chapter 11 Reorganizations," *Journal of Financial Economics*, 35 (June 1994), 349–70; Frank J. Fabozzi, Jane Tripp Howe, Takashi Makabe, and Toshihide Sudo, "Recent Evidence on the Distribution Patterns in Chapter 11 Reorganizations," *Journal of Fixed Income*, 2 (March 1993), 6–23; and Allan C. Eberhart, William T. Moore, and Rodney L. Rosenfeldt, "Security Pricing and Deviations from the Absolute Priority Rule in Bankruptcy Proceedings," *Journal of Finance*, 45 (December 1990), 1457–69.

Vulture Capitalists Bargaining also comes into play among various creditor classes. Certain investors, known as **vulture capitalists**, will acquire a significant percent of a particular class of debt. If this investor controls one-third or more of the class, the vulture can block the reorganization plan proposed. The vulture's purpose is simple: extract value from the other creditor classes to the class in which the vulture has an investment. If operations of the distressed company can be improved and firm value actually enhanced, so much the better. Blocking strategies by management and other security classes are aided by the possibility of a "cram down," but bankruptcy judges are reluctant to impose such.

The role of the vulture is controversial. Some contend that they serve no economically useful purpose. As the name implies, they prey on the fallen and use bullying tactics to extract value from other parties, known as **bondmail.** Others contend that because vulture investors have no previous involvement, they do not have an emotional, financial, or regulatory "sunk cost" in the proceedings. They can break the log jam between various parties and get things moving in a reorganization. In addition, it is argued, they are more able to bring about operational changes and discipline management, not carrying past baggage. In an empirical study, Edith S. Hotchkiss and Robert M. Mooradian find that postrestructuring operating performance is greater when there is vulture involvement (board membership, chairman, CEO, or outright control).[15] In addition, the authors find positive excess stock and bond returns around the announcement of a vulture's purchase of debt or equity. The authors contend that vulture investors add value, though an alternative explanation may be that they simply are good at selecting undervalued situations. In another study, Brian L. Betker finds that where a vulture investor gains a meaningful stake in a Chapter 11 reorganized company, the direct restructuring costs, as a percentage of prebankruptcy total assets, are lower than for Chapter 11 reorganizations overall.[16]

Prepackaged Bankruptcy

Sometimes, management will arrange a *prepackaged bankruptcy*, which falls somewhere between a workout and a formal, extended bankruptcy. It works as follows. At the time of filing a bankruptcy petition, the distressed company also files a reorganization plan. Management has previously struck an agreement with most creditors as to the terms of the plan. The advantage of prepackaged bankruptcy is that it reduces the time in reorganization and the costs. Also, certain problems with creditors who hold out can be reduced.[17] Finally, the **prepack,** as opposed to an informal workout, permits more flexible use of net operating loss carryforwards for tax purposes.[18] This is a cash-flow advantage to the firm. Because of these advantages, increasing numbers of distressed firms are turning to prepacks in Chapter 11 filings.

Prepackaged bankruptcy is quicker and more efficient, but difficult if creditors are dispersed.

---

[15]Edith S. Hotchkiss and Robert M. Mooradian, "Vulture Investors and the Market for Control of Distressed Firms," *Journal of Financial Economics*, 43 (March 1997), 373–99.

[16]Brian L. Betker, "The Administrative Costs of Debt Restructurings: Some Recent Evidence," *Financial Management*, 26 (Winter 1997), 56–68.

[17]For an analysis of the benefits of prepackaged bankruptcy, see John J. McConnell and Henri Servaes, "The Economics of Pre-packaged Bankruptcy," *Journal of Applied Corporate Finance*, 4 (Summer 1991), 93–97; and Elizabeth Tashjian, Ronald C. Lease, and John J. McConnell, "Prepacks: An Empirical Analysis of Prepackaged Bankruptcies," *Journal of Financial Economics*, 40 (January 1996), 135–62.

[18]Brian L. Betker, "An Empirical Examination of Prepackaged Bankruptcy," *Financial Management*, 24 (Spring 1995), 3–18. In a subsequent paper, "The Administrative Costs of Debt Restructuring: Some Recent Evidence," *Financial Management*, 26 (Winter 1997), 56–68. Betker finds that the direct costs of Chapter 11 reorganizations as a percent of pre-bankruptcy total assets is lower in the case of prepacks (2.85%) than it is for overall reorganizations (3.93%).

The essential ingredient for prepackaged bankruptcy is a workable number of responsible creditors. If the number of creditors is large and they have conflicting interests, obtaining their cooperation is all but impossible. In other situations, the efficiency gains of prepackaged bankruptcy can be compelling to creditors. This attests to the costs of bankruptcy and the frequent violation of the rule of absolute priority.

A Summing Up

Through various devices, management often is able to cut equity holders into a slice of the pie to which they otherwise would not be entitled. This does not make for economic efficiency and is at odds with what occurs in a number of advanced industrial countries where creditors are supreme. However, it is reality in the United States. Secured creditors give little or nothing, provided the assets have more value than their loan. It is unsecured creditors who give ground.

Management/equity holders obviously want to preserve the company and in an option-pricing context will want to increase the volatility of firm value, hoping to gain on the upside. This works to the detriment of debt holders, as we illustrated in Chapter 9. It is not that management benefits personally in situations of financial distress. Many are replaced, and those who remain often receive substantial cuts in salary and bonuses.[19] Still, the end result is equity holders gaining at the expense of creditors, and management benefiting via their stock positions and sometimes by preservation of their jobs.

The sad part is that so many companies that are restructured through legal reorganization do not survive. The odds simply are too much against them. If we are concerned with economic efficiency, liquidation is the preferable alternative. Simply to demonstrate some probability of succeeding, no matter how negligible, is not sufficient reason to preserve an ailing company in the face of the considerable costs associated with its extension. The rehabilitation process cannot be effective when bankruptcy judges allow so many companies to go the Chapter 11 reorganization route. Much of the grief associated with subsequent financial distress could be avoided with more rational gatekeeping on the part of bankruptcy judges.

Summary

Corporate restructuring transactions fall into the broad categories of divestiture, ownership restructuring, and distress restructuring. Voluntary divestitures have several motivations: (1) expected efficiency gains, sometimes through strategic realignment; (2) information effects to correct asymmetric information between investors and management; (3) wealth transfers from debt holders to equity holders; and (4) tax reasons.

Voluntary liquidations, sell-offs, spin-offs, and equity carve-outs have similar characteristics and some that are different. A voluntary liquidation involves the sale of the overall company. A sell-off usually involves the sale of a business unit for cash or securities. In contrast,

[19]See Stuart C. Gilson and Michael R. Vetsuypens, "CEO Compensation in Financially Distressed Firms: An Empirical Analysis," *Journal of Finance*, 48 (June 1993), 425–58.

a spin-off involves distribution of common stock in the business unit to stockholders of the company spinning off the unit. In both the sell-off and the spin-off, the company divests itself of all ownership and control. In an equity carve-out, common stock in a business unit is sold to the public, but the company usually keeps majority ownership and control. In all three situations, there typically is a positive return to stockholders around the announcement date, after isolating the effect of market movements.

When a company goes private, it is transformed from public ownership to private ownership by a small group of investors, including management. There are a number of motivations for going private, and some reasons for expecting economic gain. The empirical evidence suggests sizable premiums being paid to the public stockholders, similar to those for mergers. One means for going private is the leveraged buyout. Here a large amount of debt is used to finance a cash purchase of a division of a company or a company as a whole. Both senior debt secured by assets and junior subordinated debt are employed. The latter is known as mezzanine financing and usually comes with warrants or some other type of equity link. With the moderate equity base, an adverse change in operations or in interest rates can result in default. A leveraged recapitalization is similar to an LBO in that leverage is employed. However, the cash raised through debt is used to pay a large dividend to stockholders. They continue to hold stock, known as stub shares, and the company remains a public corporation.

Companies in financial distress have a limited number of options. Preferable is some kind of workout with creditors on a voluntary basis—extension, composition, or even liquidation. Legal proceedings are cumbersome and costly. Chapter 7 of the bankruptcy law deals with liquidation through the courts, and Chapter 11 with the reorganization of a company by paring down its fixed charges. For both, there are standard procedures for filing a petition with the bankruptcy court, appointing a trustee, proving claims, and disposition of the matter. For a reorganization plan to be approved it must be fair, equitable, and feasible.

In recent years, the rule of absolute priority, which concerns the order of settlement of claims, has been violated. This can work to the advantage of equity holders, and it clearly is to the detriment of creditors. Management has an upper hand in being able to propose a reorganization plan and threatening to delay things to the detriment of firm, and creditor, value. As a result, management often is able to extract concessions from creditors and obtain new stock for equity holders in the reorganized company. Sometimes a prepackaged bankruptcy can be arranged with creditors, where they agree to a reorganization plan prior to a bankruptcy petition being filed.

Self-Correction Problems

1. What are the similarities and differences among sell-offs, spin-offs, and equity carve-outs? Is one method better than the others? Why would a company want to divest itself of a business unit?

2. Rumpole Bailey Company recently has become subject to a hostile takeover attempt. Management is considering either a leveraged buyout or a leveraged recapitalization. With the LBO, it would initially own 30 percent of the stock, but this would be diluted if mezzanine lenders were to exercise their warrants. These warrants, upon exercise, give holders 30 percent of the total shares. Management presently owns 400,000 shares of the 10 million shares outstanding. With a leveraged recap, it would receive 6 shares of "stub" stock for each old share owned, but no dividend, while public stockholders would receive one new share for each old share owned plus a large cash dividend.

    a. In the case of the LBO, after exercise of the warrants, what will be management's proportion of ownership of the company?

    b. If a leveraged recap were to occur, what would be management's proportion of ownership?

    c. Are there other factors to consider? What are they?

3. Tokay Enterprises is considering going private through a leveraged buyout by management. Management presently owns 21 percent of the 5 million shares outstanding. Market price per share is $20, and it is felt that a 40 percent premium over the present price will be necessary to entice public stockholders to tender their shares in a cash offer. Management intends to keep their shares and to obtain senior debt equal to 80 percent of the funds necessary to consummate the buyout. The remaining 20 percent will come from junior subordinated debentures. Terms on the senior debt are 2 percent above the prime rate, with principal reductions of 20 percent of the initial loan at the end of each of the next 5 years. The junior subordinated debentures bear a 13 percent interest rate and must be retired at the end of 6 years with a single balloon payment. The debentures have warrants attached that enable the holders to purchase 30 percent of the stock at the end of year 6. Management estimates that earnings before interest and taxes will be $25 million per year. Because of tax-loss carry-forwards, the company expects to pay no taxes over the next 5 years. The company will make capital expenditures in amounts equal to its depreciation.

    a. If the prime rate is expected to average 10 percent over the next 5 years, is the leveraged buyout feasible?

    b. What if it averaged only 8 percent?

    c. What minimal EBIT is necessary to service the debt?

4. Tara Plantation Company has run into financial difficulty and is facing possible reorganization. It currently has the following capital structure (in thousands):

	Book Value
Long-term bonds	$ 40,000
General unsecured debt	30,000
Preferred stock	10,000
Common stock	20,000
Total	$100,000

Unfortunately, the trustee under Chapter 11 estimates that Tara has a value of only $75 million as a going concern, not the $100 million shown on the books. The trustee has recommended the following capital structure for the reorganized company (in thousands):

Long-term bonds	$10,000
Unsecured debt	20,000
Preferred stock	5,000
Common stock	40,000
Total	$75,000

If this plan is accepted by the claimholders and confirmed by the bankruptcy court, what will be the distribution of the new securities to the holders of old claims?

 Problems

1. R. Leonard Company has three divisions, and the total market value (debt and equity) of the firm is $71 million. Its debt-to-total-market-value ratio is .40, and bond indentures provide the usual protective covenants. However, they do not preclude the sale of a division. Leonard has decided to divest itself of its Eltron division for a consideration of $20 million. In addition to this payment to Leonard, the buyer will assume $5 million of existing debt of the division. The full $20 million will be distributed to Leonard Company stockholders. In other words, are the remaining debt holders of Leonard Company better or worse off? Why? In theory, are the equity holders better or worse off?

2. Lorzo-Perez International has a subsidiary, the DelRay Sorter Company. The company believes the subsidiary on average will generate $1 million per year in annual net cash flows, after necessary capital expenditures. These annual net cash flows are projected into the far future (assume infinity). The required rate of return for the subsidiary is 12 percent. If the company were to invest an additional $10 million now, it is believed that annual net cash flows could be increased from $1 million to $2 million. Exson Corporation has expressed an interest in DelRay, because it is in the sorter business and believes it can achieve some economies. Accordingly, it has made a cash offer of $10 million for the subsidiary. Should Lorzo-Perez (a) continue the business as is? (b) invest the additional $10 million? (c) sell the subsidiary to Exson? (Assume the subsidiary is entirely equity financed.)

3. Biglow Carpet Company is considering divesting itself of its linoleum division. It is considering either a sell-off, a spin-off, or an equity carve-out, where the carve-out would be for 48 percent of the value of the division. Event studies for similar situations suggest the following abnormal returns around the announcement date: sell-offs, 1 percent; spin-offs, 3 percent; equity carve-outs, 1 percent. Which method would you advise the company to use? Are there considerations other than these data that would influence your decision?

4. Hogs Breath Inns, a chain of restaurants, is considering going private. The president, Clint Westwood, believes that with the elimination of stockholder servicing costs and other costs associated with public ownership, the company could save $800,000 per annum before taxes. In addition, the company believes management incentives and hence performance will be higher as a private company. As a result, annual profits are expected to be 10 percent greater than the present after-tax profits of $9 million. The effective tax rate is 30 percent, the price/earnings ratio of the stock is 12, and there are 10 million shares outstanding.

    a. What is the present market price per share?

    b. What is the maximum dollar premium above this price that the company could pay in order to take the company private?

5. Bulaweyo Industries wishes to sell its valve division for $10 million. Management of the division wishes to buy it and has arranged a leveraged buyout.

The management will contribute $1 million in cash. A senior lender will advance $7 million secured by all the assets of the company. The rate on the loan is 2 percent above the prime rate, which is presently 12 percent. The loan is payable in equal annual principal installments over 5 years, with interest for the year payable at the end of each year. A junior subordinated loan of $2 million also has been arranged, and this loan is due at the end of 6 years. The interest rate is fixed at 15 percent, and interest payments only are due at the end of each of the first 5 years. Interest and principal are due at the end of the sixth year. In addition, the lender has received warrants exercisable for 50 percent of the stock. The valve division expects earnings of $3.4 million before interest and taxes in each of the first 3 years and $3.7 million in each of the next 3 years. The tax rate is $33\frac{1}{3}$ percent, and the company expects capital expenditures and investments in receivables and inventories to equal depreciation charges in each year. All debt servicing must come from profits. (Assume also that the warrants are not exercised and that there is no cash infusion as a result.)

a. If the prime rate stays at 12 percent on average throughout the 6 years, will the enterprise be able to service the debt properly?

b. If the prime rate were to rise to 20 percent in the second year and average that for years 2 through 6, would the situation change?

6. USB Corporation is considering a leveraged recapitalization. Currently, its balance sheet consists of the following (in millions):

Total assets	$941
Total debt	295
Shareholders' equity	$646

There are 20 million shares outstanding, of which management owns 1 million. The leveraged recap involves $703 million in new debt, paying public stockholders a cash dividend of $37 per share, and giving them one new share of stub stock for each old share of stock owned. Management will receive no cash dividend but will get nine new shares of stock for each old share held.

a. What will the balance sheet look like after the leveraged recap? What will give the shares value?

b. What proportional ownership will management have after the transaction compared with what it had before?

c. Determine the after-recap value per share implicit in cash-dividend and exchange-offer differentials between management and public stockholders. Assume there is no control value and that management and stockholders are indifferent between having cash dividends or value in the shares they own.

7. Merry Land, an amusement park in Atlanta, has experienced increased difficulty in paying its bills. Although the park has been marginally profitable over the years, the current outlook is not encouraging, as profits during the last 2 years have been negative. The park is located on reasonably valuable real es-

tate and has an overall liquidating value of $5 million. After much discussion with creditors, management has agreed to a voluntary liquidation. A trustee, who is appointed by the various parties to liquidate the properties, will charge $200,000 for his services. The Merry Land Company owes $300,000 in back property taxes. It has a $2 million mortgage on certain amusement park equipment that can be sold for only $1 million. Creditor claims are as follows:

Party	Book Value Claim
General creditors	$1,750,000
Mortgage bonds	2,000,000
Long-term subordinated debt	1,000,000
Common stock	5,000,000

What amount is each party likely to receive in liquidation?

8. The Greenwood Corporation is in Chapter 11. The trustee has estimated that the company can earn $1.5 million before interest and taxes (40 percent) in the future. In the new capitalization, he feels that debentures should bear a coupon of 10 percent and have coverage of 5 times, income bonds (12 percent) should have overall coverage of 2 times, preferred stock (10 percent) should have after-tax coverage of 3 times, and common stock should be issued on a price/earnings ratio basis of 12 times. Determine the capital structure that conforms to the trustee's criteria.

9. Facile Fastener Company had the following liabilities and equity position when it filed for bankruptcy under Chapter 11 (in thousands):

Accounts payable	$ 500
Accrued wages	200
Bank loan, 12% rate (secured by receivables)	600
Current liabilities	$1,300
13% First-mortgage bonds	500
15% Subordinated debentures	1,700
Total debt	$3,500
Common stock and paid-in capital	500
Retained earnings	420
Total liabilities and equity	$4,420

After straightening out some operating problems, the company is expected to be able to earn $800,000 annually before interest and taxes. Based on other going-concern values, it is felt that the company as a whole is worth five times its EBIT. Court costs associated with the reorganization will total $200,000, and the expected tax rate is 40 percent for the reorganized company. As trustee, suppose you have the following instruments to use for the long-term capitalization of the company: 13 percent first-mortgage bonds, 15 percent capital notes, 13 percent preferred stock, and common stock. With the new capitalization, the capital notes should have an overall coverage ratio, after bank loan interest, of four times, and preferred stock should have a coverage ratio after interest and taxes of two times. Moreover, it is felt that common stock equity should equal at least 30 percent of the total assets of the company.

    a. What is the total valuation of the company after reorganization?

    b. If the maximum amounts of debt and preferred stock are employed, what will be the new capital structure and current liabilities of the company?

    c. How should these securities be allocated, assuming a rule of absolute priority?

Solutions to Self-Correction Problems

1. In sell-offs and spin-offs, the company divests itself entirely of the business unit. In an equity carve-out, only a portion of the equity ownership of the unit is divested, through a sale of stock to the public. Usually, this portion is a minority interest, and the company continues to manage the business unit. With a sell-off and an equity carve-out, the company receives a consideration for the business unit, usually cash. With a spin-off, it receives no such consideration. Rather, stock in the business unit is distributed to stockholders. The most appropriate method depends on the circumstances and what the company wishes to accomplish by the transaction. As discussed in the chapter, the motives to divest a business unit are several. There may be an economic gain in the business unit being more valuable to someone else than it is to the company. If there is asymmetric information between management and investors, it may be possible to achieve a favorable information effect, and valuation, by divesting. A wealth transfer from old debt holders to stockholders will sometimes occur if lenders have a lesser claim after the transaction. Finally, there may be tax advantages to the divestiture.

2.   a. $30\% \times (1 - .30) = 21\%$

    b.

Management shares after recap	2.4 million
Public stockholder shares after recap	9.6 million
Total shares after the recap	12.0 million

Proportion of ownership by management = 2.4/12.0 = 20%

Management obtains a slightly lesser ownership position with the leveraged recap than with the LBO.

    c. With the leveraged recap, the company remains a public corporation and management can trade its shares. With an LBO, it owns stock in a private company and such stock is illiquid. There are certain costs for the public corporation and, perhaps, an undue focus on quarterly earnings, which would not be the case with the private-company LBO. The leveraged recap can be consummated without putting the company up for sale and obligating the board of directors to accept the highest offer. However, with the leveraged recap, 80 percent of the stock will stay in public hands, so the company still could be subject to hostile takeover attempts. However, the high degree of leverage may serve as a deterrent.

3. a. Shares owned by outsiders = 5 million × .79 = 3,950,000
    Price to be offered = $20 × 1.40 = $28 per share
    Total buyout amount = 3,950,000 shares × $28 = $110,600,000

    Senior debt = $110,600,000 × .80 = $88,480,000
    Annual principal payment = $88,480,000/5 = $17,696,000
    Junior debt = $110,600,000 × .20 = $22,120,000

    Annual EBIT to service debt:

Senior debt interest	$88,480,000 × .12 =	$10,617,600
Senior debt principal		17,696,000
Junior debt interest	$22,120,000 × .13 =	2,875,600
Total EBIT necessary		$31,189,200

    During the first 5 years, EBIT of $25 million will not be sufficient to service the debt.

    b. $88,480,000 × .10 = $8,848,000, which together with the two other amounts above, comes to $29,419,600. Still, expected EBIT will not be sufficient to service the debt.

    c. $31,189,200

4. Long-term bondholders:

Long-term bondholders:	Long-term bonds	$20,000
	Unsecured debt	10,000
	Preferred stock	10,000
General unsecured creditors:	Common stock	30,000
Preferred stock-holders:	Common stock	5,000
		$75,000

Common stockholders receive nothing in this reorganization, if the rule of absolute priority holds. If they are able to extract concessions from creditors through various threats of delay, the above distribution would be changed to give them some stock.

Selected References

ALDERSON, MICHAEL J., and BRIAN L. BETKER, "Liquidation Costs and Capital Structure," *Journal of Financial Economics*, 39 (September 1995), 45–69.

ALLEN, JEFFREY W., and JOHN J. McCONNELL, "Equity Carve-Outs and Managerial Discretion," *Journal of Finance*. 53 (February 1998), 163–86.

ANDRADE, GEGOR, and STEVEN N. KAPLAN, "How Costly Is Financial Distress? Evidence from Highly Leveraged Transactions that Became Distressed," *Journal of Finance*, 53 (October 1998), 1443–93.

ASQUITH, PAUL, and THIERRY A. WIZMAN, "Event Risk, Covenants, and Bondholder Returns in

Leveraged Buyouts," *Journal of Financial Economics,* 27 (September 1990), 195–213.

BERGER, PHILIP G., and ELI OFEK, "Bustup Takeovers of Value-Destroying Diversified Firms," *Journal of Finance,* 51 (September 1996), 1175–200.

BETKER, BRIAN L., "The Administrative Costs of Debt Restructurings: Some Recent Evidence," *Financial Management,* 26 (Winter 1997), 56–68.

———— "An Empirical Examination of Prepackaged Bankruptcy," *Financial Management,* 24 (Spring 1995), 3–18.

CHAPLINSKY, SUSAN, GREG NIEHAUS and LINDA VAN DE GUCHT, "Employee Buyouts: Causes, Structure, and Consequences," *Journal of Financial Economics.* 48 (June 1998), 283–332.

CHATTERGEE, DRIS, UPINDER D. DHILLON, and GABRIEL G. RAMIREZ, "Resolution of Financial Distress: Debt Restructuring via Chapter 11, Prepackaged Bankruptcies, and Workouts," *Financial Management,* 25 (Spring 1996), 5–18.

CUSATIS, PATRICK J., JAMES A. MILES, and J. RANDALL WOOLRIDGE, "Restructuring through Spinoffs: The Stock Market Evidence," *Journal of Financial Economics,* 33 (June 1993), 293–311.

DALEY, LANE, VIKAS MEHROTA, and RANJINI SIVAKUMAR, "Corporate Focus and Value Creation: Evidence from Spinoffs," *Journal of Financial Economics* 45 (August 1997), 257–81.

DEANGELO, HARRY, LINDA DEANGELO, and EDWARD M. RICE, "Going Private: Minority Freezeouts and Stockholder Wealth," *Journal of Law and Economics,* 27 (June 1984), 367–401.

DENIS, DAVID J., and DIANE K. DENIS, "Causes of Financial Distress Following Leveraged Recapitalizations," *Journal of Financial Economics,* 37 (February 1995), 129–57.

DENIS, DAVID J., and TIMOTHY A. KRUSE, "Managerial Discipline and Corporate Restructuring following Performance Declines," *Journal of Financial Economics,* 55 (March 2000), 391–424.

DESAI, HEMANG, and PREM C. JAIN, "Firm Performance and Focus: Long-run Stock Market Performance Following Spinoffs," *Journal of Financial Economics.* 54 (October 1999), 75–101.

DICHEV, ILIA D., "Is the Risk of Bankruptcy a Systematic Risk?" *Journal of Finance,* 53 (June 1998), 1131–47.

DONALDSON, GORDON, *Corporate Restructuring.* Cambridge, MA: Harvard Business School Press, 1994.

EBERHART, ALLAN C., WILLIAM T. MOORE, and RODNEY L. ROSENFELDT, "Security Pricing and Deviations from the Absolute Priority Rule in Bankruptcy Proceedings," *Journal of Finance,* 45 (December 1990), 1457–69.

FRANKS, JULIAN R., and WALTER N. TOROUS, "A Comparison of Financial Recontracting in Distressed Exchanges and Chapter 11 Reorganiza-

tions," *Journal of Financial Economics,* 35 (June 1994), 349–70.

GILSON, STUART C., "Managing Default: Some Evidence on How Firms Choose between Workouts and Bankruptcy," *Journal of Applied Corporate Finance,* 4 (Summer 1991), 62–70.

————, "Transactions Costs and Capital Structure Choice: Evidence from Financially Distressed Firms," *Journal of Finance.* 52 (March 1997),

GILSON, STUART C., and MICHAEL R. VETSUYPENS, "CEO Compensation in Financially Distressed Firms: An Empirical Analysis," *Journal of Finance,* 48 (June 1993), 425–58.

GUPTA, ATUL, and LEONARD ROSENTHAL, "Ownership Structure, Leverage and Firm Value: The Case of Leveraged Recapitalizations," *Financial Management,* 20 (Autumn 1991), 69–83.

HITE, GAILEN L., and JAMES E. OWERS, "Security Price Reactions around Corporate Spin-off Announcements," *Journal of Financial Economics,* 12 (December 1983), 409–36.

HITE, GAILEN L., and MICHAEL R. VETSUYPENS, "Management Buyouts of Divisions and Shareholder Wealth," *Journal of Finance,* 44 (June 1989), 953–80.

HOTCHKISS, EDITH SHWALB, "Postbankruptcy Performance and Management Turnover," *Journal of Finance,* 50 (March 1995), 3–21.

HOTCHKISS, EDITH S., and ROBERT M. MOORADIAN, "Vulture Investors and the Market for Control of Distressed Firms," *Journal of Financial Economics,* 43 (March 1997), 373–99.

JAIN, PREM C., "The Effect of Voluntary Sell-off Announcements on Shareholder Wealth," *Journal of Finance,* 40 (March 1985), 209–24.

KAPLAN, STEVEN, "The Effects of Management Buyouts on Operating Performance and Value," *Journal of Financial Economics,* 24 (October 1989), 217–54.

KAPLAN, STEVEN N., and RICHARD S. RUBACK, "The Valuation of Cash Flow Forecasts: An Empirical Analysis," *Journal of Finance,* 50 (September 1995), 1059–93.

KHANNA, NAVEEN, and ANNETTE B. POULSEN, "Managers of Financially Distressed Firms: Villains or Scapegoats?" *Journal of Finance,* 50 (July 1995), 919–40.

KLEIN, APRIL, "The Timing and Substance of Divestiture Announcements," *Journal of Finance,* 41 (July 1986), 685–96.

KRISHNASWAMI, SUDHA, and VENKAT SUBRAMANIAM, "Information Asymmetry, Valuation, and the Corporate Spin-off Decision," *Journal of Financial Economics,* 53 (July 1999), 72–112.

MAKSIMOVIC, VOJISLAV, and GORDON PHILLIPS, "Asset Efficiency and Realloaction Decisions of Bankrupt Firms," *Journal of Finance,* 53(October 1998), 1495–1532.

MARIAS, LAURENTIUS, KATHERINE SCHIPPER, and ABBIE SMITH, "Wealth Effects of Going Private for Senior Securities," *Journal of Financial Economics,* 23 (June 1989), 155–91.

MICHAELY, RONI, and WAYNE H. SHAW, "The Choice of Going Public: Spin-offs vs. Carve-outs," *Financial Management,* 24 (Autumn 1995), 5–21.

MILES, JAMES A., and JAMES D. ROSENFELD, "The Effect of Voluntary Spin-off Announcements on Shareholder Wealth," *Journal of Finance,* 38 (December 1983), 1597–1606.

NANDA, VIKRAM, "On the Good News in Equity Carve-Outs," *Journal of Finance,* 46 (December 1991), 1717–37.

PULVINO, TODD C., "Effects of Bankruptcy Court Protection on Asset Sales," *Journal of Financial Economics,* 52 (May 1999), 151–86.

SCHIPPER, KATHERINE, and ABBIE SMITH, "Effects of Recontracting on Shareholder Wealth," *Journal of Financial Economics,* 12 (December 1983), 437–67.

———, "A Comparison of Equity Carve-outs and Seasoned Equity Offerings," *Journal of Financial Economics,* 15 (January–February 1986), 153–86.

SLOVIN, MYRON B., MARIE E. SUSHKA, and STEVEN R. FERRARO, "A Comparison of the Information Conveyed by Equity Carve-outs, Spin-offs, and Asset Sell-offs," *Journal of Financial Economics,* 37 (January 1995), 89–104.

TASHJIAN, ELIZABETH, RONALD C. LEASE, and JOHN J. MCCONNELL, "Prepacks: An Empirical Analysis of Pre-packaged Bankruptcies," *Journal of Financial Economics,* 40 (January 1996), 135–62.

VIJH, ANAND M., "The Spinoff and Merger Ex-Date Effects," *Journal of Finance,* 49 (June 1994), 581–609.

———, "Long-term Returns from Equity Carve-outs," *Journal of Financial Economics,* 51 (February 1999), 273–308.

WESTON, J. FRED, KWANG S. CHUNG, and JUAN A. SIU, *Takeovers, Restructuring, and Corporate Governance,* 2nd ed. Upper Saddle River, NJ: Prentice Hall, 1998.

Wachowicz's Web World is an excellent overall Web site produced and maintained by my coauthor of *Fundamentals of Financial Management,* John M. Wachowicz Jr. It contains descriptions of and links to many finance Web sites and articles. *www.prenhall.com/wachowicz.*

International Financial Management

The last 15 years have witnessed a globalization of business, not only in foreign sales but also in manufacturing/service facilities and in finance. There has been an explosion in international investments, through mutual funds and other intermediaries by the individual and through direct security investment by the institution. Capital raising is increasingly occurring across national boundaries. The financial manager must search for "best price" in a global marketplace, sometimes with currency and other hedges. To accommodate the underlying demands of investors and capital raisers, financial institutions and instruments have changed dramatically. Financial deregulation, first in the United States and then in Europe and Asia, has prompted increased integration of world financial markets. As a result of the rapidly changing scene, the financial manager today must be global in his or her perspective. While the concepts developed earlier in this book are applicable here, the environment in which decisions are made is different. In this chapter, we develop an understanding of this environment and describe how a company goes about protecting itself. ■

SOME BACKGROUND

The motivation to invest capital in a foreign operation, of course, is to provide a return in excess of that required. There may be gaps in foreign markets where excess returns can be earned. Domestically, competitive pressures may be such that only a normal rate of return can be earned. Although expansion into foreign markets is the reason for most investment abroad, there are other reasons. Some firms invest in order to produce more efficiently. Another country may offer lower labor and other costs, and a company will choose to locate production facilities there in the quest for lower operating costs. The electronics industry has moved toward foreign production facilities for this saving. Finally, some companies invest abroad to secure necessary raw materials. Oil companies and mining companies in particular invest abroad for this reason. All of these pursuits—markets, production facilities, and raw materials—are in keeping with an objective of securing a higher rate of return than is possible through domestic operations alone.

International Capital Budgeting

The relevant cash inflows for a foreign investment are those that can be **repatriated** to the parent. If the expected return on investment is based on nonremittable cash flows that build up in a foreign subsidiary, the investment is unlikely to be attractive. If cash flows can be freely repatriated, however, capital budgeting is straightforward. The U.S. firm would

1. Estimate expected cash flows in the foreign currency.
2. Compute their U.S. dollar equivalents at the expected exchange rate (foreign currency per dollar).
3. Determine the net present value of the project using the U.S. required rate of return, adjusted upward or downward for any risk premium effect associated with the foreign investment.

Suppose Jacklin Jersey Company is considering an investment in Malaysia costing 1.5 million ringgits. The product has a short life, 4 years, and the required rate of return on repatriated U.S. dollars is 15 percent. The ringgit, now 3.75 to the dollar, is expected to depreciate over time. That is, a dollar is expected to be worth more ringgits in the future than it is worth now. Table 25-1 illustrates the three steps used to calculate dollar cash flows and their net present value, which we see to be approximately $77,000.

Although the calculations are straightforward, obviously much goes into the assumptions concerning projected cash flows, projected exchange rates, and the required rate of return. Learning about these things is the purpose of this chapter.

Risk Factors

With respect to required returns, international diversification is a consideration. Recall from our discussion of portfolio risk in Chapter 3 that the key element is the correlation among projects in the asset portfolio. By combining projects with low degrees of correlation with each other, a firm is able to reduce risk in relation to expected return. Since domestic investment projects tend to be correlated with each other, most being highly dependent on the state of the economy, foreign investments have an advantage. The economic cycles of different countries do not tend

TABLE 25-1

Expected Cash Flows for Jacklin Jersey Company's Malaysian Project (in thousands)

	Year				
	0	1	2	3	4
Expected cash flow (in ringgits)	−1,500	500	800	700	600
Exchange rate (R/$)	3.75	3.79	3.84	3.90	3.97
Expected cash flow (in dollars)	−400	132	208	179	151

Net present value at 15 percent = $77

to be completely synchronized, so it is possible to reduce risk relative to expected return by investing across countries. The idea is simply that returns on investment projects tend to be less correlated among countries than they are in any one particular country.

Foreign Diversification   Whether foreign diversification by a company benefits its stockholders depends on whether capital markets between countries are at least partially segmented. If they are not, there is little reason to believe that foreign diversification by a company will increase its value. This notion is the same as that for diversification of assets involving domestic projects, which was discussed earlier. If capital markets are perfect, investors can effectively replicate any asset diversification by the firm. Therefore, such diversification adds nothing at the margin to shareholder wealth. If currency restrictions, investment barriers, legal restrictions, lack of information, and other capital market imperfections of this sort exist, capital markets between countries may be segmented. Under these circumstances, foreign diversification may enhance shareholder wealth.

Does Diversification Pay?   Thus, whether stocks are better regarded as being traded in domestic markets, where the market models (CAPM or APT) would hold, or in an international market is the question. The former implies at least a partially segmented capital market, whereas the latter suggests an integrated one with the relevant market portfolio being worldwide. The situation is illustrated in Fig. 25-1. With a domestic portfolio of stocks, one is able to reduce total risk through diversification in the manner shown by the top line. This illustration corresponds to Fig. 3-9, which dealt with the relationship among total, systematic, and unsystematic risk. With an integrated market for securities, the investor is able to reduce risk more quickly and further by diversifying across international stocks as opposed to only domestic ones. This suggests that the cost of capital for a company whose stock is held by investors with broad international diversification will be lower than if only "home country" investors are involved.

Diversification
will reduce risk if global markets are partially segmented.

FIGURE 25-1
Domestic versus international stock diversification

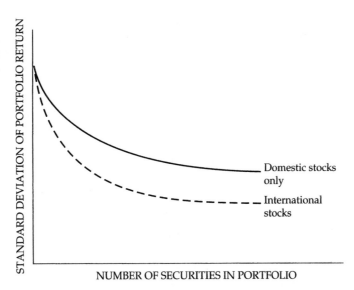

NUMBER OF SECURITIES IN PORTFOLIO

This suggests that the cost of capital for a company in a global stock market context may be lower than that measured when only the domestic capital market is considered. If the cash flows of a company are correlated more closely with the domestic economy than they are with the global economy, the global beta for a company's stock will be lower than its domestic beta.[1] As a result, its measured required return on equity will be lower. In the context of the CAPM calculations in Chapter 3, we would substitute the return on the global market portfolio, as typefied by the Morgan Stanley Capital International index, for that on the U.S. market portfolio, where we used the S&P 500 stock index.

Some of the things that make direct foreign investments different from domestic investments are taxation and political risk. Before we get into currency exposure of a company, we consider these topics.

International finance is like domestic finance, but there are institutional differences, political risk, and exchange-rate risk.

Taxation

Because of different tax laws and different treatments of foreign investment, the taxation of a multinational firm is complex. Our purpose is to discuss some of the salient aspects of the problem.

Taxation by U.S. Government If a U.S. corporation carries on business abroad through a branch or division, the income from that operation is reported on the company's U.S. tax form and is taxed in the same way as domestic income. If business is carried on through a foreign subsidiary, the income normally is not taxed in the United States until it is distributed to the parent in the form of dividends. The advantage here, of course, is that the tax is deferred until the parent receives a cash return. In the meantime, earnings are reinvested in the subsidiary to finance expansion. Unlike dividends from a domestic corporation (70 percent exempt), dividends received by a U.S. corporation from a foreign subsidiary are fully taxable.

Taxation by Foreign Governments Every country taxes income of foreign companies doing business in that country. The type of tax imposed varies. Some of these countries differentiate between income distributed to stockholders and undistributed income, with a lower tax on distributed income. Less-developed countries frequently have lower taxes and provide certain other tax incentives to encourage foreign investment.

The taxation policies of foreign governments are not only varied but also highly complex. The definition of what constitutes taxable income is different for different countries, and the tax rate varies among countries. Certain nations, such as Luxembourg, Panama, and the Bahamas, have low tax rates on corporate profits in order to encourage foreign investment, whereas the tax rates in most advanced industrial countries are high. The picture is complicated further by the numerous tax treaties that the United States has with other nations. Although the U.S. government restricts use of a low-tax country as a tax haven, enough latitude remains so that companies still devise complicated legal structures to take advantage of such havens.

To avoid double taxation, the United States gives a federal income **tax credit for foreign taxes** paid by a U.S. corporation. If a foreign country has a tax rate of less than that of the U.S. corporation, it will pay combined taxes at the full U.S. tax rate. Part of the taxes are paid to the foreign government, the other part to the U.S.

---

[1]See Rene M. Stulz, "Globalization, Corporate Finance, and the Cost of Capital," *Journal of Applied Corporate Finance*, 12 (Fall 1999), 8–25.

government. Suppose a foreign branch of a U.S. corporation operates in a country where the income tax rate is 27 percent. The branch earns $2 million and pays $540,000 in foreign income taxes. Suppose the $2 million earnings are subject to a 35 percent tax rate in the United States, or $700,000 in taxes. The company receives a tax credit of $540,000; thus, it pays only $160,000 in U.S. taxes on earnings of its foreign branch. If the foreign tax rate were 50 percent, the company would pay $1 million in foreign taxes on those earnings, nothing in U.S. taxes. Here, total taxes paid are obviously higher.

Moreover, the size of foreign tax credit may be constrained. The United States taxes companies on their worldwide income and permits a foreign tax credit only to the extent that the foreign source income would have been taxed in the United States. Suppose 30 percent of a multinational company's total income is attributable to foreign sources. If its pre-credit U.S. tax liability is $10 million, only $3 million in foreign tax credits may be used to offset the U.S. tax liability. If the company pays more in foreign taxes, it will be subject to double taxation on that portion. A number of countries have withholding taxes on dividend distributions to foreign investors. To the extent the investor pays little or no taxes domestically, such as occurs with institutional investors, there is no ability to neutralize the withholding tax and it serves as a disincentive to foreign investment.

It is clear that tax planning for an international operation is complex and highly technical. From time to time, various special tax incentives come into existence to help export industries, the Foreign Sales Corporation (FSC) being a current example. Other tax provisions, both U.S. and foreign, are constantly changing. The advice of tax experts and legal counsel, both foreign and domestic, should be sought at the time the foreign operation is organized.

Political Risk

A multinational company faces political risks that can range from mild interference to complete confiscation of all assets. Interference includes laws that specify a minimum percentage of nationals who must be employed in various positions, required investment in environmental and social projects, and restrictions on the convertibility of currencies. The ultimate political risk is expropriation, such as that which occurred in Chile in 1971, when the country took over the copper companies. Between mild interference and outright expropriation, there may be discriminatory practices, such as higher taxes, higher utility charges, and the requirement to pay higher wages than a national company. In essence, they place the foreign operation of the U.S. company at a competitive disadvantage. However, the situation is not one-directional. Certain developing countries give foreign companies concessions to invest such that they may have more favorable costs than a domestic company.

Because political risk has a serious influence on the overall risk of an investment project, it must be assessed realistically. Essentially, the job is one of forecasting political instability. How stable is the government involved? What are the prevailing political winds? What is likely to be a new government's view of foreign investment? How efficient is the government in processing requests? How much inflation and economic stability are there? How strong and equitable are the courts? Answers to these questions should give considerable insight into the political risk involved in an investment. Some companies have categorized countries according to their political risk. If a country is classified in the undesirable category, probably no investment will be permitted, no matter how high its expected return.

Once a company decides to invest, it should take steps to protect itself. By co-operating with the host country in hiring nationals, making the "right" types of investment, and in other ways being desirable, political risk can be reduced. A **joint venture** with a company in the host country can improve the public image of the operation. Indeed, in some countries a joint venture may be the only way to do business, because direct ownership, particularly of manufacturing, is prohibited. The risk of expropriation also can be reduced by making the subsidiary dependent on the parent for technology, markets, and/or supplies. A foreign government is reluctant to expropriate when the enterprise is not self-sustaining. Although every effort should be made to protect an investment once it is made, often when sharp political changes occur nothing can be done. The time to look hardest at political risk is before the investment is made.

TYPES OF EXPOSURE

The company with foreign operations is at risk in various ways. Apart from political danger, risk fundamentally emanates from changes in exchange rates. In this regard, the **spot rate** represents the number of units of one currency that can be exchanged for another. Put differently, it is the price of one currency relative to another. The currencies of the major countries are traded in active markets, where rates are determined by the forces of supply and demand. Quotations can be in terms of the domestic currency or in terms of the foreign currency. If the U.S. dollar is the domestic currency and the British pound the foreign, a quotation might be 0.629 pounds per dollar or 1.59 dollars per pound. The result is the same, for one is the reciprocal of the other.

Currency risk can be thought of as the volatility of the exchange rate of one currency for another. In Fig. 25-2, it is illustrated for the U.S. dollar/British pound sterling exchange rate. As shown, the dollar strengthened in value (fewer dollars per pound) from 1981 to 1985, and then weakened in value to 1988, after which it fluctuated until the 1992 European correction when it fell in value. In recent years, it has fluctuated around 1.60.

We must distinguish a spot exchange rate, which involves the immediate delivery of one currency for another, from a **forward exchange rate.** Forward transactions involve an agreement today for settlement in the future. It might be the delivery of 1,000 pounds 90 days hence, where the settlement rate is 1.58 dollars per pound. The forward exchange rate usually differs from the spot exchange rate for reasons we will explain shortly.

FIGURE 25-2

Exchange rate:
U.S. dollars/British
pound sterling

With these definitions in mind, there are three types of exposure with which we are concerned:

1. Translation exposure
2. Transactions exposure
3. Economic exposure

Translation exposure
is the effect of an exchange-rate change on the accounting balance sheet and income statement.

The first, **translation exposure**, is the change in accounting income and balance sheet statements caused by changes in exchange rates. As the topic of accounting exposure is technical, we treat it in the Appendix that follows.

Transactions exposure has to do with settling a particular transaction, like a receivable, at one exchange rate when the obligation was originally recorded at another. Finally, economic exposure involves changes in expected future cash flows, and hence economic value, caused by a change in exchange rates. For example, if we budget 2 million Euros, the currency of the European Monetary Union, to build an extension to our German plant and the exchange rate now is 0.95 Euros per dollar, this corresponds to €2.0 million x .95 = $1.9 million. When we go to pay for materials and labor, the Euro might unexpectedly strengthen, say to 1.00 to the U.S. dollar. The plant now has a dollar cost of €2.0 million x 1.00 = $2.0 million. The difference of $100,000 represents an economic loss.

Having briefly defined these three exposures, we investigate the last two in detail (the first being in the Appendix). This will be followed by how exposure can be managed.

Transactions Exposure

Transactions exposure
is the effect of an exchange-rate change upon the value of a single transaction.

Transactions exposure involves the gain or loss that occurs when settling a specific foreign transaction. The transaction might be the purchase or sale of a product, the lending or borrowing of funds, or some other transaction involving the acquisition of assets or the assumption of liabilities denominated in a foreign currency. Though any transaction will do, the term *transactions exposure* usually is employed in connection with foreign trade, that is, specific imports or exports on open account credit.

Suppose a Swiss franc receivable of SF1,053 is booked when the exchange rate is 1.62 SF to the dollar. Payment is not due for 2 months. In the interim, the Swiss franc weakens in value and the exchange rate goes to 1.65. As a result, there is a transactions loss. Before, SF1,053/1.62 = $650. When payment is received, SF1,053/1.65 = $638.18. Thus, we have a transactions loss of $11.82. If the Swiss franc were to strengthen in value, say to 1.60, there would be a transactions gain. We would have SF1,053/1.60 = $658.13. With this example in mind, it is easy to produce examples of other types of transactions losses and gains.

ECONOMIC EXPOSURE

Perhaps the most important of the three exposures—translation, transactions, and economic—is the last. **Economic exposure** is the change in value of a company that accompanies an *unanticipated* change in exchange rates. Note that we distinguish anticipated from unanticipated. Anticipated changes in exchange rates already are reflected in the market value of the firm. Economic exposure is not as precise as translation or transactions exposures. It relates to both the existing balance sheet of the foreign subsidiary as well as expected future cash flows.

Degrees of Exposure on Existing Assets and Liabilities

Economic exposure
is the effect of an unanticipated change in exchange rates on the economic value of the firm.

When there is a change in exchange rate, this affects the economic value of a foreign subsidiary's balance sheet. Not all assets and liabilities are equally exposed. For example, inventories may be less exposed than monetary assets, such as cash, marketable securities, and accounts receivable. Hekman has derived a framework for categorizing assets and liabilities as to their degree of exposure.[2] To illustrate her approach, suppose we had a Singapore subsidiary, Tan Lee Feu Limited, that had the balance sheet shown in the first column of Table 25-2. The Singaporean dollar assets and liabilities are converted to their U.S. dollar equivalents. In the second column, market values appear. The last asset requires explanation. For book-value purposes, it is net property, plant, and equipment (cost less cumulative depreciation). For the market-value column, it is the total value of the subsidiary less the market value of the other assets. As such, it is a residual.

The next task in the Hekman framework is to assign an exposure coefficient to each asset and liability. A coefficient of 1.0 means the market value of the balance sheet item is entirely exposed. When exchange rates change (Singaporean dollar in relation to the U.S. dollar), the full brunt of the change is felt. If the Singaporean dollar weakens (more Singaporean dollars to U.S. dollars) by 10 percent and the item involved is receivables, the U.S. dollar market value declines by 10 percent, and vice versa. A coefficient of 0.0 means the market value of the balance sheet item is unexposed. When the Singaporean dollar weakens by 10 percent in value, there is no change in the market value of the balance

TABLE 25-2
Balance Sheet of the Tan Lee Feu Subsidiary (in millions)

	Book Value	Market Value	Exposure Coefficient	Exposure
Cash	$ 1.5	$ 1.5	1.0	$ 1.5
Marketable securities	5.6	5.6	1.0	5.6
Receivables	16.3	16.3	1.0	16.3
Inventories	21.8	24.2	.6	14.5
Value of market position and operating capacity	34.1	71.9	0.3	21.6
Total assets	$79.3	$119.5		$59.5
Accounts payable	$14.9	$ 14.9	1.0	$14.9
Accruals	8.7	8.7	1.0	8.7
Debt	17.0	15.8	1.0	15.8
Total liabilities	$40.6	$ 39.4		$39.4
Shareholders' equity	38.7	80.1		
Total	$79.3	$119.5		

Net aggregate market-value exposure = +$20.1

---

[2]Christine R. Hekman, "Measuring Foreign Exchange Exposure: A Practical Theory and Its Application," *Financial Analysts Journal*, 39 (September–October 1983), 59–65; and Hekman, "Don't Blame Currency Values for Strategic Errors," *Midland Corporate Finance Journal*, 4 (Fall 1986), 45–55.

sheet item as expressed in U.S. dollars. An example here is a commodity whose price is set in world markets completely apart from Singapore and the United States. For coefficients between these two extremes, the item is partially exposed.

In Table 25-2, monetary assets—cash, marketable securities, and accounts receivable—and all monetary liabilities have an exposure coefficient of 1.0. They are totally exposed. Real assets, however, are only partially exposed. Because the Singaporean plant produces fabricated products sold in Southeast Asia, the inventory exposure coefficient is 0.6. If the inventory were heavily commodity oriented, the coefficient would be lower, maybe 0.2. The inventory coefficient depends on sourcing, competitive position, technology, and things of this sort.

Finally, the exposure coefficient for market position/operating capacity is due to some of these same factors. For the Tan Lee Feu subsidiary, it is estimated to be 0.3. Thus, the value of the future operations is only moderately exposed to changes in the Sing. $/U.S. $ exchange rate. Just because an operation is located in Singapore does not mean that it is highly sensitive to the value of the Singapore dollar. To be sure, the labor component of costs will be sensitive, but raw materials are likely to come from other markets. If the finished product is sold in non-Singaporean markets, there may be little sensitivity here as well. The key is whether prices can be adjusted to provide a U.S. dollar margin. If the goods are priced in world markets, which are U.S. dollar sensitive, the market position/operating capacity value of the subsidiary will be relatively insensitive to the Sing. $/U.S. $ exchange rate.

Aggregate Economic Exposure

When the market-value column is multiplied by the exposure coefficient column, we obtain the exposed market value for the various balance sheet items. Liability exposure, of course, offsets asset exposure. Thus, we subtract total liability exposure from total asset exposure to obtain net aggregate market-value exposure. In our case, net aggregate market-value exposure is seen at the bottom of the table to be $20.1 million. This compares with the market value of shareholders' equity of $80.1 million.

It is useful to put things on a relative basis with the following:

$$\text{Aggregate exposure coefficient} = \frac{\text{Net aggregate market-value exposure}}{\text{Market value of equity}} \qquad (25\text{-}1)$$

For our example, the aggregate exposure coefficient for the Tan Lee Feu subsidiary is

$$\text{Aggregate exposure coefficient} = \frac{\$20.01}{\$80.1} = 25.1\%$$

This means that its exposure is asset sensitive. If the Singaporean dollar should weaken by 10 percent, the subsidiary's U.S. dollar value will decline by $10\% \times .251 = 2.51$ percent, and vice versa. If the aggregate exposure coefficient were negative, the subsidiary would be liability sensitive and a weakening in value of the Singaporean dollar would result in a rise in U.S. dollar value of the subsidiary. For most situations, there will be net asset sensitivity. Typically, the more global the markets served, the less the overall exposure.

We see that this framework can be used to assess the economic exposure of the existing balance sheet of a foreign subsidiary. This is one part of the economic exposure picture.

EXPOSURE OF EXPECTED FUTURE CASH FLOWS

The other, usually more important part has to do with what happens to the economic value of expected future cash flows when there is an unanticipated change in exchange rates. The relevant cash flows here are expected future repatriated cash flows from the foreign subsidiary, the framework for calculating them having been presented at the outset of the chapter. To determine whether there is currency exposure, the place to begin is with whether a natural hedge exists.

Natural Hedges

> **A natural hedge** exists whenever the effect of an exchange-rate change is offset by an opposite change in local currency margins.

The relationship between revenues (prices) and costs of a foreign subsidiary sometimes provides a **natural hedge,** giving a company ongoing protection from exchange-rate fluctuations. The key is the extent to which cash flows adjust naturally to currency changes. A perfect natural hedge would exist when local-currency cash flows increase or decrease in such a manner as to exactly offset the weakening or strengthening of that currency. As a result, the value of expected repatriated U.S. dollar cash flows would remain unchanged. Obviously, few natural hedges ever prove to be perfect, so it is a matter of approximation.

One way to explore the likelihood of a natural hedge is to determine whether the subsidiary's revenue and cost functions are sensitive to global or to domestic market conditions. At the extremes there are four situations:

Scenario	Globally Determined	Domestically Determined
1. Pricing	×	
Cost	×	
2. Pricing		×
Cost		×
3. Pricing	×	
Cost		×
4. Pricing		×
Cost	×	

In the first category, we might have a copper fabricator in Taiwan. Its principal cost is copper, the raw material, whose price is determined in global markets and quoted in dollars. Moreover, the fabricated product produced is sold in markets dominated by global pricing. Therefore, the subsidiary has little exposure to exchange-rate fluctuations. In other words, there is a natural hedge. The second category might correspond to a cleaning service company in Belgium. The dominant cost component is labor, and both it and the pricing of the service are determined domestically. As domestic inflation hits costs, the subsidiary is able to pass along the increase in its pricing to customers. Margins, expressed in U.S. dollars, are relatively insensitive to the combination of domestic inflation and exchange-rate changes. This situation also constitutes a natural hedge.

The third situation might involve a British-based international consulting firm. Pricing is largely determined in global markets, whereas costs, again mostly labor, are determined in the domestic market. As the foreign currency (pound sterling in this case) strengthens relative to the dollar, costs rise in relation to prices and margins suffer. The opposite occurs if the foreign currency weakens in value; margins improve. The subsidiary is exposed. Finally, the last category might correspond to a Japanese importer of foreign foods. Costs are determined globally, whereas prices are largely domestically determined. When the yen strengthens in value, prices rise in relation to costs, resulting in improved margins. This is a favorable outcome, but should the yen weaken in value, the opposite occurs. Although scenarios 3 and 4 both involve exposure, they are opposite in direction.

A company's strategic positioning of its international operations largely determines its natural exposure. Such exposure can be modified by sourcing differently and by changing marketing emphasis on a country-by-country basis.

Degree of Natural Exposure

The degree of exchange-rate exposure of a foreign subsidiary is that which remains after any natural hedge. Suppose that the price of a product is domestically determined, whereas its cost is globally determined. (We assume that the U.S. dollar is the metric for global costing and pricing.) The combination of domestic pricing and global costing means that as the foreign currency appreciates in value, prices rise relative to costs. As a result, the value of expected repatriated cash flows increases as the foreign currency appreciates. This is shown in Fig. 25-3. Now suppose that the pricing of the product is globally determined, whereas its cost is domestically determined. In this situation, an appreciation in the foreign currency causes cost to rise relative to price and there is a cost/price squeeze. As a result, the value of repatriated cash flows declines as the foreign currency appreciates. This is illustrated in Fig. 25-3. If *both* costs and prices are determined either domestically or globally, we have a natural hedge. As a result, the value of the repatriated cash flows is invariant with respect to unanticipated changes in the exchange rate.

Of course it may be that costs and/or prices are partially domestically determined and partially globally determined. Example: Costs consist of raw materials and energy, which are determined in global markets, and labor and services, which are determined in domestic markets. The more mixed the situation, the flatter the relationship line in Fig. 25-3. With a complete offset, we would have a natural hedge—the horizontal line in the figure. Thus, the direction and the degree of currency exposure are determined by whether the line goes up or down with currency appreciation and its flatness or steepness.

> **Exposure** can be approximated by determining whether pricing and costs are more sensitive to local-market or global-market conditions.

Only the residual exposure remains after we take account of any natural hedge that represents exchange-rate risk. Remember the definition of a natural hedge is that the cash-flow margins in local currency (prices minus costs) expand or contract in such a way as to offset the effect of a change in exchange rates. If a foreign currency were to depreciate in value, repatriated cash flows would be less, all other things the same. However, if local currency cash flows expand, they may offset this deleterious effect. If you do have a natural hedge, no further hedges should occur. If you overlay a currency hedge, for example, you are undoing the natural hedge in place and, at the margin, taking on currency risk.

Once the direction and degree of net exchange-rate exposure are determined, management needs to decide whether it wishes to hedge the residual (after natural hedge) risk. The devices available? Operating, financing, and currency-market hedges. We explore each in turn.

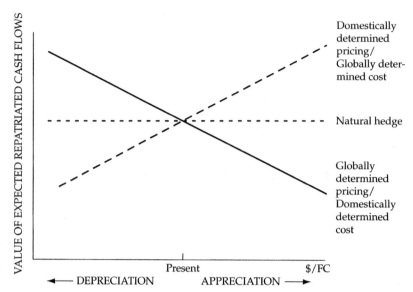

VALUE OF EXPECTED REPATRIATED CASH FLOWS

Domestically determined pricing/ Globally determined cost

Natural hedge

Globally determined pricing/ Domestically determined cost

Present $/FC

←— DEPRECIATION   APPRECIATION —→

FIGURE 25-3

Relationship between value of a foreign subsidiary and the exchange rate

Operating Hedges

In our context, operating hedges consist of cash management among countries through intracompany accounts. If a company knew a currency were going to fall in value, it would want to do a number of things. First, it should reduce its cash to a minimum by purchasing inventories or other real assets. Moreover, the company should try to avoid extended trade credit. As quick a turnover as possible of receivables into cash is desirable. In contrast, it should try to obtain extended terms on its accounts payable. It may also want to borrow in the local currency to replace advances made by the U.S. parent. The last step will depend on relative interest rates. If the currency were going to appreciate in value, opposite steps should be undertaken. Without knowledge of the future direction of currency value movements, aggressive policies in either direction are inappropriate. Under most circumstances, we are unable to predict the future, so the best policy may be one of balancing monetary assets against monetary liabilities in order to neutralize the effect of exchange-rate fluctuations.

Timing Payments   A company with multiple foreign operations can protect itself against foreign exchange risks by adjusting transfer of funds commitments between countries. Accelerating the timing of payments made or received in foreign currencies is called **leading,** and decelerating the timing is called **lagging.** For example, assume that your company has foreign subsidiaries in Britain and Sweden. Further assume that you think the pound sterling will soon be revalued upward relative to the Swedish krona. The Swedish subsidiary purchases approximately $100,000 of goods each month from the British subsidiary. Normal billing calls for payment 3 months after delivery of the goods. Instead of this arrangement, you now instruct the Swedish subsidiary to lead by paying for the goods on delivery, in view of the likely revaluation upward of the pound.

In addition to these arrangements, the multinational company also can adjust intracompany dividends and royalty payments. Sometimes the currency in which a sale is billed is varied in keeping with anticipated foreign exchange movements. Transfer pricing of components or of finished goods, which are exchanged between the parent and various foreign affiliates, can be varied. (However, the tax authorities in most countries look very closely at transfer prices to ensure that taxes are not being avoided.) In all of these cases as well as others, intracompany payments are arranged so that they fit into the company's overall management of its currency exposure.

Reinvoicing Centers   Some multinational companies establish a **reinvoicing center** to manage intracompany and third-party foreign trade. The multinational's exporting subsidiaries sell goods to the reinvoicing center, which resells (reinvoices) them to importing subsidiaries or third-party buyers. While title to the goods initially passes to the reinvoicing center, the goods move directly from the selling unit to the buying unit or independent customer. Generally, the reinvoicing center is billed in the selling unit's home currency and then bills the purchasing unit in that unit's home currency. In this way the reinvoicing center can centralize and manage all intracompany foreign exchange transactions exposure. This arrangement also facilitates the netting of obligations among units, thereby reducing the total volume of foreign exchange transactions. Finally, a reinvoicing center allows for more coordinated control over *leading* or *lagging* arrangements between affiliates.

International Financing

If a company is exposed in one currency and is hurt when that currency weakens in value (scenario 4), it can borrow in that country to offset the exposure. In the context of the framework presented earlier, asset sensitive exposure would be balanced with borrowings. Monetary assets and monetary liabilities both have an exposure coefficient of 1.0, so they serve as offsets. A wide variety of sources of external financing are available to the foreign affiliate. These range from commercial bank loans within the host country to loans from international lending agencies. In this section, we consider the chief sources of external financing.

Commercial Bank Loans and Trade Bills   One of the major sources of financing abroad, commercial banks perform essentially the same financing function as domestic banks—a topic discussed in Chapter 16. One subtle difference is that banking practices in Europe allow longer-term loans than are available in the United States. Another is that loans tend to be on an overdraft basis. That is, a company writes a check that overdraws its account and is charged interest on the overdraft. Many of these banks are known as merchant banks, which simply means that they offer a full menu of financial services to business firms. Corresponding to the growth in multinational companies, international banking operations of U.S. banks have accommodated. All the principal cities of the world have branches or offices of a U.S. bank.

In addition to commercial bank loans, discounting trade bills is a common method of short-term financing. Although this method of financing is not used extensively in the United States, it is widely used in Europe to finance both domestic and international trade. More will be said about the instruments involved later in the chapter.

Eurodollar Financing   A **Eurodollar** is defined as a dollar deposit held in a bank outside the United States. Since the late 1950s, an active market has developed for these deposits. Foreign banks and foreign branches of U.S. banks, mostly in Europe, bid actively for Eurodollar deposits, paying interest rates that fluctuate in keeping with supply and demand. The deposits are in large denominations, frequently $100,000 or more, and the banks use them to make dollar loans to quality borrowers. The loans are made at a rate in excess of the deposit rate; the differential varies according to the relative risk of the borrower. Essentially, borrowing and lending Eurodollars is a wholesale operation, with far fewer costs than are usually associated with banking. The market itself is unregulated, so supply and demand forces have free rein.

The Eurodollar market is a major source of short-term financing for the working capital requirements of the multinational company. The interest rate on loans is based on the Eurodollar deposit rate and bears only an indirect relationship to the prime rate. Typically, rates on loans are quoted in terms of the London interbank offered rate, commonly called **LIBOR**. The greater the risk, the greater the spread above LIBOR. A prime borrower will pay about $\frac{1}{2}$ percent over LIBOR for an intermediate term loan. One should realize that LIBOR is more volatile than the U.S. prime rate, owing to the sensitive nature of supply and demand for Eurodollar deposits.

Bond Financing   The Eurocurrency market must be distinguished from the **Eurobond market.** The latter market is more traditional, with underwriters placing securities. Though a bond issue is dominated in a single currency, it is placed in multiple countries. Once issued, it is traded over the counter in multiple countries and by a number of security dealers. A Eurobond is different from a **foreign bond,** where a bond is issued by a foreign government or corporation in a local market. Such a bond is sold in a single country and falls under the security regulations of that country. *Yankee bonds* are issued by non-Americans in the U.S. market; *Samurai bonds* are issued by non-Japanese in the Japanese market. Similarly, there are British *Bulldog bonds,* Spanish *Matador bonds,* and Dutch *Rembrandt bonds,* all issued by nondomestics in those countries. With Eurobonds, foreign bonds, and domestic bonds of different countries, there are numerous differences in terminology, in the way interest is computed, and in features. We do not address these differences, as that would require a separate book.

Many debt issues in the international arena are floating-rate notes (FRNs). These instruments have a variety of features, often involving multiple currencies. Some instruments are indexed to price levels or to commodity prices. Others are linked to an interest rate, such as LIBOR. The reset interval may be annual, semiannual, quarterly, or even more frequent. Still other instruments have option features.

Currency-Option and Multiple-Currency Bonds   Certain bonds provide the holder with the right to choose the currency in which payment is received, usually prior to each coupon or principal payment. Typically this option is confined to two currencies, though it can be more. For example, a 5 percent bond might be issued in Japanese yen with semiannual coupons. The bond might have the option to receive payment in either yen or in pounds sterling. The exchange rate is fixed at the time of issue. The bondholder obviously will choose the payment that is most advantageous at the time. If the pound should appreciate relative to the yen, holders will elect payment in pounds; if it should depreciate, they will choose yen. As with any option, it benefits the holder in being able to choose the stronger currency.

Another option feature is a *conversion option,* which permits an instrument denominated in one currency to be converted into an instrument denominated in another. A Japanese company might issue a U.S. dollar bond, which is convertible into shares of stock quoted in yen. The exchange rate of yen into dollars is fixed at the time of issuance (via the combined conversion/exchange ratio). Thus, two options are involved: (1) a conversion option of the bond into so many shares of common stock (see Chapter 21), and (2) a currency option. If the yen rises in value relative to the U.S. dollar, the investor benefits in being able to exchange a dollar asset, the bond, into a yen asset, common stock.

Bond issues sometimes are floated in multiple currencies. Known as a **"currency cocktail,"** the market value of the bond is less volatile than that of a bond denominated in a single currency. With a **dual currency bond,** interest and principal payments are made in different currencies. For example, a Swiss bond might call for interest payments in Swiss francs and principal payments in U.S. dollars. In this case, the value of the bond is found by (1) discounting the interest payments to present value using a Swiss interest rate and (2) discounting the principal payment at maturity to present value using a dollar interest rate. We see, then, that a variety of currency features are possible.

CURRENCY MARKET HEDGES

Yet another means to hedge currency exposure is through one of several currency markets—forward contracts, futures contracts, currency options, and currency swaps. Let us see how these markets work to protect us.

Forward Exchange Market

In the forward exchange market, one buys a **forward contract** for the exchange of one currency for another at a specific future date and at a specific exchange ratio. This differs from the **spot market,** where currencies are traded for immediate delivery. A forward contract provides assurance of being able to convert into a desired currency at a price set in advance.

> **Currency hedges** include futures and forward contracts, options, and swaps.

Suppose Xicon, a U.S. company, is selling equipment to a Canadian company through its Montreal branch for Can.$1 million with terms of 90 days. Upon payment, Xicon intends to convert the Canadian dollars into U.S. dollars. The spot and 90-day forward rates of U.S. dollars in terms of Canadian dollars were the following:

Spot rate (U.S.$/Can. $)	0.700
90-day forward rate	0.697

The spot rate is simply the current market-determined exchange rate for Canadian dollars. In our example, one Canadian dollar is worth 70 U.S. cents. A foreign currency sells at a **forward discount** if its forward price is less than its spot price. In our example, the Canadian dollar sells at a discount. If the forward price exceeds the spot price, it is said to sell at a **forward premium.**

If Xicon wants to avoid foreign exchange risk, it should sell 1 million Canadian dollars forward 90 days. When it delivers the Canadian dollars 90 days hence, it will receive $697,000. If the spot price stays at 70 cents, of course, Xicon would be better off not having sold Canadian dollars forward. They would be worth $700,000. Instead, it is out $3,000. The annualized cost of this protection is

$$\left(\frac{.003}{.700}\right)\left(\frac{365}{90}\right) = 1.74\%$$

Foreign Currency Exchange

To buy foreign products or services or to invest in other countries, companies and individuals may first have to buy the currency of the country with which they are doing business. Generally, exporters prefer to be paid for their goods and services either in their own currency (Japanese in yen and Germans in marks, for example) or in U.S. dollars, which are accepted all over the world. For example, when the French buy oil from Saudi Arabia, they may pay in U.S. dollars, not French francs or Saudi dinars, even though the United States is not involved in the transaction. The **foreign exchange market**, or "FX" market, is where the buying and selling of different currencies takes place. The price of one currency in terms of another country's currency is called an **exchange rate**.

The market itself is actually a worldwide network of traders, connected by telephone lines and computer screens—there is no central headquarters. The three major centers of trading, which handle more than half of all FX transactions are Great Britain, the United States, and Japan. Transactions in Singapore, Switzerland, Hong Kong, Germany, France, and Australia account for most of the rest of the market. Trading goes on 24 hours a day; at 8 a.m. in London, the trading day is ending in Tokyo, Singapore, and Hong Kong. At 1 p.m. in London, the New York market opens for business. In the afternoon, traders in San Francisco can do business with their colleagues in the Far East.

Forward markets are well suited for hedging transactions exposure.

For stable pairs of currencies, the discount or premium of the forward rate over the spot rate varies from zero to 8 percent on an annualized basis. For somewhat less stable currencies, the discount or premium will be higher. For an unstable currency, the discount may go as high as 20 percent. Much beyond this point of instability, the forward market for the currency ceases to exist. In summary, the forward exchange market allows a company to ensure against devaluation or market-determined declines in value. The forward market is particularly suited for hedging transactions exposure.

Price Quotations Quotations on selected foreign exchanges at a moment in time are shown in Table 25-3. The spot rates reported in the first column indicate the conversion rate into dollars. The exchange-rate quotations contained in such papers as the *Wall Street Journal* and the *New York Times* are for very large transactions. As a traveler, you cannot buy or sell foreign currency at nearly as good a rate. Often you will pay several percent more when you buy, and receive several percent less when you sell. Alas, the hardships of dealing in less than $1 million!

In the first column of the table, the conversion rate of one unit of a foreign currency into U.S. dollars is shown. Near the top, we see that the Australian dollar is worth 0.5982 U.S. dollars. To determine how many Australian dollars $1 will buy, we take the reciprocal, 1/.5982 = A$1.6718. Forward rates are shown for the British pound, the Canadian dollar, the Japanese yen, and the Swiss franc. The relationships between the forward and the spot rates indicate that all of these currencies are at forward rate premiums relative to the U.S. dollar. That is, they are worth more dollars on future delivery than they are now.

The Euro

About halfway down Table 25-3, there appears the **Euro**. This is a common currency for the European Monetary Union (**EMU**), which includes such countries as Ger-

TABLE 25-3
Foreign Exchange Rates, April 10, 2000

	U.S. Dollars to Buy 1 Unit	Units Required to Buy One $
Argentina (peso)	$1.0002	.9998
Australia (dollar)	.5982	1.6718
Brazil (real)	.5739	1.7425
Britain (pound)	1.5845	.6311
30-day forward	1.5847	.6310
90-day forward	1.5850	.6309
180-day forward	1.5862	.6304
Canada (dollar)	.6839	1.4621
30-day forward	.6844	1.4611
90-day forward	.6854	1.4590
180-day forward	.6870	1.4577
Chile (peso)	.0020	505.0500
China (renminbi)	.1208	8.2798
Czech Republic (koruna)	.0265	37.7610
Euro	.9623	1.0392
Hong Kong (dollar)	.1284	7.7870
India (rupee)	.0229	43.6100
Japan (yen)	.0094	106.4400
30-day forward	.0094	105.9100
90-day forward	.0095	104.8100
180-day forward	.0097	103.1100
Malaysia (ringgit)	.2632	3.8000
Mexico (peso)	.1071	9.3330
Saudi Arabia (riyal)	.2666	3.7506
Singapore (dollar)	.5822	1.7175
Switzerland (franc)	.6113	1.6359
30-day forward	.6130	1.6312
90-day forward	.6166	1.6218
180-day forward	.6219	1.6080
Taiwan (dollar)	.0330	30.3000
Thailand (baht)	.0263	38.0350
Venezuela (bolivar)	.0015	671.2500

many, France, Italy, Netherlands, Belgium, Spain, Austria, Portugal, and Ireland. On January 1, 1999, currency conversion rates between the "legacy" currencies and the Euro were established. For a while the legacy currencies traded separate from the Euro but at previously established conversion ratios with each other. As time went on, most currency hedging transactions involving EMU countries occurred in Euros. The Euro was introduced with much fanfare and began trading January 1, 1999, at $1.17 to the Euro, even touching as high as 1.19. However, there was a steady decline in value until parity was breached in late 1999. We see in Table 25-3 that its value in April 2000 was 0.9623 dollars to the Euro.

Currency Futures

Closely related to the use of a forward contract is a **futures contract**. Currency futures markets exist for the major currencies of the world—the Australian dollar, the Canadian dollar, the British pound, the Euro, the Swiss franc, the Japanese yen, the Mexican peso, and, of course, the U.S. dollar. A futures contract is a standardized agreement that calls for delivery of a currency at some specified future date—the third Wednesday of March, June, September, or December.

Many contracts are traded on an exchange, the major one in the U.S. being the Chicago Mercantile Exchange. The clearinghouse of the exchange interposes itself between the buyer and the seller. This means that all transactions are with the clearinghouse, not direct between the two parties. Very few contracts involve actual delivery at expiration. Rather, buyers and sellers of a contract independently take offsetting positions to close out a contract. The seller cancels a contract by buying another contract; the buyer, by selling another contract.

Each day, the futures contract is **marked-to-market** in the sense that it is valued at the closing price. Price movements affect the buyer and seller in opposite ways. Every day there is a winner and a loser, depending on the direction of price movement. The loser must come up with more margin (a small deposit), while the winner can draw off excess margin. Futures contracts are different from forward contracts in this regard; the latter need to be settled only at expiration. Another difference is that only a set number of maturities are available. Finally, futures contracts come only in multiples of standard-size contracts—for example, multiples of 12.5 million yen. Forward contracts can be for almost any size.

The two instruments, however, are used for the same hedging purpose. Suppose Poipu Manufacturing Company will collect a 250,000 Swiss franc receivable 90 days hence. If we now are in the middle of March, it could sell June futures contracts that call for the delivery of Swiss francs for dollars. In this way, the company locks in a certain conversion ratio today. This is the same principle as with a forward contract; the future conversion ratio of one currency for another is set in advance. The futures markets are reasonably liquid, and this affords the company flexibility in reversing a position if conditions should change.

Currency Options

Forward and futures contracts provide a "two-sided" hedge against currency movements. That is, if the currency involved moves in one direction, the forward or futures position offsets it. **Currency options,** in contrast, enable the hedging of "one-sided" risk. Only adverse currency movements are hedged, either with a call option to buy the foreign currency or with a put option to sell it. The holder has the right, but not the obligation, to buy or sell the currency over the life of the contract. If not exercised, of course, the option expires. For this protection, one pays a premium.

There are both options on spot market currencies and options on currency futures contracts. Because currency options are traded on a number of exchanges throughout the world, one is able to trade with relative ease. The use of currency options and their valuation are largely the same as described in Chapter 5 for stock options, so we do not repeat that discussion. The value of the option, and hence the premium paid, depend importantly on exchange-rate volatility.

Currency Swaps

Swaps are
a long-term
hedging vehicle.

Yet another device for shifting risk is the **currency swap.** In a currency swap, two parties exchange debt obligations denominated in different currencies. Each party agrees to pay the other's interest obligation. At maturity, principal amounts are exchanged, usually at a rate of exchange agreed on in advance. An illustration is shown in Fig. 25-4, involving a British company and a U.S. company. The annual interest obligations are 9 percent in British pounds and 8 percent in U.S. dollars. Maturity is 3 years, the exchange rate fixed in the swap is 1.60 dollars to the pound, and the amount of debt involved is 1 million pounds. On an annual basis, the U.S. company pays the British company £90,000 in interest, (£1 million × .09), while the British company pays the U.S. company $128,000, (£1 million × 1.60 × .08). At the end of 3 years, the principal amounts of $1.6 million and £1 million are exchanged back.

Only Differences Are Paid   The exchanges themselves are **notional** in that only cash-flow differences are paid. If the exchange rate in the first year stays at 1.60 dollars to the pound, the British company owes the U.S. company $128,000 in interest, which translates into £80,000. The U.S. company owes the British company £90,000 in interest, but it pays only the difference of £10,000. In the second year, suppose the pound appreciates to 1.70 dollars to the pound. In this situation, the British company owes the U.S. company the equivalent of £75,294, ($128,000/1.70), in interest. The differential the U.S. company now pays is £90,000 − £75,294 = £14,706. If at the end of 3 years the exchange rate were again 1.70 dollars to the pound, the interest differential owed by the U.S. company would again be £14,706. With respect to principal, the British company owes the U.S. company the equivalent of £941,176 ($1.6 million/1.70). As the U.S. company owes £1 million in principal, the principal differential payment it must make is £58,824.

As with an interest-rate swap (see Chapter 22), there is not an actual exchange of principal. If one party defaults, there is no loss of principal per se. There is, however, the opportunity cost associated with currency movements after the

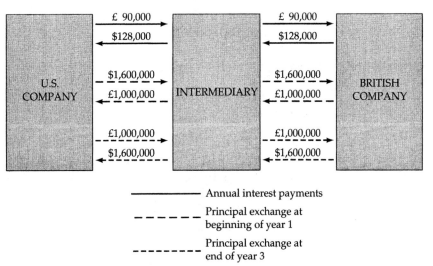

FIGURE 25-4

Illustration of a currency swap (fixed rate to fixed rate)

swap's initiation. These movements affect both interest and principal payments, as we have seen. In this respect, currency swaps are more risky than interest-rate swaps, where the exposure is only to interest. The example just cited is a fixed rate–to–fixed rate exchange of borrowings.

Currency/Interest-Rate Swaps Currency swaps can be, and often are, combined with interest-rate swaps. In Chapter 22, we examined the mechanics and valuation of interest-rate swaps. With a combined swap, there is an exchange of fixed-rate for floating-rate payments where the two payments are in different currencies. For example, a Japanese company might swap a 3-year, fixed-rate Euro-currency–denominated liability for a 3-year British pound liability with the floating rate tied to LIBOR. From the standpoint of the Japanese company, there is a combination Euro/British pound currency swap, together with a fixed/floating interest-rate swap. A number of extensions are possible: more than two currencies, options, and other features. As can be imagined, things get complicated rather quickly.

Hedging Exposure: A Summing Up

We have seen that there are a number of ways that exchange-rate risk exposure can be hedged. The place to begin is to determine if your company has a natural hedge. If it does, then to lay on a financing or a currency hedge actually increases your exposure. That is, you will have undone a natural hedge that your company has by virtue of the business it does abroad and the sourcing of such business. As a result, you will have created a net risk exposure where little or none existed before. That is a bad thing to do. Tell us you won't do that!

So the first step is to estimate your net, residual exchange-rate risk exposure after taking account of any natural hedges that your company may have. If you have a net exposure, then the question is whether you wish to hedge it and how. Cash management and intracompany account adjustments are only temporary measures, and they are limited in the magnitude of their effect. Financing hedges provide a means to hedge on a longer-term basis, as do currency swaps. Currency forward, futures, and options contracts with reasonable pricing usually are available only out 3 years or so. While longer-term contracts can be arranged through investment banks, called over-the-counter contracts, the premium paid is often large. How you hedge your net exposure, if at all, should be a function of the suitability of the hedging device and its cost, topics considered in the sections above.

SHOULD EXPOSURE BE MANAGED?

In the previous sections, we have looked at ways to manage a company's exposure to exchange-rate fluctuations. If international product and financial markets were perfect and complete, it would not be optimal for a company to engage in any of the defensive tactics just considered. The transaction costs of such moves would be a net drain to suppliers of capital. Instantaneous price adjustments would occur in both markets, and suppliers of capital would not be concerned with the variability of cash flows and earnings of an individual firm. It is only when we admit to imperfections and incompleteness in such markets that a case can be made for the various hedging strategies discussed.

Hedging and Security-Investment Risk When it comes to international investments, certain scholars argue that one should always hedge currency exposure.

The idea is that one can achieve substantial reductions in risk with no significant loss of expected return.[3] The average expected return on a currency hedge is zero, and transaction costs are said to be minimal. Seemingly this is a compelling case for 100 percent hedging. However, Black makes a powerful theoretical argument for bearing some unhedged currency risk.[4] Moreover, empirical evidence on global stock and bond portfolios suggests that complete, 100 percent hedging does not produce superior investment results. Over the longer run, hedging tends to undo purchasing power parity, with the result that portfolio return variance is increased.[5]

Should a Corporation Self-Insure?

Back to corporate finance. A large company with numerous foreign transactions may wish to engage in self-insurance and not hedge currency fluctuations. However, costs of bankruptcy and agency costs make extensive exposure, particularly for the smaller firm, unwise. For reasons of imperfections and incompleteness in international product and financial markets, then, most companies manage their currency-risk exposure. Certainly, a degree of self-insurance occurs, but few companies are willing to risk everything on future exchange rates. The real issue is not so much whether a company manages currency-risk exposure or not, but the degree of its management. It may well overemphasize such management in an attempt to ensure managerial survival when shareholders would be better off with a degree of self-insurance.

MACRO FACTORS GOVERNING EXCHANGE-RATE BEHAVIOR

Fluctuations in exchange rates are continual and often defy explanation, at least in the short run. In the longer run, however, there are linkages between domestic and foreign inflation and between interest rates and foreign exchange rates. These relationships provide an underlying theory of international product and financial market equilibrium. We first present the theory, which assumes free trade and an absence of imperfections, and then touch on the empirical evidence.

The Law of One Price

Simply put, the **law of one price** says that a commodity will sell for the same price regardless of where it is purchased. More formally, for a single good

$$P^{FC} = P^{\$} \times S^{FC/\$} \tag{25-2}$$

where P^{FC} is the price of the good in a foreign currency, $P^{\$}$ is the price of the good in the United States, and $S^{FC/\$}$ is the spot exchange rate of the foreign currency per dollar.

If it is cheaper to buy wheat from Argentina than it is from a U.S. producer, after transportation costs and after adjusting the Argentine price for the exchange rate, a rational U.S. buyer will purchase Argentine wheat. This action, together with commodity arbitrage, will cause the Argentine wheat price to rise relative to

---

[3]This argument is associated with Andre F. Perold and Evan C. Schulman, "The Free Lunch in Currency Hedging: Implications for Investment Policy and Performance Standards," *Financial Analysts Journal*, 44 (May–June 1988), 45–50.

[4]Fischer Black, "Equilibrium Exchange Rate Hedging," *Journal of Finance*, 45 (July 1990), 899–908.

[5]Kenneth A. Froot, "Currency Hedging over Long Horizons," working paper, National Bureau of Economic Research (May 1993).

the U.S. price and, perhaps, for the peso exchange rate to strengthen. The combination of rising Argentine wheat prices and a changing peso value raises the dollar price of Argentine wheat to the U.S. buyer. Theory would have it that these transactions would continue until the dollar cost of wheat was the same. At that point, the purchaser would be indifferent between U.S. and Argentine wheat. For that matter, an Argentine buyer of wheat also would be indifferent. For this to hold, of course, transportation and transaction costs must be zero, and there must be no impediments to trade.

Purchasing Power Parity

Purchasing power parity works through differences in inflation between countries.

The law of one price is really a way to express **purchasing power parity (PPP)**. Invoking the law of one price, PPP says that the rate of exchange between currencies of two countries is directly related to the differential rate of inflation between them. Any change in the differential rate of inflation is offset by an opposite movement in the spot exchange rate. From Eq. (25-2), PPP implies

$$1 + P^{\wedge FC} = [1 + P^{\wedge \$}] \times [1 + S^{\wedge (FC/\$)}] \tag{25-3}$$

where the $^\wedge$ represents the rate of change in the price level or in the exchange rate. Rearranging yields

$$\frac{1 + P^{\wedge FC}}{1 + P^{\wedge \$}} = 1 + S^{\wedge (FC/\$)} \tag{25-4}$$

If the annual rate of inflation is 2 percent in the United States and 3 percent in Canada, the implication is

$$\frac{1.03}{1.02} = 1.0098$$

or that the Canadian dollar should depreciate in value relative to the U.S. dollar by approximately 1 percent on an annualized basis. If instead the rate of inflation in the U.S. were 4 percent, we would have

$$\frac{1.03}{1.04} = .9904$$

which means the U.S. dollar should decline in value, relative to the Canadian dollar, by approximately 1 percent a year.

As an approximation to Eq. (25-4), many people use

$$P^{\wedge FC} - P^{\wedge \$} = S^{\wedge (FC/\$)} \tag{25-5}$$

in which the exchange rate change is directly related to the inflation differential. In the context of this formula, purchasing power parity is illustrated in Fig. 25-5. (Eq. 25-5) has been used in an expectational sense. For example, suppose we expect inflation in the United States to exceed the average for the European Monetary Union by 2 percent and that the spot exchange rate now is 1.10 dollars to the Euro. At the end of 1 year, PPP would imply the exchange rate would be 1.10(1.02)

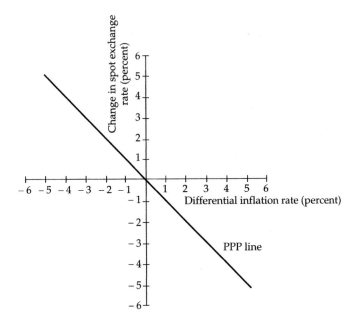

FIGURE 25-5

Approximation of purchasing power parity (PPP) between two countries

= 1.122 $/€. Again, remember that this is only an approximation. For greater accuracy, we should use Eq. (25-4).

How closely a country's exchange rate corresponds to purchasing power parity depends on the price elasticity of exports and imports. To the extent exports are traded in world competitive markets, there usually is close conformity to PPP. Commodities and fabricated products like steel and clothing are highly price sensitive. In general, products in mature industries conform more closely to PPP than products in newer industries with emerging technology. To the extent a country's inflation is dominated by nontraded goods, like services, there tends to be less conformity to PPP. We know also that PPP does not work well when a country intervenes in the exchange-rate market, either propping up its currency or keeping it artificially low.

Interest-Rate Parity

Our last concept concerns the interest-rate differential between two countries. **Interest-rate parity** suggests that if interest rates are higher in one country than they are in another, the former's currency will sell at a discount in the forward market. Expressed differently, interest-rate differentials and forward-spot exchange-rate differentials are offsetting. How does it work? The starting point is the relationship between nominal interest rates and inflation. The **Fisher effect** implies that the nominal rate of interest is comprised of the real rate plus the rate of inflation expected to prevail over the life of the instrument. Thus

$$r = R + P^\wedge \tag{25-6}$$

where r is the nominal rate, R the inflation-adjusted real rate of interest, and $P^\wedge$ the rate of inflation per annum expected over the life of the instrument.[6]

---

[6]Mathematically, the correct expression is $r = R + P^\wedge + RP^\wedge$. Unless the inflation rate is large, most ignore the cross product term.

International Fisher Effect In an international context, sometimes called the *international Fisher effect*, the equation suggests that differences in interest rates between two countries serve as a proxy for differences in expected inflation. For example, if the nominal interest rate were 6 percent in the United States but 8 percent in Australia, the expected differential in inflation would be 2 percent. That is, inflation in Australia is expected to be 2 percent higher than in the United States. Does this hold exactly? Though there is disagreement as to the precise relationship between nominal interest rates and inflation, most people feel that expected inflation for a country has an important effect on interest rates in that country. The more open the capital markets, the closer the conformity to an international Fisher effect.

Remember from purchasing power parity that exchange rates were directly tied to the inflation differential between two countries. Through the common link of inflation differentials, it figures that exchange-rate differentials should be related to interest-rate differentials. The mechanism by which this manifests itself is the difference between the spot rate of exchange and the forward exchange rate.

With interest-rate parity, forward discounts and premiums are driven by differences in interest rates.

IRP Illustration To illustrate interest-rate parity, consider the relationship between the U.S. dollar ($) and the British pound (£) both now and 90 days in the future; the theorem suggests that

$$\frac{F(£/\$)}{S(£/\$)} = \frac{1 + r_£}{1 + r_\$}$$

where $F(£/\$)$ is the current 90-day forward exchange rate in pounds per dollar, $S(£/\$)$ is the current spot exchange rate in pounds per dollar, $r_£$ is the nominal British interbank Euromarket interest rate, expressed in terms of the 90-day return, and $r_\$$ is the nominal U.S. interbank Euromarket interest rate, expressed in terms of the 90-day return.

If the nominal interest rate in Britain were 8 percent and nominal U.S. rate were 6 percent, these annualized rates translate into 3-month rates of 2 percent and 1.5 percent, respectively. If the current spot rate were .625 pounds per dollar, we would have

$$\frac{F(£/\$)}{.625} = \frac{1.02}{1.015}$$

Solving for the implied forward rate

$$1.015F(£/\$) = .6375$$
$$F(£/\$) = .6281$$

Thus, the implied forward rate is .6281 British pounds per U.S. dollar. The pound is at a forward rate discount from the spot rate of .625 pounds to the dollar. That is, a pound is worth less in terms of dollars in the forward market, $1/.6281 = \$1.592$, than it is in the spot market, $1/.625 = \$1.60$. The discount is $(.6281 - .625)/.625 = .005$. With interest-rate parity, the discount must equal the relative difference in interest rates, and indeed, this is the case, for $(1.02 - 1.015)/1.015 = .005$. If the interest rate in Britain were less than that in the United States, the implied forward rate in our example would be less than the spot rate. In this case, the British pound is at a forward premium. For example, if the U.S. interest rate (annualized) were 7 percent and the British interest rate 5 percent, the implied 3-month forward rate for British pounds would be

$$\frac{F(£/\$)}{.625} = \frac{1.0125}{1.0175}$$

Solving for $F(£/\$)$, we have

$$1.0175F(£/\$) = .6328$$
$$F(£/\$) = .6219$$

Therefore, the forward rate is at a premium in the sense that it is worth more in terms of dollars in the forward market than it is in the spot market.

Covered Interest Arbitrage

If interest-rate parity did not occur, presumably arbitragers would be alert to the opportunity for profit. In our first example, had the British pound 90-day forward been .634 instead of .6281, an arbitrager, recognizing this deviation, would borrow in Britain at 8 percent interest for 3 months. If the amount involved were £100,000, the amount due at the end of 3 months would be £100,000(1.02) = £102,000. Upon receipt of the pound loan, the arbitrager should convert the £100,000 into dollars in the spot market. At an exchange rate of .625, he or she would have $160,000. This amount should be invested at 6 percent for 3 months. At the end of 3 months, the arbitrager would have $160,000(1.015) = $162,400. To cover the loan's repayment in pounds, the arbitrager should buy British pounds 3 months forward. He or she would need £102,000 to repay the loan. At a 3-month forward rate of .634 pounds per U.S. dollar, it would require £102,000/.634 = $160,883.

In this series of transactions, which is known as **covered interest arbitrage,** the profit is equal to the receipt of funds from investment less the repayment of the loan. For our example

$$\text{Arbitrage profit} = \$162,400 - \$160,883 = \$1,517$$

Arbitrage actions of this sort increase the demand for British pounds in the forward market and increase the supply of dollars. Moreover, borrowing in Britain will tend to increase interest rates there, while lending in the United States will lower American rates. The combination of these forces will work to reduce the interest-rate differential as well as reduce the discount for the British pound forward exchange rate. Arbitrage actions will continue until interest-rate parity is established and there is zero profit potential on covered interest arbitrage.

Interest-Rate Parity Approximation

On an annualized basis, interest-rate parity can be expressed as

$$\frac{F^{FC/\$} - S^{FC/\$}}{S^{FC/\$}} = r_{FC} - r_{\$} \tag{25-7}$$

where the forward rate and the two interest rates are for 1-year contracts/instruments. Using our earlier example for British pounds, where the current spot exchange rate is .625 and U.K. and U.S. interest rates are 8 percent and 6 percent, respectively, the implied discount in the 1-year forward market is 2 percent of the spot rate. This means that the forward rate is greater than the spot rate by 2 percent; more pounds per dollar in the future implies a weaker pound over time. The absolute, as opposed to the percentage, discount using Eq. (25-7) is

$$R^{£/\$} - S^{£/\$} = (.08 - .06).625 = .0125$$

Thus, the implied forward rate of pounds per dollar 1 year hence is .625+ .0125 = .6375.

This simple formula tells us that interest-rate differentials are a proxy for forward exchange-rate/spot exchange-rate differentials, and vice versa. Eq. 25-7 is expressed graphically in Fig. 25-6. The upper right-hand quadrant represents a foreign currency discount because the forward exchange rate of the foreign currency per dollar exceeds the spot rate. That is, the foreign currency is expected to depreciate in terms of dollars. In contrast, the lower left-hand quadrant represents a foreign currency premium, for the forward exchange rate is less than the spot rate.

At a moment in time, covered interest-rate parity tends to prevail for the United States, the European Monetary Union, Britain, Switzerland, Japan and a few other advanced industrial countries. That is, there is a precise offsetting relationship between differences in interest rates between two countries and the forward exchange rate relative to the spot rate. The difference between the forward and spot exchange rates, and whether one country's currency is at a premium or a discount relative to the other, are driven by differences in short-term interest rates. In turn, these differences are determined primarily by actions of central banks. Whichever country has the lower interest rate, that currency will trade at a forward-rate premium relative to the other country's currency.

Empirical Evidence Concerning IRP

Does this mean that IRP prevails between all sets of currencies at all times? For European and other currencies, where there is largely an absence of imperfections, IRP generally holds within the limits of transaction costs. While the relationship is strong for short-term interest rates, it weakens for longer maturities. For countries with restrictions on exchange, and tax and other imperfections, IRP is not expected because covered interest arbitrage is not possible.

Looking at IRP another way, known as uncovered interest rate parity, the question is whether the change in the actual exchange rate between two countries equals that previously implied by the interest-rate differential. In other words, does an unbiased expectations hypothesis hold? Evidence through the early 1990s rejected this equality.

High-interest-rate countries provided a higher net return, taking account of exchange-rate changes, than did low-interest-rate countries.[7] Although the currency of a high-interest-rate country may depreciate over time, it was not enough

---

[7]Geert Bekaert and Robert J. Hodrick, "On Biases in the Measurement of Foreign Exchange Risk Premiums," *Journal of International Money and Finance,* 12 (1993), 115–38; and Piet Sercu and Raman Uppal, *International Financial Markets and the Firm* (Cincinnati, OH: South-Western, 1995), Chap. 14. For a review of the evidence, see Charles Engel, "The Forward Discount Anomaly and the Risk Premium: A Survey of Recent Evidence," working paper, National Bureau of Economic Research (October 1995).

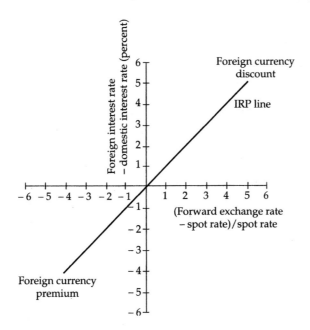

FIGURE 25-6
Approximation of
interest-rate parity
between two
countries (IRP)

to offset the yield advantage over the low-interest-rate country. However, the evidence from the mid-1990s on was not so clear. During this timeframe the equality more nearly prevailed.

STRUCTURING INTERNATIONAL TRADE TRANSACTIONS

Foreign trade differs from domestic trade with respect to the instruments and documents employed. Most domestic sales are on open-account credit; the customer is billed and has so many days to pay. In international trade, sellers are seldom able to obtain as accurate or as thorough credit information on potential buyers as they are in domestic sales. Communication is more cumbersome, and transportation of the goods is slower and less certain. Moreover, the channels for legal settlement in cases of default are more complicated and more costly to pursue. For these reasons, procedures for international trade differ from those for domestic trade. There are three key documents: an order to pay, or draft; a bill of lading, which involves the physical movement of the goods; and a letter of credit, which guarantees the creditworthiness of the buyer. We examine each in turn. This is followed by other means for facilitating trade: countertrading, factoring, and forfaiting.

A number of devices
facilitate trade transactions: trade drafts, bills of lading, letters of credit, countertrading, factoring, and forfaiting.

The Trade Draft

The international draft, sometimes called a bill of exchange, is simply a written statement by the exporter ordering the importer to pay a specific amount of money at a specific time. Although the word *order* may seem harsh, it is the customary way of doing business internationally. The draft may be either a **sight draft** or a **time draft**. A sight draft is payable on presentation to the party to whom the draft is addressed. This party is known as the *drawee*. If the drawee, or importer, does not pay the amount specified on presentation of the draft, he or she defaults, and redressment is achieved through the letter of credit arrangement to be discussed later. A time draft is not payable until a specified future date. For example, a time draft might be payable 90 days after sight, an example of which is shown in Fig. 25-7.

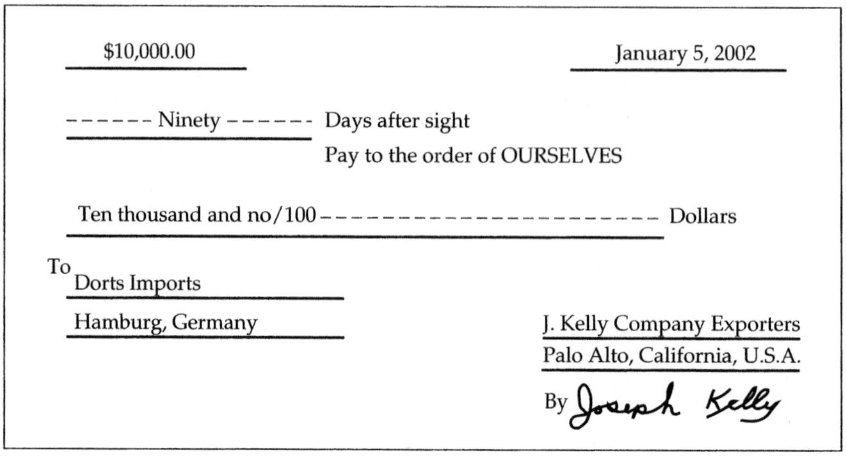

$10,000.00	January 5, 2002

- - - - - - Ninety - - - - - - Days after sight

Pay to the order of OURSELVES

Ten thousand and no/100 - Dollars

To
Dorts Imports

Hamburg, Germany

J. Kelly Company Exporters
Palo Alto, California, U.S.A.

By *Joseph Kelly*

FIGURE 25-7
Time draft

Several features should be noted about the draft. First, it is an unconditional order in writing signed by the drawer, the exporter. It specifies an exact amount of money that the drawee, the importer, must pay. Finally, it specifies an exact interval after sight at which time this amount must be paid. Upon presentation of the time draft to the drawee, it is accepted. The **acceptance** can be by either the drawee or a bank. If the drawee accepts the draft, he or she acknowledges in writing on the back of the draft the obligation to pay the amount specified 90 days hence. The draft then is known as a trade acceptance. If a bank accepts the draft, it is known as a **bankers' acceptance.** The bank accepts responsibility for payment and thereby substitutes its creditworthiness for that of the drawee.

If the bank is large and well known—and most banks accepting drafts are—the instrument becomes highly marketable upon acceptance. As a result, the drawer, or exporter, does not have to hold the draft until the due date; he or she can sell it in the market. In fact, an active market exists for bankers' acceptances of well-known banks. A 90-day draft for $10,000 may be accepted by a well-known bank. Say that 90-day interest rates in the bankers' acceptance market are 8 percent. The drawer then could sell the draft to an investor for $9,800, or $10,000 − [$10,000 × .08(90/360)]. At the end of 90 days, the investor would present the acceptance to the accepting bank for payment and would receive $10,000. Thus, the existence of a strong secondary market for bankers' acceptances has facilitated international trade by providing liquidity to the exporter.

Bills of Lading

A **bill of lading** is a shipping document used in the transportation of goods from the exporter to the importer. It has several functions. First, it serves as a receipt from the transportation company to the exporter, showing that specified goods have been received. Second, it serves as a contract between the transportation company and the exporter to ship the goods and deliver them to a specific party at a specific point of destination. Finally, the bill of lading can serve as a document of title. It gives the holder title to the goods. The importer cannot take title until receipt of the bill of lading from the transportation company or its agent. This bill will not be released until the importer satisfies all the conditions of the draft.

The bill of lading accompanies the draft, and the procedures by which the two are handled are well established. Banks and other institutions able to handle these documents efficiently exist in virtually every country. Moreover, the procedures by which goods are transferred internationally are well grounded in international law. These procedures allow an exporter in one country to sell goods to an unknown importer in another and not release possession of the goods until paid, if there is a sight draft, or until the obligation is acknowledged, if there is a time draft.

Letters of Credit

A commercial **letter of credit** is issued by a bank on behalf of the importer. In the document, the bank agrees to honor a draft drawn on the importer, provided the bill of lading and other details are in order. In essence, the bank substitutes its credit for that of the importer. Obviously, the local bank will not issue a letter of credit unless it feels the importer is creditworthy and will pay the draft. The letter of credit arrangement pretty much eliminates the exporter's risk in selling goods to an unknown importer in another country.

Illustration of a Confirmed Letter   The arrangement is strengthened further if a bank in the exporter's country *confirms* the letter of credit. A New York exporter wishes to ship goods to a Brazilian importer located in Rio de Janeiro. The importer's bank in Rio regards the importer as a sound credit risk and is willing to issue a letter of credit guaranteeing payment for the goods when they are received. Thus, the Rio bank substitutes its credit for that of the importer. The contract is now between the Rio bank and the beneficiary of the letter of credit, the New York exporter. The exporter may wish to work through her bank, because she has little knowledge of the Rio bank. She asks her New York bank to confirm the Rio bank's letter of credit. If the New York bank is satisfied with the creditworthiness of the Rio bank, it will agree to do so. When it does, it obligates itself to honor drafts drawn in keeping with the letter of credit arrangement.

Thus, when the exporter ships the goods, she draws a draft in accordance with the terms of the letter of credit arrangement. She presents the draft to her New York bank and the bank pays her the amount designated, assuming all the conditions of shipment are met. As a result of this arrangement, the exporter has her money, with no worries about payment. The New York bank then forwards the draft and other documents to the Rio bank. Upon affirming that the goods have been shipped in a proper manner, the Rio bank honors the draft and pays the New York bank. In turn, it goes to the Brazilian importer and collects from him once the goods have arrived in Rio and are delivered.

Facilitation of Trade   From the description, it is easy to see why the letter of credit facilitates international trade. Rather than extending credit directly to an importer, the exporter relies on one or more banks, and their creditworthiness is substituted for that of the importer. The letter itself can be either *irrevocable* or *revocable*, but drafts drawn under an irrevocable letter must be honored by the issuing bank. This obligation can be neither canceled nor modified without the consent of all parties. On the other hand, a revocable letter of credit can be canceled or amended by the issuing bank. A revocable letter specifies an arrangement for payment but is no guarantee that the draft will be paid. Most letters of credit are irrevocable, and the process described assumes an irrevocable letter.

The three documents described—the draft, the bill of lading, and the letter of credit—are required in most international transactions. Established procedures exist for doing business on this basis. Together, they afford the exporter protection in selling goods to unknown importers in other countries. They also give the importer assurance that the goods will be shipped and delivered in a proper manner.

Countertrading

In addition to the documents used to facilitate a standard transaction, there are more customized means for financing trade. One method is the **countertrade.** A countertrade agreement is where the selling party accepts payment in the form of goods as opposed to currency. When exchange restrictions and other difficulties preclude payment in hard currencies, such as dollars and yen, it may be necessary to accept goods instead. These goods may be produced in the country involved, but this need not be the case. Countertrading is nothing more than bartering. One needs to be mindful that there are risks in accepting goods in lieu of a hard currency. Quality and standardization on receipt may differ from what was promised. There may be volatility in prices, if indeed a viable market exists at all. Although the method involves risk, countertrade associations and consultants, together with other infrastructure, have developed to facilitate this means of trade.

Factoring

Factoring exports is like factoring domestic receivables, which we took up in Chapter 16. The factor assumes the credit risk, so the exporter is assured of being paid. The typical fee is around 2 percent of the value of the overseas shipment. Before the receivable is collected, a cash advance is possible for upward to 90 percent of the shipment's value. For such an advance, the exporter pays interest, and this is over and above the factor's fee. Most factors will not do business with an exporter unless the volume is reasonably large, say at least $2 million in annual transactions. Also, the factor can reject certain accounts that it deems too risky. For accounts that are accepted, the main advantage to the exporter is the peace of mind that comes in entrusting collections to a factor with international contacts and experience.

Forfaiting

Forfaiting is a means of financing trade which resembles factoring. An exporter who is owed money evidenced by a longer-term note, as opposed to a receivable, sells the note to a financial institution at a discount. The discount reflects the length of time the note has to maturity as well as the credit risk of its drawer. Usually the note is for 6 months or longer and involves larger transactions. A financial institution would not engage in forfaiting a $9,600 note but might if it were for $180,000. In addition to an interest rate embraced in the discount, the financial institution often charges a commitment fee. Forfaiting brokers exist for arranging deals, but one can go directly to a financial institution. One advantage to forfaiting is that it is relatively quick to arrange, often taking no more than 2 weeks.

 Summary

The financial manager is increasingly becoming involved in global product and financial markets. The globalization movement means that investment and financing decisions must be made in an international arena. Capital budgeting, for example, embraces estimates of future rates of exchange between two currencies. Owing to market segmentation, foreign projects sometimes afford risk-reduction properties that are not available in domestic projects. If capital markets are partially segmented, diversification of stock internationally may reduce portfolio risk further than can be accomplished through domestic stock diversification. Expansion abroad is undertaken to go into new markets, acquire less costly production facilities, and secure raw materials. A number of factors make foreign investment different from domestic investment. Taxation is different, and there are risks present in political conditions.

A company faces three types of risk in its foreign operations: translation exposure, transactions exposure, and economic exposure. *Translation exposure* is the change in accounting income and balance sheet statements caused by changes in exchange rates. *Transactions exposure* relates to settling a particular transaction, like open account credit, at one exchange rate when the obligation was booked at another. *Economic exposure* has to do with the impact of changing exchange rates on the existing balance sheet of a foreign subsidiary and on the expected future repatriated cash flows. Two frameworks were presented for measuring the degree of economic exposure. The first aggregated the individual exposure coefficients for all balance sheet items.

The second measured the degree of net exposure for expected future cash flows. This was net of any natural hedge, where local currency margins adjust naturally to offset a change in exchange rates. A natural hedge depends on the degree to which prices and costs are globally determined or domestically determined. A relationship can be plotted between the value of repatriated cash flows and the exchange rate. The direction of the line and its steepness tells us whether or not we are hurt if the foreign currency appreciates (depreciates) in value and the degree of exposure. Net exposure is that which remains after any natural hedge.

A company can protect itself against any net exposure by several devices. If the exposure is short-term in nature, it can adjust intracompany accounts in what is known as an operating hedge. For longer-term exposure, it can undertake a hedge by financing in different currencies. The major sources of international financing are commercial banks, discounted trade drafts, Eurodollar loans, and international bonds. The last includes Eurobonds, foreign bonds, floating-rate notes linked to LIBOR, currency-option bonds, and multiple-currency bonds.

Finally, there are currency hedges, which include forward contracts, futures contracts, currency options, and currency swaps. For the first, one buys a forward contract for the exchange of one currency for another at a specific future date and at an exchange ratio set in advance. For this protection, there is a cost that is determined by the difference in the forward and spot exchange rates. Currency futures contracts are like forward contracts in function, but there are differences in settlement and other features. Currency options afford protection against "one-sided" risk. Finally, currency swaps are an important longer-term risk-shifting device. Here, two parties exchange debt obligations in different currencies. Often currency swaps are combined with interest-rate swaps.

Certain underlying theories provide a better understanding of the relationship between inflation, interest rates, and exchange rates. Purchasing power parity is the idea that a basket of goods should sell at the same price internationally, after factoring into account exchange rates. Relative inflation has an important influence on exchange rates and on relative interest rates. Interest-rate parity suggests that the difference between forward and spot currency exchange rates can be explained by differences in nominal interest rates between two countries.

Three principal documents are involved in international trade. The *draft* is an order by the exporter to the importer to pay a specified amount of money either upon presentation of the draft or a certain number of days after presentation. A *bill of lading* is a shipping document that can serve as a receipt, as a shipping contract, and as title to the goods involved. A *letter of credit* is an agreement by a bank to honor a draft drawn on the importer. It greatly reduces the risk to the exporter and may be confirmed by another bank. These three documents greatly facilitate international trade. Trade may be financed by countertrading, factoring, and forfaiting.

Appendix: Translation Exposure

Translation exposure relates to the accounting treatment of changes in exchange rates. Statement No. 52 of the Financial Accounting Standards Board deals with the translation of foreign currency changes on the balance sheet and income statement. Under these accounting rules, a U.S. company must determine a functional currency for each of its foreign subsidiaries. If the subsidiary is a stand-alone operation that is integrated within a particular country, the functional currency may be the local currency; otherwise, it is the dollar.[8] Where high inflation occurs (over 100 percent per annum), the functional currency must be the dollar regardless of the conditions given.

The functional currency used is important because it determines the translation process. If the local currency is used, all assets and liabilities are translated at the **current rate of exchange.** Moreover, translation gains or losses are not reflected in the income statement, but rather are recognized in owners' equity as a translation adjustment. The fact that such adjustments do not affect accounting income is appealing to many companies. If the functional currency is the dollar, however, this is not the case. Gains or losses are reflected in the income statement of the parent company using what is known as the **temporal method.** In general, the use of the dollar as the functional currency results in greater fluctuations in accounting income, but in smaller fluctuations in balance sheet items than does the use of the local currency. Let us examine the differences.

Differences in Methods

With the dollar as the functional currency, balance sheet and income statement items are categorized as to historical exchange rates or as to current exchange rates. Cash, receivables, liabilities, sales, expenses, and taxes are translated using current exchange rates, whereas inventories, plant and equipment, equity, cost of goods sold, and depreciation are translated at

the historical exchange rates existing at the time of the transactions. This differs from the situation where the local currency is used as the functional currency; here all items are translated at current exchange rates.

To illustrate, a company we shall call Richmond Precision Instruments has a subsidiary in the Kingdom of Spamany where the currency is the liso. At the first of the year, the exchange rate is 8 lisos to the dollar, and that rate has prevailed for many years. During 20x2, however, the liso declines steadily in value to 10 lisos to the dollar at year end. The average exchange rate during the year is 9 lisos to the dollar. Table 25A-1 shows the balance sheet and the income statement for the foreign subsidiary at the beginning and at the end of the year and the effect of the method of translation.

Taking the balance sheet first, the 12/31/x1 date serves as a base, and the dollar statement in column 3 is simply the liso amounts shown in column 1 divided by the exchange rate of 8 lisos to the dollar. For the two separate dollar statements at 12/31/x2, shown in the last two columns, we see that cash, receivables, current liabilities, and long-term debt are the same for both methods of accounting. These amounts are determined on a current exchange rate basis by dividing the amounts shown in column 2 by the exchange rate at year end of 10 lisos to the dollar. For the local functional currency statement, column 4, inventories and fixed assets are determined in the same manner, that is, by use of the current exchange rate. For the dollar functional currency statement, inventories and fixed assets are valued using historical exchange rates. Because cost of goods sold equals beginning inventory, the ending inventory is purchased throughout the year. Assuming steady purchases, we divide the ending liso amount by the average exchange rate (9 to 1) to obtain $500,000. Using historical exchange rates again,

---

[8]Various criteria are used to determine if the foreign subsidiary is self-contained, including whether sales, labor, other costs, and debt are primarily dominated in the local currency. Also, the nature and magnitude of intercompany transactions are important. Under certain circumstances, it is possible for a foreign currency other than the local one to be used.

TABLE 25A-1
Foreign Subsidiary, Richmond Precision Instruments

| | In Lisos | | In Dollars | | |
| | | | | Local Functional Currency | Dollar Functional Currency |
	12/31/x1	12/31/x2	12/31/x1	12/31/x2	12/31/x2
Balance Sheet (in thousands)					
Cash	L 600	L 1,000	$ 75	$ 100	$ 100
Receivables	2,000	2,600	250	260	260
Inventories (FIFO)	4,000	4,500	500	450	500
Current assets	6,600	8,100	825	810	860
Net fixed assets	5,000	4,400	625	440	550
Total	L 11,600	L 12,500	$1,450	$1,250	$1,410
Current liabilities	L 3,000	L 3,300	$ 375	$ 330	$ 330
Long-term debt	2,000	1,600	250	160	160
Common stock	600	600	75	75	75
Retained earnings	6,000	7,000	750	861	845
Accumulated translation adjustment				−176	
Total	L 11,600	L 12,500	$1,450	$1,250	$1,410
Income Statement (in thousands with rounding)					
Sales		L 10,000		$1,111	$1,111
Cost of goods sold		4,000		444	500
Depreciation		600		67	75
Expenses		3,500		389	389
Taxes		900		100	100
Operating income		L 1,000		$ 111	$ 47
Translation gain					48
Net income		L 1,000		$ 111	$ 95
Translation adjustment = −$176					

net fixed assets are determined by dividing the liso amount at year end by the earlier 8 lisos to the dollar exchange rate. The common stock account is carried at the base amount under both methods.

Finally, the change in retained earnings is a residual. (We defer until the discussion of the income statement the accumulated translation adjustment item.) Because of the upward adjustment in inventories and fixed assets, total assets are higher with the dollar functional currency (temporal method) than they are with the local functional currency (current method). The opposite would occur in our example if the liso increased in value relative to the dollar. We see that there is substantially more change in total assets when a local functional currency is used than when a dollar functional currency is employed.

The opposite occurs for the income statement. In our example, sales are adjusted by the average exchange rate that prevailed during the year (9 to 1) for both accounting methods. For column 4, local functional currency, all cost and expense items are adjusted by this exchange rate. For the last column, dollar functional currency, cost of goods sold, and depreciation are translated at historical exchange rates (8 to 1), whereas the other items are translated at the current average rate (9 to 1). We see that operating income and net income are larger when the local functional currency is used than when the functional currency is the dollar. For the latter method, the translation gain is factored in, so that net income agrees with the change in retained earnings from 12/31/x1 to 12/31/x2. We see that this change is $845 − $750 = $95. In contrast, when the functional currency is local, the translation adjustment occurs after the income figure of $111. The adjustment is that amount, −$176, that, together with net income, brings the liability and net worth part of the balance sheet into balance. This amount then is added to the sum of past translation adjustments to obtain the new accumulated translation adjustment figure that appears on the balance sheet. As we assume past adjustments total zero, this item becomes −$176.

Thus, the translation adjustments for the two methods are in opposite directions. Should the liso increase in value relative to the dollar, the effect would be the reverse of that illustrated: Operating income would be higher if the functional currency were the dollar.

Implications

Because translation gains or losses are not reflected directly on the income statement, reported operating income tends to fluctuate less when the functional currency is local than when it is the dollar. However, the variability of balance sheet items is increased, owing to the translation of all items by the current exchange rate. Because many corporate executives are concerned with accounting income, FASB No. 52 is popular, as long as a subsidiary qualifies for a local functional currency. However, this accounting method also has its drawbacks. For one thing, it distorts the balance sheet and the historical cost numbers. Moreover, it may cause return on asset calculations and other measures of return to be meaningless. It is simply inconsistent with the nature of other accounting rules, which are based on historical costs. Most financial ratios are affected by the functional currency employed, so the financial analyst must be careful when foreign subsidiaries account for a sizable portion of a company's operations. The method also has been criticized for not allowing proper assessment of the parent's likely future cash flows. In summary, there is no universally satisfactory way to treat foreign currency translations, and the accounting profession continues to struggle with the issue.

Self-Correction Problems

1. The following exchange rates prevail in the foreign currency market:

	U.S. Dollars Required to Buy One Unit
Spamany (liso)	.100
Britland (ounce)	1.500
Chilaquay (peso)	.015
Trance (franc)	.130
Shopan (ben)	.005

Determine the number of:

    a. Spamany lisos that can be acquired for $1,000.

    b. Dollars that 30 Britland ounces will buy.

    c. Chilaquay pesos that $900 will acquire.

    d. Dollars that 100 Trench francs will purchase.

    e. Shopan ben that $50 will acquire.

2. Zike Athletic Shoe Company sells to a wholesaler in Germany. The purchase price of a shipment is 50,000 Euros with terms of 90 days. Upon payment, Zike will convert the Euros to dollars. The present spot rate for dollars per Euro is 0.980, whereas the 90-day forward rate is 0.984.

    a. If Zike were to hedge its foreign exchange risk, what would it do? What are the transactions necessary?

    b. Is the Euro at a premium or at a discount?

    c. What is the implied difference in interest rates between the two currencies? (Use interest-rate parity assumptions.)

3. (Appendix) Fog Industries, Inc., has a subsidiary in Lolland where the currency is the guildnote. The exchange rate at the beginning of the year is 3 guildnotes to the dollar; at the end of the year, it is 2.5 guildnotes, as the guildnote strengthens in value. The subsidiary's balance sheets at the two points in time and the income statement for the year are as follows (in thousands):

	In Guildnotes	
	12/31/x1	**12/31/x2**
Balance Sheet		
Cash	300	400
Receivables	1,800	2,200
Inventories (FIFO)	1,500	2,000
Net fixed assets	2,100	1,800
Total	5,700	6,400
Current liabilities	2,000	1,900
Common stock	600	600
Retained earnings	3,100	3,900
Total	5,700	6,400

Income Statement	
Sales	10,400
Cost of goods sold	6,000
Depreciation	300
Expenses	2,400
Taxes	900
Operating income	800

The historical exchange rate for the fixed assets is 3 guildnotes to the dollar. The historical cost exchange rate for inventories and cost of goods sold, using the dollar as the functional currency, is 2.70. Using the guildnote, it is 2.60 for cost of goods sold purposes. The average exchange rate for the year is 2.75 guildnotes to the dollar, and sales, depreciation, expenses, and taxes paid are steady throughout the year. Also assume no previous translation adjustments. On the basis of this information, determine to the nearest thousand dollars the balance sheet and income statement for 12/31/x2, assuming that the functional currency is the guildnote. Assuming that it is the dollar, what are the differences?

 Problems

1. The following spot rates are observed in the foreign currency market:

Currency	Foreign Currency per U.S. Dollar
Britain (pound)	.62
Netherlands (guilder)	1.90
Sweden (krona)	6.40
Switzerland (franc)	1.50
Italy (lira)	1,300.00
Japan (yen)	140.00

On the basis of this information, compute to the nearest second decimal the number of:
   a. British pounds that can be acquired for $100.
   b. Dollars that 50 Dutch guilders (a European Monetary Union legacy currency) will buy.
   c. Swedish krona that can be acquired for $40.
   d. Dollars that 200 Swiss francs can buy.
   e. Italian lira (an EMU legacy currency) that can be acquired for $10.
   f. Dollars that 1,000 Japanese yen will buy.

2. The U.S. Imports Company purchased 100,000 deutschemarks (an EMU legacy currency) worth of machines from a firm in Dortmund, Germany. The value of the dollar in terms of the mark has been decreasing. The firm in Dortmund offers 2/10, net 90 terms. The spot rate for the mark is $.55; the 90-day forward rate is $.56.
   a. Compute the dollar cost of paying the account within the 10 days.
   b. Compute the dollar cost of buying a forward contract to liquidate the account in 90 days.
   c. The differential between parts a and b is the result of the time value of money (the discount for prepayment) and protection from currency value fluctuation. Determine the magnitude of each of these components.

3. Loco Boost Vehicles, Inc., is considering a new plant in the Netherlands. The plant will cost 26 million guilders. Incremental cash flows are expected to be 3 million guilders per year for the first 3 years, 4 million guilders the next 3, 5 million guilders in years 7 through 9, and 6 million guilders in years 10 through 19, after which the project will terminate with no residual value. The

present exchange rate is 1.90 guilders per dollar. The required rate of return on repatriated dollars is 16 percent.

    a. If the exchange rate stays at 1.90, what is the project's net present value?

    b. If the guilder appreciates to 1.84 for years 1–3, to 1.78 for years 4–6, to 1.72 for years 7–9, and to 1.65 for years 10–19, what happens to the net present value?

4. Fleur du Lac, a French company, has shipped goods to an American importer under a letter of credit arrangement, which calls for payment at the end of 90 days. The invoice is for $124,000. Presently the exchange rate is 5.70 French francs (an EMU legacy currency) to the dollar. If the French franc were to strengthen by 5 percent by the end of 90 days, what would be the transaction's gain or loss in French francs? If it were to weaken by 5 percent, what would happen? (*Note:* Make all calculations in francs per dollar.)

5. Itoh Selangor Berhad is the Malaysian subsidiary of USD Corporation. Presently the subsidiary has the following balance sheet items expressed in U.S. dollar equivalents using book values (in millions):

Monetary assets	$24
Inventories	16
Value of operating capacity	30
Total assets	$70
Monetary liabilities	$40
Shareholders' equity	30
Total liabilities and equity	$70

The market values of monetary assets and liabilities are the same as book values, whereas inventories are 1.25 times book value and the value of operating capacity is 1.667 times book value. Suppose the exposure coefficients for these two assets are .5 and .2, respectively, for the Malaysian ringgit/U.S. dollar exchange rate. Using the Hekman framework, what is the net aggregate market value exposure for the subsidiary and its aggregate exposure coefficient (on equity)?

6. Wheat sells for $4.00 a bushel in the United States. The price in Canada is Can.$4.56. The exchange rate is 1.2 Canadian dollars to 1 U.S. dollar. Does purchasing power parity exist? If not, what changes would need to occur for it to exist?

7. Presently, the dollar is worth 140 Japanese yen in the spot market. The interest rate in Japan on 90-day government securities is 4 percent; it is 8 percent in the United States.

    a. If the interest-rate parity theorem holds, what is the implied 90-day forward exchange rate in yen per dollar?

    b. What would be implied if the U.S. interest rate were 6 percent?

8. Cordova Leather Company is in a 38 percent U.S. tax bracket. It has sales branches in Algeria and in Spain, each of which generates earnings of $200,000 before taxes. If the effective income tax rate is 52 percent in Algeria and 35 percent in Spain, what total U.S. and foreign taxes will Cordova pay on the above earnings?

9. McDonnoughs Hamburger Company wishes to lend $500,000 to its Japanese subsidiary. At the same time, Yasufuku Heavy Industries is interested in making a medium-term loan of approximately the same amount to its U.S. subsidiary. The two parties are brought together by an investment bank for the purpose of making parallel loans. McDonnoughs will lend $500,000 to the U.S. subsidiary of Yasufuku for 4 years at 13 percent. Principal and interest are payable only at the end of the fourth year, with interest compounding annually. Yasufuku will lend the Japanese subsidiary of McDonnoughs 70 million yen for 4 years at 10 percent. Again the principal and interest (annual compounding) are payable at the end. The current exchange rate is 140 yen to the dollar. However, the dollar is expected to decline by 5 yen to the dollar per year over the next 4 years.

   a. If these expectations prove to be correct, what will be the dollar equivalent of principal and interest payments to Yasufuku at the end of 4 years?

   b. What total dollars will McDonnoughs receive at the end of 4 years from the payment of principal and interest on its loan by the U.S. subsidiary of Yasufuku?

   c. Which party is better off with the parallel loan arrangement? What would happen if the yen did not change in value?

10. The government of Zwill presently encourages investment in the country. Comstock International Mining Corporation, a U.S. company, is planning to open a new copper mine in Zwill. The front-end investment is expected to be $25 million, after which cash flows are expected to be more than sufficient to cover further capital needs. Preliminary exploration findings suggest that the project is likely to be very profitable, providing an expected internal rate of return of 34 percent, based on business considerations alone. The government of Zwill, like that of many countries, is unstable. The management of Comstock, trying to assess this instability and its consequences, forecasts a 10 percent probability that the government will be overthrown and a new government will expropriate the property with no compensation. The full $25 million would be lost, and the internal rate of return would be −100 percent. There also is a 15 percent probability that the government will be overthrown but that the new government will make partial payment for the properties; this would result in an internal rate of return of −40 percent. Finally, there is a 15 percent probability that the present government will stay in power, but that it will change its policy on repatriation of profits. More specifically, it will allow the corporation to repatriate its original investment, $25 million, but all other cash flows generated by the project would have to be reinvested in the host country forever. These probabilities still leave a 60 percent chance that a 34 percent internal rate of return will be achieved. Given these political risks, approximate the likely return to Comstock. Should the mining venture be undertaken?

Solutions to Self-Correction Problems

1. a. $1,000/.100 = 10,000 lisos
    b. 30 × $1,500 = $45
    c. $900/.015 = 60,000 pesos
    d. 100 × $.13 = $13
    e. $50/.005 = 10,000 ben

2.   a. It would hedge by selling Euros forward 90 days. Upon delivery of 50,000 Euros in 90 days, it would receive €50,000 x 0.984 = $49,200. If it were to receive payment today, Zike would get €50,000 x 0.980 = $49,000.

      b. The Euro is at a premium because the 90-day forward rate of dollars per Euro is greater than the current spot rate.

      c. [(0.980 − 0.984)/0.980] x [365/90] = −0.0166. The differential in interest rates is approximately −1.66 percent. This means that if interest-rate parity holds, interest rates in the United States should be approximately 1.66 percent higher than 90-day Euro denominated interest rates for European Monetary Union countries.

3. In dollars, December 31, 20x2:

	Functional Currency Guildnote	Functional Currency Dollar
Balance Sheet		
Cash	$ 160	$ 160
Receivables	880	880
Inventories	800	741
Net fixed assets	720	600
Total	$2,560	$2,381
Current liabilities	$ 760	$ 760
Common stock	200	200
Retained earnings ($1,033 at 12/31/x1)	1,198	1,421
Accumulated translation adjustment	402	
Total	$2,560	$2,381
Income Statement		
Sales	$3,782	$3,782
Cost of goods sold	2,308	2,222
Depreciation	109	100
Expenses	873	873
Taxes	327	327
Operating income	$ 165	$ 260
Translation gain		128
Net income	$ 165	$ 388

Translation adjustment = $402

When the guildnote is used as the functional currency, all balance sheet items except common stock and retained earnings are translated at the current exchange rate, 2.50. All income statement items are translated at the average exchange rate for the year, 2.75, except cost of goods sold, which is translated at 2.60. Net income is a residual, after deducting costs and expenses from sales. Retained earnings are net income, $165, plus retained earnings at the beginning of the year, $1,033, to give $1,198. The translation adjustment is that amount necessary to bring about an equality in the two totals on the balance sheet. It is $402. For the dollar as the functional currency, inventories and cost of goods sold are translated at the historical exchange rate of 2.70, and fixed assets and depreciation at the historical exchange rate of 3.00. Other items are translated in the same manner as with the other method. Retained earnings are a balancing factor to bring equality between the balance sheet totals. Operating income is a residual. The translation gain is that amount necessary to make net income equal to the change in retained earnings: $1,421 − $1,033 = $388 − $260 = $128. Depending on the accounting method, income is more variable with the dollar as the functional currency, whereas balance sheet totals are more variable with the guildnote as the functional currency.

Selected References

ABUAF, NISO, and PHILIPPE JORION, "Purchasing Power Parity in the Long Run," *Journal of Finance*, 45 (March 1990), 157–74.

BEKAERT, GEERT, and ROBERT J. HODRICK, "On Biases in the Measurement of Foreign Exchange Risk Premiums," *Journal of International Money and Finance*, 12 (1993), 115–38.

BLACK, FISCHER, "Equilibrium Exchange Rate Hedging," *Journal of Finance*, 45 (July 1990), 899–908.

CLARKE, ROGER G., and MARK P. KRITZMAN, *Currency Management: Concepts and Practices*. Charlottesville, VA: Research Foundation of the Institute of Chartered Financial Analysts, 1996.

COPELAND, TOM, and MAGGIE COPELAND, "Managing Corporate FX Risk: A Value Maximizing Approach," *Financial Management*, 28 (Autumn 1999), 68–75.

GODFREY, STEPHEN, and RAMON ESPINOSA, "A Practical Approach to Calculating Costs of Equity for Investments in Emerging Markets," *Journal of Applied Corporate Finance*, 9 (Fall 1996), 80–89.

GRIFFIN, JOHN M., and G. ANDREW KAROLYI, "Another Look at the Role of the Industrial Structure of Markets for International Diversification Strategies," *Journal of Financial Economics*, 50 (December l998), 351–74.

HEKMAN, CHRISTINE R., "Measuring Foreign Exchange Exposure: A Practical Theory and Its Application," *Financial Analysts Journal*, 39 (September–October 1983), 59–65.

———, "Don't Blame Currency Values for Strategic Errors," *Midland Corporate Finance Journal*, 4 (Fall 1986), 45–55.

LESSARD, DONALD, "International Portfolio Diversification: A Multivariate Analysis for a Group of Latin American Countries," *Journal of Finance*, 28 (June 1973), 619–34.

LINS, KARL, and HENRI SERVAES, "International Evidence on the Value of Corporate Diversification," *Journal of Finance*, 54 (December 1999), 2215–39.

MELLO, ANTONIO S., "Strategic Hedging," *Journal of Applied Corporate Finance*, 12 (Fall 1999), 43–54.

PEROLD, ANDRE F., and EVAN C. SCHULMAN, "The Free Lunch in Currency Hedging: Implications for Investment Policy and Performance Standards," *Financial Analysts Journal*, 44 (May–June 1988), 45–50.

SHAPIRO, ALAN C., *Multinational Financial Management*, 6th ed. Upper Saddle River, NJ: Prentice Hall, 1999.

SOLNIK, BRUNO, "Global Asset Management," *Journal of Portfolio Management*, 24 (Summer 1998), 43–51.

———, "The International Pricing of Risk: An Empirical Investigation of the World Capital Market Structure," *Journal of Finance*, 29 (May 1974), 365–78.

STULZ, RENE M., "Globalization of Capital Markets and the Cost of Capital," *Journal of Applied Corporate Finance*, 8 (Fall 1995), 30–38.

———, "Globalization, Corporate Finance, and the Cost of Capital," *Journal of Applied Corporate Finance*, 12 (Fall 1999), 8–25.

VAN HORNE, JAMES C., *Financial Market Rates and Flows*, 6th ed. Upper Saddle River, NJ: Prentice Hall, 2001, Chap. 14.

Wachowicz's Web World is an excellent overall Web site produced and maintained by my coauthor of *Fundamentals of Financial Management*, John M. Wachowicz Jr. It contains descriptions of and links to many finance Web sites and articles. *www.prenhall.com/wachowicz*.

Appendix: Present-Value Tables and Normal Probability Distribution Table

TABLE A
Present Value of One Dollar Due at the End of n Years

N	1%	2%	3%	4%	5%	6%	7%	8%	9%	10%	N
1	.99010	.98039	.97007	.96154	.95238	.94340	.93458	.92593	.91743	.90909	1
2	.98030	.96117	.94260	.92456	.90703	.89000	.87344	.85734	.84168	.82645	2
3	.97059	.94232	.91514	.88900	.86384	.83962	.81630	.79383	.77218	.75131	3
4	.96098	.92385	.88849	.85480	.82270	.79209	.76290	.73503	.70843	.68301	4
5	.95147	.90573	.86261	.82193	.78353	.74726	.71299	.68058	.64993	.62092	5
6	.94204	.88797	.83748	.79031	.74622	.70496	.66634	.60317	.59627	.56447	6
7	.93272	.87056	.81309	.75992	.71068	.66506	.62275	.58349	.54703	.51316	7
8	.92348	.85349	.78941	.73069	.67684	.62741	.58201	.54027	.50187	.46651	8
9	.91434	.83675	.76642	.70259	.64461	.59190	.54393	.50025	.46043	.42410	9
10	.90529	.82035	.74409	.67556	.61391	.55839	.50835	.46319	.42241	.38554	10
11	.89632	.80426	.72242	.64958	.58468	.52679	.47509	.42888	.38753	.35049	11
12	.88745	.78849	.70138	.62460	.55684	.49697	.44401	.39711	.35553	.31863	12
13	.87866	.77303	.68095	.60057	.53032	.46884	.41496	.36770	.32618	.28966	13
14	.86996	.75787	.66112	.57747	.50507	.44230	.38782	.34046	.29925	.26333	14
15	.86135	.74301	.64186	.55526	.48102	.41726	.36245	.31524	.27454	.23939	15
16	.85282	.72845	.62317	.53391	.45811	.39365	.33873	.29189	.25187	.21763	16
17	.84438	.71416	.60502	.51337	.43630	.37136	.31657	.27027	.23107	.19784	17
18	.83602	.70016	.58739	.49363	.41552	.35034	.29586	.25025	.21199	.17986	18
19	.82774	.68643	.57029	.47464	.39573	.33051	.27651	.23171	.19449	.16351	19
20	.81954	.67297	.55367	.45639	.37689	.31180	.25842	.21455	.17843	.14864	20
21	.81143	.65978	.53755	.43883	.35894	.29415	.24151	.19866	.16370	.13513	21
22	.80340	.64684	.52189	.42195	.34185	.27750	.22571	.18394	.15018	.12285	22
23	.79544	.63416	.50669	.40573	.32557	.26180	.21095	.17031	.13778	.11168	23
24	.78757	.62172	.49193	.39012	.31007	.24698	.19715	.15770	.12640	.10153	24
25	.77977	.60953	.47760	.37512	.29530	.23300	.18425	.14602	.11597	.09230	25

Continued

N	11%	12%	13%	14%	15%	16%	17%	18%	19%	20%	N
1	.90090	.89286	.88496	.87719	.86957	.86207	.85470	.84746	.84034	.83333	1
2	.81162	.79719	.78315	.76947	.75614	.74316	.73051	.71818	.70616	.69444	2
3	.73119	.71178	.69305	.67497	.65752	.64066	.62437	.60863	.59342	.57870	3
4	.65873	.63552	.61332	.59208	.57175	.55229	.53365	.51579	.49867	.48225	4
5	.59345	.56743	.54276	.51937	.49718	.47611	.45611	.43711	.41905	.40188	5
6	.53464	.50663	.48032	.45559	.43233	.41044	.38984	.37043	.35214	.33490	6
7	.48166	.45235	.42506	.39964	.37594	.35383	.33320	.31392	.29592	.27908	7
8	.43393	.40388	.37616	.35056	.32690	.30503	.28478	.26604	.24867	.23257	8
9	.39092	.36061	.33288	.30751	.28426	.26295	.24340	.22546	.20897	.19381	9
10	.35218	.32197	.29459	.26974	.24718	.22668	.20804	.19106	.17560	.16151	10
11	.31728	.28748	.26070	.23662	.21494	.19542	.17781	.16192	.14756	.13459	11
12	.28584	.25667	.23071	.20756	.18691	.16846	.15197	.13722	.12400	.11216	12
13	.25751	.22917	.20416	.18207	.16253	.14523	.12989	.11629	.10420	.09346	13
14	.23199	.20462	.18068	.15971	.14133	.12520	.11102	.09855	.08757	.07789	14
15	.20900	.18270	.15989	.14010	.12289	.10793	.09489	.08352	.07359	.06491	15
16	.18829	.16312	.14150	.12289	.10686	.09304	.08110	.07078	.06184	.05409	16
17	.16963	.14564	.12522	.10780	.09293	.08021	.06932	.05998	.05196	.04507	17
18	.15282	.13004	.11081	.09456	.08080	.06914	.05925	.05083	.04367	.03756	18
19	.13768	.11611	.09806	.08295	.07026	.05961	.05064	.04308	.03669	.03130	19
20	.12403	.10367	.08678	.07276	.06110	.05139	.04328	.03651	.03084	.02608	20
21	.11174	.09256	.07680	.06383	.05313	.04430	.03699	.03094	.02591	.02174	21
22	.10067	.08264	.06796	.05599	.04620	.03819	.03162	.02622	.02178	.01811	22
23	.09069	.07379	.06014	.04911	.04017	.03292	.02702	.02222	.01830	.01509	23
24	.08170	.06588	.05322	.04308	.03493	.02838	.02310	.01883	.01538	.01258	24
25	.07361	.05882	.04710	.03779	.03038	.02447	.01974	.01596	.01292	.01048	25

Continued

N	21%	22%	23%	24%	25%	26%	27%	28%	29%	30%	N
1	.82645	.81967	.81301	.80645	.80000	.79365	.78740	.78125	.77519	.76923	1
2	.68301	.67186	.66098	.65036	.64000	.62988	.62000	.61035	.60093	.59172	2
3	.56447	.55071	.53738	.52449	.51200	.49991	.48819	.47684	.46583	.45517	3
4	.46651	.45140	.43690	.42297	.40906	.39675	.38440	.37253	.36111	.35013	4
5	.38554	.37000	.35520	.34411	.32768	.31488	.30268	.29104	.27993	.26933	5
6	.31863	.30328	.28878	.27509	.26214	.24991	.23833	.22737	.21700	.20718	6
7	.26333	.24859	.23478	.22184	.20972	.19834	.18766	.17764	.16822	.15937	7
8	.21763	.20376	.19088	.17891	.16777	.15741	.14776	.13878	.13040	.12259	8
9	.17986	.16702	.15519	.14428	.13422	.12493	.11635	.10842	.10109	.09430	9
10	.14864	.13690	.12617	.11635	.10737	.09915	.09161	.08470	.07836	.07254	10
11	.12285	.11221	.10258	.09383	.08590	.07869	.07214	.06617	.06075	.05580	11
12	.10153	.09198	.08339	.07567	.06872	.06245	.05680	.05170	.04709	.04292	12
13	.08391	.07539	.06780	.06103	.05498	.04957	.04472	.04039	.03650	.03302	13
14	.06934	.06180	.05512	.04921	.04398	.03934	.03522	.03155	.02830	.02540	14
15	.05731	.05065	.04481	.03969	.03518	.03122	.02773	.02465	.02194	.01954	15
16	.04736	.04152	.03643	.03201	.02815	.02478	.02183	.01926	.01700	.01503	16
17	.03914	.03403	.02962	.02581	.02252	.01967	.01719	.01505	.01318	.01156	17
18	.03235	.02789	.02408	.02082	.01801	.01561	.01354	.01175	.01022	.00889	18
19	.02673	.02286	.01958	.01679	.01441	.01239	.01066	.00918	.00792	.00684	19
20	.02209	.01874	.01592	.01354	.01153	.00983	.00839	.00717	.00614	.00526	20
21	.01826	.01536	.01294	.01902	.00922	.00780	.00661	.00561	.00476	.00405	21
22	.01509	.01259	.01052	.00880	.00738	.00619	.00520	.00438	.00369	.00311	22
23	.01247	.01032	.00855	.00710	.00590	.00491	.00410	.00342	.00286	.00239	23
24	.01031	.00846	.00695	.00573	.00472	.00390	.00323	.00267	.00222	.00184	24
25	.00852	.00693	.00565	.00462	.00378	.00310	.00254	.00209	.00172	.00142	25

Continued

N	31%	32%	33%	34%	35%	36%	37%	38%	39%	40%	N
1	.76336	.75758	.75188	.74627	.74074	.73529	.72993	.72464	.71942	.71429	1
2	.58272	.57392	.56532	.55692	.54870	.54066	.53279	.52510	.51757	.51020	2
3	.44482	.43479	.42505	.41561	.40644	.39745	.38890	.38051	.37235	.36443	3
4	.33956	.32939	.31959	.31016	.30107	.29231	.28387	.27573	.26788	.26031	4
5	.25920	.24953	.24029	.23146	.22301	.21493	.20720	.19980	.19272	.18593	5
6	.19787	.18904	.18067	.17273	.16520	.15804	.15124	.14479	.13865	.13281	6
7	.15104	.14321	.13584	.12890	.12237	.11621	.11040	.10492	.09975	.09486	7
8	.11530	.10849	.10214	.09620	.09064	.08545	.08058	.07603	.07176	.06776	8
9	.08802	.08219	.07680	.07179	.06714	.06283	.05882	.05509	.05163	.04840	9
10	.06719	.06227	.05774	.05357	.04973	.04620	.04293	.03992	.03714	.03457	10
11	.05129	.04717	.04341	.03998	.03684	.03397	.03134	.02893	.02672	.02469	11
12	.03915	.03574	.03264	.02984	.02729	.02498	.02887	.02096	.01922	.01764	12
13	.02989	.02707	.02454	.02227	.02021	.01837	.01670	.01519	.01383	.01260	13
14	.02281	.02051	.01845	.01662	.01497	.01350	.01219	.01101	.00995	.00900	14
15	.01742	.01554	.01387	.01240	.01109	.00993	.00890	.00789	.00716	.00643	15
16	.01329	.01177	.01043	.00925	.00822	.00730	.00649	.00578	.00515	.00459	16
17	.01015	.00892	.00784	.00691	.00609	.00537	.00474	.00419	.00370	.00328	17
18	.00775	.00676	.00590	.00515	.00451	.00395	.00346	.00304	.00267	.00234	18
19	.00591	.00512	.00443	.00385	.00334	.00290	.00253	.00220	.00192	.00167	19
20	.00451	.00388	.00333	.00287	.00247	.00213	.00184	.00159	.00138	.00120	20
21	.00345	.00294	.00251	.00214	.00183	.00157	.00135	.00115	.00099	.00085	21
22	.00263	.00223	.00188	.00160	.00136	.00115	.00098	.00084	.00071	.00061	22
23	.00201	.00169	.00142	.00119	.00101	.00085	.00072	.00061	.00051	.00044	23
24	.00153	.00128	.00107	.00089	.00074	.00062	.00052	.00044	.00037	.00031	24
25	.00117	.00097	.00080	.00066	.00055	.00046	.00038	.00032	.00027	.00022	25

TABLE B
Present Value of One Dollar Per Year, *n* Years at r%

Year	1%	2%	3%	4%	5%	6%	7%	8%	9%	10%	Year
1	.9901	.9804	.9709	.9615	.9524	.9434	.9346	.9259	.9174	.9091	1
2	1.9704	1.9416	1.9135	1.8861	1.8594	1.8334	1.8080	1.7833	1.7591	1.7355	2
3	2.9410	2.8839	2.8286	2.7751	2.7232	2.6730	2.6243	2.5771	2.5313	2.4868	3
4	3.9020	3.8077	3.7171	3.6299	3.5459	3.4651	3.3872	3.3121	3.2397	3.1699	4
5	4.8535	4.7134	4.5797	4.4518	4.3295	4.2123	4.1002	3.9927	3.8896	3.7908	5
6	5.7955	5.6014	5.4172	5.2421	5.0757	4.9173	4.7665	4.6229	4.4859	4.3553	6
7	6.7282	6.4720	6.2302	6.0020	5.7863	5.5824	5.3893	5.2064	5.0329	4.8684	7
8	7.6517	7.3254	7.0196	6.7327	6.4632	6.2098	5.9713	5.7466	5.5348	5.3349	8
9	8.5661	8.1622	7.7861	7.4353	7.1078	6.8017	6.5152	6.2469	5.9852	5.7590	9
10	9.4714	8.9825	8.5302	8.1109	7.7217	7.3601	7.0236	6.7101	6.4176	6.1446	10
11	10.3677	9.7868	9.2526	8.7604	8.3064	7.8868	7.4987	7.1389	6.8052	6.4951	11
12	11.2552	10.5753	9.9539	9.3850	8.8632	8.3838	7.9427	7.5361	7.1607	6.8137	12
13	12.1338	11.3483	10.6349	9.9856	9.3935	8.8527	8.3576	7.9038	7.4869	7.1034	13
14	13.0038	12.1062	11.2960	10.5631	9.8986	9.2950	8.7454	8.2442	7.7861	7.3667	14
15	13.8651	12.8492	11.9379	11.1183	10.3796	9.7122	9.1079	8.5595	8.0607	7.6061	15
16	14.7180	13.5777	12.5610	11.6522	10.8377	10.1059	9.4466	8.8514	8.3125	7.8237	16
17	15.5624	14.2918	13.1660	12.1656	11.2740	10.4772	9.7632	9.1216	8.5436	8.0215	17
18	16.3984	14.9920	13.7534	12.6592	11.6895	10.8276	10.0591	9.3719	8.7556	8.2014	18
19	17.2261	15.6784	14.3237	13.1339	12.0853	11.1581	10.3356	9.6036	8.9501	8.3649	19
20	18.0457	16.3514	14.8774	13.5903	12.4622	11.4699	10.5940	9.8181	9.1285	8.5136	20
21	18.8571	17.0111	15.4149	14.0291	12.8211	11.7640	10.8355	10.0168	9.2922	8.6487	21
22	19.6605	17.6580	15.9368	14.4511	13.1630	12.0416	11.0612	10.2007	9.4424	8.7715	22
23	20.4559	18.2921	16.4435	14.8568	13.4885	12.3033	11.2722	10.3710	9.5802	8.8832	23
24	21.2435	18.9139	16.9355	15.2469	13.7986	12.5503	11.4693	10.5287	9.7066	8.9847	24
25	22.0233	19.5234	17.4131	15.6220	14.0939	12.7833	11.6536	10.6748	9.8226	9.0770	25

Continued

Year	11%	12%	13%	14%	15%	16%	17%	18%	19%	20%	Year
1	.9009	.8929	.8850	.8772	.8696	.8621	.8547	.8475	.8403	.8333	1
2	1.7125	1.6901	1.6681	1.6467	1.6257	1.6052	1.5852	1.5656	1.5465	1.5278	2
3	2.4437	2.4018	2.3612	2.3216	2.2832	2.2459	2.2096	2.1743	2.1399	2.1065	3
4	3.1024	3.0373	2.9745	2.9137	2.8550	2.7982	2.7432	2.6901	2.6386	2.5887	4
5	3.6959	3.6048	3.5172	3.4331	3.3522	3.2743	3.1993	3.1272	3.0576	2.9906	5
6	4.2305	4.1114	3.9976	3.8887	3.7845	3.6847	3.5892	3.4976	3.4098	3.3255	6
7	4.7122	4.5638	4.4226	4.2883	4.1604	4.0386	3.9224	3.8115	3.7057	3.6046	7
8	5.1461	4.9676	4.7988	4.6389	4.4873	4.3436	4.2072	4.0776	3.9544	3.8372	8
9	5.5370	5.3282	5.1317	4.9464	4.7716	4.6065	4.4506	4.3030	4.1633	4.0310	9
10	5.8892	5.6502	5.4262	5.2161	5.0188	4.8332	4.6586	4.4941	4.3389	4.1925	10
11	6.2065	5.9377	5.6869	5.4527	5.2337	5.0286	4.8364	4.6560	4.4865	4.3271	11
12	6.4924	6.1944	5.9176	5.6603	5.4206	5.1971	4.9884	4.7932	4.6105	4.4392	12
13	6.7499	6.4235	6.1218	5.8424	5.5831	5.3423	5.1183	4.9095	4.7147	4.5327	13
14	6.9819	6.6282	6.3025	6.0021	5.7245	5.4675	5.2293	5.0081	4.8023	4.6106	14
15	7.1909	6.8109	6.4624	6.1422	5.8474	5.5755	5.3242	5.0916	4.8759	4.6755	15
16	7.3792	6.9740	6.6039	6.2651	5.9542	5.6685	5.4053	5.1624	4.9377	4.7296	16
17	7.5488	7.1196	6.7291	6.3729	6.0472	5.7487	5.4746	5.2223	4.9897	4.7746	17
18	7.7016	7.2497	6.8399	6.4674	6.1280	5.8178	5.5339	5.2732	5.0333	4.8122	18
19	7.8393	7.3658	6.9380	6.5504	6.1982	5.8775	5.5845	5.3162	5.0700	4.8435	19
20	7.9633	7.4694	7.0248	6.6231	6.2593	5.9288	5.6278	5.3527	5.1009	4.8696	20
21	8.0751	7.5620	7.1016	6.6870	6.3125	5.9731	5.6648	5.3837	5.1268	4.8913	21
22	8.1757	7.6446	7.1695	6.7429	6.3587	6.0113	5.6964	5.4099	5.1486	4.9094	22
23	8.2664	7.7184	7.2297	6.7921	6.3988	6.0442	5.7234	5.4321	5.1668	4.9245	23
24	8.3481	7.7843	7.2829	6.8351	6.4338	6.0726	5.7465	5.4509	5.1822	4.9371	24
25	8.4217	7.8431	7.3300	6.8729	6.4641	6.0971	5.7662	5.4669	5.1951	4.9476	25

Continued

Year	21%	22%	23%	24%	25%	26%	27%	28%	29%	30%	Year
1	.8264	.8197	.8130	.8065	.8000	.7937	.7874	.7813	.7752	.7692	1
2	1.5095	1.4915	1.4740	1.4568	1.4400	1.4235	1.4074	1.3916	1.3761	1.3609	2
3	2.0739	2.0422	2.0114	1.9813	1.9520	1.9234	1.8956	1.8684	1.8420	1.8161	3
4	2.5404	2.4936	2.4483	2.4043	2.3616	2.3202	2.2800	2.2410	2.2031	2.1662	4
5	2.9260	2.8636	2.8035	2.7454	2.6893	2.6351	2.5827	2.5320	2.4830	2.4356	5
6	3.2446	3.1669	3.0923	3.0205	2.9514	2.8850	2.8210	2.7594	2.7000	2.6427	6
7	3.5079	3.4155	3.3270	3.2423	3.1611	3.0833	3.0087	2.9370	2.8682	2.8021	7
8	3.7256	3.6193	3.5179	3.4212	3.3289	3.2407	3.1564	3.0758	2.9986	2.9247	8
9	3.9054	3.7863	3.6731	3.5655	3.4631	3.3657	3.2728	3.1842	3.0997	3.0190	9
10	4.0541	3.9232	3.7993	3.6819	3.5705	3.4648	3.3644	3.2689	3.1781	3.0915	10
11	4.1769	4.0354	3.9018	3.7757	3.6564	3.5435	3.4365	3.3351	3.2388	3.1473	11
12	4.2785	4.1274	3.9852	3.8514	3.7251	3.6060	3.4933	3.3868	3.2859	3.1903	12
13	4.3624	4.2028	4.0530	3.9124	3.7801	3.6555	3.6381	3.4272	3.3224	3.2233	13
14	4.4317	4.2646	4.1082	3.9616	3.8241	3.6949	3.5733	3.4587	3.3507	3.2487	14
15	4.4890	4.3152	4.1530	4.0013	3.8593	3.7261	3.6010	3.4834	3.3726	3.2682	15
16	4.5364	4.3567	4.1894	4.0333	3.8874	3.7509	3.6228	3.5026	3.3896	3.2832	16
17	4.5755	4.3908	4.2190	4.0591	3.9099	3.7705	3.6400	3.5177	3.4028	3.2948	17
18	4.6079	4.4187	4.2431	4.0799	3.9279	3.7861	3.6536	3.5294	3.4130	3.3037	18
19	4.6346	4.4415	4.2627	4.0967	3.9424	3.7985	3.6642	3.5386	3.4210	3.3105	19
20	4.6567	4.4603	4.2786	4.1103	3.9539	3.8083	3.6726	3.5458	3.4271	3.3158	20
21	4.6750	4.4756	4.2916	4.1212	3.9631	3.8161	3.6792	3.5514	3.4319	3.3198	21
22	4.6900	4.4882	4.3021	4.1300	3.9705	3.8223	3.6844	3.5558	3.4356	3.3230	22
23	4.7025	4.4985	4.3106	4.1371	3.9764	3.8273	3.6885	3.5592	3.4384	3.3254	23
24	4.7128	4.5070	4.3176	4.1428	3.9811	3.8312	3.6918	3.5619	3.4406	3.3272	24
25	4.7213	4.5139	4.3232	4.1474	3.9849	3.8342	3.6943	3.5640	3.4423	3.3286	25

Continued

Year	31%	32%	33%	34%	35%	36%	37%	38%	39%	40%	Year
1	.7634	.7576	.7519	.7463	.7407	.7353	.7299	.7246	.7194	.7143	1
2	1.3461	1.3315	1.3172	1.3032	1.2894	1.2760	1.2627	1.2497	1.2370	1.2245	2
3	1.7909	1.7663	1.7423	1.7188	1.6959	1.6735	1.6516	1.6302	1.6093	1.5889	3
4	2.1305	2.0957	2.0618	2.0290	1.9969	1.9658	1.9355	1.9060	1.8772	1.8492	4
5	2.3897	2.3452	2.3021	2.2604	2.2200	2.1807	2.1427	2.1058	2.0699	2.0352	5
6	2.5875	2.5342	2.4828	2.4331	2.3852	2.3388	2.2939	2.2506	2.2086	2.1680	6
7	2.7386	2.6775	2.6187	2.5620	2.5075	2.4550	2.4043	2.3555	2.3083	2.2628	7
8	2.8539	2.7860	2.7208	2.6582	2.5982	2.5404	2.4849	2.4315	2.3801	2.3306	8
9	2.9419	2.8681	2.7976	2.7300	2.6653	2.6033	5.5437	2.4866	2.4317	2.3790	9
10	3.0091	2.9304	2.8553	2.7836	2.7150	2.6495	2.5867	2.5265	2.4689	2.4136	10
11	3.0604	2.9776	2.8987	2.8236	2.7519	2.6834	2.6180	2.5555	2.4956	2.4383	11
12	3.0995	3.0133	2.9314	2.8534	2.7792	2.7084	2.6409	2.5764	2.5148	2.4559	12
13	3.1294	3.0404	2.9559	2.8757	2.7994	2.7268	2.6576	2.5916	2.5286	2.4685	13
14	3.1522	3.0609	2.9744	2.8923	2.8144	2.7403	2.6698	2.6026	2.5386	2.4775	14
15	3.1696	3.0764	2.9883	2.9047	2.8255	2.7502	2.6787	2.6106	2.5457	2.4839	15
16	3.1829	3.0882	2.9987	2.9104	2.8337	2.7575	2.6852	2.6164	2.5509	2.4885	16
17	3.1931	3.0960	3.0065	2.9209	2.8398	2.7629	2.6899	2.6206	2.5546	2.4918	17
18	3.2008	3.1039	3.0124	2.9260	2.8443	2.7668	2.6934	2.6236	2.5573	2.4941	18
19	3.2067	3.1090	3.0169	2.9299	2.8476	2.7697	2.6959	2.6258	2.5592	2.4958	19
20	3.2112	3.1129	3.0202	2.9327	2.8501	2.7718	2.6977	2.6274	2.5606	2.4970	20
21	3.2147	3.1158	3.0227	2.9349	2.8519	2.7734	2.6991	2.6285	2.5616	2.4979	21
22	3.2173	3.1180	3.0246	2.9365	2.8533	2.7746	2.7000	2.6294	2.5623	2.4985	22
23	3.2193	3.1197	3.0260	2.9377	2.8543	2.7754	2.7008	2.6300	2.5628	2.4989	23
24	3.2209	3.1210	3.0271	2.9386	2.8550	2.7760	2.7013	2.6304	2.5632	2.4992	24
25	3.2220	3.1220	3.0279	2.9392	2.8556	2.7765	2.7017	2.6307	2.5634	2.4994	25

TABLE C
Normal Probability Distribution Table*

Number of Standard Deviations From Mean (X)	Area to the Left or Right (One Tail)	Number of Standard Deviations From Mean (X)	Area to the Left or Right (One Tail)
.00	.5000	1.55	.0606
.05	.4801	1.60	.0548
.10	.4602	1.65	.0495
.15	.4404	1.70	.0446
.20	.4207	1.75	.0401
.25	.4013	1.80	.0359
.30	.3821	1.85	.0322
.35	.3632	1.90	.0287
.40	.3446	1.95	.0256
.45	.3264	2.00	.0228
.50	.3085	2.05	.0202
.55	.2912	2.10	.0179
.60	.2743	2.15	.0158
.65	.2578	2.20	.0139
.70	.2420	2.25	.0122
.75	.2264	2.30	.0107
.80	.2119	2.35	.0094
.85	.1977	2.40	.0082
.90	.1841	2.45	.0071
.95	.1711	2.50	.0062
1.00	.1577	2.55	.0054
1.05	.1469	2.60	.0047
1.10	.1357	2.65	.0040
1.15	.1251	2.70	.0035
1.20	.1151	2.75	.0030
1.25	.1056	2.80	.0026
1.30	.0968	2.85	.0022
1.35	.0885	2.90	.0019
1.40	.0808	2.95	.0016
1.45	.0735	3.00	.0013
1.50	.0668		

*Area of normal distribution that is X standard deviations to the left or right of the mean.

Index